Network Programm and Automation Fundamentals

Khaled Abuelenain, CCIE No. 27401

Jeff Doyle, CCIE No. 1919

Anton Karneliuk, CCIE No. 49412

Vinit Jain, CCIE No. 22854

Cisco Press

Hoboken, New Jersey

Network Programmability and Automation Fundamentals

Published by:
Cisco Press

ScoutAutomatedPrintCode

Library of Congress Control Number: 2020922839

ISBN-13: 978-1-58714-514-8
ISBN-10: 1-58714-514-6

Warning and Disclaimer

This book is designed to provide information about network programmability and automation. Every effort has been made to make this book as complete and as accurate as possible, but no warranty or fitness is implied.

The information is provided on an "as is" basis. The authors, Cisco Press, and Cisco Systems, Inc. shall have neither liability nor responsibility to any person or entity with respect to any loss or damages arising from the information contained in this book or from the use of the discs or programs that may accompany it.

The opinions expressed in this book belong to the author and are not necessarily those of Cisco Systems, Inc.

Trademark Acknowledgments

All terms mentioned in this book that are known to be trademarks or service marks have been appropriately capitalized. Cisco Press or Cisco Systems, Inc. cannot attest to the accuracy of this information. Use of a term in this book should not be regarded as affecting the validity of any trademark or service mark.

Feedback Information

At Cisco Press, our goal is to create in-depth technical books of the highest quality and value. Each book is crafted with care and precision, undergoing rigorous development that involves the unique expertise of members from the professional technical community.

Readers' feedback is a natural continuation of this process. If you have any comments regarding how we could improve the quality of this book or otherwise alter it to better suit your needs, you can contact us through email at feedback@ciscopress.com. Please make sure to include the book title and ISBN in your message.

We greatly appreciate your assistance.

Editor-in-Chief: Mark Taub

Director, ITP Product Management: Brett Bartow

Alliances Manager, Cisco Press: Arezou Gol

Managing Editor: Sandra Schroeder

Development Editor: Ellie C. Bru

Project Editor: Mandie Frank

Copy Editor: Kitty Wilson

Technical Editors: Jeff Tantsura, Viktor Osipchuk

Editorial Assistant: Cindy Teeters

Designer: Chuti Prasertsith

Composition: codeMantra

Indexer: Ken Johnson

Proofreader: Abigail Bass

Americas Headquarters
Cisco Systems, Inc.
San Jose, CA

Asia Pacific Headquarters
Cisco Systems (USA) Pte. Ltd.
Singapore

Europe Headquarters
Cisco Systems International BV Amsterdam,
The Netherlands

Cisco has more than 200 offices worldwide. Addresses, phone numbers, and fax numbers are listed on the Cisco Website at **www.cisco.com/go/offices.**

Credits

Figure/Text Selection	Attribution/Credit
"HTTP is not designed to be a transport protocol. It is a transfer protocol in which the messages reflect the semantics of the Web architecture by performing actions on resources through the transfer and manipulation of representations of those resources [Section 6.5.2]"	© Roy Thomas Fielding, 2000
"This specification [HTTP/2.0] is an alternative to, but does not obsolete, the HTTP/1.1 message syntax. HTTP's existing semantics remain unchanged."	Hypertext Transfer Protocol Version 2
"a sequence of octets, along with representation metadata describing those octets that constitutes a record of the state of the resource at the time when the representation is generated."	Uniform Resource Identifier (URI): Generic Syntax, Copyright © The Internet Society (2005)
"While RFC 2396, section 1.2, attempts to address the distinction between URIs, URLs and URNs, it has not been successful in clearing up the confusion."	IETF (Internet Engineering Task Force). Architectural Principles of Uniform Resource Name Resolution, ed. K. Sollins. 1998
1. Device state metrics; **2.** Data from shared services such as DDI (DNS, DHCP and IPAM) and Active Directory; **3.** Network flows from sources such as NetFlow; and **4.** Configuration data normalized into key value pairs.	Shamus McGillicudy, "A Network Source of Truth Promotes Trust in Network Automation," Enterprise management Associates, May 2020
"Deliver working software frequently, from a couple of weeks to a couple of months, with a preference to the shorter timescale".	©2020 Agile Alliance
"allows client/server applications to communicate over the Internet in a way that is designed to prevent eavesdropping, tampering, and message forgery."	Copyright (c) 2020 IETF
"the most important security protocol on the internet"	Copyright (c) 2020 IETF
"there was more TLS 1.3 use in the first five months after RFC 8446 was published than in the first five years after the last version of TLS was published as an RFC"	Copyright (c) 2020 IETF

Figure 1-6	CI/CD	©2021 Red Hat, Inc. www.redhat.com
Figure 6-2	Accessing a Django Application in a Web Browser	© 2005-2021 Django Software Foundation
Figure 7-1	The SupportApache-small.png Image, as It Appears in a Web Browser	Copyright © 2020 The Apache Software Foundation
Figure 7-6	The Postman Interface	©2020 Postman, Inc.
Figure 7-7	A GET Request Using Postman	©2020 Postman, Inc.
Figure 7-8	Viewing the Response Headers in Postman	©2020 Postman, Inc.
Figure 13-1	GitHub Website with YANG Modules	© 2020 GitHub, Inc.
Figure 17-3	Comparing the Body of the Response in the Developer Sandbox and Postman	Screenshot of Comparing the body of the response in the Developer Sandbox and Postman ©2020 Postman, Inc.
Figure 18-3	Converting a username:password Tuple to Base64 Format	Screenshot of Converting username:password tuple to Base64 format © Cisco systems
Figure 18-4	Arista YANG Modules	Screenshot of Arista YANG modules © 2020 GitHub, Inc.
Figure 19-3	Available Ansible Module Categories	Copyright © 2020 Red Hat, Inc.

About the Authors

Khaled Abuelenain, CCIE No. 27401 (R&S, SP), is currently the Consulting Director at Acuative, a Cisco Managed Services Master Partner. Khaled has spent the past 18 years designing, implementing, operating, and automating networks and clouds. He specializes in service provider technologies, SD-WAN, data center technologies, programmability, automation, and cloud architectures. Khaled is especially interested in Linux and OpenStack.

Khaled is a contributing author of the best-selling Cisco Press book *Routing TCP/IP, Volume II*, 2nd edition, by Jeff Doyle. He also blogs frequently on network programmability and automation on blogs.cisco.com. Khaled is also a member of the DevNet500 group, being one of the first 500 individuals in the world to become DevNet certified.

Khaled lives in Riyadh, Saudi Arabia, and when not working or writing, he likes to run marathons and skydive. He can be reached at kabuelenain@gmail.com, on Twitter at @kabuelenain or on LinkedIn at linkedin.com/in/kabuelenain.

Jeff Doyle, CCIE No. 1919, is a Member of Technical Staff at Apstra. Specializing in IP routing protocols, complex BGP policy, SDN/NFV, data center fabrics, IBN, EVPN, MPLS, and IPv6, Jeff has designed or assisted in the design of large-scale IP and IPv6 service provider networks in 26 countries over 6 continents.

Jeff is the author of *CCIE Professional Development: Routing TCP/IP, Volumes I and II* and *OSPF and IS-IS: Choosing an IGP for Large-Scale Networks*; a co-author of *Software-Defined Networking: Anatomy of OpenFlow*; and an editor and contributing author of *Juniper Networks Routers: The Complete Reference*. Jeff is currently writing *CCIE Professional Development: Switching TCP/IP*. He also writes for Forbes and blogs for both *Network World* and *Network Computing*. Jeff is one of the founders of the Rocky Mountain IPv6 Task Force, is an IPv6 Forum Fellow, and serves on the executive board of the Colorado chapter of the Internet Society (ISOC).

Anton Karneliuk, CCIE No. 49412 (R&S, SP), is a Network Engineer and Manager at THG Hosting, responsible for the development, operation, and automation of networks in numerous data centers across the globe and the international backbone. Prior to joining THG, Anton was a team lead in Vodafone Group Network Engineering and Delivery, focusing on introduction of SDN and NFV projects in Germany. Anton has 15 years of extensive experience in design, rollout, operation, and optimization of large-scale service providers and converged networks, focusing on IP/MPLS, BGP, network security, and data center Clos fabrics built using EVPN/VXLAN. He also has several years of full-stack software development experience for network management and automation.

Anton holds a B.S. in telecommunications and an M.S. in information security from Belarusian State University of Informatics and Radio Electronics. You can find him actively blogging about network automation and running online training at Karneliuk.com. Anton lives with his wife in London.

Vinit Jain, CCIE No. 22854 (R&S, SP, Security & DC), is a Network Development Engineer at Amazon, managing the Amazon network backbone operations team. Previously, he worked as a technical leader with the Cisco Technical Assistance Center (TAC), providing escalation support in routing and data center technologies. Vinit is a speaker at various networking forums, including Cisco Live! events. He has co-authored several Cisco Press titles, such as *Troubleshooting BGP*, and *Troubleshooting Cisco Nexus Switches and NX-OS*, *LISP Network Deployment and Troubleshooting*, and has authored and co-authored several video courses, including *BGP Troubleshooting*, the *CCNP DCCOR Complete* video course, and the *CCNP ENCOR Complete* video course. In addition to his CCIEs, Vinit holds multiple certifications related to programming and databases. Vinit graduated from Delhi University in mathematics and earned a master's in information technology from Kuvempu University in India. Vinit can be found on Twitter as @VinuGenie.

About the Technical Reviewers

Jeff Tantsura, CCIE No. 11416 (R&S), has been in the networking space for over 25 years and has authored and contributed to many RFCs and patents and worked in both service provider and vendor environments.

He is co-chair of IETF Routing Working Group, chartered to work on new network architectures and technologies, including protocol-independent YANG models and next-generation routing protocols. He is also the co-chair of the RIFT (Routing in Fat Trees) Working Group, chartered to work on a new routing protocol that specifically addresses fat tree topologies typically seen in the data center environment.

Jeff serves on the Internet Architecture Board (IAB). His focus has been on 5G transport and integration with RAN, IoT, MEC, low-latency networking, and data modeling. He's also a board member of San Francisco Bay Area ISOC chapter.

Jeff is Head of Networking Strategy at Apstra, a leader in intent networking, where he defines networking strategy and technologies.

Jeff also holds the certification Ericsson Certified Expert IP Networking.

Jeff lives in Palo Alto, California, with his wife and youngest child.

Viktor Osipchuk, CCIE No. 38256 (R&S, SP), is a Senior Network Engineer at Google, focusing on automation and improving one of the largest production networks in the world. Before joining Google, Viktor spent time at DigitalOcean and Equinix, helping to architect and run their worldwide infrastructures. Viktor spent many years at Cisco, supporting customers and focusing on automation, telemetry, data models, and APIs for large-scale web and service provider deployments. Viktor has around 15 years of diverse network experience, an M.S. in telecommunications, and associated industry certifications.

Dedications

Khaled Abuelenain: To my mother, the dearest person to my heart, who invested all the years of her life so I can be who I am today. I owe you more than any words can express. To my father, my role model, who always led by example and showed me the real meaning of work ethic. Nothing I do or say will ever be enough to thank you both.

And to the love of my life, my soulmate, and my better half, Mai, for letting me work and write while you take care of, literally, everything else. This book would not have happened if not for your phenomenal support, patience and love. I will forever be grateful for the blessing of having you in my life.

Jeff Doyle: I would like to dedicate this book to my large and growing herd of grandchildren: Claire, Samuel, Caroline, Elsie, and Amelia. While they are far too young to comprehend or care about the contents of this book, perhaps someday they will look at it and appreciate that Grampa is more than a nice old man and itinerant babysitter.

Anton Karneliuk: I dedicate this book to my family, which has tremendously supported me during the writing process. First of all, many thanks to my amazing wife, Julia, who took on the huge burden of sorting out many things for our lives, allowing me to concentrate on the book. You acted as a navigation star during this journey, and you are my beauty. I'd also like to thank my parents and brother for me helping me form the habit of working hard and completing the tasks I've committed to, no matter how badly I want to drop them.

Vinit Jain: I would like to dedicate this book to the woman who has been a great influence and inspiration in my life: Sonal Sethia (*Sonpari*). You are one of the most brilliant, talented, courageous, and humble people I have ever known. You have always inspired me to push myself beyond what I thought I was capable of. You have been there for me during difficult times and believed in me when even I did not. You are my rock. This is a small token of my appreciation, gratitude, and love for you. I am really glad to have found my best friend in you and know that I will always be there for you.

Acknowledgments

Khaled: First and foremost, I would like to thank Jeff Doyle, my co-author, mentor, and friend, for getting me started with writing, and for his continuous assistance and guidance. Jeff has played a fundamental role in my professional life as well as in the lives of many other network engineers; he probably doesn't realize the magnitude of this role! Despite all that he has done for this industry and the network engineering community, Jeff remains one of the most humble and amiable human beings I have ever come across. Thank you, Jeff, I owe you a lot!

I am grateful to Anton and Vinit for agreeing to work with me on this project. It has been challenging at times, but it has been seriously fun most of the time.

I would also like to thank Jeff Tantsura and Viktor Osipchuk for their thorough technical reviews and feedback. I bothered Viktor very frequently with discussions and questions over email, and never once did he fail to reply and add a ton of value!

I especially want to thank Brett Bartow and Eleanor Bru for their immense support and phenomenal patience. And I'm grateful to Mandie Frank, Kitty Wilson, and everyone else at Cisco Press who worked hard to get this book out to the light. Such an amazing team.

Jeff Doyle: I would like to express my thanks to my friend Khaled Abuelenain for bringing me into this project, and thanks to Anton and Vinit for letting me be a part of their excellent work. Thanks also to Brett Bartow and everyone at Pearson, whom I've worked with for many years and continue to tell everyone who will listen that this is the best publishing team any technical writer could hope to work for. Finally, thanks to my wife Sara who, as always, puts up with my obsessiveness. When she sees me sitting and staring into nothingness she knows there's writing going on in my head.

Anton: Special thanks to Schalk Van Der Merwe, CTO, and Andrew Mutty, CIO, at The Hut Group for believing in me and giving me freedom and responsibility to implement my automation ideas in a high-scale data center environment. Thanks to all my brothers-in-arms from The Hut Group hosting networks for constantly sharing with me ideas about what use cases to focus on for automation. I want to thank my previous manager in Vodafone Group, Tamas Almasi, who supported me during my initial steps in network automation and helped me create an appropriate mindset during numerous testbeds and proofs of concept. Last but not least, I'm very grateful to Khaled Abuelenain for his invitation to co-author this book and the whole author and technical reviewer team; it was a pleasure to work with you.

Vinit: A special thanks to Khaled for asking me to co-author this book and for being amazingly patient and supportive of me as I faced challenges during this project. I would like to thank Jeff Doyle and Anton Karneliuk for their amazing collaboration on this project. I learned a lot from all of you guys and look forward to working with all of you in the future.

I would also like to thank our technical reviewers, Jeff Tantsura and Viktor Osipchuk, and our editor, Eleanor Bru, for your in-depth verification of the content and insightful input to make this project a successful one.

This project wouldn't have been possible without the support of Brett Bartow and other members of the editorial team.

Contents at a Glance

Contents

Icons Used in This Book

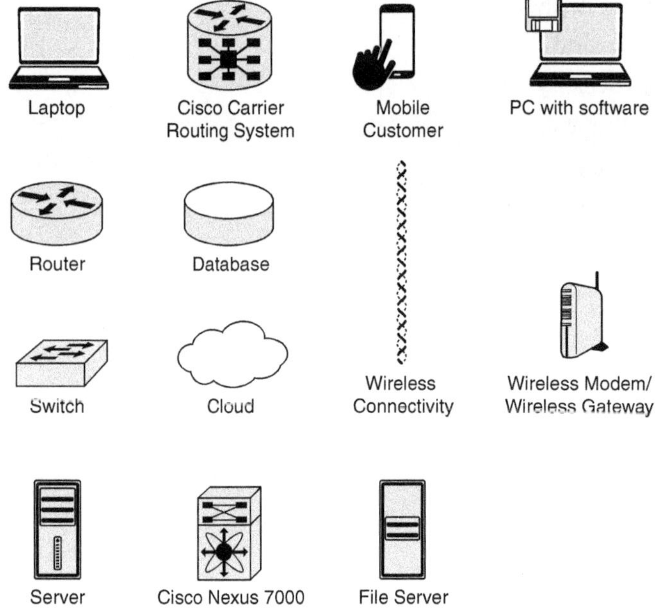

Command Syntax Conventions

The conventions used to present command syntax in this book are the same conventions used in Cisco's Command Reference. The Command Reference describes these conventions as follows:

- **Boldface** indicates commands and keywords that are entered literally as shown. In actual configuration examples and output (not general command syntax), boldface indicates commands that are manually input by the user (such as a **show** command).
- *Italics* indicate arguments for which you supply actual values.
- Vertical bars (|) separate alternative, mutually exclusive elements.
- Square brackets [ ] indicate optional elements.
- Braces { } indicate a required choice.
- Braces within brackets [{ }] indicate a required choice within an optional element.

Note This book covers multiple operating systems, and in each example, icons and router names indicate the OS that is being used. IOS and IOS XE use router names like R1 and R2 and are referenced by the IOS router icon. IOS XR routers use router names like XR1 and XR2 are referenced by the IOS XR router icon.

Introduction

For more than three decades, network management has been entirely based on the command-line interface (CLI) and legacy protocols such as SNMP. These protocols and methods are severely limited. The CLI, for example, is vendor specific, lacks a unified data hierarchy (sometimes even for platforms from the same vendor), and was designed primarily as a human interface. SNMP suffers major scaling problems, is not fit for writing configuration to devices, and overall, is very complex to implement and customize.

In essence, automation aims at offloading as much work from humans as possible and delegating that work to machines. But with the aforementioned legacy interfaces and protocols, machine-to-machine communication is neither effective nor efficient; and at times, close to impossible.

Moreover, device configuration and operational data have traditionally lacked a proper hierarchy and failed to follow a data model. In addition, network management workflows have always been far from mature, compared to software development workflows in terms of versioning, collaboration, testing, and automated deployments.

Enter network programmability. Programmability revolves around programmable interfaces, commonly referred to as application programming interfaces (APIs). APIs are interfaces that are designed primarily to be used for machine-to-machine communication. A Python program accessing a network router to retrieve or push configuration, without human intervention, is an example of a machine-to-machine interaction. Contrast this with the CLI, where a human needs to manually enter commands on a device and then visually inspect the output.

Network equipment vendors (for both physical and virtual equipment) are placing ever-increasing emphasis on the importance of managing their equipment using programmable interfaces, and Cisco is at the forefront of this new world. This new approach to managing a network provides several benefits over legacy methods, including the following:

- Normalizing the interface for interaction with network platforms by abstracting communication with these platforms and breaking the dependency of this communication on specific network OS scripting languages (for example, NX-OS, IOS XR, and Junos OS)
- Providing new methods of interacting with network platforms and, in the process, enabling and aligning with new technologies and architectures, such as SDN, NFV, and cloud
- Harnessing the power of programming to automate manual tasks and perform repetitive tasks efficiently
- Enabling rapid infrastructure and service deployment by using workflows for service provisioning
- Increasing the reliability of the network configuration process by leveraging error checking, validation, and rollback and minimizing human involvement in the configuration process

- Using common software development tools and techniques for network configuration management, such as software development methodologies, versioning, staging, collaboration, testing, and continuous integration/continuous delivery

This book covers all the major programmable interfaces used in the market today for network management. The book discusses the protocols, tools, techniques, and technologies on which network programmability is based. Programming, operating systems, and APIs are not new technologies. However, programmable interfaces on network platforms, and using these programmable interfaces to fully operate and maintain a network, along with the culture accompanying these new methods and protocols, may be (relatively) new. This book explains, in detail, all the major components of this new ecosystem.

Goals and Methods of This Book

This is a "fundamentals" book aimed at transitioning network engineers from a legacy network-based mindset to a software-based (and associated technologies) mindset. A book covering fundamentals generally struggles to cover as many subjects as possible with just enough detail. The fine balance between breadth and depth is challenging, but this book handles this challenge very well.

This book introduces the emerging network programmability and automation ecosystem based on programmable interfaces. It covers each protocol individually, in some significant detail, using the relevant RFCs as guiding documents. Protocol workflows, messages, and other protocol nuances tend to be dry, and at times boring, so to keep things interesting, practical examples are given wherever possible and relevant. You, the reader, can follow and implement these examples on your machine, which can be as simple as a Linux virtual machine with Python Version 3.x installed, and free tools to work with APIs, such as Postman and cURL. This book makes heavy use of the Cisco DevNet sandboxes, so in the majority of cases, you do not need a home lab to test and experiment with physical equipment.

A whole section of the book is dedicated to putting the knowledge and skills learned throughout the book to good use. One chapter covers programming Cisco platforms and another covers programming non-Cisco platforms. A third chapter in that same section is dedicated exclusively to Ansible. This book provides an abundance of hands-on practice.

The last chapter provides a way forward, discussing tools and technologies that you might want to explore after you are done with this book.

Who This Book Is For

This book is meant for the following individuals and roles, among others:

- Network architects and engineers who want to integrate programmability into their network designs
- NOC engineers monitoring and operating programmable networks or those who rely on network management systems that utilize programmability protocols

- Network engineers designing, implementing, and deploying new network services
- Software engineers or programmers developing applications for network management systems
- Network and software engineers working with networks or systems involving SDN, NFV, or cloud technologies
- Network engineers pursuing their Cisco DevNet certifications

Whether you are an expert network engineer with no prior programming experience or knowledge, or a software engineer looking to utilize your expertise in the network automation domain, after reading this book, you will fully understand the most commonly used protocols, tools, technologies, and techniques related to the subject, and you will be capable of effectively using the newly learned material to design, implement, and operate full-fledged programmable networks and the associated network automation systems.

How This Book Is Organized

This book covers the information you need to transition from having a focus on networking technology to focusing on software and network programmability. This book covers six main focus areas:

- Operating systems: Linux
- Software development: Python
- Transport: HTTP, REST, and SSH
- Encoding: XML, JSON, and YAML
- Modeling: YANG
- Protocols: NETCONF, RESTCONF, gRPC, and service provider programmability
- Practical programmability: Cisco platforms, non-Cisco platforms, and Ansible

Each chapter in this book either explicitly covers one of these focus areas or prepares you for one of them. Special consideration has been given to the ordering of topics to minimize forward referencing. Following an introduction to the programmability landscape, Linux is covered first because to get anything done in network programmability, you will almost always find yourself working with Linux. The book next covers Python because the vast majority of the rest of the book includes coverage of Python in the context of working with various protocols. The following chapters present an organic flow of topics: transport, encoding, modeling, and the protocols that build on all the previous sections. For example, understanding NETCONF requires you to understand SSH, XML, and YANG, and understanding RESTCONF requires that you understand HTTP, XML/JSON, and YANG. Both NETCONF and RESTCONF require knowledge of Python, most likely running on a Linux machine.

How This Book Is Structured

The book is organized into nine parts, described in the following sections.

PART I, "Introduction"

Chapter 1, "The Network Programmability and Automation Ecosystem": This chapter introduces the concepts and defines the terms that are necessary to understand the protocols and technologies covered in the following chapters. It also introduces the network programmability stack and explores the different components of the stack that constitute a typical network programmability and automation toolbox.

PART II, "Linux"

Chapter 2, "Linux Fundamentals": Linux is the predominant operating system used for running software for network programmability and automation. Linux is also the underlying operating system for the vast majority of network device software, such as IOS XR, NX-OS, and Cumulus Linux. Therefore, to be able to effectively work with programmable devices, it is of paramount importance to master the fundamentals of Linux. This chapter introduces Linux, including its architecture and boot process, and covers the basics of working with Linux through the Bash shell, such as working with files and directories, redirecting input and output, performing system maintenance, and installing software.

Chapter 3, "Linux Storage, Security, and Networks": This chapter builds on Chapter 2 and covers more advanced Linux topics. It starts with storage on Linux systems and the Linux Logical Volume Manager. It then covers Linux user, group, file, and system security. Finally, it explains three different methods to manage networking in Linux; the **ip** utility, the NetworkManager service, and network configuration files.

Chapter 4, "Linux Scripting": This chapter builds on Chapters 2 and 3 and covers Linux scripting using the Bash shell. The chapter introduces the **grep**, **awk**, and **sed** utilities and covers the syntax and semantics of Bash scripting. The chapter covers comments, input and output, variables and arrays, expansion, operations and comparisons, how to execute system commands from a Bash script, conditional statements, loops, and functions. It also touches on the Expect programming language.

PART III, "Python"

Chapter 5, "Python Fundamentals": This chapter assumes no prior knowledge of programming and starts with an introduction to programming, covering some very important software and computer science concepts, including algorithms and object-oriented programming. It also discusses why programming is a foundational skill for learning network programmability and covers the fundamentals of the Python programming language, including installing Python Version 3.x, executing Python programs, input and output, data types, data structures, operators, conditional statements, loops, and functions.

Chapter 6, "Python Applications": This chapter builds on Chapter 5 and covers the application of Python to different domains. The chapter illustrates the use of Python for creating web applications using Django and Flask, for network programmability using NAPALM and Nornir, and for orchestration and machine learning. The chapter also covers some very important tools and protocols used in software development in general, such as Git, containers, Docker and virtual environments.

PART IV, "Transport"

Chapter 7, "HTTP and REST": This is one of the most important chapters in this book. It introduces the HTTP protocol and the REST architectural framework, as well as the relationship between them. This chapter covers HTTP connections based on TCP. It also covers the anatomy of HTTP messages and dives into the details of HTTP request methods and response status codes. It also provides a comprehensive explanation of the most common header fields. The chapter discusses the syntax rules that govern the use of URIs and then walks through working with HTTP, using tools such as Postman, cURL, and Python libraries, such as the **requests** library.

Chapter 8, "Advanced HTTP": Building on Chapter 7, this chapter moves to more advanced HTTP topics, including HTTP authentication and how state can be maintained over HTTP connections by using cookies. This chapter provides a primer on cryptography for engineers who know nothing on the subject and builds on that to cover TLS, and HTTP over TLS (aka HTTPS). It also provides a glimpse into HTTP/2 and HTTP/3, and the enhancements introduced by these newer versions of HTTP.

Chapter 9, "SSH": Despite being a rather traditional protocol, SSH is still an integral component of the programmability stack. SSH is still one of the most widely used protocols, and having a firm understanding of the protocol is crucial. This chapter discusses the three sub-protocols that constitute SSH and cover the lifecycle of an SSH connection: the SSH Transport Layer Protocol, User Authentication Protocol, and Connection Protocol. It also discusses how to set up SSH on Linux systems as well as how to work with SSH on the three major network operating system: IOS XR, IOS XE, and NX-OS. Finally, it covers SFTP, which is a version of FTP based on SSH.

PART V, "Encoding"

Chapter 10, "XML": This chapter covers XML, the first of three encoding protocols covered in this book. XML is the oldest of the three protocols and is probably the most sophisticated. This chapter describes the general structure of an XML document as well as XML elements, attributes, comments, and namespaces. It also covers advanced XML topics such as creating document templates using DTD and XML-based schemas using XSD, and it compares the two. This chapter also covers XPath, XSLT, and working with XML using Python.

Chapter 11, "JSON": JSON is less sophisticated, newer, and more human-readable than XML, and it is therefore a little more popular that XML. This chapter covers JSON data formats and data types, as well as the general format of a JSON-encoded document. The chapter also covers JSON Schema Definition (JSD) for data validation and how JSD coexists with YANG.

Chapter 12, "YAML": YAML is frequently described as a superset of JSON. YAML is slightly more human-readable than JSON, but data encoded in YAML tends to be significantly lengthier than its JSON-encoded counterpart. YAML is a very popular encoding format and is required for effective use of tools such as Ansible. This chapter covers the differences between XML, JSON, and YAML and discusses the structure of a YAML document. It also explains collections, scalers, tags, and anchors. Finally, the chapter discusses working with YAML in Python.

PART VI, "Modeling"

Chapter 13, "YANG": At the heart of the new paradigm of network programmability is data modeling. This is a very important chapter that covers both generic modeling and the YANG modeling language. This chapter starts with a data modeling primer, explaining what a data model is and why it is important to have data models. Then it explains the structure of a data model. This chapter describes the different node types in YANG and their place in a data model hierarchy. It also delves into more advanced topics, such as augmentations and deviations in YANG. It describes the difference between open-standard and vendor-specific YANG models and where to get each type. Finally, the chapter covers a number of tools for working with YANG modules, including **pyang** and **pyangbind**.

PART VII, "Protocols"

Chapter 14, "NETCONF and RESTCONF": NETCONF was the first protocol developed to replace SNMP. RESTCONF was developed later and is commonly referred to as the RESTful version of NETCONF. Building on earlier chapters, this chapter takes a deep dive into both NETCONF and RESTCONF. The chapter covers the protocol architecture as well as the transport, message, operations, and content layers of each of the two protocols. It also covers working with these protocols using Python.

Chapter 15, "gRPC, Protobuf, and gNMI": The gRPC protocol was initially developed by Google for network programmability that borrows its operational concepts from the communications models of distributed applications. This chapter provides an overview of the motivation that drove the development of gRPC. It covers the communication flow of gRPC and protocol buffers (Protobuf) used to serialize data for gRPC communications. The chapter also shows how to work with gRPC using Python. The chapter then takes a deep dive into gNMI, a gRPC-based specification. Finally, the chapter shows how gRPC and gNMI are used to manage a Cisco IOS XE device.

Chapter 16, "Service Provider Programmability": Service providers face unique challenges due to the typical scale of their operations and the stringent KPIs that must be imposed on their networks, especially given the heated race to adopt 5G and associated technologies. This chapter discusses how such challenges influence the programmability and automation in service provider networks and provides in-depth coverage of Segment Routing, BGP-LS, and PCEP.

PART VIII, "Programmability Applications"

Chapter 17, "Programming Cisco Platforms": This chapter explores the programmability capabilities of several Cisco platforms, covering a wide range of technology domains. In addition, this chapter provides several practical examples and makes heavy use of Cisco's DevNet sandboxes. This chapter covers the programmability of IOS XE, IOS XR, NX-OS, Meraki, DNA Center, and Cisco's collaboration platforms, with a use case covering Webex Teams.

Chapter 18, "Programming Non-Cisco Platforms": This chapter covers the programmability of a number of non-Cisco platforms, such as the Cumulus Linux and Arista EOS platforms. This chapter shows that the knowledge and skills gained in the previous chapters are truly vendor neutral and global. In addition, this chapter shows that programmability using APIs does in fact abstract network configuration and management and breaks the dependency on vendor-specific CLIs.

Chapter 19, "Ansible": This chapter covers a very popular tool that has become synonymous with network automation: Ansible. As a matter of fact, Ansible is used in the application and compute automation domains as well. Ansible is a very simple, yet extremely powerful, automation tool that provides a not-so-steep learning curve, and hence a quick and effective entry point into network automation. This is quite a lengthy chapter that takes you from zero to hero in Ansible.

PART IX, "Looking Ahead"

Chapter 20, "Looking Ahead": This chapter builds on the foundation covered in the preceding chapters and discusses more advanced technologies and tools that you might want to explore to further your knowledge and skills related to network programmability and automation.

PART VIII Programmability Applications

Chapter 1

The Network Programmability and Automation Ecosystem

We all have that one story we tell on ourselves about some stupid mistake that brought down a network segment or even an entire network. Here's mine.

Thirty years ago, I was sitting in an office in Albuquerque, logged in to a router in Santa Fe, making some minor, supposedly nondisruptive modifications to the WAN interface. I wanted to see the changes I had made to the config, and I got as far as typing **sh** of the IOS **show** command before realizing I was still in interface config mode and needed to back out of it before entering the show command. But instead of backspacing or taking some other moderately intelligent action, I reflexively hit Enter.

The router, of course, interpreted **sh** as **shutdown**, did exactly what it was told to do, and shut down the WAN interface—the only interface by which the router was remotely accessible. There was no warning message. No "You don't want to do that, you idiot." The WAN interface just went down, leaving me no choice but to drive the 60 miles to Santa Fe to get physical access to the router, endure the sour looks of the workers in the office I had isolated, and turn the interface back up.

There are other stories. Like the time not too many years after The Santa Fe Incident when I mistyped a router ID, causing the OSPF network to have duplicate RIDs and consequently misbehave in some interesting ways. I think that one later became a troubleshooting exercise in one of my books.

My point is that configuration mistakes cause everything from annoying little link failures to catastrophic outages that take hours or days to correct and put your company on the front pages of the news. Depending on the study you read, human error accounts for 60% to 75% of network outages.

Every network outage has a price, whether it's the cost of a little branch office being offline for an hour or a multinational corporation suffering millions of dollars in lost revenue and damaged reputation.

Even when we're not making configuration mistakes, we *Homo sapiens* tend to be a troublesome and expensive feature of any network.

The cost of building a network (CAPEX) has always been outweighed by the cost of running that network (OPEX). And that operational cost is more than just paying people to configure, change, monitor, and troubleshoot the network. There are costs associated with direct human operations, such as the following:

- Configuration mistakes, large and small, which are exacerbated by working under pressure during network outages
- Failure to comply with configuration standards
- Failure to even *have* configuration standards
- Failure to see and correctly interpret network telemetry that indicates impending trouble
- Failure to maintain accurate network documentation
- Having network experts constantly in "firefighting mode" rather than performing steady-state network analysis and advanced planning

It's important to emphasize that network automation and programmability do not necessarily mean reducing the workforce, although workers are going to require some retraining. At its best, automation makes network staff more valuable by removing their daily "firefighting drills," allowing them to spend their time thinking about the 3- and 5-year network plan; evaluating new technologies, vendor solutions, and industry trends; analyzing whether the network can better serve company objectives; and just keeping a better eye on the big picture.

Pilots of Boeing 777s report that on an average flight, they spend just 7 minutes manually flying the plane. They are quick to emphasize, however, that while the autopilot is doing the flying, the pilots are still very much in control. They input instructions and expectations, and then supervise the automated processes. The autopilot performs the mundane physical tasks necessary to fly the plane, and it probably performs those tasks more quickly and accurately than most pilots do. The pilots, freed from the distractions of manual flying, apply their expertise to monitoring approaching weather and flight patterns, keeping an eye on the overall health of the plane, and even looking over the shoulder of the autopilot to be sure it is correctly executing the instructions they gave it. The pilot's role is expanded, not diminished.

The pilot tells the airplane what he wants (that is, programming), and the plane does what it is told (that is, automation). We don't have this level of artificial intelligence and machine learning in our networks yet, but that's where we're headed.

First, a Few Definitions

There's a fair amount of confusion around the concepts discussed in this book. Is automation just a part of network management? Are automation and programmability the same thing? How does orchestration fit in? And does SDN really stand for "Still Does Nothing"?

Network Management

The terms *automation*, *programmability*, *orchestration*, *virtualization*, *SDN*, and *intent*—all of which are defined in this section—apply, in one way or another, to network management. So let's start by defining that:

Network management is how you make a network meet whatever expectations you have of it.

This is about as simple a definition that you can get, but behind this one sentence is arrayed an extensive repository of systems, processes, methodologies, rules, and standards pertaining to the management of all aspects of the network.

One framework for sorting out all the aspects of a network to be managed is FCAPS, which represents the following areas:

- Fault management
- Configuration management
- Accounting management
- Performance management
- Security management

It's doubtful that you would be reading this book if you didn't already know what these five areas represent. You probably also know that there are deep aspects of each. Configuration management, for example, covers not just provisioning but configuration standards and procedures, change management, configuration change tracking, reference designs, configuration file archiving, and the specialized systems to support all that stuff.

You probably also hear ITIL discussed regularly in the context of network management. ITIL, which stands for Information Technology Infrastructure Library, is a library of principles, processes, and procedures that support FCAPS but that also goes beyond that framework to apply to personnel and organizations, IT products, partners, suppliers, practices, and services that go into managing the network. Whereas FCAPS is system oriented, ITIL is services and governance oriented.

The outline of the ITIL 4 management practices provide an example of the complexity of ITIL:

- General management practices
  - Architecture management
  - Continual service improvement
  - Information security management

    - Knowledge management
    - Measurement and reporting
    - Organizational change management
    - Portfolio management
    - Project management
    - Relationship management
    - Risk management
    - Service financial management
    - Strategy management
    - Supplier management
    - Workforce and talent management
- Service management practices
    - Availability management
    - Business analysis
    - Capacity and performance management
    - Change control
    - Incident management
    - IT asset management
    - Monitoring and event management
    - Problem management
    - Release management
    - Service catalog management
    - Service configuration management
    - Service continuity management
    - Service design
    - Service desk
    - Service level management
    - Service request management
    - Service validation and testing

- Technical management practices
  - Deployment management
  - Infrastructure and platform management
  - Software development and management

This is quite a list, and it covers only the top-level topics. Fortunately for our definitions, we don't have to go into all of them. I just wanted to show you how extensive and formalized network management can be. For the purposes of this book we don't need to go into the highly structured, highly detailed ITIL specifications. Most of the topics in this book support the simpler FCAPS framework; in fact, most topics in the book support configuration management.

Managing a network system means interacting with the system in some way. It usually involves the following:

- Accessing the CLI via SSH (don't use Telnet!) or directly via a console port for configuration, monitoring, and troubleshooting
- Monitoring (and sometimes changing) the system through Simple Network Management Protocol (SNMP) agents and Management Information Bases (MIBs)
- Collecting system logs via syslog
- Collecting traffic flow statistics with NetFlow or IP Flow Information Export (IPFIX)
- Sending information to and extracting information from network devices through Application Programming Interfaces (APIs), whether the APIs are RESTful (such as RESTCONF) or not (such as NETCONF or gRPC)

Automation

Automation, very simply, means using software to perform a task you would otherwise do manually. And automation is nothing new or unfamiliar to you. Routing protocols, for example, are automation programs that save you the work of manually entering routes at every network node. DNS is an automation program that saves you from having to look up the IP address of any destination you want to talk to. You get the point.

Automation software might be built into a network node, might be a purchased software platform, or might be a program or script you create yourself.

That last bit -- creating your own automation routines -- is what this book is all about: It gives you the fundamentals to be able to understand and operate the underlying protocols used by products, as well as utilize those protocols in your scripts and programs.

Besides the obvious benefit of making life easier, automation provides the following advantages:

- Fast rollout of network changes
- Relief from performing routine repetitive tasks
- Consistent, reliable, tested, standards-compliant system changes
- Reduced human errors and network misconfigurations
- Better integration with change control policies
- Better network documentation and change analysis

Out of all of these advantages, you might be inclined to choose speed of deployment as the most important. Being able to deploy a network change "with a push of a button" definitely is less expensive than visiting each network node and manually reconfiguring. The time savings increase dramatically as the number of affected nodes increases.

However, consistent and reliable network changes, along with reduced human error (that is, accuracy) are of even greater benefit than speed of deployment. The significance of accuracy becomes more obvious as the number of times a change has to be implemented increases. Implementing a network change on five devices can be done fairly accurately using primitive tools and elevated vigilance. This may not be possible when implementing the same change on 1000 devices. Speed saves operational expense during deployment, but accuracy provides cumulative benefits over the life of the network.

Orchestration

Orchestration, in the traditional musical sense, is the composition of musical parts for a diversity of instruments. When the instrumentalists play their individual parts together—usually under the direction of a conductor—you get Beethoven's Fifth or the theme to *Lion of the Desert* or *Lawrence of Arabia*.

Orchestration in the IT sense is very much the same: Individual elements work together, following their own instructions, to create a useful service or set of services. For example, the deployment of a certain application in a data center is likely to require compute, storage, security, and network resources. Orchestration enables you to coordinate and deploy all of those resources to accomplish one goal.

Does this sound like automation? Well, yes and no. It's true that the differences between automation and orchestration can sometimes get fuzzy, but here's the difference:

- *Automation* is the performance of a single task, such as a configuration change across a set of switches or routers or the deployment of a virtual machine on a server, without manual (human) intervention.
- *Orchestration* is the coordination of many automated tasks, in a specific sequence, across disparate systems to accomplish a single objective. Another term for this is *workflow*.

So, automation performs individual tasks, and orchestration automates workflows. Both automation and orchestration save time and reduce human error.

A wealth of orchestration tools are available on the market, including the following:

- VMware vRealize Orchestrator, for VMWare environments
- OpenStack Heat, for OpenStack
- Google Cloud Composer, for (you guessed it) orchestrating Google Cloud
- Cisco Network Services Orchestrator (NSO), which, as the name implies, focuses on network services
- RedHat Ansible, which is usually used as a simple automation tool but can also perform some workflow automation
- Kubernetes, a specialized platform for orchestrating containerized workloads and services

Programmability

It's an understandable misconception that programmability is a part of automation. After all, most automation does not work unless you give it operating parameters. A routing protocol, for instance, doesn't do anything unless you tell it what interfaces to run on, perhaps what neighbors to negotiate adjacencies with, and what authentication factors to use.

Is network programmability, then, just providing instructions to automation software? No, that's configuration.

Programmability is the ability to customize your network to your own standards, policies, and practices. Programmability enables you to operate your network and the services it supports as a complete entity, built to support the specifics of your business. In this age in which most businesses depend on their applications and are built around their networks, that's huge.

Isn't that the way it should always have been? Your network should comply to your requirements; you should not have to adjust your requirements to comply to your network. Once you can customize your network to your own standards, you have the power to innovate, to quickly adapt to competitive challenges, and to create advantages over your competitors. These are all far more important advantages than just operational savings, reduced downtime, and faster problem remediation. (Although you get all that, too.)

But programmability, as a technical marketing term today, has a slightly different meaning. Programmability, used in this context, is the ability to monitor devices, retrieve data, and configure devices through a *programmable interface*, which is a software interface to your device through which other software can speak with your device. This interface is formally known as an *Application Programming Interface* (*API*).

What is the difference between a legacy interface such as the CLI and an API? For one, a CLI was created with a human operator in mind. A human types commands into the terminal and receives output to the screen. On the other hand, an API is used by other software, such as automation products or custom Python scripts to speak with a device without any human interaction, apart from writing the Python script itself or configuring the device parameters on that automation product.

APIs are covered in a lot of detail in this book because they are a foundational building block for any software-to-software interaction. Instead of reading an exhaustive comparison between legacy interfaces and APIs, you will see for yourself the major advantages of interacting with your network through programmable interfaces as you progress through the chapters of this book.

Virtualization and Abstraction

Virtualization is one of those words you've known and understood throughout your career. First there are those *V* acronyms: VPN, VPLS, VLAN, VXLAN, VC, VM, VRF, VTEP, OTV, NVE, VSAN, and more. There is often virtualization even when the word itself isn't used. TCP, for example, provides a virtual point-to-point connection over connectionless IP by using handshaking, sequence numbers, and acknowledgments.

Virtualization is the creation of a service that behaves like a physical service but is not. We use virtualization to share resources, such as consolidating multiple data networks over a shared MPLS cloud, communicating routing tables (VRFs) for multiple isolated networks and security zones over a shared MP-BGP core, implementing multiple VLANs on one physical LAN, or creating virtualized servers on a single physical server. The motivation might be to create a bunch of different services when you have only one physical resource to work with, or it might be to more efficiently use that resource by divvying it up among multiple users, each of whom gets the impression that they are the only one using the resource.

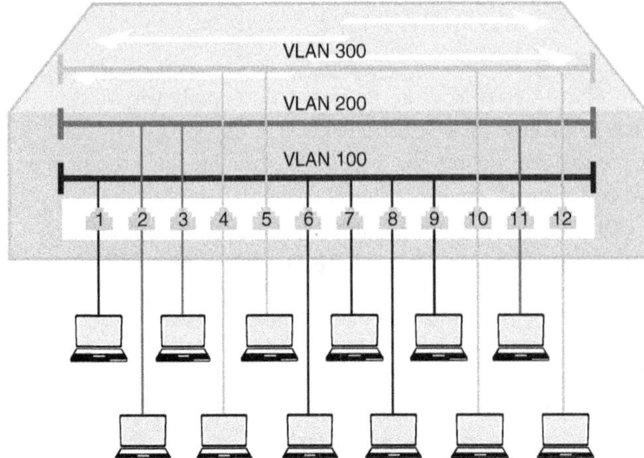

Figure 1-1 *VLANs Connected to a Switch Are Not Aware of Each Other*

Boiling all this down to a simple definition, virtualization is a software-only or software-defined service built on top of one or more hardware devices. In the case of a virtualized network, the network might look quite different from the underlying physical network. For example, in Figure 1-1, from the individual perspectives of VLANs 100, 200, and 300, each is connected to a single switch, and none is aware of the other two VLANs. In Figure 1-2, the Layer 3 VPNs Red, Green, and Blue are built on top of a single MPLS infrastructure but are aware only of their own VPN peers.

And here are a couple more definitions related to the networks pictured here: An *overlay* network is a software-defined network running over a physical *underlay* network. You'll encounter overlays and underlays particularly in data center networking.

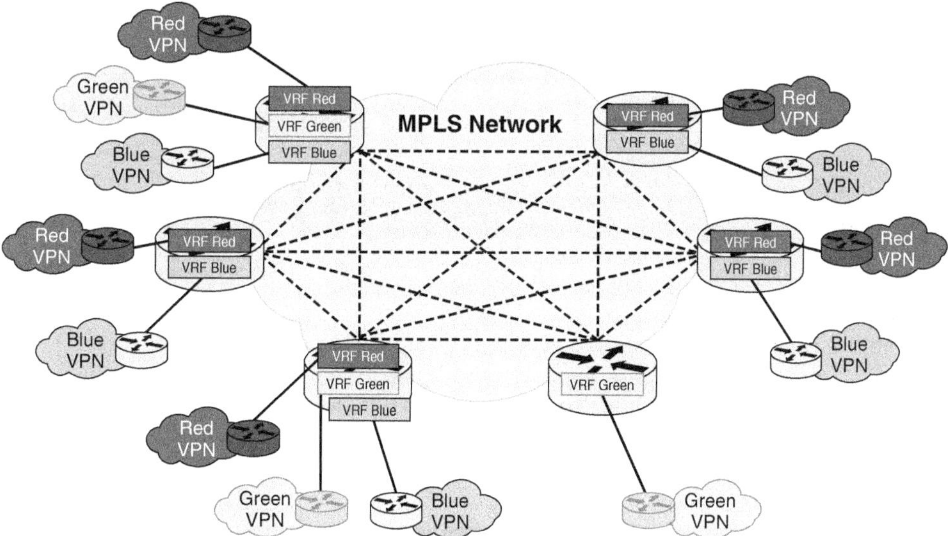

Figure 1-2 *VPNs Built on a Single MPLS Infrastructure That Are Aware Only of Their Own VPN Peers*

Abstraction is a term you may not understand clearly, although you have certainly heard it used in the context of *network abstractions*. You also likely use the concept often when you're whiteboarding some network, and you draw a cloud to represent the Internet, an MPLS core, or some other part of a network, where you just mean that packets go in at one edge and come out at some other edge.

Abstraction goes hand-in-hand with virtualization because we build virtualized services on top of abstractions. The "whiteboard cloud" example illustrates this: Our whiteboard discussion is focused on the details of ingress and egress packet flows, not on the magic that happens in the cloud to get the packets to the right place.

Virtual machines are, for instance, built on an abstraction of the underlying physical server (see Figure 1-3). The server abstraction is the CPU, storage, memory, and I/O allotted to the VM rather than the server itself.

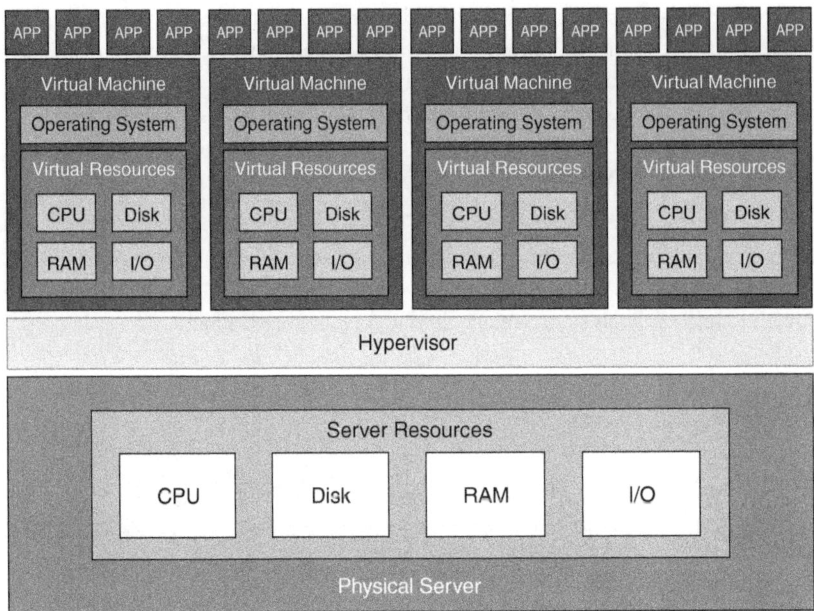

Figure 1-3 *A Server Abstracted into the Components Allotted to Each VM*

Another example, sticking with servers, is a container platform such as Docker (see Figure 1-4), which packages up application code and its dependencies into containers that are isolated from the underlying server hardware. The advantage of both VMs and containerized applications is that they can be deployed, changed, and moved independently of the physical infrastructure.

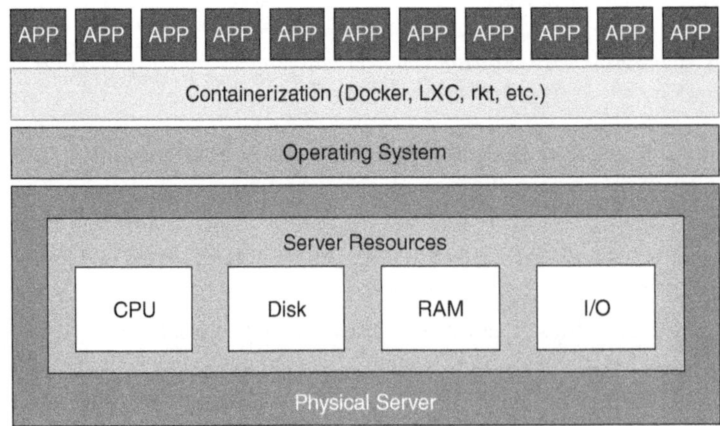

Figure 1-4 *Using Containers to Abstract Away the Underlying Server and Operating System for Individual Applications*

Network abstraction is the same idea but with more elements. By adding an "abstraction layer"—or abstracting away the network—you focus only on the virtualized network: adding, changing, and removing services independently of the network infrastructure (see Figure 1-5). Just as a VM uses some portion of the actual server resources, virtual network services use some portion of the physical network resources. Network abstraction can also allow you to change infrastructure elements without changing the virtual network.

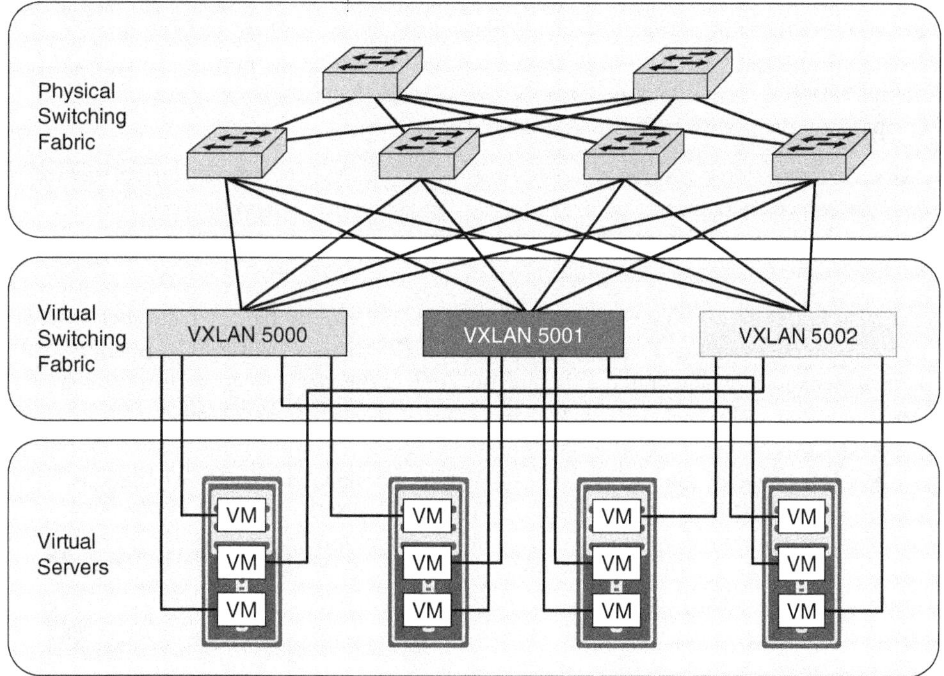

Figure 1-5 *Data Center Infrastructure Abstracted Away by VXLAN*

A network abstraction layer is essential for efficient automation and programmability because you want to be able to control your network independently of the specifics of vendors and operating systems. One of the things you will learn in Chapter 6, "Python Applications," for example, is how to use a Python library called NAPALM (Network Automation and Programmability Abstraction Layer with Multivendor Support). In Chapter 13, "YANG," you'll learn about YANG, a network modeling language (that is, a language for specifying a model, or an abstraction, of the network).

The abstraction, or model, of the network serves as a *single source of truth* for your automation and orchestration. Do you have enough resources for a service that is about to be deployed? What's the available bandwidth? How will RIBs and FIBs change, and is there enough memory capacity to support the changes? What effect will the added service have on existing Layer 2 or Layer 3 forwarding behavior?

Without a single source of truth, the "intelligent" part of your automation or orchestration must reach out and touch every element in the network to gather the information it needs for pre-deployment verification. Each element is its own source of truth and might or might not express its truth consistently with other elements—especially in multivendor networks. A single source of truth, if built properly, continuously collects network state and telemetry to provide a real-time, accurate, and relevant model of the network. Every service you want to deploy can then be verified against this abstraction before it is deployed, increasing your confidence and decreasing failures.

But don't confuse this perspective of a single source of truth with a Configuration Management Database (CMDB), which is a repository of what the network state *should* be and, therefore, is not updated from the live network. Instead, the live network state is compared to the CMDB to verify its compliance.

Network abstraction gives rise to *Network as Code* (NaC) or the broader *Infrastructure as Code*, which encompasses network, storage, and compute. NaC is the code that ties together network abstraction, virtualization, programming, and automation to create an intelligent interface to your network.

NaC also brings networking into the DevOps realm and enables the application of proven software practices such as Continuous Integration/Continuous Delivery/Continuous Deployment (CI/CD), illustrated in Figure 1-6. Among the many tools you can use for developing NaC is RedHat Ansible, which is covered in Chapter 19, "Ansible."

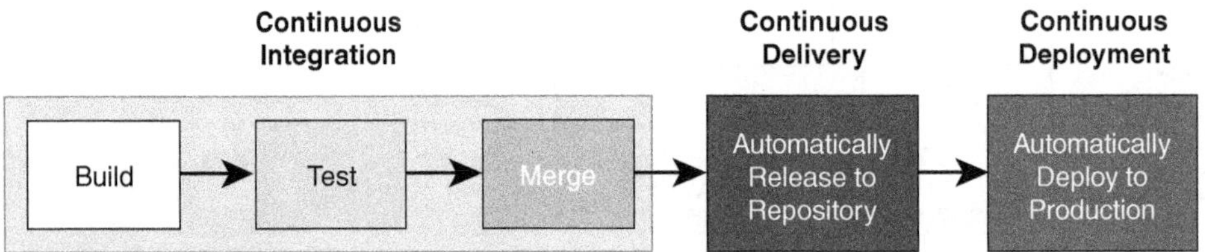

Figure 1-6 *CI/CD*

With your new network code developed, tested, and merged with existing code and passed to the virtualization layer, the last bit of the workflow is to translate the generalized code into verified, vendor- and operating system–specific configurations and push them to physical network elements. Interactive scripts using languages such as Expect, TCL, and Perl were—and sometimes still are—used to log in to the network devices and configure them; these scripts just automate the actions an operator would take to manually configure the device via the CLI.

These days, automation tools interact with networking devices through APIs, which are themselves abstractions of the underlying physical device. The difference is that the APIs reside on the individual devices and are specific to their own device. Automation software usually communicates with the APIs via eXtensible Markup Language (XML) or JavaScript Object Notation (JSON), covered in Chapters 10, "Extensible Markup Language (XML) and XML Schema Definition (XSD)," and 11, "JavaScript Object Notation (JSON) and JSON Schema Definition (JSD)." You'll find that even the CLIs of modern routers and switches are actually applications running on top of the local APIs rather than direct interfaces to the operating systems.

Software-Defined Networking

Software-Defined Networking (SDN) isn't covered in this book, but all this discussion of automation, programmability, network abstraction, and APIs merits at least a mention of SDN.

The "SDN 101" concept of the technology is that SDN is a centralized control plane on top of a distributed forwarding plane. Instead of a network of switches and routers that each have their own control planes, SDN "pops the control planes off" and centralizes them in one controller or a controller cluster. The control plane is greatly simplified because individual control planes no longer have to synchronize with each other to maintain consistent forwarding behavior.

This concept embodies much of what we've been discussing in the previous sections: separation of physical infrastructure from service workflows, a network abstraction layer, and a single source of truth. Incorporating everything we've previously discussed provides a more refined definition of SDN:

SDN is a conceptual framework in which networks are treated as abstractions and are controlled programmatically, with minimal direct touch of individual network components.

This definition still adheres to the idea of centralized control, but it encompasses a wider set of SDN solutions, such as SD-WAN, that virtualizes the Wide-Area Network and places it under centralized control and subject to vendor SDN solutions such as Cisco's Application Centric Infrastructure (ACI) and VMware's NSX. The definition also takes in products such as Cisco's Network Services Orchestrator (NSO) that don't really fit in the more traditional definition of SDN.

Note ACI and NSX are often lumped together when giving examples of SDN solutions. While they do many of the same things, there are also some significant differences in how they work and what they do. For instance, ACI has a different approach to network abstraction from the approach described here.

Intent-Based Networking

Intent-Based Networking (IBN) is the next evolutionary step beyond SDN. Like SDN, it isn't covered in this book, but it is certainly based on the concepts described so far. Chapter 20, "Looking Ahead," has more to say about IBN; you'll also get some exposure to it in the discussion of Cisco DNA Intent APIs in Chapter 17, "Programming Cisco Platforms."

SDN gives you a centralized control point for your network, but you still have to provide most of the intelligence to deploy or change the underlay and overlay. In other words, you still have to tell the control plane how to do what you want it to do.

IBN adds an interpretive layer on top of the control plane that enables you to just express *what* you want—that is, your intent—and IBN translates your expressed intent into *how* to do it. Depending on the implementation, the IBN system either then pushes the developed configurations to a controller for deployment to the infrastructure or (more often) acts as the control plane itself and pushes configurations directly to the infrastructure.

Once your intent is configured (*intent fulfillment*), an IBN system uses closed-loop telemetry and state tables to monitor the network and ensure that it does not drift from your expressed intent (*intent assurance*).

IBN is still in its infancy as this book is being written, but it holds enormous potential for transforming the way we operate our networks. You'll learn more about this in Chapter 20.

Your Network Programmability and Automation Toolbox

All of the definitions so far in this chapter bring us to an important question: What tools does an adept network engineer and architect need to carry? And with that question we arrive at the entire purpose of this book.

One of the reasons for spending so much time on definitions is to be able to classify various tools and to understand the relationships among those classifications. Figure 1-7 offers one perspective on how you might classify tools within the functions discussed in the previous section and a number of functions not discussed in this chapter.

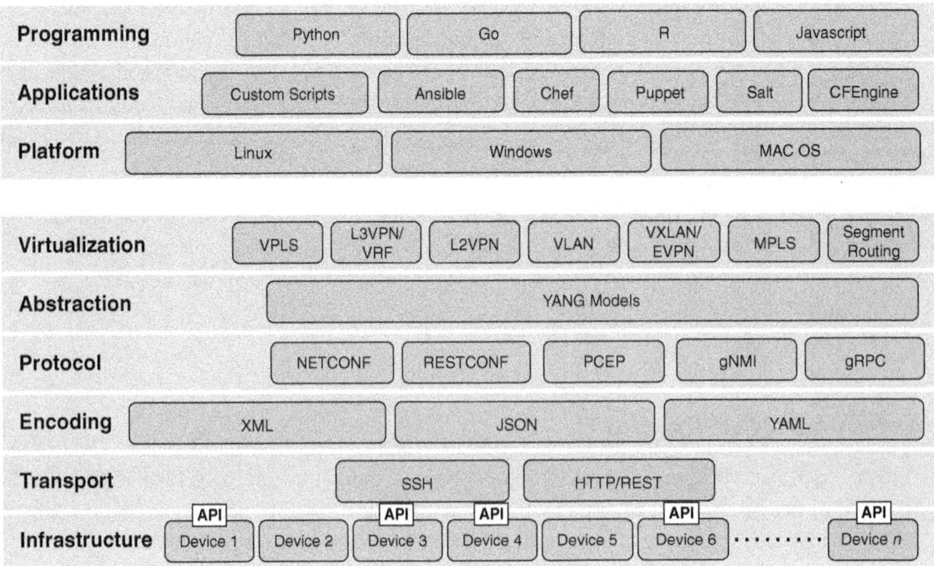

Figure 1-7 *The Network Programmability and Automation Ecosystem*

Before going further, it's important to note that Figure 1-7 is just *one* perspective. The order in which the Application, Automation, Platform, Virtualization, and Abstraction layers appear and how they interact can vary according to the network environment. What's more important are the tools available to you within the various layers.

It's also important to note that I've provided examples of more tools than are covered in this book. And that gets us to why the authors of this book have chosen the tools we have for you to learn.

Python

At the top of the programmability and automation ecosystem are programming languages. Python, Go, R, and JavaScript are given as examples in Figure 1-7. There are, of course, other programming languages that could be added here, C and C++ being the most prominent of them, although they are used more by people making their living at software development than by people making their living at other things—like networking—who need to be able to write programs and scripts to make their job easier. There are also a number of languages that we could add to the list, such as Perl, Expect, and TCL, that are still around to one degree or another but that have been overshadowed by newer, more powerful languages. Like Python.

Which brings us to why this book exclusively covers Python: It's by far the most widely used programming language for network automation, supporting a terrific number of libraries, modules, and packages specific to networking. Python is easy to learn, easy to use, and easy to debug, which fits the bill for networkers who just need to get their job done without having to become professional programmers. That said, Python is far from a "beginner" language. It's used extensively by companies such as Facebook, Netflix, Instagram, Reddit, Dropbox, and Spotify. Google software developers even have a saying: "Use Python where we can, C++ where we must."

Python is versatile, working equally well for scripting and as a glue language (for tying together modules written in other languages). It's also highly portable to different platforms. Once you know a little Python, you might even find yourself using it for quick little tasks such as running math calculations.

Finally, the more you use packaged automation products such as Ansible or Cisco ACI or interact with network devices through their APIs rather than directly with their CLI, the more you'll find Python to be an essential tool in your toolbox. Chapter 5, "Python Fundamentals," covers the basics of Python, and Chapter 6, "Python Applications," covers some useful libraries and tools that you will want to use when automating your network using Python.

Ansible

The next category of tools in your programmability and automation toolbox is applications. And first on that list are custom scripts. If you are already wielding a programming language such as Python to perform your job, you almost certainly have a collection of scripts that you use to automate everyday repetitive tasks. The more proficient you are, the more useful your scripts become. You'll learn how to script some of the boring parts of your job in this book.

Also in the applications category are a number of prebuilt automation platforms that you can either download for free or purchase: Ansible, Salt, Chef, Puppet, and CFEngine are examples, but there are many others. What they have in common is that they all began life as platforms for automating server management. If you're in a DevOps shop or any environment that orchestrates large numbers of end systems, your organization probably already has a favorite automation platform from this list.

We've chosen Ansible as the automation engine to familiarize you with in this book. Not only is Ansible open source and available for the very reasonable price of free, it is the most popular automation framework among networkers. It's easy to learn and integrates well as a Python module; in fact, Ansible is written in Python. Even if you end up using some other framework within your organization, having a grounding in Ansible is valuable and will give you a head start in understanding the concepts of any of this class of automation platforms. Ansible is covered in Chapter 19.

Linux

The next tool in the lineup is the platform on which you're doing your programming and running your automation. Not the hardware itself but the operating system on the hardware. Figure 1-7 lists the three most well-known operating systems: Linux, Windows, and macOS. For each of these, there are specific versions and distributions. For example, Linux includes Fedora, CentOS, SuSE, Ubuntu, and many others. Under Windows are the many incarnations of Windows Server, Windows 7, 8, 10, and so on. There are also platform-specific operating systems on which your automation applications can run (for example, Cisco IOS XE and NX-OS).

Recall the earlier comment about Figure 1-7 being just one perspective on how the programmability and automation ecosystem is organized. The Programming, Applications, and Platform tools might be running on a management server. They might be running on your laptop. One or more of the layers might be running directly on top of an infrastructure device or themselves might be part of the infrastructure. So, don't take Figure 1-7 as the only way the various elements of the ecosystem might interact with each other.

For network programmability and automation, you need to have a strong working knowledge of Linux. Three chapters in this book are dedicated to Linux: Chapter 2, "Linux Fundamentals," Chapter 3, "Linux Storage, Security, and Networks" and Chapter 4, "Linux Scripting." Here are just a few of the reasons Linux needs to be part of your toolbox:

- Linux is the most widely used operating system in IT environments, running more than two-thirds of the servers on the Internet. Linux is used as a server OS and also for the following:
  - Automation
  - Virtualization and containers

- Programming and scripting
- Software-Defined Networking
- Big Data systems
- Cloud computing

- Linux supports a huge number of built-in networking features.
- Linux supports a huge number of development tools, such as Git.
- Linux supports a number of automation tools and supporting capabilities, including almost everything shown in Figure 1-7.
- Python interpreters (along with many other languages) run natively on Linux, and many Linux distributions come with Python already built in.
- The vast majority of network operating systems today (such as Cisco NX-OS, IOS XE, and IOS XR) run as applications on top of some Linux distribution. Some entire cloud platforms, such as OpenStack, are supported in Linux. Even macOS is very Linux-like under the hood.
- Although there are paid versions of Linux, such as Red Hat Enterprise Linux (RHEL), what you're primarily paying for is support. Linux distributions for the most part are free to download and use.
- Because Linux is open source, with enormous development support worldwide, the source code is tremendously reliable, stable, and secure.

Virtualization

"Wait a minute," you might say, "the services you show for the virtualization layer run on individual infrastructure devices. What are they doing separated from the infrastructure?"

You're right, the services themselves run on network devices. But what all of them represent are different forms of virtualized overlays to the physical underlay network. Think of the overlay and the underlay as the top and bottom of your network data plane. Between them are sandwiched all the layers that implement the virtualized overlay onto the physical underlay.

YANG

You've already read about abstraction in this chapter: Abstraction means a generic model of your network. Hence, it is closely associated with the virtualization layer. In Figure 1-7, the only modeling language shown is YANG (Yet Another Next Generation). There are other data modeling languages, such as Unified Modeling Language (UML) and NEMO (NEtwork MOdeling), but YANG is used so extensively for network modeling that it is the only language shown Figure 1-7. You'll learn all about using YANG in Chapter 13.

Protocols

The protocols layer dictates a programmatic interface for accessing or building the abstraction of a network. Protocols may be RESTful, such as RESTCONF, or not, such as NETCONF or gRPC. A protocol uses a particular encoding for its messages. NETCONF, for example, uses XML only, whereas RESTCONF supports both XML and JSON. A protocol uses a particular transport to reach a device. RESTCONF uses HTTP, while NETCONF uses SSH. A protocol uses Remote Procedure Calls (RPCs) to install, manipulate, and delete configurations based on your model or retrieve configuration or operational data based on your model. Models are described in YANG. The protocols shown in Figure 1-7 are all covered in this book in Chapters 14, "NETCONF and RESTCONF," 15, "gRPC, Protobuf, and gNMI," and 16, "Service Provider Programmability."

Encoding the Protocols

The protocols themselves need a common language to communicate with the infrastructure, and this is the purpose of the encoding layer. eXtensible Markup Language (XML), JavaScript Object Notation (JSON), and Yet Another Markup Language (YAML) are the most common encoding languages in use for network automation and configuration management.

One of the major advantages of encoding languages is that they provide *structured* input and output to which data models easily map. Encoding languages provide data in a standard format, where a piece of data usually has a name or tag, and a value, where the tag is defined in a data model in a well-defined hierarchy. When you need to search for data, you search for the tag and then simply read the value. This paradigm maps well to programming data structures such as arrays. In contrast, with the ASCII format of typical network configuration files, you have to parse through text files and match strings to be able to find a piece of information. You'll learn about all three of the encoding languages in this book in Chapters 10, 11, and 12, "YAML."

Transporting the Protocols

After your protocol is encoded, it must be transported to the discrete network nodes. As a networker, you're certainly familiar with the concept of transporting data across a network—particularly via UDP and TCP. Secure Shell (SSH) and Hypertext Transfer Protocol (HTTP) are the most common transports for getting data to and from network devices.

Notice in Figure 1-7 that some devices at the infrastructure level have APIs, and some do not. As the name implies, an API exposes a programmatic interface to applications that need to communicate with the device, such as for automation, configuration management, telemetry collection, and security monitoring. An API becomes a communication socket from an application to the device.

Not all network devices have APIs; old devices often do not have them, for example. When a device does not have an API, an application needs to mimic a human operator by logging in through the CLI. In fact, most scripts 20 or more years ago did just this: Telnet or SSH to the device (20 years ago it was most likely Telnet) and then perform a series of commands in the device OS's expected syntax, look for the correct response, go to the next command, and so on. It was much like cutting and pasting a configuration to the command line.

CLI-centric scripts are a major operational headache for two reasons:

- **Unstructured data:** When you use a CLI, you know what you're looking for and can quickly adapt to variations in the data you see. Suppose, for example, that you need to see the administrative state of an interface. You type **show interface** or some similar command and read the output. Your mind is immensely adaptable and capable of quickly reading through the data and finding the data that you need. Scripts cannot do that as easily. They must parse the data they receive to find what they need.
- **Changing CLIs:** A script expects to find the information it needs in a certain place and in a certain format. If you upgrade your OS or (heaven forbid) change the device to a different OS altogether, the data might be presented differently, and your script has to be rewritten to accommodate the change.

For all that headache, using CLI-oriented automation scripts is still better than managing a large infrastructure manually.

The value of APIs is that they deliver structured data. While CLIs are designed for human operators, APIs are designed for applications. There can still be headaches, but they're greatly reduced.

Software and Network Engineers: The New Era

If you talk about automation and related concepts such as SDN and IBN, you get a couple different responses:

- **Older engineers:** "So I need to be a programmer now? Are software developers going to take my job if I don't?"
- **Newer engineers:** "I've invested enormous time and money into earning the certifications that will set me on the career path I want. Most of my study time has been spent configuring and troubleshooting through the CLI. Is all that a waste of time?"

We have good news and bad news for you, whether you're an old network hand or an engineer proudly displaying your freshly earned certifications. The bad news is that yes, if you want to keep up with where the industry is going, you need to acquire some programming skills and understand the protocols supporting modern automation trends. That's what this book is here for, along with a mountain of other resources to help you get up to speed. If you're a seasoned engineer, none of this is different from what you've done your entire career: keeping up with new technologies by keeping up with the latest RFCs, reading the right trade journals and blogs, and attending industry events like Cisco Live and your regional network operators' groups. If you're just starting out, you're already in deep learning mode, and you'll find that enhancing your growing skill set is not that hard at all. And we guarantee that it makes you more valuable as an engineer.

The good news is that no, automation and programmability do not mean that your jobs are going to be eliminated or taken over by software developers. Software developers' programming abilities go far beyond what's needed for networking, and for the most part, they know little about networking itself. You only have to know enough about programming to make your own job easier. As mentioned at the beginning of this chapter, automating the mundane parts of your job just means you have more time to utilize your deep knowledge of networking. The network is better for it, and you are most certainly the better for it.

So let's get started adding some shiny new tools to your toolbox!

Chapter 2

Linux Fundamentals

Chapter 1, "The Network Programmability and Automation Ecosystem," discusses where operating systems (such as Windows, UNIX, and Linux) fit in the big picture of programmability and automation. As indicated in Chapter 1, today Linux is the predominant operating system used by developers and network engineers alike—and for good reasons. This chapter is dedicated to Linux fundamentals. It starts with an assumption that you know nothing about Linux. By the end of the chapter, you will have gained enough knowledge and hands-on experience to successfully install, operate, and maintain a Linux-based system. This system will be the first building block in the development environment you will use to apply most of the material covered in subsequent chapters of this book.

The Story of Linux

This section introduces the Linux operating system: how it started, where it stands today, and where it is headed in the future. It also touches on the architecture of the operating system and introduces the concept of Linux distributions.

History

The Linux operating system was first developed in 1991 by a Finnish computer science student at the University of Helsinki called Linus Torvalds. His motivation was to provide a free alternative to the UNIX-like operating system MINIX that would run on Intel's 80386 chipset. The majority of the Linux kernel was written in the C programming language.

The first release of Linux consisted of only a kernel. A *kernel* is the lowest-level software component of an operating system and is the layer that acts as an interface between the hardware and the rest of the operating system. A kernel on its own is not very useful. Therefore, the Linux kernel was bundled with a set of free software utilities developed under a project called *GNU* (which is a recursive acronym for GNU's Not Unix). In 1992, Linux was relicensed using the *General Public License Version 2* (*GPLv2*), which is also a part of the GNU project. Together, the kernel and GNU utilities made up the Linux operating system. A group of developers worked on developing the Linux kernel as well as integrating the kernel with GNU software components in order to release the first stable version of Linux, Linux 1.0, in March 1994. In the following few years, most of the big names in the industry, such as IBM, Oracle, and Dell, announced their support for Linux.

Even though Linux is licensed under the GPL and is, therefore, free, companies have built businesses around Linux and made a lot of money out of it. Companies like Red Hat make money by packaging the free Linux kernel along with other software components, bundled with subscription-based support services. This product is then sold to customers who do not want to have to depend on the goodwill of the open source community to receive support for their Linux servers that are running mission-critical applications.

Linux Today

Today, Linux is supported on virtually any hardware platform, and most commercial application developers provide versions of their software that run on Linux. Linux powers more than half of the servers on the Internet. More than 85% of smartphones shipped in 2017 ran on Android, a Linux-based operating system. More smart TVs, home appliances, and even cars are running some version of Linux every day. All supercomputers today run on Linux. Most network devices today either run on Linux or on a Linux-like network operating system (NOS), and many vendors expose a Linux shell so that network engineers can interact directly with it. The Linux shell is covered in detail later in this chapter.

Linux Development

Linux is an open-source operating system that is developed collaboratively by a vast number of software developers all over the world and sponsored by a nonprofit organization called the Linux Foundation.

Developers interested in introducing changes to the Linux kernel submit their changes to the relevant mailing list in units called *patches*. The developers on the mailing list respond with feedback on a patch, and the patch goes through a cycle of enhancements and feedback. Once a patch is ready to be integrated into the kernel, a Linux maintainer who is responsible for one section of the kernel signs off on the patch and forwards it to Linus Torvalds, who is also a Linux Foundation fellow, for final approval. If approved, the patch is integrated into the next release of the Linux kernel. A new major release of the kernel is made available approximately every three months.

When Linux was released in March 1994, the kernel consisted of just 176,250 lines of code. At the time of writing this book, version 5.0 of the Linux kernel consists of more than 25 million lines of code.

Linux Architecture

A detailed discussion of the Linux OS architecture is beyond the scope of this book. However, this section describes a few of the important characteristics of the different Linux OS components.

Figure 2-1 provides an architectural block diagram of Linux. It shows that applications are in the top layer, presenting the software interface through which the user interacts with the device, hardware is at the bottom, and the kernel is in between.

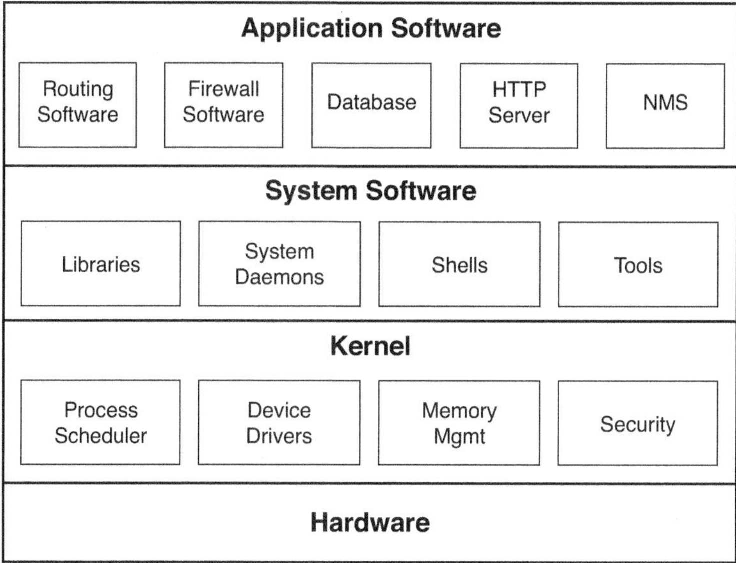

Figure 2-1 *Architectural Block Diagram of Linux*

The kernel is the part of the operating system that interfaces the different software components with the hardware. It translates instructions from the application software to a language that the hardware understands through the *device drivers* that are part of the Linux kernel. So, if a user decides to send a paper print request, this instruction is received by the application, passed to the kernel, and then passed straight to the hardware driver. The same applies to networking: When a user tries to visit an Internet web page, or if an application such as BGP on a router tries to establish peering with a distant router (assuming that the NOS is based on Linux), the browser or BGP opens a network socket (request) that the kernel handles, and translates the request into instructions that the device driver of the network card can understand. This all happens before the request gets converted into electrical signals leaving the system over the network cable.

The operating system needs to make sure that applications and the kernel do not share valuable system resources and, in doing so, disrupt each other's operations. Therefore, each is run in its own *space*—that is, a different segregated and protected part of memory. The kernel has its own allocation of memory, the *kernel space*, to prevent the kernel from crashing the system if something goes wrong. Alternatively, when a user executes an application, it runs in what is called *user space*, or *userland*, where each running application and its data are stored.

Applications come from different sources, and they may be poorly and/or recklessly developed, leading to software bugs. When you run such applications separately from kernel space, they can't interact with the kernel resources, which means they can't cause the system to halt or crash.

Figure 2-2 illustrates the communication between the application software, the different components of Linux, and the hardware. It also highlights the important architectural concepts of kernel and user space.

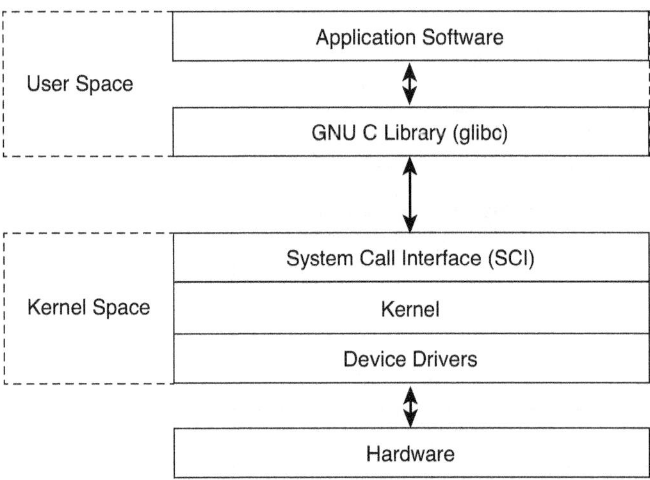

Figure 2-2 *Communication Between Applications, Linux, and System Hardware*

Applications and daemons must make what is called a *system call* to the kernel in order to access hardware resources such as memory or network devices. A *daemon* is an application that provides a specific service such as HTTP, NTP, or log collection and runs in the background (without hogging the user interface). Daemon process names typically end with the letter d, such as **httpd** or **syslogd**. When a daemon is performing a system-level function such as log collection, the daemon is commonly referred to as a *system daemon*. Daemons are covered in further detail later in this chapter and in Chapter 3, "Linux Storage, Security, and Networks."

A system call is made by using a group of subroutines provided by a library called the *GNU C library* (*glibc*). These subroutines access the kernel through the kernel's *system call interface* (*SCI*). The kernel's SCI and the GNU C library are collectively known as the *Linux application programming interface* (*Linux API*). The kernel accesses the hardware via device drivers. If this sounds a little overwhelming to you, do not worry. All the components just mentioned are simply pieces of software, each providing a particular function.

The Linux kernel is a *monolithic kernel*, which means the kernel functionality is run in the kernel space, including, for example, the device drivers. This is in contrast to the *microkernel* architecture, in which only a minimal set of services are run in the kernel space, while the rest of the services are run in the user space.

The kernel includes software modules for the following:

- Process scheduling
- Interprocess communication (IPC)
- Memory management
- Network services
- Management of virtual files
- Device drivers
- File system drivers
- Security
- System call interfaces that are used by applications in the user space to make system calls to the kernel

Loadable kernel modules (*LKMs*) are software packages that are not part of the kernel but that are loaded into the kernel space in order to extend the functionality of the kernel, without requiring rebuilding and rebooting of the kernel every time this functionality is required.

Software components that are commonly a part of a Linux operating system installation but that are *not* part of the Linux kernel typically include the following:

- Daemons
- Window system for implementing the WIMP (windows, icons, menus, pointer) user interface
- Vendor-proprietary device drivers
- User applications such as word processing applications and Internet browsers
- Command shells that accept commands from the users, parse and validate these commands, and then interpret these commands into a lower-level language to be passed to the Linux kernel for execution
- Utilities that provide common system tasks through the shell, such as the **ls**, **sort**, and **cp** utilities

Many of these components are revisited and covered in more detail later in this chapter.

Linux Distributions

A Linux *distribution*, usually referred to as a *distro*, is the actual package of software that you install on a device as the Linux OS. As mentioned in the previous section, a kernel on its own is not very useful, and in order to have a functioning, usable operating system, the kernel is packaged with other software components that run in the user space. Some distros come fully loaded with bleeding-edge software packages and drivers, which translates into a significant OS footprint. Other distros are composed of minimal software packages. A Linux distro is typically tailored for a specific audience or function, such as the scientific community or the software developer community, or to run application servers, such as email or web servers. A distro typically includes a kernel, loadable kernel modules, and other software components that run in the user space.

There are more than 300 different distros in active development today. However, there are fewer than 10 distro "families" from which all other distros are spun off. These are the major distro families:

- **Slackware:** This is the parent distro for SuSE.
- **Debian:** This is the parent distro for Ubuntu.
- **Red Hat:** This is the parent distro for Red Hat Enterprise Linux (RHEL), CentOS, and Fedora.
- **Enoch:** This is the parent distro for Gentoo.
- **Arch:** This is a Linux distro optimized for the x86_64 architecture and follows a "do-it-yourself" philosophy.
- **Wind River:** This is the Linux distro on which Cisco's NX-OS, IOS XE, and IOS XR run as applications.
- **Android:** This is the operating system running on more than 70% of smart mobile phones today.

Knowledge of any particular distro can be ported to any other distro without the steep learning curve associated with studying a subject for the first time. For the purpose of this book, the distro of choice is CentOS, a member of the Red Hat family that targets server environments and is a free version of RHEL (Red Hat Enterprise Linux) but without the support provided by Red Hat. RHEL and CentOS have been developed from the start with commercial use in mind. At the time of writing, the latest version of CentOS is 8.x. Detailed steps for installing CentOS 8.2 on different platforms are provided in the online documentation for the OS.

The Linux Boot Process

After you install Linux on a computer, when you power up the computer, the Linux OS goes through a boot process in which the different components of the OS are loaded into memory. Before you begin to use Linux, you need to have a basic understanding of what happens from the minute you power on your computer until the login screen appears and the OS is ready to be used. This section helps you learn what you need to know, without going into too much detail. The discussion focuses on the Intel x86 architecture since modern servers predominantly use CPUs based on x86 architecture. Figure 2-3 provides a high-level view of the process.

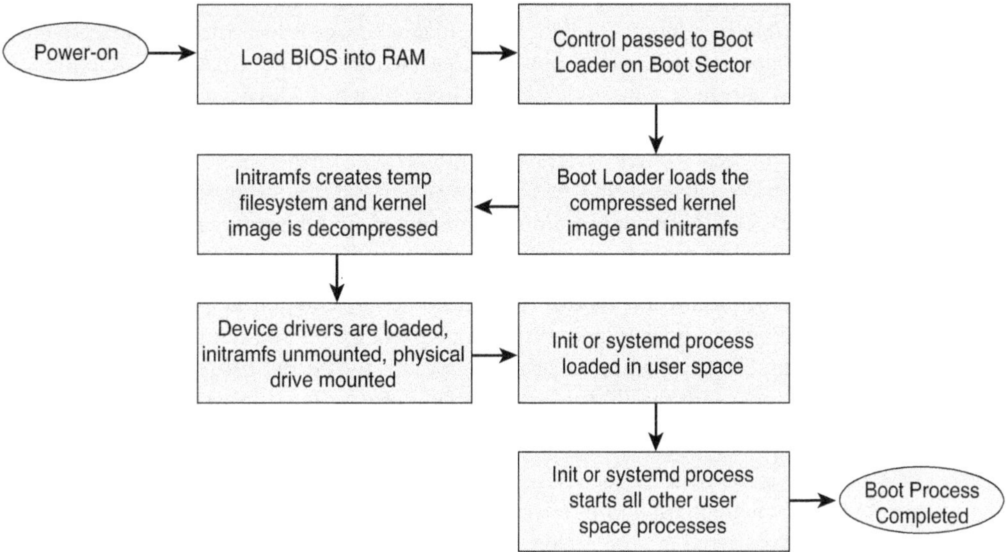

Figure 2-3 *The Linux OS Boot Process*

When you press the power-on button of your computer, system software, or *firmware*, saved on non-volatile flash memory on the computer's motherboard, is run in order to initialize the computer's hardware and do *power-on self-tests* (*POST*) to confirm that the hardware is functioning properly. This firmware is called the *BIOS*, which stands for *basic input/output system*. After the hardware is initialized and the POST completed, based on the boot order that is set in the BIOS configuration, the BIOS starts searching for a *boot sector* on each of the drives listed in the configuration, in the order configured. The boot sector comes in several types, based on the drive type you are booting from. However, the BIOS has no understanding of the kind of boot sector it is accessing or the partitioning of the drive on which the boot sector resides. All it knows is that the boot sector is a *bootable* sector (because of the *boot sector signature* in its last 2 bytes), and it passes control to whatever software resides there (in this case, the *boot loader*). A *master boot record* (*MBR*) is a special type of boot sector that resides before the first partition and not on any one partition.

The boot loader then assumes control. The boot loader's primary function is to load the kernel image into memory and pass control to it in order to proceed with the rest of the boot process. A boot loader can also be configured to present the user with options in multi-boot environments, where the loader prompts the user to choose which of several different operating systems to boot. There are several boot loaders available, such as LILO, GRUB, and SYSLINUX, and the choice of which one to use depends on what needs to be achieved. Boot loaders can work in one or more stages, where the first stage is usually OS independent and the later stages are OS specific. Different boot loaders can also be *chain-loaded* (by configuration), one after the other, depending on what you (or the software implementation) need to do.

The boot loader searches for a kernel image to load based on the boot loader's configuration and, possibly, user input. Once the correct kernel image is identified, it is loaded into memory in compressed state. The boot loader also loads an *initial RAM disk* function called **initrd** or **initramfs**, which is a software image that provides a temporary file system in memory and allows the kernel to decompress and create a root file system without mounting any physical storage devices. (This is discussed further in the next section.) The kernel then decompresses in RAM and loads hardware device drivers as loadable kernel modules. Then **initrd** or **initramfs** is unmounted, and the physical drive is mounted instead.

Recall from earlier in this chapter that the Linux software components are classified as kernel space programs or user space programs. Up to this this point, no user space programs have run. The first user space program to run is the *parent process*, which is the **/usr/sbin/init** process or the **/lib/systemd/systemd** process in some systems. All other user space processes or programs are invoked by the **init** (or **systemd**) process.

Based on which components you chose to install, the **init** process starts a command shell and, optionally, a graphical user interface. At this point, you are prompted to enter your username and password in order to log in to the system.

To switch from the GUI to the command shell and back on CentOS, you need to log in to the GUI that boots up by default and then press Alt+Ctrl+F2 (or any function key from F3 to F6). The GUI then switches to full command-line mode. To switch back to the GUI, press Alt+Ctrl+F1. CentOS starts five command-line terminals and one graphical user interface.

A Linux Command Shell Primer

An *interpreter* is a program that accepts commands written in a high-level language, such as Python, and coverts them into lower-level code, either to be executed directly by the hardware or to be passed on to another program (such as the Python virtual machine) for further processing. Similarly, a *command shell* is a program that accepts commands from the user, parses and validates those commands, one by one, and then interprets the commands into a lower-level language to be passed to the Linux kernel for execution. Of course, the Linux shell communications model is a little more involved than this. This section focuses on the user interface of the command shell.

But why use the command-line interface (CLI) when you can use the graphical user interface (GUI)? There is nothing wrong with the GUI, but whether you want to use the CLI or the GUI depends primarily on what you are trying to accomplish. This book is about network automation and programmability. You will never tap into the true power of automation that Linux provides without relying heavily on the CLI (aka the command shell), whose use is described throughout this chapter. The significant value that automation provides applies to repeatable tasks; the key word here is *repeatable*. Automation in essence involves breaking up a task into smaller, repeatable tasks and then applying automation to those tasks, and this is where the CLI comes into play. Chapter 4, "Linux Scripting," builds on the CLI commands covered in this chapter and shows how to use Linux scripting to automate repeatable tasks, among other things.

There are numerous shells available today, some of which are platform independent and others that are available for particular operating systems only. Some shells are GPL licensed, and others are not. The shell covered here is the *Bash shell*, where Bash stands for *Bourne-again shell*. Bash is a UNIX shell and command language written by Brian Fox for the GNU Project as a free software replacement for the Bourne shell, and it is the default shell on the vast majority of Linux distros in active development today.

To get started with Bash, log in to a CentOS machine and start the Terminal program, which is the interface to the Bash shell. You can start Terminal in several ways; the most straightforward method on CentOS 8 is to press on **Activities** at the top left corner of the screen. A search window will appear. Type terminal and press on the icon for Terminal that appears right under the search text box.

If you created the user NetProg during the installation and have logged in as that user, you should see a prompt similar to the one in Example 2-1.

Example 2-1 *The Terminal Program Prompt*

```
[NetProg@localhost ~]$
```

Throughout this chapter, the Terminal program window will be referred to as Terminal, the terminal, the Bash shell, the command-line shell, or just the shell, interchangeably. The command prompt in Terminal is a great source of information. The username of the current user is shown first. In this case, it is user NetProg. Then, after the @ comes the computer (host) name, which in this case is the default localhost. Next comes the ~ (tilde), which represents the home directory of the current user, NetProg. Each user in Linux has a home directory that is named after the user and is always located under the /home directory. In this case, this directory is /home/NetProg. If you use the **pwd** command, which stands for *print working directory*, the shell prints out the current working directory, which in this case is /home/NetProg, as you can see in Example 2-2. This is referred to as the *working directory*.

Example 2-2 *Using the pwd Command*

```
[NetProg@localhost ~]$ pwd
/home/NetProg
```

The last piece of information that you can extract from the prompt is the fact that this is not user root, signified by the $ sign at the end of the prompt line. Example 2-3 introduces the command **su**, which stands for *switch user*. When you type **su** and press Enter, you are prompted for the root password that you set during the CentOS installation. Notice that the prompt changes to a # when you switch to user root.

Example 2-3 *Using the su Command*

```
[NetProg@localhost ~]$ su
Password:
[root@localhost NetProg]# pwd
/home/NetProg
```

The basic syntax for the **su** command is **su** {*username*}. When no username is specified in the command, it defaults to user root. Notice also in Example 2-3 that while the current user changed to root, the current directory is not the home directory of user root. In fact, it is the home directory of user NetProg, as shown in the **pwd** command output in Example 2-3. To switch to user root as well as the home directory for root, you use the **su** command with the - option, as shown in Example 2-4.

Example 2-4 *Using the su - Command*

```
[NetProg@localhost ~]$ su -
Password:
[root@localhost ~]# pwd
/root
```

If a user wants to run a command that requires root privileges, the user has two options. The first is to use the **su -** command to switch to the root user, and then execute the command as root. The second option is to use the **sudo** utility using the syntax **sudo** {*command*}. The sudo utility is used to execute a command as a superuser, granted that the user invoking the **sudo** command is authorized to do so. In other words, the user invoking the **sudo** command should be a member of the superusers group on the system, more formally known as the *sudoers* group. When the sudo utility is invoked, the invoking user is checked against the sudoers group, and if she is a member, the user is prompted to enter her password. If the authorization is successful, the command that requires root privileges is executed. More on users and groups in Chapter 3.

Whenever you need to clear the terminal screen, you use the command **clear.** This command clears the current terminal screen and all of the scroll back buffer except for one screen length of buffer history.

When you press the up arrow once at the terminal prompt, the last command you entered is recalled. Pressing the up arrow once more recalls the command before that. Each time you press the arrow key, one older command is recalled. To see a list of your previously entered commands, type the command **history**, which lists, by default, the last 1000 commands you entered. The number of previously entered commands that can be retained is configurable. If you are using the Bash shell, the history is maintained in the ~/.bash_history file.

Finding Help in Linux

Before proceeding any further, let's look at how to find help in Linux. Covering every option and argument of every command in Linux in this single chapter would simply not be possible. However, Linux provides an easy way to get help that enables you to further investigate and experiment with the commands covered in the subsequent sections and chapters so you can expand your knowledge beyond what is covered here. Linux has built-in documentation for virtually every Linux command and feature. It makes comprehensive information readily available to Linux users.

The simplest way to get help for a command is by using the **--help** option, right after the command. Example 2-5 shows the help provided for the command **ls**, which stands for *list*. As stated in the help output, this command is used to "List information about the FILEs (the current directory by default)." As you can see, the output from the command **help** is quite detailed. The output in Example 2-5 has been truncated for brevity. Don't worry if some or most of this output does not make much sense to you at this point.

Example 2-5 *Help for the ls Command*

```
[NetProg@localhost ~]$ ls --help
Usage: ls [OPTION]... [FILE]...
List information about the FILEs (the current directory by default).
Sort entries alphabetically if none of -cftuvSUX nor --sort is specified.

Mandatory arguments to long options are mandatory for short options too.
  -a, --all                  do not ignore entries starting with .
  -A, --almost-all           do not list implied . and ..
      --author               with -l, print the author of each file
  -b, --escape               print C-style escapes for nongraphic characters
      --block-size=SIZE      scale sizes by SIZE before printing them; e.g.,
                               '--block-size=M' prints sizes in units of
                               1,048,576 bytes; see SIZE format below
  -B, --ignore-backups       do not list implied entries ending with ~

--------- OUTPUT TRUNCATED FOR BREVITY ---------
```

To illustrate the output of the command **ls** and how the **help** output from Example 2-5 can be put to good use, Example 2-6 shows the output of the command when entered while in the home directory of user NetProg. Three different variations of arguments are used. The first is plain vanilla **ls**. The second is **ls -l**, which forces **ls** to use a long listing format. The final variation is **ls -la**, which tells **ls** to not ignore entries starting with a period, which are hidden files and directories; this argument basically tells **ls** to list all files and directories, including hidden ones.

Example 2-6 *Using Three Different Variations of the ls Command*

```
[NetProg@localhost ~]$ ls
Desktop  Documents  Downloads  Music  Pictures  Public  Templates  Videos

[NetProg@localhost ~]$ ls -l
total 32
drwxr-xr-x. 2 NetProg NetProg 4096 Feb 13 04:48 Desktop
drwxr-xr-x. 2 NetProg NetProg 4096 Feb 13 04:48 Documents
drwxr-xr-x. 2 NetProg NetProg 4096 Feb 13 04:48 Downloads
drwxr-xr-x. 2 NetProg NetProg 4096 Feb 13 04:48 Music
drwxr-xr-x. 2 NetProg NetProg 4096 Feb 13 04:48 Pictures
drwxr-xr-x. 2 NetProg NetProg 4096 Feb 13 04:48 Public
drwxr-xr-x. 2 NetProg NetProg 4096 Feb 13 04:48 Templates
drwxr-xr-x. 2 NetProg NetProg 4096 Feb 13 04:48 Videos

[NetProg@localhost ~]$ ls -la
total 80
drwx------. 14 NetProg NetProg 4096 Feb 13 04:48 .
drwxr-xr-x.  5 root    root    4096 Feb 13 04:07 ..
-rw-------.  1 NetProg NetProg    4 Feb 13 04:08 .bash_history
-rw-r--r--.  1 NetProg NetProg   18 Jan  4 12:45 .bash_logout
-rw-r--r--.  1 NetProg NetProg  193 Jan  4 12:45 .bash_profile
-rw-r--r--.  1 NetProg NetProg  231 Jan  4 12:45 .bashrc
drwx------.  9 NetProg NetProg 4096 Feb 13 04:48 .cache
drwxr-xr-x. 11 NetProg NetProg 4096 Feb 13 04:48 .config
drwxr-xr-x.  2 NetProg NetProg 4096 Feb 13 04:48 Desktop
drwxr-xr-x.  2 NetProg NetProg 4096 Feb 13 04:48 Documents
--------- OUTPUT TRUNCATED FOR BREVITY ---------
```

Again, don't worry if some of this output does not make sense to you. The **ls** command is covered in detail later in this chapter, in the section "File and Directory Operations."

The second way Linux provides help to users is through the *manual pages*, also known as the *man pages*. Man pages are documentation pages for Linux built-in commands and programs. Applications that are not built-in also have the option to add their own man pages during installation. To access the man pages for a command, you enter **man** {*command*}. Example 2-7 shows the first man page for the **ls** command.

Example 2-7 *The First Man Page for the ls Command*

```
LS(1)                           User Commands                          LS(1)

NAME
       ls - list directory contents

SYNOPSIS
```

```
       ls [OPTION]... [FILE]...

DESCRIPTION
       List  information  about  the FILEs (the current directory by default).
       Sort entries alphabetically if none of -cftuvSUX nor --sort  is  specified.

       Mandatory  arguments  to  long  options are mandatory for short options
       too.

       -a, --all
              do not ignore entries starting with .

       -A, --almost-all
              do not list implied . and ..

       --author
              with -l, print the author of each file

       -b, --escape
              print C-style escapes for nongraphic characters

       --block-size=SIZE
              scale sizes by SIZE before printing them; e.g., '--block-size=M'
              prints sizes in units of 1,048,576 bytes; see SIZE format below

       -B, --ignore-backups
              do not list implied entries ending with ~

Manual page ls(1) line 1 (press h for help or q to quit)
```

You should use the down arrow or Enter key to scroll down through the man page one line at a time. You should press the spacebar or Page Down key to scroll down one page at a time. To scroll up, you should either use the up arrow key to scroll one line at a time or the Page Up key to scroll up one page at a time. To exit the man page, press q. To search through the man pages, type / followed by the search phrase you are looking for. What you type, including the /, appears at the bottom of the page. If you press Enter, the phrase you are looking for is highlighted throughout the man pages. The line containing the first search result appears at the top of the page. You should press the letter n to move forward through the search results or N (capital n) to move backward to previous search results. To get to the top of the man page, you should press g, and to go to the end of the man page, you should press G (capital g). Being able to jump to the start or end of a man page with a single keypress is handy when you're dealing with a man page that is thousands of lines long.

All available man pages on a Linux distro are classified into sections, and the number of sections depends on the distro you are using. CentOS has nine sections. Each section consists of the man pages for a different category of components of the Linux OS. In Example 2-7, notice the LS(1) on the first line of the output, on both the left and right sides. This indicates that this man page is for the command **ls**, and this is Section 1 of the man pages.

From the output of the **man man** command, which brings up the manual pages for the **man** command itself, you can see that the man pages are classified into the following sections:

- **Section 1:** Executable programs or shell commands
- **Section 2:** System calls (that is, functions provided by the kernel)
- **Section 3:** Library calls (that is, functions within program libraries)
- **Section 4:** Special files (usually found in /dev)
- **Section 5:** File formats and conventions, such as /etc/passwd
- **Section 6:** Games
- **Section 7:** Miscellaneous (including macro packages and conventions), such as man(7) and groff(7)
- **Section 8:** System administration commands (usually only for root)
- **Section 9:** Kernel routines (nonstandard)

Why are the man pages categorized into different sections? Consider this scenario: **tar** is both a command that executes the utility to archive files and also a file format for archived files. The man pages for the archiving utility are provided in Section 1 (executable programs or shell commands), while the man pages for the file format are provided in Section 5 (file formats and conventions). When you type **man tar**, you invoke the man pages for the **tar** utility under Section 1, by default. In order to invoke the man pages for the **tar** file format, you need to type **man 5 tar**. And to see all possible man pages for a specific phrase, you use the form **man -k** {*phrase*}, as shown in Example 2-8 for the phrase **tar**. Note that the phrase **tar** was enclosed in quotes with an ^ before and a **$** after **tar**. This is an example of putting regular expressions to good use to avoid getting results that you do not need. In this case, you are only looking for the phrase **tar** and not for words that start or end with **tar** or any other variation of **tar** such as words that contain **tar** in them. Regular expressions are discussed in detail in Chapter 4. For now, you just need to know that regular expressions make it possible to match on certain strings using special symbols, such as the ^ symbol, which represents the beginning of a line, and the **$** symbol, which represents the end of a line.

Example 2-8 *Man Pages in Different Sections for tar*

```
[NetProg@localhost ~]$ man -k "^tar$"
tar (1)              - an archiving utility
tar (5)              - format of tape archive files
```

An interesting—and maybe more intuitive—alternative to the man pages is the GNU *info* documentation. The info pages are help pages similar to the man pages, but the info pages are more detailed, documentation-style (rather than command-reference-style) hypertext documents, named *nodes*. The hyperlinks in the info pages enhance the experience of a user looking for information or help. The GNU info files can be accessed using either the **info** or **pinfo** commands. You can pass a phrase to one of these commands as an argument, where the phrase is what you are looking for. Or you can just type the command with no argument and then search the output for what you are looking for by typing / and then the search phrase. You can navigate through the info files by using the up and down arrow keys. You can go to the next node by pressing n or to the previous node by pressing p. Experiment with the GNU info pages by trying to locate the help for the commands covered so far and comparing the info pages with the man pages.

Files and Directories in Linux

By now, you should be familiar with the Linux Bash shell prompt and know where to go to find help. This section takes a closer look at the Linux file system, files, and directories.

The Linux File System

A disk (or any other storage medium, for that matter) is organized into one or more partitions. A *partition* is simply a logical section or slice of a disk. Each partition is logically separated from the other. In order to start using a particular partition, you need to create a file system on that partition. A file system defines how data is stored and retrieved from a disk. It defines a block of related data that has a beginning and an end and, most importantly, a name by which the block of data is identified. This block of data is called a *file*. Files are further grouped into directories, and directories are grouped into other directories, creating a tree-like hierarchy. Among other things, a file system does the following:

- Defines the size of the *allocation unit*, which is the minimum amount of physical storage space that can be allocated to a file
- Manages the space allocation to files, which may be composed of discontiguous allocations, as files are created, deleted, or changed in size
- Defines how to map between files and directories
- Defines the naming schemes of files and how to map the names to the actual locations of the files on the physical medium
- Maintains the metadata for files and directories—that is, the information about those files or directories (for example, file size, and time of last modification)

Linux supports several file systems, including ext2, ext3, ext4, XFS, Btrfs, JFS, and NTFS.

Linux organizes its files and directories following the *Filesystem Hierarchy Standard (FHS)*, which was developed specifically for Linux. This standard ensures that the different Linux distros follow the same guidelines when implementing their file system hierarchy so that application developers can develop software that is portable between distros and meet other needs for standardization. The detailed standard can be found at http://refspecs.linuxbase.org/fhs.shtml.

Figure 2-4 illustrates the very basic directory tree structure in Linux. This hierarchy starts at the root, represented by a /, and all other files and directories branch from this root directory.

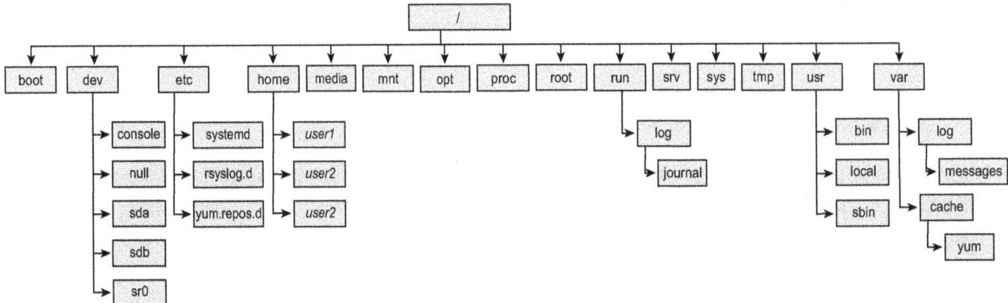

Figure 2-4 *The Linux Directory Tree Structure, Starting at the Root (/) Directory and Branching Out*

Everything in Linux is represented by a file somewhere in the file hierarchy. It is important that you become familiar with the Linux file system hierarchy and know which files to view or edit in order to get a particular task accomplished. Your knowledge will gradually increase as you progress through this chapter and Chapter 3. For now, the following is a high-level description of the main default directories on a CentOS Linux system:

- /: This is the root directory that is at the top of the file hierarchy and from which all other directories branch. This is not to be confused with the /root directory, which is the home directory of user root.
- **boot:** This directory contains the boot loader, kernel image, and initial RAM disk files.
- **dev:** This directory contains all the files required to access the devices. For example, when a hard disk is mounted on the system, the path to this disk is something similar to /dev/sda.
- **etc:** This directory contains the system configuration files and the configuration files of any application installed using the package management system of the distro being used (yum or dnf in the case of CentOS).
- **home:** Each user in Linux has a home directory that is named after the user's username. All home directories for all users reside under this home directory. A user's home directory contains all the subdirectories and files owned by this user. User NetProg's home directory, for example, is /home/NetProg.

- **media:** This directory contains subdirectories that are used as mount points for (temporary) *removable media* such as floppy disks and CD-ROMs.
- **mnt:** This directory is provided so that the system administrator can temporarily mount a file system, as needed.
- **opt:** This directory is reserved for the installation of add-on application software packages.
- **proc:** This directory is used for the storage and retrieval of process information as well as other kernel and memory information.
- **root:** This is the home directory of the user root that has superuser privileges. Note that this is not the root directory, which is the / directory.
- **run:** This directory contains files that are re-created each time the system reboots. The information in these files is about the running system and is as old as the last time the system was rebooted.
- **srv:** This directory contains site-specific data that is served by this system.
- **sys:** This directory contains information about devices, drivers, and some kernel features. Its underlying structure is determined by the particular Linux kernel being used.
- **tmp:** This directory contains temporary files that are used by users and applications. All the contents of this directory are flushed every configurable period of time (which is, by default, 10 days for CentOS).
- **usr:** This directory contains the files for installed applications. Application-shared libraries are also placed here. This directory contains the following subdirectories:
  - **usr/bin:** This subdirectory contains the binary files for the commands that are used by any user on the system, such as **pwd**, **ls**, **cp**, and **mv**.
  - **usr/sbin:** This subdirectory contains the command binary files for commands that may be executed by users of the system with administrator privileges.
  - **usr/local:** This directory is used for the installed application files, similar to the Program Files directory in Windows.
- **var:** This directory contains files that are constantly changing in size, such as system log files.
- **.:** The dot is a representation of the current working directory. The value of . is equivalent to the output of the **pwd** command.
- **..:** The double-dot notation is a representation of the parent directory of the working directory. That is, the directory that is one level higher in the file system hierarchy than the working directory.

File and Directory Operations

This section introduces a number of commands for navigating, creating, deleting, copying, and viewing files and directories using the Linux command-line shell.

Navigating Directories

The command **cd** stands for *change directory* and is used to change the working directory from one directory to another. The syntax for **cd** is **cd** {*path*}, where *path* is the destination that you want to become your working directory. The *path* argument can be provided in one of two forms: either as a *relative path* or as an *absolute path*. Example 2-9 illustrates the use of both forms.

The relative path can be used when the destination directory is a subdirectory under the current working directory. In this case, the first part of the path (which is the absolute path to the current working directory) is implied. In Example 2-9, because the current working directory is /home/NetProg and you want to navigate to /home/NetProg/LinuxStudies, you can use the command **cd LinuxStudies**, where the first part of the path, /home/NetProg/, is implied because this is the current working directory. Obviously, the relative path does not work if you need to navigate to a directory that is not under your current working directory. In Example 2-9, for example, you could not navigate to /home/NetProg/Documents from /home/NetProg/LinuxStudies by simply entering **cd Documents.** In this case, the absolute path *must* be used.

Example 2-9 *Relative and Absolute Paths*

```
[NetProg@localhost ~]$ ls
Desktop     Downloads     Music     Public     Videos
Documents   LinuxStudies  Pictures  Templates

! Using the relative path to navigate to LinuxStudies
[NetProg@localhost ~]$ cd LinuxStudies
[NetProg@localhost LinuxStudies]$ pwd
/home/NetProg/LinuxStudies

! Now the relative path does not work when attempting to navigate to
  /home/NetProg/Documents
[NetProg@localhost LinuxStudies]$ cd Documents
-bash: cd: Documents: No such file or directory

! Using the absolute path to navigate to Documents
[NetProg@localhost LinuxStudies]$ cd /home/NetProg/Documents
[NetProg@localhost Documents]$ pwd
/home/NetProg/Documents
```

At any point in your navigation, entering **cd** without any arguments takes you back to your home directory, characterized by the tilde (~) in the command prompt.

When you have navigated to the desired directory, you typically need to display its contents. The **ls** command stands for *list* and, as the name implies, **ls** is used to list the directory contents of the current working directory. When used without any options, it lists the files, side by side, without displaying any information apart from the file or subdirectory name. The **-a** option causes **ls** to display all files, including hidden files. The name of a hidden file starts with a dot (.). The **-l** option displays the files in a list format, along with the attributes of each file. The **-i** option adds the *inode number* to the displayed information. Example 2-10 displays the output of the **ls** command with all three options added, inside the home directory of user NetProg.

Example 2-10 *ls Command Output*

```
[NetProg@localhost ~]$ ls -lai
total 84
31719425 drwx------. 14 NetProg NetProg 4096 Feb 13 17:41 .
       2 drwxr-xr-x.  5 root    root    4096 Feb 13 04:07 ..
31719432 -rw-------.  1 NetProg NetProg  293 Feb 14 09:55 .bash_history
31719426 -rw-r--r--.  1 NetProg NetProg   18 Jan  4 12:45 .bash_logout
31719427 -rw-r--r--.  1 NetProg NetProg  193 Jan  4 12:45 .bash_profile
31719428 -rw-r--r--.  1 NetProg NetProg  231 Jan  4 12:45 .bashrc
31719433 drwx------.  9 NetProg NetProg 4096 Feb 13 04:48 .cache
31719434 drwxr-xr-x. 11 NetProg NetProg 4096 Feb 13 04:48 .config
31719485 drwxr-xr-x.  2 NetProg NetProg 4096 Feb 13 04:48 Desktop
31719489 drwxr-xr-x.  2 NetProg NetProg 4096 Feb 13 04:48 Documents
31719486 drwxr-xr-x.  2 NetProg NetProg 4096 Feb 13 04:48 Downloads

--------- OUTPUT TRUNCATED FOR BREVITY ---------
```

A lot of information can be extracted from the output in Example 2-10. The phrase **total 84** indicates the total number of disk blocks allocated to store all the files in that directory. The second two lines of the output are for the current directory (.) and the directory one level above the current directory (..).

To elaborate on the use of the . and .., assume that the current working directory is /home/NetProg/LinuxStudies, and you want to navigate to /home/NetProg/Documents. You have two options: Either enter **cd /home/NetProg/Documents**, which is the absolute path, or use the shorthand notation **cd ../Documents**, where the .. substitutes for /home/NetProg. You use the dot (.) notation similarly but for the current working directory. The value of using shorthand notation for the current working directory may not be immediately obvious, considering the availability of relative paths. However, by the end of Chapter 4 you will see how useful this notation is.

Next, all the files and subdirectories are listed; by default, they appear in alphabetical order. As noted earlier, the name of a hidden file or directory starts with a dot (.). The information from the beginning of each line all the way up to the file or directory name is collectively known as the *file* or *directory attributes*. Here is a description of each attribute:

- **Inode number:** The inode number is also called the file *serial number* or file *index number*. As per the **info** description for **ls**, the inode number is a number that "uniquely identifies each file within a particular file system."
- **File type:** This first character right after the inode number defines the file type. Three characters are commonly used in this field:
  - - stands for a regular file.
  - **d** stands for a directory.
  - **l** stands for a soft link.

  There are several other file types that are not discussed here.
- **File permissions:** Also called the file mode bits, the file permissions define who is allowed to read (r), write (w), or execute (x) the file. Users are classified into three categories: the owner of the file (u), the group of the file (g), and everyone else, or other (o). File permissions are covered in detail later in this chapter. For now, you need to know that the first three letters belong to the file owner, the second three belong to the group of the file, and the last three belong to everyone else. So, **rwxr-xr--** means that the file owner with permissions **rwx** can read, write, and execute the file. Users who are members of the same group as the file group, with permissions **r-x**, can read and execute the file but not write to it. Everyone else, with permissions **r--**, can only read the file but can neither write to it nor execute it. While the meaning of write, read, and execute are self-explanatory for files, they may not be so obvious for directories. Reading from a directory means listing its contents using the **ls** command, and writing to a directory means creating files or subdirectories under that directory. Executing directory X means changing the current working directory to directory X by using the **cd** command.
- **Alternate access method:** Notice the dot (.) right after the file permissions. This dot means that you have alternate means to set permissions for this file, such as using *access control lists* (*ACL*). ACLs are covered in detail in Chapter 3.
- **Number of hard links:** The number to the right of the file permissions is the total number of hard links to a file or to all files inside a directory. This is discussed in detail in section "Hard and Soft Links," later in this chapter.
- **File/directory owner:** This is the name of the file owner. In Example 2-10, it is NetProg.

- **File/directory group:** This is the file's group name. In Example 2-10, it is also NetProg. The file owner may or may not be part of this group. For example, the file owner could be NetProg, the group of the file could be Sales, and user NetProg may not be a member of the group Sales. Chapter 3 discusses how file access works in each case.
- **Size:** This is the file size, in bytes.
- **Time stamp:** This is the time when the file was last modified.

Viewing Files

In this section you will see how to display the contents of files on the terminal by using the commands **cat**, **more**, **less**, **head**, and **tail.**

The **cat** command, which stands for *concatenate*, writes out a file to *standard output* (that is, the screen). Example 2-11 shows how to use the **cat** command to display the output of the PIM.txt file.

Example 2-11 *cat Command Output*

```
[NetProg@localhost LinuxStudies]$ cat PIM.txt
!
Router-1# show ip pim neighbor
PIM Neighbor Table
Mode: B - Bidir Capable, DR - Designated Router, N - Default DR Priority,
      P - Proxy Capable, S - State Refresh Capable, G - GenID Capable
Neighbor          Interface                Uptime/Expires    Ver   DR
Address                                                            Prio/Mode
192.168.10.10     TenGigabitEthernet1/2    7w0d/00:01:26     v2    1 / G
192.168.20.20     TenGigabitEthernet2/1    2w2d/00:01:32     v2    1 / P G





PE-L3Agg-Mut-303-3# show ip pim interface

Address          Interface                Ver/   Nbr    Query  DR     DR
                                          Mode   Count  Intvl  Prior
192.168.10.11    TenGigabitEthernet1/2    v2/S   1      30     1      192.168.10.10
192.168.20.21    TenGigabitEthernet2/1    v2/S   1      30     1      192.168.20.20
!
[NetProg@localhost LinuxStudies]$
```

Several useful options can be used with **cat.** For example, **cat -n** inserts a line number at the beginning of each line. **cat -b**, on the other hand, inserts a line number for non-empty lines only. **cat -s** is the squeeze option, which squeezes more than one consecutive empty lines into a single empty line. Example 2-12 shows the output of the **cat** command on the file PIM.txt, using the **-sn** option to squeeze any consecutive empty lines in the file into one empty line and then number all lines, including the empty lines. For a more comprehensive list of options, you can visit the **cat** info page by using the command **info coreutils cat.**

Example 2-12 *cat -sn Command Output*

```
[NetProg@localhost LinuxStudies]$ cat -sn PIM.txt
  1  !
  2  Router-1# show ip pim neighbor
  3  PIM Neighbor Table
  4  Mode: B - Bidir Capable, DR - Designated Router, N - Default DR Priority,
  5        P - Proxy Capable, S - State Refresh Capable, G - GenID Capable
  6  Neighbor         Interface              Uptime/Expires    Ver   DR
  7  Address                                                        Prio/Mode
  8  192.168.10.10    TenGigabitEthernet1/2  7w0d/00:01:26     v2    1 / G
  9  192.168.20.20    TenGigabitEthernet2/1  2w2d/00:01:32     v2    1 / P G
 10
 11  PE-L3Agg-Mut-303-3# show ip pim interface
 12
 13  Address         Interface               Ver/   Nbr    Query  DR     DR
 14                                          Mode   Count  Intvl  Prior
 15  192.168.10.11   TenGigabitEthernet1/2   v2/S   1      30     1      192.168.10.10
 16  192.168.20.21   TenGigabitEthernet2/1   v2/S   1      30     1      192.168.20.20
 17  !
[NetProg@localhost LinuxStudies]$
```

One of the major drawbacks of **cat** is that the file being displayed is output to the screen all at once, without a pause. The next two commands, **more** and **less**, provide a more readable form of output, where just one section of the file is displayed on the screen, and then the user is prompted for input in order to proceed with the following section of the file, and so forth. Therefore, both of these commands are handy tools for displaying files that are longer than the current screen length. **more** is the original utility and is very compact, so it is ideal for systems with limited resources. However, the major drawback of **more** is that it does not allow you to move backward in a file; you can only move forward. Therefore, the **less** utility was eventually developed to allow users to move forward and backward over the content of a file. Over time, several developers contributed to the **less** program, adding more features in the process. One other distinctive feature of **less** is that it does not have to read the whole file before it starts displaying output; it is therefore much faster than many other programs, including the prominent **vi** text editor.

Example 2-13 shows the **more** command being used to display the contents of the file InternetRoutes.txt.

Example 2-13 *more Command Output*

```
[NetProg@localhost LinuxStudies]$ more InternetRoutes.txt
Codes: L - local, C - connected, S - static, R - RIP, M - mobile, B - BGP
       D - EIGRP, EX - EIGRP external, O - OSPF, IA - OSPF inter area
       N1 - OSPF NSSA external type 1, N2 - OSPF NSSA external type 2
       E1 - OSPF external type 1, E2 - OSPF external type 2
       i - IS-IS, su - IS-IS summary, L1 - IS-IS level-1, L2 - IS-IS level-2
       ia - IS-IS inter area, * - candidate default, U - per-user static route
       o - ODR, P - periodic downloaded static route, H - NHRP
       + - replicated route, % - next hop override

Gateway of last resort is 67.16.148.37 to network 0.0.0.0

S*    0.0.0.0/0 [1/0] via 67.16.148.37
      1.0.0.0/8 is variably subnetted, 2511 subnets, 16 masks
B        1.0.4.0/22 [200/100] via 67.16.148.37, 6d02h
B        1.0.4.0/24 [200/100] via 67.16.148.37, 6d02h
B        1.0.5.0/24 [200/100] via 67.16.148.37, 6d02h
B        1.0.6.0/24 [200/100] via 67.16.148.37, 6d02h
B        1.0.7.0/24 [200/100] via 67.16.148.37, 6d02h
B        1.0.16.0/24 [200/150] via 67.16.148.37, 7w0d
--More--(0%)
```

Notice the text --More--(0%) at the end of the output, which indicates how much of the file has been displayed so far. You can perform the following operations while viewing a file by using **more**:

- In order to keep scrolling down the file contents, press the Enter key to scroll one line at a time or press the Spacebar to scroll one screenful at a time.
- Type a number and press s to skip that number of lines forward in the file.
- Similarly, type a number and then press f to skip forward that number of screens.
- If you press =, the line number where you are currently located is displayed in place of the percentage at the bottom of the screen. This is the line number of the last line of the output at the bottom of the screen.
- To search for a specific pattern using regular expressions, type /{*pattern*} and press Enter. The output jumps to the first occurrence of the pattern you are searching for.
- To quit the output and return to the terminal prompt, press q.

Now let's look at an example of using the **less** command. Example 2-14 shows the contents of the InternetRoutes.txt file displayed using **less**. Notice the filename at the end of the output.

Example 2-14 *less Command Output*

```
Codes: L - local, C - connected, S - static, R - RIP, M - mobile, B - BGP
       D - EIGRP, EX - EIGRP external, O - OSPF, IA - OSPF inter area
       N1 - OSPF NSSA external type 1, N2 - OSPF NSSA external type 2
       E1 - OSPF external type 1, E2 - OSPF external type 2
       i - IS-IS, su - IS-IS summary, L1 - IS-IS level-1, L2 - IS-IS level-2
       ia - IS-IS inter area, * - candidate default, U - per-user static route
       o - ODR, P - periodic downloaded static route, H - NHRP
       + - replicated route, % - next hop override

Gateway of last resort is 67.16.148.37 to network 0.0.0.0

S*    0.0.0.0/0 [1/0] via 67.16.148.37
      1.0.0.0/8 is variably subnetted, 2511 subnets, 16 masks
B        1.0.4.0/22 [200/100] via 67.16.148.37, 6d02h
B        1.0.4.0/24 [200/100] via 67.16.148.37, 6d02h
B        1.0.5.0/24 [200/100] via 67.16.148.37, 6d02h
B        1.0.6.0/24 [200/100] via 67.16.148.37, 6d02h
B        1.0.7.0/24 [200/100] via 67.16.148.37, 6d02h
B        1.0.16.0/24 [200/150] via 67.16.148.37, 7w0d
InternetRoutes.txt
```

The following are some operations you can perform while viewing the file by using **less**:

- Use Enter, e, or j to scroll forward through the file one line at a time or use the Spacebar or z to scroll forward one screenful at a time.
- Press y to scroll backward one line at a time or b to scroll backward one screen at a time. Type a number before the y or b to scroll that many lines or screens, respectively.
- Press g to go to the beginning of the file or G to go to the end of the file.
- Press = to see the filename and the range of line numbers currently displayed on the screen, out of the total number of lines in the file, partial and full data size information, as well as your location in the file as a percentage.
- To search for a specific pattern using regular expressions, type /{*pattern*} and press Enter. The output jumps to the first occurrence of the pattern you are searching for.
- To quit the output and return to the terminal prompt, press q.

For a complete list of operations you can perform while viewing the file by using **less**, visit the man or info pages for the **less** command.

It is generally recommended to use **less** instead of **more** because the latter is not under current development right now. Keep in mind, however, that you might run into systems with limited resources that support only **more**.

The final two commands covered in this section are **head** and **tail**. As their names may imply, these simple commands or utilities print a set number of lines from the start of the file or from the end of the file. Example 2-15 shows both commands being used to display selected output from the start or end of the InternetRoutes.txt file.

Example 2-15 *head and tail Command Output*

```
! displaying the first 15 lines of the file
[NetProg@localhost LinuxStudies]$ head -n 15 InternetRoutes.txt
Codes: L - local, C - connected, S - static, R - RIP, M - mobile, B - BGP
       D - EIGRP, EX - EIGRP external, O - OSPF, IA - OSPF inter area
       N1 - OSPF NSSA external type 1, N2 - OSPF NSSA external type 2
       E1 - OSPF external type 1, E2 - OSPF external type 2
       i - IS-IS, su - IS-IS summary, L1 - IS-IS level-1, L2 - IS-IS level-2
       ia - IS-IS inter area, * - candidate default, U - per-user static route
       o - ODR, P - periodic downloaded static route, H - NHRP
       + - replicated route, % - next hop override

Gateway of last resort is 67.16.148.37 to network 0.0.0.0

S*    0.0.0.0/0 [1/0] via 67.16.148.37
      1.0.0.0/8 is variably subnetted, 2511 subnets, 16 masks
B        1.0.4.0/22 [200/100] via 67.16.148.37, 6d02h

! displaying the last 10 lines of the file
[NetProg@localhost LinuxStudies]$ tail -n 10 InternetRoutes.txt
B        110.204.0.0/17 [200/100] via 67.16.148.37, 6d02h
B        110.204.128.0/17 [200/100] via 67.16.148.37, 6d02h
B        110.205.0.0/16 [200/100] via 67.16.148.37, 6d02h
B        110.205.0.0/17 [200/100] via 67.16.148.37, 6d02h
B        110.205.128.0/17 [200/100] via 67.16.148.37, 6d02h
B        110.206.0.0/17 [200/100] via 67.16.148.37, 6d02h
B        110.206.128.0/17 [200/100] via 67.16.148.37, 6d02h


Connection closed by foreign host.
[NetProg@localhost LinuxStudies]$
```

The first section of the output in Example 2-15 shows how to extract the first 15 lines of the file by using **head**, and the second section of the output shows how to display the last 10 lines of the same file by using **tail**. A very useful variation is to use the **head** command with a negative number, such as **-20**, after the **-n** option. When this form is used, it means that all of the file is to be displayed *except for* the last 20 lines. Instead of using number of lines, you can specify the first or last number of bytes of the file to be displayed (using **head** or **tail**, respectively) by replacing the option **-n** with **-c**. Finally, to keep a *live* view of a file, you can use the **tail** command with the **-f** option. With this option, if a new line is added to the file, it appears on the screen. This comes in handy when viewing log files that are expected to change, and these changes need to be monitored as they happen; this is a very common scenario when troubleshooting system incidents. To quit live mode, press Ctrl+c.

File Operations

This section covers the most common file operations: creating, copying, deleting, and moving files.

In Example 2-16, the directory LinuxStudies has three empty subdirectories under it. The example shows how to use the **touch** command to create a file and call it PolicyMap.txt. When you pass a filename to the **touch** command as an argument, that file is created if it does not already exist. If the file already exists, the access and modification time stamps of the file are changed to the time when the **touch** command was issued. You can see this file in the output of the **ls** command.

Example 2-16 *Creating a File by Using touch*

```
[NetProg@localhost LinuxStudies]$ ls -l
total 12
drwxrwxr-x. 2 NetProg NetProg 4096 Feb 17 12:14 configurations
drwxrwxr-x. 2 NetProg NetProg 4096 Feb 17 12:19 operational
drwxrwxr-x. 2 NetProg NetProg 4096 Feb 17 12:06 temp

[NetProg@localhost LinuxStudies]$ touch PolicyMap.txt

[NetProg@localhost LinuxStudies]$ ls -l
total 12
drwxrwxr-x. 2 NetProg NetProg 4096 Feb 17 12:14 configurations
drwxrwxr-x. 2 NetProg NetProg 4096 Feb 17 12:19 operational
-rw-rw-r--. 1 NetProg NetProg    0 Feb 17 12:22 PolicyMap.txt
drwxrwxr-x. 2 NetProg NetProg 4096 Feb 17 12:06 temp
[NetProg@localhost LinuxStudies]$
```

Note three things in Example 2-16:

- The file created is empty and has a size of zero bytes.
- The file's time stamp is the time at which the **touch** command was issued.
- Linux is case sensitive. The files PolicyMap.txt and policymap.txt are two entirely different files. The same case sensitivity applies to commands.

Example 2-17 shows how to copy the file PolicyMap.txt to the operational directory by using the **cp** command. Because this is a copy operation, now both the LinuxStudies directory and the subdirectory operational contain copies of the file, as shown by using the **ls -l** command in each of the directories. Remember that the dot (.) and double dot (..) notations, combined with relative paths, are often used to refer to the current working directory and the parent directory, respectively. The file is then deleted from the LinuxStudies directory by using the **rm** command. Issuing the **ls** command again shows that the file was indeed deleted. Following that, the file is moved (not copied) with the **mv** command from the operational subdirectory to the configurations subdirectory. Issuing the **ls** command in both directories shows that the file was moved to the latter, and the former is empty now. Finally, the file is renamed PolicyMapConfig.txt: The **mv** command renames and moves the old file to the new one, in the same location. The **ls** command, issued one final time, confirms that the file renaming was successful.

Example 2-17 *File Operations: Copy, Delete, and Move*

```
! File copy operation
[NetProg@localhost LinuxStudies]$ cp PolicyMap.txt operational
[NetProg@localhost LinuxStudies]$ ls -l
total 16
drwxrwxr-x. 2 NetProg NetProg 4096 Feb 17 12:14 configurations
drwxrwxr-x. 2 NetProg NetProg 4096 Feb 17 12:19 operational
-rw-rw-r--. 1 NetProg NetProg    0 Feb 17 12:24 PolicyMap.txt
drwxrwxr-x. 2 NetProg NetProg 4096 Feb 17 12:06 temp
[NetProg@localhost LinuxStudies]$ ls -l operational
total 4
-rw-rw-r--. 1 NetProg NetProg 361 Feb 17 12:24 PolicyMap.txt

! File delete operation
[NetProg@localhost LinuxStudies]$ rm PolicyMap.txt
[NetProg@localhost LinuxStudies]$ ls -l
total 12
drwxrwxr-x. 2 NetProg NetProg 4096 Feb 17 12:14 configurations
drwxrwxr-x. 2 NetProg NetProg 4096 Feb 17 12:19 operational
drwxrwxr-x. 2 NetProg NetProg 4096 Feb 17 12:06 temp
[NetProg@localhost LinuxStudies]$ cd operational/
[NetProg@localhost operational]$ ls -l
total 4
-rw-rw-r--. 1 NetProg NetProg 361 Feb 17 12:24 PolicyMap.txt

! File move operation
[NetProg@localhost operational]$ mv PolicyMap.txt ../configurations/
[NetProg@localhost operational]$ ls -l
total 0
```

```
[NetProg@localhost operational]$ cd ../configurations/
[NetProg@localhost configurations]$ ls -l
total 4
-rw-rw-r--. 1 NetProg NetProg 361 Feb 17 12:24 PolicyMap.txt

! Renaming a file by moving it to the same location but with a different name
[NetProg@localhost configurations]$ mv PolicyMap.txt PolicyMapConfig.txt
[NetProg@localhost configurations]$ ls -l
total 4
-rw-rw-r--. 1 NetProg NetProg 361 Feb 17 12:24 PolicyMapConfig.txt
[NetProg@localhost configurations]$
```

A more secure alternative to the command **rm** is the command **shred**, which overwrites the file a configurable number of times (three by default) in order to eliminate the possibility of recovering the deleted file even via direct hardware access.

The following is a summary of the commands used for file operations:

- **touch** {*file_name*}: Use this syntax to create a file.
- **cp** {*source*} {*destination*}: Use this syntax to copy a file to another location.
- **mv** {*source*} {*destination*}: Use this syntax to move a file from one location to another:
- **mv** {*old_file_name*} {*new_file_name*}: Use this syntax to rename a file. The old and new files could be collocated in the same directory or located in different directories.
- **rm** {*file_name*}: Use this syntax to delete a file.
- **shred** {*file_name*}: Use this syntax to securely delete a file.

When operating on files, it is important to be careful about what the current directory is, what the destination directory is, and where the file currently resides. When using the commands listed here, you need to use absolute paths, relative paths, or no path at all—whichever is applicable at the time. Also, notice the use of the shorthand dot and double dot notations in the previous examples and how they make a command line both shorter and easier.

Directory Operations

This section discusses directory operations. Some of the commands in this section are the same as those used with files, but they have added options for directories. Some of the commands in this section are exclusive to directories.

The next few examples demonstrate how to create a directory, copy it to a new location, move it to a new location, and rename it. The examples also show what you need to do to delete a directory in two different cases: either the directory is empty or it is not.

Example 2-18 shows two directories being created under the LinuxStudies directory with the **mkdir** command: EmptyDir and NonEmptyDir. By using the **cp** command, the file PolictMapConfig.txt is then copied to the directory NonEmptyDir (not shown in the example). One directory is now empty, and the other directory contains one file.

Example 2-18 *Creating Directories*

```
[NetProg@localhost LinuxStudies]$ ls
configurations  operational  temp
[NetProg@localhost LinuxStudies]$ mkdir EmptyDir
[NetProg@localhost LinuxStudies]$ mkdir NonEmptyDir
[NetProg@localhost LinuxStudies]$ ls
configurations  EmptyDir  NonEmptyDir  operational  temp
[NetProg@localhost LinuxStudies]$
```

The next example shows a different hierarchy: A new directory is created, and the two directories created in the previous example are moved into it. In Example 2-19, a new directory called MasterDir is created using the **mkdir** command and then the **mv** command is used to move both directories under the newly created MasterDir directory. The output of the **ls** command shows that both directories were successfully moved to the new location.

Example 2-19 *Moving Directories*

```
[NetProg@localhost LinuxStudies]$ mkdir MasterDir
[NetProg@localhost LinuxStudies]$ ls
configurations  EmptyDir  MasterDir  NonEmptyDir  operational  temp
[NetProg@localhost LinuxStudies]$ mv EmptyDir MasterDir
[NetProg@localhost LinuxStudies]$ mv NonEmptyDir MasterDir
[NetProg@localhost LinuxStudies]$ ls MasterDir
EmptyDir  NonEmptyDir
[NetProg@localhost LinuxStudies]$
```

Example 2-20 shows a new directory called MasterDirReplica being created. The **cp** command is then used in an attempt to copy both EmptyDir and NonEmptyDir to the new directory. As shown in the example, the operation fails; the error message indicates that when copying directories, you need to issue the **cp** command with the **-r** option, which stands for *recursive*. When the **cp** command is issued with the correct option, the copy operation is successful, as indicated by the output of the **ls** command. Notice that the **-r** option needs to be added to the **cp** command, whether the directory is empty or not.

Example 2-20 *Copying Directories*

```
[NetProg@localhost LinuxStudies]$ mkdir MasterDirReplica
[NetProg@localhost LinuxStudies]$ ls
configurations  MasterDir  MasterDirReplica  operational  temp
[NetProg@localhost LinuxStudies]$ cp MasterDir/EmptyDir MasterDirReplica
cp: -r not specified; omitting directory 'MasterDir/EmptyDir'
[NetProg@localhost LinuxStudies]$ cp MasterDir/NonEmptyDir MasterDirReplica
cp: -r not specified; omitting directory 'MasterDir/NonEmptyDir'
[NetProg@localhost LinuxStudies]$ cp -r MasterDir/EmptyDir MasterDirReplica
[NetProg@localhost LinuxStudies]$ cp -r MasterDir/NonEmptyDir MasterDirReplica
[NetProg@localhost LinuxStudies]$ ls MasterDirReplica/
EmptyDir  NonEmptyDir
[NetProg@localhost LinuxStudies]$
```

The command to delete an *empty* directory in Linux is **rmdir**. For historical reasons, **rmdir** works only for empty directories, and the command **rm -r** is required to delete *non-empty* directories. In Example 2-21, an attempt is made to delete both the EmptyDir and NonEmptyDir directories by using the **rmdir** command, but as expected, it does not work on the directory NonEmptyDir. Using **rm -r** works fine, and the final **ls** command shows that.

Example 2-21 *Deleting Directories*

```
[NetProg@localhost LinuxStudies]$ ls MasterDir
EmptyDir  NonEmptyDir
[NetProg@localhost LinuxStudies]$ rmdir MasterDir/EmptyDir
[NetProg@localhost LinuxStudies]$ ls MasterDir
NonEmptyDir
[NetProg@localhost LinuxStudies]$ rmdir MasterDir/NonEmptyDir
rmdir: failed to remove 'MasterDir/NonEmptyDir': Directory not empty
[NetProg@localhost LinuxStudies]$ ls MasterDir
NonEmptyDir
[NetProg@localhost LinuxStudies]$ rm -r MasterDir/NonEmptyDir
[NetProg@localhost LinuxStudies]$ ls MasterDir
[NetProg@localhost LinuxStudies]$
```

Finally, Example 2-22 shows the use of the **mv** command to rename the directory NonEmptyDir to NonEmptyDirRenamed.

Example 2-22 *Renaming Directories*

```
[NetProg@localhost MasterDirReplica]$ ls
EmptyDir  NonEmptyDir
[NetProg@localhost MasterDirReplica]$ mv NonEmptyDir NonEmptyDirRenamed
[NetProg@localhost MasterDirReplica]$ ls
EmptyDir  NonEmptyDirRenamed
```

The following is a summary of the commands used for directory operations:

- **mkdir** {*directory_name*}: Use this syntax to create directories.
- **cp -r** {*source*} {*destination*}: Use this syntax to copy directories to another location.
- **mv** {*source*} {*destination*}: Use this syntax to move directories from one location to another.
- **mv** {*old_dir_name*} {*new_dir_name*}: Use this syntax to rename directories. A renamed directory could be collocated (in the same path) with the original directory, or it could be in a different path (moved and renamed in the same operation).
- **rmdir** {*directory_name*}: Use this syntax to delete empty directories.
- **rm -r** {*directory_name*}: Use this syntax to delete non-empty directories.

Hard and Soft Links

Linux provides the facility to create a link from one file to another file. A *link* is basically a relationship between two files. This relationship means that changes to one file affect the linked file in one way or another. There are two types of links in Linux: hard links and soft, or symbolic, links. You create links in Linux by using the **ln** command. A link is created between the original file, referred to as the *target*, and a newly created file, referred to as the *link*.

Hard Links

You create a hard link between a target and a link by using the syntax (in its simplest form) **ln** {*target-file*} {*link-file*}. A hard link is characterized by the following:

- Any changes to the contents of the target file are reflected in the link file and vice versa.
- Any changes to the target file attributes, such as the file permissions, are reflected in the link file and vice versa.
- Deleting the target file does *not* delete the link file.
- A target file can have one or more link files linked to it. The target and all its hard links have the same inode number.
- Hard links are allowed for files only, not for directories.

Example 2-23 shows a hard link named HL-1-to-Access-List.txt created to the file Access-List.txt. The command **ls -li** is used to list the files in the directory LinuxStudies, including the file attributes. Notice that apart from the different name, the hard link file is basically a replica of the target: Both have the same file size, permissions, and inode number. Then a second hard link, named HL-2-to-Access-List.txt, is created. Notice the number 1 to the right of the file permissions of the original target, Access-List.txt, before any hard links are created. This number increments by 1 every time a hard link is created.

Then the first hard link is deleted. Notice that the target file and the second hard link stay intact. The target file is deleted, and the second hard link stays intact. As mentioned previously, deleting the target or one of the hard links does not affect the other hard links.

Example 2-23 *Creating and Deleting Hard Links*

```
[NetProg@localhost ~]$ cd LinuxStudies
[NetProg@localhost LinuxStudies]$ ls -li
total 2304
57934070 -rw-r--r--. 1 NetProg NetProg     470 Feb 14 10:08 Access-List.txt
57934069 -rw-r--r--. 2 NetProg NetProg 2353097 Feb 14 10:09 showrun.txt

! Create the first hardlink
[NetProg@localhost LinuxStudies]$ ln Access-List.txt HL-1-to-Access-List.txt
[NetProg@localhost LinuxStudies]$ ls -li
total 2308
57934070 -rw-r--r--. 2 NetProg NetProg     470 Feb 14 10:08 Access-List.txt
57934070 -rw-r--r--. 2 NetProg NetProg     470 Feb 14 10:08 HL-1-to-Access-List.txt
57934069 -rw-r--r--. 2 NetProg NetProg 2353097 Feb 14 10:09 showrun.txt

! Create the second hard link
[NetProg@localhost LinuxStudies]$ ln Access-List.txt HL-2-to-Access-List.txt
[NetProg@localhost LinuxStudies]$ ls -li
total 2312
57934070 -rw-r--r--. 3 NetProg NetProg     470 Feb 14 10:08 Access-List.txt
57934070 -rw-r--r--. 3 NetProg NetProg     470 Feb 14 10:08 HL-1-to-Access-List.txt
57934070 -rw-r--r--. 3 NetProg NetProg     470 Feb 14 10:08 HL-2-to-Access-List.txt
57934069 -rw-r--r--. 2 NetProg NetProg 2353097 Feb 14 10:09 showrun.txt

! Remove the first hard link - target and second hard link stay intact
[NetProg@localhost LinuxStudies]$ rm HL-1-to-Access-List.txt
[NetProg@localhost LinuxStudies]$ ls -li
total 2308
57934070 -rw-r--r--. 2 NetProg NetProg     470 Feb 14 10:08 Access-List.txt
57934070 -rw-r--r--. 2 NetProg NetProg     470 Feb 14 10:08 HL-2-to-Access-List.txt
57934069 -rw-r--r--. 2 NetProg NetProg 2353097 Feb 14 10:09 showrun.txt

! Delete the target - second hard link stays intact
[NetProg@localhost LinuxStudies]$ rm Access-List.txt
[NetProg@localhost LinuxStudies]$ ls -li
total 2304
57934070 -rw-r--r--. 1 NetProg NetProg     470 Feb 14 10:08 HL-2-to-Access-List.txt
57934069 -rw-r--r--. 2 NetProg NetProg 2353097 Feb 14 10:09 showrun.txt
[NetProg@localhost LinuxStudies]$
```

Example 2-24 shows how hard-linked files change together. Reverting to the original state where we have the file Access-List.txt and two hard links to it, using the command **chmod**, the permissions of the target are changed from **-rw-r--r--** to **-rw-rw-r--**. This command is covered in detail in Chapter 3. For now, notice the new permissions that change for the target as well as all the hard links. To take this a step further, the permissions are changed for the second hard link to **-rw-rw-rw-**. Notice now how the permissions change for the target as well as the other hard link.

Example 2-24 *How Attributes Are Reflected Across Hard Links*

```
[NetProg@localhost LinuxStudies]$ ls -li
total 2312
57934070 -rw-r--r--. 3 NetProg NetProg     470 Feb 14 10:45 Access-List.txt
57934070 -rw-r--r--. 3 NetProg NetProg     470 Feb 14 10:45 HL-1-to-Access-List.txt
57934070 -rw-r--r--. 3 NetProg NetProg     470 Feb 14 10:45 HL-2-to-Access-List.txt
57934069 -rw-r--r--. 2 NetProg NetProg 2353097 Feb 14 10:09 showrun.txt

! Changing the file permissions for the target
[NetProg@localhost LinuxStudies]$ chmod g+w Access-List.txt
[NetProg@localhost LinuxStudies]$ ls -li
total 2312
57934070 -rw-rw-r--. 3 NetProg NetProg     470 Feb 14 10:45 Access-List.txt
57934070 -rw-rw-r--. 3 NetProg NetProg     470 Feb 14 10:45 HL-1-to-Access-List.txt
57934070 -rw-rw-r--. 3 NetProg NetProg     470 Feb 14 10:45 HL-2-to-Access-List.txt
57934069 -rw-r--r--. 2 NetProg NetProg 2353097 Feb 14 10:09 showrun.txt

! Changing the file permissions for the second hard link
[NetProg@localhost LinuxStudies]$ chmod o+w HL-2-to-Access-List.txt
[NetProg@localhost LinuxStudies]$ ls -li
total 2312
57934070 -rw-rw-rw-. 3 NetProg NetProg     470 Feb 14 10:45 Access-List.txt
57934070 -rw-rw-rw-. 3 NetProg NetProg     470 Feb 14 10:45 HL-1-to-Access-List.txt
57934070 -rw-rw-rw-. 3 NetProg NetProg     470 Feb 14 10:45 HL-2-to-Access-List.txt
57934069 -rw-r--r--. 2 NetProg NetProg 2353097 Feb 14 10:09 showrun.txt
[NetProg@localhost LinuxStudies]$
```

Similarly, content changes in one file are automatically reflected in the target and all other hard links, as shown in Example 2-25. The command **cat** displays the contents of file Access-List.txt on the terminal, and then **cat** is used again to display the contents of HL-1-to-Access-List.txt. The contents of the two files are, as expected, the same. Now the text editor **vi** is used to add a new line at the top of access list Test-Access-List with sequence number 5 in the file Access-List.txt. The file contents are then viewed using **cat** to confirm that the changes were successfully saved. Viewing the contents of both hard-linked files shows that the new line was also added to the ACL Test-Access-List in both files.

Example 2-25 *How Content Changes Are Reflected Across Hard Links*

```
[NetProg@localhost LinuxStudies]$ ls -li
total 2312
57934145 -rw-rw-r--. 3 NetProg NetProg     512 Feb 14 14:45 Access-List.txt
57934145 -rw-rw-r--. 3 NetProg NetProg     512 Feb 14 14:45 HL-1-to-Access-List.txt
57934145 -rw-rw-r--. 3 NetProg NetProg     512 Feb 14 14:45 HL-2-to-Access-List.txt
57934069 -rw-r--r--. 2 NetProg NetProg 2353097 Feb 14 10:09 showrun.txt

! Identical file content before editing
[NetProg@localhost LinuxStudies]$ cat Access-List.txt
!
ipv4 access-list Test-Access-List
 10 permit ipv4 192.168.10.0 0.0.0.255 any
 20 permit ipv4 192.168.20.0 0.0.3.255 any
 30 permit ipv4 192.168.30.0 0.0.0.255 any
!
[NetProg@localhost LinuxStudies]$ cat HL-1-to-Access-List.txt
!
ipv4 access-list Test-Access-List
 10 permit ipv4 192.168.10.0 0.0.0.255 any
 20 permit ipv4 192.168.20.0 0.0.3.255 any
 30 permit ipv4 192.168.30.0 0.0.0.255 any
!

! Content changes in target are automatically reflected in both hard links
[NetProg@localhost LinuxStudies]$ vi Access-List.txt
[NetProg@localhost LinuxStudies]$ cat Access-List.txt
!
ipv4 access-list Test-Access-List
 5 permit ipv4 192.168.10.0 0.0.0.255 any
 10 permit ipv4 192.168.10.0 0.0.0.255 any
 20 permit ipv4 192.168.20.0 0.0.3.255 any
 30 permit ipv4 192.168.30.0 0.0.0.255 any
!
[NetProg@localhost LinuxStudies]$ cat HL-1-to-Access-List.txt
!
ipv4 access-list Test-Access-List
 5 permit ipv4 192.168.10.0 0.0.0.255 any
 10 permit ipv4 192.168.10.0 0.0.0.255 any
 20 permit ipv4 192.168.20.0 0.0.3.255 any
 30 permit ipv4 192.168.30.0 0.0.0.255 any
!
```

```
[NetProg@localhost LinuxStudies]$ cat HL-2-to-Access-List.txt
!
ipv4 access-list Test-Access-List
 5 permit ipv4 192.168.10.0 0.0.0.255 any
 10 permit ipv4 192.168.10.0 0.0.0.255 any
 20 permit ipv4 192.168.20.0 0.0.3.255 any
 30 permit ipv4 192.168.30.0 0.0.0.255 any
!
[NetProg@localhost LinuxStudies]$
```

In very simple terms, a hard link creates a new *live* copy of a file that changes as the target or any of the other hard links change. More accurately, a hard link creates a new pointer to the same inode that has a different name (filename). The inode number is the same across all hard-linked files, and hard links cannot span different file systems because inode numbers may not be unique across different file systems on separate partitions.

One last thing to note in the output of the **ls -l** command is that each file by default has one hard link that must be present before you create any hard links to the file manually. This hard link is the original target file. This reinforces the concept that a hard link is just a pointer to the same inode number, and the first pointer to a particular inode number is the target itself.

One use case for hard links is the utility to distribute data. Consider a configuration file or a device inventory with one or more hard links, each being used by a different device or application. Every time the file or one of the hard links is updated by one of the applications or devices, the updates are automatically reflected in all the other files. Think of all the possibilities that this functionality provides in the real world of automation!

Soft Links

A soft link, commonly referred to as a symbolic link, or symlink for short, does not create a live copy of a target file as a hard link does. Instead, a symbolic link, as the name implies, is just a pointer, or a shortcut, to the original file, not the inode, as is the case with hard links. Symlinks are created using the command **ln -s** {*target_file*} {*link_file*}. Symlinks are characterized by the following:

- The target file and the link file have different inode numbers.
- Symlink file permissions are always rwxrwxrwx, regardless of the permissions of the target file.
- Symlinks have the letter **l** to the left of the file permissions in the output of the **ls -l** command and an arrow pointing to the target file at the end of the line of the same output.
- A symlink does not disappear when the target file is deleted. Instead, the output of the command **ls -l** shows the target file highlighted in red and flashing to indicate that the symlink is broken.

- The symlink references the target file by name. If the target file is replaced by any other file that has the same name, the symlink points to that new file.
- Unlike hard links, symlinks can be created for directories as well as files.

Example 2-26 shows symlinks at work. First, a symlink named SL-1-to-Access-List.txt is created for the file Access-List.txt. Notice the different inode numbers and file permissions between the target and link files. Notice also the **l** that is prepended to the file permissions of the soft link and the arrow pointing to the target at the end of the line; both the **l** and the arrow indicate that this is a soft link. The target is then deleted using the **rm** command. However, the soft link file still appears in the output of the **ls** command. On a computer screen, the target would also be highlighted in red to indicate a broken link. Next in the example, a new empty file is created using the **touch** command, but it has the same name as the file that was deleted, Access-List.txt. When the **ls** command is issued, it shows that the symlink is operational again, and it points to the newly created text file. To further confirm that the symlink is working, the **cat** command is issued, and it shows both files being empty. The **vi** editor is then used to add an ACL, Access-List-Test, to the symlink file, and after the **cat** command is issued for both files, it turns out that the changes made to the symlink have been reflected to the target, Access-List.txt.

Example 2-26 *Symlinks at Work*

```
[NetProg@localhost LinuxStudies]$ ln -s Access-List.txt SL-1-to-Access-List.txt
[NetProg@localhost LinuxStudies]$ ls -li
total 2312
57934145 -rw-rw-r--. 3 NetProg NetProg    512 Feb 14 14:45 Access-List.txt
57934143 lrwxrwxrwx. 1 NetProg NetProg     15 Feb 14 14:55 SL-1-to-Access-List.txt
  -> Access-List.txt

! Deleting the target does not delete the symlink
[NetProg@localhost LinuxStudies]$ rm Access-List.txt
[NetProg@localhost LinuxStudies]$ ls -li
total 2308
57934143 lrwxrwxrwx. 1 NetProg NetProg     15 Feb 14 14:55 SL-1-to-Access-List.txt
  -> Access-List.txt

! Creating a new file with the same name as the deleted target reinstates the
  symlink
[NetProg@localhost LinuxStudies]$ touch Access-List.txt
[NetProg@localhost LinuxStudies]$ ls -li
total 2308
57934146 -rw-rw-r--. 1 NetProg NetProg      0 Feb 14 14:58 Access-List.txt
57934143 lrwxrwxrwx. 1 NetProg NetProg     15 Feb 14 14:55 SL-1-to-Access-List.txt
  -> Access-List.txt

[NetProg@localhost LinuxStudies]$ cat Access-List.txt
```

```
[NetProg@localhost LinuxStudies]$ cat SL-1-to-Access-List.txt

[NetProg@localhost LinuxStudies]$ vi SL-1-to-Access-List.txt
[NetProg@localhost LinuxStudies]$ cat SL-1-to-Access-List.txt
!
ipv4 access-list Test-Access-List
 10 permit ipv4 192.168.10.0 0.0.0.255 any
 20 permit ipv4 192.168.20.0 0.0.0.255 any
 30 permit ipv4 192.168.30.0 0.0.0.255 any
!
[NetProg@localhost LinuxStudies]$ cat Access-List.txt
!
ipv4 access-list Test-Access-List
 10 permit ipv4 192.168.10.0 0.0.0.255 any
 20 permit ipv4 192.168.20.0 0.0.0.255 any
 30 permit ipv4 192.168.30.0 0.0.0.255 any
!
[NetProg@localhost LinuxStudies]$
```

Soft links provide similar functionality to Windows shortcuts. One use case for symlinks is to consolidate all your work in one directory. The directory contains symlinks to all files from other directories. Changes made to any symlink are reflected to the original file, and you do not have to move the original file from its place in the file system.

Input and Output Redirection

Earlier in this chapter, you briefly learned about the GNU utilities that are bundled with the Linux kernel to form the Linux operating system. Utilities are a collection of software tools that enable a user to perform common system tasks without having to write their own tool set.

All the commands introduced so far in this chapter (as well as in the remainder of this chapter) are actually utilities, and each is invoked via the respective command. For example, the **ls**, **cat**, **more**, **less**, **head**, **tail**, **cp**, **mv**, **rm**, **mkdir**, **rmdir**, and **ln** commands covered so far are actually utilities, and you run each utility by typing the corresponding command in the shell. Most utilities are grouped together in packages. When a package is installed, all constituent utilities are installed. Two popular packages are **coreutils** and **util-linux**.

The true power of Linux lies not only in its architecture but in the vast number of utilities that come prepackaged with it, new utilities that can be easily installed and immediately add to the power and usability of the system, and, finally, the option of programming your own custom utilities. Utilities are introduced in this section because input and output redirection are arguably two of the most powerful features of Linux that act on utilities. Redirection stretches the flexibility and usability of utilities and combines the workings of two or more utilities in ways unique to Linux, as you will see in this section.

The Linux and UNIX philosophy has been inspired by the experience of the software development leaders who developed programming languages. Ken Thomson and Dennis Ritchie developed the C language as well as UNIX. Ken and Dennis, among others, realized early on that the operating system should present an interface to the user that facilitates a productive and interactive experience. Mimicking programming languages, they wanted the user to be able to filter input/output of programs and apply control to the flow of standard input, output, and errors between these utilities.

The UNIX forefathers applied software engineering methods traditionally used in programming languages to their operating system user experience. These engineering methods are reflected in the powerful command-line utilities of both UNIX and Linux, along with pipes and redirection, to smoothly integrate tools.

The power of the UNIX and Linux command line is achieved with the following design philosophies:

- Make each program do one thing well. To do a new job, build afresh rather than complicate old programs by adding new features.
- Expect the output of every program to become the input to another, as yet unknown, program. Don't clutter output with extraneous information.

Thanks to these design philosophies for the command line, an administrator is immediately equipped with a powerful and infinitely flexible tool chain for all sorts of operations.

The community of Linux developers around the world is continuously contributing to the long list of available utilities, creating small blocks that can work together to produce powerful results, making it easy to automate mundane administrative tasks. A good way to demonstrate this power is by showing an advanced example that illustrates the full potential of utilities and pipes. Example 2-27 is a relatively complex example that pings the gateways in the Linux routing table and inserts the unreachable ones in a file. This file is then sent via email. In this example, the output of one command is piped to another using the **|** (pipe) symbol.

Note You do not need to worry about the particular semantics of this example as its goal is to illustrate the sheer power of piping the output of one command to be used as input to another command.

Example 2-27 *A Relatively Complex Example of Piping*

```
[NetProg@localhost]$ netstat -nr | awk '{print $2}' | grep -o '[0-9]\{1,3\}\.[0-9]\
  {1,3\}\.[0-9]\{1,3\}\.[0-9]\{1,3\}' | xargs -n1 ping -c1  | grep  -b1 100 |
  mail -s "Unreachable gateways" netprog@thenetdev.com
```

This section covers input and output redirection in detail. For now, here is a brief explanation of each command in Example 2-27:

- **netstat -nr:** Displays the routing table and pipes it to the next command (**awk**).
- **awk '{print $2}':** Filters the second column only (gateways) from the output of the previous command (**netstat**), and pipes the result to the next command (**grep**).
- **grep -o '[0-9]\{1,3\}\.[0-9]\{1,3\}\.[0-9]\{1,3\}\.[0-9]\{1,3\}':** Only shows IP addresses from the output of the previous command (**awk**) and pipes the result to the next command (**xargs**).
- **xargs -n1 ping -c1:** Pings IP addresses that were provided by the previous command (**grep**) and pipes the ping results to the next command (**grep**).
- **grep -b1 100:** Filters the unreachable IP addresses from the ping performed in the previous command (**xargs**) and pipes the result to the next command (**mail**).
- **mail -s "Unreachable IPs" -t netprog@thenetdev.com:** Sends an email with the output of the previous command (**grep**) with the subject "Unreachable IPs" to user NetProg's email address.

In Linux, for each command that you execute or utility that you run, there are three files, each of which contains a different *stream* of data:

- **stdin (standard input):** This is the file that the command reads to get its input. stdin has the file handle 0.
- **stdout (standard output):** This is the file to which the command sends its output. stdout has the file handle 1.
- **stderr (standard error):** This is the file to which the command sends any errors, also known as exceptions. stderr has the file handle 2.

A file handle is a number assigned to a file by the OS when that file is opened.

stdin is, by default, what you type on your keyboard. Similarly, stdout and stderr are, by default, displayed onscreen.

Input and output redirection are powerful capabilities in Linux that are very important pieces of the automation puzzle. Output that is normally seen onscreen can be redirected to a file. Output from a command can also be split into regular output and error, which can then be redirected separately. The contents of a file or the output of a command can be redirected to another command as input to that command.

The **sort** utility accepts input through stdin (via the keyboard), sorts the input in alphabetical order, and then sends the output to stdout (to the screen). In Example 2-28, after the user types the command **sort** and presses Enter, the shell waits for input from the user through the keyboard. The user types the letters q, w, e, r, t, and y on the keyboard, one by one, pressing Enter after each letter, to start a new line. The user then executes the **sort** command by pressing the Ctrl+d key combination. As shown in the example, the lines are sorted in alphabetical order, as expected.

Example 2-28 *Using the sort Utility and Providing the Input Through the Default stdin Stream, the Keyboard*

```
[NetProg@localhost LinuxStudies]$ sort
q
w
e
r
t
y ! Press ctrl+d here
e
q
r
t
w
y
[NetProg@localhost LinuxStudies]$
```

Input redirection can be used to change a command's stdin to a file instead of the keyboard. One way to do this is to specify the file as an *argument* to the command. Another way is to use the syntax {*command*} **<** {*file*}, where the contents of *file* are used as input to *command*. Example 2-29 shows how stdin to the **sort** command is changed to the file qwerty.txt using both methods.

Example 2-29 *Changing stdin for the* **sort** *Command from the Keyboard to a File by Providing the File as an Argument, and by Using Input Redirection*

```
[NetProg@localhost LinuxStudies]$ cat qwerty.txt
q
w
e
r
t
y
[NetProg@localhost LinuxStudies]$ sort qwerty.txt
e
q
r
t
w
y
[NetProg@localhost LinuxStudies]$ sort < qwerty.txt
```

```
e
q
r
t
w
y
[NetProg@localhost LinuxStudies]$
```

How to change stdout and stderr may be a bit more obvious than how to change stdin because the output from commands is usually expected to appear on the screen. Output redirection can be used to redirect the output to a file instead. In Example 2-30, the output from the **sort** command is output to the file qwerty-sorted.txt, and then the **cat** command is used to display the contents of the sorted file.

Example 2-30 *Redirecting Stdout to the File qwerty-sorted.txt with the >*

```
[NetProg@localhost LinuxStudies]$ ls
configurations  operational  QoS.txt  qwerty.txt  temp
[NetProg@localhost LinuxStudies]$ sort qwerty.txt > qwerty-sorted.txt
[NetProg@localhost LinuxStudies]$ ls
configurations  operational  QoS.txt  qwerty-sorted.txt  qwerty.txt  temp
[NetProg@localhost LinuxStudies]$ cat qwerty-sorted.txt
e
q
r
t
w
y
[NetProg@localhost LinuxStudies]$
```

Notice that file qwerty-sorted.txt did not exist before the **sort** command was executed. The file was created before it was used to store the redirected output. Similarly, if the file had existed before the command was executed, it would have been overwritten.

What if you need to append the output to the file instead of overwriting it ? Example 2-31 shows how to append output to an existing file by using the **>>** notation. As you saw earlier, the **cat** command outputs the contents of a file to the screen. In Example 2-31, instead of displaying the contents of QoS.txt on the screen, the **cat** command with the **>>** notation is used to redirect the file's contents to the qwerty-sorted.txt file, but this time the output is appended to the existing content of qwerty-sorted.txt instead of overwriting it.

Example 2-31 *Appending Command Output by Using >>*

```
[NetProg@localhost LinuxStudies]$ cat QoS.txt >> qwerty-sorted.txt
[NetProg@localhost LinuxStudies]$ cat qwerty-sorted.txt
e
q
r
t
w
y
!
policy-map MOBILE_RAN_QOS_OUT
!
class MOBILE_VOICE_CLASS
priority level 1
police rate percent 50
conform-action transmit
exceed-action drop
!
set cos 5
!
class MOBILE_BROADBAND
bandwidth percent 35
set cos 3
random-detect default
!
class class-default
bandwidth percent 15
set cos 0
random-detect default
!
end-policy-map
!
[NetProg@localhost LinuxStudies]$
```

stderr is also, by default, displayed on the screen. If you want to redirect stderr to a file instead, you use the syntax {*command*} **2>** {*file*}, where the regular output goes to the screen, while the errors or exception messages are redirected to the file specified in the command. Example 2-32 shows how the error message from issuing the **stat** command on a nonexistent file is redirected to file error.txt. The **stat** command gives you important information about the file, such as the file size, inode number, permissions, user ID of the file owner, group ID of the file, and what time the file was last accessed, modified (content changed), and changed (metadata such as permissions changed).

Example 2-32 *Redirecting stderr to a File by Using 2>*

```
[NetProg@localhost LinuxStudies]$ stat QoS.txt
  File: QoS.txt
  Size: 361             Blocks: 8          IO Block: 4096   regular file
Device: fd03h/64771d    Inode: 31719574    Links: 1
Access: (0664/-rw-rw-r--)  Uid: ( 1001/ NetProg)   Gid: ( 1001/ NetProg)
Context: unconfined_u:object_r:user_home_t:s0
Access: 2018-02-23 18:04:59.919457898 +0300
Modify: 2018-02-23 18:00:21.881647657 +0300
Change: 2018-02-23 18:00:21.881647657 +0300
 Birth: -
[NetProg@localhost LinuxStudies]$ stat WrongFile.txt
stat: cannot stat 'WrongFile.txt': No such file or directory
[NetProg@localhost LinuxStudies]$ stat WrongFile.txt 2> error.txt
[NetProg@localhost LinuxStudies]$ cat error.txt
stat: cannot stat 'WrongFile.txt': No such file or directory
[NetProg@localhost LinuxStudies]$
```

So far, you have seen how to redirect stdout to a file and how to do the same for stderr—but not both together. To redirect both stdout and stderr to a file, you use the syntax {*command*} **&>** {*file*}. Example 2-33 shows the **cat** command being used to concatenate three files: QoS.txt, WrongFile.txt, and qwerty.txt. However, one of these files, WrongFile.txt, does not exist, and so an error message is generated. As a result, the contents of QoS.txt and qwerty.txt are concatenated, and then both stdout and stderr are redirected to the same file, OutandErr.txt.

Example 2-33 *Redirecting Both stdout and stderr to OutandErr.txt*

```
[NetProg@localhost LinuxStudies]$ cat QoS.txt WrongFile.txt qwerty.txt &>
  OutandErr.txt
[NetProg@localhost LinuxStudies]$ cat OutandErr.txt
!
policy-map MOBILE_RAN_QOS_OUT
 !
 class MOBILE_VOICE_CLASS
  priority level 1
  police rate percent 50
   conform-action transmit
   exceed-action drop
  !
  set cos 5
 !
 class MOBILE_BROADBAND
  bandwidth percent 35
```

```
  set cos 3
  random-detect default
 !
 class class-default
  bandwidth percent 15
  set cos 0
  random-detect default
 !
 end-policy-map
!
cat: WrongFile.txt: No such file or directory
q
w
e
r
t
y
[NetProg@localhost LinuxStudies]$
```

To split stdout and stderr into their own separate files, you can use the syntax {*command*} **>** {*output_file*} **2>** {*error_file*}, as shown in Example 2-34.

Example 2-34 *Redirecting stdout and stderr Each to Its Own File*

```
[NetProg@localhost LinuxStudies]$ cat QoS.txt WrongFile.txt qwerty.txt > output.txt
  2> error.txt
[NetProg@localhost LinuxStudies]$ cat output.txt
!
policy-map MOBILE_RAN_QOS_OUT
 !
 class MOBILE_VOICE_CLASS
  priority level 1
  police rate percent 50
   conform-action transmit
   exceed-action drop
  !
  set cos 5
 !
 class MOBILE_BROADBAND
  bandwidth percent 35
  set cos 3
  random-detect default
 !
```

```
  class class-default
   bandwidth percent 15
   set cos 0
   random-detect default
  !
  end-policy-map
!
q
w
e
r
t
y
[NetProg@localhost LinuxStudies]$ cat error.txt
cat: WrongFile.txt: No such file or directory
[NetProg@localhost LinuxStudies]$
```

To ignore or discard an error altogether and not save it to a file, you can simply redirect it to /dev/null. The file /dev/null is a special device file that discards any data redirected to it.

You can also append both stdout and stderr to an existing file by using the syntax *{command}* **>>** *{file}* **2>&1**.

As mentioned earlier in the chapter, Linux provides a facility to redirect the output of one command to be used as input for another command. This is done using the **|** (pipe) operator. Example 2-35 shows how the output of the **stat** command for the QoS.txt file is piped to the **sort** command, which sorts the output in alphabetical order. The result is then piped again to the **head** command to extract the first line of the output.

Example 2-35 *Piping Command Output to Another Command*

```
[NetProg@localhost LinuxStudies]$ stat QoS.txt
  File: QoS.txt
  Size: 361            Blocks: 8          IO Block: 4096   regular file
Device: fd03h/64771d    Inode: 31719574    Links: 1
Access: (0664/-rw-rw-r--)  Uid: ( 1001/ NetProg)   Gid: ( 1001/ NetProg)
Context: unconfined_u:object_r:user_home_t:s0
Access: 2018-02-23 18:04:59.919457898 +0300
Modify: 2018-02-23 18:00:21.881647657 +0300
Change: 2018-02-23 18:00:21.881647657 +0300
 Birth: -

! Stat output piped to sort
[NetProg@localhost LinuxStudies]$ stat QoS.txt | sort
```

```
Access: (0664/-rw-rw-r--)  Uid: ( 1001/ NetProg)   Gid: ( 1001/ NetProg)
Access: 2018-02-23 18:04:59.919457898 +0300
 Birth: -
Change: 2018-02-23 18:00:21.881647657 +0300
Context: unconfined_u:object_r:user_home_t:s0
Device: fd03h/64771d      Inode: 31719574     Links: 1
  File: QoS.txt
Modify: 2018-02-23 18:00:21.881647657 +0300
  Size: 361       .   Blocks: 8          IO Block: 4096   regular file

! Double piping to sort and then head
[NetProg@localhost LinuxStudies]$ stat QoS.txt | sort | head -n 1
Access: (0664/-rw-rw-r--)  Uid: ( 1001/ NetProg)   Gid: ( 1001/ NetProg)
[NetProg@localhost LinuxStudies]$
```

You have seen how stdout is by default displayed on the screen and how to redirect it to a file. But can you display it on the screen and simultaneously redirect it to a file? Yes. You can use the pipe operator coupled with the **tee** command to do just that. In Example 2-36, the output of the command **ls -l** is piped to the **tee** command, and as a result, the output is both displayed on the screen and saved to the file lsoutput.txt.

Example 2-36 *Piping Command Output To the* ***tee*** *Command to Display It on the Screen As Well As Save It To File lsoutput.txt*

```
[NetProg@localhost LinuxStudies]$ ls -l | tee lsoutput.txt
total 40
-rw-rw-r--. 1 NetProg NetProg   46 Feb 23 20:28 colors.txt
drwxrwxr-x. 2 NetProg NetProg 4096 Feb 23 16:59 configurations
-rw-rw-r--. 1 NetProg NetProg   61 Feb 23 18:15 error.txt
-rw-rw-r--. 1 NetProg NetProg  475 Feb 23 19:43 Existing.txt
drwxrwxr-x. 2 NetProg NetProg 4096 Feb 17 12:34 operational
-rw-rw-r--. 1 NetProg NetProg  419 Feb 23 19:25 OutandErr.txt
-rw-rw-r--. 1 NetProg NetProg  361 Feb 23 18:00 QoS.txt
-rw-rw-r--. 1 NetProg NetProg  373 Feb 23 18:08 qwerty-sorted.txt
-rw-rw-r--. 1 NetProg NetProg   12 Feb 23 17:28 qwerty.txt
drwxrwxr-x. 2 NetProg NetProg 4096 Feb 17 15:03 temp

[NetProg@localhost LinuxStudies]$ cat lsoutput.txt
total 40
-rw-rw-r--. 1 NetProg NetProg   46 Feb 23 20:28 colors.txt
drwxrwxr-x. 2 NetProg NetProg 4096 Feb 23 16:59 configurations
-rw-rw-r--. 1 NetProg NetProg   61 Feb 23 18:15 error.txt
-rw-rw-r--. 1 NetProg NetProg  475 Feb 23 19:43 Existing.txt
drwxrwxr-x. 2 NetProg NetProg 4096 Feb 17 12:34 operational
```

```
-rw-rw-r--. 1 NetProg NetProg  419 Feb 23 19:25 OutandErr.txt
-rw-rw-r--. 1 NetProg NetProg  361 Feb 23 18:00 QoS.txt
-rw-rw-r--. 1 NetProg NetProg  373 Feb 23 18:08 qwerty-sorted.txt
-rw-rw-r--. 1 NetProg NetProg   12 Feb 23 17:28 qwerty.txt
drwxrwxr-x. 2 NetProg NetProg 4096 Feb 17 15:03 temp
[NetProg@localhost LinuxStudies]$
```

The **tee** command overwrites the output file (in this case, the lsoutput.txt file). You can use the **tee** command with the **-a** option to append to the file instead of overwriting it.

Archiving Utilities

An archiving utility takes a file or a group of files as input and encodes the file or files into one single file, commonly known as an archive. The archiving utility also makes it possible to add files to the archive, remove files from the archive, update the files in the archive, or de-archive the archive file into its constituent files. Archiving utilities have historically been used for backup purposes and to package several files into one file that can be easily distributed, downloaded, and so on. The most commonly used archiving utility in Linux is the **tar** utility, which stands for *tape archive*. Archive files produced by the **tar** utility have a .tar extension and are commonly referred to as tarballs.

In contrast to an archiving utility, a compression utility takes a file or a group of files as input and compresses the file or files into another format that is smaller than the original file. This compression is *lossless*, meaning that no information is lost in the process. The compressed file can be decompressed and returned to its original state without any data or metadata being lost. In Linux, the most popular compression utilities are **gzip**, **bzip2**, and **xz**. The performance of compression utilities is measured based on several criteria, two of which are how quickly the compression happens and the compression ratio (which is how small the new compressed file is in comparison with the original uncompressed file). The **xz** utility is the best when it comes to compression ratio, but it is the slowest. The **gzip** utility is the fastest but has the lowest (worst) compression ratio. As you have already concluded, **bzip2** lies in the middle with respect to speed and compression ratio.

We cover archiving and compression utilities together in this section because a very common use case involves compressing files using one of the compression utilities listed here and then archiving the compressed files by using the **tar** utility. In addition to covering these utilities, this section also illustrates how compression and archiving can be performed using a single command.

Example 2-37 shows how to use the **gzip** utility to compress the InternetRoutes.txt file. You simply issue the command **gzip InternetRoutes.txt**, and the utility creates another file, InternetRoutes.txt.gz, which is the compressed file, and removes the original uncompressed file. To decompress the file back to its original form, you use the command **gunzip InternetRoutes.txt.gz**. What if you want to keep the original file as well as the compressed file after compression? You use **gzip** with the **-k** option, which stands for *keep*, as shown in the example. Similarly, you can use the **-k** option with **gunzip** to decompress the file and keep the compressed file intact.

Example 2-37 *Using the gzip Utility to Compress a Text File*

```
[NetProg@localhost LinuxStudies]$ ls -l
total 17212
-rw-rw-r--. 1 NetProg NetProg 17622037 Feb 24 12:27 InternetRoutes.txt

[NetProg@localhost LinuxStudies]$ gzip InternetRoutes.txt
[NetProg@localhost LinuxStudies]$ ls -l
total 1268
-rw-rw-r--. 1 NetProg NetProg 1296408 Feb 24 12:27 InternetRoutes.txt.gz

[NetProg@localhost LinuxStudies]$ gunzip InternetRoutes.txt.gz
[NetProg@localhost LinuxStudies]$ ls -l
total 17212
-rw-rw-r--. 1 NetProg NetProg 17622037 Feb 24 12:27 InternetRoutes.txt

[NetProg@localhost LinuxStudies]$ gzip -k InternetRoutes.txt
[NetProg@localhost LinuxStudies]$ ls -l
total 18480
-rw-rw-r--. 1 NetProg NetProg 17622037 Feb 24 12:27 InternetRoutes.txt
-rw-rw-r--. 1 NetProg NetProg  1296408 Feb 24 12:27 InternetRoutes.txt.gz

[NetProg@localhost LinuxStudies]$ rm InternetRoutes.txt
[NetProg@localhost LinuxStudies]$ ls -l
total 1268
-rw-rw-r--. 1 NetProg NetProg 1296408 Feb 24 12:27 InternetRoutes.txt.gz

[NetProg@localhost LinuxStudies]$ gunzip -k InternetRoutes.txt.gz
[NetProg@localhost LinuxStudies]$ ls -l
total 18480
-rw-rw-r--. 1 NetProg NetProg 17622037 Feb 24 12:27 InternetRoutes.txt
-rw-rw-r--. 1 NetProg NetProg  1296408 Feb 24 12:27 InternetRoutes.txt.gz
[NetProg@localhost LinuxStudies]$
```

Notice in the example that the size of the original uncompressed file is approximately 17 MB, and the size of the compressed file is approximately 1.2 MB; this represents a compression ratio of about 13.6.

Example 2-38 shows how the **bzip2** utility is used to compress the same InternetRoutes.txt file by using the command **bzip2 InternetRoutes.txt** and then uncompress the file by using the command **bunzip2 InternetRoutes.txt.bz2**.

Example 2-38 *Using the bzip2 Utility to Compress a Text File*

```
[NetProg@localhost LinuxStudies]$ ls -l
total 17212
-rw-rw-r--. 1 NetProg NetProg 17622037 Feb 24 12:27 InternetRoutes.txt

[NetProg@localhost LinuxStudies]$ bzip2 -kv InternetRoutes.txt
  InternetRoutes.txt: 19.386:1,  0.413 bits/byte, 94.84% saved, 17622037 in,
  909025 out.
[NetProg@localhost LinuxStudies]$ ls -l
total 18100
-rw-rw-r--. 1 NetProg NetProg 17622037 Feb 24 12:27 InternetRoutes.txt
-rw-rw-r--. 1 NetProg NetProg   909025 Feb 24 12:27 InternetRoutes.txt.bz2

[NetProg@localhost LinuxStudies]$ rm InternetRoutes.txt
[NetProg@localhost LinuxStudies]$ ls -l
total 888
-rw-rw-r--. 1 NetProg NetProg 909025 Feb 24 12:27 InternetRoutes.txt.bz2

[NetProg@localhost LinuxStudies]$ bunzip2 InternetRoutes.txt.bz2
[NetProg@localhost LinuxStudies]$ ls -l
total 17212
-rw-rw-r--. 1 NetProg NetProg 17622037 Feb 24 12:27 InternetRoutes.txt
[NetProg@localhost LinuxStudies]$
```

Notice that the **-k** option also works with **bzip2**, and when used, the original uncompressed file is left intact. This option works equally well with **bunzip2** to leave the compressed file intact. As shown in Example 2-38, the **-v** option, which stands for *verbose*, provides some information and statistics on the compression process. It is worth noting that the verbose option is available for the vast majority of Linux commands, and it is available for use with all archiving and compression utilities in this chapter. If you look at the sizes of the original and compressed files, you see that the compression ratio in the example is approximately 19.4, which is in line with the verbose output.

Example 2-39 shows how to use the **xz** utility to compress the same InternetRoutes.txt file, using the command **xz InternetRoutes.txt**, and then uncompress the file by using the command **xz -d InternetRoutes.txt.xz**. The **-v** option is used here as well to provide some insight into the compression process.

Example 2-39 *Using the xz Utility to Compress a Text File*

```
[NetProg@localhost LinuxStudies]$ ls -l
total 17212
-rw-rw-r--. 1 NetProg NetProg 17622037 Feb 24 12:27 InternetRoutes.txt

[NetProg@localhost LinuxStudies]$ xz -v InternetRoutes.txt
InternetRoutes.txt (1/1)
  100 %        711.9 KiB / 16.8 MiB = 0.041   2.3 MiB/s       0:07
[NetProg@localhost LinuxStudies]$ ls -l
total 712
-rw-rw-r--. 1 NetProg NetProg 728936 Feb 24 12:27 InternetRoutes.txt.xz

[NetProg@localhost LinuxStudies]$ xz -dv InternetRoutes.txt.xz
InternetRoutes.txt.xz (1/1)
  100 %        711.9 KiB / 16.8 MiB = 0.041
[NetProg@localhost LinuxStudies]$ ls -l
total 17212
-rw-rw-r--. 1 NetProg NetProg 17622037 Feb 24 12:27 InternetRoutes.txt
[NetProg@localhost LinuxStudies]$
```

As you can see from the output in Example 2-39, **xz** provides a compression ratio of about 24.2, which is the best compression ratio so far. However, the **xz** utility takes a substantial amount of time (7 seconds, according to the verbose output) to compress the file. As shown in the earlier examples, compression using **gzip** is almost instantaneous, while **bzip2** takes a couple of seconds to compress the same file.

As mentioned at the beginning of this section, **tar** is an archiving utility that is used to group several files into a single archive file. Example 2-40 shows how **tar** is used to archive three files into one. To archive a number of files, you issue the command **tar -cvf** {*Archive_File.tar*} {*file1*} {*file2*} .. {*fileX*}. The option c is for *create*, **v** is for *verbose*, and **f** is for stating the archive *filename* in the command. To view the constituent files of the archive, you use the command **tar -tf** {*Archive_File.tar*}. This does not extract the files in the archive. It only lists the files that make up the archive, as shown by the **ls -l** command in the example, right after this command is used. Finally, in order to extract the files from the archive, you use the command **tar -xvf** {*Archive_File.tar*}.

Example 2-40 *Using the tar Utility to Archive Three Files into One*

```
[NetProg@localhost LinuxStudies]$ ls -l
total 17260
-rw-rw-r--. 1 NetProg NetProg 17622037 Feb 24 12:27 BGP.txt
-rw-rw-r--. 1 NetProg NetProg    43147 Feb 24 13:33 IPRoute.txt
-rw-r--r--. 1 NetProg NetProg      796 Feb 24 13:33 QoS.txt
```

```
! Archive three files into one tarball
[NetProg@localhost LinuxStudies]$ tar -cvf Archive.tar BGP.txt IPRoute.txt QoS.txt
BGP.txt
IPRoute.txt
QoS.txt
[NetProg@localhost LinuxStudies]$ ls -l
total 34520
-rw-rw-r--. 1 NetProg NetProg 17674240 Feb 24 15:22 Archive.tar
-rw-rw-r--. 1 NetProg NetProg 17622037 Feb 24 12:27 BGP.txt
-rw-rw-r--. 1 NetProg NetProg    43147 Feb 24 13:33 IPRoute.txt
-rw-r--r--. 1 NetProg NetProg      796 Feb 24 13:33 QoS.txt

[NetProg@localhost LinuxStudies]$ rm BGP.txt IPRoute.txt QoS.txt
[NetProg@localhost LinuxStudies]$ ls -l
total 17260
-rw-rw-r--. 1 NetProg NetProg 17674240 Feb 24 15:22 Archive.tar

! Display the constituent files in the archive without de-archiving the tarball
[NetProg@localhost LinuxStudies]$ tar -tf Archive.tar
BGP.txt
IPRoute.txt
QoS.txt
[NetProg@localhost LinuxStudies]$ ls -l
total 17260
-rw-rw-r--. 1 NetProg NetProg 17674240 Feb 24 15:22 Archive.tar

! De-archive the tarball into its constituent files
[NetProg@localhost LinuxStudies]$ tar -xvf Archive.tar
BGP.txt
IPRoute.txt
QoS.txt
[NetProg@localhost LinuxStudies]$ ls -l
total 34520
-rw-rw-r--. 1 NetProg NetProg 17674240 Feb 24 15:22 Archive.tar
-rw-rw-r--. 1 NetProg NetProg 17622037 Feb 24 12:27 BGP.txt
-rw-rw-r--. 1 NetProg NetProg    43147 Feb 24 13:33 IPRoute.txt
-rw-r--r--. 1 NetProg NetProg      796 Feb 24 13:33 QoS.txt
[NetProg@localhost LinuxStudies]$
```

Notice that the size of the archive file is actually a little bigger than the sizes of the constituent files added together. This is because archiving utilities do not compress files. Moreover, the archive file contains extra metadata that is required for describing the archive file contents and metadata related to the archiving process.

Luckily, the **tar** command can be used with certain options to summon compression utilities to compress the files before archiving them:

- To compress the files using the **gzip** utility before the **tar** archive is created, use the syntax **tar -zcvf** {*archive-file.tar.gz*} {*file1*} {*file2*} .. {*fileX*}. To de-archive the tarball and then decompress the constituent files, use the syntax **tar -zxvf** {*archive-file.tar.gz*}.
- To compress the files using the **bzip2** utility before the **tar** archive is created, use the syntax **tar -jcvf** {*archive-file.tar.bz2*} {*file1*} {*file2*} .. {*fileX*}. To de-archive the tarball and then decompress the constituent files, use the syntax **tar -jxvf** {*archive-file.tar.bz2*}.
- To compress the files using the **xz** utility before the **tar** archive is created, use the syntax **tar -Jcvf** {*archive-file.tar.xz*} {*file1*} {*file2*} .. {*fileX*}. To de-archive the tarball and then decompress the constituent files, use the syntax **tar -Jxvf** {*archive-file.tar.xz*}.

Example 2-41 shows the **tar** command being used with the **-J** option, which summons the **xz** utility to compress the files before **tar** archives these files. Then the same option is used to decompress the files after they are extracted from the **tar** archive.

Example 2-41 *Using the tar Utility with xz to Compress and Archive Three Files into One*

```
[NetProg@localhost LinuxStudies]$ ls -l
total 17260
-rw-rw-r--. 1 NetProg NetProg 17622037 Feb 24 12:27 BGP.txt
-rw-rw-r--. 1 NetProg NetProg    43147 Feb 24 13:33 IPRoute.txt
-rw-r--r--. 1 NetProg NetProg      796 Feb 24 13:33 QoS.txt

[NetProg@localhost LinuxStudies]$ tar -Jcvf Archive.tar.xz BGP.txt
  IPRoute.txt QoS.txt
BGP.txt
IPRoute.txt
QoS.txt
[NetProg@localhost LinuxStudies]$ ls -l
total 17980
-rw-rw-r--. 1 NetProg NetProg   735548 Feb 24 16:01 Archive.tar.xz
-rw-rw-r--. 1 NetProg NetProg 17622037 Feb 24 12:27 BGP.txt
-rw-rw-r--. 1 NetProg NetProg    43147 Feb 24 13:33 IPRoute.txt
-rw-r--r--. 1 NetProg NetProg      796 Feb 24 13:33 QoS.txt

[NetProg@localhost LinuxStudies]$ rm BGP.txt IPRoute.txt QoS.txt
[NetProg@localhost LinuxStudies]$ ls -l
total 720
```

```
-rw-rw-r--. 1 NetProg NetProg 735548 Feb 24 16:01 Archive.tar.xz

[NetProg@localhost LinuxStudies]$ tar -Jxvf Archive.tar.xz
BGP.txt
IPRoute.txt
QoS.txt
[NetProg@localhost LinuxStudies]$ ls -l
total 17980
-rw-rw-r--. 1 NetProg NetProg   735548 Feb 24 16:01 Archive.tar.xz
-rw-rw-r--. 1 NetProg NetProg 17622037 Feb 24 12:27 BGP.txt
-rw-rw-r--. 1 NetProg NetProg    43147 Feb 24 13:33 IPRoute.txt
-rw-r--r--. 1 NetProg NetProg      796 Feb 24 13:33 QoS.txt
[NetProg@localhost LinuxStudies]$
```

Notice that the size of the **tar** file is now smaller in size than the sizes of the constituent files added together. This is due to the compression preceding the archiving. Notice also that the archive file is named with file extension .tar.xz. This is not mandatory, and the command works just fine if the archive is just a filename with no extension. However, this extension enables a user to identify the file as a **tar** archive that has been compressed using the **xz** compression utility.

Linux System Maintenance

This section discusses general maintenance of a Linux system. In order to maintain a healthy Linux system as well as troubleshoot and resolve system incidents, you need to understand how to do the following:

- Manage jobs and processes
- Monitor utilization of CPU, memory, and other resources
- Collect system information
- Locate, read, and analyze system logs

The following sections discuss these points in some depth. For further details, you can consult the man or info pages for each command.

Job, Process, and Service Management

In operating systems jargon, a *thread* is a sequence of instructions that are executed by the CPU. A thread is a basic building block and cannot be broken up into smaller components to be executed simultaneously.

A *process* is a group of threads. Two or more of those threads may be executed simultaneously in a multithreaded system in order to run a process faster. A process has its own address space in memory. Linux virtualizes memory such that each process thinks that it has exclusive access to all the physical memory on the system even though it actually only has access to its own process address space. Utilities such as **ls**, **cp**, and **cat** run as processes.

A *job* may be composed of two or more processes. For example, running the command **ls** starts a process, while piping **ls** to **less** using the command **ls | less** starts a job composed of more than one process.

A *service* is composed of one or more processes and provides a specific function; examples are the HTTP, NTP, and SSH services. A service is also usually run in the background and is therefore referred to as a *daemon*. Service names in Linux almost always end with the letter d. Services are briefly introduced earlier in this chapter.

As you progress through this section, the differences between processes, jobs, and services will become more apparent.

The command **ps** lists the processes currently running on the system. Without any options or arguments, the command lists the running processes associated with the current user and terminal, as shown in Example 2-42.

Example 2-42 *ps Command Output*

```
[NetProg@localhost ~]$ ps
  PID TTY          TIME CMD
 2897 pts/0    00:00:00 bash
 2954 pts/0    00:00:00 ps
[NetProg@localhost ~]$
```

For each process, the **ps** command output lists the following fields:

- **PID:** This is the process ID, which is a number that uniquely identifies each process.
- **TTY:** This is the terminal number from which the process was started. pts/0 in the output stands for pseudo-terminal slave 0. The first terminal window you open will be pts/0, the second pts/1, and so forth.

Note Use of the terms "master" and "slave" is ONLY in association with the official terminology used in industry specifications and standards, and in no way diminishes Pearson's commitment to promoting diversity, equity, and inclusion, and challenging, countering and/or combating bias and stereotyping in the global population of the learners we serve.

- **TIME:** This is the total amount of time the process spent consuming the CPU throughout the duration of its lifetime.
- **CMD:** This is the process name.

For more detailed output, several options can be added to the **ps** command. Adding the **-A** or **-e** options lists all processes running on the system for all users and all TTY lines, as shown in Example 2-43. The output is in the same format as the vanilla **ps** command output. In order to compare the output from both commands, you can pipe the output to **wc -l**. The command **wc** stands for *word count*, and when used with the **-l** option, the command returns the number of lines in the command argument (in this case, the output of the **ps** command). As you can see, both commands return 189 lines of output. The purpose of this example is two-fold: to display the output of the **ps** command using both options and to introduce the very handy command **wc -l**.

Example 2-43 *ps -e and ps -A Commands*

```
[NetProg@localhost ~]$ ps -e
  PID TTY          TIME CMD
    1 ?        00:00:02 systemd
    2 ?        00:00:00 kthreadd
    3 ?        00:00:00 ksoftirqd/0
    5 ?        00:00:00 kworker/0:0H
    7 ?        00:00:00 migration/0
    8 ?        00:00:00 rcu_bh
    9 ?        00:00:01 rcu_sched
   10 ?        00:00:00 watchdog/0
   12 ?        00:00:00 kdevtmpfs

-------- OUTPUT TRUNCATED FOR BREVITY --------

[NetProg@localhost ~]$ ps -A
  PID TTY          TIME CMD
    1 ?        00:00:02 systemd
    2 ?        00:00:00 kthreadd
    3 ?        00:00:00 ksoftirqd/0
    5 ?        00:00:00 kworker/0:0H
    7 ?        00:00:00 migration/0
    8 ?        00:00:00 rcu_bh
    9 ?        00:00:01 rcu_sched
   10 ?        00:00:00 watchdog/0
   12 ?        00:00:00 kdevtmpfs

--------- OUTPUT TRUNCATED FOR BREVITY ---------

[NetProg@localhost ~]$ ps -e | wc -l
189
[NetProg@localhost ~]$ ps -A | wc -l
189
[NetProg@localhost ~]$
```

Notice in Example 2-43 that the TTY field shows a question mark (?) throughout the output. This indicates that these processes are not associated with a terminal window, referred to as a *controlling terminal*.

The command **ps -u** lists all the processes owned by the *current* user and adds to the information displayed for each process. To display the processes for any *other* user, you use the syntax **ps -u** {*username*}. Example 2-44 shows the output of **ps -u**, which lists the processes owned by the user NetProg (the current user).

Example 2-44 *ps -u Command Output*

```
[NetProg@localhost ~]$ ps -u
USER        PID %CPU %MEM    VSZ   RSS TTY      STAT START   TIME COMMAND
NetProg    4312  0.0  0.0 116564  3280 pts/1    Ss   12:22   0:00 bash
NetProg    4517  0.0  0.0 116564  3280 pts/2    Ss   12:33   0:00 bash
NetProg    5609  0.0  0.0 119552  2284 pts/2    S+   13:59   0:00 man ps
NetProg    5620  0.0  0.0 110260   944 pts/2    S+   13:59   0:00 less -s
NetProg    7990  0.0  0.0 119552  2284 pts/1    S+   17:40   0:00 man ps
NetProg    8001  0.0  0.0 110260   948 pts/1    S+   17:40   0:00 less -s
NetProg    8827  0.0  0.0 116564  3288 pts/0    Ss   18:28   0:00 bash
NetProg   10108  0.0  0.0 151064  1792 pts/0    R+   19:49   0:00 ps -u
[NetProg@localhost ~]$
```

Notice that the output of **ps -u** adds seven more fields to the output:

- **User:** The user ID of the process owner
- **%CPU:** The CPU time the process used divided by the process runtime (process lifetime), expressed as a percentage
- **%MEM:** The ratio of the main memory used by the process (resident set size) to the total amount of main memory on the system, expressed as a percentage
- **VSZ:** Virtual memory size, the amount of virtual memory used by the process, expressed in kilobytes
- **RSS:** Resident set size, the amount of main memory (RAM) used by the process, expressed in kilobytes
- **STAT:** The state of the process
- **START:** The start time of the process

The process STAT field contains 1 or more of the 14 characters describing the state of the process. For example, state S indicates that the process is in the sleep state (that is, waiting for an event to happen in order to resume running, such as waiting for input from the user). The **+** indicates that the process is running in the foreground rather than running in the background.

Processes are grouped into *process groups*, and one or more process groups make up a *session*. All the processes in one pipeline, such as **cat**, **sort**, and **tail** in **cat file.txt | sort | tail -n 10**, are in the same process group and have the same process group ID (PGID). The process whose PID is the same as its PGID is the *process group leader*, and it is the first member of the process group. On the other hand, all process groups started by a shell are in the same session, and they have the same session ID (SID). The process whose PID is the same as its SID is the *session leader*. In Example 2-44, as expected, the two shell processes (**bash**) are session leaders, as indicated by the s in their STAT field. To check the PID, PGID, and SID of a process all at once, issue the command **ps -j**.

To list all processes that have a specific name, use the -C option. In Example 2-45, **ps -C bash** lists all processes that are named **bash**.

Example 2-45 *ps -C bash Command Output*

```
[NetProg@localhost ~]$ ps -C bash
  PID TTY          TIME CMD
 4312 pts/1    00:00:00 bash
 4517 pts/2    00:00:00 bash
 8827 pts/0    00:00:00 bash
[NetProg@localhost ~]$
```

Finally, to see the parent process ID (PPID) of a process, you can use the option **-f**. As the name implies, the parent process is the process that started this process. In Example 2-46, the command **ps -ef | head -n 10** is used to display the first 10 processes in the list, along with the **PPID** of each process.

Example 2-46 *ps -ef | head -n 10 Command Output*

```
[NetProg@localhost ~]$ ps -ef | head -n 10
UID         PID  PPID  C STIME TTY          TIME CMD
root          1     0  0 09:29 ?        00:00:02 /usr/lib/systemd/systemd --switched-
  root --system --deserialize 21
root          2     0  0 09:29 ?        00:00:00 [kthreadd]
root          3     2  0 09:29 ?        00:00:00 [ksoftirqd/0]
root          5     2  0 09:29 ?        00:00:00 [kworker/0:0H]
root          7     2  0 09:29 ?        00:00:00 [migration/0]
root          8     2  0 09:29 ?        00:00:00 [rcu_bh]
root          9     2  0 09:29 ?        00:00:00 [rcu_sched]
root         10     2  0 09:29 ?        00:00:00 [watchdog/0]
root         12     2  0 09:29 ?        00:00:00 [kdevtmpfs]
[NetProg@localhost ~]$
```

Note that the process with PID 0 is the kernel, and the process with PID 1 is the **systemd** process, or the **init** process in some systems (recall the Linux boot process?). Knowing this, the output in Example 2-46 should make more sense.

As you have seen from the output of **ps -e | wc -l** in Example 2-43, the list of running processes can be very long. While the output can be piped to **grep** in order to list specific lines of the command output, the use of the command **pgrep** may be a little more intuitive. Example 2-47 shows the output of the command **pgrep -u NetProg -l bash**, showing all processes owned by user NetProg and named **bash**.

Example 2-47 *pgrep -u NetProg -l bash Command Output*

```
[NetProg@localhost ~]$ pgrep -u NetProg -l bash
3173 bash
5815 bash
6561 bash
6667 bash
6730 bash
[NetProg@localhost ~]$
```

You can start and stop processes by using the **kill** command. The **kill** command sends 1 of 64 signals to a process or process group. This signal may be a **SIGTERM** signal to request the process to terminate gracefully, or it may be a **SIGKILL** signal to force the termination of the process. The signals **SIGSTOP** and **SIGCONT** are also used to pause and resume a process, respectively. To view all the available signals, you can issue the command **kill -l**, as shown in Example 2-48. The default signal **SIGTERM** is used if no signal is explicitly specified in the command. The command **kill** may be used with the signal numeric value or signal name.

Example 2-48 *Using **kill -l** to List Signals Used with the **kill** Command*

```
[NetProg@localhost ~]$ kill -l
 1) SIGHUP       2) SIGINT       3) SIGQUIT      4) SIGILL       5) SIGTRAP
 6) SIGABRT      7) SIGBUS       8) SIGFPE       9) SIGKILL     10) SIGUSR1
11) SIGSEGV     12) SIGUSR2     13) SIGPIPE     14) SIGALRM     15) SIGTERM
16) SIGSTKFLT   17) SIGCHLD     18) SIGCONT     19) SIGSTOP     20) SIGTSTP
21) SIGTTIN     22) SIGTTOU     23) SIGURG      24) SIGXCPU     25) SIGXFSZ
26) SIGVTALRM   27) SIGPROF     28) SIGWINCH    29) SIGIO       30) SIGPWR
31) SIGSYS      34) SIGRTMIN    35) SIGRTMIN+1  36) SIGRTMIN+2  37) SIGRTMIN+3
38) SIGRTMIN+4  39) SIGRTMIN+5  40) SIGRTMIN+6  41) SIGRTMIN+7  42) SIGRTMIN+8
43) SIGRTMIN+9  44) SIGRTMIN+10 45) SIGRTMIN+11 46) SIGRTMIN+12 47) SIGRTMIN+13
48) SIGRTMIN+14 49) SIGRTMIN+15 50) SIGRTMAX-14 51) SIGRTMAX-13 52) SIGRTMAX-12
53) SIGRTMAX-11 54) SIGRTMAX-10 55) SIGRTMAX-9  56) SIGRTMAX-8  57) SIGRTMAX-7
58) SIGRTMAX-6  59) SIGRTMAX-5  60) SIGRTMAX-4  61) SIGRTMAX-3  62) SIGRTMAX-2
63) SIGRTMAX-1  64) SIGRTMAX
[NetProg@localhost ~]$
```

Example 2-49 shows how to pause, resume, and kill the process **bash** with process ID 3173. The **-p** option is used with the **ps** command to list a specific process using its PID.

Example 2-49 *Pausing, Resuming, and Killing the Process **bash** Using the **kill** Command*

```
[NetProg@localhost ~]$ ps -C bash
  PID TTY          TIME CMD
 3173 pts/1    00:00:00 bash
 5815 ?        00:00:00 bash
 8501 pts/3    00:00:00 bash
 8980 pts/4    00:00:00 bash
 9233 pts/2    00:00:00 bash
[NetProg@localhost ~]$ ps -up 3173
USER       PID %CPU %MEM    VSZ   RSS TTY      STAT START   TIME COMMAND
NetProg   3173  0.0  0.0 116696  3440 pts/1    Ss   11:41   0:00 bash
[NetProg@localhost ~]$ kill -SIGSTOP 3173
[NetProg@localhost ~]$ ps -up 3173
USER       PID %CPU %MEM    VSZ   RSS TTY      STAT START   TIME COMMAND
NetProg   3173  0.0  0.0 116696  3440 pts/1    Ts   11:41   0:00 bash
[NetProg@localhost ~]$ kill -SIGCONT 3173
[NetProg@localhost ~]$ ps -up 3173
USER       PID %CPU %MEM    VSZ   RSS TTY      STAT START   TIME COMMAND
NetProg   3173  0.0  0.0 116696  3440 pts/1    Ss   11:41   0:00 bash
[NetProg@localhost ~]$ kill -SIGTERM 3173
[NetProg@localhost ~]$ ps -up 3173
USER       PID %CPU %MEM    VSZ   RSS TTY      STAT START   TIME COMMAND
NetProg   3173  0.0  0.0 116696  3440 pts/1    Ss   11:41   0:00 bash
[NetProg@localhost ~]$ kill -SIGKILL 3173
[NetProg@localhost ~]$ ps -up 3173
USER       PID %CPU %MEM    VSZ   RSS TTY      STAT START   TIME COMMAND
[NetProg@localhost ~]$ ps -C bash
  PID TTY          TIME CMD
 5815 ?        00:00:00 bash
 8501 pts/3    00:00:00 bash
 8980 pts/4    00:00:00 bash
 9233 pts/2    00:00:00 bash
[NetProg@localhost ~]$
```

As you can see from Example 2-49, when process **bash** with PID 3137 receives the **SIGSTOP** signal, its state changes from Ss (interruptible sleep, indicated by S, and session leader, indicated by s) to Ts (stopped by job control signal, indicated by T, and session leader, indicated by s).

The process returns to the Ss state when it receives the **SIGCONT** signal. When the **SIGTERM** signal is then used in an attempt to terminate the process, its state does not change; therefore, **SIGKILL** is used, and it successfully forces the process to terminate. It should be noted, however, that it is generally not recommended to terminate a process by using the **SIGKILL** signal unless the process is suspected to be malicious or is not properly responding.

Jobs, on the other hand, can be displayed by using the **jobs** command. The **jobs** command lists all jobs run by the current shell. In Example 2-50, a simple **for** loop is used to create a job that runs indefinitely. (Loops and control structures in Bash are covered in Chapter 4.) In addition, you can enter the command **gedit** to start the text editor program. An & is added at the end of both command lines shown in Example 2-50. This instructs the shell to run both jobs in the background, so the running process will not hog the shell prompt, and the prompt will be available for you to enter other commands. A third job is created by running the **ping** command to google.com in the foreground. The **ping** command is then stopped (paused) by using the Ctrl+z key combination. The command **jobs** then lists all three jobs.

Example 2-50 *Using the jobs Command to Display Job Status*

```
[NetProg@localhost ~]$ jobs
[NetProg@localhost ~]$ i=0; while true; do ((i++)); sleep 5; done &
[1] 19332
[NetProg@localhost ~]$ gedit &
[2] 19347
[NetProg@localhost ~]$ ping google.com
PING google.com (172.217.18.46) 56(84) bytes of data.
64 bytes from ham02s12-in-f46.1e100.net (172.217.18.46): icmp_seq=1 ttl=63 time=220 ms
64 bytes from ham02s12-in-f46.1e100.net (172.217.18.46): icmp_seq=2 ttl=63 time=280 ms
^Z
[3]+  Stopped                 ping google.com
[NetProg@localhost ~]$ jobs
[1]   Running        while true; do ((i++)); sleep 5; done &
[2]-  Running        gedit &
[3]+  Stopped        ping google.com
[NetProg@localhost ~]$
```

The number in brackets in Example 2-50 is the job number, and the number after that is the PID. The jobs in the example are numbered 1 to 3. The first two jobs are in Running state, and the ping job is in the Stopped state. To list the running jobs only, you use the **jobs -r** command, and to display the stopped jobs only, you use the **jobs -s** command.

To resume a stopped process, you bring the process to the foreground by using the command **fg** {*job_number*}. To send it to the background again, you use the command **bg** {*job_number*}. When the job is running in the foreground, you can stop it by using the Ctrl+c key combination. Example 2-51 shows a **ping** process brought to the foreground and stopped.

Example 2-51 *Bringing a ping Job to the Foreground and Stopping It*

```
[NetProg@localhost ~]$ jobs
[1]   Running        while true; do ((i++)); sleep 5; done &
[2]-  Running        gedit &
[3]+  Stopped        ping google.com
[NetProg@localhost ~]$ fg 3
ping google.com
64 bytes from ham02s12-in-f46.1e100.net (172.217.18.46): icmp_seq=3 ttl=63 time=5463 ms
64 bytes from ham02s12-in-f46.1e100.net (172.217.18.46): icmp_seq=4 ttl=63 time=5261 ms
64 bytes from ham02s12-in-f46.1e100.net (172.217.18.46): icmp_seq=5 ttl=63 time=4698 ms
64 bytes from ham02s12-in-f46.1e100.net (172.217.18.46): icmp_seq=6 ttl=63 time=5178 ms
^C
--- google.com ping statistics ---
11 packets transmitted, 6 received, 45% packet loss, time 633961ms
rtt min/avg/max/mdev = 220.614/3517.335/5463.953/2321.238 ms, pipe 6
[NetProg@localhost ~]$
```

If a job is running in the background and you want to stop it without bringing it to the foreground first, you use the **kill** command in exactly the same way you use it with processes. Example 2-52 shows the **kill** command being used to terminate the two running jobs. Notice that the **-l** option is used with the **jobs** command to add a PID column to the output.

Example 2-52 *Terminating a Job Using the **kill** Command*

```
[NetProg@localhost ~]$ jobs -l
[1]- 19332 Running    while true; do ((i++)); sleep 5; done &
[2]+ 19347 Running    gedit &
[NetProg@localhost ~]$ kill 19332
[1]-  Terminated      while true; do ((i++)); sleep 5; done
[NetProg@localhost ~]$ jobs
[2]+  Running         gedit &
[NetProg@localhost ~]$ kill 19347
[2]+  Terminated      gedit
[NetProg@localhost ~]$ jobs
[NetProg@localhost ~]$
```

To view service status, start and stop services, and carry out other service-related operations, you can use the command **systemctl**. The general syntax of the command is **systemctl** {*options*} {*service_name*}. These are the most common options for this command:

- **status:** Displays the status of the service
- **start:** Starts the service

- **stop:** Stops the service
- **enable:** Enables the service so that it is automatically started at system startup
- **disable:** Disables the service so that it is not automatically started at system startup

Example 2-53 shows how to check the status of the **httpd** service, start it, stop it, and enable it.

Example 2-53 *Using the systemctl Command to View and Change the Status of the httpd Service*

```
[NetProg@localhost ~]$ systemctl status httpd
● httpd.service - The Apache HTTP Server
   Loaded: loaded (/usr/lib/systemd/system/httpd.service; disabled; vendor preset:
  disabled)
   Active: inactive (dead)
     Docs: man:httpd(8)
           man:apachectl(8)
[NetProg@localhost ~]$ sudo systemctl enable httpd
[sudo] password for NetProg:
Created symlink from /etc/systemd/system/multi-user.target.wants/httpd.service to /
  usr/lib/systemd/system/httpd.service.
[NetProg@localhost ~]$ systemctl status httpd
● httpd.service - The Apache HTTP Server
   Loaded: loaded (/usr/lib/systemd/system/httpd.service; enabled; vendor preset:
  disabled)
   Active: inactive (dead)
     Docs: man:httpd(8)
           man:apachectl(8)
[NetProg@localhost ~]$ sudo systemctl start httpd
[NetProg@localhost ~]$ systemctl status httpd
● httpd.service - The Apache HTTP Server
   Loaded: loaded (/usr/lib/systemd/system/httpd.service; enabled; vendor preset:
  disabled)
   Active: active (running) since Sun 2018-04-08 17:35:40 +03; 3s ago
     Docs: man:httpd(8)
           man:apachectl(8)
 Main PID: 2921 (httpd)
   Status: "Processing requests..."
   CGroup: /system.slice/httpd.service
           ├─2921 /usr/sbin/httpd -DFOREGROUND
           ├─2925 /usr/sbin/httpd -DFOREGROUND
           ├─2926 /usr/sbin/httpd -DFOREGROUND
           ├─2927 /usr/sbin/httpd -DFOREGROUND
           ├─2928 /usr/sbin/httpd -DFOREGROUND
           └─2929 /usr/sbin/httpd -DFOREGROUND
```

```
Apr 08 17:35:40 localhost.localdomain systemd[1]: Starting The Apache HTTP Ser....
Apr 08 17:35:40 localhost.localdomain httpd[2921]: AH00558: httpd: Could not r...e
Apr 08 17:35:40 localhost.localdomain systemd[1]: Started The Apache HTTP Server.
Hint: Some lines were ellipsized, use -l to show in full.
[NetProg@localhost ~]$ sudo systemctl stop httpd
[sudo] password for NetProg:

[NetProg@localhost ~]$ systemctl status httpd
● httpd.service - The Apache HTTP Server
   Loaded: loaded (/usr/lib/systemd/system/httpd.service; enabled; vendor preset:
  disabled)
   Active: inactive (dead) since Sun 2018-04-08 17:41:14 +03; 8s ago
     Docs: man:httpd(8)
           man:apachectl(8)
  Process: 3132 ExecStop=/bin/kill -WINCH ${MAINPID} (code=exited, status=0/SUCCESS)
  Process: 2921 ExecStart=/usr/sbin/httpd $OPTIONS -DFOREGROUND (code=exited,
  status=0/SUCCESS)
 Main PID: 2921 (code=exited, status=0/SUCCESS)
   Status: "Total requests: 0; Current requests/sec: 0; Current traffic:   0 B/sec"

Apr 08 17:35:40 localhost.localdomain systemd[1]: Starting The Apache HTTP Ser....
Apr 08 17:35:40 localhost.localdomain httpd[2921]: AH00558: httpd: Could not r...e
Apr 08 17:35:40 localhost.localdomain systemd[1]: Started The Apache HTTP Server.
Apr 08 17:41:13 localhost.localdomain systemd[1]: Stopping The Apache HTTP Ser....
Apr 08 17:41:14 localhost.localdomain systemd[1]: Stopped The Apache HTTP Server.
Hint: Some lines were ellipsized, use -l to show in full.
[NetProg@localhost ~]$
```

In Example 2-53, the **httpd** service is both inactive and disabled. When the **enable** option is used, the **httpd** service changes its state to enabled, which means the service will be automatically started when the system is booted. However, the service is still inactive; that is, it is *not* currently running. When you use the **start** option, the **httpd** service becomes active. Finally, the service is stopped using the **stop** option. Note that starting and stopping the service is independent of the service's enabled/disabled status. The former describes the *current* status of the service, while the latter describes whether the service should be started automatically at system startup time.

Resource Utilization

Resource utilization, at a very basic level, refers to CPU, memory, and storage utilization. While checking disk space on a system tends to be a straightforward process, checking the CPU and memory utilization can be quite challenging if you don't know exactly what tools to use. The single most important Linux command to use to check resource utilization is **top**.

Example 2-54 shows the output of the **top** command. The list of processes is live—that is, updated in real time as the output is being viewed. The output is also limited by the shell window size. The bigger the window, the longer the list of processes that you can view.

Example 2-54 *Output of the top Command*

```
top - 23:52:06 up 3 min,  3 users,  load average: 0.23, 0.34, 0.16
Tasks: 205 total,   1 running, 204 sleeping,   0 stopped,   0 zombie
%Cpu(s):  0.9 us,  0.6 sy,  0.0 ni, 98.5 id,  0.0 wa,  0.0 hi,  0.0 si,  0.0 st
KiB Mem :  8010152 total,  6713388 free,   783364 used,   513400 buff/cache
KiB Swap:  5242876 total,  5242876 free,        0 used.  6940600 avail Mem

  PID USER      PR  NI    VIRT    RES    SHR S  %CPU %MEM     TIME+ COMMAND
 2051 NetProg   20   0 2520892 226276  47980 S   4.3  2.8   0:17.71 gnome-shell
 1183 root      20   0  354540  55024  10848 S   2.6  0.7   0:05.44 X
 2675 NetProg   20   0  723988  25624  15312 S   1.3  0.3   0:02.18 gnome-terminal-
 2788 NetProg   20   0  157860   2368   1532 R   1.0  0.0   0:01.06 top
 2789 NetProg   20   0  157944   2316   1532 S   1.0  0.0   0:01.00 top
 1992 NetProg   20   0  214904   1312    880 S   0.3  0.0   0:00.41 VBoxClient
    1 root      20   0  193708   6844   4068 S   0.0  0.1   0:01.85 systemd
    2 root      20   0       0      0      0 S   0.0  0.0   0:00.00 kthreadd
    3 root      20   0       0      0      0 S   0.0  0.0   0:00.02 ksoftirqd/0
    4 root      20   0       0      0      0 S   0.0  0.0   0:00.00 kworker/0:0

--------- OUTPUT TRUNCATED FOR BREVITY ---------
```

The following is a list of keys that, when pressed, change the formatting of the output while the **top** command is running:

- **m:** Pressing this key shows memory usage, as a percentage.
- **t:** Pressing this key shows CPU usage, as a percentage.
- **1:** Pressing this key shows all processors on the system.
- **Shift+m:** Pressing this key combination sorts processes by memory usage, in descending order.
- **Shift+p:** Pressing this key combination sorts processes by CPU usage, in descending order.
- **Shift+r:** Pressing this key combination sorts processes by PID.
- **k-**{*PID*}-{*Signal_No*|*Signal_Name*}: Pressing **k** starts a dialog above the first column of the process list. This dialog requests a PID. After you type a PID and press Enter, it requests the signal you want to send to that process. This can be used to send any of the 64 signals to any of the processes on the system.

Example 2-55 shows the output you get when you use the **top** command and press 1 followed by **t**. As you can see, all four processors on the system are listed, with the percentage utilization of each.

Example 2-55 *Output of the* **top** *Command Showing Each of the Four CPUs Being Used*

```
top - 00:06:33 up 17 min,  4 users,  load average: 0.11, 0.08, 0.10
Tasks: 201 total,   2 running, 198 sleeping,   1 stopped,   0 zombie
%Cpu0  :   6.8/2.3     9[|||||                                          ]
%Cpu1  :   8.2/0.0     8[||||                                           ]
%Cpu2  :   4.2/2.1     6[|||                                            ]
%Cpu3  :   1.9/0.0     2[|                                              ]
KiB Mem :  8010152 total,  6692660 free,   803756 used,   513736 buff/cache
KiB Swap:  5242876 total,  5242876 free,        0 used.  6920176 avail Mem

  PID USER      PR  NI    VIRT    RES    SHR S  %CPU %MEM     TIME+ COMMAND
 2051 NetProg   20   0 2521404 226756  47984 S  31.4  2.8   0:44.63 /usr/bin/gn+
 1183 root      20   0  359576  59968  10900 S   9.8  0.7   0:15.58 /usr/bin/X +
 2675 NetProg   20   0  725372  27116  15320 D   3.9  0.3   0:07.04 /usr/libexe+
  692 root      20   0    6472    652    540 S   2.0  0.0   0:00.16 /sbin/rngd +
 1992 NetProg   20   0  214904   1312    880 S   2.0  0.0   0:02.36 /usr/bin/VB+
 2212 NetProg   20   0 1520856  28752  17476 S   2.0  0.4   0:01.20 /usr/libexe+
 2788 NetProg   20   0  157888   2404   1564 R   2.0  0.0   0:06.34 top
    1 root      20   0  193708   6844   4068 S   0.0  0.1   0:02.05 /usr/lib/sy+

--------- OUTPUT TRUNCATED FOR BREVITY ---------
```

When troubleshooting an incident, it is sometimes useful to have **top** run with a refresh rate that is faster than the default. The command **top -d** {*N*} runs **top** and refreshes the output every *N* seconds. *N* does not have to be an integer; it can be a fraction of a second.

System Information

Linux provides several ways to collect information describing the hardware and software of the system it is running on, as well as set and change this information, where applicable.

The **date** command, as shown in Example 2-56, displays the date and time configured on the system. Adding the **-R** option to the command displays the same information in RFC 2822 format.

Example 2-56 *Output of the date Command*

```
[NetProg@localhost ~]$ date
Sun Apr  8 01:38:48 +03 2018
[NetProg@localhost ~]$ date -R
Sun, 08 Apr 2018 01:38:53 +0300
[NetProg@localhost ~]$
```

From left to right, the first command output in Example 2-56 displays the following information:

- Day of the week
- Month
- Day
- Time, in *hh:mm:ss* format
- Time zone
- Year

Another command you can use to view and set the system time and date is the **timedatectl** command, shown in Example 2-57.

Example 2-57 *Output of the timedatectl Command*

```
[NetProg@localhost ~]$ timedatectl
      Local time: Sun 2018-04-08 11:40:50 +03
  Universal time: Sun 2018-04-08 08:40:50 UTC
        RTC time: Sun 2018-04-08 08:40:48
       Time zone: Asia/Riyadh (+03, +0300)
     NTP enabled: no
NTP synchronized: no
 RTC in local TZ: no
      DST active: n/a
[NetProg@localhost ~]$
```

The **uptime** command displays how long the system has been running as well as CPU load average. Example 2-58 shows the output from the **uptime** command.

Example 2-58 *Output of the uptime Command*

```
[NetProg@localhost ~]$ uptime
 22:39:25 up 41 min,  2 users,  load average: 0.02, 0.06, 0.11
[NetProg@localhost ~]$
```

The **uptime** command output in Example 2-56 displays the following information:

- The system time when the command was issued (in this example, 10:39:25 p.m.)
- How long the system has been up (in this case 41 minutes)
- How many users are logged in (in this case 2 users)
- The load average over the past 1 minute, 5 minutes, and 15 minutes

The load average is an indication of the average system utilization over a specific duration. The load average factors in all processes that are either using the CPU or waiting to use the CPU (runnable state), as well as processes waiting for I/O access, such as disk access (uninterruptable state). If one process is in either of these states for a duration of 1 minute, then the load average over 1 minute is 1 for a single-processor system.

The output of the **uptime** command shows the load average over the past 1, 5, and 15 minutes. A 0.2 in the first load average field of the output of the **uptime** command indicates an average load of 20% over the past 1 minute if the system has a single processor. For multiprocessor systems, the load average should be divided by the number of processors in the system. Therefore, a 0.2 value in a system with four processors means a load average of 5%. A value of 1 in a four-processor system indicates a load average of 25%.

When you have multiple processors on a system, you can view detailed processor information by viewing the contents of the file /proc/cpuinfo. Example 2-59 displays part of the contents of this file. The cpuinfo file lists each processor and details for each of them. Processors are numbered 0 to the number of processors minus 1. A quick way to display the number of processors on a system is to use the command **cat /proc/cpuinfo | grep processor | wc -l**.

Example 2-59 *CPU Information from the /proc/cpuinfo File*

```
[root@localhost ~]# cat /proc/cpuinfo
processor       : 0
vendor_id       : GenuineIntel
cpu family      : 6
model           : 158
model name      : Intel(R) Core(TM) i7-7700HQ CPU @ 2.80GHz
stepping        : 9
cpu MHz         : 2837.118
cache size      : 6144 KB
physical id     : 0
siblings        : 4
core id         : 0
cpu cores       : 4
apicid          : 0
initial apicid  : 0
fpu             : yes
fpu_exception   : yes
```

```
cpuid level     : 22
wp              : yes
flags           : fpu vme de pse tsc msr pae mce cx8 apic sep mtrr pge mca cmov pat
  pse36 clflush mmx fxsr sse sse2 ht syscall nx rdtscp lm constant_tsc rep_good nopl
  xtopology nonstop_tsc pni pclmulqdq ssse3 cx16 sse4_1 sse4_2 x2apic movbe popcnt
  aes xsave avx rdrand hypervisor lahf_lm abm 3dnowprefetch avx2 rdseed clflushopt
bogomips        : 5674.23
clflush size    : 64
cache_alignment : 64
address sizes   : 39 bits physical, 48 bits virtual
power management:

processor       : 1
vendor_id       : GenuineIntel
cpu family      : 6
model           : 158
model name      : Intel(R) Core(TM) i7-7700HQ CPU @ 2.80GHz

--------- OUTPUT TRUNCATED FOR BREVITY ---------

[root@localhost ~]# cat /proc/cpuinfo | grep processor | wc -l
4
[root@localhost ~]#
```

You can also view processor information by using the command **dmidecode**. You can use this command to display information about a variety of system resources, including CPU and memory. The command **dmidecode -t** lists the resources that the command can provide information on, as shown in Example 2-60.

Example 2-60 *dmidecode Command Options*

```
[root@localhost ~]# dmidecode -t
dmidecode: option requires an argument -- 't'
Type number or keyword expected
Valid type keywords are:
  bios
  system
  baseboard
  chassis
  processor
  memory
  cache
  connector
  slot
[root@localhost ~]#
```

For example, to display the details of the system memory, you can use the command **dmidecode -t memory**, as shown in Example 2-61.

Example 2-61 *Getting Memory Information by Using the **dmidecode -t memory** Command*

```
[root@localhost ~]# dmidecode -t memory
# dmidecode 3.1
Getting SMBIOS data from sysfs.
SMBIOS 3.0.0 present.

Handle 0x0003, DMI type 16, 23 bytes
Physical Memory Array
    Location: System Board Or Motherboard
    Use: System Memory
    Error Correction Type: None
    Maximum Capacity: 32 GB
    Error Information Handle: Not Provided
    Number Of Devices: 2

Handle 0x0004, DMI type 17, 40 bytes
Memory Device
    Array Handle: 0x0003
    Error Information Handle: Not Provided
    Total Width: 64 bits
    Data Width: 64 bits
    Size: 16384 MB
    Form Factor: SODIMM
    Set: None
    Locator: ChannelA-DIMM0
    Bank Locator: BANK 0
    Type: DDR4
    Type Detail: Synchronous Unbuffered (Unregistered)
    Speed: 2400 MT/s
    Manufacturer: 0443
    Serial Number: 124AB741
    Asset Tag: None
    Part Number: RMSA3300MH78HBF-2666

--------- OUTPUT TRUNCATED FOR BREVITY ---------
```

The output in Example 2-61 shows that the system has 32 GB of memory in two DDR4 SODIMM modules.

Additional tools can be used to display information about the system hardware and drivers. Two such tools, which are commonly available on most distros, are **dmesg** and **lspci.**

dmesg (which stands for *display message* or *driver message*) is a commonly used command that displays all messages from the kernel ring buffer. The output of this command typically contains the messages produced by the device drivers. This would be the first place to look when you suspect hardware or driver problems. Example 2-62 shows sample output of the **dmesg** command, which in this case is filtering the output for the word **usb.**

Example 2-62 *USB Device Driver Messages from the dmesg Command*

```
[root@localhost ~]# dmesg | grep -i usb
[    0.189199] ACPI: bus type USB registered
[    0.189213] usbcore: registered new interface driver usbfs
[    0.189220] usbcore: registered new interface driver hub
[    0.189226] usbcore: registered new device driver usb
[    0.749477] ehci_hcd: USB 2.0 'Enhanced' Host Controller (EHCI) Driver
[    0.749505] ohci_hcd: USB 1.1 'Open' Host Controller (OHCI) Driver
[    0.749521] usbcore: registered new interface driver usb-storage
[    0.749539] usbcore: registered new interface driver usbserial
[    0.749543] usbcore: registered new interface driver usbserial_generic
[    0.749548] usbserial: USB Serial support registered for generic
[    0.750640] usbcore: registered new interface driver usbhid
[    0.750641] usbhid: USB HID core driver
[root@localhost ~]#
```

The **lspci** utility displays information about PCI buses in the system and devices connected to them. By default, it shows a brief list of devices. Example 2-63 shows the use of the **lspci** command with the **-tv** options to display verbose output in a tree-like format.

Example 2-63 *Verbose Tree-Like Output of the lspci -tv Command*

```
[root@localhost ~]# lspci -tv
-[0000:00]-+-00.0  Intel Corporation 440FX - 82441FX PMC [Natoma]
           +-01.0  Intel Corporation 82371SB PIIX3 ISA [Natoma/Triton II]
           +-01.1  Intel Corporation 82371AB/EB/MB PIIX4 IDE
           +-02.0  InnoTek Systemberatung GmbH VirtualBox Graphics Adapter
           +-04.0  InnoTek Systemberatung GmbH VirtualBox Guest Service
           +-05.0  Intel Corporation 82801AA AC'97 Audio Controller
           +-07.0  Intel Corporation 82371AB/EB/MB PIIX4 ACPI
           +-08.0  Intel Corporation 82545EM Gigabit Ethernet Controller (Copper)
           +-09.0  Intel Corporation 82545EM Gigabit Ethernet Controller (Copper)
           +-0a.0  Intel Corporation 82545EM Gigabit Ethernet Controller (Copper)
           \-11.0  Intel Corporation 82545EM Gigabit Ethernet Controller (Copper)
[root@localhost ~]#
```

System Logs

Most system log files, including the following, are stored in the /var/log directory:

- **lastlog:** Lists users and services, as well as the last successful login of each
- **messages:** Stores general system log messages
- **secure:** Stores user login information, including failed attempts
- **yum.log:** Stores YUM logs (YUM is covered in the next section of this chapter.)

Under the /var/log directory are other directories, such as the httpd directory, which contains the access and error log files for the **httpd** service. Some log files have the same name, such as secure, with a date appended to it. This indicates that the same log file is being rotated by the system. *Rotation* means periodically archiving a file by appending a date to it and then starting a fresh log file with the same name, without the appended date. Eventually, based on the system settings, rotated files are deleted.

Most log files can be viewed using any of the file view commands covered earlier in this chapter, including **cat**, **more**, **less**, **head**, or **tail**. The **tail** command is commonly used to check the most recent messages in a file, using the syntax **tail -n** {*N*} {*log_file*}, where *N* is the number of messages to view, starting from the end of the file. Another useful alternative is the command **tail -f** {*log_file*}, which runs the **tail** process in the foreground and maintains a live view of the log file and displays any changes to the log file in real time.

Some log files are binary files and cannot be viewed using regular file view utilities. An example is the lastlog file. To view this file, you use the **lastlog** command.

The default protocol used to log events in Linux is the syslog protocol, and the two services responsible for logging syslog messages are **rsyslogd** and **journald.**

The first service responsible for receiving syslog messages and populating the corresponding log files is **rsyslogd.** The configuration file for **rsyslogd** is /etc/rsyslog.conf, which is shown in Example 2-64.

Example 2-64 *Default Content of the rsyslog.conf File*

```
[root@localhost ~]# cat /etc/rsyslog.conf
# rsyslog configuration file

# For more information see /usr/share/doc/rsyslog-*/rsyslog_conf.html
# If you experience problems, see http://www.rsyslog.com/doc/troubleshoot.html

#### MODULES ####

# The imjournal module bellow is now used as a message source instead of imuxsock.
$ModLoad imuxsock # provides support for local system logging (e.g. via logger
  command)
$ModLoad imjournal # provides access to the systemd journal
```

```
#$ModLoad imklog # reads kernel messages (the same are read from journald)
#$ModLoad immark  # provides --MARK-- message capability

# Provides UDP syslog reception
#$ModLoad imudp
#$UDPServerRun 514

# Provides TCP syslog reception
#$ModLoad imtcp
#$InputTCPServerRun 514

#### GLOBAL DIRECTIVES ####

# Where to place auxiliary files
$WorkDirectory /var/lib/rsyslog

# Use default time stamp format
$ActionFileDefaultTemplate RSYSLOG_TraditionalFileFormat

# File syncing capability is disabled by default. This feature is usually not
  required,
# not useful and an extreme performance hit
#$ActionFileEnableSync on

# Include all config files in /etc/rsyslog.d/
$IncludeConfig /etc/rsyslog.d/*.conf

# Turn off message reception via local log socket;
# local messages are retrieved through imjournal now.
$OmitLocalLogging on

# File to store the position in the journal
$IMJournalStateFile imjournal.state

#### RULES ####

# Log all kernel messages to the console.
# Logging much else clutters up the screen.
kern.*                                                 /dev/console

# Log anything (except mail) of level info or higher.
# Don't log private authentication messages!
*.info;mail.none;authpriv.none;cron.none                /var/log/messages

--------- OUTPUT TRUNCATED FOR BREVITY ---------
```

The configuration file is split into sections, and each section covers one aspect of the **rsyslogd** configuration.

The section titled "Include all config files in /etc/rsyslog.d/" (highlighted in Example 2-64) configures **rsyslogd** to read any file with a .conf extension in the /etc/rsyslog.d/ directory and load any configuration in that file. In other words, for any extra configuration required, you can write this configuration to a .conf file and save it under the /etc/rsyslog.d/ directory.

The section titled "RULES" (also highlighted in Example 2-64) instructs **rsyslogd** to redirect syslog messages to specific files based on each message's facility and/or severity. The facility of a syslog message indicates where the message originated. For example, all syslog messages from the kernel have kern listed as the facility. Under the "RULES" section in the configuration file, you can see that any message with the facility kern and *any* severity, represented by the string **kern.***, will be directed to the file /dev/console, and any message with severity **info** from any facility, represented by the string ***.info**, will be directed to file /var/log/messages.

To disable any configuration in the file without deleting it, you use **#** to comment out the configuration.

Let's now examine a specific syslog message from the messages log file. The first part of the message shown in Example 2-65 is the timestamp, followed by the host name, then the service or process that generated the message, and finally the message content.

Example 2-65 *Sample Syslog Message*

```
Apr  9 13:01:30 localhost systemd: Started Fingerprint Authentication Daemon.
```

The second service that receives syslog messages is the **journald** service. The difference between **journald** and **rsyslogd** is that **journald** receives and stores all syslog messages for all facilities and severities in one file, named system.journal. The file resides in the directory **/run/log/journal/**{*arbitrary_number*}. This file is a binary file, which means it cannot be viewed using the regular utilities such as **cat** and **tail**; instead, the log file can be viewed using the **journalctl** command. By default the contents of the log file are wiped out with every reboot of the system.

Example 2-66 shows part of the log file stored by **journald**.

Example 2-66 *Syslog Messages Stored by* **journald** *in system.journal*

```
-- Logs begin at Mon 2018-04-09 09:22:55 +03, end at Mon 2018-04-09 15:24:39 +03. --
Apr 09 09:22:55 localhost.localdomain systemd-journal[106]: Runtime journal is using
  8.0M (max allowed 391.1
Apr 09 09:22:55 localhost.localdomain kernel: Initializing cgroup subsys cpuset
Apr 09 09:22:55 localhost.localdomain kernel: Initializing cgroup subsys cpu
```

```
Apr 09 09:22:55 localhost.localdomain kernel: Initializing cgroup subsys cpuacct
Apr 09 09:22:55 localhost.localdomain kernel: Linux version 3.10.0-693.21.1.el7.
  x86_64 (builder@kbuilder.dev
Apr 09 09:22:55 localhost.localdomain kernel: Command line: BOOT_IMAGE=/vmlinuz-
  3.10.0-693.21.1.el7.x86_64 r
Apr 09 09:22:55 localhost.localdomain kernel: e820: BIOS-provided physical RAM map:
Apr 09 09:22:55 localhost.localdomain kernel: BIOS-e820: [mem 0x0000000000000000-
  0x000000000009fbff] usable

--------- OUTPUT TRUNCATED FOR BREVITY ---------
```

The following are several variations of the **journalctl** command that you can use to make the output more relevant to your requirements:

- **journalctl -n** {*N*}: Displays the last *N* log messages in the log file
- **journalctl -p** {*severity*}: Displays messages with a particular severity
- **journalctl --since** {**today|yesterday**}: Displays messages logged today or logged since yesterday
- **journalctl --since** {*date/time_1*} **--until** {*date/time_2*}: Displays messages logged from *date/time_1* through *date/time_2*
- **journalctl -f**: Displays a live view of the log file

Installing and Maintaining Software on Linux

There are several ways to install and maintain programs on Linux, from manual compilation and installation of source code to using high-level package managers. Package management constitutes one of the most notable differences between Linux distros. In keeping with the rest of this chapter, this section covers software and package management for the Red Hat family, so it applies to all distros branching out from Red Hat, such as CentOS and Fedora. The same concepts apply to other distros, but the file formats and the package management programs may be different.

The following are some important components of software and package management on Linux:

- **Source code:** Source code is a list of human-readable instructions that a programmer writes. Source code is run through a compiler to turn it into machine code that an OS can understand and execute.
- **Compile:** Compilation is the process of converting high-level source code into machine code that can be passed to the Linux kernel for direct execution without the need for other software.

- **Package management software:** Package management software is used to install, remove, or update programs on an operating system without the need to manually compile the source code of the program and then place each of the compiled files in its respective directory for correct program execution. Recall the **tar** archiving utility. Typically all files required to install a certain application on the computer are grouped into one archive file called a *package*. Package managers verify the integrity of a package, de-archive the package, and, at a minimum, identify software dependencies required to install the package. Many package managers also resolve these dependencies automatically. The package manager then places each file from the archive into the correct directory for proper program execution and, finally, updates any configuration files as required. A package manager also maintains a database that tracks the installed software so that the process of uninstalling software from the system is as automated as the process of installing it.
- **Software dependencies:** When one software or program requires that another software or program be installed first, before that first software can be installed, there is a *software dependency* between the programs. The real complication with software dependencies arises when one program has a dependency on a number of other programs that, in turn, each, have their own dependencies, and so forth. A package includes its list of dependencies in the metadata from which the package manager gets the information it requires to flag, and possibly resolve, these dependencies.
- **RPM:** RPM is a recursive acronym and stands for RPM Package Manager; it was previously known as Red Hat Package Manager before other distros besides Red Hat started using it. The archive files managed by this manager have the .rpm file extension. RPM has some limitations, the most significant being the inability to resolve software dependencies (although it can detect them and alert the user).
- **YUM:** YUM, which stands for Yellowdog Updater Modified, is a high-level package manager that is based on the RPM file format. YUM is different from RPM in that it automatically resolves dependencies by downloading and installing all the software required to complete a program installation. Whereas RPM acts directly on .rpm files, YUM uses software repositories to download packages and all their dependencies.
- **DNF:** DNF, which stands for Dandified YUM, is a next-generation YUM package manager. DNF introduces several enhancements over YUM and is the default package manager on Fedora and CentOS 8.
- **Depsolve:** This is the dependency resolution module for YUM. When *depsolve* or *depsolving* is a part of a message you receive while using a package manager, you know the message is related to software dependency resolution.
- **Libsolv:** This is an external dependency resolver used by DNF.
- **Software repository:** Also known as a *repo* for short, a software repository is a location on a local disk, on a network, or on the Internet that contains a group of

packages, either for a specific software, programming language, or operating system. Simply put, a repo is a collection of RPM files. High-level package managers such as YUM and DNF search all configured repos for packages that the user wishes to install. The package manager also automatically searches those repos for packages required for resolving software dependencies. A local repo exists on the system as a file with a .repo extension. The repos configured on the system are typically listed in the /etc/yum.repos.d/ directory.

Understanding each of the items in this list and where it fits in the puzzle will make the rest of this section easier to digest. The rest of the chapter builds on these terms, providing a more comprehensive understanding of software maintenance on Linux systems.

Manual Compilation and Installation

Before the advent of package managers, the only way to install programs on a Linux OS was by downloading the source code, compiling it, and then placing each compiled file in the correct directory. Configuration files then had to be amended manually, such as adding paths to the **PATH** environment variable. This process was usually different for different programs, and the process was provided by the application developer as a custom installation process, typically in a readme file. The process of manual compilation and installation typically involves four steps:

Step 1. Download and extract the archive files that make up the program installation package. The archive files are commonly provided as tarballs.

Step 2. Run the **configure** script provided by the application developer as part of the application installation package. The **configure** script detects the specific hardware and software it is to run on. The script then creates a file named makefile that contains all required instructions to compile and install the program on that particular system. Running the **configure** script is as simple as issuing the **./configure** command in the directory in which the tarball was extracted.

Step 3. Using the makefile generated by the **configure** script in step 2, invoke the **make** utility by using the **make** command to compile the application source code, generate new libraries, or link existing shared libraries. **make** is a Linux utility that is used to determine automatically which pieces of a large program need to be recompiled and issue the commands to recompile them.

Step 4. Issue the **make install** command under the same installation directory used in steps 2 and 3. The **install** option causes **make** to execute the "install" part of the makefile and installs the application by moving each compiled binary file generated in the previous step into its respective directory.

This manual process can still be used to install applications on a Linux system. However, this method is usually used by programmers and application developers who have specialized requirements, such as customizing open-source software before installing (or redistributing) it. For day-to-day software maintenance, Linux system administrators and users can use higher-level methods that are more streamlined and use the RPM, YUM, and DNF utilities, as described in the following subsections.

RPM

RPM is a package manager that automates the process of manual compilation and installation described in the previous section. All the compiled files that constitute a program are archived in an RPM file. When the **rpm** utility is used to install a program, the utility verifies the integrity of the RPM file and determines the software dependencies from the RPM file metadata. It then prompts the user to resolve those dependencies. When dependencies do not exist or when all dependencies have been resolved, the **rpm** utility de-archives the RPM file, places each compiled file in the correct directory, and updates all relevant configuration files.

The **rpm** utility is invoked using the **rpm** command with an option to run one of several basic modes. Table 2-1 lists some of the most commonly used basic modes, briefly describes each mode, and lists the option to use in order to invoke **rpm** in that mode.

Table 2-1 *RPM Basic Modes*

Mode	Description	Option
Query	Provide information on the package	-q
Verify	Verifies whether a package is installed correctly	-V
Install	Installs a package	-i
Upgrade	Upgrades a package: Installs the package if a previous version is not installed, and if a previous version is installed, it is uninstalled first	-U
Freshen	Upgrades a package only if a previous version exists	-F
Uninstall	Removes all files installed by the package	-e

Example 2-67 shows how to query an installed package by using the command **rpm -qi** {*package_name*}. The **-q** option indicates query mode, and the **-i** option in this case stands for information. If you omit the **-i** option, the command returns the package name only. Example 2-67 uses the **gedit** text editor program that is installed by default on CentOS to showcase the command.

Note that the first option used with the **rpm** command defines the mode. So **rpm -q** runs query mode, and **rpm -i** runs install mode. Any options that follow the mode are defined according to the mode of operation. For example, the command **rpm -qi** operates in query mode, since the first option is **-q**. The **-i** option that follows does not mean that RPM is operating in install mode; it means that the information option is specified for the query mode. As noted previously, if you omit the **-i** option, the command returns the package name only.

Example 2-67 *Querying the gedit Package by Using rpm -qi gedit*

```
[NetProg@localhost ~]$ rpm -q gedit
gedit-3.22.0-3.el7.x86_64
[NetProg@localhost ~]$ rpm -qi gedit
Name         : gedit
Epoch        : 2
Version      : 3.22.0
Release      : 3.el7
Architecture: x86_64
Install Date: Wed 20 Dec 2017 04:57:34 PM +03
Group        : Unspecified
Size         : 14304200
License      : GPLv2+ and GFDL
Signature    : RSA/SHA256, Thu 10 Aug 2017 07:03:22 PM +03, Key ID 24c6a8a7f4a80eb5
Source RPM   : gedit-3.22.0-3.el7.src.rpm
Build Date   : Mon 07 Aug 2017 06:34:42 AM +03
Build Host   : c1bm.rdu2.centos.org
Relocations  : (not relocatable)
Packager     : CentOS BuildSystem <http://bugs.centos.org>
Vendor       : CentOS
URL          : https://wiki.gnome.org/Apps/Gedit
Summary      : Text editor for the GNOME desktop
Description :
gedit is a small, but powerful text editor designed specifically for
the GNOME desktop. It has most standard text editor functions and fully
supports international text in Unicode. Advanced features include syntax
highlighting and automatic indentation of source code, printing and editing
of multiple documents in one window.

gedit is extensible through a plugin system, which currently includes
support for spell checking, comparing files, viewing CVS ChangeLogs, and
adjusting indentation levels. Further plugins can be found in the
gedit-plugins package.
[NetProg@localhost ~]$
```

In order to query a package that is *not installed*, you add the **-p** option to the **-qi** options used in Example 2-67. The **-p** option instructs the **rpm** utility to extract the information from the RPM package itself, so whether it is installed or not is irrelevant. The Google Chrome package is downloaded from the Internet and queried in Example 2-68 without being installed.

Example 2-68 *Querying the Google Chrome Package by Using rpm -qpi {rpm_file}*

```
[NetProg@localhost Downloads]$ ls
google-chrome-stable_current_x86_64.rpm
[NetProg@localhost Downloads]$ rpm -qi google-chrome-stable_current_x86_64.rpm
package google-chrome-stable_current_x86_64.rpm is not installed
[NetProg@localhost Downloads]$ rpm -qpi google-chrome-stable_current_x86_64.rpm
warning: google-chrome-stable_current_x86_64.rpm: Header V4 DSA/SHA1 Signature,
  key ID 7fac5991: NOKEY
Name        : google-chrome-stable
Version     : 65.0.3325.181
Release     : 1
Architecture: x86_64
Install Date: (not installed)
Group       : Applications/Internet
Size        : 188171280
License     : Multiple, see https://chrome.google.com/
Signature   : DSA/SHA1, Tue 20 Mar 2018 08:25:11 AM +03, Key ID a040830f7fac5991
Source RPM  : google-chrome-stable-65.0.3325.181-1.src.rpm
Build Date  : Tue 20 Mar 2018 08:01:42 AM +03
Build Host  : lin64-4-m0.official.chromium.org
Relocations : /opt
Packager    : Chrome Linux Team <chromium-dev@chromium.org>
Vendor      : Google Inc.
URL         : https://chrome.google.com/
Summary     : Google Chrome
Description :
The web browser from Google

Google Chrome is a browser that combines a minimal design with sophisticated
  technology to make the web faster, safer, and easier.
[NetProg@localhost Downloads]$
```

Two more options that can be used in query mode are **-ql**, which lists all files installed by that package (including the full path), and **-qR**, which lists all other packages on which this package has a dependency. Adding the **-p** option to either of these options provides the same information for a package that is *not installed*. Issuing the **rpm** command with the **-qa** option (without any arguments) queries (and lists) all installed packages on the system.

To install a package, use the command **rpm -i** {*package_name*}. If the package or an older version of the package is already installed on the system, the command fails to execute and returns an error. The **rpm -U** {*package_name*} command updates the package; that is, it installs the package, whether an older version exists or not. If an older version does not exist, a fresh installation is done. If an older version is already installed, the old version is updated to the newer version being installed. The **rpm -F** {*package_name*} command freshens the package; that is, it installs the package only if an older version is already installed. Otherwise, the command execution fails and returns an error. The **-v** option, which stands for *verbose*, provides you with extra information on the installation process.

Example 2-69 shows an attempt to install the Google Chrome browser using the **rpm -i** {*package_name*} command. Recall that **rpm** tests for dependencies and alerts the user to them but does not actually resolve them. In this case, the installation fails because, for Google Chrome to work, two additional packages need to be installed first. One of the dependencies, libXss.so.1()(64bit), is a shared library, as indicated by the .so in the name. The RPM for this library is downloaded and installed with no issues. The RPM for the second dependency, /usr/bin/lsb_release, is also downloaded, but during an installation attempt, a failed dependency message indicates that this second dependency has two dependencies of its own and that two additional packages need to be installed before it is possible to proceed any further. This situation, where one dependency has one or more dependencies, and those dependencies, in turn, have their own dependencies, is referred to as *dependency hell*. This is why we referred to this as *an attempt* to install Google Chrome; the installation was not completed due to the complexity of dependency resolution.

Note that an RPM package can contain an arbitrary set of files. Most RPM files are *binary RPMs* (*BRPMs*) that contain compiled versions of software. There are also *source RPMs* (*SRPMs*) that contain the source code used to build a binary package. These have an appropriate tag in the file header that distinguishes them from normal BRPMs, causing them to be extracted to /usr/src on installation.

Example 2-69 *Installing the Google Chrome Package by Using* ***rpm -i*** *{rpm_file}*

```
[NetProg@localhost Downloads]$ rpm -i google-chrome-stable_current_x86_64.rpm
warning: google-chrome-stable_current_x86_64.rpm: Header V4 DSA/SHA1 Signature,
  key ID 7fac5991: NOKEY
error: Failed dependencies:
    /usr/bin/lsb_release is needed by google-chrome-stable-65.0.3325.181-1.x86_64
    libXss.so.1()(64bit) is needed by google-chrome-stable-65.0.3325.181-1.x86_64

! Dependencies are downloaded and an attempt is made to install them
[NetProg@localhost Downloads]$ ls -l
total 50932
-rw-rw-r--. 1 NetProg NetProg 52087337 Mar 21 09:48 google-chrome-stable_current_
  x86_64.rpm
-rw-rw-r--. 1 NetProg NetProg    24120 Mar 23 21:50 libXScrnSaver-1.2.2-
  6.1.el7.x86_64.rpm
-rw-rw-r--. 1 NetProg NetProg    38428 Mar 23 21:52 redhat-lsb-core-4.1-
  27.el7.centos.1.x86_64.rpm
```

```
! The first package in the dependency list is installed fine
[NetProg@localhost Downloads]$ sudo rpm -iv libXScrnSaver-1.2.2-6.1.el7.x86_64.rpm
warning: libXScrnSaver-1.2.2-6.1.el7.x86_64.rpm: Header V3 RSA/SHA256 Signature,
  key ID f4a80eb5: NOKEY
Preparing packages...
libXScrnSaver-1.2.2-6.1.el7.x86_64

! The second package in the dependency list: installation fails because it has a
  dependency of its own
[NetProg@localhost Downloads]$ sudo rpm -iv redhat-lsb-core-4.1-
  27.el7.centos.1.x86_64.rpm
warning: redhat-lsb-core-4.1-27.el7.centos.1.x86_64.rpm: Header V3 RSA/SHA256
  Signature, key ID f4a80eb5: NOKEY
error: Failed dependencies:
    redhat-lsb-submod-security(x86-64) = 4.1-27.el7.centos.1 is needed by
      redhat-lsb-core-4.1-27.el7.centos.1.x86_64
    spax is needed by redhat-lsb-core-4.1-27.el7.centos.1.x86_64
[NetProg@localhost Downloads]$
```

YUM

Unlike RPM, which acts on RPM files directly, YUM is a package manager that utilizes software repositories. In this context, a software repo is simply a collection of RPM files. A centralized repo provides highly available, secure, consistent, and efficient means to download and install software. Consider, for example, a company with hundreds of hosts running on Linux. All the hosts have access to a central server cluster on which the software repo resides. Downloading from a software repo does not require root privileges on the server hosting the repo; therefore, administrative access to the repo is restricted, and the repo is secure. All hosts accessing the repo have access to the same versions of the same RPM archives; therefore, software consistency is maintained throughout. The process of configuring a repo on a machine is a one-time process, after which the configured repos are searched automatically for software when software installation is initiated on the local host. Moreover, a script can be configured locally on each server to download and update the software on the local host at preset times of day, which keeps all company servers updated and patched regularly. A software repo can be configured on a local machine, on a server on the network, or on a publicly available server over the Internet.

YUM also detects and automatically resolves dependencies by recursively reading RPM archive metadata, then searching for and downloading all required dependencies, and then performing the same actions for all identified dependencies until all dependencies are resolved. YUM searches for packages in all configured repositories.

You invoke YUM by using the **yum** command, which requires root privileges. Information may be retrieved using one of the command modes listed in Table 2-2. Note that *REGEX* in the table refers to *regular expression*.

Note If you are a network engineer, you have probably worked with regular expressions before. If not, do not worry as regular expressions are covered in some detail in Chapter 4. For now, you need to know that a regular expression is a sequence of symbols and characters that is used to represent one or more strings. It is typically used in programming when a single expression needs to represent several different strings that follow the same set of rules. For example, the regular expression **^Net[0-9].$** would match on the strings **Net5Q** and **Net8X** but not **QNet2E**, **Net9DP**, or **NetPS**. In regular expressions, the caret (^) stands for the beginning of a line, and the dollar sign ($) stands for the end of a line. Two numbers separated by a hyphen (-) and enclosed in brackets represent a single number out of this range (inclusive). The dot (.) represents any single character. Therefore, the regular expression **^Net[0-9].$** represents any string that starts with **Net**, since the ^ sign represents the start of the line. This should be followed by any single number from zero to nine represented by the range in the brackets. The word that matches this regular expression ends in any single character represented by the dot. Nothing should follow, since the **$** sign represents the end of the line. **QNet2E**, **Net9DP**, and **NetPS** would not match because **QNet2E** violates the beginning-of-the-line rule with the **Q** at the beginning, **Net9DP** violates the end-of-the-line rule with the extra **P** at the end, and **NetPS** does not have a single number from the zero to nine range after **Net**.

Table 2-2 *YUM Commands to Query and Retrieve Package Information*

Command	Description
yum list	Lists all installed and available packages on the system
yum list {*REGEX*}	Lists all installed and available packages whose names match the regular expression *REGEX*
yum list installed	Lists all installed packages
yum list available	Lists all available packages
yum search {*REGEX*}	Lists all packages that have the expression whose names or summary fields match the regular expression *REGEX*, and if no results are returned, the description and URL of the packages are searched
yum search all {*REGEX*}	Works the same as **yum search** {*REGEX*}, but all four fields are searched without waiting for the search to fail on the first two fields, so it typically returns more results
yum info {*REGEX*}	Returns detailed information on packages whose names match *REGEX*. The returned information includes the package name, architecture, version, size, repo, summary, and description
yum provides {*file_name*}	Returns the package that provides this file
yum group info {*group_name*}	Provides information for this group

Command	Description
yum history	Provides a list of the past YUM transactions
yum history info {*transaction_id*}	Provides detailed information on a specific transaction in the history

Example 2-70 shows the output of the **yum list gedit** command, which displays all installed and available packages that have **gedit** in the package name.

Example 2-70 *Output from the yum list Command*

```
[NetProg@localhost ~]$ yum list gedit
Loaded plugins: fastestmirror, langpacks
Loading mirror speeds from cached hostfile
 * base: mirror.airenetworks.es
 * extras: mirror.airenetworks.es
 * updates: mirror.airenetworks.es
Installed Packages
gedit.x86_64          2:3.22.0-3.el7                  @anaconda
Available Packages
gedit.i686            2:3.22.0-3.el7                  base
[NetProg@localhost ~]$
```

The output in this example shows that there is one installed package, and there is one package that is available but not installed.

When the package name is not known but something *is* known about the package, you can use the command **yum search** {*REGEX*} to search for packages that have a specific expression in the package name or summary. Example 2-71 shows how to search for all packages that have the phrase **text editor** in either the name or the summary of the package.

Example 2-71 *Output from the yum search Command*

```
[NetProg@localhost ~]$ yum search 'text editor'
Loaded plugins: fastestmirror, langpacks
Determining fastest mirrors
 * base: centoss5.centos.org
 * extras: centos.aumix.net
 * updates: centose5.centos.org
========================= N/S matched: text editor =========================
emacs.x86_64 : GNU Emacs text editor
emacs-nox.x86_64 : GNU Emacs text editor without X support
gedit.i686 : Text editor for the GNOME desktop
```

```
gedit.x86_64 : Text editor for the GNOME desktop
gedit-devel.i686 : Support for developing plugins for the gedit text editor
gedit-devel.x86_64 : Support for developing plugins for the gedit text
                   : editor
kate.x86_64 : Advanced Text Editor
kdelibs-ktexteditor.i686 : KDE4 Text Editor component library
kdelibs-ktexteditor.x86_64 : KDE4 Text Editor component library
kwrite.x86_64 : Text Editor
nano.x86_64 : A small text editor
perl-Syntax-Highlight-Engine-Kate.noarch : Port to Perl of the syntax
     ...: highlight engine of the Kate text editor
sed.x86_64 : A GNU stream text editor

  Name and summary matches only, use "search all" for everything.
[NetProg@localhost ~]$
```

If the search returns no results, the expression used in the command is used to match on the description or URL of the package. To search all four fields without waiting for the search to return no values on the first two fields, you use the command **yum search all** {*REGEX*}.

When you need detailed information about a package, you can use the command **yum info** {*REGEX*}. Example 2-72 shows output from the command **yum info gedit**. It displays detailed information for the two packages found that have **gedit** in their name. Note that in this case, the two packages displayed provide the same application, **gedit**, but each package is for a different architecture. Therefore, only one of them is installed, and the other is available.

Example 2-72 *Output from the yum info Command*

```
[NetProg@localhost ~]$ yum info gedit
Loaded plugins: fastestmirror, langpacks
Loading mirror speeds from cached hostfile
* base: mirror.airenetworks.es
 * extras: mirror.airenetworks.es
 * updates: ct.mirror.garr.it
Installed Packages
Name         : gedit
Arch         : x86_64
Epoch        : 2
Version      : 3.22.0
Release      : 3.el7
Size         : 14 M
Repo         : installed
From repo    : anaconda
```

```
Summary     : Text editor for the GNOME desktop
URL         : https://wiki.gnome.org/Apps/Gedit
License     : GPLv2+ and GFDL
Description : gedit is a small, but powerful text editor designed specifically for
            : the GNOME desktop. It has most standard text editor functions and
              fully
            : supports international text in Unicode. Advanced features include
              syntax
            : highlighting and automatic indentation of source code, printing and
              editing
            : of multiple documents in one window.
            :
            : gedit is extensible through a plugin system, which currently includes
            : support for spell checking, comparing files, viewing CVS ChangeLogs,
              and
            : adjusting indentation levels. Further plugins can be found in the
            : gedit-plugins package.

Available Packages
Name        : gedit
Arch        : i686
Epoch       : 2
Version     : 3.22.0
Release     : 3.el7
Size        : 2.4 M
Repo        : base/7/x86_64
Summary     : Text editor for the GNOME desktop
URL         : https://wiki.gnome.org/Apps/Gedit
License     : GPLv2+ and GFDL
Description : gedit is a small, but powerful text editor designed specifically for
            : the GNOME desktop. It has most standard text editor functions and
              fully
            : supports international text in Unicode. Advanced features include
              syntax
            : highlighting and automatic indentation of source code, printing and
              editing
            : of multiple documents in one window.
            :
            : gedit is extensible through a plugin system, which currently includes
            : support for spell checking, comparing files, viewing CVS ChangeLogs,
              and
            : adjusting indentation levels. Further plugins can be found in the
            : gedit-plugins package.
[NetProg@localhost ~]$
```

To install a package on the system, you use the command **yum install** {*package_name*}. The command **sudo** needs to precede that if the user doing the installation is not the user root.

In Example 2-73, the Apache web server is installed on the system. First, assuming that the package name of the Apache server is not known, **yum search 'http server'** is used to list the packages that have the phrase **http server** in the package summary. Then **yum info httpd.x86_64** is used to display complete information for package httpd.x86_64. From the summary and description, you can see that **httpd** is in fact the Apache web server package, or just Apache for short. Once the package is identified to be the correct one, **sudo yum install httpd** is used to install it.

Example 2-73 *Installing httpd by Using sudo yum install httpd*

```
! Search for a package containing the phrase 'http server' in its summary
[NetProg@localhost ~]$ yum search 'http server'
Loaded plugins: fastestmirror, langpacks
Loading mirror speeds from cached hostfile
 * base: mirror.airenetworks.es
 * extras: mirror.airenetworks.es
 * updates: mirrors.prometeus.net
====================== N/S matched: http server ================================
httpd.x86_64 : Apache HTTP Server
httpd-devel.x86_64 : Development interfaces for the Apache HTTP server
httpd-manual.noarch : Documentation for the Apache HTTP server
httpd-tools.x86_64 : Tools for use with the Apache HTTP Server
mod_auth_openidc.x86_64 : OpenID Connect auth module for Apache HTTP Server
mod_ldap.x86_64 : LDAP authentication modules for the Apache HTTP Server
mod_nss.x86_64 : SSL/TLS module for the Apache HTTP server
mod_proxy_html.x86_64 : HTML and XML content filters for the Apache HTTP Server
mod_revocator.x86_64 : CRL retrieval module for the Apache HTTP server
mod_security.x86_64 : Security module for the Apache HTTP Server
mod_session.x86_64 : Session interface for the Apache HTTP Server
mod_ssl.x86_64 : SSL/TLS module for the Apache HTTP Server
perl-HTTP-Daemon.noarch : Simple HTTP server class

  Name and summary matches only, use "search all" for everything.

! Display detailed information for the package
[NetProg@localhost ~]$ yum info httpd.x86_64
Loaded plugins: fastestmirror, langpacks
Loading mirror speeds from cached hostfile
 * base: mirror.airenetworks.es
```

```
 * extras: mirror.airenetworks.es
 * updates: mirrors.prometeus.net
Available Packages
Name        : httpd
Arch        : x86_64
Version     : 2.4.6
Release     : 67.el7.centos.6
Size        : 2.7 M
Repo        : updates/7/x86_64
Summary     : Apache HTTP Server
URL         : http://httpd.apache.org/
License     : ASL 2.0
Description : The Apache HTTP Server is a powerful, efficient, and extensible
            : web server.

! Install the package
[NetProg@localhost ~]$ sudo yum install httpd
[sudo] password for NetProg:
Loaded plugins: fastestmirror, langpacks
base                                                    | 3.6 kB  00:00:00
extras                                                  | 3.4 kB  00:00:00
updates                                                 | 3.4 kB  00:00:00
(1/4): base/7/x86_64/group_gz                           | 156 kB  00:00:04
(2/4): extras/7/x86_64/primary_db                       | 184 kB  00:00:04
(3/4): base/7/x86_64/primary_db                         | 5.7 MB  00:00:24
(4/4): updates/7/x86_64/primary_db                      | 6.9 MB  00:00:32
Loading mirror speeds from cached hostfile
 * base: mirror.crazynetwork.it
 * extras: mirror.airenetworks.es
 * updates: mirror.crazynetwork.it
Resolving Dependencies
--> Running transaction check
---> Package httpd.x86_64 0:2.4.6-67.el7.centos.6 will be installed
--> Processing Dependency: httpd-tools = 2.4.6-67.el7.centos.6 for package:
  httpd-2.4.6-67.el7.centos.6.x86_64
--> Processing Dependency: /etc/mime.types for package: httpd-2.4.6-
  67.el7.centos.6.x86_64
--> Running transaction check
---> Package httpd-tools.x86_64 0:2.4.6-67.el7.centos.6 will be installed
---> Package mailcap.noarch 0:2.1.41-2.el7 will be installed
--> Finished Dependency Resolution
```

```
Dependencies Resolved
=====================================================================================
 Package          Arch          Version                        Repository      Size
=====================================================================================
Installing:
 httpd            x86_64        2.4.6-67.el7.centos.6          updates         2.7 M
Installing for dependencies:
 httpd-tools      x86_64        2.4.6-67.el7.centos.6          updates         88 k
 mailcap          noarch        2.1.41-2.el7                   base            31 k

Transaction Summary
=====================================================================================
Install  1 Package (+2 Dependent packages)

Total download size: 2.8 M
Installed size: 9.6 M
Is this ok [y/d/N]: y
Downloading packages:
No Presto metadata available for base
updates/7/x86_64/prestodelta                                    | 957 kB  00:00:02
(1/3): mailcap-2.1.41-2.el7.noarch.rpm                          |  31 kB  00:00:00
(2/3): httpd-tools-2.4.6-67.el7.centos.6.x86_64.rpm             |  88 kB  00:00:01
(3/3): httpd-2.4.6-67.el7.centos.6.x86_64.rpm                   | 2.7 MB  00:00:07
-------------------------------------------------------------------------------------
Total                                                 181 kB/s | 2.8 MB  00:00:15
Running transaction check
Running transaction test
Transaction test succeeded
Running transaction
  Installing : httpd-tools-2.4.6-67.el7.centos.6.x86_64                          1/3
  Installing : mailcap-2.1.41-2.el7.noarch                                       2/3
  Installing : httpd-2.4.6-67.el7.centos.6.x86_64                                3/3
  Verifying  : mailcap-2.1.41-2.el7.noarch                                       1/3
  Verifying  : httpd-2.4.6-67.el7.centos.6.x86_64                                2/3
  Verifying  : httpd-tools-2.4.6-67.el7.centos.6.x86_64                          3/3

Installed:
  httpd.x86_64 0:2.4.6-67.el7.centos.6

Dependency Installed:
  httpd-tools.x86_64 0:2.4.6-67.el7.centos.6          mailcap.noarch 0:2.1.41-2.el7

Complete!
[NetProg@localhost ~]$
```

In Example 2-73, you can see that YUM automatically determines the dependencies for installing the Apache web server, searches the configured repos for these extra packages, downloads them, and automatically installs them as part of the installation process. This is a big change from RPM's dependency resolution process, and it would not be possible unless YUM depended on repos to get the required RPM archives.

In order to uninstall the **httpd** package, the command **sudo yum remove httpd** is used, as shown in Example 2-74.

Example 2-74 *Uninstalling httpd by Using sudo yum remove httpd*

```
[NetProg@localhost ~]$ sudo yum remove httpd
Loaded plugins: fastestmirror, langpacks
Resolving Dependencies
--> Running transaction check
---> Package httpd.x86_64 0:2.4.6-67.el7.centos.6 will be erased
--> Finished Dependency Resolution

Dependencies Resolved
=====================================================================================
 Package          Arch              Version                        Repository    Size
=====================================================================================
Removing:
 httpd            x86_64            2.4.6-67.el7.centos.6          @updates      9.4 M

Transaction Summary
=====================================================================================
Remove  1 Package

Installed size: 9.4 M
Is this ok [y/N]: y
Downloading packages:
Running transaction check
Running transaction test
Transaction test succeeded
Running transaction
  Erasing    : httpd-2.4.6-67.el7.centos.6.x86_64                                 1/1
  Verifying  : httpd-2.4.6-67.el7.centos.6.x86_64                                 1/1

Removed:
  httpd.x86_64 0:2.4.6-67.el7.centos.6

Complete!
[NetProg@localhost ~]$
```

To update a package on the system, you use the command **sudo yum update** {*package_name*}, and to update all packages installed on the system, you use the command **sudo yum update.**

Let's now move on to managing repositories. You can use the command **yum repolist all** to list all repositories configured on the system. If you drop the keyword **all**, the command lists only the enabled repos, as shown in Example 2-75.

Example 2-75 *Listing Repos on CentOS 7 by Using yum repolist (all)*

```
[NetProg@localhost ~]$ yum repolist
Loaded plugins: fastestmirror, langpacks
Loading mirror speeds from cached hostfile
 * base: mirror.crazynetwork.it
 * extras: ct.mirror.garr.it
 * updates: mirror.crazynetwork.it
repo id                             repo name                                status
base/7/x86_64                       CentOS-7 - Base                           9,591
extras/7/x86_64                     CentOS-7 - Extras                           444
updates/7/x86_64                    CentOS-7 - Updates                        2,411
repolist: 12,446
[NetProg@localhost ~]$ yum repolist all
Loaded plugins: fastestmirror, langpacks
Loading mirror speeds from cached hostfile
 * base: mirror.crazynetwork.it
 * extras: ct.mirror.garr.it
 * updates: mirror.crazynetwork.it
repo id                            repo name                          status
C7.0.1406-base/x86_64              CentOS-7.0.1406 - Base             disabled
C7.0.1406-centosplus/x86_64        CentOS-7.0.1406 - CentOSPlus       disabled
C7.0.1406-extras/x86_64            CentOS-7.0.1406 - Extras           disabled
C7.0.1406-fasttrack/x86_64         CentOS-7.0.1406 - CentOSPlus       disabled
C7.0.1406-updates/x86_64           CentOS-7.0.1406 - Updates          disabled
C7.1.1503-base/x86_64              CentOS-7.1.1503 - Base             disabled
C7.1.1503-centosplus/x86_64        CentOS-7.1.1503 - CentOSPlus       disabled
C7.1.1503-extras/x86_64            CentOS-7.1.1503 - Extras           disabled
C7.1.1503-fasttrack/x86_64         CentOS-7.1.1503 - CentOSPlus       disabled
C7.1.1503-updates/x86_64           CentOS-7.1.1503 - Updates          disabled
C7.2.1511-base/x86_64              CentOS-7.2.1511 - Base             disabled
C7.2.1511-centosplus/x86_64        CentOS-7.2.1511 - CentOSPlus       disabled
C7.2.1511-extras/x86_64            CentOS-7.2.1511 - Extras           disabled
C7.2.1511-fasttrack/x86_64         CentOS-7.2.1511 - CentOSPlus       disabled
C7.2.1511-updates/x86_64           CentOS-7.2.1511 - Updates          disabled
C7.3.1611-base/x86_64              CentOS-7.3.1611 - Base             disabled
C7.3.1611-centosplus/x86_64        CentOS-7.3.1611 - CentOSPlus       disabled
C7.3.1611-extras/x86_64            CentOS-7.3.1611 - Extras           disabled
```

```
C7.3.1611-fasttrack/x86_64      CentOS-7.3.1611 - CentOSPlus     disabled
C7.3.1611-updates/x86_64        CentOS-7.3.1611 - Updates        disabled
base/7/x86_64                   CentOS-7 - Base                  enabled: 9,591
base-debuginfo/x86_64           CentOS-7 - Debuginfo             disabled
base-source/7                   CentOS-7 - Base Sources          disabled
c7-media                        CentOS-7 - Media                 disabled
centosplus/7/x86_64             CentOS-7 - Plus                  disabled
centosplus-source/7             CentOS-7 - Plus Sources          disabled
cr/7/x86_64                     CentOS-7 - cr                    disabled
extras/7/x86_64                 CentOS-7 - Extras                enabled:   444
extras-source/7                 CentOS-7 - Extras Sources        disabled
fasttrack/7/x86_64              CentOS-7 - fasttrack             disabled
updates/7/x86_64                CentOS-7 - Updates               enabled: 2,411
updates-source/7                CentOS-7 - Updates Sources       disabled
repolist: 12,446
[NetProg@localhost ~]$
```

The number to the right of the repo status in Example 2-75 is the number of packages available through that repo. Each repo in the list has a configuration file in the directory /etc/yum.repos.d that you can manually edit to change the configuration of that repo.

To enable one of the disabled repos from the list in Example 2-75, you can use the command **yum-config-manager --enable** {*repo_name*}. To disable a repo, you can use the command **yum-config-manager --disable** {*repo_name*}. Alternatively, you can edit the repo configuration file so that the value of the field enabled= is changed to 0 for disabled or 1 for enabled.

To add a new repo, use the command **yum-config-manager --add-repo=**{*repo_url*}. Example 2-76 shows how to add the EPEL repo to CentOS 7. EPEL stands for *Extra Packages for Enterprise Linux*, and is a Fedora special interest group that maintains the EPEL repo. The repo contains extra packages that were originally developed for the Fedora distro but that work with other distros, including CentOS, Scientific Linux, and Red Hat. After adding the repo using its URL, the command **yum repolist** confirms that the repo has been added, is enabled, and contains 12,499 packages. Furthermore, the repo configuration file is created in the /etc/yum.repos.d directory.

Example 2-76 *Adding the EPEL Repo to CentOS 7*

```
[NetProg@localhost ~]$ sudo yum-config-manager --add-
  repo="https://dl.fedoraproject.org/pub/epel/7/x86_64/"
[sudo] password for NetProg:
Loaded plugins: fastestmirror, langpacks
adding repo from: https://dl.fedoraproject.org/pub/epel/7/x86_64/
[dl.fedoraproject.org_pub_epel_7_x86_64_]
name=added from: https://dl.fedoraproject.org/pub/epel/7/x86_64/
```

```
baseurl=https://dl.fedoraproject.org/pub/epel/7/x86_64/
enabled=1
[NetProg@localhost ~]$ yum repolist
Loaded plugins: fastestmirror, langpacks
Loading mirror speeds from cached hostfile
 * base: centosh5.centos.org
 * extras: centosq4.centos.org
 * updates: centosh5.centos.org
repo id                              repo name                              status
base/7/x86_64                        CentOS-7 - Base                         9,591
dl.fedoraproject.org_pub_epel_7_x86_64_ added from: https://dl.fedoraproject.org/
  pub/ep 12,449
extras/7/x86_64                      CentOS-7 - Extras                         446
updates/7/x86_64                     CentOS-7 - Updates                      2,416
repolist: 24,902
[NetProg@localhost ~]$ ls /etc/yum.repos.d/
CentOS-Base.repo       CentOS-fasttrack.repo  CentOS-Vault.repo
CentOS-CR.repo         CentOS-Media.repo      dl.fedoraproject.org_pub_epel_7_
                                              x86_64_.repo
CentOS-Debuginfo.repo  CentOS-Sources.repo
[NetProg@localhost ~]$
```

For EPEL and some other popular repos, there are alternative ways to add a repo on the system. For example, you can install the EPEL repo by using the command **yum install epel-release**, which is an RPM package available through the default CentOS-7 - Extras repo.

Creating a local repo on your machine involves four steps:

Step 1. Create a directory on the local machine that will hold all the RPM archives that will be available through that repo.

Step 2. Create and build the repo configuration file under the /etc/yum.repos.d directory.

Step 3. Run the command **createrepo** {*rpm_archives_directory*} to build the repo. Building the repo using this command creates a subdirectory named repodata that contains the metadata required for the repo.

Step 4. Run the command **yum clean all** to clear the YUM cache and the command **yum update** to update the cache with the new repo data.

Example 2-77 shows how to create a local repo named LocalRepo. The command **mkdir LocalRepo** is used to create directory LocalRepo in the user's home directory. The RPM package for Google Chrome is copied to the newly created directory. Then the file LocalRepo.repo is created under the directory /etc/yum.repos.d and edited to include a minimal configuration that includes the repo name, the base URL, and the enabled and gpgcheck switches. The **echo** command is used to add additional lines to the file, and the

cat command is used at the end to verify the final content of the file. Alternatively, the file could have been edited using **vi** or some other text editor. Due to the default permissions of both the /etc/yum.repo.d directory and all files created under it, the .repo files can only be edited by the root user—not any other user, even if it is in the root group. (You will learn more about users and groups in Chapter 3.) The command **createrepo LocalRepo** is used to build the repo. Then **yum clean all** and **yum update** are used to clear the YUM cache and then update it with the new repo information. For more information on the repo configuration file, check the man page for yum.conf.

Example 2-77 *Adding a Local Repo*

```
[NetProg@localhost ~]$ mkdir LocalRepo
[NetProg@localhost ~]$ cp Downloads/google-chrome-stable_current_x86_
  64.rpm LocalRepo/
[NetProg@localhost ~]$ ls -l | grep LocalRepo
drwxrwxr-x. 2 NetProg NetProg  53 Mar 30 16:34 LocalRepo
[NetProg@localhost ~]$ su -
Password:
Last login: Fri Mar 30 16:34:54 +03 2018 on pts/0
[root@localhost ~]# touch /etc/yum.repos.d/LocalRepo.repo
[root@localhost ~]# cd /etc/yum.repos.d/
[root@localhost yum.repos.d]# echo "[LocalRepo]" > LocalRepo.repo
[root@localhost yum.repos.d]# echo "Name=LocalRepo" >> LocalRepo.repo
[root@localhost yum.repos.d]# echo "Baseurl=file:///home/NetProg/LocalRepo" >>
  LocalRepo.repo
[root@localhost yum.repos.d]# echo "Enabled=1" >> LocalRepo.repo
[root@localhost yum.repos.d]# echo "Gpgcheck=0" >> LocalRepo.repo
[root@localhost yum.repos.d]# cat LocalRepo.repo
[LocalRepo]
Name=LocalRepo
Baseurl=file:///home/NetProg/LocalRepo
Enabled=1
Gpgcheck=0
[NetProg@localhost ~]$ createrepo /home/NetProg/LocalRepo/
Spawning worker 0 with 1 pkgs
Workers Finished
Saving Primary metadata
Saving file lists metadata
Saving other metadata
Generating sqlite DBs
Sqlite DBs complete
[NetProg@localhost ~]$ yum clean all
Loaded plugins: fastestmirror, langpacks
Cleaning repos: LocalRepo base extras updates
Cleaning up everything
```

```
Maybe you want: rm -rf /var/cache/yum, to also free up space taken by orphaned data
  from disabled or removed repos
Cleaning up list of fastest mirrors
[NetProg@localhost ~]$ yum update
Loaded plugins: fastestmirror, langpacks
LocalRepo                                               | 2.9 kB    00:00
base                                                    | 3.6 kB    00:00
extras                                                  | 3.4 kB    00:00
updates                                                 | 3.4 kB    00:00
(1/5): LocalRepo/primary_db                               | 3.6 kB  00:00
(2/5): base/7/x86_64/group_gz                             | 156 kB  00:01
(3/5): extras/7/x86_64/primary_db                         | 185 kB  00:01
(4/5): base/7/x86_64/primary_db                           | 5.7 MB  00:29
(5/5): updates/7/x86_64/primary_db                        | 6.9 MB  00:32
Determining fastest mirrors
 * base: centosq4.centos.org
 * extras: centosn4.centos.org
 * updates: centosq4.centos.org
No packages marked for update
[NetProg@localhost ~]$ yum repolist
Loaded plugins: fastestmirror, langpacks
Loading mirror speeds from cached hostfile
 * base: centosq4.centos.org
 * extras: centosn4.centos.org
 * updates: centosq4.centos.org
repo id                            repo name                              status
LocalRepo                          LocalRepo                                   1
base/7/x86_64                      CentOS-7 - Base                         9,591
extras/7/x86_64                    CentOS-7 - Extras                         446
updates/7/x86_64                   CentOS-7 - Updates                      2,416
repolist: 12,454
[NetProg@localhost ~]$
```

As you can see from the **yum repolist** output, the repo has been configured and has one file. In order to test the functionality of the new repo, the Chrome package that has been copied to the new repo is then installed. Example 2-78 uses the command **yum info google-chrome*** to list the package information. The * at the end of the command is required when you do not have the full package name. Alternatively, as discussed earlier, **yum search chrome** can be used to locate the package first. As the output in Example 2-78 shows, the package is in the repo LocalRepo. Then the **yum install google-chrome** command is used to install the package.

Example 2-78 *Installing Google Chrome from LocalRepo*

```
[NetProg@localhost ~]$ yum info google-chrome*
Loaded plugins: fastestmirror, langpacks
Loading mirror speeds from cached hostfile
 * base: centoss5.centos.org
 * extras: centosg4.centos.org
 * updates: centost5.centos.org
Available Packages
Name        : google-chrome-stable
Arch        : x86_64
Version     : 65.0.3325.181
Release     : 1
Size        : 50 M
Repo        : LocalRepo
Summary     : Google Chrome
URL         : https://chrome.google.com/
License     : Multiple, see https://chrome.google.com/
Description : The web browser from Google
            :
            : Google Chrome is a browser that combines a minimal design with
            : sophisticated technology to make the web faster, safer, and easier.

[NetProg@localhost ~]$ sudo yum install google-chrome-stable
[sudo] password for NetProg:
Loaded plugins: fastestmirror, langpacks
LocalRepo                                                    | 2.9 kB  00:00:00
Loading mirror speeds from cached hostfile
 * base: centosq4.centos.org
 * extras: centosn4.centos.org
 * updates: centosq4.centos.org
Resolving Dependencies
--> Running transaction check
---> Package google-chrome-stable.x86_64 0:65.0.3325.181-1 will be installed
--> Processing Dependency: /usr/bin/lsb_release for package: google-chrome-
  stable-65.0.3325.181-1.x86_64
--> Running transaction check
---> Package redhat-lsb-core.x86_64 0:4.1-27.el7.centos.1 will be installed
--> Processing Dependency: redhat-lsb-submod-security(x86-64) = 4.1-27.el7.centos.1
  for package: redhat-lsb-core-4.1-27.el7.centos.1.x86_64
--> Processing Dependency: spax for package: redhat-lsb-core-4.1-27.el7.
  centos.1.x86_64
--> Running transaction check
---> Package redhat-lsb-submod-security.x86_64 0:4.1-27.el7.centos.1 will be
  installed
```

```
---> Package spax.x86_64 0:1.5.2-13.el7 will be installed
--> Finished Dependency Resolution

Dependencies Resolved
=====================================================================================
 Package                      Arch      Version                  Repository    Size
=====================================================================================
Installing:
 google-chrome-stable         x86_64    65.0.3325.181-1          LocalRepo     50 M
Installing for dependencies:
 redhat-lsb-core              x86_64    4.1-27.el7.centos.1      base          38 k
 redhat-lsb-submod-security   x86_64    4.1-27.el7.centos.1      base          15 k
 spax                         x86_64    1.5.2-13.el7             base         260 k

Transaction Summary
=====================================================================================
Install  1 Package (+3 Dependent packages)

Total size: 50 M
Total download size: 50 M
Installed size: 180 M
Is this ok [y/d/N]: y
Downloading packages:
Running transaction check
Running transaction test
Transaction test succeeded
Running transaction
  Installing : spax-1.5.2-13.el7.x86_64                                          1/4
  Installing : redhat-lsb-submod-security-4.1-27.el7.centos.1.x86_64             2/4
  Installing : redhat-lsb-core-4.1-27.el7.centos.1.x86_64                        3/4
  Installing : google-chrome-stable-65.0.3325.181-1.x86_64                       4/4
Redirecting to /bin/systemctl start atd.service
  Verifying  : google-chrome-stable-65.0.3325.181-1.x86_64                       1/4
  Verifying  : redhat-lsb-submod-security-4.1-27.el7.centos.1.x86_64             2/4
  Verifying  : spax-1.5.2-13.el7.x86_64                                          3/4
  Verifying  : redhat-lsb-core-4.1-27.el7.centos.1.x86_64                        4/4

Installed:
  google-chrome-stable.x86_64 0:65.0.3325.181-1

Dependency Installed:
  redhat-lsb-core.x86_64 0:4.1-27.el7.centos.1
  redhat-lsb-submod-security.x86_64 0:4.1-27.el7.centos.1
```

```
  spax.x86_64 0:1.5.2-13.el7

Complete!

[NetProg@localhost ~]$ yum info google-chrome*
Loaded plugins: fastestmirror, langpacks
google-chrome                                               |  951 B  00:00:00
google-chrome/primary                                       | 1.9 kB  00:00:01
Loading mirror speeds from cached hostfile
 * base: centoss5.centos.org
 * extras: centosg4.centos.org
 * updates: centost5.centos.org
google-chrome                                                                3/3
Installed Packages
Name        : google-chrome-stable
Arch        : x86_64
Version     : 65.0.3325.181
Release     : 1
Size        : 179 M
Repo        : installed
From repo   : LocalRepo
Summary     : Google Chrome
URL         : https://chrome.google.com/
License     : Multiple, see https://chrome.google.com/
Description : The web browser from Google
            :
            : Google Chrome is a browser that combines a minimal design with
            : sophisticated technology to make the web faster, safer, and easier.
[NetProg@localhost ~]$
```

As you can see, YUM is smart enough to search and locate the google-chrome package in the LocalRepo repo, resolve the dependencies, and search and locate those dependencies in the base repo. This means that a package could be in one repo and its dependencies in another, and YUM will take care of the whole installation process.

DNF

DNF, also known as Dandified YUM, is a next-generation YUM package manager. At the time of writing, the latest version of DNF is 2.7.5, and work on Version 3 has begun. DNF is currently the default package manager on Fedora and CentOS 8 but not on earlier versions of CentOS. DNF offers several enhancements over YUM, mainly related to performance and stability, especially with dependency resolution. DNF is not covered in detail in this section, but you can use **man dnf** or **info dnf** on a Fedora or CentOS 8 distro to check it out.

Summary

Although a lot of essential material is covered in this chapter, this chapter does not even scratch the surface of Linux administration. Our goal in this chapter is to make you feel comfortable enough to start diving into more advanced topics in Chapter 3, which covers Linux storage, security, and networks. Toward this goal, this chapter covers the following topics:

- The history of Linux, its status today, and the Linux development process
- Linux distros and Linux architecture
- The Linux boot process
- The Linux Bash shell
- How to find help in Linux
- The Linux file hierarchy
- File and directory operations
- Input and output redirection
- Archiving and compression
- Linux system maintenance
- Software installation and maintenance

Chapter 3

Linux Storage, Security, and Networks

Chapter 2, "Linux Fundamentals," covers Linux basics, and by now, you should be familiar with the Linux environment and feel comfortable performing general system maintenance tasks. This chapter takes you a step further in your Linux journey and covers storage, security, and networking.

Linux Storage

Many network engineers struggle with concepts such as what mounting a volume means and the relationship between physical and logical volumes. This section covers everything you need to know about storage to effectively manage a Linux-based environment, whether it is your development environment or the underlying Linux system on which a network operating system is based, such as IOS XR and NX-OS.

Physical Storage

The /dev directory contains device files, which are special files used to access the hardware on a system. A program trying to access a device uses a device file as an interface to the device driver of that device. Writing data to a device file is the same as sending data to the device represented by that device file, and reading data from a device file is the same as receiving data from that device. For example, writing data to the printer device file prints this data, and reading data from the device file of a hard disk partition is the same as reading data from that partition on the disk.

Example 3-1 shows the output of the **ls -l** command for the /dev directory. Notice that, unlike other directories, the first bit of the file permissions is one of five characters:

- - for regular files
- **d** for directories

- l for links
- c for character device files
- b for block device files

You learned about the first three of these bits in Chapter 2, and the other two are covered here.

Example 3-1 *Contents of the /dev Directory*

```
[netdev@server1 dev]$ ls -l
total 0
-rw-r--r--. 1 root    root          0 Aug 10 00:28 any_regular_file
crw-r--r--. 1 root    root     10, 235 Aug 10 00:19 autofs
drwxr-xr-x. 2 root    root        140 Aug 10 00:18 block
drwxr-xr-x. 2 root    root         60 Aug 10 00:18 bsg
drwxr-xr-x. 3 root    root         60 Aug 10 00:19 bus
drwxr-xr-x. 2 root    root       2940 Aug 10 00:20 char
drwxr-xr-x. 2 root    root         80 Aug 10 00:18 cl
crw-------. 1 root    root      5,   1 Aug 10 00:20 console
lrwxrwxrwx. 1 root    root         11 Aug 10 00:18 core -> /proc/kcore
drwxr-xr-x. 6 root    root        120 Aug 10 00:19 cpu
crw-------. 1 root    root     10,  62 Aug 10 00:19 cpu_dma_latency
drwxr-xr-x. 6 root    root        120 Aug 10 00:18 disk
brw-rw----. 1 root    disk    253,   0 Aug 10 00:19 dm-0
brw-rw----. 1 root    disk    253,   1 Aug 10 00:19 dm-1

--------- OUTPUT TRUNCATED FOR BREVITY ---------
```

Character device files provide *unbuffered* access to hardware. This means that what is written to the file is transmitted to the hardware device right away, byte by byte. The same applies to read operations. Think of data sent to the device file of an audio output device or data read from the device file representing your keyboard. This data should not be buffered.

On the other hand, block device files provide *buffered* access; that is, data written to a device file is buffered by the kernel before it is passed on to the hardware device. The same applies to read operations. Think of data written to or read from a partition on your hard disk. This is typically done in data blocks, not individual bytes.

However, note that the *device file* type (as seen in the /dev directory) is not necessarily the same as the *device* type. Storage devices such as hard disks are block devices, which means that data is read from and written to the device in fixed-size blocks. Although this may sound counterintuitive, block devices may be accessed using character device files on some operating systems, such as BSD. This is not the case with Linux, where block devices are always associated with block device files. The difference between block devices and block device files is sometimes a source of confusion.

The first step in analyzing a storage and file system is getting to know the hard disks. Each hard disk and partition has a corresponding device file in the /dev directory. By listing the contents of this directory, you find the sda file for the first hard disk, and, if installed, sdb for the second hard disk, sdc for the third hard disk, and so forth. Partitions are named after the hard disk that the partition belongs to, with the partition number appended to the name. For example, the *first* partition on the *second* hard disk is named sdb1. The hard disk naming convention follows the configuration in the /lib/udev/rules.d/60-persistent-storage.rules file, and the configuration is per hard disk type (ATA, USB, SCSI, SATA, and so on). Example 3-2 lists the relevant files in the /dev directory on a CentOS 7 distro. As you can see, this system has two hard disks. The first hard disk is named sda and has two partitions—sda1 and sda2—and the second is named sdb and has three partitions—sdb1, sdb2, and sdb3.

Example 3-2 *Hard Disks and Partitions in the /dev Directory*

```
[root@localhost ~]# ls -l /dev | grep sd
brw-rw----. 1 root    disk      8,    0 Jun  8 04:55 sda
brw-rw----. 1 root    disk      8,    1 Jun  8 04:55 sda1
brw-rw----. 1 root    disk      8,    2 Jun  8 04:55 sda2
brw-rw----. 1 root    disk      8,   16 Jun  8 04:55 sdb
brw-rw----. 1 root    disk      8,   17 Jun  8 04:55 sdb1
brw-rw----. 1 root    disk      8,   18 Jun  8 04:55 sdb2
brw-rw----. 1 root    disk      8,   19 Jun  8 04:55 sdb3
```

Notice the letter b at the beginning of each line of the output in Example 3-2. This indicates a block device file. A character device file would have the letter c instead.

The command **fdisk -l** lists all the disks and partitions on a system, along with some useful details. Example 3-3 shows the output of this command for the same system as in Example 3-2.

Example 3-3 *Using the fdisk -l Command to Get Hard Disk and Partition Details*

```
[root@localhost ~]# fdisk -l

Disk /dev/sda: 26.8 GB, 26843545600 bytes, 52428800 sectors
Units = sectors of 1 * 512 = 512 bytes
Sector size (logical/physical): 512 bytes / 512 bytes
I/O size (minimum/optimal): 512 bytes / 512 bytes
Disk label type: dos
Disk identifier: 0x000b4fba
```

```
   Device Boot      Start         End      Blocks   Id  System
/dev/sda1   *        2048     2099199     1048576   83  Linux
/dev/sda2         2099200    52428799    25164800   8e  Linux LVM

Disk /dev/sdb: 107.4 GB, 107374182400 bytes, 209715200 sectors
Units = sectors of 1 * 512 = 512 bytes
Sector size (logical/physical): 512 bytes / 512 bytes
I/O size (minimum/optimal): 512 bytes / 512 bytes
Disk label type: dos
Disk identifier: 0x149c8964

   Device Boot      Start         End      Blocks   Id  System
/dev/sdb1            2048    41945087    20971520   83  Linux
/dev/sdb2        41945088    83888127    20971520   83  Linux
/dev/sdb3        83888128   115345407    15728640   83  Linux

Disk /dev/mapper/centos-root: 23.1 GB, 23081254912 bytes, 45080576 sectors
Units = sectors of 1 * 512 = 512 bytes
Sector size (logical/physical): 512 bytes / 512 bytes
I/O size (minimum/optimal): 512 bytes / 512 bytes

Disk /dev/mapper/centos-swap: 2684 MB, 2684354560 bytes, 5242880 sectors
Units = sectors of 1 * 512 = 512 bytes
Sector size (logical/physical): 512 bytes / 512 bytes
I/O size (minimum/optimal): 512 bytes / 512 bytes
[root@localhost ~]#
```

In addition to physical disks /dev/sda and /dev/sdb and their respective partitions, the command output in Example 3-3 lists two other disks: /dev/mapper/centos-root and /dev/mapper/centos-swap. These are two logical volumes. (Logical volumes are discussed in detail in the next section.) Notice that there is an asterisk (*) under the title Boot for partition /dev/sda1. As you may have guessed, this indicates that this is the partition on which the boot sector resides, containing the boot loader. The boot loader is the software that will eventually load the kernel image into memory during the system boot process, as you have read in Section "The Linux Boot Process" in Chapter 2.

In addition to displaying existing partition details, **fdisk** can create new partitions and delete existing ones. For example, after a third hard disk, sdc, is added to the system, the **fdisk** utility can be used to create two partitions, sdc1 and sdc2, as shown in Example 3-4.

Example 3-4 *Creating New Hard Disk Partitions by Using the fdisk Utility*

```
! Current status of the sdc hard disk: no partitions exist
[root@localhost ~]# fdisk -l /dev/sdc

Disk /dev/sdc: 21.5 GB, 21474836480 bytes, 41943040 sectors
Units = sectors of 1 * 512 = 512 bytes
Sector size (logical/physical): 512 bytes / 512 bytes
I/O size (minimum/optimal): 512 bytes / 512 bytes

! Using fdisk to create two new partitions on sdc
[root@localhost ~]# fdisk /dev/sdc
Welcome to fdisk (util-linux 2.23.2).

Changes will remain in memory only, until you decide to write them.
Be careful before using the write command.

Device does not contain a recognized partition table
Building a new DOS disklabel with disk identifier 0x4cd00767.

Command (m for help): m
Command action
   a   toggle a bootable flag
   b   edit bsd disklabel
   c   toggle the dos compatibility flag
   d   delete a partition
   g   create a new empty GPT partition table
   G   create an IRIX (SGI) partition table
   l   list known partition types
   m   print this menu
   n   add a new partition
   o   create a new empty DOS partition table
   p   print the partition table
   q   quit without saving changes
   s   create a new empty Sun disklabel
   t   change a partition's system id
   u   change display/entry units
   v   verify the partition table
   w   write table to disk and exit
   x   extra functionality (experts only)

Command (m for help): n
Partition type:
   p   primary (0 primary, 0 extended, 4 free)
   e   extended
```

```
Select (default p): p
Partition number (1-4, default 1):
First sector (2048-41943039, default 2048):
Using default value 2048
Last sector, +sectors or +size{K,M,G} (2048-41943039, default 41943039): +5G
Partition 1 of type Linux and of size 5 GiB is set

Command (m for help): n
Partition type:
   p   primary (1 primary, 0 extended, 3 free)
   e   extended
Select (default p):
Using default response p
Partition number (2-4, default 2):
First sector (10487808-41943039, default 10487808):
Using default value 10487808
Last sector, +sectors or +size{K,M,G} (10487808-41943039, default 41943039):
Using default value 41943039
Partition 2 of type Linux and of size 15 GiB is set

Command (m for help): w
The partition table has been altered!

Calling ioctl() to re-read partition table.
Syncing disks.

! Status after creating the two new partitions sdc1 and sdc2
[root@localhost ~]# fdisk -l /dev/sdc

Disk /dev/sdc: 21.5 GB, 21474836480 bytes, 41943040 sectors
Units = sectors of 1 * 512 = 512 bytes
Sector size (logical/physical): 512 bytes / 512 bytes
I/O size (minimum/optimal): 512 bytes / 512 bytes
Disk label type: dos
Disk identifier: 0x4cd00767

   Device Boot      Start         End      Blocks   Id  System
/dev/sdc1            2048    10487807     5242880   83  Linux
/dev/sdc2        10487808    41943039    15727616   83  Linux3
[root@localhost ~]#
```

The interactive dialogue of the **fdisk** utility is self-explanatory. After the **fdisk /dev/sdc** command is issued, you can enter **m** to see all available options. You can enter **n** to start the new partition dialogue. Note the different methods to specify the size of the partition. If you go with the default option (by simply pressing Enter), the command uses all the remaining space on the disk to create that particular partition.

Before a hard disk partition can be used to store data, the partition needs to be formatted; that is, a file system has to be created. (File systems are discussed in some detail in Chapter 2.) At the time of writing, the two most common file systems used on Linux are ext4 and xfs. A partition is formatted using the **mkfs** utility. In Example 3-5, the sdc1 partition is formatted to use the ext4 file system, and sdc2 is formatted to use the xfs file system.

Example 3-5 *Creating File Systems by Using the **mkfs** Command*

```
[root@localhost ~]# mkfs -t ext4 /dev/sdc1
mke2fs 1.42.9 (28-Dec-2013)
Filesystem label=
OS type: Linux
Block size=4096 (log=2)
Fragment size=4096 (log=2)
Stride=0 blocks, Stripe width=0 blocks
327680 inodes, 1310720 blocks
65536 blocks (5.00%) reserved for the super user
First data block=0
Maximum filesystem blocks=1342177280
40 block groups
32768 blocks per group, 32768 fragments per group
8192 inodes per group
Superblock backups stored on blocks:
      32768, 98304, 163840, 229376, 294912, 819200, 884736

Allocating group tables: done
Writing inode tables: done
Creating journal (32768 blocks): done
Writing superblocks and filesystem accounting information: done

[root@localhost ~]# mkfs -t xfs /dev/sdc2
meta-data=/dev/sdc2              isize=512    agcount=4, agsize=982976 blks
         =                       sectsz=512   attr=2, projid32bit=1
         =                       crc=1        finobt=0, sparse=0
data     =                       bsize=4096   blocks=3931904, imaxpct=25
         =                       sunit=0      swidth=0 blks
naming   =version 2              bsize=4096   ascii-ci=0 ftype=1
log      =internal log           bsize=4096   blocks=2560, version=2
         =                       sectsz=512   sunit=0 blks, lazy-count=1
realtime =none                   extsz=4096   blocks=0, rtextents=0
[root@localhost ~]#
```

To specify a file system type, you use **mkfs** with the **-t** option. Keep in mind that the command output depends on the file system type used with the command.

The final step toward making a partition usable is to mount that partition or file system. Mounting is usually an ambiguous concept to engineers who are new to Linux. As discussed in Chapter 2, the Linux file hierarchy always starts at the root directory, represented by /, and branches down. For a file system to be accessible, it has to be *mounted* to a *mount point*—that is, attached (mounted) to the file hierarchy at a specific path in that hierarchy (mount point). The mount point is the path in the file hierarchy that the file system is attached to and through which the contents of that file system can be accessed. For example, mounting the /dev/sdc1 partition to the /Operations directory maps the content of /dev/sdc1 to, and makes it accessible through, the /Operations directory, for both read and write operations. Example 3-6 shows the /Operations directory being created and the sdc1 partition being mounted to it.

Example 3-6 *Mounting /dev/sdc1 to /Operations*

```
[root@localhost ~]# mkdir /Operations
[root@localhost ~]# mount /dev/sdc1 /Operations
```

To display all the mounted file systems, you use the **df** command, as shown in Example 3-7. The option **-h** displays the file system sizes in human-readable format.

Example 3-7 *Output of the df -h Command*

```
[root@localhost ~]# df -h
Filesystem               Size  Used Avail Use% Mounted on
/dev/mapper/centos-root   22G  5.3G   17G  25% /
devtmpfs                 3.9G     0  3.9G   0% /dev
tmpfs                    3.9G     0  3.9G   0% /dev/shm
tmpfs                    3.9G  9.4M  3.9G   1% /run
tmpfs                    3.9G     0  3.9G   0% /sys/fs/cgroup
/dev/sda1               1014M  333M  682M  33% /boot
tmpfs                    783M   32K  783M   1% /run/user/1000
/dev/sdc1                4.8G   20M  4.6G   1% /Operations
[root@localhost ~]#
```

Each row in the output in Example 3-7 is a separate file system. The entry /dev/mapper/centos-root is a logical volume (and is discussed in detail in the next section). The following few entries are tmpfs file systems, which are temporary file systems created in memory (not on disk) for cache-like operations due to the high speed of RAM, as compared to the low speed of hard disks. An entry exists in the list for partition /dev/sda1 that is mounted to directory /boot. Then the entry at the bottom is for /dev/sdc1 that was mounted to directory /Operations as shown in Example 3-6.

To unmount the /dev/sdc1 file system, you use the **umount /dev/sdc1** command. You can also use the mount point, in which case the command is **umount /Operations**. Note that the command is **umount**, not *unmount*. Adding the letter *n* is a very common error.

The mounting done by using the **mount** command is not persistent. In other words, once the system is rebooted, the volumes mounted using the **mount** command are no longer mounted. For persistent mounting, an entry needs to be added to the /etc/fstab file. Example 3-8 shows the contents of the /etc/fstab file after the entry for /dev/sdc1 is added.

Example 3-8 *Editing the /etc/fstab File for Persistent Mounting*

```
! Adding an entry for /etc/sdc1 using the echo command
[root@localhost ~]# echo "/dev/sdc1 /Operations    ext4 defaults 0 0" >> /etc/fstab

! After adding an entry for /etc/sdc1
[root@localhost ~]# cat /etc/fstab
#
# /etc/fstab
# Created by anaconda on Sat May 26 04:28:54 2018
#
# Accessible filesystems, by reference, are maintained under '/dev/disk'
# See man pages fstab(5), findfs(8), mount(8) and/or blkid(8) for more info
#
/dev/mapper/centos-root /              xfs     defaults        0 0
UUID=dfe65618-19ab-458d-b5e3-dafdb59b4e68 /boot      xfs    defaults    0 0
/dev/mapper/centos-swap swap           swap    defaults        0 0
/dev/sdc1 /Operations           ext4   defaults    0 0

! Command mount -a immediately mounts all file systems listed in fstab
[root@localhost ~]# mount -a
```

The command **mount -a** immediately mounts all file systems listed in /etc/fstab.

The /etc/fstab file has one entry for each file system that is to be mounted at system boot. It is important to understand the entries in the /etc/fstab file because this is the file that defines what file systems a system will have mounted right after it boots and the options that each of these file systems will be mounted with. Each line has the following fields:

- The first field can be either the file system path, the universal unique identifier (UUID), or the label. You can learn the UUID (and type) of all file systems by using the command **blkid**. You can show the label by using the command **tune2fs -l** {*file_system*} for ext2/3/4 file systems or **xfs_admin -l** {*file_system*} for xfs file systems. Using the file system path, which is /dev/sdc1 in this case, is pretty straightforward. However, when a system has tens of hard disks installed, it would be wiser to use the partition UUIDs. A UUID is a unique number that identifies a partition. The UUID does not change if the hard disk containing the partition is moved to another system, and hence it is universal. Using a UUID eliminates the possibility of errors in the /etc/fstab file.

- The second field is the file system mount point, which is /Operations in this case.
- The third field is the file system type, which is ext4 in this example.
- The fourth field is the mounting options. In this example, defaults indicates that the default mounting options will be used. You can also add non-default mounting options such as acl for ACL support. You add options in a comma-separated list.
- The fifth field indicates which file systems are to be backed up by the **dump** utility. The zero value in this case indicates that this file system will not be automatically backed up.
- The sixth field is used by the **fsck** utility to determine whether to check the health of the file system. The **fsck** utility checks file systems with a nonzero value in this field, in order, starting with the file system that has the value one. A zero in this field tells the **fsck** utility not to check that file system.

fdisk is not the only Linux utility available to manipulate disk partitions. Two other popular utilities for disk partitioning are **gdisk** and **parted.** You can use the man pages for these utilities to explore them and use a non-production environment (ideally a virtual machine) to experiment with using them. You may run into a distro that has one of them implemented but not the other. The more utilities you are familiar with, the better.

Logical Volume Manager

Linux generally uses the concept of logical volumes to provide storage to users. Logical volumes abstract the storage that is available to a user from the actual physical disks. Logical volumes on Linux are managed by system software called *Logical Volume Manager* (*LVM*). LVM operates by grouping physical disks or disk partitions, each referred to as a *physical volume* (*PV*), such as /dev/sda or /dev/sdb2, into a *volume group* (*VG*). LVM then manages a VG as one pool of storage that is split by the LVM into one or more *logical volumes* (*LVs*). Figure 3-1 illustrates these concepts.

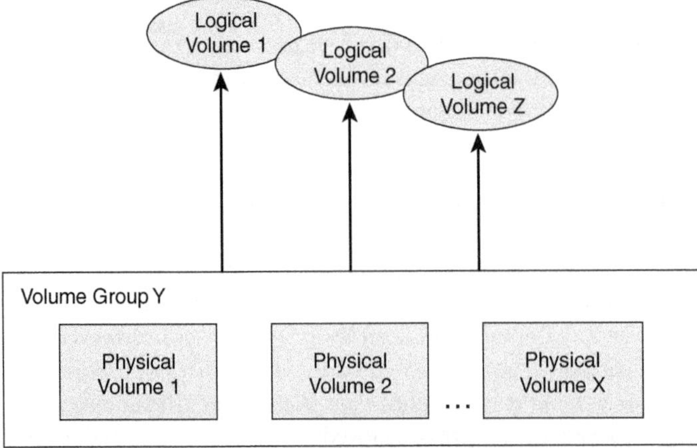

Figure 3-1 *Physical Volumes, Volume Groups, and Logical Volumes*

To better understand the concept of logical volumes, keep in mind the following:

- The different PVs that constitute a VG do not have to be equal in size.
- The different PVs that constitute a VG may be different disks, or different partitions on the same disk, or different partitions on different disks.
- Two different partitions on the *same* disk may be members of two different VGs.
- The LVs that are created from a VG do not correlate to the PVs that constitute the VG in either size or number.

Using LVs created by LVM provides several advantages over using physical storage directly. The most significant benefit is the disassociation between user data and specific physical storage volumes. From a capacity perspective, capacity can be added to and removed from a logical volume without having to repartition a physical disk to create a bigger or smaller partition, and a file system is not limited by the size of the physical disk that it resides on. From a performance perspective, data may be striped across several physical volumes (for added throughput) transparently from the user. These are just a few of the advantages.

The following steps are involved in creating a logical volume that is ready to use:

Step 1. Using the command **pvcreate** {*physical_disk/partition*}, label the physical volumes that will constitute the volume group as LVM physical volumes.

Step 2. Using the command **vgcreate** {*vg_name*} {*pv1*} {*pv2*} .. {*pvN*}, create the VG by using the physical volumes *pv1*, *pv2*,...*pvN*.

Step 3. Using the command **lvcreate -n** {*lv_name*} **-L** {*lv_size*} {*vg_name*}, create the logical volume named *lv_name* from the volume group named *vg_name*.

Step 4. Create the file system of choice on the new logical volume by using the **mkfs** command, exactly as you would on a physical partition.

Step 5. Mount the new file system by using the **mount** command exactly as you would mount a file system created on a physical partition.

In Example 3-9, two disks, sdb and sdc, are each divided into two partitions as follows:

- sdb1: 12 GB
- sdb2: 8 GB
- sdc1: 15 GB
- sdc2: 10 GB

Example 3-9 *The Four Partitions That Will Be Used to Create a Volume Group*

```
[root@server1 ~]# fdisk -l | grep -E sd[b,c]
Disk /dev/sdc: 26.8 GB, 26843545600 bytes, 52428800 sectors
/dev/sdc1            2048    31459327    15728640   83  Linux
/dev/sdc2        31459328    52428799    10484736   83  Linux
Disk /dev/sdb: 21.5 GB, 21474836480 bytes, 41943040 sectors
/dev/sdb1            2048    25167871    12582912   83  Linux
/dev/sdb2        25167872    41943039     8387584   83  Linux
[root@server1 ~]#
```

After each of the four partitions is labeled as a PV, all four partitions are added to the VG VGNetProg, which has a total capacity of 40 GB. The volume group capacity is then used to create two logical volumes—LVNetAutom with a capacity of 10 GB and LVNetDev with a capacity of 30 GB—as shown in Example 3-10.

Example 3-10 *Creating Physical Volumes, Volume Groups, and Logical Volumes*

```
! Label the physical volumes
[root@server1 ~]# pvcreate /dev/sdb1 /dev/sdb2 /dev/sdc1 /dev/sdc2
  Physical volume "/dev/sdb1" successfully created.
  Physical volume "/dev/sdb2" successfully created.
  Physical volume "/dev/sdc1" successfully created.
  Physical volume "/dev/sdc2" successfully created.

! Create the volume group
[root@server1 ~]# vgcreate VGNetProg /dev/sdb1 /dev/sdb2 /dev/sdc1 /dev/sdc2
  Volume group "VGNetProg" successfully created

! Create the two logical volumes
[root@server1 ~]# lvcreate -n LVNetAutom -L 10G VGNetProg
  Logical volume "LVNetAutom" created.
[root@server1 ~]# lvcreate -n LVNetDev -L 30G VGNetProg
  Logical volume "LVNetDev" created.
[root@server1 ~]#
```

Example 3-11 shows the **pvdisplay** command being used to display the details of the physical volumes.

Example 3-11 *Displaying Physical Volume Details by Using the* ***pvdisplay*** *Command*

```
[root@server1 ~]# pvdisplay /dev/sdb1
  --- Physical volume ---
  PV Name               /dev/sdb1
  VG Name               VGNetProg
  PV Size               12.00 GiB / not usable 4.00 MiB
  Allocatable           yes
  PE Size               4.00 MiB
  Total PE              3071
  Free PE               511
  Allocated PE          2560
  PV UUID               dPYPj6-Wv1i-iX7H-3iH0-oCnE-OzkA-2LcJ1x
[root@server1 ~]# pvdisplay /dev/sdb2
  --- Physical volume ---
  PV Name               /dev/sdb2
  VG Name               VGNetProg
  PV Size               <8.00 GiB / not usable 3.00 MiB
  Allocatable           yes
  PE Size               4.00 MiB
  Total PE              2047
  Free PE               765
  Allocated PE          1282
  PV UUID               ftOYQo-a19G-0Gs6-01ir-i6M5-Yj1N-TRREDR
[root@server1 ~]# pvdisplay /dev/sdc1
  --- Physical volume ---
  PV Name               /dev/sdc1
  VG Name               VGNetProg
  PV Size               15.00 GiB / not usable 4.00 MiB
  Allocatable           yes (but full)
  PE Size               4.00 MiB
  Total PE              3839
  Free PE               0
  Allocated PE          3839
  PV UUID               DYW0TD-vXGl-8Ssr-BCcy-SLQQ-mkfi-rvQFVd
[root@server1 ~]# pvdisplay /dev/sdc2
  --- Physical volume ---
  PV Name               /dev/sdc2
  VG Name               VGNetProg
  PV Size               <10.00 GiB / not usable 3.00 MiB
  Allocatable           yes (but full)
  PE Size               4.00 MiB
  Total PE              2559
  Free PE               0
  Allocated PE          2559
  PV UUID               n1snhx-aevL-X5ay-la43-1jlo-83uC-LIkIT7
[root@server1 ~]#
```

Example 3-12 shows the **vgdisplay** command being used to display the volume group that has been created.

Example 3-12 *Displaying Volume Group Details by Using the **vgdisplay** Command*

```
[root@server1 ~]# vgdisplay VGNetProg
  --- Volume group ---
  VG Name               VGNetProg
  System ID
  Format                lvm2
  Metadata Areas        4
  Metadata Sequence No  3
  VG Access             read/write
  VG Status             resizable
  MAX LV                0
  Cur LV                2
  Open LV               0
  Max PV                0
  Cur PV                4
  Act PV                4
  VG Size               44.98 GiB
  PE Size               4.00 MiB
  Total PE              11516
  Alloc PE / Size       10240 / 40.00 GiB
  Free  PE / Size       1276 / 4.98 GiB
  VG UUID               PSi3RJ-9lkc-1ZFE-oCVA-RaXC-HDh5-K0VuV3
[root@server1 ~]#
```

Example 3-13 shows the **lvdisplay** command being used to display the logical volumes that have been created. A logical volume is addressed using its full path in the /dev directory, as shown in the example.

Example 3-13 *Displaying Logical Volume Details by Using the **lvdisplay** Command*

```
[root@server1 ~]# lvdisplay /dev/VGNetProg/LVNetAutom
  --- Logical volume ---
  LV Path                /dev/VGNetProg/LVNetAutom
  LV Name                LVNetAutom
  VG Name                VGNetProg
  LV UUID                Y09QdN-J8Fw-s3Nb-RB84-bBPs-1USv-tzMfAw
  LV Write Access        read/write
  LV Creation host, time server1, 2018-08-05 21:57:42 +0300
  LV Status              available
  # open                 0
  LV Size                10.00 GiB
```

```
  Current LE             2560
  Segments               1
  Allocation             inherit
  Read ahead sectors     auto
  - currently set to     8192
  Block device           253:2
[root@server1 ~]# lvdisplay /dev/VGNetProg/LVNetDev
  --- Logical volume ---
  LV Path                /dev/VGNetProg/LVNetDev
  LV Name                LVNetDev
  VG Name                VGNetProg
  LV UUID                Z9VRTv-CUe6-uSa8-S821-jGY5-ymKh-zsKfHZ
  LV Write Access        read/write
  LV Creation host, time server1, 2018-08-05 21:58:17 +0300
  LV Status              available
  # open                 0
  LV Size                30.00 GiB
  Current LE             7680
  Segments               3
  Allocation             inherit
  Read ahead sectors     auto
  - currently set to     8192
  Block device           253:3
[root@server1 ~]#
```

Note that you can issue the **pvdisplay**, **vgdisplay**, and **lvdisplay** commands without any arguments to display all physical volumes, all volume groups, and all logical volumes, respectively, that are configured on the system.

To delete a physical volume, volume group, or logical volume, you use the commands **pvremove**, **vgremove**, or **lvremove**, respectively.

After logical volumes are created, you use the **mkfs** command to format the LVNetAutom LV as an ext4 file system and the LVNetDev LV as an xfs file system, as shown in Example 3-14.

Example 3-14 *Creating File Systems on the new Logical Volumes by Using the* ***mkfs*** *Command*

```
[root@server1 ~]# mkfs -t ext4 /dev/VGNetProg/LVNetAutom
mke2fs 1.42.9 (28-Dec-2013)
Filesystem label=
OS type: Linux
Block size=4096 (log=2)
Fragment size=4096 (log=2)
Stride=0 blocks, Stripe width=0 blocks
```

```
655360 inodes, 2621440 blocks
131072 blocks (5.00%) reserved for the super user
First data block=0
Maximum filesystem blocks=2151677952
80 block groups
32768 blocks per group, 32768 fragments per group
8192 inodes per group
Superblock backups stored on blocks:
    32768, 98304, 163840, 229376, 294912, 819200, 884736, 1605632

Allocating group tables: done
Writing inode tables: done
Creating journal (32768 blocks): done
Writing superblocks and filesystem accounting information: done
[root@server1 ~]# mkfs -t xfs /dev/VGNetProg/LVNetDev
meta-data=/dev/VGNetProg/LVNetDev isize=512    agcount=4, agsize=1966080 blks
         =                       sectsz=512   attr=2, projid32bit=1
         =                       crc=1        finobt=0, sparse=0
data     =                       bsize=4096   blocks=7864320, imaxpct=25
         =                       sunit=0      swidth=0 blks
naming   =version 2              bsize=4096   ascii-ci=0 ftype=1
log      =internal log           bsize=4096   blocks=3840, version=2
         =                       sectsz=512   sunit=0 blks, lazy-count=1
realtime =none                   extsz=4096   blocks=0, rtextents=0
[root@server1 ~]#
```

Finally, in Example 3-15, both logical volumes are mounted, which means they are usable for storing and retrieving data.

Example 3-15 *Mounting Both Logical Volumes by Using the* ***mount*** *Command*

```
[root@server1 ~]# mkdir /Automation
[root@server1 ~]# mkdir /Development
[root@server1 ~]# ls /
Automation  dev          hd3  lib64  opt          root  srv  usr
bin         Development  home media  proc         run   sys  var
boot        etc          lib  mnt    Programming  sbin  tmp

[root@server1 ~]# mount /dev/VGNetProg/LVNetAutom /Automation
[root@server1 ~]# mount /dev/VGNetProg/LVNetDev /Development/
[root@server1 ~]# df -h
Filesystem                      Size  Used Avail Use% Mounted on
/dev/mapper/centos-root          44G  6.7G   38G  16% /
devtmpfs                        3.9G     0  3.9G   0% /dev
```

```
tmpfs                             3.9G     0  3.9G   0% /dev/shm
tmpfs                             3.9G  8.8M  3.9G   1% /run
tmpfs                             3.9G     0  3.9G   0% /sys/fs/cgroup
/dev/sda1                        1014M  233M  782M  23% /boot
tmpfs                             783M   20K  783M   1% /run/user/1001
/dev/mapper/VGNetProg-LVNetAutom  9.8G   37M  9.2G   1% /Automation
/dev/mapper/VGNetProg-LVNetDev     30G   33M   30G   1% /Development
[root@server1 ~]#
```

Of course, the mounting done in Example 3-15 is not persistent. To mount both logical volumes during system boot, two entries need to be added to the /etc/fstab file—one entry for each LV.

You may have noticed in the output of the **df -h** command in Example 3-15 that each LV appears as a subdirectory to the directory /dev/mapper. The *device mapper* is a kernel space driver that provides the generic function of creating mappings between different storage volumes. The term *generic* is used here because the mapper is not particularly aware of the constructs used by LVM to implement logical volumes. LVM uses the device mapper to create the mappings between a volume group and its constituent logical volumes, without the device mapper explicitly knowing that the latter is a logical volume (rather than a physical one).

The examples in this section show only the very basic functionality of LVM—that is, creating the basic building blocks for having and using logical volumes on a system. However, the real power of LVM becomes clear when you use advanced features such as increasing or decreasing the size of a logical volume, without having to delete the volume and re-create it, or the several options for high availability of logical volumes. Red Hat has a 147-page document titled "Logical Volume Manager Administration" on managing logical volumes. You can check out the document for RHEL 8 at https://access.redhat.com/documentation/en-us/red_hat_enterprise_linux/8/html/configuring_and_managing_logical_volumes/index.

Linux Security

Linux security is a massive and complex topic so it is important to establish the intended scope of this section early on. The purpose of this section is two-fold. The first purpose is to familiarize you with basic Linux security operations that would enable you to effectively manage your development environment without being stumped. For example, you can't execute a script unless your user on the system has the privileges to execute that script, based on the script's file permissions and your group memberships. The second purpose of this section is to show you how to accomplish a minimal level of hardening for your development environment. Using an unsecured device to run scripts that access network devices—and possibly push configuration to those devices—is not a wise thing to do. Accordingly, this section covers user, group, file, and directory security, including access control lists. This chapter also covers the Linux firewall.

User and Group Management

Linux is a multiuser operating system, which means that more than one user can access a single Linux system at a time.

For a user to access a Linux system, the user's account must be configured on the system. The user will then have a username and user ID (UID). A user with an account on the system is a member of one or more groups. Each group has a group name and a group ID (GID). By default, when a user is created on the system, a new group is also created; it has the same name as the username, and this becomes the primary group of the user. A user typically has a password, and each group also has a password.

Each user has a *home* directory that contains that user's files. One way that Linux maintains user segregation and security is by maintaining permissions on files and directories and allowing users with the appropriate authorization level to set those permissions. File permissions are classified into permissions for the owner of the file, the group of the file, and everyone else. The root user and any other user with root privileges can access all resources on the system, including other users' files and directories. The root user and users with root privileges are members of a group named wheel.

You can find user information by using the command **id** {*username*}, as shown in Example 3-16 for user NetProg.

Example 3-16 *Getting User Information by Using the* **id** *Command*

```
[root@localhost ~]# id NetProg
uid=1001(NetProg) gid=1002(NetProg) groups=1002(NetProg),10(wheel)
[root@localhost ~]#
```

User NetProg's UID is 1001. The output in Example 3-16 shows that the user's default (primary) group has the same name as the username. User NetProg in the example is also a member of the wheel group and therefore has root privileges that can be invoked by using the **sudo** {*command*} command, where *command* requires root privileges to be executed. The number to the left of each group name is the group ID.

User information is also stored in the /etc/passwd file, and group information is stored in the /etc/group file. Hashed user passwords are stored in the file /etc/shadow, and hashed group passwords are stored in the file /etc/gshadow. Example 3-17 displays the last five entries of each of the files.

Example 3-17 *Last Five Entries from the /etc/passwd, /etc/group, /etc/shadow, and /etc/gshadow Files*

```
! Sample entries from the /etc/passwd file
[netdev@server1 ~]$ tail -n 5 /etc/passwd
netdev:x:1000:1000:Network Developer:/home/netdev:/bin/bash
vboxadd:x:970:1::/var/run/vboxadd:/bin/false
cockpit-wsinstance:x:969:969:User for cockpit-ws instances:/nonexisting:/sbin/
  nologin
```

```
flatpak:x:968:968:User for flatpak system helper:/:/sbin/nologin
rngd:x:967:967:Random Number Generator Daemon:/var/lib/rngd:/sbin/nologin
[netdev@server1 ~]$

! Sample entries from the /etc/group file
[netdev@server1 ~]$ tail -n 5 /etc/group
netdev:x:1000:
vboxsf:x:970:
cockpit-wsinstance:x:969:
flatpak:x:968:
rngd:x:967
[netdev@server1 ~]$

! file /etc/shadow requires root privileges to be read
[netdev@server1 ~]$ tail -n 5 /etc/shadow
tail: cannot open '/etc/shadow' for reading: Permission denied
[netdev@server1 ~]$

! Sample entries from the /etc/shadow file
[netdev@server1 ~]$ sudo tail -n 5 /etc/shadow
[sudo] password for netdev:
netdev:$6$.JUG9NvdC/NzqiYq$zpCkMR3eENFgk906PjFVLJ526qFRI9L2n13rFApiyPS0lgb2F1CTjJvc1
  dqvvE3XV91q2fK.p3hvlEYtKciD2.:18489:0:99999:7:::
vboxadd:!!:18473::::::
cockpit-wsinstance:!!:18473::::::
flatpak:!!:18473::::::
rngd:!!:18473::::::
[netdev@server1 ~]$

! file /etc/gshadow requires root privileges to be read
[netdev@server1 ~]$ tail -n 5 /etc/gshadow
tail: cannot open '/etc/gshadow' for reading: Permission denied
[netdev@server1 ~]$

! Sample entries from the /etc/gshadow file
[netdev@server1 ~]$ sudo tail -n 5 /etc/gshadow
netdev:!::
vboxsf:!::
cockpit-wsinstance:!::
flatpak:!::
rngd:!::
[netdev@server1 ~]$
```

Each line in the /etc/passwd file is a record containing the information for one user account. Each record is formatted as follows: *username*:x:*user_id*:*primary_group_id*:*user_extra_information*:*user_home_directory*:*user_default_shell*.

The /etc/passwd and /etc/group files can be read by any user on the system but can only be edited by a user with root privileges. For this reason, as a security measure, the second field in the record, which historically contained the user password hash, now shows only the letter x. The user password hashes are now maintained in the /etc/shadow file, which can only be read by users with root privileges. The same arrangement is true for the /etc/group and the /etc/gshadow files. Whenever a user does not have a password, the x is omitted. Two consecutive colons in any record indicate missing information for the respective field.

Each line in the /etc/group file is a record containing information for one group. Each record is formatted as follows: *groupname*:x:*group_id*:*group_members*. The last field is a comma-separated list of non-default users in the group. For example, the record for the netdev group shows all users who are members of the group netdev except the user netdev itself.

Each line in the /etc/shadow file is a record containing the password information for one user. Each record is formatted as follows: *username*:*password_hash*:*last_changed*:*min*:*max*:*warn*:*expired*:*disabled*:*reserved*.

The field *last_changed* is the number of days between January 1, 1970, and the date the password was last changed. The field *min* is the minimum number of days to wait before the password can be changed. The value 0 indicates that it may be changed at any time. The field *max* is the number of days after which the password must be changed. The value 99999 means that the user can keep the same password practically forever. The field *warn* is the number of days to send a warning to the user prior to the password expiring. The field *expired* is the number of days after the password expires before the account should be disabled. The field *disabled* is the number of days since January 1, 1970, that an account has been disabled. The last field is reserved.

Finally, each line in the /etc/gshadow file is a record that contains the password information for one group. Each record is formatted as follows: *groupname*:*group_password_hash*:*group_admins*:*group_members*. The *group_password_hash* field contains an exclamation symbol (!) if no user is allowed to access the group by using the **newgrp** command. (This command is covered later in this section.)

You use the command **useradd** {*username*} to create a new user, and the command **passwd** {*username*} to set or change the password for a user. After switching to user root by using the **su** command in Example 3-18, the **id NetDev** command is used to verify that user NetDev does not already exist. The new user NetDev is then created by issuing the command **useradd NetDev**.

Next, the example shows the **su** command being used to attempt to log in as user NetDev. Notice that although a password was requested, no password will actually work. This is because, by default, when a new user is created, a password entry is created in the /etc/shadow file, but until this password is actually set by using the **passwd** command, you cannot log in as the user because the *default* password hash in the shadow file is an invalid hash. The example shows the password being removed altogether with the command **passwd -d NetDev**. Only at this point are you able to log in without getting a password prompt. The password is then set using the command **passwd NetDev**, and a warning is displayed because the password entered was **Cisco123**. Once the password is set, it is possible to log in as the user in question. Note that creating a user also creates a home directory—in this case /home/NetDev—as shown in the output of the **pwd** command. The files /etc/passwd, /etc/group, and /etc/shadow are also updated to reflect the new user details, as shown in the example.

Example 3-18 *Creating a New User and Setting the Password*

```
[NetProg@localhost ~]$ su -
Password:
Last login: Sun Apr 15 14:26:29 +03 2018 on pts/1
[root@localhost ~]#

! Verify whether the user NetDev exists
[root@localhost ~]# id NetDev
id: NetDev: no such user
[root@localhost ~]#

! Add user NetDev and log in to it
[root@localhost ~]# useradd NetDev
[root@localhost ~]# exit
Logout
[NetProg@localhost ~]$

! Authentication will fail due to invalid "default" hash
[NetProg@localhost ~]$ su NetDev
Password:
su: Authentication failure
[NetProg@localhost ~]$

! Switch back to user root and remove the password
[NetProg@localhost ~]$ su -
Password:
Last login: Sun Apr 15 14:27:07 +03 2018 on pts/1
[root@localhost ~]# passwd -d NetDev
Removing password for user NetDev.
passwd: Success
[root@localhost ~]# exit
logout
```

```
[NetProg@localhost ~]$ su NetDev
[NetDev@localhost NetProg]$ exit
Exit
[NetProg@localhost ~]$

! Switch to user root and set the password manually then test
[NetProg@localhost ~]$ su -
Password:
Last login: Sun Apr 15 14:28:12 +03 2018 on pts/1
[root@localhost ~]# passwd NetDev
Changing password for user NetDev.
New password:
BAD PASSWORD: The password fails the dictionary check - it is based on a dictionary
  word
Retype new password:
passwd: all authentication tokens updated successfully.
[root@localhost ~]# exit
logout
[NetProg@localhost ~]$ su NetDev
Password:
[NetDev@localhost NetProg]$

! Check the home directory and other details for user NetDev
[NetDev@localhost NetProg]$ cd
[NetDev@localhost ~]$ pwd
/home/NetDev
[NetDev@localhost ~]$ id NetDev
uid=1002(NetDev) gid=1003(NetDev) groups=1003(NetDev)
[NetDev@localhost ~]$ tail -n 1 /etc/passwd
NetDev:x:1002:1003::/home/NetDev:/bin/bash
[NetDev@localhost ~]$ tail -n 1 /etc/group
NetDev:x:1003:
[NetDev@localhost ~]$

! Switch to user root and check file /etc/shadow
[NetDev@localhost ~]$ su -
Password:
Last login: Sun Apr 15 14:50:37 +03 2018 on pts/0
[root@localhost ~]# tail -n 1 /etc/shadow
NetDev:$6$y27JA0id$i8Wze1ShSptxy5wRS8f7fOkPeeAezo2cayDl/
  sqikRkYp2VseEXNrzwqDQXqvMeAqzMs2Jd./jj5fm05PK.Wi/:17636:0:99999:7:::
[root@localhost ~]# exit
logout
[NetDev@localhost ~]$
```

A user can change her own password by simply typing **passwd** without any arguments. The user is then prompted to enter the current password and then the new password and then to confirm the new password.

To delete a user, you use the command **userdel** {*username*}. This command deletes the user from the system; to delete that user's home directory and print spool as well, you use the option **-r** with the command. You use the option **-f** to force the delete action even if the user is still logged in.

You can add groups separately from users by using the command **groupadd** {*group_name*}. You can use the option **-g** to set the GID manually instead of allowing automatic assignment of the next available GID. You delete groups by using the command **groupdel** {*group_name*}. Example 3-19 shows how to create a new group called engineers and set its GID to 1111.

Example 3-19 *Creating a New Group engineers*

```
[root@localhost ~]# tail -n 2 /etc/group
NetProg:x:1002:
NetDev:x:1003:
[root@localhost ~]# groupadd -g 1111 engineers
[root@localhost ~]# tail -n 3 /etc/group
NetProg:x:1002:
NetDev:x:1003:
engineers:x:1111:
[root@localhost ~]#
```

To delete a group, you use the command **groupdel** {*group_name*}. You change a group's details by using the command **groupmod**. The command **groupmod -g** {*new_gid*} {*group_name*} changes the group gid to *new_gid*, and the command **groupmod -n** {*new_name*} {*old_name*} changes the group's name from *old_name* to *new_name*. Finally, you change the group password by using the command **gpasswd** {*group_name*}. In Example 3-20, the group engineers is changed to NetDevOps, and its GID is changed to 2222. Then its password is modified to Cisco123.

Example 3-20 *Modifying Group Details*

```
[root@localhost ~]# tail -n -1 /etc/group
engineers:x:1111:
[root@localhost ~]#

! Change the group name to NetDevOps
[root@localhost ~]# groupmod -n NetDevOps engineers
[root@localhost ~]# tail -n -1 /etc/group
NetDevOps:x:1111:
[root@localhost ~]#
```

```
! Change the gid to 2222
[root@localhost ~]# groupmod -g 2222 NetDevOps
[root@localhost ~]# tail -n -1 /etc/group
NetDevOps:x:2222:
[root@localhost ~]#

! Change the group password to Cisco123
[root@localhost ~]# gpasswd NetDevOps
Changing the password for group NetDevOps
New Password:
Re-enter new password:
[root@localhost ~]#
```

A user has one primary group and one or more secondary groups. A user's primary group is the group that the user is placed in when logging in. You modify user group membership by using the command **usermod.** To change a user's primary group, you use the syntax **usermod -g** {*primary_group*} {*username*}. To change a user's secondary group, you use the syntax **usermod -G** {*secondary_group*} {*username*}; note that this command removes all secondary group memberships for this user and adds the group *secondary_group* specified in the command. To add a user to a secondary group while maintaining his current group memberships, you use the syntax **usermod -aG** {*new_secondary_group*} {*username*}. To lock a user account, you use the option **-L** with the **usermod** command, and to unlock an account, you use the **-U** option with this command. Example 3-21 shows how to change the primary group of user NetDev from NetDev to NetOps and add the wheel group to the list of secondary groups to give the user root privileges through the **sudo** command.

Example 3-21 *Modifying User Details*

```
[root@localhost ~]# id NetDev
uid=1002(NetDev) gid=1003(NetDev) groups=1003(NetDev)
[root@localhost ~]# usermod -g NetOps NetDev
[root@localhost ~]# id NetDev
uid=1002(NetDev) gid=2222(NetOps) groups=2222(NetOps)
[root@localhost ~]# usermod -aG wheel NetDev
[root@localhost ~]# id NetDev
uid=1002(NetDev) gid=2222(NetOps) groups=2222(NetOps),10(wheel)
[root@localhost ~]#
```

Notice that when the **-g** option is used to change the primary group, the secondary group is also changed. This is because user NetDev was only a member of a single group, NetDev, and that group was both the user's primary group and secondary group. When the primary and secondary groups are different, the **-g** option changes only the primary group of the user.

File Security Management

Chapter 2 describes the output of the **ls -l** command and introduces file permissions, also known as the file mode bits. This section builds on that introduction and expands on how to manage access to files and directories by modifying their permissions. It also discusses changing the file owner (user) and group. Keep in mind that in Linux, everything is represented by a file. Therefore, the concepts discussed here have a wider scope than what seems to be obvious. Also, whenever a reference is made to a file, the same concept applies to a directory, unless explicitly stated otherwise.

Example 3-22 shows the output of **ls -l** for the NetProg home directory.

Example 3-22 *Output of the ls -l Command*

```
[NetProg@localhost ~]$ ls -l
total 0
drwxr-xr-x. 2 NetProg NetProg  40 Apr  9 09:41 Desktop
drwxr-xr-x. 2 NetProg NetProg   6 Mar 31 17:34 Documents
drwxr-xr-x. 2 NetProg NetProg   6 Mar 31 17:34 Downloads
drwxr-xr-x. 2 NetProg NetProg   6 Mar 31 17:34 Music
drwxr-xr-x. 2 NetProg NetProg   6 Mar 31 17:34 Pictures
drwxr-xr-x. 2 NetProg NetProg   6 Mar 31 17:34 Public
drwxrwxr-x. 2 NetProg NetProg 183 Apr  7 22:53 Scripts
drwxr-xr-x. 2 NetProg NetProg   6 Mar 31 17:34 Templates
-rw-rw-r--. 1 NetProg NetProg   0 Apr  9 17:51 Testfile.txt
drwxr-xr-x. 2 NetProg NetProg   6 Mar 31 17:34 Videos
[NetProg@localhost ~]$
```

Here is a quick recap on the file permissions: The very first bit indicates whether this is a file (-), a directory (d), or a link (l). Then the following 3 bits define the permissions for the file owner. By default, the owner is the user who created the file. The following 3 bits define the permissions for the users who are members of the file group. By default, this is the primary group of the user who created the file. The last 3 bits define the permissions for everyone else, referred to as *other*. The letter r stands for read permission, w for write permission, and x for execute permission.

The dot right after the mode bits indicates that this file has an SELinux context. SELinux is a kernel security module that defines the access rights of every user, application, process, and file on the system. SELinux then governs the interactions of these entities using a security policy, where an entity referred to as a subject attempts to access another entity referred to as an object. SELinux is an important component of Linux security but is beyond the scope of this book. When a file or a directory has a + symbol in place of the dot (.), it means the file has an access control list (ACL) applied to it. ACLs, which are covered later in this chapter, provide more granular access control to files on a per-user basis.

The output of the **ls -l** command also displays the file owner (more formally referred to as user) and the file group.

File permissions can be represented (and modified) by either using *symbolic* notation or *octal* notation.

Symbolic notation is the type of notation described so far, where user, group, and others are represented by u, g, and o, respectively, and the access permissions are write, read, and execute, represented by w, r, and x, respectively. The following syntax is used to set the file permissions: **chmod [u=**{*permissions*}**][,g=**{*permissions*}**][,o=**{*permissions*}**]** {*file_name*}.

Example 3-23 shows how to modify the file permissions for file TestFile.txt to the following:

- **User:** Read, write, and execute
- **Group:** Read and write
- **Other:** No access

Example 3-23 *Setting File Permissions by Using Symbolic Notation*

```
! Current file permissions
[NetProg@localhost ~]$ ls -l Testfile.txt
-rw-rw-r--. 1 NetProg NetProg 0 Apr  9 17:51 Testfile.txt
[NetProg@localhost ~]$

! Change the file permissions as listed
[NetProg@localhost ~]$ chmod u=rwx,g=rw,o= Testfile.txt

! New file permissions
[NetProg@localhost ~]$ ls -l Testfile.txt
-rwxrw----. 1 NetProg NetProg 0 Apr  9 17:51 Testfile.txt
[NetProg@localhost ~]$
```

Notice that in order to remove all permissions for one of the categories, you just leave the right side of the = symbol blank.

One of the challenges with the symbolic notation syntax as used in Example 3-23 is that you have to know beforehand what permissions the file already has and make sure to align the current permissions with the new permissions you are trying to set. For example, if a file already has read and write permissions set for the file group and you would like to add the execute permission, you have to know this fact prior to the change, and then you need to make sure you do not delete the already existing write or read permissions while setting the execute permission. In order to just add or remove permissions for a specific category, without explicitly knowing or considering the existing permissions, you replace the = symbol in the previous syntax with either a + or a - symbol, as follows: **chmod** [u[+|-]{*permissions*}][,g[+|-]{*permissions*}][,o[+|-]{*permissions*}] {*file_name*}.

In Example 3-24 the permissions for the file TestFile.txt are modified as follows:

- **User:** Unchanged
- **Group:** Write permission removed and execute permission added
- **Other:** Execute permission added

Notice that when using this syntax, you do not need to know what permissions the file already has. You only need to consider the changes that you want to implement.

Example 3-24 *Adding and Removing File Permissions by Using Symbolic Notation*

```
[NetProg@localhost ~]$ ls -l Testfile.txt
-rwxrw----. 1 NetProg NetProg 0 Apr  9 17:51 Testfile.txt
[NetProg@localhost ~]$ chmod g-w,g+x,o+x Testfile.txt
[NetProg@localhost ~]$ ls -l Testfile.txt
-rwxr-x--x. 1 NetProg NetProg 0 Apr  9 17:51 Testfile.txt
[NetProg@localhost ~]$
```

Notice that you can mix the + and - symbols in the same command and for the same category, as shown in Example 3-24 for the file group, where **g-w** is used to remove the write permission for the group, and **g+x** is used to add the execute permission for the group.

When a certain permission has to be granted or revoked from all categories, the letter a is used to collectively mean u, g, and o. The letter a in this case stands for *all*. The letter a may be dropped altogether, and the command then applies to all categories. For example, the command **chmod +w Example.py** adds the write permission to all categories for the file Example.py.

Octal notation, on the other hand, uses the following syntax: **chmod** {*user_permission*}{*group_permission*}{*other_permission*} {*file_name*}. The *user*, *group*, and *other* categories are represented by their positions in the command. The permission granted to each category is represented as a numeric value that is equal to the summation of each permission's individual value. To elaborate, note the following permission values:

- Read=4
- Write=2
- Execute=1

To set the read permission only, you need to use the value 4; for write permission only, you use the value 2; and for execute permission only, you use the value 1. To set all permissions for any category, you need to use 4+2+1=7. To set the read and write permissions only, you need to use 4+2=6, and so forth. Example 3-25 illustrates this concept and uses octal notation to set the read, write, and execute permissions for both user and group, and set only the execute permission for the category other for file Testfile.txt.

Example 3-25 *Setting File Permissions Using Octal Notation*

```
[NetProg@localhost ~]$ ls -l Testfile.txt
-rwxr-x--x. 1 NetProg NetProg 0 Apr  9 17:51 Testfile.txt
[NetProg@localhost ~]$ chmod 771 Testfile.txt
[NetProg@localhost ~]$ ls -l Testfile.txt
-rwxrwx--x. 1 NetProg NetProg 0 Apr  9 17:51 Testfile.txt
[NetProg@localhost ~]$
```

The number **7** in each of the first two positions in the command **chmod 771 Testfile.txt** represents the sum of 4, 2, and 1 and is used to set all permissions for user and group. The number **1** in the last position sets the execute only permission for other.

While octal notation looks snappier than symbolic notation, it does not provide the option of adding or removing permissions without considering the existing file permissions, as provided by the **+** and **-** symbols used with symbolic notation.

Besides modifying file and directory permissions, you can control access to a file or directory by changing the file's user and/or group through the **chown** command. The command syntax is **chown** {*user*}:{*group*} {*file*}. Example 3-26 shows how to change the *user* and *group* of file TestFile.txt to NetDev and networks, respectively.

Example 3-26 *Changing File User and Group by Using the chown Command*

```
[root@localhost ~]# ls -l /home/NetProg/Testfile.txt
-rwxrwx--x. 1 NetProg NetProg 0 Apr  9 17:51 /home/NetProg/Testfile.txt
[root@localhost ~]# chown NetDev:networks /home/NetProg/Testfile.txt
[root@localhost ~]# ls -l /home/NetProg/Testfile.txt
-rwxrwx--x. 1 NetDev networks 0 Apr  9 17:51 /home/NetProg/Testfile.txt
[root@localhost ~]#
```

You use the **-R** option (which stands for *recursive*) with both the **chmod** and the **chown** commands if the operation is being performed on a directory, and you want the changes to also be made to all subdirectories and files in that directory.

By default, any file or directory created by a user is assigned to the primary group of that user. For example, if user NetDev is in the NetOps group, any file created by user NetDev has NetDev as the file user and NetOps as the file group. You can change this default behavior by either using the **sg** command when creating the file or by logging in to another group by using the command **newgrp**. If that other group is one of the user's secondary groups, no password is required. If that other group is not one of the user's secondary groups, the user is prompted for a password.

Example 3-27 shows the default behavior when creating a file. In this case, a new file named NewFile is created by user NetDev. As expected, the file user is NetDev, and the file group is NetOps.

Example 3-27 *Default User and Group of a Newly Created File*

```
[NetDev@localhost ~]$ id NetDev
uid=1002(NetDev) gid=2222(NetOps) groups=2222(NetOps),10(wheel)
[NetDev@localhost ~]$ touch NewFile
[NetDev@localhost ~]$ ls -l NewFile
-rw-r--r--. 1 NetDev NetOps 0 Apr 17 00:59 NewFile
[NetDev@localhost ~]$
```

Example 3-28 shows how to use the **sg** command to create file NewFile_1 but under the group networks.

Example 3-28 *Using the sg Command to Create a File Under a Different Group*

```
[NetDev@localhost ~]$ id NetDev
uid=1002(NetDev) gid=2222(NetOps) groups=2222(NetOps),10(wheel)
[NetDev@localhost ~]$ sg networks 'touch NewFile_1'
Password:
[NetDev@localhost ~]$ ls -l NewFile_1
-rw-r--r--. 1 NetDev networks 0 Apr 17 01:03 NewFile_1
[NetDev@localhost ~]$
```

Notice that the command **touch** *{file_name}*, which itself is an argument to the **sg** command, has to be enclosed in quotes because it is a multi-word command. Notice also that because the user NetDev is not a member in the networks group, as you can see from the output of the **id** command, the user is prompted for the group password, which was set earlier by using the command **gpasswd networks**.

Alternatively, the user can log in to another group by using the command **newgrp** and create a file or directory under that group. Example 3-29 shows the user NetProg logging in to group systems and not being prompted for a password since this is one of NetProg's secondary groups. When the file NewFile_2 is created, the user of the file is NetProg, and the group is systems, not NetProg.

Example 3-29 *Using the newgrp Command to Log In to a Different Group*

```
[NetProg@localhost ~]$ id NetProg
uid=1001(NetProg) gid=1002(NetProg) groups=1002(NetProg),10(wheel),2224(systems)
[NetProg@localhost ~]$ newgrp systems
[NetProg@localhost ~]$ touch NewFile_2
[NetProg@localhost ~]$ ls -l NewFile_2
-rw-r--r--. 1 NetProg systems 0 Apr 17 01:15 NewFile_2
[NetProg@localhost ~]$
```

Access Control Lists

So far in this chapter, you have seen how to set file and directory access permissions for either user, or collectively for group, or other. What if you want to set those permissions individually for a specific user who is not the file owner or for a group of users who belong to a group other than the file group? File mode bits do not help in such situations. Using the file mode bits, the only user whose permissions can be changed individually is the file or directory owner (user) and the only group of users whose permissions can be changed collectively are the users who are members of the file or directory group.

Access control lists (*ACLs*) provide more granular control over file and directory access. ACLs allow a system administrator (or any other user who has root privileges) to set file and directory permissions for any user or group on the system.

Before you can configure ACLs, three prerequisites must be met:

- The kernel must support ACLs for the file system type on which ACLs will be applied.
- The file system on which ACLs will be used must be mounted with the ACL option.
- The ACL package must be installed.

Most common distros today—including CentOS 7 and Red Hat Enterprise Linux (RHEL) 7 and later versions—have these prerequisites configured by default, and you do not need to do any further configuration.

If you are running a different distro or an older version of CentOS, you can check the first prerequisite by using either the **findmnt** or **blkid** command to determine the file system type on your system. The command **findmnt** works only if the file system has been mounted, and **blkid** works whether it is mounted or not. Then you need to inspect the kernel configuration file /boot/conf-<*version.architecture*> to determine whether ACLs have been enabled for this file system type. Example 3-30 shows the relevant output for the file system on the sda1 partition.

Example 3-30 *ACL Support for the sda1 File System*

```
[root@server1 ~]# findmnt /dev/sda1
TARGET SOURCE    FSTYPE OPTIONS
/boot  /dev/sda1 xfs    rw,relatime,seclabel,attr2,inode64,noquota
[root@server1 ~]# cat /boot/config-3.10.0-693.el7.x86_64 | grep ACL
CONFIG_EXT4_FS_POSIX_ACL=y
CONFIG_XFS_POSIX_ACL=y
CONFIG_BTRFS_FS_POSIX_ACL=y
CONFIG_FS_POSIX_ACL=y
CONFIG_GENERIC_ACL=y
CONFIG_TMPFS_POSIX_ACL=y
CONFIG_NFS_V3_ACL=y
CONFIG_NFSD_V2_ACL=y
CONFIG_NFSD_V3_ACL=y
CONFIG_NFS_ACL_SUPPORT=m
CONFIG_CEPH_FS_POSIX_ACL=y
CONFIG_CIFS_ACL=y
[root@server1 ~]#
```

The kernel configuration file lists different configuration options, each followed by an = symbol and then the letter y, n, or m. The letter y means that this option (module) was configured as part of the kernel when the kernel was first compiled. In this example, CONFIG_XFS_POSIX_ACL=y means that the kernel supports ACLs for the xfs file system. The letter n indicates that this module was not compiled into the kernel, and the letter m means that this module was compiled as a loadable kernel module (introduced in Chapter 2).

The second prerequisite is that the partition on which the ACLs will be used has to be mounted with the ACL option. By default, on ext3/4 and xfs file systems, ACL support is enabled. In older CentOS versions and other distros where the ACL option is not enabled by default, the file system can be mounted with the ACL option by using the syntax **mount -o acl** {*partition*} {*mount_point*}. On the other hand, if the ACL option is enabled by default, and you want to disable ACL support while mounting the file system, you can use the **noacl** option with the **mount** command. As discussed in the previous section, mounting using the **mount** command is non-persistent. For persistent mounting with the ACL option, you can add an entry to the /dev/fstab file (or amend an existing entry) and add the **acl** option (right after the **defaults** keyword). The /dev/fstab file is discussed in detail earlier in this chapter.

Finally, by using the **yum info acl** command, you can confirm whether the ACL package has been installed. The **yum** command is covered in detail in Chapter 2.

When ACL support has been established, you can use the command **getfacl** {*filename*|*directory*} to display the ACL configuration for a file or directory. Example 3-31 shows the output of the **getfacl** command for the directory /Programming and then for the file NewFile.txt.

Example 3-31 *Output of the getfacl Command*

```
[root@localhost /]# ls -ld Programming
drwxr-xr-x. 2 root root 25 Jun  9 05:46 Programming
[root@localhost /]# ls -l Programming
total 0
-rw-r--r--. 1 root root 0 Jun  9 05:46 NewFile.txt
[root@localhost /]# getfacl Programming
# file: Programming
# owner: root
# group: root
user::rwx
group::r-x
other::r-x
[root@localhost /]# getfacl Programming/NewFile.txt
# file: Programming/NewFile.txt
# owner: root
# group: root
user::rw-
group::r--
other::r–
[root@localhost /]#
```

As you can see from the output in Example 3-31, both the directory and file are owned by the user root, and the group of both is also root. So far, there is no additional information provided by the **getfacl** command beyond what is already displayed by **ls -l**; the format is the only difference.

For the file NewFile.txt, the user NetProg is not the file owner and is not a member of the file group. As per the permissions for *other*, the user NetProg should be able to only read the file but not write to it or execute it. In Example 3-32, the user NetProg attempts to write to the file NewFile.txt by using the **echo** command, but a "Permission denied" error message is displayed. The **setfacl -m u:NetProg:rw /Programming/Newfile.txt** command grants write permission to the user NetProg. When the write operation is attempted again, it is successful due to the new elevated permissions.

Example 3-32 *Changing the Permissions for the User NetProg by Using setfacl*

```
! Echo(write) operation fails since NetProg has no write permissions
[NetProg@localhost /]$ echo "This is a write test" > /Programming/NewFile.txt
bash: /Programming/NewFile.txt: Permission denied

! Grant user NetProg write permission (requires root permissions)
[NetProg@localhost /]$ su
Password:
```

```
[root@localhost /]# setfacl -m u:NetProg:rw /Programming/NewFile.txt
[root@localhost /]# getfacl /Programming/NewFile.txt
getfacl: Removing leading '/' from absolute path names
# file: Programming/NewFile.txt
# owner: root
# group: root
user::rw-
user:NetProg:rw-
group::r--
mask::rw-
other::r--

! Write operation now successful
[root@localhost /]# su NetProg
[NetProg@localhost /]$ echo "This is a write test" > /Programming/NewFile.txt
[NetProg@localhost /]$ cat /Programming/NewFile.txt
This is a write test
[NetProg@localhost /]$ ls -l /Programming/NewFile.txt
-rw-rw-r--+ 1 root root 21 Jun  9 07:24 /Programming/NewFile.txt
[NetProg@localhost /]$
```

Notice the **+** symbol that now replaces the dot to the right of file permission bits at the end of Example 3-32. This indicates that an ACL has been applied to this file. The new write permission has been granted to the user NetProg only, and not to any other user. This was done without amending the file permissions for the user, group, or other categories. It was also done without modifying the group memberships of the user NetProg. The same permission could also be applied to a group instead of an individual user. The level of granularity provided by ACLs should be clear by now.

The **setfacl** command used in Example 3-32 was issued with the option **-m**, which is short for *modify* and is used to apply a new ACL or modify an existing ACL. To remove an ACL, you use the option **-x** instead of **-m**; the remainder of the command remains the same, except that the ACL in the command is an existing ACL that is now being removed.

In Example 3-32 you can see the three-field argument **u:NetProg:rw**. When setting an ACL for a user, the first field is u, as in the example. For a group, the first field would be g, and for other, the first field would be o. The second field is the user or group name, which is NetProg in this example. If the ACL is for other, this field remains empty. The third field is the permissions you wish to grant to the user or group.

Finally, after the three-field argument is the name of the directory or file to which the ACL is applied. Note that whether a full path or only a relative path is required depends on the current working directory relative to the location of the file or directory to which the ACL is being applied. The same rules apply here as with any other Linux command that operates on a file or directory.

Therefore, the general syntax of the **setfacl** command to add, modify, or remove an ACL is **setfacl** {**-m**|**-x**} {**u**|**g**|**o**}:{*username*|*group*}:{*permissions*} {*file*|*directory*}. To remove all ACL entries applied to a file, you use the option **-b** followed by the filename, omitting the three-field argument.

In Example 3-32, notice the text mask::rw- in the output of the **getfacl** command, after the ACL has been applied. The mask provides one more level of control over the permissions granted by the ACL. Say that after granting several users different permissions to a file, you decide to remove a specific permission, such as the write permission, from *all* named users. The ACL mask then comes in handy. The permissions in the mask override the permissions for all named users and the file group. For example, if the mask permissions are r-x and the user NetProg has been granted rwx permissions, that user's effective permissions are r-x after the mask is set. The effective mask permissions are applied using the command **setfacl -m m:**{*permissions*} {*filename*}. In Example 3-33, the user NetProg has permissions rw-, and so does the mask. The mask is modified to r--. Notice the effective permissions that appear on the right side of the output of the **getfacl** command after the mask has been modified. After you remove the write permission from the mask, NetProg's write attempt to the file fails.

Example 3-33 *Changing the Mask Permissions by Using setfacl*

```
! Set the effective rights mask
[root@localhost /]# setfacl -m m:r /Programming/NewFile.txt
[root@localhost /]# getfacl /Programming/NewFile.txt
getfacl: Removing leading '/' from absolute path names
# file: Programming/NewFile.txt
# owner: root
# group: root
user::rw-
user:NetProg:rw-        #effective:r--
group::r--
mask::r--
other::r--

! Write operation to file by user NetProg now fails
[root@localhost /]# su NetProg
[NetProg@localhost /]$ echo "Testing mask permissions" > /Programming/NewFile.txt
bash: /Programming/NewFile.txt: Permission denied
[NetProg@localhost /]$
```

When ACLs are applied to directories, by default, these ACLs are not inherited by files and subdirectories in that directory. In order to achieve inheritance, the option **-R** has to be added to the same **setfacl** command used earlier. In Example 3-34, an ACL setting rwx permissions for the user NetProg is applied to the directory Programming. Attempting to write to file NewFile.txt under the directory by user NetProg fails because the write permission has not been inherited by the file.

Example 3-34 *ACLs Are Not Inherited by Default by Subdirectories and Files Under a Directory*

```
! Apply an acl to the /Programming directory
[root@localhost ~]# setfacl -m u:NetProg:rwx /Programming
[root@localhost ~]# getfacl /Programming
getfacl: Removing leading '/' from absolute path names
# file: Programming
# owner: root
# group: root
user::rwx
user:NetProg:rwx
group::r-x
mask::rwx
other::r-x

! The acl is not applied to NewFile.txt under the directory
[root@localhost ~]# getfacl /Programming/NewFile.txt
getfacl: Removing leading '/' from absolute path names
# file: Programming/NewFile.txt
# owner: root
# group: root
user::rw-
group::r--
other::r--

! And the write operation fails as expected
[root@localhost ~]# su - NetProg
[NetProg@localhost ~]$ echo "This is a write test" > /Programming/NewFile.txt
bash: /Programming/NewFile.txt: Permission denied
[NetProg@localhost ~]$
```

After the ACL has been removed and then reapplied in Example 3-35 using the **-R** option, the user NetProg can write to the file successfully. The **getfacl** command also shows that the ACL has been applied to the file as if the **setfacl** command had been applied to the file directly.

Example 3-35 *ACL Inheritance by Subdirectories and Files Under a Directory Using the -R Option*

```
! Clear the acl from the /Programming directory
[root@localhost ~]# setfacl -b /Programming

! Apply the acl to directory /Programming using the -R option
[root@localhost ~]# setfacl -R -m u:NetProg:rwx /Programming
[root@localhost ~]# getfacl /Programming
getfacl: Removing leading '/' from absolute path names
# file: Programming
# owner: root
# group: root
user::rwx
user:NetProg:rwx
group::r-x
mask::rwx
other::r-x

! The acl is inherited by the file NewFile.txt
[root@localhost ~]# getfacl /Programming/NewFile.txt
getfacl: Removing leading '/' from absolute path names
# file: Programming/NewFile.txt
# owner: root
# group: root
user::rw-
user:NetProg:rwx
group::r--
mask::rw-
other::r--

! And the write operation is successful
[root@localhost ~]# su - NetProg
[NetProg@localhost ~]$ echo "This is to test inheritance" > /Programming/NewFile.txt
[NetProg@localhost ~]$ cat /Programming/NewFile.txt
This is to test inheritance
[NetProg@localhost ~]$
```

It is important to remember that the ACL applied to a directory and inherited by all subdirectories and files will *not* be applied to any files created *after* the ACL has been applied. Only the files that existed before the ACL was applied will be affected.

The ACLs described so far are called access ACLs. Another type of ACLs, called default ACLs, may be used with directories (only) if the requirement is that all files and subdirectories, when created, should inherit the parent directory ACLs. The syntax for applying a default ACL is **setfacl -m d:{u|g|o}:**{*username|group*}**:**{*permissions*} {*directory*}. Try to experiment with default ACLs and note how newly created files inherit the directory ACL without your having to explicitly issue the **setfacl** command after the file or subdirectory has been created.

The same concepts discussed previously for a single user apply to a group when you set the ACL for a group of users other than the file or directory group by using the letter **g** along with the group name in the **setfacl** command instead of a **u** with the username.

In addition to using the **setfacl** command to set permissions for a specific user or group, you can use this command to set permissions for the file user, group, or other categories, similar to what can be accomplished using the **chmod** command as shown in the previous section. Note that if the **setfacl** command is used to apply an ACL to a file or directory, it is recommended that you *not* use **chmod.**

When a file or directory is copied or moved, ACLs are moved along with the file or directory.

Linux System Security

CentOS 7 and later versions come with a default built-in firewall service named **firewalld.** This service functions in a similar manner to a regular firewall in terms of providing *security zones* with different *trust levels.* Each zone constitutes a group of permit/deny rules for incoming traffic. Each physical interface on the server is bound to one of the firewall zones. However, **firewalld** provides only a subset of the services provided by a full-fledged firewall.

You can check the status of the **firewalld** service and start, stop, enable, and disable the service just as you would any other service on Linux by using the **systemctl** command. Example 3-36 shows the status of the **firewalld** service: In this example, you can see that it is active and enabled.

Example 3-36 *The firewalld Service Status*

```
[NetProg@localhost ~]$ systemctl status firewalld
● firewalld.service - firewalld - dynamic firewall daemon
   Loaded: loaded (/usr/lib/systemd/system/firewalld.service; enabled; vendor
     preset: enabled)
   Active: active (running) since Sat 2018-04-21 21:37:06 +03; 30min ago
     Docs: man:firewalld(1)
 Main PID: 787 (firewalld)
   CGroup: /system.slice/firewalld.service
           └─787 /usr/bin/python -Es /usr/sbin/firewalld --nofork --nopid

Apr 21 21:37:05 localhost.localdomain systemd[1]: Starting firewalld - dynamic
  firewall daemon...
Apr 21 21:37:06 localhost.localdomain systemd[1]: Started firewalld - dynamic
  firewall daemon.

--------- OUTPUT TRUNCATED FOR BREVITY ---------
```

The **firewalld** service has a set of zones created by default when the service is first installed; these zones are sometimes referred to as the *base* or *predefined* zones. Custom zones can also be created and deleted. However, base zones cannot be deleted. One zone is designated as the default zone and is the zone to which all interfaces are bound, by default, unless the interface is explicitly moved to another zone. By default, the default zone is the public zone. Each zone has a set of rules attached to it and a list of interfaces bound to it. Rules and interfaces can be added to or removed from a zone.

Example 3-37 shows how to list the base zones of **firewalld** by using the command **firewall-cmd --get-zones** and how to identify the default zone by using the command **firewall-cmd --get-default-zone.**

Example 3-37 *Listing the Base and Default Zones of a Firewall*

```
[root@localhost ~]# firewall-cmd --get-zones
block dmz drop external home internal public trusted work
[root@localhost ~]# firewall-cmd --get-default-zone
public
[root@localhost ~]#
```

You can change the default zone by using the command **firewall-cmd --set-default-zone=**{*zone_name*}.

You can list the details of a zone by using the command **firewall-cmd --list-all --zone=**{*zone_name*}, as shown in Example 3-38. To list the details of the default zone, you omit the **--zone=**{*zone_name*} option.

Example 3-38 *Listing Zone Details*

```
[root@localhost ~]# firewall-cmd --list-all --zone=internal
internal
  target: default
  icmp-block-inversion: no
  interfaces:
  sources:
  services: ssh mdns samba-client dhcpv6-client
  ports:
  protocols:
  masquerade: no
  forward-ports:
  source-ports:
  icmp-blocks:
  rich rules:

[root@localhost ~]# firewall-cmd --list-all
public (active)
```

```
  target: default
  icmp-block-inversion: no
  interfaces: enp0s3 enp0s9 enp0s10 enp0s8
  sources:
  services: ssh dhcpv6-client
  ports:
  protocols:
  masquerade: no
  forward-ports:
  source-ports:
  icmp-blocks:
  rich rules:
[root@localhost ~]#
```

Example 3-39 shows how to add rules to the zone dmz to permit specific incoming traffic on interfaces bound to this zone. The first rule added permits traffic from the source IP address 10.10.1.0/24 by using a *source-based* rule. Then BGP traffic on TCP port 179 is permitted by using a *port-based* rule. HTTP service is then permitted by defining a *service-based* rule. Finally, interface enp0s9 is removed from the public zone and bound to the dmz zone. Notice how the rules appear when the details of the zone are listed at the end of the example.

Example 3-39 *Adding Rules to Zone **dmz***

```
[root@localhost ~]# firewall-cmd --list-all --zone=dmz
dmz
  target: default
  icmp-block-inversion: no
  interfaces:
  sources:
  services: ssh
  ports:
  protocols:
  masquerade: no
  forward-ports:
  source-ports:
  icmp-blocks:
  rich rules:

[root@localhost ~]# firewall-cmd --zone=dmz --add-source=10.10.1.0/24
success
[root@localhost ~]# firewall-cmd --zone=dmz --add-port=179/tcp
success
```

```
[root@localhost ~]# firewall-cmd --zone=dmz --add-service=http
success
[root@localhost ~]# firewall-cmd --zone=dmz --add-interface=enp0s9
The interface is under control of NetworkManager, setting zone to 'dmz'.
success
[root@localhost ~]# firewall-cmd --zone=dmz --list-all
dmz (active)
  target: default
  icmp-block-inversion: no
  interfaces: enp0s9
  sources: 10.10.1.0/24
  services: ssh http
  ports: 179/tcp
  protocols:
  masquerade: no
  forward-ports:
  source-ports:
  icmp-blocks:
  rich rules:
[root@localhost ~]#
```

Note that in order to remove a rule, instead of using the **--add** option, you use the **--remove** option. For example, to remove the rule for TCP port 179, you use the command **firewall-cmd --zone=dmz --remove-port=179/tcp.**

Much like running and startup configurations on routers and switches, **firewalld** supports both runtime and permanent configurations. A *runtime configuration* is not persistent and is lost after a reload. A *permanent configuration* is persistent but takes effect only after a reload when the configuration has been changed. Any configuration commands that have been executed are reflected in the runtime configuration. To make a configuration permanent, you use the option **--permanent** with the command. You reload the **firewalld** service by using the command **firewall-cmd --reload.**

Linux Networking

Linux provides several methods for managing network devices and interfaces on a system. Usually, a system administrator can accomplish the same task using several different methods. A network device or an interface is managed by the kernel, and each method accesses the Linux kernel via a different path. There are three popular methods for managing Linux networking:

- Using the command-line **ip** utility
- Using the NetworkManager service
- Using network configuration files

This section covers these three methods listed. It should be fairly easy to use the help resources on your Linux distro, such as the man and info pages, to learn about any utility not covered here.

Note Keep in mind that some commands and utilities for managing Linux networking, such as **ifconfig**, **netstat**, **arp**, and **route**, are considered legacy utilities. These utilities have not been updated for years and have been deprecated on some distros but are still available on others. Even if any of these commands are available in the distro you are using, we do not recommend using them; instead, use the methods described in this section. Basically, the way legacy utilities function, particularly how these utilities speak with the kernel, is not very efficient. You will probably run into these legacy utilities at some point while working on Linux. For example, at the time of this writing, all four legacy utilities mentioned here are still supported on the Bash shells exposed by IOS XR and NX-OS.

The ip Utility

ip is a command-line utility that is part of the **iproute2** group of utilities. It is invoked using the command **ip** [*options*] {*object*} {*action*}. This syntax is quite intuitive in that the *action* in the command indicates what action you would want to apply to an *object*. For example, the command **ip link show** applies the action **show** to the object **link**. As you may have guessed, this command displays the state of all network interfaces (links) on the system, as shown in Example 3-40. To limit the output to one specific interface, you can add **dev** {*intf*} to the end of the command, as also shown in the example.

Note The man pages for the **ip** command refer to the *action* part in the previous syntax as *command*. We took the liberty to call it *action* in the upcoming few paragraphs in order to avoid the obvious confusion that will result from calling it *command*.

Example 3-40 *Output of the Command ip link show*

```
[NetProg@localhost ~]$ ip link show
1: lo: <LOOPBACK,UP,LOWER_UP> mtu 65536 qdisc noqueue state UNKNOWN mode DEFAULT
  qlen 1
    link/loopback 00:00:00:00:00:00 brd 00:00:00:00:00:00
2: enp0s3: <BROADCAST,MULTICAST,UP,LOWER_UP> mtu 1500 qdisc pfifo_fast state UP mode
  DEFAULT qlen 1000
    link/ether 08:00:27:a7:32:f7 brd ff:ff:ff:ff:ff:ff
3: enp0s8: <BROADCAST,MULTICAST,UP,LOWER_UP> mtu 1500 qdisc pfifo_fast state UP mode
  DEFAULT qlen 1000
    link/ether 08:00:27:83:40:75 brd ff:ff:ff:ff:ff:ff
4: enp0s9: <BROADCAST,MULTICAST,UP,LOWER_UP> mtu 1500 qdisc pfifo_fast state UP mode
  DEFAULT qlen 1000
    link/ether 08:00:27:b4:ce:55 brd ff:ff:ff:ff:ff:ff
```

```
5: enp0s10: <BROADCAST,MULTICAST,UP,LOWER_UP> mtu 1500 qdisc pfifo_fast state UP
  mode DEFAULT qlen 1000
    link/ether 08:00:27:48:59:02 brd ff:ff:ff:ff:ff:ff
6: virbr0: <NO-CARRIER,BROADCAST,MULTICAST,UP> mtu 1500 qdisc noqueue state DOWN
  mode DEFAULT qlen 1000
    link/ether 52:54:00:ea:c5:d4 brd ff:ff:ff:ff:ff:ff
7: virbr0-nic: <BROADCAST,MULTICAST> mtu 1500 qdisc pfifo_fast master virbr0 state
  DOWN mode DEFAULT qlen 1000
    link/ether 52:54:00:ea:c5:d4 brd ff:ff:ff:ff:ff:ff
[NetProg@localhost ~]$ ip link show dev enp0s3
2: enp0s3: <BROADCAST,MULTICAST,UP,LOWER_UP> mtu 1500 qdisc pfifo_fast state UP mode
  DEFAULT qlen 1000
    link/ether 08:00:27:a7:32:f7 brd ff:ff:ff:ff:ff:ff
[NetProg@localhost ~]$
```

Table 3-1 lists some of the objects that are commonly used with the **ip** command.

Table 3-1 *Objects That Are Commonly Used with the* **ip** *Command*

Object	Description
address	IPv4 or IPv6 protocol address
link	Network interface
route	Routing table entry
maddress	Multicast address
neigh	ARP entry

As of this writing, there are 19 objects that can be acted upon by using the **ip** command. A full list of objects can be found in the man pages for the **ip** command. Objects can be written in full or in abbreviated form, such as **address** or **addr.** The actions that can be used with the **ip** command are limited to three options listed in Table 3-2.

Table 3-2 *Actions That Can Be Used with the* **ip** *Command*

Action	Description
add	Adds the object
delete	Deletes the object
show (or list)	Displays information about the object

The keyword **show** or **list** can be dropped from a command, and the command will still be interpreted as a **show** action. For example, the command **ip link show** is equivalent to just **ip link**.

The **ip addr** command lists all interfaces on the system, each with its IP address information, and the **ip maddr** command displays the multicast information for each and every interface. The **ip neigh** command displays the ARP table. The ARP table consists of a list of neighbors on each interface on the local network. The examples in this section show how to use these **show** commands.

You can bring an interface on Linux up or down by using the command **ip link set** {*intf*} {**up|down**}. The **set** action is only applicable to the link object and therefore was not listed in Table 3-2. Example 3-41 shows how to bring interface enp0s8 down and then up again. Note that changing networking configuration on Linux, including toggling an interface's state, requires root privileges. The **show** commands, however, do not. To keep Example 3-41 short and avoid the frequent password prompt, all commands in the example are issued by the root user. However, running commands as root in general is *not* a recommended practice. On a production network, make sure to avoid logging in as root. It is best practice to log in with your regular user account and use the **sudo** command whenever a command requires root privileges to execute, as explained in Chapter 2.

Example 3-41 *Toggling Interface State*

```
[root@localhost ~]# ip link show dev enp0s8
3: enp0s8: <BROADCAST,MULTICAST,UP,LOWER_UP> mtu 1500 qdisc pfifo_fast state UP mode
  DEFAULT qlen 1000
    link/ether 08:00:27:83:40:75 brd ff:ff:ff:ff:ff:ff
[root@localhost ~]# ip link set enp0s8 down
[root@localhost ~]# ip link show dev enp0s8
3: enp0s8: <BROADCAST,MULTICAST> mtu 1500 qdisc pfifo_fast state DOWN mode DEFAULT
  qlen 1000
    link/ether 08:00:27:83:40:75 brd ff:ff:ff:ff:ff:ff
[root@localhost ~]# ip link set enp0s8 up
[root@localhost ~]# ip link show dev enp0s8
3: enp0s8: <BROADCAST,MULTICAST,UP,LOWER_UP> mtu 1500 qdisc pfifo_fast state UP mode
  DEFAULT qlen 1000
    link/ether 08:00:27:83:40:75 brd ff:ff:ff:ff:ff:ff
[root@localhost ~]#
```

You can add an IP address to an interface by using the command **ip addr add** {*IP_address*} **dev** {*intf*}. By replacing the action **add** with **del**, you remove the IP address. In Example 3-42, IP address 10.1.0.10/24 is added to interface enp0s8, and then the original IP address, 10.1.0.1/24, is removed. The **ip addr show dev enp0s8** command is used to inspect the interface IP address before and after the change.

Example 3-42 *Adding and Removing IP Addresses on Interfaces*

```
[root@localhost ~]# ip addr show dev enp0s8
3: enp0s8: <BROADCAST,MULTICAST,UP,LOWER_UP> mtu 1500 qdisc pfifo_fast state UP qlen
  1000
    link/ether 08:00:27:83:40:75 brd ff:ff:ff:ff:ff:ff
    inet 10.1.0.1/24 brd 10.1.0.255 scope global enp0s8
       valid_lft forever preferred_lft forever
    inet6 fe80::8b8:d663:847f:79d9/64 scope link
       valid_lft forever preferred_lft forever
[root@localhost ~]# ip addr add 10.1.0.10/24 dev enp0s8
[root@localhost ~]# ip addr show dev enp0s8
3: enp0s8: <BROADCAST,MULTICAST,UP,LOWER_UP> mtu 1500 qdisc pfifo_fast state UP qlen
  1000
    link/ether 08:00:27:83:40:75 brd ff:ff:ff:ff:ff:ff
    inet 10.1.0.1/24 brd 10.1.0.255 scope global enp0s8
       valid_lft forever preferred_lft forever
    inet 10.1.0.10/24 scope global secondary enp0s8
       valid_lft forever preferred_lft forever
    inet6 fe80::8b8:d663:847f:79d9/64 scope link
       valid_lft forever preferred_lft forever
[root@localhost ~]# ip addr del 10.1.0.1/24 dev enp0s8
[root@localhost ~]# ip addr show dev enp0s8
3: enp0s8: <BROADCAST,MULTICAST,UP,LOWER_UP> mtu 1500 qdisc pfifo_fast state UP qlen
  1000
    link/ether 08:00:27:83:40:75 brd ff:ff:ff:ff:ff:ff
    inet 10.1.0.10/24 scope global enp0s8
       valid_lft forever preferred_lft forever
    inet6 fe80::8b8:d663:847f:79d9/64 scope link
       valid_lft forever preferred_lft forever
[root@localhost ~]#
```

Notice that the IP address 10.1.0.10/24 is added as a secondary address, as long as another IP address is configured on the interface. When the original IP address is removed, the new IP address becomes the primary address.

Notice the mtu value in the output of the **ip addr show** command in Example 3-42. By default the mtu is set to 1500 bytes. To change that value, you use the command **ip link set** {*intf*} **mtu** {*mtu_value*}.

A very useful feature that any network engineer would truly appreciate is interface promiscuous mode. By default, when an Ethernet frame is received on an interface, that frame is passed on to the upper layers for processing only if the destination MAC address of the frame matches the MAC address of the interface (or if the destination MAC address is a broadcast address). If the MAC addresses do not match, the frame is ignored. This renders packet sniffing applications such as Wireshark and features such as port mirroring unusable. In promiscuous mode, an interface accepts any and all incoming packets, whether the packets are addressed to that interface or not. You can enable promiscuous mode by using the command **ip link set** {*intf*} **promisc on**.

In the routing table, the list of routes on the system can be displayed by using the command **ip route**. Example 3-43 shows that the routing table is empty when no IP addresses are configured on any of the interfaces. When the IP address 10.2.0.30/24 is configured on interface enp0s3, one entry, corresponding to that interface, is added to the routing table.

Example 3-43 *Viewing a Routing Table by Using the* **ip route** *Command*

```
[NetProg@server4 ~]$ ip addr
1: lo: <LOOPBACK,UP,LOWER_UP> mtu 65536 qdisc noqueue state UNKNOWN qlen 1
    link/loopback 00:00:00:00:00:00 brd 00:00:00:00:00:00
    inet 127.0.0.1/8 scope host lo
       valid_lft forever preferred_lft forever
    inet6 ::1/128 scope host
       valid_lft forever preferred_lft forever
2: enp0s3: <BROADCAST,MULTICAST,UP,LOWER_UP> mtu 1500 qdisc pfifo_fast state UP qlen
  1000
    link/ether 08:00:27:2c:61:d0 brd ff:ff:ff:ff:ff:ff
    inet6 fe80::a00:27ff:fe2c:61d0/64 scope link
       valid_lft forever preferred_lft forever
[NetProg@server4 ~]$ ip route

[NetProg@server4 ~]$ sudo ip addr add 10.2.0.30/24 dev enp0s3
[sudo] password for NetProg:
[NetProg@server4 ~]$ ip addr show dev enp0s3
2: enp0s3: <BROADCAST,MULTICAST,UP,LOWER_UP> mtu 1500 qdisc pfifo_fast state UP qlen
  1000
    link/ether 08:00:27:2c:61:d0 brd ff:ff:ff:ff:ff:ff
    inet 10.2.0.30/24 scope global enp0s3
       valid_lft forever preferred_lft forever
    inet6 fe80::a00:27ff:fe2c:61d0/64 scope link
       valid_lft forever preferred_lft forever
[NetProg@server4 ~]$ ip route
10.2.0.0/24 dev enp0s3 proto kernel scope link src 10.2.0.30
[NetProg@server4 ~]$
```

Routing tables on Linux systems are very similar to routing tables on routers. In fact, a Linux server could easily function as a router. In order to display routing table functionality in Linux, server1 in the topology in Figure 3-2 is used as a router to route traffic between server2 and server3. server2 is connected to network 10.1.0.0/24, and server3 is connected to network 10.2.0.0/24. All three servers are configured such that server1 routes between the two networks, and eventually server2 should be able to ping server3.

Figure 3-2 *Server1 Configured to Route Between server2 and server3, Each on a Different Subnet*

IP addressing needs to be configured first. server1 is configured with IP addresses ending with .10, server2 with an IP address ending in .20, and server3 with an IP address ending in .30, as shown in Example 3-44.

Example 3-44 *Configuring IP Addresses on the Interfaces Connecting The Three Servers*

```
! server1
[root@server1 ~]# ip addr add 10.1.0.10/24 dev enp0s8
[root@server1 ~]# ip addr add 10.2.0.10/24 dev enp0s9
[root@server1 ~]# ip addr show enp0s8 | grep "inet "
    inet 10.1.0.10/24 scope global enp0s8
[root@server1 ~]# ip addr show enp0s9 | grep "inet "
    inet 10.2.0.10/24 scope global enp0s9
[root@server1 ~]#

! server2
[root@server2 ~]# ip addr add 10.1.0.20/24 dev enp0s3
[root@server2 ~]# ip addr show enp0s3 | grep "inet "
    inet 10.1.0.20/24 scope global enp0s3
[root@server2 ~]#

! server3
[root@server3 ~]# ip addr add 10.2.0.30/24 dev enp0s3
[root@server3 ~]# ip addr show dev enp0s3 | grep "inet "
    inet 10.2.0.30/24 scope global enp0s3
[root@server3 ~]#
```

A ping to the directly connected server is successful on all three servers. However, when server2 attempts to ping server3, the ping fails, as shown in Example 3-45.

Example 3-45 *Pinging the Directly Connected Interfaces Is Successful but Pinging server3 From server2 Is Not*

```
! Pinging the directly connected interfaces

! server2 to server1
[root@server2 ~]# ping -c 1 10.1.0.10
PING 10.1.0.10 (10.1.0.10) 56(84) bytes of data.
64 bytes from 10.1.0.10: icmp_seq=1 ttl=64 time=0.796 ms

--- 10.1.0.10 ping statistics ---
1 packets transmitted, 1 received, 0% packet loss, time 0ms
rtt min/avg/max/mdev = 0.796/0.796/0.796/0.000 ms
[root@server2 ~]#

! server3 to server1
[root@server3 ~]# ping -c 1 10.2.0.10
PING 10.2.0.10 (10.2.0.10) 56(84) bytes of data.
64 bytes from 10.2.0.10: icmp_seq=1 ttl=64 time=1.13 ms

--- 10.2.0.10 ping statistics ---
1 packets transmitted, 1 received, 0% packet loss, time 0ms
rtt min/avg/max/mdev = 1.139/1.139/1.139/0.000 ms
[root@server3 ~]#

! Pinging server2 to server3 and vice versa is not successful

! server2 to subnet 10.2.0.0/24
[root@server2 ~]# ping 10.2.0.10
connect: Network is unreachable
[root@server2 ~]# ping 10.2.0.30
connect: Network is unreachable
[root@server2 ~]#

! server3 to subnet 10.1.0.0/24
[root@server3 ~]# ping -c 1 10.1.0.10
connect: Network is unreachable
[root@server3 ~]# ping -c 1 10.1.0.20
connect: Network is unreachable
[root@server3 ~]#
```

You are probably very familiar with the **ping** command. **ping** works on Linux exactly as it does on network devices: by sending one or more ICMP packets to the destination and either receiving an ICMP reply if the ping is successful (one reply per packet sent)

or receiving an ICMP unreachable packet or no response at all if the ping is not. The command in Example 3-45 uses the **-c 1** option to send a single ICMP packet, which is enough to test the reachability of the destination.

Example 3-46 shows how to use the command **ip route add 10.2.0.0/24 via 10.1.0.10** on server2 and the command **ip route add 10.1.0.0/24 via 10.2.0.10** on server3 to add routes to the routing tables of each server. The general syntax for adding a route to the routing table is **ip route add** {*destination*}{*/mask*} **via** {*nexthop*}. The routes instruct each server to use server1 as the next hop to reach the remote network. After the routes are added, server2 and server3 are able to ping server1's interface on the remote network, but they are still not able to ping each other.

Example 3-46 *Adding Routing Table Entries for Remote Subnets on server2 and server3. server2 and server3 Can Ping the Remote Subnets on server1, But Still Cannot Ping Each Other*

```
! server2
[root@server2 ~]# ip route add 10.2.0.0/24 via 10.1.0.10
[root@server2 ~]# ip route
10.1.0.0/24 dev enp0s3 proto kernel scope link src 10.1.0.20
10.2.0.0/24 via 10.1.0.10 dev enp0s3
[root@server2 ~]# ping -c 1 10.2.0.10
PING 10.2.0.10 (10.2.0.10) 56(84) bytes of data.
64 bytes from 10.2.0.10: icmp_seq=1 ttl=64 time=0.822 ms

--- 10.2.0.10 ping statistics ---
1 packets transmitted, 1 received, 0% packet loss, time 0ms
rtt min/avg/max/mdev = 0.822/0.822/0.822/0.000 ms
[root@server2 ~]# ping -c 1 10.2.0.30
PING 10.2.0.30 (10.2.0.30) 56(84) bytes of data.

--- 10.2.0.30 ping statistics ---
1 packets transmitted, 0 received, 100% packet loss, time 0ms
[root@server2 ~]#

! server3
[root@server3 ~]# ip route add 10.1.0.0/24 via 10.2.0.10
[root@server3 ~]# ip route
10.1.0.0/24 via 10.2.0.10 dev enp0s3
10.2.0.0/24 dev enp0s3 proto kernel scope link src 10.2.0.30
[root@server3 ~]# ping -c 1 10.1.0.10
PING 10.1.0.10 (10.1.0.10) 56(84) bytes of data.
64 bytes from 10.1.0.10: icmp_seq=1 ttl=64 time=0.865 ms
```

```
--- 10.1.0.10 ping statistics ---
1 packets transmitted, 1 received, 0% packet loss, time 0ms
rtt min/avg/max/mdev = 0.865/0.865/0.865/0.000 ms
[root@server3 ~]# ping -c 1 10.1.0.20
PING 10.1.0.20 (10.1.0.20) 56(84) bytes of data.

--- 10.1.0.20 ping statistics ---
1 packets transmitted, 0 received, 100% packet loss, time 0ms
[root@server3 ~]#
```

Forwarding between the interfaces on server1 is disabled by default for security reasons. Therefore, the remaining step is to enable forwarding in the kernel of server1 by toggling the default value of 0 in file /proc/sys/net/ipv4/ip_forward to 1 by using either the command **echo 1 > /proc/sys/net/ipv4/ip_forward** or the command **/sbin/sysctl -w net.ipv4.ip_forwad=1**. After either command is used, forwarding is enabled, and both servers can ping each other successfully, as shown in Example 3-47.

Example 3-47 *Enabling Routing on Server1 Resulting in Successful ping Between server2 and server3*

```
! Enabling routing on server1
[root@server1 ~]# echo 1 > /proc/sys/net/ipv4/ip_forward
[root@server1 ~]# cat /proc/sys/net/ipv4/ip_forward
1

! server2 to server3 ping is successful
[root@server2 ~]# ping -c 1 10.2.0.30
PING 10.2.0.30 (10.2.0.30) 56(84) bytes of data.
64 bytes from 10.2.0.30: icmp_seq=1 ttl=63 time=0.953 ms
--- 10.2.0.30 ping statistics ---
1 packets transmitted, 1 received, 0% packet loss, time 0ms
rtt min/avg/max/mdev = 0.953/0.953/0.953/0.000 ms
[root@server2 ~]#

! server3 to server2 ping is successful
[root@server3 ~]# ping -c 1 10.1.0.20
PING 10.1.0.20 (10.1.0.20) 56(84) bytes of data.
64 bytes from 10.1.0.20: icmp_seq=1 ttl=63 time=1.39 ms

--- 10.1.0.20 ping statistics ---
1 packets transmitted, 1 received, 0% packet loss, time 0ms
rtt min/avg/max/mdev = 1.394/1.394/1.394/0.000 ms
[root@server3 ~]#
```

Note that two commands to achieve the same result are mentioned here. The first method gets the job done by editing a file, and the second gets the same job done by using the command **sysctl**. Which one you should use depends on several factors, the first of which is personal preference. Another issue is whether you know which file in the /proc/sys/ directory contains the kernel setting (sometimes referred to as a *kernel tunable*) that you need to change. If you do not know the file, you can simply use the **sysctl** command to target the parameter directly, regardless of where it is located. You can list all kernel tunables by using the command **/sbni/sysctl -a**.

Note *You* in this case does not necessarily have to literally mean you. It may refer to the automation script or tool that you are using to get the job done. Using a particular tool to amend a file may be more efficient than issuing a command; the reverse may be the case for another tool. Always choose the method that is most efficient and effective for your specific environment.

To remove a routing table entry, you use the syntax **ip route delete** {*destination*}{*/mask*} **via** {*nexthop*}. You can also have routes point to exit interfaces rather than next hops by using the syntax **ip route add** {*destination*}{*/mask*} **dev** {*intf*}. You can add a default route by using the syntax **ip route add default via** {*next_hop*} **dev** {*intf*}.

One final note on the **ip** utility is that any configuration performed using the commands discussed in this section is not persistent. Any changes to the configuration disappear after a system reboot. Persistent configuration is discussed in the following sections.

The NetworkManager Service

NetworkManager is the default network management service on several Linux distros, including Red Hat and Fedora. Because NetworkManager is a service, you can check its status, and you can start, stop, enable, or disable it as you can any other service on Linux by using the **systemctl** command. For example, the command **systemctl status network-manager** displays the current status of the service. To poll NetworkManager for information or push configuration to it, you can use one of several user interfaces:

- **Graphical user interfaces (GUIs):** There are two main graphical user interface tools that interact with NetworkManager. The first is the Network Control Center, which is accessible via the Settings menu. The Settings window has an icon labeled Network that opens the network control center, which provides basic network configuration. The other GUI tool is the Connection Editor and is used to configure more advanced settings. You can start the Connection Editor from the terminal by entering the command **nm-connection-editor**.
- **NetworkManager command-line interface (nmcli):** The NetworkManager CLI is a command-line utility that you can use to control NetworkManager. You can use this interface to NetworkManager via the **nmcli** command in the Bash shell.

- **NetworkManager text user interface (nmtui):** Similar to the interface used to configure a computer's BIOS settings or old DOS-based programs, the **nmtui** provides an interface to NetworkManager that displays graphics in text mode. You start the text user interface by issuing the **nmtui** command in the shell.
- **API:** NetworkManager provides an API that can be used by applications for programmatic access to NetworkManager.

Because the majority of automation is typically performed through CLI tools (and API calls) and not the GUI, this section cover NetworkManager configuration via the **nmcli** interface.

NetworkManager deals with objects called connections. A *connection* is a representation of a link to the outside world and may represent, for example, a wired connection, a wireless connection, or a VPN connection. To display the current status of all network connections on a system, use the command **nmcli con show**, as shown in Example 3-48.

Example 3-48 *Listing All Connections on a System*

```
[root@server1 ~]# nmcli con show
NAME                UUID                                  TYPE            DEVICE
Wired connection 1  d8323782-5cf2-3afc-abcd-e603605ac4f8  802-3-ethernet  --
Wired connection 2  669fefb4-bc57-3d19-b83b-2b2125e0036b  802-3-ethernet  --
[root@server1 ~]#
```

The output in Example 3-48 indicates that there are two connections, named Wired connection 1 and Wired connection 2. These connections are not bound (applied) to any interfaces, as indicated by the -- in the last column. Both connections are of type Ethernet. A connection is uniquely identified by its universally unique identifier (UUID). Although not shown in the command output, a connection can either be active or inactive. To activate an inactive connection, you use the command **nmcli con up** {*connection_name*}. To deactivate a connection, you replace the keyword **up** with the keyword **down**.

Each connection is known as a *connection profile* and contains several attributes or properties that you can set. These properties are known as *settings*. Connection profile settings are created and then applied to a device or device type. Settings are represented in a dot notation. For example, a connection's IPv4 addresses are represented by the setting **ipv4.addresses**. To drill down on the details for a specific connection and list its settings and their values, you can use the command **nmcli con show** {*connection_name*}. Example 3-49 lists the connection profile settings for Wired connection 1. The output is truncated due to the length of the list. A full list of settings and their meanings can be found in the man pages for the **nmcli** command.

Note Use of the terms "master" and "slave" is ONLY in association with the official terminology used in industry specifications and standards, and in no way diminishes Pearson's commitment to promoting diversity, equity, and inclusion, and challenging, countering and/or combating bias and stereotyping in the global population of the learners we serve.

Example 3-49 *Connection Attributes for Wired Connection 1*

```
[root@server1 ~]# nmcli con show "Wired connection 1"
connection.id:                          Wired connection 1
connection.uuid:                        d8323782-5cf2-3afc-abcd-e603605ac4f8
connection.stable-id:                   --
connection.interface-name:              --
connection.type:                        802-3-ethernet
connection.autoconnect:                 yes
connection.autoconnect-priority:        -999
connection.autoconnect-retries:         -1 (default)
connection.timestamp:                   1525512827
connection.read-only:                   no
connection.permissions:                 --
connection.zone:                        --
connection.master:                      --
connection.slave-type:                  --
connection.autoconnect-slaves:          -1 (default)
connection.secondaries:                 --
connection.gateway-ping-timeout:        0
connection.metered:                     unknown
connection.lldp:                        -1 (default)
802-3-ethernet.port:                    --
802-3-ethernet.speed:                   0
802-3-ethernet.duplex:                  --
802-3-ethernet.auto-negotiate:          no
802-3-ethernet.mac-address:             08:00:27:83:40:75
802-3-ethernet.cloned-mac-address:      --
802-3-ethernet.generate-mac-address-mask:--
802-3-ethernet.mac-address-blacklist:   --
802-3-ethernet.mtu:                     auto
802-3-ethernet.s390-subchannels:        --
802-3-ethernet.s390-nettype:            --
802-3-ethernet.s390-options:            --
802-3-ethernet.wake-on-lan:             1 (default)
802-3-ethernet.wake-on-lan-password:    --
ipv4.method:                            auto
ipv4.dns:                               --
ipv4.dns-search:                        --
ipv4.dns-options:                       (default)
ipv4.dns-priority:                      0
ipv4.addresses:                         --
ipv4.gateway:                           --
ipv4.routes:                            --

--------- OUTPUT TRUNCATED FOR BREVITY ---------
```

To list the devices (aka interfaces) on the system and the status of each one, you use the command **nmcli dev status** for all devices or the command **nmcli dev show** {*device_name*} for a specific device, as shown in Example 3-50.

Example 3-50 *Device Status Using the nmcli dev status and nmcli dev show Commands*

```
[root@server1 ~]# nmcli dev status
DEVICE  TYPE      STATE         CONNECTION
enp0s8  ethernet  disconnected  --
enp0s9  ethernet  disconnected  --
lo      loopback  unmanaged     --
[root@server1 ~]# nmcli dev show enp0s8
GENERAL.DEVICE:                         enp0s8
GENERAL.TYPE:                           ethernet
GENERAL.HWADDR:                         08:00:27:83:40:75
GENERAL.MTU:                            1500
GENERAL.STATE:                          30 (disconnected)
GENERAL.CONNECTION:                     --
GENERAL.CON-PATH:                       --
WIRED-PROPERTIES.CARRIER:               on
[root@server1 ~]#
```

As you can see from the outputs in Examples 3-49 and 3-50, connections and devices are mutually exclusive. A connection profile may or may not be applied to a device after it is created.

In Example 3-51, both of the wired connections are deleted, and one new connection named NetDev_1 is created. NetDev_1 is of type ethernet and is applied to device enp0s8. Connections are deleted using the command **nmcli con del** {*connection_name*}. You create new connections and configure their settings by using the command **nmcli con add** {*connection_name*} {*setting*} {*value*}. In Example 3-51, the type, ifname, ip4, and gw4 settings are set to Ethernet, enp0s8, 10.1.0.10/24, and 10.1.0.254, respectively. Note that in this command, *setting* can either be entered in the full dot format or in abbreviated format. For example, the IP address can be set using either **ip4** or **ipv4.address**.

Example 3-51 *Deleting and Creating Connections*

```
[root@server1 ~]# nmcli con show
NAME                UUID                                  TYPE            DEVICE
Wired connection 1  d8323782-5cf2-3afc-abcd-e603605ac4f8  802-3-ethernet  --
Wired connection 2  669fefb4-bc57-3d19-b83b-2b2125e0036b  802-3-ethernet  --
[root@server1 ~]# nmcli con del "Wired connection 1"
Connection 'Wired connection 1' (d8323782-5cf2-3afc-abcd-e603605ac4f8) successfully
  deleted.
[root@server1 ~]# nmcli con del "Wired connection 2"
```

```
Connection 'Wired connection 2' (669fefb4-bc57-3d19-b83b-2b2125e0036b) successfully
  deleted.
[root@server1 ~]# nmcli con show
NAME  UUID  TYPE  DEVICE
[root@server1 ~]# nmcli con add con-name NetDev_1 type ethernet ifname enp0s8 ip4
  10.1.0.10/24 gw4 10.1.0.254
Connection 'NetDev_1' (a8ac9116-697a-4a0a-85a2-63428d6e75a3) successfully added.
[root@server1 ~]# nmcli con show
NAME      UUID                                  TYPE            DEVICE
NetDev_1  a8ac9116-697a-4a0a-85a2-63428d6e75a3  802-3-ethernet  enp0s8
[root@server1 ~]# nmcli con show --active
NAME      UUID                                  TYPE            DEVICE
NetDev_1  a8ac9116-697a-4a0a-85a2-63428d6e75a3  802-3-ethernet  enp0s8
[root@server1 ~]# nmcli dev status
DEVICE  TYPE      STATE         CONNECTION
enp0s8  ethernet  connected     NetDev_1
enp0s9  ethernet  disconnected  --
lo      loopback  unmanaged     --
[root@server1 ~]# nmcli dev show enp0s8
GENERAL.DEVICE:                         enp0s8
GENERAL.TYPE:                           ethernet
GENERAL.HWADDR:                         08:00:27:83:40:75
GENERAL.MTU:                            1500
GENERAL.STATE:                          100 (connected)
GENERAL.CONNECTION:                     NetDev_1
GENERAL.CON-PATH:                       /org/freedesktop/NetworkManager/ActiveCon-
  nection/359
WIRED-PROPERTIES.CARRIER:               on
IP4.ADDRESS[1]:                         10.1.0.10/24
IP4.GATEWAY:                            10.1.0.254
IP6.ADDRESS[1]:                         fe80::8c1f:4c4a:51a5:6423/64
IP6.GATEWAY:                            --
[root@server1 ~]# ping 10.1.0.20 -c 3
PING 10.1.0.20 (10.1.0.20) 56(84) bytes of data.
64 bytes from 10.1.0.20: icmp_seq=1 ttl=64 time=0.604 ms
64 bytes from 10.1.0.20: icmp_seq=2 ttl=64 time=0.602 ms
64 bytes from 10.1.0.20: icmp_seq=3 ttl=64 time=0.732 ms

--- 10.1.0.20 ping statistics ---
3 packets transmitted, 3 received, 0% packet loss, time 2011ms
rtt min/avg/max/mdev = 0.602/0.646/0.732/0.060 ms
[root@server1 ~]#
```

Notice that once a connection has been created and the device enp0s8 has been bound to it (all in the same command), the connection and device both come up, and that results in the device successfully pinging server2 on the other end of the link.

After a connection is created, you can modify its settings by using the command **nmcli con mod** {*connection_name*} {*setting*} {*value*}. When modifying a setting, the full dot format is required in the command. If the shorthand format is used, the new value in the command may be added to the existing value of the setting. For example, if the shorthand format is used to modify the IP address, the new IP address in the command is added to the device as a secondary IP address. On the other hand, if the full dot format is used, the IP address in the command replaces the IP address configured on the device. Example 3-52 shows how to modify the IP address of device enp0s8 to 10.1.0.100/24.

Example 3-52 *Deleting and Creating Connections*

```
[root@server1 ~]# nmcli con show NetDev_1 | grep ipv4.addr
ipv4.addresses:                         10.1.0.10/24
[root@server1 ~]# nmcli dev show enp0s8 | grep IP4.ADD
IP4.ADDRESS[1]:                         10.1.0.10/24
[root@server1 ~]# nmcli con mod NetDev_1 ip4 10.1.0.100/24

! The new IP address is added as a secondary address due to the shorthand format
[root@server1 ~]# nmcli con show NetDev_1 | grep ipv4.addr
ipv4.addresses:                         10.1.0.10/24, 10.1.0.100/24

! The new IP address is not reflected to the device enp0s8
[root@server1 ~]# nmcli dev show enp0s8 | grep IP4.ADD
IP4.ADDRESS[1]:                         10.1.0.10/24

[root@server1 ~]# nmcli con up NetDev_1
Connection successfully activated (D-Bus active path: /org/freedesktop/
  NetworkManager/ActiveConnection/366)

! After resetting the con, the new IP address now is reflected to the device
[root@server1 ~]# nmcli dev show enp0s8 | grep IP4.ADD
IP4.ADDRESS[1]:                         10.1.0.10/24
IP4.ADDRESS[2]:                         10.1.0.100/24

! Using the full dot format will replace the old IP address with the new one
[root@server1 ~]# nmcli con mod NetDev_1 ipv4.address 10.1.0.100/24
[root@server1 ~]# nmcli con up NetDev_1
Connection successfully activated (D-Bus active path: /org/freedesktop/
  NetworkManager/ActiveConnection/367)
[root@server1 ~]# nmcli con show NetDev_1 | grep ipv4.addr
ipv4.addresses:                         10.1.0.100/24
[root@server1 ~]# nmcli dev show enp0s8 | grep IP4.ADD
IP4.ADDRESS[1]:                         10.1.0.100/24
[root@server1 ~]#
```

Note that each time a change is made to a connection using **nmcli**, the connection needs to be reactivated in order for the changes to be reflected to the device.

Adding routes using **nmcli** is different than adding routes using the **ip** utility in that when using **nmcli**, routes are added per interface and not globally. You add routes by using the syntax **nmcli con mod** {*intf*} **+ipv4.routes** {*destination*} **ipv4.gateway** {*next_hop*}. Therefore, to accomplish the same task that was done earlier by using the **ip** utility (to add a route on server2 to direct traffic destined for network 10.2.0.0/24 using the next hop 10.1.0.10 on server1), you use the following command: **nmcli con mod enp0s3 +ipv4.routes 10.2.0.0/24 ipv4.gateway 10.1.0.10.**

Unlike with the **ip** utility, changes made through **nmcli** are, by default, persistent and will survive a system reload.

It is important to understand the difference between the **ip** utility and NetworkManager. The **ip** utility is a program. When you use the **ip** command, you run this program, which makes a system call to the kernel, either to retrieve information or configure a component of the Linux networking system.

On the other hand, NetworkManager is a system daemon. It is software that runs (lurks) in the background, by default, and oversees the operation of the Linux network system. NetworkManager may be used to configure components of the network or to retrieve information about the network by using a variety of methods discussed earlier in this section—one of them being **nmcli**.

The nuances of how the **ip** utility interacts with NetworkManager are not discussed in detail here. All you need to know for now is that changes to the network that are made via the **ip** utility are detected and preserved by NetworkManager. There is no conflict between them. As mentioned at the very beginning of this section, different software on Linux can achieve the same result via different communication channels with the kernel. However, any software that needs access to the network will eventually have to go through the kernel.

Network Scripts and Configuration Files

The third method for configuring network devices and interfaces is to modify network scripts and configuration files directly. Different files in Linux control different components of the networking ecosystem, and editing these files was the only way to configure networking on Linux before NetworkManager was developed. Configuration files and scripts can still be used instead of, or in addition to, NetworkManager.

On Linux distros in the Red Hat family, configuration files for network interfaces are located in the /etc/sysconfig/network-scripts directory, and each interface configuration file is named ifcfg-**<*intf_name*>**. The first script that is executed on system bootup is /etc/init.d/network. When the system boots up, this script reads through all interface configuration files whose names start with ifcfg. Example 3-53 shows the ifcfg file for the enp0s8 interface.

Example 3-53 *Interface Configuration File for Interface enp0s8*

```
[root@server1 network-scripts]# cat ifcfg-enp0s8
TYPE=Ethernet
PROXY_METHOD=none
BROWSER_ONLY=no
BOOTPROTO=dhcp
DEFROUTE=yes
IPV4_FAILURE_FATAL=no
IPV6INIT=yes
IPV6_AUTOCONF=yes
IPV6_DEFROUTE=yes
IPV6_FAILURE_FATAL=no
IPV6_ADDR_GEN_MODE=stable-privacy
NAME=NetDev_1
UUID=a8ac9116-697a-4a0a-85a2-63428d6e75a3
DEVICE=enp0s8
ONBOOT=yes
[root@server1 network-scripts]#
```

The filename just needs to be prefixed with ifcfg. The network script simply scans the directory and reads any file whose name has this prefix. Therefore, you can safely assume that the configuration file is for the interface *or* connection. However, while the filename has to start with ifcfg, there is general consensus that the value in the DEVICE field (interface) should follow the ifcfg prefix.

The TYPE field in the file indicates the connection type, which is **Ethernet** in this case. The BOOTPROTO field is set to **dhcp**, which means the connection gets an IP address via DHCP. If a static IP address is required on the interface, then dhcp is replaced with none. The interface associated with this configuration is also shown in the DEVICE field (enp0s8 in this case), and the ONBOOT field indicates that this connection is to be brought up at system bootup. When a static IP address is required on the interface, the fields IPADDR, PREFIX, and GATEWAY and their respective values are added to the file.

When **ONBOOT=yes** is set, the /etc/init.d/network script checks whether this interface is managed by NetworkManager. If it is and the connection has already been activated, no further action is taken. If the connection has not been activated, the script requests NetworkManager to activate the connection. In case the connection is not managed by NetworkManager, the network script activates the connection by running another script, /usr/sbin/ifup. The ifup script checks the field TYPE in the ifcfg file, and based on that, it calls *another* type-specific script. For example, if the type of the connection is Ethernet, the ifup-eth script is called. Linux requires type-specific scripts because different connection types require different configuration parameters. For example, the concept of an SSID (wireless network name) does not exist for an Ethernet connection. Similarly, to bring down an interface for an unmanaged interface, the ifdown script is called. The vast majority of interface types are managed by NetworkManager by default, unless the line **NM_CONTROLLED=no** has been added to the ifcfg file.

While the recommended method for configuring interfaces is to use the **nmcli** utility, as discussed in the previous section, you can also configure interfaces by editing the corresponding ifcfg file.

Static routes configured on a system have configuration files named **route-<*intf_name*>** in the same directory as the interface configuration files. As you have probably guessed, the name has to be prefixed with **route**. However, the **-<*intf_name*>** is just a naming convention, and the file may have any name as long as the prefix **route** is there. The routing entries in the file may have one of two formats:

- The **ip** command arguments format:

  {*destination*}/{*mask*} via {*next_hop*} [dev *interface*]

  With this format, specifying the interface using [**dev** *interface*] is optional.

- The network/netmask directives format:

  ADDRESS{*N*}:{*destination*}

  NETMASK{*N*}:{*netmask*}

  GATEWAY{*N*}:{*next_hop*}

  where *N* is the routing table entry starting with 0 and incrementing by 1 for each entry, without skipping any values. In other words, if the routing table has four entries, the entries are numbered from 0 to 3.

Going back to the network of three servers in Figure 3-2, where server1 is required to route between server2 on subnet 10.1.0.0/24 and server3 on subnet 10.2.0.0/24: the static routes previously configured in order to route between the servers are deleted, after which the ping from server2 to server3 fails, as shown in Example 3-54.

Example 3-54 *Ping Fails Due To Lack of Static Routes on server2 and server3*

```
! No routes in routing table of server2 to remote subnet 10.2.0.0/24
[root@server2 ~]# ip route
10.1.0.0/24 dev enp0s3 proto kernel scope link src 10.1.0.20 metric 100
[root@server2 ~]#

! Ping to the directly connected interface on server1 is successful
[root@server2 ~]# ping -c 1 10.1.0.10
PING 10.1.0.10 (10.1.0.10) 56(84) bytes of data.
64 bytes from 10.1.0.10: icmp_seq=1 ttl=64 time=0.828 ms

--- 10.1.0.10 ping statistics ---
1 packets transmitted, 1 received, 0% packet loss, time 0ms
rtt min/avg/max/mdev = 0.828/0.828/0.828/0.000 ms
[root@server2 ~]#
```

```
! Ping to server3 on subnet 10.2.0.0/24 is not successful
[root@server2 ~]# ping -c 1 10.2.0.30
connect: Network is unreachable
[root@server2 ~]#

! No routes in routing table of server3 to remote subnet 10.1.0.0/24
[root@server3 ~]# ip route
10.2.0.0/24 dev enp0s3 proto kernel scope link src 10.2.0.30 metric 100
[root@server3 ~]#

! Ping to the directly connected interface on server1 is successful
[root@server3 ~]# ping -c 1 10.2.0.10
PING 10.2.0.10 (10.2.0.10) 56(84) bytes of data.
64 bytes from 10.2.0.10: icmp_seq=1 ttl=64 time=0.780 ms

--- 10.2.0.10 ping statistics ---
1 packets transmitted, 1 received, 0% packet loss, time 0ms
rtt min/avg/max/mdev = 0.780/0.780/0.780/0.000 ms
[root@server3 ~]#

! Ping to server2 on subnet 10.1.0.0/24 is not successful
[root@server3 ~]# ping -c 1 10.1.0.20
connect: Network is unreachable
[root@server3 ~]#
```

The file route-enp0s3 is created under the directory /etc/sysconfig/network-scripts/ on both servers. A routing entry is added to the routing configuration file on server2 by using the **ip** command arguments format, and a routing entry is added to the file on server3 by using the network/netmask directives format, as shown in Example 3-55.

Example 3-55 *Routing Configuration Files Added on Both server2 and server3*

```
! server2

! No routing configuration files in the directory
[root@server2 ~]# cd /etc/sysconfig/network-scripts/
[root@server2 network-scripts]# ls -l | grep "route"
[root@server2 network-scripts]#

! Create the file route-enp0s3 and populate it with a route to the remote subnet
  10.2.0.0/24 using the IP Command Arguments format
[root@server2 network-scripts]# touch route-enp0s3
[root@server2 network-scripts]# echo "10.2.0.0/24 via 10.1.0.10" >> route-enp0s3
[root@server2 network-scripts]# ls -l | grep " route"
-rw-r--r--. 1 root root    26 Aug 17 15:52 route-enp0s3
```

```
[root@server2 network-scripts]# cat route-enp0s3
10.2.0.0/24 via 10.1.0.10
[root@server2 network-scripts]#

! Restart the network service and check the routing table
[root@server2 network-scripts]# systemctl restart network
[root@server2 network-scripts]# ip route
10.1.0.0/24 dev enp0s3 proto kernel scope link src 10.1.0.20 metric 100
10.2.0.0/24 via 10.1.0.10 dev enp0s3 proto static metric 100
[root@server2 network-scripts]#

! server3

! No routing configuration files in the directory
[root@server3 ~]# cd /etc/sysconfig/network-scripts/
[root@server3 network-scripts]# ls -l | grep " route"

! Create the file route-enp0s3 and populate it with a route to the remote subnet
  10.1.0.0/24 using the Network/Netmask Directives format
[root@server3 network-scripts]# touch route-enp0s3
[root@server3 network-scripts]# echo "ADDRESS0=10.1.0.0" >> route-enp0s3
[root@server3 network-scripts]# echo "NETMASK0=255.255.255.0" >> route-enp0s3
[root@server3 network-scripts]# echo "GATEWAY0=10.2.0.10" >> route-enp0s3
[root@server3 network-scripts]# ls -l | grep " route"
-rw-r--r--. 1 root root    60 Aug 17 16:04 route-enp0s3
[root@server3 network-scripts]# cat route-enp0s3
ADDRESS0=10.1.0.0
NETMASK0=255.255.255.0
GATEWAY0=10.2.0.10
[root@server3 network-scripts]#

! Restart the network service and check the routing table
[root@server3 network-scripts]# systemctl restart network
[root@server3 network-scripts]# ip route
10.1.0.0/24 via 10.2.0.10 dev enp0s3 proto static metric 100
10.2.0.0/24 dev enp0s3 proto kernel scope link src 10.2.0.30 metric 100
[root@server3 network-scripts]#
```

The ping test is now successful, and server2 can reach server3, as shown in Example 3-56.

Example 3-56 *Ping from server2 to server3 and Vice Versa Is Successful Now*

```
[root@server2 network-scripts]# ping -c 1 10.2.0.30
PING 10.2.0.30 (10.2.0.30) 56(84) bytes of data.
64 bytes from 10.2.0.30: icmp_seq=1 ttl=63 time=2.11 ms

--- 10.2.0.30 ping statistics ---
1 packets transmitted, 1 received, 0% packet loss, time 0ms
rtt min/avg/max/mdev = 2.119/2.119/2.119/0.000 ms
[root@server2 network-scripts]#

[root@server3 network-scripts]# ping -c 1 10.1.0.20
PING 10.1.0.20 (10.1.0.20) 56(84) bytes of data.
64 bytes from 10.1.0.20: icmp_seq=1 ttl=63 time=1.58 ms

--- 10.1.0.20 ping statistics ---
1 packets transmitted, 1 received, 0% packet loss, time 0ms
rtt min/avg/max/mdev = 1.585/1.585/1.585/0.000 ms
[root@server3 network-scripts]#
```

The network script is run as a service and, like any other service, can be controlled by using the command **systemctl** {**start**|**stop**|**restart**|**status**} **network**. To enable/disable the network service at startup, you use the command **chkconfig network** {**on**|**off**}. Keep in mind that after a configuration file is changed, the network service has to be restarted for the changes to take effect. It goes without saying that any configuration done via amending the network configuration files is persistent and will remain intact after a system reload.

Network Services: DNS

Domain Name System (*DNS*) is a hierarchical naming system used on the Internet and some private networks to assign domain names to resources on the network. Domain names tend to be easier to remember than IP addresses. Using domain names provides the additional capability to resolve a domain name to multiple IP addresses for purposes such as high availability or routing user traffic based on the geographically closest server.

DNS uses the concept of a *resolver*, commonly referred to as a *DNS server*, which is a server or a database that contains mappings between domain names and the information related to each of those domain names, such as the IP addresses. These mappings are called *records*. DNS is hierarchical and distributed. The majority of DNS servers maintain records for only some domain names and then initiate queries to other DNS servers for the rest of the domain names, for which it does not maintain records.

Performing a DNS query means sending a request to a DNS server to resolve the domain name and return the data associated with that domain name. To resolve a domain name on Linux to its corresponding information, including its IP address, you use the **dig** command, which stands for *domain information groper*. Example 3-57 shows **dig** being used to resolve google.com to its public IP address. The public IP address received from the DNS response is highlighted in the example.

Example 3-57 *Using the dig Command to Resolve google.com*

```
[root@server1 ~]# dig google.com

; <<>> DiG 9.9.4-RedHat-9.9.4-51.el7_4.2 <<>> google.com
;; global options: +cmd
;; Got answer:
;; ->>HEADER<<- opcode: QUERY, status: NOERROR, id: 38879
;; flags: qr rd ra; QUERY: 1, ANSWER: 1, AUTHORITY: 0, ADDITIONAL: 1

;; OPT PSEUDOSECTION:
; EDNS: version: 0, flags:; udp: 4096
;; QUESTION SECTION:
;google.com.                     IN      A

;; ANSWER SECTION:
google.com.             264      IN      A         216.58.207.14

;; Query time: 31 msec
;; SERVER: 192.168.8.1#53(192.168.8.1)
;; WHEN: Fri Aug 17 17:16:06 +03 2018
;; MSG SIZE  rcvd: 55
[root@server1 ~]#
```

In Example 3-57, the DNS server used for the name resolution is 192.168.8.1. The IP address of this DNS server is configured in the /etc/resolv.conf file, shown in Example 3-58. To configure other DNS servers, you list each server's IP address on a new line in this file.

Example 3-58 *List of DNS Servers in the /etc/resolv.conf File*

```
[root@server1 ~]# cat /etc/resolv.conf
# Generated by NetworkManager
nameserver 192.168.8.1
[root@server1 ~]#
```

Manual DNS entries are configured in the /etc/hosts file. If an entry for a domain name is found in that file, the DNS servers are not consulted for resolution. There is one caveat, though: The **dig** command still requests the name resolution from the DNS server configured in /etc/resolv.conf. However, the **ping** command and also the web browsers on the system use the hosts file, and, therefore, use the manual entry there. Try to add a manual entry for google.com in the hosts file, pointing to an IP address that is not reachable and then try to use **dig**, use **ping**, and browse to google.com and notice how each of these behave differently.

Summary

This chapter takes Linux administration a step further and covers storage, security, and networking. It discusses the following topics:

- Partitioning, formatting, and managing physical storage
- Creating physical volumes, volume groups, and logical volumes using LVM
- User and group security management
- File security management, including permission bits and ACLs
- Linux system security, including the Linux firewall
- Managing Linux networking by using the **ip** utility
- Managing Linux networking by using the NetworkManager CLI (**nmcli**)
- Managing Linux networking via network scripts and configuration files
- Network services such as DNS

Chapter 4, "Linux Scripting," builds on this chapter and covers Linux scripting, which is one big step towards automation.

Chapter 4

Linux Scripting

Recall from Chapter 1, "The Network Programmability and Automation Ecosystem," and Chapter 2, "Linux Fundamentals," that automation has been described as a process of breaking down a big task into smaller, *repeatable* tasks and then attempting to automate each of those repeatable tasks by doing the heavy lifting only once and having a tool repeat the task for you. This chapter gives you your first real taste of automation using programmability: writing scripts in the Bash programming language, more commonly referred to as the Bash scripting language. Scripts (whether in Bash or any other language) are written once and can, theoretically, be executed an infinite number of times.

A *shell* is a program that parses and interprets commands and then passes the (interpreted) commands to the kernel for execution. Commands are typically entered into the shell individually, through what is commonly known as *interactive mode*: You type a command, and you get the result instantly. Piping and redirection add to the sophistication of what can be achieved interactively with the shell. Scripting takes this a step further, by allowing you to type a sequence of commands in a file and then pass the file to the shell for execution, without having to manually enter the commands through the CLI one by one. With high-level programming languages like Python, Java, or Go, the resulting sequence of commands is commonly called a *program*. In case of Bash, such a sequence is commonly referred to as a *script* because Bash is not a full-fledged programming language. Bash is typically used to glue together different components into a script, where each of the components may be a program on its own (for example, a Linux utility).

Scripts can run system commands such as **pwd**, **ls**, and **cat**. Scripts typically use *variables* that hold values that can change throughout the execution of the script. They may also contain constructs for *conditional* execution of code (running a line or block of code only if a particular condition is true) or constructs for *looping* (running the same line or block of code more than once). Scripts can read *input* from the keyboard or a file, and they can *output* to the screen or to a file. These examples just scratch the surface of what a Bash script may contain or what it can do.

This chapter starts by covering three new utilities: **grep**, **awk**, and **sed**. These advanced but simple utilities are heavily used in scripting. Then, after introducing the general structure of a Bash script, the chapter covers the following topics:

- Comments
- Input and output
- Variables and arrays
- Expansion, operations, and comparisons
- System commands
- Conditional statements
- Loops
- Functions

Finally, this chapter touches on Expect, a programming language that is frequently used to extend the capabilities of Bash with respect to interacting with a user running a script. Expect comes in handy, for example, when logging in to a device requires a username and password to be entered by the user.

The *GNU Bash Manual* is published by the Free Software Foundation (FSF) at https://www.gnu.org/software/bash/manual/. As you read this chapter, consult the manual any time you need more detailed coverage of the subjects presented here.

Regular Expressions and the grep Utility

Regular expressions are briefly introduced in Chapter 3, "Linux Storage, Security, and Networks." If you are a network engineer or a software developer, chances are that you have already had some exposure to regular expressions. If not, do not worry, as they are thoroughly covered in this section.

A *regular expression*, or *regex* for short, is basically a sequence of characters, commonly referred to as a *pattern*. The pattern is used to search through text to find matches. Each character in a pattern may be a literal or a metacharacter. A *literal* represents itself; for example, the regex pattern **zz** would match any occurrence of the literal zz, such as **zz**, o**zz**, or bli**zz**ard. A *metacharacter* has a special meaning; for example, the plus symbol (**+**) means one or more occurrences of the character that precedes it. For example, the regex **12+** would match the number 1 followed by one or more occurrences of the number 2, such as **12**, **122**, or **1222**. The concept is very simple, yet extremely powerful and provides limitless use cases. This section covers how the **grep** utility can be used to search through a file for lines that match some criteria expressed by using regular expressions.

Note A regex pattern may use square brackets ([ ]), curly braces ({}) or parenthesis (()) as part of the pattern itself, as you will see shortly in this chapter. For this reason, and to avoid confusion, the standard code conventions used in the rest of the book will not be used throughout this chapter. Instead, keywords that need to be typed literally as shown will appear in **bold** and placeholders for arguments for which you should supply actual values will be entered in *italic*. Any other symbol or character will be entered literally as shown.

The **grep** utility, originally created by Ken Thompson for UNIX, searches a file for text that matches one or more patterns and then prints out the lines containing matches to stdout. Although the general syntax of the command is **grep** *options patterns file_name*, the command is commonly coupled with redirection (piping) to search through the output of another command in order to display only the lines that have pattern matches.

The **grep** utility accepts several flavors of regular expressions, based on the options used in the command:

- **grep -G** *pattern*: Interprets the pattern in the command as a GNU/standard regular expression
- **grep -E** *pattern*: Interprets the pattern in the command as an extended regular expression
- **grep -F** *pattern*: Interprets the pattern in the command as a fixed regular expression
- **grep -P** *pattern*: Interprets the pattern in the command as a Perl regular expression

grep -G supports basic regular expressions, which can use any of the following metacharacters:

- **^**: Represents the beginning of a line
- **$**: Represents the end of a line
- **.**: Represents any single character except a newline character
- *****: Represents zero or more occurrences of the preceding character
- **[***literals***]**: Represents a single character that matches any one of the enclosed literals. For example, **[abc]** is equivalent to "match either **a** or **b** or c"
- **[***first_literal-last_literal***]**: Represents a single character that matches any character in the range between the brackets (inclusive). For example **[a-f] is equivalent to "match any letter from a to f" and [1-5] is equivalent to "match any number from 1 to 5"**
- **\<** or **\b**: Represents the beginning of a word
- **\>** or **\b**: Represents the end of a word

- ****: Represents the escape character

In addition to all the options supported with the **-G** option, the **grep -E** command also supports the following metacharacters:

- **?**: Represents zero or one occurrences of the preceding character
- **+**: Represents one or more occurrences of the preceding character
- **{*N*}** or **{*N*,*M*}**: Represents strings with *N* repetitions or between *N* and *M* repetitions
- **|**: Represents the OR operator
- **( )**: Represents a capture group

Each of these metacharacters is explained in detail in this section. Because the **grep** command with the **-E** option supports both basic and extended regular expressions, the examples throughout this section use the **-E** option.

Note **grep -E** may be replaced by the command **egrep**, and **grep -F** may be replaced by the command **fgrep**. However, the **egrep** and **fgrep** commands are deprecated and are mentioned here in case you run into a legacy system or code that uses either of them.

The **grep** utility searches text files for text that matches a particular regex pattern and then prints out (or, more formally, outputs to stdout) the whole line where a match is found. In fact, **grep** stands for *global regular expression print*. In Example 4-1, the file named data-file is used to showcase the use of **grep** and regular expressions.

Example 4-1 *Data File for Testing Regular Expressions with grep*

```
[NetProg@server1 grep-scripts]$ cat data-file
KhaledAbuelenain 11 Anton 22 Cairo 33 jeff
Jeff 111 Doyle 222 Colorado AbuelenainKhaled 333
Vinit 1111 Jain 2222 Palo Alto 3333 JeffDoyle 4444
11111 Khaled 22222 Ca:ro Dusseldorf 33333 Anton
Anton Karneliuk Ca9ro Jeff
```

Example 4-2 shows how to search for all lines containing the pattern **Jeff**. No metacharacters are used in this example.

Example 4-2 *Printing the Lines Containing Matches to the Pattern Jeff*

```
[NetProg@server1 grep-scripts]$ grep 'Jeff' data-file
Jeff 111 Doyle 222 Colorado AbuelenainKhaled 333
Vinit 1111 Jain 2222 Palo Alto 3333 JeffDoyle 4444
Anton Karneliuk Ca9ro Jeff
```

Although **grep** prints the whole line where a match is found, on a monitor the *matching pattern* is typically colored differently, usually in a shade of red. However, this is configurable and implementation specific. In the examples in this section, the matches are highlighted in gray shading. As you can see in Example 4-2, running the **grep** command results in three matches, and three lines containing the pattern **Jeff** have been printed out. Notice two things here. First, it doesn't matter where in the line the pattern **Jeff** appears; regardless of whether it is at the beginning of the line, in the middle, or at the end, it will match. The second thing to notice is that any occurrence of the pattern will result in a match, whether it is a standalone word or a part of another word, such as JeffDoyle.

Now say that you need to find the same word but only when it is at the beginning of a line. Example 4-3 illustrates the use of the caret symbol (^) to match a pattern only if the line begins with it. Similarly, the dollar symbol (**$**) is used to find the lines that end with the pattern **Jeff**.

Example 4-3 *Using ^ and $ to Find Lines That Start and End with a Pattern*

```
[NetProg@server1 grep-scripts]$ grep -E ^Jeff data-file
Jeff 111 Doyle 222 Colorado AbuelenainKhaled 333

[NetProg@server1 grep-scripts]$ grep -E Jeff$ data-file
Anton Karneliuk Ca9ro Jeff
```

Notice that the first line in the file ends with the name jeff. However, the name begins with a lowercase j, while the pattern used for matching has an uppercase J. **grep** is case sensitive. Example 4-4 provides two solutions that allow you to work around this behavior. The first solution is to use the option **-i**, which makes **grep** case insensitive. The other solution is to use a character class.

Example 4-4 *Using Either The* **-i** *Option Or a Character Class to Match on Uppercase and Lowercase Letters*

```
! Using the -i option to make grep case insensitive
[NetProg@server1 grep-scripts]$ grep -E -i Jeff data-file
KhaledAbuelenain 11 Anton 22 Cairo 33 jeff
Jeff 111 Doyle 222 Colorado AbuelenainKhaled 333
Vinit 1111 Jain 2222 Palo Alto 3333 JeffDoyle 4444
Anton Karneliuk Ca9ro Jeff

! Using a character class
[NetProg@server1 grep-scripts]$ grep -E [Jj]eff data-file
KhaledAbuelenain 11 Anton 22 Cairo 33 jeff
Jeff 111 Doyle 222 Colorado AbuelenainKhaled 333
Vinit 1111 Jain 2222 Palo Alto 3333 JeffDoyle 4444
Anton Karneliuk Ca9ro Jeff
```

A character class allows you to specify alternatives to match on for a *particular character position*. In Example 4-4, any word that begins with either **j** or **J** matches. Different options are entered side by side between brackets. For example, at a specific position in a string, in order to match one of the following letters: a, b, c, or d, you can use the character class **[abcd]** in that position in the pattern. In addition, a character class can provide ranges. To match any small character in the alphabet, you can use the character class **[a-z]**, and in order to match any alphanumeric character (character or number), you can use the character class **[a-zA-Z0-9]**.

Now what if you need to match the beginning of a word or the end of a word? The data file contains several occurrences of the name Khaled. Example 4-5 shows how to use the character sequences **\<** and **\>** to match the pattern **Khaled** only if it starts or ends a word, respectively. Both can be used together to match a pattern if the pattern is a word on its own, as also shown in the example.

Example 4-5 *Matching the Beginning and Ending of Words by Using \< and \>*

```
! Matching the pattern Khaled
[NetProg@server1 grep-scripts]$ grep -E Khaled data-file
KhaledAbuelenain 11 Anton 22 Cairo 33 jeff
Jeff 111 Doyle 222 Colorado AbuelenainKhaled 333
11111 Khaled 22222 Ca:ro Dusseldorf 33333 Anton

! Matching the pattern Khaled if it is the beginning of a word only
[NetProg@server1 grep-scripts]$ grep -E '\<Khaled' data-file
KhaledAbuelenain 11 Anton 22 Cairo 33 jeff
11111 Khaled 22222 Ca:ro Dusseldorf 33333 Anton

! Matching the pattern Khaled at the end of a word only
[NetProg@server1 grep-scripts]$ grep -E 'Khaled\>' data-file
Jeff 111 Doyle 222 Colorado AbuelenainKhaled 333
11111 Khaled 22222 Ca:ro Dusseldorf 33333 Anton

! Matching the pattern Khaled on its own
[NetProg@server1 grep-scripts]$ grep -E '\<Khaled\>' data-file
11111 Khaled 22222 Ca:ro Dusseldorf 33333 Anton
```

Notice that the regex pattern is enclosed in single quotation marks when **\<** and **\>** notations are used. This is because the backslash followed by a character has a special meaning, and for this special meaning to be applied, single quotation marks must be used. This is called *expansion*. Several expansion types exist. (You'll learn more about expansion later in this chapter.)

The dot (.) is used in a regex pattern to represent a single character. In Example 4-6, the dot is used in the pattern **Ca.ro**. As you can see, it matches **Cairo**, **Ca9ro**, and **Ca:ro**. It basically matches the letters **Ca**, followed by any single character, followed by the letters **ro**.

Example 4-6 *Using a Dot to Match Any Single Character*

```
[NetProg@server1 grep-scripts]$ grep -E Ca.ro data-file
KhaledAbuelenain 11 Anton 22 Cairo 33 jeff
11111 Khaled 22222 Ca:ro Dusseldorf 33333 Anton
Anton Karneliuk Ca9ro Jeff
```

Repetition metacharacters are characters that are used in a regex pattern to indicate a certain number of repetitions on the literal that immediately precedes the repetition character. For example, when a regex is composed of the letter A followed by a repetition character, that regex will match on zero or more repetitions of the letter A, depending on which repetition character is used. Four repetition notations are mentioned earlier in this section and are repeated here for convenience:

- *: Represents zero or more occurrences of the preceding character
- ?: Represents zero or one occurrences of the preceding character
- +: Represents one or more occurrences of the preceding character
- {*N*} or {*N*,*M*}: Represents words with *N* repetitions or between *N* and *M* repetitions of the preceding character.

Example 4-7 uses some of these notations to illustrate the concept of repetition in patterns.

Example 4-7 *Using Repetition Characters*

```
! The full data file
[NetProg@server1 grep-scripts]$ cat data-file
KhaledAbuelenain 11 Anton 22 Cairo 33 jeff
Jeff 111 Doyle 222 Colorado AbuelenainKhaled 333
Vinit 1111 Jain 2222 Palo Alto 3333 JeffDoyle 4444
11111 Khaled 22222 Ca:ro Dusseldorf 33333 Anton
Anton Karneliuk Ca9ro Jeff

! Using the asterisk symbol (*) to match zero or more occurrences of '2'
[NetProg@server1 grep-scripts]$ grep -E 2* data-file
KhaledAbuelenain 11 Anton 22 Cairo 33 jeff
Jeff 111 Doyle 222 Colorado AbuelenainKhaled 333
Vinit 1111 Jain 2222 Palo Alto 3333 JeffDoyle 4444
11111 Khaled 22222 Ca:ro Dusseldorf 33333 Anton
Anton Karneliuk Ca9ro Jeff

! Using the asterisk symbol (*) to match a '2' followed by zero or more occurrences
  of '2'
[NetProg@server1 grep-scripts]$ grep -E 22* data-file
KhaledAbuelenain 11 Anton 22 Cairo 33 jeff
Jeff 111 Doyle 222 Colorado AbuelenainKhaled 333
```

```
Vinit 1111 Jain 2222 Palo Alto 3333 JeffDoyle 4444
11111 Khaled 22222 Ca:ro Dusseldorf 33333 Anton

! Using the plus symbol (+) to match one or more occurrences of '2'
[NetProg@server1 grep-scripts]$ grep -E 2+ data-file
KhaledAbuelenain 11 Anton 22 Cairo 33 jeff
Jeff 111 Doyle 222 Colorado AbuelenainKhaled 333
Vinit 1111 Jain 2222 Palo Alto 3333 JeffDoyle 4444
11111 Khaled 22222 Ca:ro Dusseldorf 33333 Anton
```

In the second section of Example 4-7, **grep** uses the regex **2***, which translates to zero or more occurrences of 2. This will basically match all lines because *no occurrences* of 2 will match *everything*. This is why the last line in the output is a match. In the second section, a tighter condition using the regex **22*** states that a word will match if it contains a 2 followed by zero or more occurrences of 2. This means that a single 2 or any number of consecutive 2s will result in a match. This is the same criterion specified in the last section in the example, but the last section uses a plus symbol (**+**) to match on any word that contains one or more occurrences of 2. As you can see, in this case, the regex pattern **22*** is equivalent to the regex pattern **2+**.

It is interesting to note that the dot (.) is frequently used with the asterisk (as in .*) to indicate any number of any characters—that is, anything (or everything). This character sequence matches any word that has zero or more occurrences of any character. Of course, this is not very useful unless it is used as part of a larger regex in which, perhaps, it is used to indicate *anything* followed by, preceded by, or enclosed by a more meaningful pattern. In Example 4-8, this notation is used in the regex **Doyle.*3** to match the second line in the data file. The pattern simply matches on the string **Doyle** and the number **3**, on the same line, with anything in between.

Example 4-8 *Using the .* Notation to Match Anything/Everything*

```
[NetProg@server1 grep-scripts]$ grep -E Doyle.*3 data-file
Jeff 111 Doyle 222 Colorado AbuelenainKhaled 333
```

Understanding how the other repetition characters work may be slightly more challenging because **grep** outputs the whole line in which a match is found. Example 4-9 displays a new data file that contains a different number of consecutive 1s on each line.

Example 4-9 *Data File for Testing the Repetition Characters ? and + and the Notations {N} and {N,M}*

```
[NetProg@server1 grep-scripts]$ cat data-file-2
123
1123
11123
111123
1111123
```

```
23132
231132
2311132
23111132
231111132
```

First, the question mark (?) is used in Example 4-10 in the regex **11?23**. This pattern will match any sequence of characters that starts with the literal 1, followed by *zero or one* occurrence of 1, followed by the literal 23. Although this actually only matches 123 and 1123, the first five lines of the file all appear to match. Notice the highlighting in Example 4-10: The highlighted part of the line is the part that actually matches the regex (and is typically differently colored on a monitor). However, if the results are redirected to an output file and the matches appear all in the same font color, the results may be misleading. This would not be the case if the literal preceding the matching sequence were anything except the literal 1, as you will see in the next example.

Example 4-10 *Using the ? Repetition Character*

```
[NetProg@server1 grep-scripts]$ grep -E 11?23 data-file-2
123
1123
11123
111123
1111123
```

Example 4-11 presents another instance of the usage of the question mark that may seem more intuitive. The regex pattern **2311?32** is used to match any occurrence of the literal 231, followed by *zero or one* occurrence of 1, followed by the literal 32. As you can see, only **23132** and **231132** match this pattern.

Example 4-11 *Using the ? Repetition Character – A More Intuitive Example*

```
[NetProg@server1 grep-scripts]$ grep -E 2311?32 data-file-2
23132
231132
```

Moving on to the plus symbol (+), in Example 4-12 **grep** is used to find matches to the pattern **2311+32** in the same data file used in Example 4-11. The regex translates to any sequence of characters that starts with the literal 231, followed by *one or more* occurrences of the literal 1, followed by the literal 32. This results in the matches shown in the example. Notice that **23132** does *not* match the pattern.

Example 4-12 *Using the + Repetition Character*

```
[NetProg@server1 grep-scripts]$ grep -E 2311+32 data-file-2
231132
2311132
23111132
231111132
```

As mentioned earlier, the repetition notation {*N*} is used to find any *N* number of occurrences of the character immediately preceding it. The notation {*N*,*M*} provides a range for the number of occurrences. Leaving out the upper range is equivalent to infinity. The question mark (?) is equivalent to {0,1}, the plus symbol (+) is equivalent to {1,}, and the asterisk symbol (*) is equivalent to {0,}. For example, the pattern **1[0-9]{1,2}** will match any number that starts with a 1 followed by either a single digit between 0 and 9, or two digits, each of them between 0 and 9. In other words, the matching criteria **[0-9]** can occur once, or twice. Therefore, this pattern will match any number between 10 and 19 in addition to any number between 100 and 199.

To print out the lines that do *not* contain a particular regex, you use the option **-v** with **grep**. In Example 4-13, all lines that do *not* contain the pattern **Jeff** are printed out. Notice that jeff with a small j does not match this criterion because **grep** is case sensitive. So the line containing the string jeff will *not* be excluded.

Example 4-13 *Using grep -v to Select Lines That Do Not Contain a Certain Pattern*

```
[NetProg@server1 grep-scripts]$ grep -E -v Jeff data-file
KhaledAbuelenain 11 Anton 22 Cairo 33 jeff
11111 Khaled 22222 Ca:ro Dusseldorf 33333 Anton
```

Use of regular expressions is not limited to the **grep** command. As you will see later in this chapter, regular expressions are a global concept that is used extensively in Linux scripting.

The following are a few more options you can use with the **grep** command to extend its functionality:

- -c: Returns the number of lines in which matches were found
- -n: Returns the lines with matches and prepends each line with its line number from the original input file
- -A *N*: Returns the line(s) with matches along with the *N* trailing lines from the original input file
- -B *N*: Returns the line(s) with matches along with the *N* leading lines from the original input file
- -C *N*: Returns the line(s) with matches along with *N* leading and *N* trailing lines from the original input file

In all the previous examples, a filename was provided to the **grep** command for a file containing the text to search through. When a filename is not provided to **grep**, the command behaves in one of two ways. Either **grep** searches text provided through stdin (from the keyboard) or it searches through the files in the current working directory. The second case applies if either the **-r** or **-R** options are used, indicating recursive searches. Make sure to visit the man page for **grep** for a wealth of other options and use cases.

The AWK Programming Language

AWK is a full-fledged programming language. AWK was created by (and named after) Alfred V. Aho, Peter J. Weinberger, and Brian W. Kernighan, who also wrote a book titled *The AWK Programming Language* in 1988. AWK is based on a simple paradigm: Find a pattern in the input and then perform an action.

Like any other programming language, AWK can manipulate variables and has, among other features, flow control constructs. However, the coverage of AWK in this section focuses on single-line operations that use the **awk** command and can be integrated into Bash scripts. The power of **awk** is in its capability to process the contents of spreadsheet-like text files formatted into rows and columns. Much like **grep**, **awk** makes it possible to search text for matching patterns. It also has the capability to take actions such as print out data in a specific column position in the matching text. Moreover, it can execute other operations that are commonly done by spreadsheet processing programs, such as arithmetic operations on values extracted from the text. These are just a few basic examples of the capabilities of **awk**.

Note On some systems, when you try to access the man pages of the **awk** command, you are redirected to the man pages of **gawk**, which is the GNU version of **awk**. Similarly, if you use the **ls -l** command on the /usr/bin directory, you might see that the /usr/bin/awk file is actually a soft link to /usr/bin/gawk. Do not let this confuse you. It simply means that the version of **awk** on the system (in this case CentOS 8) is actually the GNU version (or implementation) named **gawk**, which is an enhanced version of **awk**. A newer version of awk called **nawk** (for *new awk*) is also available, but it is not available on CentOS 8 by default.

The basic syntax of the command-line version of awk is **awk** '*/search-pattern/{action}*' *filename*. As in **grep**, an **awk** search pattern utilizes regular expressions. The command can be used to only match on a pattern or to only take an action, or both. In Example 4-14, the output of **ls -l** for the directory /dev is saved in the file awk-data-ls to be used for testing the functionality of **awk**.

Example 4-14 *Data File to Test awk*

```
[NetProg@server1 awk-scripts]$ ls -l /dev > awk-data-ls
[NetProg@server1 awk-scripts]$ cat awk-data-ls
total 0
crw-------. 1 root    root     10, 235 Sep 21 18:29 autofs
drwxr-xr-x. 2 root    root         320 Sep 21 18:29 block
drwxr-xr-x. 2 root    root         120 Sep 21 18:29 bsg
crw-------. 1 root    root     10, 234 Sep 21 18:29 btrfs-control
drwxr-xr-x. 3 root    root          60 Sep 21 18:29 bus
lrwxrwxrwx. 1 root    root           3 Sep 21 18:29 cdrom -> sr0
drwxr-xr-x. 2 root    root          80 Sep 21 18:29 centos
drwxr-xr-x. 2 root    root        3060 Sep 21 18:29 char
crw-------. 1 root    root      5,   1 Sep 21 18:30 console
lrwxrwxrwx. 1 root    root          11 Sep 21 18:29 core -> /proc/kcore
drwxr-xr-x. 6 root    root         140 Sep 21 18:29 cpu
crw-------. 1 root    root     10,  61 Sep 21 18:29 cpu_dma_latency
crw-------. 1 root    root     10,  62 Sep 21 18:29 crash

--------- OUTPUT TRUNCATED FOR BREVITY ---------
```

In Example 4-15, **awk** is used to search for and print the line containing the file sdb2 using the regex pattern **sdb2**. Then **awk** is used to search for and print out a list of all files that are symlinks, identified by the letter **l** at the start of the line using the regex pattern **^l**.

Example 4-15 *Printing the Line Containing the Pattern sdb2 and Then a List of Symlinks in the File awk-data-ls*

```
[NetProg@server1 awk-scripts]$ awk '/sdb2/' awk-data-ls
brw-rw----. 1 root    disk      8,  18 Sep 21 18:29 sdb2

[NetProg@server1 awk-scripts]$ awk '/^l/' awk-data-ls
lrwxrwxrwx. 1 root    root           3 Sep 21 18:29 cdrom -> sr0
lrwxrwxrwx. 1 root    root          11 Sep 21 18:29 core -> /proc/kcore
lrwxrwxrwx. 1 root    root          13 Sep 21 18:29 fd -> /proc/self/fd
lrwxrwxrwx. 1 root    root          25 Sep 21 18:29 initctl -> /run/systemd/initctl/
                                                              fifo
lrwxrwxrwx. 1 root    root           4 Sep 21 18:29 rtc -> rtc0
lrwxrwxrwx. 1 root    root          15 Sep 21 18:29 stderr -> /proc/self/fd/2
lrwxrwxrwx. 1 root    root          15 Sep 21 18:29 stdin -> /proc/self/fd/0
lrwxrwxrwx. 1 root    root          15 Sep 21 18:29 stdout -> /proc/self/fd/1
[NetProg@server1 awk-scripts]$
```

Recall from the previous section that regular expressions use the caret symbol (^) to match the beginning of a line, so that the regex **^l** will match any line that starts with the letter l. Example 4-16 uses the **print** action to print out only the filenames, which is the data in the ninth column in Example 4-15.

Example 4-16 *Printing Only the Ninth Column After Matching on the Pattern ^l*

```
[NetProg@server1 awk-scripts]$ awk '/^l/ {print $9}' awk-data-ls
cdrom
core
fd
initctl
rtc
stderr
stdin
stdout
[NetProg@server1 awk-scripts]$
```

The column number is specified using the syntax $*column_number* inside the action parentheses right after the action (**print** in this case), as highlighted in Example 4-16. The default *field separator* used by **awk** is the whitespace, so one column is distinguished from another by a whitespace. Therefore, in order to print out the filenames as well as the target of the symlink, you need to print out three columns: the filename, the right arrow and the target. These are columns 9, 10 and 11. The command **awk** '/^l/ {**print $9,$10,$11**}' **awk-data-ls** is used in Example 4-17 to print out the three required columns.

Example 4-17 *Printing Only the Ninth, Tenth, and Eleventh Columns*

```
[NetProg@server1 awk-scripts]$ awk '/^l/ {print $9,$10,$11}' awk-data-ls
cdrom -> sr0
core -> /proc/kcore
fd -> /proc/self/fd
initctl -> /run/systemd/initctl/fifo
rtc -> rtc0
stderr -> /proc/self/fd/2
stdin -> /proc/self/fd/0
stdout -> /proc/self/fd/1
[NetProg@server1 awk-scripts]$
```

What if the fields in a file are separated by something other than a whitespace? Consider, for example, the popular CSV format, in which the fields are separated by commas rather than whitespaces. In this case, the field separator can be changed by using the **-F** option, and the command is **awk -F** , '*/pattern/ {action}' filename*. Notice the comma (,) after the **-F** option in the command.

To process the text in a file based on column position, you need to make sure that the column numbers in a file are uniform. For example, in the file used in the previous examples, some devices in the /dev directory have a major number and a minor number, and some others have only a minor number. Therefore, for example, if you print out column 5, you will get a different piece of information for each row. To print out the number of columns (fields) per line in the file, you use the command **awk '{print NF}'** *filename*. In Example 4-18, the number of columns is printed out for the data file. The output of **awk** is piped to the command **sort -u**, which removes redundant output. As you can see, the number of columns varies between 2, 9, 10, and 11.

Example 4-18 *Using print NF to Print Out the Number of Fields*

```
[NetProg@server1 awk-scripts]$ awk '{print NF}' awk-data-ls | sort -u
10
11
2
9
[NetProg@server1 awk-scripts]$
```

Finally, say that there is a requirement to print out the minor number (fifth column) of all symlinks and multiply that by a number, such as 512. Example 4-19 illustrates how you can use **awk** to perform arithmetic operations on the data in the file. The minor number is printed first, followed by the string "----" and, finally, the result of the multiplication.

Example 4-19 *Performing Arithmetic Operations Using awk*

```
[NetProg@server1 awk-scripts]$ awk '/^l/ {print $5,"----",$5*512}' awk-data-ls
3 ---- 1536
11 ---- 5632
13 ---- 6656
25 ---- 12800
4 ---- 2048
15 ---- 7680
15 ---- 7680
15 ---- 7680
[NetProg@server1 awk-scripts]$
```

Keep in mind that, like any other command in Linux, **awk** can be used with **grep** and **sed** (covered in the next section) through piping. Typically, **grep** is preferred for the search operation, and **sed** can be used for text manipulation. The output of any of the commands can be piped to any other command, as long as the output of one command is valid input for the other.

The sed Utility

sed, which stands for *stream editor*, is a utility that reads text from a file line by line, from stdin, or from a pipe; processes this text in some way; and outputs the edited version. The output of **sed** may be directed to stdout, piped to a new file, or written back to the source file. **sed** is an important utility that you need to be familiar with because it allows you to integrate into your scripts powerful text editing capabilities that are not feasible using visual text editors.

sed allows you to search a file for a match on a particular pattern, expressed using a regex, or to specify a particular line or range of lines. Much like **grep** and **awk**, **sed** processes the whole line containing a match. After the lines to be processed are identified, an action is taken. The following are some common actions with **sed**:

- Printing (**p**)
- Substitution (**s**)
- Deleting (**d**)
- Writing to files (**w**)
- Appending (**a**)
- Changing (**c**)
- Inserting (**i**)

The general syntax for **sed** is **sed** *options 'line_identification action' filename.* Example 4-20 provides a simple example of the print action.

Example 4-20 *Data File to Test sed and Using the* **-n** *Option to Illustrate the Workflow of sed*

```
! File show-bgp used to test sed
[NetProg@server1 sed-scripts]$ cat show-bgp
*>i5.41.131.0/24    196.201.61.245                100     0 16637 39386 25019 39891 i
*>i5.41.132.0/24    196.201.61.245                100     0 16637 39386 25019 39891 i
*>i5.41.133.0/24    196.201.61.245                100     0 16637 39386 25019 39891 i
*>i5.41.134.0/24    196.201.61.245                100     0 16637 39386 25019 39891 i
*>i5.41.135.0/24    196.201.61.245                100     0 16637 39386 25019 39891 i

! Attempting to print the first line of the file (without -n)
[NetProg@server1 sed-scripts]$ sed '1p' show-bgp
*>i5.41.131.0/24    196.201.61.245                100     0 16637 39386 25019 39891 i
*>i5.41.131.0/24    196.201.61.245                100     0 16637 39386 25019 39891 i
*>i5.41.132.0/24    196.201.61.245                100     0 16637 39386 25019 39891 i
*>i5.41.133.0/24    196.201.61.245                100     0 16637 39386 25019 39891 i
*>i5.41.134.0/24    196.201.61.245                100     0 16637 39386 25019 39891 i
*>i5.41.135.0/24    196.201.61.245                100     0 16637 39386 25019 39891 i

! Attempting to print the first line of the file (with -n)
[NetProg@server1 sed-scripts]$ sed -n '1p' show-bgp
*>i5.41.131.0/24    196.201.61.245                100     0 16637 39386 25019 39891 i
```

File show-bgp contains five text lines that are routes extracted from the Internet routing table. The command **sed '1p' show-bgp** is used to attempt to print the first line of the file. As you can see, the line number, **1**, is followed by the action, **p**, in the command, inside single quotation marks. However, the output is not what you would expect. **sed** prints out the *whole file* and duplicates the first line. If you add the **-n** option to the command, it prints only the first line, as required.

This section dives right into using the **-n** option because understanding the behavior in Example 4-20 is your path to understanding the workflow of **sed**: When **sed** reads a line from a file, that line is saved in memory in a *pattern buffer*. When the processing of this one line is complete, the pattern buffer is emptied and then populated with the next line to be processed.

By default, the **sed** command prints out the contents of the pattern buffer. Because the whole file passes through the pattern buffer line by line, **sed** prints out each of these lines and eventually prints the whole file. In addition, the **1p** in the command in the example instructs **sed** to print out the first line, which means the first line is printed out twice. The **-n** option causes **sed** *not* to print out the content of the pattern buffer, which means only the first line is printed out.

To elaborate on this, in Example 4-21 the command **sed ' ' show-bgp** prints the whole file. The whitespace between the double quotation marks means no selection of lines and no action is to be taken. This, in turn, means that only the pattern buffer—equivalent to the whole file—is printed out. **sed -n ' ' show-bgp** prints out nothing because each line is placed in the pattern buffer, no action is taken on it, the line is discarded, and then the next line is placed in the pattern buffer, and so on.

Example 4-21 *The -n Option Instructing sed to Not Print the Contents of the Pattern Buffer*

```
! The default behavior of sed is to print out the whole file
[NetProg@server1 sed-scripts]$ sed ' ' show-bgp
*>i5.41.131.0/24    196.201.61.245                100    0 16637 39386 25019 39891 i
*>i5.41.132.0/24    196.201.61.245                100    0 16637 39386 25019 39891 i
*>i5.41.133.0/24    196.201.61.245                100    0 16637 39386 25019 39891 i
*>i5.41.134.0/24    196.201.61.245                100    0 16637 39386 25019 39891 i
*>i5.41.135.0/24    196.201.61.245                100    0 16637 39386 25019 39891 i

! Using the -n option to not print the contents of the pattern buffer
[NetProg@server1 sed-scripts]$ sed -n ' ' show-bgp
[NetProg@server1 sed-scripts]$
```

Now that the meaning of the **-n** option is clear, Example 4-22 displays how to print the whole file, a single line, and a range of lines. It also illustrates the use of the **$** symbol to indicate the last line of the file and, finally, the use of the *begin*,**+***N* notation to specify a number of lines *N* to process after a specific line number indicated by *begin*.

Example 4-22 *Selecting Specific Lines to Print*

```
! Print out the whole file
[NetProg@server1 sed-scripts]$ sed -n 'p' show-bgp
*>i5.41.131.0/24     196.201.61.245              100     0 16637 39386 25019 39891 i
*>i5.41.132.0/24     196.201.61.245              100     0 16637 39386 25019 39891 i
*>i5.41.133.0/24     196.201.61.245              100     0 16637 39386 25019 39891 i
*>i5.41.134.0/24     196.201.61.245              100     0 16637 39386 25019 39891 i
*>i5.41.135.0/24     196.201.61.245              100     0 16637 39386 25019 39891 i
[NetProg@server1 sed-scripts]$

! Print out the third line only
[NetProg@server1 sed-scripts]$ sed -n '3p' show-bgp
*>i5.41.133.0/24     196.201.61.245              100     0 16637 39386 25019 39891 i

! Print out the last line of the file using the $ sign
[NetProg@server1 sed-scripts]$ sed -n '$p' show-bgp
*>i5.41.135.0/24     196.201.61.245              100     0 16637 39386 25019 39891 i

! Print out lines 3 and 4
[NetProg@server1 sed-scripts]$ sed -n '3,4p' show-bgp
*>i5.41.133.0/24     196.201.61.245              100     0 16637 39386 25019 39891 i
*>i5.41.134.0/24     196.201.61.245              100     0 16637 39386 25019 39891 i

! Print out line 3 till the last line
[NetProg@server1 sed-scripts]$ sed -n '3,$p' show-bgp
*>i5.41.133.0/24     196.201.61.245              100     0 16637 39386 25019 39891 i
*>i5.41.134.0/24     196.201.61.245              100     0 16637 39386 25019 39891 i
*>i5.41.135.0/24     196.201.61.245              100     0 16637 39386 25019 39891 i

! Print out line 2 and another 2 line afterwards
[NetProg@server1 sed-scripts]$ sed -n '2,+2p' show-bgp
*>i5.41.132.0/24     196.201.61.245              100     0 16637 39386 25019 39891 i
*>i5.41.133.0/24     196.201.61.245              100     0 16637 39386 25019 39891 i
*>i5.41.134.0/24     196.201.61.245              100     0 16637 39386 25019 39891 i
```

To delete a line instead of printing it out, you use the **d** action. In Example 4-23 lines 2 and 3 are deleted, and the rest of the file is printed out. Notice that in this case the **-n** option is not used because the purpose of the example is to show the whole file and omit the deleted lines. The **-n** option is also used in the example, and the output is empty because the lines have been deleted.

Example 4-23 *Using the d Action to Delete Lines from a File*

```
! Omitting the -n option
[NetProg@server1 sed-scripts]$ sed '2,3d' show-bgp
*>i5.41.131.0/24     196.201.61.245                100     0 16637 39386 25019 39891 i
*>i5.41.134.0/24     196.201.61.245                100     0 16637 39386 25019 39891 i
*>i5.41.135.0/24     196.201.61.245                100     0 16637 39386 25019 39891 i

! Adding the -n option
[NetProg@server1 sed-scripts]$ sed -n '2,3d' show-bgp
[NetProg@server1 sed-scripts]$
```

It is important to note that the **sed** command does not write anything to the disk using any of the commands introduced so far. In order to store the results of the processing done by the **sed** command, you need to either pipe the output to a file or use the **w** action as in **sed -n** '*processing* **w** *results_file*' *file_to_be_processed*. Example 4-24 illustrates both methods of writing the results to disk.

Example 4-24 *Writing the Results of sed to Disk*

```
! Printing out lines 2 and 3 using the p action with piping
[NetProg@server1 sed-scripts]$ sed -n '2,3p' show-bgp > results-using-pipe
[NetProg@server1 sed-scripts]$ cat results-using-pipe
*>i5.41.132.0/24     196.201.61.245                100     0 16637 39386 25019 39891 i
*>i5.41.133.0/24     196.201.61.245                100     0 16637 39386 25019 39891 i

! Printing out lines 2 and 3 using the w action
[NetProg@server1 sed-scripts]$ sed -n '2,3 w results-using-w' show-bgp
[NetProg@server1 sed-scripts]$ cat results-using-w
*>i5.41.132.0/24     196.201.61.245                100     0 16637 39386 25019 39891 i
*>i5.41.133.0/24     196.201.61.245                100     0 16637 39386 25019 39891 i
```

To overwrite the source file instead of creating a new file containing the results, you simply specify the source file's name in either of the commands in Example 4-24, instead of using a new filename. For example, using piping, instead of using the command **sed -n '2,3p' show-bgp > results-using-pipe** as in Example 4-24, you use the command **sed -n '2,3p' show-bgp > show-bgp** to write the results of the processing back to the show-bgp file, which is the source file. A word of caution though: Make sure you don't overwrite the file with the wrong data and always make backups of important files before attempting to write any data to them.

Instead of specifying line numbers, the **sed** command can identify specific lines in a file by searching for a match to a pattern expressed as a regex. The syntax of the command in that case is **sed** '*/pattern/ action*' *filename*. In Example 4-25, **sed** is used to print out all text lines that have either **1** or **2** as the first octet and **.23** as the second octet, from a file containing a list of miscellaneous BGP routes extracted from the Internet routing table.

Example 4-25 *Identifying the Lines to Be Processed by Matching on a Regex Pattern*

```
[NetProg@server1 sed-scripts]$ sed -n '/[12]\.23\./ p' bgp-routes-misc
 *   1.23.220.0/24  138.187.128.20   500000  300  0 (65000) 6453 4755 45528 i
 *   1.23.224.0/24  138.187.128.20   500000  300  0 (65000) 6453 4755 45528 i
 *   1.23.225.0/24  138.187.128.20   550000  300  0 (65000) 9498 45528 i
 *   1.23.226.0/24  138.187.128.20   500000  300  0 (65000) 6453 4755 45528 i
 *   1.23.227.0/24  138.187.128.20   500000  300  0 (65000) 6453 9498 45528 i
 *   2.23.144.0/20  138.187.128.38   601000  300  0 (65000) 3320 1299 ?
 *   2.23.160.0/22  138.187.128.79   500000  300  0 (65000) 6453 20940 20940 16625 i
 *   2.23.164.0/23  138.187.128.79   500000  300  0 (65000) 6453 20940 20940 16625 i
```

The regex pattern used should be familiar to you by now. The **[12]** character class matches a string with either **1** or **2**. The characters **\.** are used to escape the dot and match on a literal dot. This is followed by the number **23** and then another **\.** that matches another dot. Therefore, the regex **[12]\.23\.** will match on any IP address starting with 1.23 or 2.23, which is exactly what is listed in the output in Example 4-25. Note that **sed** can match on a simple literal such as **3356** to print out all routes containing 3356 in their AS paths, as shown in Example 4-26.

Example 4-26 *Identifying the Lines to be Processed by Matching on the Literal 3356*

```
[NetProg@server1 sed-scripts]$ sed -n '/3356/ p' bgp-routes-misc
 *   4.55.0.0/16    138.187.128.38    500000   300     0 (65000) 3356 i
 *   4.128.0.0/9    138.187.128.4     500000   300     0 (65000) 3356 i
 *   5.24.64.0/19   138.187.128.4     550000   300     0 (65000) 3356 34984 16135 i
```

To perform several operations using the same **sed** command, you use the **-e** option. In Example 4-27, the routes originating in each of the two ASs 3356 and 16625 are identified using two regular expressions, and the results of the match operations are written to different text files.

Example 4-27 *Multiple Operations Using the -e Option*

```
[NetProg@server1 sed-scripts]$ sed -n -e '/3356 i/ w 3356.txt' -e '/16625 i/ w
  16625.txt' bgp-routes-misc

[NetProg@server1 sed-scripts]$ cat 3356.txt
 *   4.55.0.0/16    138.187.128.38   500000  300  0 (65000) 3356 i
 *   4.128.0.0/9    138.187.128.4    500000  300  0 (65000) 3356 i

[NetProg@server1 sed-scripts]$ cat 16625.txt
 *   2.16.12.0/23   138.187.128.50      250  300  0 (65000) 20940 16625 i
 *   2.23.160.0/22  138.187.128.79   500000  300  0 (65000) 6453 20940 20940 16625 i
 *   2.23.164.0/23  138.187.128.79   500000  300  0 (65000) 6453 20940 20940 16625 i
```

The next action is substitution, which is performed by using the **s** action. Substitution is similar to the find and replace function in text editors. The syntax for substitution is **s/***regex***/***replacement***/***flags*, and this goes into the *action* part of the generic **sed** syntax: **sed** *options 'line_identification action' filename*. In Example 4-28, substitution is used to replace the number 4 with the letter R in the line corresponding to route 5.41.133.0.

Example 4-28 *Using Substitution to Replace the Number 4 with the Letter R on the Line Matching the Route 5.41.133.0*

```
! Original file before the substitution
[NetProg@server1 sed-scripts]$ cat show-bgp
*>i5.41.131.0/24     196.201.61.245                  100     0 16637 39386 25019 39891 i
*>i5.41.132.0/24     196.201.61.245                  100     0 16637 39386 25019 39891 i
*>i5.41.133.0/24     196.201.61.245                  100     0 16637 39386 25019 39891 i
*>i5.41.134.0/24     196.201.61.245                  100     0 16637 39386 25019 39891 i
*>i5.41.135.0/24     196.201.61.245                  100     0 16637 39386 25019 39891 i

! Substitution without the g flag
[NetProg@server1 sed-scripts]$ sed '/5.41.133.0/ s/4/R/' show-bgp
*>i5.41.131.0/24     196.201.61.245                  100     0 16637 39386 25019 39891 i
*>i5.41.132.0/24     196.201.61.245                  100     0 16637 39386 25019 39891 i
*>i5.R1.133.0/24     196.201.61.245                  100     0 16637 39386 25019 39891 i
*>i5.41.134.0/24     196.201.61.245                  100     0 16637 39386 25019 39891 i
*>i5.41.135.0/24     196.201.61.245                  100     0 16637 39386 25019 39891 i

! Substitution with the g flag
[NetProg@server1 sed-scripts]$ sed '/5.41.133.0/ s/4/R/g' show-bgp
*>i5.41.131.0/24     196.201.61.245                  100     0 16637 39386 25019 39891 i
*>i5.41.132.0/24     196.201.61.245                  100     0 16637 39386 25019 39891 i
*>i5.R1.133.0/2R     196.201.61.2R5                  100     0 16637 39386 25019 39891 i
*>i5.41.134.0/24     196.201.61.245                  100     0 16637 39386 25019 39891 i
*>i5.41.135.0/24     196.201.61.245                  100     0 16637 39386 25019 39891 i
```

Notice that the substitution command is used with and without the **g** (global) flag (highlighted in Example 4-28). Without the **g** flag, only the first occurrence of the matching pattern is replaced. With the **g** flag, all occurrences in the line are replaced. You can see in the example that with the **g** flag, each 4 on the line is replaced with an R.

Substitution is one of the most commonly used actions with **sed**. Example 4-28 shows how to search for a value and change it in a BGP table. While this example helps explain how substitution works with **sed**, it is not a very useful thing to do. Alternatively, a very common (and popular) use case for **sed** involves parsing through a device configuration file and replacing certain fields (such as IP addresses or VLANs) with new values of your own to be used to configure another device. Example 4-29 shows a file containing interface configuration retrieved from one device. **sed** is then used to amend the interface description and dot1q encapsulation and save the new configuration in a new file named intf-config-RTR-01.conf.

Example 4-29 *Using Substitution to Generate New Configuration Files*

```
! Original file before the substitution
[NetProg@server1 sed-scripts]$ cat intf-config-template
!
interface GigabitEthernet100/0/0/1 l2transport
 description *** This is the OLD description ***
 encapsulation dot1q 100
 rewrite ingress tag pop 1 symmetric
 ethernet-services access-group INGRESS-POLICY ingress
 ethernet-services access-group EGRESS-POLICY egress
!

! Changing the intf description and encapsulation
[NetProg@server1 sed-scripts]$ sed -e 's/desc.*/description *** NEW description
  AFTER sed ***/' -e 's/encap.*/encapsulation dot1q 200/' intf-config-template >
  intf-config-RTR-01.conf

! New configuration file ready to be applied to RTR-01
[NetProg@server1 sed-scripts]$ cat intf-config-RTR-01.conf
!
interface GigabitEthernet100/0/0/1 l2transport
 description *** NEW description AFTER sed ***
 encapsulation dot1q 200
 rewrite ingress tag pop 1 symmetric
 ethernet-services access-group INGRESS-POLICY ingress
 ethernet-services access-group EGRESS-POLICY egress
!
```

Later in this chapter you will see how you can use Expect to automate the process of logging in to a device, executing commands in that open session, and then logging out. When you couple this with **sed**'s substitution capabilities and the Bash scripting that you will learn starting in the next section, there is a lot you can accomplish with respect to configuration management automation using only Linux, Bash, and Expect.

Several other actions are possible with **sed**, using actions such as the change action (**c**), where a whole line is replaced by another; the insert action (**i**), where a line is inserted in the file at a specific line number; and the append action (**a**), which adds a line after a specific line number. For a list of all actions that are possible with **sed**, see the **sed** man page.

General Structure of Shell Scripts

A *shell script* is simply a Linux file. Such a file should always start with a *hashbang*, which is the character sequence **#!**. The hashbang is then followed by the absolute path of the shell program that is supposed to run this script. For example, **#!/bin/bash** means that the code in the script should be parsed and interpreted using the Bash shell, whose absolute path is /bin/bash. The character sequence **#!** at the beginning of the script tells the program loader (which is the part of the kernel responsible for loading programs into memory) two important things. First, it indicates that this is a shell script (not a compiled executable). Second, it indicates that the path following the **#!** (in this case /bin/bash) is where the program (the shell) that will parse and interpret this script is located. The script will be passed as an argument to the shell that the hashbang points to, regardless of where the script is run from or what the default shell of the user who runs the script is.

Note that omitting the hashbang in a script may result in unexpected behavior; the behavior depends on what shell it is being run from. If a shell script without a hashbang is run from a Bash shell, the shell spawns a subshell to execute the script.

To write scripts that are portable from one system to another and from one distro to another, it is good practice to place something on that first line that does not need to be changed as the script is run on different systems. The absolute path to the Bash shell binary on different systems might be different. Therefore, it is recommended to use **#!/usr/bin/env bash** instead of the absolute path. This tells the program loader to pass the script to the Bash shell whose exact path is specified in the **PATH** environment variable in the /usr/bin/env file. In order to view the **PATH** environment variable and confirm that the path to the Bash shell is there, you use the command **env | grep "PATH"**. The **env** file is a binary executable, so it cannot be viewed using regular file viewing utilities such as **cat**, **more**, or **less**.

The Linux OS usually does not use file extensions to determine file types. File extensions in Linux are primarily used by humans to quickly identify file types. They are also used for interoperability with other operating systems. Think of a tarball created on a Linux system and de-archived on a Windows machine. File extensions are also used by some applications running on top of the Linux OS. A shell script can be saved in a file with any valid Linux filename and extension. This book follows the common practice of using the .bash extension for Bash script files.

Files containing shell scripts need to be executable. Depending on whether a script is run by the file owner, a user who is a member of the file group, or someone who is neither this nor that (other), an **x** (execute permission) has to be reflected in the file mode bits for the corresponding category. Recall that the **chmod** command is used for that, using the syntax **chmod u|g|o|a+x** *filename*, where **u** is for user, **g** is for group, **o** is for other, and **a** is for all. Note that in case the file has to be executable for all, the **a** option can be omitted, and the command becomes **chmod +x** *filename*.

In case a script already exists, or if you have a template that you frequently use to create new scripts (by copying and renaming the template), you can use the **-p** option with the **cp** command to preserve the original file permissions so that if the template or the original script is already executable, you do not have to issue the **chmod** command to make it so.

When the script is complete and the file is saved and made executable, the next step is to run the script. You run a script by typing its name in the shell. However, if two files on the system happen to have the same name, how does the program loader differentiate between both and then choose one of them? If the full path of the script file (whether relative or absolute) was used for execution, there is no doubt about which file will be executed. If only the name of the file is given, the system consults the **PATH** environment variable and searches for the filename in all the paths listed in the **PATH** variable, in order. The first file it finds is then executed. The current working directory (identified by the **pwd** command) plays no part here. Therefore, in order to execute a shell script, you need to either provide the path to the file or make sure your scripts are in a directory listed in the **PATH** environment variable.

Example 4-30 shows a simple Bash script, which is just the hashbang followed by a sequence of commands. At different points, the script uses the **echo** command to output text enclosed in quotation marks. The script also uses the **pwd** command to print the current working directory before and after issuing the **cd ..** command, which navigates to the parent directory. The command **ls -l | wc -l** uses piping to print the number of lines in the output of **ls -l**. The script also uses the **sleep** command to pause the execution of the next line of code for a number of seconds (provided as a parameter to the **sleep** command). Note the use of the **#** symbol to insert comments in the script. These commented lines are for informational purpose only, and the shell ignores them.

Example 4-30 *Simple Bash Script*

```
[NetProg@server1 Scripts]$ cat BasicScript.bash
#!/usr/bin/env bash
# This is the first section of the script
echo "The current working directory is.."
pwd
echo "The script sleeps for 3 seconds here"
sleep 3
# This is the second section of the script
echo
cd ..
echo "The current working directory now is.."
pwd
echo "The number of lines in the output of the ls -l cmd is.."
ls -l | wc -l
echo "The script sleeps for 5 seconds here"
sleep 5
```

This script was created by the vim text editor, but any text editor—such as nano, gedit, or emacs—could be used instead. The script is then run by using the shorthand notation **./BasicScript.bash**, as shown in Example 4-31. (Remember to make sure the file is executable before running it.)

Example 4-31 *Executing the Bash Script*

```
[NetProg@server1 Scripts]$ ./BasicScript.bash
The current working directory is..
/home/NetProg/Scripts
The script sleeps for 3 seconds here

The current working directory now is..
/home/NetProg
The number of lines in the output of the ls -l cmd is..
10
The script sleeps for 5 seconds here
[NetProg@server1 Scripts]$
```

The interpreter ignores commented lines that are part of the script. Comments are added to a script for better readability and easier maintenance. Comments in Bash are identified by the **#** symbol right before the comment. The **#** can be at the start of a line, which causes the whole line to be ignored, or after a line of code, so that only the text after the **#** is ignored. Example 4-32 provides two examples of comments.

Example 4-32 *Comments at the Beginning of a Line and at the End of a Line of Code*

```
[NetProg@server1 Scripts]$ cat Comments.bash
#!/usr/bin/env bash
# This is a script to illustrate
# common usage of comments in Bash

Random_Num_1=123 # This is the first Random Number
Random_Num_2=321 # This is the second Random Number

echo -e "The 1st random number is $Random_Num_1\n"
#echo -e "The 2nd random number is $Random_Num_2\n"

#This is the end of the script

[NetProg@server1 Scripts]$ ./Comments.bash
The 1st random number is 123

[NetProg@server1 Scripts]$
```

Note that the only line in Example 4-32 that starts with a **#** symbol and is not a comment is the line that starts with the hashbang at the very beginning of the script.

Output and Input

A script runs the same logic every single time it is run. However, the input to the script may change each time the script is executed, possibly producing different results. Therefore, an important part of any scripting language is the capability to output the results of running the script, if any. Equally important is the capability of passing input to the script. In this section you will see how to pass input to a Bash script in a few different ways and how to display the output to stdout.

Output

As shown earlier in this chapter, you use the **echo** command to print characters to the screen. The very basic syntax of the **echo** command is **echo** *options* "*text*". By default, the **echo** command outputs the text inside the quotation marks, followed by a newline character. Example 4-33 shows a script composed of three **echo** commands. The first **echo** command prints the text "This is the first line" followed by a newline character, such that the second **echo** command starts its output at the beginning of the following line. The second **echo** command outputs the text "This is the second line", followed by a newline character, such that the third **echo** command outputs its line of text at the beginning of the third line, and so forth.

Example 4-33 *Using the echo Command Without Any Options*

```
[NetProg@server1 ~]$ cat Echo_Vanilla.bash
#! /usr/bin/env bash
echo "This is the first line"
echo "This is the second line"
echo "This is the third line"

[NetProg@server1 ~]$ ./Echo_Vanilla.bash
This is the first line
This is the second line
This is the third line
[NetProg@server1 ~]$
```

The default behavior can be changed by using the **-n** option with the **echo** command. Using this option, the three lines of text are output on the same line, as shown in Example 4-34.

Example 4-34 *Using the echo Command with the -n Option*

```
[NetProg@server1 ~]$ cat Echo_NewLine.bash
#!/usr/bin/env bash
echo -n "This is the first line"
echo -n "This is the second line"
echo -n "This is the third line"

[NetProg@server1 ~]$ ./Echo_NewLine.bash
This is the first lineThis is the second lineThis is the third line[NetProg@server1 ~]$
```

By default, the **echo** command prints the text inside the quotation marks as is. For the **echo** command to use the backslash character (\) as an *escape character*, you use the option **-e**. Using the backslash as an escape character means that the character right after the backslash has a special meaning. For example, the **\n** option instructs the **echo** command to insert a new line. Special characters include, but are not limited to, the following escape sequences:

- **\n:** Newline
- **\t:** Horizontal tab
- **\v:** Vertical tab
- **\b:** Backspace
- **\\:** Prints the backslash

For example, to insert a horizontal tab anywhere in the text enclosed in quotation marks, you use the **\t** escape character. However, without the **-e** option, **\t** is printed as is instead of inserting a tab. Example 4-35 shows a script with new line, horizontal tab, and backslash escape characters used with and without the **-e** option. Notice the different results when running the script, except for the double backslash character sequence (****).

Example 4-35 *Using Escape Characters with the echo Command With and Without the -e Option*

```
[NetProg@server1 ~]$ cat EscapeCharacters.bash
#!/usr/bin/env bash
echo "This is the \n, \t and \\ characters WITHOUT the -e option"
echo -e "Using the -e option you can insert a new line:\n [This is the text after
  the new line]"
echo -e "And a horizontal tab: \t [This is the text after the tab]"
echo -e "And an actual backslash: \\"

[NetProg@server1 ~]$ ./EscapeCharacters.bash
This is the \n, \t and \ characters WITHOUT the -e option
Using the -e option you can insert a new line:
 [This is the text after the new line]
And a horizontal tab:      [This is the text after the tab]
And an actual backslash: \
```

To print out the value of a variable by using the **echo** command, you precede the variable with the **$** sign inside double quotation marks. The value of a variable is not printed out if single quotation marks are used. To execute a system command and print out the result, the **echo** command uses the format **$(***system_command***)**. Example 4-36 demonstrates how to assign a value to variable **server_hostname** and then print it out using the **echo** command. Then the output of the **pwd** command is printed out using **$(pwd)**. Variables are covered in detail later in this chapter.

Example 4-36 *Printing Out Variable Values and System Commands*

```
[NetProg@server1 Scripts]$ cat EchoWithVariable.bash
#!/usr/bin/env bash
server_hostname=Server1
echo "The server hostname is $server_hostname"
echo "And the current working directory is: $(pwd)"

[NetProg@server1 Scripts]$ ./EchoWithVariable.bash
The server hostname is Server1
And the current working directory is: /home/NetProg/Scripts
```

Note Single quotation marks preserve the literal value of the characters enclosed within quotation marks. Double quotation marks also preserve the literal value of the characters within the quotation marks, except for the dollar symbol (**$**), the single quotation marks ('), and the backslash (****). Notice how the double backslash escape sequence (****) in Example 4-35 appeared as a single backslash (****) regardless of whether the **-e** option was used or not. You will learn later in this chapter how each of these symbols translates into a special meaning inside the double quotation marks. You can also refer to Section 3.2.1 of the *GNU Bash Manual* for further details on the use of quotation marks in scripts.

POSIX, which stands for Portable Operating System Interface, is a family of standards specified by the IEEE for maintaining compatibility between operating systems. For the **echo** command to be used portably across POSIX-compliant operating systems, the **-n** option and escape characters must not be used. Because of this and the limitations of **echo**, particularly with formatted output, the IEEE encourages the use of the **printf** command instead of **echo**. (See https://pubs.opengroup.org/onlinepubs/009695399/utilities/echo.html for more information.)

The **printf** command is a very common command in the C and C++ programming languages. The general syntax of the **printf** command is **printf** "*format*" "*arguments*". In Example 4-37 **printf** is used in its most basic form: to print out a string to stdout.

Example 4-37 *Basic Usage of the printf Command to Print Out a String*

```
NetProg@server1 Scripts]$ cat printf.bash
#!/usr/bin/env bash
printf "This is a simple string"

! Executing the script
[NetProg@server1 Scripts]$ ./printf.bash
This is a simple string[NetProg@server1 Scripts]$
```

The most visible difference between **echo** and **printf** is the fact that, unlike **echo**, **printf** does not print a trailing newline. Therefore, as you can see in the output in Example 4-37, the command prompt appears on the same line as the script output. When you add the newline character, as in Example 4-38, the **printf** command emulates the functionality of **echo**.

Example 4-38 *Printing Out a String and a Trailing Newline Character*

```
[NetProg@server1 Scripts]$ cat printf.bash
#!/usr/bin/env bash
printf "This is a simple string\n"

[NetProg@server1 Scripts]$ ./printf.bash
This is a simple string
[NetProg@server1 Scripts]$
```

printf is more commonly used as shown in Example 4-39.

Example 4-39 *Using a Placeholder to Print Out the String Arguments*

```
[NetProg@server1 Scripts]$ cat printf.bash
#!/usr/bin/env bash
printf "%s-%s-%s-%s\n" "Khaled" "Jeff" "Vinit" "Anton"

[NetProg@server1 Scripts]$ ./printf.bash
Khaled-Jeff-Vinit-Anton
[NetProg@server1 Scripts]$
```

The **printf** command is followed by the format field in double quotation marks, containing a series of the character combination **%s** with dashes in between. **%s** is a *placeholder* that is used as a directive to indicate that a string will be placed in this position. The first placeholder uses the first argument, and the string **Khaled** is printed. Then a dash is printed as is, followed by the second argument, **Jeff**, in place of the second **%s**, and so forth. As a result, the arguments are printed side by side with a dash in between, as you can see in the output in Example 4-39.

Example 4-40 shows an alternative way to print the four arguments from Example 4-39. A single placeholder is used, this time followed by the escape sequence **\n** for a new line. The placeholder iterates through the argument list, one argument at a time, printing each, followed by a new line, with the result shown in the example.

Example 4-40 *Using a Single Placeholder and the Newline (\n) Character to Print All Arguments*

```
# [NetProg@server1 Scripts]$ cat printf.bash
#!/usr/bin/env bash
printf "%s\n" "Khaled" "Jeff" "Vinit" "Anton"

[NetProg@server1 Scripts]$ ./printf.bash
Khaled
Jeff
Vinit
Anton
[NetProg@server1 Scripts]$
```

The **printf** command uses the placeholders **%d** to print integers and **%f** to print floating-point numbers. With floating-point numbers, you can specify the decimal places in the output. Example 4-41 shows how to use **printf** to print floating-point numbers to a precision of two decimal places.

Example 4-41 *Printing Floating-Point Numbers with Two Decimal Places*

```
[NetProg@server1 Scripts]$ cat printf.bash
#!/usr/bin/env bash
printf "%0.2f\t" 10 13.4 19.5492 19.5443
printf "\n"

[NetProg@server1 Scripts]$ ./printf.bash
10.00   13.40   19.55   19.54
```

As you can see, when the argument is an integer or has a single decimal point, the **printf** command amends the format to be two decimal points by adding the necessary zeros. If the number has more decimal places than what is specified by the format string, the number is rounded up or down. For example, in Example 4-41, 19.549 is rounded up to 19.55, and 19.544 is rounded down to 19.54.

Input

In the context of automation, the purpose of a script is to automate a repeatable task, where the task is the processing performed by the script. And while the processing does not change (because the task is repeatable), the data being processed does change. Therefore, a script almost always requires a data set to process. There are three primary methods through which a script receives data:

- In the form of an argument passed to the script when the script is first executed
- In the form of user input during the execution of the script
- In the form of data read from a file during the execution of the script

Arguments are passed to a script in exactly the same way that arguments are passed to any Linux command. *filename* is the argument to the **cat** command in **cat** *filename*. Similarly, arguments are passed to a script in the form *scriptname argument1 argument2 .. argumentN* when running the script from the shell, where *argumentN* is the last argument. And then, from inside the script, the argument values are accessed using **${1}**, **${2}**, **..**, **${*N*}**. In Example 4-42, the **Arguments.bash** script accepts three arguments and, using the **echo** command, prints out the argument values as output. Notice that **${0}** prints out the script name, and **$#** prints out the number of arguments passed to the script.

Example 4-42 *Passing Argument to the Arguments.bash Script When First Executing It*

```
[NetProg@server1 Scripts]$ cat Arguments.bash
#!/usr/bin/env bash
echo "This is the first argument: ${1}"
echo "This is the second argument: ${2}"
echo "This is the third argument: ${3}"
echo "This is the script name: ${0}"
echo "This script received $# arguments"

[NetProg@server1 Scripts]$ ./Arguments.bash Khaled Jeff Vinit
This is the first argument: Khaled
This is the second argument: Jeff
This is the third argument: Vinit
This is the script name: ./Arguments.bash
This script received 3 arguments
```

The second way to pass data to a script is by using the **read** command. This command pauses a script indefinitely until the user inputs a line of data and presses the Enter key. Common syntax of the **read** command is **read -p** "*message*" *variable1 variable2 .. variableN*. Example 4-43 shows how to use the **read** command to read the user's first and last names and then output the user's full name by using the **echo** command.

Example 4-43 *Reading User Input Using the **read** command*

```
[NetProg@server1 Scripts]$ cat InOut.bash
#!/usr/bin/env bash
read -p "Please enter your first name: " firstname
read -p "Please enter your last name: " lastname
echo "$firstname $lastname"

[NetProg@server1 Scripts]$ ./InOut.bash
Please enter your first name: Khaled
Please enter your last name: Abuelenain
Khaled Abuelenain
```

The operation of the **read** command is slightly more complex than Example 4-43 indicates. The **read** command actually accepts a line of text from the user, and this line of text is terminated when the user presses the Enter key. This line of text is then split into words, each word separated from the next by a space, which is called the *inter-field separator* (*IFS*). Then the first word is assigned to the first variable, the second word is assigned to the second variable, and so forth. Rewriting the script in the previous example, Example 4-44 uses a single **read** command to accept the first and last names from the user and still assign them to two different variables.

Example 4-44 *Reading User Input with a Single **read** Command*

```
[NetProg@server1 Scripts]$ cat InOut-1.bash
#!/usr/bin/env bash
read -p "Please enter your first and last names separated by a space: " firstname
  lastname
echo "$firstname $lastname"

[NetProg@server1 Scripts]$ ./InOut-1.bash
Please enter your first and last names separated by a space: Khaled Abuelenain
Khaled Abuelenain
```

What if the input from the user produces more words than there are variables in the command? In this case, each variable is assigned a word from the user input until the last variable remains, and that last variable is then assigned all remaining words. For example, if the user inputs a line that is composed of five words, and the **read** command has only three variables, the first and second variables are assigned the first and second words, respectively, and the third variable is assigned the remaining three words. What if the number of variables exceeds the number of words in the user input? In this case, starting with the first variable, each variable is assigned a word, until the words run out, and then the rest of the variables are assigned empty values.

The **read** command has several options, including the following:

- **-s**: Makes user input silent (that is, it does not appear on the screen as it is typed). This is a very handy option for reading passwords into a script.
- **-i** *default_value*: Allows you to specify a default value that is assigned to a variable(s) if no data is entered by the user.
- **-t** *timeout*: Causes the **read** command to not wait indefinitely for the user to enter input. Instead, the command times out after *timeout* seconds.
- **-r**: Causes the **read** command to interpret the backslash and any characters that follow, in the user input, as is (rather than as an escape character, which is the default behavior). It is generally good practice to use the **-r** option, unless there is an explicit requirement not to, such as when giving the user the option to use the backslash to input special characters into a script.
- **-n** *nchar*: Instructs the **read** command to accept *nchar* characters instead of waiting for the user to press the Enter key to end the input line. However, the Enter key can still be used if fewer characters than *nchar* are to be read.
- **-a** *array_variable*: Causes the words of the file (provided as an argument to the **read** command) to be assigned as values to the sequential indexes of the array variable *array_variable*. (Arrays are covered in detail later in this chapter.)

The third source of input to a script is a file. A script reads from a file line by line by using the **read** command coupled with redirection, as discussed in Chapter 3. Example 4-45 shows a simple script that reads from a single-line file named authors and then prints this line by using the **echo** command.

Example 4-45 *Reading from a File Using the read Command*

```
! The single-line file authors
[NetProg@server1 Scripts]$ cat authors
Khaled Jeff Vinit Anton

! The script FileAccess.bash
[NetProg@server1 Scripts]$ cat FileAccess.bash
#!/usr/bin/env bash
echo "Accessing File ${1}"
read line < "${1}"
echo "$line"

! Executing the script
[NetProg@server1 Scripts]$ ./FileAccess.bash authors
Accessing File authors
Khaled Jeff Vinit Anton
```

When the script is executed, the file authors is passed to it as an argument, and then the notation **${1}** is used to address this first (and only) argument to the script. Redirection is then used to redirect the file authors as the input source to the **read** command instead of the default stdin (keyboard).

Note The data file **authors** in Example 4-45 was intentionally made a one-line file. Reading through multiple-line files requires knowledge of conditional statements and looping constructs. Processing a file word by word requires knowledge of array variables. Conditional statements, looping constructs, and array variables are covered later in this chapter.

Variables

Data processed by a script is largely saved in memory while the script is running. A variable is an object used to identify a specific location in memory. The value of the variable is the value saved in that memory location. A variable has several characteristics that may differ from one programming language to the other. The following are some of the common variable characteristics in Bash:

- A variable has a name. Like everything else in Linux, a variable name in Bash is case sensitive. A variable name can include any alphanumeric character (letter or number) or an underscore, but it cannot contain a special character. However, it can only start with a letter or an underscore.
- A variable does *not* have to be declared before it is used in a Bash script. You can assign a value to a variable right away, or you can declare it first by using the **declare** command and, in the process, set some of its properties, also known as *attributes*.
- A variable is assigned a value by using the syntax *variable_name*=*variable_value*. There must be no spaces before or after the = sign.
- In Bash, a variable value is accessed using the syntax **$***variable_name*. For example, **echo $Author** would print out the value of the variable **Author**.
- A variable typically has a type. In Bash, variable types are loosely defined. If a variable is not declared before being assigned a value, it can hold a value of any type. If a variable's value is an integer, then some arithmetic operations are allowed on it. The variable type is implied by its value as soon as the value is assigned to it. Moreover, the variable type changes as values of different types are assigned to it unless it is declared before being used. Bash generally provides the following variable types:
  - Integer
  - String
  - Constant

- Indexed array
- Associative array

Numbers that have fractional parts (not whole numbers) are processed by a computer using the floating-point number system. Bash does not have a floating-point variable type and does not support floating-point arithmetic operations. A workaround using the **bc** program is discussed later in this section.

Integers and Strings

A one-dimensional variable is a variable that at any point in time has a single value. One-dimensional variables may hold integers, strings, or constants. Example 4-46 shows two variables named **testvar** and **testVar** being assigned different values and then the **echo** command being used to expand the values of these variables using no quotation marks, single quotation marks, and double quotation marks.

Example 4-46 *Simple Variable Value Assignment and Expansion*

```
[NetProg@server1 Scripts]$ cat Variables.bash
#!/usr/bin/env bash
testvar=10
testVar=20
echo No Quotes: The value of testvar is $testvar and the value of testVar is
  $testVar
echo 'Single Quotes: The value of testvar is $testvar and the value of testVar is
  $testVar'
echo "Double Quotes: The value of testvar is $testvar and the value of testVar is
  $testVar"

[NetProg@server1 Scripts]$ ./Variables.bash
No Quotes: The value of testvar is 10 and the value of testVar is 20
Single Quotes: The value of testvar is $testvar and the value of testVar is $testVar
Double Quotes: The value of testvar is 10 and the value of testVar is 20
```

In Example 4-46, notice first that because variable names are case sensitive, **testvar** and **testVar** are two different, unrelated variables. Also notice that the variable values are not expanded if single quotation marks are used. Using single quotation marks is referred to as *strong* quoting, while using double quotation marks is referred to as *weak* quoting.

If some text directly follows a variable value without whitespace in between, the variable name must be enclosed in braces. For example, if the value of variable **bw** has to be followed by the string GB, then the syntax to print out the value of **bw** is **echo "${bw}GB"**. This tells the **echo** command that **GB** is not part of the variable name. If variable **bw** has a value of **10**, then the **echo** command output is **10GB**.

As mentioned earlier in this section, a variable type depends on the value assigned to the variable, and the type of the variable changes as values of different types are assigned to it. Example 4-47 shows how the variable **testvar** is assigned an integer and then a string without any errors. Then both values are printed out just fine—again without any errors.

Example 4-47 *The Same Variable Assigned Values with Different Data Types*

```
[NetProg@server1 Scripts]$ cat Variables1.bash
#!/usr/bin/env bash
testvar=10
echo -e "The value of testvar is $testvar - type:integer \n"
testvar=Cairo
echo "The value of testvar is $testvar - type:string"

[NetProg@server1 Scripts]$ ./Variables1.bash
The value of testvar is 10 - type:integer

The value of testvar is Cairo - type:string
```

In Bash, you can declare a variable before it is assigned a value by using the **declare** command. The syntax of the **declare** command is **declare** *options variable_name***=***variable_value*. As you can see from the syntax, a variable may also be assigned a value in the **declare** command. Declaring variables is mandatory in some programming languages, where a variable accepts data of only one specific type and not any other. In Bash, you can declare a variable to accept only integer values by using the **-i** option, or you can declare a variable as a constant (that is, read only) by using the **-r** option. You can use the **-l** option to convert any uppercase letters in a variable value to lowercase, and you can use the **-u** option to do just the opposite. Each of these options sets the corresponding property of a variable, called a *variable attribute*. Although it may sound counterintuitive, any attribute set using any of the previously mentioned options may be *unset* by replacing the option with the **+** option in the **declare** command. You can view attributes set for a variable by using the **declare** command with the **-p** option.

Example 4-48 illustrates the use of the **declare** command. Variable **var1** is declared with the **-l** option and is not assigned a value. Variable **var2** is declared as an integer using the **-i** option and is assigned the value **200**. Finally, variable **var3** is declared as a constant using the **-r** option and is given the value **Alexandria**. A string is assigned to **var1** and, as expected, all uppercase letters are converted to lowercase. Then an attempt is made to assign a string to **var2**, and while the assignment does not generate an error, the **echo** command outputs a 0 instead of the correct variable value because **var2** was declared as an integer but is being assigned a value of type string. Finally, an attempt is made to assign an integer value to **var3**, which generates an error, as highlighted in Example 4-48, because **var3** was declared as a constant.

Example 4-48 *Variable Declaration Using the declare Command*

```
[NetProg@server1 Scripts]$ cat Variables2.bash
#!/usr/bin/env bash
declare -l var1
declare -i var2=200
declare -r var3=Alexandria
var1=ThIsIsATeSTSTRInG
echo "The value of var1 is $var1"
var2=TestString
echo "The value of var2 is $var2"
var3=Sinai
echo "The value of var3 is $var3"
echo "The attributes of var1 are: $(declare -p var1)"

[NetProg@server1 Scripts]$ ./Variables2.bash
The value of var1 is thisisateststring
The value of var2 is 0
./Variables2.bash: line 15: var3: readonly variable
The value of var3 is Alexandria
The attributes of var1 are: declare -l var1="thisisateststring"
```

Notice that in order to execute the **declare** command and display its result using **echo**, you use **$(declare -p var1)** inside the double quotation marks of the **echo** command. The same applies to any system command. This is an example of *command substitution*: A system command's output is used in some context, such as in the output of the **echo** command, or assigned to a variable. For instance, to assign the output of the command to the variable **Var1**, you use **Var1=$(declare -p var1)**.

Arithmetic operations in Bash are performed using *arithmetic expansion*. The notation **$((*expression*))** is used to evaluate the arithmetic expression between the double parentheses. The result can then be processed using the **echo** *variable* command. In Example 4-49, the result of dividing nine by two is evaluated using arithmetic expansion and then assigned to the variable **expr**. The value of **expr** is then printed out to stdout.

Example 4-49 *Simple Integer-Based Arithmetic Operations*

```
[NetProg@server1 Scripts]$ cat arithmetic.bash
#!/usr/bin/env bash
expr=$((9/2))
echo "The value of 9/2 is: $expr"

[NetProg@server1 Scripts]$ ./arithmetic.bash
The value of 9/2 is: 4
```

Notice that although the result of dividing nine by two should be 4.5, the result of the arithmetic expansion in the script output has been truncated to 4. As stated earlier in this section, Bash does not have a floating-point data type and does not support floating-point operations. However, a workaround involves using the **bc** utility. To assign the precise result of an arithmetic operation to a variable, you can use the syntax *variable*=**$echo("scale=***decimal_places* **;** *expr*" **| bc)**. The **scale** option sets the number of decimal places required in the output. A whitespace before or after the semicolon (for readability) is optional. Example 4-50 shows the **bc** utility being used to output the value of some arithmetic operations to a precision set by **scale**.

Example 4-50 *The Use of the* **scale** *Command with Addition, Subtraction, Multiplication, and Division*

```
[NetProg@server1 Scripts]$ cat bcutiliy.bash
#!/usr/bin/env bash
Add1=$(echo "1.2+3.546789" | bc)
Add2=$(echo "scale=3 ; 1.2+3.546789" | bc)
Subt1=$(echo "10-3.546789" | bc)
Subt2=$(echo "scale=3 ; 10-3.546789" | bc)
Mult1=$(echo "1.234*5.678" | bc)
Mult2=$(echo "scale=10 ; 1.234*5.678" | bc)
Div1=$(echo "10/3" |bc)
Div2=$(echo "scale=7 ; 10/3" | bc)
echo $Add1
echo $Add2
echo $Subt1
echo $Subt2
echo $Mult1
echo $Mult2
echo $Div1
echo $Div2

[NetProg@server1 Scripts]$ ./bcutiliy.bash
4.746789
4.746789
6.453211
6.453211
7.006
7.006652
3
3.3333333
```

Notice that the **bc** utility does not always respect the **scale** setting in the command. With addition and subtraction, regardless of whether the scale is set, it is ignored, and the scale that is used for the result is the same as that of the highest-precision number in the arithmetic operation. For multiplication, the scale that is set is honored, and if the scale is not set, the scale of the highest-precision number in the multiplication is used. Not setting a scale with division results in using the default scale of zero. Otherwise, the scale setting is honored.

Indexed and Associative Arrays

An *array* is a data structure that consists of one or more *elements*. A variable representing the array data structure is typically just called an *array*. Each array element stores one of the array's values. For example, the array **capitals** may hold three values: **Cairo**, **Washington**, and **Minsk**. Each of the array elements is identified either by its position in the array, called the *index*, or by a unique value, called a *key*. An *indexed array* uses indexes to identify its elements. An *associative array* uses keys to identify its elements.

If the array **capitals** were an indexed array, one way the elements would be identified is by **capitals[0]**, **capitals[1]**, and **capitals[2]**, where the numbers enclosed in brackets are the array element indexes, and **capitals[0]** would hold the value **Cairo**, **capitals[1]** would hold the value **Washington**, and **capitals[2]** would hold the value **Minsk**. Note that the first element has an index of 0. However, the actual elements holding values do not have to be consecutive, and not all elements have to be assigned values. The elements holding the three values could be **capitals[3]**, **capitals[18]**, and **capitals[179]**. The elements not holding values, such as **capitals[0]** or **capitals[100]**, have the value **null**. This will become clear after you study the next example.

In the case of an associative array, the elements of the array may be identified by **capitals[Egypt]**, **capitals[USA]**, and **capitals[Belarus]**, where **Egypt**, **USA**, and **Belarus** are the array elements *keys*. You can guess what the value of each element would be.

When a variable is assigned a value using the syntax *variable*[*index*]=*value*, the variable is automatically treated as an indexed array, and you can simply start assigning values to its elements by using this syntax. Alternatively, you can use the **declare** command to declare an array before values are assigned to its elements by using the syntax **declare -a|-A** *array_name*, where the **-a** option is for indexed arrays, and the **-A** option is for associative arrays.

While the benefit of declaring an indexed array is questionable (it *might* speed up subsequent array operations), it is mandatory for associative arrays. You can use the **declare** command to declare *and* initialize the array's elements with values by using the syntax **declare -a** *array_name*=(*value1 value2 ... valueN*) for indexed arrays or **declare -A** *array_name*=([*key1*]=*value1* [*key2*]=*value2* ... [*keyN*]=*valueN*) for associative arrays. On the other hand, to access element values, the syntax **${***array_name*[*index*]**}** is used for indexed arrays and **${***array_name*[*key*]**}** for associative arrays. Indexed arrays and associative arrays are very similar in operation except that the former uses an index to address each of its elements, and the latter uses a key for this. This chapter focuses on indexed arrays and highlights the differences between indexed arrays and associative arrays, where applicable.

Example 4-51 displays some examples of basic array operations.

Example 4-51 *Declaring Arrays, Initializing Them Without Declaration, and Printing Their Values by Using the echo Command*

```
[NetProg@server1 Scripts]$ cat Arrays1.bash
#!/usr/bin/env bash
declare -a authors=(Khaled Jeff Vinit Anton) # Declare and initialize an indexed array
declare -A last_names # Declare an associative array

# Assign values to array capitals (without declaration) using element indices
# Element indices don't have to be consecutive numbers
capitals[2]=Cairo
capitals[10]="Washington DC" # Double quotes used due to whitespace
capitals[50]=Minsk
capitals[53]=999

# Assign values to the elements of last_name using the element keys
last_names[Kh]=Abuelenain
last_names[Je]=Doyle
last_names[Vi]=Jain
last_names[An]=Karneliuk

echo "The value of capitals[1] is ${capitals[1]}"
echo "The value of capitals[2] is ${capitals[2]}"
echo "The value of capitals[10] is ${capitals[10]}"
echo "The value of capitals[50] is ${capitals[50]}"
echo "The value of capitals[53] is ${capitals[53]}"

Sum=$((${capitals[53]}+123))

echo "The value capitals[53]+123 is $Sum"
echo "The number of elements in capitals is ${#capitals[@]}"
echo -e "The index values of capitals are ${!capitals[@]}\n"
echo "The value of the 2nd element of authors is ${authors[1]}"
echo "The value of the 3rd element of last_names is ${last_names[Vi]}"
echo "The key values of last_names are ${!last_names[@]}"
echo "All values of last_names are ${last_names[@]}"

[NetProg@server1 Scripts]$ ./Arrays1.bash
The value of capitals[1] is
The value of capitals[2] is Cairo
The value of capitals[10] is Washington DC
The value of capitals[50] is Minsk
The value of capitals[53] is 999
The value capitals[53]+123 is 1122
The number of elements in capitals is 4
The index values of capitals are 2 10 50 53
```

```
The value of the 2nd element of authors is Jeff
The value of the 3rd element of last_names is Jain
The key values of last_names are kh Je Vi An
All values of last_names are Abuelenain Doyle Jain Karneliuk
```

As you can see in Example 4-51, to access all elements of the array, you use the syntax **${*array_name*[@]}**. The command **echo "${!*array_name*[@]}"** prints out the index numbers in the case of an indexed array or the key values in case of an associative array, and **echo "${#*array_name*[@]}"** prints out the number of elements in the array. Alternatively, **echo "${#*array_name*[*N*]}"** prints out the length of the *N*th element. Using *array_name*[*] is equivalent to using *array_name*[@] in all the previous examples.

Notice in Example 4-51 that the first three elements of the array **capitals** are strings, and the fourth element is an integer. Elements of the same array may each hold a value of a different type. To prove this further, the number 123 is added to the value of **capitals[53]**, and the result of this arithmetic operation is assigned to the variable **Sum** and printed out.

You can add a new array element by simply making an assignment using the array name and index (or key). Alternatively, for indexed arrays, you can use the syntax *array_name*+=(*new_element_value*) to add a new element that has an index number that is 1 more than the last index used in the array. For associative arrays, the equivalent syntax is *array_name*+=([*new_element_key*]=*new_element_value*). To remove an element from an array, you use the command **unset** *array_name*[*index*|*key*]. To delete an entire array, you use @ instead of *index* or *key* in the command. Example 4-52 shows how to add and remove array elements.

Example 4-52 *Adding and Removing Array Elements*

```
[NetProg@server1 Scripts]$ cat Arrays2.bash
#!/usr/bin/env bash
capitals[0]=Cairo
capitals[1]="Washington DC"
capitals[5]=Minsk
echo -e "The array capitals is currently: ${capitals[@]}\n"
capitals+=("Riyadh")
echo -e "The array capitals is now: ${capitals[@]}\n"
echo -e "And the list of indices is ${!capitals[@]}\n"
unset capitals[5]
echo -e "The array elements are now: ${capitals[@]}\n"
echo -e "And the list of indices becomes: ${!capitals[@]}\n"

[NetProg@server1 Scripts]$ ./Arrays2.bash
The array capitals is currently: Cairo Washington DC Minsk

The array capitals is now: Cairo Washington DC Minsk Riyadh
```

```
And the list of indices is 0 1 5 6

The array elements are now: Cairo Washington DC Riyadh

And the list of indices becomes: 0 1 6
```

The command **capitals+=("Riyadh")** adds a new element to the array. The array value in this case is, obviously, **Riyadh**, and the assigned index is the next available index number, **6**. The command **unset capitals[5]** is used to delete the element whose index is **5** and value is **Minsk**.

Arrays can be concatenated and the result assigned to a third array. Example 4-53 concatenates the arrays **capitals1** and **capitals2** and assigns the result to the array **capitals3**.

Example 4-53 *Concatenating Arrays*

```
[NetProg@server1 Scripts]$ cat Arrays4.bash
#!/usr/bin/env bash
capitals1=(Cairo Washington Minsk)
capitals2=(London Dusseldorf)
capitals3=(${capitals1[@]} ${capitals2[@]})
echo -e "Array capitals1 has the elements: ${capitals1[@]}\n"
echo -e "And array capitals2 has the elements: ${capitals2[@]}\n"
echo -e "Concatenate them into capitals3: ${capitals3[@]}\n"

[NetProg@server1 Scripts]$ ./Arrays4.bash
Array capitals1 has the elements: Cairo Washington Minsk

And array capitals2 has the elements: London Dusseldorf

Concatenate them into capitals3: Cairo Washington Minsk London Dusseldorf
```

Arrays in any programming language allow for very complex data manipulation operations. Try to experiment with arrays to familiarize yourself with this fascinating data type.

Conditional Statements

When you need to execute a command or perform an action in programming only if a certain condition exists, you use conditional statements. Conditional statements may be a part of a larger construct that evaluates a condition, and if the condition is true, one or more commands are executed. However, if the condition is not true, further testing may be performed and other alternative commands executed. There are two primary conditional constructs in Bash:

- if-then-elif-then-else-fi (which we refer to as the if-then construct for brevity)
- case-in-esac

The if-then Construct

The flow through an if-then construct is very intuitive: The **if** keyword tests whether a condition is true, and if it is, the **then** keyword executes one or more commands. The **fi** keyword then marks the end of the construct. Example 4-54 shows the syntax of the if-then construct in its simplest form.

Example 4-54 *if-then Construct in Its Simplest Form: if-then-fi*

```
if [[ condition ]]
then
        command-block
fi
```

In Example 4-54, notice the mandatory whitespace between the condition and the double brackets. Example 4-55 shows a simple if-then-fi construct in which the user is prompted to enter his or her username. The **if** statement tests whether the username is equal to the string **NetProg**. If it is, a message is output to stdout using the **echo** command. Otherwise, nothing happens, and the script exits.

Example 4-55 *Testing User Input and Output Message if Condition Is True*

```
[NetProg@server1 Scripts]$ cat if-then.bash
#!/usr/bin/env bash
read -p "Please enter your username: " username
if [[ $username = "NetProg" ]]
then
  echo "Hello $username"
fi

! This is the execution result when the condition evaluates to true
[NetProg@server1 Scripts]$ ./if-then.bash
Please enter your first name: NetProg
Hello NetProg
[NetProg@server1 Scripts]$

! This is the execution result when the condition evaluates to false
[NetProg@server1 Scripts]$ ./if-then.bash
Please enter your first name: OtherUser
[NetProg@server1 Scripts]$
```

To avoid situations similar to the one shown in Example 4-55, where nothing happens if the condition tested is false, the if-then construct is designed to accommodate more complex algorithms than what you have seen so far. Example 4-56 shows the full syntax of the if-then construct.

Example 4-56 *The Full Syntax of the if-then Construct*

```
if [[ condition ]]
then
        command-block
elif [[ alternative-condition ]]
then
        command-block-2
else
        default-command-block
fi
```

This is how the logic flows:

1. The **if** keyword tests whether *condition* is true. If it is, execute the command(s) in *command-block*.
2. If *condition* tested by the **if** keyword is not true, the **elif** keyword tests whether *alternative-condition* is true or not. If *alternative-condition* is true, execute the command(s) in *command-block-2*.
3. If more than one **elif** block exists, move to an **elif** block if and only if the previous **elif** block's *alternative-condition* evaluates to false.
4. If *alternative-condition* tested by the last **elif** keyword is not true, go to the **else** block and execute the command(s) in *default-command-block*.
5. Exit the construct at the **fi** keyword.

The if-then construct is very flexible in that it can test for a single condition and execute one command block using a simple if-then-fi construct, as shown in Example 4-55. Or you can add to that an **else** block *without* an **elif** block so that the construct becomes if-then-else-fi. Alternatively, you may require a construct that uses **if** and **elif** blocks without an **else** block, so that the construct becomes if-then-elif-then-fi. And then you may have a full construct employing **if**, **elif**, and **else** blocks—that is, an if-then-elif-then-else-fi construct. The construct may also have more than one **elif** block testing for further alternative conditions, where each **elif** block is executed if the condition in the previous **elif** is false.

In any case, and regardless of what blocks are included in the code, only one command block is executed in any one run of the program. Either the execution block under the **if** keyword is executed or the block under *one of the* **elif** keywords is executed, or the block under the **else** keyword is executed. But never are two (or more) of these blocks executed in the same script run.

Example 4-57 enhances the script from Example 4-56 so that, if the username is not NetProg, it uses **elif** to test whether the username is NetDev. If the username is neither NetProg nor NetDev, a message is output to stdout by using an **else** statement.

Example 4-57 *Using the Full if-then-elif-then-else-fi Construct to Test User Input*

```
[NetProg@server1 Scripts]$ cat if-then-elif-else.bash
#!/usr/bin/env bash
read -p "Please enter your username: " username
if [[ $username = "NetProg" ]]
then
  echo "Hello $username"
elif [[ $username = "NetDev" ]]
then
  echo "Hello $username - please log out and log in using the NetProg account"
else
  echo "This access is not authorized - please log out immediately !"
fi

! Script execution results for three different user inputs
[NetProg@server1 Scripts]$ ./if-then-elif-else.bash
Please enter your username: NetProg
Hello NetProg

[NetProg@server1 Scripts]$ ./if-then-elif-else.bash
Please enter your username: OtherUser
This access is not authorized - please log out immediately !

[NetProg@server1 Scripts]$ ./if-then-elif-else.bash
Please enter your username: NetDev
Hello NetDev - please log out and log in using the NetProg account
[NetProg@server1 Scripts]$
```

In order for the if-then statement to make a decision, an expression has to be evaluated to be either true or false. Comparison operators are used to compare two values to each other, and the end result is either true or false. Strings, numbers, and files have different sets of comparison or evaluation operators that are used to evaluate a condition to be either true or false. This evaluation of a condition using comparison or evaluation operators may then be used in any programming construct requiring such an evaluation, including the if-then conditional statement. Table 4-1 lists the string comparison operators supported in Bash.

Table 4-1 *String Operators in Bash*

Operator	Description
<	Less than
>	Greater than
=	Equal to
==	Equal to
!=	Not equal to
-z	True if the length of the string is zero
-n	True if the length of the string is nonzero

String values used for comparisons are based on alphabetical order. For example, strings that start with the letter a are less than strings that start with the letter b, and those that start with the letter c are greater than those that start with the letter b, and so forth. Example 4-58 illustrates the use of some string comparison operators.

Example 4-58 *Using String Comparison Operators*

```
[NetProg@server1 Scripts]$ cat stringcompare.bash
#!/usr/bin/env bash
if [[ abcd < e ]]
then
  echo "abcd is less than e"
else
  echo "e is less than abcd"
fi
if [[ X = Y ]]
then
  echo "X is equal to Y"
else
  echo "X is not equal to Y"
fi
if [[ "Cairo" != "Colorado" ]]
then
  echo "Cairo is in Egypt, Colorado is in the US !"
fi
if [[ -n "Cairo" ]]
then
  echo "The string \"Cairo\" has non-zero length!"
fi
if [[ -z "" ]]
then
  echo "The empty quotes are a string with zero length"
fi
```

```
[NetProg@server1 Scripts]$ ./stringcompare.bash
abcd is less than e
X is not equal to Y
Cairo is in Egypt, Colorado is in the US !
The string "Cairo" has non-zero length!
The empty quotes are a string with zero length
```

Both the single equal sign (=) and the double equal sign (==) are used for evaluating equality in conditional statements. In the context of this book, which covers Bash scripting fundamentals, you can assume that they behave in an identical manner. There are, of course, subtle differences between them that are not covered here. Feel free to refer to the *GNU Bash Manual* for further elaboration.

Table 4-2 lists the arithmetic operators supported in Bash.

Table 4-2 *Arithmetic Operators in Bash*

Operator	Description
-lt	Less than
-gt	Greater than
-le	Less than or equal to
-ge	Greater than or equal to
-eq	Equal to
-ne	Not equal to

Integers are compared based on their numeric value. For example, 1 is less than 2, and 2 is less than 12. Example 4-59 illustrates the use of some of the integer comparison operators.

Example 4-59 *Using Integer Comparison Operators*

```
[NetProg@server1 Scripts]$ ./intcompare.bash
#!/usr/bin/env bash
if [[ 1 -lt 2 ]]
then
  echo "1 is less than 2"
else
  echo "2 is less than 1"
fi
if [[ 2 -gt 12 ]]
then
  echo "2 is greater than 12"
else
  echo "2 is less than 12"
```

```
fi
if [[ 135 -ne 246 ]]
then
  echo "135 and 246 are not equal !"
fi

[NetProg@server1 Scripts]$ ./intcompare.bash
1 is less than 2
2 is less than 12
135 and 246 are not equal !
```

Table 4-3 lists some of the file evaluation operators supported in Bash.

Table 4-3 *File Comparison Operators in Bash*

Operator	Description
-a or -e	True if file exists
-d	True if file is a directory
-f	True if file is a regular file
-r	True if file exists and is readable
-s	True if file is not zero in size
-w	True if file exists and is writable
-x	True if file exists and is executable

Example 4-60 illustrates the use of some of the file evaluation operators.

Example 4-60 *Using File Comparison Operators in Bash*

```
[NetProg@server1 Scripts]$ cat fileeval.bash
#!/usr/bin/env bash
if [[ -f /home/NetProg/Scripts/intcompare.bash ]]
then
  echo -e "The file intcomparison.bash exists and is a regular file !\n"
fi
if [[ -x stringcompare.bash ]]
then
  echo -e "The file stringcomparison.bash exists and is executable !\n"
fi

[NetProg@server1 Scripts]$ ./fileeval.bash
The file intcomparison.bash exists and is a regular file !

The file stringcomparison.bash exists and is executable !
```

The case-in Construct

The case-in conditional construct compares the value of a variable (or a word) to one or more expressions and executes the command block corresponding to the matching value. Example 4-61 shows the general syntax of this construct.

Example 4-61 *General Syntax of the case-in Construct*

```
case $variable in
        first-value)
                command-block-1
                ;;
        second-value)
                command-block-2
                ;;
        Nth-value)
                command-block-N
                ;;
        *)
                default-command-block
                ;;
esac
```

The case-in construct is very flexible and provides more than what immediately meets the eye. Each section of the construct corresponding to a testing value is called a *clause*. Each clause starts with a testing value, is followed by a command block, and ends with double semicolons (;;), a semicolon and an ampersand (;&), or double semicolons and an ampersand (;;&), each indicating a different course of action.

Each testing value ends in a closing parenthesis. The value may be a constant, a variable, or a regular expression. Following the testing value is a command block that is executed if *variable* is equal to the testing value.

If the clause ends in double semicolons (;;), the construct exits if a match is found. If the clause ends in double semicolons and an ampersand (;;&), then even if a match is found, the testing continues with the testing value in the next clause. If a clause ends in a semicolon and an ampersand (;&), the command block of the next clause is executed without testing.

This is how the logic flows:

1. The **case** keyword tests whether *variable* and *first-value* are equal. If they are, the commands in *command-block-1* are executed. If they are not equal, *command-block-1* is skipped and *variable* is compared to *second-value*.

2. In case *command-block-1* is executed and the first clause ends in double semicolons (;;), the construct exits, and the execution is complete.

3. In case *command-block-1* is executed and the first clause ends in a semicolon and an ampersand (;&), *command-block-2* is also executed without *variable* being compared to *second-value.*

4. In case *command-block-1* is executed and the first clause ends in double semicolons and an ampersand (;;&), *second-value* is compared to *variable*, and if they match, the commands in *command-block-2* are executed. If they don't match, the commands are skipped.

5. These steps repeat until the last clause is reached, signified by the *). An asterisk matches any value, so if the logic reaches this point in the construct, the commands in the *default-command-block* are executed.

6. The construct ends with the **esac** keyword.

Example 4-62 shows a simple multiple-choice quiz that tests the input from a user against two possible answers and provides default output in the event that the user's input does not match either of the testing values.

Example 4-62 *The case-in Construct Used to Conduct a Simple Quiz*

```
[NetProg@server1 Scripts]$ cat case-in.bash
#!/usr/bin/env bash
read -p "What is the Capital of Colombia ?  " Capital
case $Capital in
     Bogota)
      echo -e "Yes you are right - the capital of Colombia is Bogota\n"
      ;;
     Medellin)
      echo -e "Close but not correct\n"
      ;;
     *)
      echo -e "You need a geography lesson !\n"
      ;;
esac

[NetProg@server1 Scripts]$ ./case-in.bash
What is the Capital of Colombia ?  New York
You need a geography lesson !

[NetProg@server1 Scripts]$ ./case-in.bash
What is the Capital of Colombia ?  Medellin
Close but not correct

[NetProg@server1 Scripts]$ ./case-in.bash
What is the Capital of Colombia ?  Bogota
Yes you are right - the capital of Colombia is Bogota
```

Keep in mind that you may end any of the clauses in double semicolons (;;), in double semicolons and an ampersand (;;&), or in a semicolon and an ampersand (;&). This list of choices is *not* exclusive to the first clause only.

Loops

When you need to execute a command or a sequence of commands multiple times in a script, looping constructs come into play. A looping construct repeats a sequence of actions as long as a particular condition evaluates to true. Three looping constructs are commonly used in Bash:

- for-do-done
- while-do-done
- until-do-done

The for-do Loop

The for-do loop has two general forms, as shown in Example 4-63.

Example 4-63 *The for-do Loop General Syntax*

```
! The first form of the for-do loop
for VAR in list-of-values
do
  command-block
done

! The second form of the for-do loop
for (( expr1 ; expr2 ; expr3 ))
do
  command-block
done
```

The for-do loop starts with the **for** keyword and an argument that takes one of two forms. It also contains a command block that may be one or more commands and starts with the **do** keyword and ends with the **done** keyword.

In the first form, the variable *VAR* is assigned the values that follow the **in** keyword, one by one, and the commands in *command-block* are executed once for each value. Keep in mind that the commands may or may not reference or use the variable *VAR*. For example, the values may be the strings **Khaled** and **Jeff**, and *command-block* would be **echo "Hello World"**. The result of running the script would then be the string **Hello**

World printing out two times without any reference to the two values. Example 4-64 shows the for-do loop being used to iterate through a list of values and then print out those values.

Example 4-64 *Printing a Sequence of Values by Using a for-do Loop*

```
[NetProg@server1 Scripts]$ cat for-do.bash
#!/usr/bin/env bash
count=1
for authors in Khaled Jeff Vinit Anton
do
  echo "Author-${count} is $authors"
  (( count++ ))
done

[NetProg@server1 Scripts]$ ./for-do.bash
Author-1 is Khaled
Author-2 is Jeff
Author-3 is Vinit
Author-4 is Anton
```

Say that you want to have a user input a number, and then you want to print out all numbers from zero up to that number, in order. You would want to iterate through the values, starting from zero up to the number that the user has entered that will be stored in a variable. Assume that variable is called **maxnumber**. The first form of the for-do loop would not permit iterating through a list of values starting with zero and ending with **$maxnumber**. But the second form of the for-do loop would.

The second form of the for-do loop has a similar format to the for-do loop in the C programming language. The **for** keyword is followed by three expressions in double parentheses (arithmetic expansion), and separated by semicolons. The logic of these expressions is as follows:

1. The first expression is evaluated once. The result of this evaluation does not affect the loop.
2. The second expression is then evaluated.
3. If the result of evaluating the second expression is zero, exit the loop. Otherwise, proceed to the next step.
4. If the result of evaluating the second expression is a nonzero value, the commands in *command-block* are executed, and then the third expression is evaluated.
5. Repeat steps 2 through 4.

The for-do loop in Example 4-65 illustrates this logic.

Example 4-65 *Printing Numbers from 1 to a Maximum Number by Using a for-do Loop*

```
[NetProg@server1 Scripts]$ cat for-do-1.bash
#!/usr/bin/env bash
read -p "Enter maximum number: " max
for ((i=1; i<=$max; i++))
do
  echo "$i"
done

[NetProg@server1 Scripts]$ ./for-do-1.bash
Enter maximum number: 3
1
2
3
```

In this example, the user enters the number **3** when prompted for input by the **read** command. Starting with the for keyword, the expression in the first field is evaluated. The variable **i** is set to **1**. This is done only once, regardless of how many times the loop iterates.

Then the expression in the second field is evaluated: Is **i** less than or equal to **max**? Yes, it is, so the commands in the body of the loop are executed. In this case, the **echo** command outputs the value of **i**, which is **1**.

On the loop's second iteration, the third expression is evaluated, which results in incrementing the value of **i** to **2**. Note that the expression *variable*++ increments the value of *variable* by **1**. Then the second expression is evaluated again: Is **i** still less than or equal to **max**? Yes, it is, so the **echo** command executes a second time, printing out the value of **i**, which is now **2**.

On the loop's third iteration, the third expression is evaluated, incrementing the value of **i** to **3**. The second expression is now evaluated: Is **i** still less than or equal to **max**? Yes, it is, so the **echo** command prints out the number **3**.

Finally, the third expression is evaluated, and the value of **i** is incremented to **4**. When the second expression is evaluated, **i**, which is **4** now, is not less than or equal to **max**. Therefore, the second expression evaluates to false, the loop exits, and the script finishes execution.

An interesting example for the use of the for loop is to parse through a file, word by word, and perform some processing on these words, such as a search and replace operation. Example 4-66 combines the second form of the for loop with arrays, covered earlier in this chapter, to do just that.

Example 4-66 *Parsing Through a File Word by Word*

```
! The contents of the file DataFile
[NetProg@server1 Scripts]$ cat DataFile
The for-do loop starts with the keyword for and an argument that takes up one of
  two forms.

! The Script content
[NetProg@server1 Scripts]$ cat for-do-2.bash
#!/usr/bin/env bash
Content=( $(cat ./DataFile) )
for ((i=0 ; i<${#Content[@]} ; i++))
do
  echo "${Content[$i]}"
done

! Script execution result
[NetProg@server1 Scripts]$ ./for-do-2.bash
The
for-do
loop
starts
with
the
keyword
for
and
an
argument
that
takes
up
one
of
two
forms.
```

In Example 4-66, the file DataFile contains a line from this chapter as a sample test. The script uses *command substitution* to assign the output of the **cat** command to the array **Content**. Then a **for** loop sets **i=0** and iterates as long as **i** is less than the value of **${#Content[@]}**—which is the number of elements in the array **Content**. Through each iteration, the **echo** command prints the value of the element **Content[$i]** and the **for** loop increments the value of **i**. The value of **Content[1]** is the first word in the file, **Content[2]** is the second, and so forth, effectively printing each word in the file on a separate line. Think of all the processing possibilities, apart from printing out the words to the screen, that you can accomplish by mapping each word in a text file to an element in array.

The while-do Loop

Example 4-67 shows the general syntax of the while-do loop.

Example 4-67 *The while-do Loop General Syntax*

```
while condition
do
  command-block
done
```

The while-do loop is as simple as its syntax: While *condition* is true, execute the command(s) in *command-block*. Example 4-68 shows the same algorithm previously implemented using the for-do loop but this time using the while-do loop. The script requests an integer from a user and outputs to stdout all numbers, in order, from 0 to that number.

Example 4-68 *Printing a Sequence of Numbers by Using a while-do Loop*

```
[NetProg@server1 Scripts]$ cat while-do.bash
#!/usr/bin/env bash
read -p "Please enter any integer: " maxnumber
count=0
while [[ count -le maxnumber ]]
do
  echo $count
  (( count++ ))
done

[NetProg@server1 Scripts]$ ./while-do.bash
Please enter any integer: 11
0
1
2
3
4
5
6
7
8
9
10
11
[NetProg@server1 Scripts]$
```

The until-do Loop

Example 4-69 shows the general syntax of the until-do loop.

Example 4-69 *The until-do Loop General Syntax*

```
until condition
do
  command-block
done
```

Unlike the while-do loop, which executes the commands in *command-block* if and only if *condition* is true, the until-do loop actually breaks when *condition* is true; until this happens, the commands in *command-block* keep executing. Example 4-70 is a rewrite of the algorithm in Example 4-68 that outputs a sequence of numbers using the until-do loop.

Example 4-70 *Using an until-do Loop to Print Numbers from 0 to a Maximum Number*

```
[NetProg@server1 Scripts]$ cat until-do.bash
#!/usr/bin/env bash
read -p "Please enter any integer: " maxnumber
count=0
until [[ count -eq maxnumber ]]
do
  echo $count
  (( count++ ))
done

[NetProg@server1 Scripts]$ ./until-do.bash
Please enter any integer: 7
0
1
2
3
4
5
6
[NetProg@server1 Scripts]$
```

In the output in Example 4-70, notice that the numbers printed are 0 to 6, which is one less than the number that the user actually entered (7). The reason for this is that on the last loop iteration, the variable **count** is equal to 6. Its value is output to stdout by the **echo** command and then incremented to 7. On the following loop iteration, the variable **count** is actually equal to the value in the variable **maxnumber** (that is, 7); therefore, the commands in the command block are not executed, and the loop is terminated. In order to print all numbers up to and including the number entered by the user, the condition has to be changed to **[[count -gt maxnumber]]**, which evaluates to true only if **count** is *greater* than **maxnumber**.

Functions

Programming languages provide a programming construct called a *function*, which is a segment of code inside a script that is identified by a name, has a start and an end, can be passed arguments, and has a return status that is passed back to the calling script.

Why would you want to use functions in a script? Functions are highly efficient when a certain task has to be repeated more than once. When you use a function, the code for accomplishing a task is written once, and the function is called any number of times required, which saves you the effort of writing the same code more than once.

Example 4-71 shows the syntax for writing a function inside a script.

Example 4-71 *General Syntax of Functions*

```
function_name() {
  function_code
}
```

A function typically contains code that otherwise would exist in the body of the main script. Arguments are passed to the function the same way arguments are passed to the main script. The first argument value is then stored in **$1**, the second argument value in **$2**, and so forth. Example 4-72 shows a script that has a function named **print_values()** that prints to stdout all numbers between the first and last arguments passed to it, inclusive.

Example 4-72 *The print_values() Function*

```
[NetProg@server1 Scripts]$ cat main-script.bash
#!/usr/bin/env bash

# function code starts here inside the main script
print_values() {
  for (( i=$1 ; i<=$2 ; i++))
  do
    echo -n "$i "
  done
  echo
}
# function code ends here  - still inside the main script

read -p "Please enter the first number and last number: " START END

print_values $START $END
```

The last two lines of the script request the user to input two values, which are assigned to the variables **START** and **END**. The values of these two variables are then passed to the function **print_values()** as arguments. The function uses the value of the first argument, **$1**, as the starting value of the variable **i** in the **for** loop, and the second argument, **$2**, to evaluate the condition. When the variable **i** is greater than the second argument, the **for** loop exits. The body of the loop simply prints out the value of the variable **i** at every loop iteration. The loop is evaluated in Example 4-73 using the values 1 and 10.

Example 4-73 *Running a Script Using 1 and 10 as the Two Arguments for the Function print_values()*

```
[NetProg@server1 Scripts]$ ./main-script.bash
Please enter the first number and last number: 1 10
1 2 3 4 5 6 7 8 9 10
```

When a function completes execution, it returns a value, called the *exit status*, to the calling script. By default, if the function executes successfully and without errors, the value of the exit status is zero. If some error occurs, the exit status returned is a non-zero value. The returned value is stored in **$?**. In Example 4-74, the command **echo $?** is added to the script, and the execution result shows that the value of **$?** is **0**.

Example 4-74 *Printing the Exit Status of the Function* **print_values()** *by Using $?*

```
[NetProg@server1 Scripts]$ cat main-script-1.bash
#!/usr/bin/env bash
print_values() {
  for (( i=$1 ; i<=$2 ; i++))
  do
    echo -n "$i "
  done
echo
}

read -p "Please enter the first number and last number: " START END

print_values $START $END

echo $? # Printing out the exit status

[NetProg@server1 Scripts]$ ./main-script-1.bash

Please enter the first number and last number: 1 10
1 2 3 4 5 6 7 8 9 10
0
```

You can change the exit status by using the command **return** *status_value*. In more complex scripts, you can use a conditional statement to return one of many possible exit status values to the script calling the function. Each value has a different meaning beyond just the simple success/fail of the function.

In Example 4-75, the script from Example 4-74 is updated with **return 100** so that **echo $?** prints out **100** instead of **0**.

Example 4-75 *Printing the Return Status of the Function **print_values()** by Using $?*

```
[NetProg@server1 Scripts]$ cat main-script-2.bash
#!/usr/bin/env bash
print_values() {
  for (( i=$1 ; i<=$2 ; i++))
  do
    echo -n "$i "
  done
echo
return 100
}

read -p "Please enter the first number and last number: " START END

print_values $START $END

echo $? # Returning a custom exit status instead of 0

[NetProg@server1 Scripts]$ ./main-script-2.bash
Please enter the first number and last number: 1 10
1 2 3 4 5 6 7 8 9 10
100
```

Variables inside a function block are, by default, global variables. A *global variable* is a variable that exists throughout the whole life of a script. A global variable retains its value and can be used anywhere in the script. The code block in which a variable is visible is called the *variable scope*. Alternatively, a local variable is visible only inside one specific code block, such as a function. In Example 4-75, the variable **i** used in the **for** loop is, by default, a global variable. In Example 4-76, the value of **i** is printed outside the function block, and as you can see, its value, **11**, is intact.

Example 4-76 *Printing the Value of The Global Variable **i** Outside The Function Where It Is Used*

```
[NetProg@server1 Scripts]$ ./main-script-3.bash
#!/usr/bin/env bash
print_values() {
  for (( i=$1 ; i<=$2 ; i++))
```

```
  do
    echo -n "$i "
  done
echo
}

read -p "Please enter the first number and last number: " START END

print_values $START $END

echo $i

[NetProg@server1 Scripts]$ ./main-script-3.bash
Please enter the first number and last number: 1 10
1 2 3 4 5 6 7 8 9 10
11
```

You can change a variable from global to local by using the **local** keyword to declare the variable. In Example 4-77, the variable **i** is declared as a local variable inside the function. When the function exits, **i** becomes an undeclared variable, and **echo $i** returns a null value.

Example 4-77 *Attempting to Print the Value of The Local Variable **i** Outside The Function Where It Is Declared*

```
[NetProg@server1 Scripts]$ cat main-script-4.bash
#!/usr/bin/env bash
print_values() {
local i
  for (( i=$1 ; i<=$2 ; i++))
  do
    echo -n "$i "
  done
echo
}

read -p "Please enter the first number and last number: " START END

print_values $START $END

echo $i

[NetProg@server1 Scripts]$ cat main-script-4.bash
Please enter the first number and last number: 1 10
1 2 3 4 5 6 7 8 9 10

[NetProg@server1 Scripts]$
```

Bash functions do not have the capability to return any values to the calling script apart from the exit status. Therefore, in order to transfer values from functions back to the calling script, you need to do one of three things: Either use global variables, which is *not* a recommended practice, or pipe the output produced by the function (such as the output of the **echo** command in the previous few examples) or alternatively, you can use the syntax *variable***=$(***function_name function_args***)** to assign the output produced by a function to a variable.

Expect

Expect is a programming language that streamlines and automates interactive operations. A very popular example of an interactive operation is providing a device with the required login credentials. This section does not cover the Expect language in detail, but it covers a number of commands that, when integrated with a Bash script, make interactive operations much easier to code. Four commonly used commands that are used to achieve this functionality are covered in this section: **spawn**, **expect**, **send**, and **interact**.

Much like a Bash script, an Expect script is run using an interpreter. By default, the Expect interpreter is not installed on CentOS 8 and can be installed by using the command **yum install expect** in admin mode. To invoke the Expect interpreter, you need to begin an Expect script with **#!usr/bin/env expect** and then provide the body of the script.

You use the **spawn** command to run another script, process, or utility. For example, **spawn ./somescript.bash** simply runs the script named **somescript.bash.** The command **spawn ssh 10.0.0.1** runs the **ssh** command to connect to IP address 10.0.0.1.

Examples 4-78 and 4-79 show how the **expect** and **send** commands work in an Expect script to "speak" to a Bash script. In Example 4-78, the Bash script expect-1.bash is used to read the first and last names of the user using the **read** command and then print out the user's full name by using the **echo** command. Earlier in this chapter, you learned that such input is typically provided by the user through **stdin** (the keyboard).

Example 4-78 *A Bash Script expect-1.bash Requesting Input from the User*

```
#!/usr/bin/env bash
read -p "Enter your firstname: " firstname
read -p "Enter your lastname: " lastname
echo "Your full name is $firstname $lastname"
```

However, in this case, there is no user. The user functionality will be emulated using an Expect script. In Example 4-79, an Expect script executes the Bash script shown in Example 4-78 by using the **spawn** command, and then *expects* the strings printed out by the Bash script using the **expect** command, and finally, sends the responses back to the Bash script by using the **send** command.

Example 4-79 *An Expect Script "Speaking" with the Bash Script from the Example 4-78*

```
#!/usr/bin/env expect
spawn ./expect-1.bash
expect "Enter your firstname: "
send "Khaled\r"
expect "Enter your lastname: "
send "Abuelenain\r"
expect eof
```

After it executes the Bash script **./expect-1.bash**, the Expect script waits for the string **"Enter your firstname: "** from the spawned (that is, executed) script, and when it receives it, it sends the string **"Khaled\r"**, which acts as input to the Bash script. Note that the **\r** escape character, which represents a carriage return, is the equivalent of pressing the Enter key. The same goes for the following **expect** and **send** commands. Finally, the last statement, **expect eof**, lets the Bash script run until the end of file (that is, the end of the Bash script) has been encountered, at which point the Expect script is complete, and control is passed back to the shell. Example 4-80 shows the result of running the Expect script.

Example 4-80 *The Result of Running the Expect Script*

```
[NetProg@server1 Scripts]$ ./expect-1.exp
spawn ./expect-1.bash
Enter your firstname: Khaled
Enter your lastname: Abuelenain
Your full name is Khaled Abuelenain
[NetProg@server1 Scripts]$
```

The **interact** command, on the other hand, lets the user interact with the spawned script. In Example 4-81, the Expect script from Example 4-80 has been amended to have the user enter his or her last name instead of sending a preset last name saved in the script.

Example 4-81 *Using the* ***interact*** *Command to Allow User Input to the Expect Script*

```
#!/usr/bin/env expect
spawn ./expect-1.bash
expect "Enter your firstname: "
send "Khaled\r"
expect "Enter your lastname: "
interact
```

Example 4-82 shows the result of running the script. Note that the last name **SomeOtherName** was entered manually from the keyboard.

Example 4-82 *Running the Script Using the* ***interact*** *Command and Entering the Last Name Manually from the Keyboard*

```
[NetProg@server1 Scripts]$ ./expect-1.exp
spawn ./expect-1.bash
Enter your firstname: Khaled
Enter your lastname: SomeOtherName
Your full name is Khaled SomeOtherName
[NetProg@server1 Scripts]$
```

Example 4-83 puts the Expect language to good use and shows a script that logs in to a public route server via Telnet, sends the username and password, and then issues the command **show ip route connected.** The script then hands over control to the user by using the **interact** command. However, if no input is received from the user within 10 seconds, the Expect script sends the command **exit** to the route server, ending the Telnet session.

Example 4-83 *Logging In to a Public Server by Using Expect and Collecting the Output of the Command* ***show ip route connected***

```
#!/usr/bin/env expect
log_file ip_route_connected
spawn telnet route-server.opentransit.net
expect "Username: "
send "rview\r"
expect "Password: "
send "Rview\r"
expect "OAKRS1#"
send "show ip route connected\r"
interact timeout 10 { send "exit\r" }
```

Example 4-84 shows the output that results from running the script shown in Example 4-83. The script sends the highlighted sections and the hidden password automatically, without user interaction.

Example 4-84 *The Result of Executing the Expect Script from Example 4-83*

```
[NetProg@server1 Scripts]$ ./expect-rview.exp
spawn telnet route-server.opentransit.net
Trying 204.59.3.38...
Connected to route-server.opentransit.net.
Escape character is '^]'.
C

&&&&&&&&&&&&&&&&&&&&&&&&&&&&&&&&&&&&&&&&&&&&&&&&&&&&&&&&&&&&&&&&&&&&&&&
         route-server.opentransit.net -- & Opentransit
                        IPv4/IPv6 views
```

```
This router keeps peering sessions with all the Opentransit Backbone Routers,
throughout the Opentransit IP Backbone as follows:

[IPv4/IPv6 view]

IPv4: 193.251.245.1          IPv6: 2001:688:0:1::158 Dallas
IPv4: 193.251.245.3          IPv6: 2001:688:0:1::1c  Los Angeles
IPv4: 193.251.245.7          IPv6: 2001:688:0:1::55  London
IPV4: 193.251.245.9          IPv6: 2001:688:0:1::41  Palo Alto
IPv4: 193.251.245.10         IPv6: 2001:688:0:1::4e  Paris
IPv4: 193.251.245.16         IPv6: 2001:688:0:1::168 New York
IPv4: 193.251.245.19         IPv6: 2001:688:0:1::4b  Barcelona
IPv4: 193.251.245.28         IPv6: 2001:688:0:1::8   Frankfurt
IPv4: 193.251.245.37         IPv6: 2001:688:0:1::    Frankfurt
IPv4: 193.251.245.49         IPv6: 2001:688:0:1::19  London
IPv4: 193.251.245.53         IPv6: 2001:688:0:1::1e  Chicago
IPv4: 193.251.245.57         IPv6: 2001:688:0:1::45  Miami
IPv4: 193.251.245.66         IPv6: 2001:688:0:1::44  Geneva
IPV4: 193.251.245.69         IPV6: 2001:688:0:1::56  Singapore
IPv4: 193.251.245.76         IPv6: 2001:688:0:1::d   New York
IPv4: 193.251.245.78         IPv6: 2001:688:0:1::22  Madrid
IPv4: 193.251.245.81         IPv6: 2001:688:0:1::4   Barcelona
IPv4: 193.251.245.88         IPv6: 2001:688:0:1::f   London
IPv4: 193.251.254.92         IPv6: 2001:688:0:1::24  Paris
IPv4: 193.251.245.96         IPv6: 2001:688:0:1::3E  Brussels
IPv4: 193.251.245.134        IPv6: 2001:688:0:1::4a  Zurich
IPv4: 193.251.245.147        IPv6: 2001:688:0:1::2A  HongKong
IPv4: 193.251.245.163        IPv6: 2001:688:0:1::18  New York
IPv4: 193.251.245.170        IPv6: 2001:688:0:1::2f  Madrid
IPv4: 193.251.245.181        IPv6: 2001:688:0:1::3C  Singapore
IPv4: 193.251.245.196        IPv6: 2001:688:0:1::57  Frankfurt
IPv4: 193.251.245.216        IPv6: 2001:688:0:1::16  Miami
IPv4: 193.251.245.251        IPv6: 2001:688:0:1::30  Amsterdam
IPv4: 193.251.245.252        IPv6: 2001:688:0:1::12  Ashburn

For questions about this route-server, send email to: opentransit.iptac@orange.com

*** Log in with username 'rviews', password 'Rviews' ***

User Access Verification

Username: rviews
Password:
OAKRS1#show ip route connected
```

```
Codes: L - local, C - connected, S - static, R - RIP, M - mobile, B - BGP
       D - EIGRP, EX - EIGRP external, O - OSPF, IA - OSPF inter area
       N1 - OSPF NSSA external type 1, N2 - OSPF NSSA external type 2
       E1 - OSPF external type 1, E2 - OSPF external type 2, m - OMP
       n - NAT, Ni - NAT inside, No - NAT outside, Nd - NAT DIA
       i - IS-IS, su - IS-IS summary, L1 - IS-IS level-1, L2 - IS-IS level-2
       ia - IS-IS inter area, * - candidate default, U - per-user static route
       H - NHRP, G - NHRP registered, g - NHRP registration summary
       o - ODR, P - periodic downloaded static route, l - LISP
       a - application route
       + - replicated route, % - next hop override, p - overrides from PfR

Gateway of last resort is 204.59.3.37 to network 0.0.0.0

      193.251.245.0/24 is variably subnetted, 7 subnets, 2 masks
C        193.251.245.248/32 is directly connected, Loopback0
      204.59.3.0/24 is variably subnetted, 2 subnets, 2 masks
C        204.59.3.36/30 is directly connected, GigabitEthernet0/0/0
L        204.59.3.38/32 is directly connected, GigabitEthernet0/0/0
OAKRS1#exit
Connection closed by foreign host.

[NetProg@server1 Scripts]$
```

Notice the command **log_file** right after the hashbang in Example 4-83. This command saves all output to the file **ip_route_connected**. If you issue the command **cat ip_route_connected**, you see an exact replay of everything that was output to stdout during the session, starting with the **spawn** command. The session log is appended to the log file every time the script is executed.

Summary

This chapter builds on what you have learned in Chapters 2 and 3, covering how to automate a series of tasks using the Bash shell scripting language. This chapter covers the following topics:

- **grep**
- **awk**
- **sed**
- Comments
- Input and output using the **echo**, **printf**, and **read** commands
- Passing arguments to shell scripts

- Executing system commands
- Variables: integers, strings, and constants
- Indexed and associative arrays
- Expansions, operations, and comparisons
- Conditional statements:
  - if-then-elif-then-else-fi
  - case-in-esac
- Looping constructs:
  - for-do-done loop
  - while-do-done loop
  - until-do-done loop
- Functions
- The Expect scripting language

At this point in the book, you have a fairly good grounding as a Linux professional. You can effectively manage a development environment based on Linux that you will need to run your automation scripts. You also know how to do basic management tasks for a network operating system that exposes a Linux shell, such as IOS XR, NX-OS, and IOS XE, as you will see in Chapters 17, "Programming Cisco Platforms," and 18, "Programming non-Cisco Platforms." The rest of this book revisits Linux quite often, and as you progress through the chapters, the applications of Linux in network programmability will become more and more evident.

Chapter 5

Python Fundamentals

Computer programming has gained a lot of popularity in past three decades, but what exactly is programming? Computers were designed to take sets of instructions from humans and perform those tasks. For instance, users can instruct a computer to perform a series of calculations on the numbers that can be defined statically or via user input. A computer is instructed to perform calculations via programming. Thus, *programming* can be defined as instructing a computer to perform various tasks. The complexities of the tasks can vary based on what a user is trying to achieve. A task may be as simple as performing some basic mathematical operations such as addition or subtraction between two numbers or as complex as rendering and clearing the noise in an image.

If programming is instructing a computer to perform various tasks, what is a program? A computer software *program* is a specific set of ordered instructions for a computer to perform. To conceptualize a software program, think of the process of preparing tea. A person has to go through a set of steps (instructions) in order to prepare tea. The steps may vary from person to person based on the kind of tea being made, but some steps always remain the same. For instance, the following steps can be followed to prepare tea:

1. Boil the water.
2. Add tea leaves and the hot water to a tea pot and wait 3–4 minutes.
3. Pour the brewed tea into cups.
4. Add sugar and milk to each cup, as needed.

Steps 1 to 3 are common to most styles of preparing tea, but only a person who prefers sweetened tea or milk tea needs to follow step 4. As you can see, the steps for preparing tea need to be followed in a particular order. The same goes for a computer program. Let us take a simple example of reversing a string, a task that can be done in different ways. Example 5-1 shows a function for calculating the sum of the first n integers. In this example, the integer n is passed as a parameter to the **sum()** function. This function iterates through all the integers from 1 to n, starting from 0 and adding the integer at the ith position to the sum of 1 up to $i - 1$ integers. The iteration of integers from 1 to n is done via a **for** loop. (**for** loops are explained later in this chapter.)

Example 5-1 *Python Function to Return the Sum of the First* n *Integers*

```
def sum(n: int):
    sum = 0
    for i in range (1, n+1):
        sum = sum + i
    return sum
```

Why do you need to perform this task programmatically when a human can do it by hand quickly and also apply better mathematical formulas to get to the result? Keep in mind that Example 5-1 demonstrates a function that calculates the sum of the first *n* integers. This task is easy when *n* is a smaller integer, but it gets more time-consuming and complex when the value of *n* is higher, such as the integer value 998,786. With a large integer like 998,786, performing the task manually is definitely going to be time-consuming and involve a substantial chance of human error. Performing tasks programmatically reduces or even eliminates the chance of human error, especially with tasks that are repetitive and complex. A program essentially needs only sound logic and an optimized series of steps.

Scripting Languages Versus Programming Languages

Before we dive into network programmability, it is important to understand the difference between scripting languages and programming languages. Engineers are often confused about the difference between scripting languages and programming languages. Simply put, *programming languages* are languages that need a compiler to convert their code into native machine code, whereas *scripting languages* are interpreted instead of being compiled into machine code. Because the code is compiled into machine code, programming languages run faster compared to scripting languages.

Scripting is a subset of programming that is primarily focused on automating the execution of tasks. These tasks can be some machine-level tasks (system tasks) or user-defined tasks that are usually developed through programming logic. A task can be simply defined as a procedure that is nothing but a set of steps; in order for a computer to perform a task, a procedure must be defined. In the earlier example of preparing a cup of tea, the task was to prepare the tea, and the steps laid out the procedure. As stated previously, scripting languages are interpreted, which means they require an interpreter to convert their code into native machine code. Scripting languages can also be used for the purpose of extracting data from a data set. Some common examples of scripting languages are JavaScript, Perl, and Python.

Let's look at an example of web application development. In end-to-end web application development, there are primarily three layers for which development occurs:

- **Front end:** The front end involves everything a user sees in a browser and is primarily a combination of Hypertext Markup Language (HTML), CSS, and JavaScript.
- **Middleware:** The middleware or middle layer is where you define the logic or create APIs to allow the front end to interact with the back end. For instance, a web application to gather registration information from users as input would be sent to the

middleware, and the middleware would make a call to the database or the back end to store the data.

- **Back end:** The back end either consists of server-side scripts or databases. The server-side scripts process the data and return a response based on the processed data to the front-end clients.

Figure 5-1 illustrates the layers in a typical web application.

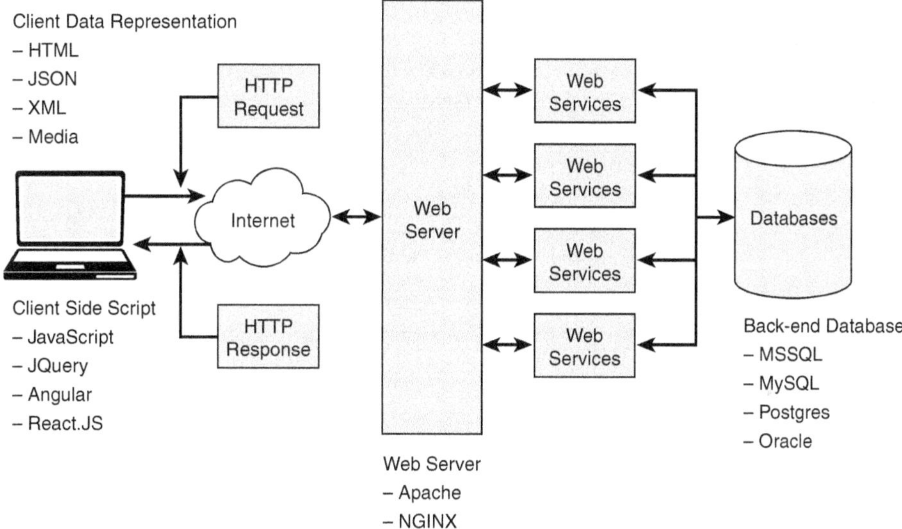

Figure 5-1 *Typical Web Application Layers*

The use of scripting languages such as JavaScript in the front end helps in performing validations on user input, whereas back-end programming logic tells the application what it needs to do with the data it received from the front-end user interface. The validation of front-end input data helps ensure that the back-end logic or database does not return an error due to an invalid data type or data format. The automation of front-end validation through scripting saves a lot of time and resources during data processing. If there were no validation happening in the front end, a software developer would have to write the validator and its logic in the back-end code, which would put more load on the server processing the data. If the data were already validated before being received by the back-end application, the back-end code would just focus on performing the task to store or update the data in the database.

In contrast to scripting languages, programming languages are compiled into a more compact standalone form that is machine consumable. A programming language consists of three primary components:

- Pseudocode (that is, human-readable code)
- Compiler
- Machine-readable compiled code

Pseudocode allows programmers to write their logic in an easily readable and understandable format. The pseudocode is then compiled by the compiler into a machine-readable format. A computer system understands or processes data in binary or assembly code. Most compilers compile the code into assembly code, which can be executed. For example, a typical C program goes through a series of transformations and optimizations before being executed in hardware. The source code file is processed through the C compiler (for instance, gcc) and transforms the pseudocode into an ASCII-based assembly file, which is then converted by an assembler into an object file. The object file is then processed via a linker and converted into an executable file, which loads the program into the memory of the system when executed. In this process, the end result is an executable file (.exe), which is machine consumable. Figure 5-2 illustrates the process of compiling C language pseudocode into a machine-understandable executable file.

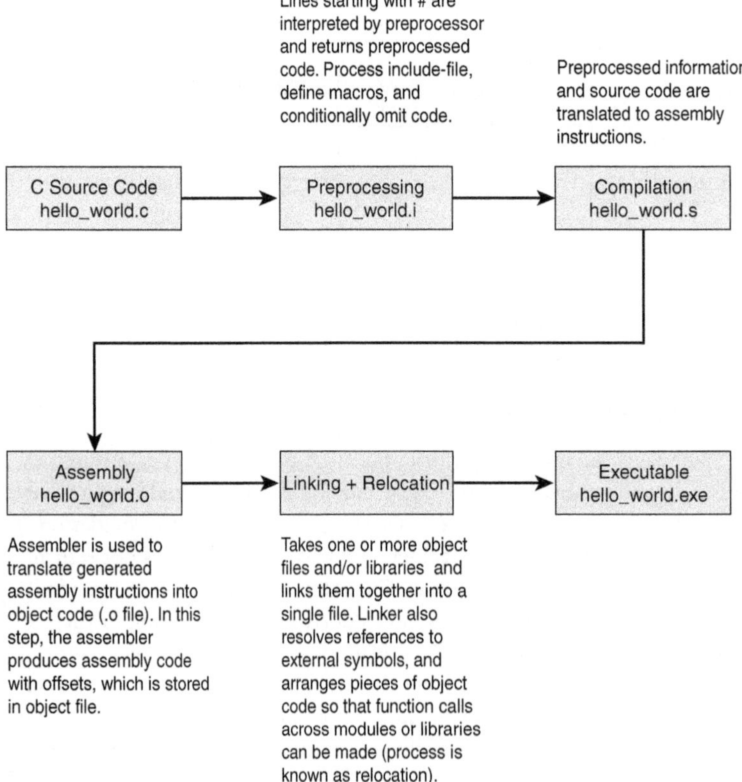

Figure 5-2 *Compiling C into an Executable File*

With programming languages, the complete pseudocode is compiled into native machine code at once. So, when a program is executed, memory allocation occurs for the whole program, regardless of whether a function is being called within the code. This is one of the reasons a scripting language may make more efficient use of system resources during execution, as the memory allocation happens only for the function calls that are made by the user. Some examples of well-known programming languages are C, C++, and Java. Most programming languages can also be used for accessing low-level hardware details, which is not directly possible via scripting languages. The different capabilities of the scripting and programming languages easily help developers identify their respective use cases.

Network Programmability

Now that you understand the need for programming, you might wonder how programming helps with network devices. For many years, network infrastructure components were manually configured, using laborious, monotonous techniques (such as using the CLI) that are prone to human error. Over the years, the demand for network and service availability across the network has changed, as has the infrastructure. Organizations now demand event-driven reactive action to mitigate network outages in order to minimize downtime. Manually performing tasks to maintain high availability of network services is neither scalable nor cost-effective. Automation and programmable network devices can cost-effectively provide the network availability and scalability needed in today's networks.

Note When we talk about network programmability and its benefits, it's important to understand that we are automating the management plane and not changing the control plane or data plane behavior.

Network programmability refers to the ability to alter the way in which network devices were traditionally managed and control flow via the software that is operated independently from the network hardware. Using network programmability, network engineers can easily reconfigure the network infrastructure at scale. Providing programmable open interfaces allows organizations and service providers to keep pace with the rapid demands of business services.

Network programmability may be used, for example, in scenarios where a network engineer needs to automate the configuration of a large number of devices or validate the software or firmware version for device upgrades or dynamic provisioning of services such as adding a new MPLS VPN customer or enable traffic shaping functionality across the network. Programmable networks have many benefits, including the following:

- **Reduced operational expenses (opex):** According to industry estimates, the major cost in any given enterprise or data center is the cost of technical personnel required to manage the infrastructure. Hardware expenses have been declining over the years, but the cost to manage the infrastructure has been growing steadily. Automating infrastructure management and service deployment reduces the time an IT professional needs to spend on a day-to-day basis and also the number of IT professionals who need to be engaged. Automation therefore reduces opex and also saves a lot of time and reduces human error.

- **Customization:** Network programmability makes it possible to customize the management plane of network devices based on an organization's business requirements. This in turn helps the organization increase its productivity and speed up its service delivery timeline. Customization of device behavior allows for faster turnaround time and makes it possible to monetize the network quickly. By writing custom automation tools and scripts, network engineers can identify network issues quickly and also automate the solutions to fix those network issues—thus making the network self-healing.
- **Reduced human error:** Even today, most network engineers and IT teams use manual methods for provisioning services. Despite the use of approved change or maintenance windows, configuration changes may be prone to errors and may lead to outages. Automating tasks reduces the chance of typos and other errors and leads to better and faster service delivery.
- **Increased opportunity for innovation:** When automation and programmability are in place and most of the routine elements are taken care of, IT engineers have more time and resources to innovate and come up with ideas to solve complex networking problems.
- **Operational flexibility:** Network programmability not only provides an opportunity for innovation but also adds to operational flexibility by freeing up resources. Where there were once multiple resources required to perform a task, with network automation and programmability, fewer resources are required for the task. Programmability thus provides flexibility for the operations team to spends its resources performing other tasks.

A programmable network device allows a user to perform changes in the network by using remote software and application programming interfaces (APIs). An API acts as a middle layer that enables communication between a front-end application and the back end. In terms of a network, the back end is the network device hardware to which changes are made. APIs enable network engineers to make changes to a scaled environment using a programming language such as Python or Java. The front-end application, such as a Python application, connects to the devices and uses the open APIs on those devices to make the changes, eliminating the need for manual intervention.

Two terms confuse many people: network programming and network programmability. *Network programming* is a field of programming that deals with socket programming (that is, programming for Layer 3 and Layer 4 protocols). Through network programming, users can interact with TCP and UDP protocols, send and receive data, maintain connections/sessions, or even create their own networking protocols. *Network programmability*, on the other hand, is the ability to interact with the base network operating system and leverage its APIs to make changes to the device, monitor the device, or enhance an existing feature. The capability of a programmable network is limited to what the network operating system allows you to do with it. Modern network operating systems are designed with open APIs, which allow users to modify the behavior of the system or automate its tasks.

Computer Science Concepts

Many companies, universities, and individuals have defined computer science in various ways. What exactly is computer science? In order to understand the science behind computers, let's take an example of humans. When a baby is born, it has no skill set or predefined instructions. Over a period of time, a baby is transformed into a full-grown adult who is capable of thinking and making decisions, taking actions, performing tasks, and so on. This is all made possible through language. During the phases of the transformation to adulthood, a person learns language—at least a first language and potentially other languages, such as sign language or a second language taught as part of schooling—and the language or languages help the person understand other people. The person needs to understand language in order to understand other individuals speaking that language and learn as well as adapt to the environment of people around them.

In order to be useful to humans, computers must be able to perform the tasks humans want them to perform. A computer that is unable to perform a task is of no use to a person. A human can use a programming language to make computers understand what tasks to perform. *Computer science* is the art of teaching a computer what to do and how to do it.

Like a spoken language, a programming language has fundamental building blocks. Each programming language has its own set of paradigms and libraries that help achieve functionalities as basic as how to take input and how to print the output and what writing format to use. A programmer has to learn the basics before it is possible to advance to a level where he or she can create a set of instruction sets and libraries for the computers to achieve various tasks. Using libraries, a computer learns how a user wants it to perform a certain task. When a computer uses a library to understand tasks, the computer knows exactly what it needs to do and how it needs to do it.

Computers are not capable of understanding the language of code. With human language, translators bridge the gap between those who speak two different languages. Similarly, computers and humans understand different languages: Computers understand machine language, and humans understand pseudocode. Much as with human languages, computer languages require translators: In order to make a computer understand pseudocode, a compiler acts as a translator, converting pseudocode into machine-understandable code.

Over the years, as the community of developers and programmers grew, the community came to need a set of rules to ensure that code follows certain standards. Maintaining and following coding standards helps reduce the complexity of the code and, therefore, the number of errors. When followed, coding standards also help keep code consistent and make it easier to manage code, thus making the code easy to understand and allowing other developers to build on top of the existing code. One set of coding standards is the object-oriented programming (OOP) paradigm.

Object-Oriented Programming

The OOP paradigm took shape from a new approach to programming that started around 1960, when the first object-oriented language, Simula, was developed by the researchers at the Norwegian Computing Center. In 1970, Alan Kay and his research team developed the first pure OOP language, Smalltalk. Over the next couple decades, more articles about object-oriented design and methods were published.

Before starting to build any software application, it is important to understand its requirements and lay down the fundamental building blocks of the application. Each block in an object-oriented architecture is treated as an object. In the OOP paradigm, an object is used to represent a real-life entity or phenomenon. Thus, in the initial phase of building a software application, it is important to lay down all the objects and model them in a way that helps a computer system understand how any two objects will interact with each other. The process of identifying or gathering software requirements and developing specifications in terms of a system's object model and interactions is known as *object-oriented analysis* (OOA). The objects are integrated with both data and functions that describe the properties of the objects and also the method by which two objects can communicate; this is computer modeling.

Modeling can also be understood as the process of representing real-world objects as a set of mathematical equations or expressions. These equations help us understand how the interaction between objects is going to happen. This modeling technique is not just used for representing the objects and their interactions but also in the field of simulations. Most of the simulation software applications out there use computer modeling to analyze outcomes for different scenarios. These scenarios can be based on different mathematical equations, laws of physics, and so on. For instance, a road accident model might simulate the impact on each structural member in an automobile while also simulating the total amount of energy consumed by one moving mass colliding with another.

When the requirements are gathered and the model has been created for the software application, the next phase is to start writing code and bringing the application to life. This is where OOP comes into play. OOP is a programming paradigm that is based on objects and aims to incorporate advantages such as modularity and reusability. In OOP, a class is a user-defined extensible code template that is used for creating an object and providing initial values for member variables for initializing the states and also for implementing behaviors using functions or methods. The behavior and properties of an object are defined within a class, which can then be used as the object. In addition to revolving around objects and classes, OOP has a strong foundation built on the following primary concepts:

- **Inheritance:** *Inheritance* allows objects to inherit the properties of existing objects. A class that is used as the basis for inheritance is called a superclass or base class or parent class, and a class that inherits from a superclass is called a derived class or subclass. Using inheritance, a subclass can access the properties and functions of the base class and can also override those functions or properties. For example, a class named Surgeon is inherited from a class named Doctor. In this case, a member of Surgeon will be a member of Doctor, but a member of Doctor may not be a member of Surgeon. There are different levels and ways to implement inheritance in programming languages. Some of them are as follows:

  - **Single inheritance:** In single inheritance, a class is inherited from just its parent class.
  - **Multiple inheritance:** In multiple inheritance, a class is derived from more than one parent class; that is, the subclass or child class inherits features from multiple parent classes.
  - **Multi-level inheritance:** In this type of inheritance, a class is inherited from a child class. For example, class C is inherited from a derived class B, which is inherited from parent class A.
  - **Hierarchical inheritance:** Hierarchical inheritance comes into play when multiple child classes or subclasses inherit properties from the same parent class.

- **Polymorphism:** *Polymorphism* means a state of having many forms or shapes. In the context of OOP, polymorphism refers to the ability of the language to process objects differently based on their data types. In the context of a programming language, polymorphism represents multiple implementations of a method or function but with different parameters. Based on the parameters (which may or may not be of different data types), the implementation of the function is made different.
- **Abstraction:** *Abstraction* is one of the most fundamental concepts of OOP languages. Abstraction is a method or process of hiding unnecessary details of an object from the user and revealing only the relevant data or features. For instance, while making coffee using a coffee machine, the inner process of the coffee machine is hidden from the user. The coffee machine only takes input of coffee, water, and milk and, based on the type of coffee selected, it yields the prepared coffee to the user, hiding the unnecessary or unwanted details from the user. Similarly, the inner functionality of an object class should not be revealed; only the functions and properties of the class are revealed. For example, when a user tries to log in to a web portal, the authentication mechanism of the portal is hidden from the user. Based on the input on the login page, the user is either successfully authenticated or denied access.
- **Encapsulation:** Whereas abstraction is all about hiding the implementation, *encapsulation* deals with hiding information. Encapsulation allows users to hide or restrict access to some of the components of the objects to the outside world. It means that the internal representation of an object is hidden from outside view. OOP languages allow various levels of restrictions that can be applied to restrict the accessibility of object components from other classes or functions outside the class.

Object-oriented programming languages include C++, Java, C#, Python, Ruby, and PHP.

Algorithms

A computer *algorithm* can be thought of as a recipe or procedure with precise steps to be followed by a computer in order to achieve a goal or solve a problem. Algorithms are the science behind computer science. They are the building blocks in making a computer do tasks the way you want it to. If programmers know or can create some optimal algorithms and know when to apply them, they can develop very useful and robust software applications. Sometimes a very complex and efficient algorithm can be developed by integrating multiple simple or complex algorithms into one. The procedure described in an algorithm is considered most optimal or useful when the task can be completed with the minimal number of steps and by consuming the fewest resources in the system.

To understand how to write algorithms, let's take an example of an algorithm to reverse a string. In order to achieve the goal of reversing a string, you might think of an algorithm or procedure. There are multiple ways to achieve the task, but let's consider using these two algorithms:

- Using loops:
  1. Create a temporary variable, such as rstr, with an empty string. Note that adding a new symbol or character to the variable means that you are creating a new string variable.
  2. List each character of the input string by splitting the string.
  3. Run a loop beginning with the first character of the string and continuing to the end.
  4. At each iteration, add (append) rstr to the current character and assign the value to rstr.
  5. When the loop is complete, return the value of rstr. This value will be your reversed string.
- Using a recursive lookup:
  1. Create a function named reverse with a base condition to return the string if the length of the string is 0.
  2. If the length is not 0, the function is recursively called to slice the string except for the first character. (Slicing is described shortly.)
  3. The first character is concatenated to the end of the sliced string.

With slicing, three values are taken into account:

- Start index
- Stop index
- Step

Using these three values, a slicing function is created to iterate through the string by beginning with the starting index within the string and enumerating the characters in the string with the value of step until it reaches the stop index. For instance, say that the string apple is to be sliced from the starting index of 1 and ending index of 4 with a step value of 1; the sliced string value will be ppl. Note that in most programming languages, a string starts with an index value of 0. Thus, with the string apple, index 1 is the character p, and index 4 is character e. Thus, slicing will start with character p and return characters until the slicing reaches e. As soon as it reaches index 4, it will stop and not include that index as part of the sliced string.

In the earlier example of reversing a string, two different algorithms were used to achieve the reversed string, and both of those methods work for the task. Which one you use depends on which one is more optimized for a particular scenario. By comparing the execution times and resources required for various algorithms, you can determine how well the algorithms are written and decide which one to use.

Note To measure the execution time of a process, a program, or a command, you can use the GNU **time** program on Linux or UNIX machines. Example 5-2 shows the execution times for the two string-reversing algorithms mentioned previously (written in Python code). The GNU **time** program displays three values:

- **real:** The total execution time taken by the command or program
- **user:** The total execution time taken by the command or program in user mode
- **sys:** The total execution time taken by the command or program in kernel mode

Example 5-2 *Execution Times of Different Algorithms*

```
root@rnd-srvr:~/python# /usr/bin/time -f "\t%E real,\t%U user,\t%S sys"
  ./first.py
        0:00.04 real,   0.03 user,      0.00 sys
```

```
root@rnd-srvr:~/python# /usr/bin/time -f "\t%E real,\t%U user,\t%S sys"
  ./second.py
        0:00.04 real,   0.04 user,      0.00 sys
```

You can also use the **-v** option to display more detailed (verbose) information about the execution.

To build algorithms in any programming language, programmers have to define and use various data structures and data types to perform actions on the particular kind of data. Unless a program knows what kind of data it is dealing with, it cannot perform the correct operation on the data, thus making the program either useless or error prone. We discuss data structures and data types further in the next section.

Python Fundamentals

Python is an easy-to-learn, easy-to-use, and powerful programming language that allows easy integration with other programming languages. In fact, the first words of the official Python tutorial were "Python is an easy to learn, powerful programming language." Python, which was created in 1991, was named for the British comedy group Monty Python. Over the years since then, so much development has gone into Python that there are now more than 190,000 Python packages, and many of them are incredibly useful. Python is being used to create web applications, artificial intelligence applications, data science applications, and scientific applications.

The following are some of the core features that make Python one of the most powerful languages:

- **Easy to learn:** Even if you are a complete beginner and have not learned any programming language before, with Python, you can hit the ground running once you have learned the basics, which are fairly simple to understand. You just need to build the logic, know the basics, and get familiar with Python syntax.
- **Easy to integrate:** Python can easily integrate with third-party applications and also with code written in different programming languages. This integration makes it possible to reuse existing code (even code written in different languages) and helps reduce application development time.
- **Platform independent:** With Python, users don't have to write code based on the platform. Using Python, developers create cross-platform applications that can be seamlessly used without the burden of recompiling the code between platforms.
- **Powerful:** Thanks to the massive repository of available Python packages, you can import the necessary package and perform extremely complex data analysis in minutes—or even seconds. The many available packages create endless possibilities for what you can do with your data; this is one reason Python is popular in data science and machine learning.

There are two well-known versions of Python: Python 2 and Python 3. Python 2 reached end-of-life on January 1, 2020. Multiple branches of Python 3 are available to developers for download, including 3.6, 3.7, 3.8, and 3.9. (At the time of writing, the latest versions of Python 3 are 3.6.12, 3.7.9, 3.8.6, and 3.9.1.) Many Python 2 applications are still running, but because it is end-of-life, this chapter focuses on Python 3. However, most of the content in this chapter is still relevant to Python 2.

Python Installation

You can download and install Python at www.python.org/downloads. You can download the relevant installer for your operating system and then follow the installation steps in order to install Python. The distribution that you download from the www.python.org

website is the standard distribution; that is, it has the standard package that comes with Python by default. To install additional packages, you have to use the Python package manager named **pip**, which is based on Python 2, or **pip3**, which is based on Python 3. The **pip** or **pip3** package manager makes it a lot easier to install or uninstall or even roll back packages in the event of any instability. You can install packages by using the command **pip install** *package_name*. Once this command is executed, the specified package is downloaded, along with its dependencies. Example 5-3 illustrates the installation of a **pip3** package manager on CentOS using the command **yum install -y python3** and the **numpy** package using the **pip3** package manager.

Example 5-3 *pip3 Installation and Package Installation*

```
[root@rnd-srvr ~]# yum install -y python3
Loaded plugins: fastestmirror
Loading mirror speeds from cached hostfile
 * base: repos-lax.psychz.net
 * extras: mirror.sjc02.svwh.net
 * updates: mirror.sjc02.svwh.net
base                                                      | 3.6 kB     00:00
docker-ce-stable                                          | 3.5 kB     00:00
extras                                                    | 2.9 kB     00:00
updates                                                   | 2.9 kB     00:00
Resolving Dependencies
--> Running transaction check
---> Package python3.x86_64 0:3.6.8-10.el7 will be installed
--> Processing Dependency: python3-libs(x86-64) = 3.6.8-10.el7 for package:
  python3-3.6.8-10.el7.x86_64
--> Processing Dependency: python3-setuptools for package: python3-3.6.8-
  10.el7.x86_64
--> Processing Dependency: python3-pip for package: python3-3.6.8-10.el7.x86_64
--> Processing Dependency: libpython3.6m.so.1.0()(64bit) for package:
  python3-3.6.8-10.el7.x86_64
--> Running transaction check
---> Package python3-libs.x86_64 0:3.6.8-10.el7 will be installed
---> Package python3-pip.noarch 0:9.0.3-5.el7 will be installed
---> Package python3-setuptools.noarch 0:39.2.0-10.el7 will be installed
--> Finished Dependency Resolution

Dependencies Resolved

================================================================================
 Package                Arch          Version               Repository    Size
================================================================================
 Installing:
 python3                x86_64        3.6.8-10.el7          base          69 k
```

```
Installing for dependencies:
 python3-libs              x86_64        3.6.8-10.el7         base          7.0 M
 python3-pip               noarch        9.0.3-5.el7          base          1.8 M
 python3-setuptools        noarch        39.2.0-10.el7        base          629 k

Transaction Summary
================================================================================
Install  1 Package (+3 Dependent packages)

Total download size: 9.4 M
Installed size: 48 M
Downloading packages:
(1/4): python3-libs-3.6.8-10.el7.x86_64.rpm                 | 7.0 MB   00:06
(2/4): python3-pip-9.0.3-5.el7.noarch.rpm                   | 1.8 MB   00:00
(3/4): python3-setuptools-39.2.0-10.el7.noarch.rpm          | 629 kB   00:00
(4/4): python3-3.6.8-10.el7.x86_64.rpm                      |  69 kB   00:08
--------------------------------------------------------------------------------
Total                                              1.1 MB/s | 9.4 MB   00:08
Running transaction check
Running transaction test
Transaction test succeeded
Running transaction
  Installing : python3-libs-3.6.8-10.el7.x86_64                             1/4
  Installing : python3-3.6.8-10.el7.x86_64                                  2/4
  Installing : python3-setuptools-39.2.0-10.el7.noarch                      3/4
  Installing : python3-pip-9.0.3-5.el7.noarch                               4/4
  Verifying  : python3-setuptools-39.2.0-10.el7.noarch                      1/4
  Verifying  : python3-libs-3.6.8-10.el7.x86_64                             2/4
  Verifying  : python3-3.6.8-10.el7.x86_64                                  3/4
  Verifying  : python3-pip-9.0.3-5.el7.noarch                               4/4

Installed:
  python3.x86_64 0:3.6.8-10.el7

Dependency Installed:
  python3-libs.x86_64 0:3.6.8-10.el7          python3-pip.noarch 0:9.0.3-5.el7
  python3-setuptools.noarch 0:39.2.0-10.el7

Complete!
```

```
[root@rnd-srvr ~]# pip3 install numpy
```

```
Collecting numpy
  Downloading
  https://files.pythonhosted.org/packages/92/e6/45f71bd24f4e37629e9db5fb75caab919507
  deae6a5a257f9e4685a5f931/numpy-1.18.0-cp36-cp36m-manylinux1_x86_64.whl (20.1MB)

! Output omitted for brevity

Installing collected packages: numpy
Successfully installed numpy-1.18.0
```

Note The **easy_install** package manager works the same way as **pip**, although it is less widely used than **pip**.

You can also use distributions known as the scientific distributions to install Python (for example, Anaconda, Canopy, WinPython). These distributions not only install Python but also install some additional useful packages that can be useful for data scientists or machine learning programmers. Also, these distributions come with additional tools and integrated development environments (IDEs).

As a beginner, you can install the standard distribution, and when you are comfortable with Python, you may want to work with an advanced distribution.

Python Code Execution

The major difference between programming languages like C or C++ and Python is that Python is an interpreted language, whereas C and C++ are compiled languages. *Compiled languages* are languages in which pseudocode gets compiled into machine code, which is executed directly on a computer's processor. Unlike compiled languages, interpreted languages are not translated into machine code beforehand. Rather, translation happens at runtime. Python is a scripting language, and when the code is executed, it is converted into bytecode. The bytecode is interpreted by the Python interpreter and is then executed line by line. If you are compiling Python code, the .py file (the source code file) is compiled into bytecode and saved with the .pyc extension. The .pyc file, when executed, follows the same line-by-line execution. Before we get further into the compilation of Python code, however we need to talk about how Python works internally.

Python code is read by a parser. The Python parser takes input in the form of a token stream. Before Python code is executed, it goes through the following steps:

- **Tokenizer:** Converts Python code into a token stream.
- **Lexical analyzer:** Takes care of useful spaces and indentation in the pseudocode. All the syntax validation happens here.

- **Bytecode generator:** Generates bytecode for the Python code and performs optimization, if any.
- **Bytecode interpreter:** Interprets the bytecode stream and also maintains the state of the Python execution environment.

Once the bytecode is generated, it is cached in memory. For instance, if there is a recursive call to a function in the code, the program skips tokenization, lexical analysis, and bytecode generation for code that Python has already loaded into memory. Although it might seem like this process would be fast and would save time on repetition of steps, it is still slower than an application compiled into a machine code.

Note The default and most widely used implementation of Python, which is written in C and Python, is called CPython.

Eventually we will dive in to the Python compilation and execution processes, but for now we will take time to examine some Python code. Python code can be run in an interpreter or can be saved in a file with .py extension and then run using the **python** or **python3** executable with the filename as the parameter.

Example 5-4 shows a simple Python program. In this example, a file named first.py, which prints text to standard output using the built-in **print()** function, is created. The command **python3 first.py** is then used to execute the Python code. One way to test or write Python code is directly into the interpreter. This method is useful when programmers want to do a quick validation of their logic and code. To get into the interpreter, you use the command **python** or **python3** to invoke the interpreter and allow user input. Example 5-4 illustrates how to print the text on the standard output device using the interpreter.

Example 5-4 *A Simple Python Program*

```
[root@rnd-srvr python]# ls
first.py
[root@rnd-srvr python]# cat first.py
print("Hello, This is my first Python application")

root@rnd-srvr:~/python# python3 first.py
Hello, This is my first Python application
```

```
[root@rnd-srvr python]# python3
Python 3.6.8 (default, Jan 14 2019, 11:02:34)
[GCC 8.0.1 20180414 (experimental) [trunk revision 259383]] on linux
Type "help", "copyright", "credits" or "license" for more information.
>>>
>>> print("Hello, This is my first Python application")
Hello, This is my first Python application
```

An alternate way to run a Python program written in a .py file is to add an entry to set the executable within the file by using a shebang—for example, **#!/bin/python** or **#!/bin/python3**. This method is primarily used for portability of the application and ensures that when the file is executed, the application specified in the shebang is invoked. Example 5-5 illustrates the use of a shebang in the Python code file and the use of the **chmod linux** command to add execute permissions to the file. The file is then executed using the syntax *./path-to-file*. After it is executed, the validation time of the code is checked by using the GNU **time** application (on a Linux system).

Example 5-5 *Executable Python File*

```
[root@rnd-srvr python]# cat first.py
#!/bin/python3

print("Hello, This is my first Python application")

! Use the chmod linux command to give execute permissions to the file.
[root@rnd-srvr python]# chmod +x first.py
[root@rnd-srvr python]# ./first.py
Hello, This is my first Python application

[root@rnd-srvr python]# time ./first.py
Hello, This is my first Python application

real    0m0.025s
user    0m0.019s
sys     0m0.006s
```

Note In Linux or UNIX-like operating systems, . (a dot, or period) represents the current directory. When the goal is to run the executable file in the current directory and the directory is not in **$PATH**, prepending ./ to the filename tells the shell where the executable is.

As mentioned earlier, Python code is compiled into bytecode. The Python bytecode is a lower-level and platform-independent representation of the source code. The bytecode is interpreted via the Python interpreter and converted into machine code at runtime; if a particular section of code is not called in the program, it is not interpreted from bytecode to machine code. Usually, when a user executes a Python code in the interpreter, the process does not create precompiled bytecode by default. The process happens all in memory.

In order to precompile Python pseudocode into bytecode, you can import a package named **py_compile**. This package has a function named **compile(*filename*)** that takes the filename as the parameter and compiles it into a bytecode file with a .pyc extension and saves it in the **__pycache__** directory in the local path where the pseudocode file is present. The bytecode is then executed by the appropriate virtual machine. The virtual machine is the runtime environment of Python and is always present as part of the Python system. The bytecode file, which is not in readable format (at least not completely), can then be passed on to the Python application for further execution, as shown in Example 5-6.

Example 5-6 *Using the py_compile library to Compile Python Code*

```
[root@rnd-srvr python]# python3
Python 3.6.8 (default, Jan 14 2019, 11:02:34)
[GCC 8.0.1 20180414 (experimental) [trunk revision 259383]] on linux
Type "help", "copyright", "credits" or "license" for more information.
>>>
>>> import py_compile
>>> py_compile.compile("first.py")
'__pycache__/first.cpython-36.pyc'
>>> exit()

[root@rnd-srvr python]# ls
first.py   __pycache__
[root@rnd-srvr python]# cd __pycache__/
[root@rnd-srvr __pycache__]# ls
first.cpython-36.pyc

[root@rnd-srvr __pycache__]# cat first.cpython-36.pyc
3
Ãb]5„n@s
        edÉ□□d□S)□z*Hello, This is my first Python applicationN)□/print©r□r□first.
  py<module>□s

[root@rnd-srvr __pycache__]# python3 first.cpython-36.pyc
Hello, This is my first Python application
```

Note If you receive a .pyc file (a bytecode file) and you want to decode the bytecode to pseudocode, you can install the package named **uncompyle6** by using the command **pip3 install uncompyle6**. Once it is installed, you can use the command **uncompyle6 -o** ***your_filename*.pyc** to create a .py file from the .pyc file.

Each time the Python interpreted program is executed, the interpreter converts the bytecode into machine code and pulls in the runtime libraries. This can be viewed by using the **-v** or **-verbose** option with the Python interpreted program. Example 5-7 illustrates the use of the **-verbose** option when running the first.py Python program. Notice that, initially, multiple system or runtime libraries are imported. When the import process is complete, the Python runtime environment moves to interpreter mode and executes the code. When the code execution is completed, the runtime cleanup process is initiated to dispose of or destroy all the resources from the memory.

Example 5-7 *Python Code Execution*

```
[root@rnd-srvr python]# python3 -v first.py
import _frozen_importlib # frozen
import _imp # builtin
import sys # builtin
import '_warnings' # <class '_frozen_importlib.BuiltinImporter'>
import '_thread' # <class '_frozen_importlib.BuiltinImporter'>
import '_weakref' # <class '_frozen_importlib.BuiltinImporter'>
import '_frozen_importlib_external' # <class '_frozen_importlib.FrozenImporter'>
import '_io' # <class '_frozen_importlib.BuiltinImporter'>
import 'marshal' # <class '_frozen_importlib.BuiltinImporter'>
import 'posix' # <class '_frozen_importlib.BuiltinImporter'>
import _thread # previously loaded ('_thread')
import '_thread' # <class '_frozen_importlib.BuiltinImporter'>
import _weakref # previously loaded ('_weakref')
import '_weakref' # <class '_frozen_importlib.BuiltinImporter'>
# installing zipimport hook
import 'zipimport' # <class '_frozen_importlib.BuiltinImporter'>
# installed zipimport hook
# /usr/lib/python3.6/encodings/__pycache__/__init__.cpython-36.pyc matches /usr/lib/
  python3.6/encodings/__init__.py
# code object from '/usr/lib/python3.6/encodings/__pycache__/__init__.cpython-
  36.pyc'
# /usr/lib/python3.6/__pycache__/codecs.cpython-36.pyc matches /usr/lib/python3.6/
  codecs.py
# code object from '/usr/lib/python3.6/__pycache__/codecs.cpython-36.pyc'
import '_codecs' # <class '_frozen_importlib.BuiltinImporter'>
import 'codecs' # <_frozen_importlib_external.SourceFileLoader object at
  0x7f2d4d2b7358>
# /usr/lib/python3.6/encodings/__pycache__/aliases.cpython-36.pyc matches /usr/lib/
  python3.6/encodings/aliases.py
# code object from '/usr/lib/python3.6/encodings/__pycache__/aliases.cpython-36.pyc'
import 'encodings.aliases' # <_frozen_importlib_external.SourceFileLoader object at
  0x7f2d4d2c4cf8>
import 'encodings' # <_frozen_importlib_external.SourceFileLoader object at
  0x7f2d4d32ae80>
# /usr/lib/python3.6/encodings/__pycache__/utf_8.cpython-36.pyc matches /usr/lib/
  python3.6/encodings/utf_8.py
```

```
# code object from '/usr/lib/python3.6/encodings/__pycache__/utf_8.cpython-36.pyc'
import 'encodings.utf_8' # <_frozen_importlib_external.SourceFileLoader object at
  0x7f2d4d2d3b00>
import '_signal' # <class '_frozen_importlib.BuiltinImporter'>

<snip>

import 'site' # <_frozen_importlib_external.SourceFileLoader object at
  0x7f2d4d2e4ef0>
Python 3.6.8 (default, Jan 14 2019, 11:02:34)
[GCC 8.0.1 20180414 (experimental) [trunk revision 259383]] on linux
Type "help", "copyright", "credits" or "license" for more information.
Hello, This is my first Python application
# clear builtins._
# clear sys.path
# clear sys.argv
# clear sys.ps1
# clear sys.ps2
# clear sys.last_type
# clear sys.last_value
# clear sys.last_traceback
# clear sys.path_hooks
# clear sys.path_importer_cache
# clear sys.meta_path
# clear sys.__interactivehook__
# clear sys.flags
# clear sys.float_info
# restore sys.stdin
# restore sys.stdout
# restore sys.stderr
# cleanup[2] removing builtins
# cleanup[2] removing sys
# cleanup[2] removing _frozen_importlib
# cleanup[2] removing _imp
# cleanup[2] removing _warnings
# cleanup[2] removing _thread
# cleanup[2] removing _weakref
# cleanup[2] removing _frozen_importlib_external
# cleanup[2] removing _io
# cleanup[2] removing marshal
# cleanup[2] removing posix
# cleanup[2] removing zipimport
# cleanup[2] removing encodings
```

```
<snip>

# destroy abc
# destroy errno
# destroy posixpath
# cleanup[3] wiping stat
# cleanup[3] wiping _stat
# destroy _stat
# cleanup[3] wiping genericpath
# cleanup[3] wiping importlib._bootstrap
# cleanup[3] wiping sys
# cleanup[3] wiping builtins
# destroy os
# destroy stat
# destroy genericpath
```

Most Python code testing and verification is done in Python interpreter shell because it is an easy and excellent way to see how Python code works. A user can type the code right into the interpreter shell and get the results right away. Example 5-8 shows some basic examples of dealing with numeric and string data in the Python interpreter shell.

Example 5-8 *Dealing with Numeric and String Data in the Python Shell*

```
[root@rnd-srvr python]# python3
Python 3.6.8 (default, Jan 14 2019, 11:02:34)
[GCC 8.0.1 20180414 (experimental) [trunk revision 259383]] on linux
Type "help", "copyright", "credits" or "license" for more information.
>>> 10
10
>>> 10 + 10
20

>>> a = 'Python'
>>> a
Python

>>> print(a)
Python

>>> exit()
root@rnd-srvr:~#
```

Python Data Types

Python data types are the basic code building blocks that are used to build larger blocks of code. Operations can be performed on the data based on the data type. For instance, for an integer data type, a user can perform an operation such as addition or multiplication. Following are the built-in data types for Python along with their classes:

- Numeric data types:
  - int
  - float
  - complex
  - fractions
  - decimal
- String
  - str
- Boolean
  - bool
- Lists
  - list
- Dictionaries
  - dict
- Tuples
  - tup
- Sets
  - set
  - frozen sets

We will look in more detail at Python data types later in this section, but first we need to take a detour into variables.

Variables

A Python *variable* is a pointer to the memory location—referred to as an envelope or a bucket—where information can be maintained and from which it can be referenced. When a variable is created, it is assigned a data type based on the type of data it will be used to store. In other programming languages such as Java, users usually have to assign a data type while declaring a variable, but this is not the case with Python. Python uses dynamic typing, which means a variable can be reassigned to different data types. This makes Python a very flexible programming language compared to programming languages that are statically typed.

Based on the data type of a variable, certain actions can be performed on the variable. For instance, with the integer data type, operations such as addition, subtraction, and multiplication can be performed on the data. With string variables, concatenation can be performed. If an operation of one data type is performed on the variable or value of another data type, an error is returned.

There are a few rules to keep in mind when defining variable names:

- **Should not start with a number:** The name of a variable should not start with a number. Variables need to start with letters (for example, **a**, **a1**, **abc**, **xyz**).
- **No spaces:** There should not be any spaces in a variable name. An underscore character (_) can be used instead of a space when defining a variable (for example, **user_id**, **first_name**).
- **No symbols:** When defining a variable name, the following symbols cannot be used:

  : ' " , < > / ? | \ ( ) ! @ # $ % ^ & * ~ - +
- **No reserved names:** A variable name should not be the same as any reserved name, such as **None**, **True**, or **filter**.

Although there is no rule about using uppercase or lowercase when defining a variable, it is considered a best practice to use lowercase for variable names. It's imperative to remember that variable names are case sensitive.

Note The *Style Guide for Python Code*, commonly referred to as PEP 8, spells out rules and best practices for Python code. It can be found at https://www.python.org/dev/peps/pep-0008/.

Example 5-9 demonstrates dynamic data type allocation for a variable. In this example, the variable **a** is assigned an integer value. The data type of the variable can be found using the built-in function **type()**, which takes the variable name as a parameter. This function can be used to identify the data types at different sections of the code block to avoid any bugs due to unexpected data types. Later in this example, the same variable **a** is assigned the string value **'Python'**. This example also illustrates the operations performed on the variable based on data type. Notice that when the values assigned to the variable **a** are of type int, only numeric calculations can be performed on the data. When a string value is assigned to the same variable and you try to perform numeric operations on the variable, you get an error.

Example 5-9 *Python Dynamic Data Type Allocation*

```
[root@rnd-srvr ~]# python3
Python 3.6.8 (default, Jan 14 2019, 11:02:34)
[GCC 8.0.1 20180414 (experimental) [trunk revision 259383]] on linux
Type "help", "copyright", "credits" or "license" for more information.
>>> a = 10
>>> a
10

>>> type(a)
<class 'int'>

>>> a + 2
12
>>> a = 'Python'
>>> type(a)
<class 'str'>

>>> len(a)
6

>>> a + len(a)
Traceback (most recent call last):
  File "<stdin>", line 1, in <module>
TypeError: must be str, not int

>>> 'Hello ' + a
'Hello Python'

>>> exit()
root@rnd-srvr:~#
```

Note Use the **exit()** function in Python to exit the interpreter and return to the Bash shell or terminal.

A variable defined in Python has either a local or global scope. When a user wants to use the same variable for the rest of the program or module, a global variable is defined. When a variable is specific to a code block such as a function or a method, a local variable is defined.

It is possible to delete an entire variable by using the **del** statement. Once a variable is deleted, a Python program returns an error if a user tries to reference or access that deleted variable again (unless it is created again). Example 5-10 displays the use of **del** keyword for deleting a variable.

Example 5-10 *Deleting a Python Variable*

```
[root@rnd-srvr ~]# python3
Python 3.6.8 (default, Jan 14 2019, 11:02:34)
[GCC 8.0.1 20180414 (experimental) [trunk revision 259383]] on linux
Type "help", "copyright", "credits" or "license" for more information.
>>> a = 10
>>> a
10
>>> del a
>>> a
Traceback (most recent call last):
  File "<stdin>", line 1, in <module>
NameError: name 'a' is not defined
```

Numbers

In Python, the most commonly used numeric data types are:

- **int** (integer): Represents a whole number
- **float** (floating point number): Represents a number with a decimal point

Mathematical operations can be performed with numeric data types. The numeric data types are used where a program is dealing with mathematical calculations between two or more numeric inputs. The calculations can be either simple or complex in nature, but the mathematical fundamentals remain the same. In Example 5-8, you already saw a few simple mathematical operations, including addition, subtraction, multiplication, and division between two numbers. Example 5-11 shows more numeric calculations between the two variables **a** and **b**; the result is stored in a new variable, **c**. In Example 5-11, notice the operator **+=**. This operator adds a number to a variable and assigns the value back to the variable itself. For example, the statement **a += 1** would represent a = a + 1. Another thing to note in Example 5-11 is that the division operator between two integer variables returns a floating point result.

Example 5-11 *Numeric Operations Between Variables*

```
[root@rnd-srvr ~]# python3
Python 3.6.8 (default, Jan 14 2019, 11:02:34)
[GCC 8.0.1 20180414 (experimental) [trunk revision 259383]] on linux
Type "help", "copyright", "credits" or "license" for more information.
```

```
>>> a = 10
>>> b = 20
>>> c = a + b
>>> c
30
>>> a += 1    # This represents a = a + 1
>>> c
30
>>> a
11
>>> c = a + b
>>> c
31
>>> c -= a    # This represents c = c - a
>>> c
20
>>> c = a * b
>>> c
220
>>> c = c / b
>>> c
11.0
```

Another operator that can be used with numeric data is the modulo (%) operator. The modulo operator returns the remainder from the division of one argument by a second operator. This operator can be very handy for determining whether a given number is an even number or an odd number. For an even number, % 2 returns the result **0**, and for an odd number, it returns the result **1**. Example 5-12 illustrates the use of the modulo operator.

Example 5-12 *Using the Modulo Operator in Python*

```
>>> a = 10
>>> b = 11
>>> a % 2
0
>>> b % 2
1
>>> c = 14
>>> c % 3
2
```

All the operations that can be performed on an integer can also be performed on floating point input data. When performing numeric operations, if one of the inputs is a floating point number, the result is also a floating point number, and it belongs to the class **float** in Python. To convert one type of data into another type—that is, to convert integer data to floating point number or vice versa—you use the **int()** function or the **float()** function with the parameter of the input data. These functions convert the integer data to floating point data by adding a decimal point or convert floating point data to an integer by getting rid of the decimal point. Example 5-13 demonstrates different operations on floating point data and the conversion of integer into floating point data and vice versa.

Note During the conversion from floating point to integer, value is lost, so this conversion may not be helpful when developing applications that require extensive and accurate mathematical calculations.

Example 5-13 *Operations on Integer and Floating Point Data*

```
>>> a = 11.5
>>> b = 12
>>> c = a + b
>>> c
23.5
>>> type(a)
<class 'float'>
>>> type(b)
<class 'int'>
>>> type(c)
<class 'float'>
>>> int(a)
11
>>> float(b)
12.0
>>> a % 2
1.5
>>> b % 2
0
```

Python can not only just deal with integers and floating point numbers but also complex numbers. A complex number, say **z**, is stored using rectangular coordinates and is divided into two parts: a real part and an imaginary part. Complex numbers in Python are written with a **j** as the imaginary part. You can use *variable-name*.**imag** and *variable-name*.**real** to view the imaginary and real fields of a complex number.

Complex numbers are not used with regular mathematics but are highly useful for performing scientific calculations. To perform mathematical operations on complex numbers, the **cmath** library can be imported; this library has predefined functions for dealing with complex numbers. Example 5-14 illustrates the use of some complex numbers in Python.

Example 5-14 *Complex Numbers in Python*

```
>>> a = 1+5j
>>> a
(1+5j)
>>> type(a)
<class 'complex'>
>>> a = -1
>>> b = 0
>>> c = complex(a,b)
>>> c
(-1+0j)
>>> c.imag
0.0
>>> c.real
-1.0

>>> import cmath
>>> cmath.phase(c)
3.141592653589793

>>> import math
>>> math.atan2(c.imag, c.real)
3.141592653589793
```

Note To learn more about mathematical functions for complex numbers, refer to the cmath library functions at https://docs.python.org/3/library/cmath.html.

Strings

A string is a sequence of characters, represented in Python as class **str**. String literals are written using either single quotation or double quotation marks, as in these examples:

- 'Hello'
- "Python"
- "Welcome to Python"

Strings in Python can be assigned to variables, and different operations and functions that are applicable to strings can then be applied on those variables. It's important to keep in mind that Python strings are immutable; that is, a Python string is not changeable, and its state cannot be modified after the string is created. Although you can assign a string variable again, you cannot modify a string object.

The + sign, which is used for performing addition with integer literals, can also be used to concatenate strings. Example 5-15 shows several concatenation operations between string variables. You can see in this example that the concatenation fails if one of the variables is a non-string literal. Example 5-15 also demonstrates the use of the **id()** function, which allows you to verify the address of a variable. Notice that when the string variable c is assigned a new variable, the address location of the variable changes.

Example 5-15 *Concatenation Operations Between Strings*

```
>>> a = 'Hello'
>>> b = 'Python'
>>> c = a + b
>>> c
'HelloPython'
>>> id(c)
4483299760
>>> b = 99
>>> c = a + b
Traceback (most recent call last):
  File "<stdin>", line 1, in <module>
TypeError: must be str, not int
>>> c = a + str(b)
>>> c
'Hello99'
>>> id(c)
4483299952
```

A string is an ordered sequences of characters, and characters within a string can be accessed using their index values, so users can grab subsections of a string. Recall from earlier in this chapter that indexing allows users to access a single character from a string. The index of a string literal starts with 0 and goes up to $n - 1$, where n is the total number of characters in the string. Similarly, strings support negative indexing, which is useful when a user wants to traverse through the characters in the string not from the starting index but from the end. Figure 5-3 displays both the positive and negative indexes of a string.

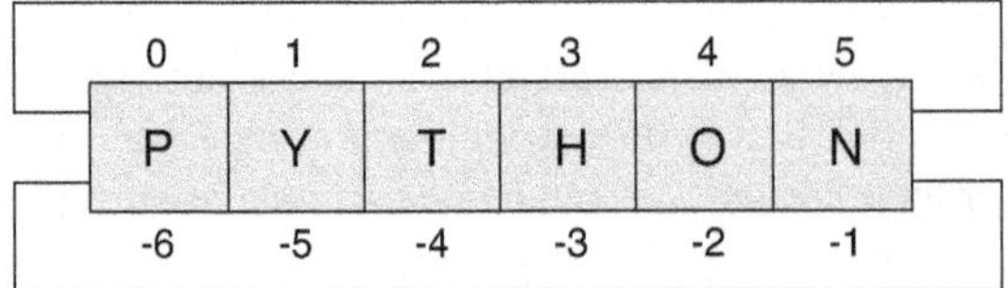

Figure 5-3 *String Indexes*

String indexing is achieved using the [] notation after the string or string variable. Example 5-16 demonstrates how to access different characters from within a string using both positive and negative indexes. If an index beyond the last index is mentioned, the code returns the error "index out of range."

Example 5-16 *Indexing on String Data*

```
>>> a = 'Hello'
>>> len(a)
5
>>> a[3]
'l'
>>> a[0] + a[1] + a[2] + a[3] + a[4]
'Hello'
>>> a[-5] + a[-4] + a[-3] + a[-2] + a[-1]
'Hello'
>>> a[5]
Traceback (most recent call last):
  File "<stdin>", line 1, in <module>
IndexError: string index out of range
```

Indexing allows you to grab a single character from a string. In order to grab multiple characters or a substring from within a string, you can use slicing. As discussed earlier in this chapter, slicing takes in three parameters, which are all optional:

- Start index
- Stop index
- Step

The start index is where the slicing begins. The stop index is the last index at which a character is captured. Step allows the user to navigate through a substring hop by hop, based on the step number. For example, if the current index is 1 and the step is specified as 2, then the next index value will be 3, followed by 5, and so on. If no number is specified for step, the default value, 1, is used. Example 5-17 illustrates how to slice a substring from the string saved in the variable c. It also shows the use of slicing with a step value of 2, start index 2, and stop index 6. This example captures the character from index 1 followed by index 3 and finally index 5, and it returns the substring **'el9'**.

Example 5-17 *Slicing Using Positive Indexes*

```
>>> c
'Hello99'
>>> c[3:6]
'lo9'
>>> c[1:6:2]
'el9'
```

Slicing can also be performed using negative indexes. For a slicing operation, the starting index should be 0 or some other number that is lower than the stop index, and the stop index cannot be a number lower than -1. Example 5-18 demonstrates slicing using negative indexes. In this example, the starting index -6 is equal to the positive index 1, and the stop index -1 is equal to the index value 6 and step value 2, which means choosing every alternate character in the string.

Example 5-18 *Slicing Using Negative Indexes*

```
>>> c
'Hello99'
>>> c[3:6]
'lo9'
>>> c[-4:-1]
'lo9'
>>> c[1:6:2]
'el9'
>>> c[-6:-1:2]
'el9'
```

Some predefined functions, including the following, can be called on string literals:

- **str.strip()**: Strips or removes any whitespace at the beginning and at the end of the string.
- **str.lower()**: Converts the whole string to lowercase.
- **str.upper()**: Converts the whole string to uppercase.
- **str.replace()**: Takes two parameters: the substring to replace and the string to be replaced with. The **replace()** function finds the substring specified in the parameter and replaces it with the string specified as the second parameter.

Example 5-19 illustrates the use of these functions on a string assigned to the variable **a**.

Example 5-19 *Using String Functions*

```
>>> a = ' Hello, This is Python '
>>> a.strip()
'Hello, This is Python'
>>> a.lower()
' hello, this is python '
>>> a.upper()
' HELLO, THIS IS PYTHON '
>>> a.replace('Py', 'Hacka')
' Hello, This is Hackathon '
```

Along with some of the functions shown in Example 5-19, the **str** class has a **format()** function that allows multiple substitutions and formatting of the string. The **format()** function takes input variables as parameters, and these variables can be substituted in the string at places where placeholders appear. A placeholder is defined by a pair of curly braces ({}), and curly braces can also be placed with the index of the variables in the **format()** function, as shown in Example 5-20. Example 5-20 demonstrates multiple ways to use the **str.format()** function with the string. Note that the input value in the **format()** function can be an integer, a floating point number, a string, or a character that is either directly passed or passed via a variable.

Example 5-20 *Formatting String Data*

```
>>> age = 33
>>> txt = "My name is Andrew, my age is {}".format(age)
>>> txt
'My name is Andrew, my age is 33'

>>> txt = "My name is Andrew, my age is {}"
>>> print(txt.format(age))
My name is Andrew, my age is 33

>>> name = ' Andrew '

>>> txt = 'My name is {}, my age is {}'.format(name,age)
>>> txt
'My name is Andrew, my age is 33'

>>> txt = 'My name is {}, my age is {}'
>>> print(txt.format(name,age))
My name is Andrew, my age is 33

>>> txt = 'My name is {1}, my age is {0}'
>>> print(txt.format(age,name))
My name is Andrew, my age is 33
```

Operators

So far in this chapter, various operations have been performed on integers and string literals. Operators make different operations possible, and Python supports several types of operators:

- Arithmetic operators
- Bitwise operators
- Assigning operators
- Logical operators
- Identity operators
- Membership operators

Table 5-1 provides a list of arithmetic and bitwise operators.

Table 5-1 *Arithmetic and Bitwise Operators*

Operator	Description	Example
+	Arithmetic operator for addition	a + b
-	Arithmetic operator for subtraction	a - b
*	Arithmetic operator for multiplication	a * b
/	Arithmetic operator for division	a / b
%	Arithmetic operator for modulo	a % b
**	Arithmetic operator for exponentiation	a ** b
& (AND)	Bitwise operator that sets each bit to 1 if both bits are 1	a & b
| (OR)	Bitwise operator that sets each bit to 1 if one of the two bits is 1	a | b
^ (XOR)	Bitwise operator that sets each bit to 1 if only one of the bits is 1	a ^ b
~ (NOT)	Bitwise operator that inverts all the bits (that is, sets 0 to 1 and 1 to 0)	a ~ b
<< (left shift)	Bitwise operator that shifts left by pushing 0s in from the right and letting the leftmost bits fall off	a << b
>> (signed right shift)	Bitwise operator that shifts right by pushing copies of the leftmost bit in from the left and letting the rightmost bits fall off	a >> b

Understanding the operators shown in Table 5-1 is important for Python programming as these operators help build the logic and are also used for defining data structures. You have seen most of the arithmetic operators listed in Table 5-1 earlier in this chapter. We now examine the exponential operator and other bitwise operators. The exponential operator is a programmatical representation of **(a)**^{b} or the **(a * a * a ... * a)** mathematical operation, where **a** is multiplied by itself **b** times.

Python bitwise operators treat numbers as strings of bits. In other words, the numbers are represented in binary format—that is, in two's complement binary—and the bitwise operations are performed on those binary numbers. The two's complement binary format is similar to binary representation of positive numbers but slightly different for negative numbers. A negative number, such as **(-x)**, in bit pattern is written as the value **(x - 1)** and then complemented; that is, the bits are switched from 1 to 0 and 0 to 1. Table 5-2 provides some examples of binary representation of both positive and negative numbers.

Table 5-2 *Representing Positive and Negative Numbers in Two's Complement*

Number	Two's Complement Binary
1	1
2	10
5	101
9	1001
-5	complement (5 - 1) = complement (4) = complement (00000100) = 11111011
-1	complement (1 - 1) = complement (0) = 11111111

Note At one time, Python used 8-bit numbers for bitwise operations, but it does not anymore. Python now supports an infinite number of bits for bitwise operation. This makes Python applications easily portable as you do not need to worry about underlying bit support on the native operating system.

The easiest way to understand bitwise operations is to use binary representation of every number and perform the operations. When you understand the operators, you will start to understand the operations. Example 5-21 illustrates the use of different bitwise operators and the arithmetic operator **. The following different bitwise operations are shown in Example 5-21:

- 2 & 3
  - In binary: 10 & 11, which is 10
    - Result: 2

- **2 | 3**
  - In binary: 10 | 11, which is 11
    - Result: 3
- 2 ^ 3
  - In binary: 10 ^ 11, which is 01
    - Result: 1
- 2 << 3
  - In binary: 10 << 3, which is 10000
    - Result: 16
- 2 >> 3
  - In binary: 10 >> 3, which is 00
    - Result: 0
- (2 << 3) >> 2
  - In binary: 10000 >> 2, which is 00100
    - Result: 4

Example 5-21 *Using Arithmetic and Bitwise Operators*

```
>>> a = 2
>>> b = 3
! Arithmetic Operator
>>> a ** b
8
! Bitwise Operator
>>> a & b
2
>>> a | b
3
>>> a ^ b
1
>>> a << b
16
>>> a >> b
0
>>> (a << b) >> a
4
```

= is the primary assignment operator, but Python, like other programming languages, allows for a combinational assignment. Basically, the assignment operator works in conjunction with other arithmetic or bitwise operators. First, the arithmetic or bitwise operation is applied on the variable, and then the result is assigned to the variable. Table 5-3 shows a variety of combinational assignments.

Table 5-3 *Assignment Operators*

<table>
<tr><th>Operator</th><th>Example</th><th>Same As</th></tr>
<tr><td>=</td><td>x = 10</td><td>x = 10</td></tr>
<tr><td>+=</td><td>x += 10</td><td>x = x + 10</td></tr>
<tr><td>-=</td><td>x -= 10</td><td>x = x - 10</td></tr>
<tr><td>*=</td><td>x *= 10</td><td>x = x * 10</td></tr>
<tr><td>/=</td><td>x /= 10</td><td>x = x / 10</td></tr>
<tr><td>%=</td><td>x %= 10</td><td>x = x % 10</td></tr>
<tr><td>**=</td><td>x **= 10</td><td>x = x ** 10</td></tr>
<tr><td>&=</td><td>x &= 10</td><td>x = x & 10</td></tr>
<tr><td>|=</td><td>x |= 10</td><td>x = x | 10</td></tr>
<tr><td>^=</td><td>x ^= 10</td><td>x = x ^ 10</td></tr>
<tr><td>>>=</td><td>x >>= 3</td><td>x = x >> 3</td></tr>
<tr><td><<=</td><td>x <<= 5</td><td>x = x << 5</td></tr>
</table>

Python and several other programming languages also have comparison operators. A comparison operator is used with conditional statements such as **if-else**. A comparison operator is used to perform a comparison between two values or variables; when used with statements such as **if-else**, it allows you to perform certain steps based on the result.

Comparison operators are not used to compare objects. To compare objects in Python, you use identity operators. The identity operators are **is**, which returns **True** if the objects are the same (that is, if the two objects point to the same address location in memory), and **is not**, which returns **True** if the objects are not the same or if they point to different address locations in the memory. Both the comparison and identity operators return Boolean values—that is, either **True** or **False**.

If there are multiple conditions to be validated within a statement or loop, logical operators can be used along with comparison or identity operators. A logical operator returns a Boolean value by comparing the result from the comparison operators or identity operators between two values or objects. There are three logical operators:

- **and:** The **and** operator returns **True** if the result from each of the comparison statements is **True**. The Python interpreter first validates whether the result of the first statement is **True**, and if it is, then it progresses on to validating the second statement.

- **or**: The **or** operator returns **True** if the result from the comparison statements is **True**. If the result of the first statement is **True**, the Python interpreter doesn't even validate the second operator because the comparison has already resulted in **True**.
- **not**: The **not** operator reverses the result of the comparison between values or objects.

Table 5-4 describes the comparison operators, identity operators, and logical operators and provides examples of how to use them.

Table 5-4 *Python Comparison, Identity, and Logical Operators*

Operator	Description	Example
==	Comparison operator: Equal to.	**a == b**
!=	Comparison operator: Not equal to.	**a != b**
>	Comparison operator: Greater than.	**a > b**
<	Comparison operator: Less than.	**a < b**
>=	Comparison operator: Greater than or equal to.	**a >= b**
<=	Comparison operator: Less than or equal to.	**a <= b**
is	Identity operator: Used for object comparison. Returns **True** if both variables are the same object.	**a is b**
is not	Identity operator: Used for object comparison. Returns **True** if both variables are not the same object.	**a is not b**
and	Logical operator: Returns **True** if both statements are true.	**(a > x) and (b < y)**
or	Logical operator: Returns **True** if one of the statements is true.	**(a > x) or (b < y)**
not	Logical operator: Returns the reverse result. If true, returns **False** and vice versa.	**not((a > x) or (b < y))**

The membership operators, which are used to validate whether a sequence is present in an object, can be used with conditional statements to return a Boolean value or loops to iterate through the object. There are two membership operators: **in** and **not in**. The **in** membership operator returns **True** if a value is present in the sequence and **False** otherwise; the **not in** operator returns **True** if a sequence was not present in the object and **False** otherwise. Table 5-5 describes the membership operators and provides examples.

Table 5-5 *Membership Operators*

Operator	Description	Example
in	Returns **True** if the value present in the sequence, **False** otherwise	**a in b**
not in	Used for validating if a value exists in a sequence or not. Returns **True** if the value is not present in the sequence, **False** otherwise	**a not in b**

Python Data Structures

Some of the fundamental needs in writing software programs are to manage the data, perform computations, organize the data, and store the data. *Data structures* provide the means to represent related data to be used later within a program. Different types of data structures are used, depending on the kind of data and the manageability of the data. Python has the four built-in data structures:

- List
- Dictionary
- Tuple
- Set

List

A list is an ordered sequence that can hold a variety of object types that are changeable. Lists are defined inside square brackets ([]), with commas separating objects in the list. A list in Python is similar to an array in other programming languages, such as Java or PHP. It allows users to store an enumerated set of items in one place and access them using their position (that is, the index in the list). To illustrate the concept of indexing in a list, the following example shows a list named **colors** that enumerates the colors of the rainbow:

```
colors = ['violet', 'indigo', 'blue', 'green', 'yellow', 'orange',
'red']
```

Each item in the list is a color name (value) and has a specific position (index). The list named **colors** can simply be expressed in an ordered sequence, as shown in Figure 5-4. Because Python uses zero-based indexing, the first element, **violet**, has the index value 0, and the last element, **red**, has the index value 6. The first element in the list is often called the *head end* of the list, and the last element is called the *tail end*. Programs typically access the elements from the head end comes; however, if a program needs to start with the end of a list or the penultimate element, it starts enumerating elements from the tail end of the list. In such a scenario, negative indexing can be used. In negative indexing, -1 corresponds to the last element of the list, and the programs keeps on decrementing to the first element.

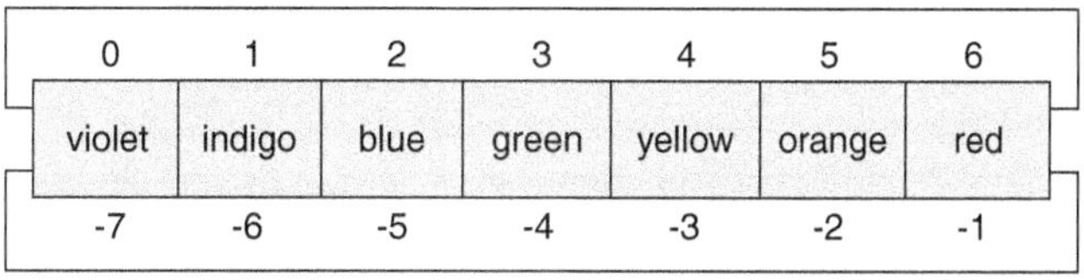

0	1	2	3	4	5	6
violet	indigo	blue	green	yellow	orange	red
-7	-6	-5	-4	-3	-2	-1

Figure 5-4 *A List with Indexes and Values*

Each member item in a list can individually be accessed using its index number, as shown in Example 5-22. In this example, there are two lists: **list1** and **list2**, each with five different values that can be accessed using the index value of the list. For instance, the fourth index of **list1** returns the value **5**. The **len()** function can also be used to assess the depth of the list. The **+** operator is used to perform concatenation of two lists—and not an arithmetic operation on the members of lists. The arithmetic **+** operation can be performed on members of a list accessed using their index values, as shown at the end of Example 5-22.

Example 5-22 *Accessing List Data and List Operations*

```
>>> list1 = [1,2,3,4,5]
>>> list2 = [6,7,8,9,10]
>>> list1
[1, 2, 3, 4, 5]
>>> list2
[6, 7, 8, 9, 10]
>>> list1[4]
5
>>> list2[3]
9
>>> len(list1)
5
>>> list1 + list2
[1, 2, 3, 4, 5, 6, 7, 8, 9, 10]
>>> list1
[1, 2, 3, 4, 5]
>>> list2
[6, 7, 8, 9, 10]
>>> list3 = list1 + list2
>>> list3
[1, 2, 3, 4, 5, 6, 7, 8, 9, 10]
>>> list1[0] + list1[1] + list2[3] + list2[4]
22
```

Note Python list members can also be accessed using negative indexing. With Python lists, the indexing begins with -1 and below and goes from right to left. There is no index 0 with negative indexing. The indexing in a list works the same way as indexing in string variables.

Indexes can be used not only to access list members but are also to assign values. When assigning values, only the index part of a list can be used. A value assignment to a new list index is not allowed. Support for indexes also provides the capability of performing list slicing. *List slicing* works the same way as string slicing, but it returns the submembers of the list after slicing. Example 5-23 demonstrates value assignment on different list indexes and list slicing.

Example 5-23 *Value Assignment and Slicing in a Python List*

```
>>> list1[0] = 11
>>> list2[2] = 18
>>> list1
[11, 2, 3, 4, 5]
>>> list2
[6, 7, 18, 9, 10]
>>> list1[1:]
[2, 3, 4, 5]
>>> list1[2:4]
[3, 4]
>>> list1[0::2]
[1, 3, 5]
```

Note Python list value assignment and list slicing using negative indexes work the same way as for strings.

Python lists have predefined functions: **list.append()** adds a new member to a list, and **list.pop()** removes an existing member from a list. The **list.append()** function takes a parameter as the value and appends the value to the last index of the list. The **list.pop()** function can be used with or without a parameter. If used without a parameter, the **list.pop()** function removes the last member from the list. Otherwise, the **list.pop()** function takes the parameter of the index that needs to be removed or popped from the list. Example 5-24 demonstrates the use of the **list.append()** and **list.pop()** functions.

Example 5-24 *Using List Functions*

```
>>> list3
[1, 2, 3, 4, 5, 6, 7, 8, 9, 10]
>>> list3.append(20)
>>> list3
[1, 2, 3, 4, 5, 6, 7, 8, 9, 10, 20]
>>> list3.pop()
20
>>> list3
[1, 2, 3, 4, 5, 6, 7, 8, 9, 10]
>>> list3.pop(4)
5
>>> list3
[1, 2, 3, 4, 6, 7, 8, 9, 10]
```

One of the benefits that the Python list data structure provides is sorting capabilities, which are provided by the **list.sort()** and **list.reverse()** functions. The **list.sort()** and **list.reverse()** function works for lists holding both numeric values and character/string values. Example 5-25 displays the use of both the **list.sort()** and **list.reverse()** functions.

Example 5-25 *Using the list.sort() and list.reverse() Functions*

```
>>> list_num = [1,2,5,8,3,4,6]
>>> list_char = ['d','e','g','a','f','b']
>>> list_num.sort()
>>> list_num
[1, 2, 3, 4, 5, 6, 8]
>>> list_char.sort()
>>> list_char
['a', 'b', 'd', 'e', 'f', 'g']
>>> list_num.reverse()
>>> list_num
[8, 6, 5, 4, 3, 2, 1]
>>> list_char.reverse()
>>> list_char
['g', 'f', 'e', 'd', 'b', 'a']
```

Python list members can be of type **list**, which means that users can create nested list data structures. The operations on the list members depend on the class type of the returned value. If the returned value of an index is also a list, then another set of square brackets with index values can be used to access the members of the inner list. Example 5-26 illustrates how nested lists look and how data within the nested lists can be fetched.

Example 5-26 *Using Nested Lists*

```
>>> nested_list = [1,2,3,[4,5],[7,8,9],['a','b']]
>>> nested_list
[1, 2, 3, [4, 5], [7, 8, 9], ['a', 'b']]
>>> nested_list[3]
[4, 5]
>>> nested_list[3][1]
5
>>> nested_list[5][0]
'a'
>>> type(nested_list)
<class 'list'>
>>> type(nested_list[3])
<class 'list'>
>>> type(nested_list[3][0])
<class 'int'>
>>> type(nested_list[5][0])
<class 'str'>
```

Dictionaries

A *dictionary* is an unordered collection of objects that are changeable and indexed. Unlike lists, dictionaries use key/value pairs for storing objects. Starting with Version 3.7, Python dictionaries are ordered. These key/value pairs allow users to easily access the data without knowing the index location of an object. In Python, dictionaries are written within curly brackets and use colons to signify the keys and their associated values, and the key/value pairs are separated by commas. One question that usually arises is when to choose a dictionary over a list. On dictionary objects, operations such as indexing, slicing, and sorting cannot be performed. The data can be stored at any location in a dictionary, and the user just needs to know the key to fetch the data. A value in a dictionary can be accessed by specifying the key within square brackets. Example 5-27 shows a dictionary named **my_dict** with three key/value pairs. The value for a referenced key can be modified by using the assignment operator **=**.

Example 5-27 *Using Python Dictionaries*

```
>>> my_dict
{'key1': 0, 'key2': 1, 'key3': 2}
>>> my_dict['key1']
0
>>> my_dict['key3']
2
```

```
>>> my_dict.get('key2')
1
>>> my_dict['key1'] = 'Zero'
>>> my_dict
{'key1': 'Zero', 'key2': 1, 'key3': 2}
```

In Python, data insertion on dictionaries can simply be done using the keys and assigning values to those keys. It is not necessary to have a specified key preexist in a dictionary, but it is imperative to remember that keys are immutable. Dictionaries allow for storing values of different kinds, including a Python list or a dictionary itself. Users can use the **type()** function to identify the class type of the returned value and can perform actions or call predefined functions based on the data types. Example 5-28 illustrates how to handle a dictionary with different data types and edit or add new key/value pairs.

Example 5-28 *Dictionaries of Different Data Types*

```
>>> mydict = {1:'Hello' , 2:'Python', 'key3': ['a','b','c'], 'key4':{'n1':'v1',
  'n2':'v2'}}
>>> mydict[1]
'Hello'
>>> mydict[2]
'Python'
>>> mydict['key3']
['a', 'b', 'c']
>>> type(mydict['key3'])
<class 'list'>
>>> mydict['key3'][1]
'b'
>>> mydict['key4']
{'n1': 'v1', 'n2': 'v2'}
>>> type(mydict['key4'])
<class 'dict'>
>>> mydict['key4']['n2']
'v2'
>>> type(mydict['key4']['n2'])
<class 'str'>
>>> mydict['key4']['n2'].upper()
'V2'
>>> mydict['key4']['n2'] = 'New Value'
>>> mydict['key4']['n2']
'New Value'
>>> mydict[5] = 'Value 5'
>>> mydict
{1: 'Hello', 2: 'Python', 'key3': ['a', 'b', 'c'], 'key4': {'n1': 'v1', 'n2':
  'New Value'}, 5: 'Value 5'}
```

Python has predefined functions for dictionary data structures. **dict.keys()**, **dict.values()**, and **dict.items()** are the three key functions for the dictionary class. The **dict.keys()** function yields all the keys present in the dictionary. This function can be useful for iterating through a whole dictionary via a loop or validating the presence of a key within a dictionary. The **dict.values()** function returns all the values present in a given dictionary. Similar to the **dict.keys()** function, the **dict.values()** function can be useful for iterating through the values present in a given dictionary. Finally, the **dict.items()** function returns the key/value pairs. Note that all three of these functions return the values in the form of an array or a list. Example 5-29 shows the result from the use of all three of these functions.

Example 5-29 *Using Dictionary Functions*

```
>>> mydict.keys()
dict_keys([1, 2, 'key3', 'key4', 5])
>>> mydict.values()
dict_values(['Hello', 'Python', ['a', 'b', 'c'], {'n1': 'v1', 'n2': 'New Value'},
  'Value 5'])
>>> mydict.items()
dict_items([(1, 'Hello'), (2, 'Python'), ('key3', ['a', 'b', 'c']), ('key4',
  {'n1': 'v1', 'n2': 'New Value'}), (5, 'Value 5')])
```

The key/value pairs can be deleted by simply deleting the key using the **del** keyword. The **del** keyword takes in the dictionary parameter with the key that is to be deleted. Example 5-30 illustrates how to delete a specific key/value pair in a dictionary. In this example, notice that the key 1 has the value **'Hello'**. After calling the **del** keyword on key 1 of the dictionary, you can no longer see key 1 present in the dictionary.

Example 5-30 *Deleting a Specific Dictionary (Key/Value) Entry*

```
>>> mydict
{1: 'Hello', 2: 'Python', 'key3': ['a', 'b', 'c'], 'key4': {'n1': 'v1', 'n2': 'v2'}}
>>> del mydict[1]

>>> mydict
{2: 'Python', 'key3': ['a', 'b', 'c'], 'key4': {'n1': 'v1', 'n2': 'v2'}}
```

Tuples

A Python *tuple* is a collection of data in an ordered and immutable form, so once a tuple is created, the data inside the tuple cannot be modified. This data structure comes in handy in cases where an application needs static or read-only data. Python tuples are represented in parentheses and can hold data of different data types. If an attempt is made to modify data stored in a tuple, a type error is returned, stating that the object does not support item assignment. Example 5-31 illustrates the creation of a tuple and how data at different indexes can be fetched. Note that based on the data type of the data within the tuple, Python functions can be called. For instance, if data is of type **str**, then functions such as **str.upper()** and **str.reverse()** can be called on the data at a given index of a tuple.

Example 5-31 *Handling Python Tuples*

```
>>> tup1 = (1,2,3,'Hello','This is Python3')
>>> tup1
(1, 2, 3, 'Hello', 'This is Python3')
>>> type(tup1)
<class 'tuple'>
>>> tup1[0]
1
>>> tup1[3]
'Hello'
>>> tup1[0] = 'Hello'
Traceback (most recent call last):
  File "<stdin>", line 1, in <module>
TypeError: 'tuple' object does not support item assignment

>>> type(tup1[3])
<class 'str'>
>>> tup1[3].upper()
'HELLO'
```

Although the data within a tuple cannot be modified, it is possible to join two different tuples and create a third tuple. This is done by using the **+** operator between the two tuples. You can also delete a tuple but not the data within the tuple. You use the **del** keyword to delete a tuple. Example 5-32 demonstrates both the joining of two tuples and the deletion of a tuple.

Example 5-32 *Joining Tuples and Deleting a Tuple*

```
>>> tup1 = (1,2,3)
>>> tup2 = ('a', 'b', 'c')
>>> tup3 = tup1 + tup2
>>> tup3
(1, 2, 3, 'a', 'b', 'c')
>>> del tup3
>>> tup3
Traceback (most recent call last):
  File "<stdin>", line 1, in <module>
NameError: name 'tup3' is not defined
```

Sets

A *set* is an unordered and unindexed collection of unique data elements. Because a set is unindexed, the data items in the set cannot be accessed by any index. The only way to access the elements of a set is in a **for** loop, using membership operators such as **in** or **not in**. The class set has three key functions to perform update, add, and delete operations on the elements of the set: **set.add()**, **set.update()**, and **set.remove()**. To add an element to a set, you use the **set.add()** function. Similarly, you can update the elements in a set, but you cannot update a specific element with a newer value. The **set.update()** function updates a whole set—that is, all the elements in the set. To remove a specific element in a set, you can call the **set.remove()** function. Example 5-33 shows how to create a new set and how different operations can be performed on the set with the **set.add()**, **set.update()**, and **set.remove()** functions.

Example 5-33 *Defining Sets and Performing Operations on Sets*

```
>>> set1 = {'a',2,3,4,'e'}
>>> set2 = {1,2,3,4,5}
>>> set3 = {'a','b','c','d','e'}
>>> set1
{2, 3, 'e', 4, 'a'}
>>> set1.add(6)
>>> set1
{2, 3, 'e', 4, 6, 'a'}
>>> set2.update([1,2,4,6,5,7])
>>> set2
{1, 2, 3, 4, 5, 6, 7}
>>> set2.remove(7)
>>> set2
{1, 2, 3, 4, 5, 6}
```

Note You can use the **set.pop()** function to remove the last item from a set. Because a set is unordered in nature, you do not know which item this function will remove.

Much like other data structures, sets can be combined with other sets; the function for this is **set.union()**. This function returns a new set that is a union of all the elements of two sets. Note that with the **set.union()** function, the elements returned from two sets are unique. If there are overlapping elements, the **set.union()** function returns only the common element as a single element. The **set.clear()** function is used to empty all the elements from a set. The **set.difference()** function returns a set showing all the differences between two sets. Example 5-34 illustrates the use of all the three of these functions.

Example 5-34 *Using Set Functions*

```
>>> set4 = set1.union(set2)
>>> set4
{1, 2, 3, 'e', 4, 6, 5, 'a'}

! Empty the elements in the set using clear() function.
>>> set4.clear()
>>> set4
set()

>>> set1.difference(set2)
{'a', 'e'}
```

Control Flow

In a program, *control flow* refers to the order in which a code block is executed. In Python, control flow is driven by conditional statements, loops, and function calls. The control flow syntax includes colons and indentation (whitespace) used to separate the parts of a code block that will be executed when a certain condition is met or when the execution control of the code is with the loop or a function call. Python code is structured using indentation, which sets it apart from other programming languages. Each line of code within a code block is aligned vertically as part of a function or a loop. If a code block has nested code blocks within it, the indentation moves further to the right, and the alignment follows. A block ends on a line that is less indented than the code lines in the code block. A colon in the code declares the beginning of an indentation block or code block. Example 5-35 shows a nested code block with conditional statements and loop statements. At this point, you are not expected to know how to use the conditional statements or loops; this example just presents how a nested code block can be written. In this example, there is an **if-else** statement at the top level, and there is a nested **if-else** statement within that code block.

Example 5-35 *Nested Code Block with Conditional Statements*

```
>>> a = 10
>>> b = 20
>>> c = 21
>>> if a > b:
...     print('{} is greater than {}'.format(a,b))
...     if a > c:
...         print('{} is greater than {}'.format(a,c))
...     else:
...         print('{} is greater than {}'.format(c,a))
```

```
... else:
...     print('{} is greater than {}'.format(b,a))
...     if c > b:
...         print('{} is greater than {}'.format(c,b))
...     else:
...         print('{} is greater than {}'.format(b,c))
...

! When the code executes, below output is printed.

20 is greater than 10
21 is greater than 20
```

Note There is no limit on the depth of the code blocks that can be written, but when writing code, focus should be given to the performance of the code within a code block.

if-else Statements

A Python **if-else** statement provides the functionality of conditional code execution. A Python program with an **if-else** statement evaluates an expression, returns a Boolean value (**True** or **False**), and executes the code block if the expression is **True.** If the expression is **False**, the code block is not executed, and the **else** section of the code block is executed (if present). In Python, the control flow of the **if** statement is indicated by the colon (:) and structured using indentation. The first unindented line marks the end of the code block. This unindented line can be the beginning of the **else** statement or a continuation of the parent code block. Figure 5-5 illustrates **if-else** control flow.

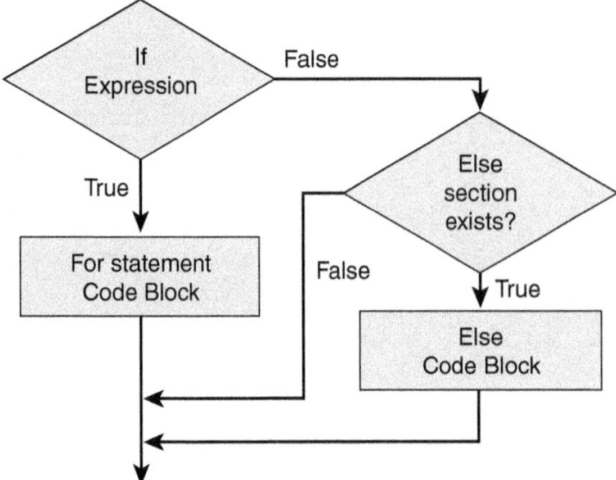

Figure 5-5 *if-else Statement Flow Diagram*

if-else statements can be nested within other **if-else** statements; that is, an **if-else** statement can appear within the code block of an **if** or an **else** statement. Example 5-36 illustrates nested **if-else** statements by comparing the values of three numeric variables **a**, **b**, and **c**. In this example, the first **if** expression validates whether the value of **a** is greater than the value of **b**. If that holds true, further conditions are validated. In this example, because the value of **a** is less than the value of **b**, the control goes to the code block of the **else** statement. Within the **else** statement code block, further evaluation is done to see if the value of **c** is greater than value of **b**; because it is, the code block within the **if** statement is executed.

Example 5-36 *Nested if-else Statements*

```
a = 10
b = 20
c = 21
if a > b:
    print('{} is greater than {}'.format(a,b))
    if a > c:
        print('{} is greater than {}'.format(a,c))
    else:
        print('{} is greater than {}'.format(c,a))
else:
    print('{} is greater than {}'.format(b,a))
    if c > b:
        print('{} is greater than {}'.format(c,b))
    else:
        print('{} is greater than {}'.format(b,c))
```

```
! Output from above code.

20 is greater than 10
21 is greater than 20
```

In Example 5-36, even though there are nested **if-else** statements, the code execution becomes complex. The same task can be reduced with a smaller number of validations by using logical operators and validating multiple expressions in a single expression and then using the result to execute the respective code block of the **if** or **else** statement. Also, if more than one expression is to be evaluated, an **elif** statement (which is actually an **else-if** statement) can be used. Example 5-37 demonstrates the use of logical operators in evaluating multiple conditions in a single expression and the use of an **elif** statement to evaluate more than one primary expression in an **if-else** statement.

Example 5-37 *Using Logical Operators with an if-else Statement*

```
a = 10
b = 20
c = 21
if a > b and a > c:
    print('{} is greater than {} and {}'.format(a,b,c))
elif b > a and b > c:
    print('{} is greater than {} and {}'.format(b,a,c))
else:
    print('{} is greater than {} and {}'.format(c,a,b))
```

```
! Output from above code.

21 is greater than 10 and 20
```

In all the previous examples, the values of the variables were always preassigned. However, a dynamic program allows users to enter values at runtime and then uses that input to perform validations or take actions. In order to take user input, you use the **input()** function, which takes the parameter as a string (text) to be displayed on the terminal window and waits for the user input. When the user has input a value, it can be stored in another variable for later use or can be consumed right away. To understand how to build different building blocks of a program, examine the Python code shown in Example 5-38. In this example, two lists, named **person** and **age**, are created; the two lists have the same lengths such that someone at a given index in the **person** list has a matching age at the same index in the **age** list. This program takes user input for a name and validates the input against the **person** list. Based on this input, different **if-elif-else** conditions are evaluated, and the program prints either the person's age or indicates whether the person is a teenager or a senior citizen.

Example 5-38 *An if-else Statement with a List*

```
person = ['Jason','Ray','Chris','Juan']
age = [23,51,19,63]
name = input('Enter your name : ')
if name in person:
    p_age = age[person.index(name)]
    if p_age > 60:
        print('{} is a Senior Citizen'.format(name))
    elif p_age < 20:
        print('{} is a teenager'.format(name))
    else:
        print('Age of {} is {}'.format(name, p_age))
```

```
else:
    print('{} is not on our list'.format(name))
```

```
! First Execution
Enter your name : Ray
Age of Ray is 51
```

```
! Second Execution
Enter your name : Andrew
Andrew is not on our list
```

```
! Third Execution
Enter your name : Juan
Juan is a Senior Citizen
```

```
! Fourth Execution
Enter your name : Chris
Chris is a teenager
```

Managing data in Python lists is easy, but it may not be the right choice in Example 5-38. For instance, if the length of the **person** list differed from the length of the **age** list, the application would not function properly. This can easily happen due to human error in a scenario where the application is also allowing the user to add a new person to the list along with the person's age. When developing applications, it is important to use the right type of data structure to reduce the chances of human error.

To expand on the application that validates a person's name and age, say that new user input can be saved into the data structure and made available for later validation. In Example 5-39, a data structure of type dictionary is created with the person's name as the key and age as the value. The program ensures that the age is correctly mapped to a person. In Example 5-39, if the input name does not exist in the keys, a new key is created, and the user input is used to map the name to the person's age. This example also illustrates the use of membership operators to validate whether a name exists in keys. Notice how different code blocks with **if-else** statements are being used to further enhance the functionality of the application.

Example 5-39 *An if-else with Dictionaries*

```
person = {
    'Jason': 23,
    'Ray': 51,
    'Chris': 19,
    'Juan': 63,
}
```

```
name = input('Enter your name : ')
if name not in person.keys():
    response = input('Do you want to enter your name on our list? yes or no : ')
    if response.lower() == 'yes':
        new_age = input('Enter your Age : ')
        person[name] = new_age
        print("You have been added to our list.\n ")
        print("Current List: \n")
        print(person)
    else:
        print("You have not been added to our list")
        print("Current List: \n")
        print(person)
else:
    p_age = person[name]
    if p_age > 60:
        print('{} is a Senior Citizen'.format(name))
    elif p_age < 20:
        print('{} is a teenager'.format(name))
    else:
        print('Age of {} is {}'.format(name, p_age))
```

```
! First Execution
Enter your name : Andrew
Do you want to enter your name on our list? Yes or No : Yes
Enter your Age : 33
You have been added to our list.

Current List:

{'Jason': 23, 'Ray': 51, 'Chris': 19, 'Juan': 63, 'Andrew': '33'}
```

```
! Second Execution
Enter your name : Juan
Juan is a Senior Citizen
```

```
! Fourth Execution
Enter your name : Vincent
Do you want to enter your name on our list? Yes or No : No
You have not been added to our list
Current List:

{'Jason': 23, 'Ray': 51, 'Chris': 19, 'Juan': 63}
```

for Loops

if-else statements are used to validate one or more expressions and then perform actions, but when the code block is completed, the program doesn't iterate through that code block again. However, loops allow programmers to iterate through a code block *n* number of times. A **for** loop is used to enumerate over a sequence of objects of different data types and data structures, such as lists, dictionaries, and tuples. When the program enumerates through the last member of the sequence, the program exits the code block to continue further execution of the program or exit the program. To understand the flow of a program with a **for** loop, examine the flow diagram shown in Figure 5-6.

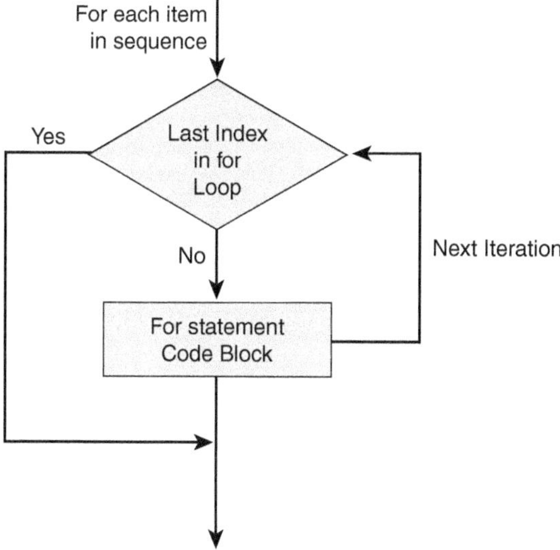

Figure 5-6 *Python for Loop Flow Diagram*

A **for** loop can use identity operators or membership operators to enumerate through the sequence of objects. Taking the previous example further, the **for** loop can be used to enumerate through the keys and print the age of each person, as shown in Example 5-40.

Example 5-40 *Using for Loops*

```
person = {
    'Jason': 23,
    'Ray': 51,
    'Chris': 19,
    'Juan': 63,
}

name = input('Enter your name : ')
```

```
if name not in person.keys():
    response = input('Do you want to enter your name on our list? Yes or No : ')
    if response == 'Yes':
        new_age = input('Enter your Age : ')
        person[name] = new_age
        print("You have been added to our list.\n ")
        print("Current List: \n")
        for name in person.keys():
            print("Age of {} is {}\n".format(name,person[name]))
    else:
        print("You have not been added to our list")
        print("Current List: \n")
        for name in person.keys():
            print("Age of {} is {}\n".format(name,person[name]))
else:
    p_age = person[name]
    if p_age > 60:
        print('{} is a Senior Citizen'.format(name))
    elif p_age < 20:
        print('{} is a teenager'.format(name))
    else:
        print('Age of {} is {}'.format(name, p_age))
```

```
! Output
Enter your name : Andrew
Do you want to enter your name on our list? Yes or No : Yes
Enter your Age : 33
You have been added to our list.

Current List:

Age of Jason is 23

Age of Ray is 51

Age of Chris is 19

Age of Juan is 63

Age of Andrew is 33
```

Let's consider another example of a **for** loop. This one enumerates through a sequence of numbers and prints their values. The sequence of numbers is generated using the built-in

range() function, which takes as parameters the start and end values and generates only one number at a time. Using the membership operators, the loop can iterate through the sequence of numbers generated by the **range()** function. One important thing to note is that, after each completion of the iteration, the value is incremented by one, or if it is enumerated by another sequential object, the flow moves to the next object in the sequence. Example 5-41 shows how to enumerate through the numbers 1 to 10 and print the iteration number. The **for** loop also allows the use of an **else** statement along with a **for-in** statement, which means that once the **for-in** statement has enumerated through all the objects, the control flow moves to the **else** block. The **for** statement **for i in range(1, 10)** is equivalent to **for i in [1, 2, 3, 4, 5, 6, 7, 8, 9]**.

Example 5-41 *Using a for Loop with the range() Function*

```
for i in range(1, 10):
    print('Iteration # {}'.format(i))
else:
    print('The for loop is over')
```

```
! Output
Iteration # 1
Iteration # 2
Iteration # 3
Iteration # 4
Iteration # 5
Iteration # 6
Iteration # 7
Iteration # 8
Iteration # 9
The for loop is over
```

for loops also allow for nested looped statements. Example 5-42 demonstrates the use of nested **for** loops. In this example, at every iteration of the outer loop, the inner loop runs its iterations. When the outer **for** loop completes, control is moved to the **else** control block.

Example 5-42 *Nested for Loops*

```
for i in range(1, 6):
    print('Iteration # {}'.format(i))
    for j in range(1,3):
        print('Nested Iteration # {}.{}'.format(i,j))
else:
    print('The for loop is over')
```

```
! Output
Iteration # 1
Nested Iteration # 1.1
Nested Iteration # 1.2
Iteration # 2
Nested Iteration # 2.1
Nested Iteration # 2.2
Iteration # 3
Nested Iteration # 3.1
Nested Iteration # 3.2
Iteration # 4
Nested Iteration # 4.1
Nested Iteration # 4.2
Iteration # 5
Nested Iteration # 5.1
Nested Iteration # 5.2
The for loop is over
```

while Loops

A Python **while** loop executes a code block as long as the condition in the **while** statement is true. A **while** statement can be used in conjunction with logical operators, and it keeps executing the code in the **while** block as long as the **while** statement result holds true. A **while** statement can also have an **else** block, in which case the **while** block moves the control to the **else** block when the condition doesn't hold true. Going back to the example of validating a person and his age and adding a new person's information to the dictionary or list, the **while** loop, as shown in Example 5-43, ensures that the program keeps running as long as the running state is set to **True.** As soon as the running state is set to **False**, the program terminates. The running state in this case depends on user input to continue the program or exit.

Example 5-43 *Using while Loops*

```
person = {
    'Jason': 23,
    'Ray': 51,
    'Chris': 19,
    'Juan': 63,
}

running = True

while running:
```

```
    name = input('\nEnter your name : ')
    if name not in person.keys():
        response = input('Do you want to enter your name on our list? Yes or No : ')
        if response == 'Yes':
            new_age = input('Enter your Age : ')
            person[name] = new_age
            print("You have been added to our list.\n ")
            print("Current List: \n")
            for name in person.keys():
                print("Age of {} is {}\n".format(name,person[name]))
        else:
            print("You have not been added to our list")
            print("Current List: \n")
            for name in person.keys():
                print("Age of {} is {}\n".format(name,person[name]))
    else:
        p_age = person[name]
        if p_age > 60:
            print('{} is a Senior Citizen'.format(name))
        elif p_age < 20:
            print('{} is a teenager'.format(name))
        else:
            print('Age of {} is {}'.format(name, p_age))
    cont = input('Do you wish to continue? y or n : ')
    if not(cont.lower() == 'y'):
        running = False
```

```
! Output
Enter your name : Andrew
Do you want to enter your name on our list? Yes or No : Yes
Enter your Age : 33
You have been added to our list.

Current List:


Age of Jason is 23


Age of Ray is 51


Age of Chris is 19


Age of Juan is 63
```

```
Age of Andrew is 33

Do you wish to continue? y or n : y

Enter your name : Vincent
Do you want to enter your name on our list? Yes or No : No
You have not been added to our list
Current List:

Age of Jason is 23

Age of Ray is 51

Age of Chris is 19

Age of Juan is 63

Age of Andrew is 33

Do you wish to continue? y or n : n
```

Note The main difference between a **for** loop and a **while** loop is that a **for** loop keeps running until it enumerates through all the members in a list, whereas the **while** loop keeps repeating the code block until the statement returns **False.**

Functions

By using different data structures of different data types and using control flow statements, you can easily write Python programs to perform certain tasks. You can create a program that reads the word count in a document or even a full-blown calculator by using Python. But one of the challenges with simply writing a program is that blocks of code become repetitive, and repetitive code reduces the performance of the code. One way to optimize the code is to create reusable pieces of code that can be used in multiple programs. For instance, a piece of code that performs a calculation between two or more numbers can be used in a calculator and can also be used in a word count program. Python functions make it possible to solve such problems.

Python *functions* are code blocks that can be referenced by their names anywhere in a program. Once a function is called in a program, the block of code within the function is executed. Throughout this chapter, you have seen multiple examples of predefined

Python library functions that provide different functionalities. Functions are probably the most important building block of any software application in any programming language that provides reusability. Functions not only provide code reusability but also makes a program more readable and understandable.

A Python function is defined by using the **def** keyword followed by the identifier name of the function followed by a pair of parentheses. The parentheses may contain a list of variables called *arguments*. A program can contain multiple functions with the same identifier name but with different ranges or types of arguments. To understand what a function code block looks like, examine the representation of the function named **funcname()** in Example 5-44. There are two definitions for the function in this example: one with empty parameters and one with parameters. Two definitions of the same function name can be completely different from one another and can perform different actions when called upon.

Example 5-44 *Function Representations*

```
def funcname():
    # Code block belonging to function
    . . .
    . . .
# End of Function code block

def funcname(params...):
    # Code block belonging to function
    . . .
    . . .
# End of Function code block

funcname()  # Calling function name
funcname(params...])  # Calling function name
```

Functions can be used to perform certain tasks and also to return values. To return values, you use the **return** keyword. The return value can be of any object type. (In the earlier example of people and their ages, for example, functions could be used to perform different tasks and integrated into the flow.) Example 5-45 shows three functions being created. First, the function named **person_in_list()** is created and used with the parameters **name** and **age**. This function adds a new person to the dictionary named **person** and returns the updated dictionary. The function **validate_person()** is defined and takes the parameter **name.** This function prints the age of the person, based on the provided name. The **name** variable in the parameter is used as the key in the dictionary. Finally, the **print_persons()** function is defined to print the current list of people in the **person** dictionary. Notice in Example 5-45 that the **person_in_list()** function is being called within the **for** loop statement. This is the case because the function returns the **person** dictionary, and the **dict.keys()** function is called on this function name based on its return value. Even though this **for** loop is performing the same task as the **print_persons()** function, this example demonstrates how a function returning a value can be used. Alternatively, the **print_persons()** function could be reused instead of using the **for** loop.

Example 5-45 *Defining Functions and Calling Functions in a Code Block*

```
person = {
    'Jason': 23,
    'Ray': 51,
    'Chris': 19,
    'Juan': 63,
}
# Defining a function to return person in the list
def person_in_list(name, age):
    person[name] = age
    return person

# Defining a function to validate person's age based on their information
def validate_person(name):
    p_age = person[name]
    if p_age > 60:
        print('{} is a Senior Citizen'.format(name))
    elif p_age < 20:
        print('{} is a teenager'.format(name))
    else:
        print('Age of {} is {}'.format(name, p_age))

# Defining a function to print the person's age
def print_persons():
    print("Current List: \n")
    for name in person.keys():
        print("Age of {} is {}\n".format(name,person[name]))



running = True

while running:
    name = input('Enter your name : ')
    if name not in person.keys():
        response = input('Do you want to enter your name on our list? Yes or No : ')
        if response == 'Yes':
            new_age = input('Enter your Age : ')
            for name in person_in_list(name,new_age).keys():
                print("Age of {} is {}\n".format(name,person[name]))
```

```
        else:
            print("You have not been added to our list")
            print_persons()

    else:
        validate_person(name)
    cont = input('Do you wish to continue? y or n : ')
    if not(cont == 'y' or cont == 'Y' or cont == 'yes' or cont == 'Yes'):
        running = False
```

```
! Output
Enter your name : Chris
Chris is a teenager
Do you wish to continue? y or n : y
Enter your name : Andrew
Do you want to enter your name on our list? Yes or No : Yes
Enter your Age : 33
Age of Jason is 23
Age of Ray is 51

Age of Chris is 19

Age of Juan is 63

Age of Andrew is 33

Do you wish to continue? y or n : n
```

Summary

This chapter discusses the fundamentals of programming and computer science concepts such as object-oriented programming and algorithms. It covers the following topics:

- How scripting languages are used to control applications without the need to compile them
- How programming languages are compiled into machine code to provide an interface between instructions and a machine
- How network programmability can be used to enhance the manageability of a network device
- How network automation can be used to reduce the chance of human error and reduce the deployment time for the network services

- How code execution occurs in a Python program
- The various Python data types, data structures, and control flow, such as **if-else** statements and **for** and **while** loops
- Functions to enable reusability of code and make it more readable

References

Python documentation: docs.python.org

GNU Smalltalk User's Guide: www.gnu.org/software/smalltalk/manual/html_node/Overview.html

Chapter 6

Python Applications

When Python was initially developed in 1989, it was built on the fundamental of Don't Repeat Yourself (DRY) principle. Over the years, Python has evolved as one of the most popular programming languages and can be used to develop a host of applications such as web applications, text and image processing applications, machine learning, or even Enterprise-level applications. But before digging into the various applications of Python, it is important as a developer to set up the development environment to simplify and organize the process of application development.

Organizing the Development Environment

Software programmers often face challenges such as understanding and writing code, building logic, and linking different pieces of code together. In addition to these challenges, there are a few other challenges programmers and software developers often face, including the following:

- **Maintaining version control:** Developing a software/web application usually involves multiple team members, and during the course of the development, it becomes immensely difficult to track the changes made every day by different team members. Version control helps restore code to the last known good state so that if any defects are introduced in a new version of the code, the last known good code can be called up to restore the services. In addition, version control can help track feature enhancements across releases.
- **Different environments:** Every project that comes across a developer's desk has different requirements, such as different software versions and different third-party packages. Modifying the existing environment to match different project requirements is not an efficient way of settings up the environment. Rather, the packages, software versions, and so on should be isolated to respective project requirements.

- **Replicating the production environment:** There will always be instances (at different stages of the development process or during production) when software applications may run into defects. Defects can either be corner cases that may result from how an application was deployed or the way the production environment was set up. In such scenarios, the first step would be to identify the difference between the testing/development environment and the production environment and then to replicate the exact problem or defect that occurred during production. Mimicking the production environment or the environment where a problem occurred can be a challenging task as it requires matching the exact versions of other applications, such as third-party tools and databases. This becomes more challenging when a programmer wants to replicate a problem without making changes to the existing development environment.
- **Reusable code:** The key to being a good and efficient programmer is to write reusable code in the form of modules that can later be integrated or used in other modules.

The following subsections cover some of the tools and technologies that can help overcome these challenges.

Git

Git is an open-source tool that is used for distributed version control and to efficiently manage everything from small-scale projects to large-scale projects. Git also helps with collaboration between multiple team members. Git was originally developed in 2005 by Linus Torvalds, and today, an astounding number of projects rely on it. Apart from version control, Git provides several other benefits:

- **Performance:** The Git tool is optimized for high performance when committing new changes, branching, merging, and comparing past versions of a project. The distributed nature of Git also provides significant performance benefits. The built-in algorithms of Git use the common attributes of real source code file trees and their modifications over time. The Git tool focuses on the content of a file rather than the name of the file. Git uses a combination of delta encoding, compression, and storage of directory contents and version metadata objects.
- **Security:** Git provides and maintains data integrity by securing all the data in the repository using a secure hashing algorithm called SHA1 that protects the code and the change history against any malicious or accidental changes and makes it fully traceable.
- **Flexibility:** Git supports multiple nonlinear development workflows and is compatible with various existing systems and protocols. Git not only maintains history of the code files and changes but also history based on branches as well as tags.

Git is one of the main tools that developers use for maintaining version control for ongoing projects, especially when working in a team. Git's version control relies on repositories. A *repository* can be thought of as a primary folder where everything associated with a specific project is maintained. A repository can have subfolders or files within it. By using Git, you can maintain both a local copy as well as an online copy of all the files in the repository. Multiple online Git servers, including GitHub, BitBucket, and GitLab, can be used for repositories and are generally used by individuals to share or maintain code. You can create public repositories that are accessible to everyone, repositories for selected users, and private repositories on a project-by-project basis. When it comes to managing code within an organization, it typically makes sense to have a local Git server where all the code commits for the team can be done.

Setting up a Git server requires a few simple steps:

1. Generate an SSH key on the client machine.
2. Install Git by using the command **yum install git**.
3. Add a user and create an authorized_keys file under the .ssh directory of the user.
4. Copy the public key on the client machine to the Git server.

Example 6-1 shows these steps being used to set up a Git server on CentOS.

Example 6-1 *Setting Up a Git Server on CentOS*

```
! Generating SSH Key on client
[root@node2 ~]# ssh-keygen -C "dev@gmail.com"
Generating public/private rsa key pair.
Enter file in which to save the key (/root/.ssh/id_rsa): /root/.ssh/id_dev_rsa
Enter passphrase (empty for no passphrase):
Enter same passphrase again:
Your identification has been saved in /root/.ssh/id_dev_rsa.
Your public key has been saved in /root/.ssh/id_dev_rsa.pub.
The key fingerprint is:
SHA256:oXUbsjEhDw8syKeJ/MG2MYaAwtzf/psmSyYrIyl4bbI dev@gmail.com
The key's randomart image is:
+---[RSA 2048]----+
|+... .+ .        |
|+oo.o .* .       |
|+.o+... O o      |
|.ooB . + B o     |
|  + = o S .      |
|   o   .         |
|. ... . o.       |
|ooooo =. o.      |
|..E+o. .+o.      |
+----[SHA256]-----+
```

```
! Installing Git on CentOS Server
 [root@master-node ~]# yum install -y git
```

```
! Add user git on Server
[root@master-node ~]# useradd git
```

```
! Change password for user git
[root@master-node ~]# passwd git
Changing password for user git.
New password:
Retype new password:
passwd: all authentication tokens updated successfully.

! Create authorized_keys file under .ssh directory

[root@master-node ~]# su git
Password:
[git@master-node ~]# mkdir ~/.ssh && touch ~/.ssh/authorized_keys
```

```
! Copy Public key On Client machine to remote server
[root@node2 ~]# cat .ssh/id_dev_rsa.pub | ssh root@172.16.102.131 "cat >>
  /home/git/.ssh/authorized_keys"
The authenticity of host '172.16.102.131 (172.16.102.131)' can't be established.
ECDSA key fingerprint is SHA256:sTsJgHuf+SLBIePL+LLGtA9eG50xZsva18aFvzxjLBQ.
ECDSA key fingerprint is MD5:4d:eb:46:c2:00:26:e5:c0:04:ed:80:e1:e1:e7:72:06.
Are you sure you want to continue connecting (yes/no)? yes
Warning: Permanently added '172.16.102.131' (ECDSA) to the list of known hosts.
root@172.16.102.131's password:
[root@node2 ~]#
```

Once the Git server is set up, you can start using it. To use a Git server, you need to first create an empty repository on the Git server by using the command **git init -bare** *project-name.git*. A set of commands can be used to perform the initial setup on the server. Table 6-1 lists some of the commands that are required during Git setup and initialization.

Table 6-1 *Git Setup and Initialization Commands*

Command	Description
git config --global user.name "*firstname lastname*"	Sets up a name that appears in the version history
git config --global user.email "*email-address*"	Sets up an email address that will be associated with each history marker
git init	Initializes an existing directory as a Git repository

A number of commands can be used to add repositories and copy files to a Git server from a client machine. Table 6-2 lists and describes these command.

Table 6-2 *Commands for Updating Local Repos and Fetching Updates from Remote Repos*

Command	Description
git pull	Fetches and merges any commits from the tracked remote branch
git remote add *alias url*	Adds a Git URL as an alias for the remote Git repository
git push *alias branch*	Transmits local branch commits to a branch in a remote repository
git merge *alias/branch*	Merges a remote branch into the current branch to bring it up to date
git fetch *alias*	Fetches all branches from the remote Git repository
git add *file*	Adds a file in the current state to the next commit
git commit -m *"commit-description"*	Commits staged content to a new commit snapshot

Note These are not the only Git-related commands. More commands are available to modify history, track changes, inspect and compare changes, handle staging and snapshots, and so on. For more details on the Git commands, see http://education.github.com and other Git portals.

Example 6-2 illustrates the use of Git commands on a server as well as on a client machine to stage a commit from the client machine to the remote server. To set up a bare or empty repository on the server, you use the command **git init** with the **-bare** option. A bare Git repository has no working directory, whereas a non-bare Git repository is initialized with a working directory. Bare repositories are useful when you are working as part of a team, and you want a repository to act as a central repository, to which all team members can move their work. (For more information on the commands used in this example, refer to Table 6-1 and Table 6-2.)

Example 6-2 *Setting Up a Git Repository and Using Git on a Client Machine*

```
! Setup a Bare (empty) repository on Server
[git@prime-node ~]$ mkdir project && cd project
[git@prime-node project]$ git init --bare project.git
Initialized empty Git repository in /home/git/project/project.git/
[git@master-node project]$
```

```
[root@node2 ~]# mkdir project
[root@node2 ~]# cd project/
[root@node2 project]# git init
Initialized empty Git repository in /root/project/.git/
```

```
[root@node2 project]# git add .
[root@node2 project]# git commit -m 'initial commit'
# On branch master
#
# Initial commit
#
nothing to commit (create/copy files and use "git add" to track)
[root@node2 project]# git remote add origin
  ssh://git@172.16.102.131:/home/git/project/project.git

[root@node2 project]# touch initial
[root@node2 project]# git add initial
[root@node2 project]# git commit -m 'initial commit'
[master (root-commit) aad844f] initial commit
 1 file changed, 0 insertions(+), 0 deletions(-)
 create mode 100644 initial
[root@node2 project]# git push -u origin master
Counting objects: 3, done.
Writing objects: 100% (3/3), 203 bytes | 0 bytes/s, done.
Total 3 (delta 0), reused 0 (delta 0)
To git@master-node:/home/git/project/project.git
 * [new branch]      master -> master
Branch master set up to track remote branch master from origin.
```

Once the repository has been updated on the server, it can be cloned to another directory on the same client or on another client. The **git clone** command allows you to clone the Git repository, which consists of the last updated files on the repository, as shown in Example 6-3.

Example 6-3 *Cloning a Git Repository*

```
[root@node2 ~]# mkdir new_proj
[root@node2 ~]# cd new_proj/
[root@node2 new_proj]# git clone git@master-node:/home/git/project/project.git
Cloning into 'project'...
remote: Counting objects: 3, done.
remote: Total 3 (delta 0), reused 0 (delta 0)
Receiving objects: 100% (3/3), done.
[root@node2 new_proj]# ls -al
total 0
drwxr-xr-x. 3 root root  21 Dec 28 22:39 .
dr-xr-x---. 6 root root 231 Dec 28 22:38 ..
drwxr-xr-x. 3 root root  33 Dec 28 22:39 project
[root@node2 new_proj]# cd project/
```

```
[root@node2 project]# ls
initial
[root@node2 project]# pwd
/root/new_proj/project
```

Git workflow can be summarized in three simple phases, which are demonstrated in Example 6-2 and Example 6-3:

- **Commit:** After saving the files, you are required to commit the changes to the repository. The committed work is saved as a version of the repository, which can now be saved on the online repository.
- **Pull:** Before saving the changes on a remote or online repository, a pull of the existing repository is required to ensure that the files are completely up to date with the online repository.
- **Push:** When the local copy of the repository is up to date, you can push the changes to the online repository.

Docker

There have been many advancements over the years in programming languages, but even with modern programming languages, programmers still face steep challenges in setting up their development environments. It is imperative for a development team to use the same development environment so that integration of the application isn't affected due to the differences. When it comes to setting up the development environment, there are many variables involved, such as different operating systems, different versions of Python, virtual environments, and third-party modules; the problem is magnified for users working as a team. Similar challenges arise when replicating a problem that is occurring in a production environment.

All the challenges just mentioned can be resolved easily with the help of virtualization. A cloud provider such as Amazon Web Services (AWS) provides virtual instances of servers that can be dynamically added and removed as required. With virtualization, it is largely the software behind the scenes that is changed rather than the actual hardware. Virtual instances of servers are provided to the end users using virtual machines. The downside of using virtual machines is that they lack speed and large amounts of CPU, memory, and storage resources. A typical virtual machine with a standard operating system requires at least a single CPU core, 1 to 2 GB of storage, and 2 to 4 GB of random-access memory (RAM). Thus, a machine running five virtual machines would require at least 5 CPU cores, 5 to 10 GB of storage, and 10 to 20 GB of RAM. Even though CPU, storage, and RAM are not as expensive as they once were, these resources can still result in high costs.

Docker provides a lightweight virtualization solution that isolates an entire operating system via Linux containers. With containers, you can virtualize the environment on the upper layers of Linux, which speeds up deployment and also segregates the upper layers from the rest of the environment. Figure 6-1 illustrates container virtualization with Docker.

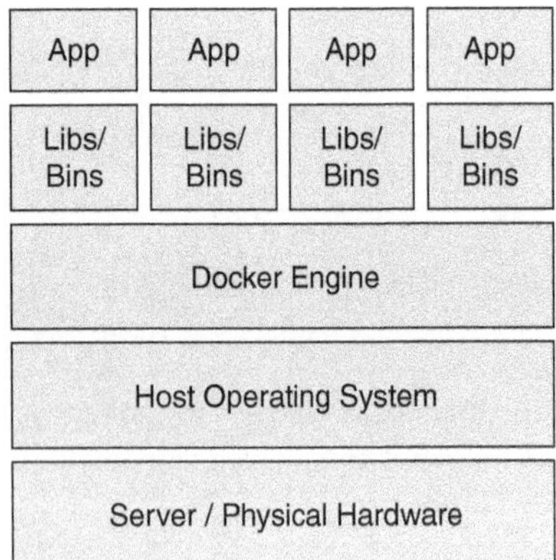

Figure 6-1 *Container Virtualization*

At the time of writing, the CentOS software repository does not maintain a default repository for the Docker application. To install the Docker application, the default repository should be updated to the location of the Docker repository. To begin the installation of Docker on CentOS, you need to install a few prerequisite packages. The **yum-utils** package provides the **yum-config-manager** utility, which allows users to add a repository. Docker uses the **devicemapper** storage driver, and the **device-mapper-persistent-data** and **lvm2** packages are required by **devicemapper.** Once these packages are installed using the **yum** package manager, you can add the **docker-ce** repository by using the **yum-config-manager** utility as shown in Example 6-4. You can then install the **docker-ce** package by using the **yum** package manager. The **docker-ce** package comes with other dependencies, such as the **docker-cli**, **container-selinux**, and **containered.io** packages. The **container-selinux** package provides support for SELinux security for containers, and the **containered.io** package provides a standard runtime environment for containers.

Example 6-4 *Installing Docker on CentOS*

```
[root@rnd-srvr ~]# yum install -y yum-utils device-mapper-persistent-data lvm2
[root@rnd-srvr ~]# yum-config-manager \
>     --add-repo \
>     https://download.docker.com/linux/centos/docker-ce.repo
Loaded plugins: fastestmirror
adding repo from: https://download.docker.com/linux/centos/docker-ce.repo
grabbing file https://download.docker.com/lin

[root@rnd-srvr ~]# yum install -y docker-ce
Loaded plugins: fastestmirror
Loading mirror speeds from cached hostfile
 * base: repos-lax.psychz.net
 * extras: mirror.sjc02.svwh.net
 * updates: mirror.sjc02.svwh.net
```

```
docker-ce-stable                                          | 3.5 kB   00:00
(1/2): docker-ce-stable/x86_64/updateinfo                 |   55 B   00:05
(2/2): docker-ce-stable/x86_64/primary_db                 |  37 kB   00:05
Resolving Dependencies
--> Running transaction check
---> Package docker-ce.x86_64 3:19.03.5-3.el7 will be installed
--> Processing Dependency: container-selinux >= 2:2.74 for package: 3:docker-ce-
  19.03.5-3.el7.x86_64
--> Processing Dependency: containerd.io >= 1.2.2-3 for package: 3:docker-ce-
  19.03.5-3.el7.x86_64
--> Processing Dependency: docker-ce-cli for package: 3:docker-ce-19.03.5-
  3.el7.x86_64
--> Running transaction check
---> Package container-selinux.noarch 2:2.107-3.el7 will be installed
---> Package containerd.io.x86_64 0:1.2.10-3.2.el7 will be installed
---> Package docker-ce-cli.x86_64 1:19.03.5-3.el7 will be installed
--> Finished Dependency Resolution

Dependencies Resolved

================================================================================
 Package              Arch      Version              Repository          Size
================================================================================
Installing:
 docker-ce            x86_64    3:19.03.5-3.el7      docker-ce-stable    24 M
Installing for dependencies:
 container-selinux    noarch    2:2.107-3.el7        extras              39 k
 containerd.io        x86_64    1.2.10-3.2.el7       docker-ce-stable    23 M
 docker-ce-cli        x86_64    1:19.03.5-3.el7      docker-ce-stable    39 M

Transaction Summary
================================================================================
Install  1 Package (+3 Dependent packages)

Total download size: 87 M
Installed size: 362 M
Downloading packages:
(1/4): container-selinux-2.107-3.el7.noarch.rpm          |  39 kB   00:05
warning: /var/cache/yum/x86_64/7/docker-ce-stable/packages/containerd.io-1.2.10-
  3.2.el7.x86_64.rpm: Header V4 RSA/SHA512 Signature, key ID 621e9f35: NOKEY
Public key for containerd.io-1.2.10-3.2.el7.x86_64.rpm is not installed
(2/4): containerd.io-1.2.10-3.2.el7.x86_64.rpm           |  23 MB   00:07
(3/4): docker-ce-19.03.5-3.el7.x86_64.rpm                |  24 MB   00:07
(4/4): docker-ce-cli-19.03.5-3.el7.x86_64.rpm            |  39 MB   00:02
--------------------------------------------------------------------------------
Total                                           9.3 MB/s |  87 MB   00:09
Retrieving key from https://download.docker.com/linux/centos/gpg
```

```
Importing GPG key 0x621E9F35:
 Userid     : "Docker Release (CE rpm) <docker@docker.com>"
 Fingerprint: 060a 61c5 1b55 8a7f 742b 77aa c52f eb6b 621e 9f35
 From       : https://download.docker.com/linux/centos/gpg
Running transaction check
Running transaction test
Transaction test succeeded
Running transaction
  Installing : 2:container-selinux-2.107-3.el7.noarch                        1/4
  Installing : containerd.io-1.2.10-3.2.el7.x86_64                           2/4
  Installing : 1:docker-ce-cli-19.03.5-3.el7.x86_64                          3/4
  Installing : 3:docker-ce-19.03.5-3.el7.x86_64                              4/4
  Verifying  : containerd.io-1.2.10-3.2.el7.x86_64                           1/4
  Verifying  : 1:docker-ce-cli-19.03.5-3.el7.x86_64                          2/4
  Verifying  : 2:container-selinux-2.107-3.el7.noarch                        3/4
  Verifying  : 3:docker-ce-19.03.5-3.el7.x86_64                              4/4

Installed:
  docker-ce.x86_64 3:19.03.5-3.el7

Dependency Installed:
  container-selinux.noarch 2:2.107-3.el7  containerd.io.x86_64 0:1.2.10-3.2.el7
  docker-ce-cli.x86_64 1:19.03.5-3.el7

Complete!
[root@rnd-srvr ~]#
```

Note Along with Docker, the tool Docker Compose can be used to help automate commands. To install this tool, you use the command **pip3 install docker-compose.** When you install Docker Compose, other tools are installed along with it, such as PyYAML, Cryptography, jsonschema, and importlib-metadata.

After Docker is installed, you can verify the Docker version by using the command **docker --version.** Similarly, you can use the command **docker-compose --version** to validate the version of the Docker Compose tool, as shown in Example 6-5. Along with verifying the version, you can use the command **docker info** to get detailed information about the Docker setup on the system. The **docker info** command provides a summary of all the containers in different states, including runtime information, storage information, security information, information on registries, and any proxy information used by the Docker daemon.

Example 6-5 *Verifying the Docker and Docker Compose Versions*

```
[root@rnd-srvr ~]# docker --version
Docker version 19.03.5, build 633a0ea
[root@rnd-srvr ~]# docker-compose --version
docker-compose version 1.25.0, build b42d419
[root@rnd-srvr ~]# docker info
Containers: 8
 Running: 0
 Paused: 0
 Stopped: 8
Images: 9
Server Version: 1.13.1
Storage Driver: overlay2
 Backing Filesystem: xfs
 Supports d_type: true
 Native Overlay Diff: true
Logging Driver: journald
Cgroup Driver: systemd
Plugins:
 Volume: local
 Network: bridge host macvlan null overlay
Swarm: inactive
Runtimes: docker-runc runc
Default Runtime: docker-runc
Init Binary: /usr/libexec/docker/docker-init-current
containerd version:  (expected: aa8187dbd3b7ad67d8e5e3a15115d3eef43a7ed1)
runc version: 9c3c5f853ebf0ffac0d087e94daef462133b69c7 (expected:
  9df8b306d01f59d3a8029be411de015b7304dd8f)
init version: fec3683b971d9c3ef73f284f176672c44b448662 (expected:
  949e6facb77383876aeff8a6944dde66b3089574)
Security Options:
 seccomp
  WARNING: You're not using the default seccomp profile
  Profile: /etc/docker/seccomp.json
  selinux
Kernel Version: 3.10.0-1062.9.1.el7.x86_64
Operating System: CentOS Linux 7 (Core)
OSType: linux
Architecture: x86_64
Number of Docker Hooks: 3
CPUs: 1
Total Memory: 487 MiB
Name: rnd-srvr
ID: IEFM:3N2G:HYZT:PDBE:DOBK:NR7I:OEMB:MDIH:IC2Q:VEQ3:LEUM:ADAF
```

```
Docker Root Dir: /var/lib/docker
Debug Mode (client): false
Debug Mode (server): false
Http Proxy: http://proxy.cisco.com:80/
Https Proxy: http://proxy.cisco.com:80/
Registry: https://index.docker.io/v1/
WARNING: bridge-nf-call-iptables is disabled
WARNING: bridge-nf-call-ip6tables is disabled
Experimental: false
Insecure Registries:
 127.0.0.0/8
Live Restore Enabled: false
Registries: docker.io (secure)
```

The Docker engine is a client/server application with three main components:

- **Server:** Docker is a long-running program represented by a daemon process. It listens to API requests and manages objects such as images, containers, networks, and volumes.
- **REST API:** An API interface allows applications to interact with a daemon process and provide them with instructions.
- **Client:** The client is represented by the command-line interface (CLI) command **docker**. When you execute the **docker run** command, the client sends the request to **dockerd** (the Docker daemon process), which executes the request.

To begin using Docker and get an idea of how it works, you can run a hello world container by using the command **docker run hello-world**. Successful execution of this container helps you verify the successful installation of the Docker software. When you execute the **docker run** command, the Docker client and Docker daemon go through the following steps:

1. The Docker client contacts the Docker daemon.
2. The Docker daemon pulls the hello world image from Docker Hub (http://hub.docker.com).
3. The Docker daemon creates a new container from that image to run the executable.
4. The Docker daemon streams the output to the Docker client, which is then sent to the terminal.

The public Docker repository at Docker Hub contains various images of different applications and operating systems. Example 6-6 illustrates the execution of the **hello-world** Docker image and the CentOS image that is pulled from Docker Hub. Note that the images are not pulled from the repository every time they are executed. The images are pulled the first time and stored on the disk. The next time the Docker daemon tries to spin up a container, it first checks the local storage to see if it has the image, and if it finds the image, it spins up the container using that image. The **docker** command can be executed with various options. One of the most commonly used options is **-it**, which is a combination of the two options **-i** and **-t**; it tells the Docker daemon that you want an interactive session with a TTY attached. The command option **bash** enables Bash shell access to the container. When the shell is exited, the container stops and releases the resources.

Example 6-6 *Executing hello-world and centos Containers*

```
[root@rnd-srvr ~]# docker run hello-world
Unable to find image 'hello-world:latest' locally
Trying to pull repository docker.io/library/hello-world ...
latest: Pulling from docker.io/library/hello-world
1b930d010525: Pull complete
Digest: sha256:4fe721ccc2e8dc7362278a29dc660d833570ec2682f4e4194f4ee23e415e1064
Status: Downloaded newer image for docker.io/hello-world:latest
[86886.763550] docker0: port 1(vethf57043d) entered blocking state
[86886.764829] docker0: port 1(vethf57043d) entered disabled state
[86886.766195] device vethf57043d entered promiscuous mode
[86886.767555] IPv6: ADDRCONF(NETDEV_UP): vethf57043d: link is not ready
[86886.768973] docker0: port 1(vethf57043d) entered blocking state
[86886.770252] docker0: port 1(vethf57043d) entered forwarding state
[86886.773996] docker0: port 1(vethf57043d) entered disabled state
[86886.936805] SELinux: mount invalid.  Same superblock, different security
  settings for (dev mqueue, type mqueue)
[86887.042984] IPv6: ADDRCONF(NETDEV_UP): eth0: link is not ready
[86887.045667] IPv6: ADDRCONF(NETDEV_CHANGE): eth0: link becomes ready
[86887.047194] IPv6: ADDRCONF(NETDEV_CHANGE): vethf57043d: link becomes ready
[86887.048679] docker0: port 1(vethf57043d) entered blocking state
[86887.049948] docker0: port 1(vethf57043d) entered forwarding state
[86887.051307] IPv6: ADDRCONF(NETDEV_CHANGE): docker0: link becomes ready

Hello from Docker!
This message shows that your installation appears to be working correctly.

To generate this message, Docker took the following steps:
 1. The Docker client contacted the Docker daemon.
 2. The Docker daemon pulled the "hello-world" image from the Docker Hub.
    (amd64)
 3. The Docker daemon created a new container from that image which runs the
    executable that produces the output you are currently reading.
 4. The Docker daemon streamed that output to the Docker client, which sent it
    to your terminal.

To try something more ambitious, you can run an Ubuntu container with:
 $ docker run -it ubuntu bash
```

```
Share images, automate workflows, and more with a free Docker ID:
 https://hub.docker.com/

For more examples and ideas, visit:
 https://docs.docker.com/get-started/

[root@rnd-srvr ~]#
```

```
[root@rnd-srvr ~]# docker run -it centos bash
Unable to find image 'centos:latest' locally
Trying to pull repository docker.io/library/centos ...
latest: Pulling from docker.io/library/centos
729ec3a6ada3: Pull complete
Digest: sha256:f94c1d992c193b3dc09e297ffd54d8a4f1dc946c37cbeceb26d35ce1647f88d9
Status: Downloaded newer image for docker.io/centos:latest
[87022.416608] docker0: port 1(vetha10bb9d) entered blocking state
[87022.417940] docker0: port 1(vetha10bb9d) entered disabled state
[87022.421141] device vetha10bb9d entered promiscuous mode
[87022.422546] IPv6: ADDRCONF(NETDEV_UP): vetha10bb9d: link is not ready
[87022.423952] docker0: port 1(vetha10bb9d) entered blocking state
[87022.425243] docker0: port 1(vetha10bb9d) entered forwarding state
[87022.427503] docker0: port 1(vetha10bb9d) entered disabled state
[87022.589013] SELinux: mount invalid.  Same superblock, different security
  settings for (dev mqueue, type mqueue)
[87022.644691] IPv6: ADDRCONF(NETDEV_UP): eth0: link is not ready
[87022.646575] IPv6: ADDRCONF(NETDEV_CHANGE): eth0: link becomes ready
[87022.648045] IPv6: ADDRCONF(NETDEV_CHANGE): vetha10bb9d: link becomes ready
[87022.649560] docker0: port 1(vetha10bb9d) entered blocking state
[87022.650827] docker0: port 1(vetha10bb9d) entered forwarding state
[root@fb6a5b14bcdb /]#
[root@fb6a5b14bcdb /]# ls -al
total 0
drwxr-xr-x.   1 root root  17 Dec 31 09:22 .
drwxr-xr-x.   1 root root  17 Dec 31 09:22 ..
-rwxr-xr-x.   1 root root   0 Dec 31 09:22 .dockerenv
lrwxrwxrwx.   1 root root   7 May 11  2019 bin -> usr/bin
drwxr-xr-x.   5 root root 360 Dec 31 09:22 dev
drwxr-xr-x.   1 root root  66 Dec 31 09:22 etc
drwxr-xr-x.   2 root root   6 May 11  2019 home
lrwxrwxrwx.   1 root root   7 May 11  2019 lib -> usr/lib
lrwxrwxrwx.   1 root root   9 May 11  2019 lib64 -> usr/lib64
drwx------.   2 root root   6 Sep 27 17:13 lost+found
drwxr-xr-x.   2 root root   6 May 11  2019 media
drwxr-xr-x.   2 root root   6 May 11  2019 mnt
drwxr-xr-x.   2 root root   6 May 11  2019 opt
```

```
dr-xr-xr-x. 104 root root   0 Dec 31 09:22 proc
dr-xr-x---.   2 root root 162 Sep 27 17:13 root
drwxr-xr-x.   1 root root  21 Dec 31 09:22 run
lrwxrwxrwx.   1 root root   8 May 11  2019 sbin -> usr/sbin
drwxr-xr-x.   2 root root   6 May 11  2019 srv
dr-xr-xr-x.  13 root root   0 Dec 30 09:12 sys
drwxrwxrwt.   7 root root 145 Sep 27 17:13 tmp
drwxr-xr-x.  12 root root 144 Sep 27 17:13 usr
drwxr-xr-x.  20 root root 262 Sep 27 17:13 var
[root@fb6a5b14bcdb /]# cat /etc/centos-release
CentOS Linux release 8.0.1905 (Core)
[root@fb6a5b14bcdb /]# exit
exit
[root@rnd-srvr ~]#
```

You can also pull Docker images by using the command **docker pull** *image-name*. This command pulls an image from the registry and stores it locally but does not execute the image. Example 6-7 demonstrates the process of pulling the **alpine** image from the Docker Hub registry and listing downloaded images by using the **docker images** command.

Example 6-7 *docker pull and docker images Command Output*

```
[root@rnd-srvr ~]# docker pull alpine:latest
Trying to pull repository docker.io/library/alpine ...
latest: Pulling from docker.io/library/alpine
c9b1b535fdd9: Pull complete
Digest: sha256:ab00606a42621fb68f2ed6ad3c88be54397f981a7b70a79db3d1172b11c4367d
Status: Downloaded newer image for docker.io/alpine:latest
```

```
[root@rnd-srvr ~]# docker images
REPOSITORY             TAG        IMAGE ID        CREATED         SIZE
docker.io/alpine       latest     e7d92cdc71fe    2 days ago      5.59 MB
docker.io/python       3          038a832804a0    3 weeks ago     932 MB
docker.io/centos       latest     0f3e07c0138f    2 days ago      220 MB
docker.io/hello-world  latest     fce289e99eb9    12 months ago   1.84 kB
```

A few other commands are useful with Docker. Table 6-3 lists some of the commands that can be useful with Docker clients.

Table 6-3 *Docker Commands*

Command	Description
docker image ls	Lists all the images locally stored with Docker Engine. (It is similar to the **docker images** command.)
docker image rm *image*	Deletes an image from the local image store.
docker push *image*	Pushes an image to a registry.
docker container run --name *name* **-p** *port-ext*:*port-int image*	Runs a container with the specified image. The **--name** option allows you to specify the name of the running container. The **-p** option exposes the external port (*port-ext*) that is mapped to the internal port inside the container (*port-int*).
docker container ls	Lists the running containers. Use this command with the **-all** option to include the stopped containers in the output.
docker container stop *name*	Stops the running container that has the specified name. When using this command, the container is stopped using **SIGTERM**.
docker container kill *name*	Stops the running container that has the specified name. When using this command, the container is stopped using **SIGKILL**.
docker container logs [*options*] *name*	Fetches the logs of a container. Use the **--tail** *number* option to print the last specified number of lines.
docker attach *name*	Enters the shell of a specified running container.
docker rm *name*	Deletes the container that has the specified name.

Now that you have seen how to use the Docker client and the Docker daemon, you need to learn how to dockerize an application (in this case, a Python application). *Dockerizing* an application means converting the application to run within a Docker container. The first step in dockerizing an application is to create a Dockerfile. A Docker image consists of stacked read-only layers, each of which represents a Dockerfile instruction. The Dockerfile instructions are laid out using layers, as described in Table 6-4.

Table 6-4 *Dockerfile Instructions*

Instruction	Usage	Description
FROM	FROM *image* FROM *image:tag* FROM *image@digest*	This is the first non-comment instruction in the Dockerfile. Can appear multiple times within a single Dockerfile in order to create multiple images. The *tag* and *digest* values are optional. If they are omitted, the Docker builder assumes the latest values by default.
LABEL	LABEL *key=value* [*key=value*] . . .	The **LABEL** instruction adds metadata to an image.
RUN	RUN *command* RUN "*executable*", "*param1*","*param2*"	**RUN** allows you to run commands using a base image that does not contain the specified shell executable. The default shell can be modified using the **SHELL** command.
CMD	CMD "*executable*", "*param1*","*param2*" CMD *command param1 param2*	There can be only one **CMD** instruction in a Dockerfile. The **CMD** instruction provides defaults for an executing container. These defaults can include an executable or can commit the executable. The defaults specified with **CMD** can be overridden by a user specifying arguments to the Docker **RUN** command.
ADD	ADD *src src . . . dest* ADD "*src*","*src*" . . . "*dest*" (used in cases where paths include whitespace)	**ADD** copies new files, directories, or remote file URLs from *src* and adds them to the file system of the image at the path *dest*. If *src* is a file or directory, then it must be relative to the source directory that is being used while building the Docker image. *dest* is an absolute path or a path relative to **WORKDIR**.
COPY	COPY *src src . . . dest* COPY "*src*","*src*" . . . "*dest*" (used in cases where paths include whitespace)	**COPY** copies new files, directories, or remote file URLs from *src* and adds them to the filesystem of the image at the path *dest*. If *src* is a file or directory, then it must be relative to the source directory that is being used while building the Docker image. *dest* is an absolute path or a path relative to **WORKDIR**. **COPY** works the same as **ADD** but without the **tar** and remote URL handling.

Instruction	Usage	Description
ENTRYPOINT	ENTRYPOINT "*executable*", "*param1*","*param2*" ENTRYPOINT *command param1 param2*	**ENTRYPOINT** allows a user to configure a container that will run as an executable. It overrides all elements specified under the **CMD** instruction.
VOLUME	VOLUME "*path*", . . . VOLUME *path* [*path* . . .]	**VOLUME** is used to expose any database storage area, configuration storage, or files/ folders created by the Docker container.
USER	USER [*username* | *UID*]	**USER** allows you to set the *username* or *UID* to use when running an image and for any **RUN**, **CMD**, and **ENTRYPOINT** instructions that follow in the Dockerfile.
WORKDIR	WORKDIR *path-to-workdir*	**WORKDIR** sets the working directory for any **RUN**, **CMD**, **COPY**, **ADD**, and **ENTRYPOINT** instructions specified in the Dockerfile. It can be used multiple times in one Dockerfile.
ONBUILD	ONBUILD *Dockerfile INSTRUCTION*	**ONBUILD** is executed only after the current Dockerfile build is complete. Any *INSTRUCTION* specified under **ONBUILD** executes in any child image derived from the current image.
ENV	ENV *key=value* [*key=value* ...] ENV *key value*	The **ENV** instruction sets the environment variable *key* to the value *value*. Environment variables defined using **ENV** always override an **ARG** instruction with the same key value.
ARG	ARG *name=default-value*	**ARG** defines a variable that you can pass at build time, such as when using the **docker build** command with the **--build-arg** *varname=value* flag.

Example 6-8 illustrates the process of dockerizing a Python application that uses the **numpy** library. In this example, the **FROM** instruction set specifies the use of Python 3 for the Dockerfile, adds the hist.py file to the Dockerfile by using the **ADD** instruction, runs the command **pip3 install numpy** by using **RUN** instruction, and executes the Python code by using the **python3** command specified under the **CMD** instruction. Once the Dockerfile is built, the command **docker build** is used to create a Dockerfile named **plotter**. When the docker image is built, the command **docker run plotter**, where **plotter** is the name of the container, is used to run the container.

Example 6-8 *Dockerizing a Python Application*

```
! Creating a Dockerfile
[root@rnd-srvr plotter]# touch Dockerfile

! Dockerfile is edited with the following contents
FROM python:3
ADD hist.py /
RUN pip3 install numpy
CMD [ "python3", "./hist.py" ]
```

```
! hist.py File
import numpy as np

greyhounds = 10

grey_height = 28 + 4 * np.random.randn(greyhounds)

print(grey_height)
```

```
[root@rnd-srvr plotter]# docker build -t plotter .
Sending build context to Docker daemon 3.072 kB
Step 1/4 : FROM python:3
Trying to pull repository docker.io/library/python ...
3: Pulling from docker.io/library/python
8f0fdd3eaac0: Pull complete
d918eaefd9de: Pull complete
43bf3e3107f5: Pull complete
27622921edb2: Pull complete
dcfa0aa1ae2c: Pull complete
bf6840af9e70: Pull complete
21f900120cf5: Pull complete
644b4ceca849: Pull complete
50f0ac11639a: Pull complete
Digest: sha256:58666f6a49048d737eb24478e8dabce32774730e2f2d0803911a2c1f61c1b805
Status: Downloaded newer image for docker.io/python:3
 ---> 038a832804a0
Step 2/4 : ADD hist.py /
 ---> a1aa56c4a003
Removing intermediate container 8a0ffc6ae9e7
Step 3/4 : RUN pip3 install numpy
[171502.757410] docker0: port 1(vethe9cc10a) entered blocking state
[171502.761254] docker0: port 1(vethe9cc10a) entered disabled state
 ---> Running in 2d2c56d17289
[171502.778704] device vethe9cc10a entered promiscuous mode
```

```
[171502.780834] IPv6: ADDRCONF(NETDEV_UP): vethe9cc10a: link is not ready
[171502.782820] docker0: port 1(vethe9cc10a) entered blocking state
[171502.784738] docker0: port 1(vethe9cc10a) entered forwarding state
[171502.796246] docker0: port 1(vethe9cc10a) entered disabled state

[171502.934059] SELinux: mount invalid.  Same superblock, different security
  settings for (dev mqueue, type mqueue)
[171503.001974] IPv6: ADDRCONF(NETDEV_UP): eth0: link is not ready
[171503.005056] IPv6: ADDRCONF(NETDEV_CHANGE): eth0: link becomes ready
[171503.007321] IPv6: ADDRCONF(NETDEV_CHANGE): vethe9cc10a: link becomes ready
[171503.009437] docker0: port 1(vethe9cc10a) entered blocking state
[171503.011278] docker0: port 1(vethe9cc10a) entered forwarding state
Collecting numpy
  Downloading
  https://files.pythonhosted.org/packages/f5/4d/cbea29c189e2a9c5d3e2d76307be15f
  7f864a073cdb6c1abbc8e4311afbc/numpy-1.18.0-cp38-cp38-manylinux1_x86_64.whl (20.6MB)
Installing collected packages: numpy
Successfully installed numpy-1.18.0
[171534.064076] docker0: port 1(vethe9cc10a) entered disabled state
[171534.079041] docker0: port 1(vethe9cc10a) entered disabled state
[171534.082044] device vethe9cc10a left promiscuous mode
[171534.083874] docker0: port 1(vethe9cc10a) entered disabled state
 ---> f36b3a2a503a
Removing intermediate container 2d2c56d17289
Step 4/4 : CMD python3 ./hist.py
 ---> Running in cd9f08d4e70c
 ---> d90c530f9c87
Removing intermediate container cd9f08d4e70c
Successfully built d90c530f9c87
```

```
[root@rnd-srvr plotter]# docker run plotter
[172184.450904] docker0: port 1(vethc2445d5) entered blocking state
[172184.453092] docker0: port 1(vethc2445d5) entered disabled state
[172184.457887] device vethc2445d5 entered promiscuous mode
[172184.459767] IPv6: ADDRCONF(NETDEV_UP): vethc2445d5: link is not ready
[172184.461788] docker0: port 1(vethc2445d5) entered blocking state
[172184.463616] docker0: port 1(vethc2445d5) entered forwarding state
[172184.475302] docker0: port 1(vethc2445d5) entered disabled state
[172184.597108] SELinux: mount invalid.  Same superblock, different security
  settings for (dev mqueue, type mqueue)
[172184.643800] IPv6: ADDRCONF(NETDEV_UP): eth0: link is not ready
[172184.645876] IPv6: ADDRCONF(NETDEV_CHANGE): eth0: link becomes ready
[172184.647860] IPv6: ADDRCONF(NETDEV_CHANGE): vethc2445d5: link becomes ready
[172184.649851] docker0: port 1(vethc2445d5) entered blocking state
[172184.651668] docker0: port 1(vethc2445d5) entered forwarding state
```

```
[30.24019652 25.82537121 29.06987139 23.12124747 26.15472775 24.82905669
 24.32525392 26.372184   24.0266377  25.66512881]
[root@rnd-srvr plotter]# [172185.041128] docker0: port 1(vethc2445d5) entered
  disabled state
[172185.049379] docker0: port 1(vethc2445d5) entered disabled state
[172185.051577] device vethc2445d5 left promiscuous mode
[172185.053236] docker0: port 1(vethc2445d5) entered disabled state

[root@rnd-srvr plotter]#
```

Note In the event that the repository that holds the packages you want to download resides behind a proxy server, other system and environment variables have to be updated. You use the **ENV** command in the Dockerfile as shown here to update the system variables:

```
ENV http_proxy http://proxy-srvr.xyz.com:8080/
ENV https_proxy http://proxy-srvr.xyz.com:8080/
```

The virtualenv Tool

Python, like most other languages, has a unique way of storing and managing packages. Even though everything is stored and maintained properly, it becomes challenging to maintain packages that are solely used on a project-by-project basis. Once an application is developed and ready for deployment, it is hard to remember which packages and versions are required. Also, it is challenging to keep the development environment separate from the production environment. To overcome these challenges, you can use **virtualenv**.

virtualenv is a tool for creating isolated Python virtual environments to manage Python packages for different projects. This means that each project can have its own dependencies, regardless of the dependencies of the system or other projects running in different virtual environments. In addition, these virtual environments allow programmers to maintain separate Python versions for individual projects. Example 6-9 demonstrates how to install **virtualenv** by using **pip3** package manager.

Example 6-9 *Installing virtualenv*

```
[root@node2 ~]# pip3 install virtualenv
WARNING: Running pip install with root privileges is generally not a good idea.
  Try `pip3 install --user` instead.
Collecting virtualenv
  Downloading
  https://files.pythonhosted.org/packages/05/f1/2e07e8ca50e047b9cc9ad56cf4291f4e041fa
  73207d000a095fe478abf84/virtualenv-16.7.9-py2.py3-none-any.whl (3.4MB)



Installing collected packages: virtualenv
Successfully installed virtualenv-16.7.9
[root@rnd-srvr project]#
```

To create a virtual environment with **virtualenv**, you use the command **virtualenv** *name*. This command creates a directory with the specified name and installs Python packages into that directory. If you specify a dot (.) instead of a name, the current directory is used to set up the virtual environment. Inside the directory, four subdirectories are created:

- **bin:** Contains the files that interact with the virtual environment.
- **include:** Contains the C headers that compile the Python packages.
- **lib:** Holds a copy of the Python version along with a site packages folder where each dependency is installed.
- **lib64:** Holds a copy of the Python version along with a site packages folder where each dependency is installed.

Note **lib64** site packages are preferred over **lib** site packages on 64-bit systems.

Another way to create a virtual environment is by using the **python3** command. You can use the command **python3 -m venv** *name* to create a virtual environment with the specified name. Example 6-10 shows how to create a virtual environment using both the **virtualenv** command and the **python3 -m venv** command. To use the virtual environment, you need to call the **activate** script, which is located in the **bin** directory of the virtual environment. You can do this by using the command **source** *venv*/**bin/activate**, where *venv* is the name of the virtual environment. In Example 6-10, notice that the changes made to the site packages within the virtual environment are not reflected to the global packages, so you can maintain separate environments for different projects.

Example 6-10 *Creating Virtual Environments*

```
[root@rnd-srvr project]# virtualenv env
Using base prefix '/usr'
  No LICENSE.txt/LICENSE found in source
New python executable in /root/project/env/bin/python3
Also creating executable in /root/project/env/bin/python
Installing setuptools, pip, wheel...

done.
[root@rnd-srvr project]#
[root@rnd-srvr project]# source env/bin/activate
(env) [root@rnd-srvr project]# python --version
Python 3.6.8
(env) [root@rnd-srvr project]# python3 --version
Python 3.6.8
(env) [root@rnd-srvr project]# deactivate
[root@rnd-srvr project]# python --version
Python 2.7.5
```

```
[root@rnd-srvr project]# python3 --version
Python 3.6.8
```

```
[root@rnd-srvr project]# python3 -m venv newenv
[root@rnd-srvr project]# ls
env  newenv  test.py
[root@rnd-srvr project]# source newenv/bin/activate
(newenv) [root@rnd-srvr project]# python --version
Python 3.6.8
(newenv) [root@rnd-srvr project]# pip3 install --upgrade pip
Cache entry deserialization failed, entry ignored
Collecting pip
  Downloading
  https://files.pythonhosted.org/packages/00/b6/9cfa56b4081ad13874b0c6f96af8ce16cfbc
  1cb06bedf8e9164ce5551ec1/pip-19.3.1-py2.py3-none-any.whl (1.4MB)

Installing collected packages: pip
  Found existing installation: pip 9.0.3
    Uninstalling pip-9.0.3:
      Successfully uninstalled pip-9.0.3
Successfully installed pip-19.3.1
(newenv) [root@rnd-srvr project]# pip3 --version
pip 19.3.1 from /root/project/newenv/lib64/python3.6/site-packages/pip (python 3.6)
(newenv) [root@rnd-srvr project]# deactivate
[root@rnd-srvr project]# pip3 --version
pip 9.0.3 from /usr/lib/python3.6/site-packages (python 3.6)
[root@rnd-srvr project]#
```

Note It is possible to use **pipenv** instead of **virtualenv. pipenv** automatically creates and manages a virtual environment for projects and allows you to manage packages from a pip-file (that is, add or remove packages as they are installed or uninstalled). With **pipenv**, you are not required to use **pip/pip3** and **virtualenv** separately.

Python Modules

A Python *module* is a file that contains Python code with definitions and statements. Python modules allow you to logically organize code by grouping classes, functions, and variables; modules also help you write reusable code. A Python module can be used and called by using the **import** statement, which takes a list of modules as parameters, as shown here:

```
import module1 [, module2 [, ... , moduleN]
```

When Python code is being executed and the interpreter encounters an **import** statement, it imports the module into the current code so that the definitions and the statements part of the module become accessible to the current code. Example 6-11 shows an example of using the module **mymod**, which is defined in the file mymod.py. The **mymod** module defines the function **say_hello()**, which takes a name (as a string) as the parameter. When the **mymod** module is imported into the test.py file, the **say_hello()** function becomes accessible in test.py, and you can call it by referencing the module name as shown in Example 6-11. Note that the module is loaded only once, regardless of the number of times it has been imported in the Python code. Once it is loaded, the definitions and statements within the module are accessible throughout the program.

Example 6-11 *Using Modules with import Statements*

```
! mymod.py in /root/python directory
[root@rnd-srvr python]# cat mymod.py

def say_hello(name):
        print('Hello ' + name)
```

```
! test.py in /root/python directory
[root@rnd-srvr python]# cat test.py
import mymody

mymody.say_hello('John')
```

```
[root@rnd-srvr python]# python3 test.py
Hello John
```

The **import** statements import all the methods and classes into the Python interpreter. In Python, a module is always fully imported into the **sys.modules** mapping. Using a **from-import** statement in Python is another way of importing a module. The main difference when using a **from-import** statement is that it binds a name pointing directly to the attribute contained in the module. The complete module still gets imported using this **import** statement format. The **from-import** statement takes the list of functions/definitions as parameters, as shown here:

```
from module-name import name1 [, name2 [,..., nameN]
```

Note To import all non-private names without having to specify them using commas (,), you can use the wildcard character * after the **import** keyword, as shown here:

```
from module-name import *
```

Example 6-12 demonstrates the use of a **from-import** statement. Note that in this example, the module **mymod** is present in the directory named **hello**, and the module has functions named **say_hello()** and **say_bye()**. The **from-import** statement in this example directly binds a reference to the **say_hello()** function, but the rest of the function is still accessible to a programmer who wants to access it.

Example 6-12 *Using a from-import Statement*

```
! mymod.py in /root/python/hello directory
[root@rnd-srvr python]# cat hello/mymod.py

def say_hello(name):
        print('Hello ' + name)

def say_bye(name):
        print('Bye ' + name)
```

```
! test.py in /root/python directory
[root@rnd-srvr python]# cat test.py
from hello.mymod import say_hello

say_hello('John')
```

```
[root@rnd-srvr python]# python3 test.py
Hello John
```

Another way to implement modules is by using classes. Example 6-13 illustrates the use of a class defined in a module. **__init__** is a reserved method in Python classes that is used as a constructor (which is a concept in object-oriented programming). The method is called when an instance of the class is created that allows the class to initialize its attributes. The **__init__** method can be called with just **self** as the argument or along with extra arguments. The **self** keyword represents an instance of the class and helps in accessing the attributes and methods of the class in Python. In Example 6-13, a constructor of the **Hello** class is created with the string parameter **name**. When the constructor is called, it sets the name attribute of the **Hello** class to the value specified in the parameter. Thus, when **mymodule.Hello()** is called with 'John' as the parameter, the **name** attribute of class **Hello** is set to the value 'John'. Since an object is created here by calling the constructor named **test** for the class **Hello**, you can now access the method **say_hello()** by using the same object.

Example 6-13 *A Python Module with a Class and a Constructor*

```
! mymodule.py in /root/python/hello directory
[root@rnd-srvr python]# cat hello/mymodule.py

class Hello:
    def __init__(self, name):
        self.name = name

    def say_hello(self):
        print('Hello ' + self.name)
```

```
! test.py in /root/python directory
```

```
[root@rnd-srvr python]# cat test.py
from hello import mymodule

test = mymodule.Hello('John')
test.say_hello()
```

```
[root@rnd-srvr python]# python3 test.py
Hello John
```

From the examples in this section, it is clear that modules make it possible to reuse the code within a project. The next section dives into various applications of the Python programming language.

Python Applications

The use of Python has increased greatly in the past several decades. Due to its emphasis on the DRY (Don't Repeat Yourself) principle and ease of readability, Python has been adopted by developers across multiple application domains. Because of Python's wide acceptance, the Python Package Index lists thousands of third-party modules that can be used to develop robust, highly scalable, and secure applications. Today Python is being widely used in multiple application domains, including the following:

- Web application development
- Desktop applications
- Business applications (ERP, CRM, and so on)
- Machine learning and artificial intelligence
- Data science and data visualization
- Automation and orchestration
- Audio and video applications

The following sections discuss some of these domains.

Web/API Development

A web application is a client/server program in which the client runs on the browser. The application is hosted on a remote server and delivered over the Internet or across the network through a browser interface. A web application has two major components:

- **Front end:** Refers to the user interface, where the information or data is displayed to the user.
- **Back end:** Refers to the application and database where the logic is implemented for the actions that need to be performed on the data and how the data will be sent to the front-end application.

Some web applications are also developed with three-layer architecture, which has a front end for user interaction, a back end for databases, and a middle layer for logic and validation. Multiple web development frameworks, including these, make it possible to develop web applications using Python:

- Django
- Pyramid
- Flask
- Bottle
- FastAPI

The following sections discuss how to install and use Django and Flask for web/API development.

Django

Django is a high-level web framework based on Python that makes it possible to rapidly develop scalable and secure web applications. Django follows a pragmatic design that allows developers to incrementally add functionality to a web application without having to impact other components or other sections of the code. It takes care of most of the web development hassle and allows developers to focus on writing modular apps. In addition, Django has support for multiple databases, such as MySQL and Postgres, which makes it easier to build a back-end database and logic without having users directly interact with the database itself. At the time of writing, some high-profile and highly scalable websites—such as Instagram, National Geographic, and OpenStack—are using Django in their back ends to some extent.

Currently, Django supports its users with three different trains. The latest versions of Django are 3.0.3, 2.2.10, and 1.11.28. The Django web framework can be installed using the Python package manager, **pip** or **pip3**. Once Django is installed, you can start creating projects by issuing the command **django-admin startproject** *project-name*. Example 6-14 shows the installation of Django Version 2.2.10 in a virtual environment and the creation of a new project.

Example 6-14 *Installing Django and Starting a New Django Project*

```
[root@rnd-srvr opt]# virtualenv web
[root@rnd-srvr opt]# source web/bin/activate
(web) [root@rnd-srvr opt]# pip3 install django==2.2.10
Collecting django==2.1.1
  Downloading https://files.pythonhosted.org/packages/ca/7e/fc068d164b32552ae3a8f8d
  5d0280c083f2e8d553e71ecacc21927564561/Django-2.2.10-py3-none-any.whl (7.3MB)
|,ñà,ñà,ñà,ñà,ñà,ñà,ñà,ñà,ñà,ñà,ñà,ñà,ñà,ñà,ñà,ñà,ñà,ñà,ñà,ñà,ñà,ñà,ñà,ñà,ñà,ñà,ñà,ñ
  à,ñà,ñà,ñà,ñà| 7.3MB 3.8MB/s
Requirement already satisfied: pytz in ./web/lib/python3.6/site-packages (from
  django==2.2.10) (2019.3)
```

```
Installing collected packages: django
Successfully installed django-2.2.10

! Creating a project in Django
(web) [root@rnd-srvr opt]# django-admin startproject Demo1
```

Every Django project starts with a manage.py file in its project root directory. The **manage.py** script allows you to run administrative tasks such as Django's **django-admin**. As mentioned earlier, Django applications allow you to interact with the databases. The database tables are defined using models. Updating models created in Django on the database requires migrations. Django migration allows for propagation of changes made to the models into the database schema. These migrations are automatic, but it is important for developers to understand and know when to make these migrations. The following commands can be used with manage.py as parameters to perform migration operations:

- **migrate:** Applies migrations.
- **makemigrations:** Makes new migrations, based on changes made to the models.
- **sqlmigrate:** Displays SQL statements for migrations.
- **showmigrations:** Lists projects' migrations and their status.

When migrations are performed for an application, the next step is to test the application. For testing web applications or web APIs, Django comes with its own web server. You can invoke Django's web server by using the **runserver** command to manage.py. The **runserver** command can be executed with options such as *IP-address:port*, where *IP-address* can be the IP address of one of the physical network interface cards (NICs) or 0.0.0.0, which allows client machines to send requests on any IP address configured on the server.

Example 6-15 illustrates how to perform migrations and test a web application by enabling Django's web server on port 8080.

Example 6-15 *Performing Django Migrations and Running a Django Application Web Server*

```
(web) [root@rnd-srvr Demo1]# pwd
/opt/Demo1
(web) [root@rnd-srvr Demo1]# ls
db.sqlite3  Demo1  manage.py
(web) [root@rnd-srvr Demo1]# python manage.py migrate
Operations to perform:
  Apply all migrations: admin, auth, contenttypes, sessions
Running migrations:
  Applying contenttypes.0001_initial... OK
  Applying auth.0001_initial... OK
  Applying admin.0001_initial... OK
```

```
  Applying admin.0002_logentry_remove_auto_add... OK
  Applying admin.0003_logentry_add_action_flag_choices... OK
  Applying contenttypes.0002_remove_content_type_name... OK
  Applying auth.0002_alter_permission_name_max_length... OK
  Applying auth.0003_alter_user_email_max_length... OK
  Applying auth.0004_alter_user_username_opts... OK
  Applying auth.0005_alter_user_last_login_null... OK
  Applying auth.0006_require_contenttypes_0002... OK
  Applying auth.0007_alter_validators_add_error_messages... OK
  Applying auth.0008_alter_user_username_max_length... OK
  Applying auth.0009_alter_user_last_name_max_length... OK
  Applying sessions.0001_initial... OK
(web) [root@rnd-srvr Demo1]# python manage.py runserver 172.16.102.134:8080
Performing system checks...

System check identified no issues (0 silenced).
January 03, 2020 - 08:55:04
Django version 2.1.1, using settings 'Demo1.settings'
Starting development server at http://172.16.102.134:8080/
Quit the server with CONTROL-C.
Invalid HTTP_HOST header: '172.16.102.134:8080'. You may need to add
  '172.16.102.134' to ALLOWED_HOSTS.
Bad Request: /
[03/Jan/2020 08:55:13] "GET/HTTP/1.1" 400 59543
```

Note Multiple command options are available for use with manage.py. To get a list of all the available commands, use the command **python3 manage.py --help**.

Notice that in Example 6-15, even though the web application is running on the server at port 8080, any request made to the server is treated as a bad request. This is due to the permissions and settings on the Django application. To change the settings of the Django project, you need to edit the settings.py file that is generated for each project. The settings.py file resides in the project directory and contains all the configurations for a Django installation. The settings.py file includes the following sections:

- **Core settings:** Contains settings such as allowed hosts, admin settings, and absolute URL overrides.
- **Auth:** Contains settings for Django authentication models and back ends.
- **Messages:** Contains settings for Django messages.
- **Sessions:** Contains settings for managing sessions in a Django application.
- **Static files:** Contains settings for static URLs, static file directories, and so on.

The bad request shown in Example 6-15 can be resolved by changing the **ALLOWED_ HOSTS** settings in the settings.py file as shown in Example 6-16. This setting takes in a list of strings representing the host or domain names that the Django site can serve. The default setting for this field is an empty list ([]), or the field can be set to a particular IP address or a domain name, such as *example.com* or even * (which means the application will match any value). Example 6-16 shows that changing the settings.py file so that it matches any host allows the application to respond to the **GET** request coming from the HTTP client.

Example 6-16 *Editing Changes in the Settings.py File and Running a Django Application*

```
(web) [root@rnd-srvr Demo1]# cd Demo1/
(web) [root@rnd-srvr Demo1]# ls
__init__.py  settings.py  urls.py  wsgi.py

! Edit the settings.py file to allow All hosts using '*' or specific hosts by
  specifying the IP address range

(web) [root@rnd-srvr Demo1]# cat settings.py
"""
Django settings for Demo1 project.

Generated by 'django-admin startproject' using Django 2.1.1.

For more information on this file, see
https://docs.djangoproject.com/en/2.1/topics/settings/

For the full list of settings and their values, see
https://docs.djangoproject.com/en/2.1/ref/settings/
"""

import os

# Build paths inside the project like this: os.path.join(BASE_DIR, ...)
BASE_DIR = os.path.dirname(os.path.dirname(os.path.abspath(__file__)))


# Quick-start development settings - unsuitable for production
# See https://docs.djangoproject.com/en/2.1/howto/deployment/checklist/

# SECURITY WARNING: keep the secret key used in production secret!
SECRET_KEY = 'i69x735220ef*qz^qr&ix0bw8-bwp@^))5u1x134ztd)&*t@_5'
```

```
# SECURITY WARNING: don't run with debug turned on in production!
DEBUG = True

ALLOWED_HOSTS = ['*']

# Application definition

INSTALLED_APPS = [
    'django.contrib.admin',
    'django.contrib.auth',
    'django.contrib.contenttypes',
    'django.contrib.sessions',
    'django.contrib.messages',
    'django.contrib.staticfiles',
]

! Output omitted for brevity
```

```
(web) [root@rnd-srvr Demo1]# python manage.py runserver 172.16.102.134:8080
Performing system checks...

System check identified no issues (0 silenced).
January 03, 2020 - 08:59:34
Django version 2.1.1, using settings 'Demo1.settings'
Starting development server at http://172.16.102.134:8080/
Quit the server with CONTROL-C.
[03/Jan/2020 08:59:41] "GET/HTTP/1.1" 200 16348
[03/Jan/2020 08:59:41] "GET /static/admin/css/fonts.css HTTP/1.1" 200 423
Not Found: /favicon.ico
[03/Jan/2020 08:59:41] "GET /favicon.ico HTTP/1.1" 404 1976
[03/Jan/2020 08:59:41] "GET /static/admin/fonts/Roboto-Bold-webfont.woff
  HTTP/1.1" 200 82564
[03/Jan/2020 08:59:41] "GET /static/admin/fonts/Roboto-Regular-webfont.woff
  HTTP/1.1" 200 80304
[03/Jan/2020 08:59:41] "GET /static/admin/fonts/Roboto-Light-webfont.woff
  HTTP/1.1" 200 81348
```

When you access a Django application in a browser, if you see a web page like the one shown in Figure 6-2, you know that the Django framework was successfully installed.

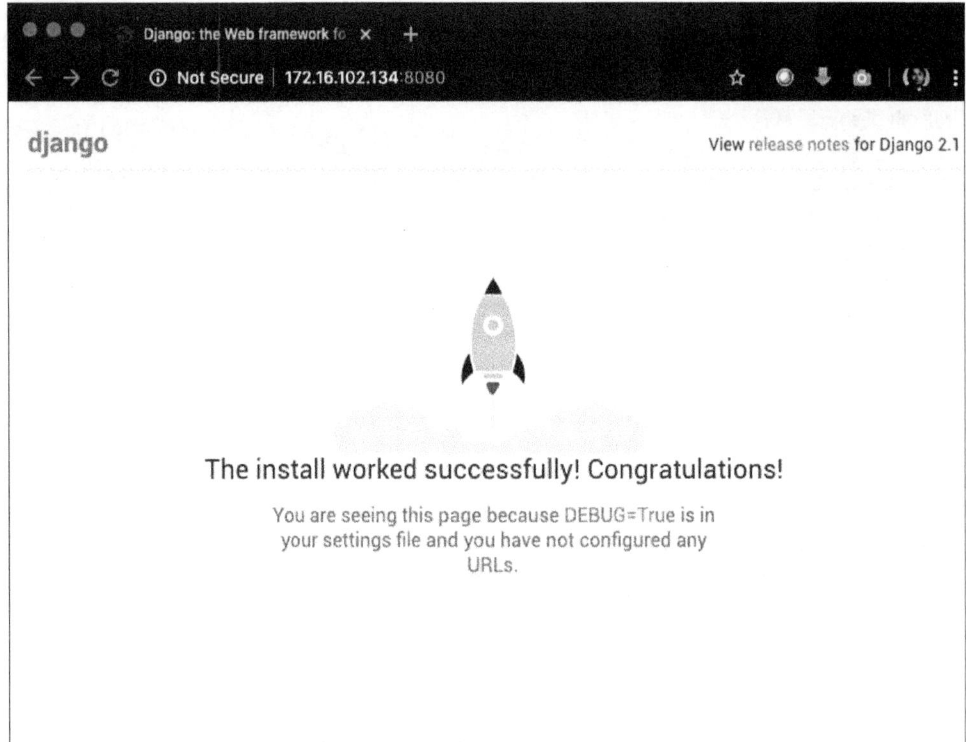

Figure 6-2 *Accessing a Django Application in a Web Browser*

The Django framework can be used to build a web application, but Django Rest Framework (DRF) is very handy for creating APIs. It is possible to build APIs using the Django framework, but DRF provides several useful functions, such as serializers, filtering, and OAuth support. DRF allows developers to create RESTful APIs and use serializers to convert HTTP requests into valid Django objects and vice versa when a response is received from a data source. Example 6-17 shows the installation of DRF and also illustrates how to create an app inside a Django project by using the command **django-admin startapp** *app-name*. After an app is created, in order to use DRF, both *app-name* and *rest_framework* should be added to the **INSTALLED_APPS** list in the settings.py file.

Example 6-17 *Installing DRF and Creating a Django App*

```
(web) [root@rnd-srvr Demo1]# pip3 install djangorestframework
Collecting djangorestframework
  Downloading
  https://files.pythonhosted.org/packages/be/5b/9bbde4395a1074d528d6d9e0cc161d3b99bd
  9d0b2b558ca919ffaa2e0068/djangorestframework-3.11.0-py3-none-any.whl (911kB)
Requirement already satisfied: django>=1.11 in /opt/web/lib/python3.6/site-packages
  (from djangorestframework) (2.1.1)
Requirement already satisfied: pytz in /opt/web/lib/python3.6/site-packages (from
  django>=1.11->djangorestframework) (2019.3)
```

```
Installing collected packages: djangorestframework
Successfully installed djangorestframework-3.11.0
(web) [root@rnd-srvr Demo1]# django-admin startapp demoapp
(web) [root@rnd-srvr Demo1]# ls
db.sqlite3  Demo1  demoapp  manage.py
```

```
! Edit the INSTALLED_APPS sections in settings.py file inside Demo1 Directory.
INSTALLED_APPS = [
    'django.contrib.admin',
    'django.contrib.auth',
    'django.contrib.contenttypes',
    'django.contrib.sessions',
    'django.contrib.messages',
    'django.contrib.staticfiles',
    'demoapp',
    'rest_framework',
]
```

The next step is to build the back end and logic for **demoapp**. Each app within Django contains the following files:

- **models.py**: This file defines the structure of the user data.
- **serializer.py**: This file uses Serializer to allow complex data such as query sets and model instances to be converted into native Python data types. This data can be then rendered into XML or JSON formats.
- **views.py**: This file allows you to define views or view sets. Views are Python functions that take in web requests and return web responses.
- **urls.py**: This file, which is present in both the project directory and the app directory, allows you to define a URL route for the app as well as the project.

Example 6-18 illustrates a basic employee model that takes in first name, last name, and data creation time as input and saves that in the back-end database. In this example, notice the use of the dot (.) in the **import** statement; this dot indicates a relative import, starting with the current package.

Example 6-18 *Building a Demo App*

```
! models.py

from django.db import models
from django.utils import timezone

class Employee(models.Model):
```

```
    firstName = models.CharField(max_length=400)
    lastName = models.CharField(max_length=400)
    created_at = models.DateTimeField(default=timezone.now)
```

```
! serializer.py

from rest_framework import serializers
from .models import Employee

class EmpSerializer(serializers.HyperlinkedModelSerializer):

    class Meta:
        model = Employee
        fields = ('id', 'firstName', 'lastName', 'created_at')
```

```
! views.py

from django.shortcuts import render
from rest_framework import viewsets
from .models import Employee
from .serializer import EmpSerializer

class EmpViewSet(viewsets.ModelViewSet):

    queryset = Employee.objects.all()
    serializer_class = EmpSerializer
```

```
! urls.py under demoapp

from rest_framework import routers
from . import views

router = routers.DefaultRouter()
router.register(r'Employees', views.EmpViewSet)

# Wire up our API using automatic URL routing.
# Additionally, we include login URLs for the browsable API.
urlpatterns = [
    path('', include(router.urls))]
```

```
! urls.py under Demo1 project folder

from django.contrib import admin
from django.urls import path, include
```

```
urlpatterns = [
    path('admin/', admin.site.urls),
    path('api/', include('demoapp.urls'))],
```

Note The details of how to write code in each file are beyond the scope of this book. The goal of this example is to illustrate how a web application/web API can be developed using Django and DRF. To read more about Django, see www.djangoproject.com.

When the demo app is complete, you execute the **runserver** command again and test the API either in a browser or by using a tool such as Postman.

Note Postman is a collaboration platform for API development. It allows you to test the APIs without having to write the code for the front end and visualize what the data response is going to look like from the server.

Flask

Flask is a Python-based microframework for building web applications and APIs. It is called a *microframework* because it does not provide a database abstraction layer or validation layer as Django does. Like most other Python libraries, the Flask package can be installed from the Python Package Index (PyPI). You may also want to install **flask-sqlalchemy** in order to allow a Flask application to interact with the SQL database. Example 6-19 shows the installation of the Flask package in a virtual environment. Note that there are a few other packages that get installed as part of the Flask installation.

Example 6-19 *Installing Flask in a Virtual Environment*

```
[root@rnd-srvr opt]# virtualenv flask
Using base prefix '/usr'
  No LICENSE.txt/LICENSE found in source
New python executable in /opt/flask/bin/python3
Also creating executable in /opt/flask/bin/python
Installing setuptools, pip, wheel...
done.
[root@rnd-srvr opt]# source flask/bin/activate
(flask) [root@rnd-srvr opt]#
(flask) [root@rnd-srvr opt]# pip3 install flask
Collecting flask
  Downloading
  https://files.pythonhosted.org/packages/9b/93/628509b8d5dc749656a9641f4caf13540e2c
  dec85276964ff8f43bbb1d3b/Flask-1.1.1-py2.py3-none-any.whl (94kB)


Collecting itsdangerous>=0.24
```

```
  Downloading
  https://files.pythonhosted.org/packages/76/ae/44b03b253d6fade317f32c24d100b3b35c22
  39807046a4c953c7b89fa49e/itsdangerous-1.1.0-py2.py3-none-any.whl
Collecting Jinja2>=2.10.1
  Downloading
  https://files.pythonhosted.org/packages/65/e0/eb35e762802015cab1ccee04e
  8a277b03f1d8e53da3ec3106882ec42558b/Jinja2-2.10.3-py2.py3-none-any.whl (125kB)

Collecting click>=5.1
  Downloading
  https://files.pythonhosted.org/packages/fa/37/45185cb5abbc30d7257104c434fe0b07e5a1
  95a6847506c074527aa599ec/Click-7.0-py2.py3-none-any.whl (81kB)

Collecting Werkzeug>=0.15
  Downloading
  https://files.pythonhosted.org/packages/ce/42/3aeda98f96e85fd26180534d36570e4d1810
  8d62ae36f87694b476b83d6f/Werkzeug-0.16.0-py2.py3-none-any.whl (327kB)

Collecting MarkupSafe>=0.23
  Downloading
  https://files.pythonhosted.org/packages/b2/5f/23e0023be6bb885d00ffbefad2942bc51a6203
  28ee910f64abe5a8d18dd1/MarkupSafe-1.1.1-cp36-cp36m-manylinux1_x86_64.whl
Installing collected packages: itsdangerous, MarkupSafe, Jinja2, click, Werkzeug,
  flask
Successfully installed Jinja2-2.10.3 MarkupSafe-1.1.1 Werkzeug-0.16.0 click-7.0
  flask-1.1.1 itsdangerous-1.1.0
(flask) [root@rnd-srvr opt]#
```

Unlike with Django, developers can build APIs quickly on Flask. All you need to begin developing an API in Flask is an entry point and a function with the URL route. The entry point of an application is at __**main**__, which indicates a top-level script. __**name**__ is a variable that defines whether the script is being run as the main module or as an imported module. In the __**main**__ section, you can define the host IP address and port number to access the web application or API and also enable Debugs if required. Once an entry point is defined, the app routing can be done using the **route** directive, which takes in the parameter as the path to access the API; a function is defined beneath this directive. Example 6-20 shows a simple Flask application that runs on port 5000 and prints "My First Flask Application." When the application is executed, you can use the **curl** command to test the response from the web server running on port 5000.

Example 6-20 *A Simple Flask Application*

```
! App.py

#!/opt/flask/bin/python

from flask import Flask

app = Flask(__name__)
```

```
@app.route('/')
def index():
    return "My First Flask Application"


! Define the entry point of the App
if __name__ == '__main__':
    app.debug = True
    app.run(host = '0.0.0.0',port=5000)
```

```
(flask) [root@rnd-srvr Demo2]# chmod a+x app.py
(flask) [root@rnd-srvr Demo2]# ./app.py
 * Serving Flask app "app" (lazy loading)
 * Environment: production
   WARNING: This is a development server. Do not use it in a production deployment.
   Use a production WSGI server instead.
 * Debug mode: on
 * Running on http://0.0.0.0:5000/ (Press CTRL+C to quit)
 * Restarting with stat
 * Debugger is active!
 * Debugger PIN: 162-511-044
10.24.70.54 - - [05/Jan/2020 07:30:15] "GET/HTTP/1.1" 200 -
10.24.70.54 - - [05/Jan/2020 07:30:15] "GET/HTTP/1.1" 200 -
10.24.70.54 - - [05/Jan/2020 07:30:15] "GET/HTTP/1.1" 200 -
10.24.70.54 - - [05/Jan/2020 07:30:16] "GET /favicon.ico HTTP/1.1" 404 -
```

```
! Testing the API using CURL

[root@node2 ~]# curl -i http://172.16.102.134:5000/
HTTP/1.1 200 OK
Server: Werkzeug/0.16.0 Python/3.6.8
Date: Sun, 05 Jan 2020 07:37:01 GMT
Content-Length: 26
Content-Type: text/html; charset=utf-8
Via: 1.1 sjc5-dmz-wsa-3.cisco.com:80 (Cisco-WSA/X)
Connection: keep-alive
Proxy-Connection: keep-alive

My First Flask Application
[root@node2 ~]#
```

Every application is built around a single purpose: handling data (that is, performing actions such as adding, deleting, or updating data). Because Flask is based on Python, developers can leverage other libraries and packages to perform actions on data. Most modern applications represent data in JSON format because it is easy to manage data in JSON. By using Flask, you can work on either data that is stored in a database table or in-memory data. Example 6-21 shows an example of handling in-memory data and a simple API to get all the JSON data stored in a variable. In this example, the variable **employees** is defined and contains the ID, first name, last name, and title of the employee. Then an API with the path api/v1.0/employees is created; it can be accessed using the HTTP **GET** method, which returns a JSON representation of the data via the **jsonify()** function that is part of the Flask package. Once the app is executed, you can access the employee data by using **curl** and specifying the path of the API.

Example 6-21 *Accessing In-Memory Employee Data*

```
#!/opt/flask/bin/python

from flask import Flask, jsonify

app = Flask(__name__)

employees = [
    {
        'id': 1,
        'firstname': u'John',
        'lastname': u'Doe',
        'title': u'CEO'
    },
    {
        'id': 2,
        'firstname': u'Jason',
        'lastname': u'Bruch',
        'title': u'CFO'
    }
]

@app.route('/api/v1.0/employees', methods=['GET'])
def get_employees():
    return jsonify({'employees': employees})

if __name__ == '__main__':
    app.debug = True
    app.run(host = '0.0.0.0',port=5000)
```

```
[root@node2 ~]# curl -i http://172.16.102.134:5000/api/v1.0/employees
HTTP/1.1 200 OK
Server: Werkzeug/0.16.0 Python/3.6.8
```

```
Date: Sun, 05 Jan 2020 08:35:28 GMT
Content-Length: 242
Content-Type: application/json
Via: 1.1 wsa.xyz.com:80
Connection: keep-alive
Proxy-Connection: keep-alive

{
  "employees": [
    {
      "firstname": "John",
      "id": 1,
      "lastname": "Doe",
      "title": "CEO"
    },
    {
      "firstname": "Jason",
      "id": 2,
      "lastname": "Bruch",
      "title": "CFO"
    }
  ]
}
```

Fetching all the data from a variable is easy, but web applications are usually required to fetch specific data and perform actions on that data. Example 6-22 shows how to get the ID of the employee in the URL and translate it in the *emp_id* argument in the function. With the **get_employee(***emp_id***)** function, a search is performed on the **employee** array. If the ID that is received as the argument does not exist, an HTTP 404 error is received, indicating that the resource is not found. If an entry is found, it is returned and printed in JSON format.

Example 6-22 *Retrieving Data Based on ID*

```
from flask import abort

app = Flask(__name__)

! Output omitted for brevity

@app.route('/api/v1.0/employees/<int:emp_id>', methods=['GET'])
def get_employee(emp_id):
    emp = [emp for emp in employees if emp['id'] == emp_id]
    if len(emp) == 0:
        abort(404)
```

```
    return jsonify({'Employee': emp[0]})
```

```
[root@node2 ~]# curl -i http://172.16.102.134:5000/api/v1.0/employees/1
HTTP/1.1 200 OK
Server: Werkzeug/0.16.0 Python/3.6.8
Date: Sun, 05 Jan 2020 09:19:02 GMT
Content-Length: 110
Content-Type: application/json
Via: 1.1 sjc12-dmz-wsa-5.cisco.com:80 (Cisco-WSA/X)
Connection: keep-alive
Proxy-Connection: keep-alive

{
  "Employee": {
    "firstname": "John",
    "id": 1,
    "lastname": "Doe",
    "title": "CEO"
  }
}
```

```
[root@node2 ~]# curl -i http://172.16.102.134:5000/api/v1.0/employees/3
HTTP/1.1 404 Not Found
Server: Werkzeug/0.16.0 Python/3.6.8
Date: Sun, 05 Jan 2020 09:20:20 GMT
Content-Length: 232
Content-Type: text/html
Via: 1.1 sjc5-dmz-wsa-3.cisco.com:80 (Cisco-WSA/X)
Connection: keep-alive
Proxy-Connection: keep-alive

<!DOCTYPE HTML PUBLIC "-//W3C//DTD HTML 3.2 Final//EN">
<title>404 Not Found</title>
<h1>Not Found</h1>
<p>The requested URL was not found on the server. If you entered the URL manually
  please check your spelling and try again.</p>
[root@node2 ~]#
```

The previous examples demonstrate the use of HTTP **GET** methods to fetch data from the web server. To add or update existing data on the server, HTTP **POST** or **PUT** methods are required. Example 6-23 illustrates the creation of an API to perform the HTTP **POST** operation on the in-memory employee data. In this example, the **route()** method sets the HTTP method as **POST**. As the name suggests, the role of the **add_employee()**

function in Example 6-23 is to add a new employee to the employees list. **request.json** has the request data only if that data came marked as JSON. The code checks whether the request data is present, and if it is present, it checks to ensure that the **'firstName'** field is not missing. If all the necessary fields are present, the function appends the data present in **request.data** to the **employees** list.

> **Note** When testing **POST** methods in API calls using **curl**, it is important to mention the content type as application/JSON; otherwise, the code will be unable to find any data in **request.json.**

Example 6-23 *Inserting Data by Using the HTTP POST Method*

```
from flask import request

@app.route('/api/v1.0/employees', methods=['POST'])
def add_employee():
    if not request.json or not 'firstName' in request.json:
        abort(400)
    employee = {
        'id': employees[-1]['id'] + 1,
        'firstName': request.json['firstName'],
        'lastName': request.json['lastName'],
        'title': request.json['title']
    }
    employees.append(employee)
    return jsonify({'employee': employee}), 201
```

```
[root@node2 ~]# curl -i -H "Content-Type: application/json" -X POST -d
  '{"firstName":"Billy", "lastName":"Mathews", "title":"Software Engineer"}'
  http://172.16.102.134:5000/api/v1.0/employees


HTTP/1.1 201 Created
Server: Werkzeug/0.16.0 Python/3.6.8
Date: Sun, 05 Jan 2020 09:35:53 GMT
Content-Length: 126
Content-Type: application/json
Via: 1.1 sjc12-dmz-wsa-2.cisco.com:80 (Cisco-WSA/X)
Connection: keep-alive
Proxy-Connection: keep-alive

{
  "employee": {
    "firstName": "Billy",
    "id": 3,
```

```
    "lastName": "Mathews",
    "title": "Software Engineer"
  }
}
```

```
[root@node2 ~]# curl -i http://172.16.102.134:5000/api/v1.0/employees
HTTP/1.1 200 OK
Server: Werkzeug/0.16.0 Python/3.6.8
Date: Sun, 05 Jan 2020 09:38:05 GMT
Content-Length: 360
Content-Type: application/json
Via: 1.1 sjc12-dmz-wsa-1.cisco.com:80 (Cisco-WSA/X)
Connection: keep-alive
Proxy-Connection: keep-alive

{
  "employees": [
    {
      "firstname": "John",
      "id": 1,
      "lastname": "Doe",
      "title": "CEO"
    },
    {
      "firstname": "Jason",
      "id": 2,
      "lastname": "Bruch",
      "title": "CFO"
    },
    {
      "firstName": "Billy",
      "id": 3,
      "lastName": "Mathews",
      "title": "Software Engineer"
    }
  ]
}
```

Other web development frameworks are available as well, but Django and Flask are the most commonly used web development frameworks. You can begin using Flask very quickly and with very few lines of code. With Django, you need to do some homework even for a simple "Hello world" program. However, as an application grows, managing a project and its flow is much simpler in Django than in Flask. Basically, you can use Django to develop large-scale applications, and you can use Flask for lightweight applications or applications that have very low turnaround time.

Network Automation

Another field in which Python has gained a lot of interest in the past few years is network automation. Most companies have huge open budgets for managing and maintaining network infrastructure. Most network outages occur due to human error when deploying new services or while making changes in the existing environment. In addition, a network operating system may run into software defects that cause massive network outages; it is tricky to identify the problem in such situations. Even if the root cause of an outage is known, the network operations team has to manually check on the network devices from time to time in order to ensure that the network is stable and that known issues are not occurring. Another potentially problematic area of network administration is manual application of patches to devices throughout a network. Manually applying patches can take up to several weeks or even months. All these challenges can be solved with network automation tools, and these tools can also help save time and minimize operational costs.

To build a foundation for network automation, it is important to understand that there are primarily two key players around which the architecture needs to be built:

- Human interface
- Network infrastructure

Automation tasks are created to reduce manual work that requires human interaction. However, automation tasks often require that some inputs as well as validations be performed through human interaction. Most automation tasks involve configuration and monitoring. A human interface may be needed to perform data management, and the data is then provided as an input to the configuration management module, which in turn interacts with the network devices to perform the configuration tasks. Data management can be performed by maintaining data in various formats, such as YAML, JSON, and XML, but the data exchange between the modules or components is usually in JSON or XML format.

A network device collects and maintains live as well as historical data for various features and components. This data can be used by collection tools to provide insights into the device. For instance, a configuration change might change the data flow on the device, and it is important that network operators and administrators be able to see the change and its reflection on the network. Network devices are capable of providing more visibility into the network through **show** commands, historical data, and telemetry data that can be used for various purposes. Data retrieved from telemetry or by using **show** commands and in combination with historical data can be used for further verification and testing and can then be displayed on the user interface, which makes it easier to manage the network and know its state. The data can also be sent to the data management module so that improvements can be made if the data shows signs of problems. This closed-loop architecture ensures that the visibility and data from the network devices can be used to make further changes to devices and improve the state of the network. Figure 6-3 provides a flow diagram that illustrates the closed-loop network architecture.

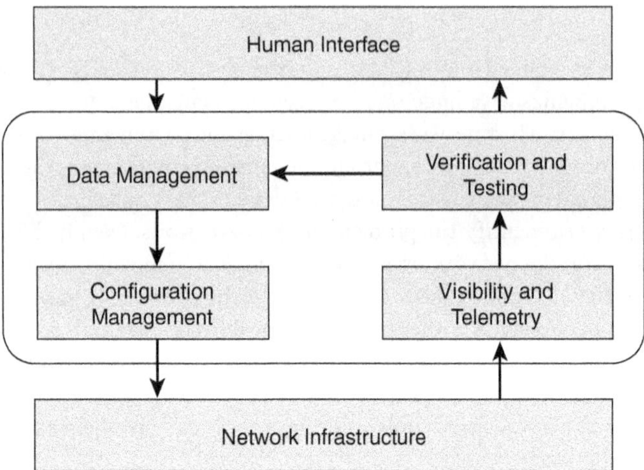

Figure 6-3 *Network Automation Architecture*

Multiple open-source libraries and automation frameworks available on PyPI, including NAPALM and Nornir, contain Python functions that allow you to interact with various network operating systems through a unified API. The next few sections cover various automation frameworks and demonstrate how and where these frameworks can be useful.

NAPALM

NAPALM (Network Automation and Programmability Abstraction Layer with Multivendor Support) provides functions that allow you to perform configuration operations such as commit or rollback operations and also to retrieve state data from network devices, regardless of the network operating system. The NAPALM library contains methods to establish connections to network devices and can work in conjunction with automation tools such as Ansible to manage a group of devices in a network at once. The NAPALM library provides support for various network operating systems, including Cisco IOS, IOS XR, and NX-OS; Juniper Junos OS; and Arista EOS. You can install the NAPALM library by using the Python package manager **pip**, using the command **pip install napalm**. Once the library is installed, you can use the **get_network_driver()** function from the NAPALM library to access the various network operating system drivers. Example 6-24 illustrates the use of the NAPALM library to access various network drivers.

Example 6-24 *Accessing Various Network Drivers by Using the NAPALM Library*

```
>>> from napalm import get_network_driver
>>> get_network_driver('ios-xr')
<class 'napalm.iosxr.iosxr.IOSXRDriver'>
>>> get_network_driver('ios')
<class 'napalm.ios.ios.IOSDriver'>
>>> get_network_driver('junos')
<class 'napalm.junos.junos.JunOSDriver'>
```

Note that the NAPALM library requires some preliminary configuration, such as management IP address and SSH configuration, in order to access the devices. Before we can dive in to the fundamentals of building a network automation tool, it is imperative to understand the importance of a networking devices inventory database, which usually contains the following information:

- Device name (hostname)
- Management IP address
- Network operating system
- Username/password

This information can be leveraged to establish a connection to a network device using a matching network driver and authentication credentials. Network databases can be created in different formats, including JSON and YAML. To illustrate the use of the NAPALM library, this section shows how to build a database in JSON format. Examine the hosts.json file shown in Example 6-25. In this JSON file, two hosts are defined, along with their management IP addresses, the network operating system type, and the username and password. A Python program can read in this JSON-based host database file to determine whether the specified host is a valid host.

Example 6-25 *Building a Host Database in JSON Format*

```
! hosts.json
{
  "xe-1": {
    "IP": "172.16.102.136",
    "type": "ios",
    "user": "cisco",
    "password": "cisco"
    },
    "nx-2": {
    "IP": "172.16.102.137",
    "type": "nxos",
    "user": "admin",
    "password": "admin"
    }
}
```

After defining the host database file, you can fetch the configuration from the network devices. The NAPALM library provides a **get_config()** function that fetches the configuration of a specified network device. Example 6-26 illustrates the use of the NAPALM library to fetch the network configuration. In this example, the Python program takes the parameters **get_config** and **hostname** for the configuration that is to be returned. If the hostname does not match with the host database file, an error is returned. When the hostname specified in the parameter matches the one specified in the host database JSON file, the relevant driver is loaded as per the host database, and a connection to the device is established. Then the program uses the device object to call the **get_config()** method to fetch the configuration from the device.

Example 6-26 *Fetching the Device Configuration by Using the NAPALM get_config() Function*

```
! napalm_example.py


import sys
import json
from napalm import get_network_driver



def err_report(*err_list):
    error_msg = ' '.join(str(x) for x in err_list)
    sys.exit(error_msg.rstrip("\n\r"))



if len(sys.argv) != 3:
    err_report("Usage: get_config hostname")

hostname = sys.argv[2]

try:
    with open('hosts.json', 'r') as f:
        device_db = json.load(f)
except (ValueError, IOError, OSError) as err:
    err_report('Could not read the host file: ', err)

try:
    device_info = device_db[hostname.lower()]
except KeyError:
    err_report("Unknown Device '{}'".format(hostname))

driver = get_network_driver(device_info['type'])
with driver(device_info['IP'], device_info['user'], device_info['password']) as
  device:
    config = device.get_config()
    print(config['running'])
```

```
(venv) [root@rnd-srvr napalm]# python napalm_example.py get_config xe-1
Building configuration...
```

```
Current configuration : 7221 bytes
!
! Last configuration change at 06:57:17 UTC Sun Mar 22 2020
!
version 16.11
service timestamps debug datetime msec
service timestamps log datetime msec
service call-home
platform qfp utilization monitor load 80
no platform punt-keepalive disable-kernel-core
platform console serial
!
hostname XE-1
!
! Output omitted for brevity
```

Note Errors in the program are handled through **try** and **except** blocks. A **try** block contains the code that may possibly return an error, and the **except** block holds the code to handle the error that is returned.

The NAPALM library can also be used to perform configuration-related operations on the network devices. The following operations can be performed:

- **Replace:** Allows you to replace the existing running configuration with an entirely new configuration.
- **Merge:** Allows you to merge configuration changes from a file to the running configuration on the device.
- **Compare:** Compares the newly proposed configuration with the existing one. Only applies to replace operation and not to merge operation.
- **Discard:** Resets the merge configuration file to an empty file, thus not allowing the new configuration to be applied on the device.
- **Commit:** Commits the proposed configuration to the network device. In other words, used to deploy a staged configuration.
- **Rollback:** Rolls back (reverts) the running configuration to the saved configuration prior to the last commit.

All these operations can be achieved through predefined functions in the NAPALM library. Some of these functions are illustrated in Example 6-27. In this example, a new loopback is proposed to be configured from the file config.txt. The newly proposed configuration is a merge candidate for the existing running configuration and can be loaded by using the **load_merge_candidate()** function. This function takes the filename or the configuration itself as the parameter. Once the merged config is loaded, the **compare_config()** function can be used to compare the newly proposed configuration with the existing configuration. (Note that only the delta configuration can be committed to the device.) The configuration can be committed by using the **commit_config()** function and can be discarded by using the **discard_config()** function.

Example 6-27 *Fetching Device Configuration by Using the NAPALM get_config() Function*

```
! config.txt
interface loopback100
  ip address 100.1.1.1 255.255.255.255
exit
```

```
! napalm_example.py

! Output omitted for brevity
driver = get_network_driver(device_info['type'])
with driver(device_info['IP'], device_info['user'], device_info['password']) as
  device:
    # config = device.get_config()
    # print(config['running'])
    device.load_merge_candidate(filename='config.txt')
    diffs = device.compare_config()
    if diffs != "":
        print(diffs)
        yesno = input('\nDo you wish to apply the changes? [y/N] ').lower()
        if yesno == 'y' or yesno == 'yes':
            print("Applying changes...")
            device.commit_config()
        else:
            print("Discarding changes...")
            device.discard_config()
    else:
        print("Configuration already present on the device")
        device.discard_config()
```

```
(venv) [root@rnd-srvr napalm]# python napalm_example.py merge_config xe-1

+ interface loopback100
+  ip address 100.1.1.1 255.255.255.255

Do you wish to apply the changes? [y/N] y
Applying changes...
```

By using the NAPALM library, you can easily manage the network devices: You can fetch information and apply changes to the network devices.

Note Refer to the NAPALM library documentation at https://napalm.readthedocs.io to explore all the available functions in the library.

Nornir

Nornir is a pure Python-based automation framework that takes care of managing the network and host inventory and provides a common framework to write plug-ins for network devices and hosts. The Nornir library requires a minimum Python version of 3.6.2 and can be installed using the Python package manager. An important and interesting fact about Nornir is that it is multithreaded. You can execute tasks simultaneously and in parallel on multiple hosts. Parallelization is triggered by running a task via **nornir.core.Nornir.run** and setting the global variable **num_workers**, which defaults to 20 worker threads. If **num_workers** is set to **1**, the tasks are handled by a single worker thread and are executed one after another, in a simple loop. This can be time-consuming, but it can be very useful during debugging.

Note The complete Nornir documentation can be found at https://nornir.readthedocs.io.

Now, before we dig into the Nornir framework, it is important to understand the files required to initialize Nornir. Nornir can be initialized by using a configuration file or by using code or by using a combination of both. Along with the configuration file, two other files are referenced within the configuration file:

- Host inventory file
- Group file

Both of these files are YAML based. The host inventory file is similar to the host database, which consists of the hostname, management IP address, port number, username and password, platform, and other information. The group file is used to assign common characteristics to the hosts. The hosts are part of a defined group, and additional characteristics that are common to multiple hosts are assigned to those groups. For instance, there might be 10 hosts in the host inventory file, which may be part of ASN 100, and there might be 5 other hosts that are part of ASN 200. In such a case, rather than define repeated information to 10 hosts, you can group the hosts together, and the ASN value can be assigned within the group. Example 6-28 illustrates how to configure the host.yaml, group.yaml, and config.yaml files that are used to initialize Nornir.

Example 6-28 *Inventory and Configuration Files for Nornir*

```
! hosts.yaml
---
XE-1:
    hostname: 172.16.102.136
    port: 22
    username: cisco
    password: cisco
    platform: ios
    groups:
        - xe-routers

XR-3:
    hostname: 172.16.102.138
    port: 22
    username: genie
    password: sonpari
    platform: iosxr
    groups:
        - xr-routers

NX-2:
    hostname: 172.16.102.137
    port: 443
    username: admin
    password: admin
    platform: nxos
    groups:
        - nx-routers
```

```
! groups.yaml
---
global:
    data:
        domain: domain.local
        asn: 65000

xe-routers:
    groups:
        - global

nx-routers:
    groups:
        - global
```

```
xr-routers:
    data:
        asn: 100
```

```
! config.yaml
---
core:
    num_workers: 20
inventory:
    plugin: nornir.plugins.inventory.simple.SimpleInventory
    options:
        host_file: "hosts.yaml"
        group_file: "groups.yaml"
```

Once the inventory and configuration files are defined, you can initialize Nornir by using the **InitNornir()** function defined under the **nornir** package. You then have the flexibility to use either the NAPALM library part of the Nornir framework or the Netmiko library, which can be used to send commands to the network devices. Example 6-29 demonstrates how to initialize Nornir by using the configuration file. Once Nornir is initialized, you can use the **run()** command to assign tasks for the worker threads. One of the tasks that can be used to gather information from network devices is **napalm_get**, which is defined under **nornir.plugins.tasks.networking**. It has options for following parameters:

- **getters:** Getters are the calls that are made to the devices to fetch information from them.
- **getters_options:** This parameter is used when passing multiple getters.
- ****kwargs:** This parameter specifies any additional arguments required by the getters. ****kwargs** is used to pass a variable-length argument list. The ** before **kwargs** allows you to pass any number of keyword arguments.

The Example 6-29 illustrates the use of the **get_facts** getter, which fetches from a network device information much as **show** commands do, including the hostname, fully qualified domain name (FQDN), and interface information.

Example 6-29 *Initializing Nornir*

```
! run_nornir.py
from nornir import InitNornir
from nornir.plugins.tasks.networking import napalm_get
from nornir.plugins.functions.text import print_result


nr = InitNornir(config_file="config.yaml")
```

```
result = nr.run(
            napalm_get,
            getters=['get_facts'])


print_result(result)
```

```
(nornir) [root@rnd-srvr nornir]# python3 run-nornir.py
napalm_get*********************************************************************
* NX-2 ** changed : False *****************************************************
vvvv napalm_get ** changed : False vvvvvvvvvvvvvvvvvvvvvvvvvvvvvvvvvvvvvvvvvvvvvvvv
  INFO
{ 'facts': { 'fqdn': 'NX-2',
             'hostname': 'NX-2',
             'interface_list': [ 'mgmt0',
                                 'Ethernet1/1',
                                 'Ethernet1/2',
                                 'Ethernet1/3',
                                 'Ethernet1/4',
                                 'Ethernet1/5',
                                 'Ethernet1/6',
                                 'Ethernet1/7',
                                 'Ethernet1/8',
],
             'model': 'Nexus9000 9000v Chassis',
             'os_version': '',
             'serial_number': '9IWWC65KRZ5',
             'uptime': 47743,
             'vendor': 'Cisco'}}
^^^^ END napalm_get ^^^^^^^^^^^^^^^^^^^^^^^^^^^^^^^^^^^^^^^^^^^^^^^^^^^^^^^^^^^^^^
* XE-1 ** changed : False *****************************************************
vvvv napalm_get ** changed : False vvvvvvvvvvvvvvvvvvvvvvvvvvvvvvvvvvvvvvvvvvvvvvvv
  INFO
{ 'facts': { 'fqdn': 'XE-1.not set',
             'hostname': 'XE-1',
             'interface_list': [ 'GigabitEthernet1',
                                 'GigabitEthernet2',
                                 'GigabitEthernet3',
                                 'GigabitEthernet4',
                                 'GigabitEthernet5',
                                 'GigabitEthernet6',
                                 'GigabitEthernet7',
                                 'GigabitEthernet8'],
             'model': 'CSR1000V',
```

```
            'os_version': 'Virtual XE Software '
                          '(X86_64_LINUX_IOSD-UNIVERSALK9-M), Version '
                          '16.11.1b, RELEASE SOFTWARE (fc2)',
            'serial_number': '9OJVU3ML6ZM',
            'uptime': 47700,
            'vendor': 'Cisco'}}
^^^^ END napalm_get ^^^^^^^^^^^^^^^^^^^^^^^^^^^^^^^^^^^^^^^^^^^^^^^^^^^^^^^^^^^^^
* XR-3 ** changed : False *****************************************************
vvvv napalm_get ** changed : False vvvvvvvvvvvvvvvvvvvvvvvvvvvvvvvvvvvvvvvvvvvvv
  INFO
{ 'facts': { 'fqdn': 'XR-3',
             'hostname': 'XR-3',
             'interface_list': [ 'GigabitEthernet0/0/0/0',
                                 'GigabitEthernet0/0/0/1',
                                 'GigabitEthernet0/0/0/2',
                                 'GigabitEthernet0/0/0/3',
                                 'GigabitEthernet0/0/0/4',
                                 'GigabitEthernet0/0/0/5',
                                 'GigabitEthernet0/0/0/6',
                                 'GigabitEthernet0/0/0/7',
                                 'MgmtEth0/RP0/CPU0/0',
                                 'Null0'],
             'model': 'R-IOSXRV9000-CC',
             'os_version': '6.6.2',
             'serial_number': '18C5B2EF3A6',
             'uptime': 47500,
             'vendor': 'Cisco'}}
^^^^ END napalm_get ^^^^^^^^^^^^^^^^^^^^^^^^^^^^^^^^^^^^^^^^^^^^^^^^^^^^^^^^^^^^^
(nornir) [root@rnd-srvr nornir]#
```

Other tasks are available in Nornir, such as **napalm_configure** (which is also defined under **nornir.plugins.takss.networking**). **napalm_configure** can be used in conjunction with Jinja templates, which are covered in the following section.

Templating with Jinja2

Jinja is a modern templating language for Python that is modeled after Django. Jinja templates can be used to dynamically generate content/snippets. The name Jinja2 identifies the latest version of Jinja. Jinja2 templates allow you to easily interact with the Python program and use the data received from functions to quickly generate dynamic content. Jinja provides several benefits, including the following:

- Template inheritance
- Optimal just-in-time compilation

- Easy debuggability
- Configurable syntax

Jinja2 is commonly used with web frameworks such as Flask, and it is also used as a template language by configuration management tools such as Ansible and network automation frameworks such as Nornir. This section refers to Jinja2 templates as simply Jinja templates.

Jinja can generate any text-based format, such as HTML, XML, or CSV. A Jinja template is a simple text file that can be stored in a file with any extension. A Jinja template may contain variables, statements (such as **if-else** statements), expressions, and comments. A few delimiters can be used in Jinja:

- {% . . . %}: For statements
- {{ . . . }}: For expressions (used to print template output)
- {# . . . #}: For comments (which are not included in template output)
- # . . . ##: For line statements

Example 6-30 illustrates how to use statements and expressions in a Jinja template. In this example, a Jinja template is created to generate a configuration for a Nexus switch based on a config.yaml file. Within the config.yaml file, multiple VLANs are defined, along with ports that are acting as either trunk ports or access ports. For each VLAN, an SVI needs to be created. In the Jinja template, a **for** statement is used to generate the configurations of multiple VLANs, and then another **for** statement is used to configure the interfaces. Within this **for** statement, another **if-else** statement is used to validate whether the interface should be an access port or a trunk port. Finally, another **for** statement creates the SVIs. In this example, the Jinja template is used with the Netmiko library to connect to the remote Nexus switch and configure it.

Example 6-30 *Using a Jinja2 Template with the Netmiko Library*

```
! switchport-template.j2
hostname {{ name }}

feature interface-vlan

# For loop to iterate through vlan list and use it to create multiple vlans on the
  device
{% for vlan, name in vlans.items() %}
vlan {{ vlan }}
name {{ name }}
{% endfor %}

{% for interface in interfaces %}

interface {{ interface.id }}
```

```
description Link to {{ interface.remote_server }} port {{ interface.port }}
{% if interface.mode == "trunk" -%}
  switchport mode trunk
  {% else -%}
  switchport mode access
  switchport access vlan {{ interface.vlan }}
  {% endif -%}
  no shutdown
{% endfor %}

{% for vlan, name in vlans.items() %}
interface vlan {{ vlan }}
ip address 10.1.{{ vlan }}.1/24
no shutdown
{% endfor %}
```

```
! config.yaml
name: NX-1
vlans:
  10: Management
  100: Data
  200: Voice
interfaces:
  - id: Eth1/1
    mode: trunk
    remote_server: NX-2
    port: Eth1/1
  - id: Eth1/2
    mode: access
    remote_server: Srvr2
    vlan: 100
    port: 1
```

```
! app.py
import yaml
from jinja2 import Environment, FileSystemLoader
from netmiko import ConnectHandler

configs = yaml.load(open('./config.yaml'), Loader=yaml.FullLoader)

env = Environment(loader = FileSystemLoader('./'), trim_blocks=True,
  lstrip_blocks=True)
template = env.get_template('switchport-template.j2')

cfg = template.render(configs)
```

```
with open("configs.txt", "w") as f:
    f.write(cfg)

with ConnectHandler(ip = "172.16.102.137",
                    port = "22",
                    username = "admin",
                    password = "admin",
                    device_type = "cisco_nxos") as ch:

                    config_set = cfg.split("\n")
                    output = ch.send_config_set(config_set)
                    print(output)
```

```
(jinja) [root@rnd-srvr jinja]# python3 app.py
config term
Enter configuration commands, one per line. End with CNTL/Z.

NX-2(config)# hostname NX-1
NX-1(config)# feature interface-vlan
NX-1(config)#
NX-1(config)# vlan 10
NX-1(config-vlan)# name Management
NX-1(config-vlan)# vlan 100
NX-1(config-vlan)# name Data
NX-1(config-vlan)# vlan 200
NX-1(config-vlan)# name Voice
NX-1(config-vlan)# interface Eth1/3
NX-1(config-if)# description Link to NX-2 port Eth1/1
NX-1(config-if)# switchport mode trunk
NX-1(config-if)# no shutdown
NX-1(config-if)# interface Eth1/4
NX-1(config-if)# description Link to Srvr2 port 1
NX-1(config-if)# switchport mode access
NX-1(config-if)# switchport access vlan 100
NX-1(config-if)# no shutdown
NX-1(config-if)# interface vlan 10
NX-1(config-if)# ip address 10.1.10.1/24
NX-1(config-if)# no shutdown
NX-1(config-if)# interface vlan 100
NX-1(config-if)# ip address 10.1.100.1/24
NX-1(config-if)# no shutdown
NX-1(config-if)# interface vlan 200
NX-1(config-if)# ip address 10.1.200.1/24
NX-1(config-if)# no shutdown
```

```
NX-1(config-if)# end
(jinja) [root@rnd-srvr jinja]# cat configs.txt
hostname NX-1

feature interface-vlan

vlan 10
name Management
vlan 100
name Data
vlan 200
name Voice

interface Eth1/3
description Link to NX-2 port Eth1/1
switchport mode trunk
no shutdown

interface Eth1/4
description Link to Srvr2 port 1
switchport mode access
  switchport access vlan 100
no shutdown

interface vlan 10
ip address 10.1.10.1/24
no shutdown
interface vlan 100
ip address 10.1.100.1/24
no shutdown
interface vlan 200
ip address 10.1.200.1/24
no shutdown
```

As mentioned earlier, Jinja templates can also be used with Nornir for network automation purposes. The next few examples illustrate the use of Jinja templates with Nornir. Example 6-31 examines the changes in the groups.yaml file where the groups **xe-routers**, **nx-routers**, and **xr-routers** are assigned site names, ASNs, loopback interface IP addresses, and BGP-related information that will be used by Jinja templates to generate the configurations. Note that the hosts.yaml file remains the same as shown in Example 6-28.

Example 6-31 *A groups.yaml File for Nornir*

```
---
global:
    data:
        domain: domain.local

xe-routers:
    data:
      site: SJC
      asn: 65001
      nos: xe
      loopback0: 1.1.1.1
      networks:
        - net: 1.1.1.1
          mask: 255.255.255.255
        - net: 192.168.1.0
          mask: 255.255.255.0
      neighbors:
        - ip: 10.1.2.2
          remote_asn: 65002
          peering_type: ebgp
        - ip: 10.10.10.10
          remote_asn: 65001
          peering_type: ibgp
    groups:
        - global


nx-routers:
    data:
      site: RTP
      asn: 65002
      nos: nxos
      loopback0: 2.2.2.2
      networks:
        - net: 2.2.2.2
          mask: 255.255.255.255
        - net: 192.168.2.0
          mask: 255.255.255.0
      neighbors:
        - ip: 10.1.2.1
          remote_asn: 65001
```

```
          peering_type: ebgp
        - ip: 10.2.3.3
          remote_asn: 65003
          peering_type: ebgp
        - ip: 20.20.20.20
          remote_asn: 65002
          peering_type: ibgp
    groups:
        - global

xr-routers:
    data:
      site: RCDN
      asn: 65003
      nos: xr
      loopback0: 3.3.3.3
      networks:
        - net: 3.3.3.3
          mask: 255.255.255.255
        - net: 192.168.3.0
          mask: 255.255.255.0
      neighbors:
        - ip: 10.2.3.2
          remote_asn: 65002
          peering_type: ebgp
        - ip: 30.30.30.30
          remote_asn: 65003
          peering_type: ibgp
    groups:
        - global
```

After the group file is updated, the next step is to create the Jinja templates. Example 6-32 shows three different templates for different network operating systems: Cisco IOS XE, NX-OS, and IOS XR. Another way to do this would be to use an **if-else** statement within the Jinja templates to differentiate between the configuration snippets for different network operating systems. In Example 6-32, each template creates a loopback0 interface and assigns an IP address to it and then configures BGP with the specified ASN and configures both the network and neighbor statements. Note that BGP configuration is somewhat similar in IOS XR and NX-OS but is quite different in IOS XE. These Jinja templates are a perfect example of how you can use automation tools to apply configurations at scale.

Example 6-32 *Jinja Templates for Cisco IOS XE, NX-OS, and IOS XR*

```
interface loopback0
ip address {{ host.loopback0 }} 255.255.255.255

router bgp {{ host.asn }}
bgp router-id {{ host.loopback0 }}

{% for nei in host.neighbors %}
  neighbor {{ nei.ip }} remote-as {{ nei.remote_asn }}
   {% if nei.peering_type == "ibgp" -%}
     neighbor {{ nei.ip }} update-source loopback0
   {% endif -%}
   address-family ipv4 unicast
   neighbor {{ nei.ip }} activate
   exit
{% endfor %}
address-family ipv4 unicast
{% for net in host.networks %}
  network {{ net.net }} mask {{ net.mask }}
{% endfor %}
End
```

```
interface loopback0
ip address {{ host.loopback0 }}/32

feature bgp
router bgp {{ host.asn }}
router-id {{ host.loopback0 }}

 address-family ipv4 unicast
{% for net in host.networks %}
  network {{ net.net }} mask {{ net.mask }}
{% endfor %}

{% for nei in host.neighbors %}
  neighbor {{ nei.ip }}
   remote-as {{ nei.remote_asn }}
   {% if nei.peering_type == "ibgp" -%}
     update-source loopback0
   {% endif -%}
   address-family ipv4 unicast
{% endfor %}
```

```
interface loopback0
```

```
ip address {{ host.loopback0 }}/32

router bgp {{ host.asn }}
bgp router-id {{ host.loopback0 }}

 address-family ipv4 unicast
{% for net in host.networks %}
  network {{ net.net }} {{ net.mask }}
{% endfor %}

{% for nei in host.neighbors %}
  neighbor {{ nei.ip }}
   remote-as {{ nei.remote_asn }}
   {% if nei.peering_type == "ibgp" -%}
     update-source loopback0
   {% endif -%}
   address-family ipv4 unicast
{% endfor %}
```

After creating the Jinja templates, you can follow these steps to easily configure the network devices:

1. Create a task that uses the Jinja template.
2. Invoke **napalm_configure** within the task.
3. Initialize Nornir by using the **InitNornir()** function.
4. Run the task by using the **run()** method.

Example 6-33 shows a function named **load_config()** being created with the parameter **task**. Within this function, you can start multiple tasks by using the **task.run()** method. The first task transforms inventory data (data from hosts and group files) to configuration data via Jinja templates and then saves the compiled configuration into a host variable. The next task deploys the compiled configuration to the device by using NAPALM. In this example, notice that the **path** value begins with an **f** string. The benefit of using an **f** string is that it evaluates at program runtime.

Example 6-33 *Using Jinja Templates with NAPALM and Nornir*

```
from nornir import InitNornir
from nornir.plugins.tasks.data import load_yaml
from nornir.plugins.tasks import text
from nornir.plugins.tasks.networking import napalm_configure
from nornir.plugins.functions.text import print_result

def load_config(task):
```

```
    r = task.run(task=text.template_file, template='bgp_config.j2',
  path=f'templates/{task.host["site"]}')
    task.host["template_config"] = r.result
    task.run(task=napalm_configure, name="Loading configuration for the device",
  configuration=task.host["template_config"])


nr = InitNornir(config_file="config.yaml")
sjc = nr.filter(site="SJC")
result = sjc.run(load_config)
print_result(result)
```

Once the Python file is executed, all the devices that are part of the site SJC are configured based on their respective network operating systems. Example 6-34 displays the output of the Python program and the changes that will be committed to the devices in the SJC site.

Example 6-34 *Output from a Python Program with Jinja, Nornir, and NAPALM*

```
load_config*********************************************************************
* NX-2 ** changed : True *******************************************************
vvvv load_config ** changed : False vvvvvvvvvvvvvvvvvvvvvvvvvvvvvvvvvvvvvvvvvvvvv
  INFO
---- template_file ** changed : False -------------------------------------------
  INFO
interface loopback0
ip address 2.2.2.2/32

feature bgp
router bgp 65002
router-id 2.2.2.2

 address-family ipv4 unicast
  network 2.2.2.2 mask 255.255.255.255
  network 192.168.2.0 mask 255.255.255.0

  neighbor 10.1.2.1
   remote-as 65001
   address-family ipv4 unicast
  neighbor 10.2.3.3
   remote-as 65003
   address-family ipv4 unicast
  neighbor 20.20.20.20
   remote-as 65002
   update-source loopback0
   address-family ipv4 unicast
```

```
---- Loading configuration for the device ** changed : True --------------------
  INFO
interface loopback0
ip address 2.2.2.2/32
feature bgp
router bgp 65002
router-id 2.2.2.2
 address-family ipv4 unicast
  network 2.2.2.2 mask 255.255.255.255
  network 192.168.2.0 mask 255.255.255.0
  neighbor 10.1.2.1
   remote-as 65001
   address-family ipv4 unicast
  neighbor 10.2.3.3
   remote-as 65003
   address-family ipv4 unicast
  neighbor 20.20.20.20
   remote-as 65002
   update-source loopback0
   address-family ipv4 unicast
^^^^ END load_config ^^^^^^^^^^^^^^^^^^^^^^^^^^^^^^^^^^^^^^^^^^^^^^^^^^^^^^^^^^^^^
* XE-1 ** changed : True *********************************************************
vvvv load_config ** changed : False vvvvvvvvvvvvvvvvvvvvvvvvvvvvvvvvvvvvvvvvvvvvvv
  INFO
---- template_file ** changed : False -------------------------------------------
  INFO

interface loopback0
ip address 1.1.1.1 255.255.255.255

router bgp 65001
bgp router-id 1.1.1.1

  neighbor 10.1.2.2 remote-as 65002
   address-family ipv4 unicast
   neighbor 10.1.2.2 activate
   exit
  neighbor 10.10.10.10 remote-as 65001
   neighbor 10.10.10.10 update-source loopback0
   address-family ipv4 unicast
   neighbor 10.10.10.10 activate
   exit
address-family ipv4 unicast
  network 1.1.1.1 mask 255.255.255.255
```

```
  network 192.168.1.0 mask 255.255.255.0
end

---- Loading configuration for the device ** changed : True -------------------
  INFO
+interface loopback0
+ip address 1.1.1.1 255.255.255.255
+router bgp 65001
+bgp router-id 1.1.1.1
+  neighbor 10.1.2.2 remote-as 65002
+address-family ipv4 unicast
+  network 1.1.1.1 mask 255.255.255.255
^^^^ END load_config ^^^^^^^^^^^^^^^^^^^^^^^^^^^^^^^^^^^^^^^^^^^^^^^^^^^^^^^^^^
load_config********************************************************************
* XR-3 ** changed : True *******************************************************
vvvv load_config ** changed : False vvvvvvvvvvvvvvvvvvvvvvvvvvvvvvvvvvvvvvvvvvvv
  INFO
---- template_file ** changed : False ------------------------------------------
  INFO
interface loopback0
ip address 3.3.3.3/32

router bgp 65003
bgp router-id 3.3.3.3

 address-family ipv4 unicast
  network 3.3.3.3 255.255.255.255
  network 192.168.3.0 255.255.255.0

  neighbor 10.2.3.2
   remote-as 65002
   address-family ipv4 unicast
  neighbor 30.30.30.30
   remote-as 65003
   update-source loopback0
   address-family ipv4 unicast

---- Loading configuration for the device ** changed : True -------------------
  INFO
---
+++
@@ -13,6 +13,9 @@
   active
   destination transport-method http
  !
```

```
+!
+interface Loopback0
+ ipv4 address 3.3.3.3 255.255.255.255
 !
 interface MgmtEth0/RP0/CPU0/0
  shutdown
@@ -46,6 +49,24 @@
   0.0.0.0/0 172.16.102.1
  !
 !
+router bgp 65003
+ bgp router-id 3.3.3.3
+ address-family ipv4 unicast
+  network 3.3.3.3/32
+  network 192.168.3.0/24
+ !
+ neighbor 10.2.3.2
+  remote-as 65002
+  address-family ipv4 unicast
+  !
+ !
+ neighbor 30.30.30.30
+  remote-as 65003
+  update-source Loopback0
+  address-family ipv4 unicast
+  !
+ !
+!
 xml agent tty
  iteration off
 !
^^^^ END load_config ^^^^^^^^^^^^^^^^^^^^^^^^^^^^^^^^^^^^^^^^^^^^^^^^^^^^^^^^^^^^
```

You can use NAPALM and Nornir along with Ansible to perform configuration and device management.

Orchestration

So far in this chapter, we have looked at how open-source Python libraries can be leveraged for network automation tasks. But there is more to what Python can do. You can also leverage Python for orchestration. Today, most cloud-based solutions use Docker containers, and most of the applications that are deployed in the cloud use orchestration tools such as Kubernetes (also known as K8s) that allow cloud architects to quickly deploy container applications with just few clicks. Keeping track of different resources to manage these orchestration tools and validating container applications for testing can be tedious. Moreover, it can be difficult at times to remember the Docker/containers or Kubernetes commands and use them properly during the development phase. To ease these tasks, both Docker and Kubernetes come with Python libraries that can be used within a Python program to get access to these tools and their respective CLIs as library functions and use them to deploy and test cloud applications.

Docker

For Docker, you can install a Docker package by using the Python package manager. Once it is installed, you can use the **import** keyword to import the Docker library. On a system with a Docker package installed, a Docker daemon is already running. In order to connect to the docker daemon, you are first required to initiate a client. You can use the **from_env()** function to connect to the Docker daemon using the default environment settings. You can then use the client instance to access the list of images or containers, pull a Docker image, or even initiate a container from the pulled image. Following are some of the Docker library functions that you can use:

- **client.images.list():** Lists all the Docker images on the local system.
- **client.images.pull(*image-name*):** Pulls a Docker image from the global repository.
- **client.containers.list():** Lists all the containers.
- **client.containers.get(*container-name* | *container-id*):** Gets a container by name or ID.
- **client.containers.run(*image*, *command=None*, ***kwargs*):** Runs a container.
- **client.containers.start(***kwargs*):** Starts a container. Doesn't support **attach** options.
- **client.containers.stop(***kwargs*):** Stops a container.

Example 6-35 illustrates how to use some of the functions available in the Docker library. In this example, the latest **alpine** image is pulled from the repository, a container is run by calling the **client.containers.run()** function, and the command **ifconfig** is passed in the argument. Notice that when the **client.containers.run()** function is called, all the logs are printed on the terminal, along with the **ifconfig** output from the container. When the job is complete—that is, when the **ifconfig** output is printed to the terminal—the container is disposed from memory. Also notice the use of the **dir()** function in Example 6-35. **dir()** is a powerful built-in function in Python 3 that returns a list of the attributes and methods available for any object. This function can be very useful when you are not familiar with all the functions available or accessible using an object.

Example 6-35 *Pulling a Docker Image and Running a Container Using the Docker Library*

```
(docker) [root@rnd-srvr docker]# python
Python 3.6.8 (default, Aug  7 2019, 17:28:10)
[GCC 4.8.5 20150623 (Red Hat 4.8.5-39)] on linux
Type "help", "copyright", "credits" or "license" for more information.
>>> import docker
>>> dir(docker)
['APIClient', 'DockerClient', '__builtins__', '__cached__', '__doc__', '__file__',
  '__loader__', '__name__', '__package__', '__path__', '__spec__', '__title__',
  '__version__', 'api', 'auth', 'client', 'constants', 'credentials', 'errors',
  'from_env', 'models', 'tls', 'transport', 'types', 'utils', 'version',
  'version_info']
>>> client = docker.from_env()
>>> client.images.list()
[<Image: 'plotter:latest'>, <Image: 'docker.io/python:3'>, <Image:
  'docker.io/centos:latest'>, <Image: 'docker.io/hello-world:latest'>]
>>> dir(client.images)
['__call__', '__class__', '__delattr__', '__dict__', '__dir__', '__doc__', '__eq__',
  '__format__', '__ge__', '__getattribute__', '__gt__', '__hash__', '__init__',
  '__init_subclass__', '__le__', '__lt__', '__module__', '__ne__', '__new__',
  '__reduce__', '__reduce_ex__', '__repr__', '__setattr__', '__sizeof__', '__str__',
  '__subclasshook__', '__weakref__', 'build', 'client', 'create', 'get',
  'get_registry_data', 'list', 'load', 'model', 'prepare_model', 'prune',
  'prune_builds', 'pull', 'push', 'remove', 'search']
>>> client.images.pull('alpine:latest')
<Image: 'docker.io/alpine:latest'>
>>> client.images.list()
[<Image: 'plotter:latest'>, <Image: 'docker.io/python:3'>, <Image:
  'docker.io/alpine:latest'>, <Image: 'docker.io/centos:latest'>, <Image:
  'docker.io/hello-world:latest'>]
>>> dir(client.containers)
['__call__', '__class__', '__delattr__', '__dict__', '__dir__', '__doc__', '__eq__',
  '__format__', '__ge__', '__getattribute__', '__gt__', '__hash__', '__init__',
  '__init_subclass__', '__le__', '__lt__', '__module__', '__ne__', '__new__',
  '__reduce__', '__reduce_ex__', '__repr__', '__setattr__', '__sizeof__',
  '__str__', '__subclasshook__', '__weakref__', 'client', 'create', 'get', 'list',
  'model', 'prepare_model', 'prune', 'run']
>>> client.containers.run('alpine:latest', 'ifconfig')
[1524800.223807] docker0: port 1(vethc88c6ef) entered blocking state
[1524800.231275] docker0: port 1(vethc88c6ef) entered disabled state
[1524800.251101] device vethc88c6ef entered promiscuous mode
[1524800.256202] IPv6: ADDRCONF(NETDEV_UP): vethc88c6ef: link is not ready
[1524800.258182] docker0: port 1(vethc88c6ef) entered blocking state
[1524800.260075] docker0: port 1(vethc88c6ef) entered forwarding state
[1524800.269984] docker0: port 1(vethc88c6ef) entered disabled state
[1524800.522753] SELinux: mount invalid.  Same superblock, different security
  settings for (dev mqueue, type mqueue)
[1524800.629330] IPv6: ADDRCONF(NETDEV_UP): eth0: link is not ready
```

```
[1524800.632217] IPv6: ADDRCONF(NETDEV_CHANGE): eth0: link becomes ready
[1524800.634336] IPv6: ADDRCONF(NETDEV_CHANGE): vethc88c6ef: link becomes ready
[1524800.636374] docker0: port 1(vethc88c6ef) entered blocking state
[1524800.638209] docker0: port 1(vethc88c6ef) entered forwarding state
[1524800.816280] docker0: port 1(vethc88c6ef) entered disabled state
[1524800.825025] docker0: port 1(vethc88c6ef) entered disabled state
[1524800.827276] device vethc88c6ef left promiscuous mode
[1524800.828927] docker0: port 1(vethc88c6ef) entered disabled state


b'eth0      Link encap:Ethernet  HWaddr 02:42:AC:11:00:02  \n          inet
  addr:172.17.0.2  Bcast:0.0.0.0  Mask:255.255.0.0\n          inet6 addr:
  fe80::42:acff:fe11:2/64 Scope:Link\n          UP BROADCAST RUNNING MULTICAST
  MTU:1500  Metric:1\n          RX packets:2 errors:0 dropped:0 overruns:0
  frame:0\n          TX packets:1 errors:0 dropped:0 overruns:0 carrier:0\n
  collisions:0 txqueuelen:0 \n          RX bytes:176 (176.0 B)  TX bytes:90
  (90.0 B)\nlo        Link encap:Local Loopback  \n          inet addr:127.0.0.1
  Mask:255.0.0.0\n          inet6 addr: ::1/128 Scope:Host\n          UP LOOPBACK
  RUNNING  MTU:65536  Metric:1\n          RX packets:0 errors:0 dropped:0
  overruns:0 frame:0\n          TX packets:0 errors:0 dropped:0 overruns:0
  carrier:0\n          collisions:0 txqueuelen:1000 \n          RX bytes:0 (0.0 B)
  TX bytes:0 (0.0 B)\n'
>>>
```

Note For more details and information about the different methods and attributes available in the Docker library, refer to the documentation at https://docker-py.readthedocs.io/en/stable/index.html.

Kubernetes

Fundamentally, Kubernetes is a system for running multiple instances of containerized applications across a cluster of machines, providing redundancy to the applications. Kubernetes manages the complete lifecycle of the containerized applications and services, providing scalability and high availability. Kubernetes brings together individual physical or virtual machines into a cluster, using a shared network to establish communication between the nodes. All the Kubernetes components, capabilities, and workloads are configured on this cluster. One of the nodes is given the role of the primary server. This primary server acts as the brain for the cluster and exposes APIs for users and clients. The other machines are designated as nodes, and they are responsible for accepting and running workloads using local and external resources.

Kubernetes provides JSON REST APIs in order to control a Kubernetes cluster. APIs are available in multiple languages, including Python. Once the Kubernetes package is installed, you can easily import the Kubernetes library and use the client. Within the Kubernetes library, you can use both the client and configuration-related APIs. You use the **config.load_kube_config()** method to load authentication and cluster-related information from the **kube-config** and store it in **kubernetes.client.configuration**. Youcan then use the **client.CoreV1API()** method to access the client APIs. There are various methods available as part of the client APIs. One of the methods, **list_pod_all_namespace()**, returns a list of pods available in each namespace on the cluster. Example 6-36 demonstrates how to access the Kubernetes client APIs and use the **list_pod_all_namespaces()** method to iterate through and list the pods in all namespaces.

Example 6-36 *Using the Kubernetes Client to Invoke the **list_pod_all_namespaces()** Method*

```
(kubernetes) root@node1:~# python
Python 3.6.9 (default, Nov  7 2019, 10:44:02)
[GCC 8.3.0] on linux
Type "help", "copyright", "credits" or "license" for more information.
>>> from kubernetes import client, config
>>>
>>> config.load_kube_config()
>>> api = client.CoreV1Api()
>>> pods = api.list_pod_all_namespaces()
>>> for pod in pods.items:
...    print("%s: %s" % (pod.metadata.namespace,pod.metadata.name))
...
default: wordpress-9f7965d6-6fzhl
default: wordpress-mysql-746dd7c4db-p5clw
kube-system: calico-kube-controllers-648f4868b8-zvj85
kube-system: calico-node-fnmqf
kube-system: calico-node-hjtb9
kube-system: calico-node-tb4fs
kube-system: coredns-6955765f44-4dvxk
kube-system: coredns-6955765f44-74178
kube-system: etcd-kubernetes-node1
kube-system: kube-apiserver-kubernetes-node1
kube-system: kube-controller-manager-kubernetes-node1
kube-system: kube-proxy-d95c7
kube-system: kube-proxy-lpzjt
kube-system: kube-proxy-zrtct
kube-system: kube-scheduler-kubernetes-node1
kubernetes-dashboard: dashboard-metrics-scraper-76585494d8-8nvhb
kubernetes-dashboard: kubernetes-dashboard-5996555fd8-ncjv7
```

Note Explanation of how Kubernetes works is beyond the scope of this book. If you are interested in learning about Kubernetes, check out the documentation available at https://kubernetes.io.

Along with the client API, the Kubernetes library also provides the **watch** APIs. These APIs can be very handy for tracking the events in a given namespace and can be used to created controllers in Python. Example 6-37 illustrates the use of a **watch** API to create a stream and list all the events along with the metadata name within a namespace. In this example, you can see that event information is printed whenever an event is triggered within the namespace.

Example 6-37 *Using a watch API*

```
>>> from kubernetes import watch
>>> dir(watch)
['Watch', '__builtins__', '__cached__', '__doc__', '__file__', '__loader__',
  '__name__', '__package__', '__path__', '__spec__', 'watch']
>>> w = watch.Watch()
>>> dir(w)
['__class__', '__delattr__', '__dict__', '__dir__', '__doc__', '__eq__',
  '__format__', '__ge__', '__getattribute__', '__gt__', '__hash__', '__init__',
  '__init_subclass__', '__le__', '__lt__', '__module__', '__ne__', '__new__',
  '__reduce__', '__reduce_ex__', '__repr__', '__setattr__', '__sizeof__',
  '__str__', '__subclasshook__', '__weakref__', '_api_client', '_raw_return_type',
  '_stop', 'get_return_type', 'get_watch_argument_name', 'resource_version',
  'stop', 'stream', 'unmarshal_event']
>>> for event in w.stream(api.list_namespace):
...     print("%s: %s" % (event['type'], event['object'].metadata.name))
...
ADDED: kube-system
ADDED: kubernetes-dashboard
ADDED: default
ADDED: kube-node-lease
ADDED: kube-public
ADDED: test1
MODIFIED: test1
MODIFIED: test1
DELETED: test1
ADDED: test2
MODIFIED: test2
MODIFIED: test2
DELETED: test2
```

```
root@node1:~# kubectl get namespaces
NAME                   STATUS   AGE
default                Active   20d
kube-node-lease        Active   20d
kube-public            Active   20d
kube-system            Active   20d
kubernetes-dashboard   Active   20d
```

```
root@node1:~# kubectl create namespace test1
namespace/test1 created
root@node1:~# kubectl delete namespace test1
namespace "test1" deleted
root@node1:~# kubectl create namespace test2
namespace/test2 created
root@node1:~# kubectl delete namespace test2
namespace "test2" deleted
root@node1:~# exit
```

One or more containers in Kubernetes are encapsulated into an object known as a *pod*. In Kubernetes, the pod is the basic deployment unit. In general, a pod represents one or more containers that are controlled as a single application. By using the Kubernetes library, you can create new pods through a Python program. First, you define a YAML file that contains pod-related information such as the following:

- **version**
- **kind**
- **metadata**
- **specs**
  - **containers**
  - **image**
  - **ports**

It is easy to create pods in Kubernetes by using the client APIs. For example, you can use the **create_namespaced_pod()** method and the manifest provided in the YAML file to create a pod and then specify the namespace in which to create the pod. Once the pod is created, you can view the status as well as details of the containers by using the **read_namespaced_pod()** method. Example 6-38 demonstrates how to create a pod with a container running an Nginx web server.

Example 6-38 *Creating a Pod by Using Python*

```
! newpod.yaml
apiVersion: v1
kind: Pod
metadata:
  name: nginx-webserver
spec:
   containers:
   - name: nginx
     image: nginx:1.15.4
     ports:
```

```
    - containerPort: 80
```

```
! app.py
from kubernetes import client, config
import yaml

config.load_kube_config()
api = client.CoreV1Api()


pod_manifest = yaml.load(open('./newpod.yaml'), Loader=yaml.FullLoader)
print('Creating a POD with NGINX Container. . .')
api.create_namespaced_pod(body=pod_manifest, namespace='default')
print('Status of the Container: %s' % api.read_namespaced_pod("nginx-webserver",
  "default").status.phase)
print('Details of the Container: \n', api.read_namespaced_pod("nginx-webserver",
  "default").status.container_statuses)
```

```
(kubernetes) root@kubernetes-node1:~/apps/kubernetes# python app.py
Creating a POD with NGINX Container. . .
Status of the Container: Running
Details of the Container:
[{'container_id':
  'docker://3abe710710e5d161289c5aa993f2411657ef0966f568f8ee474c7b0da5a493aa',
 'image': 'nginx:1.15.4',
 'image_id': 'docker-
 pullable://nginx@sha256:e8ab8d42e0c34c104ac60b43ba60b19af08e19a0e6d50396bdfd4cef0
 347ba83',
 'last_state': {'running': None, 'terminated': None, 'waiting': None},
 'name': 'nginx',
 'ready': True,
 'restart_count': 0,
 'state': {'running': {'started_at': datetime.datetime(2020, 1, 18, 7, 9, 34,
 tzinfo=tzutc())},
          'terminated': None,
          'waiting': None}}]
```

Note Many functions available in the Kubernetes library can be leveraged to perform most of the tasks in a Kubernetes cluster. Refer to the GitHub documentation of the Python library at https://github.com/kubernetes-client/python for details.

Machine Learning

Humans have advanced through learning: We have learned to adapt, to speak, and to create new things based on our necessities and desires. Our brains have evolved to analyze the changing environment and adjust accordingly. All the technological developments and advancements we have made over the ages seem rather miraculous. Over the years, to ease and reduce our manual tasks, we have innovated millions of machines, and many others are continuing to be developed. The basic source of all this development is the human brain, which has self-learning and self-evolving capabilities.

For decades, computers were programmed to perform certain tasks, but they could not perform any task beyond what was programmed. With more and more tasks being performed using computers, an enormous amount of data that was captured and stored was never being used. Today, so much data is being generated that it is not practically possible to manually analyze it all. In order to be more efficient in analyzing data, it is important to develop software applications that can automatically analyze the data and make some sense out of it. This is where machine learning comes into play.

Machine learning is an application of techniques and algorithms to find patterns in massive amounts of data to learn from it and then make determinations or predictions. In other words, it is the science behind making computers learn automatically and taking actions without explicit programming. Machine learning is based on examples and experiences rather than hard-coded logic, which restricts what a program can do or achieve. There are primarily three types of learning in machine learning:

- **Supervised learning:** In this type of learning, the machine depends on external resources to train the learning agent in the machine learning system. In this method, the data is labeled (or classified).
- **Unsupervised learning:** In this type of learning, the data is not preclassified or labeled. The system is exclusively guided by the data, without any external knowledge, throughout the learning process.
- **Reinforcement learning:** In this type of learning, the system is built for an environment that can learn and act and choose optimal actions to achieve its goals. Reinforcement learning is most applicable when the goal is optimization.

Each of these learning methods supports several algorithms. Sometimes a new algorithm needs to be created. Python supports multiple well-known libraries, including scikit-learn and TensorFlow, which can be used to implement these machine learning techniques.

Let's consider an example of supervised learning. In this example, we will be dealing with a *classifier*, which is a labeling mechanism that takes data as input and assigns a label as output. Once the data is classified, you can train the classifiers based on the labeled data. Once a classifier is trained, it can take data input and make a prediction based on what it has learned from the training set. Thus, you can break down a supervised learning into a recipe of a few simple steps:

1. Collect training data.
2. Train the classifier.
3. Make predictions.

Let's look at a particular example of supervised learning in Python, using the scikit-learn library. Example 6-39 shows a simple example of finding peaches and oranges based on their characteristics (where peaches are heavier and green in color, whereas oranges are lighter in weight and orange in color). Using this data, the example creates a feature set based on weight and color. The color green is represented as 0, and the color orange is represented as 1. In Example 6-39, the first three items of the **fruit_features** variable are labeled 0, which represents peaches; the next three items, which are lower in weight and have orange color as their characteristic, are labeled 1, which represents oranges. For this example, the Decision Tree algorithm is used to train the classifier. The classifier is initialized by calling the **tree.DecisionTreeClassifier()** method. At this point, the classifier is a set of rules and has no training data; that is, at this point, it does not know about peaches or oranges. Then, the **fit()** method trains the classifier by finding patterns in the data and building a decision tree based on that. When the classifier is trained, the **predict()** method takes test data as an argument and returns a prediction. Based on the input provided in the **predict()** method in this example, the decision tree algorithm predicts that the fruit is a peach.

Example 6-39 *Classification Using a Decision Tree Algorithm*

```
from sklearn import tree

fruit_features = [[140, 0], [150, 0],[145, 0], [110, 1], [120, 1], [105, 1]]
labels = [0, 0, 0, 1, 1, 1]

clf = tree.DecisionTreeClassifier()
clf.fit(fruit_features, labels)
print(clf.predict([[130, 0]]))
```

```
(venv) [root@rnd-srvr ml]# python simple-classification.py
[0]
```

This is a very basic example with a small data set. Real-world applications typically involve massive amounts of data, and it is critical to choose an appropriate algorithm for the kind of data.

Note Covering all algorithms as well as all the machine learning methods is beyond the scope of this book.

Summary

This chapter covers various applications of Python, including the following:

- How to organize development environments using tools such as Git, Docker, and virtual environments
- Various applications of Python, including web/API development, network automation, orchestration, and machine learning
- Python frameworks such as Django and Flask
- The use of open-source libraries such as NAPALM and Nornir to perform network automation and management
- How to use the Docker and Kubernetes libraries to orchestrate container applications dynamically using Python code
- How machine learning works

Chapter 7

HTTP and REST

HTTP Overview

This chapter discusses the first protocol in the transport layer of the network programmability stack: Hypertext Transfer Protocol (HTTP). As you probably already know, HTTP is one of the primary protocols used over the Internet and intranets for client/server communication. As discussed in Chapter 1, "The Network Programmability and Automation Ecosystem," the protocols in the transport layer of the programmability stack enable network devices to expose an API using protocols such as NETCONF and RESTCONF or native REST APIs through which the device can be managed. This chapter covers HTTP in detail.

Note Do not confuse the transport layer of the seven-layer OSI networking model with the transport layer of the network programmability stack. In the OSI model, HTTP is an application layer protocol. The two models do not contradict one another. The difference is only in the layer naming.

In his doctoral dissertation defining the REST framework, Roy Fielding bluntly stated that "HTTP is not designed to be a *transport* protocol. It is a *transfer* protocol in which the messages reflect the semantics of the Web architecture by performing actions on resources through the transfer and manipulation of representations of those resources [Section 6.5.2]." Despite that, the industry refers to the layer of the network programmability stack that houses HTTP and SSH as the transport layer.

As you will see later in this chapter, HTTP actually requires TCP to operate, and TCP is classified as a transport protocol in the OSI model. There is no reason for you to get confused by the naming of the layers. You just need to identify the functional role of a protocol within the ecosystem. (If you reread this note when you're done reading the rest of the chapter, it will probably make a little more sense than it does now.)

To understand what HTTP is, you need to understand hyperlinks. A *hyperlink* is a reference or pointer to data, referred to as the *resource* or the *target* of the hyperlink. As you may already know, a hyperlink may be a link on an Internet web page that you can click to browse to a different web page, or perhaps a specific location on the same page. Hyperlinks are not exclusive to the Internet— or even networks in general. A hyperlink may exist in a document that takes you to a different section in that same document or to a different document on the local system storage. The text that you click on is called the *anchor text* of the hyperlink.

Hypertext is simply text that contains one or more hyperlinks. The term hypertext was coined by Ted Nelson in 1965 (see https://www.w3.org/WhatIs.html) to describe non-linear text. *Non-linear* means that no specific hierarchy exists for the links between the documents. In 1989, while he was working for CERN, Sir Timothy Berners-Lee introduced the concept of a client/server protocol that utilizes hypertext, and he wrote the first web client and server implementation that used this concept. The protocol he described was used to fetch the data that a hyperlink pointed to. That protocol eventually became HTTP. Today, Sir Timothy is best known as the inventor of the World Wide Web.

HTTP first appeared as Version 0.9, followed by Versions 1.0, then 1.1, and finally 2.0. Versions 0.9 and 1.0 are obsolete now, and the current version that is widely used is HTTP/1.1. HTTP/1.1 was initially described in RFC 2068, and then in RFC 2616, which was obsoleted by the series of RFCs numbered sequentially from 7230 to 7235, inclusive. Each of these RFCs describes a different set of operational and functional aspects of HTTP/1.1, as follows:

- RFC 7230, “Message Syntax and Routing”
- RFC 7231, “Semantics and Content”
- RFC 7232, “Conditional Requests”
- RFC 7233, “Range Requests”
- RFC 7234, “Caching”
- RFC 7235, “Authentication”

RFC 7540, which describes HTTP/2.0, states, “This specification [HTTP/2.0] is an alternative to, but does not obsolete, the HTTP/1.1 message syntax. HTTP’s existing semantics remain unchanged.” This means that HTTP/2.0 does not change the message format of HTTP/1.1. It simply introduces some enhancements to HTTP/1.1. Therefore, this chapter primarily covers HTTP/1.1. HTTP/2.0 enhancements are covered in Chapter 8, “Advanced HTTP”.

In a nutshell, HTTP is a client/server protocol, where the client sends a request to an HTTP server requesting information and the server sends back a response. The server response may include the information requested by the client, or it may indicate some error with the request in its response to the client. The client may also use HTTP to send information to the server.

Although HTTP is classified as a transport layer protocol in the network programmability stack, more formally, according to the OSI model, HTTP is an application layer protocol that uses TCP at the transport layer of the OSI model. Unlike TCP, HTTP is connectionless. IANA has allocated TCP/UDP port 80 for HTTP. By default, an HTTP server listens on TCP port 80, but the port number is typically configurable. The fine details of HTTP connectivity are discussed in detail in the section "The HTTP Connection," later in this chapter.

An HTTP transaction starts with a TCP connection attempt from a client to a server. If and when the connection is established, the client sends HTTP requests to the server. Each client request uses a *universal resource identifier* (*URI*) to identify the target server and *resource* (on the server) that the transaction pertains to, such as a web page, text file, or JPEG image. A URI is a hierarchical address that is composed of several segments separated by forward slash (/) symbols. The fine details of URI construction and the differences between a URI, URL, and URN are covered in detail in the section "Resource Identification," later in this chapter. For now, we refer to all resource addresses as *URIs*.

The client request also includes one of several available methods. A *method* specifies the purpose behind a client request. For example, a client uses the GET method to indicate that the request sent to the server is for fetching the resource identified by the URI in the request. Alternatively, clients use PUT or POST methods to send information to the server—specifically, to the location identified by the URI in the request. Client methods are covered in detail in the section "HTTP Transactions," later in this chapter. Example 7-1 shows a typical GET client request.

Example 7-1 *The Content of a GET Request Message to www.apache.org*

```
GET / HTTP/1.1
Host: www.apache.org
Connection: keep-alive
Upgrade-Insecure-Requests: 1
User-Agent: Mozilla/5.0 (X11; Fedora; Linux x86_64) AppleWebKit/537.36 (KHTML, like
  Gecko) Chrome/70.0.3538.77 Safari/537.36
Accept: text/html,application/xhtml+xml,application/xml;q=0.9,image/webp,image/
  apng,*/*;q=0.8
Accept-Encoding: gzip, deflate
Accept-Language: en-US,en;q=0.9,ar;q=0.8,es;q=0.7,ms;q=0.6
```

Notice that the first line of the message consists of the client method, followed by a forward slash (/), and then the HTTP version. The forward slash tells the server to fetch everything at www.apache.org—in other words, the whole web page. If the client wanted to fetch only the image located at http://www.apache.org/images/SupportApache-small.png, the client would send the GET message shown in Example 7-2. As you can see, the (relative) URI in the start line of the message points to the image (that is, the resource).

Example 7-2 *The Content of the GET Request Message to Fetch Only One Particular Image from www.apache.com*

```
GET /images/SupportApache-small.png HTTP/1.1
Host: www.apache.org
Connection: keep-alive
Upgrade-Insecure-Requests: 1
User-Agent: Mozilla/5.0 (Windows NT 10.0; Win64; x64) AppleWebKit/537.36 (KHTML,
  like Gecko) Chrome/70.0.3538.102 Safari/537.36
Accept: text/html,application/xhtml+xml,application/xml;q=0.9,image/webp,image/
  apng,*/*;q=0.8
Accept-Encoding: gzip, deflate
Accept-Language: en-US,en;q=0.9,ar;q=0.8,es;q=0.7,ms;q=0.6
```

After the start line, the client request lists a number of header fields that provide further information about the client, the connection, the specific request, or the payload body, if one exists. By the end of this chapter, you will understand what each field means and how it is used. In Example 7-2, the headers section of the request message starts with the Host header and ends with the Accept-Language header.

But how does this apply to network programmability? The GET method is typically used to fetch configuration or operational data on a network device running an HTTP daemon. A client may send a GET request to a URI that identifies the BGP configuration on a router in order to retrieve that configuration. Or a client may send a POST request to update the VLAN configuration on an interface on a switch. You will better understand how this is accomplished as you progress through this chapter, and you will get an even clearer picture as you progress through this book.

When the HTTP server receives and processes the client's request, it sends an HTTP response back to the client. The server response includes a *status code* that indicates the status of the client request. For example, status code 200 means that the server has processed the request successfully, and the notorious status code 404 indicates that the server could not find the resource referenced by the client (such as a web page) in the URI in the request. Example 7-3 shows the server response to the GET request in Example 7-2 (minus the actual message body, which is the SupportApache-small.png image shown in Figure 7-1).

Example 7-3 *The Content of the Response Message to the GET Message in Example 7-2*

```
HTTP/1.1 200 OK
Date: Sat, 17 Nov 2018 13:43:49 GMT
Server: Apache/2.4.18 (Ubuntu)
Last-Modified: Fri, 01 Jun 2018 15:46:08 GMT
ETag: "17954-56d967b8bc599"
Accept-Ranges: bytes
Content-Length: 96596
```

```
Cache-Control: max-age=3600
Expires: Sat, 17 Nov 2018 14:43:49 GMT
Keep-Alive: timeout=30, max=100
Connection: Keep-Alive
Content-Type: image/png
```

Notice that the status code (200 in this case) and the HTTP version of the server are stated in the first line of the message. Much as in a request message, the start line of the response message is followed by a list of header fields, each used to convey further information pertaining to the server, the connection, the resource, the payload body in the message, or the response message. Header fields are covered in detail in the section "HTTP Messages," later in this chapter.

You can enter the full URI in a web browser to fetch and display the image SupportApache-small.png, as shown in Figure 7-1.

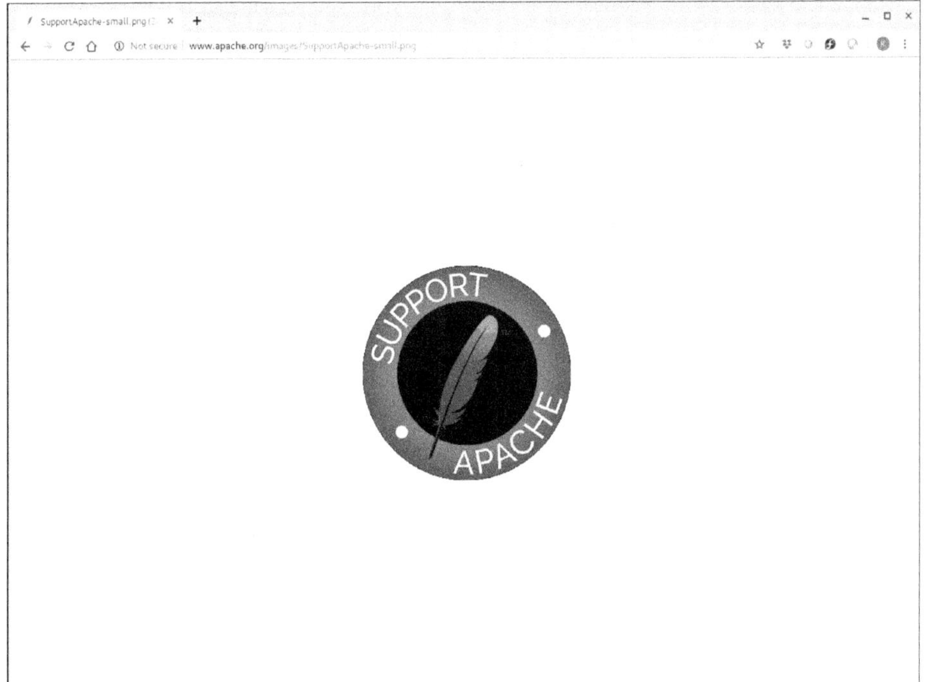

Figure 7-1 *The SupportApache-small.png Image, as It Appears in a Web Browser*

Following the start line and headers section in a request or response HTTP message, comes the optional message body, also referred to as the payload body or entity body. The message body is the part of the HTTP message that contains the actual data or content.

The following section discusses the REST software architecture and lays a foundation for almost all the concepts presented in this chapter. The chapter then covers client/server connections based on TCP, along with the transport enhancements leveraged by HTTP/1.1. Then the chapter presents an overview of HTTP request methods and response status codes. The section that follows covers the format and content of HTTP messages and HTTP headers. The next section covers how resources are identified by HTTP and URI syntax. The last three sections of the chapter take a more hands-on approach and cover Postman, Bash, and Python, and how they can be used to construct and send HTTP requests and examine the responses.

The REST Framework

A resource that a client targets in a request could be of any kind: a text document, an image, or an application. Regardless of the resource type, HTTP provides the same (uniform) interface for clients to operate on that resource. This means that the behavior of HTTP does not change based on the resource type. Therefore, instead of dealing with a resource, HTTP uses the concept of *representations*.

When a client sends a GET request to a router requesting the configuration of an interface, the router may return that information in its response, encoded in JSON. While the interface configuration *is* the resource, that configuration encoded in JSON is a representation of that resource. The same information encoded in XML is yet another representation of the same resource. Just as the current configuration on the interface describing the *current state* of the resource may have more than one representation (JSON, XML, and so on), if a client attempts to change this configuration to a *desired state*, that desired state would be yet another representation of the same resource: the interface configuration. Therefore, a representation is used to express a past, current, or desired state of a resource in a format that can be transported by HTTP. JSON, XML, and YAML are all formats (that is, encodings) that may be used to represent a resource. (These formats are discussed in Chapters 10, "XML," 11, "JSON," and 12, "YAML.")

REST, which stands for *Representational State Transfer,* is a framework, a specification, or an architectural style that was developed by Roy Fielding in his 2000 doctoral dissertation on programming software interfaces, commonly referred to as application programming interfaces (APIs). The REST framework specifies six constraints for programming REST APIs, five of them mandatory and one optional:

- Client/server
- Stateless
- Cacheable
- Uniform interface
- Layered system
- Code-on-Demand (optional)

An API that adheres to these constraints is said to be a *RESTful API*.

Note Fielding's dissertation is publicly available at https://www.ics.uci.edu/~fielding/pubs/dissertation/top.htm.

At this point, it is important to clarify the relationship between REST and HTTP. REST is an architectural style for programming software interfaces (APIs). HTTP, on the other hand, is an application layer protocol (in the OSI model) that is leveraged to implement APIs that adhere to the constraints dictated by the REST framework. HTTP is the only protocol designed specifically for transferring resource representations. Instead of explaining the REST framework independently, the following few paragraphs explain how HTTP implements the REST constraints.

As you already know by now, HTTP is a *client/server* protocol; it therefore adheres to the first constraint.

When a server sends back a response to a client request, this particular transaction is completed, and no state information pertaining to this transaction is maintained on the server. Any one client request contains all information required to fully understand and process this request, independent of any previous requests. Therefore, HTTP is a *stateless* protocol and hence adheres to the second constraint on the list.

HTTP resources *may* be cached at intermediate cache servers along the path between the client and server. Resources should be labeled as cacheable or not. HTTP defines a number of header fields to support this functionality. Therefore, *cacheable* resources is a feature of HTTP, so it satisfies the third constraint.

As stated at the beginning of this section, the interface provided by HTTP to resources does not differ, regardless of the resource type. Therefore, HTTP adheres to the fourth constraint by providing a *uniform* interface for clients to address resources on servers.

The fifth constraint dictates that a system leveraging RESTful APIs should be able to support a layered architecture. A layered architecture segregates the functional components into a number of hierarchical layers, where each layer is only aware of the existence of the adjacent layers and communicates only with those adjacent layers. For example, a client may be interacting with a proxy server, not the actual HTTP server, while not being aware of this fact. On the other end of the connection, a server processing and responding to client requests in the front end may rely on a database server in the back end to store the resources.

The final constraint, which is an optional constraint, is support for Code-on-Demand (CoD)—the capability of downloading software from the server to the client to be executed by the client, such as Java applets or JavaScript code downloaded from a website and run by the client web browser.

To appreciate why the REST framework and its application to RESTful APIs using HTTP are very popular, look at its biggest implementation: the Internet. While REST APIs may not be the best fit for some use cases, they have proven to be a massive success in terms of reliability, simplicity, scalability, and performance for Internet-scale applications. Today, the vast majority of services provided over the Internet leverage REST APIs, such as services from Google and social media companies such as Twitter and Facebook.

RFC 3986 formally defines a representation as "a sequence of octets, along with representation metadata describing those octets that constitutes a record of the state of the resource at the time when the representation is generated." Therefore, a representation in HTTP is composed of not only the message body (or the entity body) but also of metadata used to describe the representation in the body of that message to help interpret this representation. For example, a client would not know if a certain representation returned by a server is encoded in JSON or XML unless some metadata stated that information. This representation metadata is stored in header fields in HTTP. These header fields are covered in detail in the section "The HTTP Entity Header Fields," later in this chapter.

The HTTP Connection

This section discusses the first building block of HTTP: the client/server connection that leverages TCP to provide a reliable transport for HTTP request and response messages. It also covers the enhancements leveraged by HTTP/1.1 related to that connection.

Client/Server Communication

HTTP is a connectionless application layer protocol that uses TCP at the transport layer. Before clients and servers can engage in an HTTP transaction, a TCP connection must be set up. Figure 7-2 illustrates the process of TCP connection establishment, followed by the HTTP transactions, and finally the TCP connection teardown.

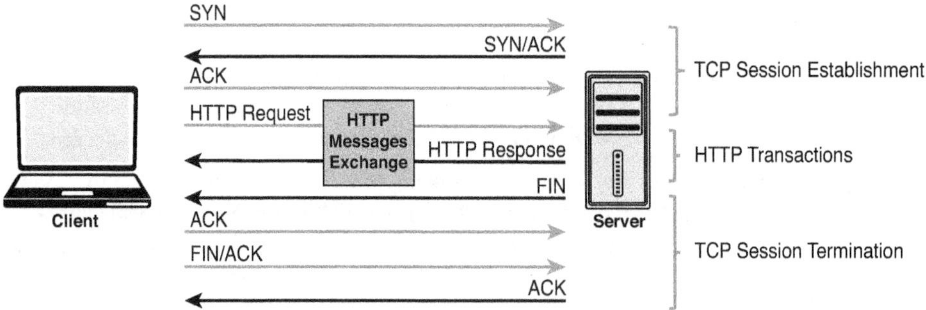

Figure 7-2 *TCP Connection Establishment and Termination with HTTP Message Exchange In Between*

A TCP connection is established through a three-way handshake. Before a client can attempt to connect to a server, the server must first bind to and listen on a port to open it up for connections. It starts with the client sending a SYN message (a TCP segment with the SYN flag set) to the server on the port that the server is listening on. By default, an HTTP daemon on the server binds and listens on port 80. If the server is ready to set up the TCP connection, it responds with a TCP segment with the SYN and ACK flags set. As the final step, before the connection gets established, the client acknowledges the server's segment via an ACK message.

After the TCP connection is established, HTTP transactions can take place. To recap, the client sends one or more messages, each called a request. Each request contains a method identifying the purpose of the request. The server response contains a status code that indicates the status of the request. Each client or server message typically also contains a number of header fields and sometimes a message body containing the resource representation being exchanged in the transaction.

When the HTTP transactions are completed, either the client or server starts the TCP connection termination by sending a TCP segment with the FIN flag set. The other side replies with an ACK message followed by a segment that has both the FIN and ACK flags set. Finally, the side that initiated the connection termination sends a segment with the ACK flag set, marking the termination of the TCP connection.

Note Here we have described the ideal scenario where all goes well. Other scenarios for the TCP connection establishment and termination exist, but because TCP is not the subject of this chapter, the scenario already described is sufficient.

How does the client determine the IP address and port on which the TCP connection is to be established? This is decided by a layer other than HTTP. When you enter a URI in the browser address bar, that URI is resolved by DNS to an IP address. The resolution is either done by checking the browser or OS cache, checking a manual entry in the /etc/hosts file on Linux systems, or sending a DNS request to the DNS server configured on the system. If a port number is not explicitly specified, the default port 80 is used. When using a browser, you can specify a non-default port by entering a colon followed by the non-default port number right after the URI. To connect to www.portquiz.net on port 1234, for example, you enter the following in the address bar: http://www.portquiz.net:1234/.

So what is the Host header field doing in the HTTP message in Example 7-1? Keep in mind that the HTTP message (a GET request in that case) comes into the picture only *after* the TCP session has been established and is irrelevant before that. An HTTP server may have several *virtual hosts* configured on it, all using the same IP address but responding to different URIs. This is a common scenario with shared hosting: Several URIs reside on the same server, sharing the same IP address. The Host header field is a request header field that is used by the server receiving the request to identify which virtual host on that server should receive the request.

HTTP/1.1 Connection Enhancements

As mentioned at the beginning of this chapter, HTTP started with Version 0.9, and it has evolved to Version 2.0. HTTP/1.1 is the version primarily used today, and this version leverages some very important enhancements, including persistent connections, pipelining, and compression.

Persistent Connections

HTTP/1.1 uses *persistent connections* for HTTP transactions. Prior to the use of persistent connections, a client would initiate a TCP connection, send a request, and receive the response from the server, and then the TCP connection would be terminated. Each HTTP request would solicit the establishment of a separate TCP connection. On the other hand, persistent connections used by HTTP/1.1 allow one single TCP connection to be established, followed by one or more HTTP request/response pairs to be exchanged, and then finally a TCP connection termination. Obviously, persistent connections increase the efficiency of the protocol by saving the resources required to establish and then terminate one TCP connection per HTTP request—most notably network, compute, and memory resources required to process the typically vast number of TCP sessions in nonpersistent connections. This efficiency reflects on the client and server, as well as the intermediate devices such as switches, routers, firewalls, and load balancers that need to process the additional traffic required to set up and terminate those TCP sessions.

Note Switches are, by definition, L2 devices that only understand and can process L2 frames. Routers are, by definition, L3 devices that only understand and can process L3 packets. TCP, on the other hand, is an L4 protocol. Therefore, devices operating purely as switches or routers have no visibility into the TCP datagrams encapsulated inside the L2 and L3 headers, but still have to process this traffic at lower layers (L2 and L3). Therefore, more TCP traffic means more processing for L2 and L3 devices along the traffic path of the TCP connections.

The general header field Connection in the GET message in Example 7-1 has the value keep-alive, indicating that the client wishes to use a persistent connection for this request. Since persistence is the default behavior in HTTP/1.1, whether the Connection field is used or not, the connection is persistent by default. However, when the Connection header field has the value close, this indicates that the client or server using this value wishes to close this TCP session as soon as the current request/response transaction is completed.

HTTP/1.0 supports persistence, but it is not the default behavior. With this version, the client and server must explicitly use the value keep-alive in the Connection header field if a persistent connection is desired.

Pipelining

A further enhancement in HTTP/1.1 is *pipelining*, which allows more than one request to be sent to the server before the server responds to any of those requests. And while the server may, in some cases, process these requests simultaneously, the server is expected to reply to client requests in the order in which the requests are received. Persistence, which is discussed in the previous section, is a prerequisite to pipelining. While its positive impact may not be immediately obvious, pipelining shortens the round-trip delay and hence provides tangible latency improvements.

Note In HTTP/2, pipelining has been replaced by multiplexing, and the Transfer-Encoding header must not be used.

Compression

HTTP *compression*, introduced with version 1.0, decreases the overall number of bytes that need to be transferred and processed during an HTTP transaction. This has a direct positive impact on performance since fewer bytes require less bandwidth and fewer resources and, hence, faster performance on systems with limited resources. Compression can happen at two different levels: at the entity level or at the message level.

Entity compression is the encoding and decoding of a resource that occurs on the server and client sides, regardless of the HTTP transactions taking place. An image or a video that resides on a server may be encoded/compressed regardless of whether that image or video will be part of the content transferred using HTTP. Entity compression is signaled between client and server using the Content-Encoding header field. Static content on the server (which does not change very frequently or at all) may be encoded ahead of any HTTP transactions. Alternatively, dynamic content is usually encoded as the HTTP transaction is happening.

Message compression, on the other hand, is the compression of the HTTP message body, as requests and responses are being exchanged back and forth between client and server. Message compression is signaled using the Transfer-Encoding header field. Transfer encoding is a hop-by-hop value, whereas content encoding is an end-to-end value.

Note IANA maintains a registry of all available transfer and content encoding schemes at https://www.iana.org/assignments/http-parameters/http-parameters.xhtml.

HTTP Transactions

An HTTP transaction involves a client sending an HTTP request message and, ideally, the server responding with a server HTTP response message. A request message contains an HTTP method that defines the action that the client wishes to take on the resource identified by the request URI. The server, in its response message, uses a status code to indicate the result of processing the client request. A request/response pair constitutes an HTTP transaction. This section discusses, in some detail, client request methods and server response status codes, and the next section covers the format and the rest of the content of HTTP messages.

Client Requests

RFC 7231 defines the following client requests:

- GET
- HEAD
- POST
- PUT
- DELETE
- CONNECT
- OPTIONS
- TRACE

An HTTP method is said to be *safe* if using this method means that no state change will happen on the server. In other words, a safe method is a read-only method. GET, HEAD, OPTIONS, and TRACE are safe methods.

When sending the same request multiple times has the same effect as sending it only once, the method used in the request is said to be *idempotent*. For example, when a resource is created using the PUT method, sending the same request just re-creates the resource. The net effect of sending the request once or hundreds of times is the same. The same applies to deleting a resource. All the safe methods as well as PUT and DELETE are idempotent methods.

Cacheable methods are methods whose responses may be saved and re-sent by intermediate cache servers. GET, HEAD, and POST are cacheable methods.

GET

The most basic use of HTTP is to retrieve one or more objects from an HTTP server. These objects may constitute components of a web page or may be a part of a configuration on a network device that exposes a REST API. In order to retrieve information from a server, the client uses the GET method. In REST terminology, the GET method is used to request the current representation of the resource, identified by the URI in the start line of the HTTP request. Because a GET request is used to fetch data, a GET request typically has no payload body; it has only headers.

The response to a GET request may be cached by a cache server. This is controlled by the Cache-Control general header field. If the GET request is processed by the server and the representation requested is returned in the response, the status code in the response is "200 OK." If a current representation of the requested resource does not exist, the server uses status code "404 Not Found" in its response. Alternatively, the server may use status code "410 Gone" to indicate that a current representation has not been found and probably never will; that is, it indicates that the condition is likely to be permanent.

Two different GET requests are discussed in the "HTTP Overview" section, earlier in this chapter: one for a full web page (refer to Example 7-1) and one for a specific image on the same web page (refer to Example 7-2).

HEAD

A client request using the HEAD method returns exactly the same response from the server as a request using the GET method, minus the actual payload body. The server returns only headers. The headers returned in the response constitute the metadata of the representation of the resource that was targeted in the request. These returned headers are typically used for testing and validation. Like a GET request, a HEAD request typically has no payload.

The response to a HEAD request may be cached, and the caching is controlled by the Cache-Control header field.

POST

The POST method is used when a client intends to send information to a server for processing. Although that would not be the best use of HTTP, a client may send two numbers to a script running on a server by using the POST method. The script would then add these two numbers and return the sum back to the client in a response message. Or it might create a new resource at a "subordinate" URI at which the result is saved, and return the new resource URI in the response message with the response code "201 Created."

The resource that processes the information is specified in the URI of the request message. Subsequently, the POST method may amend an existing resource or create a new resource, or it may not result in any resource-specific changes.

POST is the primary method used to send information to Cisco switches through their REST APIs, such as for login authentication or configuration updates. Example 7-4 provides an example of using the POST method to configure a static route for destination 192.168.1.0/24 with the next hop 10.10.20.254.

Example 7-4 *Using a POST Message to Configure a Static Route on a Nexus Switch*

```
POST /api/mo/sys/ipv4/inst/dom-default.json HTTP/1.1
Content-Type: text/plain
User-Agent: PostmanRuntime/7.26.8
Accept: */*
Host: sbx-nxos-mgmt.cisco.com
Accept-Encoding: gzip, deflate, br
Connection: keep-alive
Content-Length: 462
Cookie: <cookie-value>

{
  "ipv4Dom": {
    "attributes": {
      "name": "default"
    },
    "children": [
      {
        "ipv4Route": {
          "attributes": {
            "prefix": "192.168.1.0/24"
          },
          "children": [
            {
              "ipv4Nexthop": {
                "attributes": {
```

```
                    "nhAddr": "10.10.20.254",
                    "nhIf": "unspecified",
                    "nhVrf": "management",
                    "tag": "1000"
                  }
                }
              }
            ]
          }
        }
      ]
    }
  }
```


The URI in Example 7-4 targets the default routing domain identified by the object dom-default, which is the resource in this example. Each VRF instance on the switch has its own routing domain. The default routing domain is the global routing table. Chapter 11 discusses JSON encoding in detail. Chapter 14, "NETCONF and RESTCONF," discusses how to target resources and construct URIs using the RESTCONF protocol. Chapter 17, "Programming Cisco Platforms," describes how to identify and construct URIs to target the different resources that map to objects, specifically on a (programmable) Nexus switch, using a RESTful API named NX-API REST. Therefore, do not worry yourself with the specifics of the message in the example. The purpose of this example is to display the high-level anatomy of an HTTP request that uses the POST method to perform configuration changes on a network device.

The representation in the request body is the static route configuration, formatted in JSON. This representation starts right after the empty line following the Cookie header field. The POST request updates the resource with the newly added route. In other words, the POST request adds the new route to the default routing table. Once the update is accepted and the route is added, a "200 OK" response is sent back to the client, as shown in Example 7-5.

Example 7-5 *The "200 OK" Response Indicating That the Route Was Successfully Added*

```
HTTP/1.1 200 OK
Server: nginx/1.13.12
Date: Sat, 07 Nov 2020 20:11:12 GMT
Content-Type: application/json
Content-Length: 13
Connection: keep-alive
Access-Control-Allow-Headers: Origin, X-Requested-With, Content-Type, Accept,
  devcookie
Access-Control-Allow-Origin: http://127.0.0.1:8000
Access-Control-Allow-Methods: POST,GET,OPTIONS
Strict-Transport-Security: max-age=31536000; includeSubDomains
X-Frame-Options: SAMEORIGIN
X-XSS-Protection: 1; mode=block
```

```
X-Content-Type-Options: nosniff
Content-Security-Policy: block-all-mixed-content; base-uri 'self'; default-src
  'self'; script-src 'self' 'unsafe-inline'; style-src 'self' 'unsafe-inline';
  img-src 'self' data:; connect-src 'self'; font-src 'self'; object-src 'none';
  media-src 'self'; form-action 'self'; frame-ancestors 'self';

{"imdata":[]}
```

Example 7-6 shows the list of static routes before and after the HTTP request. The new route to 192.168.1.0/24 is added to the static routes configuration and reflected in the routing table.

Example 7-6 *Static Routes on the Switch Before and After the POST Request*

```
! Before sending the POST request
sbx-ao# show ip route
IP Route Table for VRF "default"
'*' denotes best ucast next-hop
'**' denotes best mcast next-hop
'[x/y]' denotes [preference/metric]
'%<string>' in via output denotes VRF <string>

10.98.98.0/24, ubest/mbest: 1/0, attached
    *via 10.98.98.1, Lo98, [0/0], 00:10:50, direct
10.98.98.1/32, ubest/mbest: 1/0, attached
    *via 10.98.98.1, Lo98, [0/0], 00:10:50, local

! After sending the POST request
sbx-n9kv-ao# show ip route
IP Route Table for VRF "default"
'*' denotes best ucast next-hop
'**' denotes best mcast next-hop
'[x/y]' denotes [preference/metric]
'%<string>' in via output denotes VRF <string>
10.98.98.0/24, ubest/mbest: 1/0, attached
    *via 10.98.98.1, Lo98, [0/0], 00:13:06, direct
10.98.98.1/32, ubest/mbest: 1/0, attached
    *via 10.98.98.1, Lo98, [0/0], 00:13:06, local
192.168.1.0/24, ubest/mbest: 1/0
    *via 10.10.20.254%management, [1/0], 00:00:05, static, tag 1000
```

Another POST request is an authentication request to a Nexus switch. But unlike the previous request, this one does not create or change any resources. Example 7-7 shows a request sent to a Nexus switch for authenticating with the switch and receiving a cookie that is then used to authenticate all subsequent requests to the switch.

Example 7-7 *Authentication Request Message with No Resources Created or Amended*

```
POST /api/aaaLogin.json HTTP/1.1
Content-Type: application/json
Cache-Control: no-cache
User-Agent: PostmanRuntime/7.26.8
Accept: */*
Host: sbx-nxos-mgmt.cisco.com
Accept-Encoding: gzip, deflate, br
Connection: keep-alive
Content-Length: 116

{
     "aaaUser": {
       "attributes": {
         "name": "admin",
         "pwd": "Admin_1234!"
        }
    }
}
```

The resource URI in the start line of the request message is /api/aaaLogin.json, and the message body contains the information (representation)—in this case, the login credentials. No resources are created or changed in this case. Note that the URI is a relative URI reference that becomes an absolute URI when appended with the scheme (HTTPS) and authority (sbx-nxos-mgmt.cisco.com) to become https://sbx-nxos-mgmt.cisco.com/api/aaaLogin.json. (Relative and absolute URI references are covered later in this chapter.)

Note This example and the next few examples present the functionality of the different request methods. You are not yet expected to understand much of the content in the HTTP messages presented, so do not worry. The meaning of each of the lines will become clear as you progress through the chapter and the rest of the book.

PUT

The PUT method will replace the state of a resource with the representation in the request payload. If the resource did not exist in the first place, the resource is created. If the method in the static route example in the previous section were a PUT instead of a POST, all static routes would be replaced by the static route configuration represented in the payload body of the request. The resource in this case is, again, the default routing domain (table). Example 7-8 shows a PUT request for the destination 192.168.2.0/24 and next hop 10.10.20.254.

Example 7-8 *Using a PUT Request to Configure a Static Route on a Nexus Switch*

```
PUT /api/mo/sys/ipv4/inst/dom-default.json HTTP/1.1
Content-Type: text/plain
User-Agent: PostmanRuntime/7.26.8
Accept: */*
Host: sbx-nxos-mgmt.cisco.com
Accept-Encoding: gzip, deflate, br
Connection: keep-alive
Content-Length: 462
Cookie: <cookie-value>

{
  "ipv4Dom": {
    "attributes": {
      "name": "default"
    },
    "children": [
      {
        "ipv4Route": {
          "attributes": {
            "prefix": "192.168.2.0/24"
          },
          "children": [
            {
              "ipv4Nexthop": {
                "attributes": {
                  "nhAddr": "10.10.20.254",
                  "nhIf": "unspecified",
                  "nhVrf": "management",
                  "tag": "2000"
                }
              }
            }
          ]
        }
      }
    ]
  }
}
```

The response shown in Example 7-9 is again "200 OK," meaning that the request has been accepted and processed. If the target resource did not exist, the PUT request would create the resource, and in that case, the status code in the server response might be "201 Created." That does not apply in this case, however, because the resource—the default routing table—is a data structure that will always exist on the switch and cannot be deleted and re-created through any interface on the router (CLI or API).

Example 7-9 *The "200 OK" Response to the PUT Request*

```
HTTP/1.1 200 OK
Server: nginx/1.13.12
Date: Sat, 07 Nov 2020 20:18:51 GMT
Content-Type: application/json
Content-Length: 13
Connection: keep-alive
Access-Control-Allow-Headers: Origin, X-Requested-With, Content-Type, Accept,
  devcookie
Access-Control-Allow-Origin: http://127.0.0.1:8000
Access-Control-Allow-Methods: POST,GET,OPTIONS
Strict-Transport-Security: max-age=31536000; includeSubDomains
X-Frame-Options: SAMEORIGIN
X-XSS-Protection: 1; mode=block
X-Content-Type-Options: nosniff
Content-Security-Policy: block-all-mixed-content; base-uri 'self'; default-src
  'self'; script-src 'self' 'unsafe-inline'; style-src 'self' 'unsafe-inline';
  img-src 'self' data:; connect-src 'self'; font-src 'self'; object-src 'none';
  media-src 'self'; form-action 'self'; frame-ancestors 'self';

{"imdata":[]}
```

Example 7-10 shows that the PUT method replacing all static routes with the representation in the request, which is the single static route for 192.168.2.0/24.

Example 7-10 *Static Routes on a Switch Before and After a PUT Request*

```
! Before sending the PUT request
sbx-n9kv-ao# show ip route
IP Route Table for VRF "default"
'*' denotes best ucast next-hop
'**' denotes best mcast next-hop
'[x/y]' denotes [preference/metric]
'%<string>' in via output denotes VRF <string>

10.98.98.0/24, ubest/mbest: 1/0, attached
    *via 10.98.98.1, Lo98, [0/0], 00:13:06, direct
10.98.98.1/32, ubest/mbest: 1/0, attached
    *via 10.98.98.1, Lo98, [0/0], 00:13:06, local
192.168.1.0/24, ubest/mbest: 1/0
   *via 10.10.20.254%management, [1/0], 00:00:05, static, tag 1000

! After sending the PUT request
sbx-n9kv-ao# show ip route
IP Route Table for VRF "default"
```

```
'*' denotes best ucast next-hop
'**' denotes best mcast next-hop
'[x/y]' denotes [preference/metric]
'%<string>' in via output denotes VRF <string>

192.168.2.0/24, ubest/mbest: 1/0
    *via 10.10.20.254%management, [1/0], 00:00:05, static, tag 2000
```

Instead of targeting the resource dom-default that represents the entire default routing domain, you could instead target just the specific route that you want to operate on. In the case of the static route for 192.168.2.0/24, the resource URI would be https://sbx-nxos-mgmt.cisco.com/api/mo/sys/ipv4/inst/dom-default/rt-[192.168.2.0/24].json.

DELETE

The DELETE method deletes the resource targeted by the URI. Example 7-11 deletes the static route for destination 192.168.1.0/24 by using the URI for that specific route (rather than by targeting the default routing domain, as in the previous examples). The request has no body; it has only headers.

Example 7-11 *Using a DELETE Request to Delete the Static Route to 192.168.1.0/24*

```
DELETE /api/mo/sys/ipv4/inst/dom-default/rt-[192.168.1.0/24].json HTTP/1.1
User-Agent: PostmanRuntime/7.26.8
Accept: */*
Host: sbx-nxos-mgmt.cisco.com
Accept-Encoding: gzip, deflate, br
Connection: keep-alive
Cookie: <cookie-value>
```

The response is, again, "200 OK," as shown in Example 7-12.

Example 7-12 *The "200 OK" Response to the DELETE Request*

```
HTTP/1.1 200 OK
Server: nginx/1.13.12
Date: Sat, 07 Nov 2020 20:48:41 GMT
Content-Type: application/json
Content-Length: 13
Connection: keep-alive
Access-Control-Allow-Headers: Origin, X-Requested-With, Content-Type, Accept,
  devcookie
Access-Control-Allow-Origin: http://127.0.0.1:8000
Access-Control-Allow-Methods: POST,GET,OPTIONS
```

```
Strict-Transport-Security: max-age=31536000; includeSubDomains
X-Frame-Options: SAMEORIGIN
X-XSS-Protection: 1; mode=block
X-Content-Type-Options: nosniff
Content-Security-Policy: block-all-mixed-content; base-uri 'self'; default-src
  'self'; script-src 'self' 'unsafe-inline'; style-src 'self' 'unsafe-inline';
  img-src 'self' data:; connect-src 'self'; font-src 'self'; object-src 'none';
  media-src 'self'; form-action 'self'; frame-ancestors 'self';

{"imdata":[]}
```

As you can see in Example 7-13, the static route for 192.168.1.0/24 was deleted from the switch.

Example 7-13 *Static Routes on the Switch Before and After the DELETE Request*

```
! Before sending the DELETE request
sbx-n9kv-ao# show ip route
IP Route Table for VRF "default"
'*' denotes best ucast next-hop
'**' denotes best mcast next-hop
'[x/y]' denotes [preference/metric]
'%<string>' in via output denotes VRF <string>

10.98.98.0/24, ubest/mbest: 1/0, attached
    *via 10.98.98.1, Lo98, [0/0], 00:20:50, direct
10.98.98.1/32, ubest/mbest: 1/0, attached
    *via 10.98.98.1, Lo98, [0/0], 00:20:50, local
192.168.1.0/24, ubest/mbest: 1/0
    *via 10.10.20.254%management, [1/0], 00:00:08, static, tag 1000

! After sending the DELETE request
sbx-n9kv-ao# show ip route
IP Route Table for VRF "default"
'*' denotes best ucast next-hop
'**' denotes best mcast next-hop
'[x/y]' denotes [preference/metric]
'%<string>' in via output denotes VRF <string>

10.98.98.0/24, ubest/mbest: 1/0, attached
    *via 10.98.98.1, Lo98, [0/0], 00:22:09, direct
10.98.98.1/32, ubest/mbest: 1/0, attached
    *via 10.98.98.1, Lo98, [0/0], 00:22:09, local
```

A DELETE method deletes the resource altogether. A subsequent GET request to the deleted resource should return the response code "404 Not Found."

CONNECT

The CONNECT method is used to create a tunnel from a client to a server. It is specifically used in situations where a proxy server is used to connect a client to the outside world. The server that the client is attempting to connect to is the *request target*.

Say that Client-1 needs to establish a TCP connection to Server-1 on port 80, and Client-1 is configured to forward all its HTTP requests to Proxy-1. In this case, the CONNECT method is used as follows:

Step 1. Client-1 sends the CONNECT request to Proxy-1, indicating that the request target is Server-1 and that the port is 80.

Step 2. The proxy server attempts to set up a TCP session to Server-1 on port 80.

Step 3. When and if a successful connection from Proxy-1 to Server-1 is established, Proxy-1 sends a "200 OK" message back to the client, indicating that the tunnel to the request target is up.

Step 4. From this point onward, for messages between Client-1 and Server-1, Proxy-1 functions strictly as a two-way relay.

Step 5. Proxy-1 closes its connection when it detects a closed connection from either side. When this happens, the proxy server forwards any pending data that came from the side that closed the connection and closes its own connections.

But why would a client need to establish a tunnel to a remote server? This tunnel could eventually be secured using TLS in order to implement HTTPS, as you will see in Chapter 8. Moreover, the client could request that the tunnel use some TCP port other than 80, such that the messages from the client to the proxy are wrapped in HTTP, unwrapped at the proxy, and forwarded to the request target as a protocol other than HTTP, as determined by the TCP port used.

Cisco network devices running a version of IOS XR, NX-OS, or IOS XE do *not* support the CONNECT method.

OPTIONS

The OPTIONS method is used in a request when the client needs to know the options and/or requirements for communicating with a resource. For example, a read-only resource might only accept/support the GET and HEAD methods, such as operational data from a router. On the other hand, the resources constituting the router configuration might additionally support the POST, PUT, and DELETE methods. In each case, the server would respond with the supported methods (for that particular resource) listed in the Allow header field.

The OPTIONS method can also be used to determine the capabilities of a server (for example, whether the server supports HTTP/1.1). This is similar to testing reachability using a ping.

Example 7-14 shows an OPTIONS request where the target is a JPEG image. The response in the same example shows the allowed methods listed in the value of the Allow header field.

Example 7-14 *Using the OPTIONS Method to Query the Allowed Methods for a Specific Resource*

```
! Client request using the OPTIONS method
OPTIONS /home/netdev/Downloads/Postman/app/resources/app/html/thenetdev.com/
  NetDev.jpg
Cache-Control: no-cache
Postman-Token: e937c593-ebb2-4179-9d35-6bfc2e20661f
User-Agent: PostmanRuntime/7.4.0
Accept: */*
Host: thenetdev.com
Accept-Encoding: gzip, deflate
Content-Length:

! Server Response indicating the allowed methods
HTTP/1.1 200 OK
Date: Sat, 22 Dec 2018 17:08:58 GMT
Server: Apache/2.4.6 (CentOS)
Allow: GET,HEAD,POST,OPTIONS,TRACE
Content-Length: 0
Keep-Alive: timeout=5, max=100
Connection: Keep-Alive
Content-Type: image/jpeg
```

TRACE

A client request using the TRACE method is looped by the final recipient of the request back to the client after excluding some header fields. The loopback functionality allows the client to know exactly what information the target server receives when it sends a request to it. The response (that is, the looped-back message) is a "200 OK" message with the client's original request included in the response body and the Content-Type header set to the value message/http.

Server Status Codes

Servers use status codes to indicate the status of attempts to understand and process client requests. A client may be requesting a web page or the running configuration of a router, content that the server would ideally return in a response message back to the client. In this case, the status code would indicate a successful request, typically using a 2xx code. The content that the client requested might not be available, or the method in the client request might not be allowed for the specific resource targeted in the URI, in which case the server would return a 4xx status code, such as the notorious "403 Forbidden" code that you would receive when requesting a resource that you are not authorized to access.

RFC 7231 defines the following status code categories for HTTP/1.1:

- 1xx: Informational
- 2xx: Successful
- 3xx: Redirection
- 4xx: Client error
- 5xx: Sever error

Table 7-1 lists all server codes defined in RFCs 7230 to 7235, along with the meaning of each one.

Table 7-1 *Server Response Codes Listed in RFC 7231*

Code	Meaning
100	Continue
101	Switching Protocols
200	OK
201	Created
202	Accepted
203	Non-Authoritative Information
204	No Content
205	Reset Content
206	Partial Content
300	Multiple Choices
301	Moved Permanently
302	Found
303	See Other
304	Not Modified
305	Use Proxy
307	Temporary Redirect
400	Bad Request
401	Unauthorized
403	Forbidden

Code	Meaning
404	Not Found
405	Method Not Allowed
406	Not Acceptable
407	Proxy Authentication Required
408	Request Timeout
409	Conflict
410	Gone
411	Length Required
412	Precondition Failed
413	Payload Too Large
414	URI Too Long
415	Unsupported Media Type
416	Range Not Satisfiable
417	Expectation Failed
426	Upgrade Required
500	Internal Server Error
501	Not Implemented
502	Bad Gateway
503	Service Unavailable
504	Gateway Timeout
505	HTTP Version Not Supported

A detailed description of each status code and its associated triggers is beyond the scope of this book and is not a prerequisite for a comprehensive understanding of network programmability. Therefore, this section discusses the most common codes briefly. For further information, see Section 6 of RFC 7231, Section 4 of RFC 7232, Section 4 of RFC 7233, and Section 3 of RFC 7235.

Note The list shown in Table 7-1 is not exhaustive. A full list of server response codes that is maintained by IANA is available at https://www.iana.org/assignments/http-status-codes/http-status-codes.xhtml.

1xx: Informational Status Codes

1xx status codes indicate informational server responses. The purpose of these messages is to convey the current (interim) status of the connection or transaction before the final response is sent to the client.

A client may send a request that should include a message body, and instead of sending the (potentially big) message body, it sends only the start line and headers. For example, with a POST request to a router that contains lengthy configuration, the client may use the Expect header field with the value 100-continue to indicate to the server that there is a message body to follow in the next message. If the received portion is okay, the server sends back a response with the status code "100 Continue" to inform the client that the status line and headers are okay and that it is expecting the body in the next message. If the client were to send several hundred lines of configuration in a POST request without being authenticated, the message body would be sent in vain. In the event that the server has a problem with the start line and/or headers, it reverts to the client with one of the 4xx error codes.

The client or server may indicate to the other side a preference to switch the application layer protocol used in a connection to another protocol. The other protocol may be another version of HTTP or an entirely different protocol (that understands the HTTP semantics of the current message). This is accomplished using the Upgrade request header field. When a client lists one or more protocols that it wishes to switch to, the server may respond with a "101 Switching Protocols" status code to indicate that it agrees to switch to one of the protocols in the Upgrade header field of the request, and it includes an Upgrade header field of its own in the 101 response to specify which protocol it will switch to immediately after the empty line that terminates the 101 response.

2xx: Successful Status Codes

2xx status codes indicate that client requests have been successfully received and processed.

Status code "200 OK" means that the request was successfully received and processed and that a payload body is present in this response message, containing a representation that depends on the request method. For example, a 200 response to a GET request contains a payload that is a representation of the resource targeted by the URI in the request. Every 200 response has a payload, except for responses to CONNECT requests.

In the event that the processing of a request results in creating a resource, status code "201 Created" is used. The newly created resource may be referenced by adding a Location header field in the response with a value that is the URI of the new resource. If no Location header field is added to the response, the new resource's URI is the same as the target URI in the request.

Status code "202 Accepted" is used when the server successfully accepts a request but has not processed it yet. A server may, for example, do batch processing at preset times of day, and there is no point in keeping an active connection to each and every client that sends input to this batch process.

Status code "203 Non-Authoritative Information" is used in successful responses when the response is coming from a proxy server, not the origin server, and the content in the payload has been modified by that proxy.

The status codes "204 No Content" and "205 Reset Content" both indicate successful responses that have no payload. The difference between them is that 204 does not imply a change of "document view," as is the case when a user saves a document. A 204 response to a request to save indicates that the document has been saved successfully, but the view does not change. However, with a 205 response, the view is reset; for example, when a user fills the fields of an online form and submits the data in a request, the fields of the form are reset to empty fields for the next record to be entered. A 205 response resets the form.

3xx: Redirection Status Codes

3xx status codes indicate that the server is expecting further action from the client before the request can be processed successfully. This further action is most likely to be another request initiated by the client, using another URI provided by the server (hence the Redirection label). Redirection heavily utilizes the Location header field, as you will see shortly.

When a server can provide more than one choice of representation for a resource targeted by the client in the request URI, status code "300 Multiple Choices" is used in the response. Each of these different representations has a more specific URI than that in the request URI. These different choices are provided back to the client in the payload body of the response, and the Location header field contains the server's preferred choice, if one exists.

Status codes "301 Moved Permanently," "302 Found," and "307 Temporary Redirect" are used in the server response to indicate to the client that the resource referenced by the client in the request URI is available at a different URI. This different URI is provided in the Location header field.

Status code "303 See Other" is used by the server to redirect the client to a totally different resource. The URI for this other resource is provided in the Location header field.

In the event that the request from the client is received by a cache server, and the cache server needs to redirect the client to another URI representing a previously cached version of the resource, that URI is provided in the Location header field, in a response that uses a "304 Not Modified" status code.

A server may send a 3xx redirect response to a request that uses any HTTP method. When a client receives a 3xx response, it may automatically re-send the original request by using the new URI communicated by the server in its response, or it may ignore the redirection advice from the server.

4xx: Client Error Status Codes

Servers use 4xx status codes in responses to tell clients that they believe there is something wrong with the received requests. The representation in the response includes further elaboration on this error condition.

Status code "400 Bad Request" is a general status code indicating that there is something wrong with the received request, and hence this request will not be processed.

Status code "402 Payment Required" is reserved and not currently used.

Status code "403 Forbidden" is used in a response when there is nothing wrong with the request syntax or semantics and the server has understood the request, but the client is not authorized to access the resource targeted in the request URI. Due to the obvious security vulnerability presented by this status code, the server may respond with status code "404 Not Found" in order to hide the fact that the resource exists in the first place. Using a PUT, POST, or DELETE method on a resource, for example, from a client with read-only authorization credentials would typically trigger a 403 response code.

Status code "404 Not Found" means that the server did not find or is not allowed to disclose a current representation of the resource targeted by the request URI. If this status is permanent—that is, if the resource is not available and will not be available in the foreseeable future—status code "410 Gone" may be used instead.

Status code "405 Method Not Allowed" is the typical response when a client uses a method that is not supported by the target resource, such as using a PUT or POST request method with a read-only resource. A response with this status code must also include the Allow entity header field, which tells the client which methods are supported by this resource.

When a client sends a request to a server, it may include proactive negotiation header fields, such as the Accept header field. These header fields, which are discussed further later in this chapter, provide information on the preferred representation that the client wishes to receive from the server for the resource targeted in its request URI. When the server is not able to provide a representation that meets the restrictions or constraints in those header fields, it responds with a status code "406 Not Acceptable."

When a client takes too long to complete a request, the server closes the connection with the client by sending a "408 Request Timeout" response that has a Connection header field with the value close.

When a client does not include the Content-Length header field in its request but the server requires it, the server responds with a "411 Length Required" status code.

Status codes "413 Payload Too Large," "414 URI Too Long," and "415 Unsupported Media Type" are self-explanatory.

As discussed earlier, in the section "1xx: Informational Status Codes," the Expect header field has one and only one valid value, which is 100-continue. If the client uses any other values for this field in its request, the server should respond with the status code "417 Expectation Failed."

Finally, a server uses status code "426 Upgrade Required" to inform the client that it needs to upgrade the protocol used for this transaction. The protocol that the client should upgrade to is indicated in the Upgrade header field of the response. Recall that status code 101 is used by the *server* in its response when the *client* has a requirement for upgrading the protocol and the client uses the Upgrade header field in its request.

5xx: Server Error Status Codes

Servers use 5xx status codes in responses to tell clients that there is a problem from the server's side, and due to this problem, the client request will not be processed. The representation in the response includes further elaboration on the error condition.

Status code "500 Internal Server Error" is a general status code indicating that the server encountered an unexpected error condition, and hence this request will not be processed.

Status code "501 Not Implemented" is the response a server uses when a client requests an operation on a resource, and while there may be nothing wrong with the operation requested, the server is not configured to perform that operation. While this error code may seem identical to error code "405 Method Not Allowed," there is a subtle difference between them. A server uses error code 405 when the method used in the client request *is known* by the origin server *but not supported by the target resource.* A server uses error code 501, on the other hand, when it *does not recognize the request method* and is not capable of supporting it for *any resource.*

Proxy servers having issues with upstream servers use status codes "502 Bad Gateway" and "504 Gateway Timeout" in their responses to the clients to inform the clients of those problems.

When a transient issue is stopping a server, temporarily, from processing new requests (such as being already overloaded with requests or having high resource utilization), the server responds to client requests with a "503 Service Unavailable" status code.

A server responding with status code "505 HTTP Version Not Supported" due to the fact that the client is using an HTTP version that is not supported by the server, includes a representation in the response that elaborates on the reasons and alternatives.

Server Status Codes on Cisco Devices

Not all clients are required to understand all status codes defined in the HTTP RFCs; they only need to understand the classes, such as 1xx, 2xx, and so on. Moreover, status codes are extensible. This means that a vendor may only leverage the status codes that are required to implement its own ecosystem of programmability and that it may add to the already defined list of codes, provided that it follows the proper registration procedure for those status codes it creates, as defined in Section 8.2 of RFC 7231.

Cisco network devices do not use the full range of server status codes. Chapter 14 shows status codes used by the RESTCONF protocol on Cisco devices, and Chapter 17 demonstrates a native RESTful API exposed by programmable Nexus switches and the use of status codes by the API.

HTTP Messages

As you already know, an HTTP message is either a client request or a server response. In either case, the message is composed of a start line followed by zero or more header fields and, optionally, a message body containing a resource representation. The general format of an HTTP message, whether a request or response, is shown in Figure 7-3.

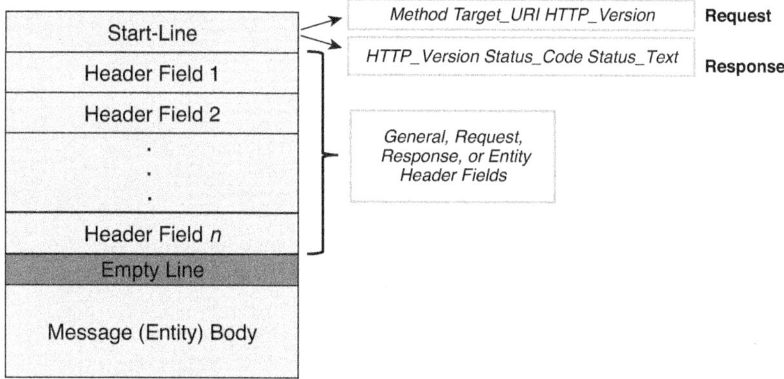

Figure 7-3 *The HTTP Message Format*

The start line in a request message is formatted as follows:

```
{Method} {Target_URI} {HTTP_Version}
```

Here is an example:

```
GET /images/SupportApache-small.png HTTP/1.1
```

The start line in a response message is formatted as follows:

```
{HTTP_Version} {Status_Code} {Status_Text}
```

Here is an example:

```
HTTP/1.1 200 OK
```

The start line is followed by a carriage return and line feed (CRLF), which basically moves the cursor to the beginning of a new line. It is called a CRLF for historic reasons, from the time when moving to the next line (line feed) was different from moving to the start of the line (carriage return).

Following the start line and trailing CRLF is the headers section, which is composed of a number of header fields, each formatted as {*name*}:{*value*}. The header field names are not case sensitive, but the values may be case sensitive, depending on the semantics of the specific header field.

Whitespaces are not allowed between the field name and the colon due to the security risks that this poses. An optional whitespace may be inserted before and/or after the field value for readability.

A header field with the same name may appear more than once on separate lines in a message, with different values. These different lines may be combined into one line, with comma-separated values. For example, the header field Accept-Encoding may appear like this:

```
Accept-Encoding: gzip

Accept-Encoding: deflate
```

Or it might be combined into a single line, like this:

```
Accept-Encoding: gzip, deflate
```

Header fields provide detailed information about the client, server, connection, payload body, or message itself. RFC 2616 classifies HTTP message header fields into four types:

- **General header fields:** These are generic fields that describe values not specific to the message type (request or response), such as the system date or the connection parameters.
- **Request header fields:** These fields are found only in request messages and are request specific, such as the Host (server) or the User-Agent (client) details.
- **Response header fields:** These fields are only found in response messages and are response specific, such as the Last-Modified or Set-Cookie header fields.
- **Entity header fields:** These fields define the properties of the representation in the message body. Both request and response messages may contain entity header fields.

Figure 7-4 illustrates some of the header fields covered in this chapter, along with their types.

Note RFC 2616 has been made obsolete by RFCs 7230 through 7235, and in those new RFCs, the distinction by header field type is not very clear. For example, there is no mention of a general header category, and some of the previously identified general header fields are classified now as request header fields, such as the Connection and Cache-Control headers. This book sticks with the RFC 2616 classification due to its good logic. We do not mean that the current HTTP RFCs follow "bad logic"; however, we think RFC 2616 provides a better entry point to understanding HTTP for a reader just getting started with the protocol.

An HTTP message typically has a number of general header fields and either request header fields or response header fields, but not both, depending on whether the message is a request or a response. If the message has a payload, it also has a number of entity header fields.

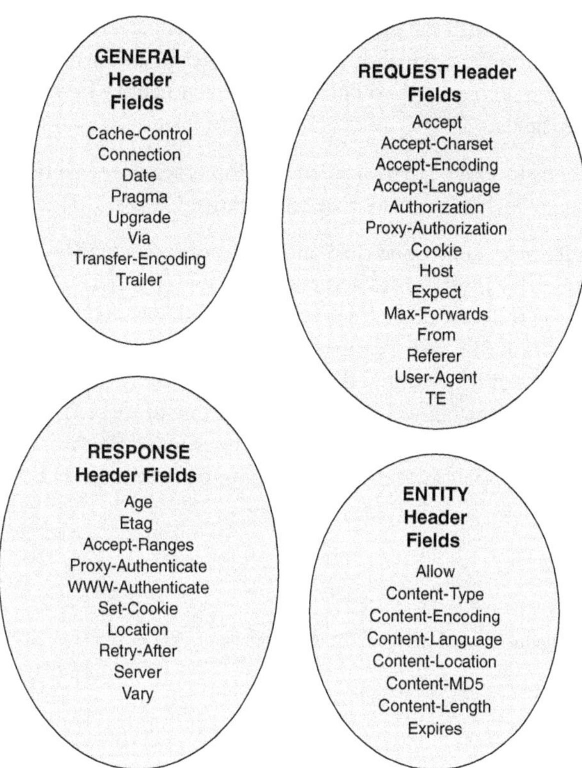

Figure 7-4 *HTTP Header Fields and Their Types*

Note that while RFC 7230 provides some guidance on good-practice ordering of header fields, it describes the ordering of the fields as "not significant." Therefore, you typically see HTTP messages with fields belonging to the different header types in no particular order. Consider the headers sections in the GET request to www.apache.org discussed earlier in this chapter, repeated in Example 7-15 for convenience.

Example 7-15 *The Content of the GET Request Message to www.apache.org*

```
GET / HTTP/1.1
Host: www.apache.org
Connection: keep-alive
Upgrade-Insecure-Requests: 1
User-Agent: Mozilla/5.0 (X11; Fedora; Linux x86_64) AppleWebKit/537.36 (KHTML, like
  Gecko) Chrome/70.0.3538.77 Safari/537.36
Accept: text/html,application/xhtml+xml,application/xml;q=0.9,image/webp,image/
  apng,*/*;q=0.8
Accept-Encoding: gzip, deflate
Accept-Language: en-US,en;q=0.9,ar;q=0.8,es;q=0.7,ms;q=0.6
```

The headers section in the message starts with the Host header field, which is a request header field, followed by the Connection field, which is a general header field. Then the next five fields are all request header fields again. And because there is no entity in the message, there are no entity header fields.

Each header field in the message ends in a CRLF. The headers section is separated from the message body by an empty line, which is basically two consecutive CRLFs.

There are permanent message header field names, and there are provisional message header field names. The latter may be defined by third parties and registered with the IETF. An updated list of all header fields can be found at https://www.iana.org/assignments/message-headers/message-headers.xhtml. RFC 3864 defines the procedure to register a new provisional header field name. As of this writing, there are approximately 340 permanent header fields, and while knowing what each and every one of these fields is used for may come in handy, it is not necessary for the scope and purpose of network programmability. The following sections briefly cover the most common header fields for each header type.

HTTP General Header Fields

The following are some of the commonly used general header fields:

- Cache-Control
- Pragma
- Connection
- Date
- Upgrade
- Via
- Transfer-Encoding
- Trailer

Cache Servers: Cache-Control and Pragma

The first two header fields, Cache-Control, and Pragma, provide directives and information related to cache servers. A *cache server* is a server that stores responses from an *origin server* and, upon receiving a request from a client, responds to the client on behalf of the origin server (caching is covered in RFC 7234.) These three header fields provide metadata related to cache server operation in case any of these servers exist along the path between the client and the server.

Both clients and servers can use the Cache-Control header field to provide *directives* to all cache servers along the communications path. Directives are classified into either request directives or response directives.

Examples of request directives are no-cache, only-if-cached, no-store, and no-transform. The no-cache directive indicates that the client does not want to receive a cached response. On the other hand, the only-if-cached directive indicates that the client only wishes to receive a cached response. The client uses the no-store directive to request that the cache server delete the client request as soon as the request is satisfied and not cache any responses to that request unless that response was already cached before the client request was received. The no-transform directive indicates that the cache server should not transform the payload received from the origin server in any way (such as by changing an image format to save space on the cache).

Unlike the previous directives, the other request directives, max-age, max-stale, and min-refresh, are given values in the header field since they specify client requirements related to the *freshness* of the response. Using these directives, the Cache-Control header field is formatted as follows:

```
Cache-Control: [{directive} = {value}]
```

Response directives also include no-cache, no-store, and no-transform, which have the same meanings as when used as request directives. However, the no-cache directive may be specified for one or more fields only instead of for the whole message. In this case, the Cache-Control header field is formatted as follows:

```
Cache-Control: no-cache = "{field_name}"
```

The directives public and private in a response specify whether the response is intended for a single user or for the public. They also provide restrictions on caching the response by public and private caches. Much like the no-cache directive, the private directive may be specified for only one field or more than one field, and not necessarily for the whole message.

The other response directives are must-revalidate and proxy-revalidate, which specify that the response may not be reused without being revalidated with the origin server first, and max-age and s-maxage, which are used to specify how long before a response becomes *stale* (that is, expires and cannot be used).

The Pragma header field has a single possible value, no-cache, which means the same thing as the no-cache directive in the Cache-Control header field. The Pragma field provides backward compatibility with HTTP/1.0, since Cache-Control was implemented only starting with HTTP/1.1.

The Pragma field is used primarily in client requests. When both the Pragma and Cache-Control header fields are included in a request, both having the value no-cache, HTTP/1.1 caches just ignore the Pragma field.

Because the Cache-Control header field allows for directives other than the no-cache directive, it is common for clients to use the Pragma field for the no-cache directive and then use the Cache-Control field for other directives that target only HTTP/1.1 caches.

Connection

The Connection header field is used for HTTP connection management, and may have the value close or the value keep-alive. The Connection header field is discussed in the section "HTTP/1.1 Connection Enhancements," earlier in this chapter. The Connection header field may also have the value upgrade as explained in the upcoming section discussing the Upgrade header field.

Date

The Date header field contains the message origination date. The date format preferred by RFC 7231 is a fixed-length, single-zone (UTC) subset of the date and time specification used by the Internet Message Format, as per RFC 5322. It is case sensitive and formatted as follows:

```
Date: {day_name}, {day_number} {month_name} {year} {hour}:{minute}:
{second} GMT
```

These are the fields in the Date header:

- *day_name*: This field should be one of the following three-letter day names: Sun, Mon, Tue, Wed, Thu, Fri, or Sat.
- *day_number*: This field is the two-digit day of the month.
- *month*: This field is one of the following three-letter month names: Jan, Feb, Mar, Apr, May, Jun, Jul, Aug, Sep, Oct, Nov, or Dec.
- *year*: This is the four-digit year number.
- *hour*: This is the two-digit hour, in 24-hour format.
- *minute*: This is the two-digit minute.
- *second:* This is the two-digit second.

The following is an example of a Date field from an earlier example in this chapter:

```
Date: Sat, 22 Dec 2018 17:08:58 GMT
```

Upgrade

The Upgrade header field is discussed earlier in this chapter, in the section "1xx: Informational Status Codes." A client or a server can use the Upgrade header field to indicate a wish to switch to an application layer protocol other that HTTP/1.1. Note that when the Upgrade header field is used, the Connection header field in the same message should have the value upgrade. The Upgrade header cannot be used to switch the transport protocol used (TCP in this case).

Via

The Via header field indicates that there are intermediate recipients of the HTTP message between the client and the server, in either direction, such as a proxy server. Each recipient receives the message, adds an entry to the Via header field, and then forwards it upstream toward its destination, whether the destination is the origin server (in the case of a request) or the client (in the case of a response).

Each recipient adds to the Via field the protocol name and protocol version it uses, its host URI, and the TCP port used. The protocol name may be dropped if it is HTTP, and the port may be dropped if it is the default TCP port 80. The host name may also be replaced with a *pseudonym* if the intermediary wishes to keep its host URI confidential. The general format of the Via field is as follows:

```
Via: [Protocol_Name]/{Protocol_Version} {Host_URI}:[Port]
```

For example, if a client sends a request to a server, passing through a proxy with host name proxy.example.com that uses protocol HTTP/1.1 and TCP port 80, the proxy server can add this Via header field before forwarding the request upstream toward the origin server:

```
Via: 1.1 proxy.example.com
```

Transfer-Encoding

The Transfer-Encoding header field is a comma-separated list of the coding schemes that are applied to the message body (not the headers section). The following coding schemes are currently supported by HTTP/1.1:

- chunked
- compress
- deflate
- gzip

RFC 7230 states that transfer encoding is applied to the payload body to ensure "safe transport" through a network. The primary purpose of transfer encoding is two-fold: to decrease the size of the message for more efficient transport through the network and to properly delimit HTTP messages, keeping in mind that there are no defined limits for an HTTP message size.

The chunked coding scheme breaks up the message payload body into smaller pieces, or chunks. Each chunk consists of a chunk size field indicating the chunk size, in bytes, followed by one or more optional chunk extensions that provide per-chunk metadata, and finally the chunk data. The last chunk has a chunk size of zero. An optional trailer containing header fields may follow the last chunk. A recipient knows that the chunked message transmission is complete when it receives a chunk with a chunk size of zero followed by an empty line, with an optional trailer in between. A client that is willing to receive the optional trailer following the last chunk in a response from the server should include the TE request header field in its request with the value trailers (the TE request header field is covered in the next section).

The compress, deflate, and gzip coding schemes are compression coding schemes that decrease the overall size of the message payload body.

A typical Transfer-Encoding header field would be as follows:

```
Transfer-Encoding: deflate, chunked
```

Any recipient along the path of the message can amend the message body coding and change the Transfer-Encoding header field to reflect these changes.

Trailer

When using the chunked transfer encoding, the Trailer header field lists the header fields that are included in the optional trailer after the last chunk, in the event that the sender opts to include that trailer. Note that some header fields are not allowed in the trailer due to security and other considerations.

Client Request Header Fields

The following are some of the commonly used request header fields:

- Accept
- Accept-Charset
- Accept-Encoding
- Accept-Language
- Authorization
- Proxy-Authorization
- Cookie
- Host
- Expect
- Max-Forwards
- From
- Referer
- User-Agent
- TE

Content Negotiation Header Fields: Accept, Accept-Charset, Accept-Encoding and Accept-Language

In cases where a server may provide the same information to a client using different representations, *content negotiation* allows the client to express its preferences or limitations with respect to which representation the server provides in its response.

The Accept, Accept-Charset, Accept-Encoding, and Accept-Language request header fields (referred to as the Accept-X header fields) enable a client to engage in content negotiation with the server.

Several algorithms are defined for content negotiation, including proactive and reactive negotiation. In reactive negotiation, the server provides the client with a list of options to choose from. Proactive negotiation, on the other hand, requires the client to make its preferences known to the server in its request.

The Accept-X header fields allow the client to express its preferences to the server when engaged in proactive content negotiation. If the server cannot honor the client preferences, the server may respond with the next best match, or it may respond to the client with a "406 Not Acceptable" response.

Each Accept-X header field is formatted as a comma-separated list of all the preferred values for that particular header field. Then an optional weight may be assigned to each value by using a qvalue that indicates the client's preference for that value. The qvalue is a number ranging from 0.001 to 1, where 0.001 is the least preferred and 1 is the most preferred. If the qvalue is omitted, the default value of 1 is assumed. A qvalue of 0 means that this value is explicitly not acceptable. Here is an example of an Accept-X header field:

```
Accept-X: Value1; q=0.7, Value2; q=0.4, Value3, Value4; q=0
```

This means the server should send the representation that uses Value3, and if such a representation does not exist, it should send the representation that uses Value1, and finally, it should send the representation that uses Value2. Value4 is explicitly not acceptable.

The Accept header field is used to indicate the media types that the client is willing to accept. The Accept-Charset header field is used to indicate the charsets that the client is willing to accept. The Accept-Encoding header field is used to indicate the content codings that the client is willing to accept. The Accept-Language header field is used to indicate the set of natural languages (not computer languages) that the client is willing to accept. Media types, content codings, and language tags are explained in the section "Representation Metadata Header Fields: Content-X," later in this chapter.

Client Authentication Credentials: Authorization, Proxy-Authorization and Cookie

When a client attempts to apply a method to a resource requiring authentication, the server challenges the client in a response using status code "403 Forbidden" and its own response header fields (explained in the next section). At that point, the client uses the Authorization or Proxy-Authorization header fields to send its authentication credentials back to the server. The difference between the two header fields is that the Authorization header is used to respond to a challenge from the origin server, whereas the Proxy-Authorization header is used to respond to a challenge from a proxy server.

A client uses the Cookie header field to send a cookie to the server that was received earlier from the server in order to maintain the state of the HTTP session.

HTTP authentication is covered in RFC 7235, and HTTP state management is covered in RFC 6265. Both HTTP authentication and HTTP state management are discussed in detail in Chapter 8.

Host

The Host header field, which is explained in the section "Client/Server Communication," earlier in this chapter, is used to specify which virtual host on a particular IP address the request pertains to.

Expect

The Expect header field, which is discussed in the section "1xx: Informational Status Codes," earlier in this chapter, has one possible value: 100-continue. A client uses this field to indicate to the server that the request body will follow in another message, and in the meantime, the client is expecting a response using the 100 status code.

Max-Forwards

The Max-Forwards header field indicates the maximum number of forwards allowed by proxies for a particular request. This field is used with the TRACE and OPTIONS request methods and acts much like a TTL value. Every proxy receiving the request is required to decrement the value of the Max-Forwards header field and forward it toward its final recipient. If the proxy finds that the Max-Forwards field is equal to zero, it must not forward the request any further but must respond to the client in place of the origin server (the final recipient of the request). This behavior is similar to the functioning of the **traceroute** utility.

Request Context: From, Referer and User-Agent

The From, Referer, and User-Agent header fields provide further information related to the request context.

If the privacy settings allow it, the From header field contains the email address of a human who may be contacted by the authority controlling the server, if needed.

The Referer header field is used to indicate where the client request is being sent from. For example, when you are browsing a web page and click a hyperlink on that page to navigate to another web page, the Referer is the URI of the web page that you were originally browsing.

The User-Agent header field contains information on the user agent used to send the client request. The user agent may be, for example, the browser from which a GET request is initiated, such as Google Chrome, or a more specialized program used to tailor client requests, such as Postman.

TE

The TE header field indicates which transfer coding schemes a client is willing to accept from the server besides chunked. (It is mandatory for any HTTP/1.1 client to accept the chunked coding scheme.) This header field also indicates whether it will accept a trailer after the last chunk in a chunked message that may be optionally added by the server. Therefore, the TE header field may have the value compress, deflate, gzip, trailers, or a comma-separated list of some or all of these values. Absence of the TE field or an empty TE field indicates that the client only accepts the chunked coding scheme. See the section "Transfer-Encoding," earlier in this chapter.

Server Response Header Fields

The following are some of the commonly used response header fields:

- Age
- ETag
- Last-Modified
- Proxy-Authenticate
- WWW-Authenticate
- Set-Cookie
- Location
- Retry-After
- Vary
- Server

Age

When a cache server responds directly to a request using a previously cached response, without checking with the origin server first, this response has to include the Age header field. The Age field has a value equal to the number of seconds since that response was generated or since it was last validated from the origin server.

Validator Header Fields: ETag and Last-Modified

Validator header fields are used to convey metadata values that are used to validate the state of a representation. This validation is necessary for the proper operation of HTTP functions such as conditional requests and caching.

Conditional requests are client requests in which some preconditions are specified. If these preconditions are met, as tested by the server, the method in the client request is applied to the resource. If not, a response is sent back to the client with an appropriate status code, such as "412 Precondition Failed." Note that if the preconditions are not met, the response does not necessarily have to be a 4xx code. It could, for example, be a 2xx code. This may happen in situations in which the client is attempting to change the status of a resource by using POST, PUT, or DELETE methods, and the end result of applying the client method already matches the current state of the resource (in other words, when nothing needs to be done).

In situations in which multiple representations exist for the same resource, the ETag header field is used in a response message to differentiate between those different representations. The value of the ETag field appears as a quoted string in the response message.

The Last-Modified header field has a value equal to what the origin server believes to be the last time a representation was modified. The Last-Modified field is a time stamp, and its format is similar to that of the Date header field discussed in the section "HTTP General Header Fields."

Response Authentication Challenges: *X*-Authenticate and Set-Cookie

When a client is attempting to apply a method to a resource that requires authentication, a server uses the header fields WWW-Authenticate or Proxy-Authenticate to transmit authentication challenges to the client. The client then provides the authentication credentials in its own request header fields (explained in a previous section). The difference between the two fields is that the WWW-Authenticate field is used by the origin server, and the Proxy-Authenticate field is used by a proxy server.

A server uses the Set-Cookie header field to transmit cookies to the client, which is one of many ways to maintain state information for an HTTP session.

Both HTTP authentication and state management using cookies are covered in detail in Chapter 8.

Response Control Header Fields: Location, Retry-After, and Vary

Control header fields provide essential information that is required for the correct functioning of HTTP.

The Location header field is discussed in some detail in the section "Server Status Codes," earlier in this chapter. The value of this header field is a URI that identifies the location of a resource. Which resource it identifies depends on the specific semantics of the associated request and response. In other words, what resource this header points to depends on what method is used in the request and what status code is returned in the response. Refer to the section "Server Status Codes" for more details.

In cases in which a client may send a follow-up request, such as after the receipt of a "503 Service Unavailable" or a 3xx (redirect) response, the Retry-After header field is used to inform the client when would be a good time to either try again or to send the redirect request. This header field may contain a date or the number of seconds to wait, expressed as a non-negative decimal integer.

The Vary header field is primarily used by cache servers to decide whether a response from the origin server may be cached and used for subsequent responses to requests for the same resource. The origin server populates this header field with the header names that it used from the request, besides the request method, the request target and the Host header field, to decide which representation for a particular resource to use in its response.

The Vary header field may have a value of an asterisk (*) or a comma-separated list of header field names. An asterisk signals that any header field in the request may influence the representation in the response; therefore, an asterisk is a directive to *not* cache this request since each request may warrant a different response.

Otherwise, the cache server knows which header fields influence the choice of representation by the origin server, and it can decide, based on the values of the same header fields in future requests, whether to use a cached response or to forward the request to the origin server to generate a fresh response.

Response Context: Server

Response context header fields provide further information that is good to know but not necessary or mandatory for the correct functioning of HTTP.

An origin server may generate a Server response header field that contains information on the software used on the server. For example, a server might indicate the operating system installed, the distro and/or version of that OS, or the kind of HTTP server that responded to the request that triggered that particular response (for example, Apache or NGNIX).

The information in the Server header field helps clients work around incompatibilities or limitations in the server software.

The HTTP Entity Header Fields

The following are some of the commonly used entity header fields :

- Allow
- Content-Encoding
- Content-Location
- Content-Type
- Content-Language
- Content-Length
- Expires

Control Header Fields: Allow

The Allow header field is a control header field that a server uses to inform a client which methods are supported by a specific resource typically in response to an OPTIONS client request. The Allow field is a comma-separated list of all allowed methods. As discussed in the section "Status Codes 4xx: Server Error," earlier in the chapter, this header must be included in all "405 Method Not Allowed" responses.

Representation Metadata Header Fields: Content-*X*

The following header fields constitute the representation metadata:

- Content-Type
- Content-Encoding
- Content-Language
- Content-Location

The value of the Content-Type header field indicates the media type of the representation in the message body. Media types are defined in RFC 2046 as text, image, audio, video, or application. Media types are classified by a type and subtype separated by a front slash (/). A subtype provides further information, such as what the application is, the format of the audio or video, or whether the text is plain or rich. Examples of types/subtypes are text/plain, text/html, image/jpeg, audio/x-wav, video/mpeg, and application/msword. An asterisk in place of a subtype (type/*) indicates all subtypes of that type. Similarly, */* indicates all media types. The general format of the header field is

```
Content-Type: {type}/{subtype}; {parameter}={value}
```

The full header field for the utf-32 charset for the type text and subtype plain is as follows:

```
Content-Type: text/plain; charset=utf-32
```

The value of the Content-Encoding header field indicates any lossless coding that has been applied to the representation in the message body. The receiving peer (client or server) uses the value of this header field to know how to decompress/decode the representation. RFC 7231 defines three coding schemes:

- compress and x-compress
- deflate
- gzip and x-gzip

Note A full, up-to-date list of coding schemes can be found at https://www.iana.org/assignments/http-parameters/http-parameters.xhtml.

The following is an example of the Content-Encoding header field:

```
Content-Encoding: gzip
```

As mentioned earlier in this chapter, content encoding is a property of the original entity (resource) residing on the server regardless of the HTTP transactions involving this entity, in contrast to transfer encoding, which is property of the HTTP message. However, both encodings reflect a transformation that has been applied to the data in the message body, and have nothing to do with the HTTP message headers.

The Content-Language header field indicates the natural human language used by the representation, called the *language tag*. The values of this header field exclude computer languages.

The language tag is composed of a primary language subtag, such as en for English and ar for Arabic, and, optionally, one or more subtags that identify a specific variant of that language, such as us for U.S. English or arz for Egyptian Arabic. Subtags are separated by hyphens. This header field can include multiple language tags, separated by commas. For example, a text document that contains both U.S. English and Egyptian Arabic would require the following Content-Language header field:

```
Content-Language: en-us, ar-arz
```

Note The Content-Language header is not specific to text documents. It may be applied to any content type.

The Content-Location header field may have one of several potential meanings, depending on whether it is used by a client in a request or by a server in a response and depending on other details of the HTTP transaction in which it is used.

The value of the Content-Location header field in an HTTP message is a URI. This URI may or may not be the same as the target URI in the HTTP request (when both are resolved to absolute form, described later in this chapter). If they are the same, then this URI points to the location of the resource for which a representation is enclosed in the message body.

Three cases are highlighted in RFC 7231, where the Content-Location field in a *response* message has a significant meaning if it has a value different from that of the target URI.

The first case pertains to content negotiation. A resource on a server may have several possible representations that could be sent to requesting clients. For example, the representation could be JSON, XML, or HTML; the representation may use deflate or gzip compression; and the representation may be in one language or another. On the other hand, the client may use a generic URI for that resource in a GET or HEAD request. Based on a negotiation algorithm, the server chooses one of several representations and sends it to the client in its response. In this case, the response includes a Content-Location header field that specifies the location of the more specific representation of that resource enclosed in the message.

For example, if the target URI in the client request is www.example.com/documents/foo, the Content-Location value in the response may be www.example.com/documents/foo.xyz, which is a version of the resource, for example, encoded in JSON and compressed using gzip. The payload of the response also constitutes the actual representation.

The client may express its requirements/preferences for one representation over another by using other header fields in the request, such as the Accept header field, and the server then runs the negotiation algorithm based on that field.

The second case pertains to a state-changing method, such as when the client request uses the PUT method, and a resource is created. In this case, the server sends a "201 Created" response and includes a Content-Location header field with the URI of the newly created resource. The payload of the response message also constitutes a representation of the newly created resource.

The third case also involves the client sending out a request that involves a state changing method, and the server, in its response, reports the status of this request. For example, if an online payment is performed, and a receipt is generated as part of a response, the receipt is sent back to the customer in the response message payload, and the Content-Location header field points to the location of the receipt on the server for future downloads.

A common source of confusion is the difference between the Location and Content-Location header fields. The Content-Location header field typically points to the same resource as the Location header field, except that the Content-Location field is more specific and points to a location that corresponds to a specific representation of a resource, not the general (perhaps representation agnostic) location of the resource. Therefore, a response message may contain both header fields.

Content-Length

In HTTP, there is no predefined limit on the size of a message payload body. Therefore, the Content-Length header field indicates the size of the payload body, in bytes, for the recipient to be able to determine when the message has been fully received.

If this header field is required by the server and the client does not provide it, the server responds to the client with a "411 Length Required" response message.

Expires

The Expires header field in a response message indicates the date/time after which the response becomes stale. The Expires field is a time stamp in a format similar to the Date header field. An invalid value in this field, especially the value 0, indicates that the response already expired. Much like the Pragma general header field, the Expires header field is used when a recipient does not implement the Cache-Control header field, and it is therefore ignored in the event that the message has a Cache-Control header field with the max-age or the s-maxage directives. The Expires header field is typically discussed in the context of cache servers, but since RFC 2616 classifies the Expires header field as an entity header field, it is covered here for consistency.

Resource Identification

Up to this point in the chapter, the term *URI* has been used for a hierarchical address used to target a resource or representation. However, the terms URL and URN are also used in the industry, often incorrectly. This section defines these terms and attempts to clear up the confusion that usually accompanies their use in the literature and industry. This section also defines the rules that constitute correct URI syntax.

URI, URL, and URN

Both a client and a server use a URI to identify a resource. URI, which stands for uniform resource identifier, was defined by a number of RFCs, including RFC 3986, which updates some earlier RFCs and makes others obsolete.

URIs should be uniform. This means that what a valid URI should look like is governed by a set of syntax rules. Uniformity provides the benefit that a URI is interpreted in exactly the same manner regardless of the context in which it is used.

A resource may be a document, an image, a video, or any other physical or abstract object, and a URI is used to uniquely identify that resource within a certain context or scope. Despite the concept of uniformity, the context in which a URI is used is still important. Why is that? Think of http://localhost/. This is a URI that uniquely identifies the local machine, and it has significance in the context of the local machine only. However, due to uniformity, it has the same meaning regardless of what machine it is used on.

A URI is expressed as a sequence of characters, roughly composed of two parts: the scheme and a string that is formatted according to the standards dictated by that particular scheme. The scheme is the access network protocol, such as HTTP, FTP, or Telnet. The scheme and the string that follows are separated by a colon. The general syntax of a URI is discussed in detail in the next section.

URL stands for uniform resource locator. A URL is a URI that maps to a specific access mechanism (that is, network protocol). In this case, the scheme is the network protocol, such as FTP, HTTP, HTTPS, gopher, mailto, or Telnet. By specifying the access mechanism, a URL points to the location of the resource—hence the word *locator* in the name. URLs were originally referenced in RFC 1630 and then defined in RFC 1738, which was made obsolete by a series of RFCs for various network protocols, titled "The {*Protocol*} URI Scheme." For example, RFC 4248 specifies the URI Telnet scheme and is titled "The telnet URI Scheme," and RFC 6068 defines the URI mailto scheme and is titled "The 'mailto' URI Scheme." As you can see, URLs are a subset of URIs.

URN stands for uniform resource name and refers to URIs starting with the URN scheme. The latest RFC discussing URNs is RFC 8141, dated April 2017. A URN points to a resource, regardless of its location. In other words, a URN references a resource, persistently, regardless of where that resource is located, and it points to this same resource even if the location of that resource changes or the resource ceases to exist. Think of a document located on a server over the Internet, to which a URN points, persistently, even if that document is moved to a different server (a different location).

To achieve this abstraction, a URN references a specific *namespace* in the URN string, using a namespace ID (NID), and a namespace-specific portion, referred to as the NSS, such that the URN string is formatted **urn:**{*NID*}:{*NSS*}. Examples of namespaces are IETF, PIN, ISBN, and IEEE.

Note A full list of namespaces can be found at https://www.iana.org/assignments/urn-namespaces/urn-namespaces.xhtml.

Resolving a URN to actually point to a specific resource is a much more involved process than the more straightforward process of resolving a URL, and it is not entirely standardized. The simplest method would be to create a mapping from a URN to a locator, similar to a URL, and update this mapping to a new URL if the original URL is no longer valid or changes in any way. In this case, the URN used by the client to access the resource does not change, while the mapping from the URN to the locator (that was changed), is transparent to the client.

All URLs and URNs are URIs. In other words, URLs and URNs are each a subset of the universal set of URIs. It is quite common to be confused about the difference between these three terms. As a matter of fact, the informational RFC 3305 titled "Report from the Joint W3C/IETF URI Planning Interest Group: Uniform Resource Identifiers (URIs), URLs, and Uniform Resource Names (URNs): Clarifications and Recommendations" states that "While RFC 2396, section 1.2, attempts to address the distinction between URIs, URLs and URNs, it has not been successful in clearing up the confusion." Furthermore, RFC 3305 defines a contemporary view of this subject by saying that because URLs and URNs are simply URIs with specific schemes, these two classifications need not be used at all, and all references to the subject may consistently use the term URI only.

For the purpose of this book, and for the sake of keeping the terminology simple, we follow the recommendations of RFC 3305 and use only the term URI.

URI Syntax

Parsing a URI and extracting the parameters required to use the URI to operate on the associated resource is referred to as URI *resolution*. After resolution is completed, using the URI to operate on the resource is referred to as *dereferencing* the URI. For different systems to successfully resolve and dereference URIs, a common set of rules are required to govern how a URI is constructed. There are generic syntax rules that apply to all schemes, and there are scheme-specific rules that further restrict the generic rules for each scheme.

URI Components

A URI is constructed from the following components: scheme, authority, path, query, and fragment. The authority component is composed of the user information, host, and port subcomponents. RFC 3986 specifies that the scheme and path components are required (mandatory) in every URI, and the authority, query, and fragment components are optional. However, the path component may be empty if the authority component is present.

Figure 7-5 illustrates the format of a generic URI.

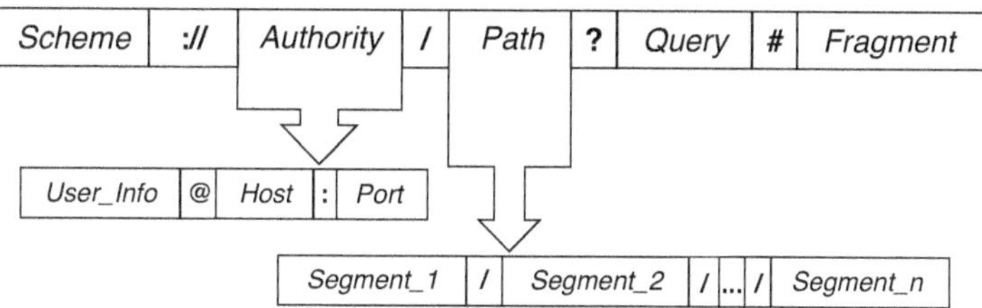

Figure 7-5 *Generic Format of a URI*

Scheme

The scheme, as discussed earlier, is the access mechanism for the resource referenced by the URI. For the purposes of network programmability, you are limited to using the defined URI schemes. However, URI schemes are extensible (that is, new schemes may be defined). A scheme name should start with a letter and may include letters, decimals, or any of the +, -, or . characters. HTTP, FTP, and mailto are examples of schemes in use today.

Authority

The authority component of a URI identifies the body that provides governance of (that is, has control over) the namespace used in the URI. The authority component starts right after the double slash (//) following the scheme and is terminated by a slash (/) when followed by a path, by a question mark (?) when followed by a query, or by a pound symbol (#) when followed by a fragment. The authority component may also be the last part of a URI, with nothing following it.

The authority component may be further broken down into other subcomponents: user information (userinfo for short), host, and port. The format of a generic authority component is [*userinfo*@]{{*host*}:[*port*]}, where both the *userinfo* and *port* subcomponents are optional.

For example, in the URI https://developer.cisco.com/startnow/#coding-apis-v0, the authority is developer.cisco.com. In this case, there is no userinfo or port subcomponent, and the authority is terminated by a slash because it is followed by the path component.

Although it is a little counterintuitive, the URI mailto:netdev@example.com has no Authority component. The string netdev@example.com is actually the path component. How would you draw this conclusion? Remember that the authority is always preceded by a double slash (//), regardless of the scheme. In the URI https://netdev@example.com:1234/anypath, the authority is netdev@example.com:1234.

The *userinfo* subcomponent is not frequently used in HTTP, but when it is, it provides a username that is used for authorization purposes.

The *host* subcomponent is either an IPv4 or IPv6 address or a registered host name. If *host* matches the IPv4 dotted-decimal format, it is parsed as an IPv4 address. If it is enclosed in square brackets, then it is considered an IPv6 address. If neither of these two conditions apply, it is parsed as a registered host name.

The *generic* URI syntax does not mandate an authority component to be present in a URI. However, it is mandatory to have an authority component in an HTTP URI.

The *port* component specifies the protocol port used and is defined per scheme. In HTTP, it is the port used for the TCP connection, and it defaults to port 80 when not explicitly stated.

Path

The path component is composed of different segments, each separated from the next by a slash (/). The path has a hierarchical format, where the path segments decrease in significance and increase in specificity from left to right, similar to file locations on a computer system.

The format of a generic path component is /[*segment_1*]/[*segment_2*]/.../[*segment_n*]. The path component begins with a slash (/) and is terminated by a question mark (?) when followed by a query, a pound symbol (#) when followed by a fragment, or nothing when the end of the path component marks the end of the URI.

Along with the query component, the path identifies a unique resource within the scope of the scheme and authority of the URI.

Query

The query component starts with a question mark (?) and is either terminated by a pound symbol (#) when followed by the fragment component or nothing when it is the last component in the URI. The query component provides non-hierarchical data that is required (in addition to the hierarchical data provided by the path) in order to uniquely identify a resource. An example of a query would be a specific parameter/value pair that identifies a specific record in a database, such as ?Name=NetDev. Some schemes, such as HTTP, allow the use of a query component, and other schemes, such as FTP, do not.

Fragment

The fragment component, if present in a URI, starts with the pound symbol (#) and is the last component in the URI. A fragment provides information that allows for the identification of a secondary resource that relates to the primary resource identified by the path and query.

A very common example of the use of fragments is when the resource is an HTML page, where the fragment component is used to identify a specific element on the page to which the browser scrolls when the page is first displayed. For example, the URI https://developer.cisco.com/docs/nx-os/#!getting-started/introduction opens the Open NX-OS documentation and scrolls to the Introduction under the Getting Started section, identified by the fragment #!getting-started/introduction.

As another example, when the resource is a comma-separated values document, the fragment identifies specific rows, columns, or cells. For example, the URI http://example.com/sheet.csv#col=10 identifies the tenth column in the resource sheet.csv on the server (authority) example.com.

Unlike the rest of the URI components, a fragment is dereferenced by the client, not the server, and the fragments are not sent to the server in the first place. When a resource is an HTML page, the client browser dereferences the fragment to know how to display the page to the user. As such, fragments are not scheme-specific and only depend on the media type of the resource referenced by the URI.

Characters

A URI is basically a set of characters used to identify a resource. Some characters, such as the slash (/), have special meanings when used in a URI and are referred to as *reserved* characters. Other characters, such the letters of the alphabet, just represent themselves and are referred to as *unreserved* characters. Together, the reserved and unreserved character sets are referred to as the *allowed* character set.

URIs frequently use the percent-encoding scheme. In this scheme, a character is encoded into its U.S. ASCII hexadecimal equivalent and used in the URI preceded by a percent symbol (%). For example, the + symbol is encoded into %2B. The next few sections explain when and why percent encoding of characters is utilized in URIs.

Reserved Characters

Some characters are used in a URI to separate or delimit the different components of the URI discussed in the previous sections. The characters used to delimit a component (such as the scheme or the authority), which are referred to as gen-delims, are :, /, ?, #, [,], and @. For example, the Query component is delimited by the ? character. The characters used inside a component and used to delimit subcomponents, which are referred to as sub-delims, are !, $, &, ', (,), *, +, ;, =, and ,. For example, the equal sign (=) is often used to delimit a parameter and its value inside a component.

When a reserved character must be used in a URI and not interpreted as a delimiting character, its percent-encoded value must be used. For example, an ampersand (&) is used in a URI to delimit the pairs in a sequence of parameter/value pairs. Therefore, if a URI contains an ampersand that should *not* be interpreted as a delimiter, the string %26 should be used instead.

Unreserved Characters

All characters that you are allowed to use in a URI and that have no special meaning are called *unreserved characters*. The set of unreserved characters is composed of all letters, decimal digits, the hyphen (-), period (.), underscore (_), and tilde (~).

Non-allowed Characters

Characters that are neither in the reserved nor unreserved character sets, such as non-English characters, are encoded into UTF-8 and then inserted into the URI by using the percent-encoded format. For example, if a URI contains the character "LATIN SMALL LETTER E WITH ACUTE" (é), which is frequently used in the French language, the string %c3a9 is used in the URI to represent it.

Absolute and Relative References

A URI is a sequence of characters used to uniquely identify, or refer to, a resource. The URI is not the resource itself, and it also does not specify how the URI is used to act on the resource that it refers to. Therefore, this sequence of characters is more formally referred to as a *URI reference.*

URI references exist in two different formats: absolute and relative.

An *absolute URI reference* is what you have seen so far throughout this chapter. For example, http://apache.org/img/support-apache.jpg is an absolute URI composed of a scheme, an authority, and a path. An absolute reference such as this has a distinctive hierarchy and is unique from any other absolute reference. An absolute reference has all the information required to resolve and eventually dereference the URI.

Say that the image support-apache.jpg under the directory img is moved from the server apache.org to another server, such as example.com. In this case, the absolute path becomes http://example.com/img/support-apache.jpg. Now imagine if this and tens or hundreds of other URI references are used in HTML code. In such a case, all these absolute references need to be updated with the new server address. That would be a mundane task and is one of the use cases for utilizing relative URI references.

A relative reference refers to a resource in relation to a specific context or a base URI. The base URI, at a minimum, is the scheme, but it might be the scheme and authority, or even a scheme, an authority, and a partial path. For our sample URI reference, if the context is http://apache.org, the relative reference would be /img/support-apache.jpg. Another relative reference on same web page is /img/the-apache-way.jpg. If the web page is moved to example.com, the relative references in the HTML code do not need to be updated since these references are relative to the server on which the HTML code is running.

Before a relative URI reference can be resolved, a reference resolution algorithm is applied to obtain the target URI. This algorithm is explained in a lot of detail in Section 5 of RFC 3986.

Postman

Several programs are available to assist with developing, testing, and sharing APIs. One such program, which is widely used, is Postman. The program's developers refer to Postman as an *API development environment* (*ADE*). You can use Postman to design, test, debug, and fine-tune the performance of APIs. You can use Postman to test an API that you have coded yourself or to test an API provided by someone else such as the APIs provided by Google, Facebook, or Twitter. For example, you can use an API provided by Google Maps to retrieve the latitude and longitude of an address provided to the Maps API as a parameter. Since the majority of network device vendors expose APIs on their devices to be consumed by third parties, Postman can be used to make API calls to a network device to either retrieve configuration or operational data or to actually configure the device.

Postman enables you to execute individual API calls (requests) or to group API calls into *collections* and run all the APIs in a collection sequentially, using a facility called *Collection Runner*. An individual API call to retrieve the routing table on a device may be executed individually. Alternatively, a group of API calls to retrieve the routing table, CDP neighbor information, and interface configurations may be executed one after the other, automatically, as one collection.

Running a collection is not the only action that can be taken on a group of saved requests. A collection can be mocked and monitored as well. Mocking a collection means providing the expected presaved results for an API call. Developers of an API can use these presaved results to observe the response to a request, even if the HTTP server is not ready yet, and cannot provide actual responses. Monitoring, on the other hand, involves running a collection periodically, at a set frequency, and sending alerts to the user when specific triggers occur.

It is possible to run Java scripts from inside Postman before and after API calls. Environment variables with different scopes can also be used to store values from one API call to be used in another API call. Postman also provides advanced facilities such as automated API documentation and automatic API testing for continuous integration and continuous deployment (CI/CD) scenarios. It can also be used to publish APIs to other developers so they can collaborate on API development. These are only a few of the features provided by Postman.

Despite Postman's advanced features, this section only shows how to use Postman to construct HTTP request messages, send those messages to a server, and then examine the responses received. In other words, in this section, Postman is used as an HTTP client, and it provides the advantage of granular visibility into the contents of requests and responses.

The HTTP server in this case may be anything from a Windows or Linux machine to a Cisco switch or router. The important thing is that this server or network device must be running an HTTP server, such as the Apache web server. For the purpose of this chapter, an Open NX-OS sandbox from Cisco DevNet is used for testing. NX-OS is based on a Linux distro called Wind River, customized under a project called the Yocto Project. NX-OS also runs an NGINX web server that handles the HTTP transport for the APIs exposed by the box. NX-OS provides several APIs through which configuration and operational data can be sent to and from the switch—some RESTful and some not. NX-OS programmability is covered in more detail in Chapter 17.

Downloading and Installing Postman

Postman was originally developed as an extension to Google Chrome. Now the Chrome extension has been deprecated, and two version of Postman are being actively developed. One is a native app that is available for the Windows, Linux, and Mac OS X operating systems. The other version is a web app that you may run from your browser.

To download and install the native Postman app, go to the URI https://www.postman.com/downloads/. The web page will automatically detect your operating system and provide a big orange button labeled "Download the App". Click the Download button and a window pops up, asking for the location to save the file. Choose a location and click OK. The downloaded file is a .gzip tar archive. Keep in mind that the download web page may change with time.

After the file has been downloaded to the location of your choice, extract the files using the command **tar -xvf Postman-linux-x64-**{*version*}**.tar.gz**. A new subdirectory named Postman is created. The executable file that runs Postman is a file inside the Postman directory, also called Postman. To run Postman, use the command **./Postman**. (Review Chapter 2, "Linux Fundamentals," for a refresher on these commands.)

At this point, you can start using the program. However, to make Postman accessible from the desktop, on a CentOS 8 system, via the Applications/Programming menu or by pressing on the Activities menu and searching for Postman through the Search box (or the vertical shortcuts bar at the left of the screen), you need to create a file and name it **Postman.desktop** under the directory ~/.local/share/applications. Add the lines shown in Example 7-16 to the file, replacing [*YOUR_INSTALL_DIR*] with the path to the directory in which the downloaded file was extracted.

Example 7-16 *The Content of the Postman.desktop File*

```
[Desktop Entry]
Encoding=UTF-8
Name=Postman
Exec=[YOUR_INSTALL_DIR]/Postman/app/Postman %U
Icon=[YOUR_INSTALL_DIR]/Postman/app/resources/app/assets/icon.png
Terminal=false
Type=Application
Categories=Development;
```

The Postman Interface

When you run Postman, a launch window appears. Uncheck the "Show This Window on Launch" box in the bottom-left corner and close the window. The normal Postman interface appears, as shown in Figure 7-6.

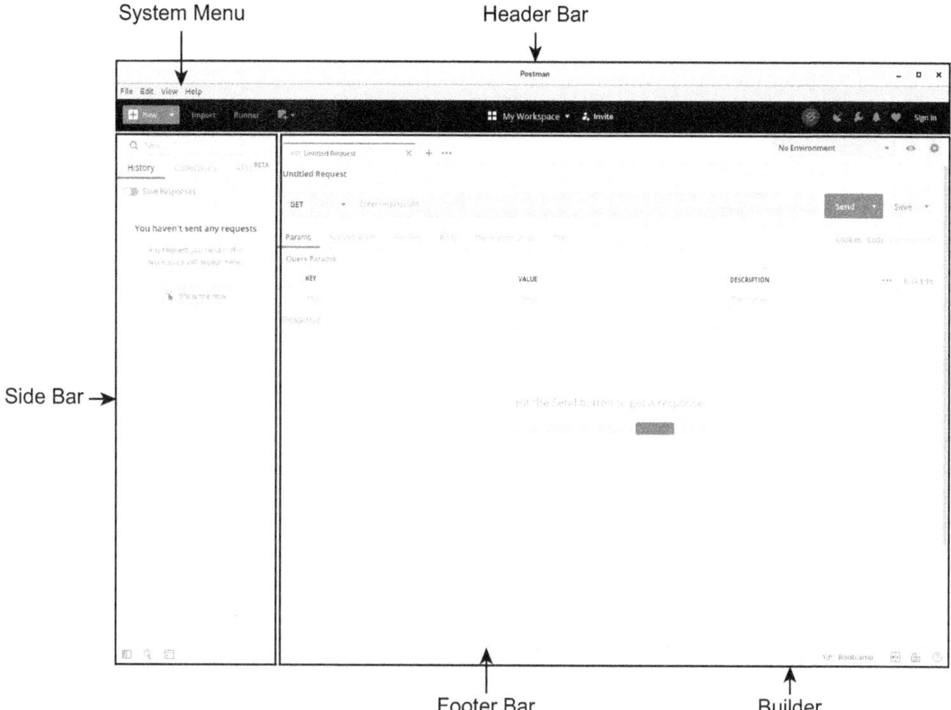

Figure 7-6 *The Postman Interface*

As indicated in the figure, the workspace is composed of a system menu and header bar at the top of the workspace, a sidebar to the left of the workspace, and the main operations area, called the Builder, in the center. In addition, there is a footer bar at the bottom of the workspace.

Note: Before proceeding with the description of the Postman interface, keep in mind that Postman is a very dynamic program and the interface and features seem to change on a *daily* basis. So please take the description here with a grain of salt. The discussion here is based on version 7.24.0. If at the time of reading this a newer interface is released, you may download the version on which this description is based from https://dl.pstmn.io/download/version/7.24.0/linux64. Once you are confident with what you have learnt here, go ahead and upgrade to the latest version. Porting your knowledge to a newer user interface will not be challenging at all.

The header bar is a toolbar with a number of buttons and menus that perform different functions. From left to right, these are the buttons and menus:

- **New button:** Used to create different Postman objects, such as requests and collections.

- **Import button:** Used to import objects, such as collections, into the current workspace. Several formats can be used to import objects, such as a JSON file or a direct import from a URI.
- **Runner button:** Used to start the Collection Runner, which is used to run all requests in a collection automatically.
- **Open New button:** Used to open a new request tab, a new Postman window, or a new Collection Runner window.
- **Workspaces menu button:** Used to manage workspaces. A new workspace has no collections or history entries. A workspace may be a personal or team workspace. With a team workspace, more than one person can access the workspace and can have default read-only access to the collections in that workspace. The access can be elevated for any workspace team member to be able to edit a collection.
- **Invite button:** Used to invite someone to collaborate on a workspace.
- **Sync icon:** Used to sync a user's objects, including workspaces and the collections inside them, between all the computers on which the user is using Postman. When the sync process is in progress, the icon is blue. When it turns orange, all computers are up to date.
- **Interceptor/Proxy icon:** Used to manage proxy or interceptor settings when Postman is used to intercept HTTP messages by acting as a proxy server to the source of the requests.
- **Settings icon:** Used to open a menu for settings and support resources.
- **Notifications icon:** Used to open the list of application notifications.
- **Heart icon:** Used to go to an external web page from which you can share Postman posts on social media.
- **Manage accounts icon:** Used to access user and profile options.

The sidebar has three tabs:

- **History tab:** The History tab shows a list of HTTP requests that have previously been executed.
- **Collections tab:** Collections are used to group saved requests together and, optionally, to act on a whole collection as one entity, such as to run all requests in a collection automatically, using Collection Runner, share the collection with another user or team workspace, or mock or monitor the collection.
- **APIs tab:** The APIs tab is used for end-to-end API design, implementation, and testing.

The footer bar is the thin bar at the bottom of the workspace that has a number of buttons. From left to right, these are the buttons:

- **Hide Side Bar:** Used to toggle between hiding and showing the sidebar.
- **Find:** Used to search for text strings in the current workspace.
- **Postman Console:** Used to open the Postman Console, which provides a "raw" view of requests and responses.
- **Learning Center (Bootcamp):** Used to open a list of tasks that you may want to learn. When you choose a task from the list, a group of balloon windows walk you through the task on the Postman interface.
- **Two Pane View:** Used to toggle between single-pane and double-pane views.
- **Keyboard Shortcuts:** Used to manage the keyboard shortcuts for common tasks.
- **Help:** Used to open a list of help and support options.

The Builder is the place where most of the action takes place, such as building, sending, and saving requests and viewing and analyzing responses. You will learn more about the Builder as you learn how to construct and send requests in the next section.

Using Postman

The Builder section of the Postman workspace is composed of tabs, and each tab corresponds to a different HTTP request. To the right of the tabs are a drop-down list and two buttons for managing the environment. An environment defines the scope of your variables. (Environments and variables are relatively advanced topics that are not covered in this book.)

By default, when you start Postman, the tabs that were open in your last session appear in the Builder. To create a new request, click the plus (+) icon to the right of the tab heads. When you run Postman for the first time, by default a new tab opens.

The new tab is divided into two sections: the upper section for requests and the lower section for responses (see Figure 7-6).

At the top left of the Request section is a drop-down list for the HTTP request method, which is GET by default. The URI for the request goes into the text box to its right.

To put Postman to the test, open a new tab, choose GET from the method drop-down list, type the URI http://www.apache.org/img/the-apache-way.jpg into the URI text box, and click the Send button. Figure 7-7 shows the result.

As you can see, the GET request fetches the image the-apache-way.jpg and displays it in the bottom half of the Postman window, under the Body tab. To view the Response headers, click Headers, and you see the tab shown in Figure 7-8.

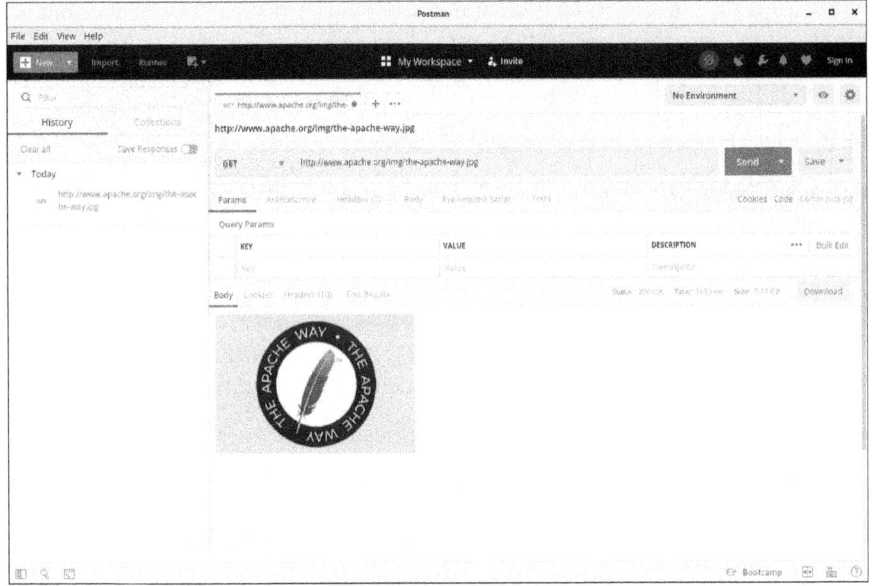

Figure 7-7 *A GET Request Using Postman*

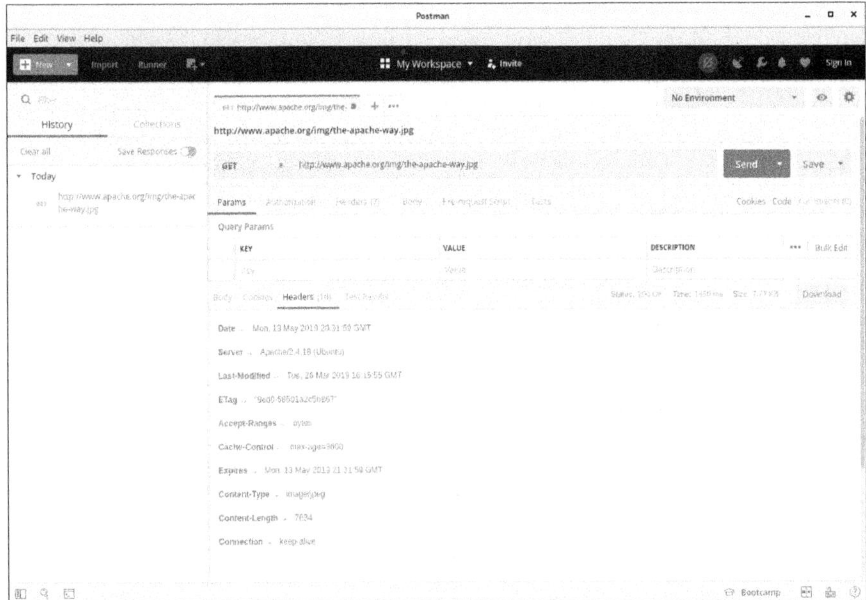

Figure 7-8 *Viewing the Response Headers in Postman*

You can use Postman to fully manage a networking device that exposes a RESTful interface or, at a minimum, an interface that uses HTTP at the transport layer, such as RESTCONF, as you will see in Chapter 14. Postman is not a very scalable method for management, but you can use it to test an API call before you use that call in a more scalable environment, such as Python code. To give you a glimpse of the possibilities, this section shows the Cisco DevNet Nexus sandbox used to display how Postman can be used to pull and push configuration to an NX-OS device.

Before attempting any requests, you need to authenticate to the switch. Authenticating to NX-OS involves using the POST method and the URI https://sbx-nxos-mgmt.cisco.com/api/aaaLogin.json. The switch credentials are provided in the body of the request. To implement this on Postman, choose the POST method from the drop-down list and enter the URI in the corresponding text box. The credentials sent to the Nexus switch are included in the body of the message. To compose the message body, click the Body button below the URI text box, choose the Raw radio button, and paste the text shown in Example 7-17 into the text box.

Example 7-17 *The Body of the POST Request for Authenticating with the NX-OS Box*

```
{
     "aaaUser": {
       "attributes": {
         "name": "admin",
         "pwd": "Admin_1234!"
        }
    }
}
```

Before you send the request, make sure to disable SSL Certificate Verification in the Postman settings by pressing on the wrench icon at the top right side of the screen, choosing Settings from the drop-down menu, and toggling the option "SSL certificate verification" to OFF. Disabling this setting prevents Postman from searching for a saved certificate for the server on your local machine. This is a safe action in this situation because the server in this case is a trusted device from Cisco DevNet. When you click the Send button to the right of the URI text box, Postman constructs the HTTP request and sends it over to the Nexus switch. If authentication is successful, you should see a response similar to what is shown in Example 7-18 in the bottom half of the screen.

Example 7-18 *The Response to the Authentication POST Request Indicating Successful Authentication to the NX-OS Box*

```
{
    "imdata": [
        {
            "aaaLogin": {
                "attributes": {
                      "token": "wJ5C2J+Mehlx7B5xVDzFhI80cY8MxELzhgFiWzShsfg5YR8ieb4Byv
RdgSAFYLOniht3gB656Wr6JSOvnfiUJ9q+2uI25E5ioQOB5Uo5aNF+sp+LTNLDBIr/7HSPddhfzDI8OkNt
J+NtUzm2gQUkjRqLg7ZFUlx1XTOnbX3uJjU=",
```

```
        "siteFingerprint": "",
        "refreshTimeoutSeconds": "600",
        "guiIdleTimeoutSeconds": "1200",
        "restTimeoutSeconds": "1282698853",
        "creationTime": "1554845704",
        "firstLoginTime": "1554845704",
        "userName": "admin",
        "remoteUser": "false",
        "unixUserId": "0",
        "sessionId": "VFN391T+vuoBAAAAFwAAAA==",
        "lastName": "",
        "firstName": "",
        "version": "0.9(14HEAD${version.patch})",
        "buildTime": "Tue Jul 17 15:13:26 PDT 2018",
        "controllerId": "0"
    },
    "children": [
        {
            "aaaUserDomain": {
                "attributes": {
                    "name": "all",
                    "rolesR": "admin",
                    "rolesW": "admin"
                },
                "children": [
                    {
                        "aaaReadRoles": {
                            "attributes": {}
                        }
                    },
                    {
                        "aaaWriteRoles": {
                            "attributes": {},
                            "children": [
                                {
                                    "role": {
                                        "attributes": {
                                            "name": "network-admin"
                                        }
                                    }
                                }
                            ]
                        }
                    }
```

```
                        ]
                    }
                }
            ]
        }
    }
  ]
}
```


When authentication is successful, the switch sends back a cookie that will be used to authenticate all subsequent HTTP requests. This is the value of the token in the output in Example 7-18, and it is also the value of the Set-Cookie header field that can be viewed under the Headers tab in the Response section of the Postman window. Cookies are covered in detail in Chapter 8.

To retrieve any configuration from the switch, a GET request is used with the appropriate URI. As you read through this book, you will learn how to construct URIs for performing particular tasks on a number of different platforms. For now, the BGP configuration on the switch is represented by the URI https://sbx-nxos-mgmt.cisco.com/api/mo/sys/bgp/inst.json. Therefore, open a new Request tab, choose the GET method if it is not already chosen, enter the URI into the corresponding text box, and click the Send button.

In the Response section of the Builder, you should see output similar to the output shown in Example 7-19. This is a JSON dictionary that contains all the information pertaining to the BGP instance running on the switch.

Example 7-19 *The Response to the GET Request for the Switch BGP Configuration*


```
{
    "totalCount": "1",
    "imdata": [
        {
            "bgpInst": {
                "attributes": {
                    "activateTs": "2019-05-09T21:13:28.527+00:00",
                    "adminSt": "enabled",
                    "affGrpActv": "0",
                    "asPathDbSz": "0",
                    "asn": "65535",
                    "attribDbSz": "120",
                    "childAction": "",
                    "createTs": "2019-05-09T21:12:56.487+00:00",
                    "ctrl": "fastExtFallover",
                    "disPolBatch": "disabled",
                    "disPolBatchv4PfxLst": "",
                    "disPolBatchv6PfxLst": "",
```

```
                    "dn": "sys/bgp/inst",
                    "epeActivePeers": "0",
                    "epeConfiguredPeers": "0",
                    "fabricSoo": "unknown:unknown:0:0",
                    "flushRoutes": "disabled",
                    "isolate": "disabled",
                    "lnkStClnt": "inactive",
                    "lnkStSrvr": "inactive",
                    "medDampIntvl": "0",
                    "memAlert": "normal",
                    "modTs": "2018-09-18T18:42:44.190+00:00",
                    "name": "bgp",
                    "numAsPath": "0",
                    "numRtAttrib": "1",
                    "operErr": "",
                    "persistentOnReload": "true",
                    "srgbMaxLbl": "none",
                    "srgbMinLbl": "none",
                    "status": "",
                    "waitDoneTs": "2019-05-09T21:13:28.527+00:00"
                }
            }
        }
    ]
}
```


A similar JSON dictionary in a request body used with the POST method is used to configure the switch. Chapter 17 covers this in more detail.

Consider these two very useful hints when using Postman:

- From the View system menu, you can choose Show Postman Console to open the Postman Console in a separate window. The Console provides you with a message-oriented view of your HTTP transactions. The transactions are listed in the window in collapsed form. When you click the arrow to the left of a transaction to expand it, you see the option Show Raw Log to the right of the message details. You can click this option to get a raw view of the HTTP request and response messages that is great for studying and experimenting with HTTP.
- You can use Postman to convert an HTTP request into code such as Python code. Toward the right side of the Request section in the Builder area of the Postman window is a link labeled Code. You can click it to open the Generate Code Snippet window, which lists a number of programming and scripting languages. You can choose any of the languages to display the code corresponding to the HTTP request to the right of the screen in that language.

HTTP and Bash

HTTP runs over TCP, and by default, an HTTP server listens to HTTP requests on TCP port 80. For a client, sending an HTTP request to an HTTP server is as simple as opening a TCP connection to that web server on port 80 and sending a properly constructed HTTP request. This can be done by simply starting a Telnet session to the server on port 80, and when the session is established, you can send the request line of the request, which consists of the method, the URI, and the HTTP version. Example 7-20 shows Telnet being used to establish a TCP session to www.example.com and then a GET request being sent to the server to retrieve the contents of the web page.

Example 7-20 *A GET Request Sent to www.example.com Using Telnet*

```
[netprog@localhost ~]$ telnet www.example.com 80
Trying 93.184.216.34...
Connected to www.example.com.
Escape character is '^]'.
GET http://www.example.com/ HTTP/1.1


HTTP/1.1 200 OK
Accept-Ranges: bytes
Cache-Control: max-age=604800
Content-Type: text/html; charset=UTF-8
Date: Sat, 26 Jan 2019 23:13:11 GMT
Etag: "1541025663+ident"
Expires: Sat, 02 Feb 2019 23:13:11 GMT
Last-Modified: Fri, 09 Aug 2013 23:54:35 GMT
Server: ECS (dca/2468)
Vary: Accept-Encoding
X-Cache: HIT
Content-Length: 1270

<!doctype html>
<html>
<head>
    <title>Example Domain</title>

    <meta charset="utf-8" />
    <meta http-equiv="Content-type" content="text/html; charset=utf-8" />

--------- OUTPUT TRUNCATED FOR BREVITY ---------

[netprog@localhost ~]$
```

As you can see, the server responds with a "200 OK" message and includes the HTML code that constitutes the contents of the www.example.com web page.

Additionally, the start line sent to the server may be followed by any number of header fields. When the server detects an empty line (two CRLFs), it knows that the header section is complete.

With Telnet, you cannot send a payload body in a request. However, you can use a program named cURL (which stands for Client URL) to send HTTP client requests (including a message body) to an HTTP server. Daniel Stenberg wrote the cURL program (originally named httpget) in 1997 to transfer data between a client and server. cURL supports a number of protocols, including FTP, SCP, HTTP, HTTPS, and LDAP. cURL is supported on a large number of operating systems, including Linux and Windows.

On Linux, the cURL program is executed using the command **curl**. The syntax of the **curl** command depends on which HTTP method you use in the request.

To send a GET request, you use the very basic syntax **curl** {*URI*}. Example 7-21 shows a GET request to www.example.com.

Example 7-21 *A GET Request to www.example.com Using curl*

```
[netprog@localhost ~]$ curl www.example.com
<!doctype html>
<html>
<head>
    <title>Example Domain</title>

    <meta charset="utf-8" />
    <meta http-equiv="Content-type" content="text/html; charset=utf-8" />
    <meta name="viewport" content="width=device-width, initial-scale=1" />

--------- OUTPUT TRUNCATED FOR BREVITY ---------

[netprog@localhost ~]$
```

The output of the **curl** {*URI*} command is the HTML code of the web page www.example.com, which is the payload body of the HTTP response. By default, **curl** sends its output to stdout. To send the output to a file, you use the **-o** option and provide the filename. In Example 7-22, the payload body of the returned response is saved to the file example-file.html.

Example 7-22 *A GET Request to www.example.com Using **curl** and the **-o** Option to Save the Output to a File*

```
[netprog@localhost ~]$ curl -o example-file.html http://www.example.com
  % Total    % Received % Xferd  Average Speed   Time    Time     Time  Current
                                 Dload  Upload   Total   Spent    Left  Speed
100  1256  100  1256    0     0   3609      0 --:--:-- --:--:-- --:--:--  3609

[netdev@server1 ~]$ cat example-file.html
<!doctype html>
<html>
<head>
    <title>Example Domain</title>

--------- OUTPUT TRUNCATED FOR BREVITY ---------
```

You might notice that the output in Example 7-22 is only the payload body, and the headers in the response are not displayed. To include the response headers in the output, you use the **-i** option, as shown in Example 7-23.

Example 7-23 *A GET Request to www.example.com Using **curl** and the **-i** Option to Include the Response Headers in the Output*

```
[netprog@localhost ~]$ curl -i www.example.com
HTTP/1.1 200 OK
Age: 101828
Cache-Control: max-age=604800
Content-Type: text/html; charset=UTF-8
Date: Wed, 04 Nov 2020 19:03:18 GMT
Etag: "3147526947+ident"
Expires: Wed, 11 Nov 2020 19:03:18 GMT
Last-Modified: Thu, 17 Oct 2019 07:18:26 GMT
Server: ECS (bsa/EB15)
Vary: Accept-Encoding
X-Cache: HIT
Content-Length: 1256

<!doctype html>
<html>
<head>
    <title>Example Domain</title>

--------- OUTPUT TRUNCATED FOR BREVITY ---------
```

Of course, you can use the **-o** and the **-i** options to both include the response headers in the output and redirect the output to a file.

When troubleshooting an HTTP connection, the **-v** (for verbose) option is very handy as it provides extra information for troubleshooting. Example 7-24 shows the verbose option in action, exposing very useful information on the TCP connection before and after the request is sent, as well as the request and response headers.

Example 7-24 *A GET Request to www.example.com, Using* **curl** *and the* **-v** *Option to Show Request and Response Headers in Addition to Information on the TCP Connection*

```
[netprog@localhost ~]$ curl -v www.example.com
* Rebuilt URL to: www.example.com/
*   Trying 93.184.216.34...
* TCP_NODELAY set
* Connected to www.example.com (93.184.216.34) port 80 (#0)
> GET / HTTP/1.1
> Host: www.example.com
> User-Agent: curl/7.61.1
> Accept: */*
>
< HTTP/1.1 200 OK
< Age: 102344
< Cache-Control: max-age=604800
< Content-Type: text/html; charset=UTF-8
< Date: Wed, 04 Nov 2020 19:11:54 GMT
< Etag: "3147526947+ident"
< Expires: Wed, 11 Nov 2020 19:11:54 GMT
< Last-Modified: Thu, 17 Oct 2019 07:18:26 GMT
< Server: ECS (bsa/EB15)
< Vary: Accept-Encoding
< X-Cache: HIT
< Content-Length: 1256
<
<!doctype html>
<html>

--------- OUTPUT OMITTED FOR BREVITY ---------

</html>
* Connection #0 to host www.example.com left intact
[netprog@localhost ~]$
```

You can amend the request headers in an outgoing request by using the **-H** option. In Example 7-25, a plain GET request is sent to http://www.postman-echo/get. This is a URI provided by Postman for testing HTTP GET requests. It echoes the headers in the request message back in the response message body.

Example 7-25 *A GET Request to http://postman-echo.com/get with Default Headers*

```
[netprog@localhost ~]$ [netdev@server1 ~]$ curl -v http://postman-echo.com/get
*   Trying 52.7.61.87...
* TCP_NODELAY set
* Connected to postman-echo.com (52.7.61.87) port 80 (#0)
> GET /get HTTP/1.1
> Host: postman-echo.com
> User-Agent: curl/7.61.1
> Accept: */*
>
< HTTP/1.1 200 OK
< Date: Wed, 04 Nov 2020 21:04:47 GMT
< Content-Type: application/json; charset=utf-8
< Content-Length: 239
< Connection: keep-alive
< ETag: W/"ef-I4uCFrpgd5HbsGsiueleYG9Xpxo"
< Vary: Accept-Encoding
< set-cookie: sails.sid=s%3AwKPh6EsQdCnjIcMOaJ-Jr4TGBdtXXL1T.cPKi3r26Pr7D4nBInFod0m
  5Hvy71fN6x6AB5N6CQJTg; Path=/; HttpOnly
<
* Connection #0 to host postman-echo.com left intact
{
  "args": {},
  "headers": {
    "x-forwarded-proto": "http",
    "x-forwarded-port": "80",
    "host": "postman-echo.com",
    "x-amzn-trace-id": "Root=1-5fa3176f-3d86eb810c54ac7560f48410",
    "user-agent": "curl/7.61.1",
    "accept": "*/*"
  },
  "url": "http://postman-echo.com/get"
}
[netprog@localhost ~]$
```

In Example 7-26, the Accept header is changed from */* to **application/json**, and a new header field named **Dummy-Header** is added to the request. As you can see in the response, the headers and the values are echoed back in the response body with the same values specified in the request message. The two header fields are highlighted in the example.

Example 7-26 *A GET Request to http://postman-echo.com/get with a New Value for the Accept Header and New Header Named Dummy-Header*

```
[netprog@localhost ~]$ curl -H "Dummy-Header: Dummy Test Header" -H "Accept:
  application/json" -v http://postman-echo.com/get
*   Trying 52.7.61.87...
* TCP_NODELAY set
* Connected to postman-echo.com (52.7.61.87) port 80 (#0)
> GET /get HTTP/1.1
> Host: postman-echo.com
> User-Agent: curl/7.61.1
> Dummy-Header: Dummy Test Header
> Accept: application/json
>
< HTTP/1.1 200 OK
< Date: Wed, 04 Nov 2020 21:14:26 GMT
< Content-Type: application/json; charset=utf-8
< Content-Length: 287
< Connection: keep-alive
< ETag: W/"11f-sj15qFMYNFmdUUpOe1awH/B19Jc"
< Vary: Accept-Encoding
< set-cookie: sails.sid=s%3AbnryFdZwC_BybL5F651Vxdc_yxddw34h.Qcx%2FGrrkVjhjE85gv0JH%
  2BOBu1%2FAkTed8X%2B0gzAtmXUg; Path=/; HttpOnly
<
* Connection #0 to host postman-echo.com left intact
{
  "args": {},
  "headers": {
    "x-forwarded-proto": "http",
    "x-forwarded-port": "80",
    "host": "postman-echo.com",
    "x-amzn-trace-id": "Root=1-5fa319b2-78f9cb933edf62f91f5fcc9f",
    "user-agent": "curl/7.61.1",
    "dummy-header": "Dummy Test Header",
    "accept": "application/json"
  },
  "url": "http://postman-echo.com/get"
}
[netprog@localhost ~]$
```

Note that in both Examples 7-25 and 7-26, the message body displays the JSON message in a readable form (that is, it is *beautified*). The output that you get on the screen is not displayed in this hierarchical, human-friendly form. Countless beautifiers are available online for different encodings, such as XML, JSON, and YAML. In addition, a beautifier that is available in the Builder in Postman can beautify your text based on the encoding chosen (JSON, XML, and so on).

To send a payload body in a request, use the **-d** option. GET requests do not have a payload body, so if the **-d** option is used, the **curl** command automatically sends out the request with the POST method. Example 7-27 shows how to send a POST request to http://postman-echo.com/post. Sending a POST request to this URI echoes back the request message payload body in the response message.

Example 7-27 *A POST Request to http://postman-echo.com/post Using the -d Option to Include a Message Body in the Request*

```
[netprog@localhost ~]$ curl -d "This is sample text" -H "Content-Type: text/plain"
  -v http://www.postman-echo.com/post
*   Trying 52.7.61.87...
* TCP_NODELAY set
* Connected to www.postman-echo.com (52.7.61.87) port 80 (#0)
> POST /post HTTP/1.1
> Host: www.postman-echo.com
> User-Agent: curl/7.61.1
> Accept: */*
> Content-Type: text/plain
> Content-Length: 19
>
* upload completely sent off: 19 out of 19 bytes
< HTTP/1.1 200 OK
< Date: Thu, 05 Nov 2020 20:44:38 GMT
< Content-Type: application/json; charset=utf-8
< Content-Length: 360
< Connection: keep-alive
< ETag: W/"168-umg0RsGU/jL+WLywHjypUEP8Gl0"
< Vary: Accept-Encoding
< set-cookie: sails.sid=s%3AkLHaFrR1zr3OqsM6tEDnLz4aJcVNVqnw.wIYr4WIW%2BxydwSSK8Zw7T
  LTY%2FFo7zH4UQ3ksepMgPMs; Path=/; HttpOnly
<
* Connection #0 to host www.postman-echo.com left intact
{
  "args": {},
  "data": "This is sample text",
  "files": {},
  "form": {},
  "headers": {
```

```
    "x-forwarded-proto": "http",
    "x-forwarded-port": "80",
    "host": "www.postman-echo.com",
    "x-amzn-trace-id": "Root=1-5fa46436-40b7121e5395553327523f99",
    "content-length": "19",
    "user-agent": "curl/7.61.1",
    "accept": "*/*",
    "content-type": "text/plain"
  },
  "json": null,
  "url": "http://www.postman-echo.com/post"
}
[netprog@localhost ~]$
```

What if you need to send a POST request without a payload body? If you use the **curl** command on a URI without any options, the GET method is implied. To change the method in the outgoing request, you use the **-X** option followed by the method name. So the command for sending a POST request to www.example.com without any data would be **curl -X POST www.example.com.** The same applies to all other methods except for HEAD. To send a HEAD request, you use the **-I** option. For example, to send a HEAD request to www.example.com, you use the command **curl -I www.example.com.**

Other useful options and variations of the **curl** command include the following:

- If you include more than one URI in the command (for example, **curl www.example-1.com www.example-2.com**), the operation selected is replicated to all URIs.
- You can segregate two sections of the command, each with its own set of operations, by using the **--next** option. For example, you use the following command to get www.example-1.com and then post data to www.example-2.com: **curl www.example-1.com --next -d "sample%20data" www.example-2.com.**
- To use a port number other than the default port 80, you specify the port number (for example, 1234) in the command, as in this example: **curl www.example.com:1234.**
- To send the request to an intermediate proxy server, you use the **--proxy** option, as in this example: **curl --proxy proxy.example.com server.example.com.**

Note The official cURL manual/tutorial is available at https://curl.haxx.se/docs/manual.html.

HTTP and Python

The previous sections discuss generating HTTP requests and sending them to a server by using Postman or directly from a Bash shell on a Linux machine and then manually parsing through the responses. While these methods are sufficient for testing purposes, they are neither efficient nor scalable, and therefore they are not the best solutions for real-life scenarios. Say, for example, that you are writing a third-party application or need to integrate with one, and you need to generate HTTP requests or parse through HTTP responses as part of a bigger program that performs other functions? This section covers how to work with HTTP using Python and some commonly used libraries.

TCP Over Python: The socket Module

As discussed earlier in this chapter, HTTP servers listen to HTTP requests on TCP port 80, and a client, sending an HTTP request to an HTTP server, first establishes a TCP connection to that HTTP server on port 80 and then sends the HTTP request. In Python, this can be accomplished by using the socket module.

In the context of networks, a *socket* is a software implementation of an internal network port on the local system. A program that wishes to send data over a network requests that the operating system create a network socket. At the other end of this socket is the remote system to which data is to be transmitted. When the program wishes to send data over the network to the remote system, it sends this data to the socket that the OS created. The OS then takes care of receiving this data on the socket, processing and encoding it accordingly, and placing it on the wire to be sent to the remote system. A similar network socket is created on the remote system. The program requests a socket from the OS by talking to the OS's *socket API*.

A network socket is identified by the IP address and port on the local system. When a program requests that the OS create a socket, the OS creates the socket and assigns to it a socket descriptor, also called a *handle*. This is usually a number that uniquely identifies this socket. The program can then use this descriptor or handle whenever it wishes to send data to the socket.

These are the steps a client needs to perform to send an HTTP request to a server using the socket module:

Step 1. Using the **socket.socket()** method, the client uses the socket API to request that the OS create a socket and assign a socket handle to it.

Step 2. The client connects to the destination server by using the {*socket_handle*}.**connect()** method.

Step 3. The client sends the HTTP request contents to the server by using the {*socket_handle*}.**send()** method.

Step 4. The client receives the server response by using the {*socket_handle*}.**recv()** method.

Step 5. The client closes the connection with the server by using the {*socket_handle*}.**close()** method.

Example 7-28 shows a Python code sample that opens a network socket to www.example.com on port 80 and sends the same GET request as in the previous section.

Example 7-28 *A GET Request to www.example.com Using the Python* ***socket*** *Module*

```
#!/usr/bin/env python
import socket
my_socket_handle = socket.socket(socket.AF_INET, socket.SOCK_STREAM)
my_socket_handle.connect(('www.example.com',80))
request = 'GET http://www.example.com/ HTTP/1.1\n\n'.encode()
my_socket_handle.send(request)
data = my_socket_handle.recv(10000)
print(data.decode())
my_socket_handle.close()
```

In Example 7-28, two arguments are passed to the **socket.socket()** method in order to request a socket from the OS. The first, **socket.AF_INET**, defines the address family of the socket to be **AF_INET**. This is the family of IPv4 network sockets (as opposed to IPv6 network sockets of type **AF_INET6** or interprocess communications sockets of type **AF_UNIX**). The second argument, **socket.SOCK_STREAM**, defines the type of socket. A socket of type **SOCK_STREAM** is a TCP socket. A UDP socket would be of type **SOCK_DGRAM**. The socket handle value is assigned to the variable **my_socket_handle**.

In the second step, the client uses the **my_socket_handle.connect()** method to connect to www.example.com on port 80. This method accepts one argument, which is why double parentheses are used in the example. This argument is the URI or IP address of the server followed by a comma and then the port number.

The request line, which is currently a string, is encoded into a UTF-8 byte object using the {*string*}.**encode()** method and assigned to the variable **request**, which is used as the argument to the **my_socket_handle.send(request)** method to send the request line to the server. Notice in Example 7-28 that only the request line is sent to the server (and no headers), followed by two CRLFs, indicating the end of the headers section.

The next line of code uses the method **my_socket_handle.recv(10000)** to receive the response back from the server. The number 10000, known as the *bufsize*, is the number of bytes to be received from the server. The program in this example has been written this way to keep the code simple, but a more sophisticated form can use a loop, with a smaller bufsize, and a condition to test when no more data is being received from the server.

The data is decoded back to a string with the **string.decode()** method, and then the **print()** function is used to print the data received.

Finally, the **my_socket_handle.close()** method requests the OS to close this specific socket.

Example 7-29 shows the result of running the Example 7-28 code.

Example 7-29 *The Result of Running the Example 7-28 Python Code*

```
[NetDev@localhost HTTP]$ python http_socket.py
HTTP/1.1 200 OK
Accept-Ranges: bytes
Cache-Control: max-age=604800
Content-Type: text/html; charset=UTF-8
Date: Fri, 01 Feb 2019 23:27:58 GMT
Etag: "1541025663+gzip"
Expires: Fri, 08 Feb 2019 23:27:58 GMT
Last-Modified: Fri, 09 Aug 2013 23:54:35 GMT
Server: ECS (dca/2469)
Vary: Accept-Encoding
X-Cache: HIT
Content-Length: 1270
<!doctype html>
<html>
<head>
    <title>Example Domain</title>

    <meta charset="utf-8" />
    <meta http-equiv="Content-type" content="text/html; charset=utf-8" />
    <meta name="viewport" content="width=device-width, initial-scale=1" />
    <style type="text/css">
    body {

--------- OUTPUT TRUNCATED FOR BREVITY ---------

[NetDev@localhost HTTP]$
```

Note The socket module is covered in more detail in the Python documentation at https://docs.python.org/3/library/socket.html.

The urllib Package

The urllib package is composed of the urllib.request, urllib.parse, urllib.error, and urllib.robotparser modules. In this section you will see how to use the urllib.request module to send GET and POST HTTP requests. Note that urllib supports other schemes, not just HTTP, but to keep the discussion relevant, this section covers only HTTP.

Note Three other packages exist for Python: urllib2, urllib3, and urllib for Python 2. The four packages urllib for Python 2, urllib for Python 3, urllib2, and urllib3 are different implementations of an HTTP client. There are subtle differences between these four packages that are beyond the scope of this book. These differences are not covered here because using the requests package, covered in the next section, is the recommended method of working with HTTP in Python. urllib is covered here to illustrate the different levels of abstraction available in Python, starting with the socket module, then urllib, and finally requests.

The urllib.request module eliminates the need to open a socket manually and then encode the HTTP request. Instead, a single line of code is required to send an HTTP request to a specific URI. Example 7-30 shows a three-line Python script that sends a GET HTTP request to the web page www.example.com. Compare this script with the script in Example 7-28, which uses the socket module.

Example 7-30 *A Simple Python Script Using urllib to Send a GET Request to www.example.com*

```
import urllib.request

httphand = urllib.request.urlopen('http://www.example.com')

print(httphand.read())
```

After the module **urllib.request** is imported in the first line, a handle to the URI www.example.com is created by using the **urlopen()** function. A handle, as discussed earlier, is a reference to an object, such as a file or a URI. Then the **read()** function is used in the third line, on the handle **httphand**, to read the content of the URI—that is, to send a GET request and fetch a representation of the resource at the subject URI. Finally, the **print()** function is used to print out to the screen the content found at the URI.

Example 7-31 shows the result of running the script in Example 7-30.

Example 7-31 *The Result of Running the Python Code in Example 7-30*

```
[NetDev@localhost HTTP]$ python http_urllib.py

b'<!doctype html>\n<html>\n<head>\n    <title>Example Domain</title>\n\n    <meta
  charset="utf-8" />\n    <meta http-equiv="Content-type" content="text/html;
  charset=utf-8" />\n    <meta name="viewport" content="width=device-width,
  initial-scale=1" />\n    <style type="text/css">\n    body {\n        background-
  color: #f0f0f2;\n        margin: 0;\n        padding: 0;\n        font-family:
  "Open Sans", "Helvetica Neue", Helvetica, Arial, sans-serif;\n        \n    }\n
  div {\n        width: 600px;\n        margin: 5em auto;\n        padding: 50px;\n
  background-color: #fff;\n        border-radius: 1em;\n    }\n    a:link, a:visited
  {\n        color: #38488f;\n        text-decoration: none;\n    }\n    @media
  (max-width: 700px) {\n        body {\n            background-color: #fff;\n
  }\n        div {\n            width: auto;\n            margin: 0 auto;\n
  border-radius: 0;\n            padding: 1em;\n        }\n    }\n    </style>
  \n</head>\n\n<body>\n<div>\n    <h1>Example Domain</h1>\n    <p>This domain is
  established to be used for illustrative examples in documents. You may use this\n
  domain in examples without prior coordination or asking for permission.</p>\n
  <p><a href="http://www.iana.org/domains/example">More information...</a></p>\n
  </div>\n</body>\n</html>\n'

[NetDev@localhost HTTP]$
```

The HTML code in Example 7-31 is found at the URI www.example.com and retrieved (and printed) by the Python script.

Notice in Example 7-31 that the HTTP headers do not appear in the output, as they do with the socket module. The response headers are viewed using the {*file_handle*}.**info()** method, as shown in the script in Example 7-32.

Example 7-32 *Printing the Response Headers by Using the* ***info()*** *Method*

```
import urllib.request

httphand = urllib.request.urlopen('http://www.example.com')

print(httphand.info())
```

Example 7-33 shows the result of running the script in Example 7-21. As you can see, only the response headers are printed out, as intended by the **print(httphand.info())** line.

Example 7-33 *The Result of Running the Script in Example 7-32*

```
[NetDev@localhost HTTP]$ python Scripts/http_urllib_response_headers.py
Accept-Ranges: bytes
Cache-Control: max-age=604800
Content-Type: text/html; charset=UTF-8
Date: Mon, 13 May 2019 21:42:19 GMT
Etag: "1541025663+gzip+ident"
Expires: Mon, 20 May 2019 21:42:19 GMT
Last-Modified: Fri, 09 Aug 2013 23:54:35 GMT
Server: ECS (dcb/7EEF)
Vary: Accept-Encoding
X-Cache: HIT
Content-Length: 1270
Connection: close

[NetDev@localhost HTTP]$
```

The second thing to notice in Example 7-31 is that the HTML code prints out as a sequence of characters without any line breaks. This is due to the fact that the **urlopen()** function returns a byte object. A byte object is a sequence of bytes, in contrast to a string, which is a series of characters. The output in Example 7-31 shows the ASCII equivalent of each byte, one after the other, including the **\n** character, which represents a new line.

To decode the byte object received, you use the **decode()** function. Example 7-34 shows the same script as in Example 7-33, except that the **decode()** function is used to decode the UTF-8 byte object back to a string.

Example 7-34 *Using the **decode()** Function to Decode the Output of the **read()** Function*

```
import urllib.request

httphand = urllib.request.urlopen('http://www.example.com')

print(httphand.read().decode('utf-8'))
```

This results in the same output as in Example 7-33, except that the \n character is actually interpreted into a new line. The result is shown in Example 7-35.

Example 7-35 *The Result of Running the Python Code in Example 7-34*

```
[NetDev@localhost HTTP]$ python http_urllib.py
<!doctype html>
<html>
<head>
    <title>Example Domain</title>

    <meta charset="utf-8" />
    <meta http-equiv="Content-type" content="text/html; charset=utf-8" />
    <meta name="viewport" content="width=device-width, initial-scale=1" />
    <style type="text/css">
    body {
        background-color: #f0f0f2;
        margin: 0;
        padding: 0;
        font-family: -apple-system, system-ui, BlinkMacSystemFont, "Segoe UI",
  "Open Sans", "Helvetica Neue", Helvetica, Arial, sans-serif;

    }
    div {
        width: 600px;
        margin: 5em auto;
        padding: 50px;
        background-color: #fff;
        border-radius: 1em;
    }
    a:link, a:visited {
        color: #38488f;
        text-decoration: none;
    }
    @media (max-width: 700px) {
        body {
            background-color: #fff;
        }
        div {
            width: auto;
            margin: 0 auto;
            border-radius: 0;
            padding: 1em;
        }
    }
    </style>
```

```
</head>

<body>
<div>
    <h1>Example Domain</h1>
    <p>This domain is established to be used for illustrative examples in documents.
  You may use this domain in examples without prior coordination or asking for
  permission.</p>
    <p><a href="http://www.iana.org/domains/example">More information...</a></p>
</div>
</body>
</html>
[NetDev@localhost HTTP]$
```

The **urlopen()** function in the previous examples is used with a URI as an argument. To pass more than just the URI to the function—for example, the HTTP headers or an HTTP message body—you can use the **urlopen()** function with a *request object* as an argument instead of just using the URI. This request object includes all information required to successfully construct an HTTP request. The request object is constructed using the **Request()** class. The following is a simplified form of the **Request()** class syntax:

```
{R_Object}=urllib.request.Request({url}[,data={data}][,headers=
{headers}][,method={HTTP_method}])
```

The first argument is the URI. The second argument is the data, which is the HTTP request payload body. Data is provided as a byte object. The third argument is the HTTP headers. This is provided as a Python dictionary, where each key/value pair is the header field name and value. Finally, the last argument is the HTTP request method.

To test all the features at once, the script in Example 7-36 can be used to construct an HTTP request that attempts to authenticate to the NX-OS switch.

Example 7-36 *Using urllib to Authenticate to a Nexus Switch*

```
import urllib.request, ssl, json
gcontext = ssl.SSLContext()
uri = "https://sbx-nxos-mgmt.cisco.com/api/aaaLogin.json"
body = {
     "aaaUser": {
       "attributes": {
         "name": "admin",
         "pwd": "Admin_1234!"
        }
    }
}
encoded_to_json = json.dumps(body)
data = encoded_to_json.encode()
headers = {"Content-Type":"application/json","Cache-Control":"no-cache"}
```

```
request_object = urllib.request.Request(url=uri,data=data,headers=headers,
  method='POST')
request = urllib.request.urlopen(request_object,context=gcontext)
print('\n')
print(request.read())
```

Recall that SSL certificate checking needs to be disabled on Postman before you attempt to authenticate to a switch. This is accomplished here via the code line **gcontext = ssl.SSLContext()** and then using **context=gcontext** as an argument in the **urlopen()** function later in the code.

After you import all the required modules, you create the different components required to build the request object. First, you assign the URI to the string variable **uri.** Then you assign the request body to the variable **body** as a nested dictionary. However, the switch is expecting the body of the HTTP request to be encoded in JSON, so the **json.dumps()** method is used to convert the Python dictionary to JSON. Then the **Request()** class is expecting the data argument to be a byte object, so the JSON body is encoded into a byte object using the **encode()** method and assigned to the variable **data**. Finally, the request headers are assigned to the variable **headers** as a dictionary.

When the URI, data, and headers are properly constructed and encoded, they are passed to the **Request()** class, along with **method='POST'**, to create the request object **request_object.** Note that if no data is passed to the **Request()** class, the method defaults to GET; otherwise, the method defaults to POST, so, strictly speaking, **method='POST'** is not required, and it is added to the code for illustration purposes only.

The request object is then passed to the **urlopen()** function, resulting in an HTTP request constructed with the required parameters. Example 7-37 shows the result of running this script. Compare the response received here with the response received when the same authentication HTTP request is sent using Postman (refer to Example 7-18).

Example 7-37 *Authenticating to a Nexus Switch*

```
[NetDev@localhost ~]$ python Scripts/auth_python.py

b'{"imdata":[{"aaaLogin": {"attributes": {"token": "nnrrUpqz4P17nBD26JZkxTwf7vf3o
  v5zJQV8ahFIFNxbmdIHbChr43ASjOQM4JKRpA0jP2upEb2PUS3XeAEPvwHdpsVHpLVpF9UNwy1o94n
  6kSRRGUuN048A/Oawde9XjgQkA6UFiaeY3ehEE/iBI0+NT5hHtHYjfZYCGK6j6gg=","siteFingerpr
  int": "","refreshTimeoutSeconds": "600","guiIdleTimeoutSeconds": "1200",
  "restTimeoutSeconds": "1920151406","creationTime": "1558145939","firstLoginTime":
  "1558145939","userName": "admin","remoteUser": "false","unixUserId": "0",
  "sessionId": "VPNv91T+yeoBAAAAFwAAAA==","lastName": "","firstName": "",
  "version": "0.9(14HEAD${version.patch})","buildTime": "Tue Jul 17 15:13:26 PDT
  2018","controllerId": "0"},"children": [{"aaaUserDomain": {"attributes":
  {"name": "all","rolesR": "admin","rolesW": "admin"},"children": [{"aaaReadRoles":
  {"attributes": {}}},{"aaaWriteRoles": {"attributes": {},"children": [{"role":
  {"attributes": {"name": "network-admin"}}}]}}]}}]}}]}'
[NetDev@localhost ~]$
```

The requests Package

The requests package has been developed to further abstract and simplify the process of working with HTTP using Python. The Python Software Foundation recommends using the requests package whenever a higher-level HTTP client interface is needed.

The requests package is based on urllib3 and is not part of the standard library (as urllib and urllib2 are), so it has to be manually installed. (Third-party packages are discussed in Chapter 6, "Python Applications.") Example 7-38 shows how to install requests by using **pip3.7**.

Example 7-38 *Installing the requests Package by Using pip*

```
[NetDev@server1 ~]$ sudo pip3.7 install requests
Collecting requests
  Using cached https://files.pythonhosted.org/packages/51/bd/23c926cd341ea6b7dd0b2a0
  0aba99ae0f828be89d72b2190f27c11d4b7fb/requests-2.22.0-py2.py3-none-any.whl
Requirement already satisfied: idna<2.9,>=2.5 in /usr/local/lib/python3.7/site-
  packages (from requests) (2.7)
Requirement already satisfied: certifi>=2017.4.17 in /usr/local/lib/python3.7/
  site-packages (from requests) (2018.10.15)
Requirement already satisfied: chardet<3.1.0,>=3.0.2 in /usr/local/lib/python3.7/
  site-packages (from requests) (3.0.4)
Requirement already satisfied: urllib3!=1.25.0,!=1.25.1,<1.26,>=1.21.1 in /usr/
  local/lib/python3.7/site-packages (from requests) (1.24.1)
Installing collected packages: requests
Successfully installed requests-2.22.0
[NetDev@localhost ~]$
```

When the requests package is installed, you are ready to import it into your code.

Using the requests package is primarily based on creating a *response object* and then extracting the required information from that response object. This is the basic syntax for creating a response object:

```
{R_Object}=requests.{method}({uri}[,params={query_parameters}]
[,headers={headers}][,data={payload_body}])
```

To create an object for a GET request, you use **requests.get**, for a POST request, you use **requests.post**, and so forth.

The **params** parameter holds the value of the key/value pairs that will constitute the query part of the URI. The **headers** parameter holds the headers, and the **data** parameter holds the request payload body. All three parameters are Python dictionaries, except for the **data** parameter, which can be provided as a dictionary, a string, or a list. The parameter **data=**{*payload_body*} may be replaced by **json=**{*payload_body*}, in which case the payload is encoded into JSON automatically.

You can extract the following response information from the created object:

- {*Response_object*}.**content**: The response from the server as a byte object (not decoded).
- {*Response_object*}.**text**: The decoded response (payload body) from the server. The encoding is chosen automatically based on an educated guess.
- {*Response_object*}.**encoding**: The encoding used to convert {*Response_object*}.**content** to {*Response_object*}.**text**. You can manually set this to a specific encoding of your choice.
- {*Response_object*}.**json()**: The decoded response (payload body) from the server encoded in JSON, if the response resembles a JSON object. (Otherwise, an error is returned.)
- {*Response_object*}.**url**: The actual URI used in the request, with all the different components included as parameters in **requests.**{*method*}**()**.
- {*Response_object*}.**status_code**: The response status code.
- {*Response_object*}.**request.headers**: The request headers.
- {*Response_object*}.**headers**: The response headers.

In Example 7-39, the response object res_obj holds the response data from a POST request sent to https://httpbin.org/post with a custom header named My-Custom-Header and a payload body consisting of the string **"THIS IS THE PAYLOAD BODY"**. Then the script prints out all the listed request and response parameter values.

Example 7-39 *POST Request Using the requests Package*

```
import requests

url = 'https://httpbin.org/post'
headers = {'My-Custom-Header': 'NetDev Doing a POST'}
parameters = {'Key-1':'Value-1','Key-2':'Value-2'}
payload = "THIS IS THE PAYLOAD BODY"

res_obj = requests.post(url,params=parameters,headers=headers,data=payload)

print('The Server Response as a byte object: ','\n\n',res_obj.content,'\n')
print('The decoded response (payload) from the server: ','\n\n',res_obj.text,'\n')
print('The encoding used to convert Response_object.content to Response_object.text:
  ','\n\n', res_obj.encoding,'\n')
print('The actual URI used in the request (incl the query component): ','\n\n',
  res_obj.url,'\n')
print('The response status code: ','\n\n',res_obj.status_code,'\n')
print('The request headers: ','\n\n',res_obj.request.headers,'\n')
print('The response headers :','\n\n',res_obj.headers,'\n')
```

Example 7-40 shows the result of running the code in Example 7-39.

Example 7-40 *The Information Extracted from the Request Object*

```
[NetDev@localhost Scripts]$ python requests_simple_1.py
The Server Response as a byte object:

 b'{\n  "args": {\n    "Key-1": "Value-1", \n    "Key-2": "Value-2"\n  }, \n
  "data": "THIS IS THE PAYLOAD BODY", \n  "files": {}, \n  "form": {}, \n
  "headers": {\n    "Accept": "*/*", \n    "Accept-Encoding": "gzip, deflate", \n
  "Content-Length": "19", \n    "Host": "httpbin.org", \n    "My-Custom-Header":
  "NetDev Doing a POST", \n    "User-Agent": "python-requests/2.20.1"\n  }, \n
  "json": null, \n  "origin": "51.36.2.121, 51.36.2.121", \n  "url": "https://
  httpbin.org/post?Key-1=Value-1&Key-2=Value-2"\n}\n'

The decoded response (payload) from the server:

 {
  "args": {
    "Key-1": "Value-1",
    "Key-2": "Value-2"
  },
  "data": "THIS IS THE PAYLOAD BODY",
  "files": {},
  "form": {},
  "headers": {
    "Accept": "*/*",
    "Accept-Encoding": "gzip, deflate",
    "Content-Length": "19",
    "Host": "httpbin.org",
    "My-Custom-Header": "NetDev Doing a POST",
    "User-Agent": "python-requests/2.20.1"
  },
  "json": null,
  "origin": "51.36.2.121, 51.36.2.121",
  "url": "https://httpbin.org/post?Key-1=Value-1&Key-2=Value-2"
}

The encoding used to convert Response_object.content to Response_object.text:

 None

The actual URI used in the request (incl the query component):
```

```
https://httpbin.org/post?Key-1=Value-1&Key-2=Value-2

The response status code:

200

The request headers:

{'User-Agent': 'python-requests/2.20.1', 'Accept-Encoding': 'gzip, deflate',
 'Accept': '*/*', 'Connection': 'keep-alive', 'My-Custom-Header': 'NetDev Doing a
 POST', 'Content-Length': '19'}

The response headers :

{'Access-Control-Allow-Credentials': 'true', 'Access-Control-Allow-Origin': '*',
 'Content-Encoding': 'gzip', 'Content-Type': 'application/json', 'Date': 'Wed, 15
 May 2019 02:03:17 GMT', 'Referrer-Policy': 'no-referrer-when-downgrade', 'Server':
 'nginx', 'X-Content-Type-Options': 'nosniff', 'X-Frame-Options': 'DENY', 'X-XSS-
 Protection': '1; mode=block', 'Content-Length': '307', 'Connection': 'keep-alive'}

[NetDev@localhost Scripts]$
```

You can see from Example 7-40 that the requests package provides a more elegant solution to sending and receiving HTTP messages.

Summary

This chapter covers one of the most fundamental and extensively used protocols in web development and REST API development and use: HTTP. By now, you should be able to successfully construct HTTP requests using proper URIs, headers, and payload bodies and then navigate through the responses received. This chapter also covers the tools most commonly used today for working with HTTP. This chapter discusses the following topics:

- HTTP Overview
- The REST architectural framework and its relationship to the HTTP protocol
- The HTTP connection based on TCP and connection enhancement in HTTP/1.1
- Client request methods and server response codes
- HTTP messages and four types of header fields: general, request, response and entity header fields

- How resources are identified using URIs, URLs, and URNs, and the syntax rules of valid URIs
- Tools to automate working with HTTP and REST APIs: Postman, Telnet, cURL, and the Python socket module, urllib package, and requests package

Chapter 8 picks up where this chapter leaves off and covers advanced topics in HTTP such as authentication in HTTP, TLS and HTTPS, and HTTP/2.0.

Chapter 8

Advanced HTTP

This chapter picks up where Chapter 7, "HTTP and REST," leaves off and covers more advanced topics related to HTTP. The first section of the chapter describes the different types of HTTP authentication schemes, which provide a means to verify the identity of a client attempting to access a protected resource and, in some cases, verify the identity of the server back to the client. HTTP is stateless. Cookies provide a workaround to allow servers to maintain state information on client machines. This chapter covers cookies and their use in HTTP. This chapter also discusses the Transport Layer Security (TLS) protocol and HTTP over TLS (HTTPS). Using TLS tunnels, HTTPS provides encryption of HTTP requests and responses and, in turn, data confidentiality and integrity. Finally, this chapter covers the newer versions of HTTP, HTTP/2 and HTTP/3, and the enhancements they have introduced.

HTTP/1.1 Authentication

Authentication is a process through which the identity of a client is verified by an HTTP server and, possibly, vice versa. In addition to verifying the client identity, the HTTP server also needs to make sure that this particular client is authorized to access the resource addressed in its request to the server. The header names used in HTTP, as well as some literature, use the terms *authentication* and *authorization* interchangeably, but there are differences between them: Whereas authentication involves proving that users are who they say they are, authorization involves giving those users access to a particular resource.

There are several ways a server can authenticate clients attempting to access resources on that server. Some of these *authentication schemes* are native to HTTP, or extensions to it, and some are vendor specific. HTTP authentication in general is very extensible. For example, the Basic Authentication scheme uses the native HTTP headers WWW-Authenticate and Authorization to complete the authentication workflow. Alternatively, the product Cisco Meraki uses a vendor-defined header named X-Cisco-Meraki-API-Key to authenticate calls made to its Dashboard API. (You'll learn more about this in Chapter 17, "Programming Cisco Platforms.") The value of this header is referred to as an *API key* and is manually generated from the Meraki GUI. The API key is included in each HTTP request to that API endpoint (URI).

This section focuses on standard schemes, which usually provide the foundation for the other, non-standard, schemes. The general concepts underlying HTTP authentication are covered in RFC 7235. The IANA maintains a registry of all registered authentication schemes for HTTP at http://www.iana.org/assignments/http-authschemes. This section covers three schemes:

- Basic Authentication
- OAuth and authentication tokens
- Cookies

Authentication in HTTP may operate using a *challenge/response* model, or it may operate using a direct, *unsolicited* model. In the first model, the client attempts to access a protected resource on a server without providing credentials. The server responds with a "401 Unauthorized" response message, which is the server's way of informing the client that the resource it is trying to access is protected and needs authentication. The server response also includes further details, such as what schemes the server supports and the realm (explained shortly). This is the server *challenge*. The client then re-sends its request, but this time, it includes the required credentials in the request, using the headers relevant to the scheme used. This is the client *response*.

The unsolicited model is used when the client knows beforehand that the resource it is trying to access is protected, knows what scheme the server is using to protect the resource, and has a valid set of credentials. In this case, the client preemptively sends its request, including the credentials required for authentication. The workflow does not include a challenge – only a response.

When a client is authenticating with a proxy server, the proxy uses a "407 Proxy Authentication Required" message to challenge the client instead of a "401 Unauthorized" message.

An HTTP server may define *protection spaces*, also known as *realms*, on the server. These realms partition the server resources into different spaces, and each space may use a different authentication scheme and/or credentials. Using realms is one way to allow a server to not just authenticate a client but also authorize it to access specific resources and not others. In other words, the same client may be authorized to access resources in one realm but not in another.

Figure 8-1 illustrates the authentication workflow in HTTP.

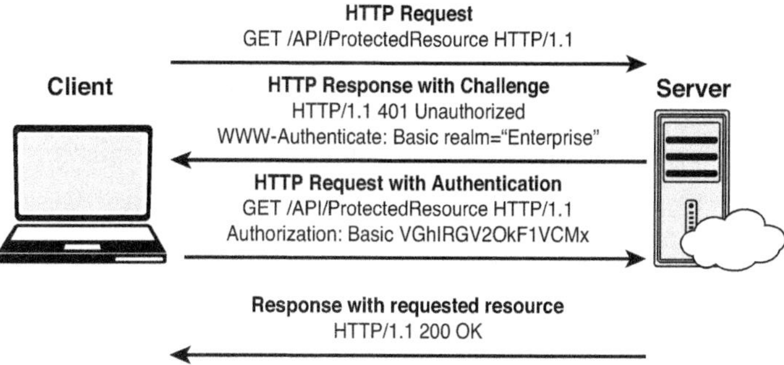

Figure 8-1 *HTTP Authentication Workflow*

The server challenge is a "401 Unauthorized" HTTP response message that includes the header WWW-Authenticate. The header field value is equal to the challenge value. The general format of the header field, which may contain one or more challenges, is as follows:

```
WWW-Authenticate: {challenge_1}[, challenge_2], ...[, challenge_n]
```

Each of the challenges in the header field has the following general format:

```
{scheme} {parameter_1}={value_1}[, {parameter_2}={value_2}[,...,]
{parameter_n}={value_n}]
```

Each challenge is composed of the scheme name followed by a whitespace and then a list of parameter name/value pairs. The following is an example of a WWW-Authenticate header containing two challenges:

```
WWW-Authenticate: Digest realm="dev", algorithm=SHA-256, Basic realm=
"prod", charset="UTF-8"
```

The first challenge in this example is for the Digest scheme and has two parameters: realm and algorithm. The second challenge is for the Basic scheme and has two parameters: realm and charset. Do not worry about the meaning of each of these parameters just yet; they are covered in detail later in this chapter. The goal here is to showcase the header field format only.

In the case of a client authenticating with a proxy server, the WWW-Authenticate header is replaced with the Proxy-Authenticate header that has the same format.

After receiving the challenge, the client should respond with the same request it sent earlier (that is, the one that triggered the challenge), but this time it should add an Authorization header field, which has the following general format:

```
Authorization: {scheme} {credentials}
```

Basic Authentication

Basic Authentication, as the name implies, is the most basic method of authenticating users attempting to access a resource on an HTTP server. Basic Authentication is covered in RFC 7617, and the scheme is identified by the scheme name Basic.

This scheme uses exactly the same response codes and header fields discussed earlier in this chapter for server HTTP challenge messages. The server uses the WWW-Authenticate header field in a "401 Unauthorized" message to challenge the client (or the Proxy-Authenticate header field in a "407 Proxy Authentication Required" message in the case of a proxy server). The general format of the WWW-Authenticate header field is as follows:

WWW-Authenticate: Basic realm="{*realm_value*}**"[, charset="UTF-8"]**

Apart from the scheme name, this scheme mandates that the protection space value be specified as the value of the realm parameter. The other parameter, charset, is optional and has only one valid value, **UTF-8**, because it is used to advise the client to use UTF-8 encoding when generating its Base64-encoded credentials to the server. (This is explained in detail shortly.) The scheme name and parameter names and values are all case insensitive, except for the realm value. The parameter values may also be expressed as quoted-string values, or tokens (without quotes).

The client responds with an HTTP request that includes the Authorization header field containing the required credentials (or a Proxy-Authorization header field in the case of authenticating with a proxy server). The Authorization header field used by the Basic scheme has the following general format:

Authorization: Basic {*base64-encoded-credentials*}

Base64 is an encoding scheme defined in RFC 4648 that was designed to represent a sequence of octets using a 65-character subset of the U.S. ASCII; this representation was not designed to be human readable. Base64 encoding is one type of *base encoding*, originally developed to support environments and systems that only support the U.S. ASCII character set. A simple search on the Internet will return several online Base64 encoders that automate the process of converting a string to its Base64 equivalent. It can be helpful to understand where the strange-looking string in the Authorization header came from and how it is generated.

The process to generate the *base64-encoded-credentials* token involves a few simple steps. Let's say that the client username is TheDev, and the password is AuT#1. The first step is to concatenate the username and password, separated by a colon—in this case, TheDev:AuT#1.

The next step is to encode this string using a data encoding scheme. There is no default encoding specified by the Base64 standard. The only restriction is that the encoding used has to be compatible with U.S. ASCII, which means that each U.S. ASCII character needs to map to one single byte. Table 8-1 shows how this works with UTF-8.

Table 8-1 *Mapping the Letters of the Username and Password to Their UTF-8 Codes*

Letter	UTF-8 Encoding (Decimal)	UTF-8 Encoding (Binary)
T	84	01010100
h	104	01101000
e	101	01100101
D	68	01000100
e	101	01100101
v	118	01110110
:	58	00111010
A	65	01000001
u	117	01110101
T	84	01010100
#	35	00100011
1	49	00110001

Note For more on UTF-8 encoding, see https://unicode.org/faq/utf_bom.html#UTF8.

The last step is to encode the string into a Base64 token. This is done in four substeps:

1. Concatenate all 12 bytes:

   ```
   010101000110100001100101010001000110010101110110001110100100000101011
   101010101010000100011001100001
   ```

2. Split the bytes into 6-bit words:

   ```
   010101-000110-100001-100101-010001-000110-010101-110110-001110-
   100100-000101-110101-010101-000010-001100-110001
   ```

3. Translate each 6-bit binary word into its decimal equivalent:

   ```
   21-6-33-37-17-6-21-54-14-36-5-53-21-2-12-49
   ```

4. Using Table 8-2, match each decimal value from step 3 to its corresponding letter:

   ```
   VGhIRGV2OkF1VCMx
   ```

   For this example, the Authentication header field is as follows:

   ```
   Authentication: Basic VGhIRGV2OkF1VCMx
   ```

Table 8-2 *Base64 Alphabet*

Value	Encoding	Value	Encoding	Value	Encoding	Value	Encoding
0	A	17	R	34	i	51	z
1	B	18	S	35	j	52	0
2	C	19	T	36	k	53	1
3	D	20	U	37	l	54	2
4	E	21	V	38	m	55	3
5	F	22	W	39	n	56	4
6	G	23	X	40	o	57	5
7	H	24	Y	41	p	58	6
8	I	25	Z	42	q	59	7
9	J	26	a	43	r	60	8
10	K	27	b	44	s	61	9
11	L	28	c	45	t	62	+
12	M	29	d	46	u	63	/
13	N	30	e	47	v		
14	O	31	f	48	w	(pad)	=
15	P	32	g	49	x		
16	Q	33	h	50	y		

As you can see, the Authentication header contains the Base64 encoding of the credentials in plaintext. Any entity capable of inspecting this HTTP response from the client can easily decode the string VGhIRGV2OkF1VCMx and learn the user credentials. This is one of the reasons Basic Authentication is almost never used on its own when security is considered to be essential. Basic Authentication is usually coupled with technologies that provide data confidentiality, such as TLS, and then used as an intermediate step in a more sophisticated authentication workflow, such as that used in OAuth 2.0. Both TLS and OAuth are covered in later sections of this chapter.

OAuth and Bearer Tokens

The OAuth protocol, or the OAuth *authorization framework*, as RFC 6749 calls it, was developed with a very specific authorization use case in mind: to enable a third-party application to access resources owned by another entity (which the RFC calls *restricted resources*) without the entity that owns these resources having to share its credentials with the application attempting to access the resources. That was a mouthful! But it is not as complicated as it sounds.

Let's consider an example. Say that you are trying to link your fitness application with your Facebook account so that the fitness app can retrieve your list of Facebook friends and check whether any of them uses the same app and then connect you together on the app. The app would also want to post your workouts to your Facebook timeline. The OAuth protocol is used to get your approval to allow the fitness app to access some or all of your Facebook data and then to authenticate and authorize the app with the Facebook authentication server. The app can then retrieve data from or post data to your Facebook account. The fitness app in this case is the third-party application attempting to access data, owned by you, residing on the Facebook server, without you having to share your Facebook credentials with the fitness app.

In order to describe the workflow for OAuth, the protocol defines four different *roles*. These roles are defined for a workflow that involves a resource hosted on a *resource server* (role 1). The resource is owned by a *resource owner* (role 2), and this owner may wish to grant a third-party application, referred to as the *client* (role 3), access to that resource; it does so by leveraging the services of an *authorization server* (role 4). We can map these roles to the previous example: The fitness app is the client. You are the resource owner. The Facebook server hosting your data is the resource server. The Facebook server that will authenticate you as the resource owner as well as the client attempting to access your data is the authorization server.

But what does all this have to do with network programmability and automation? The automation ecosystem involves a lot of *integrations*. For example, the Cisco Webex line of products depends heavily on OAuth to integrate with third-party apps. Let's say you developed an application called App X, and you need to integrate it with Webex Teams so that this app can do API calls on behalf of a user, so as to post to a space (that is, a chat room in Webex Teams) without the user providing her credentials to your app. This is a classic case for using OAuth. OAuth makes integration between applications seamless and much more secure than do other alternatives.

Note For more on Webex integrations, see https://developer.webex.com/docs/integrations.

Keep in mind that these roles are just functions and that one single entity may perform the functions of one or more roles. A client may also be the resource owner, for instance, or the resource server may be the same as the authorization server. There are therefore many variations of the OAuth workflow and quite a number of nuts and bolts to the protocol. This section covers OAuth in enough detail to help you understand the majority of the service documentation for integrations provided by network vendors and omits the fine details typically required by software developers creating or maintaining commercial-grade software.

The latest version of the OAuth protocol, Version 2.0, is defined in RFC 6749; using Bearer Tokens with the OAuth protocol is defined in RFC 6750. Although this chapter does not explicitly cover native applications, it is worth mentioning that RFC 8252 discusses the best practice of only using external user agents, such as web browsers, for making OAuth requests from native apps. (Native apps are apps running natively on a system, such as Microsoft Office applications installed on a PC; in contrast, web apps are apps that run on a remote server with only a user interface on the client machine.) The high-level workflow of OAuth involves four steps:

1. **Client Registration:** The client (that is, the third-party application) registers with the authorization server.
2. **Authorization Grant:** The client requests authorization from the resource owner and receives an *authorization grant* in response to its request. The grant may come from the resource owner directly or from the authorization server.
3. **Access Token:** The client sends the authorization grant to the authorization server and receives an *access token*.
4. **Resource Access:** The client uses the access token in its API call to the resource server in order to gain access to the protected resource(s) residing on the server and owned by the resource owner.

The high-level workflow in Figure 8-2 is adapted from the workflow in RFC 6749.

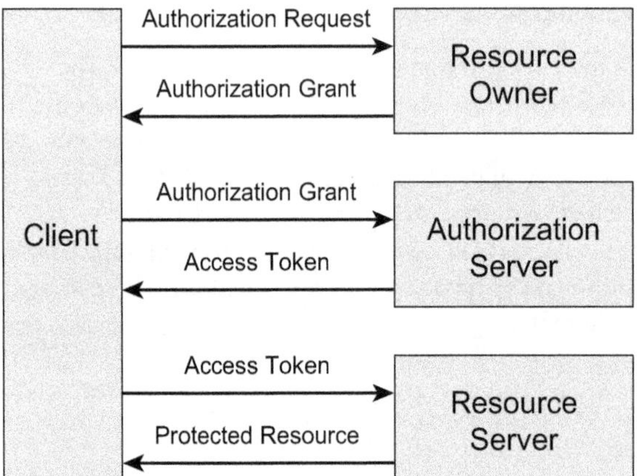

Figure 8-2 *High-Level OAuth Workflow*

The OAuth workflow described here comes in several flavors and involves a lot of fine details. A lot of abstraction is also embedded in the four steps just described. The following sections touch on each of the four steps and provide details related to network automation and programmability.

Client Registration

First, and as a prerequisite to any other OAuth-related activity, the client—whether it is a web, native, or mobile application—should register itself with the authorization server. The authorization server needs to know up front what applications are integrated with it—that is, what applications may leverage its services to request access to resources owned by other entities.

For instance, App X, which you have developed and would like to post on behalf of Webex Teams users, needs to be registered with Webex Teams (acting as the authorization server) through the registration page at https://developer.webex.com/my-apps/new/integration. The client is required to provide specific information as part of the registration process.

Each authorization server requests different registration information from the client, based on the nature of that particular integration. This is also the case with the information that the server sends back to the client. At a minimum, the client needs to specify the *redirection endpoint URI* (covered in detail in the next section). The client may also be required to provide a *token endpoint URI* (covered in detail in the "Access Token" section), an application logo, an email, a description of what the client does, and the scope. (The scope defines which resources the client needs access to, and whether this access is read-only or read/write.)

In return, the information received back from the authorization server will be, at a minimum, a *client identifier* that the server will later use to uniquely identify this particular integration and the *authorization endpoint URI* (covered in detail in the next section). The server may also send back to the client a password for authentication.

Figure 8-3 illustrates the client registration process with the authorization server.

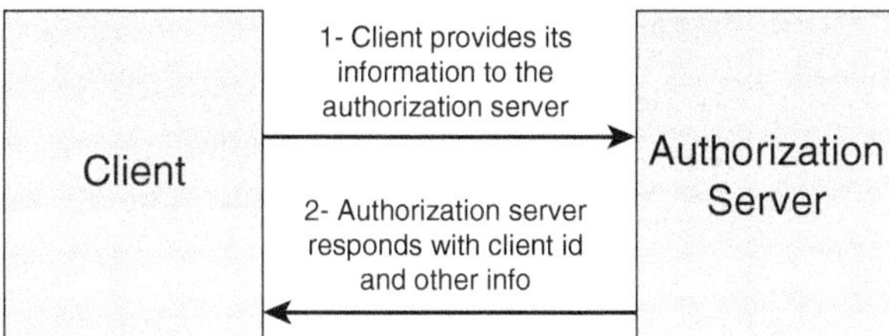

Figure 8-3 *Client Registration with the Authorization Server*

Authorization Grant

When the client is registered and integrated with the authorization server, the next step is for the client to seek authorization from the resource owner; this results, in a best-case scenario, in the resource owner issuing the authorization grant to the client. The client may request this authorization in a number of different ways, and the authorization grant that it receives back comes as one of several different grant types. This section starts with one specific use case and then branches out to describe some other variations to this particular step in the OAuth workflow.

Imagine a Webex Teams user (the resource owner) using App X (the client), mentioned earlier in this chapter, on her laptop. App X is a time-management tool. Since App X is a web application, the user accesses it through Google Chrome, which is referred to as the *user agent*, as you can see in step 1 in Figure 8-4. This figure illustrates the authorization grant workflow for this particular use case—that is, a web app attempting to integrate with Webex Teams (the authorization server).

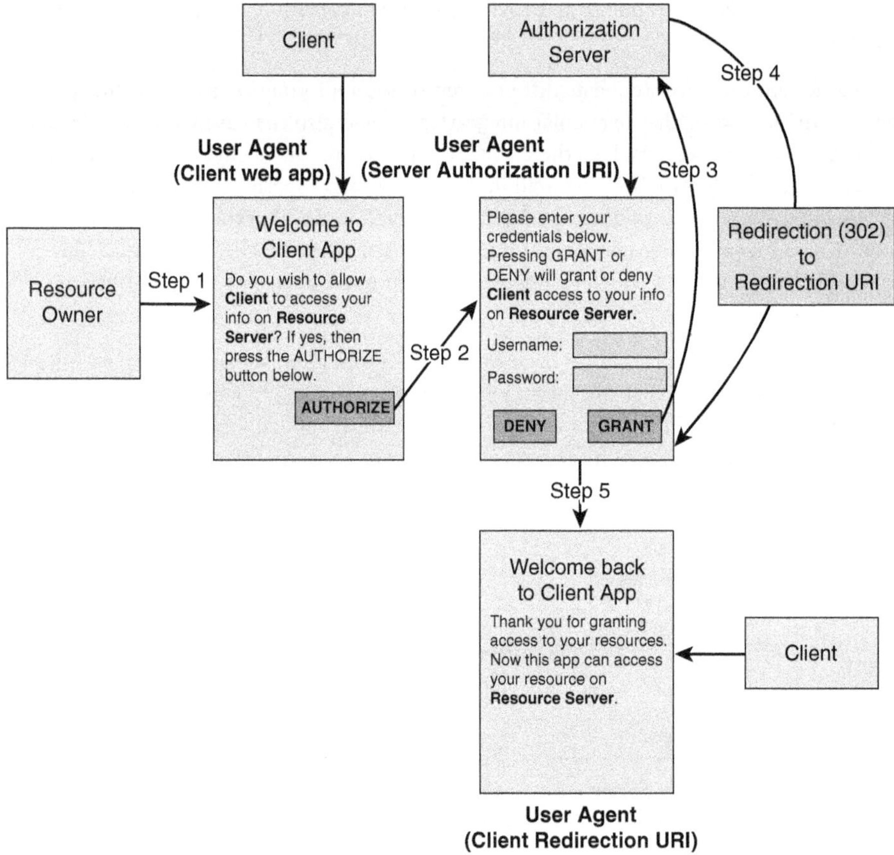

Figure 8-4 *Authorization Grant Workflow for a Web Application*

While using App X, the user decides at some point to leverage an option in the app that lets the app send messages to a Webex Teams space that is shared with the user's team at work, on behalf of the user, when the user schedules a meeting on App X. App X will be doing that through one or more API calls to the Webex Teams server (the resource server). So the user decides to click the button on the app's web page labeled, for example, AUTHORIZE, as illustrated in step 2 in Figure 8-4.

The code attached to the button on the client web page will navigate the resource owner to the authorization endpoint URI that was provided by the server to the client during registration, and at that URI, the resource owner will provide her Webex Teams account credentials. In step 3 in Figure 8-4, the user enters her credentials and clicks the button labeled GRANT. The code attached to this button sends the credentials to the authorization server (Webex Teams) for validation.

Or, to use our earlier example, the fitness app on your mobile phone would request access to your Facebook account in order to be able to post your workouts to your timeline. The resource owner (you in this case) will click a button or link that will take you to the authorization endpoint provided by the Facebook server to the fitness app during registration, and you will enter your Facebook username and password.

Back to the Webex Teams use case: If the user credentials are correct and if the user clicks the button labeled GRANT, the authorization server redirects the user to the redirection endpoint URI that the client provided to the server during the registration process. This redirection happens in step 4 in Figure 8-4 via an HTTP response from the authorization server to the user agent. In step 5, the user agent navigates back to the client application to resume her work (the redirection URI). The user or the resource owner's involvement in the OAuth workflow ends at this point.

Now that the general flow for requesting the authorization grant is clear, let's dig a little deeper, particularly into what happens in steps 2 and 4.

In step 2 in Figure 8-4, the resource owner clicks the button labeled AUTHORIZE. The code attached to this button actually generates an HTTP GET request. The target URI of this request will be the authorization endpoint URI, which is composed of the host and path parts, in addition to a number of query parameters that the client application needs to pass on to the authorization server. In the case of the Webex Teams integration with App X, the target URI will look something like this:

```
https://webexapis.com/v1/authorize?client_id={client_id}&response_
type=code[&redirect_uri={redirection_endpoint_uri}][&scope={scope}]
[&state={state}]
```

The authorization URI includes five query parameters and their values:

- **client_id:** This is the client identifier value assigned by the authorization server to this specific integration during registration.

- **response_type:** As mentioned earlier, there are several types of authorization grants. The four standard types defined by RFC 6749 (and discussed later in this section) are authorization code, implicit, resource owner password credentials, and client credentials. This query parameter specifies what type of authorization grant the client is requesting. Webex Teams integrations support only the authorization code grant type, and therefore the value of this parameter is **code**.

- **redirect_uri:** This is the redirection endpoint URI that the client provides to the authorization server during registration. It may be (optionally) included as a query parameter value for verification purposes, and it must match the value of the URI provided during registration.

- **scope:** This optional query parameter value defines the scope of the grant. Simply put, the scope parameter defines what resources and what kind of access to those resources the client gets when the whole OAuth workflow is complete. For the Webex Teams integration example, the value of this parameter defines such things as whether the client will have access to the user's teams, rooms, or people and whether the client will be able to read, write, or manage these objects, among other things. Webex Teams provides 44 different scopes, and the client may choose 1 or more scopes during the registration. The value of this query parameter is determined by the scopes the client chooses during registration.

- **state:** This optional parameter is an arbitrary value chosen by the client. The same value will be used when redirecting the resource owner's user agent back to the client application after authentication (step 4 in Figure 8-4), and it helps the client identify each resource owner that is directed to the authorization server when that owner is redirected back to the client application after the authentication process (step 5).

The HTTP response to this GET request is typically the content of the https://webexapis.com/v1/authorize web page, possibly with customized content to match the client application, based on the client_id parameter value received in the GET request. This corresponds to the web page with the GRANT and DENY buttons in Figure 8-4.

Moving on to step 4, the HTTP response from the authorization server will use a "302 Found" response code. The response will have a Location header field with a value equal to the redirection endpoint URI plus a query parameter named code that will hold the authorization grant value in the form of an *authorization code*. The net effect of this is that the user agent, Google Chrome in this case, will navigate the user back to the client application (because the redirection URI points back to a client web page) so the user can continue using the client app and the client will have received the authorization grant as a query parameter. A typical redirection URI holding the authorization code grant may look like this:

```
https://clientapp.example.com/oauth?code={authorization_code_grant_
value}&state={state}
```

So far, we have looked at only one type of authorization grant: the authorization code grant. Four types of authorization grants are defined by RFC 6749:

- **Authorization code:** This grant type is provided to the client typically in the form of an alphanumeric string. The distinctive characteristic of this type of grant, as you have seen from the description in this section, is that it is provided by the authorization server, not directly by the resource owner, to the client. This is the most common authorization grant type due to its inherent security benefits. The resource owner provides her credentials to the authorization server for authentication without exposing those credentials to the client (step 3 in Figure 8-4). The authorization code is also, typically, extracted by the client from the URI in the redirection HTTP request before the landing page is displayed to the resource owner (steps 4 and 5 in Figure 8-4) so that the authorization code is not exposed to the resource owner, and thus it is safe from any security breaches or exposures that the resource owner may be experiencing.

- **Implicit:** This is a more efficient but less secure grant type than the authorization code and is primarily targeted toward clients that have no way of authenticating themselves with the authorization server. The authorization server moves through all the steps in the previous workflow, and in step 4 in Figure 8-4, it sends an access token instead of a grant to the client. For this type, the response_type query parameter in the authorization endpoint URI has the value **token.** The use of this type is not recommended, and, as per the OAuth 2.0 Security Best Current Practice draft-ietf-oauth-security-topics (https://tools.ietf.org/html/draft-ietf-oauth-security-topics-15), the use of the implicit type has been replaced with the authorization code type with extensions for enhanced security, such as the proof key for code exchange extension (RFC 7636).

- **Resource owner password credentials:** This type of grant is exactly what its name implies. The credentials that the resource owner provides to the authorization server in the first grant type will themselves be the authorization grant that the client uses to request an access token (discussed in the next section). So instead of the client redirecting the resource owner to the authorization server to get her credentials, the client requests those credentials from the owner directly through the client application interface. This grant type is used when there is a level of trust between the resource owner and the client, such as when the client application is a highly trusted native application running on the resource owner's machine. The client will then use these credentials to request an access token from the authorization server without further involvement from the owner.

- **Client credentials:** This type of grant may be used when the client application has a way to authenticate itself with the authorization server. For example, the client may receive a client secret along with the client identifier after registration. Or perhaps the client application is the same entity as the resource owner, and that entity opts for using OAuth for authentication for some application architectural requirement. With this authorization grant type, the resource owner is not involved in the workflow at all, and the client simply sends its credentials to the authorization server to get an access token.

Note Each of these authorization grant types has a different workflow from the one described in this section. However, we discuss only the authorization code grant workflow in this chapter because it is the recommended and most commonly used authorization grant type. You can consult RFC 6749 for detailed descriptions of the other grant types.

Access Token

The client now has an authorization grant and will use it to get an access token. The client sends the grant it received (from the authorization server or directly from the client) to the *token endpoint URI* residing on the authorization server and receives an *access token* and, optionally, a *refresh token*.

The token endpoint URI is provided to the client during the registration phase or is available in the service documentation. For example, the token endpoint URI for the Webex Teams server is https://webexapis.com/v1/access_token, and this information is documented in the Webex Teams integration documentation at https://developer.webex.com/docs/integrations#getting-an-access-token.

The access token is what the client will eventually send to the resource server in order to authenticate its API calls on behalf of the resource owner (discussed in the next section). As a security measure, the authorization grant should have a lifetime, and it may only be used once to request an access token. The same applies to the access token itself: It will have a lifetime, after which it will expire and not be valid anymore, but it may be used to authenticate multiple API calls. When (or before) the access token expires, the client may use the refresh token to request a new access token from the authorization server by sending the refresh token to the token endpoint URI.

Figure 8-5 illustrates the workflow involved in using a valid access grant to receive the access and refresh tokens and then using the refresh token to get a fresh access token.

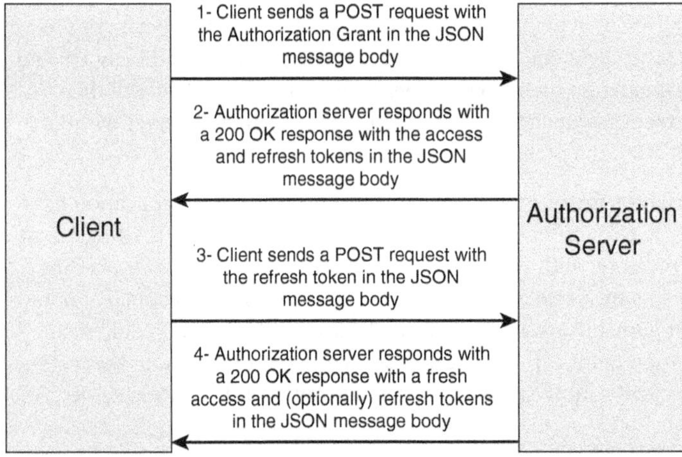

Figure 8-5 *Workflow to Issue Access and Refresh Tokens to the Client*

The request sent by the client to the authorization server to get an access token should be a POST request to the token endpoint URI with no query parameters and a JSON-encoded message body that contains the required request parameters. The parameters in the client request will be the grant_type parameter having a value of authorization_code (assuming the first grant type is used), the code parameter having a value equal to the authorization grant, and then the redirect_uri and client_id parameters.

If the client authenticates successfully with the authorization server and sends a valid authorization grant and a redirection URI that matches the one sent during the authorization grant request, the server responds to the client with a "200 OK" HTTP response message with a JSON-encoded message body.

The response message body will be composed of parameters with the values of the access token and, optionally, refresh token (access_token and refresh_token), the lifetime of the access token in seconds (expires_in), the type of the access token (token_type), and, optionally, the scope (scope). The value of the scope parameter here is mandatory if the actual scope of the provided token is different from the scope requested by the client when requesting the authorization grant. If the scopes are equal, this parameter may be omitted. The token_type parameter defines the type of token used in this OAuth workflow. The most common type is the Bearer Token type, where the value of the parameter should be Bearer.

Now if the server issued a refresh token to the client, when the access token expires the client will send an access token request to the token endpoint URI (a POST HTTP request) with no URI query parameters. The message body will include the parameter grant_type with the value refresh_token, the parameter refresh_token with a value equal to the value of the refresh token, and optionally, the scope parameter. The authorization server will respond with a "200 OK" HTTP response message that contains the details of the new access token and possibly a new refresh token. Again, the client needs to be authenticated with the authorization server in order to receive a new access token.

API Call to the Resource Server

Now that the client has a valid access token, this token is sent to the resource server in every HTTP request made by the client as a means to authorize this request. Figure 8-6 shows the workflow for accessing a resource on the resource server using the valid access token.

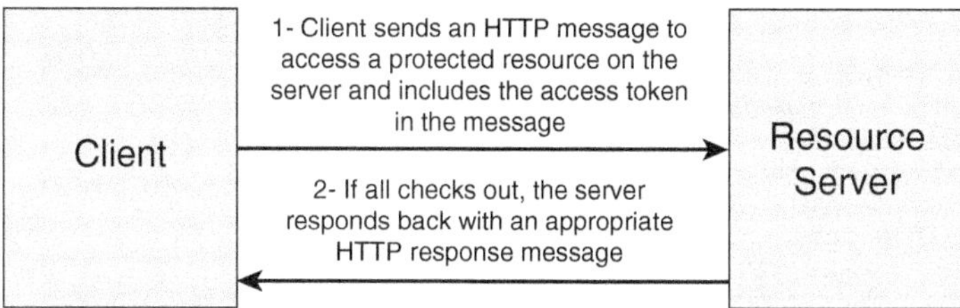

Figure 8-6 *Workflow for Accessing a Protected Resource on the Resource Server by the Client*

How the token will be included in the HTTP request message from the client depends on the token type. In the case of Bearer Tokens, the Authorization header field in the request message will use be used with the Bearer authorization scheme followed by a whitespace and then the token value, similar to the following:

```
Authorization: Bearer {access_token_value}
```

State Management Using Cookies

HTTP is a stateless protocol. This means that the server generates an HTTP response to each HTTP request it receives from a client, and this marks the end of the transaction. Of course, there are a few caveats to this statement. As you saw in Chapter 7, sometimes the server responds with codes such as the "1xx Informational" or "3xx Redirection" codes that signal the client to take further action. However, even in those cases, that further action requires a new HTTP request to be generated and sent by the client.

RFC 6265, "HTTP State Management Mechanism," defines a method by which a server can store state information on a client machine. A server does this by including a data structure called a *cookie* as the value of the Set-Cookie header field in its response to the client. The client saves the information received locally, along with some other information, such as the time the cookie was received. The client then includes a Cookie header field in its subsequent HTTP requests to that server, which the server uses to identify that particular client, in addition to other information specific to that client, such as that client's browsing preferences or location information.

Cookies are not typically used for authentication on their own and work in tandem with other authentication schemes. A typical scenario would involve the client using the Basic, Digest, or any other authentication scheme mandated by the server. Upon successful authentication, the server sends one or more cookies to the client to save specific information related to that client. Further HTTP requests from the client will not need to be authenticated as the cookie information will be sufficient to identify the client to the server. This information will remain valid until the cookie expires, in which case the client re-authenticates to the server and receives a new cookie to be used in the following HTTP requests, and so forth.

Figure 8-7 illustrates a typical workflow involving state management using cookies.

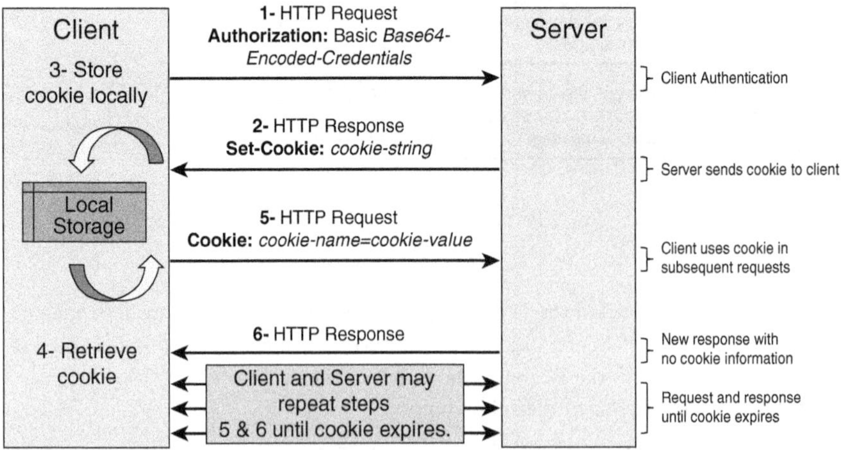

Figure 8-7 *State Management Using Cookies: A Typical Workflow*

The figure depicts six steps in the workflow. The first step is authentication. In the example, the client authenticates with the server using Basic Authentication, but it can be any authentication scheme, whether standard or proprietary. The workflow may also not involve authentication at all: The server may simply wish to tag that particular client with some information using cookies. A typical example not involving authentication is a customer visiting a public website, and that website wishing to save the customer's browsing history in order to personalize site settings or recommendations for that particular customer.

Assuming that the authentication, if any was required, was successful, the server sends back a response that includes the Set-Cookie header field, which has the following format:

```
Set-Cookie: {cookie-name}={cookie-value}[; Expires={expiry-date}]
[; Max-Age={seconds}] [; Domain={domain-value}] [; Path={path-value}]
[; Secure] [; HttpOnly]
```

cookie-name and *cookie-value* are arbitrary values.

The Expires attribute value is the expiration date of the cookie. The client may use this cookie up until the expiration date, but it may choose to discard it any time before that. The Max-Age attribute does the seemingly redundant task of indicating the cookie validity lifetime, but it does so in seconds until the cookie expires, not as a date. The Max-Age attribute has precedence over the Expires attribute if both of them are included in the Set-Cookie header. In the absence of both headers, the cookie expires at the end of the session in which the cookie has been received.

The Domain attribute defines which servers this cookie is good for. If the Domain attribute value sent back to the client is cisco.com, then this cookie should be valid for both servers: sandboxdnac.cisco.com and sbx-nxos-mgmt.cisco.com. A server should not send a Domain attribute with a value that does not encompass its own address. For example, neither server just mentioned can use the Domain value apache.org in its Set-Cookie header.

To further limit the scope of the cookie, the Path attribute indicates the path on the specific server for which the cookie is valid. For example, if the Domain value is sbx-nxos-mgmt.cisco.com and the Path value is /api/, then the cookie is valid only for all directories under https://sbx-nxos-mgmt.cisco.com/api/. If the Path attribute is missing, then the default path will be that of the request URI for which the cookie has been received.

Including the Secure attribute indicates that the server will only accept this cookie from a client over HTTPS (which is covered in the next section) and not HTTP. The HttpOnly attribute indicates that the server will only accept this cookie for API calls made using HTTP—that is, only in HTTP requests and not with any other API protocol type.

A server invalidates a cookie by sending another cookie with the same *cookie-name* and Domain and Path values but with an Expires value equal to a date that has already passed. A new cookie that has the same *cookie-name* and Domain and Path values as an existing stored cookie but with a valid Expires date value will replace the old cookie in the client storage.

A server may include more than one Set-Cookie header field in the same HTTP response.

When a client receives an HTTP response with a Set-Cookie header, depending on the application settings, the client may ignore that cookie, or it may decide to store it, as in step 3 in Figure 8-7. In the event that it decides to store it, a local copy of the cookie is created with the following attributes:

- **Cookie name:** The *cookie-name* received in the Set-Cookie header.
- **Cookie value:** The *cookie-value* received in the Set-Cookie header.
- **Expiry time:** The value of the creation time (see below) plus the Max-Age attribute, as received in the Set-Cookie header, or the value of the Expires attribute as received in the Set-Cookie header if the Max-Age attribute is not present. Max-Age always takes precedence over Expires.
- **Domain:** The *domain* received in the Set-Cookie header. If no Domain attribute was present in the Set-Cookie header, this field is left empty. If the Domain attribute in Set-Cookie is invalid, the whole cookie is ignored and not stored.
- **Path:** The *path* received in the Set-Cookie header. If no Path attribute is received from the server, then the value of this field will be equal to the path segment of the request URI from which the cookie was received. (See Chapter 7 for an explanation of the different URI segments.)
- **Creation time:** The time when the cookie was created on the client local storage.
- **Last access time:** Initially set to the value of the creation time and then updated to the system time whenever the cookie is used in a request to the server.
- **Persistent flag:** True if either the Max-Age or Expires attribute is present in the Set-Cookie header from the server. Otherwise, it is False. This flag indicates that the cookie received has a validity lifetime that is independent of the current session with the server. All cookies with this flag set to False are deleted when the current session is terminated.
- **Host-only flag:** True when the Domain attribute in the Set-Cookie header is present but empty. It means that the domain for which the cookie is valid is equal to the (canonicalized) request URI from which the cookie has been received.
- **Secure-only flag:** True if the Secure attribute is received in the Set-Cookie header.
- **Http-only flag:** True if the HttpOnly attribute is received in the Set-Cookie header.

Once a cookie has been stored by the client, it may opt to include the cookie details in its subsequent requests to the server by using the Cookie header field as in steps 4 and 5 in Figure 8-7. The request URI of the HTTP request has to match the Domain and Path attributes of the cookie as stored on the system. Moreover, if the secure-only flag is set, the cookie should not be used in requests sent over non-secure channels and if the http-only flag is set, the cookie should not be used for API calls that are made using a protocol other than HTTP.

The general format of the **Cookie** header is as follows:

```
Cookie: {cookie-1-name}={cookie-1-value}[; {cookie-2-name}={cookie-2-
value}][;...][; {cookie-n-name}={cookie-n-value}]
```

Notice that the cookie attributes are not included in the Cookie header. Notice also that, while only one Cookie header field is allowed in any one request, more than one cookie (that is, cookie name/value pair) can be included in that same Cookie header field.

In Chapter 7, you saw how to authenticate to the DevNet Nexus sandbox by sending a POST to the URI https://sbx-nxos-mgmt.cisco.com/api/aaaLogin.json and including the credentials as a JSON-encoded message body. Repeating the process again, but this time inspecting the Cookies tab in the bottom half of the Postman window, you see the list of cookies received from the switch after successful authentication. Figure 8-8 shows the Cookies tab.

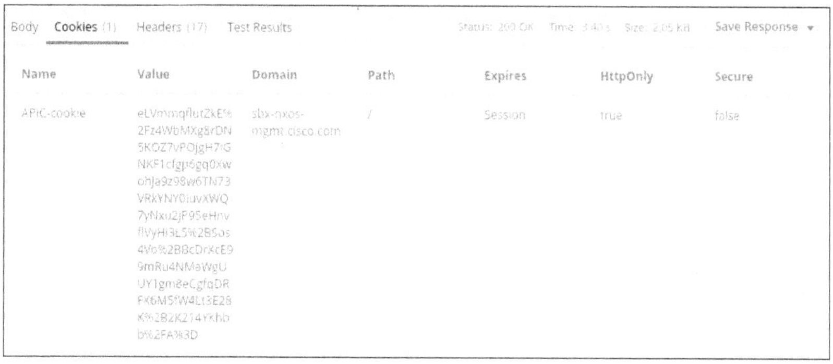

Figure 8-8 *Cookie List Received from the Nexus Sandbox After Successful Authentication*

Now if you try to send a GET request to any website of your choice, such www.amazon.com, and inspect the cookies received, you will see some interesting results. Note that these cookies were received without any authentication with the site.

Cookies are sent as plaintext, so unless the session is secure, a cookie value is visible to anyone who is able to eavesdrop on the HTTP session. Therefore, TLS is usually used to maintain data confidentiality over the wire, as described in the next section.

Transport Layer Security (TLS) and HTTPS

RFC 8446, released in August 2018, defines the Transport Layer Security (TLS) protocol Version 1.3 and summarizes the functions provided by TLS by describing it as a protocol that "allows client/server applications to communicate over the Internet in a way that is designed to prevent eavesdropping, tampering, and message forgery."

TLS is used to establish a secure channel over which a client/server application communicates, providing confidentiality, integrity, and authenticity for that application's data. TLS also provides a means to authenticate the server and, optionally, authenticate the client. An example of a client/server application that uses TLS is HTTP. HTTP over TLS is called HTTPS and is defined in RFC 2818. The IETF refers to TLS as "the most important security protocol on the internet" (see https://www.ietf.org/blog/tls13/).

The latest version of TLS is Version 1.3. TLS Version 1.0 is actually the IETF standardized version of its deprecated predecessor, the Secure Sockets Layer (SSL) protocol developed by Netscape. Although SSL has been deprecated and TLS Versions 1.0 and 1.1 have been deemed insecure, they are still supported and used on some servers over the Internet. Today, the Internet is in the process of migrating from TLS 1.2 to TLS 1.3.

TLS 1.3 has been designed from scratch, unlike TLS 1.2, which was a patched version of 1.1, which in turn was a patched version of 1.0. TLS 1.2 has been the de facto standard for most systems until very recently. However, due to the massive security and performance enhancements in TLS 1.3, it is being rapidly adopted by systems on the Internet. To describe how fast TLS 1.3 is being adopted, the IETF has stated that "there was more TLS 1.3 use in the first *five months* after RFC 8446 was published than in the first *five years* after the last version of TLS was published as an RFC" (see https://www.ietf.org/blog/tls13-adoption/).

Several cipher protocols and features in TLS 1.2 have been deemed insecure and consequently removed from TLS 1.3. RFC 7457 describes some of the known attacks on TLS. Moreover, TLS 1.3 has been designed to allow the server to start sending encrypted application data on the first round trip, a mode of operation labeled 1-RTT. Another mode allows the client to send early data on its very first *flight*, a mode labeled 0-RTT. TLS 1.3 is the version of the protocol recommended by the IETF; therefore, this chapter focuses on TLS 1.3. Reference to TLS 1.2 is made only when needed.

The objective of this section (and this book) is *not* to make you a cryptography wizard or a security expert but rather to give you a firm foundation on which you can build your understanding of HTTPS, which is necessary to be able to interact with the protocol and troubleshoot any issues that you face while making API calls.

Cryptography Primer

This section provides a primer on cryptography. It describes concepts, protocols, and technologies related to cryptography in general that are necessary to understand TLS. The concepts in this section are also tied to TLS 1.3 whenever feasible. These concepts, presented in the following section, will enable you to digest TLS specifics in no time.

Key Generation and Exchange

Encryption is a process by which either a block or a stream of data is encoded to another block or stream of data using a data structure called a *key*, such that this encrypted data cannot be decrypted back to its original form without another key that is either equal to the original key used for encryption or a different key. Endpoints that wish to encrypt and decrypt the data communicated over a channel between them need to agree on the key values used for encrypting and decrypting the data.

Therefore, when a client wishes to start an encrypted session with a server, typically the first step in the workflow is to agree on a key. Keys are used to encrypt the messages that will be exchanged between the endpoints, but a key may also be used to generate other keys. For example, a master key may be used by a system to generate two other keys: one key used for encrypting the handshake messages and another key for encrypting the application data messages after the handshake is completed. Keeping a key value confidential prevents any party that may be eavesdropping on the data exchange from decrypting the data using that key. Therefore, the first step in establishing a secure channel is to agree on an encryption key value.

Note: Use of the terms "master" and "slave" is ONLY in association with the official terminology used in industry specifications and standards, and in no way diminishes Pearson's commitment to promoting diversity, equity, and inclusion, and challenging, countering and/or combating bias and stereotyping in the global population of the learners we serve.

Keys have several different types, as you will see shortly. But first, let's discuss how both endpoints agree on a key value over an insecure channel—typically without ever having met before. Several mechanisms exist for the client and server to agree on what key type and value to use.

The simplest type of key is a pre-shared key (PSK), which as the name implies, is a key that is known to both endpoints before the connection is established. A PSK may be exchanged out of band. An example of an out-of-band PSK exchange may involve a user registering for a service via a web interface and the server sending the PSK to the user via an SMS to her mobile phone, or via a secure download link, or physically preconfigured on both endpoints by the same entity prior to the TLS session establishment. A PSK may also be exchanged in band over an already secure connection to be used for securing a future connection.

PSKs are typically used in performance-constrained systems with limited memory and/or CPU power (such as many IoT devices today) or in closed environments where the client and server are owned by the same entity. Alternatively, a PSK exchanged over a secure TLS connection may be used to bootstrap a future TLS 1.3 connection in what is referred to as *session resumption*, where the parameters used for the first session over which the PSK was exchanged are used for the new bootstrapped session. PSKs are also used for a mode called 0-RTT, in which the client sends data on its first flight to the server. This data is referred to as *early data*. A PSK, when available, is also used as the seed for generating other keys by using the *key derivation function*, as described later in this chapter.

A PSK is a *symmetric key*, meaning that the key value used by one endpoint to encrypt a message is the same as the key value used by the other peer to decrypt that message. This is not always the case. A PSK is identified by a *PSK label*. The PSK label is a PSK identifier by which the client and server can identify a particular PSK. It would not make sense to send the PSK value over an insecure channel only for it to be intercepted and learned by a third party that is eavesdropping on the connection.

An alternative method to generate a key is by using the RSA or ECDSA protocols used by X.509 certificates. A certificate is composed of a private key value and a public key value. The public key is not confidential and is available as public information, unlike the private key, whose value is only known to the server. A client that wishes to send an encrypted message to a server uses the server's public key to encrypt the message. This encrypted message can only be decrypted using the server's private key. Therefore, any third party eavesdropping on the connection and sniffing the encrypted messages (and also aware of the value of the public key) will not be able to decrypt the message.

It may sound unreasonable that the public key used to encrypt a message cannot be used to decrypt the same message, but this is the beauty of cryptography. Since the key used for encryption is different from the one used for decryption, certificates are said to use *asymmetric keys.* Asymmetric keys introduce higher latency and cost when used for the encryption and decryption of messages.

Asymmetric keys do not provide *perfect forward secrecy* (*PFS*), so a compromised server private key can be used to decrypt old messages that were encrypted and exchanged over earlier sessions. Therefore, RSA and ECDSA are *not* supported in TLS 1.3 as key exchange algorithms. They are, however, used for authentication, as you will see later in this chapter. PSKs, used on their own, also do not guarantee PFS.

A third method to generate and exchange a key value is by using a *key exchange algorithm.* Such an algorithm employs complex mathematical operations to make sure that the public information exchanged between the client and server during the negotiation phase cannot be used to deduce the final key value that will eventually be used to encrypt the data. One of the most popular (and most secure) key exchange algorithms that is also supported by TLS 1.3 is the Diffie-Hellman Ephemeral (DHE) algorithm.

Ephemeral key exchange algorithms are algorithms that generate short-lived keys. Typically a fresh key is generated for each session. Ephemeral keys guarantee PFS, unlike RSA and ECDSA, which means that a compromised key cannot be used to decrypt old messages that were encrypted and exchanged over earlier sessions that used keys other than the compromised one.

To get an idea of how the Diffie-Hellman protocol works, Figure 8-9 illustrates one of the basic implementations of the protocol.

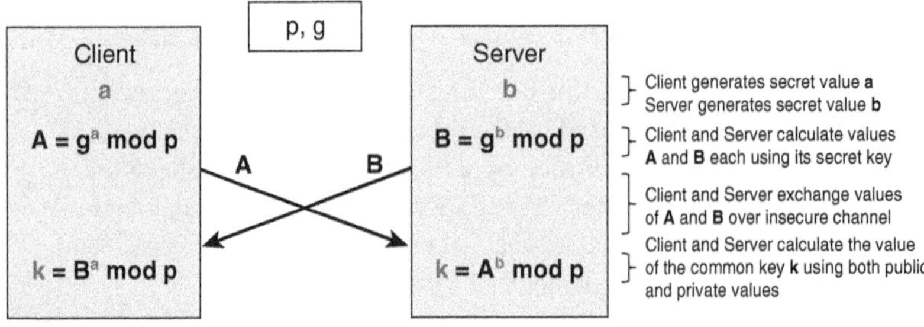

Figure 8-9 *Diffie-Hellman Protocol Implementation*

As illustrated in Figure 8-9, the Diffie-Hellman (DH) basic protocol works as follows:

1. The client and server agree on the value of the two variables **p** and **g**. The values of these variables are public (that is, known to anyone listening on this connection). The variable **p** is also a prime number. These variables have particular mathematical properties that you do not need to worry about at this point. The variable **p** is referred to as the *modulus*, and **g** is referred to as the *generator*.

2. The client and server generate values for two secret variables: **a** and **b**. The client keeps the value of the variable **a** secret (even from the server). The server keeps the value of the variable **b** secret (even from the client). The values of these variables are never transmitted over the channel.

3. The client calculates the value of the variable $\mathbf{A=g^a \bmod p}$ as shown in Figure 8-9. The server, on the other hand, calculates the value of the variable $\mathbf{B=g^b \bmod p}$ as shown in the figure.

Note The *mod* operator is a division operator, except that it returns the remainder of the operation. (X mod Y) will return the remainder after dividing X by Y. For example, 10 mod 3 will return 1, which is the remainder after dividing 10 by 3.

4. The client and server exchange the values of the variables **A** and **B**. The values of **A** and **B** are public (that is, anyone eavesdropping on the connection knows their values).

5. The client and server each calculate the value of the key **k** as shown in Figure 8-9 by using the values of the public variables **A**, **B**, and **p** as well as the secret values of variables **a** and **b**. Both the client and the server should reach the same value of the key **k**.

Now assuming that you are eavesdropping on the connection and know the values of **p**, **g**, **A**, and **B**, can you deduce the value of **k**? The answer is a little involved. If the value of **p** is large enough, it is not practically feasible to deduce the value of **k** without knowing the values of **a** and/or **b**—which is information that is kept confidential.

By now you get the idea of how two communicating endpoints can agree on the value of a secret key using a number of variables whose values are not secret. The Diffie-Hellman algorithm has two different implementations, called Finite Fields DHE (FFDHE or just DHE) and Elliptic Curve DHE (ECDHE). Each of these implementations uses a different method to generate some of the public and private values used in the key value calculation. You can read more about the DH algorithm in RFC 2631 and about ECDHE in RFCs 6090 and 8422.

RFC 7919 defines a number of Diffie-Hellman groups, each identified by a different code point. Without delving into a lot of complicated math to define what a group actually is, when a client and server agree on which group to use, they are basically agreeing on the public values to use, such as the values of the **p** and **g** variables for FFDHE. Therefore, in order for a client and server to perform a DHE key exchange, they need to agree on the

DHE group and then simply exchange the values of **A** and **B** as explained earlier. Each Diffie-Hellman group also defines the key size generated by the group, which directly corresponds to how secure the key usage is: The bigger the key, the better. For example, the named group **ffdhe2048** has a key size of 2048 bits. It also defines the value of the variables **g** and **p** as **g=2** and **p = 2^2048-2^1984+{[2^1918 * e]+560316 }*2^64 -1.** The actual value of **p** has 2104 digits!

An encrypted session typically requires more than one key, each key for a different purpose and/or phase of the session. A PSK is used to encrypt/decrypt only early data in the 0-RTT mode. Some keys are used to encrypt/decrypt the protocol handshake messages. Other keys are used to encrypt/decrypt the application data exchanged over the session after the handshake is completed. And then some keys are used to generate other keys and are not used in the encryption process. The keys used over a TLS session are collectively referred to as *keying material* (*KM*).

TLS 1.3 uses an algorithm called *HMAC-Based Extract-and-Expand Key Derivation Function* (*HKDF*), which takes different inputs to generate different keys, as required by the protocol that employs it. The components of the HKDF algorithm, and the way it generates several keys from initial input parameters, are explained in detail in RFC 5869. The different keys generated by the HKDF algorithm, for what purpose, and what inputs are involved at every stage, are collectively referred to as the *key schedule* of the protocol. The key schedule of the TLS 1.3 protocol is described in Section 7.1 of RFC 8446.

Stream and Block Data Encryption

Once the client and server agree on a key value, the second stage is to use this (symmetric) key for the actual encryption and decryption of the data exchanged between the endpoints. Algorithms that do this are commonly referred to as *ciphers*. Cipher algorithms vary in the level of security, with the more secure protocols typically coming at a higher cost both in terms of the literal cost of using a patented algorithm and in terms of compute power and memory required for the encryption and decryption processes.

Symmetric ciphers come in two types: block ciphers and stream ciphers. The difference between them lies in how the algorithm treats the data to be encrypted.

Block ciphers break down the data that will be encrypted, referred to as *plaintext*, into fixed-size blocks and encrypt each of these blocks into another block of data of the same size, referred to as *ciphertext*. If a protocol uses a block size of 128 bits, the plaintext is broken down into 128-bit blocks and encrypted into corresponding 128-bit blocks of ciphertext.

Note Don't confuse block size with key size. AES-128 and AES-256 both have a block size of 128 bits. The 128/256 in the algorithm name is the key size. The only block cipher algorithms supported by TLS 1.3 are AES-128 and AES-256.

Block cipher algorithms describe how to encrypt a single block of data. How a cipher algorithm repeats this encryption process in order to encrypt a plaintext message comprising more than one block is decided by the *mode* of operation of that block cipher. The National Institute of Standards and Technology (NIST) defined five modes in its document 800-38A, titled "Recommendations for Block Cipher Modes of Operation." This document details the algorithm, block diagram, and operation of each mode in detail. Of particular interest to TLS 1.3 are the *cipher block chaining* (*CBC*) and *counter* (*CTR*) modes.

To get an idea of why the mode of a cipher is a significant factor in the operation of the cipher, consider the CBC mode. The ciphertext of any one block j is calculated by using the following equation:

$$C_j = CIPH_K(P_j \oplus C_{j-1})$$

where C_j is the ciphertext block corresponding to the plaintext block denoted by P_j, and C_{j-1} is the ciphertext block corresponding to the *previous plaintext block*. $CIPH_K$ is the cipher algorithm using key K (such as AES), and the operator ⊕ is the XOR of the two operands. The main takeaway from this is that *encrypting a block of plaintext is dependent on the encrypted value of the previous block of plaintext*. The nature of this dependency of one plaintext block's encryption on the preceding ciphertext block is what the mode is all about. Because the very first plaintext block does not have a block preceding it, a value called the *initialization vector* (*IV*) is used instead of the value of C_{j-1}. AES encryption operating in the CBC and CTR modes is referred to as AES-CBC and AES-CTR, respectively. Apart from understanding what a mode is, there is no real need for you, at this stage, to understand the specifics of each mode.

Alternatively, stream ciphers encrypt the plaintext data stream 1 bit or byte at a time. The key used for encryption is generated via a pseudorandom bit generator that takes a value called a *seed* to produce a *keystream*. This bit generator generates a keystream with as many bits as required to encrypt all the plaintext data. The only stream cipher supported by TLS 1.3 is ChaCha20.

The Internet is full of comparison charts contrasting both types of symmetric cipher algorithms. Primarily, block ciphers use the same key to encrypt all blocks of data, while stream ciphers use a generated keystream, where each bit is encrypted with a different corresponding bit in the keystream. Block ciphers are faster when implemented in hardware, and stream ciphers are generally faster when implemented in software.

Message Integrity and Authenticity

In addition to the encryption process that targets maintaining data confidentiality, the secure channel needs to maintain data integrity and message authenticity—that is, make sure that the data being transmitted back and forth has not been tampered with in transit (integrity) and that the message received is, in fact, the message that originated from the peer on the other end and not from a man-in-the-middle (authenticity). Toward this purpose, a *message authentication code* (*MAC*) is generated by the endpoint transmitting a message, using the message content and a symmetric key as input to the MAC algorithm. This MAC is then attached to the message before it is sent. The peer receiving the message, on the other end of the connection, calculates the MAC using the (same) symmetric key and message contents and compares the MAC it calculated with the MAC received in the message. If the values match, then the message has not been tampered with.

Should the MAC be calculated for the plaintext message (before encryption) or for the ciphertext (after encryption)? And should the MAC be sent in plaintext, without encryption, or should it be encrypted first? Different protocols use different approaches.

The SSH protocol (covered in Chapter 9, "SSH"), for example, generates a MAC for the unencrypted message and sends the MAC itself without any encryption. Unfortunately, the MAC in this case can be used to learn information about the message; hence, the message encryption is compromised.

On the other hand, SSL, the predecessor of TLS, calculates the MAC for an unencrypted message, attaches this MAC to the unencrypted message, and then encrypts them both together as one payload, using the encryption key. This approach is also not the most secure way to generate and transmit a MAC.

It turns out that the most secure method is to generate a MAC for the encrypted version of the message and then send the MAC over the channel unencrypted. Although this may sound insecure, it has been mathematically proven to be the most secure approach to message authentication.

Note To see how this method has been "mathematically proven" to be the most secure method, refer to this paper by Bellare and Namprempre: http://cseweb.ucsd.edu/~mihir/papers/oem.pdf. Also you may refer to RFC 7366 for further details. Note, however, that this RFC was released prior to the TLS 1.3 RFC (8446), so it should be referenced only for comparing the MAC-then-encrypt versus the encrypt-then-MAC methods for calculating and adding a MAC to an outgoing message.

A MAC can be one of two types: a *hash function-based MAC* (*HMAC*) or a *cipher-based MAC* (*CMAC*). An HMAC is generated by using a hash function such as SHA-256. A CMAC is generated by using a block cipher algorithm such as AES. While the concept of an HMAC is generally clear, the process of generating a CMAC using a block cipher algorithm is an area of confusion for some people.

In order to clear this confusion, think of MAC generation as a separate process from message encryption (which it is). When generating a CMAC, the MAC generation process involves using a cipher block algorithm such as AES. This same cipher algorithm may or may not be used for the message encryption. If it is, then the cipher algorithm—AES in this case—is used for two different processes: MAC generation and message encryption. Because an HMAC uses a hash function that is not related to a cipher algorithm, this confusion does not exist.

There are several CMAC algorithms in existence, including the algorithm named *CMAC* recommended by NIST (see https://nvlpubs.nist.gov/nistpubs/SpecialPublications/NIST.SP.800-38b.pdf) and *CBC-MAC*, which operates exactly as the CBC mode does, except that the MAC value is *only* the ciphertext value represented by $C_j = CIPH_K(P_j \oplus C_{j-1})$, where j is the *last* block of data.

Encryption and Message Integrity and Authenticity Combined

To complicate things a little further, combining both data confidentiality and message integrity and authenticity results in *Authenticated Encryption with Associated Data (AEAD)* algorithms that perform the dual function of encryption and message authentication. The "Associated Data" part of the name refers to data that will be sent along the channel authenticated but not encrypted. This means that the value of the AD will contribute to the calculation of the MAC but will be sent across the channel as plaintext. TLS 1.3 only supports AEAD algorithms.

Recall the CTR and CBC cipher modes? Combining these two modes results in a hybrid mode called *Counter with CBC* mode (*CCM*). This mode is described in RFC 3610. AES-CCM is an AEAD protocol and is one of two modes of the AES protocol supported by TLS 1.3. AES-CCM is defined in the NIST document 800-38C. The other mode supported by TLS 1.3 is called *AES-GCM*, where GCM is short for *Galois/Counter Mode* and is defined in the NIST document 800-38D.

The AES-CCM protocol is an AEAD protocol that operates in CCM mode, which is a hybrid mode that uses the CTR mode for block encryption and the CBC mode for MAC generation (CBC-MAC which is a cipher-based MAC). The protocol workflow involves using the plaintext payload, associated data, and a value called a nonce (which is unique to that particular payload and associated data) to generate a MAC. Then it combines the MAC and the payload (not the associated data) and encrypts them to ciphertext by using the CTR mode. The result is ciphertext that includes an encrypted MAC value and plaintext associated data whose value has been accounted for in the MAC.

At the receiving end, the peer first decrypts the ciphertext into plaintext comprising the payload and MAC, calculates its own version of the MAC, compares its version with the version it received, and verifies the integrity and authenticity of the message. It should be noted that a single key value is used by AES-CCM for both the encryption (CTR mode) and MAC generation (CBC mode) processes.

AES-GCM is an AEAD protocol that operates in GCM mode, which also uses the CTR mode for block encryption, but unlike AES-CCM, it uses a hash function to generate a hash-based MAC. The hash function is called GHASH. This is not a very popular hash function because GHASH is only used with GCM and never on its own. The protocol workflow involves using the plaintext payload and a unique nonce, called an initialization vector (IV) to generate the ciphertext, and then the MAC is calculated for the ciphertext payload, the associated data, and the nonce. The MAC, referred to as a *tag*, is then sent out in plaintext, without encryption, like the associated data. Recall from the previous section that this is the most secure way to generate and send a MAC value.

At the receiving end, the peer calculates the tag value by using the received ciphertext, nonce, and associated data, and if the value matches the received tag value, it decrypts the ciphertext and produces the plaintext.

Note The GCM mode is the newer and more recommended mode of the two, although the CCM mode is still more widely used.

Finally, the ChaCha20_Poly1305 AEAD protocol uses the ChaCha20 stream cipher algorithm for encryption and the Poly1305 function to generate a hash-based MAC. The protocol workflow involves using a 256-bit key, a 32-bit *initial counter* (usually set to 1), a 96-bit nonce, and the plaintext payload as inputs to the ChaCha20 protocol to produce the ciphertext as output. Then the Poly1305 algorithm kicks in and, using the 256-bit key used by ChaCha20 and the nonce, *another* 256-bit *one-time* key is generated. This one-time key, the associated data, the ciphertext, and the lengths of the associated data and ciphertext are used as input to the Poly1305 function to produce a 128-bit MAC, also referred to as a tag.

At the receiving end, the peer calculates its own value for the tag, using the received ciphertext and associated data. If the received tag value is equal to the calculated value, the ciphertext is decrypted back to the plaintext payload.

Digital Signatures and Peer Authentication

An endpoint proves its identity to the other peer over a connection via a signature, which is a cryptographic value calculated using (as you might have already guessed) a key. Digital signature algorithms use asymmetric key pairs, each composed of a private key and a public key. The endpoint that needs to prove its identity maintains a private, confidential key. The peer that will verify the identity of the endpoint needs to know the public key of the key pair, which is not a confidential value. Digital signatures work as follows:

1. The endpoint that needs to prove its identity uses a digital signature algorithm that takes the message and private key as inputs, and it outputs a digital signature. This endpoint attaches the signature to the message and sends it over the channel.
2. At the receiving end, the peer uses a signature verification algorithm that takes the message, public key, and signature as inputs and then outputs the verification result—that is, whether or not the message, public key, and signature all match; in doing so, it effectively verifies whether the message originated from the endpoint that generated the signature and owns that public key.

Note One point to note here is that given the message and public key, the signature cannot be re-created. The only way the signature can be generated is by using the private key.

In TLS 1.3, server authentication to the client is mandatory, and client authentication to the server is optional. While certain protocols are not considered secure enough to generate keys to be used for data encryption, these same protocols may be used to generate keys used for authentication. Authentication is performed using either a PSK or a certificate that uses a digital signature. TLS 1.3 supports the digital signature algorithms RSA, ECDSA, and EdDSA. These three protocols are used to generate public and private key pairs and define signature generation and verification algorithms.

A client connecting to a server over the Internet may receive a message with a correct signature that checks out using the public key of the server. But what proves to the client that it is actually speaking with the server that claims to be who it is? A malicious party can generate a private and public key pair and share the public key with the client; because the private key was generated by the same entity, the signature checks out. This malicious party, impersonating a shopping website, for instance, may then trick the client into providing credit card information or other confidential information. For this reason, public servers over the Internet typically use X.509 certificates to authenticate themselves to clients connecting to them over TLS. These certificates are issued and signed by certificate authorities (CAs). A certificate contains information such as the certificate serial number, certification expiration date, server and organization details, server public key, and CA name and signature. Clients, such as well-known web browsers, ship preconfigured with a list of well-known and trusted CAs.

When a client receives a server certificate while, for example, loading a web page over HTTPS, it makes sure the certificate was issued by an entity that it trusts, such as a well-known CA. If it was not issued by a trusted CA (as in the case of a self-issued certificate), it may prompt the user to either proceed to the website or terminate the connection. The client also checks that the expiration date of the certificate has not passed. The certificate contains the domain name of the certificate owner, so the client can verify that it is communicating with the same domain stated in the certificate. The client then uses the server's public key listed in the certificate to verify the signature attached to each message using the verification algorithm described at the beginning of this section.

Later in this chapter you will learn more about the phase of the TLS 1.3 workflow in which the server sends its certificate to the client.

Note Before we connect the dots and discuss TLS 1.3, make sure you understand the following concepts covered in this section:

- PSK
- Key generation algorithms (FFDHE/ECDHE)
- HKDF
- Key schedule and keying material
- Block and stream cipher algorithms (such as AES-128/256 and ChaCha20)
- Block cipher modes (CCM/GCM)
- Hash functions (such as SHA-256/384)
- Message authentication code (CBC-MAC, GHMAC, and Poly1305)
- AEAD protocols
- Authentication protocols and certificates

TLS 1.3 Protocol Operation

TLS 1.3 supports only Finite Field DHE (FFDHE) and Elliptic Curve DHE (ECDHE) key exchange algorithms. TLS 1.3 also supports the use of PSKs. A PSK may either be agreed on out of band or in band over an already established secure session, to be used for another future session. A session may use a PSK alone, DHE alone, or both together.

Traditionally, a number of different protocols grouped together—that is, a specific key exchange protocol, a specific block/stream encryption protocol, a MAC protocol, and a hash function—was referred to as a *cipher suite*. Because TLS 1.3 only supports AEAD algorithms, the TLS 1.3 RFC (RFC 8446) redefines a cipher suite as only the AEAD encryption protocol along with the name of the hash function used by the HKDF. A major enhancement in TLS 1.3 is the exclusion of the vast majority of cryptographic algorithms that were deemed insecure; TLS 1.3 retains support for only five cipher suites:

- TLS_AES_128_GCM_SHA256
- TLS_AES_256_GCM_SHA384
- TLS_AES_128_CCM_SHA256
- TLS_AES_128_CCM_8_SHA256
- TLS_CHACHA20_POLY1305_SHA256

The first four of these cipher suites uses the AES block encryption protocol with one of two different key sizes (128 or 256), and one of two different modes (CCM or GCM). Three of these cipher suites use SHA-256, and one uses SHA-384 as the hash function used by the HKDF. The fifth cipher suite uses the ChaCha20 stream encryption protocol with the poly1305 MAC algorithm and the SHA-256 hash function. (By now, you should know exactly what each of these protocols does and where it fits in the picture.)

In a nutshell, TLS 1.3 performs the following tasks toward establishing a secure channel for application data, such as HTTP:

1. The peers use a PSK and/or a key generation algorithm to generate and agree on a symmetric key.
2. The HKDF generates all the keying material required by TLS moving forward, as per the key schedule of the protocol.
3. The keying material is used by the cipher specified in the cipher suite to encrypt *some* of the handshake messages and *all* the application data messages to maintain data confidentiality.
4. A MAC is generated and attached to each message to maintain message integrity and authenticity. The MAC may be generated based on the plaintext or the ciphertext, and it may use a cipher or hash function, depending on the chosen cipher suite.
5. Finally, the server is authenticated to the client, and optionally, the client is authenticated to the server, either using a PSK or certificates.

TLS comprises three sub-protocols, each managing a different phase of the protocol workflow:

- **Handshake protocol:** This protocol is responsible for negotiating the TLS version, negotiating the key exchange protocol and/or PSK, negotiating the choice of cipher suite, exchanging the public key values and establishing the shared keying material, authenticating the server to the client, and, optionally, authenticating the client to the server.
- **Record protocol:** This protocol divides the data to be transmitted from one endpoint into blocks called *records* and reconstructs the records into data at the receiving peer. The record protocol leverages the parameters established by the handshake protocol to secure the transmission of some of these records over the channel. The handshake protocol requires the record protocol to manage the transmission and receipt of the handshake messages, whether encrypted or not.
- **Alert protocol:** This protocol manages the protocol alert messages that signal connection closures or errors.

The TLS workflow has many variations, based on many variables. The TLS workflow shown in Figure 8-10 is the typical workflow when everything goes well between the client and server. The messages with a trailing asterisk (*) are optional messages that are sent in some cases, and the rest of the messages are mandatory, as discussed in the following sections.

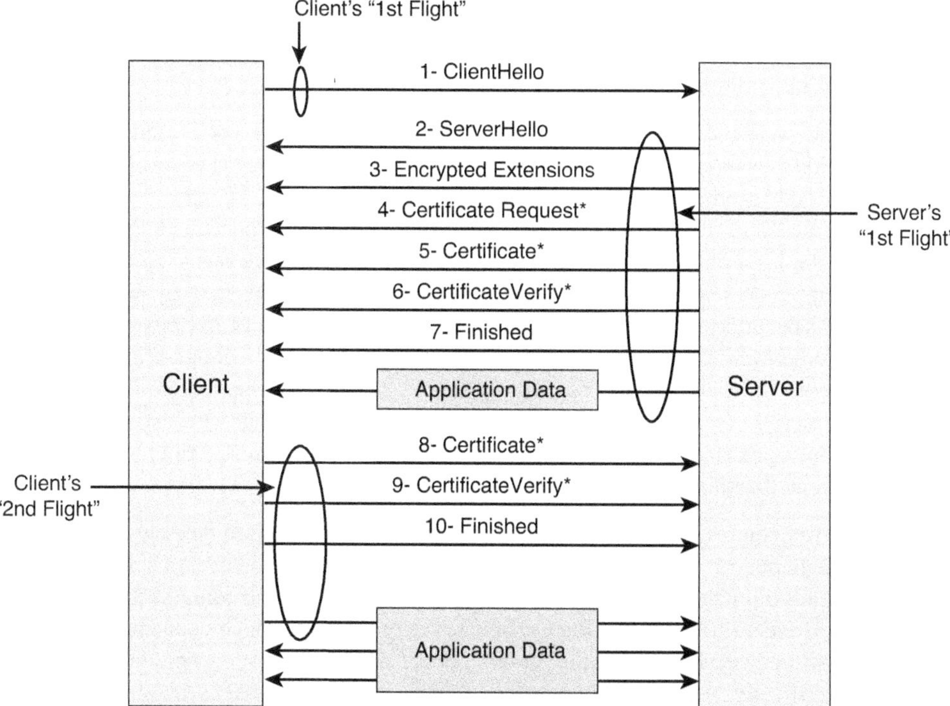

Figure 8-10 *Simple 1-RTT TLS Workflow*

The TLS Version 1.3 Handshake

In all versions of the workflow, the client initiates the TLS connection to the server by sending a ClientHello message. This message includes a few fields and several extensions. The fields are used to enable a TLS 1.3 endpoint to speak with a peer that only supports an earlier version of TLS, until the protocol version is negotiated, and the majority of information related to TLS 1.3 will be communicated via extensions.

The ClientHello is basically the client's proposed TLS version and the cryptographic protocols, modes, and parameters, such as the supported DHE groups, the public key values of some or all of these groups (such as the value of the $A=g^a$ mod p for FFDHE groups, discussed in the "Key Generation and Exchange" section), and the supported cipher suites. It also contains an extension that lists the supported signature algorithms for authentication. If a PSK (or more than one) is already known to the client and server (from an out-of-band channel or an earlier session), the PSK label is also included. The message also includes a random nonce called ClientHello.random that is unique to the particular session.

The server responds with a ServerHello message that establishes which of the client-proposed protocols and modes the server agrees to use and its own parameters for these protocols and modes, such as the value of its own public key share used by DHE (for example, the value of $B=g^b$ mod p if an FFDHE group is chosen), and which cipher suite to use. The ServerHello also uses fields and extensions in a similar fashion to the ClientHello. Up to this point, the channel is still insecure, and the parameters exchanged over it are publicly available to any third party that is listening in on the channel. But this is not a problem; this is actually how key exchange protocols such as DHE work, as you have seen earlier in this chapter.

After the server sends out the ServerHello, both the client and server have sufficient information to start generating the keying material required to start encrypting any further data exchanged over the channel. Following the ServerHello, the server sends out a second message, called the EncryptedExtensions message. As the name implies, and because this is feasible at this point in the handshake, this message is encrypted using a key called server_handshake_traffic_secret. The information in this message includes all the handshake information that is *not* necessary to establish the cryptographic parameters. In other words, the ServerHello message communicates just enough information for the server to be able to start encrypting data. Any other information required to complete the handshake is then sent encrypted. All subsequent messages are also encrypted. This is a major enhancement in TLS 1.3 over earlier versions, where the full handshake was performed without any encryption.

If the server requires a certificate from the client, it sends out a third message, the CertificateRequest message. If the server authenticates itself to the client using a certificate, it sends out a fourth message, the Certificate message, which contains the server's public key, and a fifth message, the CertificateVerify message, which contains a signature over the entire handshake using the server's private key. If the server is not authenticating using a certificate, both the Certificate and CertificateVerify messages are omitted.

Finally, the server always sends out a sixth message, the Finished message, to signal the end of the handshake protocol phase from its side. The Finished message contains a MAC that is used to verify the authenticity and integrity of the complete handshake.

Although some messages are optional and others mandatory, the messages must be sent in the order described, and this is the reason for the intentional numbering of messages (first, second, and so on). A message received out of order triggers the alert protocol at the receiving peer to issue an unexpected_message alert and abort the handshake.

The Finished message concludes a successful handshake phase from the perspective of the endpoint sending it, with the next record of data being the application data. Notice that the very first application data is sent on the server's first flight, which is practically the first round trip since the client initiated the session. For this reason, this is called the 1-RTT handshake. Besides enhanced security, one of the drivers of TLS 1.3 was better performance. The 1-RTT mode and the 0-RTT mode (which is discussed shortly) are great improvements over TLS 1.2, with which the first application data is sent after two complete round trips of handshake messages.

Application data is encrypted using a key called server_application_traffic_secret that is different from the key used to encrypt the handshake messages. Recall that TLS generates several keys called the keying material, with each key used at a different phase of the workflow. These keys are generated via the HKDF according to the protocol key schedule.

At this point in the workflow, the server is sending encrypted application data to the client. However, the client has not been authenticated yet. Recall that client authentication is optional in TLS 1.3. If the server requires that the client have a certificate and sends a CertificateRequest message, the client will send back the two messages: Certificate and CertificateVerify. Finally, the client will send its own Finished message, followed by the first transmitted application data. These three messages sent by the client contain, more or less, content similar to that of the corresponding messages sent by the server.

The first three messages are encrypted using the client_handshake_traffic_secret key, and the application data is encrypted using the client_application_traffic_secret key.

In its ClientHello, the client includes two significant extensions: the supported_groups and key_share extensions. The supported_groups extension contains an ordered list of DHE named groups supported by the client, from most preferred to least preferred. This list includes all supported groups, whether FFDHE or ECDHE. The key_share extension, on the other hand, includes the parameters for some or all of the groups listed in the former extension. This extension includes a list of records, each record specifying the group name and the parameters for the group.

For example, the supported_groups extension may comprise a list, with one entry specifying the group ffdhe2048. There should be a corresponding record in the key_share extension with the name of the group and the value of the variable A calculated as $A=g^a \bmod p$, where the values of p and g are well-known values for that particular group, and a is the secret key that the client does not share with any other entity, including the server.

The client typically includes a record in the key_share extension for every group listed in the supported_groups extension.

But what if the server agrees to use one of the groups in the supported_groups extension but does not find a record in the key_share extension? In this case, the server responds to the ClientHello with a HelloRetryRequest message. This message is sent back to the client when the server cannot find sufficient information in the ClientHello to complete the handshake. It has the same format as the ServerHello message and includes, among other extensions, the server's key_share extension for the server's chosen group. The server can only choose a group initially proposed in the first ClientHello—and not any other.

Once the client receives the new key share, it should respond with a new ClientHello that includes the client's updated (and complete) key share for the group chosen by the server. This second hello is a part of the same handshake; the session is not reset. Now if the server agrees with the client on the parameters shared in the second hello message, the workflow continues normally, as in Figure 8-10. If not, the server aborts the handshake and sends an appropriate alert message to the client.

One HelloRetryRequest message is allowed per session. If a client receives a second HelloRetryRequest in the same session, it must abort the handshake with an unexpected_message alert.

0-RTT and Early Data

As mentioned earlier in this chapter, a PSK may be used to bootstrap a TLS connection without having to perform a full handshake. A PSK may be established out of band, but it may also be generated by the server and communicated over an already secure channel to the client to be used in another future session. In the latter case, the server sends the PSK details by using a NewSessionTicket message that is encrypted using the server_application_traffic_secret key. This message is sent right after receiving the client's Finished message.

In the new session, the client communicates the PSK details in its ClientHello by using an extension called pre_shared_key. The same extension is used by the server in its ServerHello back to the client. The client may, optionally, also include a key_share extension to provide the option for the server to fall back to a full handshake, if required. In addition to the PSK, the server may still respond with a key_share in its ServerHello and use both the PSK and DHE keys to guarantee perfect forward secrecy. When using a PSK, the client and server do not need a certificate for authentication and use the PSK for that purpose. Therefore, the Certificate and CertificateVerify messages are not used. Using a PSK to bootstrap a TLS session is called *session resumption*.

When using a PSK for session resumption, the client has the option to send application data on its first flight, right after the ClientHello, without waiting for any messages from the server first. This is made possible because this *early data* is encrypted using a key called the client_early_traffic_secret that is generated directly from the PSK. The endpoints also use the PSK for authentication. It should be noted that since the early data encryption key is generated from the PSK, the early data lacks perfect forward secrecy.

This does not apply to the rest of the application data exchanged after the server Finished message. This mode of operation is called 0-RTT.

The Record Protocol

The record protocol is responsible for dividing the data to be transmitted from one endpoint into blocks called *records*, optionally protecting these records, and decrypting and reconstructing these records into data at the receiving peer. The records may be protected or not, depending on whether the messages should be encrypted or not.

Records are one of four content types: handshake, application_data, alert, or change_cipher_spec. The change_cipher_spec type is used to maintain compatibility with earlier versions of TLS only. The other three have self-explanatory names.

A TLS 1.3 record is created by dividing the plaintext data into fragments of 2^{14} bytes or less. Then the record is created by constructing a data structure that includes the data fragment, the content type, the data fragment length, and a protocol version legacy field.

If a record is to be sent unencrypted (such as in ClientHello or ServerHello messages), the plaintext record is sent to the transport layer protocol, TCP in this case, for transmission over the wire. If the protocol specifies that this record is to be sent encrypted, the AEAD protocol is used to construct an encrypted ciphertext record. The ciphertext record consists of a plaintext header (the associated data) and an encrypted body.

On the receiving end, the process is reversed in order to reconstruct the plaintext data and present it to the higher-level protocol.

HTTP over TLS (HTTPS)

TLS treats HTTP as simply application data that requires secure transport over the channel that was established by TLS. HTTP over TLS is called HTTPS and is defined in the quite outdated (but not obsolete) RFC 2818. This RFC has been updated with the more recent RFC 7230, which defines HTTP/1.1 message syntax and routing.

When using HTTPS, the client always initiates the TLS session establishment, but either the server or client may initiate the session termination. HTTPS is assigned the default port 443 when run over TCP and the scheme **https**. Apart from this, all the rules that apply to HTTP discussed in Chapter 7 also apply to HTTPS.

HTTP/2

HTTP/2 is defined in RFC 7540, released in May 2015. HTTP/3 was proposed in the Internet Draft draft-ietf-quic-http-29 in June 2020. Neither of the new versions introduces any massive changes to the syntax and semantics of the protocol compared to HTTP/1.1. For example, all versions use the same URI format, request methods, and response codes. The differences are in how each of the new protocols works behind the scenes.

HTTP/1.1 includes several performance enhancements, discussed in Chapter 7, such as connection persistence and pipelining, which enable a client to send more than one request before receiving any responses. Because in HTTP/1.1 responses have to be sent back to the client in the order in which the corresponding requests are received, pipelining still suffers *head-of-line blocking*; that is, a pending response under processing hogs the connection and prevents the server from responding to any other requests received after this one. Therefore, true concurrent request/response transactions require more than one TCP connection, which is not a very efficient solution.

HTTP/2 solves head-of-line blocking while using a single TCP connection for all transactions. HTTP/2 is based on a protocol called SPDY that was initially developed by Google. HTTP/2 uses TCP for transport and introduces major performance enhancements to HTTP/1.1, based on a newly designed binary framing format. This new framing method enables new features such as multiplexing several request/response streams on the same TCP connection, stream prioritization and dependency mapping, enhanced flow control at the HTTP layer, and server push functionality.

HTTP/3 removes the performance limitations of HTTP/2 caused by its reliance on TCP by basing the new version on an entirely new transport protocol called QUIC that was initially developed by, again, Google and since then adopted by the IETF and described in draft-ietf-quic-transport (with a number of changes to the initial Google proposal). Because HTTP/3 is still in its infancy, this section focuses almost exclusively on HTTP/2. Some protocols, such as gRPC, use HTTP/2 exclusively. Therefore, it is important to have at least a basic understanding of this protocol.

Streams, Messages, and Frames

HTTP/2 breaks down an HTTP *message*, whether a request or response, into one or more *frames*. A frame is the basic protocol unit of HTTP/2. Some frames transport the contents of request and response messages, and some other frames are used to manage the connection between the client and server. Frames have different types.

Frames that transport HTTP request and response messages contain either the request or response headers and are of type HEADERS, or they transport the message data and are of type DATA. Frames that are used to manage the connection have other types, such as SETTINGS, which is used to communicate the configuration parameters for the connection, or WINDOW_UPDATE, which is used to manage the flow control on the connection.

A group of frames belonging to the same bidirectional request/response transaction makes up a *stream*. Each frame has a 31-bit *stream identifier* that associates a frame with a particular stream. Figure 8-11 provides a simplified view of client/server communications when only one stream is being transported in each direction.

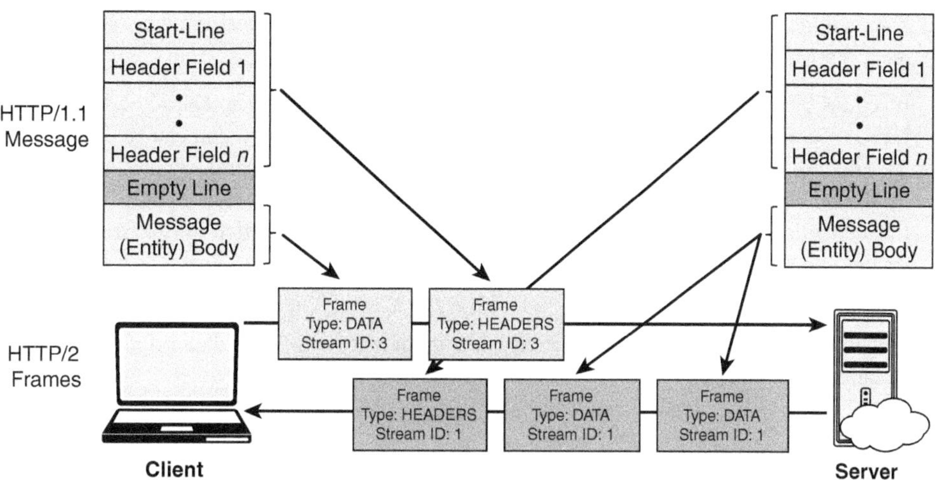

Figure 8-11 *A Simplified View of HTTP/2 Client/Server Communications*

In the figure, the client is sending the frames for the request in stream 3. The server is sending back the frames for the response in stream 1 for a request it received earlier from the client, also belonging to stream 1. You can see the HTTP/1.1 message format at the top and the corresponding HTTP/2 message format, split into frames, at the bottom. You may have noticed that both streams are odd numbered. In HTTP/2, streams initiated by the client are always odd numbered. Streams initiated by the server are always even numbered. HTTP/2 allows servers to initiate streams in server push scenarios, as you will see a little later in this chapter.

Frame Multiplexing

HTTP/2 allows more than one stream to be multiplexed on the same TCP connection. In other words, you can have one frame from one stream, followed by another frame from another stream, and then another frame from the first stream, and so on. Figure 8-12 illustrates a multistream connection.

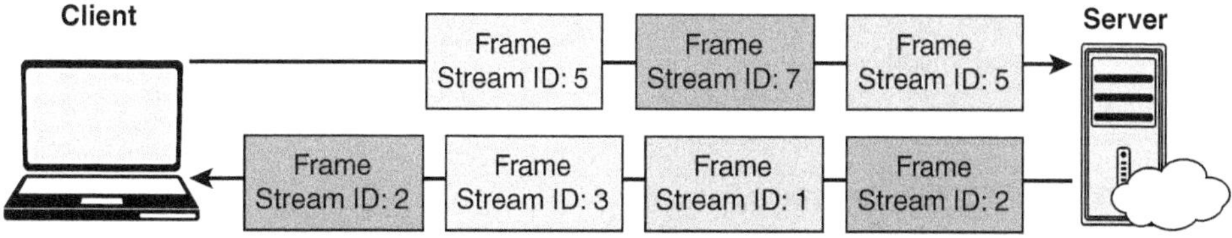

Figure 8-12 *A Multistream HTTP/2 Client/Server Connection*

HTTP/1.1 requires multiple TCP connections for concurrent streams; thanks to the ability to multiplex streams over the same connection, HTTP/2 avoids the need for multiple TCP connections for concurrent streams. HTTP/2 implements several performance enhancement features related to frame multiplexing.

It is possible to prioritize streams by setting a weight value between 0 and 256 in the HEADERS frame that starts a stream. After a stream is started, you can change its priority value by using a frame of type PRIORITY. Higher-priority streams are processed first by the server. Furthermore, one stream may depend on another stream. HTTP/2 allows this dependency of a stream on another parent stream to be specified in the HEADERS frame.

In order to minimize blocking, weight and dependencies work hand in hand to allocate all available resources to first process a dependency parent stream and then process all child streams with allocated resources relative to their weights.

Binary Message Framing

How does HTTP/2 actually implement framing and frame multiplexing, and why is this possible at all?

An HTTP/1.1 request is composed of a request line, then a headers section, followed by a data section. The start line ends with a carriage return and linefeed (CRLF), and so does each header field. The headers section is then concluded with two CRLFs (an empty line) signaling the start of the data section.

HTTP/2, on the other hand, implements a binary framing format, where the HTTP message is split into frames composed of sequences of bytes. Each frame contains headers (not the HTTP headers) that contain the frame metadata, such as the frame length, type, and stream ID, in addition to the frame payload. The frame format is illustrated in Figure 8-13.

0 – 7	8 – 15	16 – 23	24 – 31
Length (24)			
Type (8)	Flags (8)		
R (1)	Stream Identifier (31)		
Frame Payload (0...)			

Figure 8-13 *HTTP/2 Binary Frame Format*

The frame's 9-byte header contains the following fields:

- **Length:** This field is 24 bits long and indicates the frame length, in bytes. The maximum frame size is 2^{24} bytes, but the starting maximum value is 2^{14} until a bigger value is set using a SETTINGS frame type, and this applies to all streams in one direction.

- **Type:** This field is 8 bits long and indicates the frame type. The frame type may be any of the following values:
  - **DATA:** Used to transport arbitrary, variable-length sequences of bytes associated with a stream, such as the payload body of a request or response.
  - **HEADERS:** Used to start a stream or used to transport the *first* fragment of HTTP headers of a request or response message.
  - **PRIORITY:** Used to specify the proposed priority of a stream by the endpoint sending this frame type.
  - **RST_STREAM:** Sent by an endpoint to signal the immediate termination of a stream. It constitutes a 32-bit error code.
  - **SETTINGS:** Used to set the values of a number of connection parameters, such as the maximum number of allowed concurrent sessions.
  - **PUSH_PROMISE:** Used by the server to promise the delivery of a resource in server push scenarios.
  - **PING:** Used to check the reachability of the peer and measure the round-trip time. Similar to a network ping.
  - **GOAWAY:** Used to initiate a connection shutdown or serious error conditions. It practically means the endpoint is signaling its peer to stop creating and sending new streams while the endpoint is processing existing streams.
  - **WINDOW_UPDATE:** Used to manage flow control on the connection.
  - **CONTINUATION:** Used to send any header fields that do not fit in the first HEADERS frame.
- **Flags:** This field is 8 bits long and used to indicate whether certain properties are set for the frame, such as whether the frame is the last frame of a stream.
- **Reserved:** This single bit is always set to 0.
- **Stream Identifier:** This field is 31 bits and indicates the stream to which this frame belongs. While this is not practical to implement, it means that HTTP/2 can *theoretically* multiplex a little over 2 billion streams on the same TCP connection!

Other HTTP/2 Optimizations

HTTP/2 implements a flow control mechanism that is similar to TCP flow control but a bit more robust. Flow control is a receiver's way of informing the sender about how much data it can receive without its resources being overwhelmed. Therefore, it makes sense to have unidirectional flow control that is set by each endpoint individually, specifying the initial window size. This is done via the SETTINGS frame. As the streams are sent over the connection, each DATA frame received decrements the window size, and each WINDOW_UPDATE frame sent increments the window size. The WINDOW_UPDATE frame comprises a 31-bit value that specifies the increase in window size allowed by the receiver. Flow control is enabled by default on HTTP/2 connections and cannot be disabled.

Much like HTTP/1.1, HTTP/2 implements header compression. Without getting into too much detail, HTTP/2 employs compression of a combination of individual header fields by using the HPACK compression format (RFC 7541), in addition to stateful header compression, where the client and server maintain a shared compression context. A very simplified version of this stateful compression involves maintaining an indexed list for all sent header fields and their values, and then redundant headers are eventually not sent but implied at the other end of the connection.

Finally, HTTP/2 enables a mechanism called *server push*. A client may send an HTTP request targeting a specific resource, and it receives a response to that request that sufficiently satisfies the requirement of the client. However, other instances involve the client sending a request, inspecting the response, and sending other follow-up requests based on the processing performed on the initial response received. These follow-up requests may be for resources related to the one it received. A client may sometimes request a resource and wish to receive updates for that resource without having to send explicit requests for the updates. Several similar use cases exist for a server to push a response to the client based on an earlier request from that client.

When a server wishes to push a resource to the client without receiving an explicit request for that resource, the server uses a PUSH_PROMISE type frame to the client, informing the client that it will be pushing a specific resource to it. This frame is nothing but the HTTP response it will be sending minus the payload body (that is, the headers only).

Summary

This chapter covers the following topics:

- The authentication methods used by HTTP implementations: Basic Authentication and OAuth authentication using tokens
- How servers maintain state on client machines using cookies
- Cryptography and associated concepts
- TLS, which is the underlying protocol for HTTPS
- The most important concepts related to HTTP/2

Chapter 9

SSH

To establish communication between two host devices, it's natural to make connections between them. Using such connections, users can share or transfer files over the network, log in to another system remotely, or transmit commands to a remote device for execution. Networks have multiple elements that must be managed, such as routers, switches, and servers. Network administrators connect network devices via remote shell login to configure and manage the devices or retrieve information from the devices.

Various programs exist for connecting and managing network devices, such as Telnet for remote login, File Transfer Protocol (FTP) for transferring data between two devices, and rsh for remote execution of commands. But the biggest challenge with these programs is that they lack security. The three main security requirements of any remote access solution are confidentiality, integrity, and authentication. Most of the earlier technologies lack confidentiality and integrity. For instance, Telnet and FTP transmit usernames and passwords in plaintext and are thus vulnerable to attacks such as IP spoofing, denial-of-service (DoS) attacks, man-in-the-middle (MITM) attacks, and eavesdropping. To overcome the challenges of insecure remote login, the Secure Shell (SSH) protocol was developed.

SSH Overview

SSH is a UNIX-based secure network protocol for connecting to a remote computer or device. It is the most common way of connecting devices securely, and it provides command-line access to devices by spawning a remote shell. The SSH protocol was initially developed by Tatu Ylonen, in response to a hacking incident that took place in 1995 at a Finnish university. Ylonen developed SSH in order to be able to perform remote login over the Internet safely. In July 1995, Ylonen published the open-source version of SSH (Version 1), and in 1997, the IETF began to standardize SSH. The standardization process led to the development of SSH Version 2.

With SSH, the client drives the connection setup and uses a public key cryptographic method to verify the identity of the SSH server. When the setup phase is complete, SSH uses symmetric encryption and hashing algorithms to secure the communication and maintain the integrity of the data between the client and the server. Figure 9-1 illustrates how SSH works.

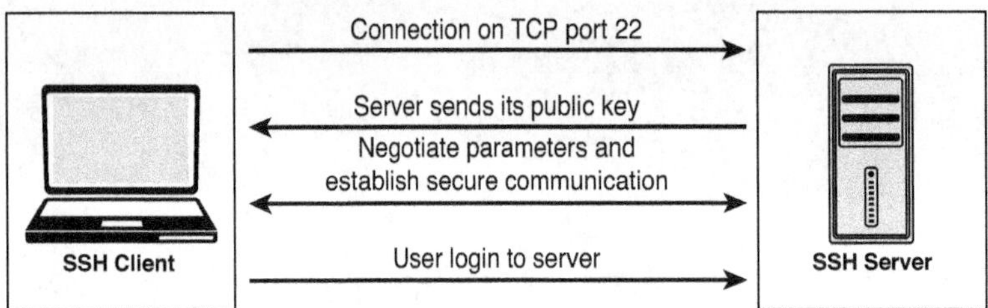

Figure 9-1 *Simplified SSH Protocol Setup Flow*

SSH meets the three main requirements of remote access as follows:

- **Confidentiality:** Data encryption provides confidentiality.
- **Authentication:** Host-based and client-based authentication are both possible.
- **Integrity:** Message authentication codes (MACs) and hashes provide integrity.

Note The open-source version of SSH is now called OpenSSH, and it is available in both Version 1 and Version 2. OpenSSH is mainly used in UNIX environments.

SSH provides the following additional features:

- Compression
- Public key authentication
- Server authentication
- Port forwarding
- X11 forwarding
- File transfer

The following sections examine SSH Version 1 (SSH1) and Version 2 (SSH2) in a bit more detail.

SSH1

SSH1 is a monolithic client/server protocol; that is, an SSH client establishes a connection to the SSH server. The IANA-allocated TCP port is port 22. When the connection is established, SSH protocol version exchange is done in ASCII format. During SSH protocol version exchange, an ASCII string in the format SSH-*protocolversion-softwareversion* is exchanged. After the exchange, the client attempts to authenticate itself to the server. For authentication purposes, there are several authentication methods:

- Kerberos
- RHosts and RHosts RSA
- Public Key Infrastructure
- Password-based authentication (One-time passwords)

Note It is important to note that the version number should match on both sides as SSH1 is not compatible with SSH2, especially when the server is running SSH1. In other words, an SSH server running SSH2 can accept connections from SSH1 clients, but a server running SSH1 cannot accept SSH2 requests.

After the authentication method between the client and the server has been negotiated, a secure connection is established. With SSH1, integrity checking is provided by means of a weak CRC-32 that is collision prone. This means that, given a CRC, somebody can provide another input that matches the same CRC value. Figure 9-2 illustrates the SSH1 protocol packet exchange between a client and a server.

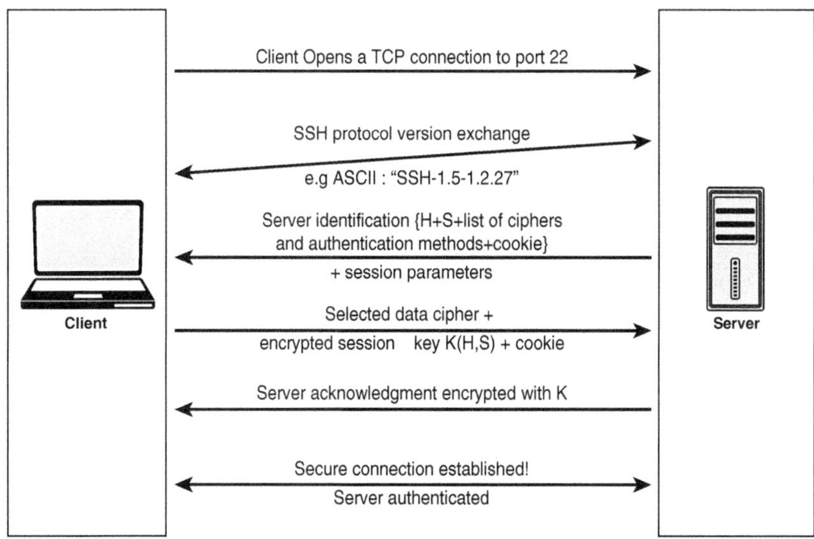

Figure 9-2 *SSH1 Protocol Packet Exchange*

With SSH1, if the client and the server negotiate for compression of the payload, the payload is compressed using the Deflate algorithm, which is used by the GNU **gzip** utility. Compression is primarily used by file transfer utilities such as Secure Copy Protocol (SCP).

SSH2

The SSH2 protocol is documented in RFCs 4250 through 4254. Unlike SSH1, SSH2 is designed in a modular way, and the protocol functionality is implemented into three separate protocol modules:

- SSH Transport Layer Protocol (SSH-TRANS)
- SSH Authentication Protocol (SSH-USERAUTH)
- SSH Connection Protocol (SSH-CONNECT)

All these protocols run on top of TCP.

Figure 9-3 illustrates the SSH2 protocol architecture. At the bottom of the protocol stack is TCP, which provides and ensures reliable connectivity across multiple networks. Next, the SSH protocol provides server authentication, confidentiality, and integrity of data. The SSH Authentication Protocol provides host-based authentication and user authentication using public keys, passwords, and so on. The SSH Connection Protocol enables session multiplexing and helps with features such as X11 and port forwarding and remote command execution.

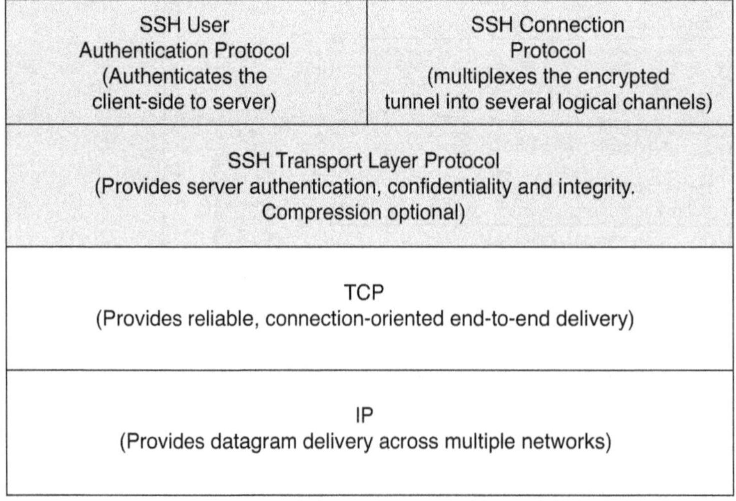

Figure 9-3 *SSH2 Layers*

SSH Transport Layer Protocol

The SSH Transport Layer Protocol (SSH-TRANS), as defined in RFC 4253, is a secure low-level transport protocol used to provide server authentication and initial key exchange and to set up strong encryption and integrity protection for the SSH protocol. The SSH-TRANS protocol provides host-based authentication and not user-based authentication. The following sequence of events happens with the SSH-TRANS protocol:

1. **Connection setup:** In this phase, the SSH connection is established—usually on an IANA-registered TCP port (port 22). The connection works over a binary-transparent transport, and the underlying TCP transport protects against any transmission errors. Once the connection is established between the client and the server, they start exchanging data in the data portion of a TCP segment. The packet is exchanged in the following format:

   - **Packet length:** This field indicates the length of the packet, in bytes.
   - **Padding length:** This field indicates the length of random padding, in bytes.
   - **Payload:** This field holds the useful contents of the packet.
   - Random padding: This field indicates the arbitrary-length padding. The purpose of random padding is to ensure that the total length—including packet length, padding length, payload, and random padding field—is a multiple of the cipher block size or 8, whichever is greater.
   - **MAC:** This field contains the Message Authentication Code (MAC) bytes if the message authentication has been negotiated; otherwise, it is set to 0 as initially the MAC algorithm is "none".

2. **Protocol version exchange:** In this step, the client sends a packet with an identification string in the following format:

   ```
   SSH-protocolversion-softwareversion SP comments CR LF
   ```

   where SP stands for space, CR stands for carriage return, and LF stands for line feed. The server responds to the client with its own identification string. During this process, the client and the server exchange SSH version and software information.

3. **Algorithm negotiation:** In this phase, each side sends an SSH_MSG_KEXINIT message that consists of a list of supported or allowed algorithms in order of preference from most to least. The algorithm negotiation also includes the exchange of packets for exchanging information on the encryption algorithm, MAC algorithm, key exchange, and the optional compression algorithm.

4. **Diffie-Hellman key exchange:** During this step, the key exchange happens via one of two Diffie-Hellman key exchange methods:

   ```
   diffie-hellman-group1-sha1 REQUIRED
   diffie-hellman-group14-sha1 REQUIRED
   ```

The Diffie-Hellman key exchange provides a shared secret that cannot be determined by either the client or the server alone. It is combined with the signature with the host key to provide host authentication. Note that RFC 4253 specifies support for alternate key exchange methods as well, but Diffie-Hellman is the method used most commonly. The output from the key exchange process is a shared key K and an exchange hash H. Both of these values are used for deriving encryption and authentication keys. The end of key exchange process is signaled by the exchange of SSH_MSG_NEWKEYS messages, including the old keys and algorithms. All messages sent after this message use the new keys and algorithms.

5. **Service request:** The client sends an SSH_MSG_SERVICE_REQUEST message to request either the SSH Authentication Protocol or the SSH Connection Protocol.

Figure 9-4 illustrates the phases of SSH-TRANS protocol packet exchange.

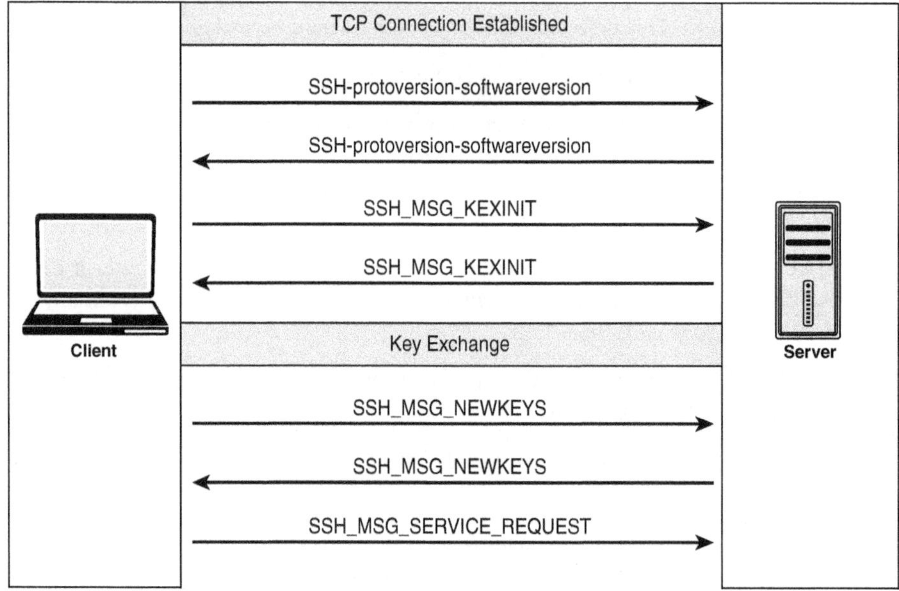

Figure 9-4 *SSH-TRANS Protocol Packet Exchange*

SSH Authentication Protocol

The SSH Authentication Protocol, defined in RFC 4252, provides the means by which a client is authenticated by a server. This protocol runs over the SSH Transport Layer Protocol and assumes that the underlying protocol already provides confidentiality and integrity of the data/packets being transmitted. The service name of this protocol is

SSH-USERAUTH. With the SSH Authentication Protocol, three types of messages are exchanged during the authentication process:

- SSH_MSG_USERAUTH_REQUEST
- SSH_MSG_USERAUTH_FAILURE
- SSH_MSG_USERAUTH_SUCCESS

The following steps are involved in the message exchange for the SSH Authentication Protocol:

1. The client sends an SSH_MSG_USERAUTH_REQUEST message with the requested method 'none'. The authentication request has the following format:

```
byte        SSH_MSG_USERAUTH_REQUEST
string      user name in ISO-10646 UTF-8 encoding
string      service name in US-ASCII
string      method name in US-ASCII
....        method specific fields
```

2. The server checks to determine whether the username received in the user authentication request is valid. If the request is invalid, the server may reject the request. If the server either rejects the authentication request or accepts the request but requires one or more authentication methods, the server sends an SSH_MSG_USERAUTH_FAILURE message with a list of one or more authentication methods to be used. The message is sent in the following format:

```
byte         SSH_MSG_USERAUTH_FAILURE
name-list    authentications that can continue
boolean      partial success
```

   The client then selects one of the authentication methods and sends an SSH_MSG_USERAUTH_REQUEST message with the method name and the required fields.

3. If the authentication succeeds and more authentication methods are required to be processed between the client and the server, the server returns to the previous step. It is important to note that the server would return the SSH_MSG_USERAUTH_FAILURE message with a partial success value of True; if it failed to return more authentication methods, the server would re-send the user authentication failure message with the partial success value set to False.

4. When all required authentication methods have succeeded, the server sends an SSH_MSG_USERAUTH_SUCCESS message, and the SSH Authentication Protocol process is complete.

Figure 9-5 illustrates the message exchange process between the client and the server for the SSH Authentication Protocol.

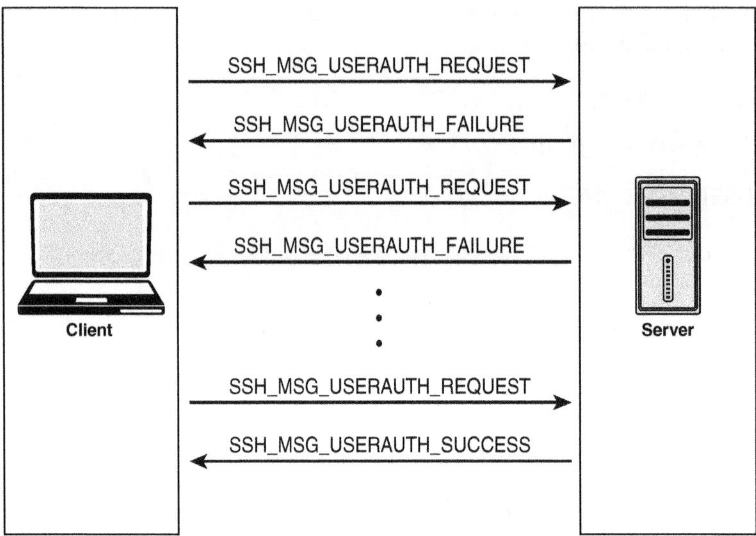

Figure 9-5 *SSH-AUTH Message Exchange*

As defined in RFC 4252, for the SSH Authentication Protocol, the server may require one or more of the following authentication methods:

- **Public key authentication (publickey):** The **publickey** method depends on the chosen public key algorithm. The client sends to the server a message signed by client's private key. On receiving the message, the server checks whether the supplied key is acceptable for authentication. Once validated, the server validates for the correct signature. If both the key and the signature are validated, only then is the user authenticated; otherwise, the authentication is rejected. This is a required authentication method, and all SSH implementations of the SSH Authentication Protocol should support this method. The public key method is exchanged with the SSH_MSG_USERAUTH_REQUEST message in the following format:

```
byte       SSH_MSG_USERAUTH_REQUEST
string     user name in ISO-10646 UTF-8 encoding
string     service name in US-ASCII
string     "publickey"
boolean    FALSE
string     public key algorithm name
string     public key blob
```

  Note that the public key algorithms are defined in the SSH transport layer protocol specification, which is defined in RFC 4253. The public key blob field may contain certificates. The server responds to the request with either the SSH_MSG_USERAUTH_FAILURE message or the SSH_MSG_USERAUTH_PK_OK message, which is in the following format:

```
byte       SSH_MSG_USERAUTH_PK_OK
```

```
string     public key algorithm name from the request
string     public key blob from the request
```

Once the algorithm is negotiated, the client sends a signature that is generated using its private key. The signature is sent in the following packet format:

```
byte       SSH_MSG_USERAUTH_REQUEST
string     user name
string     service name
string     "publickey"
boolean    TRUE
string     public key algorithm name
string     public key to be used for authentication
string     signature
```

- **Password authentication (password):** With this method, the client sends a message containing the password in plaintext. Even though the password is in plaintext, it is protected by the encryption from the SSH transport layer protocol. The password is sent with the SSH_MSG_USERAUTH_REQUEST packet in the following format:

```
byte       SSH_MSG_USERAUTH_REQUEST
string     user name
string     service name
string     "password"
boolean    FALSE
string     plaintext password in ISO-10646 UTF-8 encoding
```

The server responds with SSH_MSG_USERAUTH_SUCCESS if the authentication process is completed successfully or SSH_MSG_USERAUTH_FAILURE if the authentication fails or partially fails.

- **Host-based authentication (hostbased):** With this method, the authentication is performed on the client's host rather than on the client itself. This is useful in scenarios where sites wish to allow authentication based on the host that the user is coming from and the username on the remote host. The client sends a signature created with the private key of the client host and is checked by the server with host's public key. When the identity is established for the client's host, authorization is performed based on the username on the server and the client and the client host name. The message for host-based authentication is sent in the following format:

```
byte       SSH_MSG_USERAUTH_REQUEST
string     user name
string     service name
string     "hostbased"
string     public key algorithm for host key
string     public host key and certificates for client host
string     client host name expressed as the FQDN in US-ASCII
string     user name on the client host - ISO-10646 UTF-8 encoding
string     signature
```

The server verifies the following:

- The host key actually belongs to the client host named in the message.
- The username provided is allowed to log in.
- The signature on the given host key is correct.

SSH Connection Protocol

The SSH Connection Protocol, as defined in RFC 4254, runs on top of the SSH-TRANS and SSH-USERAUTH protocols; that is, it runs on top of a secure connection provided by the SSH-TRANS protocol and assumes that a secure authenticated connection in use is provided by the SSH-USERAUTH protocol. The secure authentication connection is also referred to as a *tunnel*, and it is used by the connection protocol to multiplex a number of logical channels.

All types of communication, such as a terminal session or a forwarded connection, are supported using separate channels, which may be opened by either side. For each channel, each side associates a unique channel number, and that number may not be the same on both sides. Channels are flow controlled, which means that no data is sent to the channel until a message is received indicating that space is available for the TCP connection. The life of a channel progresses through three stages:

- Opening a channel
- Data transfer
- Closing a channel

When either side wishes to open a channel, it allocates a local number for the channel and sends a message in the following format:

```
byte      SSH_MSG_CHANNEL_OPEN
string    channel type in US-ASCII only
uint32    sender channel
uint32    initial window size
uint32    maximum packet size
....      channel type specific data follows
```

The message contains the local channel number and the initial window size. If the remote side is able to open the channel, it returns an SSH_MSG_CHANNEL_CONFIRMATION message that contains the sender channel number, window size, and packet size values of incoming traffic in the following format:

```
byte      SSH_MSG_CHANNEL_OPEN_CONFIRMATION
uint32    recipient channel
uint32    sender channel
uint32    initial window size
```

```
uint32    maximum packet size
....      channel type specific data follows
```

It is important to remember that the window size specifies how many bytes the remote side can send before it must wait for the window size to be adjusted by either side. The window size is adjusted by sending the following message:

```
byte      SSH_MSG_CHANNEL_WINDOW_ADJUST
uint32    recipient channel
uint32    bytes to add
```

If the remote side does not support the specified channel type, it simply responds with a SSH_MSG_CHANNEL_OPEN_FAILURE message in the following format:

```
byte      SSH_MSG_CHANNEL_OPEN_FAILURE
uint32    recipient channel
uint32    reason code
string    description in ISO-10646 UTF-8 encoding [RFC3629]
string    language tag [RFC3066]
```

When the channel is open, data transfer is performed by sending an SSH_MSG_CHANNEL_DATA message that includes the recipient channel number and a block of data. The data transfer continues with the help of these messages as long as the connection is open. The channel data message is sent in the following format:

```
byte      SSH_MSG_CHANNEL_DATA
uint32    recipient channel
string    data
```

When either side wishes to terminate or close the channel, it sends an SSH_MSG_CHANNEL_CLOSE message that includes the recipient channel number.

RFC 4254 recognizes four types of channels for the SSH Connection Protocol:

- **session**
- **X11**
- **forwarded-tcpip**
- **direct-tcpip**

The channel type **session** is used for remote program execution. The program may be a shell or a file transfer application. When a session channel is opened, subsequent requests are used to start the remote program. To open a session, the following message is sent to the remote device:

```
byte      SSH_MSG_CHANNEL_OPEN
string    "session"
uint32    sender channel
```

```
uint32    initial window size
uint32    maximum packet size
```

The channel type **x11** refers to the channel for X Window System, which is a computer software system and network protocol that provides a graphical user interface (GUI) for networked computers. X Window System allows applications to run on a network server but displayed on a client desktop machine. For the **x11** channel, a message is sent in the following format:

```
byte      SSH_MSG_CHANNEL_OPEN
string    "x11"
uint32    sender channel
uint32    initial window size
uint32    maximum packet size
string    originator address (e.g., "192.168.0.100")
uint32    originator port
```

The channel types **forwarded-tcpip** and **direct-tcpip** are used for remote port forwarding and local port forwarding, respectively. To understand what these channel types do, you need to first understand what port forwarding means. In simple terms, port forwarding provides the ability to convert any insecure connection into a secure SSH connection; this is also sometimes referred to as *SSH tunneling*. Based on the port number, the incoming TCP traffic is delivered to the appropriate application. For instance, a system administrator can execute the command **ssh -L 80:demo.example.com:80 admin.example.com** to enable local port forwarding using SSH. The **-L** option with the **ssh** command is used for local port forwarding. For example, the command **ssh -L 80:demo.example.com:80 admin.example.com** opens a connection to the **admin.example.com** server and forwards any connection to port 80 on the local machine to port 80 on **demo.example.com**. Similarly, a system administrator can execute the command **ssh -R 8080:localhost:80 admin.example.com** to enable remote port forwarding. The **-R** option with the **ssh** command enables remote port forwarding. Remote port forwarding is useful in scenarios where a system administrator needs to provide access to the internal server. This command allows anyone on the remote server to connect to TCP port 8080 on the remote server. An SSH tunnel is established between the server and the client, and the client then establishes a TCP connection to port 80 on localhost.

With the **forwarded-tcpip** channel or remote forwarding, the user's SSH client acts on behalf of the server. The client, on receiving the traffic on a given destination port, forwards the traffic to the port that is mapped and sends it to the destination the user chooses. For the **forwarded-tcpip** channel, the message is sent in the following format:

```
byte      SSH_MSG_CHANNEL_OPEN
string    "forwarded-tcpip"
uint32    sender channel
uint32    initial window size
uint32    maximum packet size
string    address that was connected
```

```
uint32    port that was connected
string    originator IP address
uint32    originator port
```

With the **direct-tcpip** channel, or local forwarding, the client intercepts the selected application-level traffic based on the configured port mappings for the application and forwards it from an unsecured TCP connection to a secure SSH tunnel. The SSH server, on the other hand, sends the incoming traffic to the destination port dedicated to the client application. In the case of the **direct-tcpip** channel, the message is sent in the following format:

```
byte      SSH_MSG_CHANNEL_OPEN
string    "direct-tcpip"
uint32    sender channel
uint32    initial window size
uint32    maximum packet size
string    host to connect
uint32    port to connect
string    originator IP address
uint32    originator port
```

Note Forwarded TCP/IP channels are independent of any sessions. That is, closing a channel may not indicate that the forwarded connection will be closed.

Setting Up SSH

Almost all web and application-hosting servers or server access should be enabled with secure access using SSH. SSH is supported on all Linux/UNIX and Windows operating systems. Both Linux/UNIX and Windows-based systems support OpenSSH. When deploying SSH, users and system administrators can opt for either password-based SSH authentication or SSH key-based authentication, which involves using public and private keys to authenticate a user. The following sections look at how to deploy SSH on a CentOS 7 server with both password and SSH key-based authentication.

Setting Up SSH on CentOS

SSH can provide secure access to a server using various methods. One of the methods most commonly used by an SSH server is password-based authentication. This is an easy-to-use method, but it is not the most secure method because the passwords are usually not long enough to be resistant to brute-force attacks. Attackers can apply brute-force techniques to break the password and get access to the servers. In addition, applications, such as fail2ban provide additional security, but SSH keys are more reliable and provide more security for SSH authentication. When installing OpenSSH, password authentication is enabled by default.

Most UNIX/Linux-based operating systems have the OpenSSH package installed by default. However, if you need to manually install OpenSSH, you can use the **yum** package manager on CentOS to install the package, as shown in Example 9-1.When the package is installed, you can use the **systemctl** commands to start and enable the **sshd** process.

Example 9-1 *Installing OpenSSH on CentOS*

```
! Using yum package installer to install openssh-server and openssh-clients
# yum -y install openssh-server openssh-clients

! Using systemctl command to start sshd service
# systemctl start sshd

! Using systemctl command to automatically start sshd service at bootup
# systemctl enable sshd
```

By default, most SSH installations have password authentication enabled. This authentication method does not require any additional configuration but is not very secure. If password authentication is disabled, you need to edit the /etc/ssh/sshd_config file so that the **PasswordAuthentication** value is set to **yes**. When this value is set, you can restart the **sshd** process by using the **systemctl** command. This allows you to use password authentication for SSH login. Example 9-2 shows how to enable password authentication and perform SSH login by using this method. Notice that once the remote system has been successfully authenticated, the host is permanently added to the known hosts list in the user's .ssh/known_hosts file.

Example 9-2 *SSH Using Password Authentication*

```
[root@centos2 ~]# vi /etc/ssh/sshd_config
. . .

# To disable tunneled clear text passwords, change to no here!
# PasswordAuthentication yes
# PermitEmptyPasswords no

PasswordAuthentication yes
. . .

[root@centos2 ~]# systemctl restart sshd.service
```

```
[root@centos1 ~]# ssh root@10.1.101.101
The authenticity of host '10.1.101.101 (10.1.101.101)' can't be established.
ECDSA key fingerprint is SHA256:R5JwGwo4S844s7y9PKyZLDLKi3NfxGr0FK6Psa2YuKk.
ECDSA key fingerprint is MD5:e1:18:f6:0d:a1:7b:5e:f0:3a:76:6b:e8:23:c1:d6:49.
```

```
Are you sure you want to continue connecting (yes/no)? yes
Warning: Permanently added '10.1.101.101' (ECDSA) to the list of known hosts.
root@10.1.101.101's password:
Last login: Sun Oct 20 04:03:45 2019
[root@centos2 ~]#
[root@centos2 ~]# exit
logout
Connection to 10.1.101.101 closed.
```

```
[root@centos1 ~]# cd .ssh/
[root@centos1 .ssh]# cat known_hosts
10.1.100.1 ssh-rsa AAAAB3NzaC1yc2EAAAADAQABAAABAQCSLMuhV1sDiLV4azfbG9SPqtjWBmna09htU
J553j/PrLVkebIss58ljmFHAOZ42vPU4FyLfVmmWtPkFjdljELGTwNtA7caYRJ6LlcbD68pEV3+222D1sNQ
pq/ddFl6vcRsRIzEl5S5BIinLEjYnQEzwHNt9RrmvJHn1HPPL83YBBjBIsQrGz5hEWw72DJ/mvv1bo5eGMn
vWav2wJSZHisug/6EKgUzdRy8tuzeTk61aJgedYCaP5QgElZkin2CWnjou/GyiUsFCy1
HCfYGmzUqtkKnmYRmuYnIsAuthH6pP8TdnnFteO1v6UVmcqusTBJAWPLgcP9hWdwkWIL894Jf
10.1.101.101 ecdsa-sha2-nistp256 AAAAE2VjZHNhLXNoYTItbmlzdHAyNTYAAAAIbmlzdHAyNTYAA
ABBBFkcnWu7aiEGrC0LxNQfW/QTkRZEizhOItpuihCuKM3xv3BqZ6zCSUw9RHOWH2TdDKqafV1r7jfAgh7
2Tu3aIdQ=
[root@centos1 .ssh]#
```

As mentioned earlier, another, more secure authentication method can be used instead of password authentication. SSH key-based authentication is a more secure method of authentication as it relies on public and private keys. To enable SSH key-based authentication, the first step is to generate an SSH key on the client machine. This can be done by using the command **ssh-keygen**. The SSH key generator (**ssh-keygen**) tool, which comes with the SSH package, generates an RSA- or DSA-based key that is used for public key authentication. If an existing SSH RSA/DSA key is already present, the tool gives you an option to override the existing key. It is important to note that RSA keys are recommended over DSA keys because DSA keys are 1024 bits only, whereas RSA keys can go up to 4096 bits. By default, the **ssh-keygen** tool generates a 2048-bit RSA key as shown in Example 9-3.

Example 9-3 *Generating an SSH Key*

```
[root@centos1 ~]# ssh-keygen
Generating public/private rsa key pair.
Enter file in which to save the key (/root/.ssh/id_rsa):
/root/.ssh/id_rsa already exists.
Overwrite (y/n)? y
Enter passphrase (empty for no passphrase):
Enter same passphrase again:
Your identification has been saved in /root/.ssh/id_rsa.
Your public key has been saved in /root/.ssh/id_rsa.pub.
```

```
The key fingerprint is:
SHA256:b7jsrGEORgCyixvS8aK2hC7nLc7+Kw2LScX1rE+gW40 root@centos1.cisco.com
The key's randomart image is:
+---[RSA 2048]----+
|o                |
|.o   .           |
|. + . o          |
|.o * . o         |
|= + + = S        |
|o=.+ E o o       |
|== += = . o      |
|B.*+.+ = o       |
|.B=++.oo=        |
+----[SHA256]-----+
```

Note To implement a more secure key, it is recommended to use a larger key size—that is, 4096 bits. You can do this by using the following command:

```
ssh-keygen -b 4096
```

You can choose between using an RSA key or a DSA key by using the **-t** option with either the **rsa** or **dsa** keyword. By default, **ssh-keygen** generates an RSA key.

The **ssh-keygen** tool generates both a public key and a private key on the client machine, in the .ssh folder inside user's home directory. The public key should be copied onto the server. This can be done using the **ssh-copy-id** tool, which is installed along with the SSH package, along with *user@remote-server-address*. This tool performs an SSH login using the password authentication method and copies the public key onto the server. Example 9-4 demonstrates how the **ssh-copy-id** tool is used to copy the public key from the client machine onto the remote server.

Example 9-4 *Copying a Client Public Key onto a Server*

```
[root@centos1 ~]# cd .ssh
[root@centos1 .ssh]# pwd
/root/.ssh
[root@centos1 .ssh]# ls
authorized_keys  id_rsa  id_rsa.pub  known_hosts

[root@centos1 .ssh]# cat id_rsa.pub
ssh-rsa AAAAB3NzaC1yc2EAAAADAQABAAABAQC9NBGVjxOqYI6yXJBf9fRgevxYOn4JuWmOUAGmYJxodC+
Fs7OLdh5E/8L83q3OOJSEEDDVDtsB88vMtT3vvMB+efvhzHWaTn4fEyE56AKED53sz+vU3V4Xk8n0sfBVY
EbtpzfDvmP+IIYFX2NN15AL6DQGay3V1t9fES2hRsmswBjrHgzn1HdY/9LknzigIQWY7pQ/cdmwLGBjzCp
6fk+8y6M5evjZleobGLaGAb0mT7nbgJZ3jdGjqj1n9J8fyzc+7aszxIquJIAVW+CAEv7L4huY8c5gPUljS+
GYkzwpKuNnWp5W6FloIi0RKxkVywLX4LFzRXwou6hr3KKxcC1f root@centos1.cisco.com
```

```
[root@centos1 .ssh]#
```

```
[root@centos1 ~]# ssh-copy-id root@10.1.101.101
/bin/ssh-copy-id: INFO: Source of key(s) to be installed: "/root/.ssh/id_rsa.pub"
/bin/ssh-copy-id: INFO: attempting to log in with the new key(s), to filter out any
  that are already installed
/bin/ssh-copy-id: INFO: 1 key(s) remain to be installed -- if you are prompted now
  it is to install the new keys
root@10.1.101.101's password:

Number of key(s) added: 1

Now try logging into the machine, with:   "ssh 'root@10.1.101.101'"
and check to make sure that only the key(s) you wanted were added.
 [root@centos1 ~]#
```

When the public key has been copied on the server, the user can establish an SSH session from the client machine to the server by using the SSH keys. The public key from the client machine is copied to the authorized_keys file on the server under the .ssh directory. Example 9-5 shows an SSH session established using SSH key-based authentication on the server.

Example 9-5 *Establishing an SSH Session Using SSH Key-Based Authentication*

```
[root@centos1 ~]# ssh root@10.1.101.101
Enter passphrase for key '/root/.ssh/id_rsa':
Last login: Sun Oct 20 05:54:07 2019 from 10.1.100.100
[root@centos2 ~]# cd .ssh
[root@centos2 .ssh]# ls
authorized_keys  id_rsa  id_rsa.pub  known_hosts
[root@centos2 .ssh]# cat authorized_keys
ssh-rsa
AAAAB3NzaC1yc2EAAAADAQABAAABAQC9NBGVjxOqYI6yXJBf9fRgevxYOn4JuWmOUAGmYJxodC+
Fs7OLdh5E/8L83q3OOJSEEDDVDtsB88vMtT3vvMB+efvhzHWaTn4fEyE56AKED53sz+vU3V4Xk8n0sfBVYE
btpzfDvmP+IIYFX2NN15AL6DQGay3V1t9fES2hRsmswBjrHgzn1HdY/9LknzigIQWY7pQ/cdmwLGBjzCp6
fk+8y6M5evjZleobGLaGAb0mT7nbgJZ3jdGjqj1n9J8fyzc+7aszxIquJIAVW+CAEv7L4huY8c5gPUljS+
GYkzwpKuNnWp5W6FloIi0RKxkVywLX4LFzRXwou6hr3KKxcC1f root@centos1.cisco.com
[root@centos2 .ssh]#
```

Even after enabling SSH key-based authentication, password-based authentication is still active and should be disabled manually. However, password-based authentication should not be disabled before the SSH key-based authentication is successfully set up for the user account. You can disable password authentication for SSH by editing the sshd_config file in the /etc/ssh/ directory. Within this file, change the setting for **PasswordAuthentication** to **no**, as shown in Example 9-6. After editing the file, save and exit the file by pressing Esc+x and then Enter. After the file has been modified and saved, you need to restart the **sshd** service in order for the changes to take effect.

Example 9-6 *Disabling Password-Based Authentication*

```
[root@centos-1-srvr ~]# vi /etc/ssh/sshd_config
. . .

# To disable tunneled clear text passwords, change to no here!
# PasswordAuthentication yes
# PermitEmptyPasswords no

PasswordAuthentication no
. . .

[root@centos-1-srvr ~]# systemctl restart sshd.service
```

Enabling SSH on Cisco Devices

Secure terminal sessions are necessary not just for servers and hosts but also for network devices. Cisco devices support both Telnet and SSH-based login for performing network configuration via terminal sessions or performing validation of the output from various routing protocols. Different Cisco network operating systems have different features enabled by default. For instance, Cisco IOS/IOS XE and Cisco IOS XR software does not have SSH enabled by default, but NX-OS software does. It is recommended to use secure methods and limit login access to network devices to specific IP addresses or specific users. The following sections examine how SSH-based login can be enabled with added security configured on all three of these Cisco network operating systems.

Configuring and Verifying SSH on Cisco IOS XE

Cisco IOS XE supports both SSH1 and SSH2. You use the command **ip ssh version** [**1** | **2**] to specify which SSH version the device will be running. Because SSH1 is not standardized and is comparatively less secure than SSH2, it is recommended to run SSH2. If the command **ip ssh version** is not configured, the IOS XE device runs in default compatibility mode, which means both SSH1 and SSH2 connections will be accepted by the device.

SSH2 has been enhanced to add more capabilities to a device. Some of these capabilities include virtual routing and forwarding (VRF)-aware SSH and Diffie-Hellman (DH) group exchange support. With VRF-aware SSH, you can now use SSH to access devices on the IP addresses that are part of either a management or non-default VRF instance. Traditionally, Cisco IOS XE implementations supported 768-bit modulus for performing encryption. With the increasing need for tightened security capabilities, support for larger key sizes to accommodate DH group 14 (2048 bits) and DH group 16 (4096 bits) cryptographic applications between server and client has become necessary. Remember that the DH groups determine the strength of the key used in the key exchange process. Additional time is required to compute the key for higher group numbers as they are more secure. The command **ip ssh dh min size** can be used to configure the modulus size on an SSH server.

There are two way to enable SSH2 on Cisco IOS XE devices. One way is to assign a hostname and a domain name to a device and generate an RSA key. The other way is to use RSA key pairs instead of configuring domain names. In this method, RSA keys are generated with key labels and modulus sizes using the command **crypto key generate rsa usage-keys label** *key-label* **modulus** *modulus-size* and, then the *key-label* value is assigned to the command **ip ssh rsa keypair-name** *keypair-name*. Example 9-7 illustrates the configuration of SSH using both of these methods on a Cisco IOS XE device.

Example 9-7 *Configuring SSH2 on Cisco IOS XE*

```
! SSH Version 2 using hostname and domain name

router(config)# ip ssh version 2
Please create RSA keys to enable SSH (and of atleast 768 bits for SSH v2).

router(config)# hostname R2-A903-XE
R2-A903-XE(config)# ip domain name cisco.com
R2-A903-XE(config)# username cisco privilege 15 password cisco
R2-A903-XE(config)# crypto key generate rsa
The name for the keys will be: R2-A903-XE.cisco.com
Choose the size of the key modulus in the range of 360 to 4096 for your
  General Purpose Keys. Choosing a key modulus greater than 512 may take
  a few minutes.

How many bits in the modulus [512]: 768
% Generating 768 bit RSA keys, keys will be non-exportable...
[OK] (elapsed time was 6 seconds)

R2-A903-XE(config)# ip ssh version 2
```

```
! SSH Version 2 using RSA key pairs

Router(config)# host R1-A903-XE
R1-A903-XE(config)# username cisco privilege 15 password cisco
R1-A903-XE(config)# crypto key generate rsa usage-keys label sshkeys modulus 2048
The name for the keys will be: sshkeys

% The key modulus size is 2048 bits
% Generating 2048 bit RSA keys, keys will be non-exportable...
[OK] (elapsed time was 8 seconds)
% Generating 2048 bit RSA keys, keys will be non-exportable...
[OK] (elapsed time was 3 seconds)

R1-A903-XE(config)# ip ssh rsa keypair-name sshkeys
R1-A903-XE(config)# ip ssh version 2
```

When an external client tries to connect the IOS XE device, the complete SSH packet exchange can either be viewed using a SPAN session or by running the **debug ip ssh** command on the device. This **debug** command displays all the packet exchange related to SSH, including various SSH messages and DF algorithms. Example 9-8 illustrates a client connecting to an IOS XE device using SSH. Notice that because the RSA keys were generated with modulus 2048, DF group 14 is being selected as the key exchange algorithm.

Example 9-8 *SSH Debugging*

```
! Client on MAC connecting Cisco Device
Centos-srvr:~ root$ ssh cisco@172.16.223.26
Password:

R1-A903-XE#
```

```
R1-A903-XE# debug ip ssh
*Mar  4 03:21:26.529: SSH0: starting SSH control process
*Mar  4 03:21:26.529: SSH0: sent protocol version id SSH-2.0-Cisco-1.25
*Mar  4 03:21:26.676: SSH0: protocol version id is - SSH-2.0-OpenSSH_7.9
*Mar  4 03:21:26.676: SSH2 0: kexinit sent: kex algo = diffie-hellman-group-
  exchange-sha1,diffie-hellman-group14-sha1
*Mar  4 03:21:26.676: SSH2 0: Server certificate trustpoint not found. Skipping
  hostkey algo = x509v3-ssh-rsa
*Mar  4 03:21:26.676: SSH2 0: kexinit sent: hostkey algo = ssh-rsa
*Mar  4 03:21:26.676: SSH2 0: kexinit sent: encryption algo = aes128-ctr,aes192-
  ctr,aes256-ctr
*Mar  4 03:21:26.676: SSH2 0: kexinit sent: mac algo = hmac-sha2-256,hmac-sha2-
  512,hmac-sha1,hmac-sha1-96
*Mar  4 03:21:26.676: SSH2 0: send:packet of  length 312 (length also includes
  padlen of 4)
*Mar  4 03:21:26.677: SSH2 0: SSH2_MSG_KEXINIT sent
*Mar  4 03:21:26.677: SSH2 0: ssh_receive: 536 bytes received
*Mar  4 03:21:26.679: SSH2 0: input: total packet length of 1392 bytes
*Mar  4 03:21:26.679: SSH2 0: partial packet length(block size)8 bytes,needed
  1384 bytes,
              maclen 0
*Mar  4 03:21:26.679: SSH2 0: ssh_receive: 536 bytes received
*Mar  4 03:21:26.679: SSH2 0: partial packet length(block size)8 bytes,needed
  1384 bytes,
              maclen 0
R1-A903-XE#
*Mar  4 03:21:26.680: SSH2 0: ssh_receive: 320 bytes received
*Mar  4 03:21:26.680: SSH2 0: partial packet length(block size)8 bytes,needed
  1384 bytes,
              maclen 0
*Mar  4 03:21:26.680: SSH2 0: input: padlength 4 bytes
*Mar  4 03:21:26.680: SSH2 0: SSH2_MSG_KEXINIT received
```

```
*Mar  4 03:21:26.680: SSH2 0: kex: client->server enc:aes128-ctr mac:hmac-sha2-256
*Mar  4 03:21:26.680: SSH2 0: kex: server->client enc:aes128-ctr mac:hmac-sha2-256
*Mar  4 03:21:26.681: SSH2 0: Using kex_algo = diffie-hellman-group14-sha1
*Mar  4 03:21:26.749: SSH2 0: expecting SSH2_MSG_KEXDH_INIT
*Mar  4 03:21:26.819: SSH2 0: ssh_receive: 272 bytes received
*Mar  4 03:21:26.819: SSH2 0: input: total packet length of 272 bytes
*Mar  4 03:21:26.820: SSH2 0: partial packet length(block size)8 bytes,needed
  264 bytes,
              maclen 0
*Mar  4 03:21:26.820: SSH2 0: input: padlength 6 bytes
*Mar  4 03:21:26.820: SSH2 0: SSH2_MSG_KEXDH_INIT received
*Mar  4 03:21:26.988: SSH2 0: signature length 271
*Mar  4 03:21:26.988: SSH2 0: send:packet of  length 832 (length also includes
  padlen of 7)
*Mar  4 03:21:26.988: SSH2: kex_derive_keys complete
*Mar  4 03:21:26.989: SSH2 0: send:packet of  length 16 (length also includes padlen
  of 10)
*Mar  4 03:21:26.989: SSH2 0: newkeys: mode 1
*Mar  4 03:21:26.989: SSH0: TCP send failed enqueueing
*Mar  4 03:21:27.139: SSH2 0: SSH2_MSG_NEWKEYS sent
*Mar  4 03:21:27.139: SSH2 0: waiting for SSH2_MSG_NEWKEYS
*Mar  4 03:21:27.139: SSH2 0: ssh_receive: 16 bytes received
*Mar  4 03:21:27.139: SSH2 0: input: total packet length of 16 bytes
*Mar  4 03:21:27.139: SSH2 0: partial packet length(block size)8 bytes,needed
  8 bytes,
              maclen 0
*Mar  4 03:21:27.139: SSH2 0: input: padlength 10 bytes
*Mar  4 03:21:27.139: SSH2 0: newkeys: mode 0
*Mar  4 03:21:27.139: SSH2 0: SSH2_MSG_NEWKEYS received
*Mar  4 03:21:27.279: SSH2 0: ssh_receive: 64 bytes received
*Mar  4 03:21:27.279: SSH2 0: input: total packet length of 32 bytes
*Mar  4 03:21:27.279: SSH2 0: partial packet length(block size)16 bytes,needed
  16 bytes,
              maclen 32
*Mar  4 03:21:27.279: SSH2 0: MAC compared for #3 :ok
*Mar  4 03:21:27.279: SSH2 0: input: padlength 10 bytes
*Mar  4 03:21:27.279: SSH2 0: send:packet of  length 32 (length also includes padlen
  of 10)
*Mar  4 03:21:27.279: SSH2 0: computed MAC for sequence no.#3 type 6
*Mar  4 03:21:27.280: SSH2 0: Authentications that can continue =
  publickey,keyboard-interactive,password
*Mar  4 03:21:27.421: SSH2 0: ssh_receive: 80 bytes received
*Mar  4 03:21:27.421: SSH2 0: input: total packet length of 48 bytes
*Mar  4 03:21:27.421: SSH2 0: partial packet length(block size)16 bytes,needed
  32 bytes,
```

```
                maclen 32
*Mar  4 03:21:27.421: SSH2 0: MAC compared for #4 :ok
*Mar  4 03:21:27.421: SSH2 0: input: padlength 7 bytes
*Mar  4 03:21:27.421: SSH2 0: Using method = none
*Mar  4 03:21:27.421: SSH2 0: Authentications that can continue =
  publickey,keyboard-interactive,password
*Mar  4 03:21:27.421: SSH2 0: send:packet of  length 64 (length also includes padlen
  of 14)
*Mar  4 03:21:27.422: SSH2 0: computed MAC for sequence no.#4 type 51
*Mar  4 03:21:27.563: SSH2 0: ssh_receive: 112 bytes received
R1-A903-XE#
*Mar  4 03:21:27.563: SSH2 0: input: total packet length of 80 bytes
*Mar  4 03:21:27.563: SSH2 0: partial packet length(block size)16 bytes,needed
  64 bytes,
                maclen 32
*Mar  4 03:21:27.563: SSH2 0: MAC compared for #5 :ok
*Mar  4 03:21:27.563: SSH2 0: input: padlength 15 bytes
*Mar  4 03:21:27.563: SSH2 0: Using method = keyboard-interactive
*Mar  4 03:21:27.564: SSH2 0: send:packet of  length 48 (length also includes padlen
  of 11)
*Mar  4 03:21:27.564: SSH2 0: computed MAC for sequence no.#5 type 60
R1-A903-XE#
*Mar  4 03:21:29.999: SSH2 0: ssh_receive: 96 bytes received
*Mar  4 03:21:29.999: SSH2 0: input: total packet length of 64 bytes
*Mar  4 03:21:29.999: SSH2 0: partial packet length(block size)16 bytes,needed
  48 bytes,
                maclen 32
*Mar  4 03:21:29.999: SSH2 0: MAC compared for #6 :ok
*Mar  4 03:21:29.999: SSH2 0: input: padlength 45 bytes
*Mar  4 03:21:30.000: SSH2 0: send:packet of  length 16 (length also includes padlen
  of 10)
*Mar  4 03:21:30.000: SSH2 0: computed MAC for sequence no.#6 type 52
*Mar  4 03:21:30.000: SSH2 0: authentication successful for cisco
*Mar  4 03:21:30.145: SSH2 0: ssh_receive: 80 bytes received
! Output omitted for brevity
```

A Cisco IOS XE device can also act as an SSH client and can be used to connect to any remote device. In Example 9-9, the device R1-A903-XE is acting as a client to connect to a host named R2-A903-XE. Because on R2-A903-XE, the RSA key has been generated with modulus 768, DF group 1 is being used, as shown in Example 9-9.

Example 9-9 *A Cisco Device as SSH Client and SSH Debugging*

```
R1-A903-XE# ssh -l cisco 10.1.2.2
Password:


R2-A903-XE#
```

```
R2-A903-XE# debug ip ssh
Incoming SSH debugging is on

*Oct  8 07:54:29.525: %SYS-5-CONFIG_I: Configured from console by console
*Oct  8 07:54:31.724: SSH0: starting SSH control process
*Oct  8 07:54:31.724: SSH0: sent protocol version id SSH-2.0-Cisco-1.25
*Oct  8 07:54:31.727: SSH0: protocol version id is - SSH-2.0-Cisco-1.25
*Oct  8 07:54:31.727: SSH2 0: kexinit sent: kex algo = diffie-hellman-group-
  exchange-sha1,diffie-hellman-group14-sha1
*Oct  8 07:54:31.727: SSH2 0: Server certificate trustpoint not found. Skipping
  hostkey algo = x509v3-ssh-rsa
*Oct  8 07:54:31.727: SSH2 0: kexinit sent: hostkey algo = ssh-rsa
*Oct  8 07:54:31.727: SSH2 0: kexinit sent: encryption algo = aes128-ctr,aes192-
  ctr,aes256-ctr
*Oct  8 07:54:31.727: SSH2 0: kexinit sent: mac algo = hmac-sha2-256,hmac-sha2-
  512,hmac-sha1,hmac-sha1-96
*Oct  8 07:54:31.727: SSH2 0: send:packet of  length 312 (length also includes
  padlen of 4)
*Oct  8 07:54:31.727: SSH2 0: SSH2_MSG_KEXINIT sent
*Oct  8 07:54:31.728: SSH2 0: ssh_receive: 312 bytes received
*Oct  8 07:54:31.728: SSH2 0: input: total packet length of 312 bytes
*Oct  8 07:54:31.728: SSH2 0: partial packet length(block size)8 bytes,needed
  304 bytes,
             maclen 0
*Oct  8 07:54:31.728: SSH2 0: input: padlength 4 bytes
*Oct  8 07:54:31.728: SSH2 0: SSH2_MSG_KEXINIT received
*Oct  8 07:54:31.728: SSH2 0: kex: client->server enc:aes128-ctr mac:hmac-sha2-256
*Oct  8 07:54:31.729: SSH2 0: kex: server->client enc:aes128-ctr mac:hmac-sha2-256
*Oct  8 07:54:31.729: SSH2 0: Using kex_algo = diffie-hellman-group-exchange-sha1
*Oct  8 07:54:31.730: SSH2 0: ssh_receive: 24 bytes received
*Oct  8 07:54:31.730: SSH2 0: input: total packet length of 24 bytes
! Output omitted for brevity
```

Note It is also possible to connect to Cisco devices by using the authentication method specified in AAA configuration. AAA configuration is beyond the scope of this chapter. Refer to the Cisco documentation for AAA configuration on the appropriate Cisco platforms and software.

Configuring SSH on IOS XR

SSH on Cisco IOS XR routers is not enabled by default. The Cisco IOS XR supports SSH1 with RSA-based keys and SSH2 with both RSA and Digital Signature Algorithm (DSA). To enable SSH, the IOS XR router should have the **k9sec** package installed or have a full **k9** image installed on the system; you can verify the presence of this image by using the command **show install active summary**, as shown in Example 9-10.

Example 9-10 *show install active summary Command Output*

```
RP/0/0/CPU0:XR-2# show install active summary
Sun Oct 13 04:38:23.106 UTC
Default Profile:
  SDRs:
    Owner
  Active Packages:
    disk0:xrvr-fullk9-x-6.1.2
```

Because it is recommended to use SSH2, you should generate an RSA or DSA key. You can do this by using the command **crypto key generate** [**rsa** | **dsa**]. This command takes in the modulus values with which the RSA or DSA key can be generated. The next step is to enable the SSH server on the IOS XR device. You can do this by using the configuration command **ssh server** [**vrf** *vrf-name*] **v2** in global configuration mode. The **vrf** option allows SSH sessions to be established to an IP address within the VRF instance specified. With just these two commands, you should be able to use SSH to access the IOS XR device, as shown in Example 9-11.

Example 9-11 *Enabling SSH2 on IOS XR*

```
RP/0/0/CPU0:XR-2# crypto key generate rsa
Sun Oct 13 04:39:54.010 UTC
The name for the keys will be: the_default
  Choose the size of the key modulus in the range of 512 to 4096 for your General
  Purpose Keypair. Choosing a key modulus greater than 512 may take a few minutes.


How many bits in the modulus [2048]:
Generating RSA keys ...
Done w/ crypto generate keypair
[OK]
RP/0/0/CPU0:XR-2(config)# ssh server ?
  dscp           Cisco ssh server DSCP
  ipv4           IPv4 access list for ssh server
  ipv6           IPv6 access list for ssh server
  logging        Enable ssh server logging
```

```
  netconf         start ssh service for netconf subsystem
  rate-limit      Cisco sshd rate-limit of service requests
  session-limit   Cisco sshd session-limit of service requests
  v2              Cisco sshd force protocol version 2 only
  vrf             Cisco sshd VRF name
  <cr>
RP/0/0/CPU0:XR-2(config)# ssh server v2
RP/0/0/CPU0:XR-2(config)# commit
```

```
XE-1# ssh -l admin 10.1.2.2


IMPORTANT:  READ CAREFULLY
Welcome to the Demo Version of Cisco IOS XRv (the "Software").
The Software is subject to and governed by the terms and conditions
of the End User License Agreement and the Supplemental End User
License Agreement accompanying the product, made available at the
time of your order, or posted on the Cisco website at
www.cisco.com/go/terms (collectively, the "Agreement").
As set forth more fully in the Agreement, use of the Software is
strictly limited to internal use in a non-production environment
solely for demonstration and evaluation purposes.  Downloading,
installing, or using the Software constitutes acceptance of the
Agreement, and you are binding yourself and the business entity
that you represent to the Agreement.  If you do not agree to all
of the terms of the Agreement, then Cisco is unwilling to license
the Software to you and (a) you may not download, install or use the
Software, and (b) you may return the Software as more fully set forth
in the Agreement.


Please login with any configured user/password, or cisco/cisco



Password:


RP/0/0/CPU0:XR-2#
```

You can then use **show ssh session details** to view information about the SSH session being established on the IOS XR router. In addition, you can view TCP-related information for SSH sessions by using the **show tcp brief** command. For SSH services to run properly, you need to ensure that the IOS XR device is listening on port 22. Example 9-12 shows SSH session information using both of these commands.

Example 9-12 *Verifying SSH Sessions*

```
RP/0/0/CPU0:XR-2# show ssh session details
Sun Oct 13 04:44:12.622 UTC
SSH version : Cisco-2.0

id   key-exchange  pubkey  incipher  outcipher  inmac   outmac
--------------------------------------------------------------------
Incoming Session
0    diffie-hellman ssh-rsa aes128-ctr aes128-ctr hmac-sha1  hmac-sha1

Outgoing connection

RP/0/0/CPU0:XR-2# show tcp brief
Sun Oct 13 04:44:32.821 UTC
   PCB       VRF-ID      Recv-Q Send-Q Local Address    Foreign Address         State
0x1214c250 0x60000000       0      0  :::22            :::0                    LISTEN
0x1214853c 0x00000000       0      0  :::22            :::0                    LISTEN
0x12150f80 0x60000000       0      0  10.1.2.2:22      10.1.2.1:27233          ESTAB
0x1214be00 0x60000000       0      0  0.0.0.0:22       0.0.0.0:0               LISTEN
0x1213beec 0x00000000       0      0  0.0.0.0:22       0.0.0.0:0               LISTEN
```

You can debug an SSH connection on a server enabled on IOS XR by using the command **debug ssh server.** This **debug** command displays all the exchanges that occur between the server and the client and when the SSH client is authenticated on the SSH server. Example 9-13 illustrates the debugging of an incoming SSH connection on an SSH server running on IOS XR software and highlights some of the important information being exchanged.

Example 9-13 *Debugging SSH Server Connections on IOS XR*

```
RP/0/0/CPU0:XR-2# debug ssh server
Sun Oct 13 04:52:09.479 UTC
RP/0/0/CPU0:Oct 13 04:52:15.979 : SSHD_[1133]: sshd_conn_handler:623 type: 1,
  port: 22
RP/0/0/CPU0:Oct 13 04:52:15.979 : SSHD_[1133]: ratelimit_msecs:1000.000000,
  ratelimit_count:1, low_rate:0
RP/0/0/CPU0:Oct 13 04:52:15.979 : SSHD_[1133]: elapsed:556171.900000,
  msecs:1000.000000, count:1
RP/0/0/CPU0:Oct 13 04:52:16.019 : SSHD_[1133]: Spawned new child process 921787
RP/0/0/CPU0:Oct 13 04:52:16.039 : SSHD_[65723]: Inside init_ttylist FUNC
...
RP/0/0/CPU0:Oct 13 04:52:16.189 : SSHD_[65723]: After setting socket options,
  sndbuf65536, rcvbuf - 65536
RP/0/0/CPU0:Oct 13 04:52:16.189 : SSHD_[65723]: Connection from 10.1.2.1 port 25781
```

```
RP/0/0/CPU0:Oct 13 04:52:16.189 : SSHD_[65723]: Inside sshd_session_sem_create FUNC
RP/0/0/CPU0:Oct 13 04:52:16.189 : SSHD_[65723]: sshd_session_sem_create:
  Created/Opened the Semaphore %pid:921787 SEM Value:1:
RP/0/0/CPU0:Oct 13 04:52:16.189 : SSHD_[65723]: main: Inside the Critical Section:
  session_pid=921787, channel_id=1
RP/0/0/CPU0:Oct 13 04:52:16.189 : SSHD_[65723]: (addrem_ssh_info_tuple) ADD
  tty:XXXXX(XXXXX), user:()
RP/0/0/CPU0:Oct 13 04:52:16.189 : SSHD_[65723]: main: Exiting the Critical Section:
  session_pid=921787, channel_id=1
RP/0/0/CPU0:Oct 13 04:52:16.189 : SSHD_[65723]: Session id 0
RP/0/0/CPU0:Oct 13 04:52:16.189 : SSHD_[65723]: Exchanging versions
RP/0/0/CPU0:Oct 13 04:52:16.199 : SSHD_[65723]: ssh_version_exchange :
  client_str = SSH-1.99-Cisco-1.25  (len = 19)
RP/0/0/CPU0:Oct 13 04:52:16.199 : SSHD_[65723]: Remote protocol version 1.99,
  remote software version Cisco-1.25
RP/0/0/CPU0:Oct 13 04:52:16.199 : SSHD_[65723]: In Key exchange
RP/0/0/CPU0:Oct 13 04:52:16.209 : SSHD_[65723]: Pad_len = 4, Packlen = 308
RP/0/0/CPU0:Oct 13 04:52:16.209 : SSHD_[65723]: Calling Receive kexinit 10
RP/0/0/CPU0:Oct 13 04:52:16.209 : SSHD_[65723]: Peer Proposal : diffie-hellman-
  group-exchange-sha1,diffie-hellman-group14-sha1
RP/0/0/CPU0:Oct 13 04:52:16.209 : SSHD_[65723]: Peer Proposal : ssh-rsa
RP/0/0/CPU0:Oct 13 04:52:16.209 : SSHD_[65723]: Peer Proposal : aes128-ctr,
  aes192-ctr,aes256-ctr
...
RP/0/0/CPU0:Oct 13 04:52:16.209 : SSHD_[65723]: Peer Proposal :
RP/0/0/CPU0:Oct 13 04:52:16.209 : SSHD_[65723]: Negotiated Alg : diffie-hellman-
  group14-sha1
RP/0/0/CPU0:Oct 13 04:52:16.209 : SSHD_[65723]: Publikey Alg = ssh-rsa
RP/0/0/CPU0:Oct 13 04:52:16.209 : SSHD_[65723]: Incoming cipher = aes128-ctr
RP/0/0/CPU0:Oct 13 04:52:16.209 : SSHD_[65723]: Outgoing cipher = aes128-ctr
RP/0/0/CPU0:Oct 13 04:52:16.209 : SSHD_[65723]: Incoming mac = hmac-sha1
RP/0/0/CPU0:Oct 13 04:52:16.209 : SSHD_[65723]: Outgoing mac = hmac-sha1
RP/0/0/CPU0:Oct 13 04:52:16.209 : SSHD_[65723]: Keylen Reqd  = 20
RP/0/0/CPU0:Oct 13 04:52:16.209 : SSHD_[65723]: Waiting for KEXDH_INIT
RP/0/0/CPU0:Oct 13 04:52:16.299 : SSHD_[65723]: Pad_len = 6, Packlen = 268
RP/0/0/CPU0:Oct 13 04:52:16.299 : SSHD_[65723]: Received KEXDH_INIT
RP/0/0/CPU0:Oct 13 04:52:16.299 : SSHD_[65723]: Calling DH algorithm setting with
  group14
RP/0/0/CPU0:Oct 13 04:52:16.299 : SSHD_[65723]:  Getting the parameter inside
  (Func: set_dh_param_groups)
RP/0/0/CPU0:Oct 13 04:52:16.299 : SSHD_[65723]: After geting the parameter we are
  calling the first phase of DH
RP/0/0/CPU0:Oct 13 04:52:16.489 : SSHD_[65723]: sshd_key_exchange: Selected
  key_type is RSA
RP/0/0/CPU0:Oct 13 04:52:16.489 : SSHD_[65723]: Extracting RSA pubkey from crypto
  engine
```

```
RP/0/0/CPU0:Oct 13 04:52:16.489 : SSHD_[65723]: Retreiving 2048 bit RSA host
  key-pair
RP/0/0/CPU0:Oct 13 04:52:16.489 : SSHD_[65723]: bloblen = 279
RP/0/0/CPU0:Oct 13 04:52:16.489 : SSHD_[65723]: exponent = 3, modulus = 257
RP/0/0/CPU0:Oct 13 04:52:16.489 : SSHD_[65723]: Calculating kex hash with
  client_str = SSH-1.99-Cisco-1.25  (len = 19)
RP/0/0/CPU0:Oct 13 04:52:16.489 : SSHD_[65723]: server_str = SSH-2.0-Cisco-2.0
  (len = 17)
RP/0/0/CPU0:Oct 13 04:52:16.509 : SSHD_[65723]: Sending KEXDH_REPLY
RP/0/0/CPU0:Oct 13 04:52:16.509 : SSHD_[65723]: Sending NEWKEYS
...
RP/0/0/CPU0:Oct 13 04:52:16.629 : SSHD_[65723]: User:admin,service:ssh-
  connection,Method:none
RP/0/0/CPU0:Oct 13 04:52:16.639 : SSHD_[65723]: (sshd_authenticate) Searching RSA
  key for user:admin
RP/0/0/CPU0:Oct 13 04:52:16.639 : SSHD_[65723]: (sshd_authenticate) user:admin, rsa
  public key not found
RP/0/0/CPU0:Oct 13 04:52:16.639 : SSHD_[65723]: (sshd_authenticate) setting alarm to
  30 secs
RP/0/0/CPU0:Oct 13 04:52:16.639 : SSHD_[65723]: Waiting for Userauth req
RP/0/0/CPU0:Oct 13 04:52:19.409 : SSHD_[65723]: Pad_len = 9, Packlen = 60
RP/0/0/CPU0:Oct 13 04:52:19.409 : SSHD_[65723]: (sshd_authenticate) removing alarm
RP/0/0/CPU0:Oct 13 04:52:19.409 : SSHD_[65723]: User:admin,service:ssh-
  connection,Method:password
RP/0/0/CPU0:Oct 13 04:52:19.409 : SSHD_[65723]: Has password expired:NO
RP/0/0/CPU0:Oct 13 04:52:19.409 : SSHD_[65723]: sshd_authenticate_internal:
  username:admin, method:PASSWORD
RP/0/0/CPU0:Oct 13 04:52:19.409 : SSHD_[65723]: sshd_authenticate_internal:
  sshd.ch[id].ttyname:XXXXX, INIT_VAL:XXXXX
RP/0/0/CPU0:Oct 13 04:52:19.409 : SSHD_[65723]: sshd_authenticate_internal: Calling
  allocpty
RP/0/0/CPU0:Oct 13 04:52:19.409 : SSHD_[65723]: Connecting to VTY Server, dest
  port:16, src port:64b5
< SNIP >
RP/0/0/CPU0:Oct 13 04:52:19.439 : SSHD_[65723]: sshd_after_authenticate: Shared
  memory task table copied at(0x402880ac), authen_method:2, groups:root-system,
  cisco-support
RP/0/0/CPU0:Oct 13 04:52:19.439 : SSHD_[65723]: sshd_aaa_account:no aaa accounting
  cfg
RP/0/0/CPU0:Oct 13 04:52:19.439 : SSHD_[65723]: Done with AAA APIs
RP/0/0/CPU0:Oct 13 04:52:19.439 : SSHD_[65723]: In login_success_banner_msg
RP/0/0/CPU0:Oct 13 04:52:19.449 : SSHD_[65723]: (addrem_ssh_info_tuple) UPDATE
  session_id:0, channel_id: 1, tty:vty0(vty0), user:admin(admin), connection_type: 0
RP/0/0/CPU0:Oct 13 04:52:19.449 : SSHD_[65723]: In Interactive shell
! Output omitted for brevity
```

Configuring SSH on NX-OS

On Nexus OS (NX-OS) software, an SSH2 server is enabled by default. In addition, the NX-OS software generates an RSA key with a modulus of 1024 bits when it boots up for the first time, which makes it possible to enable SSH-based login on any NX-OS device. You can generate an RSA key with a higher modulus or other algorithms, such as DSA or Elliptic Curve DSA (ECDSA). NX-OS supports key generation with a maximum modulus of 2048 bits. To validate whether SSH has been enabled, you use the command **show feature** and filter the command output for the **sshServer** process. You use the **show ssh server** command to validate whether the SSH server has been enabled. Once you have validated that the SSH server is enabled, the next step is to verify that the RSA key is generated and, if required, generate a key with a larger size. The **show ssh key [rsa | dsa | ecdsa]** command displays the keys generated using different methods, along with a SHA-256 fingerprint. The **show ssh key md5** command, on the other hand, displays the generated key with its MD5 fingerprint. Example 9-14 shows how to verify the SSH feature and its default generated key.

Example 9-14 *Verifying the SSH Feature on NX-OS*

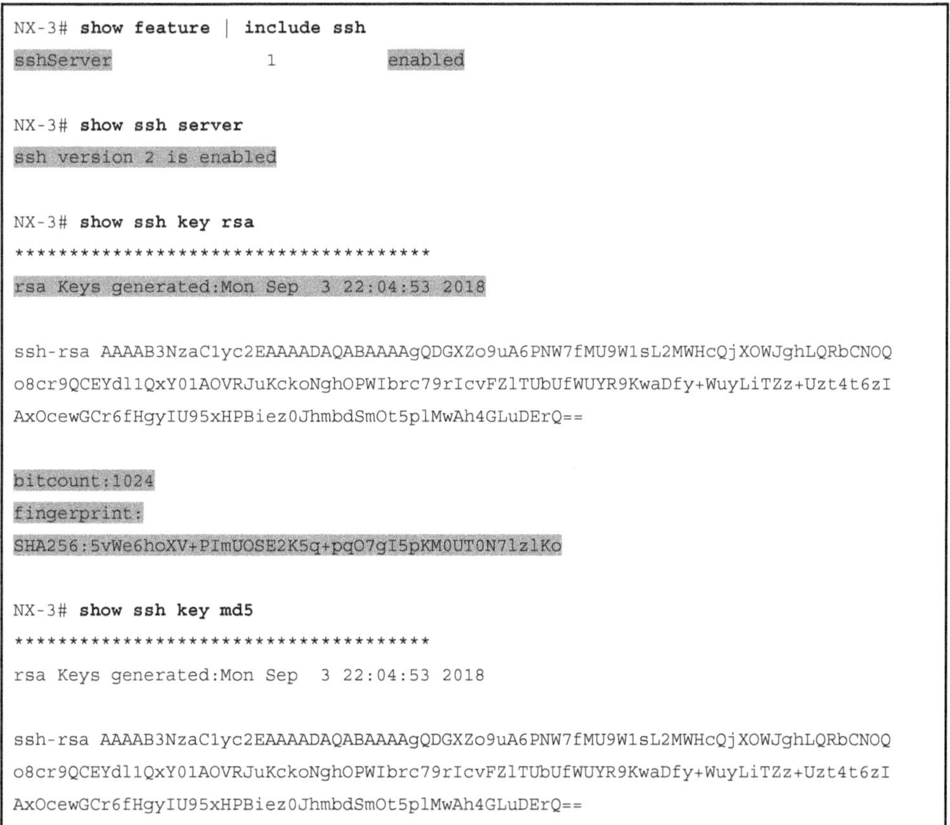

```
NX-3# show feature | include ssh
sshServer               1          enabled

NX-3# show ssh server
ssh version 2 is enabled

NX-3# show ssh key rsa
**************************************
rsa Keys generated:Mon Sep  3 22:04:53 2018

ssh-rsa AAAAB3NzaC1yc2EAAAADAQABAAAAgQDGXZo9uA6PNW7fMU9W1sL2MWHcQjXOWJghLQRbCNOQ
o8cr9QCEYdl1QxY01AOVRJuKckoNghOPWIbrc79rIcvFZlTUbUfWUYR9KwaDfy+WuyLiTZz+Uzt4t6zI
AxOcewGCr6fHgyIU95xHPBiez0JhmbdSmOt5plMwAh4GLuDErQ==

bitcount:1024
fingerprint:
SHA256:5vWe6hoXV+PImUOSE2K5q+pqO7gI5pKM0UT0N7lzlKo

NX-3# show ssh key md5
**************************************
rsa Keys generated:Mon Sep  3 22:04:53 2018

ssh-rsa AAAAB3NzaC1yc2EAAAADAQABAAAAgQDGXZo9uA6PNW7fMU9W1sL2MWHcQjXOWJghLQRbCNOQ
o8cr9QCEYdl1QxY01AOVRJuKckoNghOPWIbrc79rIcvFZlTUbUfWUYR9KwaDfy+WuyLiTZz+Uzt4t6zI
AxOcewGCr6fHgyIU95xHPBiez0JhmbdSmOt5plMwAh4GLuDErQ==
```

```
bitcount:1024
fingerprint:
MD5:8d:a9:d5:e3:fa:2a:71:2d:f3:7d:53:02:e3:26:e0:37

**************************************
could not retrieve dsa key information
**************************************
could not retrieve ecdsa key information
**************************************
```

Because a 1024-bit RSA key is not the most secure key for use with SSH, you can generate a 2048-bit SSH key by using the configuration command **ssh key rsa 2048** [**force**]. Note that the new key can be generated only once the SSH feature has been disabled. After generating the new key, you can turn the SSH feature back on by using the **feature ssh** configuration command. Example 9-15 demonstrates how to generate a key with a larger bit size and validate it with the **show ssh key rsa** command.

Example 9-15 *Generating and Verifying a New RSA key*

```
NX-3(config)# ssh key rsa 2048
rsa keys already present, use force option to overwrite them

NX-3(config)# ssh key rsa 2048 force
deleting old rsa key.....
ssh server is enabled, cannot delete/generate the keys
NX-3(config)# no feature ssh
XML interface to system may become unavailable since ssh is disabled
NX-3(config)#
NX-3(config)# ssh key rsa 2048 force
deleting old rsa key.....
generating rsa key(2048 bits).....
....
generated rsa key
NX-3(config)# feature ssh
NX-3(config)# end
```

```
NX-3# show ssh key rsa
**************************************
rsa Keys generated:Sun Oct 13 07:41:11 2019

ssh-rsa AAAAB3NzaC1yc2EAAAADAQABAAABAQC2Wk5k3+9vEkzE7qC0WAY4nSSndoonS0amc9PiKcMd
uH2/uxFdmFt/TNOyZimzvXzXJSr8nED4aSZtD/HCnitFy7EOLAQo4EsYB4R941BRik9HwOAXlv/Iuokz
```

```
irRfKfnVzpTKKQQ2mAoUGJgppl/yHTHQvPAuG+GY8fEGdIUKm7GLooIkLI6skd04va99/U3EzOTShTOG
twfkXws/pc6Cr1iOhuJZI0YlpkTLvEScE5CFZLmO2bCi8iC/L20WFUokII17TwQ5xu0rGvpcQmW+G70y
VT7YTyt+ops2A0b1o/EI6UgZ2KSVDkfM0IRdyt0zXPToMyhbuE9GvxUZoBfL

bitcount:2048
fingerprint:
SHA256:Q+BeWO9KdikEKblzakmjyqva6JveGupfByMbD4EF+yw
```


Once a client is connected to an NX-OS device, you can verify the SSH session on port 22 by using the command **show sockets connection tcp [detail]**. Note that when the SSH feature is enabled, the device is already in a listening state on port 22 for both IPv4 and IPv6 addresses. Example 9-16 displays the output of the **show sockets connection tcp** command, highlighting the SSH connection from a client machine.

Example 9-16 *show sockets connection tcp Command Output*

```
NX-3# show sockets connection tcp

Total number of netstack tcp sockets: 4
Active connections (including servers)
        Protocol State/       Recv-Q/    Local Address(port)/
                 Context      Send-Q     Remote Address(port)
[host]: tcp(4/6) LISTEN       0          *(22)
                 Wildcard     0          *(*)

[host]: tcp      LISTEN       0          *(161)
                 Wildcard     0          *(*)

[host]: tcp(4/6) LISTEN       0          *(161)
                 Wildcard     0          *(*)

[host]: tcp      ESTABLISHED  0          10.1.3.3(22)
                 default      0          10.1.3.1(16343)
```

An NX-OS device not only acts as an SSH server but can also be used as a client. The SSH client software is enabled by default. On NX-OS, you can also establish an SSH connection from the Bash shell. The Bash shell feature provides access to the Linux shell on the system, from which users and network administrators can execute Linux commands. Example 9-17 illustrates how to enable the Bash shell feature and use the Bash shell to establish a new SSH connection or verify open TCP connections used by the **sshd** process.

Example 9-17 *Establishing SSH from the Bash Shell*

```
NX-3(config)# feature bash
NX-3# run bash
bash-4.3$
bash-4.3$ lsof -nP -i TCP | grep ssh
sshd        816     11000    3u   IPv4   93874       0t0   TCP 127.0.0.1:17682 (LISTEN)
sshd      12601      root    3u   IPv6   33279       0t0   TCP *:22 (LISTEN)
sshd      12601      root    4u   IPv4   33281       0t0   TCP *:22 (LISTEN)

bash-4.3$ ssh admin@10.1.3.1
Outbound-ReKey for 10.1.3.1:22
Inbound-ReKey for 10.1.3.1:22
Password:

XE-1#
XE-1# exit
Connection to 10.1.3.1 closed by remote host.
Connection to 10.1.3.1 closed.
```

Note In Example 9-17, the use of the Bash shell is for demonstration purposes only. It is not recommended to establish SSH sessions from the Bash shell; the Bash shell should be used only for troubleshooting purposes.

Secure File Transfer

Traditionally, file transfers over the network were performed using the legacy insecure File Transfer Protocol (FTP). Developed in 1971 as part of the ARPANET protocols, FTP is one of the original programs for accessing information over the Internet. An extension to FTP, FTP Secure (FTPS), has been developed, and the Transport Layer Security (TLS) and Secure Sockets Layer (SSL) cryptographic protocols have also been added. Some of the common challenges with FTPS are that not all servers support SSL/TLS encryption, and there is not a standard way of fetching and changing file and directory attributes. Some of these challenges are easily overcome by SSH FTP.

SSH FTP (SFPT) is an extension to the already secure SSH protocol that provides easy file transfer capability. The SFTP protocol is designed on SSH standards that strictly define all aspects of operations. When transferring files over SFTP, the connection is already secured by the SSH protocol. SFTP not only deals with file transfer but also includes operations for permission, attribute manipulation, file locking, and other processes. The following are some of the advantages of using SFTP:

- **Data exchange:** The SFTP protocol formats a command and data into a special packet format and sends them through a single secure connection. This means that the server administrator does not need to open additional ports to allow file transfer, which is otherwise required for protocols such as FTP or FTPS.

- **Security:** SFTP includes all the secure functionality of SSH.
- **Operational simplicity:** Because SFTP works over SSH, it is easier to manage firewalls as there is no need to open extra ports for file transfer.
- **Integrity:** Data security and integrity are crucial for any business environment. Performing file transfer over SFTP provides data integrity thanks to SSH.

Many graphical tools, such as FileZilla, are available for configuring SFTP, but the focus of this chapter is on using the command line to configure the SFTP server and client. The first step in setting up SFTP is to ensure that SSH between the server and the client is functional. When you install OpenSSH software, the SFTP application is installed by default. To open an SFTP session, you use the following command:

```
sftp username@remote_server
```

Then, when you log in to the server with the password or SSH key, you are presented with the SFTP prompt. Example 9-18 illustrates the process of logging in to an SFTP server.

Example 9-18 *Performing SFTP Login on a Server*

```
Client1:~ centos$ sftp root@192.168.1.100
Enter passphrase for key '/Users/centos/.ssh/id_rsa':
Connected to root@167.71.231.196.
sftp>
```

Note If the server administrator has configured a non-default port number for SSH (TCP/port 22), users can connect to SFTP on a custom port number by using the following command:

```
sftp -oPort=custom_port username@remote_server
```

The SFTP shell provides access to a lot of commands that can be used for performing various operations, such as local and remote directory listing, fetching or uploading a file to the SFTP server, or changing file permissions. You can view a list of command-line options available with SFTP by using the **?** or **help** command under the SFTP shell, as shown in Example 9-19.

Example 9-19 *SFTP Help*

```
sftp> help
Available commands:
bye                                 Quit sftp
cd path                             Change remote directory to 'path'
chgrp grp path                      Change group of file 'path' to 'grp'
chmod mode path                     Change permissions of file 'path' to 'mode'
chown own path                      Change owner of file 'path' to 'own'
df [-hi] [path]                     Display statistics for current directory or
                                    filesystem containing 'path'
exit                                Quit sftp
get [-afPpRr] remote [local]        Download file
reget [-fPpRr] remote [local]       Resume download file
reput [-fPpRr] [local] remote       Resume upload file
help                                Display this help text
lcd path                            Change local directory to 'path'
lls [ls-options [path]]             Display local directory listing
lmkdir path                         Create local directory
ln [-s] oldpath newpath             Link remote file (-s for symlink)
lpwd                                Print local working directory
ls [-1afhlnrSt] [path]              Display remote directory listing
lumask umask                        Set local umask to 'umask'
mkdir path                          Create remote directory
progress                            Toggle display of progress meter
put [-afPpRr] local [remote]        Upload file
pwd                                 Display remote working directory
quit                                Quit sftp
rename oldpath newpath              Rename remote file
rm path                             Delete remote file
rmdir path                          Remove remote directory
symlink oldpath newpath             Symlink remote file
version                             Show SFTP version
!command                            Execute 'command' in local shell
!                                   Escape to local shell
```

The SFTP shell provides access to local as well as remote directories. Linux shell commands such as **pwd**, **ls**, and **cd** are used to perform file operations on remote servers, and the commands **lpwd**, **lls**, and **lcd** are used to perform file operations on the local file system. The command **pwd** is used to display the remote working directory, and **lpwd** is used to display the local working directory. Example 9-20 demonstrates the use of these commands for local and remote directory operations.

Example 9-20 *Local and Remote Directory Operations via SFTP*

```
sftp> pwd
Remote working directory: /root
sftp> ls
anaconda-ks.cfg   original-ks.cfg
sftp> lpwd
Local working directory: /Users/centos
sftp> lls
Applications            Downloads               Music                   Public
Box Sync                Dropbox                 MyJabberFiles           octave
Desktop                 Library                 Pictures                pgadmin.log
Documents               Movies                  Postman                 vmmaestro
sftp> cd /etc
sftp> pwd
Remote working directory: /etc
sftp> lcd Desktop
sftp> lpwd
Local working directory: /Users/centos/Desktop
sftp>
```

Once the local and remote paths have been set, the next step is to either fetch a remote file and save it on a local directory or upload a file from a local directory to a remote directory. This can be done using the **get** and **put** commands, as shown in Example 9-21. In this example, the command **get anaconda-ks.cfg test.cfg** fetches the file anaconda-ks.cfg from the remote SFTP server and saves it with the name test.cfg in the local directory. Similarly, the **put test.cfg** command is used to upload the test.cfg file from the local directory to the currently selected remote directory and save it with the same name.

Example 9-21 *Fetching and Uploading Files via SFTP*

```
sftp> ls
anaconda-ks.cfg   original-ks.cfg
sftp> get anaconda-ks.cfg test.cfg
Fetching /root/anaconda-ks.cfg to test.cfg
/root/anaconda-ks.cfg                                100% 6921     9.4KB/s   00:00

sftp> lls -al test.cfg
-rw-------  1 vinijain  staff  6921 Oct 18 02:35 test.cfg

sftp> put test.cfg
Uploading test.cfg to /root/test.cfg
test.cfg                                             100% 6921     1.9KB/s   00:03
sftp> ls
anaconda-ks.cfg   original-ks.cfg   test.cfg
sftp>
```

The SFTP shell also provides access to commands that allow for changing file permissions. For instance, you can change remote file permissions by using the Linux **chmod** command. Similarly, you can change the user group access of a file by using the Linux **chgrp** command from the SFTP shell. The **chgrp** Linux command takes a parameter as the group ID of the group that is assigned to the file permissions. To fetch the group ID, you can first get the /etc/group file from the server onto the local directory and then use **!** along with the **less** command to read the content of the file named group. Once the group ID has been identified, the same value can be used with the **chgrp** command, as shown in Example 9-22. Finally, you can use the **bye** or **exit** command to exit the SFTP shell.

Example 9-22 *Changing File Permissions in SFTP*

```
sftp> ls -l
-rw-------    1 root      root          6921 Aug  8 12:48 anaconda-ks.cfg
-rw-------    1 root      root          6577 Aug  8 12:48 original-ks.cfg
-rw-------    1 root      root          6921 Oct 18 10:27 test.cfg
sftp> chmod 777 test.cfg
Changing mode on /root/test.cfg
sftp> ls -l
-rw-------    1 root      root          6921 Aug  8 12:48 anaconda-ks.cfg
-rw-------    1 root      root          6577 Aug  8 12:48 original-ks.cfg
-rwxrwxrwx    1 root      root          6921 Oct 18 10:27 test.cfg
```

```
sftp> get /etc/group
Fetching /etc/group to group
/etc/group                                         100%  602     1.0KB/s   00:00
sftp> !less group
root:x:0:
bin:x:1:
daemon:x:2:
sys:x:3:
adm:x:4:centos
tty:x:5:
disk:x:6:
lp:x:7:
mem:x:8:
kmem:x:9:
wheel:x:10:centos,webadmin
cdrom:x:11:
mail:x:12:postfix
man:x:15:
dialout:x:18:
floppy:x:19:
games:x:20:
```

```
tape:x:33:
video:x:39:
ftp:x:50:
sftp> chgrp 10 test.cfg
Changing group on /root/test.cfg
sftp> ls -l
-rw-------    1 root    root        6921 Aug  8 12:48 anaconda-ks.cfg
-rw-------    1 root    root        6577 Aug  8 12:48 original-ks.cfg
-rwxrwxrwx    1 root    wheel       6921 Oct 18 10:27 test.cfg
sftp> bye
```

Setting Up SFTP on Cisco Devices

SFTP is supported across all Cisco platforms. Any network OS that supports SSH has built-in SFTP support. There are a few differences between the available SFTP options across different Cisco operating systems. On Cisco IOS XE platforms, there is no separate configuration required to enable SFTP. Once a device is configured or enabled with SSH, SFTP is enabled by default. However, network administrators can set a source interface for SSH sessions by using the command **ip ssh source-interface** *interface-type interface-number*. SFTP fetching (**get**) or uploading (**put**) operations on a file can be done using the **copy** command, as shown in Example 9-23.

Example 9-23 *SFTP on an IOS XE Router*

```
XE-1# conf t
XE-1(config)# ip ssh source-interface GigabitEthernet 3
```

```
XE-1# copy running-config sftp://alfa:Cisco!123@172.16.1.98/
Address or name of remote host [172.16.1.98]?
Destination username [alfa]?
Destination filename [xe-1-confg]?
SFTP send: Writing to /home/alfa/xe-1-confg size 4335
!
4335 bytes copied in 4.071 secs (1065 bytes/sec)
```

```
XE-1# copy sftp: bootflash:
Address or name of remote host []? 172.16.1.98
Source username [XE-1]? alfa
Source filename []? xe-1-confg
Destination filename [xe-1-confg]? XE-1.cfg
Password:
!
4335 bytes copied in 12.188 secs (356 bytes/sec)
```

```
XE-1# dir bootflash:XE-1.cfg
Directory of bootflash:/XE-1.cfg

   21  -rw-            4335  Oct 19 2019 07:28:02 +00:00  XE-1.cfg

7897796608 bytes total (7031525376 bytes free)
```

Note It is important to note that a Cisco IOS XE device cannot be configured as an SFTP server.

On IOS XR, the operating system provides access to the SFTP shell on the device itself. The SFTP shell on IOS XR has limited capability when it comes to local directory operations but provides options to perform various operations on remote files and directories. The **help** command in the SFTP shell provides a list of the commands available on IOS XR. The **get** and **put** operations are similar to the ones supported on Linux platforms. Example 9-24 shows how to access the SFTP shell on IOS XR and perform file transfer operations such as fetching and uploading files.

Example 9-24 *SFTP on IOS XR*

```
RP/0/RP0/CPU0:XR-2# sftp alfa@172.16.102.98
Sat Oct 19 18:52:30.609 UTC
Connecting to 172.16.102.98...
Password:
sftp> help
Supported SFTP commands
-----------------------
bye                                Quit SFTP
cd <path>                          Change remote host directory
chmod <mode> <path>                Change permissions
exit                               Quit SFTP
get <remote-path> [local-path]     Download file to local path
help                               Display this text
ls [-alt] [path]                   List files of remote directory
mkdir <path>                       Create a remote directory
put <local-path> [remote-path]     Upload file to remote path
pwd                                Display current remote directory
quit                               Quit SFTP
rename <old-path> <new-path>       Rename a remote file
```

```
rmdir <path>                     Remove a remote directory
rm <path>                        Remove a remote file

sftp> get xe-1-config harddisk:

/home/alfa/xe-1-config
  Transferred 4335 Bytes
  4335 bytes copied in 0 sec (2167500)bytes/sec

sftp> put harddisk:XR-2.cfg

/harddisk:/XR-2.cfg
  Transferred 520 Bytes
  520 bytes copied in 0 sec (520000)bytes/sec
sftp> bye
RP/0/RP0/CPU0:XR-2# dir harddisk:
Sat Oct 19 18:59:49.013 UTC

Directory of harddisk:
 8002 drwxr-xr-x. 2   4096 Oct 19 07:24 shutdown
16002 drwxr-xr-x. 5   4096 Oct 19 07:26 apprepo-dont-delete
24001 drwxr-xr-x. 6   4096 Oct 19 07:55 cisco_support
16001 drwxr-xr-x. 2   4096 Oct 19 07:25 ipodwdm_log
  424 -rwxr-xr-x. 1   4335 Oct 19 18:57 xe-1-config
   11 drwx------. 2   4096 Oct 19 07:24 lost+found
  416 -rwx------. 1    520 Oct 19 18:57 XR-2.cfg
   13 -rw-r--r--. 1 589824 Oct 19 07:24 .csbsc
24002 drwxr-xr-x. 2   4096 Oct 19 07:28 dumper
   12 drwxr-xr-x. 2   4096 Oct 19 07:24 tftpboot
 8001 drwxr-xr-x. 2   4096 Oct 19 07:24 nvram

1479088 kbytes total (1380492 kbytes free)
```

The NX-OS CLI is similar to the Cisco IOS XE CLI except that on Nx-OS using **sftp:** option with the **copy** command on NX-OS indirectly gets the user into the SFTP shell that is available as part of the Linux shell. **copy sftp:** *local-file-system* and **copy** *file-from-local-file-system* **sftp:** indirectly initiate **get** and **put** operations on the SFTP shell. You can see this from the CLI output when executing these commands, as shown in Example 9-25.

Example 9-25 *SFTP on NX-OS*

```
NX-3# copy sftp: bootflash:
Enter source filename: xe-1-config
Enter vrf (If no input, current vrf 'default' is considered): default
Enter hostname for the sftp server: 172.16.102.98
Enter username: alfa

The authenticity of host '172.16.102.98 (172.16.102.98)' can't be established.
ECDSA key fingerprint is SHA256:lOgTZauWMbHoQX8qbzAbJMoxRyyvvoNLBio19GZxnmc.
Are you sure you want to continue connecting (yes/no)? yes
Warning: Permanently added '172.16.102.98' (ECDSA) to the list of known hosts.
Outbound-ReKey for 172.16.102.98:22
Inbound-ReKey for 172.16.102.98:22
alfa@172.16.102.98's password:
sftp> progress
Progress meter enabled
sftp> get   xe-1-config  /bootflash/xe-1-config
/home/alfa/xe-1-config                          100% 4335     1.8KB/s   00:02
sftp> exit
Copy complete, now saving to disk (please wait)...
Copy complete.
```

```
NX-3# copy bootflash:NX-3.cfg sftp:
Enter vrf (If no input, current vrf 'default' is considered):
Enter hostname for the sftp server: 172.16.102.98
Enter username: alfa

Outbound-ReKey for 172.16.102.98:22
Inbound-ReKey for 172.16.102.98:22
alfa@172.16.102.98's password:
Connected to 172.16.102.98.
sftp> put  /bootflash/NX-3.cfg  NX-3.cfg
Uploading /bootflash/NX-3.cfg to /home/alfa/NX-3.cfg
/bootflash/NX-3.cfg                             100% 4286   787.0KB/s   00:00
sftp> exit
Copy complete, now saving to disk (please wait)...
Copy complete.
```

Alternatively, on NX-OS platforms, you can access the Bash shell and from there access the **dcos_sftp** tool, which is installed in the /isan/bin/ directory and can perform various SFTP operations. Example 9-26 shows how to access the **dcos_sftp** tool from the Bash shell.

Example 9-26 *The dcos_sftp Tool in the Bash Shell*

```
NX-3(config)# feature bash
NX-3(config)# end
NX-3# run bash
bash-4.3$
bash-4.3$ dcos_sftp
usage: dcos_sftp [-1246aCfpqrv] [-B buffer_size] [-b batchfile] [-c cipher]
          [-D sftp_server_path] [-F ssh_config] [-i identity_file] [-l limit]
          [-o ssh_option] [-P port] [-R num_requests] [-S program]
          [-s subsystem | sftp_server] host
       dcos_sftp [user@]host[:file ...]
       dcos_sftp [user@]host[:dir[/]]
       dcos_sftp -b batchfile [user@]host
bash-4.3$ which dcos_sftp
/isan/bin/dcos_sftp
```

Secure Copy Protocol

Secure Copy Protocol (SCP) is a protocol and a tool that works on top of SSH and enables you to copy files between local and remote devices or between two remote devices. SCP runs on port 22 and behaves somewhat like FTP—but with security and authentication. SCP also benefits from SSH as it allows the inclusion of both permissions and time stamps for files. Much like SFTP, SCP can be used to download files or even directories containing files. The **scp** command-line tool is native to most operating systems, including Linux, macOS, and Windows. Example 9-27 illustrates how to use the **scp** tool to copy files to and from a server and between two remote servers.

Example 9-27 *SCP on CentOS*

```
[root@centos2 centos]# scp root@10.1.100.100:test.txt new-test.txt
Enter passphrase for key '/root/.ssh/id_rsa':
test.txt                                          100%    0     0.0KB/s   00:00
```

```
[root@centos2 centos]# scp new-test.txt root@10.1.100.100:frm-centos2.txt
Enter passphrase for key '/root/.ssh/id_rsa':
new-test.txt                                      100%    0     0.0KB/s   00:00
```

```
[root@centos1 ~]# scp root@10.1.100.100:test.txt root@10.1.101.101:new-test2.txt
The authenticity of host '10.1.100.100 (10.1.100.100)' can't be established.
ECDSA key fingerprint is SHA256:6RbYWRp1qpY/1Rxg8BgYiEKllxiN5cC5JP36ChDcYo8.
ECDSA key fingerprint is MD5:8f:26:54:06:12:b0:c0:8d:1a:ad:ff:8c:80:c9:9a:d8.
Are you sure you want to continue connecting (yes/no)? yes
```

```
Warning: Permanently added '10.1.100.100' (ECDSA) to the list of known hosts.
root@10.1.100.100's password:
Enter passphrase for key '/root/.ssh/id_rsa':
test.txt                                    100%    0     0.0KB/s   00:00
Connection to 10.1.100.100 closed.
```

Note The **scp** command is also available on Cisco network operating systems. You can either use it with the **copy** command (as with SFTP) on both Cisco IOS XE or NX-OS or use the **scp** command on IOS XR to perform SCP operations. For using SCP, it is important that the remote devices are SSH enabled.

Although SCP and SFTP are both based on SSH, there are a few similarities and dissimilarities. Table 9-1 compares SCP and SFTP.

Table 9-1 *SCP and SFTP Comparison*

Feature	SFTP	SCP
Speed	SFTP is comparatively slower than SCP. SFTP much acknowledge every single packet that is exchanged between client and server.	SCP is much faster than SFTP. SCP doesn't require acknowledgements for all packets exchanged.
Functionality	SFTP can easily perform other directory operations, such as listing a directory or creating or deleting a directory, along with performing file transfers.	SCP is purely built for file transfer. It cannot perform operations such as directory listings or other directory operations.
Security	SFTP provides the same level of security as SSH.	SCP provides the same level of security as SSH.
Resuming file transfers	SFTP makes it possible to resume interrupted file transfers by using the **-a** option with the **sftp** command.	SCP does not allow you to resume interrupted file transfers.

You need to choose either the SCP or SFTP protocol based on the use case. For example, if faster transfer of data is important, then SCP is a better option, but if you have an unstable connection to the remote server, SFTP might be a better option.

Summary

This chapter covers SSH in detail, including the following topics:

- How SSH works and some of the benefits SSH provides over legacy protocols such as Telnet and rcp
- The differences between SSH1 and SSH2
- The three other protocols defined in the SSH2 RFCs that work together to provide the functionality of SSH2: SSH Transport Layer Protocol, SSH Connection Protocol, and SSH Authentication Protocol
- How to set up SSH on both Linux servers and Cisco devices
- SSH capabilities to securely transfer files to a remote server via protocols such as SFTP and SCP running over SSH

References

RFC 4251, "The Secure Shell (SSH) Protocol Architecture," https://tools.ietf.org/html/rfc4251.

RFC 4252, "The Secure Shell (SSH) Authentication Protocol," https://tools.ietf.org/html/rfc4252.

RFC 4253, "The Secure Shell (SSH) Transport Layer Protocol," https://tools.ietf.org/html/rfc4253.

RFC 4254, "The Secure Shell (SSH) Connection Protocol," https://tools.ietf.org/html/rfc4254.

Chapter 10

XML

This chapter covers the first encoding format listed in the network programmability stack: Extensible Markup Language (XML). XML is used to encode the messages of network programmability protocols. Some protocols, such as NETCONF, support only XML. XML was the first data representation language to be developed in the XML/JSON/YAML family. As you will see in this chapter, not only is XML the oldest of the three encoding schemes, but it is also the most powerful. In this chapter, you will also learn the details of XSD (XML Schema Definition), which is used to improve the capabilities of XML for complex applications.

XML Overview, History, and Usage

XML is a meta-markup language created to deal with information structures. "Meta" refers to the fact that XML has the ability to use metadata for better information handling, and "markup" means that it uses various *tags* to define the structure of the data. XML is designed to be both human readable and machine readable; it is easily readable and modifiable by humans, and when properly tagged, it is easily readable by machines.

In the world of network automation and orchestration, the data structure is one of the key elements. In fact, for all distributed applications involving any data exchange between multiple components, the data structure is crucial. The primary objective of XML is to create a proper data structure for data storage and representation. In 1998, during a time when the Internet was being developed extensively, XML was developed to complement HTML, which is focused on data visualization. XML enables a user to create any data structure, in the sense that it doesn't have any predefined tag names or values. In addition, there are limitations in terms of the data types supported by XML documents. This flexibility is very useful during the creation of applications; however, it is important to have a mechanism to check the content of the values to prevent situations such as data within an XML document being out of the range supported by the application. Therefore, further development of XML led to the introduction of XML DTD (Document Type Definition) and XML schemas, which add strict constraints to the content of XML documents to make it more formal.

The latest XML standard, released in 2008, is supported by the World Wide Web Consortium (W3C), which is in charge of updating the standard (https://www.w3.org/standards/xml/core). The IETF outlined the general guidelines of XML usage for development of IETF protocols in RFC 3470 in 2003.

Despite being a relatively old language, XML is still widely used for network automation and application communication. In network automation, the most popular application of XML is the management of network elements over NETCONF (as discussed in Chapter 14 "NETCONF and RESTCONF"). The payload of a NETCONF message is an XML document, which contains all the information needed to configure a network element or get its state.

For application-to-application communication, an XML-based protocol called SOAP (Simple Object Access Protocol) was also developed and supported by the W3C. Whereas NETCONF operates over SSH, SOAP relies on HTTP. (SOAP specifications were maintained by the XML Protocol Working Group of the W3C until the group was closed in 2009.) The REST framework, which is more commonly based on JSON data encoding, is now more commonly used than SOAP for communication between applications (see Chapter 11, "JSON").

XML Syntax and Components

XML is very flexible in terms of the data structure as all the tags you use you create yourself upon creating the structure of the data. With a NETCONF application, XML structure follows the internal structure of the database where the network operating system stores its configuration; in some cases it could be similar to the command-line interface (CLI) hierarchy, whereas in others it may vary. Despite the great flexibility, there are certain formatting rules that you need to follow to make XML syntax correct.

XML Document Building Blocks

To familiarize you with XML, Example 10-1 shows an XML document.

Example 10-1 *Basic XML Document*

```
<?xml version="1.0" encoding="UTF-8"?>
<vpn>
  <customer>NPF_cust1</customer>
  <contact>info@npf.cust1</contact>
</vpn>
```

In XML syntax, a *tag* is framed by < and > characters. There are two type of tags—the *start tag* (for example, <vpn>) and the *end tag* (for example, </vpn>)—and they are always paired. A storage unit framed by these tags is called an *element*. The topmost element is called a *root element*, and there can be only one root element per XML document.

Everything between the start and end tags is the *value* associated with the key represented by the pair of tags. Typically everything in XML should have a start tag and an end tag, but there are two exceptions to this rule:

- The document element, which is the first element in the document, starts with <?xml and ends with ?>. This element declares that a file is an XML document, and the XML processer should be used. Per W3C recommendation, the version must always be set to 1.0, and encoding must be either UTF-8 or UTF-16, with UTF-8 being the default choice (see https://www.w3resource.com/xml/declarations.php).
- The empty element tag is a tag for an element that contains no value, though it might contain an attribute. (You will learn about attributes later in this chapter.) However, in the XML encoding of some Cisco IOS XR YANG modules, you might find the empty element tag without any attribute.

In Example 10-1, you can see that the XML document is based on a parent/child relationship. The tag <vpn> is a parent for both the <customer> and <contact> entries, and <contact> and <customer> are children of <vpn>. Typically, child elements are visually marked by some spaces at the beginning of the line, which are ignored by the XML processor. Example 10-2 shows representations of data that have the same meaning for an XML processor.

Example 10-2 *Leading Spaces in XML Document*

```
! Option 1
<?xml version="1.0" encoding="UTF-8"?>
<vpn>
  <customer>NPF_cust1</customer>
  <contact>info@npf.cust1</contact>
</vpn>



! Option 2
<?xml version="1.0" encoding="UTF-8"?>
<vpn><customer>NPF_cust1</customer><contact>info@npf.cust1</contact></vpn>
```

There is no limit on the number of the parent/child relationships in an XML document, as shown in Example 10-3, which extends the XML document from Example 10-1.

Example 10-3 *XML Document with Multiple Nesting Relationships*

```
<?xml version="1.0" encoding="UTF-8"?>
<vpn>
  <customer>NPF_cust1</customer>
  <contact>info@npf.cust1</contact>
  <sites>
    <site id='1'>
      <provider_side>
        <router>DUS-1</router>
        <port>Gig1/1/1</port>
        <ipv4>10.0.0.1/30</ipv4>
        <ipv6>fc00::10:0:0:1/126</ipv6>
      </provider_side>
      <customer_side>
        <router>CUST-DUS-1</router>
        <port>xe-0/0/1</port>
        <ipv4>10.0.0.2/30</ipv4>
        <ipv6>fc00::10:0:0:2/126</ipv6>
      </customer_side>
      <enabled/>
    </site>
    <site id='2'>
      <provider_side>
        <router>FRA-1</router>
        <port>1/1/2</port>
        <ipv4>10.0.0.5/30</ipv4>
        <ipv6>fc00::10:0:0:5/126</ipv6>
      </provider_side>
      <customer_side>
        <router>CUST-FRA-1</router>
        <port>Ethernet1</port>
        <ipv4>10.0.0.6/30</ipv4>
        <ipv6>fc00::10:0:0:6/126</ipv6>
      </customer_side>
      <enabled/>
    </site>
  </sites>
</vpn>
```

As you can see in Example 10-3, multiple entities might have the same name within a single parent, each for an array or a list data structure. In total, all the children form a tree structure starting from the root element. In this example, the tag <enabled/> is an empty element tag.

You can create your own tags, but it is important to following several naming conventions:

- A tag name can contain any alphanumeric value as well as symbols (for example, -, _, :, and .).
- A tag cannot start with a number or a symbol (such as - or .).
- A tag cannot start with any variation of XML, such as xml, XML, or XmL.
- Tags are case sensitive; therefore, for example, <vpn> and <Vpn> are two completely different tags.
- There are five major approaches to tag naming:
  - **All lowercase:** For example, <vpn>
  - **All uppercase:** For example, <VPN>
  - **Camelcase:** For example, <VirtualPrivateNetwork>
  - **Lowercased first word followed by camelcase:** For example, <virtualPrivateNetwork>
  - **Words separated with an underscore:** For example, <virtual_private_network>

Although these five styles are recommended, you can use other formats as long as you follow the preceding conventions.

In Example 10-3, the tags contain all lowercase letters, numbers, and underscores.

Predefined entities are used to avoid ambiguity when using certain symbols. Several symbols can be used in XML tags, though they need to follow specific rules. For example, using the less-than (<) or greater-than (>) symbol with an opening tag would be confusing (<> or >>). Table 10-1 lists the predefined entities that allow you to express symbols without ambiguity.

Table 10-1 *Predefined Entities in XML*

Entity	Symbol	Value
<	<	Less than
>	>	Greater than
&	&	Ampersand
'	'	Single quote
"	"	Double quote

XML Attributes, Comments, and Namespaces

There is one more important concept you might have spotted in Example 10-3: attributes. For example, in that example, in <site id='1'>, site id is an attribute, and '1' is its value. A value must always be provided in either single or double quotes. An attribute is metadata, which you can think of as data about data. An attribute's value can be used to identify additional information for the XML processor about how to deal with data, but it is not the data itself, so it can't contain the value that is processed by the application.

With respect to network automation, XML attributes are widely used in NETCONF messages as shown in Example 10-4.

Example 10-4 *XML Attributes in NETCONF*

```
<interfaces>
  <interface operation="replace">
    <name>GigabitEthernet0/0/0/1</name>
    <description>local router &gt; remote router</description>
    <!-- other child tag elements -->
  </interface>
</interfaces>
```

In Example 10-4, the attribute operation instructs the NETCONF application that it should *replace* the original interface configuration with the data provided in the XML body of the NETCONF message. In addition, the predefined element in the value of the <description> tag will be rendered as *local router > remote* router after the configuration is applied to the target network device.

Example 10-4 introduces another important XML concept: comments. XML comments, like comments in any programing language, provide additional information that explains the code but that is not processed by the application. You should use comments if you work on an XML document with a team to help each other better understand the data structure. A comment in XML starts with <!-- and ends with -->. To prevent ambiguity and XML errors, a comment should not include double hyphens (--) anywhere except at the end.

Although in general XML attributes are arbitrary key/value pairs that can help the XML parser process information (and also help you structure the data by applying certain tags), there are some use cases when specific attributes are mandatory, which you will learn about later in this chapter.

As mentioned earlier in this chapter, when you work with XML, you can define your XML tags, as long as you follow the conventions outlined earlier. However, this freedom can lead to problems. Example 10-5 shows a document in which the same tag has different meanings.

Example 10-5 *The Same Tag Used Multiple Times in an XML Document*

```
<?xml version="1.0" encoding="UTF-8"?>
<vpn>
  <customer>NPF_cust1</customer>
  <contact>info@npf.cust1</contact>
  <sites>
    <site id='1'>
      <provider_side>
        <router>DUS-1</router>
        <port>Gig1/1/1</port>
        <ipv4>10.0.0.1/30</ipv4>
        <ipv6>fc00::10:0:0:1/126</ipv6>
      </provider_side>
      <customer_side>
        <router>CUST-DUS-1</router>
        <port>xe-0/0/1</port>
        <ipv4>10.0.0.2/30</ipv4>
        <ipv6>fc00::10:0:0:2/126</ipv6>
      </customer_side>
      <enabled/>
    </site>
  </sites>
  <sites>
    <site>
      <address>
        <country>Germany</country>
        <town>Berlin</town>
        <street>Unter den Linden</street>
        <house>78</house>
      </address>
    </site>
  </sites>
</vpn>
```

In Example 10-5, note that there are two <sites> tags that contain completely different data: The first one is focused on the technical information required to create a customer BGP IP MPLS VPN, whereas the second one contains the physical address. It is possible that there might be a mistake in the tag name; alternatively, the provided XML file might be used by different programs, where different information is needed. There is a way to use the same tag name in different ways within a single document: by using namespaces. An XML namespace is a specific attribute that defines XML vocabulary used to process a specific part of the XML document. Example 10-6 adds the XML namespace to the XML document from Example 10-5.

Example 10-6 *Using XML Namespaces*

```
<?xml version="1.0" encoding="UTF-8"?>
<vpn xmlns="http://network.programmability/xmldocs/namespace1">
  <customer>NPF_cust1</customer>
  <contact>info@npf.cust1</contact>
  <sites>
    <site id='1'>
    <!-- output is truncated for brevity -->
  </sites>
  <sites xmlns="http://network.programmability/xmldocs/namespace2">
    <site>
    <!-- output is truncated for brevity -->
  </sites>
</vpn>
```

In this example, the xmlns attribute's value is a URI (uniform resource indicator). xmlns is inherited, which means each child entry inherits the XML namespace from its parent. The URI is processed by the XML parser as a string, and it doesn't necessarily represent a real web page you can access on the Internet (though it might). Typically a parser uses the xmlns attribute to convey data to the corresponding software for further processing.

An application can process XML namespaces properly, but for humans, it might be hard to follow all the parent/child relationships and understand which dictionary the particular elements belongs to. To overcome this ambiguity, XML introduced the concept of prefixes, which are used to explicitly map a certain tag to a certain namespace, as illustrated in Example 10-7.

Example 10-7 *Using XML Namespaces with Prefixes*

```
<?xml version="1.0" encoding="UTF-8"?>
<pr1:vpn xmlns:pr1="http://network.programmability/xmldocs/namespace1"
  xmlns:pr2="http://network.programmability/xmldocs/namespace2">
  <pr1:customer>NPF_cust1</pr1:customer>
  <pr1:contact>info@npf.cust1</pr1:contact>
  <pr1:sites>
    <pr1:site id='1'>
    <!-- output is truncated for brevity -->
  <pr1:/sites>
  <pr2:sites>
    <pr2:site>
    <!-- output is truncated for brevity -->
  </pr2:sites>
</pr1:vpn>
```

A prefix is defined during the declaration of an XML namespace as xmlns:*prefix*—for example, xmlns:pr1 and xmlns:pr2 in Example 10-7. After the namespace has been defined, all the tags must start with an appropriate prefix value in the form *prefix:tag*—for example, pr1:vpn or pr2:sites. In Example 10-7, you can see that both of the namespaces are declared in the root element and then mapped to the respective tags using prefixes.

The W3C does not mandate the use of XML namespaces. If neither a default namespace (for example, xmlns="*URI*") nor a namespace with a prefix (for example, xmlns:*prefix*="*URI*") is defined, then an element is implicitly not related to any XML namespace. However, some protocols that rely on XML (for example, NETCONF) require the xmlns attribute to be present starting from the root element.

XML Formatting Rules

There are some more rules that you need to be aware of when you work with XML. First of all, you must always strictly follow the rules for parent/child relationships, which create your data structure. Example 10-8 shows both correct and incorrect XML documents.

Example 10-8 *XML Nesting Format*

```
! Incorrect example
<?xml version="1.0" encoding="UTF-8"?>
<vpn>
  <customer>NPF_cust1</customer>
  <contact>info@npf.cust1</contact>
  <sites>
    <site id='1'>
      <!-- Details -->
    </sites>
  </site>
</vpn>


! Correct example
<?xml version="1.0" encoding="UTF-8"?>
<vpn>
  <customer>NPF_cust1</customer>
  <contact>info@npf.cust1</contact>
  <sites>
    <site id='1'>
      <!-- Details -->
    </site>
  </sites>
</vpn>
```

In the first part of Example 10-8, the end tags </sites> and </site> are incorrectly placed. This type of mistake can easily be found by using a professional XML editor, but with a console text editor (for example, vim on Linux), it is very easy to make such a mistake. If you create your own data structure, you can avoid this mistake by creating proper tag names. Unfortunately, in many established YANG modules (for example, Cisco IOS XR), several adjacent tags are very similar (for example, the tag <interfaces> is the parent to <interface>). Incorrectly sequencing parent and child tags will result in an error in XML document processing.

Another important thing you should know about the XML format is that everything between the start tag and end tag is a value. If there are leading or trailing spaces, as in Example 10-9, they are considered values.

Example 10-9 *Space Characters in the Value Fields*

```
! Incorrect example
<?xml version="1.0" encoding="UTF-8"?>
<vpn>
  <customer> NPF_cust1</customer>
  <contact>info@npf.cust1  </contact>
</vpn>
```

In the XML document in Example 10-9, the key customer has the value *NPF_cust1*, starting with a leading space, and the key contact has the value *info@npf.cust1* with two trailing spaces. Because these spaces are considered part of the value, when the XML document is processed, any operations involving comparing the values with others may result in undesired results.

If you follow all the rules described so far in this chapter, you will create *well-formed* XML documents. An XML document must be well formed in order to be processed correctly. If an XML document contains syntax violations, it is not well formed. Such a document cannot be properly processed by an XML processor, and any application that relies on the document may fail.

With XML-based applications, a whole XML document must be parsed, analyzed, and processed before any further activity (such as changes to a network element) can be accomplished. It is therefore recommended that you keep XML documents reasonably small. Otherwise, the performance of the applications could be severely affected.

Making XML Valid

In addition to being well formed, an XML document must comply with another condition: It must be *valid*. *Validity* means that a document is properly formatted and that it contains the proper content. To be valid, a document must be well formed, and it must comply with the guidelines for the document type as expressed by the XML DTD file or the XML schema.

One of the primary goals of ensuring that XML documents are valid is to reduce the number of errors that are caused by improper tags or data types in an XML document. As mentioned earlier, XML documents with errors cannot be processed.

XML DTD

An XML Document Type Definition (DTD) defines the structure and the legal elements and attributes of an XML document. It contains or points to markup declarations that provide the grammar for a class of documents. A DTD can point to an external entity that contains markup declarations, or it can contain the markup declarations directly in an internal entity, or both. In this context, a markup declaration is an element type declaration, an attribute list declaration, an entity declaration, or a notation declaration. Basically, these declarations define which elements (that is, tags) are allowed in a specific XML document and what values they may take.

Example 10-10 extends the XML document from Example 10-1 to point to an external XML DTD document.

Example 10-10 *Basic XML Document with DTD*

```
<?xml version="1.0" encoding="UTF-8"?>
<!DOCTYPE vpn SYSTEM "vpn.dtd">
<vpn>
  <customer id="1">NPF_cust1</customer>
  <contact>info@npf.cust1</contact>
</vpn>
```

The DTD in this example starts with *<!DOCTYPE* followed by the path to the file. In Example 10-10, it is expected that the file vpn.dtd is located in the same folder as the original XML document. The DTD document should include all the tags with the data type expected in a validated XML document. Example 10-11 shows what such a DTD file might look like.

Example 10-11 *Sample DTD File*

```
<!DOCTYPE vpn [
<!ELEMENT vpn (customer,contact)>
<!ELEMENT customer (#PCDATA)>
<!ATTLIST customer id ID #REQUIRED>
<!ELEMENT contact (#PCDATA)>
]>
```

The first line of this document defines the root element of the validated document. In Example 10-10, the root element has a <vpn> tag; therefore, !DOCTYPE has the value vpn as well.

The following entries that start with !ELEMENT define the content of the tags in the original XML document:

- The element vpn consists of two other elements: customer and contact.
- The element customer must have the #PCDATA type.
- The element contact must have the #PCDATA type as well.

Note The term PCDATA derives historically from the term *parsed character data*, which could be any kind of input data.

There is another entry type defined by the !ATTLIST command, which validates the attributes attached to a certain tag.

The DTD in Example 10-11 checks the following in the original XML document:

- It ensures that the root element is vpn.
- It ensures that the element vpn has exactly two children: customer and contact.
- It ensures that each of the children (customer and contact) has some kind of textual information, including a zero string (for when there is no input).
- It ensures that the tag customer has the attribute id.

As mentioned earlier in this section, the DTD might be located in a separate file, or it might be part of the initial XML document. A joint XML document with DTD looks as shown in Example 10-12.

Example 10-12 *Joint XML and DTD File*

```
<?xml version="1.0" encoding="UTF-8"?>
<!DOCTYPE vpn [
<!ELEMENT vpn (customer,contact)>
<!ELEMENT customer (#PCDATA)>
<!ELEMENT contact (#PCDATA)>
<!ENTITY fixed_info "Configured automatically">
]>
<vpn>
  <customer>NPF_cust1</customer>
  <contact>info@npf.cust1</contact>
  <hint>&fixed_info</hint>
</vpn>
```

In addition to showing a joint XML and DTD document, Example 10-12 highlights the additional capability of the XML DTD to define some information (which is likely fixed) in the DTD part that can be inserted into the original XML document. This information is defined in the XML DTD with the !ENTITY entry followed by the *name "value"* construction. Afterward, the name defined in the !ENTITY entry is called in the XML document by using the ampersand-prepended name. In Example 10-12, the entity's name is fixed_info, so it is called with &fixed_info.

XSD

XML DTD was the first mechanism to perform validation of XML documents. However, DTD has several drawbacks, including the following:

- It uses non-XML syntax.
- It lacks support for data types.
- It lacks support for namespaces.

To overcome these drawbacks, a new approach to XML validation was created: XML Schema Definition (XSD). Today XSD is used much more often than DTD.

XSD is written in XML, and it follows the XML syntax rules described previously. Because it is used to verify the XML objects, XSD has a predefined set of tags that you can use to create a schema. Example 10-13 shows an XML document from earlier in this chapter, ready to be validated by XSD.

Example 10-13 *XML Document to Be Validated by XSD*

```
<?xml version="1.0" encoding="UTF-8"?>
<vpn xmlns="http://network.programmability/xmldocs/namespace1" xmlns:xsi="http://
  www.w3.org/2001/XMLSchema-instance" xsi:schemaLocation="http://
  network.programmability/xmldocs/namespace1 vpn.xsd">
  <customer>NPF_cust1</customer>
  <contact>info@npf.cust1</contact>
  <sites>
    <site id="1">
      <provider_side>
        <router>DUS-1</router>
        <port>Gig1/1/1</port>
        <ipv4>10.0.0.1/30</ipv4>
        <ipv6>fc00::10:0:0:1/126</ipv6>
      </provider_side>
      <customer_side>
        <router>CUST-DUS-1</router>
        <port>xe-0/0/1</port>
        <ipv4>10.0.0.2/30</ipv4>
        <ipv6>fc00::10:0:0:2/126</ipv6>
      </customer_side>
```

```
      <enabled/>
    </site>
    <site id='2'>
      <provider_side>
        <router>FRA-1</router>
        <port>1/1/2</port>
        <ipv4>10.0.0.5/30</ipv4>
        <ipv6>fc00::10:0:0:5/126</ipv6>
      </provider_side>
      <customer_side>
        <router>CUST-FRA-1</router>
        <port>Ethernet1</port>
        <ipv4>10.0.0.6/30</ipv4>
        <ipv6>fc00::10:0:0:6/126</ipv6>
      </customer_side>
      <enabled/>
    </site>
  </sites>
</vpn>
```

In Example 10-13, the root element vpn contains the following attributes:

- **xmlns="http://network.programmability/xmldocs/namespace1"**: This is the default namespace used in this XML document.
- **xmlns:xsi="http://www.w3.org/2001/XMLSchema-instance"**: This is the namespace related to the XML schema that defines the elements and data types that are used.
- **xsi:schemaLocation="http://network.programmability/xmldocs/namespace1 vpn.xsd"**: This is an attribute outside the xmlns:xsi XML namespace that points the namespace of the original XML document to the path of the XML schema used to verify the document, in the format *namespace_name schema_path*.

During the processing of the document, the XML parser takes instructions to find a proper XSD file and validate the XML document against it. Because XSD is written in XML format, the format of XSD in Example 10-14 might look familiar to you.

Example 10-14 *Initial Tag for XSD*

```
<?xml version="1.0" encoding="UTF-8"?>
<xs:scheme xmlns:xs="http://www.w3.org/2001/XMLSchema" targetNamespace=" http://
  network.programmability/xmldocs/namespace1" elementFormDefault="qualified">
<!-- The content will be created later on -->
</xs:scheme>
```

As the XSD is written in XML, it starts with the *XML declaration*, much as an ordinary XML document does. This declaration is followed by the root element, which is always called <scheme>. The W3C has developed a dictionary for XSD schemes, and the specific XML namespace in this case is called xmlns:xs="http://www.w3.org/2001/XMLSchema", and the root element <scheme> is prepended using the prefix <xs:scheme>. You can see in Example 10-14 that two attributes from that namespace are used:

- targetNamespace points to the namespace used in the validated XML document.
- elementFormDefault defines that all the elements in the validated XML documents are related to the namespace declared as targetNamespace rather than to no namespace.

After the header of the XML schema itself is created, you can start working on the actual content. The XML schema definition provides extensive capabilities in terms of content and structure verification, and you will gradually learn enough about them to be able to create XSD, which can verify the document created earlier (refer to Example 10-13).

The basic building block of XSD is an element, as shown in Example 10-15.

Example 10-15 *Element Validation in XSD*

```
! Original XML document entries
<customer>NPF_cust1</customer>
<contact>info@npf.cust1</contact>
! Relevant checks in XSD
<xs:element name="customer " type="xs:string"/>
<xs:element name="contact " type="xs:string"/>
```

In Example 10-15 you can see two key/value pairs extracted from the original XML document followed by two strings, showing how these elements would be addressed in the XSD. In the XSD, the tag describing the XML entry is <element>, and it is typically prepended by the prefix associated with the namespace (in this case, <xs:element>). As you might have noticed, <xs:element> is an empty entry tag, which means it doesn't have any value. This tag has two associated attributes:

- **name:** This attribute links this element to a particular tag in the XML document. For example, <xs:element name= "customer"> links this element to the tag <customer> in the validated XML document.
- **type:** This attribute defines the data type that this element should have. If the linked tag in the validated document has a format different from the required format, the validation check fails.

XSD has a long list of predefined data types that you can refer in your XSD schemas. Table 10-2 summarizes the most widely used XSD data types.

Table 10-2 *Most Popular XML Data Types*

Data Type	Description
string	Any set of characters allowed by XML syntax, enclosed in quotation marks (for example, "info@npf.cust1", "Customer 1")
decimal	Numeric data, possibly including a decimal point, and indication of whether the value is negative or positive (for example, 1234.45, -12, +123, -0.23)
integer	Numeric data without a decimal part but with indication of whether the value is negative or positive (for example, 123, -123)
boolean	Data type associated with Boolean logic, so the allowed values are True or False
date	Date in the format YYYY-MM-DD (for example, 2021-05-16)
time	Time of day in the format HH:MM:SS (for example, 14:30:23)

There are many others attributes that you might want to add to an XSD scheme. Two attributes are mandatory for XSD validation:

- **default:** This attribute sets the default value to the validated tag, if there is no value provided.
- **fixed:** This attribute rewrites the value of the validated tag, even if there is no value provided.

Example 10-16 shows how these two attributes would look in an XSD file.

Example 10-16 *Using Optional Attributes in the XSD Element Tag*

```
<xs:element name="customer" type="xs:string" default="Default Customer"/>
<xs:element name="contact" type="xs:string" fixed="do-not-use-this-value"/>
```

Sometimes you need to add stricter validation to an XML document, such as validation against not only a certain data type but also against a possible value. For example, in Example 10-13, you might note that the entry <router> has a hostname of the router where the customer's service is terminated. Despite the fact that the router's hostname is an arbitrary value, you should associate the service with the existing router. Therefore, you need to provide the valid router's hostname in the XML document and make sure that the XML schema can validate that.

In general, an element that has a single tag with a single value is called a *simple object*, and simple objects are typically not mentioned in an XSD document unless you need to impose further limitations, such as content verification. Say that you have a network with four routers, called FRA-1, DUS-1, BLN-1, and MNC-1. In an XSD document, you can add the validation of the <router> entry as shown in Example 10-17.

Example 10-17 *Content Validation in an XSD Document Based on Predefined Values*

```
! Validated entry
<router>FRA-1</router>


! XSD validation
<xs:element name="router">
   <xs:simpleType>
      <xs:restriction base="xs:string">
         <xs:enumeration value="FRA-1"/>
         <xs:enumeration value="DUS-1"/>
         <xs:enumeration value="BLN-1"/>
         <xs:enumeration value="MNC-1"/>
      </xs:restriction>
   </xs:simpleType>
</xs:element>
```

The tag <xs:simpleType> defines that the validated entry is a simple object. The tag <xs:restriction>, which provides the mechanism to verify the tags' values, has a single attribute base that identifies the data type to be verified. You might notice that the attribute isn't called type anymore, as it is in Example 10-16. All the tags nested in <xs:restriction> are validation rules. In Example 10-17, the rule has an enumeration type that is drop-down list of allowed values. All the possible values need to be provided separately; each value has its own entry.

There are multiple options for content validation. One of them, based on the Linux regular expression, is widely used due to its high efficiency. Example 10-18 shows such an option.

Example 10-18 *Content Validation in an XSD Document Using regexp*

```
! Validated entry
<contact>info@npf.cust1</contact>


! XSD validation
<xs:element name="contact">
   <xs:simpleType>
      <xs:restriction base="xs:string">
         <xs:pattern value="([a-zA-Z0-9\.\-\_])+\@([a-zA-Z0-9\.\-\_])+"/>
      </xs:restriction>
   </xs:simpleType>
</xs:element>
```

The validation rule in Example 10-18 is called <pattern>, and it verifies whether the entry's value matches the desired regular expression provided in the attribute <value>. In Example 10-18, the desired pattern is a character set containing uppercase and lowercase letters, numbers and characters such as ., -, and _, followed by the @ character and then the same character set. Both before and after the @, there should be at least one character. This is a standard format for mailboxes, and you might want to implement such a check to avoid problems when customer contact information is provided in an incorrect format. You can adapt Example 10-18 to make it more sophisticated and suit your needs.

Although pattern validation is applicable to the numeric data (for example, integer, decimal) as well, you might want to add numeric-specific validation rules. The following two rules are the ones that are most commonly used:

- **minInclusive:** This validation rule sets the lowest possible value for a number (for example, <xs:minInclusive value="0">).
- **maxInclusive:** This validation rule caps the range at the maximum allowed value, including the provided value itself (for example, <xs:maxInclusive value="100">).

Besides validating entry values, you might need to validate entry attributes. To do that, you use another XSD tag, <attribute>, which together with the namespace prefixes results in <xs:attribute>. This is an empty entry tag that is similar to <xs:element>, as you can see in Example 10-19.

Example 10-19 *Attribute Validation in XSD*

```
! Original XML document entries
   <site id='1'>


! Relevant checks in XSD
<xs:attribute name="id" type="xs:integer" use="required"/>
```

The mandatory attribute's name and type within the tag <xs:attribute> are the same as for the tag <xs:element>, but you can see in Example 10-19 one more optional attribute: use. By nature, attributes are not mandatory in an XML document. Therefore, if an attribute is mandatory according to the logic of an application, you should mention that in your XSD schema.

Example 10-19 has one drawback: It doesn't show how the attribute is related to the original tag. The reason is that the tag with the attribute is not a simple object like the ones covered so far. It is a complex object.

There are four types of complex elements in XML schemas:

- Empty elements
- Elements containing only other elements
- Elements containing only some text
- Elements containing mixed information

The first type is shown in Example 10-19, where it provides validation for elements that have only attributes without any textual data. The correct XSD for validation looks as shown in Example 10-20.

Example 10-20 *Complex Element for Attribute Validation in XSD*

```
! Original XML document entries
   <site id="1">


! Relevant checks in XSD
<xs:element name="site">
  <xs:complexType>
    <xs:attribute name="id" type="xs:integer" use="required"/>
  </xs:complexType>
</xs:element>
```

You can see in Example 10-20 that the entry <xs:element> has another nested entry <xs:complexType>, which in turn contains all the validations related to the entry in the XML document. In Example 10-20, it has a single attribute validation, which is the same string as provided in Example 10-19.

The second type of complex object is an element containing other elements. There are two ways such an element can be used: either to add a <complexType> entry directly to an object or to create a named <complexType> and call it by its name in a validated element. Obviously, the second option is much more scalable. To emphasize this, take a look at the validated object in Example 10-13. You can see that the elements <customer_side> and <provider_side> have the same internal content; you can therefore take advantage of the named objects of <complexType>, as shown in Example 10-21.

Example 10-21 *Complex Type for Element Validation in XSD Using Named Elements*

```
! Original XML document entries
      <provider_side>
        <router>DUS-1</router>
        <port>Gig1/1/1</port>
        <ipv4>10.0.0.1/30</ipv4>
        <ipv6>fc00::10:0:0:1/126</ipv6>
      </provider_side>
      <customer_side>
        <router>CUST-DUS-1</router>
        <port>xe-0/0/1</port>
        <ipv4>10.0.0.2/30</ipv4>
        <ipv6>fc00::10:0:0:2/126</ipv6>
      </customer_side>


! Relevant checks in XSD
<xs:element name="provider_side" type="connectivity_info"/>
<xs:element name="customer_side" type="connectivity_info"/>
<xs:complexType name="connectivity_info">
```

```
  <xs:sequence>
    <xs:element name="router" type="xs:string" use="required"/>
    <xs:element name="port" type="xs:string" use="required"/>
    <xs:element name="ipv4" type="xs:string" use="required"/>
    <xs:element name="ipv6" type="xs:string" use="required"/>
  <xs:sequence/>
</xs:complexType>
</xs:element>
```

Example 10-21 includes element <xs:complexType>, which is created as a standalone entry with the attribute name having value "connectivity_info". Inside this element is another nested element, <xs:sequence>, which contains the validated elements provided in the same form as was done earlier for the simple objects. Note that <xs:sequence> requires the validated elements to appear in the defined sequence and not randomly.

Once a named complex object is created, you can use it in the validation of elements that have further nesting. As you can see in Example 10-21, this is done with **type="connectivity_info"** in the elements that need to be validated.

Despite the fact that named complex type elements are very useful, in some cases, you can use ordinary unnamed objects to fulfil the validation requirements. Example 10-22 extends the previous example by adding one more level in the tree.

Example 10-22 *Complex Type for Element Validation in XSD for Mixed Objects*

```
! Original XML document entries
   <site id='1'>
      <provider_side>
        <router>DUS-1</router>
        <port>Gig1/1/1</port>
        <ipv4>10.0.0.1/30</ipv4>
        <ipv6>fc00::10:0:0:1/126</ipv6>
      </provider_side>
      <customer_side>
        <router>CUST-DUS-1</router>
        <port>xe-0/0/1</port>
        <ipv4>10.0.0.2/30</ipv4>
        <ipv6>fc00::10:0:0:2/126</ipv6>
      </customer_side>
   </site>


! Relevant checks in XSD
<xs:element name="site">
  <xs:complexType>
    <xs:attribute name="id" type="xs:integer" use="required"/>
    <xs:sequence>
```

```
      <xs:element name="provider_side" type="connectivity_info"/>
      <xs:element name="customer_side" type="connectivity_info"/>
    </xs:sequence>
  </xs:complexType>
</xs:element>
<xs:complexType name="connectivity_info">
  <xs:sequence>
    <xs:element name="router" type="xs:string" use="required"/>
    <xs:element name="port" type="xs:string" use="required"/>
    <xs:element name="ipv4" type="xs:string" use="required"/>
    <xs:element name="ipv6" type="xs:string" use="required"/>
  <xs:sequence/>
</xs:complexType>
</xs:element>
```

In Example 10-22, <site> is a parent element for both the <customer_side> and <provider_side> elements. You can create another element, named <xs:complexType>, to validate the site. However, you can also extend the schema created in Example 10-20 by adding the <xs:sequence> element and putting all the child elements that need to be validated directly there. If the order of the elements isn't important, you can use <xs:all> instead of <xs:sequence> to contain all the nested checks.

In certain circumstances, a validated element might have logic that it contains either one or another nested element but not both simultaneously. Say that <site> should contain either the <provider_side> or <customer_side> element. In this case, the schema's element <xs:sequence> should be replaced with the <xs:choice>, as illustrated in Example 10-23.

Example 10-23 *Complex Type for Element Validation in XSD for Mixed Objects*

```
! Relevant checks in XSD
<xs:element name="site">
  <xs:complexType>
    <xs:attribute name="id" type="xs:integer" use="required"/>
    <xs:choice>
      <xs:element name="provider_side" type="connectivity_info"/>
      <xs:element name="customer_side" type="connectivity_info"/>
    </xs:choice>
  </xs:complexType>
</xs:element>
! Further output is truncated for brevity
```

By this point, you should have an understanding of the XML Schema Definition (XSD), including the overall structure and details of building the validation entries.

Brief Comparison of XSD and DTD

Table 10-3 highlights the differences between DTD and XSD. As you can see from this comparison, when developing XML-based data structures today, you should use XSD.

Table 10-3 *DTD and XSD Comparison*

DTD	XSD
DTD syntax is different from that of XML.	XSD is written in XML, so there is no need to learn a separate language.
Data types aren't defined in DTD.	XSD defines the data types for elements.
There is no concept of namespaces in DTD.	As it is written in XML, XSD natively supports XML namespaces.
DTD is not extensible.	XSD is extensible, using standard XML.

Navigating XML Documents

So far in this chapter, you have learned about various topics related to XML documents and schemas. In this section of the chapter, you will learn how to navigate an XML document and extract the information that is necessary for XML document transformation. The transformation and associated techniques are covered later in this chapter, in the section "XML Stylesheet Language Transformations (XSLT)."

XPath

Recall that each XML document starts with at least one root element, and there may be many parent/child relationships in the hierarchy. Therefore, an XML document could be treated as a tree, where each leaf is a piece of the information that can be accessed along some branches. XPath is a key element in the navigating the XML tree and choosing the necessary data. XPath uses path expressions, which are similar to the path format used in Linux. However, XPath also has plenty of unique features.

The primary XPath building block is a node. There are seven node types defined for XPath (https://www.w3schools.com/xml/xpath_nodes.asp):

- Element
- Attribute
- Text
- Namespace
- Processing instruction
- Comment
- Document

From an XPath perspective, every XML document is a tree of nodes that starts from the root element. The connectivity between the nodes is defined by the various types of relationships. The relationships between various nodes are similar to the relationships that exist in XML documents:

- **Parent:** Each node besides the root element has a parent node. Each node can have only one parent node.
- **Children:** Each node, including the root element, may have one or more children.
- **Siblings:** All the children of the same parent are the siblings to each other.
- **Ancestors:** All the parent nodes up to the root element (for example, parent, parent's parent) are ancestors.
- **Descendants:** All the nested children down to the all leafs (for example, children, children's children) are descendants.

Table 10-4 lists and describes the XPath syntax elements.

Table 10-4 *XPath Syntax*

Expression	Description
nodename	Selects all nodes with the name *nodename*
/	Selects from the root node
//	Selects nodes in the document from the current node that match the selection, no matter where they are
.	Selects the current node
..	Selects the parent of the current node
@	Selects attributes
[ ]	Predicate element, which adds the details to the original path to make the node's choice more precise

Example 10-24 shows the XML document we use in this section to examine XPath.

Example 10-24 *XML Document for XPath Expressions*

```
<?xml version="1.0" encoding="UTF-8"?>
<vpn>
  <customer>NPF_cust1</customer>
  <contact>info@npf.cust1</contact>
  <sites>
    <site id="1">
      <provider_side>
        <router>DUS-1</router>
```

```
        <port>Gig1/1/1</port>
      </provider_side>
      <customer_side>
        <router>CUST-DUS-1</router>
        <port>xe-0/0/1</port>
      </customer_side>
      <enabled/>
    </site>
    <site id="2">
      <provider_side>
        <router>FRA-1</router>
        <port>1/1/2</port>
      </provider_side>
      <customer_side>
        <router>CUST-FRA-1</router>
        <port>Ethernet1</port>
      </customer_side>
      <enabled/>
    </site>
  </sites>
</vpn>
```

As you see, Example 10-24 provides a simplified version of a XML document shown earlier in this chapter (refer to Example 10-13).

XPath itself doesn't extract any data, as it is just a way to define the path. Therefore, XPath is widely used in XSLT, JavaScript, Python, and so on. If XPath is used with a tool, you see which element will be collected in relationship to a specific path. Example 10-25 shows a simple path expression that uses an absolute path to a node.

Example 10-25 *Simple XPath Expression with an Absolute Path*

```
Path:   /vpn/customer
Result: NPF_cust1
```

The requested path is associated with an element, and it starts from the root element vpn and continues with its child's node customer. The node contains text that is returned as a result. You can achieve the same result by using another type of selection, as shown in Example 10-26. This type of selection with the XPath syntax means that all the nodes with the name customer will be selected, regardless of where in the tree they appear.

Example 10-26 *Simple XPath Expression with an "anywhere" Selection*

```
Path:   //customer
Result: NPF_cust1
```

The end result might be less obvious if you have a list of elements with the same nodes inside, as shown in Example 10-27.

Example 10-27 *Simple XPath Expression with an Absolute Path and Multiple Outputs*

```
Path:   /vpn/sites/site/provider_side/router
Result: DUS-1
        FRA-1
```

The path expression provided doesn't specify any particular element in the list. That's why, if there are multiple elements having the same name in the XML tree, all the results will be provided. To be more specific, you can use predicates. Example 10-28 illustrates such an approach.

Example 10-28 *XPath Expression with a Predicate*

```
Path:   /vpn/sites/site[1]/provider_side/router
Result: DUS-1
```

According to the XML standard, the numbering of the elements starts with the index 1 (which is very different from Bash or Python). Therefore, the predicate [1] applied to the node site in the XPath expression indicates that the first site element is chosen from the list. However, filtering based on the element's position is not a very clean solution, as you need to know the indexing details. To overcome this, you can base the element's choice on an attribute, as shown in Example 10-29.

Example 10-29 *XPath Expression with a Predicate and an Attribute*

```
Path:   /vpn/sites/site[@id="2"]/provider_side/router
Result: FRA-1
```

In the path provided inside the predicate, the attribute search is used. Per Table 10-4, the attribute's search starts with @ followed by the name of the attribute's logical operator and the value that the attribute is compared against. The logical operator may be any of the expressions listed in Table 10-5.

Table 10-5 *XPath Logical Operator Values*

Operator	Description
=	The values are equal. This operator works for both textual and numeric data.
!=	The values are not equal. This operator works for both textual and numeric data.
>	The attribute's value is more than the value it is compared to.
<	The attribute's value is less than the value it is compared to.

You can also combine the different methods to define a path. Example 10-30 shows how you can get information about all the routers in the network.

Example 10-30 *XPath Expression with Two Methods of Path Definition*

```
Path:   /vpn/sites//router
Result: DUS-1
        CUST-DUS-1
        FRA-1
        CUST-FRA-2
```

So far you have learned how you can navigate an XML document by using XPath for flexible information choice. You will learn more about XPath later in this chapter, in examples of working with Python.

XML Stylesheet Language Transformations (XSLT)

Recall that XML is a language you can use to create data structures. However, sometimes you might need to create a sort of custom XML file based on another file or even based on multiple XML files. You can achieve this by using XSLT. XSLT is a language used to create other documents (for example, HTML, XML) based on XML input. XSLT relies heavily on XPath to collect relevant data.

The following are some of the main elements of XSLT:

- **<template>**: This element is used to create a template that transforms the initial XML document into a new format.
- **<value-of>**: This element points to a particular piece of information in the original XML document by using XPath.
- **<for-each>**: This element creates a loop over a certain set of the objects (for example, a list) and uses XPath to address it.
- **<if>**: This element settles a condition which implies that the child's elements will work only if the condition is true.

The best way to show the application of XSLT is with an example. Example 10-31 shows a basic XSLT stylesheet.

Example 10-31 *XSLT Stylesheet*

```
<?xml version="1.0" encoding="UTF-8"?>
<xsl:stylesheet version="1.0" xmlns:xsl="http://www.w3.org/1999/XSL/Transform">
  <xsl:template match="/">
    <html>
      <body>
```

```
        <table>
          <tr>
            <th>Customer</th>
            <th>Contact</th>
          </tr>
          <xsl:for-each select="vpn">
            <tr>
              <td><xsl:value-of select="customer"/></td>
              <td><xsl:value-of select="contact"/></td>
            </tr>
          </xsl:for-each>
        </table>
      </body>
    </html>
  </xsl:template>
</xsl:stylesheet>
```

The first thing you might notice in Example 10-31 is that the document starts with the XML declaration, in much the same way that all other XML documents in this chapter start. Then you see that the root element is <stylesheet>, which is a standard for the XSLT. This element has an attribute assigned that contains the namespace of the XSLT dictionary associated with the prefix xsl. As explained earlier in this chapter, this prefix prepends all the elements associated with this namespace.

The element <xsl:template> defines what will be the result of the input XML transformation. It also has the attribute match, which identifies the part of the input document to which the transformation shall be applied. In Example 10-31, the value of the attribute is /, which means the transformation will be applied to the root of the target XML document.

Inside the <xsl:template> element is a mix of HTML tags (as this template generates an HTML document) and the XSLT elements described earlier in this document. Each of the XSLT elements has the attribute select, which contains the XPath element to certain data in the target XML document.

The exact process an application goes through with XSLT transformation is beyond the scope of this chapter, as it might be created in any web framework (for example, PHP, JavaScript). However, based on the transformation of the XML document from Example 10-3, using the XSLT stylesheet from Example 10-31 results in the document shown in Example 10-32.

Example 10-32 *Result of the XSL Transformation*

```
Customer      Contact
NPF_CUST1  info@npf.cust1
```

Processing XML Files with Python

This section provides examples of processing and modifying the XML document from Example 10-3. That XML document is stored in the file input.xml, located in a directory together with the file xml_processing.py, which contains the Python code shown in Example 10-33.

Example 10-33 *Working Folder for a Python Script for XML Processing*

```
$ ls -l
total 16
-rw-r--r--  1 npf_user  npf_user  960 11 Feb 21:19 input.xml
-rwxr-xr-x  1 npf_user  npf_user  244 11 Feb 21:54 xml_processing.py
```

Note Python is covered in detail in Chapters 5, "Python Fundamentals," and 6, "Python Applications," so if you need a refresher on working with Python modules and functions, refer to those chapters.

There is a module in a standard Python 3.x package used for XML processing called **xml.etree.ElementTree.** According to the official documentation at https://docs.python.org, this module implements a simple and efficient API for parsing and creating XML data. Using this module, you can create an object by parsing the XML file read from certain paths, as shown in Example 10-34.

Example 10-34 *Creating a Python Script for XML Processing*

```
$ cat xml_processing.py
#!/usr/bin/env python

# Modules
import xml.etree.ElementTree as ET

# Body
tree = ET.parse('input.xml')
root = tree.getroot()
```

In Example 10-34 the **xml.etree.ElementTree** module for XML processing is imported in the Python script (under the name ET to simplify its usage later in the code). Next, the object **tree** is created using the method **parse** of the **ET** module from the file **input.xml.** After that, the object **root** is created from the **tree** using the **getroot** method of the element's object. The **root** object contains the whole tree from the XML document, which can be used in various shapes or forms using further methods or properties of this module. Table 10-6 highlights the most important of these methods or properties for your reference.

Table 10-6 *xml.etree.ElementTree Properties and Methods*

Property/Method	Description
tag property	Returns the name of an XML element
text property	Returns the value of a certain XML element
attrib property	Returns the attributes associated with a certain XML element
getroot() method	Returns the data tree starting from the root element of the XML document
findall() method	Returns the list of the objects associated with a certain path, provided in XPath format
find() method	Returns the first matched object associated with a certain path, provided in XPath format
get() method	Returns the value of an attribute associated with a certain XML element
set() method	Modifies an attribute's value associated with a certain XML element
append() method	Adds a sub-element at the end of the existing XML document
write() method	Saves the Python object with the XML data into a file

Let's look at an example that demonstrates how to read data from the XML document and modify it. The first operation is to get the data, as shown in Example 10-35.

Example 10-35 *Extracting Element Names and Attributes from an XML Element (Python Code and Code Execution)*

```
$ cat xml_processing.py
#!/usr/bin/env python

# Modules
import xml.etree.ElementTree as ET

# Body
tree = ET.parse('input.xml')
root = tree.getroot()

print('Building catalog for {} services:'.format(root.tag))

for site_entry in root.findall('.//sites/'):
    site_id = site_entry.get('id')

    print('{} {}'.format(site_entry.tag, site_id))


$ ./xml_processing.py
Building catalog for vpn services:
site 1
site 2
```

In Example 10-35, you can see that the Python code generates some text that includes information from the initial XML document. The first **print()** function has simple input consisting of fixed text and the name of the root element provided by the **tag** property of the **root** object.

The next part of the code is a **for** loop. Based on the information provided in Table 10-6, you know that the method **findall()** returns a list of the sub-elements on the provided XPath. The XPath in this case is **.//sites/**, which refers to the child objects of the parent element **<sites>**, which can be located anywhere in the root tree. If you examine the original XML document from Example 10-3, you might find that there are two **<site>** elements, which are siblings to each other. By using the **get()** method to search for the value of the **id** attribute, this value is extracted and assigned to the variable **site_id.** The function **print()** within the loop prints this **site_id** value together with the name of top-most tag of this sub-element returned using the **tag** property of the **site_entry** object.

Example 10-36 shows how to extract the values of the elements using Python.

Example 10-36 *Extracting Values from an XML Element*

```
$ cat xml_processing.py
#!/usr/bin/env python

# Modules
import xml.etree.ElementTree as ET

# Body
tree = ET.parse('input.xml')
root = tree.getroot()

print('Building catalog for {} services:'.format(root.tag))

for site_entry in root.findall('.//sites/'):
    site_id = site_entry.get('id')

    print('{} {}'.format(site_entry.tag, site_id))

    router_a = site_entry.find('./provider_side/router').text
    port_a = site_entry.find('./provider_side/port').text
    router_b = site_entry.find('./customer_side/router').text
    port_b = site_entry.find('./customer_side/port').text

    print('Connectivity: {} // {} <---> {} // {}'.format(router_a, port_a,
  router_b, port_b))

$ ./xml_processing.py
Building catalog for vpn services:
site 1
Connectivity: DUS-1 // Gig1/1/1 <---> CUST-DUS-1 // xe-0/0/1
site 2
Connectivity: FRA-1 // 1/1/2 <---> CUST-FRA-1 // Ethernet1
```

To get the element's value, you call the **text** property of the object. In Example 10-36, you can see that the object is a sub-element created using the **find()** method with the associated XPath. In contrast to **findall()**, which returns a list regardless of the number of entries in the list, the **find()** method always returns a single object. When you know that an element doesn't have any further children, you can safely use **find()** to collect end values. Then you can use the **text** property to get a particular value.

When the script in Example 10-36 is executed, the relevant values are collected. The report that is generated shows how the network elements are connected to each other, based on information from the XML document used.

At this point, you have learned about all the major cases and how to extract data from an XML document. The only topic left to cover is modification of an XML document.

To provide some useful context, say that you need to add to an XML document some information about a third site. There are multiple ways to provide the information about the new site. For instance, in Example 10-37, the data about the new site is provided as a Python dictionary.

Example 10-37 *A Python Dictionary with Information About a New Site*

```
$ cat xml_modification.py
#!/usr/bin/env python

# Modules
import xml.etree.ElementTree as ET

# Variables
site_data = {
                "3": {
                    "provider_side": {
                        "router": "BLN-1",
                        "port": "swp1",
                        "ipv4": "10.0.0.8/30",
                        "ipv6": "fc00::10:0:0:8/126"
                    },
                    "customer_side": {
                        "router": "CUST-BLN-1",
                        "port": "Gig1",
                        "ipv4": "10.0.0.9/30",
                        "ipv6": "fc00::10:0:0:9/126"
                    }
                }
            }

# Body
```

Note For this example, the new file xml_modification.py is created in the same folder where the previous script is located.

To create the XML element, you can use two new functions of the **ET** module: **Element()** and **SubElement()**. **Element()** creates the root XML object, and **SubElement()** adds the child's element to the parent. Example 10-38 demonstrates the process of generating the XML element out of the Python dictionary.

Example 10-38 *Converting a Python Dictionary to an XML Element*

```
$ cat xml_modification.py
#!/usr/bin/env python

# Modules
import xml.etree.ElementTree as ET

# Variables
site_data = {
                "3": {
                    "provider_side": {
                        "router": "BLN-1",
                        "port": "swp1",
                        "ipv4": "10.0.0.8/30",
                        "ipv6": "fc00::10:0:0:8/126"
                    },
                    "customer_side": {
                        "router": "CUST-BLN-1",
                        "port": "Gig1",
                        "ipv4": "10.0.0.9/30",
                        "ipv6": "fc00::10:0:0:9/126"
                    }
                }
            }

# Body
for l1_key, l1_var in site_data.items():
    XML_element_L1 = ET.Element('site')
    XML_element_L1.set('id', l1_key)

    for l2_key, l2_var in l1_var.items():
        XML_element_L2 = ET.SubElement(XML_elemnt_L1, l2_key)
```

```
        for l3_key, l3_var in l2_var.items():
            XML_element_L3 = ET.SubElement(XML_elemnt_L2, l3_key)
            XML_element_L3.text = l3_var

ET.dump(XML_element_L1)


./xml_modification.py
<site id="3"><provider_side><router>BLN-1</router><port>swp1</port>
  <ipv4>10.0.0.8/30</ipv4><ipv6>fc00::10:0:0:8/126</ipv6></provider_side>
  <customer_side><router>CUST-BLN-1</router><port>Gig1</port><ipv4>10.0.0.9/30
  </ipv4><ipv6>fc00::10:0:0:9/126</ipv6></customer_side></site>
```

The conversion of the Python dictionary to the XML element is done in a bunch of nested **for** loops created over the Python dictionary using the **items()** function. Thanks to this function, you don't need to think about the elements' names during the script creation; rather, you can offload this logic to the dictionary itself, as the dictionary key names and values are used to create both the XML element tags and values.

Then, within the loops, you can see that an XML element (root) is created using the **XML_element_L1** variable, which is the result of the **ET.Element()** function's execution. The root element tag is **site**. Then, using the **set()** method, you can set the attribute to any element.

All the XML elements nested under the root element are added using the **ET.SubElement()** function, which has two arguments for input: the name of the parent's element (e.g., **XML_elem_L2**) and the name of the element to be created (e.g., **l2_key**). Finally, to add the value to any XML element, you need to add it to the property **text** of the XML object.

All software development, including XML creation, requires careful debugging. The **ET** module has the function **dump()**, which allows you to print the output of a whole XML element, including all the levels of the hierarchy. The input to the function is, logically, the XML element itself. Therefore, the outcome of the **xml_modification.py** execution is a printed XML document.

The final stage of this journey involves integrating the created XML element into the original XML element that contains all the sites. Example 10-39 shows the full script for this final task.

Example 10-39 *Adding One XML Element to Another*

```
$ cat xml_modification.py
#!/usr/bin/env python
#
# THE OUTPUT IS TRUNCATED FOR BREVITY
#
```

```
# Body
for l1_key, l1_var in site_data.items():
    XML_element_L1 = ET.Element('site')
    XML_element_L1.set('id', l1_key)

    for l2_key, l2_var in l1_var.items():
        XML_element_L2 = ET.SubElement(XML_element_L1, l2_key)

        for l3_key, l3_var in l2_var.items():
            XML_element_L3 = ET.SubElement(XML_element_L2, l3_key)
            XML_element_L3.text = l3_var

tree = ET.parse('input.xml')
root = tree.getroot()

print('Adding elements to {} services:'.format(root.tag))

root.find('.//sites').append(XML_element_L1)
tree.write('output.xml')


$./xml_modification.py
```

Example 10-39 shows how to add one of the XML elements to another by using the **append()** method, with the new XML element provided as an input to this method and the method itself applied to the original XML element. If you need to add the new XML element to a specific path of the original element, you can do so by using the **find()** method with the appropriate XPath, as shown in Example 10-39.

After the element is modified, you can either verify it by using the **ET.dump()** function or save it to another file by using the **write()** method. Example 10-39 uses the latter approach, so you don't see anything in the console output when the Python script executes.

If you verify the file output.xml that is generated by this script, you see the output shown in Example 10-40.

Example 10-40 *The XML Element After a Merger with Another One*

```
$ cat output.xml
<vpn>
  <customer>NPF_cust1</customer>
  <contact>info@npf.cust1</contact>
  <sites>
```

```
    <site id="1">
      <provider_side>
        <router>DUS-1</router>
        <port>Gig1/1/1</port>
        <ipv4>10.0.0.1/30</ipv4>
        <ipv6>fc00::10:0:0:1/126</ipv6>
      </provider_side>
      <customer_side>
        <router>CUST-DUS-1</router>
        <port>xe-0/0/1</port>
        <ipv4>10.0.0.2/30</ipv4>
        <ipv6>fc00::10:0:0:2/126</ipv6>
      </customer_side>
      <enabled />
    </site>
    <site id="2">
      <provider_side>
        <router>FRA-1</router>
        <port>1/1/2</port>
        <ipv4>10.0.0.5/30</ipv4>
        <ipv6>fc00::10:0:0:5/126</ipv6>
      </provider_side>
      <customer_side>
        <router>CUST-FRA-1</router>
        <port>Ethernet1</port>
        <ipv4>10.0.0.6/30</ipv4>
        <ipv6>fc00::10:0:0:6/126</ipv6>
      </customer_side>
      <enabled />
    </site>
  <site id="3"><provider_side><router>BLN-
  1</router><port>swp1</port><ipv4>10.0.0.8/30</ipv4><ipv6>fc00::10:0:0:8/126
  </ipv6></provider_side><customer_side><router>CUST-BLN-1</router><port>Gig1
  </port><ipv4>10.0.0.9/30</ipv4><ipv6>fc00::10:0:0:9/126</ipv6></customer_side>
  </site></sites>
</vpn>
```

The indentations in Example 10-40 do not look quite right, but the opening and closing tags are correct, and you can see that the new element **<site id="3">** has been added exactly where it should be: right after closing of the previous **</site>** sibling. From an XML processing point of view, the XML document is generated correctly.

To verify the document, you can run the script from Example 10-36 but change the input XML file from input.xml to output.xml, as shown in Example 10-41.

Example 10-41 *Rerunning XML Processing for the Updated XML Document*

```
$ cat xml_processing.py
!
! OUTPUT IS TRUNCATED FOR BREVITY
!
tree = ET.parse('input.xml')
! FURTHER OUTPUT IS TRUNCATED FOR BREVITY
!



$ ./xml_processing.py
Building catalog for vpn services:
site 1
Connectivity: DUS-1 // Gig1/1/1 <---> CUST-DUS-1 // xe-0/0/1
site 2
Connectivity: FRA-1 // 1/1/2 <---> CUST-FRA-1 // Ethernet1
site 3
Connectivity: BLN-1 // swp1 <---> CUST-BLN-1 // Gig1
```

The output of the XML processing for the newly created site is consistent with the previous elements, which confirms that the XML modification was successful.

Summary

This chapter covers the following points:

- XML is a markup language for creating data structures, and it was the first widely used language created for this purpose.
- Generally, in contrast to HTML, XML has an arbitrary syntax, meaning that there are no predefined names for the tags.
- XML has some strict rules, such as sequencing of the opening/closing tags and beginning a document with an XML declaration.
- XML has additional (optional) metadata in the form of attributes associated with the XML elements' tags.
- XML doesn't include information about the data type inside the XML messages, so additional mechanisms are required to verify its validity.
- XML validation techniques are based on DTDs and XSD schemas.
- XSD is more flexible than DTD, and it is written in XML.

- An XML namespace provides a mapping between an XML document and an XSD file.
- To address a specific part of an XML document, you can use special links based on XPath addresses.
- XSLT can transform an initial XML document into any other document, including another XML document, an HTML document, or a document of any other format.
- The Python library **xml.etree.ElementTree** allows you to deal with XML elements, including parsing an XML document, extracting the data from the document, modifying an element, and saving elements.

Chapter 11

JSON

This chapter covers the encoding format JavaScript Object Notation (JSON). Much like XML, JSON is used to encode the messages of network programmability protocols. Whereas NETCONF supports only XML, RESTCONF and gRPC both support JSON. JSON is newer than XML. Whereas XML was primarily developed for machine-to-machine communications, JSON was developed to be human readable. JSON therefore tends to be the more popular choice for encoding when specific XML features are not required.

This chapter also covers one of the applications of JSON: JSON Schema Definition (JSD). JSD is used to construct schemas, or data models, and can be used either independently or in conjunction with YANG (which is covered in detail in Chapter 13, "YANG").

JavaScript Object Notation (JSON)

A number of RFCs define JSON, but the main one is RFC 8259, "The JavaScript Object Notation (JSON) Data Interchange Format." This RFC provides an accurate and straightforward description of what JSON is. According to this RFC, JSON is a "lightweight, text-based, language-independent data interchange format." These three characteristics all contribute to the success of the JSON:

- **Lightweight:** The structure of JSON is straightforward, and it is easy to start using JSON.
- **Text based:** You can create data in the JSON format by using any kind of text editor, as it doesn't require any specific software or application.
- **Language independent:** The vast majority of programming and scripting languages today support data in the JSON format. This is particularly important because it allows applications written in different languages to easily interoperate with each other.

Due to its capabilities, JSON is now one of the most critical and widely used data formats. For example, JSON is the number-one data structure format for managing applications through REST APIs and in RESTCONF as well, as it has a very logical and straightforward structure. Example 11-1 provides an example.

Example 11-1 *JSON Data Example*

```
{
  "book_title": "Network Programmability and Automation, Volume I",
  "publisher": "Cisco Press",
  "pages": 1232,
  "authors": ["Jeff Doyle" , "Khaled Abuelenain", "Ahmed Elbornou", "Anton
  Karneliuk"]
}
```

Example 11-1 provides a brief description of this book in JSON format. This data is easily readable and can be processed by any application (for example, Ansible) or programming language (for example, Python). The following pages describe the JSON data format.

JSON Data Format and Data Types

As already mentioned in this chapter, JSON is a data format that shows how data is stored and represented. Each JSON object is a set of key/value pairs that contains information relevant to a particular application. Example 11-2 shows a simple JSON object with a single key/value pair.

Example 11-2 *A Simple JSON Object*

```
{
  "book_title": "Network Programmability and Automation, Volume I"
}
```

A JSON object is always framed with the symbol { at the beginning and the symbol } at the end. All the key/value pairs are contained within this framing. Example 11-2 shows a single pair, where "book_title" is a key, and "Network Programmability and Automation, Volume I" is the value.

When a JSON object contains more entries than a single key/value pair, the entries are divided by commas, as illustrated in Example 11-3. The comma separator is essential because the absence of the comma triggers errors in all the applications, which means the data isn't processed.

Example 11-3 *Multiple Key/Pair Values Inside a JSON Object*

```
{
  "book_title": "Network Programmability and Automation, Volume I",
  "pages": 1232
}
```

As you can see in the examples shown so far, the key is always framed with quotation marks. However, the value isn't always framed with quotation marks; whether it is depends on the type of the value. Table 11-1 lists the six data types defined within JSON.

Table 11-1 *The JSON Data Types*

Type	Description	Example
String	Any textual data, which is processed as a string.	"some value"
Number	Any numeric data in decimal format, including all math actions.	123
Boolean	Boolean data with just two possible values: true or false.	true/false
Null	An empty value that is used when you need to have a key even if there is no value associated.	null
Object	A value for a key that is framed with { } symbols.	{"a": "b"}
Array	A value for a key that is a list containing entries in any other format. The elements of an array are separated by commas and are framed with [ ] symbols.	["c", 12, true, {"e": "f"}]

You can see in Table 11-1 that four of the basic data types provide a single value to a key. The other two data types contain more than a single value and, if necessary, make it possible to create a complex hierarchical data structure.

Example 11-4 puts all the JSON data types in context so that you can better understand them.

Example 11-4 *Using All the JSON Data Types Together*

```
{
  "book_title": "Network Programmability and Automation, Volume I",
  "publisher": "Cisco Press",
  "pages": 1232,
  "published": false,
  "release_date": null,
  "authors": ["Jeff Doyle", "Khaled Abuelenain", "Ahmed Elbornou", "Anton
  Karneliuk"],
  "sample_content": {
    "introduction": "This is an awesome book about network programmability and
  automation!",
    "chapters": [
      {
        "name": "Chapter 1",
        "description": "The Network Programmability and Automation Ecosystem"
      },
```

```
      {
        "name": "Chapter 2",
        "description": "Linux Fundamentals"
      }
    ]
  }
}
```

In the snippet shown in Example 11-4, you can see all the data types together:

- **"book_title" and "publisher":** String data type framed in quotation marks
- **"pages":** Number data type provided as just a number without quotation marks
- **"published":** Boolean data type
- **"release_date":** Null data type (because the release data isn't yet available at the time of writing)
- **"authors":** Array (or list) data type that contains the values in string data format
- **"sample_content":** JSON object nested as a value
- **"introduction" under "sample_content":** Ordinary key/value with string format
- **"chapters" under "sample_content":** Array (or list) data type that contains JSON objects as elements

As long as you follow the rules of the JSON notation, there are no boundaries in terms of how you structure your data aside from those that might be imposed by the application you are dealing with.

Note The quotation marks in the framing value are significant, and you need to be very careful with them. For example, the value **10** is a numeric data, and you can apply all math operations to it; on the other hand, **"10"** is a string value, and the rules of string processing are applied to it. Booleans and strings also require careful attention to quotation marks, as the value **true** is a Boolean type and isn't equal to **"true"**, which is a string type. The same rule applies to **null** and **"null"**. When you have a series of operations for data processing, it's particularly important to get the quotation marks right in order to get the proper result.

This short section provides all the information you need to know about the JSON data structure and types. JSON is very popular today due to the simplicity and flexibility you have already seen.

JSON Schema Definition (JSD)

Now that you know what the JSON data format is and how you can use it, the next step is to understand one of the immediate applications of JSON: JSON Schema Definition (JSD). As you will learn soon, the YANG language provides almost endless possibilities for creating data models that can be used anywhere, including in network programming. On the other hand, YANG format isn't used for representation or transmission of the actual data. There are specific reasons for that, as you are about to learn.

One of the reasons YANG format isn't used for representation or transmission of data is that presenting real information in YANG format takes a lot of space. A YANG module (or model) provides a detailed definition of all the data types used, their parameters, and so on. If both the transmitter and receiver of the information have the same YANG modules, it isn't necessary to provide all the information about data types within the message itself as doing so would be excessive. It's enough to send only the key/value pairs, which are checked for compliance using the YANG-based dictionary on the receiver side. If JSON format is used to convey those key/value pairs between applications, the JSON schema compiled from YANG modules is a perfect candidate for that "something." Using YANG directly also saves you the effort of converting data from JSON to YANG.

Based on the factors just described, YANG is used to construct data models but not to represent the real information transmitted between different network functions or applications. For such a task, other ways of representing data are used: mainly JSON schemas (covered in this chapter) and XML schemas (covered in Chapter 10, "XML"). JSON schemas and XML schemas are equally important; whereas JSON data representation is used in RESTCONF protocols, XML data representation is used in NETCONF protocols.

Earlier in this chapter, you learned about the JSON language in general, including its components and how data is represented. In this section, you will learn how JSON schemas are structured and how to create schemas from YANG modules.

Structure of the JSON Schema

The JSON schema is a representation of a data model in a specific format encoded in JSON. Currently, it exists as an IETF draft (although it is already in its seventh version) titled "JSON Schema: A Media Type for Describing JSON Documents." Because it is a draft, as the draft progresses toward becoming an RFC, some changes might be made compared to what you read in this section.

The core idea of the JSON schema is to create a clear understanding of data that is transmitted/received in JSON format. The JSON schema tries to answer questions such as these:

- What specification does the schema follow?
- What should be contained in the data model?
- What key/value pairs are mandatory? What key/value pairs are not mandatory?

- What is the data type for a specific value?
- Is the value in the allowed range?

The YANG modules seek to answer the same questions, but JSON mainly focuses on data representation.

To give you a better understanding of how the JSON schema is structured, this section focuses on building one JSON schema, step by step. For this example, say that you need to create a JSON schema for customer IP VPN service. This schema will be used by an SDN controller; because the schema is created for learning purposes, it is not directly implemented in any commercial product. Example 11-5 provides a starting point for this schema.

Example 11-5 *Basic JSON Schema Without Content*

```
{
  "$schema": "http://json-schema.org/draft-07/schema#",
  "$id": "http://network.vendor/ip-vpn.schema.json",
  "title": "IP-VPN",
  "description": "This is an arbitrary example to show you structure of the JSON
  schema based on example of IP VPN service, how it can be implemented in SDN
  controller",
  "type": "object"
}
```

There are three types of data in Example 11-5:

- **Schema keywords:** A schema keyword starts with the symbol **$**. In Example 11-5, there are two such keywords: **"$schema"** tells JSON which version of the JSON schema should be used for validation. At the time of writing, the current version of the JSON schema is draft-handrews-json-schema-02, and this is the path that is encoded. The second schema keyword is **"$id"**, and it contains the URI for the schema.
- **Schema annotation:** The schema annotation is information attached to the schema for application use. As you have already seen, the schema keywords provide some important values that any application using this JSON schema needs (that is, which JSON schema version to use and what the URI looks like), but there is no information about any content of the schema in the schema keywords. Annotations provide such information. In Example 11-5, **"title"** and **"description"** are schema annotations. Annotations are not mandatory, as they don't take part in the validation. However, using them is a good practice, and it is recommended that you use them.
- **Validation keywords:** The validation keywords add constraints (such as what data type should be used) to the schema that are used later on for the validation process. The **"type"** keyword could potentially be any JSON data type. However, the most widely used data type is the object data type. In Example 11-5, the keyword

"object", which is the value of the key **"type"**, indicates that the schema is used for validation of JSON objects.

Now we are ready to talk about what is needed to configure the IP VPN for the customer. IP VPNs are popular types of VPN services deployed in the Service Providers, which provide IP-based connectivity between a customer's router and an MPLS-based network. Example 11-6 extends the initial JSON schema with some new content for the IP VPN.

Example 11-6 *Properties in the JSON Schema*

```
{
  "$schema": "http://json-schema.org/draft-07/schema#",
  "$id": "http://network.vendor/ip-vpn.schema.json",
  "title": "IP-VPN",
  "description": "This is an arbitrary example to show you structure of the JSON
  schema based on example of IP VPN service, how it can be realized in SDN
  controller",
  "type": "object",
  "properties": {
    "ContractId": {
      "description": "This field contains customer contract ID to track customer
  services within configuration",
      "type": "integer",
      "exclusiveMinimum": 0
    },
    "CustomerName": {
      "description": "This field contains the customer name to add meta information
  to configuration, where applicable",
      "type": "string"
    },
    "CustomerContact": {
      "description": "This field contains e-mail address of the customer, which is
  used for any communication",
      "type": "string"
    },
    "Tags": {
      "description": "This field contains tags associated with the customer",
      "type": "array",
      "items": {
        "type": "string"
      }
    }
  },
  "required": [ "ContractId", "CustomerName", "CustomerContact" ]
}
```

As you can see, Example 11-6 includes new entries in the JSON schema. The key **"properties"** is called a *validation keyword* because it contains information about the content of expected JSON objects; you can think about it as a RESTCONF message received by an SDN controller. Inside **"properties"** are a variety of keys, each of which is accompanied by the schema annotation **"description"** and the validation keyword **"type"**. As discussed earlier in this chapter, there are six data types available in JSON, and the field **"type"** uses some of those types: a string, an integer, and an array. For the key **"ContractId"**, there is an additional validation keyword, **"exclusiveMinimum"**, which imposes constraints so that the value of this key can't be zero. You can find the full list of all the validation keywords in the JSON IETF draft: https://tools.ietf.org/html/draft-handrews-json-schema-validation-01.

Note SDN controllers are discussed in further detail in Chapter 16, "Service Provider Programmability." For now, you can think of an SDN controller as an application that manages your network functions.

At the end of the schema is a new validation keyword, **"required"**, which contains an array of strings with the names of the keys. These keys are mandatory, which means these values must be present in the received JSON object, or the validation won't be successful. As you can see, not all the keys are listed with **"required"**. It is possible to have additional information that might or might not be presented in the JSON object.

Repetitive Objects in the JSON Schema

The JSON schema in our example is being slowly filled in with application-oriented data, and by now you should be familiar with the basics. However, there is not yet any information about the technical details associated with the IP VPN service for which you are building the JSON schema. The next step is to create information about endpoints where the customer IP VPN service is terminated. Example 11-7 shows this information.

Example 11-7 *Definitions in the JSON Schema*

```
{
  "$schema": "http://json-schema.org/draft-07/schema#",
  "$id": "http://network.vendor/ip-vpn.schema.json",
  "title": "IP-VPN",
  "description": "This is an arbitrary example to show you structure of the JSON
  schema based on example of IP VPN service, how it can be realized in SDN
  controller",
  "type": "object",
  "properties": {
    "ContractId": {
      "description": "This field contains customer contract ID to track customer
  services within configuration",
```

```
    "type": "integer",
    "exclusiveMinimum": 0
  },
  "CustomerName": {
    "description": "This field contains the customer name to add meta information
to configuration, where applicable",
    "type": "string"
  },
  "CustomerContact": {
    "description": "This field contains e-mail address of the customer, which is
used for any communication",
    "type": "string"
  },
  "Tags": {
    "description": "This field contains tags associated with the customer",
    "type": "array",
    "items": {
      "type": "string"
    }
  },
  "VPNSites": {
    "description": "This array contains objects describing VPN endpoints for the
customer service",
    "type": "array",
    "items": {
      "$ref": "#/definitions/VPNEndpoint"
    }
  }
},
"required": [ "ContractId", "CustomerName", "CustomerContact", "VPNSites" ],
"definitions": {
  "VPNEndpoint": {
    "description": "This object contains endpoint abstraction for IP VPN service",
    "type": "object",
    "properties": {
      "EndpointHostname": {
        "description": "This field contains hostname of the router, which
terminates VPN for the customer",
        "type": "string"
      },
      "VRF": {
        "description": "This field contains hostname of the router, which
terminates VPN for the customer",
        "type": "object",
```

```
          "properties": {
            "VRFName": {
              "description": "This field contains VRF name",
              "type": "string"
            },
            "RouteDistinguisher": {
              "description": "This field contains route distinguisher associated
with VRF",
              "type": "string",
              "pattern": "^[0-9.:]+$"
            },
            "RouteTargetImport": {
              "description": "This field contains import route target associated
with VRF",
              "type": "string",
              "pattern": "^[0-9.:]+$"
            },
            "RouteTargetExport": {
              "description": "This field contains export route target associated
with VRF",
              "type": "string",
              "pattern": "^[0-9.:]+$"
            }
          },
          "required": [ "VRFName", "RouteDistinguisher", "RouteTargetImport",
"RouteTargetExport" ],
          "additionalProperties": false
        }
      },
      "required": [ "EndpointHostname", "VRF" ],
      "additionalProperties": false
    }
  }
}
```

The updated JSON schema is now more than twice as big as it was in the preceding section.

For **"properties"**, there is a new key, **"VPNSites"**, which is an array of items. However, items aren't described inline but are instead referenced using the schema keyword **"$ref"**. The schema keyword **definitions** is used to store any kind of data that can be reused anywhere in the core part of the JSON schema. This is very practical, especially in complex JSON schemas, where the same objects or properties might be used many times in different places. (The YANG language has a similar concept called *groupings*, as you will learn in Chapter 13.)

Now let's look at the definitions themselves. As you can see, the structure is precisely the same as in the main JSON schema. **"type": "object"** means that this definition is used for the description of a composite JSON object. This object has its own validation keywords, **"properties"** and **"required"**, precisely following the same logic as the master schema. This example uses *nesting*, which means there might be different levels of the parental relationship between different objects.

According to the logic of Example 11-8, the JSON object **"VPNEndpoint"** has further nesting in the form of the object **"VRF"**, which contains relevant BGP-related information on the IP VPN, including the route distinguisher and import/export route targets. If you are familiar with MPLS/BGP services, you know that route distinguishers and route targets have a specific format and limited range of characters: decimal digits, dots, and colons. That's why you see the additional validation keyword **"pattern"**, which contains the corresponding regex (regular expressions). The regular expressions allow you to perform flexible searches. In this example, the regex is designed to match any text string consisting of numbers and the dot (.) and colon (:) characters. Therefore, it would match the strings 65000:1 or 10.1.1.1:100, which are examples of IP VPN attributes in this example.

The last new relevant validation keyword is **"additionalProperties"**, which instructs the schema that no additional parameters besides those defined explicitly in the JSON schema are allowed. If any additional parameters are presented in the JSON message, the validation against the schema will fail.

Now that you know the details related to the updates in the JSON schema are explained, we can combine everything discussed to this point. A **"VPNEndpoint"** object is created in definitions, following the standard rules of the JSON schema, and then it is referenced in the main part of the JSON schema as an item within the array. The rationale behind this is that typically there are many endpoints in the IP VPN service, and they are put in an array.

The primary goal of the JSON schema in this example is to validate that the JSON object has the proper format. Example 11-8 shows the JSON object, which is constructed using the provided schema.

Example 11-8 *JSON Object for the JSON Schema of the IP VPN Service*

```
{
  "ContractId": 1,
  "CustomerName": "ACME Corp",
  "CustomerContact": "admin@acme.com",
  "Tags": [ "Very Important Client" ],
  "VPNSites": [
    {
      "EndpointHostname": "us-la-pe-01",
      "VRF": {
```

```
          "VRFName": "ACME_Corp",
          "RouteDistinguisher": "65000:1",
          "RouteTargetImport": "65000:101",
          "RouteTargetExport": "65000:101"
        }
      },
      {
        "EndpointHostname": "de-fra-pe-01",
        "VRF": {
          "VRFName": "ACME_Corp",
          "RouteDistinguisher": "65000:1",
          "RouteTargetImport": "65000:101",
          "RouteTargetExport": "65000:101"
        }
      }
    ]
}
```

Referencing External JSON Schemas

The JSON object in this example has all the possible entries, even optional tags. The **"VPNSites"** array has two objects, each describing one of the VPN termination routers. The JSON schema for customer IP VPN service is almost complete, with only one major part missing: the user-network interface, where the customer is connected to the provider network. It was intentionally not created in the previous section because the interface configuration does not exist only within the IP VPN configuration context; rather, it's independent of anything else. It is therefore possible to create a separate JSON schema for the network interface and then reference it as an external schema in another JSON schema. Example 11-9 provides an overview of a possible JSON schema for interface configuration.

Example 11-9 *Separate JSON Schema for Interface Configuration*

```
{
  "$schema": "http://json-schema.org/draft-07/schema#",
  "$id": "http://network.vendor/interface.schema.json",
  "title": "Interface",
  "description": "This is an arbitrary example of vendor-agnostic router's interface
  configuration",
  "type": "object",
  "properties": {
    "InterfaceName": {
      "description": "This field contains name of the interface",
```

```
      "type": "string"
    },
    "InterfaceMTU": {
      "description": "This field contains MTU of the interface",
      "type": "integer",
          "minimum": 64,
          "maximum": 9216
    },
    "InterfaceDescription": {
      "description": "This field contains description of the interface",
      "type": "string"
    },
    "InterfaceQoS": {
      "description": "This object contains ingress and egress QoS policies",
      "type": "object",
      "properties": {
        "IngressQoS": {
          "description": "This field contains name of ingress QoS policy",
          "type": "string"
        },
        "EgressQoS": {
          "description": "This field contains name of egress QoS policy",
          "type": "string"
        }
      },
      "additionalProperties": false
    },
    "InterfaceEncapsulation": {
      "description": "This object contains encapsulation relevant parameters",
      "type": "object",
      "oneOf": [
        { "$ref": "#/definitions/EncapsulationNull" },
        { "$ref": "#/definitions/EncapsulationDot1Q" },
        { "$ref": "#/definitions/EncapsulationQinQ" }
      ]
    }
  },
  "required": [ "InterfaceName", "InterfaceEncapsulation", "InterfaceMTU" ],
  "additionalProperties": false,
  "definitions": {
    "EncapsulationNull": {
      "description": "This object stands for null encapsulation",
      "properties": {
```

```
        "EncapsulationType": {
          "enum": [ "null" ]
        }
      },
      "required": [ "EncapsulationType" ],
      "additionalProperties": false
    },
    "EncapsulationDot1Q": {
      "description": "This object stands for dot1Q encapsulation",
      "properties": {
        "EncapsulationType": {
          "enum": [ "dot1q" ]
        },
        "Vlan1": {
          "type": "integer",
          "minimum": 1,
          "maximum": 4096
        }
      },
      "required": [ "EncapsulationType", "Vlan1" ],
      "additionalProperties": false
    },
    "EncapsulationQinQ": {
      "description": "This object stands for dot1Q encapsulation",
      "properties": {
        "EncapsulationType": {
          "enum": [ "qinq" ]
        },
        "Vlan1": {
          "type": "integer",
          "minimum": 1,
          "maximum": 4096
        },
        "Vlan2": {
          "type": "integer",
          "minimum": 1,
          "maximum": 4096
        }
      },
      "required": [ "EncapsulationType", "Vlan1", "Vlan2" ],
      "additionalProperties": false
    }
  }
}
```

This new JSON schema looks quite large, but you are already familiar with most of the keywords and concepts (such as nesting). Therefore, in this section we discuss only the new keywords you haven't already seen.

In Example 11-9, the validation keyword **"oneOf"** validates related objects against one of the entries in its array. If one of the objects matches, then validation is successful. As you can see, all the **"oneOf"** JSON objects in the example have another new validation keyword, **"enum"**, which has an associated value that is an array type. **"enum"** creates in the JSON object a predefined list of values, and only those predefined values can be used. If any other value is used, the validation will fail. Objects don't have to be similar to each other; only one key that has **enum** inside should be the same for all of them. The schema in Example 11-9 shows how convenient this is. **"enum"** is associated with the type of encapsulation, and it is necessary to provide one VLAN (Vlan1) or two VLANs (Vlan1 and Vlan2) tags for IEEE 802.1q or 802.1ad encapsulations, respectively; no additional information needs to be provided where the encapsulation type is null. This is why different JSON objects in definitions have different entries in the **"required"** validation keyword.

In addition to **"oneOf"** and **"enum"**, there are two more new validation keywords used in conjunction with the integer data type: **"minimum"** and **"maximum"**. **"minimum"** performs a greater-than-or-equal-to operation, whereas **"maximum"** performs a less-than-or-equal-to operation.

Example 11-10 shows three different JSON objects, which can be successfully validated against the provided JSON schema.

Example 11-10 *JSON Objects for the JSON Schema of the Interface*

```
{
  "InterfaceName": "GigabitEthernet0/2/0/10",
  "InterfaceDescription": "Customer ACME Corp",
  "InterfaceEncapsulation": {
    "EncapsulationType": "qinq",
    "Vlan1": 15,
    "Vlan2": 10
  },
  "InterfaceQoS": {
    "IngressQoS": "CUST_in",
    "EgressQoS": "CUST_out"
  },
  "InterfaceMTU": 9000
}



{
  "InterfaceName": "GigabitEthernet0/7/0/11",
```

```
  "InterfaceEncapsulation": {
    "EncapsulationType": "dot1q",
    "Vlan1": 1234
  },
  "InterfaceQoS": {
    "IngressQoS": "CUST_in",
    "EgressQoS": "CUST_out"
  },
  "InterfaceMTU": 9000
}



{
  "InterfaceName": "GigabitEthernet0/3/0/5",
  "InterfaceEncapsulation": {
    "EncapsulationType": "null"
  },
  "InterfaceMTU": 1514
}
```

As you see, there are some differences between the templates, based on the fact that non-mandatory fields aren't always included. Also, these examples illustrate how an enumeration works.

After the JSON schema for an interface is prepared, it can be referenced in the initial JSON schema for the IP VPN service. Example 11-11 provides a snippet of the changes needed in the initial JSON schema.

Example 11-11 *JSON Objects for the JSON Schema of the Interface with external reference*

```
! The output is truncated for brevity

            "RouteTargetExport": {
              "description": "This field contains export route target associated
  with VRF",
              "type": "string",
              "pattern": "^[0-9.:]+$"
            }
          },
          "required": [ "VRFName", "RouteDistinguisher", "RouteTargetImport",
  "RouteTargetExport" ],
          "additionalProperties": false
        },
```

```
        "Interfaces": {
          "description": "This object contains configuration of customer
interfaces",
          "type": "array",
          "minItems": 1,
          "uniqueItems": true,
          "items": {
            "$ref": "http://network.vendor/interface.schema.json"
          }
        }
      },
      "required": [ "EndpointHostname", "VRF", "Interfaces" ],
      "additionalProperties": false
    }
  }
}
```

In this example you can see a new key **"Interfaces"** in the schema for the IP VPN service, and it has the type **"array"**. This array consists of objects that are defined by an external JSON schema referenced in the schema keyword **"$ref"**. The value there is equal to the value of the keyword **"$id"** from Example 11-9. There are two more new validation keywords: **"minItems"** tells the schema there should be at least one element in the array present, and **"uniqueItems"** says that the elements must be unique.

Now we have all the pieces of the puzzle for the JSON schema describing the customer VPN. Example 11-12 shows the JSON object that is built using these schemas.

Example 11-12 *JSON Object for the Customer IP VPN Schema, Including an External Reference*

```
{
  "ContractId": 1,
  "CustomerName": "ACME Corp",
  "CustomerContact": "admin@acme.com",
  "Tags": [ "Very Important Client" ],
  "VPNSites": [
    {
      "EndpointHostname": "us-la-pe-01",
      "VRF": {
        "VRFName": "ACME_Corp",
        "RouteDistinguisher": "65000:1",
        "RouteTargetImport": "65000:101",
        "RouteTargetExport": "65000:101"
      },
```

```
    "Interfaces": [
      {
        "InterfaceName": "GigabitEthernet0/2/0/10",
        "InterfaceDescription": "Customer ACME // HQ",
        "InterfaceEncapsulation": {
          "EncapsulationType": "qinq",
          "Vlan1": 1,
          "Vlan2": 10
        },
        "InterfaceQoS": {
          "IngressQoS": "1Gbps_GOLD_in",
          "EgressQoS": "1Gbps_GOLD_out"
        },
        "InterfaceMTU": 9000
      }
    ]
  },
  {
    "EndpointHostname": "de-fra-pe-01",
    "VRF": {
      "VRFName": "ACME_Corp",
      "RouteDistinguisher": "65000:1",
      "RouteTargetImport": "65000:101",
      "RouteTargetExport": "65000:101"
    },
    "Interfaces": [
      {
        "InterfaceName": "GigabitEthernet0/3/0/13",
        "InterfaceDescription": "Customer ACME // BR1",
        "InterfaceEncapsulation": {
          "EncapsulationType": "dot1q",
          "Vlan1": 123
        },
        "InterfaceQoS": {
          "IngressQoS": "500Mbps_GOLD_in",
          "EgressQoS": "500Mbps_GOLD_out"
        },
        "InterfaceMTU": 9000
      },
      {
        "InterfaceName": "GigabitEthernet0/5/0/2",
        "InterfaceDescription": "Customer ACME // BR2",
        "InterfaceEncapsulation": {
```

```
            "EncapsulationType": "null"
          },
          "InterfaceQoS": {
            "IngressQoS": "500Mbps_GOLD_in",
            "EgressQoS": "500Mbps_GOLD_out"
          },
          "InterfaceMTU": 9000
        }
      ]
    }
  ]
}
```

If the underlying IP/MPLS and BGP network is appropriately configured, the information in Example 11-12 is enough to configure the IP VPN for the customer. Later in this chapter, you will learn how such JSON schemas are applied.

Using JSON Schemas for Data Validation

JSON schemas are used in two major cases. The first case is data modeling. The second case arises when some messages in JSON format are transmitted/received between applications, and applications need to validate JSON objects inside messages to check the following:

- Whether JSON objects have an appropriate format
- Whether all mandatory key/value pairs are present
- Whether there are any illegitimate entries

Validation is the process of comparing a JSON object to a JSON schema and determining whether it matches or not. Typically, the validation process should be built into application call flow when the receiver gets a JSON object. Nevertheless, during the development of various applications, such as network automation, it's useful to have some tools to validate the schema to avoid mistakes or typos and also to verify the JSON objects that are created. A variety of tools have been created for this task using different programming languages; many of them are available online.

The team that is working on standardization of JSON schemas for the IETF has a website (http://json-schema.org/implementations.html) that lists all the available realizations of the JSON schema validations. Example 11-13 shows how to install such a package for Python.

Example 11-13 *Installing a Python Package for JSON Schema Validation*

```
$ pip install jsonschema
Collecting jsonschema
  Downloading https://files.pythonhosted.org/packages/77/de/47e35a97b2b05c2fadbec67d
  44cfcdcd09b8086951b331d82de90d2912da/jsonschema-2.6.0-py2.py3-none-any.whl
Installing collected packages: jsonschema
Successfully installed jsonschema-2.6.0
```

Even if you install this tool by using the Python package installer, it, like many other applications written in Python, can work independently in the operating system, and you can use it outside of Python scripts. This tool is quite simple and works in such a way that there is no output if everything is okay, and it returns an error if something is wrong. This section provides examples for interface configuration for the JSON schema shown in Example 11-9. Example 11-14 shows how you prepare for JSON schema validation.

Example 11-14 *Preparing for JSON Schema Validation*

```
$ ls -l
-rw-rw-r--. 1 aaa aaa  303 Oct 28 17:40 acme_interfaces.json
-rw-rw-r--. 1 aaa aaa 2843 Oct 28 18:05 interface.schema.json



$ cat acme_interfaces.json
{
  "InterfaceName": "GigabitEthernet0/2/0/10",
  "InterfaceDescription": "Customer ACME // HQ",
  "InterfaceEncapsulation": {
    "EncapsulationType": "qinq",
    "Vlan1": 172,
    "Vlan2": 10
  },
  "InterfaceQoS": {
    "IngressQoS": "500Mbps_GOLD_in",
    "EgressQoS": "500Mbps_GOLD_out"
  },
  "InterfaceMTU": 9000
}
```

As you can see in Example 11-14, there are two files in the folder: one with the JSON schema and another that is a JSON object that can be transmitted from one application to another. It doesn't contain any mistakes or incorrect entries, so there is no output after validation is conducted, as shown in Example 11-15.

Example 11-15 *Conducting JSON Schema Validation*

```
$ jsonschema -i acme_interfaces.json interface.schema.json
$
```

Now, so you can see the real value in validating JSON objects against a JSON schema, Example 11-16 shows how an object can be modified to provide a value out of range.

Example 11-16 *Providing a Value Out of Range in a JSON Object and Its Validation*

```
$ cat acme_interfaces.json
{
  "InterfaceName": "GigabitEthernet0/2/0/10",
  "InterfaceDescription": "Customer ACME // HQ",
  "InterfaceEncapsulation": {
    "EncapsulationType": "qinq",
    "Vlan1": 172,
    "Vlan2": 10000
  },
  "InterfaceQoS": {
    "IngressQoS": "500Mbps_GOLD_in",
    "EgressQoS": "500Mbps_GOLD_out"
  },
  "InterfaceMTU": 9000
}


$ jsonschema -i acme_interfaces.json interface.schema.json
{'EncapsulationType': 'qinq', 'Vlan1': 172, 'Vlan2': 10000}: {'EncapsulationType':
  'qinq', 'Vlan1': 172, 'Vlan2': 10000} is not valid under any of the given schemas
```

Because VLAN is a 12-bit field, the possible range for VLANs is 1 to 4096. (Hexadecimal values of 0x000 and 0xFFF are reserved.) You saw this constraint imposed using validation keywords in the JSON schema earlier in this chapter. Therefore, when the validation is launched, you see output, which indicates that the provided output doesn't match any schemas.

Example 11-17 shows another case in which there is a typo in one of the keys.

Example 11-17 *A Typo in a Key in a JSON Object and Its Validation*

```
$ cat acme_interfaces.json
{
  "InterfaceName": "GigabitEthernet0/2/0/10",
  "InterfaceDescription": "Customer ACME // HQ",
  "InterfaceEncapsulation": {
```

```
    "EncapsulationType": "qinq",
    "Vlan1": 172,
    "Vlan2": 10
  },
  "InterfaceQoS": {
    "IngressQoS": "500Mbps_GOLD_in",
    "EgressQoS": "500Mbps_GOLD_out"
  },
  "IInterfaceMTU": 9000
}


$ jsonschema -i acme_interfaces.json interface.schema.json
{'InterfaceName': 'GigabitEthernet0/2/0/10', 'InterfaceDescription': 'Customer ACME
  // HQ', 'InterfaceEncapsulation': {'EncapsulationType': 'qinq', 'Vlan1': 172,
  'Vlan2': 10}, 'InterfaceQoS': {'IngressQoS': '500Mbps_GOLD_in', 'EgressQoS':
  '500Mbps_GOLD_out'}, 'IInterfaceMTU': 9000}: 'InterfaceMTU' is a required property
{'InterfaceName': 'GigabitEthernet0/2/0/10', 'InterfaceDescription': 'Customer ACME
  // HQ', 'InterfaceEncapsulation': {'EncapsulationType': 'qinq', 'Vlan1': 172,
  'Vlan2': 10}, 'InterfaceQoS': {'IngressQoS': '500Mbps_GOLD_in', 'EgressQoS':
  '500Mbps_GOLD_out'}, 'IInterfaceMTU': 9000}: Additional properties are not allowed
  ('IInterfaceMTU' was unexpected)
```

The output in Example 11-17 indicates that there are two errors. First, it shows that the required key **"InterfaceMTU"** is missing. Next, it shows that there are no additional parameters allowed, which means the typo in the key is treated as an additional parameter. You can see the same error in Example 11-18, which shows a new key added intentionally.

Example 11-18 *An Unexpected Key in a JSON Object and Its Validation*

```
$ cat acme_interfaces.json
{
  "InterfaceName": "GigabitEthernet0/2/0/10",
  "InterfaceDescription": "Customer ACME // HQ",
  "InterfaceEncapsulation": {
    "EncapsulationType": "qinq",
    "Vlan1": 172,
    "Vlan2": 10
  },
  "InterfaceQoS": {
    "IngressQoS": "500Mbps_GOLD_in",
    "EgressQoS": "500Mbps_GOLD_out"
  },
  "InterfaceMTU": 9000,
```

```
  "SomeStrangeKey": "SomeStrangeValue"
}


$ jsonschema -i acme_interfaces.json interface.schema.json
{'InterfaceName': 'GigabitEthernet0/2/0/10', 'InterfaceDescription': 'Customer ACME
  // HQ', 'InterfaceEncapsulation': {'EncapsulationType': 'qinq', 'Vlan1': 172,
  'Vlan2': 10}, 'InterfaceQoS': {'IngressQoS': '500Mbps_GOLD_in', 'EgressQoS':
  '500Mbps_GOLD_out'}, 'InterfaceMTU': 9000, 'SomeStrangeKey': 'SomeStrangeValue'}:
  Additional properties are not allowed ('SomeStrangeKey' was unexpected)
```

Such behavior isn't the default in a JSON schema. By default, such additional key/pair values are ignored and conveyed to the application. To prevent this behavior, the JSON schema defined in Example 11-9 has the validation keyword **"additionalProperties"** set to **false**.

Example 11-19 shows an error that is caused by using a value that is out of the defined range.

Example 11-19 *Using a Value That Is Out of Range in a JSON Object and Its Validation*

```
$ cat acme_interfaces.json
{
  "InterfaceName": "GigabitEthernet0/2/0/10",
  "InterfaceDescription": "Customer ACME // HQ",
  "InterfaceEncapsulation": {
    "EncapsulationType": "qinq",
    "Vlan1": 172,
    "Vlan2": 10
  },
  "InterfaceQoS": {
    "IngressQoS": "500Mbps_GOLD_in",
    "EgressQoS": "500Mbps_GOLD_out"
  },
  "InterfaceMTU": 90000
}


$ jsonschema -i acme_interfaces.json interface.schema.json
90000: 90000 is greater than the maximum of 9216
```

The error message in Example 11-19 is different from the one in Example 11-16 because in Example 11-16, it is not a single value (**Vlan2**) that is compared to its range but a bundle of parameters (**EncpasulationType**, **Vlan1**, and **Vlan2**). If there is theoretically another **enum** entry, which has another predefined range for VLANs, it will work. In

Example 11-19, it's clearly stated which value is out of range and in which direction (higher than the maximum).

Performing validation ensures that an application receives a consistent set of information in a proper format. Validation of JSON objects against JSON schemas can in some cases protect your application from malicious key/value pairs and increase the security of your objects.

Summary

In this chapter, you have learned about the JSON data format and JSON schemas, how they are built, and where they are used. This chapter covers the following details:

- The simple, powerful, language-independent JSON data format
- JSON's six data types (four primary data types and two nested data types)
- Support for JSON format in current programming and scripting languages
- The importance of paying attention to quotation marks when working with JSON data
- JSON schemas, which are used to provide a structured context for JSON objects
- JSON schemas, which define which key/pair values and in what format should be presented in a JSON object
- Reusing defined data structures called definitions and referencing external JSON schemas
- Nesting objects in a hierarchy
- Validation of JSON objects against JSON schemas to ensure that a receiving application obtains a consistent set of information in proper format

Chapter 12 discusses YAML.

Chapter 12

YAML

YAML Ain't Markup Language (*YAML*) is a user-friendly data serialization language that is useful for engineers working with data and building device configurations. YAML was first proposed in 2001 by Clark Evans. As per the initial draft, YAML was said to stand for "Yet Another Markup Language," but the name was later revised to "YAML Ain't Markup Language." As the name suggests, the creators of YAML didn't want it to become yet another random markup language but wanted to put more emphasis on data representation and human readability of data. YAML uses Unicode printable characters and has minimal structural characters, which means it is easy to use YAML to represent and understand data in a meaningful way. To date, three versions of YAML have been released, the latest of which is Version 1.2. The latest specification of YAML can be found at www.yaml.org. YAML is well supported by modern programming languages such as Python and Java.

Why do we really need another data representation language when there are already well-known data representation formats such as Extensible Markup Language (XML) and JavaScript Object Notation (JSON), which are heavily used in most network and web-based applications? After reading through this chapter and working with YAML you will realize that it is inherently easier to read and write data with YAML. Because of its exceptionally human-readable way of representing data, YAML has become an important language for IT operations and automation tools such as Ansible. Before digging into the fundamentals of YAML, let's examine the key differences between XML, JSON, and YAML:

- **Data representation:** XML is a markup language, whereas JSON and YAML are data formats. XML uses tags to define the elements and stores data in a tree structure, whereas data in JSON is stored like a map with key/value pairs. YAML, on the other hand, allows representation of data both in list or sequence format and in the form of a map with key/value pairs. JSON and YAML uses different indentation styles: JSON uses tabs, whereas YAML uses a hyphen (-) followed by whitespace.

- **Comments:** Comments makes it easier to understand and interpret data. Whereas JSON has no concept of comments, XML allows you to add comments within a document. YAML was designed for readability and thus allows comments.
- **Data types:** XML supports complex data types such as charts, images, and other non-primitive data types. JSON supports only strings, numbers, arrays, Booleans, and objects. YAML, on the other hand, supports complex data types such as dates and time stamps, sequences, nested and recursive values, and primitive data types.
- **Data readability:** It is difficult to read and interpret data written in XML, but it is fairly easy to interpret data in JSON format, and it is much easier to read data in YAML than in JSON format.
- **Usability and purpose:** XML is used for data interchange (that is, when a user wants to exchange data between two applications). JSON is better as a serialization format and is used for serving data to application programming interfaces (APIs). YAML is best suited for configuration.
- **Speed:** XML is bulky and slow in parsing, leading to relatively slow data transmission. JSON files are considerably smaller than XML files, and JSON data is quickly parsed by the JavaScript engine, enabling faster data transmission. YAML, as a superset of JSON, also delivers faster data transmission, but it's important to remember that JSON and YAML are used in different scenarios.

YAML data is stored in a file that has .yaml or .yml file extension. YAML includes important constructs that distinguish the language from the document markup, and thus there are two basic rules to remember when creating a YAML file:

- YAML is case sensitive.
- YAML does not allow the use of tabs. Use spaces instead.

As mentioned earlier, YAML provides support for various programming languages. In this chapter, we focus on using YAML-based files with Python. Later in this chapter, you will see how to use YAML files in Python code. Before we get there, the next section focuses on how different types of data are stored in YAML files.

YAML Structure

YAML allows you to easily and quickly format data in human-readable format. A YAML file begins with three hyphens (---), which separate the directives from the document. A single YAML file can contain multiple YAML documents, each beginning with three hyphens. Similarly, three dots (...) represent the end of a document (but do not start a new one). You can start a new YAML document without closing the previous one. Example 12-1 illustrates the beginning and closing of a document. In the first section of the example, notice that multiple documents are started within the same file, without the previous documents being closed. In the second section of the example, each document is closed before another document is started. Example 12-1 also illustrates the use of comments, which start with the pound sign (#). You can add comments anywhere in a document: at the beginning of the document, between the directives, or even on the same line as directives.

Example 12-1 *Starting and Closing Documents in YAML*

```
# Routing Protocols on a device
---
- OSPF
- EIGRP
- BGP

# Interfaces participating in OSPF
---
- Ethernet1/1     # Connected to Gi0/1 on R11
- Ethernet1/2     # Connected to Gi0/2 on R12
- Ethernet1/3     # Connected to Gi0/3 on R13

# Interfaces participating in EIGRP
---
- Ethernet1/4
- Ethernet1/5
```

```
# Network Events
---
- datetime: 05/17/20202 20:03:00
- event: OSPF Flap
- intf: Ethernet1/1
...
---
- time: 05/18/20202 13:45:07
- event: OSPF Flap
- intf: Ethernet1/3
...
```

YAML represents native data structures using a simple identifier called a *tag*; a single native data structure is called a *node*. Tagged nodes are rooted and connected using directed graphs, and all nodes can be reached from the root node. A node can have content in one of the three formats:

- **Sequence:** An ordered series of zero or mode nodes that may contain the same node more than once or that may even contain itself.
- **Mapping:** An ordered set of key/value node pairs.
- **Scalar:** An opaque datum that can be presented as a series of zero or more Unicode characters.

YAML Sequences and mappings are both categorized as collections. Let's now look at how data can be represented in YAML using these different formats.

Collections

YAML's block collections include sequences and mappings. When you define a block collection, you begin each entry on its own line and use indentation to define the scope of the block. You define a block sequence by beginning an entry with a hyphen (-) followed by whitespace. A mapping is a simple representation of data in key/value pairs, where a key is followed by a colon (:), a space, and then the value. Example 12-2 shows sequences and mappings in YAML.

Example 12-2 *Sequences and Mappings in YAML*

```
# Sequence of Scalars
# This sequence contains the names of nodes in the network
- rtr-R1-ios
- rtr-R2-ios-xr
- rtr-R3-nx-os
```

```
# Mapping scalars to scalars
# Below mapping represents node information such as name, OS and software version
name: rtr-R1-ios
OS: IOS-XE
version: 17.1
```

Note Maps don't have to have string keys. A key in a map can be of type integer, float, or another type. The following is an example of a map with a float key:

```
0.11: a float key
```

Refer to yaml.org for more details.

Keys in a map can also be complex. You can use a question mark (?) followed by a space to represent a complex key; the key can span multiple lines. Example 12-3 illustrates how to create complex key for mapping.

Example 12-3 *Complex Key for Mapping in YAML*

```
# Complex Key
? |
  This is a Complex key
  and span across multiple lines
: this is its value
```

YAML also provides the flexibility to represent one format of data in another format—that is, to perform cross-formatting. For instance, you can define a mapping of sequences or a sequence of mappings, as shown in Example 12-4.

Example 12-4 *Mapping of Sequences and Sequence of Mappings in YAML*

```
# Mapping of Sequences
Nodes:
  - rtr-R1
  - rtr-R2
Intf:
  - GigabitEthernet0/1
  - GigabitEthernet0/2
  - GigabitEthernet0/3
```

```
# Sequence of Mappings
-
  name: rtr-R1
  mgmt-ip: 192.168.1.1
  user: admin
-
  name: rtr-R2
  mgmt-ip: 192.168.1.2
  user: cisco
```

Along with cross-formatting, YAML supports the flow style of data representation. In the flow style, YAML uses explicit indicators instead of using indentation to denote scope. You write a flow sequence inside square brackets as comma-separated values, and you write a flow mapping inside curly braces. Example 12-5 illustrates the representation of data in a flow sequence and in a flow mapping. A flow sequence can also be understood as a sequence of sequences, and a flow mapping can be understood as a mapping of mappings.

Example 12-5 *Flow Sequence and Flow Mapping in YAML*

```
# Flow Sequence
- [node-name, mgmt-ip, user  ]
- [rtr-R1, 192.168.1.1, admin]
- [rtr-R2, 192.168.1.2, cisco]
```

```
# Flow Mapping
rtr-R1: {mgmt-ip: 192.168.1.1, user: admin}
rtr-R2: {
    mgmt-ip: 192.168.1.2,
    user: cisco
  }
```

YAML also allows mapping between sequences using complex keys. However, some parsers may return syntax errors with such mappings. Example 12-6 demonstrates the creation of a mapping between sequences using complex keys. This example shows a sequence of node names that are mapped to management IP addresses.

Example 12-6 *Mapping Between Sequences Using Complex Keys in YAML*

```
# Mapping Between Sequences using Complex Keys
? - rtr-R1
  - rtr-R2
: [192.168.1.1, 192.168.1.2]
```

Because YAML is a superset of JSON, you can create JSON-style maps and sequences in YAML. Example 12-7 shows a JSON-style representation of a sequence and maps in YAML.

Example 12-7 *JSON-Style Sequence and Maps in YAML*

```
# JSON Style Sequence and Maps
json_map: {"key": "value"}
json_seq: [3, 2, 1, "get set go"]
quotes optional: {key: [3, 2, 1, get set go]}
```

Scalars

YAML scalars are either written in literal block or in folded block styles. YAML scalars written in literal block format use the pipe character (|) literal, whereas scalars written in folded block style use the greater-than symbol (>). Literal block style preserves line breaks, and the literal continues until the end of the indentation and the leading indentation is stripped. If there are more indented lines, the following lines use the same indentation rule. Similarly, in a folded block, each line break is folded to a space unless it ends an empty or a more-indented line. For instance, a multiple-line string can be either written as a literal block using | or as a folded block using >, as shown in Example 12-8.

Example 12-8 *Scalars with Literal Block Style and Folded Block Style in YAML*

```
---
literal_block: |
    This entire block of text is the value of 'literal_block' key,
    with line breaks being preserved.

    You can keep adding more lines of text below and maintain the same
    Indentation as above.

         The 'More indented' lines are represented in the following manner -
         In this case, lines following the above line have same indentation.
```

```
---
folded_style: >
 This entire block of text is the value of 'folded_style' key.
 each linebreak is represented by a space.
```

Note It is important to remember that indentation defines the scope of a block.

YAML also include flow scalars, which are represented in plain style or quoted style. The double-quoted style provides escape sequencing, whereas single-quoted style is applicable when escaping is not needed. All flow scalars can span multiple lines. Note that the line breaks are always folded. Example 12-9 illustrates flow scalars using different styles.

Example 12-9 *Flow Scalars in YAML*

```
# Plain style flow scalar
plain:
 This is an unquoted scalar and
 it spans across multiple lines.

# Single quoted scalar
random: 'This is a single quoted text'
str: 'This is not''a # comment''.'

# Double quoted flow scalardouble-quoted: "this is a
 Quoted scalar.\n"
unicode: "The code looks good.\u263A"
```

Tags

YAML tags are used to represent native data structures as well as other data formats, such as sets and ordered maps. In addition, YAML has root nodes as well as nested nodes. The root object or root node, which continues for an entire document, is represented as a map that is equivalent to a dictionary or an object in a different language. When representing numeric data, you generally make use of integer or floating point data types, and such data is represented in the form of integer or floating point tags. Example 12-10 illustrates the representation of integer and floating point tags. Note that the integer tags include integer values, and floating point tags include decimal and exponential values.

Example 12-10 *Integer and Floating Point Tags*

```
# Integer Tags
canonical: 12345
decimal: +12789
```

```
octal: 0o17
hexadecimal: 0xEF
```

```
# Floating Point Tags
canonical: 1.23015e+3
exponential: 12.6415e+02
fixed: 9870.26
negative infinity: -.inf
not a number: .NaN
```

You can represent null, string, and Boolean values in YAML. These fall under the category of miscellaneous tags. Example 12-11 illustrates the representation of such types of data. There are a few points to remember when dealing with Boolean and string data types. A Boolean value cannot be represented as 1 as 1 is interpreted as a number, not a Boolean value. Similarly, string data is not required to be quoted but can be. Note that the null key or value can be used to represent null data being returned by the data source.

Example 12-11 *Miscellaneous Tags*

```
# Miscellaneous Tags
null:
null_value: null
true: y
false: n
booleans: [ true, false ]
string: 'hello world'
```

YAML can also parse some extra types, such as ISO-formatted date and datetime types. Usually it is possible to parse date or datetime only in programming languages or databases, but YAML allows you to represent date- and time-related data by using date and datetime literals. Example 12-12 demonstrates how to use date and datetime literals in YAML. In Example 12-12, notice that date and datetime data are represented in different ways.

Example 12-12 *Date and Datetime YAML Types*

```
---
datetime: 2020-2-15T05:45:23.1Z
datetime_with_spaces: 2019-10-17 00:02:43.10 -5
date: 2020-05-13
```

In YAML, there are also explicit tags and global tags. Explicit tags are denoted using the exclamation point (!) symbol. Explicit tags are used to explicitly represent particular data formats. For instance, the **!binary** explicit tag indicates that a string is actually a Base64-encoded representation of a binary blob. Global tags, on the other hand, are URIs and may be represented using a tag shorthand notation. Example 12-13 illustrates the representation of both explicit and global tags. Note that the primary tag handle is an exclamation point (!) symbol. Thus, the explicit tag for a string is represented in YAML as **!!str**.

Example 12-13 *Explicit and Global Tags in YAML*

```
# Explicit Tags
date-string: !!str 2020-05-10

gif-file: !!binary |
  R0lGODlhDAAMAIQAAP//9/X17unp5WZmZgAAAOfn515eXvPz7Y6OjuDg4J+fn5
  OTk6enp56enmlpaWNjY6Ooj04SEhP/++f/++f/++f/++f/++f/++f/++f/++f/+
  +f/++f/++f/++f/++f/++SH+Dk1hZGUgd2l0aCBHSU1QACwAAAAADAAMAAAFLC
  AgjoEwnuNAFOhpEMTRiggcz4BNJHrv/zCFcLiwMWYNG84BwwEeECcgggoBADs=
```

```
# Global Tags

%TAG ! tag:network.local,8080:
---
!nodes
  # Use the ! handle for presenting
  # tag:network.local,8080:node1
- !node1
 mgmt-ip: 192.168.1.1
 username: admin
 password: cisco
- !node1
 mgmt-ip: 192.168.1.2
 username: admin
 password: cisco!123
```

YAML also supports unordered sets and ordered mappings. A set is represented as a mapping where each key is associated with a null value. Ordered maps are represented as a sequence of mappings, with each mapping having one key. Example 12-14 demonstrates how to define unordered sets and ordered mappings in a YAML file.

Example 12-14 *Unordered Sets and Ordered Mappings in YAML*

```
# Sets
---
!!set
? item1
? item2
? item3
# Sets can also be written without any explicit tag
set1:
  ? item1
```

```
  ? item2
  ? item3
or: {item1, item2, item3}
# Sets are just maps with null values. set1 can also be represented as below
set2:
  item1: null
  item2: null
  item3: null
```

```
# Ordered Maps
# Below map lists the items and its prices
---
!!omap
- item1: 67
- item2: 64
- item3: 51
```

Anchors

Working with repetitive content can be tedious and tiresome, especially when you're dealing with larger data sets and when certain section of data are being repeated multiple times. To overcome such challenges, YAML provides a very handy feature known as *anchors*. An anchor acts as a reference pointer to data already defined once in the document; that reference pointer can be used multiple times later in the YAML configuration files to duplicate the same data. For instance, you can create an anchor for a value of a key and reference that anchor at another place in the document for another key to ensure that the second key has the same values as the first key. An anchor is defined by using an ampersand (&) followed by the anchor name. After the anchor name is defined, it can be referenced at another place by using *aliases*, which are represented by an asterisk (*) followed by the specified anchor name. Example 2-15 illustrates the use of anchors to duplicate the content in a YAML file.

Example 12-15 *Using Anchors in YAML*

```
# Using Anchors
key1: &val1 This is the value of both key1 and key2

key2: *val1
```

Anchors can not only be used for duplicating data but can also be used for duplicating or inheriting properties. This is achieved in YAML by using *merge keys*. A merge key, represented by a double less-than symbol (<<), is used to indicate that all the keys of one or more specified maps will be inserted into the current map. Example 12-16 demonstrates the use of merge keys in YAML.

Example 12-16 *Using Merge Key in YAML*

```
# Merge Key
login: &login
  user: admin
  pass: cisco


node1: &node1
  <<: *login
  mgmt-ip: 192.168.1.1

node: &node2
  <<: *login
  mgmt-ip: 192.168.1.2
```

YAML Example

So far, this chapter has described the fundamentals of YAML and how various YAML data representation techniques are used to represent data in a human-readable format. Now it is time to put your new knowledge into practice and create a YAML file that makes it easier to understand the data. Example 12-17 shows a configuration file for setting up and enabling networking for network devices and virtual cloud servers in a small data center. You could use this configuration with automation tools for one-click deployment of servers in the network. In this example, default credentials are defined for servers as well as network devices such as routers. Then, under the networking node, domain name and domain name server information that is going to be same across the network is specified. Under the networking node are subnodes for routers and host networks, which are then further expanded to various host profiles, such as tenant, management, storage, API, and so on. Each profile represents a specific configuration for that segment of the network. This example also shows a very efficient use of merge keys to duplicate the credentials at different places in the configuration file.

Example 12-17 *YAML Network Configuration Example*

```
SERVER_COMMON: &srvrcred {server_username: root, password: cisco!123}
DEFAULT_CRED: &login
  - user: admin
    password: Cisco@123
  - user: network-admin
    password: Cisco!123

NETWORKING:
  domain_name: cisco.com
  domain_name_servers: [172.16.101.1]
```

```
routers:
- pool: [192.168.1.2 to 192.168.1.253]
  gateway: 192.168.1.1
  <<: *login
host_networks:
- gateway: 192.168.50.1
  pool: [192.168.50.10 to 192.168.50.250]
  segments: [management, provision]
  subnet: 192.168.50.0/24
  vlan_id: 50
  <<: *srvrcred
- gateway: 10.117.0.1
  pool: [10.117.0.5 to 10.117.0.254]
  segments: [tenant]
  subnet: 10.117.0.0/24
  vlan_id: 117
  <<: *srvrcred
- gateway: 10.118.0.1
  pool: [10.118.0.5 to 10.118.0.254]
  segments: [storage]
  subnet: 10.118.0.0/24
  vlan_id: 118
- gateway: 10.35.22.1
  segments: [api]
  subnet: 10.35.22.0/24
  vlan_id: 3522
```

Handling YAML Data Using Python

All data formats are supported by and can be integrated with various programming languages. YAML is a data serialization format designed for better human readability and easy interaction with scripting languages, and it is supported by Python. When dealing with specific format of data, such as XML or JSON, a basic requirement for a library in any programming language is a parser. Python has a YAML parser known as *PyYAML*. PyYAML is a complete YAML parser for YAML Version 1.1 that supports YAML tags and provides Python-specific tags that allow programmers to represent arbitrary Python objects.

Before you can work with the PyYAML package, you need to install PyYAML. Example 12-18 demonstrates the installation of the PyYAML package inside a virtual environment. When the package is installed, you can go to the Python terminal and import the package named yaml. You can use the **dir()** method to find all the properties and methods available for the yaml object. Some of the common methods are highlighted in Example 12-18.

Example 12-18 *Installing PyYAML and Exploring the PyYAML Package*

```
[root@node1 ~]# virtualenv yaml
Using base prefix '/usr'
  No LICENSE.txt / LICENSE found in source
New python executable in /root/yaml/bin/python3
Also creating executable in /root/yaml/bin/python
Installing setuptools, pip, wheel...
done.
[root@node1 ~]# source yaml/bin/activate
(yaml) [root@node1 ~]# pip3 install pyyaml
Collecting pyyaml
  Downloading PyYAML-5.3.1.tar.gz (269 kB)
     |,ñà,ñà,ñà,ñà,ñà,ñà,ñà,ñà,ñà,ñà,ñà,ñà,ñà,ñà,ñà,ñà,ñà,ñà,ñà,ñà,ñà,ñà,ñà,ñà,ñà,
  ñà,ñà,ñà,ñà,ñà,ñà,ñà| 266 kB 10.7 MB/s eta 0:00:
     |,ñà,ñà,ñà,ñà,ñà,ñà,ñà,ñà,ñà,ñà,ñà,ñà,ñà,ñà,ñà,ñà,ñà,ñà,ñà,ñà,ñà,ñà,ñà,ñà,ñà,
  ñà,ñà,ñà,ñà,ñà,ñà,ñà| 269 kB 10.7 MB/s
Building wheels for collected packages: pyyaml
  Building wheel for pyyaml (setup.py) ... done
  Created wheel for pyyaml: filename=PyYAML-5.3.1-cp36-cp36m-linux_x86_64.whl
size=44621 sha256=10808863673407f7436cc15e471caf30cd06fd1462ac9f7f512d3c431ef37509
  Stored in directory: /root/.cache/pip/wheels/e5/9d/ad/2ee53cf262cba1ffd8afe1487eef
788ea3f260b7e6232a80fc
Successfully built pyyaml
Installing collected packages: pyyaml
Successfully installed pyyaml-5.3.1
(yaml) [root@node1 ~]#
[root@node1 demo]# python3
Python 3.7.6 (default, Dec 30 2019, 19:38:28)
[Clang 11.0.0 (clang-1100.0.33.16)] on darwin
Type "help", "copyright", "credits" or "license" for more information.
>>> import yaml
>>> dir(yaml)
['AliasEvent', 'AliasToken', 'AnchorToken', 'BaseDumper', 'BaseLoader',
  'BlockEndToken', 'BlockEntryToken', 'BlockMappingStartToken',
  'BlockSequenceStartToken', 'CollectionEndEvent', 'CollectionNode',
  'CollectionStartEvent', 'DirectiveToken', 'DocumentEndEvent',
  'DocumentEndToken', 'DocumentStartEvent', 'DocumentStartToken', 'Dumper',
  'Event', 'FlowEntryToken', 'FlowMappingEndToken', 'FlowMappingStartToken',
  'FlowSequenceEndToken', 'FlowSequenceStartToken', 'FullLoader', 'KeyToken',
  'Loader', 'MappingEndEvent', 'MappingNode', 'MappingStartEvent', 'Mark',
  'MarkedYAMLError', 'Node', 'NodeEvent', 'SafeDumper', 'SafeLoader', 'ScalarEvent',
  'ScalarNode', 'ScalarToken', 'SequenceEndEvent', 'SequenceNode',
  'SequenceStartEvent', 'StreamEndEvent', 'StreamEndToken', 'StreamStartEvent',
  'StreamStartToken', 'TagToken', 'Token', 'UnsafeLoader', 'ValueToken',
  'YAMLError', 'YAMLLoadWarning', 'YAMLObject', 'YAMLObjectMetaclass',
  '__builtins__', '__cached__', '__doc__', '__file__', '__loader__', '__name__',
  '__package__', '__path__', '__spec__', '__version__', '__with_libyaml__',
  '_warnings_enabled', 'add_constructor', 'add_implicit_resolver',
```

```
'add_multi_constructor', 'add_multi_representer', 'add_path_resolver',
'add_representer', 'compose', 'compose_all', 'composer', 'constructor',
'dump', 'dump_all', 'dumper', 'emit', 'emitter', 'error', 'events', 'full_load',
'full_load_all', 'io', 'load', 'load_all', 'load_warning', 'loader', 'nodes',
'parse', 'parser', 'reader', 'representer', 'resolver', 'safe_dump',
'safe_dump_all', 'safe_load', 'safe_load_all', 'scan', 'scanner', 'serialize',
'serialize_all', 'serializer', 'tokens', 'unsafe_load', 'unsafe_load_all',
'warnings']
```

This section focuses on some of the most common methods from the yaml package that can be used when dealing with YAML data. The first function we look at is the **yaml.dump()** function, which you use to serialize a Python object into a YAML stream. In other words, this function allows you to convert data into a more human-readable format. It produces a YAML document as a UTF-8-encoded **str** object. You can change the encoding by specifying the encoding attribute as a parameter in the **yaml.dump()** function. Example 12-19 demonstrates how to use the **yaml.dump()** method to represent some data about a user in a more readable format. The first section of the example shows some information saved inside a data variable that is in an understandable format; the second section of the example shows that serializing the data into a YAML stream makes the data even easier to understand.

Example 12-19 *Serializing a Python Object into a YAML Stream by Using the yaml.dump() Method*

```
! demo.py
import yaml

data = {
    "Name": "John Doe",
    "Age": 40,
    "Company": "XYZ",
    "Social-media": {"Facebook": "johndoe",
                     "twitter": "johndoe"},
    "Job Title": "Network Automation Engineer",
    "Skills": ["Python", "Nexus", "IOS-XE", "YAML", "JSON"]
}

print(yaml.dump(data))
```

```
[root@node1 demo]# python demo.py
Age: 40
Company: XYZ
Job Title: Network Automation Engineer
Name: John Doe
Skills:
- Python
```

```
- Nexus
- IOS-XE
- YAML
- JSON
Social-media:
  Facebook: johndoe
  twitter: johndoe
```


The **yaml.dump()** method is used to serialize a Python object and also to write the serialized YAML stream into a file. Two parameters are passed in the **yaml.dump()** function: the Python object to be converted in the YAML stream and the file to which the stream will be written (see Example 12-20).

Example 12-20 *Saving a YAML Stream to a File*

```
! demo.py
import yaml

data = {
    "Name": "John Doe",
    "Age": 40,
    "Company": "XYZ",
    "Social-media": {"Facebook": "johndoe",
                     "twitter": "johndoe"},
    "Job Title": "Network Automation Engineer",
    "Skills": ["Python", "Nexus", "IOS-XE", "YAML", "JSON"]
}

with open('test.yaml', 'w') as f:
    yaml.dump(data, f)
```

```
[root@node1 demo]# python3 demo.py
[root@node1 demo]# cat test.yaml
Age: 40
Company: XYZ
Job Title: Network Automation Engineer
Name: John Doe
Skills:
- Python
- Nexus
- IOS-XE
- YAML
- JSON
Social-media:
  Facebook: johndoe
  twitter: johndoe
```

The **yaml.dump()** method also allows you to sort a data stream based on keys. The **sort_keys** attribute, when set to **True**, sorts the keys in the YAML stream; when set to **False**, it presents the data as it was inserted in the YAML stream. Example 12-21 demonstrates the difference between sorted and unsorted YAML data streams.

Example 12-21 *Sorting YAML Data Streams*

```
import yaml

data = {
    "Name": "John Doe",
    "Age": 40,
    "Company": "XYZ",
    "Social-media": {"Facebook": "johndoe",
                     "twitter": "johndoe"},
    "Job Title": "Network Automation Engineer",
    "Skills": ["Python", "Nexus", "IOS-XE", "YAML", "JSON"]
}
print("---------Sorted----------")
print(yaml.dump(data, sort_keys=True))
print("--------Unsorted---------")
print(yaml.dump(data, sort_keys=False))
```

```
[root@node1 demo]# python3 demo.py
---------Sorted----------
Age: 40
Company: XYZ
Job Title: Network Automation Engineer
Name: John Doe
Skills:
- Python
- Nexus
- IOS-XE
- YAML
- JSON
Social-media:
  Facebook: johndoe
  twitter: johndoe

--------Unsorted---------
Name: John Doe
Age: 40
Company: XYZ
Social-media:
  Facebook: johndoe
```

```
  twitter: johndoe
Job Title: Network Automation Engineer
Skills:
- Python
- Nexus
- IOS-XE
- YAML
- JSON
```

Another important function in the yaml package is the **yaml.load()** method, which accepts a byte string, a Unicode string, an open binary file object, or an open text file object as the parameter and returns a Python object. In other words, it converts a YAML document into a Python object. Example 12-22 demonstrates how the **yaml.load()** function returns a Python object. In this example, the data.yaml file contains a mapping of sequences of routers and switches. The demo.py file opens the file data.yaml, and the object is passed as a parameter to the **yaml.load()** function. Notice that this example also has the **Loader** attribute set to **yaml.FullLoader.** The **FullLoader** parameter handles the conversion from YAML scalar values to Python dictionary format.

Example 12-22 *Using the yaml.load() Function*

```
! data.yaml
routers:
  - rtr-ios-R1
  - rtr-xr-R2
  - rtr-nx-R3
switches:
  - sw-ios-SW1
  - sw-xe-SW2
  - sw-nx-SW3
```

```
! demo.py
import yaml

with open('data.yaml') as f:
    data = yaml.load(f, Loader=yaml.FullLoader)

print(data)
print("\n----------YAML Serialized Format------------\n")
print(yaml.dump(data))
```

```
[root@node1 demo]# python3 demo.py
{'routers': ['rtr-ios-R1', 'rtr-xr-R2', 'rtr-nx-R3'], 'switches': ['sw-ios-SW1',
  'sw-xe-SW2', 'sw-nx-SW3']}
```

```
----------YAML Serialized Format------------

routers:
- rtr-ios-R1
- rtr-xr-R2
- rtr-nx-R3
switches:
- sw-ios-SW1
- sw-xe-SW2
- sw-nx-SW3
```

Note For demonstration purposes, some examples in this section use the **yaml.load()** function. However, it is not recommended to use the **yaml.load()** function when data is received from an external and untrusted source. It is thus recommended to use the **yaml.safe_load()** function. Alternatively, you can use the **yaml.load()** function but with the **Loader** value set to **yaml.SafeLoader.**

The **yaml.load()** function is useful when you need to parse through a single YAML document. However, if a string or a YAML file contains multiple documents, you should use the **yaml.load_all()** function to load all the documents. Example 12-23 illustrates the use of the **yaml.load_all()** function to load all the documents in a YAML file.

Example 12-23 *Loading Multiple YAML Documents by Using the yaml.load_all() Function*

```
! data.yaml
# First YAML Document
network-devices:
  routers:
  - rtr-ios-R1
  - rtr-xr-R2
  - rtr-nx-R3
  switches:
  - sw-ios-SW1
  - sw-xe-SW2
  - sw-nx-SW3
---
# Second YAML Document
hosts:
  - srvr1: "linux"
    patched: True
    OS: CentOS
  - srvr2: "Microsoft Windows"
```

```
    patched: False
    OS: "Windows 10"
```

```
! demo.py
import yaml

with open('data.yaml') as f:
    # yaml.load_all() loads all the YAML documents present in a YAML file
    # and returns an object, which can be further iterated
    docs = yaml.load_all(f, Loader=yaml.FullLoader)
    for doc in docs:
        for i,j in doc.items():
            print(i, "->", j)
```

```
[root@node1 demo]# python3 demo.py
network-devices -> {'routers': ['rtr-ios-R1', 'rtr-xr-R2', 'rtr-nx-R3'], 'switches':
  ['sw-ios-SW1', 'sw-xe-SW2', 'sw-nx-SW3']}
hosts -> [{'srvr1': 'linux', 'patched': True, 'OS': 'CentOS'}, {'srvr2': 'Microsoft
  Windows', 'patched': False, 'OS': 'Windows 10'}]
```

The YAML package also provides access to lower-level APIs when parsing YAML files. The **yaml.scan()** method scans through a YAML file and generates tokens that can be used to understand the kind of YAML data being worked on. As described earlier in this chapter, data is presented in YAML in three forms:

- Scalar
- Sequence
- Mapping

The tokens generated by the **scan()** method list the start and end tokens when parsing any of these three forms of data, as shown in Example 12-24. The **scan()** method is useful for debugging purposes as it allows you to take relevant actions in the code when a certain type of data is presented in YAML.

Example 12-24 *Using the yaml.scan() Method*

```
network-devices:
  routers:
  - rtr-ios-R1
  - rtr-xr-R2
  - rtr-nx-R3
  switches:
  - sw-ios-SW1
  - sw-xe-SW2
```

```
  - sw-nx-SW3
  servers:
  - srvr1: "linux"
    patched: True
    OS: CentOS
  - srvr2: "Microsoft Windows"
    patched: False
    OS: "Windows 10"
```

```
import yaml
with open('data.yaml') as f:
    data = yaml.scan(f, Loader=yaml.FullLoader)
    for tkn in data:
        print(tkn)
```

```
[root@node1 demo]# python3 demo.py
StreamStartToken(encoding=None)
BlockMappingStartToken()
KeyToken()
ScalarToken(plain=True, style=None, value='network-devices')
ValueToken()
BlockMappingStartToken()
KeyToken()
ScalarToken(plain=True, style=None, value='routers')
ValueToken()
BlockEntryToken()
ScalarToken(plain=True, style=None, value='rtr-ios-R1')
BlockEntryToken()
ScalarToken(plain=True, style=None, value='rtr-xr-R2')
BlockEntryToken()
ScalarToken(plain=True, style=None, value='rtr-nx-R3')
KeyToken()
ScalarToken(plain=True, style=None, value='switches')
ValueToken()
BlockEntryToken()
ScalarToken(plain=True, style=None, value='sw-ios-SW1')
BlockEntryToken()
ScalarToken(plain=True, style=None, value='sw-xe-SW2')
BlockEntryToken()
ScalarToken(plain=True, style=None, value='sw-nx-SW3')
KeyToken()
ScalarToken(plain=True, style=None, value='servers')
ValueToken()
```

```
BlockEntryToken()
BlockMappingStartToken()
KeyToken()
ScalarToken(plain=True, style=None, value='srvr1')
ValueToken()
ScalarToken(plain=False, style='"', value='linux')
KeyToken()
ScalarToken(plain=True, style=None, value='patched')
ValueToken()
ScalarToken(plain=True, style=None, value='True')
KeyToken()
ScalarToken(plain=True, style=None, value='OS')
ValueToken()
ScalarToken(plain=True, style=None, value='CentOS')
BlockEndToken()
BlockEntryToken()
BlockMappingStartToken()
KeyToken()
ScalarToken(plain=True, style=None, value='srvr2')
ValueToken()
ScalarToken(plain=False, style='"', value='Microsoft Windows')
KeyToken()
ScalarToken(plain=True, style=None, value='patched')
ValueToken()
ScalarToken(plain=True, style=None, value='False')
KeyToken()
ScalarToken(plain=True, style=None, value='OS')
ValueToken()
ScalarToken(plain=False, style='"', value='Windows 10')
BlockEndToken()
BlockEndToken()
BlockEndToken()
StreamEndToken()
```

As you have learned in this chapter, YAML is commonly used to build configuration files. These configuration files can be used along with Jinja templates to render configurations for various networking devices. Example 12-25 shows a BGP configuration. In this example, the data.yaml file has a number of BGP-related configurations, such as router ID, network advertisements, and neighbors. This data is rendered into a proper BGP configuration using Jinja templates. Building any configuration using YAML and Jinja involves three basic steps:

Step 1. Load the YAML data.

Step 2. Set the directory path and select the Jinja template.

Step 3. Render the data into the Jinja template to generate the configuration.

Example 12-25 demonstrates this process of generating a configuration.

Example 12-25 *Building a Configuration Using YAML and Jinja Templates*

```
! data.yaml
---
bgp:
  id: 100
  router_id: 1.1.1.1
 networks:
    - 192.168.1.1/32
    - 192.168.12.0/24
    - 192.168.13.0/24
  neighbors:
    - id: 2.2.2.2
      remote_as: 200
      afi: "ipv4 unicast"
    - id: 3.3.3.3
      remote_as: 300
      afi: "ipv4 unicast"
```

```
! templates/bgp_template.j2
router bgp {{ bgp.id }}
router-id {{ bgp.router_id }}
address-family ipv4 unicast
{% for network in bgp.networks %}
network {{ network }}
{% endfor %}
exit address-family
{% for neighbor in bgp.neighbors %}
neighbor {{ neighbor.id }}
  remote-as {{ neighbor.remote_as }}
  address-family {{ neighbor.afi }}
  exit
exit
{% endfor %}
```

```
import yaml
from jinja2 import Environment, FileSystemLoader

config_data = yaml.load(open('data.yaml'), Loader=yaml.FullLoader)
env = Environment(loader = FileSystemLoader('./templates'), trim_blocks=True,
  lstrip_blocks=True)

template = env.get_template('bgp_template.j2')
```

```
print(template.render(config_data))
```

```
[root@node1 demo]# python3 demo.py
router bgp 100
router-id 1.1.1.1
address ipv4 unicast
network 192.168.1.1/32
network 192.168.12.0/24
network 192.168.13.0/24
exit address-family
neighbor 2.2.2.2
  remote-as 200
  address-family ipv4 unicast
  exit
exit
neighbor 3.3.3.3
  remote-as 300
  address-family ipv4 unicast
  exit
exit
```

Note Chapter 6, "Python Applications," further discusses working with YAML data and Jinja templates as well as other Python libraries, such as NAPALM and Nornir.

Summary

YAML is a human-readable data serialization language used to build configurations. YAML is also a superset of JSON, and so there are many similarities between JSON and YAML. YAML allows you to represent data in three different formats:

- Scalars
- Sequence
- Mapping

In this chapter, you have learned that YAML represents native data structures using nodes and tags. Unlike other formats, such as JSON, YAML supports comments. YAML allows you to represent common data structures, such as strings, integers, floating points, and Booleans, as well as complex data structures. YAML supports anchors and merge keys, which help with duplication of data as well as inheritance.

The Python PyYAML package allows programmers to serialize Python objects into a YAML stream by using the **yaml.dump()** method and a YAML stream to a Python object by using the **yaml.load()** method. Programmers and network automation engineers can also use Jinja templates along with the PyYAML package to build configurations for network devices.

Chapter 13

YANG

This chapter discusses data modeling in general and the YANG modeling language in particular. It's very important to understand these topics, as YANG data models are very important in network automation today.

A Data Modeling Primer

Before you delve into the details of YANG, it is important that you understand the problem it attempts to solve. YANG provides a framework for *modeling* (or *structuring*) data. The following sections cover the difference between structured and unstructured data, what a data model is, why we need data models, and the problems that data modeling solves.

What Is a Data Model?

Information is everywhere. It is not an exaggeration to say that we are surrounded by various types of data all the time. Even now, you are consuming data by reading this book. If the information around you isn't structured somehow, efficient consumption and understanding of this data will be a problem. For example, the information in this book isn't related to the weather outside, or the currency exchange rate in the foreign exchange market. But this is not a problem, because different data—data in the book, data about the weather, data about the exchange rate—exists *in different contexts*.

Say that there was a mistake in this book such that one page was printed in English, another in Chinese, and a third in an unreadable font, such as Wingding. In such a case, the data would not be structured properly within *a single context*. In order to avoid such chaos, this book is created following certain rules:

- It has a clear structure defined in the table of contents at the beginning.
- All the chapters and paragraphs follow that predefined structure, without deviation.

- All the chapters are written using the same language and writing style.
- Each chapter has the same internal structure as others, starting with the introduction and ending with a summary.
- Information representation—such as fonts, font sizes, images, tables, and examples—is the same throughout the book.

Just think about this list of constraints for a moment. There is not a single word about the information that is actually contained in the book. There are only rules (constraints) and characteristics regarding *how* the information in this book *should* be composed. And that is the key, because any *data model* is a set of rules and characteristics that define how the data should be structured, formatted, and represented in order to be efficiently consumed. *Data modeling* is the process of defining those rules and characteristics. It's legitimate to say that for this book, the data modeling is done by Cisco Press; the team at Cisco Press defines the formatting, prepares the templates, and approves the table of contents before the book is written. Then, before the book is sent to print, the team reviews the content to make sure that the rules are being followed at every step of the process and that the final printed book conforms to those rules.

Another example of a data model is an application form you need to fill out to get a visa before visiting some exotic country. It provides a description of the information required from you (such as your name, surname, and birthday) and in which format each field is to be provided (for example, letters, numbers, photo). But the application form doesn't initially contain the actual data; it is you who populates this data by filling in the form. On the other hand, the data modeling for the application form is done by the government (or its subcontractors) of the country to which you are applying for a visa.

We could list examples of data models indefinitely, but the general idea of what a data model is should be clear by now.

Why Data Modeling Matters

Consider again the visa application example from the previous section. Say that after you have completed the visa application, the employees of the appropriate government service process your data. The first things they check are the *completeness* and *format* of the information provided—whether all the mandatory fields are filled in and whether all the relevant additional documents are attached, in the formats requested. The same set of data must be provided by all applicants. If the information isn't complete or if it is provided in the wrong format, the application is rejected because the data cannot be validated. If the information is complete and provided in the correct format, it's processed further in order to make a decision on granting or rejecting the visa.

As you can see from the visa application example, data models help transform informational chaos into structured data. They set explicit rules on what data should be provided by the transmitter, and in which format should the data be provided. They also set clear expectations for the receiver. If there were not such clear rules, the communication of the information and its further processing would be much more complicated—if it possible at all. Therefore, data models play a crucial role in our everyday lives, even if we don't realize that we are using them.

Now that you have some familiarity with the concept of data modeling and its applicability in general, it's time to start looking at these concepts from the perspective of network configuration and management.

Let's consider the process of provisioning of an IP VPN service for a customer. What information do you need to provision it? The answers to this question will determine the data model for the provisioning of the IP VPN service. You might want to structure the data model in the following way:

- **Field 1:** endpoint A; format: text; description: router hostname at the 1st site
- **Field 2:** port A; format: text; description: customer's attachment circuit for the 1st site
- **Field 3:** IP address A; format: numbers and special characters [.:/]; description: IP address on the customer-facing port at the 1st site
- **Field 4:** endpoint B; format: text; description: router hostname at the 2nd site
- **Field 5:** port B; format: text; description: customer's attachment circuit for the 2nd site
- **Field 6:** IP address B; format: numbers and special characters [.:/]; description: IP address on the customer-facing port at the 2nd site
- **Field 7:** RD; format: numbers and special characters [.:]; description: Route Distinguisher for the customer service
- **Field 8:** Import RTs; format: numbers and special characters [.:]; description: Import Route Targets for the customer service
- **Field 9:** Export RTs; format: numbers and special characters [.:]; description: Export Route Targets for the customer service

There might be many more optional parameters, but these nine are minimally required to establish the connectivity for a customer. (This example is covered in more detail in Chapter 11, "JSON," but for the purpose of this chapter, this high-level description is enough.) So, these nine fields constitute your data model for the IP VPN service.

Once you have a data model, you need to consider how this data model should be expressed or documented for effective use. You could create your own syntax and keywords, but you need to make sure that other applications or devices understand and support that syntax. Basically, you need a data modeling language, and it must satisfy at least the following categories:

- It should be clear and consistent in terms of syntax and keywords to avoid ambiguity.
- It should provide the possibility to create any data model for any use case.
- It should be flexible enough to extend when necessary.
- It should be product, platform, and vendor agnostic.

All these constraints are important, but the last point is of particular importance. For many years, customers were locked to certain vendor operating system implementations and had to master CLI skills for different platforms. In the era of automation and programmability, network devices cannot be operated exclusively through a CLI, especially when it comes to service provisioning/maintenance. They should be operated using standardized APIs using the same data model—and the industry is developing in that direction. For now, at least the language that is used to describe data models (and data modeling) should be the same across the industry. Thanks to collaboration within the network industry, led by the IETF, such a language exists, and it's called YANG.

YANG Data Models

You can find the original description of the YANG language in RFC 6020, "YANG: A Data Modeling Language for the Network Configuration Protocol (NETCONF)." Since that RFC was released, the networking community, led by the IETF, has significantly developed YANG, and today it is considered to be a generic data modeling language that can be used in conjunction with any type of protocol used for programming network elements, the most popular being NETCONF, RESTCONF, and gRPC. The more recent RFC 7950, "The YANG 1.1 Data Modeling Language," covers YANG Version 1.1.

So far, YANG has proven to be a sweeping success, and a number of factors have contributed to this success. First of all, YANG syntax is quite straightforward and easy to understand. The second important factor is that YANG is strongly supported by the telecommunications industry; major vendors, standardization bodies (including the Internet Engineering Task Force [IETF], Metro Ethernet Forum [MEF], and Broadband Forum [BBF]), and informal communities (including OpenConfig, a vendor-neutral working group driven by Google) are using YANG extensively to create their data models. And the third important factor is that YANG is a language, which means you can create your own YANG modules based on application requirements.

Let's consider an example that emphasizes the importance of the YANG language, particularly for data modeling and network programmability. You are familiar with the process of configuring network devices (such as routers, switches, and firewalls). You can think about the functions of those network devices, referred to as network functions (NFs), as lines of code performing different actions. These lines of configuration are basically how certain parameters (for example, IP addresses or VLAN numbers alongside encapsulation types) are mapped to certain objects (such as interfaces). In a nutshell, a data model shows the relationship between parameters and different objects. YANG provides a simple and powerful way to define such a relationship.

A *YANG module* is a tree-like structure that describes some information in a hierarchical way. The smallest component of this tree model is a single parameter in key/value format, where the key is the specific parameter, and the value is some information that describes the quality or quantity of the parameter. Going from leafs of the tree to branches and further up shows the logic involved in aggregating the smallest and most explicit components of the information tree together to describe more complex objects. (*Smallest* here refers to the fact that each of these components cannot be broken down further into constituent components.) For instance, if we think again about the earlier example of the data model for the router interface, these would be the smallest components of the information tree:

- IPv4 address
- IPv4 prefix length
- IPv6 address
- IPv6 prefix length
- Interface type
- Interface name
- Maximum transmission unit (MTU)
- Encapsulation type
- (Encapsulation) VLAN ID

This information can be structured in a hierarchical format to represent the data model of the interface, as shown in Figure 13-1.

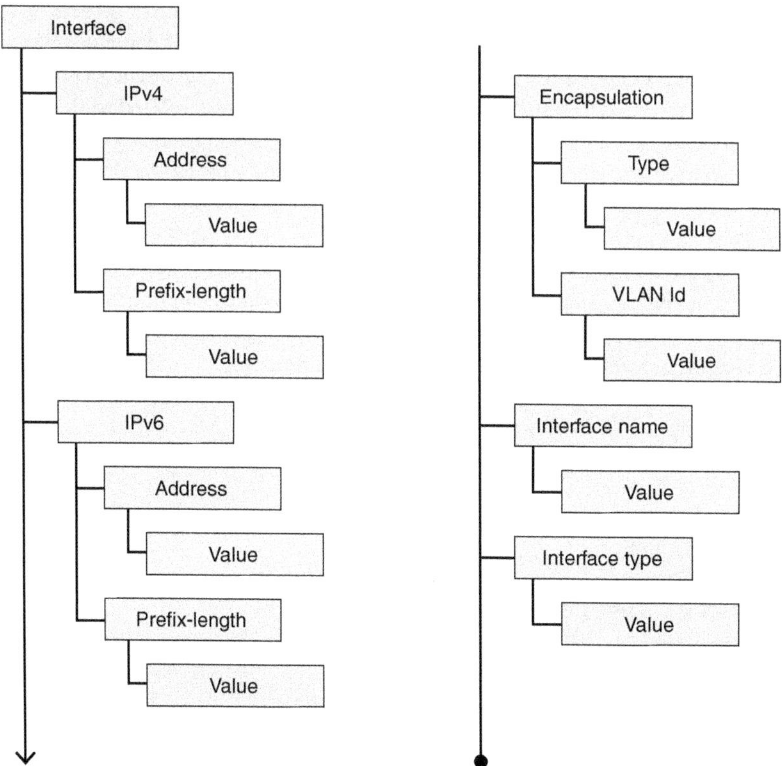

Figure 13-1 *Generic Overview of a YANG Module*

The protocols used in network programmability don't use YANG directly; rather, they use representations of YANG data models in JSON or XML format. Later in the book, you will encounter real-life scenarios of the use of YANG data models for programming network functions on Cisco IOS XE, IOS XR, and NX-OS, as well as several other non-Cisco platforms.

Structure of a YANG Module

To help you better understand YANG data modeling in the context of network programmability, this section uses examples of real YANG modules for Cisco IOS XR. To start the journey into the YANG world, first of all, you need to understand the structure of a YANG module, which has three major parts:

- Module header statements
- Revision statements
- Definition statements

The sequence of these parts is important; the module header statement must appear first in a module, and the definition statements must appear last.

Module header statements contain important information about the module in general, such as the name of the module, the XML namespace used, and additional dependencies on external YANG modules needed for the operation of the module, if any. One of the very useful features of YANG is that it's possible to have all information related to the data model in a single module, and it's also possible to split this information across several modules and reuse modules, where necessary. Example 13-1 shows the module header statements from a Cisco YANG module. Generally, each vendor has its own YANG modules (for example, Cisco, Juniper, Nokia). Further, for a vendor, there might be different flavors of operating systems, such Cisco IOS XE, IOS XR, and NX-OS, and each of these operating system flavors has its own modules as well. Finally, modules can be changed between the releases; therefore, it is very important to check your network operating system type and version before starting to work with YANG modules.

Example 13-1 *Module Header Statements in a Cisco IOS XR YANG Module*

```
$ cat Cisco-IOS-XR-ifmgr-cfg.yang

 module Cisco-IOS-XR-ifmgr-cfg {

  /*** NAMESPACE / PREFIX DEFINITION ***/
  namespace "http://cisco.com/ns/yang/Cisco-IOS-XR-ifmgr-cfg";
  prefix "ifmgr-cfg";

  /*** LINKAGE (IMPORTS / INCLUDES) ***/
```

```
import Cisco-IOS-XR-types { prefix "xr"; }

/*** META INFORMATION ***/
organization "Cisco Systems, Inc.";
contact
  "Cisco Systems, Inc.
   Customer Service
   Postal: 170 West Tasman Drive
   San Jose, CA 95134
   Tel: +1 800 553-NETS
   E-mail: cs-yang@cisco.com";

description
  "This module contains a collection of YANG definitions
   for Cisco IOS-XR ifmgr package configuration.
   This module contains definitions
   for the following management objects:
     global-interface-configuration: Global scoped configuration
       for interfaces
     interface-configurations: interface configurations
   Copyright (c) 2013-2016 by Cisco Systems, Inc.
   All rights reserved.";

                ------ The output is truncated for brevity ------
```

Much like other programming languages, and as you have seen with Bash and Python in earlier chapters, YANG provides the facility to insert comments in a YANG module. These comments are enclosed between slash characters, like this: /*** *Comment text****/. Notice in Example 13-1 that Cisco uses comments extensively to provide useful hints to module users.

The first line of Example 13-1 contains the keyword **module** to define the name of the module. In Chapter 14, "NETCONF and RESTCONF," you will learn how to get a list of all supported YANG modules on any device that is YANG capable. The common practice is to have the value with **module** exactly the same as the YANG filename. The next statement defines the namespace, which is how this particular YANG module can be called in XML-encoded messages. The **prefix** statement defines the string that is used as a prefix to access the module or to refer to definitions contained in the module. XML and XML schemas are covered in detail in Chapter 10, "XML." The **import** statement points to the other YANG modules that are required for the proper operation of the module containing the **import** statement(s). Typically, it's convenient to define some data types or groupings once and then import them to all other YANG modules that require such information. You will learn details about both data types and groupings later in this chapter. The rest of the information in the module header statements is meta-information that explains what organization released this module, how to contact the organization, and a description of the module content.

The next sections of Example 13-1, each of which starts with a **revision** statement, contains the history log of the YANG module development, which indicates which software release this particular YANG data model is applicable to and/or which changes are introduced in this version of the module compared to the previous version. You will find this information important when you try to apply the data model of one software version (such as Cisco IOS XR 5.3.1) to a device running another software version (such as Cisco IOS XR 6.4.1). Example 13-2 provides an example of the changes applied to one of the Cisco YANG modules.

Example 13-2 *revision Statements in a Cisco IOS XR YANG Module*

```
$ cat Cisco-IOS-XR-ifmgr-cfg.yang
! The output is truncated for brevity

  revision "2015-07-30" {
    description
      "Descriptions updated.";
  }

  revision "2015-01-07" {
    description
      "IOS XR 5.3.1 revision.";
  }

! The output is truncated for brevity
```

As you can see, the structure of this section is self-explanatory. Each **revision** statement is named with a date indicating when the YANG module was changed and contains a **description** field that shows an explanation of the modifications applied. There might be multiple such **revision** entries if there were several changes involved in developing this YANG module. It isn't mandatory to update these statements, but doing so is a good practice, as it makes life easier for those who are using the YANG module for configuration of network functions, as it helps them know what exactly they need to check within an updated YANG module.

Data Types in a YANG Module

Data types are the fuel on which the YANG data model engine runs. A definition of a data model comprises specific data that is expressed in certain data types and structured in a certain hierarchy. RFC 6020, which defines YANG, indicates that YANG has built-in data types and also derived data types.

Built-in Data Types

Built-in data types are types that exist in the YANG language by default and are available in all the YANG modules. You can use built-in data types in any of your models. Table 13-1 lists some of the most commonly used built-in data types to help you get a feel for what a data type is. The full list of built-in data types is available in RFC 7950.

Table 13-1 *Built-in Data Types in YANG*

Data Type	Description
binary	Any binary data
Boolean	**True** or **false**
empty	A leaf that does not have any value
enum	An enumerated string that provides a list of all allowed values for a variable (much like a drop-down menu with predefined values)
int8	An 8-bit signed integer
int16	A 16-bit signed integer
string	A human-readable string
uint8	An 8-bit unsigned integer (The difference between an unsigned integer and a signed one is that an unsigned integer cannot be negative. For example, int8 covers the range –127 to 127 [in decimal format], whereas uint8 covers the range 0 to 255.)
uint32	A 32-bit unsigned integer

To get a better understanding of how built-in data types are used, take a look at Example 13-3.

Example 13-3 *Built-in Data Types in a Cisco IOS XR YANG Module*

```
$ cat Cisco-IOS-XR-ifmgr-cfg.yang
                   ------ The output is omitted for brevity ------

      leaf bandwidth {
        type uint32 {
          range "0..4294967295";
        }
        units "kbit/s";
        description "The bandwidth of the interface in kbps";
      }
      leaf link-status {
        type empty;
```

```
      description
        "Enable interface and line-protocol state change
        alarms";
    }
    leaf description {
      type string;
      description "The description of this interface";
    }
                ------ The output is truncated for brevity ------
```

You will learn more about the keyword **leaf** later in this chapter. For now, you can just think of it as an arbitrary parameter expressed in the data type defined by the value of the keyword **type**. In addition, you can configure the range of the allowed values for this parameter by using the keyword **range**.

Derived Data Types

Despite the large number of built-in data types, you may at times need to create custom data types, referred to as derived data types. A derived data type is available only within the particular YANG module where it is defined or in any other YANG module that imports the YANG module where this data type is defined. Example 13-4 shows a derived data type defined using a built-in type.

Example 13-4 *A Derived Data Type in a Cisco IOS XR YANG Module*

```
$ cat Cisco-IOS-XR-ifmgr-cfg.yang
! The output is truncated for brevity

  typedef Interface-mode-enum {
    type enumeration {
      enum default {
        value 0;
        description "Default Interface Mode";
      }
      enum point-to-point {
        value 1;
        description "Point-to-Point Interface Mode";
      }
      enum multipoint {
        value 2;
        description "Multipoint Interface Mode";
      }
      enum l2-transport {
        value 3;
```

```
        description "L2 Transport Interface Mode";
      }
    }
    description "Interface mode enum";
  }

                ------ The output is truncated for brevity ------
```

The keyword **typedef** instructs the YANG module to create a new derived data type. This new derived data type is using the built-in data type **enumeration**, which is described in Table 13-1 as the type for enumerated strings. Each **enum** statement has the name of one of these enumerated strings and contains an associated value and description. As you might have noticed, you can add a field description almost anywhere. Using description statements extensively throughout your YANG module enhances its clarity to anyone who plans on using it. (Later in this chapter, in Example 13-6, you will see the usage of this new derived data type.)

Data Modeling Nodes

By this point, you should be familiar with the structure of a YANG module and the associated data types. The next logical step is to start building a data model. The building blocks of a data model are called *nodes*. Each node represents some object, and each node has a name and either a value or a set of child nodes. A YANG module simply defines a hierarchy of nodes and the interaction between those nodes. As per RFC 7950, Section 4.2.2, YANG defines four node types:

- Leaf nodes
- Leaf-list nodes
- Container nodes
- List nodes

The following sections discuss these node types.

Leaf Nodes

A leaf node, which is the smallest building block of a YANG data model, contains data of one particular type (for example, string) and has no possibility to nest any further data inside it. You will find a lot of leaf nodes of different data types in any YANG module. Example 13-5 shows the leaf nodes in a Cisco YANG module.

Example 13-5 *Leaf Nodes with Built-in Data Types in a Cisco IOS XR YANG Module*

```
$ cat Cisco-IOS-XR-ifmgr-cfg.yang
                   ------ The output is omitted for brevity ------

      leaf bandwidth {
        type uint32 {
          range "0..4294967295";
        }
        units "kbit/s";
        description "The bandwidth of the interface in kbps";
      }
      leaf link-status {
        type empty;
        description
          "Enable interface and line-protocol state change
          alarms";
      }
      leaf description {
        type string;
        description "The description of this interface";
      }
                  ------ The output is truncated for brevity ------
```

The keyword **leaf** defines the type of the node. A node always has a name; for example, in Example 13-5, the nodes are named **bandwidth**, **link-status**, and **description**. These names are used when you construct XML or JSON messages (as you will learn in the following chapters). Inside a **leaf** entry, you use the **type** keyword to define the data type used. This is the only mandatory parameter that must be included in all leaf nodes; the rest of the parameters are optional. So, you can optionally define the field **units**, which provides information about units of measurement for this entry, **description**, and many other parameters based on the needs of the data model.

Note Refer to RFC 7950 for a full list of the parameters defined for YANG.

Example 13-5 shows the usage of built-in data types, but there is no difference in how derived data types are used. Example 13-6 shows how the derived data type defined in Example 13-4 is used in a leaf node.

Example 13-6 *Leaf Nodes with Derived Data Type in a Cisco IOS XR YANG Module*

```
$ cat Cisco-IOS-XR-ifmgr-cfg.yang
                   ------ The output is omitted for brevity ------
```

```
    leaf interface-mode-non-physical {
      type Interface-mode-enum;
      default "default";
      description
        "The mode in which an interface is running. The
        existence of this object causes the creation of
        the software subinterface.";
    }
            ------ The output is truncated for brevity ------
```

Besides the derived data type **interface-mode-enum**, Example 13-6 shows another interesting piece of information. The keyword **default** allows you to define the default value for this parameter in case you don't define it explicitly. It makes sense to have this type of protection so that the application using this YANG module doesn't crash if you forget to specify a mandatory parameter. In Example 13-6, for example, the network device running the Cisco IOS XR SW will automatically set the interfaces type to the value defined in the keyword **default** if it is not explicitly specified.

Leaf-List Nodes

In certain cases, where a data model requires several values of a single parameter, you need to define several leaf nodes of the same type. For such a scenario, you use the leaf-list node, as shown in Example 13-7.

Example 13-7 *Leaf-List Nodes in a Cisco IOS XR YANG Module*

```
$ cat Cisco-IOS-XR-infra-policymgr-cfg.yang
            ------ The output is omitted for brevity ------

    leaf-list ipv4-dscp {
      type Dscp-range;
      max-elements 8;
      description "Match IPv4 DSCP.";
    }
    leaf-list ipv6-dscp {
      type Dscp-range;
      max-elements 8;
      description "Match IPv6 DSCP.";
    }
    leaf-list dscp {
      type Dscp-range;
      max-elements 8;
      description "Match DSCP.";
    }
            ------ The output is truncated for brevity ------
```

As shown in Example 13-7, the keyword **leaf-list** creates an entry for a leaf-list node. You use the field **type** to define the data type, exactly as you do for a leaf node. You might also want to add the optional field **max-elements**, which limits the number of leaf values in this leaf list.

Note For a comprehensive list of optional parameters available for leaf and leaf-list nodes, refer to RFC 7950.

Container Nodes

The third node type available in YANG is a container node. It doesn't have any value itself; rather, it contains any number of other nodes of any type (leaf, leaf-list, container, or list). So, if you need to group different sets of parameters related to the same object, a container node is a natural choice. Example 13-8 shows several parameters being defined simultaneously for one object.

Example 13-8 *A Container Node in a Cisco IOS XR YANG Module*

```
$ cat Cisco-IOS-XR-ifmgr-cfg.yang
                   ------ The output is omitted for brevity ------

      container encapsulation {
        description "The encapsulation on the interface";
        leaf encapsulation {
          type string;
          description "The encapsulation - e.g. hdlc, ppp";
        }
        leaf capsulation-options {
          type int32;
          description
            "The options for this capsulation, usually '0'";
        }
      }

                  ------ The output is truncated for brevity ------
```

You define a container node by using the keyword **container** followed by the name of the node. As you can see in Example 13-8, the only field that is defined directly within the container is **description**, and the rest are **leaf** entries. The container node could also nest another container, as there is no limit on the number of nested elements and levels of nesting, as shown in Example 13-9.

Example 13-9 *Container Node with a Nested Container in a Cisco IOS XR YANG Module*

```
$ cat Cisco-IOS-XR-ipv4-io-cfg.yang
                ------ The output is omitted for brevity ------

    container ipv4-network {
      description
        "Interface IPv4 Network configuration data";
      container bgp-pa {
        description
          "Interface ipv4 bgp configuration";
        container input {
          description
            "Input";
          leaf source-accounting {
            type boolean;
            description
              "BGP PA configuration on source";
          }

               ------ The output is truncated for brevity ------
```

List Nodes

Like a container node, a list node can have any number of leaf, leaf-list, container, and list nodes nested inside. The key difference is that typically list nodes are used when you need to define a similar set of parameters of many types, as in the case of configuring network interfaces or BGP neighbors. In addition, in the vast majority of cases, a list node has at least one leaf entry as a key (although this is not mandatory), and this is significant for building a tree. (See RFC 7950 Section 7.8 for further information on this particular point.) Example 13-10 shows an example of the structure of a list node.

Example 13-10 *A List Node in a Cisco IOS XR YANG Module*

```
$ cat Cisco-IOS-XR-ifmgr-cfg.yang
                ------ The output is omitted for brevity ------
        list mtu {
          key "owner";
          description "The MTU for the interface";
          leaf owner {
            type xr:Cisco-ios-xr-string;
            description
```

```
            "The Owner of the interface - eg. for
            'LoopbackX' main interface this is 'loopback'";
        }
        leaf mtu {
          type uint32 {
            range "64..65535";
          }
          mandatory true;
          description "The MTU value";
        }
      }
                ------ The output is truncated for brevity ------
```

As shown in Example 13-10, this node type is created by using the keyword **list** followed by the name. The next field, **key**, is a mandatory attribute. The key is a leaf node that must have an explicit value and that uniquely identifies an entry inside the list. The leaf identified as the key cannot have a default value since a default value would defy the whole purpose of having a unique identifier for each list entry. In addition, the optional attribute **mandatory** is used to specify that a particular leaf node must be configured.

Grouping Nodes

In some situations, you might need to use the same set of parameters (or even just one parameter) in different contexts. To achieve that, you can use a YANG construct called *grouping*. After you define a grouping, you can call it many times wherever you need it. In Example 13-11, the grouping **BFD** is created and then instantiated later in the module, under the container **bgp**. The **description** statement for the grouping indicates what this grouping accomplishes.

Example 13-11 *Reusable Node Group in a Cisco IOS XR YANG Module*

```
$ cat Cisco-IOS-XR-ipv4-bgp-cfg.yang
                ------ The output is omitted for brevity ------

  grouping BFD {
    description "Common node of global, vrf-global";

    container bfd {
      description "BFD configuration";
      leaf detection-multiplier {
        type uint32 {
          range "2..16";
        }
```

```
      description
        "Detection multiplier for BFD sessions created
        by BGP";
    }
    leaf interval {
      type uint32 {
        range "3..30000";
      }
      units "millisecond";
      description
        "Hello interval for BFD sessions created by BGP";
    }
  }
}

                ------ The output is omitted for brevity ------

container bgp {
  description "BGP configuration commands";

  list instance {
    list instance-as {
      list four-byte-as {
        container vrfs {
          list vrf {
            container vrf-global {
              uses BFD;
            }
          }
        }
      }
    }
  }
                ------ The output is truncated for brevity ------
```

Following the logic of strongly typed programming languages, any type or class of data should be defined prior to being used. You therefore create a grouping right after defining the derived data types at the beginning of a YANG module. Moreover, it's much easier to read the YANG module if you follow this convention, as you can easily follow the sequence of definitions and data usage.

You use the keyword **grouping** followed by the name of a grouping to create a context that groups a set of other node types. Later on, when you need to call a grouping of the nodes in any other context, you use the keyword **uses** followed by the name of the grouping. The **uses** statement is used to reference a grouping definition. It takes one argument, which is the name of the grouping.

Augmentations in YANG Modules

By now you should be familiar with the four YANG node types—leaf, leaf-list, container, and list—as well as with groupings. Keep in mind that for the purpose of this section, the term *node* refers to one of the four YANG node types, not to a network element itself.

The YANG language allows you to extend a parent YANG data model with additional nodes. To understand where this may be applicable, consider an interface IPv4 address: You need to configure an IP address only if the interface is active and working in routed mode, and you do not need to configure it in other cases (for example, if the interface is working in switching mode). In other words, the node representing the interface will always exist, regardless of its contents, whereas the node representing the IPv4 address may or may not exist within the interface node. This an approach is called *augmentation* in the YANG language. Example 13-12 illustrates the augmentation process for the interface IPv4 address use case.

Example 13-12 *Augmenting a Cisco IOS XR YANG Module*

```
$ cat Cisco-IOS-XR-ipv4-io-cfg.yang

  /*** NAMESPACE / PREFIX DEFINITION ***/
  namespace "http://cisco.com/ns/yang/Cisco-IOS-XR-ipv4-io-cfg";
  prefix "ipv4-io-cfg";

  /*** LINKAGE (IMPORTS / INCLUDES) ***/
  import ietf-inet-types { prefix "inet"; }
  import Cisco-IOS-XR-types { prefix "xr"; }
  import Cisco-IOS-XR-ifmgr-cfg { prefix "a1"; }

                ------ The output is omitted for brevity ------
  augment "/a1:interface-configurations/a1:interface-configuration" {
    container ipv4-network {
      description "Interface IPv4 Network configuration data";

      container addresses {
        description "Set the IP address of an interface";

        container secondaries {
          description "Specify a secondary address";
         list secondary {
            key "address";
            description "IP address and Mask";
            leaf address {
```

```
          type inet:ipv4-address-no-zone;
          description "Secondary IP address";
        }
        leaf netmask {
          type inet:ipv4-address-no-zone;
          mandatory true;
          description "Netmask";
        }
        leaf route-tag {
          type uint32 {
            range "1..4294967295";
          }
          description "RouteTag";
        }
      }
    }

    container primary {
      presence "Indicates a primary node is configured.";
      description "IP address and Mask";
      leaf address {
        type inet:ipv4-address-no-zone;
        mandatory true;
        description "IP address";
      }
      leaf netmask {
        type inet:ipv4-address-no-zone;
        mandatory true;
        description "Netmask";
      }
    }
    leaf unnumbered {
      type xr:Interface-name;
      description
        "Enable IP processing without an explicit
        address";
    }
    leaf dhcp {
      type empty;
      description "IPv4 address and Mask negotiated via DHCP";
    }
  }
 }
}
              ------ The output is truncated for brevity ------
```

The **augment** keyword followed by the name of a YANG node augments, or adds, that node to the primary module. Pay attention to the name of the augmented node, which starts with **a1**. In the **LINKAGE** section in Example 13-12, you can see the module header statements to import other YANG modules. Each of the imported modules is associated with some prefix, which is used to reference the particular YANG module within the body of the current YANG module. Following this logic, the line **import Cisco-IOS-XR-ifmgr-cfg { prefix "a1"; }** associates the imported module (**Cisco-IOS-XR-ifmgr-cfg**) with the prefix **a1**, which is then prepended (along with a colon) to the name of the augmented node (that is, **/a1:interface-configurations/a1:interface-configuration**). **augment** explicitly knows which YANG node or nodes it must extend.

The crucial point here is that an *augmented* YANG module has no knowledge that it has been augmented. This information lies solely with the *augmenting* module. The graphical representation in Figure 13-2 illustrates how augmented and augmenting YANG modules are connected to each other.

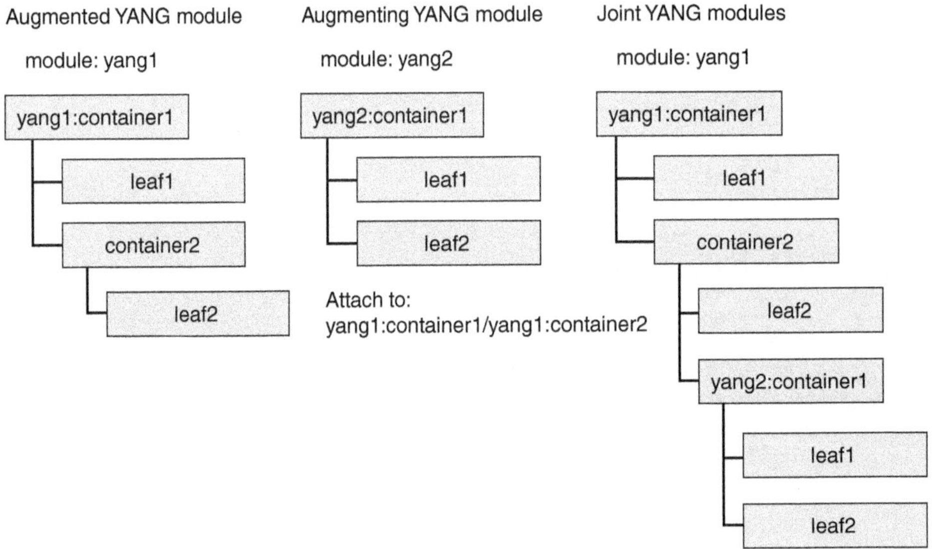

Figure 13-2 *YANG Augmentation Example*

Deviations in YANG Modules

So far in this chapter, the discussion has been about how you can create a YANG data model or extend its nodes through augmentation. Nevertheless, sometimes it might be necessary to tailor the scope of the initial YANG data models or to set some limits for just some cases or network functions.

For example, Cisco uses not only self-developed YANG models, but also third-party ones that are either standardized IETF YANG modules or community-driven OpenConfig

YANG modules. You will learn details about each of them shortly, but for now, you can think about them as just other data models. The key point is that a vendor's adaptation of a third-party YANG model (such as an IETF model) into a particular operating system version could deviate from the original representation. Another reason for deviations might be the situation where a YANG model is developed in general for a software type and version (such as Cisco IOS XR 6.4.1 or Cisco IOS XE 16.9.1), but each network hardware family has a different set of capabilities and supported protocols (such as Cisco NCS 5x00 versus ASR 9000 for IOS XR and Cisco ASR 1000 versus Cisco Catalyst 3850 for IOS XE). In such a case, the YANG data model must be adapted to match the capabilities of a particular platform.

The following list sums up the major reasons a YANG model might deviate from the original representation:

- A vendor doesn't implement in its software all the features defined in a third-party YANG model.
- A vendor has another internal data structure, and needed functions are implemented via augments somewhere else.
- A vendor references a generic YANG data model for a software type but needs to adapt it to a particular hardware platform family.

To avoid any misbehavior in all cases, you need to use the concept of deviation in the YANG language. From a structure perspective, the deviations are YANG modules, which have exactly the same structure as any other YANG modules, but these YANG modules have specific keys that explain what is not supported in particular implementations. Example 13-13 shows a list of deviations from the original OpenConfig and IETF YANG modules in Cisco IOS XE 16.9.1.

Example 13-13 *Deviations from the YANG Modules for Cisco IOS XE 16.9.1*

```
Cisco-IOS-XE-switch-deviation.yang
cisco-xe-ietf-event-notifications-deviation.yang
cisco-xe-ietf-ip-deviation.yang
cisco-xe-ietf-ipv4-unicast-routing-deviation.yang
cisco-xe-ietf-ipv6-unicast-routing-deviation.yang
cisco-xe-ietf-ospf-deviation.yang
cisco-xe-ietf-routing-deviation.yang
cisco-xe-ietf-yang-push-deviation.yang
cisco-xe-openconfig-acl-deviation.yang
cisco-xe-openconfig-bgp-deviation.yang
cisco-xe-openconfig-bgp-policy-deviation.yang
cisco-xe-openconfig-if-ethernet-deviation.yang
cisco-xe-openconfig-if-ip-deviation.yang
cisco-xe-openconfig-if-poe-deviation.yang
```

```
cisco-xe-openconfig-interfaces-deviation.yang
cisco-xe-openconfig-interfaces-switching-deviation.yang
cisco-xe-openconfig-network-instance-deviation.yang
cisco-xe-openconfig-openflow-deviation.yang
cisco-xe-openconfig-platform-deviation.yang
cisco-xe-openconfig-routing-policy-deviation.yang
cisco-xe-openconfig-spanning-tree-deviation.yang
cisco-xe-openconfig-system-deviation.yang
cisco-xe-openconfig-vlan-deviation.yang
```

Later in this chapter, you will learn where you can get the YANG modules for Cisco and other vendors. For now, it's important to understand the structure of a YANG module with deviations and how the deviations are applied to the parent module. Example 13-14 shows the deviations based on one Cisco IOS XE module.

Example 13-14 *Deviations from the IETF IP Module in Cisco IOS XE 16.9.1 for non-supported leafs*

```
$ cat cisco-xe-ietf-ip-deviation.yang
module cisco-xe-ietf-ip-deviation {
  namespace "http://cisco.com/ns/cisco-xe-ietf-ip-deviation";

  prefix ip-devs;

  import ietf-interfaces {
     prefix if;
  }

  import ietf-ip {
     prefix ip;
  }

                 ------ The output is truncated for brevity ------

  deviation /if:interfaces/if:interface/ip:ipv4/ip:enabled {
      deviate not-supported;
      description  "Not supported in IOS-XE 3.17 release.";
  }

  deviation /if:interfaces/if:interface/ip:ipv4/ip:forwarding {
      deviate not-supported;
      description  "Not supported in IOS-XE 3.17 release.";
  }
```

```
deviation /if:interfaces/if:interface/ip:ipv4/ip:mtu {
    deviate not-supported;
    description  "Not supported in IOS-XE 3.17 release.";
}

deviation /if:interfaces/if:interface/ip:ipv4/ip:neighbor {
    deviate not-supported;
    description  "Not supported in IOS-XE 3.17 release.";
}

                ------ The output is truncated for brevity ------
```

In Example 13-14, the string following the **deviation** keyword provides the path within the hierarchy of a specific YANG module where the behavior of that module, on a specific platform, will be different from that of the original module. In Example 13-14, you can see that different prefixes are used, which means the deviations are applied to augmented modules, which can't exist without parent modules. (For example, IP address augmentation can't exist outside the parent interface YANG module.)

Within the **deviation** entry is an instruction using the keyword **deviate** which states that a particular action is to be applied to the original YANG module (indicating how it should be changed). In Example 13-14, the action is **not-supported**, which tells you that this particular node isn't supported in Cisco IOS XE 16.9.1. There might be other actions; Example 13-15 shows one of them.

Example 13-15 *Deviations of the IETF IP Module in Cisco IOS XE 16.9.1 for modified leafs*

```
$ cat Cisco-IOS-XE-switch-deviation.yang
module Cisco-IOS-XE-switch-deviation {
  namespace "http://cisco.com/ns/yang/Cisco-IOS-XE-switch-deviation";
  prefix ios-sw-d;

  import Cisco-IOS-XE-native {
     prefix ios;
  }

  import Cisco-IOS-XE-policy {
     prefix ios-policy;
  }

  import Cisco-IOS-XE-switch {
```

```
    prefix ios-sw;
  }

                    ------ The output is omitted for brevity ------

  deviation "/ios:native/ios:policy/ios-policy:class-map/" +
      "ios-policy:match/ios-policy:access-group/ios-policy:index" {
    deviate replace {
      type uint32 {
        range "1..2799";
      }
    }
  }
  deviation "/ios:native/ios:policy/ios-policy:policy-map/" +
      "ios-policy:class/ios-policy:action-list/ios-policy:action-param/" +
      "ios-policy:bandwidth-case/ios-policy:bandwidth/ios-policy:bits" {
    deviate replace {
      type uint32 {
    range "100..40000000";
      }
    }
  }
! The output is truncated for brevity
```

In Example 13-15, the **deviate** keyword is coupled with the action **replace**, which means that the original leaf node is replaced by the node contained in the **deviate replace** entry.

Note For a more comprehensive list of actions, refer to RFC 6020.

YANG 1.1

YANG has evolved a lot since it was created and described in RFC 6020 in 2010. RFC 7950, "The YANG 1.1 Data Modeling Language," was released in 2016. This new RFC doesn't obsolete the original one; rather, it extends the capabilities of YANG in terms of supported features. In 2017, the IETF decided to change the structure of its YANG models to be compliant with the Network Management Datastore Architecture (NMDA); this change is defined in RFC 8342, which formally updates RFC 7950.

One of the most important changes is that YANG 1.1 modules have a stricter format and stricter character rules. It is important to check the consistency of a module with these new rules if you want to convert the module from YANG 1.0 to YANG 1.1.

You may be wondering how it is possible to know what version of YANG a particular module conforms to. Starting with Version 1.1, as specified in RFC 7950 Section 7.1.2, it's mandatory to include a YANG version statement in a header statement, as shown in Example 13-16.

Example 13-16 *YANG Version Within a Module*

```
$ cat openconfig-interfaces.yang
module openconfig-interfaces {

  yang-version "1";

  // namespace
  namespace "http://openconfig.net/yang/interfaces";

  prefix "ocif";
                   ------ The output is truncated for brevity ------
```

Although the module in Example 13-16 is developed using the YANG 1.0 language, it has the keyword **yang-version** in its header statements, which helps you (and applications using this module) understand which version rules should be applied. If the module corresponds to the newer version, the value of **yang-version** is **1.1**. If a YANG module doesn't contain this field, it automatically means that the module complies with the original YANG 1.0 version.

By now, you should be familiar with the concepts of the YANG language, the structure of a YANG module, and YANG components and data types. Understanding YANG isn't easy, and you might want to spend some time reviewing real YANG modules, such as those developed by Cisco (https://github.com/YangModels/yang) or OpenConfig (https://github.com/openconfig/public), to get a better grasp of the nuances of the language.

The rest of this chapter is dedicated to explaining the differences between Cisco native and third-party YANG modules, as well as how to use popular Python tools to explore YANG modules.

Types of YANG Modules

Various YANG modules are available, some of them open-standard modules from the IETF and OpenConfig, and others vendor-specific modules from different vendors for different hardware and software platforms. The first step in using YANG modules for model-based automation is to locate and download the YANG modules that you plan on using.

The Home of YANG Modules

The examples illustrating the YANG language shown earlier in this chapter use real Cisco and third-party YANG modules. There are two ways to get such modules:

- Extract them from a network device.
- Download them from the Internet.

You can extract modules from a network device via protocol-specific NETCONF/RESTCONF/gRPC syntax, which you will learn in the upcoming chapters covering each protocol. Generally, this is the best way to go, as it means extracting all the YANG modules, including augmentations and deviations for the particular platform that you are working on. These extracted modules can be used later on to build NETCONF/RESTCONF/gRPC messages used in your scenarios for network automation.

Downloading modules from the Internet is easier than extracting modules from a network device because the only thing you need is Internet connectivity. Different vendors have different approaches to the distribution of their YANG modules. Some of them include this information in a package together with the network operating system software. Cisco makes its YANG modules open and available for everyone, and it publishes YANG modules directly on GitHub, as shown on the Figure 13-3.

GitHub is the largest platform for open-source projects and activities, and it provides capabilities to easily save and share information, such as program code, documentation, and other text documents. Also, it has a built-in version control system and capabilities for collaboration so that several people can work on the same project simultaneously.

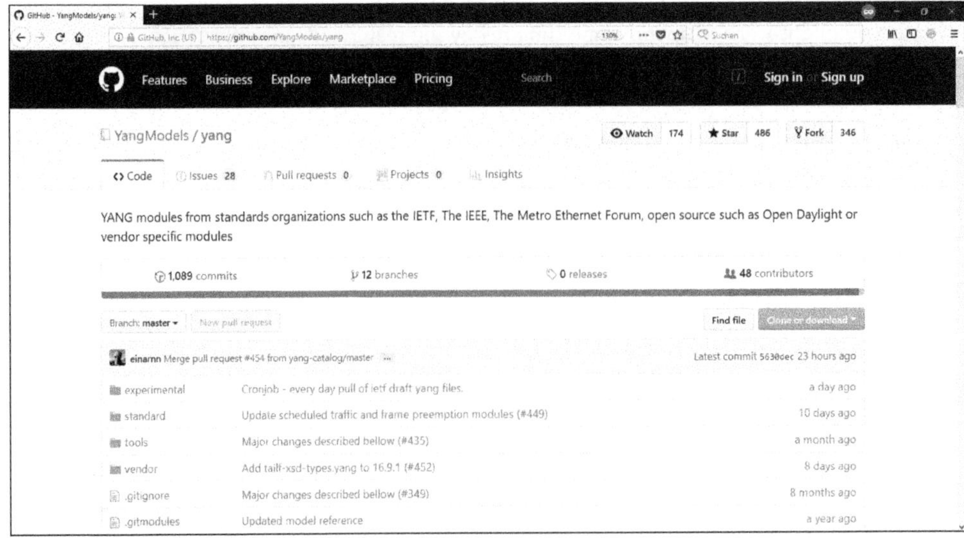

Figure 13-3 *GitHub Website with YANG Modules*

Figure 13-3 shows a page on the GitHub website that contains YANG modules from Cisco and other vendors (such as Juniper), as well as standardized IETF modules. It's possible to download files by simply clicking the button labeled Clone or Download, but there is a more convenient option: You can use the Linux **git** tool. Example 13-17 shows how to install the **git** tool on an rpm-based Linux distro such as CentOS.

Example 13-17 *Installing the* ***git*** *Tool on Linux CentOS*

```
$ sudo yum install -y git
```

The next step is to clone the repository of YANG modules locally to your PC so that you are can work with them using standard Linux tools, such as **cat**, **more**, and **vim**, as shown in Example 13-18.

Example 13-18 *Cloning YANG Modules from GitHub*

```
$ git clone https://github.com/YangModels/yang.git
Cloning into 'yang'...
remote: Enumerating objects: 2, done.
remote: Counting objects: 100% (2/2), done.
remote: Compressing objects: 100% (2/2), done.
remote: Total 21976 (delta 0), reused 1 (delta 0), pack-reused 21974
Receiving objects: 100% (21976/21976), 42.41 MiB | 2.95 MiB/s, done.
Resolving deltas: 100% (17077/17077), done.
Checking out files: 100% (20902/20902), done.
```

In the output shown in Example 13-18, you can see that all the data is cloned to the folder **yang**. Example 13-19 shows how to review what was cloned.

Example 13-19 *Verifying Downloaded YANG Modules*

```
$ ls -l yang/
total 24
drwxrwxr-x.  9 aaa aaa  127 Sep 22 17:53 experimental
-rw-rw-r--.  1 aaa aaa 9788 Sep 22 17:53 README.md
-rwxrwxr-x.  1 aaa aaa  502 Sep 22 17:53 setup.py
drwxrwxr-x.  7 aaa aaa   77 Sep 22 17:53 standard
-rwxrwxr-x.  1 aaa aaa  225 Sep 22 17:53 testall.sh
drwxrwxr-x. 15 aaa aaa 4096 Sep 22 17:53 tools
drwxrwxr-x.  6 aaa aaa   75 Sep 22 17:53 vendor
```

In Example 13-19, the hierarchy under the **yang** directory is exactly the same as in Figure 13-1. You can find more detailed explanation on the downloaded content in the README.md file by following common GitHub practice. Example 13-20 provides some excerpts from that file.

Example 13-20 *Information on Downloaded YANG Modules*

```
$ cat yang/README.md

                    ------ The output is omitted for brevity ------

YANG
=====

This repository contains a collection of YANG modules:

  * IETF standards-track YANG modules
  * OpenDaylight open source YANG modules
  * IEEE experimental YANG modules
  * Broadband Forum standard YANG modules
  * Vendor-specific YANG modules
  * Open source YANG tools

                   ------ The output is truncated for brevity ------
```

Native (Vendor-Specific) YANG Modules

So far this chapter has mostly looked at native Cisco YANG modules. This is the starting point for the development of YANG data models that all the vendors follow. The reason for that is obvious: It's much easier to develop a YANG data model around the existing configuration structure than to map third-party YANG models (such as IETF or OpenConfig models) to the configuration.

A downloaded YANG package contains all the available Cisco modules, distributed in folders based on the type of the network operating system, as shown in the Example 13-21.

Example 13-21 *YANG Modules by Operating System Type*

```
$ ls -l yang/vendor/cisco/
total 12
-rwxrwxr-x.  1 aaa aaa  564 Sep 22 17:53 check.sh
drwxrwxr-x.  2 aaa aaa   23 Sep 22 17:53 common
drwxrwxr-x. 15 aaa aaa 4096 Sep 22 17:53 nx
-rw-rw-r--.  1 aaa aaa  530 Sep 22 17:53 README.md
drwxrwxr-x. 11 aaa aaa  147 Sep 22 17:53 xe
drwxrwxr-x. 21 aaa aaa  248 Sep 22 17:53 xr
```

Cisco is famous for its excellent documentation, and it continues this tradition with YANG modules by putting notes in the README.md file, which provides plenty of useful information. Example 13-22 shows that the README.md file explains where you can find different YANG modules.

Example 13-22 *Built-in Guide for Cisco YANG Modules*

```
$ cat yang/vendor/cisco/README.md
This directory contains YANG models for Cisco platforms. There are several
  sub-directories:

* **common** - models that have some level of support across all IOS-XR, NX-OS and
  IOS-XE; there may be deviations either published by devices or available in
  OS-specific directories
* **xr** - models that are specific to IOS-XR platforms
* **nx** - models that are specific to NX-OS platforms
* **xe** - models that are specific to IOS-XE platforms

Each subdirectory may have further OS/platform-specific information in a README
  file.
```

The folder for Cisco IOS XR YANG modules contains the README.md file shown in Example 13-23.

Example 13-23 *Built-in Guide for Cisco YANG Modules - continuation*

```
$ cat yang/vendor/cisco/xr/README.md
This directory contains OS/platform-specific YANG models for Cisco's IOS-XR
  platforms.

The directory is _currently_ organized by OS-version, with each sub-directory
  containing the models for that version. The OS version number is presented as a
  single number. Thus the YANG models for IOS-XR 5.3.0 will be in the subdirectory
  named "530". Please note that this organization may change.

A README file may exist in the version subdirectories with any specific notes
  relating to the models in the directory.

Further documentation on Cisco's IOS-XR YANG-based interfaces may be found at:

* [Cisco IOS XR Data Models Configuration Guide for the NCS 5500 Series Router]
  (http://www.cisco.com/c/en/us/td/docs/iosxr/ncs5500/DataModels/b-Datamodels-cg-
  ncs5500.html)
* [Cisco Network Convergence System 5500 Series Configuration Guides](http://www.
  cisco.com/c/en/us/support/routers/network-convergence-system-5500-series/products-
  installation-and-configuration-guides-list.html)
```

As shown in Example 13-23, the README.md file provides clear explanation of the structure of the folders further down the directory hierarchy, which is arranged to have one subdirectory per Cisco IOS XR version. In each of these subdirectories, you can find all the supported YANG modules for the particular version of IOS XR. Example 13-24 shows several of the modules supported in Cisco IOS XR 6.5.1.

Example 13-24 *YANG Modules in Cisco IOS XR 6.5.1*

```
$ ls -l yang/vendor/cisco/xr/651/
total 14136
-rw-rw-r--. 1 aaa aaa  62027 Sep 22 17:53 capabilities-ncs1001.xml
-rw-rw-r--. 1 aaa aaa  66494 Sep 22 17:53 capabilities-ncs1k.xml
-rw-rw-r--. 1 aaa aaa  81766 Sep 22 17:53 capabilities-ncs5500.xml
-rw-rw-r--. 1 aaa aaa  70568 Sep 22 17:53 capabilities-ncs5k.xml
-rw-rw-r--. 1 aaa aaa  73592 Sep 22 17:53 capabilities-xrv9k.xml
-rw-rw-r--. 1 aaa aaa    591 Sep 22 17:53 capabilities-xrvr.xml
-rwxrwxr-x. 1 aaa aaa   2937 Sep 22 17:53 check-models.sh
-rw-rw-r--. 1 aaa aaa  17136 Sep 22 17:53 Cisco-IOS-XR-aaa-aaacore-cfg.yang
-rw-rw-r--. 1 aaa aaa   1871 Sep 22 17:53 Cisco-IOS-XR-aaa-diameter-base-mib-
  cfg.yang
-rw-rw-r--. 1 aaa aaa  12226 Sep 22 17:53 Cisco-IOS-XR-aaa-diameter-cfg.yang
-rw-rw-r--. 1 aaa aaa  28159 Sep 22 17:53 Cisco-IOS-XR-aaa-diameter-oper-sub1.yang
-rw-rw-r--. 1 aaa aaa   2969 Sep 22 17:53 Cisco-IOS-XR-aaa-diameter-oper.yang
-rw-rw-r--. 1 aaa aaa   6767 Sep 22 17:53 Cisco-IOS-XR-aaa-lib-cfg.yang
-rw-rw-r--. 1 aaa aaa   5621 Sep 22 17:53 Cisco-IOS-XR-aaa-lib-datatypes.yang
-rw-rw-r--. 1 aaa aaa   1040 Sep 22 17:53 Cisco-IOS-XR-aaa-li-cfg.yang

                 ------ The output is truncated for brevity ------
```

The modules listed in Example 13-24 are the actual YANG modules that you will find on a device running IOS XR Version 6.5.1. If you are building network automation based on YANG, this folder will be your starting point for the YANG models for this specific platform. Also, as mentioned earlier, you can use these modules as examples to further your studies of YANG if you don't actually have a network device to experiment on.

Cisco follows the same approach for its other network operating systems: IOS XE and NX-OS. Example 13-25 shows the YANG modules for Cisco IOS XE 16.9.1.

Example 13-25 *YANG Modules in Cisco IOS XE 16.9.1*

```
$ ls -l yang/vendor/cisco/xe/1691/
total 6252
-rw-rw-r--. 1 aaa aaa  59225 Sep 22 17:53 asr1k-netconf-capability.xml
-rw-rw-r--. 1 aaa aaa  54180 Sep 22 17:53 asr920-netconf-capability.xml
-rw-rw-r--. 1 aaa aaa  52705 Sep 22 17:53 cat3k-netconf-capability.xml
-rw-rw-r--. 1 aaa aaa  54478 Sep 22 17:53 cat9300-netconf-capability.xml
-rw-rw-r--. 1 aaa aaa  54478 Sep 22 17:53 cat9400-netconf-capability.xml
```

```
-rw-rw-r--. 1 aaa aaa  54478 Sep 22 17:53 cat9500-netconf-capability.xml
-rw-rw-r--. 1 aaa aaa  60666 Sep 22 17:53 cbr-netconf-capability.xml
-rwxrwxr-x. 1 aaa aaa   3192 Sep 22 17:53 check-models.sh
-rw-rw-r--. 1 aaa aaa  14635 Sep 22 17:53 cisco-bridge-common.yang
-rw-rw-r--. 1 aaa aaa  35576 Sep 22 17:53 cisco-bridge-domain.yang
-rw-rw-r--. 1 aaa aaa   3134 Sep 22 17:53 cisco-ethernet.yang
-rw-rw-r--. 1 aaa aaa  21338 Sep 22 17:53 cisco-ia.yang
-rw-rw-r--. 1 aaa aaa  21110 Sep 22 17:53 Cisco-IOS-XE-aaa-oper.yang
-rw-rw-r--. 1 aaa aaa  98232 Sep 22 17:53 Cisco-IOS-XE-aaa.yang
-rw-rw-r--. 1 aaa aaa   2602 Sep 22 17:53 Cisco-IOS-XE-acl-oper.yang
-rw-rw-r--. 1 aaa aaa  39943 Sep 22 17:53 Cisco-IOS-XE-acl.yang
-rw-rw-r--. 1 aaa aaa   3682 Sep 22 17:53 Cisco-IOS-XE-arp-oper.yang

                  ------ The output is truncated for brevity ------
```

Example 13-26 shows the YANG modules for Cisco NX-OS 9.2-1.

Example 13-26 *YANG Modules in Cisco IOS NX-OS 9.2-1*

```
$ ls -l yang/vendor/cisco/nx/9.2-1/
total 5468
-rwxrwxr-x. 1 aaa aaa    2153 Sep 22 17:53 check-models.sh
-rw-rw-r--. 1 aaa aaa    8665 Sep 22 17:53 cisco-nx-openconfig-acl-deviations.yang
-rw-rw-r--. 1 aaa aaa   11331 Sep 22 17:53 cisco-nx-openconfig-bgp-policy-
  deviations.yang
-rw-rw-r--. 1 aaa aaa    1081 Sep 22 17:53 cisco-nx-openconfig-if-aggregate-
  deviations.yang
-rw-rw-r--. 1 aaa aaa    1070 Sep 22 17:53 cisco-nx-openconfig-if-ethernet-
  deviations.yang
-rw-rw-r--. 1 aaa aaa   25203 Sep 22 17:53 cisco-nx-openconfig-if-ip-
  deviations.yang
-rw-rw-r--. 1 aaa aaa    2461 Sep 22 17:53 cisco-nx-openconfig-if-ip-ext-
  deviations.yang
-rw-rw-r--. 1 aaa aaa    4544 Sep 22 17:53 cisco-nx-openconfig-interfaces-
  deviations.yang
-rw-rw-r--. 1 aaa aaa   90443 Sep 22 17:53 cisco-nx-openconfig-network-instance-
  deviations.yang
-rw-rw-r--. 1 aaa aaa    2039 Sep 22 17:53 cisco-nx-openconfig-ospf-policy-
  deviations.yang
-rw-rw-r--. 1 aaa aaa    3165 Sep 22 17:53 cisco-nx-openconfig-platform-
  deviations.yang
-rw-rw-r--. 1 aaa aaa     745 Sep 22 17:53 cisco-nx-openconfig-platform-
  linecard-deviations.yang
-rw-rw-r--. 1 aaa aaa     886 Sep 22 17:53 cisco-nx-openconfig-platform-port-
  deviations.yang

! The output is truncated for brevity
```

IETF YANG Modules

In the examples in this chapter, you might have noticed that almost all the modules for Cisco NX-OS include the keyword **openconfig.** These are vendor-independent YANG data models, and we examine them later in this chapter. Cisco NX-OS also has a vendor-specific data model, which is described by the module **Cisco-NX-OS-device.yang.**

A vendor-specific YANG module works only for a certain vendor and platform. For example, YANG modules for ASR 1000 routers running Cisco IOS XE don't work on Cisco ASR 9000 running Cisco IOS XR and vice versa. In a broader context, Cisco YANG modules don't work on Nokia SR 7750 running Nokia SR OS or Juniper MX routers running Junos OS. The same is true in the other direction: Juniper YANG modules work only with Junos OS platforms, and Nokia SR OS modules work only with Nokia routers. Hence, it is necessary to develop drivers for network automation based on YANG per vendor and per device.

To overcome the issues with vendor-specific YANG modules, YANG modules should be vendor neutral and implemented by all the vendors. The IETF has been leading the standardization of the different network technologies and protocols since the pre-Internet era. (The first IETF RFC dates to 1969.) The IETF also intends to create standardized (open) YANG modules, but as of this writing, not too many open modules are being integrated into network devices. Example 13-27 shows the IETF YANG modules in Cisco IOS XR.

Example 13-27 *IETF YANG Modules in Cisco IOS XR*

```
$ ls -l yang/vendor/cisco/xr/651/ | grep 'ietf'
-rw-rw-r--. 1 aaa aaa    921 Sep 22 17:53 cisco-xr-ietf-netconf-acm-deviations.yang
-rw-rw-r--. 1 aaa aaa   1106 Sep 22 17:53 cisco-xr-ietf-netconf-monitoring-
  deviations.yang
-rw-rw-r--. 1 aaa aaa  16676 Sep 22 17:53 ietf-inet-types.yang
-rw-rw-r--. 1 aaa aaa  24295 Sep 22 17:53 ietf-interfaces.yang
-rw-rw-r--. 1 aaa aaa  12864 Sep 22 17:53 ietf-netconf-acm.yang
-rw-rw-r--. 1 aaa aaa  17518 Sep 22 17:53 ietf-netconf-monitoring.yang
-rw-rw-r--. 1 aaa aaa  26785 Sep 22 17:53 ietf-netconf.yang
-rw-rw-r--. 1 aaa aaa   4363 Sep 22 17:53 ietf-restconf-monitoring.yang
-rw-rw-r--. 1 aaa aaa   5320 Sep 22 17:53 ietf-syslog-types.yang
-rw-rw-r--. 1 aaa aaa   7035 Sep 22 17:53 ietf-yang-library.yang
-rw-rw-r--. 1 aaa aaa   4816 Sep 22 17:53 ietf-yang-smiv2.yang
-rw-rw-r--. 1 aaa aaa  18066 Sep 22 17:53 ietf-yang-types.yang
```

Compared to the number of native Cisco IOS XR modules, the number of IETF open modules is insignificant. Nevertheless, these vendor-neutral modules play an important role as they help unify different data types (such as interface types) across different vendors that implement and use these modules. One particular module, called ietf-netconf.yang, is of paramount importance. This module, which is available for each platform, describes the operation of the NETCONF protocol on that particular platform, including all available operations.

In this chapter, we have already discussed network device–level YANG modules, which are typically used for programming the network functions by using a network management system (NMS). Another type of YANG modules is used to control an NMS in terms of service provisioning by some external function (for example, a service orchestrator or OSS/BSS), and it requires a higher level of network abstraction. This level is called *service modeling*, and the YANG language is used to create a data model of the service. The IETF created YANG modules for such end-to-end services as well. For example, RFC 8299, "YANG Data Model for L3VPN Service Delivery," describes a YANG module for provisioning BGP IP VPN services. At a high level, this model describes the service characteristics, such as type of the service, access to external services out of the VPN (for example, on the Internet or in the cloud), and details of the IP addresses and circuit types for connecting the customer equipment. However, this RFC doesn't include all the information needed to configure the network devices, and it is used by an NMS as an input that should be enriched with further details and converted into a request using a device-specific YANG module.

OpenConfig YANG Modules

Although the IETF is a well-established standards development organization, its pace is sometimes quite slow compared with industry requirements. This is primarily due to the fact that all the different entities participating in the IETF must agree and come to a conclusion on each matter with which the IETF is involved. From a customer perspective, this process takes too long, especially in the context of YANG modules and associated use cases, which are developing at a significantly fast pace. Therefore, some industry heavy lifters, including Google, Comcast, Verizon, and Deutsche Telekom, got together and organized an informal working group called OpenConfig. The main intent of this initiative is to create vendor-neutral YANG modules and to push vendors to implement and support them. To keep it simple, a YANG module should be the same, regardless of vendor, so that an automation application can be developed once and then used with all network vendor equipment using the open YANG modules without much integration effort.

OpenConfig has a limited (though ever-growing) number of YANG modules. The initial focus for OpenConfig was to develop modules to help the customers deploy data centers very quickly. Now it also has support for a variety of MPLS modules, including modules for segment routing, VRF, routing protocols, route policies, and many other technologies and protocols involved in network device configuration. Nevertheless, OpenConfig still doesn't cover all possible network functions. For instance, it is not yet possible to create EVPN services by using OpenConfig YANG modules, though this might change in the future.

OpenConfig has its own page on GitHub from which you can download its YANG modules. The good news is that the process is the same as for downloading other modules from GitHub, as you can see in Example 13-28.

Example 13-28 *Downloading and Verifying OpenConfig YANG Modules*

```
$ git clone https://github.com/openconfig/public.git openconfig
Cloning into 'openconfig'...
remote: Enumerating objects: 46, done.
remote: Counting objects: 100% (46/46), done.
remote: Compressing objects: 100% (42/42), done.
remote: Total 1631 (delta 13), reused 16 (delta 4), pack-reused 1585
Receiving objects: 100% (1631/1631), 1.03 MiB | 1.34 MiB/s, done.
Resolving deltas: 100% (877/877), done.

$ ls -l openconfig/
total 16
drwxrwxr-x. 4 aaa aaa   198 Sep 23 11:24 doc
-rw-rw-r--. 1 aaa aaa 11358 Sep 23 11:24 LICENSE
-rw-rw-r--. 1 aaa aaa  1156 Sep 23 11:24 README.md
drwxrwxr-x. 3 aaa aaa    37 Sep 23 11:24 release
```

The development of OpenConfig YANG modules is primarily driven by customers, with vendors assisting with the implementation. This does not necessarily mean that the YANG modules officially published by the OpenConfig working group are all implemented by all vendors. Example 13-29 shows a comparison of the interface YANG modules officially published by OpenConfig and supported in Cisco IOS XR 6.5.1.

Example 13-29 *Official and Implemented Interface OpenConfig Modules in IOS XR*

```
$ ls -l yang/vendor/cisco/xr/651/ | grep 'openconfig-if-\|openconfig-interfaces'
-rw-rw-r--. 1 aaa aaa   1126 Sep 22 17:53 cisco-xr-openconfig-if-ethernet-
  deviations.yang
-rw-rw-r--. 1 aaa aaa   5848 Sep 22 17:53 cisco-xr-openconfig-if-ip-deviations.yang
-rw-rw-r--. 1 aaa aaa   1042 Sep 22 17:53 cisco-xr-openconfig-interfaces-
  deviations.yang
-rw-rw-r--. 1 aaa aaa   4212 Sep 22 17:53 openconfig-if-aggregate.yang
-rw-rw-r--. 1 aaa aaa   7733 Sep 22 17:53 openconfig-if-ethernet.yang
-rw-rw-r--. 1 aaa aaa  25769 Sep 22 17:53 openconfig-if-ip.yang
-rw-rw-r--. 1 aaa aaa  28225 Sep 22 17:53 openconfig-interfaces.yang
$ ls -l openconfig/release/models/interfaces/
total 108
-rw-rw-r--. 1 aaa aaa  5068 Sep 23 11:24 openconfig-if-aggregate.yang
-rw-rw-r--. 1 aaa aaa  3108 Sep 23 11:24 openconfig-if-ethernet-ext.yang
-rw-rw-r--. 1 aaa aaa 11217 Sep 23 11:24 openconfig-if-ethernet.yang
-rw-rw-r--. 1 aaa aaa  4055 Sep 23 11:24 openconfig-if-ip-ext.yang
-rw-rw-r--. 1 aaa aaa 36151 Sep 23 11:24 openconfig-if-ip.yang
-rw-rw-r--. 1 aaa aaa  1994 Sep 23 11:24 openconfig-if-poe.yang
-rw-rw-r--. 1 aaa aaa  2595 Sep 23 11:24 openconfig-if-tunnel.yang
-rw-rw-r--. 1 aaa aaa  2336 Sep 23 11:24 openconfig-if-types.yang
-rw-rw-r--. 1 aaa aaa 31942 Sep 23 11:24 openconfig-interfaces.yang
```

If you compare the output from the first command in Example 13-29 to the output from the second command, you see that Cisco IOS XR 6.5.1 implements roughly only half of the available OpenConfig modules for the interface. And almost all of the available modules have deviations tailoring the original scope to a particular platform. (Refer to the section "Deviations in YANG Modules," earlier in this chapter, for more information.) On the other hand, a true advantage of OpenConfig is that a lot of vendors support OpenConfig modules, so with proper testing, it's a really unified way of programming network functions. To emphasize this fact, some vendors, such as Arista, use OpenConfig YANG modules as their core data models and create native data models only to cover gaps where OpenConfig currently doesn't provide some needed functionality.

YANG Tools

Now that you are familiar with the YANG language and the different types of data models, the last important topic in this chapter is to YANG tools that enable you to view, edit, and use YANG models effectively.

Using pyang

Reading YANG modules directly isn't an easy task, especially if YANG modules have imported modules or just have a complex structure due to using groupings, derived data types, and so forth.

An important YANG tool is **pyang**. It's difficult to state just how important and useful this tool is with respect to network programmability using YANG. Among other tasks, **pyang** is able to do the following:

- Visualize YANG modules in human-readable output in CLI or HTML files
- Create JSON or XML schemas out of YANG modules
- Translates JSON to XML schemes
- Validate a YANG module, including imported and augmented modules and nodes

pyang is used to manage XML and JSON schemas. Chapters 10 and 11 provide information on XML and JSON This chapter shows the visualization of YANG modules using **pyang**.

pyang is part of the Python Software Foundation, and it's installed using the **pip** tool in Linux, as shown in Example 13-30. (**pip** installation is explained in Chapter 5, "Python Fundamentals.")

Example 13-30 *Installing the* **pyang** *Tool*

```
$ sudo pip install pyang
```

Alternatively, you can download the latest **pyang** software from GitHub and install it manually, but doing so is beyond the scope of this chapter.

When you have **pyang** installed, you can create a visualization of a YANG module. At the beginning of this chapter, the YANG module called **Cisco-IOS-XR-ifmgr-cfg.yang** was used a lot, and it is used in Example 13-31 as well.

Example 13-31 *Using pyang to Discover a YANG Module*

```
$ pyang -f tree -p yang/vendor/cisco/xr/651/ \
   yang/vendor/cisco/xr/651/Cisco-IOS-XR-ifmgr-cfg.yang

module: Cisco-IOS-XR-ifmgr-cfg
  +--rw global-interface-configuration
  |  +--rw link-status?   Link-status-enum
  +--rw interface-configurations
     +--rw interface-configuration* [active interface-name]
        +--rw dampening
        |  +--rw args?                 enumeration
        |  +--rw half-life?            uint32
        |  +--rw reuse-threshold?      uint32
        |  +--rw suppress-threshold?   uint32
        |  +--rw suppress-time?        uint32
        |  +--rw restart-penalty?      uint32
        +--rw mtus
        |  +--rw mtu* [owner]
        |     +--rw owner    xr:Cisco-ios-xr-string
        |     +--rw mtu      uint32
        +--rw encapsulation
        |  +--rw encapsulation?         string
        |  +--rw capsulation-options?   uint32
        +--rw shutdown?                       empty
        +--rw interface-virtual?              empty
        +--rw secondary-admin-state?          Secondary-admin-state-enum
        +--rw interface-mode-non-physical?    Interface-mode-enum
        +--rw bandwidth?                      uint32
        +--rw link-status?                    empty
        +--rw description?                    string
        +--rw active                          Interface-active
        +--rw interface-name                  xr:Interface-name
```

The syntax of the **pyang** command is as follows:

pyang -f {*format*} [-p {*path*}] {*module*}

There are different {*format*} options, each for a different representation or visualization of the information in the module. In Example 13-31, the {*format*} value is **tree**, which means the information in the YANG module is visualized in a tree-like hierarchy. The next parameter, **-p** {*path*}, informs **pyang** where to look for dependencies, such as imported modules. On the one hand, there are some predefined paths, so this attribute is optional, but typically you need to define it manually. Finally, {*module*} defines what particular module or modules should be reviewed and visualized.

It's important to note that you can simultaneously act on several modules by using **pyang**, and doing so makes sense if the modules augment each other. Example 13-32 illustrates such a case.

Example 13-32 *Using pyang to Review Augmented YANG Modules*

```
$ pyang -f tree -p yang/vendor/cisco/xr/651/ \
    yang/vendor/cisco/xr/651/Cisco-IOS-XR-ifmgr-cfg.yang \
    yang/vendor/cisco/xr/651/Cisco-IOS-XR-ipv4-io-cfg.yang

module: Cisco-IOS-XR-ifmgr-cfg
  +--rw global-interface-configuration
  |  +--rw link-status?   Link-status-enum
  +--rw interface-configurations
     +--rw interface-configuration* [active interface-name]
        +--rw dampening
        |  +--rw args?                 enumeration
        |  +--rw half-life?            uint32
        |  +--rw reuse-threshold?      uint32
        |  +--rw suppress-threshold?   uint32
        |  +--rw suppress-time?        uint32
        |  +--rw restart-penalty?      uint32
        +--rw mtus
        |  +--rw mtu* [owner]
        |     +--rw owner    xr:Cisco-ios-xr-string
        |     +--rw mtu      uint32
        +--rw encapsulation
        |  +--rw encapsulation?         string
        |  +--rw capsulation-options?   uint32
        +--rw shutdown?                                  empty
        +--rw interface-virtual?                         empty
        +--rw secondary-admin-state?                     Secondary-admin-state-enum
        +--rw interface-mode-non-physical?               Interface-mode-enum
        +--rw bandwidth?                                 uint32
        +--rw link-status?                               empty
        +--rw description?                               string
```

```
+--rw active                                    Interface-active
+--rw interface-name                            xr:Interface-name
+--rw ipv4-io-cfg:ipv4-network
|  +--rw ipv4-io-cfg:bgp-pa
|  |  +--rw ipv4-io-cfg:input
|  |  |  +--rw ipv4-io-cfg:source-accounting?        boolean
|  |  |  +--rw ipv4-io-cfg:destination-accounting?   boolean
|  |  +--rw ipv4-io-cfg:output
|  |     +--rw ipv4-io-cfg:source-accounting?        boolean
|  |     +--rw ipv4-io-cfg:destination-accounting?   boolean
|  +--rw ipv4-io-cfg:verify
|  |  +--rw ipv4-io-cfg:reachable?      Ipv4-reachable
|  |  +--rw ipv4-io-cfg:self-ping?      Ipv4-self-ping
|  |  +--rw ipv4-io-cfg:default-ping?   Ipv4-default-ping
|  +--rw ipv4-io-cfg:bgp
|  |  +--rw ipv4-io-cfg:qppb
|  |  |  +--rw ipv4-io-cfg:input
|  |  |     +--rw ipv4-io-cfg:source?        Ipv4-interface-qppb
|  |  |     +--rw ipv4-io-cfg:destination?   Ipv4-interface-qppb
|  |  +--rw ipv4-io-cfg:flow-tag
|  |     +--rw ipv4-io-cfg:flow-tag-input
|  |        +--rw ipv4-io-cfg:source?        boolean
|  |        +--rw ipv4-io-cfg:destination?   boolean
|  +--rw ipv4-io-cfg:addresses
|  |  +--rw ipv4-io-cfg:secondaries
|  |  |  +--rw ipv4-io-cfg:secondary* [address]
|  |  |     +--rw ipv4-io-cfg:address      inet:ipv4-address-no-zone
|  |  |     +--rw ipv4-io-cfg:netmask      inet:ipv4-address-no-zone
|  |  |     +--rw ipv4-io-cfg:route-tag?   uint32
|  |  +--rw ipv4-io-cfg:primary!
|  |  |  +--rw ipv4-io-cfg:address      inet:ipv4-address-no-zone
|  |  |  +--rw ipv4-io-cfg:netmask      inet:ipv4-address-no-zone
|  |  |  +--rw ipv4-io-cfg:route-tag?   uint32
|  |  +--rw ipv4-io-cfg:unnumbered?    xr:Interface-name
|  |  +--rw ipv4-io-cfg:dhcp?          empty
|  +--rw ipv4-io-cfg:helper-addresses
|  |  +--rw ipv4-io-cfg:helper-address* [address vrf-name]
|  |     +--rw ipv4-io-cfg:address     inet:ipv4-address-no-zone
|  |     +--rw ipv4-io-cfg:vrf-name    xr:Cisco-ios-xr-string
|  +--rw ipv4-io-cfg:forwarding-enable?       empty
|  +--rw ipv4-io-cfg:icmp-mask-reply?         empty
|  +--rw ipv4-io-cfg:tcp-mss-adjust-enable?   empty
|  +--rw ipv4-io-cfg:ttl-propagate-disable?   empty
```

```
     |  +--rw ipv4-io-cfg:point-to-point?          empty
     |  +--rw ipv4-io-cfg:mtu?                     uint32
     +--rw ipv4-io-cfg:ipv4-network-forwarding
        +--rw ipv4-io-cfg:directed-broadcast?   empty
        +--rw ipv4-io-cfg:unreachables?         empty
        +--rw ipv4-io-cfg:redirects?            Empty
```

In the output in Example 13-32, the augmenting YANG module has the prefix **ipv4-io-cfg** before its nodes, and this enables you to track how it's constructed. Another good thing is that the augmenting nodes are added exactly where needed, based on the **augment** keyword, as explained earlier in this chapter.

The output of **pyang** displays the structure of all the components in the YANG module (contained in the definition statements). The output also includes the data types associated with YANG node (**empty** or **unit32**, which are built-in data types, and **Interface-mode-enum**, which is a derived data type), as well as the allowed actions for the node: A node labeled **ro** is a read-only node and is a state note representing one piece of operational data, and a node labeled **rw** is a read/write node and represents configuration data. Cisco IOS XR has dedicated models for operational data only and other models for configuration data only. Example 13-33 shows the operational data YANG model that corresponds to the same entities that are configurable through the module in Example 13-32.

Example 13-33 *Using pyang to Review a single YANG Module*

```
$ pyang -f tree -p yang/vendor/cisco/xr/651/ \
    yang/vendor/cisco/xr/651/Cisco-IOS-XR-ifmgr-oper.yang

module: Cisco-IOS-XR-ifmgr-oper
  +--ro interface-dampening
  |  +--ro interfaces
  |  |  +--ro interface* [interface-name]
  |  |     +--ro if-dampening
  |  |     |  +--ro interface-dampening
  |  |     |  |  +--ro penalty?                  uint32
  |  |     |  |  +--ro is-suppressed-enabled?    boolean
  |  |     |  |  +--ro seconds-remaining?        uint32
  |  |     |  |  +--ro flaps?                    uint32
  |  |     |  |  +--ro state?                    Im-state-enum
  |  |     |  +--ro state-transition-count?        uint32
  |  |     |  +--ro last-state-transition-time?    uint32
  |  |     |  +--ro is-dampening-enabled?          boolean
  |  |     |  +--ro half-life?                     uint32
```

```
 |  |      |  +--ro reuse-threshold?            uint32
 |  |      |  +--ro suppress-threshold?         uint32
 |  |      |  +--ro maximum-suppress-time?      uint32
 |  |      |  +--ro restart-penalty?            uint32

------ The output is truncated for brevity ------
```

If you want to save the representation of a YANG module or if you prefer graphical representation rather than the CLI, you can generate the HTML representation of the YANG module by using **pyang** as well. Example 13-34 shows how to generate such a file.

Example 13-34 *Using pyang to save the output of the jstree representation of a YANG Module*

```
$ pyang -f jstree -o test.html -p openconfig/release/models/ \
    openconfig/release/models/interfaces/openconfig-interfaces.yang \
    openconfig/release/models/interfaces/openconfig-if-*
```

Compared to the earlier examples of **pyang**, the syntax in Example 13-34 is extended with optional attribute [**-o** {*output*}], which points to the file where the output should be saved. In addition, the format of the data representation set by the **-f** key is different and is now called **jstree**, where the first two letters, **js**, stand for JavaScript. You can view the HTML file that is output in any browser, as shown in Figure 13-4.

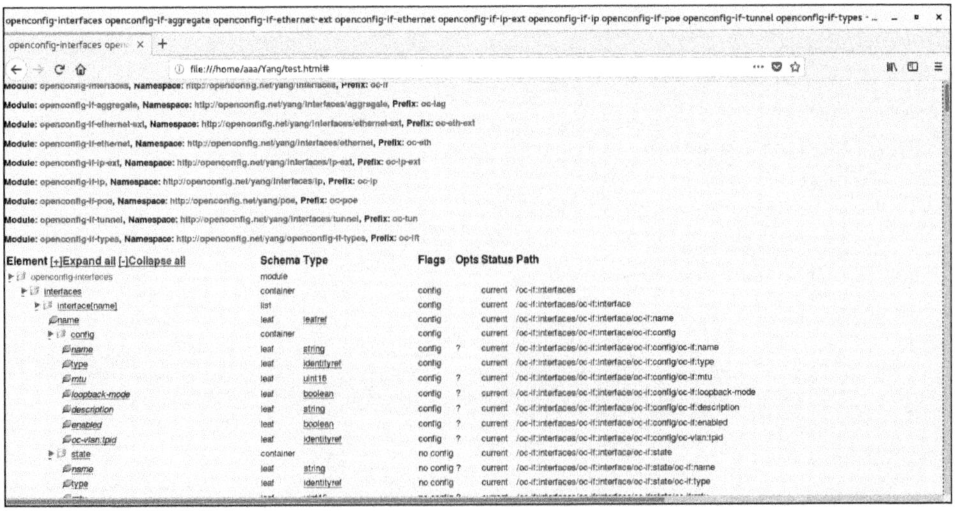

Figure 13-4 *HTML Representation of the YANG Modules Generated by YANG*

Example 13-34 generates a visualization of the OpenConfig YANG data model for the configuration of the interfaces, including all augmented YANG modules. There is some additional information, including the types of the YANG nodes, whether they are configurable, and an absolute path to the YANG node.

Using pyangbind

Chapter 5 and Chapter 6, "Python Applications," discuss the Python language and its ecosystem. **pyang** has a plug-in called **pyangbind** that helps translate YANG modules directly into Python classes so you can use Python to manage network elements through NETCONF or gNMI with YANG data modules.

In later chapters in this book, you will see some practical examples on how you can use **pyangbind**. For now, it's important to install it and gain a basic understanding of how it works. But before installing **pyangbind**, you need to make sure that all prerequisites are installed, as shown in Example 13-35 for Linux CentOS.

Example 13-35 *Installing Mandatory Packages for* ***pyangbind*** *in CentOS 7*

```
$ sudo yum -y install gcc gcc-c++ kernel-devel
$ sudo yum -y install python-devel libxslt-devel libffi-devel openssl-devel
```

After the mandatory packages are installed, you can install **pyangbuild**, as shown in Example 13-36.

Example 13-36 *Installing* ***pyangbind***

```
$ sudo pip install pyangbind
Collecting pyangbind
  Using cached https://files.pythonhosted.org/packages/2e/20/7b3f2de320d120e845bce14
  1148a23522fccb089b76ae0c76b5d5623d515/pyangbind-0.8.1.tar.gz
Requirement already satisfied: pyang in /usr/lib/python2.7/site-packages (from
  pyangbind) (1.7.5)
Collecting bitarray (from pyangbind)
  Using cached https://files.pythonhosted.org/packages/e2/1e/b93636ae36d08d0ee
  3aec40b08731cc97217c69db9422c0afef6ee32ebd2/bitarray-0.8.3.tar.gz
Requirement already satisfied: lxml in /usr/lib64/python2.7/site-packages (from
  pyangbind) (4.2.4)
Collecting regex (from pyangbind)
  Using cached https://files.pythonhosted.org/packages/2a/0a/944977367c8a6cfcfa6fcb8
  ac6b1f0f9a667c1f34194091c766b5d7c44d7/regex-2018.08.29.tar.gz
Requirement already satisfied: six in /usr/lib/python2.7/site-packages (from
  pyangbind) (1.14.0)
Requirement already satisfied: enum34 in /usr/lib/python2.7/site-packages (from
  pyangbind) (1.0.4)
Installing collected packages: bitarray, regex, pyangbind
  Running setup.py install for bitarray ... done
  Running setup.py install for regex ... done
  Running setup.py install for pyangbind ... done
Successfully installed bitarray-0.8.3 pyangbind-0.8.1 regex-2018.8.29
```

> **Note** If you haven't installed the required mandatory packages first, the setup of **pyangbind** won't be successful.

pyangbind is considered to be a plug-in for **pyang**, and they are used together. As explained earlier, **pyangbid** is used to convert YANG modules into Python classes so that they can be used in network applications. Example 13-37 shows a short bash script to run **pyangbind**.

Example 13-37 *Preparing to Run pyang*

```
$ cat test_pyangbind.sh
#!/bin/bash

PYBINDPLUGIN=`/usr/bin/env python -c 'import pyangbind; import os; print "%s/plugin"
  % os.path.dirname(pyangbind.__file__)'`
pyang --plugindir $PYBINDPLUGIN -p yang/vendor/cisco/xr/651 -f pybind -o test_
  interfaces.py yang/vendor/cisco/xr/651/Cisco-IOS-XR-ifmgr-cfg.yang

echo "Bindings successfully generated!"
```

Example 13-37 uses a Bash script to ease the structure of the **pyang** command. As you can see, the path to the directory containing **pyangbind** alongside the necessary attributes is very long and complex. Offloading it to a dedicated variable allows you to decouple the path to the plug-in from the **pybind** command itself. Then comes the **pyang** command, which you should already be familiar with. What is new here is the format used in the **pyang** command (**-f pybind**) and the path to the plug-in directory configured as **--plugindir** {*link*}. The remaining part of the **pyang** command, including the path to the folder and the actual modules, isn't new. The last part of the command sends a message to the terminal in the event that the classes are successfully generated. In Example 13-38, you can see the result of executing the **pyangbind** script.

Example 13-38 *Executing the pyangbind Script*

```
$ ./test_pyangbind.sh
Bindings successfully generated!
```

As you can see in Example 13-38, the CLI output indicates that the script was successfully executed. You now know you can check the result in the file, which was provided using the **-o** {*file*} parameter in the initial command (refer to Example 13-37). Example 13-39 shows the output of that file.

Example 13-39 *Result of the **pyangbind** Class Mapping*

```
$ cat test_interfaces.py
# -*- coding: utf-8 -*-
from operator import attrgetter
from pyangbind.lib.yangtypes import RestrictedPrecisionDecimalType
from pyangbind.lib.yangtypes import RestrictedClassType
from pyangbind.lib.yangtypes import TypedListType
from pyangbind.lib.yangtypes import YANGBool
from pyangbind.lib.yangtypes import YANGListType
from pyangbind.lib.yangtypes import YANGDynClass
from pyangbind.lib.yangtypes import ReferenceType
from pyangbind.lib.base import PybindBase
from collections import OrderedDict
from decimal import Decimal
from bitarray import bitarray
import six

# PY3 support of some PY2 keywords (needs improved)
if six.PY3:
  import builtins as __builtin__
  long = int
elif six.PY2:
  import __builtin__

class yc_global_interface_configuration_Cisco_IOS_XR_ifmgr_cfg__global_interface_
  configuration(PybindBase):
  """
  This class was auto-generated by the PythonClass plugin for PYANG
  from YANG module Cisco-IOS-XR-ifmgr-cfg - based on the path /global-interface-
  configuration. Each member element of
  the container is represented as a class variable - with a specific
  YANG type.

  YANG Description: Global scoped configuration for interfaces
  """
  __slots__ = ('_path_helper', '_extmethods', '__link_status',)

  _yang_name = 'global-interface-configuration'

  _pybind_generated_by = 'container'

  def __init__(self, *args, **kwargs):
    self._path_helper = False
```

```
    self._extmethods = False
    self.__link_status = YANGDynClass(base=RestrictedClassType(base_type=six.text_
  type, restriction_type="dict_key",
                    restriction_arg={u'default': {u'value': 0}, u'software-
  interfaces': {u'value': 2}, u'disable': {u'value': 1}},), default=six.text_
  type("default"),
is_leaf=True, yang_name="link-status", parent=self, path_helper=self._path_helper,
  extmethods=self._extmethods, register_paths=True, namespace='http://cisco.com/ns/
  yang
/Cisco-IOS-XR-ifmgr-cfg', defining_module='Cisco-IOS-XR-ifmgr-cfg', yang_type='Link-
  status-enum', is_config=True)
    load = kwargs.pop("load", None)
    if args:
      if len(args) > 1:
        raise TypeError("cannot create a YANG container with >1 argument")
      all_attr = True
      for e in self._pyangbind_elements:
        if not hasattr(args[0], e):
          all_attr = False
          break
      if not all_attr:
        raise ValueError("Supplied object did not have the correct attributes")
      for e in self._pyangbind_elements:
        nobj = getattr(args[0], e)
        if nobj._changed() is False:
          continue
        setmethod = getattr(self, "_set_%s" % e)
        if load is None:
          setmethod(getattr(args[0], e))
        else:
          setmethod(getattr(args[0], e), load=load)
  def _path(self):
    if hasattr(self, "_parent"):
      return self._parent._path()+[self._yang_name]
    else:
      return [u'global-interface-configuration']
  def _get_link_status(self):

! The output is truncated for brevity
```

Although the output in Example 13-39 is extensive, it shows you how YANG can be automatically translated to Python classes that you can use in your Python code.

Using pyang to Create JTOX Drivers

There is one more useful scenario where **pyang** can be helpful. The NETCONF protocol uses XML encoding, but for humans, it is easier to work with JSON. **pyang** has a specific output format, which is a JTOX (JSON-to-XML) driver. As the name implies, JTOX allows you to convert a JSON file to XML; this is possible if JSON is created using the same YANG module as the JTOX driver.

To implement a JTOX solution, you need to identify the YANG module or modules that will be used to create a JTOX driver. You can determine which module you need by verifying the attachment point for augmentation in YANG modules, as described earlier in this chapter (refer to Example 13-12). When you find necessary modules, you list all of them as input for **pyang**, as shown in Example 13-40. (Because the syntax of this command is explained earlier in this chapter, it isn't explained again here.)

Example 13-40 *Creating a JTOX Driver Out of Several YANG Modules*

```
$ pyang -f jtox -o cisco_if.jtox -p 612/ 612/Cisco-IOS-XR-ifmgr-cfg.yang 612/Cisco-
  IOS-XR-ipv4-io-cfg.yang 612/Cisco-IOS-XR-ipv6-ma-cfg.yang 612/Cisco-IOS-XR-
  drivers-media-eth-cfg.yang
612/Cisco-IOS-XR-drivers-media-eth-cfg.yang:13: warning: imported module Cisco-IOS-
  XR-types not used
```

The output in Example 13-40 contains a warning that some of the imported modules aren't used. This doesn't have any impact on the resulting JTOX driver, but it indicates that YANG modules probably import something that isn't referenced in this output. The reason could be that the content of the YANG module was changed, but the imported modules weren't reviewed.

Example 13-41 shows the output of the JTOX driver from Example 13-40 that is composed from several YANG modules.

Example 13-41 *JTOX Driver Created from Several YANG Modules*

```
$ cat cisco_if.jtox
{"tree": {"Cisco-IOS-XR-ifmgr-cfg:interface-configurations": ["container",
  {"interface-configuration": ["list", {"dampening": ["container", {"args": ["leaf",
  "enumeration"], "suppress-threshold": ["leaf", "uint32"], "half-life": ["leaf",
  "uint32"], "suppress-time": ["leaf", "uint32"], "reuse-threshold": ["leaf",
  "uint32"], "restart-penalty": ["leaf", "uint32"]}], "description": ["leaf",
  "string"], "secondary-admin-state": ["leaf", "enumeration"], "interface-virtual":
  ["leaf", "empty"], "Cisco-IOS-XR-drivers-media-eth-cfg:ethernet": ["container",
  {"inter-packet-gap": ["leaf", "enumeration"], "signal-fail-bit-error-rate":
  ["container", {"signal-remote-fault": ["leaf", "empty"], "signal-fail-report-
  disable": ["leaf", "empty"], "signal-fail-threshold": ["leaf", "uint32"]}],
  "duplex": ["leaf", "enumeration"], "speed": ["leaf", "enumeration"], "loopback":
  ["leaf", "enumeration"], "forward-error-correction": ["leaf", "enumeration"],
  "priority-flow-control": ["leaf", "enumeration"], "auto-negotiation": ["leaf",
  "enumeration"], "signal-degrade-bit-error-rate": ["container", {"signal-degrade-
  report": ["leaf", "empty"], "signal-degrade-threshold": ["leaf", "uint32"]}],
```

```
  "carrier-delay": ["container", {"carrier-delay-up": ["leaf", "uint32"], "carrier-
  delay-down": ["leaf", "uint32"]}], "flow-control": ["leaf", "enumeration"]}],
  "Cisco-IOS-XR-ipv6-ma-cfg:ipv6-network": ["container", {"bgp-flow-tag-policy-
  table": ["container", {"bgp-flow-tag-policy": ["container", {"source": ["leaf",
  "boolean"], "destination": ["leaf", "boolean"]}]}], "unnumbered": ["leaf",
  "string"], "addresses": ["container", {"auto-configuration": ["container",
  {"enable": ["leaf", "empty"]}], "eui64-addresses": ["container", {"eui64-address":
  ["list", {"route-tag": ["leaf", "uint32"], "prefix-length": ["leaf", "uint32"],
  "zone": ["leaf", "string"], "address": ["leaf", ["union", ["string", "string"]]]},
  [["Cisco-IOS-XR-ipv6-ma-cfg", "address"]]]}], "regular-addresses": ["container",
  {"regular-address": ["list", {"route-tag": ["leaf", "uint32"], "prefix-length":
  ["leaf", "uint32"], "zone": ["leaf", "string"], "address": ["leaf", ["union",
  ["string", "string"]]]}, [["Cisco-IOS-XR-ipv6-ma-cfg", "address"]]]}], "link-
  local-address": ["container", {"route-tag": ["leaf", "uint32"], "zone": ["leaf",
  "string"], "address": ["leaf", ["union", ["string", "string"]]]}]}], "tcp-mss-
  adjust-enable": ["leaf", "empty"], "verify": ["container", {"default-ping":
  ["leaf", "enumeration"], "self-ping": ["leaf", "enumeration"], "reachable":
  ["leaf", "enumeration"]}], "bgp-policy-accountings": ["container", {"bgp-policy-
  accounting": ["list", {"direction": ["leaf", "string"], "destination-accounting":
  ["leaf", "boolean"], "source-accounting": ["leaf", "boolean"]}, [["Cisco-
  IOS-XR-ipv6-ma-cfg", "direction"]]]}], "mac-address-filters": ["container",
  {"mac-address-filter": ["list", {"multicast-address": ["leaf", "string"]},
  [["Cisco-IOS-XR-ipv6-ma-cfg", "multicast-address"]]]}], "ttl-propagate-disable":
  ["leaf", "empty"], "unreachables": ["leaf", "empty"], "mtu": ["leaf", "uint32"],
  "bgp-qos-policy-propagation": ["container", {"source": ["leaf", "enumeration"],
!
! The output is truncated for brevity
```

As you can see, the JTOX driver in Example 13-41 is much longer than the one in Example 13-42. Despite the difference in length, the structure hasn't changed much. The only significant new point is highlighted in Example 13-42; when the augmentation should be done, it is called using the syntax { *module-name:top_container* }, in the same way that the parent module is called. You should consider this when constructing a JSON object.

Example 13-42 shows a JSON object for a fully functional Ethernet interface built using augmenting YANG modules.

Example 13-42 *A JSON Object with an Interface Configuration on Cisco IOS XR*

```
$ cat cisco_if.json
{
    "Cisco-IOS-XR-ifmgr-cfg:interface-configurations": {
        "interface-configuration": [
            {
                "active": "act",
                "interface-name": "GigabitEthernet0/0/0/0",
                "mtus": {
                        "mtu": [
```

```
                    {
                        "mtu": 1514,
                        "owner": "GigabitEthernet"
                    }
                ]
            },
            "Cisco-IOS-XR-drivers-media-eth-cfg:ethernet": {
                "carrier-delay": {
                    "carrier-delay-down": 0,
                    "carrier-delay-up": 0
                }
            },
            "Cisco-IOS-XR-ipv4-io-cfg:ipv4-network": {
                "addresses": {
                    "primary": {
                        "address": "10.11.33.33",
                        "netmask": "255.255.255.0"
                    }
                }
            },
            "Cisco-IOS-XR-ipv6-ma-cfg:ipv6-network": {
                "addresses": {
                    "regular-addresses": {
                        "regular-address": [
                            {
                                "address": "fc00::10:11:33:33",
                                "prefix-length": 112,
                                "zone": 0
                            }
                        ]
                    }
                }
            }
        }
    ]
  }
}
```

Following the syntax of the JTOX driver, the JSON object is composed using proper nodes and calling augmenting modules, where necessary. As you can see, the configuration of IPv4 and IPv6 addresses requires additional YANG modules. The same is true for Ethernet parameters, and this construction is becoming common in network programming based on YANG.

Example 13-43 shows the process of transforming a JSON object to XML and the resulting XML file.

Example 13-43 *Transforming JSON to XML by Using JTOX*

```
$ json2xml -t config -o test_book.xml cisco_if.jtox cisco_if.json
$ cat test_book.xml
<?xml version='1.0' encoding='utf-8'?>
<nc:config xmlns:drivers-media-eth-cfg="http://cisco.com/ns/yang/Cisco-IOS-XR-
  drivers-media-eth-cfg" xmlns:ifmgr-cfg="http://cisco.com/ns/yang/Cisco-IOS-XR-
  ifmgr-cfg" xmlns:ipv4-io-cfg="http://cisco.com/ns/yang/Cisco-IOS-XR-ipv4-io-cfg"
  xmlns:ipv6-ma-cfg="http://cisco.com/ns/yang/Cisco-IOS-XR-ipv6-ma-cfg" xmlns:nc=
  "urn:ietf:params:xml:ns:netconf:base:1.0" xmlns:inet="urn:ietf:params:xml:ns:
  yang:ietf-inet-types" xmlns:ip-iarm-datatypes="http://cisco.com/ns/yang/Cisco-
  IOS-XR-ip-iarm-datatypes" xmlns:xr="http://cisco.com/ns/yang/cisco-xr-types">
  <ifmgr-cfg:interface-configurations>
    <ifmgr-cfg:interface-configuration>
      <ifmgr-cfg:active>act</ifmgr-cfg:active>
      <ifmgr-cfg:interface-name>GigabitEthernet0/0/0/0</ifmgr-cfg:interface-name>
      <ifmgr-cfg:mtus>
        <ifmgr-cfg:mtu>
          <ifmgr-cfg:owner>GigabitEthernet</ifmgr-cfg:owner>
          <ifmgr-cfg:mtu>1514</ifmgr-cfg:mtu>
        </ifmgr-cfg:mtu>
      </ifmgr-cfg:mtus>
      <drivers-media-eth-cfg:ethernet>
        <drivers-media-eth-cfg:carrier-delay>
          <drivers-media-eth-cfg:carrier-delay-up>0</drivers-media-eth-cfg:carrier-
  delay-up>
          <drivers-media-eth-cfg:carrier-delay-down>0</drivers-media-eth-
  cfg:carrier-delay-down>
       </drivers-media-eth-cfg:carrier-delay>
      </drivers-media-eth-cfg:ethernet>
      <ipv4-io-cfg:ipv4-network>
        <ipv4-io-cfg:addresses>
          <ipv4-io-cfg:primary>
            <ipv4-io-cfg:netmask>255.255.255.0</ipv4-io-cfg:netmask>
            <ipv4-io-cfg:address>10.11.33.33</ipv4-io-cfg:address>
          </ipv4-io-cfg:primary>
        </ipv4-io-cfg:addresses>
      </ipv4-io-cfg:ipv4-network>
      <ipv6-ma-cfg:ipv6-network>
        <ipv6-ma-cfg:addresses>
          <ipv6-ma-cfg:regular-addresses>
            <ipv6-ma-cfg:regular-address>
```

```
              <ipv6-ma-cfg:address>fc00::10:11:33:33</ipv6-ma-cfg:address>
              <ipv6-ma-cfg:prefix-length>112</ipv6-ma-cfg:prefix-length>
              <ipv6-ma-cfg:zone>0</ipv6-ma-cfg:zone>
            </ipv6-ma-cfg:regular-address>
          </ipv6-ma-cfg:regular-addresses>
        </ipv6-ma-cfg:addresses>
      </ipv6-ma-cfg:ipv6-network>
    </ifmgr-cfg:interface-configuration>
  </ifmgr-cfg:interface-configurations>
</nc:config>
```

The most crucial point that you should pay attention to in the output of Example 13-43 is how different XML namespaces are mapped to the parts of the configuration file. Compared to Example 13-28, four different namespaces are actively used in the *<config>* context:

- xmlns:ifmgr-cfg="http://cisco.com/ns/yang/Cisco-IOS-XR-ifmgr-cfg"
- xmlns:ipv4-io-cfg="http://cisco.com/ns/yang/Cisco-IOS-XR-ipv4-io-cfg"
- xmlns:ipv6-ma-cfg="http://cisco.com/ns/yang/Cisco-IOS-XR-ipv6-ma-cfg"
- xmlns:drivers-media-eth-cfg="http://cisco.com/ns/yang/Cisco-IOS-XR-drivers-media-eth-cfg"

All the relevant information for defining these XML namespaces exists in the JTOX driver, as shown in Example 13-44.

Example 13-44 *Multiple YANG Module Definitions in a JTOX Driver*

```
$ cat cisco_if.jtox
! The output is truncated for brevity
"modules": {"Cisco-IOS-XR-ipv4-io-cfg": ["ipv4-io-cfg", "http://cisco.com/ns/yang/
  Cisco-IOS-XR-ipv4-io-cfg"], "Cisco-IOS-XR-drivers-media-eth-cfg": ["drivers-
  media-eth-cfg", "http://cisco.com/ns/yang/Cisco-IOS-XR-drivers-media-eth-cfg"],
  "Cisco-IOS-XR-ifmgr-cfg": ["ifmgr-cfg", "http://cisco.com/ns/yang/Cisco-IOS-XR-
  ifmgr-cfg"], "Cisco-IOS-XR-ip-iarm-datatypes": ["ip-iarm-datatypes", "http://
  cisco.com/ns/yang/Cisco-IOS-XR-ip-iarm-datatypes"], "ietf-inet-types": ["inet",
  "urn:ietf:params:xml:ns:yang:ietf-inet-types"], "Cisco-IOS-XR-ipv6-ma-cfg":
  ["ipv6-ma-cfg", "http://cisco.com/ns/yang/Cisco-IOS-XR-ipv6-ma-cfg"], "Cisco-IOS-
  XR-types": ["xr", "http://cisco.com/ns/yang/cisco-xr-types"]}, "annotations": {}}
```

In Example 13-44, the names of YANG modules called in the XML file that was created out of the JSON/JTOX transformation are highlighted.

Summary

This chapter covers the following topics:

- YANG is a data modeling language for creating data models that can be used anywhere, including for network management and programmability.
- The YANG data model has a tree structure.
- There are four types of nodes in a YANG tree: leaf, leaf-list, container, and list nodes.
- A grouping is a bundle of different nodes that can be reused in different contexts.
- A YANG module can contain data or can import information from other YANG modules.
- The YANG language allows you to extend a parent YANG data model with additional nodes; this is called augmentation.
- Sometimes it is necessary to tailor the scope of the initial YANG data models or to set some limits for just some cases or network functions; this is called deviation.
- Native (vendor-specific) YANG modules follow the native system's configuration structure.
- Third-party YANG modules provide a vendor-neutral view of the network devices data model across all the vendors.
- **pyang** validates and converts original YANG modules in human-readable output or in other types used in network automation applications.
- **pyangbind** makes it possible to use YANG modules directly from Python.
- JTOX is used to convert a network function configuration represented in JSON into XML format that is consumable by NETCONF.
- **json2xml** can be used for JSON-to-XML transformation based on the JTOX driver.

Chapter 14

NETCONF and RESTCONF

Protocols build on the functions provided by the transport, encoding, and modeling layers of the network programmability stack to provide a complete framework for automating the provisioning, operation, and maintenance of networks. This chapter discusses the NETCONF and RESTCONF protocols. NETCONF was developed first and provides an RPC-based API. RESTCONF, which is a RESTful protocol, was developed later and provides a subset of NETCONF functionality.

NETCONF

As you will see in this section, NETCONF relies heavily on SSH, XML, and YANG. This section also covers working with NETCONF using Python. Therefore, to make the most of this section, you need to be sure you've gone through all the relevant chapters that cover these subjects.

NETCONF Overview

In 2003, the IETF assembled the NETCONF Working Group (later renamed the Network Configuration Working Group), tasked with developing a protocol to address the shortcomings of existing practices and protocols for configuration management, such as SNMP. The working group's solution to these shortcomings was the NETCONF protocol. The background work preceding the design phase of NETCONF is documented in RFC 3535, "Overview of the 2002 IAB Network Management Workshop." The design goals from that work include the following:

- Make a distinction between configuration and state data
- Create multiple configuration data stores (candidate, running, and startup)
- Record configuration change transactions
- Ensure configuration testing and validation support

- Enable selective data retrieval with filtering
- Enable streaming and playback of event notifications
- Create an extensible procedure call mechanism

The NETCONF Working Group's activities (in chronological order) are listed at https://datatracker.ietf.org/wg/netconf/history/.

NETCONF, which stands for Network Configuration Protocol, can be used to configure a device, retrieve configuration or state data from a device, or issue exec mode commands, as long as the device is running a NETCONF server, or in other words, the device exposes a NETCONF API. Therefore, NETCONF is actually a misnomer because the protocol's function is not limited to *configuring* devices. NETCONF is formally defined in a number of RFCs. RFC 6241 covers the core protocol, which obsoletes the original RFC 4741. A number of other RFCs cover a variety of enhancements and updates to the protocol, as well as possible variations and/or implementations of the protocol. The following is a list of the RFCs for NETCONF (not including obsolete ones, as of this writing):

- RFC 5277, "NETCONF Event Notifications"
- RFC 5381, "Experience of Implementing NETCONF over SOAP (Informational)"
- RFC 5717, "Partial Lock Remote Procedure Call (RPC) for NETCONF"
- RFC 6022, "YANG Module for NETCONF Monitoring"
- RFC 6241, "Network Configuration Protocol (NETCONF)"
- RFC 6242, "Using the NETCONF Protocol over SSH"
- RFC 6243, "With-defaults Capability for NETCONF"
- RFC 6244, "An Architecture for Network Management Using NETCONF and YANG"
- RFC 7589, "Using the NETCONF Protocol over Transport Layer Security (TLS) with Mutual X.509 Authentication"
- RFC 7803, "Changing the Registration Policy for the NETCONF Capability URNs Registry (Best Current Practice)"
- RFC 8341, "Network Configuration Access Control Model"
- RFC 8526, "NETCONF Extensions to Support the Network Management Datastore Architecture"

NETCONF is a client/server session-based protocol. This means that a client initiates a connection to the server (the network device, in this case), such as an SSH connection to a particular TCP port that the server is listening on. When the server accepts the connection, both peers exchange protocol messages. Then the connection is torn down by one of the peers, either gracefully because the message exchange is complete or ungracefully because something went wrong.

After the client/server session is established, the client and server exchange hello messages, which provide information on which version of NETCONF is supported on each endpoint, as well other device capabilities. Capabilities describe which components of the NETCONF protocol, as well as which data models, the device supports. Support for some components is mandatory, and it is optional for others. Hello messages are not periodic; that is, after the initial hello message exchange, no further hello messages are exchanged.

Once the hello message exchange is completed, one or more *remote procedure call message* (rpc for short) are sent by the client. RPCs provide a programmatic method for a client to *call* (execute) a *procedure* (a piece of code) on a different device (which is why these calls are labeled *remote*). Each of the rpc messages specifies an *operation* for the server to carry out. An operation could be, for example, retrieving the running configuration of the device or editing the configuration.

The server executes the operation specified in the rpc message (or not) and responds with a *remote procedure call reply message* (rpc-reply for short) back to the client. The contents of the rpc-reply message depend on the operation requested by the client, the parameters included in the message, and whether the operation execution was successful.

The client/server session is terminated by one of the peers if one of many conditions becomes true. In a best-case scenario, the client sends an rpc message to the server, explicitly requesting that the connection be gracefully terminated. The server terminates the session, and the transport connection is torn down. On the other side of the spectrum, the transport connection may be unexpectedly lost due to a problem, and the server unilaterally kills the session.

Each of the concepts described in this section is covered in a lot of detail throughout the chapter.

Note NETCONF messages from the client encoded in XML are characterised by the root element <rpc> and the NETCONF responses back from the server, also encoded in XML, are characterised by the root element <rpc-reply>. For better readability throughout the chapter, client messages will be referred to *rpc messages* and the server responses will be referred to as *rpc-reply messages*.

Figure 14-1 illustrates the high-level operation of NETCONF.

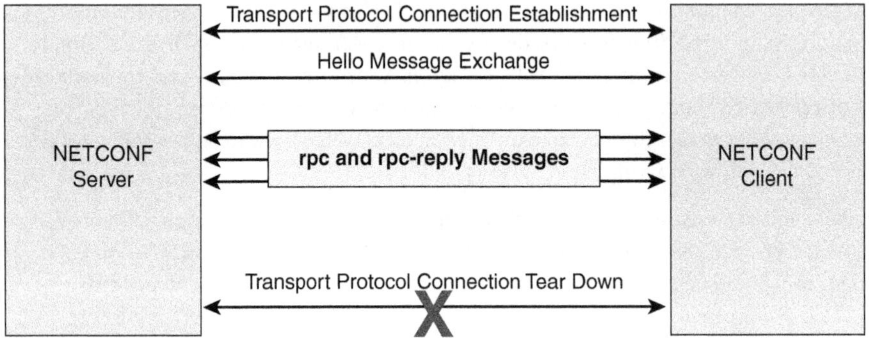

Figure 14-1 *High-Level Operation of NETCONF*

NETCONF Architecture

Like any other protocol, NETCONF is composed of several small functional components. Each of these components resides in one of the layers of a conceptual four-layer model, where each layer represents a group of similar functions. The functions contained in each layer of the model are independent of the functions in the other layers. Figure 14-2 illustrates this model.

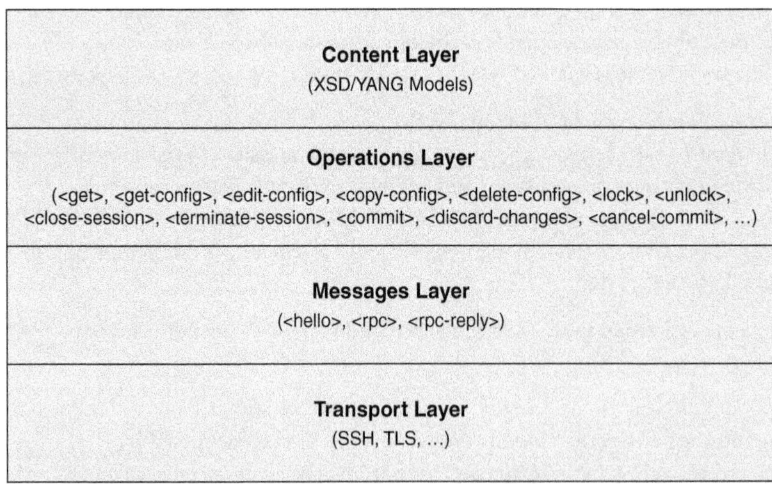

Figure 14-2 *The Four-Layer Model Encompassing All NETCONF Functions*

The transport layer at the bottom represents the functions performed by the transport protocol used by NETCONF to establish a secure, persistent connection between the client on one side and the device (server) on the other side. Although the majority of

NETCONF implementations today use SSH for transport, any transport protocol can be used, as long as this protocol satisfies a number of criteria. However, it is a mandatory requirement for any NETCONF implementation to support SSH. The section "The NETCONF Transport Layer," later in this chapter, discusses these criteria as well as the specific implementation of NETCONF over SSH.

On top of the transport layer is the messages layer. This layer encompassed the RPC paradigm used by NETCONF. Both rpc and rpc-reply messages are covered in detail later in this chapter, in the section "The NETCONF Messages Layer."

The operations layer describes all the actions, or operations, that the client can execute remotely on the device via an rpc message. An operation may retrieve configuration or state data from the device, or it might edit the running or startup configuration on the device. There are operations defined in the base NETCONF protocol, and there are extended operations that require special capabilities, which are advertised in the hello message. Client operations are discussed in detail in the section "The NETCONF Operations Layer."

The top layer of the model, the content layer, describes the actual content that goes into the messages. Any NETCONF message is a well-formed XML document, and XML documents are composed of namespaces, elements, tags, entities, and attributes. But how do the values of these document components relate to device configurations or operational data? When NETCONF first came out, the data in NETCONF messages was unstructured. A few years ago, NETCONF implementations started using document type definitions (DTDs) or XML Schema Definitions (XSDs) to define the structure of the data inside the message. Today, the data is modeled almost exclusively in YANG. NETCONF and YANG are covered in the section "The NETCONF Content Layer."

The NETCONF Transport Layer

The first layer of the NETCONF protocol stack is the transport layer, which encompasses the functions necessary to establish the client/server connection required by NETCONF to operate.

NETCONF Transport Protocol Requirements

The NETCONF standard does not mandate implementing NETCONF over SSH *only*. (See Section 2 in both RFC 6241 and RFC 6244.) NETCONF can operate over any transport protocol that satisfies a minimum number of requirements. The standard does mandate, however, that any NETCONF implementation *must*, at a minimum, support NETCONF over SSH, and it may optionally support other transport protocols as well.

For NETCONF to use any transport protocol, the transport protocol must be capable of the following characteristics and functions:

- **Connection oriented:** NETCONF is a client/server protocol, which means it requires a transport protocol that is capable of establishing a persistent connection that is long-lived for the duration of a session, involving an arbitrary number of rpc and rpc-reply messages.
- **Reliable:** Because the transport protocol is connection oriented, NETCONF requires reliability and, hence, NETCONF runs over TCP-based transport protocols only. UDP is not a supported option. For example, NETCONF over TLS is supported, but NETCONF over DTLS is not.
- **Sequenced data delivery:** Being connection oriented also implies that the transport protocol must have mechanisms to reorder any out-of-sequence frames received at either end of the connection. Think of TCP sequence and acknowledgment numbers.
- **Authentication:** NETCONF fully delegates the authentication of the client by the server, and vice versa, to the transport protocol. This process is entirely transparent to NETCONF. However, once the transport protocol authenticates a user, it passes the username of that user to the upper layers of NETCONF, and it is then referred to as the *NETCONF username*. The NETCONF stack (not the transport protocol) then takes care of the authorization of that authenticated user identified by its NETCONF username.
- **Data integrity and confidentiality:** The transport protocol must maintain data integrity against malicious or unintentional corruption. It must also implement the encryption mechanisms necessary to maintain data confidentiality.

NETCONF over SSH

As mentioned earlier, any NETCONF implementation *must* support SSH as a transport protocol. RFC 6242 (which obsoletes RFC 4742) is dedicated to NETCONF over SSH. Chapter 9, "SSH," discusses three SSH protocols: the transport, authentication, and connection protocols (also covered in RFC 4252, 4253, and 4254 respectively.) These three protocols work together to initiate the SSH session over which NETCONF operates and then to authenticate the client and server, maintain the session, and finally tear it down.

First, the transport protocol establishes an SSH transport connection from client to server. The client and server then exchange keys that are used for data integrity and encryption. The authentication protocol then kicks in, and the ssh-userauth service authenticates the user (client) to the server. Finally, the SSH connection protocol brings up the SSH session via the ssh-connection service.

After the SSH session is established, the NETCONF protocol stack invokes NETCONF as an SSH subsystem. The IANA-assigned TCP port for NETCONF is 830. However, this port is often configurable. A NETCONF over SSH session may be initiated in a number of ways. The simplest way is to use a terminal command such as:

```
[NetDev@server1~]$ ssh {username}@{device_address} -p {netconf_port}
```

Or alternatively:

```
[NetDev@server1~]$ ssh {username}@{device_address} -s
{netconf_subsystem}
```

where **-p** is used to indicate the NETCONF port configured on the system (830 if left to the default), and **-s** is used to indicate the SSH subsystem name, which is usually **netconf** on most platforms. Which method to use depends on the platform you are trying to access. Some platforms use the first method, others use the second method, and some platforms support both methods. With the first method, the client initiates a TCP session to the port specified in the command and the NETCONF server, running on the device, listens to incoming TCP connections on that same port. In the second method, the client initiates a TCP session to the default SSH port (port 22), and then the SSH server on the device hands over the connection to the NETCONF subsystem running on the device. The second method may be more handy in situations where a firewall is sitting between the client and server, and only connections to the default SSH port are permitted.

The examples in this chapter use one of the IOS XE sandboxes provided by Cisco DevNet. The NETCONF API on the router is reachable through SSH to ios-xe-mgmt-latest.cisco.com on port 10000. The sandbox is always on (that is, no reservation is required) and is available to access and use for free. With this router, you use the username developer and the password C1sco12345. This router uses the first method, so you need to use the command **ssh -p 10000 admin@ ios-xe-mgmt-latest.cisco.com** to establish a NETCONF session to the router. You can also follow the examples in this chapter by using any other method you find convenient, such as your own lab routers or the Cisco Modeling Labs (CML).

Note This router is up and running at the time of this writing, but its status may change at any time. You are strongly encouraged to check out the numerous sandboxes that Cisco provides (currently for free) at https://devnetsandbox.cisco.com/RM/Topology.

The NETCONF Messages Layer

The three types of messages defined in NETCONF are hello, rpc, and rpc-reply messages. Hello messages are the first NETCONF messages exchanged between a client and a server when a NETCONF session is opened. rpc messages are then sent by a client to request specific operations on a server, and the server responds with rpc-reply messages back to the client; the content of these messages depends on the operation in the rpc message and the result of that operation on the server.

Any valid NETCONF message must be a well-formed XML document encoded in UTF-8. A server returns an error message to the client if the client sends a NETCONF message that is either not well-formed or not encoded in UTF-8.

A NETCONF message may optionally start with an XML declaration, but the first mandatory line in the message is the root element, which must be one of three values—<hello>, <rpc>, or <rpc-reply>—depending on the type of message.

Regardless of the type of message or the version of NETCONF that is being used, the message elements are *always* defined in the namespace urn:ietf:params:xml:ns:netconf:base:1.0. Child elements down the hierarchy may possibly be defined in other namespaces. These namespaces point to the data models in which the elements are defined.

Following the root element, the child elements included in each message depend on the type of the message, the purpose of the message, and the data models referenced by the message elements. Regardless of the message type, all messages end in the character sequence]]>]]>.

Note If what you just read in the previous few paragraphs does not sound very familiar, this may be a good time to go back and review Chapter 10, "XML".

Note NETCONF is currently at Version 1.1, but at the time of this writing, Version 1.0 is still in wide use. Devices that support NETCONF Version 1.1 have the capability urn:ietf:params:netconf:base:1.1 advertised in their hello messages (as you will see in Example 14-1). NETCONF Version 1.1 uses a message framing mechanism called the *chunked framing mechanism*, in which a message is split into chunks. Each chunk includes the chunk size and chunk data, and the message is terminated using the character sequence \n##\n. To keep the examples simple, this chapter terminates messages using the character sequence]]>]]>, as this does not affect the core protocol functionality discussed in the chapter. Version 1.1 of the protocol primarily provides more capabilities beyond those provided by Version 1.0, but the core protocol remains the same. Apart from the framing mechanism, this chapter covers Version 1.1, unless otherwise stated.

Hello Messages

Once an SSH session is established by the transport layer, the client and server exchange hello messages. The messages are not exchanged in any particular order: The client and server may even send their hellos simultaneously. Example 14-1 shows a sample hello message from the DevNet Sandbox running IOS XE. The router sends this XML output to the terminal as soon as the password is entered correctly and the SSH session is established. (The router supports more than 200 capabilities, and the message is truncated here for brevity.)

Example 14-1 *Hello Message from the Server to the Client*

```
[NetDev@localhost ~]$ ssh developer@ios-xe-mgmt-latest.cisco.com -p 10000
developer@ios-xe-mgmt-latest.cisco.com's password:
<?xml version="1.0" encoding="UTF-8"?>
<hello xmlns="urn:ietf:params:xml:ns:netconf:base:1.0">
    <capabilities>
        <capability>urn:ietf:params:netconf:base:1.0</capability>
        <capability>urn:ietf:params:netconf:base:1.1</capability>
        <capability>urn:ietf:params:netconf:capability:writable-running:1.0
  </capability>
        <capability>urn:ietf:params:netconf:capability:xpath:1.0</capability>
        <capability>urn:ietf:params:netconf:capability:validate:1.0</capability>
        <capability>urn:ietf:params:netconf:capability:validate:1.1</capability>
        <capability>urn:ietf:params:netconf:capability:rollback-on-error:1.0
  </capability>
        <capability>urn:ietf:params:netconf:capability:notification:1.0</capability>
        <capability>urn:ietf:params:netconf:capability:interleave:1.0</capability>
        <capability>urn:ietf:params:netconf:capability:with-defaults:1.0?basic-
  mode=explicit&amp;also-supported=report-all-tagged</capability>
        <capability>urn:ietf:params:netconf:capability:yang-library:1.0?revision=
  2016-06-21&amp;module-set-id=730825758336af65af9606c071685c05</capability>

--------- OUTPUT OMITTED FOR BREVITY ---------

    </capabilities>
    <session-id>746</session-id>
</hello>]]>]]>
```

The hello message from the client can be as simple as the one shown in Example 14-2.

Example 14-2 *Hello Message from the Client to the Server*

```
<?xml version="1.0" encoding="UTF-8"?>
  <hello xmlns="urn:ietf:params:xml:ns:netconf:base:1.0">
    <capabilities>
      <capability>urn:ietf:params:netconf:base:1.0</capability>
    </capabilities>
  </hello>]]>]]>
```

The hello message in Example 14-2 is what you would typically copy and paste into the terminal in order to complete the NETCONF session establishment.

Capabilities are discussed in detail later in this chapter. For now, notice the element hierarchy in the hello message. The message is composed of the root element <hello>, defined in the mandatory namespace urn:ietf:params:xml:ns:netconf:base:1.0, using the attribute xmlns. Under the root element is the <capabilities> element, which in turn contains a list of sibling <capability> elements, each containing one capability supported by the device.

The hello message from the server contains a mandatory <session-id> element, which contains the session ID of that particular session. The session ID is an important parameter that comes into play when a NETCONF session attempts to kill another session, maybe because that first session has a lock on a configuration datastore, and an administrator needs to terminate that session because it is hogging the device.

The client hello message, on the other hand, does not have a <session-id> element.

rpc Messages

Example 14-3 shows a NETCONF rpc message from a client requesting the interface admin state for interface GigabitEthernet1 on the DevNet Sandbox running IOS XE.

Example 14-3 *An rpc Message for Retrieving the Admin State of Interface GigabitEthernet1*

```
<rpc xmlns="urn:ietf:params:xml:ns:netconf:base:1.0" message-id="105">
    <get>
        <filter type="subtree">
            <interfaces xmlns="http://cisco.com/ns/yang/Cisco-IOS-XE-interfaces-
  oper">
                <interface>
                    <name>GigabitEthernet1</name>
                    <admin-status />
                </interface>
            </interfaces>
        </filter>
    </get>
</rpc>]]>]]>
```

In Example 14-3, the first element in the message is the root element <rpc>, which is defined in the mandatory namespace urn:ietf:params:xml:ns:netconf:base:1.0 using the attribute xmlns. Following the root <rpc> element down in the hierarchy is the operation. In this example, the operation is get, and hence the element is <get>.

The child elements that go under the operation element (<get> in this case) depend on two main factors. The first factor is what operation is requested in the rpc message. Some operations have mandatory elements. For example, the <get-config> operation has a mandatory element named <source>, which is used to specify the source datastore from which the configuration will be retrieved. Other elements are optional. Operations and their corresponding XML elements are discussed in detail in the section "The Operations Layer," later in this chapter.

Of particular importance is the filter element. If the filter element is not included, the <get> and <get-config> operations retrieve all information, unfiltered, whether state and configuration data (in the case of the <get> operation) or configuration data only (in the case of the <get-config> operation). Filtering is also discussed in detail later in this chapter.

The second factor that determines which child elements go under the operation element is the data model that you wish to reference. In this example, the interfaces element and all its child elements are defined in the namespace http://cisco.com/ns/yang/Cisco-IOS-XE-interfaces-oper, which represents the YANG data model referenced by the specific hierarchy in the message (interfaces ➪ interface ➪ name | admin-status). The relationship between NETCONF and YANG data models is discussed in detail in the section "The Content Layer," later in this chapter.

In addition to the XML namespace declared in the <rpc> root element, another mandatory attribute is message-id. The client uses an arbitrary number in the first rpc message it sends over a session, and it increments this value with each new message it sends to the server. The server saves the value of this attribute and attaches it in the corresponding rpc-reply message so that the client can identify which rpc-reply belongs to each rpc message. This enables the message pipelining capability in NETCONF: The client can send more than one rpc message before it receives any rpc-reply messages. However, the server should process the rpc messages in the order in which they were received.

In addition to the two mandatory attributes, a client can add any number of additional attributes to the <rpc> element in an rpc message, and those attributes will be mirrored back, unchanged, in the rpc-reply message.

rpc-reply Messages

Example 14-4 shows the rpc-reply message received from the IOS XE router in response to the rpc message in Example 14-3.

Example 14-4 *An rpc-reply Message for Retrieving the Admin State of Interface GigabitEthernet1*

```
<rpc-reply xmlns="urn:ietf:params:xml:ns:netconf:base:1.0" message-id="105">
    <data>
        <interfaces xmlns="http://cisco.com/ns/yang/Cisco-IOS-XE-interfaces-oper">
            <interface>
                <name>GigabitEthernet1</name>
                <admin-status>if-state-up</admin-status>
            </interface>
        </interfaces>
    </data>
</rpc-reply>]]>]]>
```

In Example 14-4, the first element in the message is the root element, <rpc-reply>, defined in the mandatory namespace urn:ietf:params:xml:ns:netconf:base:1.0 using the attribute xmlns. The mandatory message-id attribute is also in the root element, mirroring the value received in the RPC message.

What follows the root <rpc-reply> element down in the hierarchy depends on the operation and the result of running that operation on the server. Generally speaking, three cases describe the possible elements in an rpc-reply message:

- The rpc message might contain an operation that results in data being retrieved and sent back in the rpc-reply message, such as the <get> and <get-config> operations. If the operation was executed successfully on the server, the element following the root <rpc-reply> element in the message is the <data> element, which encapsulates the retrieved data from the server. This is the case in Example 14-4.
- The rpc message might contain an operation that does not result in the retrieval of any data. For example, the <edit-config> operation requests that the configuration on the device be changed, and the <commit> operation requests that the configuration in the candidate datastore be committed to the running configuration. If the operation is successful, the element following the root <rpc-reply> element is an empty <ok> element, expressed as <ok/>.
- Some error might occur, maybe because the rpc message is not a well-formed XML document, or the operation in the rpc message is not executed on the server for some reason. In this case, the element following the root <rpc-reply> element is an <rpc-error> element.

Example 14-5 shows the rpc-reply message that is received when an error is injected into the rpc message in Example 14-3 where the value of the operation is changed from <get> to <get-INVALID-VALUE>.

Example 14-5 *An rpc-reply Message Indicating a Syntax Error in One of the Elements in the RPC Message*

```
<rpc-reply xmlns="urn:ietf:params:xml:ns:netconf:base:1.0" message-id="105">
 <rpc-error>
  <error-type>protocol</error-type>
  <error-tag>unknown-element</error-tag>
  <error-severity>error</error-severity>
  <error-path>
      /rpc
  </error-path>
  <error-info>
    <bad-element>get-INVALID-VALUE</bad-element>
  </error-info>
  </rpc-error>
</rpc-reply>]]>]]>
```

The rpc-error element has a number of child elements that elaborate on the error condition:

- **error-type:** A string value that indicates the layer at which the error was found and has one of four values: transport, rpc, protocol, and application.
- **error-tag:** A string value that describes the error. See Appendix A of RFC 6241 for a list of allowed values.
- **error-severity:** The error severity; the only allowed value is error.
- **error-app-tag:** A string value that describes the data model–specific or implementation-specific error condition.
- **error-path:** The absolute XPath to the element causing the error.
- **error-message:** A human-readable string that describes the error condition.
- **error-info:** Protocol-specific or data model–specific detailed error content.

As you can see from the sample error element in Example 14-5, not all child elements in this list are mandatory elements.

The NETCONF Operations Layer

Before we discuss the different operations defined by the NETCONF protocol, two general concepts need to be elaborated first: configuration data versus state data, and datastores.

The NETCONF protocol makes a clear distinction between configuration data and state data. Configuration data is, obviously, the configuration stored on the device. That configuration is what the device operator enters on the device in an attempt to bring the device to a desired operational state. However, the fact that specific configuration has been applied to the device does not necessarily mean that the operational state will follow. There are instances in which the state of a device does not follow the configuration on that device. Administratively enabling an interface does not necessarily mean that the interface will be in the up state. State data can either be the operational state of the different components of the device, such as the state of an interface (whether it is up or down), or it can be the statistics collected from the device, such as the interface incoming and outgoing packet count.

NETCONF supports different datastores. The concept of a datastore should be familiar to network engineers who have to save the running configuration to the startup configuration after changing the former to make sure the device will boot up from the updated configuration on the next reboot. In this case, the running configuration is one datastore, and the startup configuration is another. Some devices do not have a startup configuration datastore, and some devices support a candidate configuration datastore on which configuration changes are applied before being committed to the running configuration. What datastore is available for you to work on depends on the device. The only mandatory datastore on any device is the running configuration datastore. For example, IOS XR–based devices only have running and candidate configuration datastores and no startup configuration datastore.

An rpc message sent by a client to a server is a request for the server to execute a specific operation on the server and return an appropriate response to the client in an rpc-reply message. The operations layer defines a set of operations that are encapsulated in rpc messages that cover the scope of all allowed operations. The following sections loosely classify the operations into groups, based on what each operation is intended to accomplish.

Retrieving Data: <get> and <get-config>

The <get> and <get-config> operations are used to retrieve data from the server. The <get> operation retrieves all configuration and state data, and the <get-config> operation retrieves the configuration data from only a specific datastore.

The <source> element is a mandatory element for the <get-config> operation that indicates the configuration datastore from which the configuration will be retrieved. It can be <running>, <startup>, or <candidate>, depending on which datastores exist on the device and depending on the NETCONF capabilities supported by the device. Example 14-6 shows an rpc message to retrieve *all* the running configuration on an IOS XE router.

Example 14-6 *An rpc Message to Retrieve the Running Configuration on an IOS XE Router*

```
<rpc xmlns="urn:ietf:params:xml:ns:netconf:base:1.0" message-id="101">
  <get-config>
    <source>
      <running/>
    </source>
  </get-config>
</rpc>]]>]]>]]>]]>
```

Example 4-7 shows partial output from the router after receiving the rpc message in Example 14-6.

Example 14-7 *The rpc-reply Message Containing the Running Configuration on the IOS XE Router*

```
<?xml version="1.0" encoding="UTF-8"?>
<rpc-reply xmlns="urn:ietf:params:xml:ns:netconf:base:1.0" message-id="101">
    <data>
        <native xmlns="http://cisco.com/ns/yang/Cisco-IOS-XE-native">
            <version>16.11</version>
            <boot-start-marker />
            <boot-end-marker />
            <banner>
                <motd>
                    <banner>^C</banner>
                </motd>
            </banner>
            <memory>
                <free>
                    <low-watermark>
                        <processor>80557</processor>
                    </low-watermark>
                </free>
            </memory>
            <call-home>
                <contact-email-addr xmlns="http://cisco.com/ns/yang/Cisco-IOS-XE-
  call-home">sch-smart-licensing@cisco.com</contact-email-addr>
                <profile xmlns="http://cisco.com/ns/yang/Cisco-IOS-XE-call-home">
                    <profile-name>CiscoTAC-1</profile-name>
                    <active>true</active>

--------- OUTPUT TRUNCATED FOR BREVITY ---------
```

If the <get> or <get-config> operation is successful, the data retrieved is encapsulated in a <data> element, as you can see in Example 14-7. If there is an error processing the rpc message, an rpc-reply message with an appropriate <rpc-error> element is returned.

In very rare cases you will want to retrieve the full configuration from a datastore or all state data on a device. Unless the full configuration is required, you will use the <filter> element to specify which parts of the data you need to retrieve. Filters exist in two flavors: subtree and XPath filters.

Subtree Filters

Subtree filters indicate the XML element subtrees to include in the output. To understand this, consider the output in Example 14-7. The root element of the message is the <rpc-reply> element, followed by the <data> element, as expected. The first child element under the <data> element is the <native> element, which is followed by several elements that are child elements to <native> and sibling elements to each other. Where the <native>

element comes from is discussed in detail in the next section, "The Content Layer." For now, just accept it as one layer of hierarchy under which all configuration data exists.

Now say that you need the rpc-reply message to include only the IOS XE version, which is included in the output under the <version> element and is one layer of hierarchy under the <native> element. Then the <filter> element in the rpc message simply includes the <version> element, indicating that this element is to be included in the output data. Example 14-8 shows how the rpc message looks like in this case.

Example 14-8 *The rpc Message to Retrieve the IOS XE Version Number*

```
<rpc xmlns="urn:ietf:params:xml:ns:netconf:base:1.0" message-id="101">
  <get-config>
    <source>
        <running/>
    </source>
    <filter type="subtree">
      <native xmlns="http://cisco.com/ns/yang/Cisco-IOS-XE-native">
            <version></version>
      </native>
    </filter>
  </get-config>
</rpc>]]>]]>
```

Notice the type attribute, which should be equal to **subtree** or omitted altogether since this is the default value of the attribute. Example 14-9 shows the resulting rpc-reply message.

Example 14-9 *The rpc-reply Message, Including Only the IOS XE Version Number*

```
<?xml version="1.0" encoding="UTF-8"?>
<rpc-reply xmlns="urn:ietf:params:xml:ns:netconf:base:1.0" message-id="101">
    <data>
        <native xmlns="http://cisco.com/ns/yang/Cisco-IOS-XE-native">
            <version>16.11</version>
        </native>
    </data>
</rpc-reply>]]>]]>
```

This simple example illustrates the inclusive natures of subtree filters; that is, what you include in a filter appears in the output. Not including a <filter> element in the rpc message yields *everything*, and an empty <filter> element yields *nothing*. Example 14-8 is just meant to get you started, and subtree filters can be a little more sophisticated than that. Subtree filters can be based on five different components:

- Namespace selection
- Containment nodes

- Selection nodes
- Content match nodes
- Attribute match expressions

Namespace selection simply means pointing to the data model that defines the element hierarchy in the filter by using the **xmlns** attribute. (You don't need to worry about this just yet. The next section breaks down the relationship between YANG models, namespaces, and element hierarchies.)

Any element in an XML document that has child elements is called a *containment node*. When a subtree filter specifies a containment node in its hierarchy without any further criteria, the matching node in the data model (referenced by the namespace) is included in the output, along with all its child elements. In Example 14-10, the containment node <interface> is used to list the configuration for all interfaces on the router.

Example 14-10 *Using a Containment Node in a Subtree Filter*

```
<rpc xmlns="urn:ietf:params:xml:ns:netconf:base:1.0" message-id="101">
  <get-config>
    <source>
        <running/>
    </source>
    <filter>
      <native xmlns="http://cisco.com/ns/yang/Cisco-IOS-XE-native">
        <interface></interface>
      </native>
    </filter>
  </get-config>
</rpc>]]>]]>
```

The output under the <data> element includes the element <interface> and all its child elements and all *their* child elements, all the way to the leaf nodes, as shown in Example 14-11.

Example 14-11 *The Result of Using a Containment Node in a Subtree Filter*

```
<?xml version="1.0" encoding="UTF-8"?>
<rpc-reply xmlns="urn:ietf:params:xml:ns:netconf:base:1.0" message-id="101">
    <data>
        <native xmlns="http://cisco.com/ns/yang/Cisco-IOS-XE-native">
            <interface>
                <GigabitEthernet>
                    <name>1</name>
                    <description>MANAGEMENT INTERFACE - DON'T TOUCH ME</description>
```

```
                  <ip>
                      <address>
                          <primary>
                              <address>10.10.20.48</address>
                              <mask>255.255.255.0</mask>
                          </primary>
                      </address>
                  </ip>
                  <mop>
                      <enabled>false</enabled>
                      <sysid>false</sysid>
                  </mop>
                  <negotiation xmlns="http://cisco.com/ns/yang/
Cisco-IOS-XE-ethernet">
                      <auto>true</auto>
                  </negotiation>
              </GigabitEthernet>
              <GigabitEthernet>
                  <name>2</name>
                  <description>Network Interface</description>
                  <ip>
                      <address>
                          <primary>
                              <address>10.10.10.10</address>
                              <mask>255.255.255.0</mask>
                          </primary>
                      </address>
                  </ip>
                  <mop>
                      <enabled>false</enabled>
                      <sysid>false</sysid>
                  </mop>
                  <negotiation xmlns="http://cisco.com/ns/yang/
Cisco-IOS-XE-ethernet">
                      <auto>true</auto>
                  </negotiation>
              </GigabitEthernet>
              <GigabitEthernet>
                  <name>3</name>
                  <description>Network Interface</description>
                  <shutdown />
                  <mop>
                      <enabled>false</enabled>
                      <sysid>false</sysid>
```

```
                    </mop>
                    <negotiation xmlns="http://cisco.com/ns/yang/
  Cisco-IOS-XE-ethernet">
                        <auto>true</auto>
                    </negotiation>
                </GigabitEthernet>
            </interface>
        </native>
    </data>
</rpc-reply>]]>]]>
```

To get specific elements in the output out of a set of sibling elements, an empty leaf node, called a *selection node*, is specified in the filter. For example, if you need the interface name and description for *all* three interfaces, the containment nodes <interface> and <GigabitEthernet> are used, and then the selection nodes <name> and <description> are used to construct the filter, as shown in Example 14-12.

Example 14-12 *Using the Selection Nodes <name> and <description> in a Subtree Filter*

```
<rpc xmlns="urn:ietf:params:xml:ns:netconf:base:1.0" message-id="101">
    <get-config>
        <source>
            <running />
        </source>
        <filter>
            <native xmlns="http://cisco.com/ns/yang/Cisco-IOS-XE-native">
                <interface>
                    <GigabitEthernet>
                        <name></name>
                        <description />
                    </GigabitEthernet>
                </interface>
            </native>
        </filter>
    </get-config>
</rpc>]]>]]>
```

Note that an empty selection node can use one of two XML notations for empty elements. The first notation uses opening and closing tags with nothing in between, as the <name> element in the example does. The second notation uses just a single tag, as the <description> element does.

The result shown in Example 14-13 is a list of interfaces, with only names and descriptions included in the output.

Example 14-13 *Output Including Names and Descriptions Only for All Interfaces*

```
<?xml version="1.0" encoding="UTF-8"?>
<rpc-reply xmlns="urn:ietf:params:xml:ns:netconf:base:1.0" message-id="101">
    <data>
        <native xmlns="http://cisco.com/ns/yang/Cisco-IOS-XE-native">
            <interface>
                <GigabitEthernet>
                    <name>1</name>
                    <description>MANAGEMENT INTERFACE - DON'T TOUCH ME</description>
                </GigabitEthernet>
                <GigabitEthernet>
                    <name>2</name>
                    <description>Network Interface</description>
                </GigabitEthernet>
                <GigabitEthernet>
                    <name>3</name>
                    <description>Network Interface</description>
                </GigabitEthernet>
            </interface>
        </native>
    </data>
</rpc-reply>]]>]]>
```

What if you need to get the configuration for interface GigabitEthernet1 only but need the *full* interface configuration ? In this case, you need to use a *content match node*, which is a leaf node, but, unlike a selection node, it contains content used as the matching criteria.

Say that the leaf node <name> is to be used along with 1 as content. In this case, the filter retrieves all sibling elements having the hierarchy <native> ➪ <interface> ➪ <GigabitEthernet> that have a leaf node <name> containing the value 1. Example 14-14 shows the filter for this case.

Example 14-14 *Using a Content Match Node to Retrieve the Full Configuration of Interface GigabitEthernet1*

```
<rpc xmlns="urn:ietf:params:xml:ns:netconf:base:1.0" message-id="101">
    <get-config>
        <source>
            <running />
        </source>
        <filter>
            <native xmlns="http://cisco.com/ns/yang/Cisco-IOS-XE-native">
                <interface>
```

```
                <GigabitEthernet>
                    <name>1</name>
                </GigabitEthernet>
            </interface>
        </native>
    </filter>
  </get-config>
</rpc>]]>]]>
```

The resulting rpc-reply message contains the full configuration of interface GigabitEthernet1, as shown in Example 14-15.

Example 14-15 *The Result of Using the Content Matching Node <name> to Display the Full Configuration of Interface GigabitEthernet1*

```
<?xml version="1.0" encoding="UTF-8"?>
<rpc-reply xmlns="urn:ietf:params:xml:ns:netconf:base:1.0" message-id="101">
    <data>
        <native xmlns="http://cisco.com/ns/yang/Cisco-IOS-XE-native">
            <interface>
                <GigabitEthernet>
                    <name>1</name>
                    <description>MANAGEMENT INTERFACE - DON'T TOUCH ME</description>
                    <ip>
                        <address>
                            <primary>
                                <address>10.10.20.48</address>
                                <mask>255.255.255.0</mask>
                            </primary>
                        </address>
                    </ip>
                    <mop>
                        <enabled>false</enabled>
                        <sysid>false</sysid>
                    </mop>
                    <negotiation xmlns="http://cisco.com/ns/yang/
  Cisco-IOS-XE-ethernet">
                        <auto>true</auto>
                    </negotiation>
                </GigabitEthernet>
            </interface>
        </native>
    </data>
</rpc-reply>]]>]]>
```

If the filter matches on a specific description instead of on the name, and if it happens that two interfaces have that same description, the full configuration of both interfaces appear in the output, since the <GigabitEthernet> elements of both interfaces are sibling elements.

Finally, if one of the elements in a data model has any attributes, the values of one or more of these attributes can be used as matching criteria for a subtree filter. This works just as a content matching node works: All sibling nodes that satisfy that specific attribute value show up in the filter results, along with all child elements of these siblings.

XPath Filters

An XPath filter uses XPath expressions to filter the data retrieved from a device. XPath is covered in detail in Chapter 10, and it is revisited here in the context of NETCONF.

To use an XPath filter, you add a <filter> element under the element representing the operation, with three distinct attributes:

- **type:** This attribute has the value xpath.
- **xmlns:** This attribute has a value equal to the namespace pointing to the data model referenced by the filter.
- **select:** This attribute has a value equal to the XPath expression that is used to filter the XML tree to retrieve only the data needed.

Example 14-16 shows an rpc message that uses an XPath filter to retrieve the <name> element of *all* interfaces on the router.

Example 14-16 *An rpc Message Using an XPath Filter to Retrieve the Names of All Interfaces on the Router*

```
<rpc xmlns="urn:ietf:params:xml:ns:netconf:base:1.0" message-id="101">
    <get-config>
        <source>
            <running />
        </source>
        <filter xmlns:xyz="http://cisco.com/ns/yang/Cisco-IOS-XE-native"
                type="xpath"
                select="/xyz:native/interface/GigabitEthernet/name">
        </filter>
    </get-config>
</rpc>]]>]]>
```

Example 14-17 shows the RPC reply message that contains the interface names.

Example 14-17 *The rpc-reply Message, Including the Names of All Interfaces on the Router*

```
<?xml version="1.0" encoding="UTF-8"?>
<rpc-reply xmlns="urn:ietf:params:xml:ns:netconf:base:1.0" message-id="101">
    <data>
        <native xmlns="http://cisco.com/ns/yang/Cisco-IOS-XE-native">
            <interface>
                <GigabitEthernet>
                    <name>1</name>
                </GigabitEthernet>
                <GigabitEthernet>
                    <name>2</name>
                </GigabitEthernet>
                <GigabitEthernet>
                    <name>3</name>
                </GigabitEthernet>
            </interface>
        </native>
    </data>
</rpc-reply>]]>]]>
```

Example 14-18 shows an rpc message that uses an XPath filter to retrieve the full configuration of the interface whose <name> element has the value 1 (interface GigabitEthernet1).

Example 14-18 *An RPC Message to Retrieve the Full Configuration of Interface GigabitEthernet1*

```
<rpc xmlns="urn:ietf:params:xml:ns:netconf:base:1.0" message-id="101">
    <get-config>
        <source>
            <running />
        </source>
        <filter xmlns:xyz="http://cisco.com/ns/yang/Cisco-IOS-XE-native"
                type="xpath"
                select="/xyz:native/interface/GigabitEthernet[name='1']">
        </filter>
    </get-config>
</rpc>]]>]]>
```

Example 14-19 shows the rpc-reply message that contains the interface configuration of interface GigabitEthernet1.

Example 14-19 *The RPC Reply Message That Includes the Full Configuration of Interface GigabitEthernet1*

```
<?xml version="1.0" encoding="UTF-8"?>
<rpc-reply xmlns="urn:ietf:params:xml:ns:netconf:base:1.0" message-id="101">
    <data>
        <native xmlns="http://cisco.com/ns/yang/Cisco-IOS-XE-native">
            <interface>
                <GigabitEthernet>
                    <name>1</name>
                    <description>MANAGEMENT INTERFACE - DON'T TOUCH ME</description>
                    <ip>
                        <address>
                            <primary>
                                <address>10.10.20.48</address>
                                <mask>255.255.255.0</mask>
                            </primary>
                        </address>
                    </ip>
                    <mop>
                        <enabled>false</enabled>
                        <sysid>false</sysid>
                    </mop>
                    <negotiation xmlns="http://cisco.com/ns/yang/
  Cisco-IOS-XE-ethernet">
                        <auto>true</auto>
                    </negotiation>
                </GigabitEthernet>
            </interface>
        </native>
    </data>
</rpc-reply>]]>]]>
```

Changing Configuration: <edit-config>, <copy-config>, and <delete-config>

To change the configuration in a datastore on a device running a NETCONF server, three operations come into play: <edit-config>, <copy-config>, and <delete-config>.

The <edit-config> operation introduces changes to the configuration in a target datastore, using new configuration in the rpc message body, in addition to a suboperation that specifies how to integrate this new configuration with the existing configuration in the datastore. The <copy-config> operation is used to create or replace an entire configuration datastore. The <delete-config> operation is used to delete an entire datastore.

One of the <edit-config> operation parameters is the *target datastore*. This is the configuration datastore that the client wishes to edit, and it goes under the <target> element in the rpc message. The new configuration that the client needs to incorporate into the target datastore, referred to as the *source configuration*, typically goes under the <config> element in the rpc message (and there are more options here if the device supports the :url capability discussed later in this chapter). Example 14-20 shows an <edit-config> operation that changes the description under interface GigabitEthernet3.

Example 14-20 *Using the <edit-config> Operation to Change the Description on Interface GigabitEthernet3*

```
<rpc
    xmlns="urn:ietf:params:xml:ns:netconf:base:1.0" message-id="3">
    <edit-config>
        <target>
            <running/>
        </target>
        <config>
            <native xmlns="http://cisco.com/ns/yang/Cisco-IOS-XE-native">
                <interface>
                    <GigabitEthernet>
                        <name>3</name>
                        <description>New Description via NETCONF</description>
                    </GigabitEthernet>
                </interface>
            </native>
        </config>
    </edit-config>
</rpc>]]>]]>
```

Example 14-21 shows an rpc-reply message to a <get-config> rpc message, which confirms that the description was changed on the interface.

Example 14-21 *Confirming That the Description Was Changed on the Interface*

```
<?xml version="1.0" encoding="UTF-8"?>
<rpc-reply xmlns="urn:ietf:params:xml:ns:netconf:base:1.0" message-id="10">
    <data>
        <native xmlns="http://cisco.com/ns/yang/Cisco-IOS-XE-native">
            <interface>
                <GigabitEthernet>
                    <name>3</name>
                    <description>New Description via NETCONF</description>
                    <negotiation xmlns="http://cisco.com/ns/yang/
  Cisco-IOS-XE-ethernet">
```

```
                    <auto>true</auto>
                </negotiation>
            </GigabitEthernet>
        </interface>
    </native>
  </data>
</rpc-reply>
```

The <edit-config> operation is actually a little more sophisticated than what you have just seen in the previous two examples. The <edit-config> operation has an attribute named *operation* that defines how the source configuration integrates with the target datastore configuration (sometimes referred to as the suboperation, since <edit-config> itself is referred to as an operation).

Say that you want to configure interface Loopback100 on the router—but only if the interface does not already exist. If it does, you do not wish to overwrite it. Let's take a look at the default behavior of <edit-config> and then look at how the do-not-overwrite requirement can be satisfied.

The default mode of <edit-config> is to merge the source and target configurations—that is, to overwrite the parts of the interface configuration that you have in the rpc message and leave the rest of the configuration intact. So, if you specify a new IP address for the interface in your rpc message, the router updates the interface IP address and leaves all the other sections of the interface configuration, such as the description, intact. Example 14-22 shows an rpc-reply message to a <get-config> operation that shows the current configuration of interface Loopback100.

Example 14-22 *Current Configuration on Interface Loopback100*

```
<?xml version="1.0" encoding="UTF-8"?>
<rpc-reply xmlns="urn:ietf:params:xml:ns:netconf:base:1.0" message-id="10">
    <data>
        <native xmlns="http://cisco.com/ns/yang/Cisco-IOS-XE-native">
            <interface>
                <Loopback>
                    <name>100</name>
                    <description>Testing NETCONF edit-config</description>
                    <ip>
                        <address>
                            <primary>
                                <address>10.10.10.10</address>
                                <mask>255.255.255.255</mask>
                            </primary>
                        </address>
```

```
                    </ip>
                </Loopback>
            </interface>
        </native>
    </data>
</rpc-reply>]]>]]>
```

The current IP address on the interface is 10.10.10.10, and the description is Testing NETCONF edit-config. In Example 14-23, the new IP address 10.20.20.20/32 is applied to the interface, and the interface description is *not* changed.

Example 14-23 *Using the <edit-config> Operation to Only Change the Interface IP Address*

```
<rpc xmlns="urn:ietf:params:xml:ns:netconf:base:1.0" message-id="10">
  <edit-config>
    <target><running/></target>
    <config>
        <native xmlns="http://cisco.com/ns/yang/Cisco-IOS-XE-native">
            <interface>
                <Loopback>
                    <name>100</name>
                    <ip>
                        <address>
                            <primary>
                                <address>10.20.20.20</address>
                                <mask>255.255.255.255</mask>
                            </primary>
                        </address>
                    </ip>
                </Loopback>
            </interface>
        </native>
    </config>
  </edit-config>
</rpc>]]>]]>
```

Example 14-24 shows the new interface configuration, with the new IP address and the same description as the old configuration.

Example 14-24 *New Interface Configuration: New IP Address and Same Description*

```
<?xml version="1.0" encoding="UTF-8"?>
<rpc-reply xmlns="urn:ietf:params:xml:ns:netconf:base:1.0" message-id="10">
    <data>
        <native xmlns="http://cisco.com/ns/yang/Cisco-IOS-XE-native">
            <interface>
                <Loopback>
                    <name>100</name>
                    <description>Testing NETCONF edit-config</description>
                    <ip>
                        <address>
                            <primary>
                                <address>10.20.20.20</address>
                                <mask>255.255.255.255</mask>
                            </primary>
                        </address>
                    </ip>
                </Loopback>
            </interface>
        </native>
    </data>
</rpc-reply>]]>]]>
```

As you can see, the IP address is changed, and the interface description is left intact. The new configuration in the rpc message and the interface configuration in the datastore are *merged*.

Now let's look again at the original requirement: If Loopback100 was already configured, and you attempt to change its configuration, you want to receive an error message and leave the current configuration intact. In this case, the create suboperation is used, instead of the default merge. In Example 14-25, an rpc uses the create operation to attempt to create interface Loopback100 with interface IP address 10.30.30.30, but as expected, you receive an error message, and the interface configuration is left as is.

Example 14-25 *The Create Suboperation*

```
! rpc message with an <edit-config> operation and "create" sub-operation

<rpc xmlns="urn:ietf:params:xml:ns:netconf:base:1.0" message-id="10">
  <edit-config>
    <target><running/></target>
    <config>
        <native xmlns="http://cisco.com/ns/yang/Cisco-IOS-XE-native"
                xmlns:nf="urn:ietf:params:xml:ns:netconf:base:1.0">
```

```
            <interface>
                <Loopback nf:operation="create">
                    <name>100</name>
                    <description>Testing NETCONF edit-config</description>
                    <ip>
                        <address>
                            <primary>
                                <address>10.30.30.30</address>
                                <mask>255.255.255.255</mask>
                            </primary>
                        </address>
                    </ip>
                </Loopback>
            </interface>
        </native>
    </config>
  </edit-config>]]>]]>

! Error message received

<?xml version="1.0" encoding="UTF-8"?>
<rpc-reply xmlns="urn:ietf:params:xml:ns:netconf:base:1.0" message-id="10">
    <rpc-error>
        <error-type>application</error-type>
        <error-tag>data-exists</error-tag>
        <error-severity>error</error-severity>
        <error-path xmlns:ios="http://cisco.com/ns/yang/Cisco-IOS-XE-native"
  xmlns:nc="urn:ietf:params:xml:ns:netconf:base:1.0">
    /nc:rpc/nc:edit-
  config/nc:config/ios:native/ios:interface/ios:Loopback[ios:name='100']
  </error-path>
        <error-info>
            <bad-element>Loopback</bad-element>
        </error-info>
    </rpc-error>
</rpc-reply>]]>]]>

! interface configuration unchanged

<?xml version="1.0" encoding="UTF-8"?>
<rpc-reply xmlns="urn:ietf:params:xml:ns:netconf:base:1.0" message-id="10">
    <data>
        <native xmlns="http://cisco.com/ns/yang/Cisco-IOS-XE-native">
            <interface>
                <Loopback>
```

```
                    <name>100</name>
                    <description>Testing NETCONF edit-config</description>
                    <ip>
                        <address>
                            <primary>
                                <address>10.20.20.20</address>
                                <mask>255.255.255.255</mask>
                            </primary>
                        </address>
                    </ip>
                </Loopback>
            </interface>
        </native>
    </data>
</rpc-reply>]]>]]>
```

Notice that the <error-tag> value is data-exists. You should notice two things about the operation parameter. First, it is inserted at the element level, where the operation is required to take effect. Under the same <config> element, you can use the merge operation with one element in the hierarchy and then use the create operation with another element in the hierarchy. How the different suboperations interact together when used simultaneously under the same <config> element is implementation specific; you need to do some experimenting to fully understand it.

The other thing to note is that the suboperations are always defined in the mandatory namespace urn:ietf:params:xml:ns:netconf:base:1.0, and this is why, in the previous examples, the namespace nf is declared in the element <native>, and then the operation attribute is defined inside that namespace.

<edit-config> supports the following operation values:

- **merge:** The NETCONF server analyses the source configuration and merges it with the configuration datastore at the same level in the data model hierarchy. This is the default value if no operation attribute is defined for an element.
- **replace:** The source configuration completely replaces the configuration in the target datastore at the same hierarchy level. If the configuration does not exist, it is created.
- **create:** The source configuration is added to the target datastore configuration with the same hierarchy as presented in the rpc message—if this new configuration did *not* exist in the target datastore configuration. If it did exist, an rpc-error is returned with the <error-tag> value data-exists.
- **delete:** The target configuration matching the source configuration element that has an operation attribute equal to delete is deleted from the datastore. If a matching element in the target datastore does not exist (that is, if you try to delete configuration that does not exist) an rpc-reply message with an <rpc-error> element is returned with the <error-tag> value data-missing.

- **remove:** This operation functions exactly like the delete operation except that if a matching element in the target datastore does not exist (that is, if you are trying to delete configuration that does not exist), no rpc-error is returned.

In addition to the operation parameter, the <edit-config> operation accepts three more parameters:

- **default-operation:** This parameter sets the default operation value, which is the value used if no operation attribute is defined for an element. This can be merge, replace, or none. In the case of none, no action is taken on the target datastore unless an operation attribute is explicitly defined.
- **test-option:** This parameter requires that the device support the :validate:1.1 capability (which is covered later in this chapter). It allows the network device to validate the configuration before the <edit-config> operation is executed. The three values allowed are test-then-set (that is, validation first, followed by execution), set (direct execution without validation), and test-only (validation only without execution).
- **error-option:** This parameter tells the network device what to do if it encounters an error condition while executing an <edit-config> operation. The three allowed values are stop-on-error, continue-on-error, and rollback-on-error. If an error condition is encountered while executing an <edit-config> operation, stop-on-error stops the execution without rolling back any changes. continue-on-error causes the device to record any error conditions encountered but continues executing the operation. rollback-on-error has the device stop the execution and roll back any changes made by the current <edit-config> operation.

If the <edit-config> operation is successful, an rpc-reply message is sent back to the client with an <ok> element. Otherwise an rpc-reply message with an appropriate <rpc-error> element is returned.

Next is the <copy-config> operation. Unlike the <edit-config> operation, the <copy-config> operation replaces *all* the contents of a target datastore with the contents of another *complete* source datastore. Therefore, the operation has only two parameters: <source> and <target>. If the :url capability is supported, remote datastores identified by a URI may be used as <source> or <target>. Restrictions on which datastores are allowed as source and which are allowed as target are implementation specific.

If the <copy-config> operation is successful, an rpc-reply message is sent back to the client with an <ok> element. Otherwise, an rpc-reply message with an appropriate <rpc-error> element is returned.

Finally, the <delete-config> operation is used to delete an entire <target> datastore. The exact meaning of deleting a datastore is implementation specific, but it generally means deleting the contents of the datastore. Which datastores a client is allowed to delete is also implementation specific. For example, some implementations do not support <delete-config> with any <target> datastore on the device. Only a remote datastore accessible via a URI may be acted on using this operation. However, the NETCONF protocol forbids deleting the <running> datastore for any implementation. Example 14-26 shows a typical rpc message with a <delete-config> operation.

Example 14-26 *An rpc Message with the <delete-config> Operation Acting on the Candidate Configuration as <target>*

```
<rpc message-id="101" xmlns="urn:ietf:params:xml:ns:netconf:base:1.0">
    <delete-config>
        <target>
            <candidate/>
        </target>
    </delete-config>
</rpc>]]>]]>
```

If the operation is successful, an rpc-reply message with an <ok> element is returned. Otherwise, an rpc-reply message with an appropriate <rpc-error> element is returned.

Datastore Operations: <lock> and <unlock>

The <lock> operation is used to lock a specific datastore. Locking a datastore prevents any other entity from changing the contents of that datastore, whether it be another NETCONF session or a non-NETCONF entity such as a CLI session or SNMP. Locking the datastore also means that no other session can acquire a lock on that datastore until the current lock is released. A lock is released if the server receives an rpc message containing an <unlock> operation on the same session that issued the <lock> operation or if the session that owns the lock is terminated.

The <lock> and <unlock> operations have one mandatory parameter, which is the <target> datastore to be locked or unlocked. Example 14-27 shows two rpc messages, one to lock the candidate configuration datastore, and another to unlock it.

Example 14-27 *Two rpc Messages: One Calling the <lock> Operation, and the Other Calling the <unlock> Operation with the Candidate Configuration as the Target*

```
! lock Operation
<rpc xmlns="urn:ietf:params:xml:ns:netconf:base:1.0" message-id="1">
    <lock>
        <target>
            <candidate/>
        </target>
    </lock>
</rpc>]]>]]>

! unlock Operation
```

```
<rpc xmlns="urn:ietf:params:xml:ns:netconf:base:1.0" message-id="2">
    <unlock>
        <target>
            <candidate/>
        </target>
    <unlock>
</rpc>]]>]]>
```

If the <lock> or <unlock> operation is successful, an rpc-reply message containing an <ok> element is returned. Otherwise, the rpc-reply message contains an <rpc-error> element. A lock may fail for a number of reasons. For example, the datastore may be locked by another session. Or the target datastore may be the candidate, and while the datastore is not locked by another session, the candidate configuration may have been modified, and the modifications were neither committed nor discarded. You might want to experiment with the different error conditions and familiarize yourself with the different <rpc-error> elements received.

A session cannot unlock a configuration datastore that has been locked by another session. If a session attempts to unlock a datastore that it did not lock, it receives an error message that contains an <error-tag> element with the value lock-denied and an <error-info> element with a child <session-id> element containing the value of the session that owns the lock. The <session-id> value is an important value as it may be used in a <kill-session> operation to end the session holding the lock, as described in the next section.

Session Operations: <close-session> and <kill-session>

A NETCONF session is a persistent connection; that is, it should stay up as long as the client and server are exchanging rpc and rpc-reply messages, and after that it may be terminated.

A NETCONF session can be explicitly terminated by a client via an rpc message with a <close-session> or <kill-session> operation, or it may be implicitly terminated by the server if certain conditions are triggered, such as the failure of the underlying transport or a session timeout due to inactivity.

The <close-session> operation gracefully terminates a session. That is, it completes any operation requested *before* the <close-session> operation, releases any locks held by the session, and tears down the transport connection with the client. The <close-session> operation has no parameters.

The <kill-session> operation, on the other hand, is used by a client to immediately terminate another session. When a <kill-session> is requested, the server aborts any operation in progress for that session, stops and rolls back any confirmed commit operations, and tears down the transport connection. However, it does not roll back any other changes made over the course of the session. The <kill-session> operation has one mandatory parameter, the <session-id> element, which has a value equal to the session ID of the session that is to be terminated. A session cannot request a <kill-session> operation on itself. If it does, an error is generated.

Both <close-session> and <kill-session> operations result in an rpc-reply message with an <ok> element if successful and an <rpc-error> element if not. Example 14-28 shows an example for each operation.

Example 14-28 *Two rpc Messages: One Calling the <close-session> Operation, and the Other Calling the <kill-session> Operation for <session-id> 12345*

```
! <close-session> operation
<rpc xmlns="urn:ietf:params:xml:ns:netconf:base:1.0" message-id="1">
    <close-session/>
</rpc>]]>]]>

! <kill-session> operation
<rpc xmlns="urn:ietf:params:xml:ns:netconf:base:1.0" message-id="1">
    <kill-session>
        <session-id>12345</session-d>
    </kill-session>
</rpc>]]>]]>
```

Candidate Configuration Operations: <commit>, <discard-changes>, and <cancel-commit>

When a device supports the :candidate capability, the client may call the two operations <commit> and <discard-changes>. When the :confirmed-commit capability is also supported, two more operations are added to the list: the <confirmed-commit> and <cancel-commit> operations. These capabilities are discussed in detail later in this chapter, in the section "NETCONF Capabilities."

Some devices support a candidate configuration datastore. The candidate configuration starts off as an exact copy of the running configuration. A user or NETCONF client applies configuration changes to the candidate configuration. In NETCONF, this is accomplished by setting the <target> element representing the target datastore to <candidate> under the <edit-config> or <copy-config> operations in the rpc message. The client then has the option to call the <discard-changes> operation to discard the changes to the candidate configuration such that it reverts to its initial state before the changes, or to call a <commit> operation to copy the candidate configuration to the running configuration, effectively applying the changes to the running configuration.

Example 14-29 shows two rpc messages: one with a <commit> operation, and the other with a <discard-changes> operation.

Example 14-29 *Two rpc Messages: One Calling the <commit> Operation and the Other Calling the <discard-changes> Operation*

```
! commit operation
<rpc xmlns="urn:ietf:params:xml:ns:netconf:base:1.0" message-id="1">
    <commit/>
</rpc>]]>]]>

! discard-changes operation
<rpc xmlns="urn:ietf:params:xml:ns:netconf:base:1.0" message-id="1">
    <discard-changes/>
</rpc>]]>]]>
```

If the <commit> or <discard-changes> operations are successful, the server sends an rpc-reply message with an <ok> element. If they are not successful, the server sends back an rpc-reply message with the appropriate <rpc-error> element.

When a device also supports the :confirmed-commit capability (for example, Cisco devices running IOS XE Version 17.x and NX-OS Version 9.x), the client is allowed to call an extended <commit> operation in an rpc message called a *confirmed commit*, which is basically a conditional commit. To elaborate, the workflow for a confirmed commit is as follows:

1. The client implements changes to the candidate configuration and calls a <commit> operation that includes the <confirmed/> element.
2. A timeout timer is started. The timer is configurable and is identified in NETCONF by the element <confirm-timeout>. The default value of this timer is 10 minutes on the latest versions of IOS XE and NX-OS.
3. If the timeout timer expires without any further intervention from the client, any changes made to the candidate configuration are rolled back.
4. The client may issue three different operations *before* the timeout timer expires:
   - A <commit> operation *without* the <confirmed/> option (called a *confirming* commit) that reflects the changes to the running configuration as a regular commit would
   - Another confirmed commit operation using a <commit> with the <confirmed/> element that resets the timer to 10 minutes so that the countdown starts again
   - A <cancel-commit> operation that discards the changes to the candidate configuration and cancels the confirmed commit operation altogether, without waiting for the timeout timer to expire
5. If the <persist> option is included under the confirmed commit operation, the candidate configuration changes may be committed (the confirming commit) by any session, not necessarily by the session that called the confirmed commit. The <persist>

element is given a value in the confirmed commit operation. The other session that wishes to commit the changes is required to provide that value under the <persist-id> element of its <commit> operation.

Example 14-30 shows an rpc message calling the <commit> operation with the <confirmed/> element and the <persist> value set to 1234,XYZ. The <confirm-timeout> value is also set to 5 minutes.

Example 14-30 *An rpc Message Calling a Confirmed Commit Operation*

```
! confirmed-commit operation
<rpc xmlns="urn:ietf:params:xml:ns:netconf:base:1.0" message-id="1">
    <commit>
        <confirmed/>
        <confirm-timeout>300</confirm-timeout>
        <persist>1234,XYZ</persist>
    </commit>
</rpc>]]>]]>
```

Example 14-31 shows another session calling a confirming <commit> operation to commit the changes by the session in Example 14-30. Because the sessions are different (probably indicating two different clients), this client is required to use the value 1234,XYZ as the <persist-id> in order to be able to commit the changes.

Example 14-31 *An rpc Message Calling the <commit> Operation with a <persist-id> Value*

```
! confirming commit operation
<rpc xmlns="urn:ietf:params:xml:ns:netconf:base:1.0" message-id="1">
    <commit>
        <persist-id>1234,XYZ</persist-id>
    </commit>
</rpc>]]>]]>
```

Configuration Validation: <validate>

The <validate> operation checks the configuration in a datastore for syntax and semantic errors—that is, it *validates* that configuration. To be able to execute this operation, the device has to support the :validate capability, as explained in the section "NETCONF Capabilities," later in this chapter. Example 14-32 shows an rpc message using the <validate> operation to validate the running configuration.

Example 14-32 *An rpc Message Using the <validate> Operation to Validate the Running Configuration*

```
<rpc xmlns="urn:ietf:params:xml:ns:netconf:base:1.0" message-id="1">
    <validate>
        <source>
            <running/>
        </source>
    </validate>
</rpc>]]>]]>
```

If the configuration is valid, an rpc-reply message is returned to the client with an <ok> element. If not, an rpc-reply message is returned with an appropriate <rpc-error> element.

The NETCONF Content Layer

The previous sections in this chapter use NETCONF messages starting with the root element. Which root element a message uses depends on the message type. The root element is followed by the operation element and then a number of child XML elements that provide the necessary element values for these operations to be executed in the manner intended by the client. What XML elements follow the operation element depend on the following factors:

- **Which operation is being used in the RPC:** Some elements are mandatory for some operations, such as the <source> element for the <get-config> operation.
- **Which YANG model is being referenced:** This defines the hierarchy of the elements that constitute the content in the message body, and whether the message is an rpc or an rpc-reply message.

Chapter 13, "YANG," discusses how YANG is used to model device configuration and provide hierarchical templates to express configuration in a structured manner. This is exactly the function provided by the content layer.

To understand the correlation between the data model used and the XML hierarchy in the NETCONF message body, let's examine how the configuration of interface GigabitEthernet3 is expressed using two different models: the Cisco-IOS-XE-native and the ietf-interfaces YANG data models.

The node hierarchy from the ietf-interfaces model is shown on the left in Figure 14-3, and the actual running configuration from the router is shown on the right in the figure. Notice how the node hierarchy in the model maps to the running configuration hierarchy.

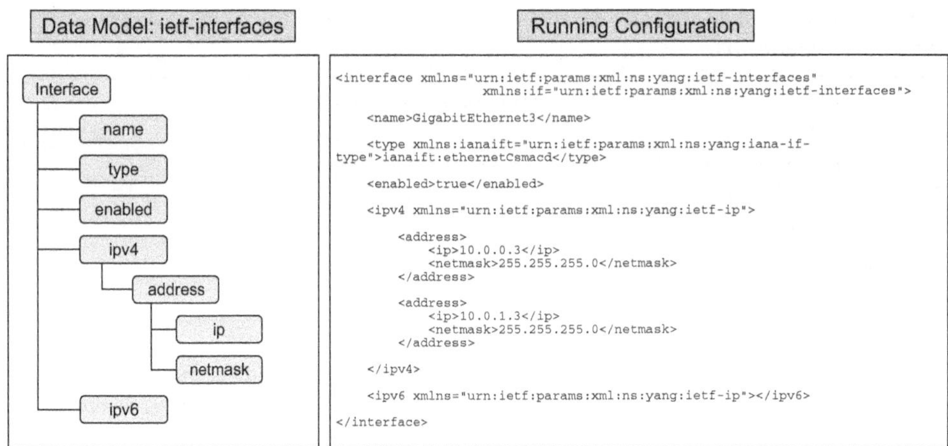

Figure 14-3 *The Configuration Hierarchy in the ietf-interfaces YANG Model Mapped to the Configuration on the Device*

The configuration shows up using this template because it was retrieved using an rpc message with a <get-config> operation that references this data model under the <filter> element, as highlighted in Example 14-33.

Example 14-33 *An rpc Message with a <get-config> Operation Referencing the YANG Model ietf-interfaces*

```
<rpc xmlns="urn:ietf:params:xml:ns:netconf:base:1.0" message-id="101">
  <get-config>
    <source><running/></source>
    <filter>
      <interfaces xmlns="urn:ietf:params:xml:ns:yang:ietf-interfaces">
        <interface>
          <name>GigabitEthernet3</name>
        </interface>
      </interfaces>
    </filter>
  </get-config>
</rpc>]]>]]>
```

Now the same interface on the same router shows up with a different configuration hierarchy when referencing the YANG model Cisco-IOS-XE-native, as shown in Figure 14-4. Notice that all values are equal. The configuration only shows up *structured* differently.

Again, the configuration shows up using this template because it was retrieved via an rpc message with a <get-config> operation that references the second data model under the <filter> element, as shown in Example 14-34.

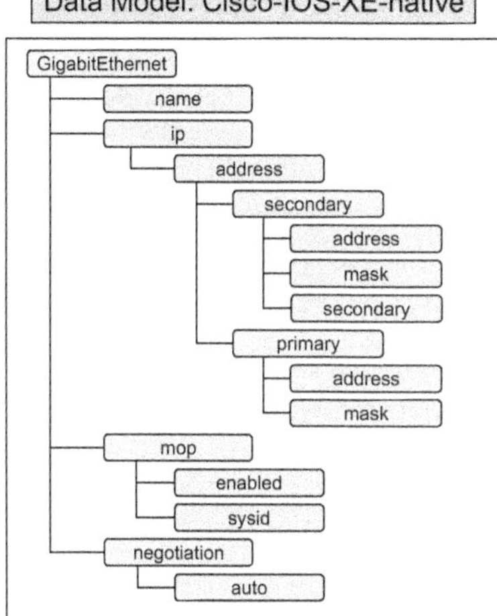

Running Configuration

```
<GigabitEthernet xmlns=http://cisco.com/ns/yang/Cisco-IOS-XE-native
                 xmlns:ios="http://cisco.com/ns/yang/Cisco-IOS-XE-
native">

    <name>3</name>

    <ip>
        <address>
            <secondary>
                <address>10.0.1.3</address>
                <mask>255.255.255.0</mask>
                <secondary/></secondary>
            <primary>
                <address>10.0.0.3</address>
                <mask>255.255.255.0</mask>
            </primary>
        </address>
    </ip>

    <mop>
        <enabled>false</enabled>
        <sysid>false</sysid>
    </mop>

    <negotiation xmlns="http://cisco.com/ns/yang/Cisco-IOS-XE-
ethernet">
        <auto>true</auto>
    </negotiation>

</GigabitEthernet>
```

Figure 14-4 *The Configuration Hierarchy in the Cisco-IOS-XE-native YANG Model Mapped to the Configuration on the Device*

Example 14-34 *An rpc Message with a <get-config> Operation Referencing the YANG Model Cisco-IOS-XE-native*

```
<rpc xmlns="urn:ietf:params:xml:ns:netconf:base:1.0" message-id="101">
  <get-config>
    <source><running/></source>
    <filter>
      <native xmlns="http://cisco.com/ns/yang/Cisco-IOS-XE-native">
        <interface>
          <GigabitEthernet>
            <name>3</name>
          </GigabitEthernet>
        </interface>
      </native>
    </filter>
  </get-config>
</rpc>]]>]]>
```

In the previous examples, the data in the message body of the rpc-reply message that is returned by the server matches the YANG data model stated in the top-level element under the <filter> element in the rpc message. The same applies to rpc messages that use operations intended to edit the configuration, such as <edit-config>: The message body constituting the new configuration also matches a specific data model.

Now that the relationship between a data model and the message body has been established, how exactly is the data model referenced in the XML-encoded body of the message? As you have seen, the YANG data model is specified as the value of the attribute xmlns, which stands for *XML namespace*. Conceptually, each YANG module defines or creates a new namespace. The exact URI for that namespace is defined inside the YANG module. This URI is the value of the attribute xmlns in the XML message body and is an attribute for the top-level element in the module, which is <interfaces> in the case of the ietf-interfaces model and <native> in the case of the Cisco-IOS-XE-native model.

RFC 6022 specifies how to discover the YANG modules supported by a device: Send a <get> rpc message to the device with a child element <netconf-state> under <filter>, as in Example 14-35.

Example 14-35 *Discovering the YANG Modules Supported by a Device by Using the <get> Operation and the <netconf-state> Element*

```
<rpc message-id="101" xmlns="urn:ietf:params:xml:ns:netconf:base:1.0">
    <get>
        <filter type="subtree">
            <netconf-state xmlns="urn:ietf:params:xml:ns:yang:ietf-netconf-
  monitoring">
                <schemas />
            </netconf-state>
        </filter>
    </get>
</rpc>
```

The resulting rpc-reply message lists all the YANG models (schemas) supported by the device, as shown in Example 14-36.

Example 14-36 *The List of YANG Models/Schemas Supported by a Device*

```
<rpc-reply xmlns="urn:ietf:params:xml:ns:netconf:base:1.0" message-id="101">
    <data>
        <netconf-state xmlns="urn:ietf:params:xml:ns:yang:ietf-netconf-monitoring">
            <schemas>
                <schema>
                    <identifier>ATM-FORUM-TC-MIB</identifier>
                    <version></version>
                    <format>yang</format>
                    <namespace>urn:ietf:params:xml:ns:yang:smiv2:ATM-FORUM-TC-
  MIB</namespace>
                    <location>NETCONF</location>
                </schema>

--------- OUTPUT OMITTED FOR BREVITY ---------
```

```
                <schema>
                    <identifier>Cisco-IOS-XE-interfaces</identifier>
                    <version>2019-03-11</version>
                    <format>yang</format>
                    <namespace>http://cisco.com/ns/yang/Cisco-IOS-XE-native
  </namespace>
                    <location>NETCONF</location>
                </schema>
                <schema>
                    <identifier>Cisco-IOS-XE-interfaces-oper</identifier>
                    <version>2018-10-29</version>
                    <format>yang</format>
                    <namespace>http://cisco.com/ns/yang/Cisco-IOS-XE-interfaces-
  oper</namespace>
                    <location>NETCONF</location>
                </schema>

--------- OUTPUT OMITTED FOR BREVITY ---------

                <schema>
                    <identifier>tailf-netconf-query</identifier>
                    <version>2017-01-06</version>
                    <format>yang</format>
                    <namespace>http://tail-f.com/ns/netconf/query</namespace>
                    <location>NETCONF</location>
                </schema>
            </schemas>
        </netconf-state>
    </data>
</rpc-reply>
```

To retrieve the actual schema content for one of the modules in the previous list, you can use the <get-schema> operation and use the <identifier>, <version>, and <format> values for that particular schema. Example 14-37 shows how to retrieve the schema contents for the Cisco-IOS-XE-interface module on the IOS XE DevNet Sandbox.

Example 14-37 *The rpc Message for Retrieving the Schema Contents for the Cisco-IOS-XE-interfaces Module Using the <get-schema> Operation*

```
<rpc message-id="101" xmlns="urn:ietf:params:xml:ns:netconf:base:1.0">
    <get-schema xmlns="urn:ietf:params:xml:ns:yang:ietf-netconf-monitoring">
        <identifier>Cisco-IOS-XE-interfaces</identifier>
        <version>2019-03-11</version>
        <format>yang</format>
    </get-schema>
</rpc>
```

Example 14-38 shows the rpc-reply message that is received as a result.

Example 14-38 *The Contents of the Cisco-IOS-XE-interfaces Schema in the rpc-reply Message*

```
<rpc-reply xmlns="urn:ietf:params:xml:ns:netconf:base:1.0" message-id="101"><data
  xmlns='urn:ietf:params:xml:ns:yang:ietf-netconf-monitoring'><![CDATA[submodule
  Cisco-IOS-XE-interfaces {
  belongs-to Cisco-IOS-XE-native {
    prefix ios;
  }
  import ietf-inet-types {
    prefix inet;
  }
  import Cisco-IOS-XE-types {
    prefix ios-types;
  }  import Cisco-IOS-XE-features {
    prefix ios-features;
  }
  import Cisco-IOS-XE-interface-common {
    prefix ios-ifc;
  }
  organization
    "Cisco Systems, Inc.";
  contact
    "Cisco Systems, Inc.
     Customer Service
     Postal: 170 W Tasman Drive
     San Jose, CA 95134
     Tel: +1 1800 553-NETS
     E-mail: cs-yang@cisco.com";
  description
    "Cisco XE Native Interfaces Yang model.
     Copyright (c) 2016-2019 by Cisco Systems, Inc.
     All rights reserved.";
  // =========================================================================
  // REVISION
  // =========================================================================
  revision 2019-03-11 {
      description
      "Modified the leafref to leaf because of pyang issue";
  }

--------- OUTPUT OMITTED FOR BREVITY ---------

      // interface Wlan-GigabitEthernet
```

```
        list Wlan-GigabitEthernet {
          description
            "WLAN GigabitEthernet";
          key "name";
          leaf name {
            type string;
          }
          uses interface-switchport-grouping;
          uses interface-common-grouping;
        }
      }
    }
  }
]]></data>
</rpc-reply>]]>]]>
```

NETCONF Capabilities

As explained earlier, the first thing that happens when a transport session is complete is the exchange of hello messages between the server and client (in no particular order). A NETCONF hello message contains a list of sibling <capability> elements, each providing a URI that represents one capability supported by the device sending out the hello message.

Some capabilities are identified as base NETCONF capabilities and are defined using URNs. In the hello message in Example 14-1 earlier in this chapter, you can see some of these base capabilities at the very beginning of the hello message. Capabilities are an extensible feature of NETCONF, and different vendors or NETCONF implementations may define their own capabilities. In any case, a capability is always defined as a URI. The next few sections discuss the base NETCONF capabilities as defined in RFC 6241. These base capabilities always have this format:

`urn:ietf:params:netconf:capability:`{*name*}`:`{*version*}

where the *version* at the end of the URN identifies the version of the capability (*not* the version of NETCONF). The shorthand notation for the capability is :{*name*}:{*version*} or just :{*name*}.

Capabilities are used to state three classes of information by the peer sending the hello message:

- The NETCONF version supported by the peer. After the hello message exchange, the peers use the lowest version number agreed on by the two peers. The current version of NETCONF is 1.1, and the previous version is 1.0. As mentioned earlier in the chapter, the NETCONF version is indicated by the **urn:ietf:params:netconf:base:1.**{*x*} capability.
- The base and extended capabilities supported by the peer.
- The data models supported by the peer.

The Writable Running Capability

A device that supports the :writable-running capability allows the client to write directly to its running configuration. In NETCONF jargon, this means that the <target> element in an <edit-config> or <copy-config> operation can be <running>. The :writable-running capability is identified by the following URN:

```
urn:ietf:params:netconf:capability:writable-running:1.0
```

The Candidate Configuration Capability

A device that supports the :candidate capability has a candidate configuration datastore. When a device has a candidate datastore, the typical workflow involves the client implementing the configuration changes on the candidate configuration first and then issuing either a <commit> operation to copy the candidate configuration to the running configuration or a <discard-changes> operation to discard the changes made to the candidate configuration.

Support for this capability means that the device can accept the element <candidate> as the <source> or <target> datastore when the operation is <get-config>, <edit-config>, <copy-config>, or <validate>.

The candidate configuration may be shared between multiple sessions. Therefore, to avoid conflicting configuration changes from different sessions, the client should use the <lock> and <unlock> operations to lock the candidate configuration during configuration changes and then to unlock it when the lock is not needed anymore.

The :candidate capability is identified by the following URN:

```
urn:ietf:params:netconf:capability:candidate:1.0
```

The Confirmed Commit Capability

A device that supports the :candidate capability may also support the :confirmed-commit capability. A device that supports the :confirmed-commit capability allows the client to call a confirmed commit operation in an rpc message.

The :confirmed-commit capability is identified by the following URN:

```
urn:ietf:params:netconf:capability:confirmed-commit:1.1
```

The Rollback-on-Error Capability

A device that supports the :rollback-on-error capability supports the option to roll back any changes if an error occurs during an <edit-config> operation. To activate this option, you place the string rollback-on-error under the <error-option> element in the rpc message. The different error options for the <edit-config> operation are covered in the section “Changing Configuration: <edit-config>, <copy-config>, and <delete-config>,” earlier in this chapter.

The :rollback-on-error capability is identified by the following URN:

```
urn:ietf:params:netconf:capability:rollback-on-error:1.0
```

The Validate Capability

The :validate capability means that a device is capable of executing the <validate> operation. This operation is covered in the section “Configuration Validation: <validate>,” earlier in this chapter.

In addition, this capability extends the <edit-config> operation to accept the <test-option> element, discussed earlier in this chapter, in the section “Changing Configuration: <edit-config>, <copy-config>, and <delete-config>.”

The :validate capability is identified by the following URN:

```
urn:ietf:params:netconf:capability:validate:1.1
```

The Distinct Startup Capability

If a device has a separate datastore for the startup configuration, the :startup capability allows the NETCONF client to operate on this startup configuration by using the element <startup/> either as <target> or <source>, depending on the operation. As is customary through the CLI, editing the running configuration does not automatically update the startup configuration. The running configuration needs to be explicitly copied to the startup configuration if the device is to boot up from the updated configuration. The same goes for NETCONF. If the running-configuration is updated, the changes are only reflected to the startup configuration after an explicit <copy-config> operation, where the <source> is <running/> and the <target> is <startup/>.

The :startup capability is identified by the following URN:

```
urn:ietf:params:netconf:capability:startup:1.0
```

The URL Capability

The :url capability allows a device to read and write to a remote XML document located at a URI (that is, a remote datastore).

The usage of this capability is slightly different for each operation. When it is used with the <edit-config> operation, the <config> element in the rpc message containing the configuration is replaced with a <url> element containing the link where the configuration resides. If you applied the configuration in Example 14-20 to a device by using a URI instead of by embedding it in the rpc message by using the <config> element, the rpc message would be similar to that shown in Example 14-39.

Example 14-39 *Using a URI and the :url Capability to Edit the Running Configuration*

```
<rpc xmlns="urn:ietf:params:xml:ns:netconf:base:1.0" message-id="1">
    <edit-config>
        <target>
            <running/>
        </target>
        <url>http://example.com/config-repo/config.xml</url>
    </edit-config>
</rpc>]]>]]>
```

In Example 14-39, the URI in the <url> element points to an XML document in which a <config> element contains the configuration in the mandatory namespace urn:ietf:params:xml:ns:netconf:base:1.0. Note that the URI does not have to point to a remote location over the Internet or even over the network. It could be a path to a file on the local file system.

When you use a URI with the <copy-config> operation, the <url> element resides under either the <source> element or the <target> element. In Example 14-40, a copy of the running configuration is backed up to a file on the local file system.

Example 14-40 *Backing Up the Running Configuration to a File on the Local File System*

```
<rpc xmlns="urn:ietf:params:xml:ns:netconf:base:1.0" message-id="1">
    <copy-config>
        <source>
            <running/>
        </source>
        <target>
            <url>file:///home/NetProg/Config_Backup_Latest</url>
        </target>
    </copy-config>
</rpc>]]>]]>
```

When the :url capability is used with the <delete-config> operation, the <url> element is always under the <target> element; when it is used with the <validate> operation, it is always under the <source> element.

The :url capability is identified by the following URN:

```
urn:ietf:params:netconf:capability:url:1.0?scheme={name-1}[,name-2]
[,...][,name-n]
```

The URI for this capability includes a scheme argument that lists all the schemes supported by the device. The following is an example of a valid :url capability URI:

```
urn:ietf:params:netconf:capability:url:1.0?scheme=http,ftp,file
```

The XPath Capability

In the section "Retrieving Data: <get> and <get-config>," earlier in this chapter, you saw that a filter can be applied to the <get> and <get-config> operations in order to select specific nodes, as per a specific data model, to be returned in the rpc-reply message. If a filter is not applied, all configuration or configuration and state data is returned. A filter may be one of two types: subtree or XPath. The capability :xpath allows a device to apply filters of type XPath to the <get> and <get-config> operations, as described earlier in this chapter.

The :xpath capability is identified by the following URN:

```
urn:ietf:params:netconf:capability:xpath:1.0
```

NETCONF Using Python: ncclient

So far in this chapter, you have seen how to construct NETCONF messages manually and send them to a network device (also manually) over an SSH connection. It is important to transition through this manual stage in order to fully understand the protocol. However, this manual method of using NETCONF is not scalable and is actually counterintuitive, considering that this book is about automation. This section shows how to use Python to communicate with a device via NETCONF by using the **ncclient** Python library.

The **ncclient** library provides the facility of emulating a NETCONF client using Python while masking some of the finer details of the protocol so that the programmer does not have to deal directly with most of the protocol specifics. This level of abstraction, which is expected from a high-level programming language library, lets the programmer focus on the task at hand instead of having to worry about things like the syntax and semantics of NETCONF.

The developers of **ncclient** claim to support all the functions of NETCONF covered in the older RFC 4741. Moreover, **ncclient** is extensible; that is, new transport protocols and protocol operations can be added to the library when needed. **ncclient** also has focused support for particular vendors, with, of course, Cisco at the very top of the list.

To use **ncclient**, you need to install the **ncclient** library. First, you install the following list of dependencies (using **yum** or **dnf** if you are on a CentOS or RHEL box):

```
setuptools 0.6+
Paramiko 1.7+
lxml 3.3.0+
libxml2
libxslt
libxml2-dev
libxslt1-dev
```

Then you need to download the Python script setup.py from the GitHub repo https://github.com/ncclient/ncclient and run it:

```
[NetDev@localhost ~]$ sudo python setup.py install
```

Or you can use **pip** to install **ncclient**:

```
[NetDev@localhost ~]$ sudo pip install ncclient
```

The **ncclient** library operates by defining a handler object called *manager* that represents the NETCONF server. The manager object has different methods defined to it, each performing a different protocol operation. To better understand **ncclient**, read through Example 14-41, and most of it will make sense right away.

Example 14-41 *Sending an rpc Message with a <get-config> Operation Using ncclient*

```
from ncclient import manager
     filter_loopback='''
        <native xmlns="http://cisco.com/ns/yang/Cisco-IOS-XE-native">
            <interface>
                <Loopback>
                    <name>100</name>
                </Loopback>
            </interface>
        </native>
       '''
with manager.connect(host='ios-xe-mgmt-latest.cisco.com',
                     port=10000,
                     username='developer',
                     password='C1sco12345',
                     hostkey_verify=False
                     ) as m:
     rpc_reply = m.get_config(source="running",filter=("subtree",filter_loopback))
     print(rpc_reply)
```

In the Python script in Example 14-41, the manager module is first imported from **ncclient**. A subtree filter is defined as a multiline string named **filter_loopback** to extract the configuration of interface Loopback100 from the router. The filter follows the same syntax rules as the subtree filters constructed earlier in this chapter.

A connection to the router is then initiated using the **manager.connect** method. The parameters passed to the method in this particular example use values specific to one of Cisco's IOS XE DevNet sandboxes. The parameters are the host address (which may also be an IP address), the port configured for NETCONF access, the username and password, and **hostkey_verify**.

When a client connects to an SSH server, the server key is stored on the client, typically in the ~/.ssh/known_hosts file. If **hostkey_verify** is set to **True**, one of the keys stored on the client has to match the key of the server that the client is trying to connect to via SSH. When set to **False**, the SSH keys on the client are not verified. For convenience, the **hostkey_verify** value is set to **False** in this example.

Then the **get_config** method, using the defined subtree filter, and parameter **source** with the value **running**, retrieves the required configuration from the running configuration datastore. The **get_config** method is also capable of using xpath filters.

Finally, the rpc-reply message received from the router is assigned to string **rpc_reply** and printed out. Example 14-42 shows this message.

Example 14-42 *The rpc-reply Message Back from the Server Containing Interface Loopback100's Configuration*

```
<?xml version="1.0" encoding="UTF-8"?>
<rpc-reply xmlns="urn:ietf:params:xml:ns:netconf:base:1.0" message-
  id="urn:uuid:ed4c62a8-10be-47ad-b8ef-8a468212a9b5"
  xmlns:nc="urn:ietf:params:xml:ns:netconf:base:1.0">
  <data>
    <native xmlns="http://cisco.com/ns/yang/Cisco-IOS-XE-native">
      <interface>
        <Loopback>
          <name xmlns:nc="urn:ietf:params:xml:ns:netconf:base:1.0">100</name>
          <description>Testing ncclient</description>
          <ip>
            <address>
              <primary>
                <address>10.10.10.10</address>
                <mask>255.255.255.255</mask>
              </primary>
            </address>
          </ip>
        </Loopback>
      </interface>
    </native>
  </data>
</rpc-reply>
```

The **manager.connect** and **get_config** methods have a few more parameters that may be used for more granular control of the functionality. Only the basic parameters are covered here.

Similarly, the **edit_config** method can be used to edit the configuration on the routers. In Example 14-43, the **edit_config** method is used to change the IP address on interface Loopback100 to 10.20.20.20/32.

Example 14-43 *Using the edit_config Method to Change the IP Address on Interface Loopback100*

```
from ncclient import manager
     config_data='''
       <config>
         <native xmlns="http://cisco.com/ns/yang/Cisco-IOS-XE-native">
           <interface>
```

```
              <Loopback>
                <name>100</name>
                <ip>
                  <address>
                    <primary>
                      <address>10.20.20.20</address>
                      <mask>255.255.255.255</mask>
                    </primary>
                  </address>
                </ip>
              </Loopback>
            </interface>
          </native>
        </config>
        '''
with manager.connect(host='ios-xe-mgmt-latest.cisco.com',
                     port=10000,
                     username='developer',
                     password='C1sco12345',
                     hostkey_verify=False
                     ) as m:
     rpc_reply = m.edit_config(target="running",config=config_data)
     print(rpc_reply)
```

The difference between the **get_config** and **edit_config** methods is that the latter requires a config parameter instead of a filter parameter, represented by the **config_data** string, and requires a target datastore instead of a source datastore.

Example 14-44 shows the output after running the script in Example 14-43, which is basically an rpc-reply message with an <ok> element. The **show run interface Loopback100** command output from the router shows the new interface configuration.

Example 14-44 *Results of Sending the rpc Message from Example 14-43*

```
! Output from the NETCONF Session
<?xml version="1.0" encoding="UTF-8"?>
<rpc-reply xmlns="urn:ietf:params:xml:ns:netconf:base:1.0" message-
  id="urn:uuid:7da14672-68c4-4d7e-9378-ad8c3957f6c1" xmlns:nc="urn:ietf:params:xml:n
  s:netconf:base:1.0">
    <ok />
</rpc-reply>

! Output from the router via the CLI showing the new interface configuration
csr1000v-1# show run interface lo100
Building configuration...
```

```
Current configuration : 99 bytes

!
interface Loopback100
 description Testing ncclient
 ip address 10.20.20.20 255.255.255.255
end
```

This section provides only a brief introduction to the **ncclient** library. For more comprehensive coverage, check out the documentation at https://ncclient.readthedocs.io/en/latest/#.

RESTCONF

RESTCONF is often referred to as the RESTful version of NETCONF because RESTCONF is compatible with NETCONF, and because specific mappings exist between several of the NETCONF and RESTCONF protocol features. However, this is not entirely true due to the inherent differences between the RPC-based API architecture on which NETCONF is based, and the REST framework on which RESTCONF is based. Also, RESTCONF implements only a subset of the NETCONF functionality. This section discusses RESTCONF in detail, as well as how it relates to NETCONF.

Note RESTCONF is a RESTful protocol, and it would be a good idea to review Chapters 7, "HTTP and REST," and 8, "Advanced HTTP," before you start with RESTCONF, to get a better understanding of the protocol.

Protocol Overview

REST is the dominant framework for programming application interfaces (APIs), and it was inevitable that someone would come up with a RESTful protocol that is compatible with NETCONF. In January 2017, the NETCONF working group in the IETF released RFC 8040, "RESTCONF Protocol." The number of RFCs covering RESTCONF is quite limited compared to the plethora of RFCs covering NETCONF. As of this writing, the list of RFCs covering RESTCONF is short:

- RFC 8040, "RESTCONF Protocol"
- RFC 8071, "NETCONF Call Home and RESTCONF Call Home"
- RFC 8527, "RESTCONF Extensions to Support the Network Management Datastore Architecture"

RESTCONF is a client/server protocol based on HTTP, so unlike NETCONF, which is based on SSH, it is not session based. Recall from Chapter 7 that the second constraint for REST APIs is that an API should be *stateless*.

A RESTCONF transaction is a regular HTTP message exchange involving a client composing and sending an HTTP request message that contains all information pertaining to that particular transaction. The server then processes the request and replies with an HTTP response message. After the response message is sent out, the server maintains no state information for that client or that transaction.

As you saw in Chapter 7, an HTTP message is basically a start line, a number of headers, and the message body. The start line of a *request* message (from the client) includes the HTTP method, a URI segment pointing to the resource (or its representation) on which the method should act, and the HTTP version used; it should look similar to:

```
GET /restconf/data?content=config HTTP/1.1
```

The start line of a *response* message includes the HTTP version, a status code indicating the result of processing the request, and a status description or text that elaborates on the status code, such as:

```
HTTP/1.1 200 OK
```

As a RESTful protocol, RESTCONF is like all the other RESTful protocols in the following respects:

- It uses HTTP for transport.
- It uses HTTP methods to perform create, read, update, and delete (CRUD) operations. These HTTP methods map to NETCONF's RPC operations.
- It uses hierarchical URIs to identify resources that represent manageable components on the server on which it is running.
- It uses headers and a message body to communicate to the server the metadata and data, respectively, that pertain to a specific transaction. An example of metadata would be the value of the Accept header in which the client indicates to the server whether it can accept data in JSON or XML format. An example of data would be the configuration that the client wishes to add to a datastore in a POST request message.

In order to understand RESTCONF and effectively work with it, you need to understand what resources RESTCONF uses and how to use HTTP methods to retrieve and manipulate data on the RESTCONF server (the network device, in this case).

Whereas NETCONF only supports XML encoding, RESTCONF supports both XML and JSON. NETCONF supports models expressed in XSD and YANG, while RESTCONF supports only YANG models.

Note RFC 7951 defines JSON encoding of data modeled with YANG.

RESTCONF does *not* have the capability to work with multiple datastores. It works with a single *conceptual* datastore. When RESTCONF is used to edit a configuration, this conceptual target datastore may be the candidate or the running configuration, depending on two factors:

- What datastores are present or supported by the device
- Whether the device is also running NETCONF in addition to RESTCONF

RESTCONF interacts with NETCONF based on a set of rules:

- If the device is not running NETCONF, RESTCONF applies edits directly to the running configuration of the device.
- If the device is running a NETCONF server besides the RESTCONF server, then only if the NETCONF server supports the :writable-running capability are the edits made by RESTCONF applied directly to the running configuration.
- If the NETCONF server supports the :candidate capability, then the edits performed by RESTCONF are applied to the candidate configuration instead. However, RESTCONF issues an automatic and immediate commit after the configuration edits are done in order to reflect the changes to the running configuration.
- If the NETCONF server supports the :startup capability, the RESTCONF edit operation updates the startup configuration, also automatically and immediately, after the configuration (running or candidate) is edited.

Note These rules are defined in Section 1.4 of RFC 8040. However, whether an equipment vendor chooses to follow these rules (and implement a standards-based version of RESTCONF/NETCONF) or not is really up to the vendor. The devices running IOS XE that were used to generate the examples for this chapter do, in fact, behave according to these rules.

While RESTCONF understands the concept of configuration locking, it cannot manipulate locks. So, if a RESTCONF client attempts to manipulate the configuration on a network device and the datastore is locked by a NETCONF server on the same device, the RESTCONF server responds to the client with an appropriate error message, typically an HTTP response message with a "409 Conflict" status code. (Remember that RESTCONF is compatible with NETCONF.)

By no means is RESTCONF intended to replace NETCONF. RESTCONF is the go-to protocol when a client wishes to access a server (device) programmatically via a RESTful API, such as web applications used to push configuration to other components in the automation toolchain. However, the constraints placed on RESTful APIs limit the use cases and applicability of these APIs to one-to-one transactions (that is, a single client to a single network device, controller, or orchestrator).

NETCONF, on the other hand, with its session-based architecture, support for different datastores, and configuration validation capabilities (recall the :validate capability and <validate> operation), is more suitable for one-to-many transactions, where a single client is used to push configuration to several network devices. This is why products such as Cisco's NSO use NETCONF when configuring network devices in the southbound direction and use RESTful APIs in the northbound direction when communicating with web portals, event management systems, or ticketing systems.

Protocol Architecture

Figure 14-5 illustrates the four-layer model of the RESTCONF protocol, representing its functional components.

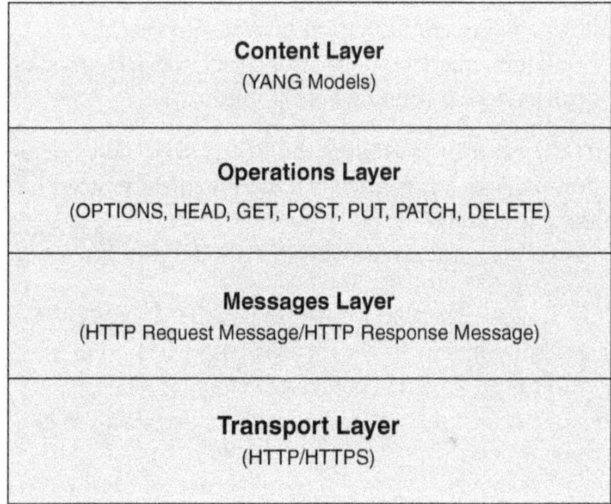

Figure 14-5 *The Four-Layer Model Encompassing All RESTCONF Functions*

The transport layer at the bottom represents the functions performed by the transport protocol used by RESTCONF—that is, HTTP. HTTP and RESTCONF are discussed in the section "The RESTCONF Transport Layer."

On top of the transport layer is the messages layer. The fact that RESTCONF uses HTTP implies that the messages used by RESTCONF are regular HTTP request and response messages. HTTP messages address resources, which represent manageable components on the device, by using URIs. HTTP messages and RESTCONF resources are discussed in the section "The RESTCONF Messages Layer."

The next layer is the operations layer. RESTful protocols like RESTCONF that are based on HTTP use HTTP methods exclusively to act on resources. The subset of HTTP methods used in RESTCONF and how these methods map to the NETCONF operations are discussed in the section "Methods and the RESTCONF Operations Layer."

The top layer of the model, the content layer, contains the same functional components of NETCONF, the YANG data models that represent the hierarchy, and characteristics of the data that are in the HTTP message body. Whatever applies to NETCONF applies to RESTCONF, except that RESTCONF does not support any schema description or modeling languages except YANG. As mentioned earlier, this YANG-modeled data may be encoded in XML or JSON format. Refer to the earlier section "The NETCONF Content Layer" for a discussion of YANG models and their relationship with the content in the message body.

The RESTCONF Transport Layer

RESTCONF uses HTTP as the transport protocol. Strictly speaking, the protocol specification mandates the use of HTTP over TLS, which is more commonly known as HTTPS. TLS and HTTPS are covered extensively in Chapter 8.

While RESTCONF delegates data confidentiality and integrity to HTTPS, the authentication process performed by HTTPS results in a value that is passed on to RESTCONF, referred to as the *RESTCONF username*, which RESTCONF uses to authorize subsequent user request messages.

All other aspects of the RESTCONF transport layer are no different from the normal operations of HTTP and HTTPS, as covered in Chapters 7 and 8.

The RESTCONF Messages Layer

RESTCONF is a RESTful protocol based on HTTP. Therefore, a RESTCONF client sends standard HTTP request messages to a RESTCONF server, and the server normally responds with an HTTP response message. The format of RESTCONF messages are no different from the format of any other HTTP messages (covered in detail in Chapter 7). For your convenience, HTTP/RESTCONF message formats are reviewed briefly in the next two sections.

Request Messages

Figure 14-6 shows the format of a typical RESTCONF request message.

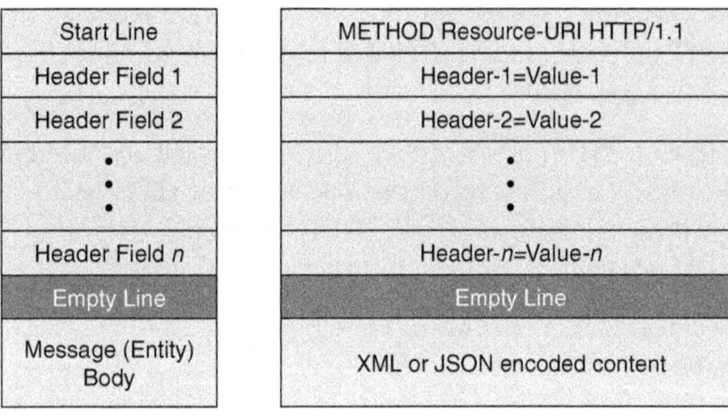

Figure 14-6 *Format of a Typical RESTCONF Request Message Matching a Typical HTTP Request Message*

An HTTP request message is composed of a start line, followed by a list of headers, an empty line marking the end of the headers section, and finally the message body.

The start line of an HTTP request message is composed of three values: the HTTP method, a URI segment representing the path to the resource, and the HTTP version, which is almost always HTTP/1.1.

Each header is formatted as {*header-name*}={*header-value*}, and each of them is on a separate line. Headers appear in a message in no particular order.

The message body is composed of XML- or JSON-encoded content. The encoding used in the body is indicated using the Content-Type header field. Two Content-Type values that you will come across very often are application/yang-data+xml and application/yang-data+json. The encoding that the client would like to receive back in the server response message is indicated in the Accept header field of the request and uses the same type values as the Content-Type header. The message body is optional.

Response Messages

Figure 14-7 shows the format of a typical RESTCONF response message.

Start Line	HTTP/1.1 Status-Code Status-Text
Header Field 1	Header-1=Value-1
Header Field 2	Header-2=Value-2
• • •	• • •
Header Field *n*	Header-*n*=Value-*n*
Empty Line	Empty Line
Message (Entity) Body	XML or JSON encoded content

Figure 14-7 *Format of a Typical RESTCONF Response Message Matching a Typical HTTP Response Message*

The only difference between the format of a request message and a response message is in the start line. The start line of a response message starts with the HTTP version, followed by the status code and then status text, both of which give brief information on the result of processing the client request. The headers section and message body are formatted exactly as in request messages.

Constructing RESTCONF Messages

To construct RESTCONF request messages successfully and understand response messages, you need to know the following:

- How to build the resource URI correctly in order to target the resource that you want to act on. This is the subject of the section "Resources."
- What method to use, coupled with the resource URI, to define what the RESTCONF operation will be. This is the subject of the section "Methods and the RESTCONF Operations Layer."
- What headers to include in the message and what their values should be. HTTP headers are comprehensively covered in Chapter 7. The use of HTTP headers in RESTCONF is covered in the next section, "RESTCONF HTTP Headers."
- What needs to go into the message body—that is, the JSON- or XML-encoded content, which depends on the YANG module referenced by the content. This is covered in the section "The NETCONF Content Layer."

RESTCONF HTTP Headers

HTTP has a huge number of defined headers that are used to communicate resource metadata back and forth between the client and the server. This section discusses the header fields that are of special relevance to RESTCONF.

A RESTCONF message body is encoded in either XML or JSON. The client and server indicate the encoding of the data in their messages by using the Content-Type header field. If the server receives an unsupported media type from the client, it responds with a "415 Unsupported Media Type" response message.

The client expresses the preferred encoding to be used in the response from the server by using the Accept header field. The server typically responds using the preferred encoding. If the preferred encoding is not supported by the server, the server responds with a "406 Not Acceptable" response message. If the Accept header is not used at all, the server either uses the encoding the client used in the request message or, if the request did not have content, the server uses an arbitrary default encoding that varies by implementation.

If a client request results in a new resource being created, the path to the new resource is identified by the Location header field in the response message.

A server responding to a retrieval request for a resource includes a Last-Modified header field, whose value is a timestamp indicating the last time the resource was modified.

The client may use the If-Modified-Since or the If-Unmodified-Since header field in its request to edit a resource only if it was *changed* or *not changed*, respectively, since a specific time. This ensures that the client is not changing a resource that has been changed by another client between the time indicated in the header field and the time the client sent its request. This, of course, applies to configuration resources only, not to state/operation resources.

A resource representation also has a unique entity tag that changes each time the resource representation is updated. This tag is communicated to the client in the ETag header field. As with the last-modified timestamp, a client can make use of the If-Match or the If-None-Match header field in a request message to make sure that the entity tag has *not changed* or *changed*, respectively, before the server edits a resource. Again, this only applies to the configuration resources, not to state/operation resources.

The Last-Modified timestamp and ETag value are also maintained for the datastore and change when the contents of the datastore change. As you will read later in this chapter, the datastore itself is a resource; therefore, each time any configuration item is edited, the Last-Modified timestamp and ETag values for the datastore resource are changed, as are the values belonging to the resource that was edited. As a matter of fact, because resources are hierarchical, when a resource is edited, the two values belonging to all resources up the hierarchy, all the way to the datastore resource, are updated as well.

RESTCONF Error Reporting

Errors in RESTCONF are communicated back to the client by using HTTP status codes in response messages. When the status code returned by a server is a 4xx or 5xx code, this is considered an error condition, and an <error> element is included in the body of the message. The <error> elements contain the same information that would be included in the <rpc-error> element if that same error happened due to a NETCONF operation. The same error fields discussed earlier in this chapter, in the section "RPC Reply Messages," are included as child elements to the <error> element in the RESTCONF response message.

Resources

A resource represents one manageable component in a device. In any HTTP-based protocol such as RESTCONF, a resource is identified by a URI. Therefore, the first step in constructing and understanding HTTP/RESTCONF messages is to be able to understand how URIs map to resources or, more accurately, resource representations. In the coming paragraphs, you will build fully functional URIs starting with the URI scheme.

As you have already read in this chapter, RESTCONF is based on HTTPS. Therefore, any RESTCONF URI starts with the scheme https://. Then comes the device IP or address and port, resulting in: **https://{*device_address*}:{*port*}/**. For example, the URI for reaching one of Cisco's IOS XE sandboxes is https://ios-xe-mgmt-latest.cisco.com:9443/, where 9443 is the (non-default) port for RESTCONF configured on the device. (See the note in the "NETCONF over SSH" section, earlier in the chapter, regarding the Cisco DevNet sandboxes.) The default port for RESTCONF is the HTTPS default port 443.

Before proceeding with a detailed discussion of RESTCONF resources, take a look at the resources hierarchy in Figure 14-8 and how it relates to the resource URI.

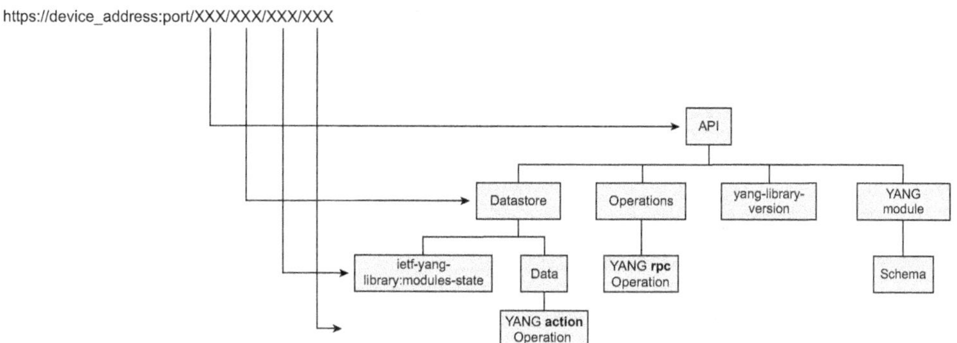

Figure 14-8 *RESTCONF Resources and Their Relationship with the Resource URI*

The API Resource

So far, the scheme, device, and RESTCONF port have been identified, but not any resources, yet. The first resource defined in RESTCONF is the protocol API itself, called the *root* or *API resource*, and it is the top-level resource in the resources hierarchy. As you can see in Figure 14-8, the API resource is at the top of the tree. When we add this to the resource URI, the URI becomes **https://**{*device_address*}**:**{*port*}**/**{*api_resource*}.

What is the value that needs to go into the URI to access the API resource? This question is answered in RFC 6415, "Web Host Metadata." The RFC states that performing a GET request to the ./well-known/host-meta URI retrieves the host-meta document formatted in XRD 1.0 (Extensible Resource Document) format. This host-meta document has the answer to this question. A GET request is sent to the Cisco IOS XE sandbox at https://ios-xe-mgmt-latest.cisco.com:9443/.well-known/host-meta using Postman, and the result is shown in Example 14-45.

Example 14-45 *GET Request to the /.well-known/host-meta URI to Retrieve the Value of the API Resource*

```
! GET request to /.well-known/host-meta
GET /.well-known/host-meta HTTP/1.1
Authorization: Basic ZGV2ZWxvcGVyOkMxc2NvMTIzNDU=
User-Agent: PostmanRuntime/7.20.1
Accept: */*
Cache-Control: no-cache
Host: ios-xe-mgmt-latest.cisco.com:9443
Accept-Encoding: gzip, deflate
Connection: keep-alive
```

```
! host-meta Document back from the server
HTTP/1.1 200 OK
Server: nginx
Date: Fri, 22 Nov 2019 12:06:11 GMT
Content-Type: application/xrd+xml
Content-Length: 107
Connection: keep-alive
Vary: Accept-Encoding

<XRD xmlns='http://docs.oasis-open.org/ns/xri/xrd-1.0'>
  <Link rel='restconf' href='/restconf'/>
</XRD>
```

In the response message body in Example 14-45, you can see the root <XRD> element and its child, the <Link> element, under it. Each <Link> element, according to RFC 6415, "conveys a link relation between the host described by the document and a common target URI." Simply put, the <Link> element in this example provides the URI /restconf/ (using the attribute href) as a link to a resource described as restconf (using the attribute rel) residing on the host on which HTTP is running. This is the path segment pointing to the API resource on that device. Applying this to the Cisco IOS XE sandbox, the API resource is identified by the URI https://ios-xe-mgmt-latest.cisco.com:9443/restconf.

Because the API resource is, in fact, a resource, sending a GET request to its URI should retrieve a representation of this resource. This is exactly what Example 14-46 shows—again using Postman.

Example 14-46 *GET Request to the API Resource*

```
! GET request to the API Resource
GET /restconf/ HTTP/1.1
Authorization: Basic ZGV2ZWxvcGVyOkMxc2NvMTIzNDU=
User-Agent: PostmanRuntime/7.20.1
Accept: */*
Cache-Control: no-cache
Host: ios-xe-mgmt-latest.cisco.com:9443
Accept-Encoding: gzip, deflate
Connection: keep-alive

! A representation of the API Resource back from the server
HTTP/1.1 200 OK
Server: nginx
Date: Fri, 22 Nov 2019 12:26:41 GMT
Content-Type: application/yang-data+xml
Transfer-Encoding: chunked
```

```
Connection: keep-alive
Cache-Control: private, no-cache, must-revalidate, proxy-revalidate
Vary: Accept-Encoding
Pragma: no-cache

<restconf xmlns="urn:ietf:params:xml:ns:yang:ietf-restconf">
  <data/>
  <operations/>
  <yang-library-version>2016-06-21</yang-library-version>
</restconf>
```

As you can see from the response message in Example 14-46, the API resource has three child (second-level) resources:

- The datastore (data) resource
- The operations (operations) resource
- The YANG library version (yang-library-version) resource

The Datastore Resource

The datastore resource represents the datastore on the device. Remember that RESTCONF defines and works with only one datastore. The datastore resource is the parent to all configuration and state data resources on the device. The datastore resource is always identified by the path segment /data. This means that in order to access the datastore resource, the resource URI becomes **https://**{*device_address*}**:**{*port*}**/**{*api_resource*}**/data.** In the case of the IOS XE sandbox, the URI for the datastore resource is https://ios-xe-mgmt-latest.cisco.com:9443/restconf/data.

A GET request sent to the datastore resource retrieves all configuration and state data on the device. The query parameter content=config is used at the end of the resource URI to limit the retrieved data to configuration data only in Example 14-47. (Query parameters are covered in detail later in this chapter.)

Example 14-47 *GET Request to the Datastore Resource*

```
! GET request to the Datastore Resource with parameter content=config
GET /restconf/data?content=config HTTP/1.1
Authorization: Basic ZGV2ZWxvcGVyOkMxc2NvMTIzNDU=
User-Agent: PostmanRuntime/7.20.1
Accept: */*
Cache-Control: no-cache
Host: ios-xe-mgmt-latest.cisco.com:9443
Accept-Encoding: gzip, deflate
Connection: keep-alive
```

```
! The contents of the Datastore Resource limited to config data only
<data xmlns="urn:ietf:params:xml:ns:yang:ietf-restconf">
    <native xmlns="http://cisco.com/ns/yang/Cisco-IOS-XE-native">
        <version>16.11</version>
        <boot-start-marker/>
        <boot-end-marker/>
        <banner>
            <motd>
                <banner>^C</banner>
            </motd>
        </banner>
        <memory>
            <free>
                <low-watermark>
                    <processor>80557</processor>
                </low-watermark>
            </free>
        </memory>
--------- OUTPUT TRUNCATED FOR BREVITY ---------
```

The Schema Resource

Unlike NETCONF, RESTCONF is not session based; therefore, there is no capability exchange between client and server. The path segment /ietf-yang-library:module-state is defined for discovering what YANG modules are supported by the server. This resource is a child resource to the datastore resource. If you send a GET request to the URI https://ios-xe-mgmt-latest.cisco.com:9443/restconf/data/ietf-yang-library:modules-state/, you get a list of supported YANG modules on the IOS XE sandbox, as shown in Example 14-48.

Example 14-48 *GET Request to the /ietf-yang-library:modules-state/ Segment to Identify the Supported YANG Modules on the Router*

```
! GET request to retrieve the list of supported YANG modules
GET /restconf/data/ietf-yang-library:modules-state/ HTTP/1.1
Authorization: Basic ZGV2ZWxvcGVyOkMxc2NvMTIzNDU=
User-Agent: PostmanRuntime/7.20.1
Accept: */*
Cache-Control: no-cache
Host: ios-xe-mgmt-latest.cisco.com:9443
Accept-Encoding: gzip, deflate
Connection: keep-alive

! Response message listing all supported modules in the message body
HTTP/1.1 200 OK
Server: nginx
```

```
Date: Sat, 07 Dec 2019 13:08:17 GMT
Content-Type: application/yang-data+xml
Transfer-Encoding: chunked
Connection: keep-alive
Cache-Control: private, no-cache, must-revalidate, proxy-revalidate
Pragma: no-cache

<modules-state xmlns="urn:ietf:params:xml:ns:yang:ietf-yang-library" xmlns:yanglib=
  "urn:ietf:params:xml:ns:yang:ietf-yang-library">
    <module-set-id>cede0ab9198ec38357734bdd25b13778</module-set-id>
--------- OUTPUT OMITTED FOR BREVITY ---------
    <module>
        <name>ietf-restconf</name>
        <revision>2017-01-26</revision>
        <schema>https://10.10.20.48:443/restconf/tailf/modules/ietf-rest-
  conf/2017-01-26</schema>
        <namespace>urn:ietf:params:xml:ns:yang:ietf-restconf</namespace>
        <conformance-type>implement</conformance-type>
    </module>
    <module>
        <name>ietf-restconf-monitoring</name>
        <revision>2017-01-26</revision>
        <schema>https://10.10.20.48:443/restconf/tailf/modules/ietf-restconf-
  monitoring/2017-01-26</schema>
        <namespace>urn:ietf:params:xml:ns:yang:ietf-restconf-monitoring</namespace>
        <conformance-type>implement</conformance-type>
    </module>
<module>
        <name>ietf-routing</name>
        <revision>2015-05-25</revision>
        <schema>https://10.10.20.48:443/restconf/tailf/modules/ietf-routing/
  2015-05-25</schema>
        <namespace>urn:ietf:params:xml:ns:yang:ietf-routing</namespace>
        <feature>multiple-ribs</feature>
        <feature>router-id</feature>
        <deviation>
            <name>cisco-xe-ietf-routing-deviation</name>
            <revision>2016-07-09</revision>
        </deviation>
        <conformance-type>implement</conformance-type>
    </module>

--------- OUTPUT OMITTED FOR BREVITY ---------

</modules-state>
```

The schema resource is a resource that identifies the schema of a specific YANG module in the list in Example 14-48. Each YANG module has a schema resource defined as a child resource. Therefore, to retrieve the schema of, say, the ietf-routing YANG module listed in Example 14-48, you perform a GET request to the URI identified in the <schema> XML node. Keep in mind that you need to replace the https://10.10.20.48:443/ path segment in Example 14-48 with your device's *public* details (10.10.20.48 is the IP address configured on the management interface on the DevNet Sandbox router and is not reachable over the Internet since it is a private IP address). In this case, in order to retrieve the schema resource for the ietf-routing YANG module on the Cisco IOS XE sandbox, you need to perform a GET request to https://ios-xe-mgmt-latest.cisco.com:9443/restconf/tailf/modules/ietf-routing/2015-05-25, as shown in Example 14-49. For the sake of brevity, the request is omitted in the example, and only the response is shown.

Example 14-49 *GET Request to the Schema Resource of the ietf-routing YANG Module*

```
! Response message showing the schema of the ietf-routing module
HTTP/1.1 200 OK
Server: nginx
Date: Sat, 07 Dec 2019 13:28:20 GMT
Content-Type: application/yang
Transfer-Encoding: chunked
Connection: keep-alive
Cache-Control: private, no-cache, must-revalidate, proxy-revalidate
Pragma: no-cache

   module ietf-routing {
     namespace "urn:ietf:params:xml:ns:yang:ietf-routing";
     prefix "rt";
     import ietf-yang-types {
       prefix "yang";
     }
     import ietf-interfaces {
       prefix "if";
     }
     organization
       "IETF NETMOD (NETCONF Data Modeling Language) Working Group";
     contact
       "WG Web:   <http://tools.ietf.org/wg/netmod/>
        WG List:  <mailto:netmod@ietf.org>
        WG Chair: Thomas Nadeau
                  <mailto:tnadeau@lucidvision.com>
        WG Chair: Juergen Schoenwaelder
                  <mailto:j.schoenwaelder@jacobs-university.de>
        Editor:   Ladislav Lhotka
```

```
               <mailto:lhotka@nic.cz>";
     description
       "This YANG module defines essential components for the management
        of a routing subsystem.

--------- OUTPUT TRUNCATED FOR BREVITY ---------
```

The Data Resource

Not to be confused with the datastore resource, which is identified by the /data path segment, a *data resource* is any piece of configuration or state data on a device that is managed as a single component. In other words, a data resource can be *uniquely* targeted using the URI in the HTTP request. A data resource maps to a data node in a YANG module—typically a leaf, leaf-list, container, or list.

A data resource is identified using a URI path segment that depends on its YANG data type.

A container is identified using the path segment /{*yang_module_name*}:{*container_name*}. We can add this to the URI segments covered so far so that the full URI for a container is **https://**{*device_address*}**:**{*port*}**/**{*api_resource*}**/data/**{*yang_module_name*}**:**{*container_name*}.

The YANG module ietf-interfaces has two top-level containers: interfaces and interfaces-state. The first represents the interface-configurable parameters, and the second represents the read-only interfaces state data and statistics. Each of them is a resource and can be accessed on the IOS XE sandbox via the URIs https://ios-xe-mgmt-latest.cisco.com:9443/restconf/data/ietf-interfaces:interfaces and https://ios-xe-mgmt-latest.cisco.com:9443/restconf/data/ietf-interfaces:interfaces-state. Example 14-50 shows a GET request message and the resulting response for the interfaces container.

Example 14-50 *GET Request to the interfaces Container in the ietf-interfaces YANG Module*

```
! Request message to the interfaces container
GET /restconf/data/ietf-interfaces:interfaces HTTP/1.1
Authorization: Basic ZGV2ZWxvcGVyOkMxc2NvMTIzNDU=
User-Agent: PostmanRuntime/7.20.1
Accept: */*
Cache-Control: no-cache
Host: ios-xe-mgmt-latest.cisco.com:9443
Accept-Encoding: gzip, deflate
Connection: keep-alive
```

```
! Response message displaying the interfaces container
HTTP/1.1 200 OK
Server: nginx
Date: Sun, 08 Dec 2019 04:07:35 GMT
Content-Type: application/yang-data+xml
Transfer-Encoding: chunked
Connection: keep-alive
Cache-Control: private, no-cache, must-revalidate, proxy-revalidate
Pragma: no-cache

<interfaces xmlns="urn:ietf:params:xml:ns:yang:ietf-interfaces"  xmlns:if="urn:ietf:
  params:xml:ns:yang:ietf-interfaces">
    <interface>
        <name>GigabitEthernet1</name>
        <description>MANAGEMENT INTERFACE - DON'T TOUCH ME</description>
        <type xmlns:ianaift="urn:ietf:params:xml:ns:yang:iana-if-
  type">ianaift:ethernetCsmacd</type>
        <enabled>true</enabled>
        <ipv4 xmlns="urn:ietf:params:xml:ns:yang:ietf-ip">
            <address>
                <ip>10.10.20.48</ip>
                <netmask>255.255.255.0</netmask>
            </address>
        </ipv4>
        <ipv6 xmlns="urn:ietf:params:xml:ns:yang:ietf-ip">
    </ipv6>
    </interface>
    <interface>
        <name>GigabitEthernet2</name>
        <description>DO NOT TOUCH ME</description>
        <type xmlns:ianaift="urn:ietf:params:xml:ns:yang:iana-if-
  type">ianaift:ethernetCsmacd</type>
        <enabled>true</enabled>
        <ipv4 xmlns="urn:ietf:params:xml:ns:yang:ietf-ip">
            <address>
                <ip>10.255.255.1</ip>
                <netmask>255.255.255.0</netmask>
            </address>
        </ipv4>
        <ipv6 xmlns="urn:ietf:params:xml:ns:yang:ietf-ip">
    </ipv6>
    </interface>
    <interface>

--------- OUTPUT OMITTED FOR BREVITY ---------

</interfaces>
```

YANG lists and leaf lists are addressed similarly. A list is addressed using the path segment /{*yang_module_name*}:{*container_name*}/{*list_name*}={*key-value-1*}[,..][,*key-value-n*], and a leaf list is addressed using the path segment /{*yang_module_name*}:{*container_name*}/{*leaf_list_name*}={*value*}. Recall from Chapter 13 that a list contains one or more instances, and each instance is differentiated from the others by one or more keys. On the other hand, a leaf list is a list of leafs, each having a single value.

In the ietf-interfaces YANG module, the <interfaces> element represents a container, under which resides the element <interface> that represents a list. To retrieve only the list instance for interface GigabitEthernet3, the URI https://ios-xe-mgmt-latest.cisco.com:9443/restconf/data/ietf-interfaces:interfaces/interface=GigabitEthernet3 is used. Note that the list key is the leaf represented by the element <name>. Example 14-51 shows the result.

Example 14-51 *Response Message to a GET Request to the List Instance for Interface GigabitEthernet3*

```
! Response message displaying the list instance for interface GigabitEthernet3
HTTP/1.1 200 OK
Server: nginx
Date: Sun, 08 Dec 2019 04:39:20 GMT
Content-Type: application/yang-data+xml
Transfer-Encoding: chunked
Connection: keep-alive
Cache-Control: private, no-cache, must-revalidate, proxy-revalidate
Pragma: no-cache

<interface xmlns="urn:ietf:params:xml:ns:yang:ietf-interfaces"
  xmlns:if="urn:ietf:params:xml:ns:yang:ietf-interfaces">
    <name>GigabitEthernet3</name>
    <description>Network Interface</description>
    <type xmlns:ianaift="urn:ietf:params:xml:ns:yang:iana-if-
  type">ianaift:ethernetCsmacd</type>
    <enabled>true</enabled>
    <ipv4 xmlns="urn:ietf:params:xml:ns:yang:ietf-ip">
        <address>
            <ip>10.10.30.1</ip>
            <netmask>255.255.255.0</netmask>
        </address>
    </ipv4>
    <ipv6 xmlns="urn:ietf:params:xml:ns:yang:ietf-ip">
  </ipv6>
</interface>
```

Finally, a leaf is addressed using the path segment /{*yang_module_name*}:{*container_name*}/{*full-path-to-leaf*}/{*leaf_name*}. To target a leaf, you include the full path to the leaf in the URI. For example, the <description> element is a leaf. Therefore, to retrieve the interface description of interface GigabitEthernet3 on the IOS XE sandbox, you use the URI https://ios-xe-mgmt-latest.cisco.com:9443/restconf/data/ietf-interfaces:interfaces/interface=GigabitEthernet3/description, as shown in Example 14-52.

Example 14-52 *Retrieving the Value of the Leaf element <description> for Interface GigabitEthernet3*

```
! Request message for leaf description for interface GigabitEthernet3
GET /restconf/data/ietf-interfaces:interfaces/interface=GigabitEthernet3/description
  HTTP/1.1
Authorization: Basic ZGV2ZWxvcGVyOkMxc2NvMTIzNDU=
User-Agent: PostmanRuntime/7.20.1
Accept: */*
Cache-Control: no-cache
Host: ios-xe-mgmt-latest.cisco.com:9443
Accept-Encoding: gzip, deflate
Connection: keep-alive

! Response message displaying the list instance for interface GigabitEthernet3
HTTP/1.1 200 OK
Server: nginx
Date: Sun, 08 Dec 2019 04:59:36 GMT
Content-Type: application/yang-data+xml
Transfer-Encoding: chunked
Connection: keep-alive
Cache-Control: private, no-cache, must-revalidate, proxy-revalidate
Pragma: no-cache

<description xmlns="urn:ietf:params:xml:ns:yang:ietf-interfaces" xmlns:if="urn:ietf:
  params:xml:ns:yang:ietf-interfaces">
  Network Interface
</description>
```

The Operations Resource

Recall from Chapter 13 that you can extend the set of NETCONF RPCs by defining new RPC operations in a YANG module by using the *rpc* statement. You can also define an operation that may be performed on a specific container or list node by using the *action* statement. Both of these constructs can be addressed in RESTCONF by using an operations resource, which is the second type of resource under the API resource (refer to Figure 14-8).

You can retrieve the list of operations defined using an rpc statement in all modules supported by the device by sending a GET request to the /operations path segment. In the case of the IOS XE sandbox, the full URI is https://ios-xe-mgmt-latest.cisco.com:9443/restconf/operations. Example 14-53 shows the response to the GET request to that URI.

Example 14-53 *Response to a GET Request to the Operations Resource*

```
! The contents of the operations resource
HTTP/1.1 200 OK
Server: nginx
Date: Mon, 25 Nov 2019 07:46:24 GMT
Content-Type: application/yang-data+xml
Transfer-Encoding: chunked
Connection: keep-alive
Cache-Control: private, no-cache, must-revalidate, proxy-revalidate
Vary: Accept-Encoding
Pragma: no-cache

<operations xmlns="urn:ietf:params:xml:ns:yang:ietf-restconf">
    <ios-xe-rpc:switch xmlns:ios-xe-rpc="http://cisco.com/ns/yang/Cisco-IOS-XE-
  rpc">/restconf/operations/Cisco-IOS-XE-rpc:switch</ios-xe-rpc:switch>
    <ios-xe-rpc:default xmlns:ios-xe-rpc="http://cisco.com/ns/yang/Cisco-IOS-XE-
  rpc">/restconf/operations/Cisco-IOS-XE-rpc:default</ios-xe-rpc:default>
    <ios-xe-rpc:clear xmlns:ios-xe-rpc="http://cisco.com/ns/yang/Cisco-IOS-XE-
  rpc">/restconf/operations/Cisco-IOS-XE-rpc:clear</ios-xe-rpc:clear>
    <ios-xe-rpc:release xmlns:ios-xe-rpc="http://cisco.com/ns/yang/Cisco-IOS-XE-
  rpc">/restconf/operations/Cisco-IOS-XE-rpc:release</ios-xe-rpc:release>
    <ios-xe-rpc:reload xmlns:ios-xe-rpc="http://cisco.com/ns/yang/Cisco-IOS-XE-
  rpc">/restconf/operations/Cisco-IOS-XE-rpc:reload</ios-xe-rpc:reload>
    <ios-xe-rpc:cellular xmlns:ios-xe-rpc="http://cisco.com/ns/yang/Cisco-IOS-XE-
  rpc">/restconf/operations/Cisco-IOS-XE-rpc:cellular</ios-xe-rpc:cellular>
    <ios-xe-rpc:license xmlns:ios-xe-rpc="http://cisco.com/ns/yang/Cisco-IOS-XE-
  rpc">/restconf/operations/Cisco-IOS-XE-rpc:license</ios-xe-rpc:license>
    <ios-xe-rpc:service xmlns:ios-xe-rpc="http://cisco.com/ns/yang/Cisco-IOS-XE-
  rpc">/restconf/operations/Cisco-IOS-XE-rpc:service</ios-xe-rpc:service>
    <ios-xe-rpc:virtual-service xmlns:ios-xe-rpc="http://cisco.com/ns/yang/Cisco-
  IOS-XE-rpc">/restconf/operations/Cisco-IOS-XE-rpc:virtual-service</ios-xe-
  rpc:virtual-service>
    <ios-xe-rpc:copy xmlns:ios-xe-rpc="http://cisco.com/ns/yang/Cisco-IOS-XE-
  rpc">/restconf/operations/Cisco-IOS-XE-rpc:copy</ios-xe-rpc:copy>
    <ios-xe-rpc:delete xmlns:ios-xe-rpc="http://cisco.com/ns/yang/Cisco-IOS-XE-
  rpc">/restconf/operations/Cisco-IOS-XE-rpc:delete</ios-xe-rpc:delete>
    <ios-xe-rpc:app-hosting xmlns:ios-xe-rpc="http://cisco.com/ns/yang/Cisco-IOS-XE-
  rpc">/restconf/operations/Cisco-IOS-XE-rpc:app-hosting</ios-xe-rpc:app-hosting>
    <ios-xe-rpc:guestshell xmlns:ios-xe-rpc="http://cisco.com/ns/yang/Cisco-IOS-XE-
  rpc">/restconf/operations/Cisco-IOS-XE-rpc:guestshell</ios-xe-rpc:guestshell>

--------- OUTPUT OMITTED FOR BREVITY ---------

</operations>
```

The response contains a number of child resources, each defining a different data model–specific RPC operation. To invoke a particular operation, a POST request is sent to the URI of the operation, formatted as **https://**{*device_address*}**:**{*port*}**/**{*api_resource*}**/operations/**{*yang_module_name*}**:**{*operation*}. For example, to reload the IOS XE sandbox, you perform a POST to the URI https://ios-xe-mgmt-latest.cisco.com:9443/restconf/operations/Cisco-IOS-XE-rpc:reload.

Note Do not try sending a POST request to the URI of the reload operation to a device in a production network unless you intend to reload the device.

An operations resource of the second type—the one defined using a YANG action statement—is defined for a specific node in the YANG module; therefore, it is addressed using the URI **https://**{*device_address*}**:**{*port*}**/**{*api_resource*}**/data/**{*path-to-data-resource*}**/**{*action*}. The available actions for any data resource cannot be discovered. Each of these actions is defined in the corresponding YANG module.

The YANG Library Version Resource

The final second-level resource under the API resource is the yang-library-version resource, which, as the name implies, indicates the version of the YANG library supported by the device. This resource is identified by the path segment /yang-library-version. Example 14-54 shows the response message to a GET request to the URI https://ios-xe-mgmt-latest.cisco.com:9443/restconf/yang-library-version.

Example 14-54 *GET Request to Retrieve the YANG Library Version Resource*

```
! The response message showing the YANG library version
HTTP/1.1 200 OK
Server: nginx
Date: Wed, 11 Dec 2019 20:27:36 GMT
Content-Type: application/yang-data+xml
Transfer-Encoding: chunked
Connection: keep-alive
Cache-Control: private, no-cache, must-revalidate, proxy-revalidate
Vary: Accept-Encoding
Pragma: no-cache

<yang-library-version xmlns="urn:ietf:params:xml:ns:yang:ietf-yang-
  library">2016-06-21</yang-library-version>
```

The message body in the response shows that the YANG library version on this device is 2016-06-21.

Methods and the RESTCONF Operations Layer

Now that you know how to construct a URI to target a specific resource, in this section you will see how to use HTTP methods to act on these resources. Methods can be roughly classified into two categories: methods to retrieve resource representations and methods to edit resources. Because RESTCONF is a RESTful protocol, much of the material in this section will sound very familiar if you have already studied Chapters 7 and 8.

Retrieving Data: OPTIONS, GET, and HEAD

You use the OPTIONS method in requests to discover which methods are supported for a specific resource. The allowed methods are returned by the server in the Allow header field of the response.

Take, for example, the two containers interfaces and interfaces-state, both defined in the YANG module ietf-interfaces. The first holds the interface configuration, and the second holds the interface (non-configurable) state data. Example 14-55 shows an OPTIONS request being sent to each resource on the IOS XE sandbox.

Example 14-55 *Using the OPTIONS Method to Discover the Allowed Methods for the interfaces and interfaces-state Resources*

```
! OPTIONS request and response for the interfaces Resource
OPTIONS /restconf/data/ietf-interfaces:interfaces/ HTTP/1.1
Authorization: Basic ZGV2ZWxvcGVyOkMxc2NvMTIzNDU=
User-Agent: PostmanRuntime/7.20.1
Accept: */*
Cache-Control: no-cache
Host: ios-xe-mgmt-latest.cisco.com:9443
Accept-Encoding: gzip, deflate
Content-Length: 0
Connection: keep-alive

HTTP/1.1 200 OK
Server: nginx
Date: Fri, 13 Dec 2019 21:32:57 GMT
Content-Type: text/html
Content-Length: 0
Connection: keep-alive
Allow: DELETE, GET, HEAD, PATCH, POST, PUT, OPTIONS
Cache-Control: private, no-cache, must-revalidate, proxy-revalidate
Accept-Patch: application/yang-data+xml, application/yang-data+json
Pragma: no-cache

! OPTIONS request and response for the interfaces-state Resource
```

```
OPTIONS /restconf/data/ietf-interfaces:interfaces-state/ HTTP/1.1
Authorization: Basic ZGV2ZWxvcGVyOkMxc2NvMTIzNDU=
User-Agent: PostmanRuntime/7.20.1
Accept: */*
Cache-Control: no-cache
Host: ios-xe-mgmt-latest.cisco.com:9443
Accept-Encoding: gzip, deflate
Content-Length: 0
Connection: keep-alive

HTTP/1.1 200 OK
Server: nginx
Date: Fri, 13 Dec 2019 21:33:04 GMT
Content-Type: text/html
Content-Length: 0
Connection: keep-alive
Allow: GET, HEAD, OPTIONS
Cache-Control: private, no-cache, must-revalidate, proxy-revalidate
Pragma: no-cache
```

The Allow header field in the first response in Example 14-55 shows that the resource accepts requests that use the DELETE, GET, HEAD, PATCH, POST, PUT, and OPTIONS methods. The second response message shows that the resource, being read-only, accepts requests that use the GET, HEAD, and OPTIONS methods only.

You have seen how GET works in other examples in this chapter. Now you will see how GET fails! If a GET request is made for a resource to which the client does not have read access, the server responds with either a "401 Unauthorized" or a "404 Not Found" message. If a GET request is made for a resource that does not exist, or for an instance of a YANG list or leaf list that does not exist, the server responds with a "404 Not Found" message.

The GET method is supported for all resource types except operations resources (that are defined in YANG modules using the rpc and action statements). If a GET request is made for an operations resource, the server responds with a "405 Method Not Allowed" message.

A GET request may be sent for a specific instance of a list or leaf list, such as a GET to the URI https://ios-xe-mgmt-latest.cisco.com:9443/restconf/data/ietf-interfaces:interfaces/interface=GigabitEthernet1, where GigbaitEthernet1 is an instance of the list interface. What if a GET request does not specify a particular instance of the list interface? If the response returned from the server is in XML, that would not be allowed, and the response status line would be "400 Bad Request," indicating an error condition. If the response is in JSON, the response would be a normal 200 OK response, and the response body would be composed of a JSON array listing *all* instances of the list or leaf list.

As you saw in Chapter 7, a client indicates the preferred encoding for the response message body by specifying this encoding in the request Accept header. Building on that, in the first part of example 14-56, the Accept header in the GET request for the interface list specifies XML as the preferred encoding for the response. As a result, the response message has a "400 Bad Request" status line. Alternatively, when the Accept header specifies JSON as the requested encoding in the second part of the example, the response message body correctly lists all interfaces in a JSON array.

Example 14-56 *Sending a GET Request for More Than One List Instance with the Accept Header Set to XML and then to JSON*

```
! GET request for the interface list with Accept header = application/yang-data+xml
GET /restconf/data/ietf-interfaces:interfaces/interface HTTP/1.1
Authorization: Basic ZGV2ZWxvcGVyOkMxc2NvMTIzNDU=
User-Agent: PostmanRuntime/7.20.1
Accept: application/yang-data+xml
Cache-Control: no-cache
Host: ios-xe-mgmt-latest.cisco.com:9443
Accept-Encoding: gzip, deflate
Connection: keep-alive

HTTP/1.1 400 Bad Request
Server: nginx
Date: Fri, 13 Dec 2019 21:51:36 GMT
Content-Type: application/yang-data+xml
Transfer-Encoding: chunked
Connection: keep-alive
Cache-Control: private, no-cache, must-revalidate, proxy-revalidate
Vary: Accept-Encoding
Pragma: no-cache

<errors xmlns="urn:ietf:params:xml:ns:yang:ietf-restconf">
    <error>
        <error-message>too many instances: 3</error-message>
        <error-tag>invalid-value</error-tag>
        <error-type>application</error-type>
    </error>
</errors>

! GET request for the interface list with Accept header = application/yang-data+json
GET /restconf/data/ietf-interfaces:interfaces/interface HTTP/1.1
Accept: application/yang-data+json
```

```
Authorization: Basic ZGV2ZWxvcGVyOkMxc2NvMTIzNDU=
User-Agent: PostmanRuntime/7.20.1
Cache-Control: no-cache
Host: ios-xe-mgmt-latest.cisco.com:9443
Accept-Encoding: gzip, deflate
Connection: keep-alive

HTTP/1.1 200 OK
Server: nginx
Date: Fri, 13 Dec 2019 21:59:25 GMT
Content-Type: application/yang-data+json
Transfer-Encoding: chunked
Connection: keep-alive
Cache-Control: private, no-cache, must-revalidate, proxy-revalidate
Pragma: no-cache

{
  "ietf-interfaces:interface": [
    {
      "name": "GigabitEthernet1",
      "description": "MANAGEMENT INTERFACE - DON'T TOUCH ME",
      "type": "iana-if-type:ethernetCsmacd",
      "enabled": true,
      "ietf-ip:ipv4": {
        "address": [
          {
            "ip": "10.10.20.48",
            "netmask": "255.255.255.0"
          }
        ]
      },
      "ietf-ip:ipv6": {}
    },
    {
      "name": "GigabitEthernet2",
      "description": "Network Interface",
      "type": "iana-if-type:ethernetCsmacd",
      "enabled": true,
      "ietf-ip:ipv4": {},
      "ietf-ip:ipv6": {}
    },
    {
```

```
        "name": "GigabitEthernet3",
        "description": "Network Interface",
        "type": "iana-if-type:ethernetCsmacd",
        "enabled": false,
        "ietf-ip:ipv4": {},
        "ietf-ip:ipv6": {}
      }
   ]
}
```

Finally, a client can use the HEAD method in place of the GET method in order to retrieve the resource metadata only. The response message for a HEAD request is exactly the same response if a GET method is used, minus the message body.

Editing Data: POST, PUT, PATCH, and DELETE

A client can use the POST method to either create a data resource or invoke an operations resource. The resource to be created is a child resource to the target resource identified by the request URI. The resource representation goes into the message body. In Example 14-57, interface Loopback123 is created under the container interfaces as an instance of the list interface.

Example 14-57 *Creating Interface Loopback123 by Using the POST Method*

```
! Interface list from the CLI before sending the POST request
csr1000v-1# show ip interface brief
Interface              IP-Address      OK? Method Status                Protocol
GigabitEthernet1       10.10.20.48     YES NVRAM  up                    up
GigabitEthernet2       unassigned      YES DHCP   up                    up
GigabitEthernet3       unassigned      YES NVRAM  administratively down down

! POST request to create interface Loopback123
POST /restconf/data/ietf-interfaces:interfaces/ HTTP/1.1
Content-Type: application/yang-data+xml
Authorization: Basic ZGV2ZWxvcGVyOkMxc2NvMTIzNDU=
User-Agent: PostmanRuntime/7.20.1
Accept: */*
Cache-Control: no-cache
Host: ios-xe-mgmt-latest.cisco.com:9443
Accept-Encoding: gzip, deflate
Content-Length: 560
Connection: keep-alive

<interface xmlns="urn:ietf:params:xml:ns:yang:ietf-interfaces"
xmlns:if="urn:ietf:p
```

```
  arams:xml:ns:yang:ietf-interfaces">
    <name>Loopback123</name>
    <description>Creating a Loopback interface using RESTCONF and POST</description>
    <type xmlns:ianaift="urn:ietf:params:xml:ns:yang:iana-if-
  type">ianaift:softwareLoopback</type>
    <enabled>true</enabled>
    <ipv4 xmlns="urn:ietf:params:xml:ns:yang:ietf-ip">
        <address>
            <ip>10.123.123.123</ip>
            <netmask>255.255.255.255</netmask>
        </address>
    </ipv4>
</interface>

HTTP/1.1 201 Created
Server: nginx
Date: Fri, 13 Dec 2019 23:20:08 GMT
Content-Type: text/html
Content-Length: 0
Location: https://ios-xe-mgmt-latest.cisco.com/restconf/data/ietf-
  interfaces:interfaces/interface=Loopback123
Connection: keep-alive
Last-Modified: Fri, 13 Dec 2019 23:20:08 GMT
Cache-Control: private, no-cache, must-revalidate, proxy-revalidate
Etag: 1576-279208-528007
Pragma: no-cache

! Interface list from the CLI after sending the POST request
csr1000v-1# show ip interface brief
Interface              IP-Address      OK? Method Status                Protocol
GigabitEthernet1       10.10.20.48     YES NVRAM  up                    up
GigabitEthernet2       unassigned      YES DHCP   up                    up
GigabitEthernet3       unassigned      YES NVRAM  administratively down down
Loopback123            10.123.123.123  YES other  up                    up
```

If the resource is created successfully, as in Example 14-57, the response has a "201 Created" status line with a Location header field pointing to the newly created resource, as highlighted in the example.

The POST method creates a new resource, and if that resource already exists, a "409 Conflict" status line is returned. Re-sending the request from Example 14-57 has this exact effect, as shown in Example 14-58.

Example 14-58 *Response Received When Attempting to Create Interface Loopback123 When It Already Exists*

```
HTTP/1.1 409 Conflict
Server: nginx
Date: Thu, 26 Dec 2019 16:38:32 GMT
Content-Type: application/yang-data+xml
Transfer-Encoding: chunked
Connection: keep-alive
Cache-Control: private, no-cache, must-revalidate, proxy-revalidate
Vary: Accept-Encoding
Pragma: no-cache

<errors xmlns="urn:ietf:params:xml:ns:yang:ietf-restconf">
  <error>
    <error-message>object already exists:
  /if:interfaces/if:interface[if:name='Loopback123']</error-message>
    <error-path>/ietf-interfaces:interfaces</error-path>
    <error-tag>data-exists</error-tag>
    <error-type>application</error-type>
  </error>
</errors>
```

If the request body contains more than one instance of a list or leaf list, a "400 Bad Request" response is returned. Accordingly, this will be the response received if you attempt to create more than one interface in the same request message.

The other use of the POST method is to invoke an operations resource, as described earlier in this chapter, in the section "The Operations Resource." In that case, the message body of the request message can be used to include the input parameters of the operation (**rpc** or **action**), if any. Similarly, the message body of the response message is used to communicate the output parameters of the operation, if any.

The PUT method also creates a resource, but unlike the POST method, PUT *replaces* a resource if it finds that it already exists. When a PUT method creates a resource, a "201 Created" response is sent back to the client. If the resource already exists and is replaced by the PUT request, a "204 No Content" response is sent back to the client.

Another subtle difference between the POST and PUT methods is that the URI in a POST request is that of the parent resource under which the new resource is created, whereas the target URI in a PUT request is that of the newly created resource itself.

Say that you want to create interface Loopack124 by using PUT. The URI to use is not https://ios-xe-mgmt-latest.cisco.com/restconf/data/ietf-interfaces:interfaces/, as it would be with the POST method. If you use that URI, you get a "400 Bad Request" response. The correct URI to use is https://ios-xe-mgmt-latest.cisco.com/restconf/data/ietf-interfaces:interfaces/interface=Loopback124, as shown in Example 14-59.

Example 14-59 *Creating Interface Loopback124 by Using the PUT Method*

```
! Interface list before the PUT request is sent
csr1000v-1#show ip interface brief
Interface              IP-Address      OK? Method Status                Protocol
GigabitEthernet1       10.10.20.48     YES NVRAM  up                    up
GigabitEthernet2       unassigned      YES DHCP   up                    up
GigabitEthernet3       unassigned      YES NVRAM  administratively down down
Loopback123            10.123.123.123  YES other  up                    up

! PUT request to create interface Loopback124
PUT /restconf/data/ietf-interfaces:interfaces/interface=Loopback124 HTTP/1.1
Content-Type: application/yang-data+xml
Authorization: Basic ZGV2ZWxvcGVyOkMxc2NvMTIzNDU=
User-Agent: PostmanRuntime/7.20.1
Accept: */*
Cache-Control: no-cache
Host: ios-xe-mgmt-latest.cisco.com:9443
Accept-Encoding: gzip, deflate
Content-Length: 560
Connection: keep-alive

<interface xmlns="urn:ietf:params:xml:ns:yang:ietf-interfaces"
  xmlns:if="urn:ietf:params:xml:ns:yang:ietf-interfaces">
    <name>Loopback124</name>
    <description>Creating a Loopback interface using RESTCONF and POST</description>
    <type xmlns:ianaift="urn:ietf:params:xml:ns:yang:iana-if-
  type">ianaift:softwareLoopback</type>
    <enabled>true</enabled>
    <ipv4 xmlns="urn:ietf:params:xml:ns:yang:ietf-ip">
        <address>
            <ip>10.123.123.124</ip>
            <netmask>255.255.255.255</netmask>
        </address>
    </ipv4>
</interface>

HTTP/1.1 201 Created
Server: nginx
Date: Fri, 13 Dec 2019 23:49:19 GMT
Content-Type: text/html
Content-Length: 0
Location: https://ios-xe-mgmt-latest.cisco.com/restconf/data/ietf-
  interfaces:interfaces/interface=Loopback124
```

```
Connection: keep-alive
Last-Modified: Fri, 13 Dec 2019 23:49:18 GMT
Cache-Control: private, no-cache, must-revalidate, proxy-revalidate
Etag: 1576-280958-904019
Pragma: no-cache

! Interface list after the PUT request is sent
csr1000v-1# show ip interface brief
Interface              IP-Address      OK? Method Status                Protocol
GigabitEthernet1       10.10.20.48     YES NVRAM  up                    up
GigabitEthernet2       unassigned      YES DHCP   up                    up
GigabitEthernet3       unassigned      YES NVRAM  administratively down down
Loopback123            10.123.123.123  YES other  up                    up
Loopback124            10.123.123.124  YES other  up                    up
```

Note that the PUT method is not intended to be used to edit a resource. The PUT method replaces a resource with the data in the message body. The PUT method removes the old configuration and places the new configuration in the datastore, effectively losing all the old configuration.

The primary way to edit a resource is using the PATCH method. The PATCH method enables you to selectively edit the target resource. Unlike the PUT and POST methods, which either create or completely replace a resource, the PATCH method operates by merging the contents in the HTTP request message body with the target resource.

The PATCH method has several flavors. The one covered in this section is named the *plain PATCH*.

Say, for example, that you need to edit the description on an interface but don't want to replace the whole interface configuration—perhaps because you do not need to worry about what the current configuration is, or you don't know what this configuration is—and you would need an extra operation to retrieve this data. In this case, the PATCH method would be a better fit than the PUT or POST methods.

Example 14-60 shows the description on interface GigabitEthernet3 before and after using the PATCH method to change the interface description.

Example 14-60 *Using the PATCH Method to Edit the Interface Description*

```
! Interface description BEFORE applying the PATCH method
csr1000v-1# show run interface Gig3
Building configuration...

Current configuration : 126 bytes
!
```

```
interface GigabitEthernet3
 description Interface Description BEFORE the PATCH method
 no ip address
 negotiation auto
end

! HTTP request message using the PATCH method and the resulting response
PATCH /restconf/data/ietf-interfaces:interfaces/interface=GigabitEthernet3 HTTP/1.1
Content-Type: application/yang-data+xml
Authorization: Basic ZGV2ZWxvcGVyOkMxc2NvMTIzNDU=
User-Agent: PostmanRuntime/7.19.0
Accept: */*
Cache-Control: no-cache
Host: ios-xe-mgmt-latest.cisco.com:9443
Accept-Encoding: gzip, deflate
Content-Length: 216
Connection: keep-alive

<interface
    xmlns="urn:ietf:params:xml:ns:yang:ietf-interfaces"
    xmlns:if="urn:ietf:params:xml:ns:yang:ietf-interfaces">
    <name>GigabitEthernet3</name>
    <description>Interface Description AFTER the PATCH method</description>
</interface>

HTTP/1.1 204 No Content
Server: nginx
Date: Mon, 18 Nov 2019 07:01:55 GMT
Content-Type: text/html
Content-Length: 0
Connection: keep-alive
Last-Modified: Mon, 18 Nov 2019 07:01:55 GMT
Cache-Control: private, no-cache, must-revalidate, proxy-revalidate
Etag: 1574-60515-423386
Pragma: no-cache

! Interface description AFTER applying the PATCH method
csr1000v-1# show run interface Gig3
Building configuration...

Current configuration : 125 bytes
!
interface GigabitEthernet3
```

```
 description Interface Description AFTER the PATCH method
 no ip address
 negotiation auto
end
```

If the PATCH method is used to edit a child resource (description) of the target resource (interface GigabitEthernet3), as in Example 14-60, keep in mind the following points:

- A plain PATCH can be used to create or update but not delete a child resource.
- If the target resource is a YANG leaf list, the PATCH method must not change the value of the leaf list instance.
- If the target resource is a YANG list instance, the key leaf values in the message body must match the key leaf values in the URI. In addition, the PATCH method must not be used to change the key leaf values.

If we apply the first restriction to Example 14-60, we see that the plain PATCH method cannot be used to delete the interface description; it can only update it. It can also be used to create an interface description if this description does not already exist.

Now consider the third restriction in the list and note that Interface GigabitEthernet3 in Example 14-60 is an instance of the list interface, whose key is the leaf name, as defined in the YANG module ietf-interfaces. Although you can use the PATCH request without including the interface name in the body, if you do include it, the value of the element <name> in the message body must be equal to the name of the interface in the URI, as you can see in Example 14-60. In addition, you cannot change the value of the key, so you cannot change the name of the interface in a PATCH request message. This might seem obvious for GigabitEthernet interfaces whose names cannot be changed anyway, but it is not so obvious for other types, such as loopback, tunnel, or VLAN interfaces.

An important point to keep in mind is that when using the PATCH method to edit a resource, the Content-Type header in the request message must match the data encoding in the message body (in this case, application/yang-data+xml). If a response has an incorrect or missing value in the Content-Type header field, the response will indicate an error, as shown in Example 14-61.

Example 14-61 *Error in Response Message Due to the Use of the Wrong Media Type in the Content-Type Header*

```
HTTP/1.1 415 Unsupported Media Type
Server: nginx
Date: Mon, 18 Nov 2019 07:51:46 GMT
Content-Type: application/yang-data+xml
Transfer-Encoding: chunked
Connection: keep-alive
```

```
Cache-Control: private, no-cache, must-revalidate, proxy-revalidate
Vary: Accept-Encoding
Pragma: no-cache

<errors xmlns="urn:ietf:params:xml:ns:yang:ietf-restconf">
  <error>
    <error-message>Unsupported media type: text/plain ; Should be one of:
  application/yang-data+xml, application/yang-data+json, application/
  yang-patch+xml, application/yang-patch+json.</error-message>
    <error-tag>malformed-message</error-tag>
    <error-type>application</error-type>
  </error>
</errors>
```

A successful PATCH operation results in a "200 OK" or "204 No Content" message, depending on whether the response message includes a body.

Finally, the DELETE method is used to delete the target resource. To delete interface Loopback124 on the IOS XE sandbox, you send to the device the request in Example 14-62.

Example 14-62 *Using the DELETE Method to Delete Interface Loopback124*

```
DELETE /restconf/data/ietf-interfaces:interfaces/interface=Loopback124 HTTP/1.1
Content-Type: application/yang-data+xml
Authorization: Basic ZGV2ZWxvcGVyOkMxc2NvMTIzNDU=
User-Agent: PostmanRuntime/7.20.1
Accept: */*
Cache-Control: no-cache
Host: ios-xe-mgmt-latest.cisco.com:9443
Accept-Encoding: gzip, deflate
Content-Length: 0
Connection: keep-alive

HTTP/1.1 204 No Content
Server: nginx
Date: Sat, 14 Dec 2019 00:08:43 GMT
Content-Type: text/html
Content-Length: 0
Connection: keep-alive
Last-Modified: Sat, 14 Dec 2019 00:08:42 GMT
Cache-Control: private, no-cache, must-revalidate, proxy-revalidate
Etag: 1576-282122-423882
Pragma: no-cache
```

A "204 No Content" response indicates that the resource has been successfully deleted.

Query Parameters

Query parameters provide you with more control over what you retrieve when you use the HEAD or GET methods or more control over what effect the POST or PUT methods have on a resource. A URI with query parameters has the following general format:

https://{*device_address*}**:**{*port*}**/**{*api_resource*}**/**{*full-path-to-resource*}**?**{*paramter_1*}**=**{*value_1*}**[&**{*parameter_2*}**=**{*value_2*}**][&..][&**{*parameter_n*}**=**{*value_n*}**]**

Vendors can define their own parameters, but Section 4.8 of RFC 8040 defines the following nine query parameters:

- **content:** This parameter is used to select whether a GET request retrieves configuration and/or non-configuration data, using one of three values: **config**, **nonconfig**, and **all**. The default value is **all**.
- **depth:** This parameter is used to select the number of levels down the resource hierarchy retrieved by a GET request; **unbounded** is the default value.
- **fields:** This parameter is used in GET requests to retrieve only a subset of the target resource child fields/nodes.
- **filter:** This parameter is used in a GET request to a server event stream resource to filter which notifications are received from that server, using XPath 1.0 expressions. Notifications and event streams are covered in Section 6 of RFC 8040.
- **insert:** When a resource is created using the POST or PUT methods, and that resource is part of a list or leaf list that is ordered by the user, this query parameter allows the user to specify where the new resource fits in the list. This parameter takes one of four values: **first**, **last**, **before**, and **after**. The default value is **last**.
- **point:** This parameter works with the insert query parameter to specify where to insert a list or leaf list entry when the **insert** parameter is either **before** or **after**. The format of the value assigned to the **point** parameter is the same as the URI string.
- **start-time:** This parameter takes a value formatted as a date and a time and is used in GET requests to trigger the notification replay feature defined in RFC 5277. The replay should start at the time specified in the parameter value.
- **stop-time:** This parameter works with the start-time parameter and indicates the last (newest) notification that should be received.
- **with-defaults:** When servers support the with-defaults capability, this query parameter used in a GET request tells the server how to respond to the client request when the data retrieved contains nodes that have a default value, as defined in the corresponding YANG module. This parameter takes one of four values: **report-all**, **trim**, **explicit**, and **report-all-tagged**. The default value depends on the server.

As you can see from the general format of the URI with query parameters, one or more parameters may be used in the same URI, separated using the ampersand (&) symbol, as long as each parameter does not appear more than once. The parameters may appear in any order. Which query parameters are allowed for a resource may depend on the particular resource, but typically, only the resource *type* is the important factor. Query parameters and their values are case sensitive.

If a parameter is given an invalid value, or if a parameter is used with a resource or method that does not support that parameter or if a parameter appears more than once in a URI, the server returns a "400 Bad Request" response.

The content query parameter tells the server whether to respond to a client GET request with configuration data and/or non-configuration data. The three possible values of this parameter are **config**, **nonconfig**, and **all**. The default value when the parameter is not used is **all**. Therefore, sending a GET request to the URI https://ios-xe-mgmt-latest.cisco.com:9443/restconf/data?content=config would return only the configuration data in the datastore on the IOS XE sandbox.

The depth query parameter tells the server how many levels down the resource hierarchy it needs to send back to the client in response to a GET request. The value of the depth parameter should be an integer. Different implementations define a depth of 1 differently. Some define depth=1 as the target resource level, and some define that depth level as the first level of child resources. Depth may also be set to **unbounded**, which is the default value if the depth parameter is omitted altogether. It basically means that the resource and all resources under it, at all levels, will be retrieved.

Example 14-63 shows the message body of the response received when sending a GET request to the URI https://ios-xe-mgmt-latest.cisco.com:9443/restconf/data/ietf-interfaces:interfaces/interface=GigabitEthernet3?depth=1 and then changing the depth to 2 and finally to **unbounded**. Notice the different levels of child nodes in each case.

Example 14-63 *Responses received when sending a GET Request with Different Depth Levels*

```
! Response received when sending a GET request using depth=1
<interface xmlns="urn:ietf:params:xml:ns:yang:ietf-interfaces"  xmlns:if="urn:ietf:p
  arams:xml:ns:yang:ietf-interfaces">
    <name>GigabitEthernet3</name>
    <description>Network Interface</description>
    <type xmlns:ianaift="urn:ietf:params:xml:ns:yang:iana-if-
  type">ianaift:ethernetCsmacd</type>
    <enabled>false</enabled>
    <ipv4 xmlns="urn:ietf:params:xml:ns:yang:ietf-ip"/>
    <ipv6 xmlns="urn:ietf:params:xml:ns:yang:ietf-ip"/>
</interface>
```

```
! Response received when sending a GET request using depth=2
<interface xmlns="urn:ietf:params:xml:ns:yang:ietf-interfaces"
  xmlns:if="urn:ietf:params:xml:ns:yang:ietf-interfaces">
    <name>GigabitEthernet3</name>
    <description>Network Interface</description>
    <type xmlns:ianaift="urn:ietf:params:xml:ns:yang:iana-if-
  type">ianaift:ethernetCsmacd</type>
    <enabled>false</enabled>
    <ipv4 xmlns="urn:ietf:params:xml:ns:yang:ietf-ip">
        <address/>
        <address/>
    </ipv4>
    <ipv6 xmlns="urn:ietf:params:xml:ns:yang:ietf-ip">
        <ipv6-router-advertisements xmlns="urn:ietf:params:xml:ns:yang:ietf-ipv6-
  unicast-routing"/>
    </ipv6>
</interface>

! Response received when sending a GET request using depth=unbounded ###
<interface xmlns="urn:ietf:params:xml:ns:yang:ietf-interfaces"
  xmlns:if="urn:ietf:params:xml:ns:yang:ietf-interfaces">
    <name>GigabitEthernet3</name>
    <description>Network Interface</description>
   <type xmlns:ianaift="urn:ietf:params:xml:ns:yang:iana-if-
  type">ianaift:ethernetCsmacd</type>
    <enabled>true</enabled>
    <ipv4 xmlns="urn:ietf:params:xml:ns:yang:ietf-ip">
        <address>
            <ip>10.0.0.3</ip>
            <netmask>255.255.255.0</netmask>
        </address>
        <address>
            <ip>10.0.1.3</ip>
            <netmask>255.255.255.0</netmask>
        </address>
    </ipv4>
    <ipv6 xmlns="urn:ietf:params:xml:ns:yang:ietf-ip">
  </ipv6>
</interface>
```

With the fields query parameter, you have the option of selecting which child elements of a resource are retrieved by a GET request. Example 14-64 shows how to retrieve only the child element <enabled> for interface GigabitEthernet3.

Example 14-64 *Using the Fields Query Parameter to Retrieve the <enabled> Child Node Only*

```
! Sending a GET request to retrieve only the <enabled> element
GET /restconf/data/ietf-
  interfaces:interfaces/interface=GigabitEthernet3?fields=enabled HTTP/1.1
Authorization: Basic ZGV2ZWxvcGVyOkMxc2NvMTIzNDU=
User-Agent: PostmanRuntime/7.21.0
Accept: */*
Cache-Control: no-cache
Host: ios-xe-mgmt-latest.cisco.com:9443
Accept-Encoding: gzip, deflate
Connection: keep-alive

! Resulting response message
HTTP/1.1 200 OK
Server: nginx
Date: Thu, 26 Dec 2019 11:16:22 GMT
Content-Type: application/yang-data+xml
Transfer-Encoding: chunked
Connection: keep-alive
Cache-Control: private, no-cache, must-revalidate, proxy-revalidate
Pragma: no-cache

<interface xmlns="urn:ietf:params:xml:ns:yang:ietf-interfaces"
  xmlns:if="urn:ietf:params:xml:ns:yang:ietf-interfaces">
  <enabled>true</enabled>
</interface>
```

As you can see, other fields do not show up. What if you need to display the interface name as well? You can specify more than one field, separated by semicolons (;), as shown in Example 14-65.

Example 14-65 *Using a Semicolon to Specify More Than One Value for the Fields Query Parameter*

```
! Sending a GET request to retrieve more than one child field
GET /restconf/data/
  ietf-interfaces:interfaces/interface=GigabitEthernet3?fields=name;enabled HTTP/1.1
Authorization: Basic ZGV2ZWxvcGVyOkMxc2NvMTIzNDU=
User-Agent: PostmanRuntime/7.21.0
Accept: */*
Cache-Control: no-cache
Host: ios-xe-mgmt-latest.cisco.com:9443
Accept-Encoding: gzip, deflate
```

```
Connection: keep-alive

### Resulting response message ###
HTTP/1.1 200 OK
Server: nginx
Date: Thu, 26 Dec 2019 11:19:03 GMT
Content-Type: application/yang-data+xml
Transfer-Encoding: chunked
Connection: keep-alive
Cache-Control: private, no-cache, must-revalidate, proxy-revalidate
Pragma: no-cache

<interface xmlns="urn:ietf:params:xml:ns:yang:ietf-interfaces" xmlns:if="urn:ietf:pa
  rams:xml:ns:yang:ietf-interfaces">
  <name>GigabitEthernet3</name>
  <enabled>true</enabled>
</interface>
```

Example 14-66 shows a more complex expression, where the interface name, status, and IP address are retrieved for *all* interfaces by sending a GET request to the URI https://ios-xe-mgmt-latest.cisco.com:9443/restconf/data/ietf-interfaces:interfaces?fields=interface(name;enabled;ietf-ip:ipv4/address/ip).

Example 14-66 *Using a Complex Expression for the Field Query Parameter to Retrieve More Than One Child Element*

```
! Sending a GET request using a complex expression for the fields query parameter
GET /restconf/data/ietf-interfaces:interfaces?fields=interface%28name;enabled;ietf-
  ip:ipv4/address/ip%29 HTTP/1.1
Authorization: Basic ZGV2ZWxvcGVyOkMxc2NvMTIzNDU=
User-Agent: PostmanRuntime/7.21.0
Accept: */*
Cache-Control: no-cache
Host: ios-xe-mgmt-latest.cisco.com:9443
Accept-Encoding: gzip, deflate
Connection: keep-alive

! The response message containing selected fields for all interfaces
HTTP/1.1 200 OK
Server: nginx
Date: Thu, 26 Dec 2019 11:27:15 GMT
Content-Type: application/yang-data+xml
Transfer-Encoding: chunked
```

```
Connection: keep-alive
Cache-Control: private, no-cache, must-revalidate, proxy-revalidate
Pragma: no-cache


<interfaces xmlns="urn:ietf:params:xml:ns:yang:ietf-interfaces"
  xmlns:if="urn:ietf:params:xml:ns:yang:ietf-interfaces">
    <interface>
        <name>GigabitEthernet1</name>
        <enabled>true</enabled>
        <ipv4 xmlns="urn:ietf:params:xml:ns:yang:ietf-ip">
            <address>
                <ip>10.10.20.48</ip>
            </address>
        </ipv4>
    </interface>
    <interface>
        <name>GigabitEthernet2</name>
        <enabled>true</enabled>
        <ipv4 xmlns="urn:ietf:params:xml:ns:yang:ietf-ip">
            <address>
                <ip>10.255.255.1</ip>
            </address>
        </ipv4>
    </interface>
    <interface>
        <name>GigabitEthernet3</name>
        <enabled>true</enabled>
        <ipv4 xmlns="urn:ietf:params:xml:ns:yang:ietf-ip">
            <address>
                <ip>10.0.0.3</ip>
            </address>
            <address>
                <ip>10.0.1.3</ip>
            </address>
        </ipv4>
    </interface>
</interfaces>
```

Notice that the following conventions are used when constructing an expression to use with the fields query parameter:

- As mentioned earlier, you can specify more than one field by separating the different child node names with semicolons (;). In Example 14-66, the semicolon is used to extract three different fields.

- You can use a slash (/) to explicitly extract a node down a hierarchy without including other nodes. In Example 14-66, only ip is extracted, using the path expression ipv4/address/ip, in the process excluding the mask.
- When a child node is defined in a different module/namespace, you specify the child node as {*namespace*}:{*child-name*} (for example, ietf-ip:ipv4).
- You use parentheses to specify the subnodes under the primary node, to specify the three different fields under the interface field.

All rules that apply to URI queries, as discussed in Chapter 7, apply to the query parameters discussed here. For example, notice that the right and left parentheses are encoded to %28 and %29, respectively, in the Example 14-66.

For a description of the remaining query parameters, see Section 4.8 of RFC 8040.

RESTCONF and Python

Because RESTCONF is a RESTful protocol, the same Python libraries discussed in Chapter 7 are used to generate and send RESTCONF requests: the **socket** module and the **urllib**, **httplib**, and **requests** packages. Example 14-67 shows a Python program that uses the **requests** package to send a POST request that creates interface Loopback111.

Example 14-67 *Creating Interface Loopback111 by Using the requests Package in Python*

```
import requests
url = 'https://ios-xe-mgmt-latest.cisco.com:9443/restconf/data/ietf-
  interfaces:interfaces/'
headers = {'Content-Type': 'application/yang-data+xml'}
payload = '''
   <interface xmlns="urn:ietf:params:xml:ns:yang:ietf-interfaces"
  xmlns:if="urn:ietf:params:xml:ns:yang:ietf-interfaces">
    <name>Loopback111</name>
    <description>Creating a Loopback interface using Python</description>
    <type xmlns:ianaift="urn:ietf:params:xml:ns:yang:iana-if-
  type">ianaift:softwareLoopback</type>
    <enabled>true</enabled>
    <ipv4 xmlns="urn:ietf:params:xml:ns:yang:ietf-ip">
        <address>
            <ip>10.111.111.111</ip>
            <netmask>255.255.255.255</netmask>
        </address>
    </ipv4>
   </interface>'''
res_obj = requests.post(url,headers=headers,data=payload,auth=('developer',
  'C1sco12345'),verify=False)
print('The request headers:','\n',res_obj.request.headers,'\n')
print('The response message body from the server is:','\n',res_obj.text,'\n')
print('The response status code:','\n',res_obj.status_code,'\n')
print('The response headers:','\n',res_obj.headers,'\n')
```

Example 14-68 shows the output from running the script.

Example 14-68 *The Output from the Four Print Statements in the Script in the Previous Example*

```
[NetDev@Server1 Scripts]$ python RESTCONF_requests.py
/usr/local/lib/python3.7/site-packages/urllib3/connectionpool.py:847:
  InsecureRequestWarning: Unverified HTTPS request is being made. Adding
  certificate verification is strongly advised. See:
  https://urllib3.readthedocs.io/en/latest/advanced-usage.html#ssl-warnings
  InsecureRequestWarning)
The request headers:
{'User-Agent': 'python-requests/2.22.0', 'Accept-Encoding': 'gzip, deflate',
  'Accept': '*/*', 'Connection': 'keep-alive', 'Content-Type': 'application/
  yang-data+xml', 'Content-Length': '556', 'Authorization': 'Basic
  ZGV2ZWxvcGVyOkMxc2NvMTIzNDU='}

The response message body from the server is:


The response status code:
201

The response headers:
{'Server': 'nginx', 'Date': 'Fri, 27 Dec 2019 13:53:04 GMT', 'Content-Type': 'text/
  html', 'Content-Length': '0', 'Location': 'https://ios-xe-mgmt-latest.cisco.com/
  restconf/data/ietf-interfaces:interfaces/interface=Loopback111', 'Connection':
  'keep-alive', 'Last-Modified': 'Fri, 27 Dec 2019 13:53:04 GMT', 'Cache-Control':
  'private, no-cache, must-revalidate, proxy-revalidate', 'Etag': '1577-454784-
  616529', 'Pragma': 'no-cache'}

[NetDev@Server1 Scripts]$
```

Notice the Location header, whose value is the URI pointing to the location of the newly created resource—in this case, interface Loopback111.

Example 14-69 shows the output from the CLI with the interface list before and after running the script.

Example 14-69 *The Interface List Before and After Running the Script Showing the Newly Created Interface Loopback111*

```
! Interface list BEFORE running the script
csr1000v-1# sh ip int bri
Interface              IP-Address      OK? Method Status                Protocol
GigabitEthernet1       10.10.20.48     YES NVRAM  up                    up
GigabitEthernet2       10.255.255.1    YES other  up                    up
GigabitEthernet3       10.0.0.3        YES manual up                    up
Loopback123            10.123.123.123  YES other  up                    up
csr1000v-1#
```

```
! Interface list AFTER running the script
csr1000v-1# show ip int bri
Interface              IP-Address      OK? Method Status                Protocol
GigabitEthernet1       10.10.20.48     YES NVRAM  up                    up
GigabitEthernet2       10.255.255.1    YES other  up                    up
GigabitEthernet3       10.0.0.3        YES manual up                    up
seLoopback111          10.111.111.111  YES other  up                    up
Loopback123            10.123.123.123  YES other  up                    up
csr1000v-1#
```

For a full discussion of the requests package and the other Python libraries for working with HTTP and RESTCONF, refer to Chapter 7.

Summary

This chapter covers the first two protocols in the network programmability stack: NETCONF and RESTCONF.

The following are the main takeaways from this chapter for NETCONF:

- At the transport layer, NETCONF requires a session-based, reliable, and secure protocol, and all implementations, at a minimum, must implement NETCONF over SSH.
- At the messages layer, NETCONF defines three types of messages: hello, rpc, and rpc-reply.
- At the operations layer, NETCONF defines several operations for retrieving data, editing data, locking and unlocking datastores, and handling session management.
- At the content layer, NETCONF uses XML exclusively for encoding the message body and follows the hierarchy defined by either an XML Schema Definition (XSD) or a YANG model.

The following are the main takeaways from this chapter for RESTCONF:

- RESTCONF is a RESTful protocol and therefore is not a stateful or session-based protocol.
- At the transport layer, RESTCONF exclusively uses HTTPS.
- At the messages layer, RESTCONF uses HTTP request and response messages.
- At the operations layer, RESTCONF defines hierarchical resources and uses URIs to target these resources. It uses HTTP methods to act on these resources.
- At the content layer, RESTCONF uses XML or JSON for encoding the message body, and it may only follow the hierarchy defined by a YANG model.

Chapter 15

gRPC, Protobuf, and gNMI

In the previous two chapters, you learned about two network management protocols, NETCONF and RESTCONF. These two protocols form the foundation of network programmability and are the two most ubiquitous protocols in today's enterprise networks—for service providers and data centers alike. However, the development of network technologies, including network automation protocols, is never in a frozen state; as new challenges arise, new solutions need to be developed to meet those challenges. This chapter introduces a new protocol that has been to developed to solve some of these newly emerging challenges: gRPC. This protocol relies on an absolutely new data serialization format named Protocol buffers (shortly Protobuf). Also, the new transport requires a new message set, new specification, which benefits from the transport at most. This role is taken by gNMI, which stands for gRPC Network Management Interface.

Requirements for Efficient Transport

One of the challenges that originated in the data center world and then later became applicable to enterprise and service provider networks as well involves multiple requirements in different dimensions that may seem, initially, contradictory:

- On one hand, there is ever-growing utilization of interfaces in data centers and service provider networks, where typical traffic rates today are on the order of hundreds of gigabits per second. Hence, there is an ever-growing need to reduce any overhead traffic, including management plane traffic, as much as possible.
- On the other hand, there is a need to collect as much operational data as possible from the network elements, including counters, routing protocols states, and the contents of MPLS FIB and MAC address tables. The need extends to analyzing this data in real time—or as close to real time as possible. In other words, there is a need for this telemetry to be continuously streamed from network devices.

- There is an additional complexity associated with streaming telemetry: Telemetry avoids the unnecessary load on network element resources, as well as unnecessary traffic on the transport media caused by request/response operations, required if streaming telemetry is not used. Originally, the concept of subscriptions was covered in RFC 5277, which addresses NETCONF event notifications. However, early production implementations of NETCONF did not implement subscriptions. Later, Cisco extended the capability of NETCONF subscriptions to some Cisco IOS XE platforms. (Refer to RFC 8640 for further details.) However, subscriptions involve huge administrative overhead on the wire due to XML encapsulation and therefore are not very efficient.

These requirements collectively drove research for a solution that would both fulfill the industry requirement and mitigate the shortcomings of the solutions implemented then. As you have already learned, network automation and programmability employs similar technologies and protocols to those used for application development and interaction. For example, NETCONF was inspired by SOAP/XML and is based on XML, and RESTCONF was inspired by and based on REST. To network programmability researchers, this indicated that a solution probably existed in the applications domain and just needed to be ported to the network programmability domain. And as expected, such a solution was found: gRPC.

History and Principles of gRPC

Some of the most complex applications shaping the Internet today, such as search engines, social media networks, and cloud infrastructures, are highly distributed by nature. This distribution is a prerequisite to provide the ability to scale and provide a sufficient level of resilience. Modern distributed applications are built using a microservices architecture (see https://microservices.io for more details). The *microservices architecture* basically refers to the splitting of a complex multicomponent application into multiple smaller applications, with each application (called a *microservice*) performing its own small subset of functions. This approach paves the way to simplify each application and remove the dependencies and spaghetti code often seen in monolithic applications, where different parts of the applications are bundled very tightly. On the other hand, in order for an overall application to work, the microservices communicate with each other using remote-procedure calls (RPCs) over a network, as each microservice has an associated IP address and TCP or UDP port. NETCONF is an RPC-based protocol (refer to Chapter 14, "NETCONF and RESTCONF"). So is gRPC. gRPC is a recursive acronym that stands for *gRPC remote-procedure call*. It is also possible to find other interpretations of the *g* part of the name gRPC, such as *general-purpose* or *Google*. Both of those are possible, as Google is the developer and core contributor/maintainer of gRPC. Currently, gRPC is a project within the Cloud Native Computing Foundation (CNCF).

Google made gRPC publicly available in 2015 but had been using the ideas of quick and highly performant RPC to manage the microservices in its data centers since the early 2000s. The name of the protocol back then was Stubby, and it was tightly bundled with Google's service architecture, so it could neither be generalized nor reused by others.

(For more details, see https://grpc.io/blog/principles/.) At the same time, in the public space, multiple developments, such as HTTP/2 and SPDY, introduced latency-reducing enhancements and optimization of handling of the requests competing for the same resources. As a result, Google reworked its Stubby protocol into gRPC, leveraging HTTP/2 and its features geared toward enhanced performance (such as binary framing, header compression, and multiplexing; see Chapter 8, "Advanced HTTP," for details) and created an open-source project that was eventually adopted by CNCF and that can be used by a wider audience.

The following concepts form the basis of gRPC:

- **Performance and speed:** One of the core goals of Stubby and, hence, gRPC is to provide fast connectivity between services, and the overall system architecture was developed to implement this concept. One example is the implementation of static paths toward resources rather than dynamic paths such as those implemented by RESTCONF. With a dynamic path, it is possible to include multiple optional queries in the URI, and they need to be parsed before call processing. In contrast, gRPC implements a *static path*, and all the queries must be part of the message body.
- **Microservices oriented:** gRPC was created to interconnect microservices that may be highly distributed across a data center or even between different data centers. It takes into account the networking components of an application, such as delays and losses.
- **Platform agnostic:** gRPC can be used on any platform or operating system, even those that have limited CPU and memory, such as mobile devices and IoT sensors.
- **Open source:** Open-source software is booming now, and for a system to be popular and widely adopted, it is important that its core functionality be open source and free to use. gRPC is open source.
- **Language independent:** gRPC was developed to be available for use in all the programming languages that have wide user bases, such as Python, Go, C/C++, Java, and Ruby. In addition, cross-platform implementation is possible, where the client and server sides are implemented in different languages (for example, a Python client and C++ servers).
- **General purpose:** Because it was built with a focus on microservices and Google architecture, gRPC is generic enough to be used as a communication system between different applications and in different scenarios (for example, the gNMI specification for network management or streaming).
- **Streaming:** gRPC supports various communication patterns, such as basic request/response operations, unidirectional streaming, and bidirectional streaming. It supports both synchronous and asynchronous operations.
- **Payload agnostic:** Originally, gRPC relied on Protocol buffers (discussed in detail later in this chapter) for both data serialization and encoding. Today, it supports any other data encoding, such as JSON or XML. However, Protocol buffers have very

dense data encoding and may provide better efficiency compared to other data encodings.

- **Metadata support:** A lot of applications, especially those communicating over the Internet (which is not a secure environment), require authentication. Application authentication is typically implemented using metadata, which is also the case with gRPC. Generally, gRPC provides the facility to transmit any metadata, which is usually a very useful feature.

- **Flow control:** Network connectivity bandwidth is often unequal inside and outside a data center. For example, the servers inside a data center might be connected with 10 Gbps interfaces, whereas customers connected to the data center from the outside may be connected to low-speed interfaces. gRPC has a built-in mechanism to be able to handle these differences to allow stable connectivity and service operation.

gRPC as a Transport

As you have already seen in this chapter, gRPC is very flexible. gRPC has the following characteristics:

- **No fixed port:** gRPC works over TCP; however, gRPC doesn't have any predefined port. The port is defined solely by the application or vendor. For example, the TCP port that is used for management of network elements via gRPC on Cisco is different from the port used by Arista, which is different from the port used by Nokia. On the one hand, such a flexibility provides an advantage in terms of security (as there are no fixed attack vectors). On the other hand, it makes managing a multivendor network more complicated.

- **No predefined calls and messages:** gRPC is a fast RPC framework. Unlike NETCONF, it doesn't have any predefined structure for its messages. Each application uses its own set of calls and messages, called a *specification*. For example, gNMI is a gRPC specification, as it defines its own set of RPC calls and associated messages.

In a nutshell, gRPC gives you great flexibility to deploy any service you need, with very few limitations. Figure 15-1 provides a high-level overview of the communications flow with gRPC.

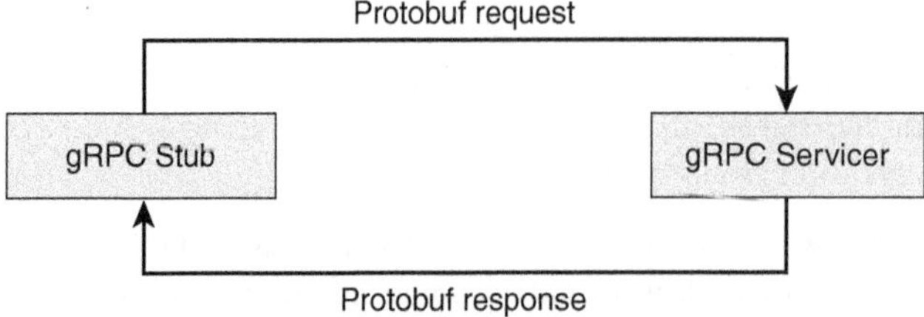

Figure 15-1 *The General gRPC Communications Flow*

In gRPC terminology, *servicer* refers to the server side of the application. Basically, it is the side that listens to customer requests, processes them, and provides responses. The gRPC client side is called *stub*, and it is the side that typically originates the requests and receives the responses from the servicer. The communication between the stub and the servicer is called a *channel*. The channel is specified by the target host address (for example, domain name, IPv4 or IPv6 addresses) and TCP port, and it is established for the duration of the communication and is typically short-lived; however, in some circumstances, it lives for a longer time.

Note The term *servicer* is a Python-specific term and refers to the interface generated from the service definition. More specifically, a servicer Python class is generated for each service and acts as the superclass of a service implementation. A *function* is generated in the servicer class for each *method* in the service. This will make more sense as you progress through the chapter. The majority of gRPC documentation refers to the two ends of the gRPC communication as stub and server or client and server. To avoid confusion and to keep things simple, the term *server* is replaced by *servicer* throughout the chapter.

In terms of communication patterns, gRPC supports the following scenarios:

- **Unary RPC:** This is one of the simplest communication methods between the stub and the servicer. It involves a single request from the stub to the servicer and a single response back from the servicer to the stub. It is the same as any NETCONF or RESTCONF request/response operation.
- **Server-side streaming RPC:** This scenario starts as a unary RPC with the stub's request; however, in the response, the servicer streams a number of messages (sometimes quite a large number of them).
- **Client-side streaming RPC:** In this scenario, the stub streams a number of messages to the servicer, and the servicer responds back with a single message.
- **Bidirectional RPC:** Both the stub and the servicer can stream a number of messages to each other. It is important for the streams to be independent of each other so that they can be implemented in an asynchronous manner. The streams may be confirmed by some sort of acknowledgment message from each side.

In addition, gRPC supports transmission of the metadata with each message, pretty much as NETCONF or RESTCONF do. One of the popular use cases for metadata is authentication of the messages; this is a mandatory part for the gNMI specification and is based on the gRPC transport.

gRPC is a programming language–neutral technology, which means it can be implemented in virtually any language. It is supported in C++, Go, Ruby, Python, Java, and many other languages. Because gRPC is language independent, the stub and the servicer can be developed and implemented in different languages and interact seamlessly with each other, as long as they follow the same specification. In this book, we focus on Python, and later in this chapter you will see Python scripts to manage network elements using gRPC from the stub's perspective.

One of the key aspects of any protocol or framework used to manage network elements is the set of calls and messages of that protocol. gRPC is very flexible, and it allows you to define your own set of calls and messages. Obviously, to make it work for management of network elements, the messages and RPC calls should be implemented in the network elements' software, which requires access to source code. Later in this chapter, you will learn about gNMI, which is the specification (that is, the set of the calls and messages) used over gRPC transport. But before that, you need to understand Protocol buffers, which are discussed next.

The Protocol Buffers Data Format

Google developed Protocol buffers (or Protobuf for short) to serve as the main language to define both the gRPC message format and RPC calls. Protocol buffers are one of the core technologies developed and used by Google to serialize data for communication between the elements of highly loaded systems. The reason they are so efficient has to do with the way the data is encoded for transmission: Only key indexes, data types, and values are converted to binary format and sent over the wire. Example 15-1 shows a sample Protobuf message.

Example 15-1 *Simple Protobuf Message*

```
syntax = "proto3";

message DeviceRoutes {
    int32 id = 1;
    string hostname = 2;
    int64 routes_number = 3;
}
```

Example 15-1 consists of two parts: **syntax** and **message**. The **syntax** section defines which version of the Protocol buffers are to be used. The most recent and widely used version is Version 3; hence, the **syntax** variable is set to **proto3**. The second section is the **message** section, which is effectively a schema, like a JSON schema or a YANG file, that defines the following:

- **Variables:** The schema defines the names of the variables that may exist in the schema. All variables are optional and may or may not exist in the actual message. In Example 15-1, **id**, **hostname**, and **routes_number** are the names of the variables.
- **Data types:** The schema associates each variable with a certain data type. In Example 15-1, **int32**, **int64**, and **string** are the data types. These data types are built-in types (see https://developers.google.com/protocol-buffers/docs/proto3#json); however, if required, you can create your own data types. For instance, you can create an **enum** type with some options or even use another message defined in the same file as a data type.
- **Indexes:** The schema identifies an index associated with each variable name, as the names aren't included in the Protobuf message sent over the wire. It is the indexes that are included. This is very different from XML and JSON data formats, where

the actual key names are transferred. The indexes are both an advantage and a disadvantage of the Protobuf: On the one hand, they allow you to save a lot of bandwidth on the wire, especially in bandwidth-hungry applications such as streaming telemetry. On the other hand, the sender and receiver must have the same schema, or it will be impossible to decode the data out of the binary stream. Indexes must be unique within the level of the message—such as **1**, **2**, and **3** in Example 15-1. In each nested level, though, they can start with **1** again.

With all these details in mind, take a look at the more complicated Protobuf messages in Example 15-2.

Example 15-2 *Complex Protobuf Schema with Multiple Messages and User-Defined Data Types*

```
syntax = "proto3";

enum AddressFamily {
    IPV4 = 0;
    IPV6 = 1;
    VPNV4 = 2;
    VPNV6 = 3;
    L2VPN = 4;
}

enum SubAddressFamily {
  UNICAST = 0;
  MULTICAST = 1;
  EVPN = 2;
}

message Routes {
    AddressFamily afi = 1;
    SubAddressFamily safi = 2;

    message Route {
        string route = 1;
        string next_hop = 2;
    }
    repeated Route route = 3;
}

message DeviceRoutes {
    int32 id = 1;
    string hostname = 2;
    int64 routes_number = 3;
    Routes routes = 4;
}
```

Although Example 15-2 is much longer than Example 15-1, it strictly follows the guidelines mentioned previously. You can see the named user-defined data types **AddressFamily** and **SubAddressFamily** created using the **enum** (enumerate) built-in data type. Each of the new data types has some allowed values, each associated with an index; the index rules stated previously are applied. These data types in turn are used in the new message **Routes**, where they are associated with the variables **afi** and **safi** and the corresponding indexes **1** and **2.** Inside the message **Routes**, a nested message **Route** is created, and it must be called in the parent message in order to be used. It is called with the index **3** because **1** and **2** are already used by **afi** and **safi.** The message name **Route** is put in the data type position and is prepended by the keyword **repeated**, which means the variable **routes** can be defined several times; this is, effectively, the Protobuf's implementation of lists or arrays.

It is also possible to call one message from another message that is not nested. Hence, you can see in the original **DeviceRoutes** message the new variable **routes**, which has data type **Routes** (after the message **Routes {}**) and index **4.**

As mentioned earlier in this chapter, Protocol buffers are used not only to define the message structure within gRPC but also to identify the structure of the RPC operations: which request message is associated with which operation type and what response message is sent back, as demonstrated in Example 15-3.

Example 15-3 *Sample gRPC Specification in Protobuf*

```
syntax = "proto3";

enum AddressFamily {
    IPV4 = 0;
    IPV6 = 1;
    VPNV4 = 2;
    VPNV6 = 3;
    L2VPN = 4;
}

enum SubAddressFamily {
  UNICAST = 0;
  MULTICAST = 1;
  EVPN2 = 2;
}

message Routes {
    AddressFamily afi = 1;
    SubAddressFamily safi = 2;

    message Route {
        string route = 1;
```

```
        string next_hop = 2;
    }
    repeated Route route = 3;
}

message DeviceRoutes {
    int32 id = 1;
    string hostname = 2;
    int64 routes_number = 3;
    Routes routes = 4;
}

message RouteRequest {
    string hostname = 1;
    AddressFamily afi = 2;
    SubAddressFamily safi = 3;
}

service RouteData {
    rpc CollectRoutes(RouteRequest) returns (DeviceRoutes) {}
}
```

Besides the additional message **RouteRequest**, you can see something completely new in Example 15-3: the **service** part. The **service** part is an abstract definition that ultimately contains the set of **rpc** operations. There should be at least one **rpc** operation per service. In Example 15-3, the **rpc** operation is called **CollectRoutes**, and it states that the client side, which is called stub in gRPC, should send the **RouteRequest** message, whereas the servicer should respond with the **DeviceRoutes** message. This is an example of the definition of *unary RPC*; however, there are three more types, as outlined earlier, and they can be defined in the following manner:

- **Server-side streaming RPC: rpc CollectRoutes(RouteRequest) returns (*stream* DeviceRoutes) {}**
- **Client-side streaming RPC: rpc CollectRoutes(*stream* RouteRequest) returns (DeviceRoutes) {}**
- **Bidirectional RPC: rpc CollectRoutes(*stream* RouteRequest) returns (*stream* DeviceRoutes) {}**

Altogether, the set of messages and services are named in the specification and stored in a **proto** file. This file is named after its format and has the extension .proto, as shown in Example 15-4.

Example 15-4 *Sample Protocol Buffers Message*

```
$ cat NPAF.proto
syntax = "proto3";

enum AddressFamily {
    IPV4 = 0;
    IPV6 = 1;
    VPNV4 = 2;
    VPNV6 = 3;
    L2VPN = 4;
}
// Further output is truncated for brevity
```

In Example 15-3, the specification is developed with the idea of route distribution between the stub and servicer. Despite the fact that the specification is application dependent, there should be some standard specifications to allow interoperability between the devices in the real world. One of the most popular specifications in the network automation world is gNMI, which is widely used in data centers. You will learn about gNMI at the end of this chapter.

Working with gRPC and Protobuf in Python

Like gRPC, the Protocol buffers are programming language independent. This means that Protocol buffers can be implemented in any popular programming language, such as C++, Go, Java, or Python. On the other hand, each programming language has its own consumption model that enables the conversion of the **proto** files into the programming language–specific structure. For example, in Python, the data construction is a set of two files with metaclasses that are created as a conversion of the single proto file. There are two files generated out of a single **proto** file because the messages and the service (RPC) part are generated in Python separately.

This conversion is done using a tool developed by Google. This tool, which is called **protoc** (Protocol Buffers Compiler), can create the proper output of the **proto** file in any desired programming language, including Python. There are multiple ways to get **protoc**, but in case of Python, the most sensible way to get it is to install the Python package with the **grpc** tools, as shown in Example 15-5.

Note All the examples in the rest of the chapter use Python Version 3.7, and backward compatibility with earlier versions isn't guaranteed.

Example 15-5 *Installing protoc for Python*

```
$ pip install grpcio grpcio_tools
Collecting grpcio
  Using cached grpcio-1.30.0-cp37-cp37m-macosx_10_9_x86_64.whl (2.8 MB)
Collecting grpcio_tools
  Using cached grpcio_tools-1.30.0-cp37-cp37m-macosx_10_9_x86_64.whl (2.0 MB)
! Some output is truncated for brevity
Successfully installed grpcio-1.30.0 grpcio-tools-1.30.0 protobuf-3.12.2 six-1.15.0
```

As part of the dependency resolution, **grpcio_tools** also installs the **protobuf** package, which is used by **protoc**. At this point, you can convert the **proto** file in the Python metaclasses by using the **protoc** method from **grpc_tools**, as shown in Example 15-6.

Example 15-6 *Converting the proto File in Python Metaclasses*

```
$ ls
npaf.proto              requirements.txt        venv

$ python3.7 -m grpc_tools.protoc -I=. --python_out=. --grpc_python_out=. npaf.proto

$ ls
npaf.proto      npaf_pb2.py             npaf_pb2_grpc.py        requirements.txt
```

Despite the fact that the module installed is **grpcio_tools**, in Python it is called **grpc_tools**. (This different naming can be confusing, but the two names refer to the same module.) You need to provide a number of arguments to this module:

- **-I:** Contains the source folder with the **proto** file.
- **--python_out:** Provides the path where the file containing the Python classes for Protobuf messages (ending with _pb2.py) is stored.
- **--grpc_python_out:** Points to the directory where the file containing the Python classes for the gRPC service (ending with _pb2_grpc.py) is located.

As mentioned earlier, each of the resulting files has its own set of associated information. The file with messages is the most complicated, as it contains the conversion of the Protobuf message format in the Python data structure using various descriptors, as demonstrated in Example 15-7.

Example 15-7 *The Auto-generated Python File with Protobuf Messages*

```
$ cat npaf_pb2.py | grep '= _descriptor'
DESCRIPTOR = _descriptor.FileDescriptor(
_ADDRESSFAMILY = _descriptor.EnumDescriptor(
_SUBADDRESSFAMILY = _descriptor.EnumDescriptor(
```

```
_ROUTES_ROUTE = _descriptor.Descriptor(
_ROUTES = _descriptor.Descriptor(
_DEVICEROUTES = _descriptor.Descriptor(
_ROUTEREQUEST = _descriptor.Descriptor(
_ROUTEDATA = _descriptor.ServiceDescriptor(
```

As you can see in Example 15-7, the names of the variables are in line with the names of the messages shown in Example 15-3. The file in Example 15-7 is generated automatically and should not be modified manually. The second auto-generated file contains the methods and classes used on the stub and the servicer sides, as you can see in Example 15-8.

Example 15-8 *The Auto-generated Python File with Protobuf Services*

```
$ cat npaf_pb2_grpc.py | grep 'class\|def'
class RouteDataStub(object):
    def __init__(self, channel):
class RouteDataServicer(object):
    def CollectRoutes(self, request, context):
def add_RouteDataServicer_to_server(servicer, server):
class RouteData(object):
    def CollectRoutes(request,
```

The names of the classes are auto-generated from the name of the service—in this case, **RouteData**—and the keyword **Stub** or **Servicer**. As you can imagine, **RouteDataStub** is a class used on the client side, and **RouteDataServicer** is used on the server side, which is listening for the customer requests. **RouteDataServicer** also has the method **CollectRoutes**, which is further defined inside the server-side script to perform any activity necessary based on the logic.

The best way to explain the logic of gRPC in Python is to show the creation of a simple application that has both servicer and stub parts. By now you should be familiar with Python and should be able to read the code of the gRPC stub provided in Example 15-9.

Example 15-9 *Sample gRPC Client*

```
#!/usr/bin/env python

# Modules
import grpc
from npaf_pb2_grpc import RouteDataStub
from npaf_pb2 import RouteRequest, DeviceRoutes

# Variables
server_data = {
    'address': '127.0.0.1',
```

```
    'port': '51111'
}

# User-defined function
def build_message():
    msg = RouteRequest()
    msg.hostname = 'router1'
    msg.afi = 0
    msg.safi = 0

    return msg

# Body
if __name__ == '__main__':
    with grpc.insecure_channel(f'{server_data["address"]}:{server_data["port"]}') as
  channel:
        stub = RouteDataStub(channel)
        request_message = build_message()

        print(f'Sending the CollectRequest to
  {server_data["address"]}:{server_data["port"]}...')
        response_message = stub.CollectRoutes(request_message)

        print(f'Received the response to CollectRequest from
  {server_data["address"]}:{server_data["port"]}:\n')
        print(response_message)
```

Example 15-9 shows a generic gRPC client that allows you to connect to a gRPC-speaking server. It requires the module called **grpc** (installed in Example 15-5 as **grpcio**) and the building blocks of your Protobuf service and messages:

- **RouteDataStub**: This class is used to send the request **CollectRoutes** to the gRPC servicer and get the response.
- **RouteRequest and DeviceRoutes:** These messages are used to structure and serialize/deserialize messages sent from the stub to the servicer and from the servicer to the stub.

In the **Variables** section of Example 15-9, you can see the simple Python dictionary **server_data**, which contains the IP address and TCP port of the gRPC server. Next is a user-defined function that constructs the data structure using the schema associated with a certain Protobuf message. The data structure, as you can see, is a number of properties of the class **RouteRequest**, which strictly follows the **RouteRequest** message in the original **proto** file: the names of the class's properties are exactly the same as the names of the variables inside the **proto** file (shown in Example 15-3). This data is saved within the function in the object **msg**, which is returned as a result of the function's execution.

In the main part of the application, you can see the object **channel** created using the function **insecure_channel** from the **grpc** module. **insecure** in this function name means that the channel is not protected by encryption (for example, an SSL certificate), and the information is transmitted and received in plaintext. Unlike RESTCONF, gRPC doesn't have an option to skip certificate verification for self-signed certificates. Therefore, you need to think about the certificates' distribution for self-signed certificates or PKI if you want to deploy **secure_channel**; this approach is recommended for production networks. The argument for **insecure_channel** is a string with the IP address and port of the gRPC servicer.

Over the gRPC channel, you need to invoke the stub itself; how it is invoked is application specific. In this case, it is invoked using the class **RouteDataStub**, which is auto-generated out of the gRPC part of the Protobuf specification. From a Python perspective, the stub is also an object that has methods named after the RPC calls in the original **proto** file for this service. The input for the method is a message in the proper format for the **proto** file (**RouteRequest** in this case), and the output is the response message (**DeviceRoute** in this case). As the response is provided, the result of the method execution is saved in the variable **response_message**, which is printed afterward.

Once you have familiarized yourself with Python's gRPC client, you should do the same with the server side; however, to be fair, it is a little bit more complicated, as you can see in Example 15-10.

Example 15-10 *Sample gRPC Server*

```
#!/usr/bin/env python

# Modules
import grpc
from npaf_pb2 import RouteRequest, DeviceRoutes
import npaf_pb2_grpc
from concurrent import futures

# Variables
server_data = {
    'address': '127.0.0.1',
    'port': '51111'
}

# Classes
class RouteDataServicer(npaf_pb2_grpc.RouteDataServicer):
    def CollectRoutes(self, request, context):
        print(request)
        return self.__constructResponse(request.hostname, request.afi, request.safi)
```

```
    def __constructResponse(self, hostname, afi, safi):
        msg = DeviceRoutes()
        msg.hostname = hostname
        msg.id = 1
        msg.routes_number = 10

        msg.routes.afi = afi
        msg.routes.safi = safi

        msg.routes.route.add(route='192.168.1.0/24', next_hop='10.0.0.1')
        msg.routes.route.add(route='192.168.2.0/24', next_hop='10.0.0.1')
        msg.routes.route.add(route='192.168.3.0/24', next_hop='10.0.0.2')

        return msg

# Body
if __name__ == '__main__':
    server = grpc.server(thread_pool=futures.ThreadPoolExecutor(max_workers=10))
    npaf_pb2_grpc.add_RouteDataServicer_to_server(RouteDataServicer(), server)

    print(f'Starting gRPC service at {server_data["port"]}...')
    server.add_insecure_port(f'{server_data["address"]}:{server_data["port"]}')
    server.start()
    server.wait_for_termination()
```

The code in Example 15-10 is a bit more complicated than the code on the client side, mainly because you need to define on the server side what should be done upon receiving the customers' requests. Let's analyze this Python script from the beginning.

To import external artifacts to the server's script, you need the same **grpc** module as in Example 15-9 because it handles the gRPC connectivity. In addition, you need to import the structure of RPC calls, and so the whole auto-generated file **npaf_pb2_grpc** is imported as well, as are the messages used with this operation; therefore, the **RouteRequest** and **DeviceRoutes** classes are imported from the file **npaf_pb2**. Finally, you should also import the **futures** library from the **concurrent** module. gRPC was developed quite recently, with performance and scalability in mind. It therefore needs to be built with multiple resources (that is, with a number of parallel threads processing the calls). Following the import of the external resources, you define the server's IP address and ports that will listen to the gRPC session. The same variable from Example 15-9 matches the one in Example 15-10 to allow the communication between the stub and the servicer.

The next section of Example 15-10 defines a class that controls how the server will behave upon receiving the calls from the customer. This class is based on the auto-generated class **RouteDataServicer** from the imported file **npaf_pb2_grpc**. It is effectively a child of the

npaf_pb2_grpc.RouteDataServicer class. This approach allows you to focus on only the relevant business logic in your script while benefiting from the session handling that is auto-generated using the **protoc** tool. Within this class, you need to have methods following the names of the RPC operations from the original service for each **proto** file. The method **CollectRoutes** has some external inputs besides its own attributes (**self**): **request** and **context**. The **request** variable contains the message body received from the client, and **context** contains various administrative information (for example, metadata, if used). In Example 15-10, this method just prints the received message and sends back the response.

The response is generated using an additional class that doesn't exist in the original specification. This is a very important concept because nothing prevents you from adding your own methods and attributes according to your requirements. This is why you see the additional private method **__constructResponse** created to build the response message. The response message must have the **DeviceRoutes** format, according to the **proto** file. Therefore, the object **msg** is instantiated from the imported **DeviceRoutes** class. The logic is as follows:

- The properties of the object following the Protobuf message are named after the variables from the **proto** file.
- If there are multiple levels of nesting, variables are stacked and interconnected with the . symbol.
- Whenever you have to deal with an entry defined as *repeated* in the **proto** file, you need to use the function **.add()**, which contains arguments. Those arguments (**route** and **next_hop** in Example 15-3) are defined in the appropriate Protobuf message in the **proto** file.

The **__constructResponse** method returns the **msg** object. Ultimately, this object contains a Protobuf message; hence, the method is called in the original method **CollectRoutes** to generate the reply message.

The last piece of the code actually brings up the gRPC servicer. To do that, the object **server** is instantiated using the **server** class from the **grpc** module, where the mandatory argument is the number of workers created to serve the gRPC requests. Afterward, the specific auto-generated function **add_RouteDataServicer_to_server** from **npaf_pb2_grpc** binds the servicer class **RouteDataServicer** you created to the gRPC object **server**. Once this is done, the method **add_insecure_port** associates the TCP socket with the server. The server listens to the incoming requests on this socket. Besides **insecure_port**, there is also a possibility to use **secure_port**, which involves using SSL certificates. At this point, the servicer is ready for operation. It is started, and to allow it to stay for a prolonged period of time, it is put in the mode **wait_for_termination()**, which prevents it from shutting down until it is explicitly terminated by the operator.

By now you should have an understanding of how the basic client and server sides of the gRPC application with your own specification works. So that you can understand it even better, Example 15-11 shows the process of the gRPC server launch.

Example 15-11 *Launching a Sample gRPC Server*

```
$ python npaf_server.py
Starting gRPC service at 51111...
```

The server part is now listening to customer requests, and you can execute the client-side script, as demonstrated in Example 15-12.

Example 15-12 *Testing the Sample gRPC Client*

```
$ python npaf_client.py
Sending the CollectRequest to 127.0.0.1:51111...
Received the response to CollectRequest from 127.0.0.1:51111:

id: 1
hostname: "router1"
routes_number: 10
routes {
  route {
    route: "192.168.1.0/24"
    next_hop: "10.0.0.1"
  }
  route {
    route: "192.168.2.0/24"
    next_hop: "10.0.0.1"
  }
  route {
    route: "192.168.3.0/24"
    next_hop: "10.0.0.2"
  }
}
```

Immediately after the client's script is executed, the gRPC stub sends the **CollectRoute** RPC to the server's address, 127.0.0.1, and port 51111, as defined in the variables. The servicer processes the request and response with the generated message. The server's script contains the **print(request)** instruction, which prints the customer's messages, which are shown in Example 15-13.

Example 15-13 *Logging gRPC Processing at the Servicer*

```
$ python npaf_server.py
Starting gRPC service at 51111...
hostname: "router1"
```

The server's method **CollectRoutes** prints the incoming message, which has the **RouteRequest** format, according to the **proto** file. There is an interesting factor here: If you look at Example 15-3, earlier in this chapter, you can see the three variables (**router**, **afi**, and **safi**), but the printed output has only one (**router**). In fact, you can call these variables as properties inside the script, and they will have a value of zero. This is the behavior of **proto3**: If the value of the variable is zero, it is not sent. Always think about efficiency when you work with Protocol buffers.

The gNMI Specification

In this chapter, you have learned about gRPC, including the transport mechanism and how it operates. One of the key things demonstrated earlier in the chapter is that gRPC provides only the transport and type of communication, and the name of the RPCs and format of the messages are application specific. Together, the gRPC services, RPCs, and messages related to a certain application are called the *specification*. gRPC Network Management Interface (gNMI) is a gRPC specification that defines the gRPC service name, RPCs, and messages.

Before we look at the details of the gNMI specification, it is worth understanding what problems it aims to solve and why it has been developed in a particular way.

Originally the only way to perform activities related to management of network elements was to use the CLI and Telnet or SSH. That process is not suitable for collecting operational data, and SNMP was introduced. For decades, SNMP has been a major mechanism for polling the various types of operational states from the network elements, and it has been used in most networks. However, SNMP's ability to change the configuration of the network elements is very limited. Some attempts were made across the industry to build XML-based network management (for example, NX-API in Cisco Nexus), but they were typically limited to particular platforms rather than being widespread.

The next major step in network management was the introduction of YANG and the module-based approach to managing the network elements. The configuration of network elements and their operational data following YANG modules became structured in hierarchical trees consisting of key/value pairs; this approach is much more suitable for management using programmability. The first standard protocol to support YANG was NETCONF; it standardized the programmable management of network elements across different vendors, and this allowed for API-based interaction with network elements, much as in any other distributed application (for example, communication between a database and a back-end server in a web application). However, the collection of the operational data using NETCONF is a bit complicated, as it must be polled by the server. Some early implementations of NETCONF agents caused very high CPU utilization on routers during requests, which made those agents suitable for configuration changes but not for continuous data polling.

The industry was experimenting with various protocols to effectively distribute operational data in YANG modules—from the network elements to the network management system relying on UDP or TCP protocols with proprietary sets of messages and communication flows. As gRPC was developed and became available for the wider public, network vendors added gRPC as another mechanism to distribute or stream the operational data in a process known as *streaming telemetry*.

As had been the case years before, the networking industry had to rely on two protocols to manage network functions in a programmable way. However, this time it was different: gRPC provided a broad framework for various communication types, including the unary type that is suitable for a traditional request/response operation, such as a configuration, and streaming in any direction suitable for the telemetry. The big consumers of the network technologies transitioned to becoming the developers themselves and started looking at how the capability of gRPC could be further applied to network management to find a single protocol that would be suitable for configuration and data collection. This development process took a couple years and resulted in gNMI. To paraphrase the official gNMI specification, gNMI is an attempt to use a single gRPC service definition to cover both configuration and telemetry and to simplify the implementation of an agent on the network devices and allow use of a single network management system (NMS) driver to interact with network devices to configure and collect operational state.

The Anatomy of gNMI

All the details of the gNMI specification are located in the single **proto** file **gnmi.proto**, which you can find in the official OpenConfig/gNMI repository at GitHub (https://github.com/openconfig/gnmi/blob/master/proto/gnmi/gnmi.proto). This file has very good and detailed documentation in the form of internal comments that help you easily understand all the parts of the **proto** file. Example 15-14 shows the structure of the gNMI service and RPCs.

Example 15-14 *gNMI Specification: Service and RPCs*

```
$ cat gnmi.proto
! Some output is truncated for brevity
service gNMI {
  rpc Capabilities(CapabilityRequest) returns (CapabilityResponse);
  rpc Get(GetRequest) returns (GetResponse);
  rpc Set(SetRequest) returns (SetResponse);
  rpc Subscribe(stream SubscribeRequest) returns (stream SubscribeResponse);
}
! Further output is truncated for brevity
```

As you can see in Example 15-14, the gNMI service consists of only one gRPC service and four RPCs, which is fewer RPC types than in NETCONF and fewer API calls than in RESTCONF. However, in terms of functionality, it can perform all the same operations. These are the four gNMI RPCs:

- **Capabilities:** This RPC aims to collect the list of supported capabilities by the network device. This list includes the version of gNMI (the most recent at this writing is 0.7.0) and the supported YANG modules so that the gNMI client knows what can be configured on the target network element or collected from it. From a results perspective, this RPC is similar to the capability exchange that happens during the NETCONF hello process described earlier in this book. This is a unary gRPC operation, which means it has a single client request followed by a single response from the server side.

- **Get:** This RPC implements a mechanism to collect some data from a network device. Depending on the requested scope, the information can be limited by scope (for example, only configuration, only operations, only states), or it is possible to collect all the information available along a certain path that is constructed based on a particular YANG module. Much like **Capabilities**, **Get** is a unary RPC operation. In NETCONF terms, this gRPC operation unites **get-config** and **get** requests.
- **Set:** This RPC is used to change the configuration of the target network device. The scope of configuration change can be quite broad; hence, to clarify it, you can either update the configuration (that is, change the value of a key) along the provided path or replace or delete it completely. Therefore, **Set** is comparable to NETCONF's **edit-config** operation with either the **merge**, **replace**, or **delete** option. Like **Capabilities** and **Get**, **Set** is a unary gRPC operation.
- **Subscribe:** This RPC creates the framework for streaming and event-driven telemetry. It allows the client to signal to the server its interest in receiving information (stream) about the values from a certain path on a regular basis. When the subscription is done, the server starts sending information until the client sends a request to unsubscribe. There is no analogue of this communication type in NETCONF (or in RESTCONF). From the gRPC operation's type standpoint, this is bidirectional streaming.

One of the key concepts in gNMI is **Path**, which is used in **Get**, **Set**, and **Subscribe** RPCs. Effectively, **Path** is very similar to a URI (refer to Chapter 14). Within any application that uses gNMI, the **Path** setting looks as shown in Example 15-15.

Example 15-15 *gNMI Specification: A Sample **Path** Value in the RESTCONF Format*

```
openconfig-interfaces:interfaces/interface[name=Loopback0]
```

The **Path** value starts with the name of the YANG module (in this case, **openconfig-interfaces**) followed by the column separator, :, and then the YANG tree, using the / separator for a parent/children relationship. When the list is part of the path, a specific entry from the list is chosen, and the path has an element identification that consists of a key/value pair in square brackets—in this case, **[name=Loopback0]**. In the early days of the gNMI specification, the **Path** value was in the string format; Example 15-15 shows a single value of the string format. However, this is not the case anymore, and in the current version of the gNMI specification, **Path** is serialized following specific Protocol buffer messages. Example 15-16 demonstrates this gNMI format.

Example 15-16 *gNMI Specification: gNMI Path Format*

```
$ cat gnmi.proto
! Some output is truncated for brevity
message Path {
  repeated string element = 1 [deprecated=true];
  string origin = 2;
  repeated PathElem elem = 3;
  string target = 4;
}

message PathElem {
  string name = 1;
  map<string, string> key = 2;
}
! Further output is truncated for brevity
```

The original string format has been deprecated. A gNMI **Path** value may contain **origin**, which refers to the YANG module in use, and multiple entries (called **elems**) of the **PathElem** messages. The **PathElem** messages define two elements of **Path: name**, which is the name of the relevant YANG leaf, leaf-list, container, or list in string format, and **key**, which is a key/value pair used in the event that it is necessary to specify the element from the list. Using this specification, **Path** is now serialized in the Protobuf binary and looks as shown in Example 15-17.

Example 15-17 *gNMI Specification: **Path** in the Protobuf Binary*

```
origin: "openconfig-interfaces"
elem {
  name: "interfaces"
}
elem {
  name: "interface"
  key {
    key: "name"
    value: "Loopback0"
  }
}
```

The Get RPC

As we continue to look at the gNMI specification, let's now consider the **Get** RPC. As you saw earlier, in Example 15-14, the **Get** request is defined by the **GetRequest** Protocol buffer message, as shown in Example 15-18.

Example 15-18 *gNMI Specification: GetRequest Message*

```
$ cat gnmi.proto
! Some output is truncated for brevity
message GetRequest {
  Path prefix = 1;
  repeated Path path = 2;
  enum DataType {
    ALL = 0;
    CONFIG = 1;
    STATE = 2;
    OPERATIONAL = 3;
  }
  DataType type = 3;
  Encoding encoding = 5;
  repeated ModelData use_models = 6;
  repeated gnmi_ext.Extension extension = 7;
}

message ModelData {
  string name = 1;
  string organization = 2;
  string version = 3;
}
! Further output is truncated for brevity
```

In Example 15-18, the variables **prefix** and **path** are combined together to provide a unique path to the resource that is being polled. Depending on the gNMI client implementation, it might be that only one of two is provided or that both are provided:

- An empty **prefix** and the **path** value **openconfig-interfaces:interfaces/interface[name=Loopback0]** result in **openconfig-interfaces:interfaces/interface[name=Loopback0]**.
- The **prefix** value **openconfig-interfaces:interfaces** and the **path** value **interface[name=Loopback0]** result in **openconfig-interfaces:interfaces/interface[name=Loopback0]** as well.
- Finally, the **prefix** value **openconfig-interfaces:interfaces/interface[name=Loopback0]** and an empty **path** also result in **openconfig-interfaces:interfaces/interface[name=Loopback0]**.

The reason for this flexibility is that a single **GetRequest** can query multiple resources simultaneously, which allows multiple path entries per message. However, gNMI, like gRPC, is all about efficiency. Therefore, the **prefix** value may contain the part of the path that is common for all the requested resources, whereas the **path** value will have the part that is different. Ultimately, **prefix** is a single entry per message, whereas **path** is a list.

Besides the path, two more elements are mandatory from a logical standpoint: the type, which defines the scope of the information to be collected, and the encoding, which defines the encoding of the information that is expected to be received. The following scopes are available for the requested information:

- **ALL** for all the information available at the provided path.
- **CONFIG** for the read/write elements in the YANG modules used.
- **STATE** for the read-only elements in the YANG modules used.
- **OPERATIONAL** for elements marked in the schema as operational. This refers to data elements whose values relate to the state of processes or interactions running on a device.

In terms of the encoding, although gNMI is defined in the Protobuf, it supports other types of encoding, as shown in Example 15-19.

Example 15-19 *gNMI Specification: Types of Data Encoding*

```
$ cat gnmi.proto
! Some output is truncated for brevity
enum Encoding {
  JSON = 0;
  BYTES = 1;
  PROTO = 2;
  ASCII = 3;
  JSON_IETF = 4;
}
! Further output is truncated for brevity
```

Example 15-19 doesn't mean, though, that the whole message is structured in the binary (**BYTES**) or **JSON** format. It means that the specific part of the response message that contains data extracted from the device will be in one of these formats. The most popular format today, which is implemented across the vast majority of network vendors, is either **JSON** or **JSON_IETF**, which refers to JSON as defined in RFC 7951.

These values are mandatory from a logical standpoint because they are required to identify what you want to collect and how to represent it. However, as you learned earlier, if a key has the value 0, which is also applicable for **enum** data, then it is not sent inside the gRPC/Protobuf. Ultimately, this means that the default encoding is **JSON**, and the default type is **ALL**.

You can use the optional **use_model** variable to further narrow down the specific YANG module by providing the full name, organization, and even version. According to the specification, the **GetRequest** message could look as shown in Example 15-20.

Example 15-20 *gNMI Specification: Sample* **GetRequest** *Message*

```
path {
  origin: "openconfig-interfaces"
  elem {
    name: "interfaces"
  }
  elem {
    name: "interface"
    key {
      key: "name"
      value: "Ethernet1"
    }
  }
}
path {
  origin: "openconfig-interfaces"
  elem {
    name: "interfaces"
  }
  elem {
    name: "interface"
    key {
      key: "name"
      value: "Loopback0"
    }
  }
}
```

The message in Example 15-20 contains two paths and uses default encoding and type parameters. If the network device that receives this request has gRPC enabled, the gNMI client may receive the response shown in Example 15-21.

Example 15-21 *gNMI Specification: Sample* **GetResponse** *Message*

```
notification {
  update {
    path {
      elem {
        name: "interfaces"
      }
      elem {
        name: "interface"
        key {
          key: "name"
          value: "Ethernet1"
```

```
          }
        }
      }
      val {
        json_ietf_val: "{\"openconfig-interfaces:config\": {\"description\": \"\",
    \"enabled\": true,\"loopback-mode\": false, \"mtu\": 0, \"name\": \"Ethernet1\",
    \"openconfig-vlan:tpid\": \"openconfig-vlan-types:TPID_0X8100\", \"type\":
    \"iana-if-type:ethernetCsmacd\"}, \"openconfig-if-ethernet:ethernet\":
    {\"config\": {\"openconfig-hercules-interfaces:forwarding-viable\": true,
    \"mac-address\": \"00:00:00:00:00:00\", \"port-speed\": \"SPEED_UNKNOWN\"},
    \"state\": {\"auto-negotiate\": false, \"counters\": {\"in-crc-errors\": \"0\",
    \"in-fragment-frames\": \"0\", \"in-jabber-frames\": \"0\", \"in-mac-control-
    frames\": \"0\", \"in-mac-pause-frames\": \"0\", \"in-oversize-frames\": \"0\",
    \"out-mac-control-frames\": \"0\", \"out-mac-pause-frames\": \"0\"}, \"duplex-
    mode\": \"FULL\", \"enable-flow-control\": false, \"openconfig-hercules-
    interfaces:forwarding-viable\": true, \"hw-mac-address\": \"08:00:27:86:de:54\",
    \"mac-address\": \"08:00:27:86:de:54\", \"negotiated-port-speed\":
    \"SPEED_UNKNOWN\", \"port-speed\": \"SPEED_UNKNOWN\",}}, \"openconfig-
    interfaces:hold-time\": {\"config\": {\"down\": 0, \"up\": 0}, \"state\":
    {\"down\": 0, \"up\": 0}}, \"openconfig-interfaces:name\": \"Ethernet1\",
    \"openconfig-interfaces:state\": {\"admin-status\": \"UP\", \"counters\":
    {\"in-broadcast-pkts\": \"0\", \"in-discards\": \"0\", \"in-errors\": \"0\",
    \"in-fcs-errors\": \"0\", \"in-multicast-pkts\": \"0\", \"in-octets\": \"0\",
    \"in-unicast-pkts\": \"0\", \"out-broadcast-pkts\": \"0\", \"out-discards\":
    \"0\", \"out-errors\": \"0\", \"out-multicast-pkts\": \"305\", \"out-octets\":
    \"29890\", \"out-unicast-pkts\": \"0\"}, \"description\": \"\", \"enabled\": true,
    \"openconfig-platform-port:hardware-port\": \"Port1\", \"ifindex\": 1,
    \"last-change\": \"1595167904282637056\", \"loopback-mode\": false, \"mtu\":
    0, \"name\": \"Ethernet1\", \"oper-status\": \"UP\", \"openconfig-vlan:tpid\":
    \"openconfig-vlan-types:TPID_0X8100\", \"type\": \"iana-if-type:ethernetCsmacd\"},
    \"openconfig-interfaces:subinterfaces\": {\"subinterface\": [{\"config\":
    {\"description\": \"\", \"enabled\": true, \"index\": 0}, \"index\": 0,
    \"openconfig-if-ip:ipv4\": {\"config\": {\"dhcp-client\": false, \"enabled\":
    false, \"mtu\": 1500}, \"state\": {\"dhcp-client\": false, \"enabled\": false,
    \"mtu\": 1500}}, \"openconfig-if-ip:ipv6\": {\"config\": {\"dhcp-client\":
    false, \"enabled\": false, \"mtu\": 1500}, \"state\": {\"dhcp-client\": false,
    \"enabled\": false, \"mtu\": 1500}}, \"state\": {\"counters\": {\"in-broadcast-
    pkts\": \"0\", \"in-discards\": \"0\", \"in-errors\": \"0\", \"in-fcs-errors\":
    \"0\", \"in-multicast-pkts\": \"0\", \"in-octets\": \"0\", \"in-unicast-pkts\":
    \"0\", \"out-broadcast-pkts\": \"0\", \"out-discards\": \"0\", \"out-errors\":
    \"0\", \"out-multicast-pkts\": \"305\", \"out-octets\": \"29890\", \"out-unicast-
    pkts\": \"0\"}, \"description\": \"\", \"enabled\": true, \"index\": 0}}]}}"
      }
    }
}
notification {
}
```

In Example 15-21, you can see that there are two **notification** sections:

- The first one contains information which indicates that the interface named in that section is configured.
- The second one is empty, which means that an interface named in the first section doesn't exist on the device.

Even without looking into the details of the corresponding **GetResponse** message, you can figure out the message structure. However, to prevent you from having any doubts, Example 15-22 shows the relevant Protocol buffers messages.

Example 15-22 *gNMI Specification: Messages Associated with the* ***GetResponse*** *Message*

```
$ cat gnmi.proto
! Some output is truncated for brevity
message GetResponse {
  repeated Notification notification = 1;
  Error error = 2 [deprecated=true];
  repeated gnmi_ext.Extension extension = 3;
}

message Notification {
  int64 timestamp = 1;
  Path prefix = 2;
  string alias = 3;
  repeated Update update = 4;
  repeated Path delete = 5;
}

message Update {
  Path path = 1;
  Value value = 2 [deprecated=true];
  TypedValue val = 3;
  uint32 duplicates = 4;
}

message TypedValue {
  oneof value {
    string string_val = 1;
    int64 int_val = 2;
    uint64 uint_val = 3;
    bool bool_val = 4;
    bytes bytes_val = 5;
    float float_val = 6;
    Decimal64 decimal_val = 7;
    ScalarArray leaflist_val = 8;
    google.protobuf.Any any_val = 9;
    bytes json_val = 10;
    bytes json_ietf_val = 11;
    string ascii_val = 12;
    bytes proto_bytes = 13;
  }
}
! Further output is truncated for brevity
```

At a high level, the **GetResponse** message consists of multiple **notification** entries, which have the format of a **Notification** message. (This is why Example 15-21 shows two **notification** entries.) The **Notification** message is a multipurpose message that is used not only in **GetResponse** but also in **SubscribeResponse** (which is used in streaming). It may contain a **timestamp** setting (depending on whether the network device vendor has implemented it), which provides the time, in nanoseconds, from the beginning of the epoch (January 1, 1970, 00:00:00 UTC). It may also include **prefix**, explained earlier, and **alias**, which may be used if supported by the network device to compress the path; when an alias is created for a path, the messages contain the value of the alias instead of a prefix, which helps reduce the length of the transmitted message. However, all those variables are optional. What is mandatory is either the **update** or **delete** variable; **update** is used to provide the information per **GetResponse** if the information exists, and **delete** contains the paths of the elements that were deleted (**delete** is not used in the current version of the specification for **GetRequest** and is used for **SetRequest** only).

Finally, the **Update** message contains the path to the resource being polled and the value stored in the variable **val**, which is further defined by the message **TypedValue**. Inside this message is the value of **val**, which is a long list of the data types. (You might notice in Example 15-21 that the response is in the **json_ietf_val** data type.)

The Set RPC

The **Set** RPC operation is generally similar to the **Get**, as it is also a unary gRPC type; however, it has its own set of messages. Example 15-23 shows the details of the **SetRequest** message.

Example 15-23 *gNMI Specification: SetRequest Message Format*

```
$ cat gnmi.proto
! Some output is truncated for brevity
message SetRequest {
  Path prefix = 1;
  repeated Path delete = 2;
  repeated Update replace = 3;
  repeated Update update = 4;
  repeated gnmi_ext.Extension extension = 5;
}
! Further output is truncated for brevity
```

Although the message in Example 15-23 is very compact, it allows you to choose the necessary operation—and it is possible to have multiple operations in a single message due to **repeated** keyword. These are the potential operations:

- **prefix:** This operation is covered earlier in this chapter, in the section "The **Get** RPC."
- **delete:** This operation contains the paths that are to be removed. You use this operation when you delete a part of the configuration on a network device.

- **replace:** This operation contains the data in the **Update** message format (refer to Example 15-22). Because the **Update** message contains the path toward the resource and **val** with the actual data to be set along the path, the logic of this operation causes the data provided to overwrite what already exists in the destination node.
- **update:** This operation also relies on the **Update** message format. However, the logic of the operation is different: The data from the **val** entry is merged with what already exists in the node that has the provided path. If nothing exists, then a new entry is created.

Example 15-21 shows a **GetRequest** for the Loopback0 interface; however, in that example, **GetRequest** is not configured on the target network function. Hence, in the **GetResponse** from Example 15-22, the notification for this request is empty. Example 15-24 illustrates the use of **SetRequest** to configure the Loopback0 interface at the target network function.

Example 15-24 *gNMI Specification: Sample* ***SetRequest*** *Message*

```
update {
  path {
    origin: "openconfig-interfaces"
    elem {
      name: "interfaces"
    }
    elem {
      name: "interface"
      key {
        key: "name"
        value: "Loopback0"
      }
    }
  }
  val {
    json_val: "{\"name\": \"Loopback0\", \"config\": {\"name\": \"Loopback0\",
  \"enabled\": true, \"type\": \"iana-if-type:softwareLoopback\", \"description\":
  \"Test IF 2\"}, \"subinterfaces\": {\"subinterface\": [{\"index\": 0, \"config\":
  {\"index\": 0, \"enabled\": true}, \"openconfig-if-ip:ipv4\": {\"addresses\":
  {\"address\": [{\"ip\": \"10.1.255.62\", \"config\": {\"ip\": \"10.1.255.62\",
  \"prefix-length\": 32, \"addr-type\": \"PRIMARY\"}}]}}}]}}"
  }
}
```

In Example 15-24, you can see the **update** entry that sets the path for the node to be configured and **val**, which contains the entry **json_val**. This entry has a value that is a JSON-encoded string containing all the key/value pairs to be set on the target device. The corresponding **SetResponse** message might look as shown in Example 15-25.

Example 15-25 *gNMI Specification: Sample* ***SetResponse*** *Message*

```
response {
  path {
    origin: "openconfig-interfaces"
    elem {
     name: "interfaces"
    }
    elem {
      name: "interface"
      key {
        key: "name"
        value: "Loopback0"
      }
    }
  }
  op: UPDATE
}
timestamp: 1595182804100815323
```

This message follows the **SetResponse** Protobuf message specification, as shown in Example 15-26.

Example 15-26 *gNMI Specification:* ***SetRequest*** *Message Format*

```
$ cat gnmi.proto
! Some output is truncated for brevity
message SetResponse {
  Path prefix = 1;
  repeated UpdateResult response = 2;
  Error message = 3 [deprecated=true];
  int64 timestamp = 4;
}

message UpdateResult {
  enum Operation {
    INVALID = 0;
    DELETE = 1;
    REPLACE = 2;
    UPDATE = 3;
  }
  int64 timestamp = 1 [deprecated=true];
  Path path = 2;
  Error message = 3 [deprecated=true];
  Operation op = 4;
}
! Further output is truncated for brevity
```

The parent message **GetResponse** contains **prefix**, **timestamp**, and **response**, formatted according to the **UpdateResult** message. In the current version of the gNMI specification (0.7.0), the **response** message contains the path of the affected resource and the result of the operation in the variable **op**, which corresponds to the **SetRequest** type: **DELETE**, **REPLACE**, or **UPDATE**.

The Capabilities RPC

You have learned details about some complicated RPCs and their associated messages. The **Capabilities** RPC is significantly easier to understand. As mentioned earlier, the **Capabilities** RPC is used to collect information about the YANG modules supported by the target network device. The **CapabilityRequest** message in Example 15-27 is the simplest Protobuf message described in this book.

Example 15-27 *gNMI Specification: CapabilityRequest Message Format*

```
$ cat gnmi.proto
! Some output is truncated for brevity
message CapabilityRequest {
}
! Further output is truncated for brevity
```

This message effectively doesn't have a variable at all. In fact, this is quite logical: When the client queries a network device about what capabilities it supports, it doesn't need to specify anything else. Example 15-28 shows the format of the **CapabilityResponse** message.

Example 15-28 *gNMI Specification: CapabilityResponse Message Format*

```
$ cat gnmi.proto
! Some output is truncated for brevity
message CapabilityResponse {
  repeated ModelData supported_models = 1;
  repeated Encoding supported_encodings = 2;
  string gNMI_version = 3;
}
! Further output is truncated for brevity
```

The **ModelData** and **Encoding** message formats (which are explained in the section "The **Get** RPC," earlier in this chapter) are provided with the keyword **repeated** because a network device might (and typically does) support multiple YANG modules or encoding formats. The variable **gNMI_version** is not repeated, though, as the network device would have a single version of the gNMI specification implemented.

A sample **CapabilityRequest** message is not shown, as this type of message doesn't contain any data. However, a **CapabilityResponse** message can be rather interesting, as shown in Example 15-29.

Example 15-29 *gNMI Specification: Sample **CapabilityResponse** Message*

```
supported_models {
  name: "openconfig-packet-match"
  organization: "OpenConfig working group"
  version: "1.1.1"
}
supported_models {
  name: "openconfig-hercules-platform"
  organization: "OpenConfig Hercules Working Group"
  version: "0.2.0"
}
supported_models {
  name: "openconfig-bgp"
  organization: "OpenConfig working group"
  version: "6.0.0"
}
!
! Some output is truncated for brevity
!
supported_encodings: JSON
supported_encodings: JSON_IETF
supported_encodings: ASCII
gNMI_version: "0.7.0"
```

From Example 15-29, you can see that the YANG modules provided in the **support_models** variable have a format similar to the format shown in Chapter 14 for NETCONF. Close to the end of the message are multiple **supported_encodings** entries, which hold information about the encoding types supported by the network device. Finally, **gNMI_version** contains the version of the gNMI specification implemented on the device.

The Subscribe RPC

The **Subscribe** RPC is used in streaming or event-driven telemetry. Per the gNMI specification, both the client and the server can stream information bidirectionally. The general flow is as follows:

1. The client signals its interest to the gNMI server, which resides on a network device, to receive the information from a certain path.
2. The server streams the information for the subscribed categories until the client unsubscribes.

The **SubscribeResponse** message format is quite simple, as it relies on the **Notification** message, which you are already familiar with (see Example 15-30).

Example 15-30 *gNMI Specification: SubscribeResponse Message Format*

```
$ cat gnmi.proto
! Some output is truncated for brevity
message SubscribeResponse {
  oneof response {
    Notification update = 1;
    bool sync_response = 3;
    Error error = 4 [deprecated=true];
  }
  repeated gnmi_ext.Extension extension = 5;
}
! Further output is truncated for brevity
```

This message contains the single entry **response**, which can be in either **Notification** or **boolean** format. The variable **update** with the **Notification** message format is used to distribute the actual data of the corresponding paths, whereas **sync_respones** indicates that all data values corresponding to the path specified in **SubscriptionList** have been transmitted at least once.

You are probably wondering what **SubscriptionList** is. It is part of **SubscribeRequest**, which is quite a complicated message, as you can see in Example 15-31.

Example 15-31 *gNMI Specification: SubscribeRequest Message Format*

```
$ cat gnmi.proto
! Some output is truncated for brevity
message SubscribeRequest {
  oneof request {
    SubscriptionList subscribe = 1;
    Poll poll = 3;
    AliasList aliases = 4;
  }
}

message Poll {
}

message SubscriptionList {
  Path prefix = 1;
  repeated Subscription subscription = 2;
  bool use_aliases = 3;
  QOSMarking qos = 4;
  enum Mode {
    STREAM = 0;
    ONCE = 1;
```

```
    POLL = 2;
  }
  Mode mode = 5;
  bool allow_aggregation = 6;
  repeated ModelData use_models = 7;
  Encoding encoding = 8;
  bool updates_only = 9;
}

message Subscription {
  Path path = 1;
  SubscriptionMode mode = 2;
  uint64 sample_interval = 3;
  bool suppress_redundant = 4;
  uint64 heartbeat_interval = 5;
}

enum SubscriptionMode {
  TARGET_DEFINED = 0;
  ON_CHANGE      = 1;
  SAMPLE         = 2;
}

message QOSMarking {
  uint32 marking = 1;
}
! Further output is truncated for brevity
```

SubscribeRequest consists of one of the three possible types: **SubscribeList**, **Poll**, or **AliasList**. **AliasList** is used to create a mapping of the paths to short names to improve the efficiency of the communication by reducing the data sent between the gNMI client (the NMS) and the gNMI server (the network device). The aliases are optional. The **Poll** message, as you can see in Example 15-31, doesn't have any further parameters. In fact, it is used in poll-based information collection, where the client sends the **Poll** messages to trigger the network device to send the update when the subscription is created.

The subscription is created inside the **SubscribeList** message, which has the following fields:

- **prefix:** This field contains the part of the path that is common for all the subscriptions.
- **Subscription:** This field (or fields) contains a path that it wants to receive the information from, and a subscription mode (defined by the target, on information change, and sampling over a certain time interval). In addition, **sample_interval** identifies

how often updates are sent from the server to the client, **suppress_redundant** optimizes the transmission in the update in such a way that the updates aren't sent if there are no changes even if the sample time comes, and **heartbeat_interval** changes the behavior of **suppress_redundant** so that the update is sent once per **sample_interval** to notify the client that the server is up and running.

- **use_aliases:** This field notifies the server about whether the aliases should be used.
- **qos:** This field tells the server which QoS marking it should use for the telemetry packets.
- **mode:** This field sets the type of the subscriptions for all the paths. The available options are **STREAM** (which means the server streams the data on the defined **sample_interval**), **POLL** (which means the server sends the updates per the client's **Poll** message), and **ONCE** (which means the server sends the response once per the client's request and then terminates the gRPC session).
- **allow_aggregation:** This field checks whether there are any data paths available for aggregation so that it can aggregate them into a single update message and send a bulk update to the client.
- **use_models:** This field makes it possible to narrow the search for the paths specified in **Subscription** to certain data models.
- **encoding:** This field sets the data format that the server should use to send updates to the client.
- **updates_only:** This field changes the way the information from the server is sent; instead of sending the state of the identified paths, it sends only updates to the states compared to the previous information distribution.

Sample messages showing the **SubscribeRequest** and the **SubscribeResponse** messages are omitted for brevity, but you can guess their content based on the examples of other messages in this chapter.

> **Note** In some of the messages shown in this chapter, you might have noticed references to the gNMI extensions. These extensions are available for future possible development of gNMI functionality and are optional to any of the messages. They aren't widely used today.

Managing Network Elements with gNMI/gRPC

Earlier in this chapter, you saw Python code that can be used to create the client side (the stub) and the server side (the servicer) of a gRPC-based application. In the case of gNMI, the servicer is already deployed on a network device. Therefore, you just need to enable it either in secure mode (using the SSL certificates and/or PKI) or insecure mode (without encryption) and create the code for the stub part. Depending on the network operating system, some of the modes (such as insecure) may be not available.

Before you enable gNMI, you need to ensure that your software supports it. If it does, you can enable gNMI on Cisco IOS XE network devices as shown in Example 15-32.

Example 15-32 *Enabling gNMI in Insecure Mode in Cisco IOS XE*

```
NPAF_R1> enable
NPAF_R1# configure terminal
NPAF_R1(config)# gnmi-yang
NPAF_R1(config)# gnmi-yang server
NPAF_R1(config)# gnmi-yang port 57400
NPAF_R1(config)# end
```

gNMI doesn't have a predefined port number; hence, different vendors implement different default values for the gNMI service. You can set this parameter to the value you like. However, if you don't set the value, Cisco IOS XE uses the default, which is TCP/50052. Refer to the official Cisco documentation to enable the secure gNMI server on Cisco IOS XE network devices. You can verify whether the service is operational as shown in Example 15-33.

Example 15-33 *Verifying That gNMI Is Operational in Cisco IOS XE*

```
NPAF_R1# show gnmi-yang state

State Status
--------------------------------
Enabled Up
```

Besides Cisco IOS XE, gNMI is supported in the latest releases of Cisco IOS XR (starting from 6.0.0) and Cisco NX OS (starting from 7.0(3)I5(1)) as well. Moreover, the vast majority of other network operating systems, such as Nokia SR OS, Arista EOS, and Juniper Junos, support gNMI as well. Therefore, you can use it as the main protocol to manage your network.

There are currently no Python libraries that work well with gNMI specifically. However, the library **grpc** (used earlier in this chapter) can help you create the proper Python scripts. If you cloned the gNMI specification from the official repository, you have the gnmi.proto file, and by using the **grpc_tools.protoc** module, you can convert the file into a set of Python metaclasses as shown in Example 15-34.

Example 15-34 *Creating Python Metaclasses for the gNMI Specification*

```
$ ls
gnmi.proto

$ python -m grpc_tools.protoc -I=. --python_out=. --grpc_python_out=. Gnmi.proto
$ ls
gnmi_pb2_grpc.py  gnmi_pb2.py  gnmi.proto

State Status
--------------------------------
Enabled Up
```

Earlier in this chapter, in Example 15-9, you saw how to create the gNMI stub for an arbitrary specification. In this section, you will create it by using the gNMI specification, leveraging explanations provided earlier in this chapter. Example 15-35 shows a script to use the **Get** RPC from the gNMI specification.

Example 15-35 *Sample gNMI Get Python Script*

```
$ cat gNMI_Client.py
#!/usr/bin/env python

# Modules
import grpc
from gnmi_pb2_grpc import *
from gnmi_pb2 import *
import re
import sys
import json

# Variables
path = {'inventory': 'inventory/inventory.json', 'network_functions':
  'inventory/network_functions'}

# User-defined functions
def json_to_dict(path):
    with open(path, 'r') as f:
        return json.loads(f.read())

def gnmi_path_generator(path_in_question):
    gnmi_path = Path()
    keys = []

    # Subtracting all the keys from the elements and storing them separately
    while re.match('.*?\[.+?=.+?\].*?', path_in_question):
```

```
        temp_key, temp_value = re.sub('.*?\[(.+?)\].*?', '\g<1>',
  path_in_question).split('=')
        keys.append({temp_key: temp_value})
        path_in_question = re.sub('(.*?\[).+?(\].*?)', f'\g<1>{len(keys) - 1}\g<2>',
  path_in_question)

    path_elements = path_in_question.split('/')

    for pe_entry in path_elements:
        if not re.match('.+?:.+?', pe_entry) and len(path_elements) == 1:
            sys.exit(f'You haven\'t specified either YANG module or the top-level
  container in \'{pe_entry}\'.')

        elif re.match('.+?:.+?', pe_entry):
            gnmi_path.origin = pe_entry.split(':')[0]
            gnmi_path.elem.add(name=pe_entry.split(':')[1])

        elif re.match('.+?\[\d+?\].*?', pe_entry):
            key_id = int(re.sub('.+?\[(\d+?)\].*?', '\g<1>', pe_entry))
            gnmi_path.elem.add(name=pe_entry.split('[')[0], key=keys[key_id])

        else:
            gnmi_path.elem.add(name=pe_entry)

    return gnmi_path


# Body
if __name__ == '__main__':
    inventory = json_to_dict(path['inventory'])

    for td_entry in inventory['network_functions']:
        print(f'Getting data from {td_entry["ip_address"]} over gNMI...\n\n')

        metadata = [('username', td_entry['username']), ('password',
  td_entry['password'])]

        channel = grpc.insecure_channel(f'{td_entry["ip_address"]}:
  {td_entry["port"]}', metadata)
        grpc.channel_ready_future(channel).result(timeout=5)

        stub = gNMIStub(channel)

        device_data =
  json_to_dict(f'{path["network_functions"]}/{td_entry["hostname"]}.json')
```

```
gnmi_message = []
for itc_entry in device_data['intent_config']:
    intent_path = gnmi_path_generator(itc_entry['path'])
    gnmi_message.append(intent_path)

gnmi_message_request = GetRequest(path=gnmi_message, type=0, encoding=0)
gnmi_message_response = stub.Get(gnmi_message_request, metadata=metadata)

print(gnmi_message_response)
```

The script shown in Example 15-35 was used to generate the **GetRequest** and **GetResponse** messages shown earlier in this chapter.

Summary

This chapter describes gRPC transport, Protobuf data encoding, and gNMI specification, including the following points:

- gRPC is a fast and robust framework created by Google to allow communication between applications.
- gRPC supports four types of communication: unary RPC, server-based streaming, client-based streaming, and bidirectional streaming.
- gRPC doesn't define any message types or formats. Each application may have its own set of messages and RPC operations.
- Protocol buffers are used to specify the services, the RPCs, and the message formats for the gRPC services.
- Protocol buffers are effectively schemas that define for each entry the data type, the name of the key, and the index that is used to identify the key upon serialization.
- By default, Protobuf uses binary serialization; however, it may support other types, such as JSON or ASCII text.
- The set of services, RPCs, and messages defined in Protobuf format for a specific gRPC service is called a specification. gNMI is a gRPC specification developed to manage network elements.
- gNMI covers network management both in terms of interacting with the network elements using the unary operation (request/response) suitable for configuration and using a bidirectional streaming operation that is suitable for collecting the live operational states.

Chapter 16

Service Provider Programmability

This chapter covers a special use case for network programmability and automation: service provider network programmability. This domain poses some unique challenges due to the special nature of typical service provider networks in terms of size, scalability, and the diverse types of interfaces and traffic that these networks are expected to transport. Service provider networks are also bound by very stringent KPIs due to the probable revenue loss associated with any downtime. These challenges have recently been amplified due to the introduction and adoption of the 5G technology. This chapter begins with a look at the software-defined networking (SDN) framework.

The SDN Framework for Service Providers

A number of challenges arise in service provider networks due to new application consumption patterns and associated development of new technologies and architectures.

Requirements for Service Provider Networks of the Future

At this writing, international standard bodies define 5G as the latest generation of mobile communication. Besides providing the fastest ever mobile broadband access to the Internet, 5G also introduces a radically new approach to mobile networking called *network slicing*. In a nutshell, a network slice is dedicated set of resources (for example, on the radio interface between a mobile phone and a cellular base station, on router buffers, on router-to-router links, on the mobile packet core), as shown on Figure 16-1.

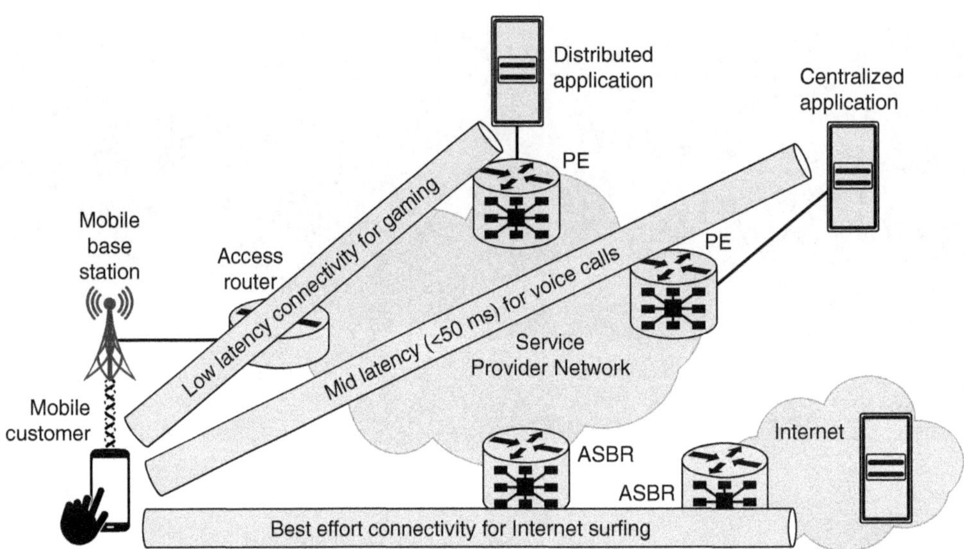

Figure 16-1 *Network Slicing*

3GPP 5G requirements call for network slicing support for various use cases, such as enhanced mobile broadband (eMBB), massive machine-type communication (mMTC), and ultra-reliable and low latency communications (URLLC). You may think that such requirements are quite trivial in the sense that QoS configuration or Multiprotocol Label Switching Traffic Engineering (MPLS-TE) has been implemented in service provider networks for ages. That is true, but network slicing has one very significant difference from traditional QoS and MPLS-TE configuration: A network slice must be created dynamically when you launch an application on your mobile phone and must be released when you switch off the application. Obviously, such a process can't exist in the traditional service provider world, where all the network changes are reviewed by change advisory boards and implemented manually (through the CLI or a GUI) by network engineers. Network slicing requires full network programmability and an integrated feedback loop so that the network configuration required to create and release the slice is done programmatically, requiring no human intervention at any stage.

The fact that service provider networks are geographically distributed adds even more complexity to the case just described. 5G network slices set a number of requirements for end-to-end KPIs regarding guaranteed bandwidth, latency, packet drops, and jitter. To fulfill those requirements, a service provider network must be able to collect a massive amount of related telemetry information, such as per-link latency, QoS buffer utilization, and actual routing topology. Then network elements must export all that information to a centralized entity, often called an SDN controller, which in turn must be capable of analyzing this information and automatically making decisions based on preprogrammed policies or API calls. Given the multidomain character of 5G networking, SDN controller hierarchy would be required to abstract the complexity by keeping detailed information within domain-specific controllers while using a multidomain controller to create an end-to-end network slice. The IETF's Traffic Engineering Architecture and Signaling (TEAS) working group has produced RFC 8453, "Framework for Abstraction and Control of TE Networks (ACTN)," which addresses this type of traffic engineering.

The case just described illustrates the direction in which service providers need to transform their networks and operational processes to keep pace with developments in business and society. This chapter explains the architecture, technology, and protocols required to achieve automation via programmability.

SDN Controllers for Service Provider Networks

It's important to understand what SDN means in the context of this chapter as SDN is commonly discussed today for solutions in different industries that solve different problems. In this chapter, we split SDN into overlay and underlay categories.

Overlay SDN covers all kinds of SDN technologies that don't affect the path of the traffic through the network and focus only on encapsulation of the traffic on an edge router (customer premises equipment [CPE] for service providers or a leaf switch in a data center) and decapsulation on another edge router. The most popular technologies are MPLS over GRE (or MPLS over UDP),VXLAN, and GENEVE. All these technologies encapsulate incoming customer traffic and then forward it over the network using standard routing mechanisms, following standard IGP/BGP path selection. For signaling of the customer routes, which might be IP prefixes, MAC addresses, or a mixture of the two, one of the most popular and useful protocols is BGP-EVPN. For the enterprise segment, the solution class is called SD-WAN, and Cisco offers Meraki and Viptela as products. In the data center field, Cisco offers ACI (Application Centric Infrastructure) as an SDN solution. Other vendors also offer solutions in this area, such as Nokia Nuage and Juniper Contrail, which are applicable both for data centers and SD-WAN deployments.

Note Although overlay SDN is valuable, it is beyond the scope of this book, so we don't discuss it further.

In contrast to overlay SDN, *underlay SDN* directly influences the path of traffic between edge routers through the use of traffic engineering technologies. It can be both traditional MPLS-TE using RSVP for path signaling or modern flavors of Segment Routing Traffic Engineering (SR-TE), which is more suitable for network programming. The real power of traffic engineering is unleashed when an SDN controller has an end-to-end view of the network and can signal a proper path (that is, a path that meets the constraints) based on this end-to-end view. To collect end-to-end topology, an SDN controller uses BGP-LS, which involves a new specific address family and distributes IS-IS or OSPF topology to the SDN controller. To signal MPLS label-switched paths (LSPs) down to edge routers, the SDN controller uses PCEP (Path Computation Element Protocol), which is defined in RFC 5450. Figure 16-2 shows these protocols working together to provide a programmable network path.

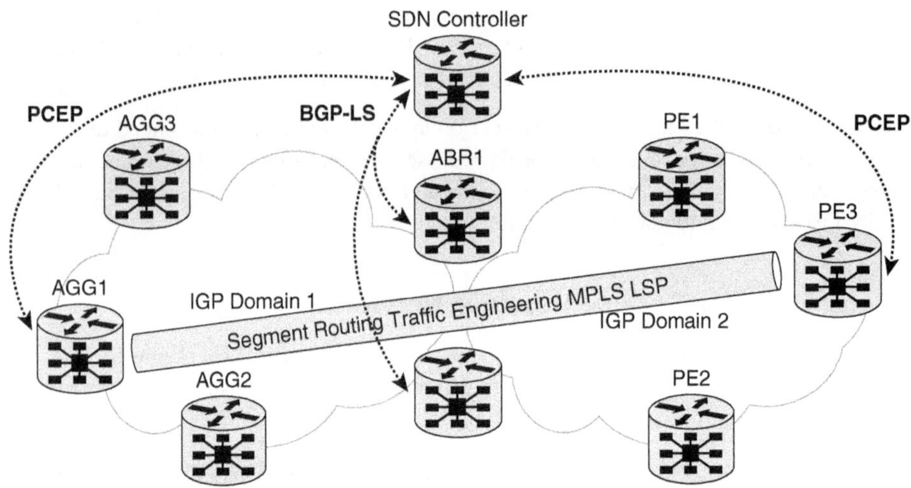

Figure 16-2 *Underlay SDN Protocol Suite*

The underlay solution works as follows:

1. The network runs a link-state IGP (IS-IS or OSPF), which is typical for service provider networks, with Segment Routing (SR) enabled. (SR is the most modern mechanism developed to perform MPLS in the network.) The original mechanism, MPLS-TE, which is a framework that allows the edge router to predefine the exact path through the network by signaling it across the routers using RSVP-TE, is generally supported as well; however, MPLS-TE is not a primary focus of this book, as it isn't primarily for service provider networks or automation. When enabled, SR ensures that there are per-node and per-link MPLS labels available.

2. Some network functions (basically, the routers that have the best view of the network, such as ABRs) establish BGP-LS sessions with the SDN controller.

3. These network functions export their link-state database created using an IGP (OSPF or IS-IS) to the SDN controller so that the SDN controller has an end-to-end view of the network topology, including routing and MPLS labels.

4. Ingress/egress network functions peer with SDN controllers using PCEP in order to get proper end-to-end MPLS LSPs.

5. Upon request, the SDN controller pushes the corresponding Segment Routing label stack (or Explicit Route Object - ERO), which is a list of the next hops (that is, IP addresses of the network functions) the MPLS-TE tunnel should take through the network to the ingress router to instantiate the MPLS LSPs.

These steps provide a rather simplified view of the process that occurs in the SDN-controlled network, but they highlight the structure of the process. The following sections describe the parts of the process in greater detail.

Segment Routing (SR)

The first major building block in service provider programmability and SDN is Segment Routing (SR). This chapter describes basic SR concepts, such as how it works on its own and with SDN controllers.

Note To learn more details about SR, you should read *Segment Routing, Part I* and *Segment Routing, Part II* by Clarence Filsfils, who has significantly contributed to the development of SR.

Segment Routing Basics

The SR technology is described in RFC 8402, "Segment Routing Architecture," which was published in July 2018. Work on SR started some time ago, and router code has supported SR for a while. Several big networks (for instance, Vodafone Germany) have been running SR for a couple years already. Figure 16-3 shows a list of IETF activities; you can see that only a few documents are standardized, and work is ongoing to extend SR capabilities.

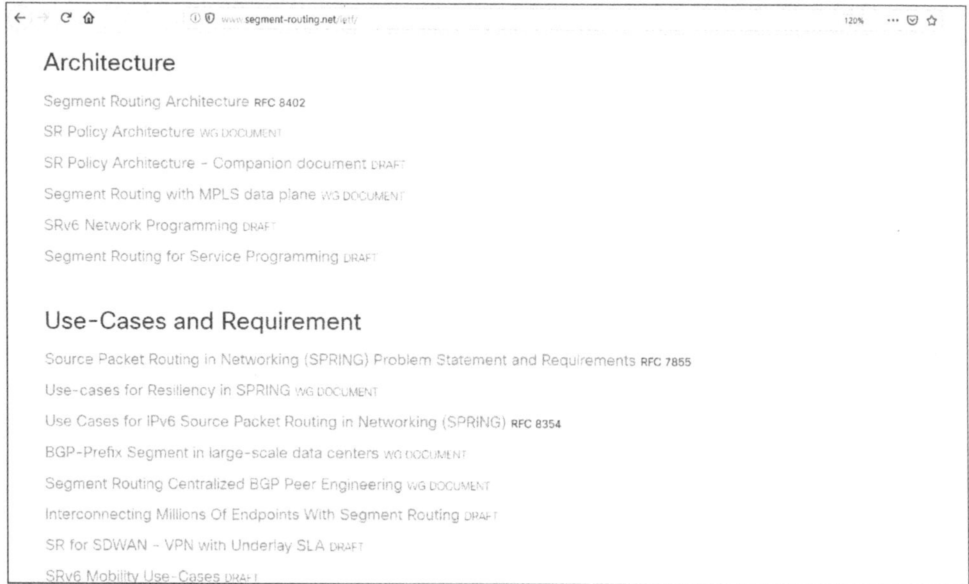

Figure 16-3 *Segment Routing IETF Drafts*

This chapter describes Segment Routing with the MPLS data plane—referred to as *SR-MPLS*. It is also possible to use Segment Routing with the IPv6 data plane, where information is encoded in the IPv6 address; this is referred to as SRv6. However, SRv6 is beyond the scope of this book.

What makes SR-MPLS the best choice for network programmability compared to other MPLS data plane protocols? Basically, SR implements a source routing paradigm. *Source routing* means that the head-end router (or ingress router in the MPLS domain) defines the full end-to-end path from itself to the tail-end route (or egress router in the MPLS domain). Once the head-end router has defined the path, the transit routers (typically called label switch routers [LSRs]) perform forwarding according to the instructions encoded in the packets. In the case of SR, MPLS labels are these instructions.

Before we can get into how SR works, it is important to understand some core definitions related to SR:

- **Segment:** This is a general instruction to a router that describes what to do with a packet. In the most common scenario, the segment value is represented as the MPLS label toward the egress router. In more sophisticated cases, segments can define egress interfaces, service chains, QoS parameters, and so on.
- **SRGB (Segment Routing Global Block):** This is a range of labels used for Segment Routing globally, which means this information is distributed across the whole SR-MPLS domain and must be consistent across this domain. For Cisco IOS XR, the default value is the range 16000 to 23999; other network operating systems (such as Juniper Junos OS, Arista EOS, and Nokia SR OS) have different default ranges.
- **SRLB (Segment Routing Local Block):** This is a range of labels used locally to each router within an SR-MPLS domain, and these labels are coming from a range other than SRGB. In Cisco IOS XR, there is no specific range for this, and the labels are assigned from the range starting from 24000—which means the range is shared with LDP, MPLS-TE, and BGP. Each Adj-SID (described later in this list) becomes the label from this range. In contrast to SRGB, these labels have local meaning. Therefore, there might be duplications of these labels within an SR-MPLS domain. Although you might think that this would lead to traffic drops, this is not the case (and you will learn why shortly).
- **Prefix-SID (Prefix Segment Identifier):** This is a segment associated with any prefix within the IGP domain. It doesn't seem necessary for this prefix to be local to the router that generates this Prefix-SID. It can be represented as an index value that is used in calculating the SR-MPLS label: label = SRGB starting label + index (for example, if the index is 11, the SR-MPLS label is 16000 + 11 = 16011). It can also be represented as an absolute label value out of the SRGB range. This parameter can be configured for each interface.
- **Node-SID (Node Segment Identifier):** This is a particular case of the Prefix-SID (with the flag *N* set) that typically represents the router itself and is usually configured at Loopback0 or any other interface that is associated with the router ID.
- **Adj-SID (Adjacency Segment Identifier):** This segment identifies unidirectional IGP adjacency (that is, a neighbor in OSPF or IS-IS).

As you examine the examples on the following pages, you will see these concepts in action and become more familiar with the ideas. Figure 16-4 shows the lab topology that is used for the following examples.

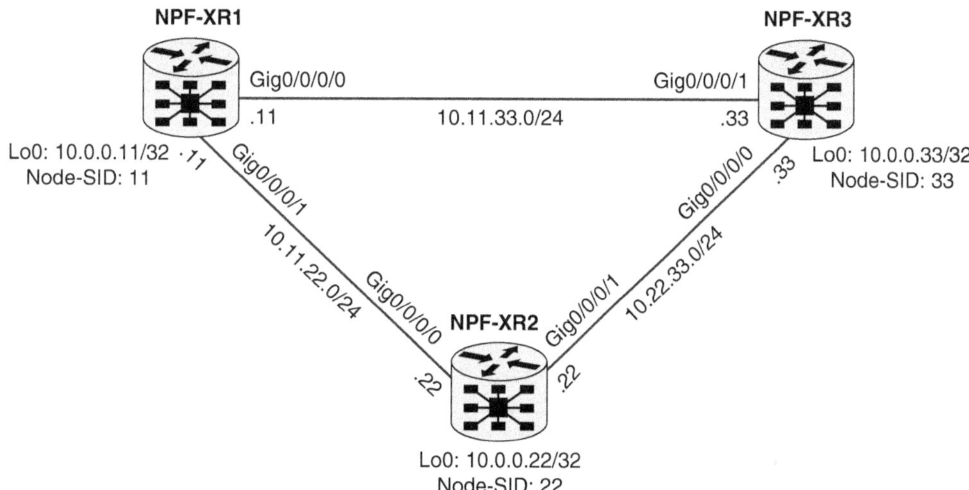

Figure 16-4 *Segment Routing Lab Topology*

This topology is quite simple. The one part you may not be familiar with is Node-SID, which, as described above, represents a router in the SR-MPLS domain and is associated with Loopback0 interfaces. Example 16-1 shows how to enable Segment Routing in this network, which is running IS-IS IGP. (OSPF is also supported.)

Example 16-1 *Configuring Segment Routing in a Network Running IS-IS*

```
RP/0/0/CPU0:NPF-XR1(config)# show conf
Sun Mar 31 18:29:09.914 UTC
Building configuration...
!! IOS XR Configuration 6.5.1
router isis CORE
 is-type level-2-only
 net 49.0000.0100.0000.0011.00
 log adjacency changes
 address-family ipv4 unicast
  metric-style wide
  advertise passive-only
  segment-routing mpls sr-prefer
 !
 interface Loopback0
  passive
```

```
  address-family ipv4 unicast
   prefix-sid index 11
  !
 !
 interface GigabitEthernet0/0/0/0
  point-to-point
  address-family ipv4 unicast
  !
 !
 interface GigabitEthernet0/0/0/1
  point-to-point
  address-family ipv4 unicast
  !
 !
!
end
```

Note If you are not familiar with IS-IS configuration and operation, see *Routing TCP/IP, Volume I* by Jeff Doyle.

Example 16-1 shows an IS-IS configuration that is quite standard for service provider networks. Note in this example that you need to enable **metric-style wide** to allow IS-IS to propagate Segment Routing information. Otherwise, the configuration of SR is straightforward: You need to enable it within the appropriate address family by using the **segment-routing mpls sr-prefer** command, where **segment-routing mpls** enables SR for IS-IS generally, and the keyword **sr-prefer** instructs the router to prefer SR labels to LDP by changing the protocol's AD (administrative distance). After that, you configure the Node-SID by issuing the command **prefix-sid index 11** within the interface/address-family context. With the keyword **index** you do not provide an absolute value but a local ID, and each router within the SR-MPLS domain calculates the SR label value on its own by using SRGB and this ID. (SRGB is not explicitly configured in this example because it is implicitly enabled with the default value 16000–23999, as mentioned earlier.)

Example 16-2 shows the output of the IS-IS information (LSDB), including Segment Routing values generated by NPF-XR1.

Example 16-2 *IS-IS Link State Information for NPF-XR1*

```
RP/0/0/CPU0:NPF-XR1# show isis database verbose NPF-XR1.00-00
Sun Mar 31 19:00:38.625 UTC

IS-IS CORE (Level-2) Link State Database
```

```
LSPID                      LSP Seq Num  LSP Checksum  LSP Holdtime/Rcvd  ATT/P/OL
NPF-XR1.00-00            * 0x00000006   0x69ce        380  /*            0/0/0
  Area Address:    49.0000
  NLPID:           0xcc
  IP Address:      10.0.0.11
  Hostname:        NPF-XR1
  Metric: 10          IS-Extended NPF-XR2.00
    Interface IP Address: 10.11.22.11
    Neighbor IP Address: 10.11.22.22
    Link Maximum SID Depth:
      Subtype: 1, Value: 10
    ADJ-SID: F:0 B:0 V:1 L:1 S:0 P:0 weight:0 Adjacency-sid:24001
  Metric: 10          IS-Extended NPF-XR3.00
    Interface IP Address: 10.11.33.11
    Neighbor IP Address: 10.11.33.33
    Link Maximum SID Depth:
      Subtype: 1, Value: 10
    ADJ-SID: F:0 B:0 V:1 L:1 S:0 P:0 weight:0 Adjacency-sid:24003
  Metric: 0           IP-Extended 10.0.0.11/32
    Prefix-SID Index: 11, Algorithm:0, R:0 N:1 P:0 E:0 V:0 L:0
    Prefix Attribute Flags: X:0 R:0 N:1
  Router Cap:      10.0.0.11, D:0, S:0
    Segment Routing: I:1 V:0, SRGB Base: 16000 Range: 8000
    SR Algorithm:
      Algorithm: 0
      Algorithm: 1
    Node Maximum SID Depth:
      Subtype: 1, Value: 10
```

The core SR components, which are shaded in Example 16-2, are as follows:

- **Adj-SIDs:** There are two of these, each associated with an IS-IS neighbor.
- **Prefix-SID:** This is configured as an index with value 11 associated with the IP address of the Loopback0 interface.
- **SRGB:** NPF-XR1 signals the SRGB range, which is 16000–23999.
- **SR Algorithm:** This is a set of constraints that must be considered by the router (or SDN controller) upon SPF calculation. Initially, there were only two values: 0 (standard SPF process without any constraints) and 1 (SPF strict calculation). Today it is possible to add arbitrary algorithm values that correspond to constraints (for example, latency, hop count, QoS).

In a Cisco implementation, each router in an SR-MPLS domain signals the same set of information, so each router can calculate the label to reach the next SR router, which is calculated as SRGB Base + Prefix-SID. Example 16-3 provides details of the MPLS FIB from NPF-XR2.

Example 16-3 *Content of the MPLS FIB at NPF-XR2*

```
RP/0/0/CPU0:NPF-XR2# show mpls forwarding
Sun Mar 31 19:22:28.845 UTC
Local  Outgoing    Prefix             Outgoing     Next Hop        Bytes
Label  Label       or ID              Interface                    Switched
------ ----------- ------------------ ------------ --------------- ------------
16011  Pop         SR Pfx (idx 11)    Gi0/0/0/0    10.11.22.11     0
16033  Pop         SR Pfx (idx 33)    Gi0/0/0/1    10.22.33.33     0
24000  Pop         SR Adj (idx 1)     Gi0/0/0/1    10.22.33.33     0
24001  Pop         SR Adj (idx 3)     Gi0/0/0/1    10.22.33.33     0
24002  Pop         SR Adj (idx 1)     Gi0/0/0/0    10.11.22.11     0
24003  Pop         SR Adj (idx 3)     Gi0/0/0/0    10.11.22.11     0
```

Let's look at the MPLS label for NPF-XR1 as an example. The Local Label value 16011 is calculated as a sum of SRGB Base of the router NPF-XR2 itself (not NPF-XR1), which is 16000, and Prefix-SID of IP address 10.0.0.11/32 learned from the IS-IS LSP of NPF-XR1, which is 11. Outgoing Label is calculated as the sum of SRGB Base from the adjacent router (NPF-XR1 in this case) and Prefix-SID of IP address 10.0.0.11/32 learned from the IS-IS LSP of NPF-XR1. You see the value Pop in this example because the egress router is directly connected, and NPF-XR2 performs a standard PHP operation.

You might wonder why each router takes a different SRGB Base value to compute the Local Label and Outgoing Label values. You need to understand what each label means. The local label is the value that the router (NPF-XR2 in this case) is looking for in incoming packets. The outgoing label value of NPF-XR2 is the local label value of NPF-XR1, which is the end destination for 10.0.0.11/32. Basically, each router calculates its own local and outgoing labels for all prefixes within the IGP domain. So, because the IS-IS database is consistent across the whole IS-IS domain, each router can calculate labels for each other router and implement traffic engineering.

There is no standardized value for SRGB in RFC 8402. This RFC recommends using the same value of SRGB across the whole SR-MPLS domain. There are a couple reasons for this, including consistency of operation and troubleshooting of the SR-MPLS operation. In reality, each vendor has a default SRGB, and to make Segment Routing interoperable between different vendors, the local calculation on each router must consider different SRGBs. To illustrate this scenario, Figure 16-5 shows the modified topology.

The default IS-IS metric for all interfaces is 10, so putting 100 on the link between NPF-XR1 and NPF-XR3 makes all the traffic between these two nodes pass NPF-XR2. On NPF-XR2, the SRGB is altered to 20000–23999, as shown in Example 16-4.

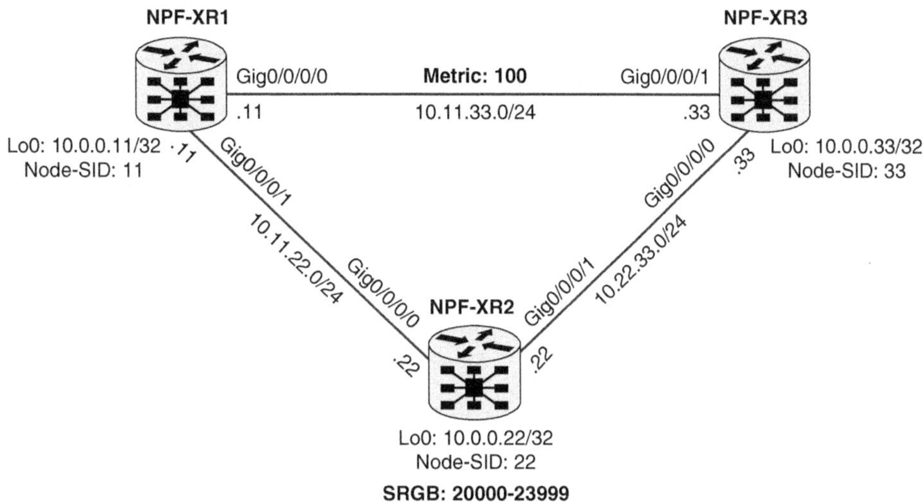

Figure 16-5 *Segment Routing Topology with a Modified Metric and SRGB*

Example 16-4 *Modifying the SRGB at NPF-XR2*

```
RP/0/0/CPU0:NPF-XR2(config)# show conf
Sun Mar 31 20:05:54.867 UTC
Building configuration...
!! IOS XR Configuration 6.5.1
router isis CORE
 segment-routing global-block 20000 23999
!
end
```

When the change is implemented, you can see in the MPLS FIB of NPF-XR2 that Local Label values are modified as shown in Example 16-5.

Example 16-5 *Updated MPLS FIB of NPF-XR2*

```
RP/0/0/CPU0:NPF-XR2# show mpls forwarding
Sun Mar 31 20:06:26.145 UTC
Local  Outgoing    Prefix             Outgoing     Next Hop        Bytes
Label  Label       or ID              Interface                    Switched
------ ----------- ------------------ ------------ --------------- ------------
20011  Pop         SR Pfx (idx 11)    Gi0/0/0/0    10.11.22.11     0
20033  Pop         SR Pfx (idx 33)    Gi0/0/0/1    10.22.33.33     0
24000  Pop         SR Adj (idx 1)     Gi0/0/0/1    10.22.33.33     0
24001  Pop         SR Adj (idx 3)     Gi0/0/0/1    10.22.33.33     0
24002  Pop         SR Adj (idx 1)     Gi0/0/0/0    10.11.22.11     0
24003  Pop         SR Adj (idx 3)     Gi0/0/0/0    10.11.22.11     0
```

The final step in this verification is to check the routing table and FIB on NPF-XR3 because the traffic to NPF-XR1 should flow over NPF-XR2. Example 16-6 shows several changes.

Example 16-6 *RIB and FIB on NPF-XR3 After Changes in the Network*

```
Routing entry for 10.0.0.11/32
  Known via "isis CORE", distance 115, metric 20, labeled SR, type level-2
  Installed Mar 31 20:08:01.783 for 00:03:10
  Routing Descriptor Blocks
    10.22.33.22, from 10.0.0.11, via GigabitEthernet0/0/0/0
      Route metric is 20
  No advertising protos.


RP/0/0/CPU0:NPF-XR3# show mpls forwarding
Sun Mar 31 20:11:21.150 UTC
Local  Outgoing    Prefix             Outgoing     Next Hop        Bytes
Label  Label       or ID              Interface                    Switched
------ ----------- ------------------ ------------ --------------- ------------
16011  20011       SR Pfx (idx 11)    Gi0/0/0/0    10.22.33.22     0
16022  Pop         SR Pfx (idx 22)    Gi0/0/0/0    10.22.33.22     0
24000  Pop         SR Adj (idx 1)     Gi0/0/0/0    10.22.33.22     0
24001  Pop         SR Adj (idx 3)     Gi0/0/0/0    10.22.33.22     0
24002  Pop         SR Adj (idx 1)     Gi0/0/0/1    10.11.33.11     0
24003  Pop         SR Adj (idx 3)     Gi0/0/0/1    10.11.33.11     0
```

As you can see, the next hop to 10.0.0.11/32 is NPF-XR2 now, and this is expected based on standard SPF calculation. Moreover, in the FIB, you can see that the Local Label value for NPF-XR3 is 16011 because the SRGB Base wasn't changed locally, and the Outgoing Label value is 20011, which reflects the change of SRGB Base on NPF-XR2. Example 16-7 shows how to use **traceroute** to check how the data plane looks when using MPLS.

Example 16-7 *Segment Routing Data Plane Verification*

```
RP/0/0/CPU0:NPF-XR3# traceroute mpls ipv4 10.0.0.11/32 source 10.0.0.33
Sun Mar 31 20:21:26.188 UTC

Tracing MPLS Label Switched Path to 10.0.0.11/32, timeout is 2 seconds

Codes: '!' - success, 'Q' - request not sent, '.' - timeout,
  'L' - labeled output interface, 'B' - unlabeled output interface,
  'D' - DS Map mismatch, 'F' - no FEC mapping, 'f' - FEC mismatch,
  'M' - malformed request, 'm' - unsupported tlvs, 'N' - no rx label,
 'P' - no rx intf label prot, 'p' - premature termination of LSP,
```

```
  'R' - transit router, 'I' - unknown upstream index,
  'X' - unknown return code, 'x' - return code 0

Type escape sequence to abort.

  0 10.22.33.33 MRU 1500 [Labels: 20011 Exp: 0]
L 1 10.22.33.22 MRU 1500 [Labels: implicit-null Exp: 0] 10 ms
! 2 10.11.22.11 10 ms
```

The outgoing MPLS label on NPF-XR3 is 20011, and NPF-XR2 performs PHP further, which is why you see implicit-null. If there were no PHP, the value would be 16011.

If the SRGB at NPF-XR2 is restored to the default value, then NPF-XR3 will have the same Local Label value as NPF-XR2, as shown in the Example 16-8. (This assumes that the changes from the Example 16-4 are reverted.)

Example 16-8 *SRGB Restored at NPF-XR2*

```
RP/0/0/CPU0:NPF-XR2# rollback configuration last 1
Sun Mar 31 21:06:49.907 UTC

Loading Rollback Changes.
Loaded Rollback Changes in 1 sec
Committing.RP/0/0/CPU0:Mar 31 21:06:51.636 UTC: isis[1011]: %ROUTING-ISIS-6-
  SRGB_INFO : SRGB info: 'Segment routing temporarily disabled on all topologies
  and address families because the global block is being modified'

4 items committed in 1 sec (4)items/sec
Updating.RP/0/0/CPU0:Mar 31 21:06:52.966 UTC: config_rollback[65725]: %MGBL-CONFIG-
  6-DB_COMMIT : Configuration committed by user 'cisco'. Use 'show configuration
  commit changes 1000000010' to view the changes.

Updated Commit database in 1 sec
Configuration successfully rolled back 1 commits.

RP/0/0/CPU0:NPF-XR3# show mpls forwarding
Sun Mar 31 21:08:37.524 UTC
Local  Outgoing    Prefix             Outgoing     Next Hop        Bytes
Label  Label       or ID              Interface                    Switched
------ ----------- ------------------ ------------ --------------- ------------
16011  16011       SR Pfx (idx 11)    Gi0/0/0/0    10.22.33.22     0
16022  Pop         SR Pfx (idx 22)    Gi0/0/0/0    10.22.33.22     0
24000  Pop         SR Adj (idx 1)     Gi0/0/0/0    10.22.33.22     0
24001  Pop         SR Adj (idx 3)     Gi0/0/0/0    10.22.33.22     0
24002  Pop         SR Adj (idx 1)     Gi0/0/0/1    10.11.33.11     0
24003  Pop         SR Adj (idx 3)     Gi0/0/0/1    10.11.33.11     0
```

The examples so far in this chapter demonstrate the standard operation of Segment Routing. A common misconception is that the ingress router uses the SR label signaled by the egress router through the whole SR-MPLS domain. In reality, each router calculates the Local and Outgoing labels itself, and these values can be different. However, if you have a single vendor, and you don't alter the default configuration, you might see that all the routers within an SR-MPLS domain have precisely the same MPLS label for a particular prefix; this is the case because the computation rules explained earlier are the same for each router. Figure 16-6 provides a higher-level view of Segment Routing with fewer details.

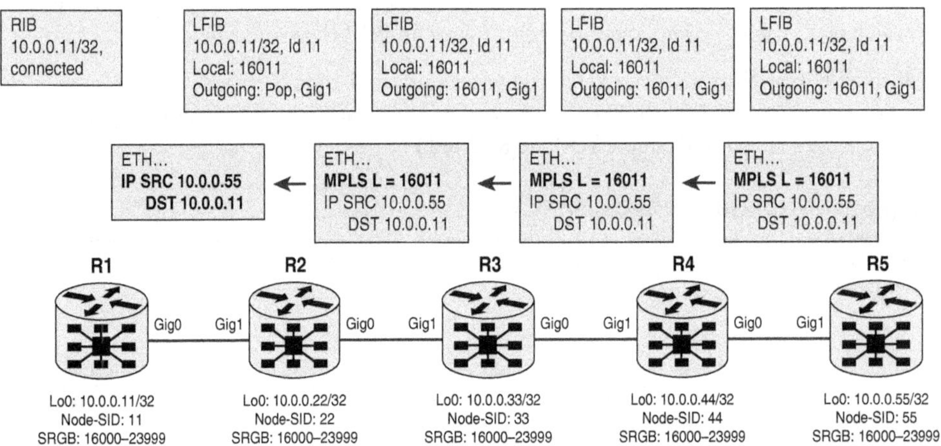

Figure 16-6 *Generic Process of Segment Routing Forwarding*

In this example, there is no additional signaling protocol in the network besides IS-IS (or OSPF, if you are running it) as all the MPLS information is encoded there. In traditional MPLS deployments, you have either LDP for non MPLS-TE cases or RSVP in case of MPLS-TE in addition to your IGP. It's important to emphasize that, by default, Segment Routing follows standard SPF procedure, and ECMP is natively built in, which improves bandwidth utilization in the network.

The calculation consistency discussed here forms a solid basis for programming network paths using SR-TE, which is discussed in the next section.

Segment Routing Traffic Engineering

So far, the focus of this chapter has been on traffic forwarding without any constraints, which is suitable for enterprise locations, data centers, and traffic that isn't sensitive to latency. In the case of service providers offering converged services, including telephony or video conferencing, latency plays a crucial role. Therefore, traffic engineering technologies are an inevitable part of network design. Moreover, this is a perfect use case for Segment Routing because all the routers in an SR domain can calculate proper MPLS labels for any given prefix in the network by using Prefix-SID and SRGB Base.

In addition, these routers know all the Adj-SID values (which are also MPLS labels), as they are signaled in IS-IS LSPs (as demonstrated in Example 16-2). Based on this information, there are two significant approaches to implementing traffic engineering using Segment Routing: via either Node-SID or Adj-SID. It is also possible to implement a third approach that mixes the first two. In the end, it's just a matter of ensuring a proper label stack on the head-end router, as this is precisely the way SR-TE works in the network. Figure 16-7 provides a high-level illustration of SR-TE on a network.

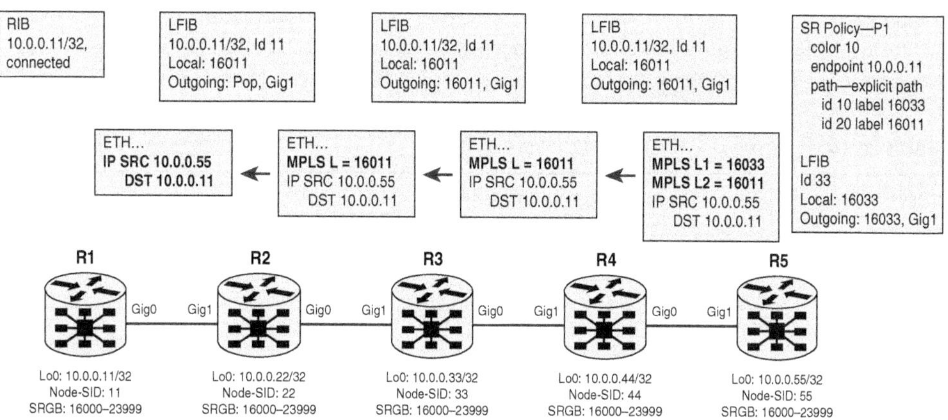

Figure 16-7 *Generic Process of Segment Routing Traffic Engineering Using Node-SID*

The critical component for SR-TE in Cisco IOS XR is SR-TE policies. Such a policy contains the following:

- **Name:** The name defines the configuration context.
- **Endpoint:** Within a policy, the endpoint defines the IPv4 address of the next hop along the route. With BGP IP VPN construction (also known as IP/MPLS VPN or L3 VPN), the endpoint is equal to the IPv4 address of the loopback used as a next hop in the BGP update.
- **Color:** The color triggers the policy for a particular route. In a nutshell, it is an opaque extended community that can be added to any route announced via any BGP address family (for example, IPv4/IPv6 unicast, VPNv4/VPNv6) by using a route policy. Although BGP is mentioned as an example here, it is also possible to use static routes. The most significant advantage of this color extended community is that it provides a possibility to distinguish routes within the same IP VPN and to provide different paths over the network.
- **Path:** The final part of the SR-TE policy is the path, which defines the way the network routes the traffic. There are three available options: dynamic, constraints, and explicit. The explicit path equals the explicit-path value in MPLS-TE, where you define the specific set of next hops using either labels or IPv4 addresses. In the case of a dynamic path, it's the router itself; or, with the help of an SDN controller, it is possible to

calculate the path using the defined metric type (either standard IGP or TE metric, or latency, and so on). The constraint is not the path itself; rather, the constraint specifies which additional parameters the router (or SDN controller) needs to take into account to compute the path. The algorithm for calculating the path under those constraints is called CSPF (Constrained Shortest Path First), and it is similar to classical SPF used in IS-IS/OSPF but with additional inputs rather than only a cost metric.

Although these details might seem complicated, the router configuration is quite straightforward. To illustrate it, we can use the reference topology from Figure 16-4 with a basic IS-IS and SR configuration and equal metrics on all the links. The SR-TE policy is configured using Node-SIDs for path definition as shown in Example 16-9.

Example 16-9 *SR-TE Policy Using Prefix-SIDs*

```
RP/0/0/CPU0:NPF-XR1# show run segment-routing
Wed Apr  3 05:58:32.600 UTC
segment-routing
 traffic-eng
  segment-list SRTE_XR1_XR3_SID
   index 10 mpls label 16022
   index 20 mpls label 16033
  !
  policy XR1_XR3_OVER_XR2_BLUE
   binding-sid mpls 1000002
   color 10 end-point ipv4 10.0.0.33
   candidate-paths
    preference 100
     explicit segment-list SRTE_XR1_XR3_SID
     !
    !
   !
  !
 !
!
```

Let's go step by step through the output shown in Example 16-9. First of all, you need to get into the configuration context for SR-TE policies by issuing the **segment-routing traffic-eng** command. You then have plenty of points to configure. Example 16-9 uses an explicit path definition, which is realized through the creation of a segment list. (The segment list is similar to an explicit path in an MPLS-TE configuration.) Inside the segment list, you need to provide either a sequence of MPLS labels or IPv4 next hops, which will be automatically converted into MPLS labels. When you complete the segment list, the next step is to create the policy itself. Inside the policy, you need to define of the following information:

- **binding-sid:** This uniquely codes the policy and represents it outside the router. Generally, it can work like any other local label, which means that if the router receives the packet labeled with this MPLS label, it replaces it with the label stack associated with the policy. In Example 16-9, the path through the network SRTE_XR1_XR3_SID is encoded using a label stack consisting of two labels: 16022 and 16033. Inside the policy XR1_XR3_OVER_XR2_blue, this path is mapped with the color and specific endpoint to the **binding-sid** value **1000002**. This binding-sid value is installed in the MPLS LFIB of the router; therefore, if NPF-XR1 receives from any neighbor the packet with label 1000002, it replaces it with two labels: 16022 and 16033. The core idea of this technology is to make the label stack that is used more shallow to cope with the hardware capability on the low-end routers.
- **color:** This, together with **end-point**, defines the set of prefixes that are tagged with this opaque extended community and the PE that these prefixes come from.
- **candidate-path:** This contains all the possible paths associated with the policy. It's possible to configure several paths with different **preference** values; if you do, the highest preference wins.
- **Path type:** The path type (dynamic, constraints, or explicit) is set within a particular path. For the explicit path type, the name of the segment list is defined; for the dynamic path type, the metric type is defined.

After you have configured a policy, you can check whether it is correct and working by using the verification command shown in Example 16-10.

Example 16-10 *Verifying the SR-TE Policy*

```
RP/0/0/CPU0:NPF-XR1# show segment-routing traffic-eng policy
Wed Apr  3 22:15:36.342 UTC

SR-TE policy database
---------------------

Name: XR1_XR3_OVER_XR2_BLUE (Color: 10, End-point: 10.0.0.33)
  Status:
    Admin: up  Operational: up for 01:20:10 (since Apr  3 20:55:26.152)
  Candidate-paths:
    Preference 100:
      Explicit: segment-list SRTE_XR1_XR3_SID (active)
        Weight: 1, Metric Type: IGP
          16022
          16033
  Attributes:
    Binding SID: 1000002
      Allocation mode: explicit
     State: Programmed
```

```
    Policy selected: yes
  Forward Class: 0
  Steering BGP disabled: no
  IPv6 caps enable: no
```

You can see in Example 16-10 that the policy is administratively and operationally up, but there are still no routes associated with the color 10. You can see how this policy works only if there are proper prefixes. In this case, you need to have BGP running, and you can extend the initial lab setup with BGP and route policy configuration as shown in Figure 16-8.

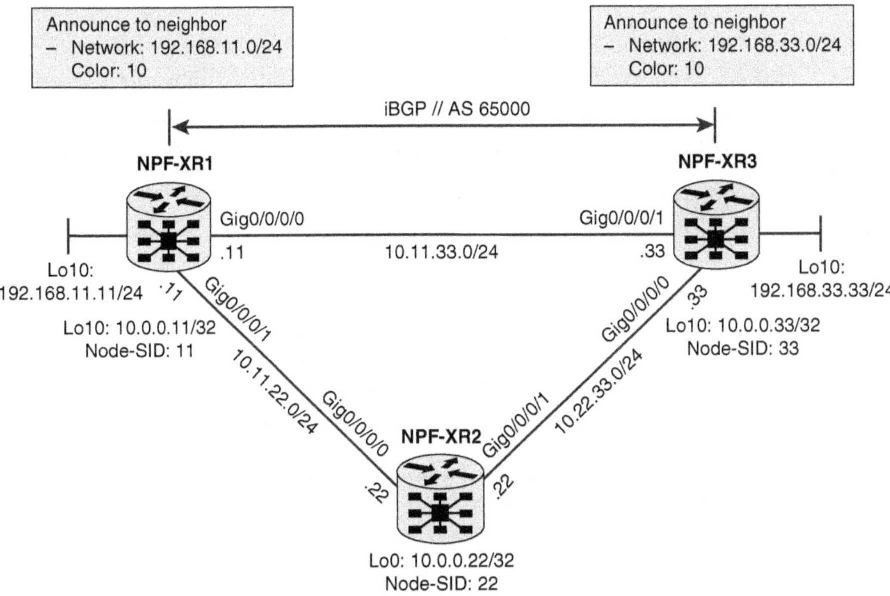

Figure 16-8 *BGP Configuration for a Color Extended Community*

The internal BGP (iBGP) peering is established between the Loopback0 interfaces of NPF-XR1 and NPF-XR3 routes within autonomous system 65000. The Loopback10 interfaces emulate customer prefixes that are advertised over BGP within the IPv4 unicast address family. These routes are tagged using the color opaque extended community. Example 16-11 shows the configuration of NPF-XR3.

Example 16-11 *BGP and Route Policy Configuration for a Color Extended Community*

```
RP/0/0/CPU0:NPF-XR3(config)# show conf
Wed Apr  3 05:58:32.600 UTC
interface Loopback10
 ipv4 address 192.168.33.33 255.255.255.0
!
```

```
extcommunity-set opaque COLOUR_BLUE
  10
end-set
!
route-policy RP_SET_COLOUR
  set extcommunity color COLOUR_BLUE
end-policy
!
router bgp 65000
 bgp router-id 10.0.0.33
 bgp log neighbor changes detail
 address-family ipv4 unicast
  network 192.168.33.0/24
 !
 neighbor 10.0.0.11
  remote-as 65000
  update-source Loopback0
  address-family ipv4 unicast
   route-policy RP_SET_COLOUR out
  !
 !
!
end
```

The configuration for NPF-XR1 isn't provided here because it is precisely the same except that it uses IPv4 addresses. Notice that the route policy operates with the community name; this is why you need to create **extcommunity-set opaque** *COMM_NAME* with the numeric value you plan to use in the SR-TE policy. Then you can create the proper route policy to call this set. The last step is to create a BGP process, announce the appropriate prefixes, and attach the route policy for the BGP neighbor within the corresponding address policy in the outgoing direction (though the incoming direction is also possible).

The SR-TE policy so far has been configured only on NPF-XR1 toward NPF-XR3, which is why the verification should be done on NFP-XR1. Example 16-12 shows the details of this verification.

Example 16-12 *Verifying the BGP Prefix Mapping to the SR-TE Policy*

```
RP/0/0/CPU0:NPF-XR1# show bgp ipv4 unicast 192.168.33.0/24
Wed Apr  3 22:22:33.514 UTC
BGP routing table entry for 192.168.33.0/24
Versions:
  Process           bRIB/RIB  SendTblVer
  Speaker                 10          10
```

```
Last Modified: Apr  3 20:55:29.543 for 01:27:03
Paths: (1 available, best #1)
  Not advertised to any peer
  Path #1: Received by speaker 0
  Not advertised to any peer
  Local
    10.0.0.33 C:10 (bsid:1000002) (metric 10) from 10.0.0.33 (10.0.0.33)
      Origin IGP, metric 0, localpref 100, valid, internal, best, group-best
      Received Path ID 0, Local Path ID 1, version 9
      Extended community: Color:10
      SR policy color 10, up, un-registered, bsid 1000002


RP/0/0/CPU0:NPF-XR1# show cef 192.168.33.00/24 detail
Wed Apr  3 22:22:35.944 UTC
192.168.33.0/24, version 21, internal 0x5000001 0x0 (ptr 0xa1416314) [1], 0x0 (0x0),
  0x0 (0x0)
 Updated Apr  3 20:55:29.212
 Prefix Len 24, traffic index 0, precedence n/a, priority 4
  gateway array (0xa13357dc) reference count 1, flags 0x2010, source rib (7),
  0 backups
                [1 type 3 flags 0x48441 (0xa13a0898) ext 0x0 (0x0)]
  LW-LDI[type=0, refc=0, ptr=0x0, sh-ldi=0x0]
  gateway array update type-time 1 Apr  3 20:55:29.212
 LDI Update time Apr  3 20:55:29.212

  Level 1 - Load distribution: 0
  [0] via 10.0.0.33/32, recursive

   via local-label 1000002, 3 dependencies, recursive [flags 0x6000]
    path-idx 0 NHID 0x0 [0xa17cbc84 0x0]
    recursion-via-label
    next hop via 1000002/1/21

    Load distribution: 0 (refcount 1)

    Hash  OK  Interface                 Address
    0     Y   XR1_XR3_OVER_XR2_BLUE     point2point
```

The first command in Example 16-12 displays the information associated with the route. From an SR-TE policy perspective, the most crucial part is **extended community: color:10**. The router analyzes this community and provides a mapping to the locally configured SR **color** and **binding-SID** values associated with the SR-TE policy. If you compare the value shown here, 1000002, with the one configured in Example 16-9, you see that these values are identical.

The second command in Example 16-12 shows the details of the CEF, including the binding-SID value again together with the name of the SR-TE policy that is in use.

The SR-TE policy for the traffic routed from NPF-XR3 to NPF-XR1 can be configured by using Adj-SIDs, as mentioned earlier. Figure 16-9 illustrates the generic process of using the SR-TE policy with Adj-SIDs.

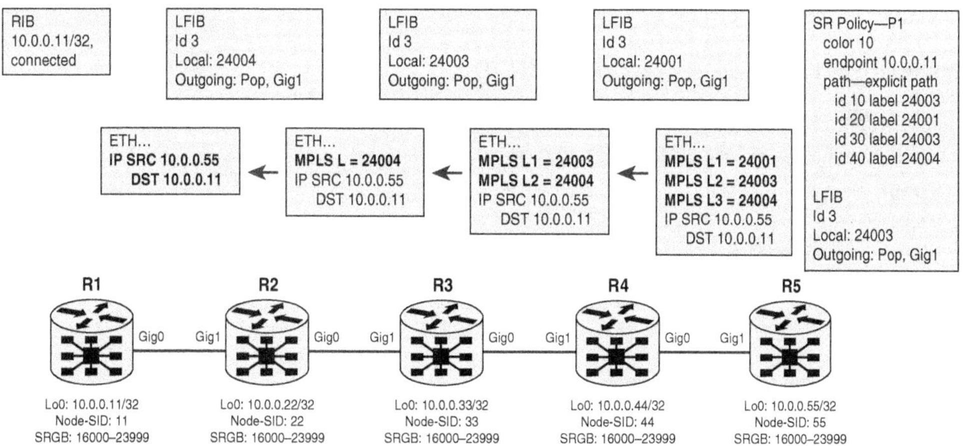

Figure 16-9 *Generic SR-TE Process Using Adj-SIDs*

As mentioned earlier, every network function in an SR-MPLS domain allocates an Adj-SID and, therefore, an MPLS label to each of its IGP neighbors. In Figure 16-9, the ID value from the LFIB table is generated dynamically and has local significance just within the node. These values are also present in Example 16-8, which provides LFIB output. You might also have spotted that the Adj-SID labels come from the standard MPLS label range, which is also where LDP, RSVP-TE, and BGP labels come from. Because the outgoing label for the Adj-SID is always Pop, the SR-TE policy must contain Adj-SIDs for all hops on the path from the head-end router to the tail-end router.

A significant advantage of the approach just described is that the resulting path is exact, without any gray areas. For instance, if you use Prefix-SID, the local label is always the same within the node, regardless of the outgoing interface; in the case of tweaked per-link metrics, this might result in a different path than expected. Such a scenario with Adj-SID is just impossible. On the other hand, the major drawback of the SR-TE policies with Adj-SIDs is that there is a large label stack associated with the path. (The label stack contains all the labels attached to the packet for transmission.) In Figure 16-9, you can see that four labels are imposed on the packet to traverse just four links. Considering that you would typically also have at least one service label (for an IP VPN or EVPN) and, possibly, an entropy label as well, the label stack can cross the hardware capabilities in terms of the label stack depth of many mid- to low-end routers. This is why you need to check what your hardware can do and decide which approach to use to reach your goal in terms of traffic engineering. For example, the label stack can be as small as 3 labels for a legacy platform and as high as 20 labels for a modern high-end router.

To solve the problem of large label stacks, the concept of MSD (Maximum SID Depth), which is described in RFC 8491, was introduced. Using this functionality, each platform participating in an SR domain advertises its MSD, which is a maximum possible allowed number of labels in a stack that the network function can process in the routing protocol used inside the SR domain (for example, OSPF or IS-IS). Despite the different SR label stack creation approach, the configuration is absolutely the same, as you can see in Example 16-13.

Example 16-13 *SR-TE Policy Using Adj-SIDs*

```
RP/0/0/CPU0:NPF-XR3# show running-config segment-routing
Thu Apr  4 20:54:46.034 UTC
segment-routing
 traffic-eng
  segment-list SRTE_XR3_XR1_ADJ
   index 10 mpls label 24003
   index 20 mpls label 24001
  !
  policy XR3_XR1_OVER_XR2_BLUE
   binding-sid mpls 1000001
   color 10 end-point ipv4 10.0.0.11
   candidate-paths
    preference 100
     explicit segment-list SRTE_XR3_XR1_ADJ
     !
    !
   !
  !
 !
!
```

The configuration in Example 16-13 is pretty much the same as the one in Example 16-9. The only difference is the way the label stack is configured, as mentioned earlier.

To understand why these labels are chosen, take a look at Example 16-14, which provides LFIB content from NPF-XR3 and NPF-XR2.

Example 16-14 *Content of the LFIB from the Head End and the Transit Routers*

```
RP/0/0/CPU0:NPF-XR3# show mpls forwarding
Thu Apr  4 21:04:51.153 UTC
Local  Outgoing    Prefix             Outgoing     Next Hop        Bytes
Label  Label       or ID              Interface                    Switched
------ ----------- ------------------ ------------ --------------- ------------
16011  Pop         SR Pfx (idx 11)    Gi0/0/0/1    10.11.33.11     1244
16022  Pop         SR Pfx (idx 22)    Gi0/0/0/0    10.22.33.22     0
```

```
24000   Pop         SR Adj (idx 1)     Gi0/0/0/1    10.11.33.11     0
24001   Pop         SR Adj (idx 3)     Gi0/0/0/1    10.11.33.11     0
24002   Pop         SR Adj (idx 1)     Gi0/0/0/0    10.22.33.22     0
24003   Pop         SR Adj (idx 3)     Gi0/0/0/0    10.22.33.22     0
1000001 Pop         No ID               XR3_XR1_OVER point2point    0


RP/0/0/CPU0:NPF-XR2# show mpls forwarding
Thu Apr  4 21:05:20.629 UTC
Local  Outgoing    Prefix             Outgoing     Next Hop        Bytes
Label  Label       or ID              Interface                    Switched
------ ----------- ------------------ ------------ --------------- -----------
16011  Pop         SR Pfx (idx 11)    Gi0/0/0/0    10.11.22.11     0
16033  Pop         SR Pfx (idx 33)    Gi0/0/0/1    10.22.33.33     0
24000  Pop         SR Adj (idx 1)     Gi0/0/0/0    10.11.22.11     0
24001  Pop         SR Adj (idx 3)     Gi0/0/0/0    10.11.22.11     0
24002  Pop         SR Adj (idx 1)     Gi0/0/0/1    10.22.33.33     0
24003  Pop         SR Adj (idx 3)     Gi0/0/0/1    10.22.33.33     0
```

The Adj-SID labels used as the SR label stack for the corresponding SR-TE policy are shaded in Example 16-14. You might wonder why these labels are marked as idx 3 rather than idx 1. The answer lies in the IS-IS database, as shown in Example 16-15.

Example 16-15 *Adj-SIDs in the IS-IS Database*

```
RP/0/0/CPU0:NPF-XR2# show isis database verbose NPF-XR2.00-00
Thu Apr  4 21:37:24.118 UTC

IS-IS CORE (Level-2) Link State Database
LSPID                 LSP Seq Num  LSP Checksum  LSP Holdtime/Rcvd  ATT/P/OL
NPF-XR2.00-00       * 0x00000009   0x7373        657  /*            0/0/0
  Area Address:   49.0000
  Metric: 10          IS-Extended NPF-XR1.00
    Interface IP Address: 10.11.22.22
    Neighbor IP Address: 10.11.22.11
    Link Maximum SID Depth:
      Subtype: 1, Value: 10
    ADJ-SID: F:0 B:0 V:1 L:1 S:0 P:0 weight:0 Adjacency-sid:24001
  Metric: 10          IS-Extended NPF-XR3.00
    Interface IP Address: 10.22.33.22
    Neighbor IP Address: 10.22.33.33
    Link Maximum SID Depth:
      Subtype: 1, Value: 10
```

```
    ADJ-SID: F:0 B:0 V:1 L:1 S:0 P:0 weight:0 Adjacency-sid:24003
  NLPID:          0xcc
  IP Address:     10.0.0.22
  Metric: 0          IP-Extended 10.0.0.22/32
    Prefix-SID Index: 22, Algorithm:0, R:0 N:1 P:0 E:0 V:0 L:0
    Prefix Attribute Flags: X:0 R:0 N:1
  Hostname:       NPF-XR2
  Router Cap:     10.0.0.22, D:0, S:0
    Segment Routing: I:1 V:0, SRGB Base: 16000 Range: 8000
    SR Algorithm:
      Algorithm: 0
      Algorithm: 1
    Node Maximum SID Depth:
      Subtype: 1, Value: 10
```

By now, you should be familiar with both types of SR-TE policy configuration. In Example 16-12, you saw the commands you can use to verify whether an SR-TE policy is used for specific routes. Therefore, verification of the output is omitted in this example. The last step is to verify the data plane operation, as shown in Example 16-16.

Example 16-16 *SR-TE Data Plane Verification*

```
RP/0/0/CPU0:NPF-XR1# traceroute 192.168.33.33 source 192.168.11.11
Thu Apr  4 21:53:22.381 UTC

Type escape sequence to abort.
Tracing the route to 192.168.33.33

 1  10.11.22.22 [MPLS: Label 16033 Exp 0] 9 msec  0 msec  0 msec
 2  10.22.33.33 0 msec  *  0 msec


RP/0/0/CPU0:NPF-XR3# traceroute 192.168.11.11 source 192.168.33.33
Thu Apr  4 21:53:35.272 UTC

Type escape sequence to abort.
Tracing the route to 192.168.11.11

 1  10.22.33.22 [MPLS: Label 24001 Exp 0] 9 msec  0 msec  0 msec
 2  10.11.22.11 0 msec  *  9 msec
```

In Example 16-16, you can see that in both SR-TE policies, the traffic passes through NPF-XR2, as planned, and this shows that the SR-TE policies are working correctly. You can also see the labels from the corresponding label stacks (Prefix-SID based and Adj-SID based), so you know that the segment lists are also working as expected.

You might wonder how everything in this section applies to you. Today, networking is moving from speaking of routers/switches to focusing on containers/services, and it's essential to be able to create a path for an application from the user to the content with an individual KPI. SR-TE makes this possible by allowing you to program the proper label stack on head-end routers or even on the end hosts within a data center. So far in this chapter, you have seen only manual configuration. Next, you will learn how to use programmable methods to collect Segment Routing information from a network and export it to SDN controllers and how to dynamically provision head-end routers in a programmatic way. Again, this programmability is built on a router's capability to program a path over the network by using SR-TE.

BGP Link State (BGP-LS)

The next step in the discovery of the programmability framework for service provider networks is to understand how the network states, including topology information and latency, can be collected. There are several ways to achieve this. The easiest way is to integrate an SDN controller in the IGP domain so that it can directly listen for IGP updates. The main drawback of this method is that the SDN controller will have visibility into only a single domain and won't be able to see the topology from other domains. The best approach today is to use a specific address family of BGP called BGP-LS.

BGP-LS Basics

BGP-LS is a new address family (or multiprotocol extension) for BGP. (The AFI/SAFI indicator is 16388/71.) RFC 7752 defines BGP-LS, and you can refer to it if you want to learn about each bit and byte.

In a nutshell, BGP-LS allows you to convert an IGP topology running IS-IS or OSPFv2/v3 into BGP routes, officially called BGP NLRI (network layer reachability information), and transmit this information to the SDN controller. The SDN controller can be located anywhere, and there is no need to connect it to the IGP domain directly. Moreover, the whole IGP topology—that is, the whole IS-IS or OSPF link state database (LSDB)—is exported over a single session, although it's recommended to have at least two sessions for redundancy. Figure 16-10 shows a high-level overview of BGP-LS peering.

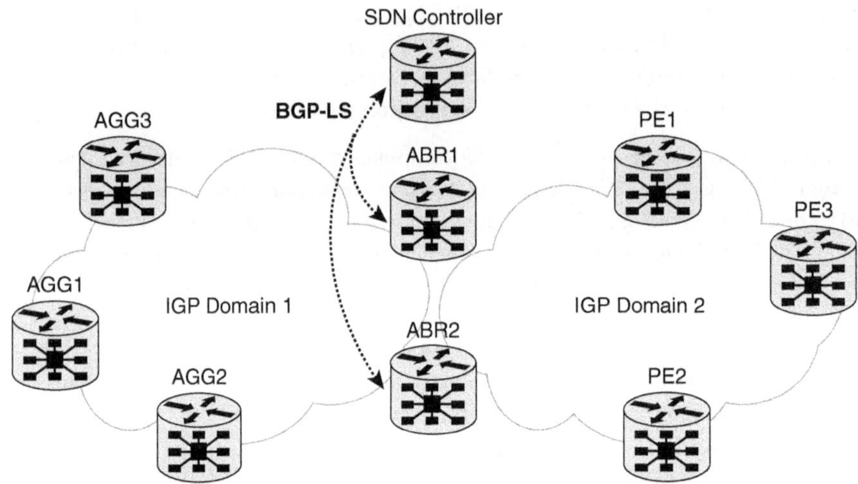

Figure 16-10 *High-Level BGP-LS Peering Architecture*

ABRs are typically the best choice for establishing BGP-LS peering with an SDN controller because ABRs have visibility in multiple IGP domains. These are the most common combinations:

- IGP Domain 1 is IS-IS process 0, level 1, and IGP Domain 2 is IS-IS process 0, level 2.
- IGP Domain 1 is IS-IS process 1, level 2, and IGP Domain 2 is IS-IS process 0, level 2.
- IGP Domain 1 is OSPF process 0, area nonzero (1, 2, and so on), and IGP Domain 2 is OSPF process 0, area 0.
- IGP Domain 1 is OSPF process 1, area 0, and IGP Domain 2 is OSPF process 0, area 0.

Other combinations are also possible.

A BGP session can be built using either an internal or external design option. Which you choose doesn't matter too much, and you should follow the logic of your network:

- If you have a single AS for all your BGP domains, it makes sense to establish an iBGP session from the ABRs to your SDN controller.
- If you have multiple AS numbers (for example, if each IGP domain has its own AS), you can have the SDN controller in its own AS as well.

You should pay attention to standard BGP rules when building connectivity to an SDN controller (for example, a split-horizon rule for iBGP, a multihop rule for eBGP).

Before configuring your first BGP-LS session, it's essential to understand some security considerations. The message flow in terms of the BGP NLRI is unidirectional from the network functions in your network running IGP to the SDN controller. You should drop all incoming BGP-LS updates on your routers and filter all the outgoing BGP-LS updates on the SDN controller (if possible).

Figure 16-11 shows a simple lab topology used to configure BGP-LS in this section.

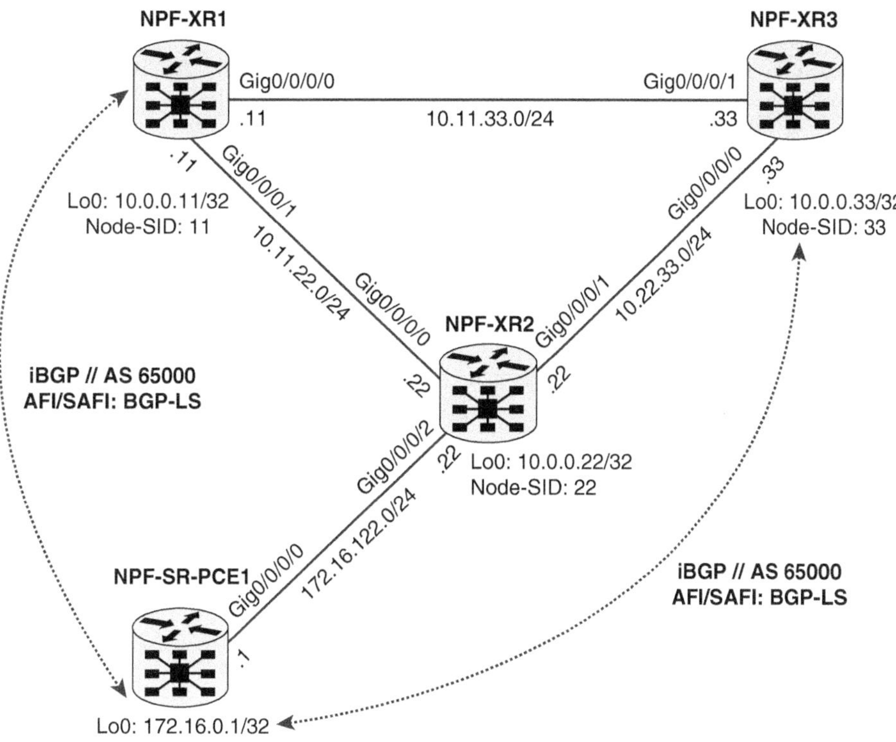

Figure 16-11 *Lab Topology for BGP-LS*

As you can see, this topology is the same as the topology used for Segment Routing earlier in this chapter (refer to Figure 16-4) —and this makes sense because the SDN controller should extend the capability of Segment Routing. The Cisco SDN controller, which calculates end-to-end MPLS paths, is called SR-PCE now; previously, it was known as XTC (XR Traffic Controller). In terms of connectivity, note the following configurations:

- The direct link between NPF-XR2 and NPF-SR-PCE1 isn't propagated into the core IS-IS process.
- NPF-XR2 has a static route pointing to NPF-XR2 Loopback0, which is propagated into the core IS-IS.
- NPF-XR2 has a default route pointing toward NPF-XR2 over a direct link.
- There are two internal BGP sessions, between NPF-SR-PCE1 and NPF-XR1 and between NPF-SR-PCE1 and NPF-XR3.
- The route filtering is applied such that NPF-XR1 and NPF-XR2 can only send BGP-LS updates, and NPF-SR-PCE1 can only receive them.

As you can see, this scenario is relatively easy from a configuration perspective. However, it requires two major code blocks: one to establish IP connectivity between network elements (that is, configure routing) and another to establish BGP-LS peering.

Example 16-17 shows the details for the first code block, which establishes IP connectivity between the network function from the lab and the SDN controller.

Example 16-17 *Configuring Basic Routing Between Routers and an SDN Controller*

```
RP/0/0/CPU0:NPF-XR2(config)# show conf
Sat Apr 20 12:48:02.226 UTC
Building configuration...
!! IOS XR Configuration 6.5.1
interface GigabitEthernet0/0/0/2
 ipv4 address 172.16.122.22 255.255.255.0
 no shutdown
!
!
prefix-set PS_SR_PCE_LO
  172.16.0.1/32
end-set
!
route-policy RP_STATIC_TO_ISIS
  if destination in PS_SR_PCE_LO then
    pass
  endif
end-policy
!
router static
 address-family ipv4 unicast
  172.16.0.1/32 GigabitEthernet0/0/0/2 172.16.122.1
 !
!
router isis CORE
 address-family ipv4 unicast
  redistribute static route-policy RP_STATIC_TO_ISIS
 !
!
end


RP/0/0/CPU0:NPF-SR-PCE1(config)# show conf
Sat Apr 20 13:02:08.597 UTC
Building configuration...
!! IOS XR Configuration 6.5.1
```

```
interface Loopback0
 ipv4 address 172.16.0.1 255.255.255.255
!
interface GigabitEthernet0/0/0/0
 ipv4 address 172.16.122.1 255.255.255.0
 no shutdown
!
router static
 address-family ipv4 unicast
  0.0.0.0/0 GigabitEthernet0/0/0/0 172.16.122.22
 !
!
end
```

Note If you are familiar with the Cisco IOS XR operating system, Example 16-17 should make sense to you, as it doesn't touch on the BGP session yet but just shows the essential connectivity. If Example 16-17 does not make sense to you, you may want to spend some time trying to brush up on Cisco IOS XR and/or Cisco NX-OS.

Example 16-18 shows the configuration of the internal BGP session for the BGP-LS address family.

Example 16-18 *Configuring BGP-LS Peering*

```
RP/0/0/CPU0:NPF-XR1(config)# show conf
Sat Apr 20 17:27:14.291 UTC
Building configuration...
!! IOS XR Configuration 6.5.1
!
route-policy RP_DROP_ALL
  drop
end-policy
!
route-policy RP_PASS_ALL
  pass
end-policy
!
router bgp 65000
 bgp router-id 10.0.0.11
 bgp log neighbor changes detail
 address-family link-state link-state
 !
```

```
 neighbor 172.16.0.1
  update-source Loopback0
  remote-as 65000
  address-family link-state link-state
   route-policy RP_DROP_ALL in
   route-policy RP_PASS_ALL out
  !
 !
!
end


RP/0/0/CPU0:NPF-SR-PCE1(config)# show conf
Sat Apr 20 17:32:59.114 UTC
Building configuration...
!! IOS XR Configuration 6.5.1.34I
!
route-policy RP_DROP_ALL
  drop
end-policy
!
route-policy RP_PASS_ALL
  pass
end-policy
!
router bgp 65000
 bgp router-id 172.16.0.1
 bgp log neighbor changes detail
 address-family link-state link-state
 !
 neighbor 10.0.0.11
  remote-as 65000
  update-source Loopback0
  address-family link-state link-state
   route-policy RP_PASS_ALL in
   route-policy RP_DROP_ALL out
  !
 !
 neighbor 10.0.0.33
  remote-as 65000
  update-source Loopback0
```

```
  address-family link-state link-state
   route-policy RP_PASS_ALL in
   route-policy RP_DROP_ALL out
  !
 !
!
end
```

Example 16-18 shows the configuration of a peering session between NPF-XR1 and NPF-SR-PCE1. (The configuration of NPF-XR3 is omitted from this section for the sake of brevity.) If you are familiar with BGP configuration on the Cisco IOS XR platform, the provided output should be quite easy to understand: You enable the proper address family within the BGP context and then enable peering with the corresponding neighbor. The configuration of the route policies isn't mandatory, but it helps to improve the stability, as explained previously. Example 16-19 shows the status of the established BGP sessions from the NPF-SR-PCE1 perspective.

Example 16-19 *Overview of BGP-LS Peering*

```
RP/0/0/CPU0:NPF-SR-PCE1# show bgp link-state link-state summary
Sat Apr 20 19:24:44.834 UTC
BGP router identifier 172.16.0.1, local AS number 65000
BGP generic scan interval 60 secs
Non-stop routing is enabled
BGP table state: Active
Table ID: 0x0   RD version: 0
BGP main routing table version 1
BGP NSR Initial initsync version 1 (Reached)
BGP NSR/ISSU Sync-Group versions 0/0
BGP scan interval 60 secs

BGP is operating in STANDALONE mode.


Process       RcvTblVer   bRIB/RIB   LabelVer  ImportVer  SendTblVer  StandbyVer
Speaker               1          1          1          1           1           0

Neighbor        Spk    AS MsgRcvd MsgSent   TblVer  InQ OutQ  Up/Down  St/PfxRcd
10.0.0.11         0 65000     111     111        1    0    0 01:48:50          0
10.0.0.33         0 65000     111     111        1    0    0 01:48:28          0
```

You can see in Example 16-19 that the status of the sessions is up, but there is no prefix received. This is correct because so far there has been no configuration that defines which IGP information should be exported to the SDN controller.

BGP-LS Route Types

Before we go further into the BGP-LS NLRI types, it's essential that you understand one more detail. Upon the export of IGP topology to the SDN controller, there must be some additional parameters that make it clear which IGP domain routes belong to. Because several IGPs might be configured on a single router, each IGP domain should have an identifier so that the SDN controller can match the routing information to a specific domain. This identifier is called an *instance identifier*, and it is part of the configuration of the export process.

Another important aspect is the idea of abstraction. IS-IS and OSPF have different structures for their link-state databases. However, an SDN controller should have an end-to-end view of the topology and should be able to program MPLS LSP regardless of the source IGP. This is why one of the core ideas of BGP-LS is to create BGP-LS routes that are as similar as possible for IS-IS and OSPF. This is achieved by using a standard BGP approach for information encoding using TLV (type length value) triples. A TLV defines a particular piece of information, where the type codes the meaning of the information, the length indicates how many subsequent octets should be analyzed, and the value is the parameter itself. TLV is a very flexible mechanism, as it makes it possible to create a single type values for certain information from both IS-IS and OSPF (for example, a router, link IP addresses) and to create additional TLV triples for IGP-specific information. All the BGP updates (not only BGP-LS) are built using the TLV approach.

There are officially four BGP-LS route types (although, technically, the third and fourth types listed here are equal but used for different address families):

- **Node NLRI:** This type represents the node in the IGP topology, which is similar to the node in the traffic engineering database (TED) with MPLS-TE.
- **Link NLRI:** This type represents the connectivity between the nodes defined in Node NLRI.
- **IPv4 topology prefix NLRI:** This type is used to encode an IPv4 address associated with any interface or redistributed from another protocol.
- **IPv6 topology prefix NLRI:** This type is used to encode an IPv6 address associated with any interface or redistributed from another protocol.

Each of these route types has some set of mandatory and optional TLV triples. Next, we will look into details of each route, using real examples. To have such routes, the routers NPF-XR1 and NPF-XR3 should export the IS-IS database into BGP-LS, as shown in Figure 16-11.

Example 16-20 shows the configuration that needs to be implemented for NPF-XR2. (Although it is not shown, the configuration for NPF-XR3 is similar.)

Example 16-20 *Distributing IS-IS to BGP-LS*

```
RP/0/0/CPU0:NPF-XR1(config-isis)# show conf
Sat Apr 20 20:34:22.082 UTC
Building configuration...
!! IOS XR Configuration 6.5.1
router isis CORE
 distribute link-state instance-id 32 level 2
!
end
```

This configuration is straightforward: Under the IGP that you want to redistribute over BGP-LS, you configure the corresponding command, including the instance identifier, and, optionally, provide some further details (for example, the IS-IS Level 2–only routes in Example 16-20). When the configuration is applied on both routers, the IS-IS routes are converted into BGP-LS updates and sent to the SDN controller. Using the verification command on NPF-SR-PCE1, you can see that routes are propagated (see Example 16-21).

Example 16-21 *Propagating the BGP-LS Routes*

```
RP/0/0/CPU0:NPF-SR-PCE1# show bgp link-state link-state summary
Sat Apr 20 20:44:56.475 UTC
BGP router identifier 172.16.0.1, local AS number 65000
BGP generic scan interval 60 secs
Non-stop routing is enabled
BGP table state: Active
Table ID: 0x0   RD version: 0
BGP main routing table version 1
BGP NSR Initial initsync version 1 (Reached)
BGP NSR/ISSU Sync-Group versions 0/0
BGP scan interval 60 secs

BGP is operating in STANDALONE mode.


Process       RcvTblVer   bRIB/RIB   LabelVer  ImportVer  SendTblVer  StandbyVer
Speaker               1          1          1          1           1           0

Neighbor        Spk    AS MsgRcvd MsgSent   TblVer  InQ OutQ  Up/Down  St/PfxRcd
10.0.0.11         0 65000     201     191        1    0    0 03:09:02         13
10.0.0.33         0 65000     201     191        1    0    0 03:08:40         13
```

As you can see in Example 16-21, NPF-XR1 and NPF-XR2 send 13 routes each. These 13 routes contain all three types of BGP-LS routes: node, link, and prefix. Example 16-22 shows some details of these routes.

Example 16-22 *Content of the BGP-LS RIB*

```
RP/0/0/CPU0:NPF-SR-PCE1# show bgp link-state link-state
Sat Apr 20 22:39:05.665 UTC
BGP router identifier 172.16.0.1, local AS number 65000
BGP generic scan interval 60 secs
Non-stop routing is enabled
BGP table state: Active
Table ID: 0x0   RD version: 0
BGP main routing table version 1
BGP NSR Initial initsync version 1 (Reached)
BGP NSR/ISSU Sync-Group versions 0/0
BGP scan interval 60 secs

Status codes: s suppressed, d damped, h history, * valid, > best
              i - internal, r RIB-failure, S stale, N Nexthop-discard
Origin codes: i - IGP, e - EGP, ? - incomplete
Prefix codes: E link, V node, T IP reacheable route, u/U unknown
              I Identifier, N local node, R remote node, L link, P prefix
              L1/L2 ISIS level-1/level-2, O OSPF, D direct, S static/peer-node
              a area-ID, l link-ID, t topology-ID, s ISO-ID,
              c confed-ID/ASN, b bgp-identifier, r router-ID,
              i if-address, n nbr-address, o OSPF Route-type, p IP-prefix
              d designated router address
   Network            Next Hop            Metric LocPrf Weight Path
* i[V][L2][I0x20][N[c65000][b0.0.0.0][s0100.0000.0011.00]]/328
                      10.0.0.11                     100      0 i
* i                   10.0.0.33                     100      0 i
* i[V][L2][I0x20][N[c65000][b0.0.0.0][s0100.0000.0022.00]]/328
                      10.0.0.11                     100      0 i
* i                   10.0.0.33                     100      0 i
* i[V][L2][I0x20][N[c65000][b0.0.0.0][s0100.0000.0033.00]]/328
                      10.0.0.11                     100      0 i
* i                   10.0.0.33                     100      0 i
* i[E][L2][I0x20][N[c65000][b0.0.0.0][s0100.0000.0011.00]][R[c65000][b0.0.0.0]
   [s0100.0000.0022.00]][L[i10.11.22.11][n10.11.22.22]]/696
                      10.0.0.11                     100      0 i
* i                   10.0.0.33                     100      0 i
* i[E][L2][I0x20][N[c65000][b0.0.0.0][s0100.0000.0011.00]][R[c65000][b0.0.0.0]
   [s0100.0000.0033.00]][L[i10.11.33.11][n10.11.33.33]]/696
                      10.0.0.11                     100      0 i
* i                   10.0.0.33                     100      0 i
* i[E][L2][I0x20][N[c65000][b0.0.0.0][s0100.0000.0022.00]][R[c65000][b0.0.0.0]
   [s0100.0000.0011.00]][L[i10.11.22.22][n10.11.22.11]]/696
                      10.0.0.11                     100      0 i
* i                   10.0.0.33                     100      0 i
```

```
* i[E][L2][I0x20][N[c65000][b0.0.0.0][s0100.0000.0022.00]][R[c65000][b0.0.0.0]
  [s0100.0000.0033.00]][L[i10.22.33.22][n10.22.33.33]]/696
                     10.0.0.11                     100      0 i
* i                  10.0.0.33                     100      0 i
* i[E][L2][I0x20][N[c65000][b0.0.0.0][s0100.0000.0033.00]][R[c65000][b0.0.0.0]
  [s0100.0000.0011.00]][L[i10.11.33.33][n10.11.33.11]]/696
                     10.0.0.11                     100      0 i
* i                  10.0.0.33                     100      0 i
* i[E][L2][I0x20][N[c65000][b0.0.0.0][s0100.0000.0033.00]][R[c65000][b0.0.0.0]
  [s0100.0000.0022.00]][L[i10.22.33.33][n10.22.33.22]]/696
                     10.0.0.11                     100      0 i
* i                  10.0.0.33                     100      0 i
* i[T][L2][I0x20][N[c65000][b0.0.0.0][s0100.0000.0011.00]][P[p10.0.0.11/32]]/400
                     10.0.0.11                     100      0 i
* i                  10.0.0.33                     100      0 i
* i[T][L2][I0x20][N[c65000][b0.0.0.0][s0100.0000.0022.00]][P[p10.0.0.22/32]]/400
                     10.0.0.11                     100      0 i
* i                  10.0.0.33                     100      0 i
* i[T][L2][I0x20][N[c65000][b0.0.0.0][s0100.0000.0022.00]][P[p172.16.0.1/32]]/400
                     10.0.0.11                     100      0 i
* i                  10.0.0.33                     100      0 i
* i[T][L2][I0x20][N[c65000][b0.0.0.0][s0100.0000.0033.00]][P[p10.0.0.33/32]]/400
                     10.0.0.11                     100      0 i
* i                  10.0.0.33                     100      0 i
```

As mentioned earlier, Example 16-22 shows 13 routes, which are classified in the following manner:

- [V] routes are node NLRIs, so they represent nodes in the IGP topology. There are three nodes (NPF-XR1, NPF-XR2, and NPF-XR3); hence, there are three node NLRIs.
- [E] routes are link NLRIs, and they describe connectivity between nodes from [V] routes. Strictly speaking, each [E] documents a half-link, meaning the link parameters from the perspective of the particular node. This is why the full bidirectional link is described by a pair of [E] routes, exactly as is done in IS-IS or OSPF. There are three nodes connected in the topology shown in Figure 16-11; therefore, there are three bidirectional links or six unidirectional (half) links, which equals six [E] routes in the BGP-LS RIB.
- [T] routes are prefix NLRIs, which contain all IPv4 or IPv6 addresses (if present in the topology) advertised in the IGP. According to the lab configuration shown in Figure 16-11, IS-IS is running only for the IPv4 address family, and only Loopback0 IP addresses are advertised. In addition, there is one static route pointing to NPF-SR-PCE1 and distributed into IS-IS, so there are four IP addresses in the IGP topology and four [T] routes in the BGP-LS RIB.

Now that you have learned about route types in general, it's a good time to look at the details that can help you figure out what information is provided.

Node NLRI

Example 16-23 shows the details of the node NLRI.

Example 16-23 *Information in a Node NLRI*

```
RP/0/0/CPU0:NPF-SR-PCE1# show bgp link-state link-state
! The output is truncated for brevity
Status codes: s suppressed, d damped, h history, * valid, > best
              i - internal, r RIB-failure, S stale, N Nexthop-discard
Origin codes: i - IGP, e - EGP, ? - incomplete
Prefix codes: E link, V node, T IP reacheable route, u/U unknown
              I Identifier, N local node, R remote node, L link, P prefix
              L1/L2 ISIS level-1/level-2, O OSPF, D direct, S static/peer-node
              a area-ID, l link-ID, t topology-ID, s ISO-ID,
              c confed-ID/ASN, b bgp-identifier, r router-ID,
              i if-address, n nbr-address, o OSPF Route-type, p IP-prefix
              d designated router address
   Network            Next Hop            Metric LocPrf Weight Path
* i[V][L2][I0x20][N[c65000][b0.0.0.0][s0100.0000.0011.00]]/328
                      10.0.0.11                     100      0 i
* i                   10.0.0.33                     100      0 i
! Further output is truncated for brevity


RP/0/0/CPU0:NPF-SR-PCE1# show bgp link-state link-state [V][L2][I0x20][N[c65000]
   [b0.0.0.0][s0100.0000.0011.00]]/328
Sun Apr 21 10:03:24.983 UTC
BGP routing table entry for [V][L2][I0x20][N[c65000][b0.0.0.0]
   [s0100.0000.0011.00]]/328
Versions:
  Process           bRIB/RIB  SendTblVer
  Speaker                  0           0
Last Modified: Apr 20 20:34:30.541 for 13:28:54
Paths: (2 available, no best path)
  Not advertised to any peer
  Path #1: Received by speaker 0
  Not advertised to any peer
  Local
    10.0.0.11 (inaccessible) from 10.0.0.11 (10.0.0.11)
      Origin IGP, localpref 100, valid, internal
```

```
    Received Path ID 0, Local Path ID 0, version 0
    Link-state: Node-name: NPF-XR1, ISIS area: 49.00.00, SRGB: 16000:8000
                SR-ALG: 0 SR-ALG: 1 , SRLB: 15000:1000 , MSD: Type 1 Value 10

Path #2: Received by speaker 0
Not advertised to any peer
Local
  10.0.0.33 (inaccessible) from 10.0.0.33 (10.0.0.33)
    Origin IGP, localpref 100, valid, internal
    Received Path ID 0, Local Path ID 0, version 0
    Link-state: Node-name: NPF-XR1, ISIS area: 49.00.00, SRGB: 16000:8000
                SR-ALG: 0 SR-ALG: 1 , SRLB: 15000:1000 , MSD: Type 1 Value 10
```

Before we look at the content of the route itself, we need to examine the route naming. The legend provided at the beginning of the full BGP-LS RIB output is very detailed and helps you easily read the route. For instance, from the route [V][L2][I0x20][N[c65000][b0.0.0.0][s0100.0000.0011.00]]/328, you can glean the following information:

- **V**: This indicates a node NLRI.
- **L2**: This indicates IS-IS Level 2.
- **I0x20**: The instance-id is 32 when configured during an export on NPF-XR1 and NPF-XR3. (0x20 in hexadecimal equals 32 in decimal.)
- **N**: This describes the local node. (There is also a remote node, which is covered later in this section.)
- **c65000**: This is the BGP ASN of the router exporting information about this node.
- **b0.0.0.0**: This is the BGP-LS identifier (which is all zeros by default); it can be altered in complex topologies.
- **s0100.0000.0011.00**: This is the node part of IS-IS NET without the area part.
- **328**: This is the overall length of the route, in bytes. It is really a cosmetic entry, as it is not meaningful from a user standpoint and is no longer visible in newer Cisco IOS XR releases. (In further route output in this chapter, this parameter is omitted from explanation.)

Even just this information gives you some insights into the topology. In addition, the second part of Example 16-23 provides further facts about the node, including the host-name and important Segment Routing parameters, such as Segment Routing Global/Local Block, supported SR algorithms, and MSD (which is type 1 with value 10). If you compare this information with the content of the IS-IS LSDB in Example 16-2, you can see that all the fields not directly related to IP addresses (IP reachability information) or links (IS-Extended) are copied to this node NLRI.

Link NLRI

Example 16-24 shows the information provided in a link NLRI, which connects node NLRIs.

Example 16-24 *Information in a Link NLRI*

```
RP/0/0/CPU0:NPF-SR-PCE1# show bgp link-state link-state
! The output is truncated for brevity
Status codes: s suppressed, d damped, h history, * valid, > best
              i - internal, r RIB-failure, S stale, N Nexthop-discard
Origin codes: i - IGP, e - EGP, ? - incomplete
Prefix codes: E link, V node, T IP reacheable route, u/U unknown
              I Identifier, N local node, R remote node, L link, P prefix
              L1/L2 ISIS level-1/level-2, O OSPF, D direct, S static/peer-node
              a area-ID, l link-ID, t topology-ID, s ISO-ID,
              c confed-ID/ASN, b bgp-identifier, r router-ID,
              i if-address, n nbr-address, o OSPF Route-type, p IP-prefix
              d designated router address
   Network            Next Hop            Metric LocPrf Weight Path
* i[E][L2][I0x20][N[c65000][b0.0.0.0][s0100.0000.0011.00]][R[c65000][b0.0.0.0]
  [s0100.0000.0022.00]][L[i10.11.22.11][n10.11.22.22]]/696
                      10.0.0.11                     100      0 i
* i                   10.0.0.33                     100      0 i
! Further output is truncated for brevity


RP/0/0/CPU0:NPF-SR-PCE1# show bgp link-state link-state [E][L2][I0x20][N[c65000]
  [b0.0.0.0][s0100.0000.0011.00]][R[c65000][b0.0.0.0][s0100.0000.0022.00]]
  [L[i10.11.22.11][n10.11.22.22]]/696
Sun Apr 21 10:31:47.446 UTC
BGP routing table entry for [E][L2][I0x20][N[c65000][b0.0.0.0][s0100.0000.0011.00]]
  [R[c65000][b0.0.0.0][s0100.0000.0022.00]][L[i10.11.22.11][n10.11.22.22]]/696
Versions:
  Process           bRIB/RIB  SendTblVer
  Speaker                  0           0
Last Modified: Apr 20 20:34:30.541 for 13:57:16
Paths: (2 available, no best path)
  Not advertised to any peer
  Path #1: Received by speaker 0
  Not advertised to any peer
  Local
    10.0.0.11 (inaccessible) from 10.0.0.11 (10.0.0.11)
      Origin IGP, localpref 100, valid, internal
      Received Path ID 0, Local Path ID 0, version 0
```

```
    Link-state: metric: 10, ADJ-SID: 24003(30) , MSD: Type 1 Value 10

Path #2: Received by speaker 0
Not advertised to any peer
Local
  10.0.0.33 (inaccessible) from 10.0.0.33 (10.0.0.33)
    Origin IGP, localpref 100, valid, internal
    Received Path ID 0, Local Path ID 0, version 0
    Link-state: metric: 10, ADJ-SID: 24003(30) , MSD: Type 1 Value 10
```

Following the same approach as for the node NLRI, for the link NLRI, we start with the route itself. From the link NLRI [E][L2][I0x20][N[c65000][b0.0.0.0][s0100.0000.0011.00]][R[c65000][b0.0.0.0][s0100.0000.0022.00]][L[i10.11.22.11][n10.11.22.22]]/696, you can glean the following information:

- **E:** This indicates a link NLRI.
- **L2:** This indicates IS-IS Level 2.
- **I0x20:** The instance-id is 32 when configured during an export on NPF-XR1 and NPF-XR3. (0x20 in hexadecimal equals 32 in decimal.)
- **N:** This describes the local node, and connectivity is described from the perspective of this node. (That is, the information is extracted from IS-IS LSP for this node.)
- **c65000:** This is the BGP ASN of the router exporting information about this node.
- **b0.0.0.0:** This is the BGP-LS identifier (which is all zeros by default), and it can be altered in complex topologies.
- **s0100.0000.0011.00:** This is the node part of IS-IS NET, without the area part.
- **R:** This is the remote node, or the link endpoint to which the local node is connected.
- **L:** This indicates that parameters of the link itself are provided.
- **i10.11.22.11:** This is the interface IP address of the local node.
- **n10.11.22.22:** This is the neighbor IP address, which is basically the interface IP address of the remote node.
- **696:** This is the overall length of the route, in bytes.

By this time, you should be starting to see that by looking at BGP-LS routes, you can construct the topology just as the SDN controller does. In the second part of the output in Example 16-24, you see further details, including metrics associated with the link, Segment Routing Adj-SID (MPLS label), and MSD. Generally, the content of the link NLRI is extracted from the IS-Extended entries of the IS-IS LSP, as shown in Example 16-2.

Prefix NLRI

The third BGP-LS route type is the prefix NLRI, which contains the IP reachability information and related parameters (see Example 16-25).

Example 16-25 *Information in a Prefix NLRI*

```
RP/0/0/CPU0:NPF-SR-PCE1# show bgp link-state link-state
! The output is truncated for brevity
Status codes: s suppressed, d damped, h history, * valid, > best
              i - internal, r RIB-failure, S stale, N Nexthop-discard
Origin codes: i - IGP, e - EGP, ? - incomplete
Prefix codes: E link, V node, T IP reacheable route, u/U unknown
              I Identifier, N local node, R remote node, L link, P prefix
              L1/L2 ISIS level-1/level-2, O OSPF, D direct, S static/peer-node
              a area-ID, l link-ID, t topology-ID, s ISO-ID,
              c confed-ID/ASN, b bgp-identifier, r router-ID,
              i if-address, n nbr-address, o OSPF Route-type, p IP-prefix
              d designated router address
   Network            Next Hop            Metric LocPrf Weight Path
* i[T][L2][I0x20][N[c65000][b0.0.0.0][s0100.0000.0011.00]][P[p10.0.0.11/32]]/400
                      10.0.0.11                     100      0 i
* i                   10.0.0.33                     100      0 i
! Further output is truncated for brevity


RP/0/0/CPU0:NPF-SR-PCE1# show bgp link-state link-state [T][L2][I0x20][N[c65000]
   [b0.0.0.0][s0100.0000.0011.00]][P[p10.0.0.11/32]]/400
Sun Apr 21 10:57:39.610 UTC
BGP routing table entry for [T][L2][I0x20][N[c65000][b0.0.0.0][s0100.0000.0011.00]]
   [P[p10.0.0.11/32]]/400
Versions:
  Process           bRIB/RIB  SendTblVer
  Speaker                  0           0
Last Modified: Apr 20 20:34:30.541 for 14:23:09
Paths: (2 available, no best path)
  Not advertised to any peer
  Path #1: Received by speaker 0
  Not advertised to any peer
  Local
    10.0.0.11 (inaccessible) from 10.0.0.11 (10.0.0.11)
      Origin IGP, localpref 100, valid, internal
      Received Path ID 0, Local Path ID 0, version 0
      Link-state: Metric: 0, PFX-SID: 11(40/0) , Extended IGP flags: 0x20
```

```
Path #2: Received by speaker 0
Not advertised to any peer
Local
  10.0.0.33 (inaccessible) from 10.0.0.33 (10.0.0.33)
    Origin IGP, localpref 100, valid, internal
    Received Path ID 0, Local Path ID 0, version 0
    Link-state: Metric: 0, PFX-SID: 11(40/0) , Extended IGP flags: 0x20
```

Following the same approach as for the node NLRI and link NLRI, for the prefix NLRI, we start with the route itself. From the prefix NLRI [T][L2][I0x20][N[c65000][b0.0.0.0][s0100.0000.0011.00]][P[p10.0.0.11/32]]/400, you can glean the following information:

- **T:** This is a prefix NLRI.
- **L2:** This indicates IS-IS Level 2.
- **I0x20:** The instance-id is 32 when configured during an export on NPF-XR1 and NPF-XR3. (0x20 in hexadecimal equals 32 in decimal.)
- **N:** This indicates a local node.
- **c65000:** This is the BGP ASN of the router exporting information about this node.
- **b0.0.0.0:** This is the BGP-LS identifier (which is all zeros by default), and it can be altered in complex topologies.
- **s0100.0000.0011.00:** This is the node part of IS-IS NET without the area part.
- **P:** This is the prefix details.
- **p10.0.0.11/32:** This is the IP prefix.
- **400:** This is the overall length of the route, in bytes.

You may have noted that the local node is the same in the routes shown in Examples 16-23 through 16-25; this means the different pieces of information are related to the same node. All these routes are coming from the IS-IS LSP generated by NPF-XR1. The second part of Example 16-25 shows additional information conveyed inside the prefix SID: metric, Segment Routing prefix SID, and extended flags. To map this information to the IS-IS LSP, you can look at the IP-Extended entries as shown in Example 16-2.

In this section, you have learned how the IGP topology, including Segment Routing information, can be converted into BGP-LS routes and sent to the SDN controller, which uses these routes to build end-to-end network topology in order to provide the proper path.

Path Computation Element Protocol (PCEP)

As mentioned earlier in this chapter, the primary goal of PCEP is to program end-to-end MPLS LSPs, taking into account various constraints, such as latency, affinity, and path disjointedness. Earlier in this chapter, in the section "Segment Routing Traffic

Engineering," you saw that MPLS LSPs can be configured and calculated locally on every edge router without a central entity that has an end-to-end view of the MPLS domain. However, this solution isn't scalable, as it would require you to manage probably hundreds of endpoints separately. An additional drawback is that each router can see only its part of the routing domain (for example, a single area for OSPF or level for IS-IS); therefore, a router simply can't calculate the path correctly. The approach with a centralized SDN controller aims to overcome these limitations by offloading the computation tasks to the SDN controller. Given that the SDN controller has already learned topology over BGP-LS, there is a need for a protocol to communicate between the router that wants to build an MPLS tunnel and the SDN controller that can compute the path for the MPLS tunnel. That is where PCEP comes in.

PCEP is a protocol used for communication between a PCE (path computation element) and a PCC (path communication client), as shown in Figure 16-12.

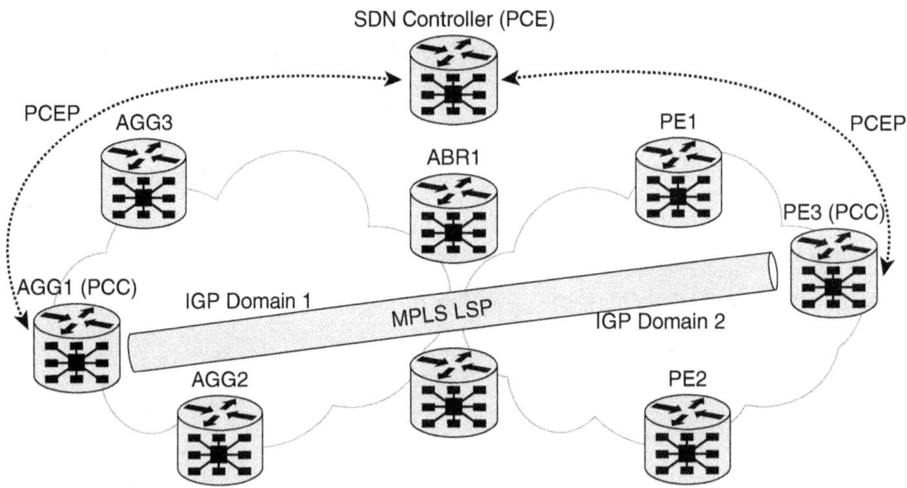

Figure 16-12 *High Level PCEP Architecture*

In Figure 16-12, PCC is an edge router that creates MPLS tunnels (the tunnel head end) but doesn't calculate the path. PCE is a function that makes the part of an SDN controller that can calculate the end-to-end MPLS path within a single MPLS domain or across multiple domains and provide this information to PCC.

There are many RFCs covering PCEP, and these are the most important of them:

- RFC 4655, "A Path Computation Element (PCE)-Based Architecture"
- RFC 5440, "Path Computation Element (PCE) Communication Protocol (PCEP)"
- RFC 8231, "Path Computation Element Communication Protocol (PCEP) Extensions for Stateful PCE"
- RFC 8281, "Path Computation Element Communication Protocol (PCEP) Extensions for PCE-Initiated LSP Setup in a Stateful PCE Model"

RFC 4655 describes general requirements and approaches to PCE deployment, including various architecture scenarios. RFC 5440 covers packet flow for the PCEP interactions, as well as the PCEP message format and their and PCEP operation in a traditional deployment, where the PCE doesn't control the MPLS LSP after initial setup. RFCs 8231 and 8281 define the extensions to PCEP for new networks, where the PCE can control the MPLS LSPs throughout its lifecycle (not only through the initial calculation and setup).

Before we get into the details of PCEP call flow, there is one more concept you should learn. Within the PCEP architecture, there are two possible ways an MPLS LSP can be established:

- **PCC initiated:** In this approach, the PCC (an ingress router) asks the PCE (an SDN controller) to calculate the path to the specific egress router. Typically, this is triggered by the configuration of the MPLS LSP on PCC with information that the PCE should use for path calculation. Two options are possible:
  - **With delegation:** The PCE takes further control of the MPLS LSP.
  - **Without delegation:** The PCE only calculates the path and doesn't take part in further MPLS LSP control.
- **PCE initiated:** With this approach, the PCE (the SDN controller) sends the order to the PCC (the ingress router) to create an MPLS LSP to the particular egress router. This is triggered by the creation of the proper configuration (SR policy) on the SDN controller.

The first mechanism is a more traditional one in terms of configuring the endpoint, and the SDN controller just does some enhancement. The second mechanism is more scalable and fits better with network programmability, as the MPLS LSP is really programmed from the central entity.

Typical PCEP Call Flow

PCEP is a connection-oriented protocol, and to a certain extent, its session-handling capabilities are similar to those of BGP. For instance, PCEP uses TCP as the transport to build the session between a PCE and a PCC, much as BGP does. The TCP port for PCEP is 4189.

Another important factor is the way a PCEP session is established. As you might have noticed in Figure 16-12, there can be many PCCs in a network (for example, all the PE routers) and fewer PCEs. This is why a PCC is configured with the PCE's IP address as the destination; the PCC initiates a PCEP session toward the PCE, and the PCE only listens for incoming connections on the defined IP address and TCP port 4189. Figure 16-13 illustrates the PCEP session establishment process.

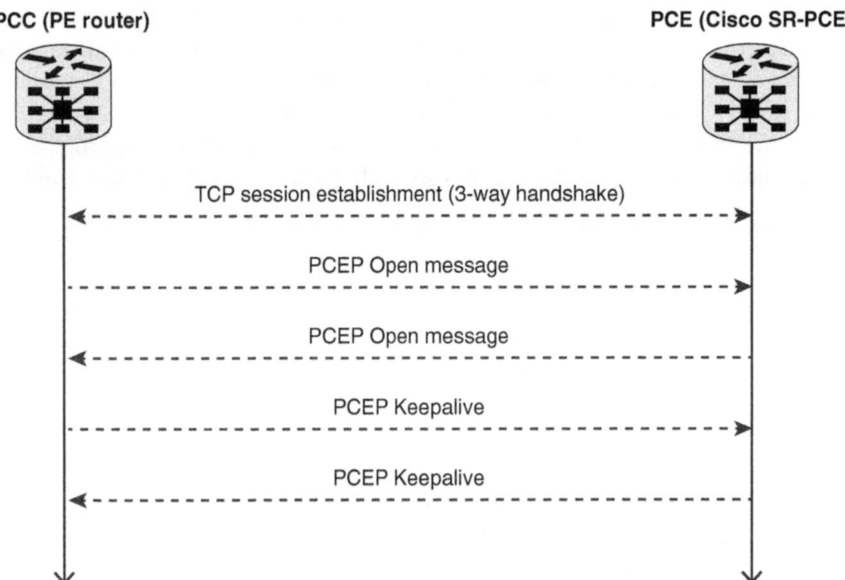

Figure 16-13 *PCEP Session Establishment*

The first step of the PCEP session establishment process is to establish the TCP session on port 4189, where the PCC initiates the PCEP session toward the PCE.

Once the TCP session is established, the PCC sends an PCEP Open message—which contains a version of PCEP, keepalive/dead timers, SID, flags, and capabilities—to the PCE, and the PCE sends its own Open message to the PCC. Much as in BGP session establishment, the transmitting/receiving process with the PCEP Open messages is asynchronous, which means it could also be the case that the PCE sends an Open message earlier than the PCC, as the source/destination TCP ports for a PCEP session are known from the initial three-way handshake process. Actually, it isn't vital who sends the Open message first. However, what is essential is that the network element must acknowledge receipt of the PCEP Open message with a PCEP Keepalive message. After both the PCE and PCC receive the PCEP Keepalive messages in response to the PCEP Open messages they sent, the PCEP session is moved to an up state.

RFC 5440 states that it is not mandatory for PCEP Keepalive messages to be sent regularly between the PCC and PCE. If the messages are sent, PCEP relies on them to track the reachability of the peer. If the messages aren't sent, PCEP relies on the TCP level (that is, the TCP session) to track whether the peer is alive. The particular implementation of the Keepalive mechanism is vendor dependent, but RFC 5440 recommends having PCEP Keepalive running. This RFC proposes to send a PCEP Keepalive message every 30 seconds (according to the keepalive timer) and to keep waiting for PCEP Keepalive messages to come four times longer than the keepalive timer (dead timer); therefore, the default value of the dead timer is 120 seconds. Cisco IOS XR has these values (that is, a 30-second keepalive timer and 120-second dead timer) in its PCEP implementation by default. If no PCEP

Keepalive messages are received within the dead interval, the PCEP session is dropped as the PCEP peer is considered to be not alive.

There are a couple more items you need to know about the PCEP Open message before going further. The PCEP Open message contains information about the PCEP capabilities supported on the network element (both PCE and PCC). Based on the available capabilities, the PCC decides what it can request or send to the PCE and vice versa. The following are several of these capabilities:

- **Stateful:** In the PCEP Open messages sent by the PCC, this capability indicates that the PCC is willing to send the status of its MPLS LSPs to the PCE. On the other hand, if the PCE sends this capability, it instructs the PCC that the PCE wants to get MPLS LSP status updates. If this capability is negotiated, the PCC sends such updates to the PCE regularly, using PCEP report messages.
- **Instantiation:** In the PCEP Open message sent by the PCC, this capability informs the PCE that PCE-initiated MPLS LSPs are supported, and, therefore, the PCE can signal them to the PCC.
- **Update:** In the PCEP Open message sent by the PCC, this capability means that the PCC supports the delegation option; hence, the PCE may control the MPLS LSP on the PCC after it's initially signaled. Further, the PCC defines in the configuration whether the particular LSP is eligible for the delegation. Although this capability informs the PCE in general that the delegation might work with this PCC, the MPLS LSPs may not all be eligible for that.
- **Segment-Routing:** This capability means that the PCC can ask for the Segment Routing–based MPLS LSPs, and the PCE can provide the Segment Routing–based MPLS LSPs.
- **SR PCE:** This capability means that the PCC and/or PCE supports the establishment of MPLS traffic engineering tunnels using Segment Routing. This capability was defined later than the others, in RFC 8664 in December 2019.

If a PCEP session is successfully established and capabilities are negotiated, the next logical step in the PCEP process is to collect the information about the MPLS LSPs configured on the PCCs. This process, called *state synchronization*, is illustrated in Figure 16-14.

During the state synchronization process, each PCC signals all the configured MPLS LSPs to the PCE using PCEP report messages (introduced in RFC 8231), which contain information about the LSPs (bandwidth, operational status, delegation/revocation intention, and so on). If the information about MPLS LSPs needs to be sent in several messages, then all the messages besides the last one are sent with the Sync flag value 1, and the last one is sent with the Sync flag value 0, indicating that the message is the last one. The PCE doesn't need to respond to these messages if there are no problems; in this case, the PCE is overloaded). If a problem occurs, the PCE sends back to the PCC the PCEP Error message and the proper error code (see RFC 5440 and RFC 8231).

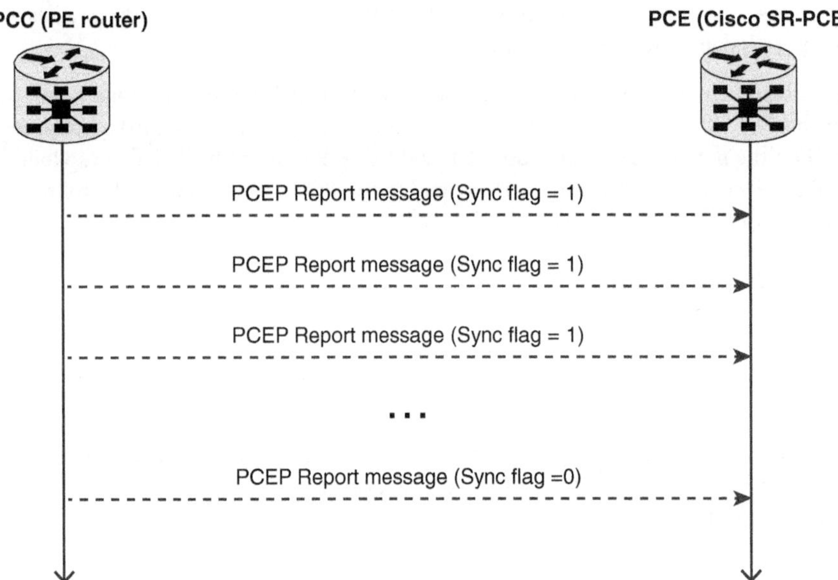

Figure 16-14 *PCEP State Synchronization*

As mentioned earlier, if the Update capability is negotiated between the PCC and PCE, the PCC can delegate control of a certain MPLS LSP to the PCE. This is usually done for inter-area scenarios because the PCE has the visibility into the whole IGP/MPLS domain or to reduce the computation efforts on the PCC. To delegate control, the PCC includes on the PCEP Report message the delegate flag set to 1 for an MPLS LSP that is to be delegated to the PCE. If the PCE accepts the delegation, it responds to the empty PCEP Update message with the MPLS LSP ID and delegation flag set to 1; if the PCE doesn't accept the delegation, it sends back the same message but with the delegation flag set to 0. Figure 16-15 shows both of these scenarios.

In the case of a successful delegation, the PCE is responsible for further control of the specific LSP. If the LSP needs to be changed—for example, if the network has changed and the new path should be used—the PCE sends the PCEP Update message with the proper content. The proper content is a new ERO (explicit route object) containing the Segment Routing label stack for SR-TE or a set of next hops for RSVP/MPLS-TE.

The last piece of information you need to know about LSP delegation is that the PCC can revoke the delegation of a specific LSP by sending a PCEP Report message with the LSP details (LSP ID, path, and so on) and the delegate flag set to 0. Alternatively, the PCE can release the delegation by sending the PCEP Update message with the LSP details and the delegation flag set to 0. In this case, the PCC takes back control and sends the PCEP Report message back to the PCE for this LSP with the delegation set to 0.

So far, you have learned about the operation of PCEP for existing MPLS LSPs with or without delegation. Next, you need to understand how the PCEP deals with the new MPLS LSPs, and there are two primary options available.

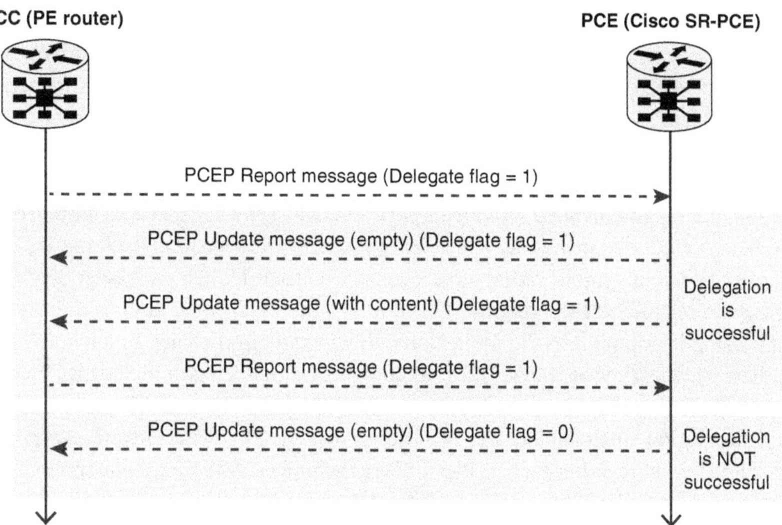

Figure 16-15 *PCEP LSP Delegation Options*

PCEP Call Flow with Delegation

For a PCC-initiated MPLS LSP (regardless of further delegation), the PCC asks the PCE to calculate the path to the particular endpoint. This is typically triggered via configuration of the SR-TE policy or MPLS-TE tunnel on the ingress router with the PCE computation. Figure 16-16 shows a PCC-initiated MPLS LSP.

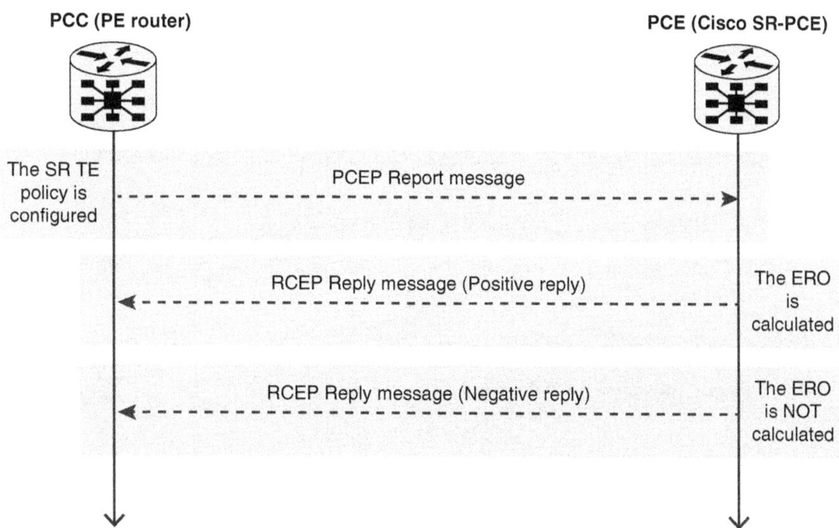

Figure 16-16 *PCC-Initiated MPLS LSP*

In Figure 16-16, you can see that the configuration of the SR-TE policy on the PCC triggers the PCEP Request message to the PCE. The PCEP Request contains the standard information for the MPLS LSP, such as the source IP address of the PCC (ingress router), the destination IP address of the egress router, the LSP ID, and the constraints (metric type, affinity, SRLG, and so on). If the PCE can find the path under the given constraints, it responds to the PCC with the PCEP Reply message with the ERO for this particular MPLS LSP. Such a message is called a *positive reply* because the MPLS LSP can be set up. If the PCE can't find the path under the given constraints, it transmits back the PCEP Reply message with the information that a path cannot be found. Such a message is called a *negative reply*. After receiving the PCEP Reply, the PCC either signals the MPLS LSP and starts using it or puts it in the operational down state (in the case of a negative reply). From here, the destiny of the MPLS LSP depends on the delegation setting. If delegation is enabled for this LSP, the process described earlier and shown in Figure 16-15 takes place. If delegation isn't enabled, the PCC sends just the PCEP Report messages with the delegate flag set to 0 for each MPLS LSP change. (RFC 8231 explains the PCC-initiated LSP both with and without delegation in more detail.)

The second primary option, as mentioned previously, is a PCE-initiated LSP. It deviates from the previous one in terms of the requestor of the LSP, as you can glean from the name. In the PCE-initiated LSP, it's the PCE that configures the particular MPLS LSP in the form of the SR-TE policy (for instance) and associates it with the PCC that should implement it. Recall that the PCC must support instantiation in order for this LSP type to work. Figure 16-17 shows the message flow for a PCE-initiated LSP.

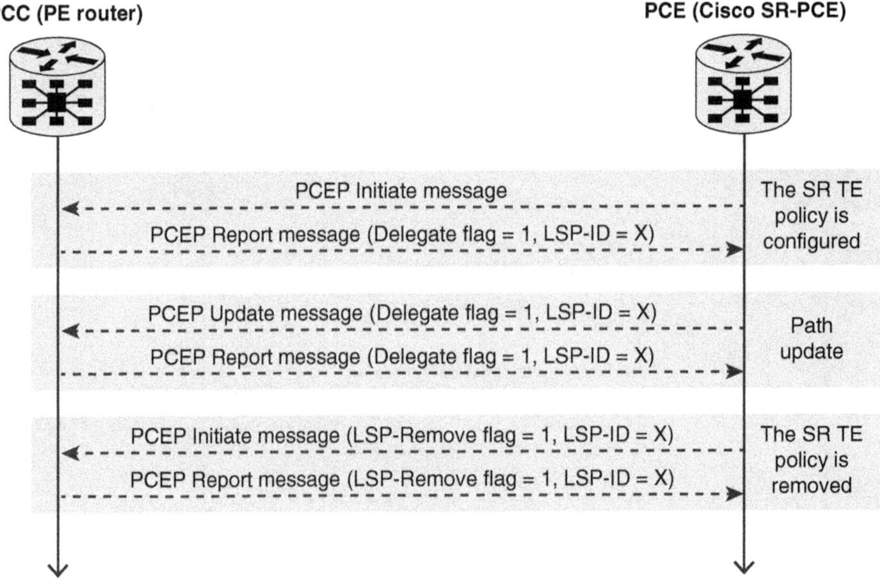

Figure 16-17 *PCE-Initiated MPLS LSP*

After the instantiation capability is negotiated between the PCC and the PCE, the PCE gets the SR-TE policy configured and associated with the particular PCC. Once the policy is configured, it triggers the PCEP to send Initiate message toward the PCC with the ERO and the symbolic name of the MPLS LSP. Based on this message, the PCC creates a new MPLS LSP and replies with the results to the PCE by using a PCEP Report message containing the MPLS LSP details, including the LSP ID generated locally by the PCC and the delegation flag set to 1. The LSP ID needs to be signaled back to have a unique identification of the MPLS LSP across the PCE and PCC; this is done through mapping of the symbolic SR-TE policy name and the LSP ID of the MPLS LDP as it is installed in the PCC.

Given that there are no options for "non-delegated" LSPs, the further operation of the PCE-initiated LSP type is the same as for the PCC-initiated and delegated LSPs. Any change in the IGP/MPLS topology affecting the path is calculated by the PCE and signaled using a PCEP Update message down to the PCC followed by the PCEP Report acknowledgment with the delegation flag set to 1 in both messages.

When the MPLS LSP isn't needed anymore, the SR-TE policy is either removed from the PCE configuration or put in the shutdown state. This action triggers the PCEP Initiate message for the particular MPLS LSP with the LSP-Remove flag (R flag) set to 1 and all the details about the MPLS LSP, including LSP ID. After receiving this message, the PCC removes the MPLS LSP from its forwarding table and confirms the deletion with a PCEP Report message with the LSP details and the R flag set to 1. (RFC 8281 provides details on the PCE-initiated MPLS LSPs.)

Configuring PCEP in Cisco IOS XR

To describe the configuration of PCEP on a Cisco IOS XR router, this section uses the same topology used earlier in this chapter. The configuration in this section relies on the previous configuration of IS-IS, Segment-Routing, and BGP-LS, so you need to be familiar with the earlier parts of this chapter. Figure 16-18 shows the details of the PCEP peering for this section.

As you can see, PCEP follows the BGP-LS peering. (In the real world, you are most likely to have a PCEP session with each PE router, and BGP-LS will be done only with ABRs.) Based on the PCEP naming convention, PCCs refer to the client nodes: NPF-XR1 and NPF-XR3 are PCCs, whereas NPF-SR-PCE is a PCE (SDN controller).

This chapter focuses on service provider programmability based on Segment Routing, so only configuration related to Segment Routing is provided. It is important to keep this in mind because the configuration context for PCEP on the PCC depends on whether MPLS-TE/RSVP or SR-TE is used. Example 16-26 shows the configuration details for PCEP on the PCC. (Only the configuration for NPF-XR1 is shown because NPF-XR3 is configured the same way.)

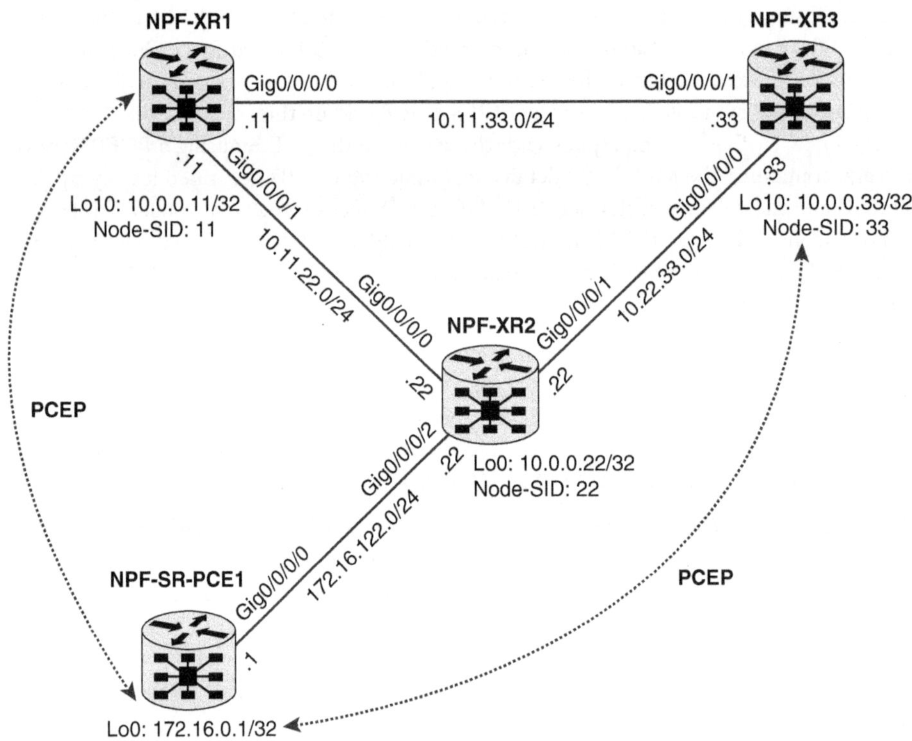

Figure 16-18 *The Lab Topology with the PCEP Lab Peering*

Example 16-26 *Configuring the PCC for SR-TE*

```
RP/0/0/CPU0:NPF-XR1(config)# show conf
Sun May 12 15:33:33.620 UTC
Building configuration...
!! IOS XR Configuration 6.5.1
segment-routing
 traffic-eng
  pcc
   source-address ipv4 10.0.0.11
   pce address ipv4 172.16.0.1
    password encrypted 002A2320
   !
   report-all
  !
 !
!
end
```

You can see in Example 16-26 that the configuration is done within the **segment-routing traffic-eng** context. You need to specify the local (PCC) and remote (PCE) addresses and the password for enhanced security (optionally), and you need to instruct the PCC to report all the available MPLS LSPs to the PCE.

The configuration of the PCE is done within another configuration context, as shown in Example 16-27.

Example 16-27 *Configuring the PCC for SR-TE*

```
RP/0/0/CPU0:NPF-SR-PCE1(config)# show conf
Sun May 12 15:39:17.471 UTC
pce
 address ipv4 172.16.0.1
 password encrypted 100A1C0956052D
 segment-routing
  traffic-eng
  !
 !
!
end
```

The **pce** configuration knob is standard for both SR-TE and MPLS-TE. You can see in Example 16-27 that there is only an IP address configured, where the PCE listens for incoming sessions. There are no other PCEP peers configured, as they are initiated on the PCC. It's crucial that the IP address configured on the PCE (**address ipv4 172.16.0.1** in Example 16-27) match the peer address on the PCC (**pce address ipv4 172.16.0.1** in Example 16-26); otherwise, PCEP sessions will not be established.

If you have configured both the PCE and the PCC correctly, the sessions follow the process shown earlier, and you can verify the state of the PCEP peering. On the PCC, you check the PCEP session state as shown in Example 16-28.

Example 16-28 *Verifying the PCEP Peering from the PCC*

```
RP/0/0/CPU0:NPF-XR1# show segment-routing traffic-eng pcc ipv4 peer detail
Sun May 12 15:46:35.656 UTC

PCC's peer database:
--------------------

Peer address: 172.16.0.1 (best PCE)
  State up
  Capabilities: Stateful, Update, Segment-Routing, Instantiation
  PCEP has been up for: 04:18:44
  Local keepalive timer is 30 seconds
```

```
 Remote keepalive timer is 30 seconds
 Local dead timer is 120 seconds
 Remote dead timer is 120 seconds
 Statistics:
   Open messages:      rx 2        | tx 2
   Close messages:     rx 0        | tx 1
   Keepalive messages: rx 674      | tx 677
   Error messages:     rx 0        | tx 0
   Report messages:    rx 0        | tx 23
   Update messages:    rx 0        | tx 0
```

In the output shown in Example 16-28, you see the state of the session, which is up. You see also the capabilities negotiated between the PCC and PCE, followed by the parameters of the keepalive/dead timers and statistics of the different PCEP messages transmitted and received.

From the PCE's perspective, you use another command that is related to the PCE configuration context, as shown in Example 16-29.

Example 16-29 *Verifying the PCEP Peering from the PCE*

```
RP/0/0/CPU0:NPF-SR-PCE1# show pce ipv4 peer detail
Sun May 12 15:51:31.121 UTC

PCE's peer database:
--------------------
Peer address: 10.0.0.11
  State: Up
  Capabilities: Stateful, Segment-Routing, Update, Instantiation
  PCEP has been up for: 04:23:42
  PCEP session ID: local 0, remote 0
  Sending KA every 30 seconds
  Minimum acceptable KA interval: 20 seconds
  Peer timeout after 120 seconds
  Maximum SID Depth: 16
  Statistics:
    Keepalive messages: rx    526 tx    526
    Request messages:   rx      0 tx      0
    Reply messages:     rx      0 tx      0
    Error messages:     rx      0 tx      0
    Open messages:      rx      1 tx      1
    Report messages:    rx     11 tx      0
    Update messages:    rx      0 tx      0
    Initiate messages:  rx      0 tx     10
 Last PCError:
```

```
    Received: None
    Sent: None

Peer address: 10.0.0.33
  State: Up
  Capabilities: Stateful, Segment-Routing, Update, Instantiation
  PCEP has been up for: 04:23:42
  PCEP session ID: local 0, remote 0
  Sending KA every 30 seconds
  Minimum acceptable KA interval: 20 seconds
  Peer timeout after 120 seconds
  Maximum SID Depth: 16
  Statistics:
    Keepalive messages: rx   526 tx   527
    Request messages:   rx     0 tx     0
    Reply messages:     rx     0 tx     0
    Error messages:     rx     0 tx     0
    Open messages:      rx     1 tx     1
    Report messages:    rx     7 tx     0
    Update messages:    rx     0 tx     0
    Initiate messages:  rx     0 tx     4
  Last PCError:
    Received: None
    Sent: None
```

On the PCE, you see the details for both PCCs connected to NPF-SR-PCE (that is, NPF-XR1 and NPF-XR3). The content in Examples 19-28 and 16-29 is quite similar, although there is a bit more information on the PCE-related maximum SID label depth of the ERO for SR-TE, and there are more packet types.

In Example 16-26, the PCC is instructed to send all the local SR-TE LSPs to the PCE. At the beginning of this chapter, you saw the configuration of the SR-TE policies on NPF-XR1 and NPF-XR3. Based on the fact that the counter of the received PCEP Report messages on the PCE isn't zero (refer to Example 16-29), you can assume that the PCCs send information about the LSPs to the PCE. This is indeed the case in this instance, and you can review these MPLS LSPs on the PCE as shown in Example 16-30.

Example 16-30 *Verifying the Reported MPLS LSPs on the PCE*

```
RP/0/0/CPU0:NPF-SR-PCE1# show pce lsp detail
Sun May 12 16:27:54.761 UTC

PCE's tunnel database:
----------------------
PCC 10.0.0.11:
```

```
Tunnel Name: cfg_XR1_XR3_OVER_XR2_BLUE
 LSPs:
  LSP[0]:
   source 10.0.0.11, destination 10.0.0.33, tunnel ID 1, LSP ID 3
   State: Admin up, Operation active
   Setup type: Segment Routing
   Binding SID: 1000002
   Maximum SID Depth: 16
   Bandwidth: signaled 0 kbps, applied 0 kbps
   PCEP information:
     PLSP-ID 0x80001, flags: D:0 S:0 R:0 A:1 O:2 C:0
   LSP Role: Single LSP
   State-sync PCE: None
   PCC: 10.0.0.11
   LSP is subdelegated to: None
   Reported path:
     Metric type: IGP, Accumulated Metric 0
      SID[0]: Node, Label 16022, Address 10.0.0.22
      SID[1]: Unknown, Label 16033,
   Computed path: (Local PCE)
     None
     Computed Time: Not computed yet
   Recorded path:
     None
   Disjoint Group Information:
     None

PCC 10.0.0.33:

Tunnel Name: cfg_XR3_XR1_OVER_XR2_BLUE
 LSPs:
  LSP[0]:
   source 10.0.0.33, destination 10.0.0.11, tunnel ID 1, LSP ID 3
   State: Admin up, Operation active
   Setup type: Segment Routing
   Binding SID: 1000001
   Maximum SID Depth: 16
   Bandwidth: signaled 0 kbps, applied 0 kbps
   PCEP information:
     PLSP-ID 0x80001, flags: D:0 S:0 R:0 A:1 O:2 C:0
   LSP Role: Single LSP
   State-sync PCE: None
   PCC: 10.0.0.33
```

```
  LSP is subdelegated to: None
  Reported path:
    Metric type: IGP, Accumulated Metric 0
     SID[0]: Adj, Label 24003, Address: local 10.22.33.33 remote 10.22.33.22
     SID[1]: Unknown, Label 24001,
  Computed path: (Local PCE)
    None
    Computed Time: Not computed yet
  Recorded path:
    None
  Disjoint Group Information:
    None
```

In Example 16-30 you can see all the MPLS LSPs currently installed in the network. The output is quite extensive and includes the symbolic tunnel name, source/destination IP addresses, the tunnel ID, the LSP ID, the PCEP PLSP-ID (because the PCC creates a unique PLSP-ID for each LSP that is constant for the lifetime of a PCEP session), the status of the delegation, the reported path (that is, RRO [recorded route object]), and more. You see also the status of those LSPs, which are admin and operational up.

Now we have reached the point where the PCE should perform the computation of the MPLS LSP; it can be either a PCC-initiated or PCE-initiated operation. The prerequisites for these computations are the routing and segment routing information. There are two ways to distribute this information: either by using IGP, where the PCE must be part of the IGP domain, or by using BGP-LS. The BGP-LS peering between the PCE and the PCCs is configured earlier in this chapter (refer to Example 16-17), and that information is used to populate the PCE. Actually, no additional configuration is required, and you can check the outcome of the topology used by PCEP as shown in Example 16-31.

Example 16-31 *Verifying the Routing Topology Used by the PCE*

```
RP/0/0/CPU0:NPF-SR-PCE1# show pce ipv4 top
Sun May 12 16:45:32.039 UTC

PCE's topology database - detail:
---------------------------------
Node 1
  Host name: NPF-XR1
  ISIS system ID: 0100.0000.0011 level-2 ASN: 65000 domain ID: 32
  Prefix SID:
    ISIS system ID: 0100.0000.0011 level-2 ASN: 65000 domain ID: 32
      Prefix 10.0.0.11, label 16011 (regular), flags: N
  SRGB INFO:
    ISIS system ID: 0100.0000.0011 level-2 ASN: 65000 domain ID: 32
```

```
    SRGB Start: 16000 Size: 8000

  Link[0]: local address 10.11.22.11, remote address 10.11.22.22
    Local node:
      ISIS system ID: 0100.0000.0011 level-2 ASN: 65000 domain ID: 32
    Remote node:
      Host name: NPF-XR2
      ISIS system ID: 0100.0000.0022 level-2 ASN: 65000 domain ID: 32
    Metric: IGP 10, TE 10, Latency 10
    Bandwidth: Total 0 Bps, Reservable 0 Bps
    Admin-groups: 0x00000000
    Adj SID: 24001 (unprotected)

  Link[1]: local address 10.11.33.11, remote address 10.11.33.33
    Local node:
      ISIS system ID: 0100.0000.0011 level-2 ASN: 65000 domain ID: 32    Remote
  node:
      Host name: NPF-XR3
      ISIS system ID: 0100.0000.0033 level-2 ASN: 65000 domain ID: 32
    Metric: IGP 10, TE 10, Latency 10
    Bandwidth: Total 0 Bps, Reservable 0 Bps
    Admin-groups: 0x00000000
    Adj SID: 24003 (unprotected)

Node 2
  Host name: NPF-XR2
! Further output is truncated for brevity
```

When you have verified that the routing information is available on the PCE, the last step is to create the MPLS LSPs.

Note SR-PCE (a Cisco IOS XR–based PCE) is actively being developed as this book goes to press. During the writing of the book, the Cisco IOS XR versions 6.5.1, 6.5.2, and 6.5.3 were used. It is important to note that not all combinations of IOS XR on the PCC and PCE work successfully. Additional complexity comes from the fact that the behavior of the PCE on the IOS XRv9000 (production SR-PCE) and IOS XRv used in VIRL is a bit different. If something isn't working in your setup, try to use another software version. We hope that the SR-PCE will be stabilized in the Cisco IOS XR 7.* software release.

As explained previously, the PCC-initiated MPLS LSP is configured on the PCC, and then the PCE calculates the path. Example 16-32 shows a sample configuration done on the PCC NPF-XR1.

Example 16-32 *Configuring the PCC-Initiated LSP on the PCC*

```
RP/0/0/CPU0:NPF-XR1(config)# show conf
Sun May 12 19:56:33.099 UTC
Building configuration...
!! IOS XR Configuration 6.5.1.34I
segment-routing
 traffic-eng
  policy XR1_XR2_PCC
   binding-sid mpls 1000012
   color 100 end-point ipv4 10.0.0.33
   candidate-paths
    preference 10
     dynamic
      pcep
      !
     metric
       type igp
      !
     !
    !
   !
  !
 !
!
end
```

The content of this configuration is explained earlier in this chapter, in the explanation of Example 16-9. The only difference here is that **candidate-path** is **dynamic**, and **pcep** should be used (so that the PCC asks the PCE to calculate the path). After you have configured the SR-TE policy, it should be visible locally on the PCC, as shown in Example 16-33.

Example 16-33 *Verifying the PCC-Initiated LSP on the PCC*

```
RP/0/0/CPU0:NPF-XR1# show segment-routing traffic-eng policy name XR1_XR2_PCC
Sun May 12 20:03:37.260 UTC

SR-TE policy database
---------------------


Name: XR1_XR2_PCC (Color: 100, End-point: 10.0.0.33)
  Status:
    Admin: up  Operational: up for 00:06:22 (since May 12 19:57:14.506)
```

```
  Candidate-paths:
    Preference 10:
      Dynamic (pce 172.16.0.1) (active)
        Metric Type: IGP,    Path Accumulated Metric: 10
          16033 [Prefix-SID, 10.0.0.33]
  Attributes:
    Binding SID: 1000012
      Allocation mode: explicit
      State: Programmed
      Policy selected: yes
    Forward Class: 0
    Steering BGP disabled: no
    IPv6 caps enable: no
```

In the details of this MPLS LSP, you can see that it's dynamic, and the PCE calculated the path (including the IP addresses of the PCE defining which PCE). Because the metric type IGP was defined, you can see it in the provided output, along with the calculated IGP metric of the whole MPLS LSP.

Because all the SR-TE LSPs are reported to the PCE according to the configuration for this chapter, you should be able to view the details on the PCE as well (see Example 16-34).

Example 16-34 *Verifying the PCC-Initiated LSP on the PCE*

```
RP/0/0/CPU0:NPF-SR-PCE1# show pce lsp name cfg_XR1_XR2_PCC detail
Sun May 12 20:04:16.541 UTC

PCE's tunnel database:
----------------------
PCC 10.0.0.11:

Tunnel Name: cfg_XR1_XR2_PCC
 LSPs:
  LSP[0]:
   source 10.0.0.11, destination 10.0.0.33, tunnel ID 6, LSP ID 2
   State: Admin up, Operation active
   Binding SID: 1000012
   Maximum SID Depth: 16
   Bandwidth: signaled 0 kbps, applied 0 kbps
   PCEP information:
     PLSP-ID 0x80006, flags: D:1 S:0 R:0 A:1 O:0 C:0
   LSP Role: Single LSP
   State-sync PCE: None
   PCC: 10.0.0.11
   LSP is subdelegated to: None
```

```
Reported path:
  Metric type: IGP, Accumulated Metric 10
   SID[0]: Node, Label 16033, Address 10.0.0.33
Computed path: (Local PCE)
  Computed Time: Sun May 12 19:57:13 UTC 2019 (00:07:03 ago)
  Metric type: IGP, Accumulated Metric 10
   SID[0]: Node, Label 16033, Address 10.0.0.33
Recorded path:
  None
Disjoint Group Information:
  None
```

As highlighted in Example 16-34, the PCEP flags are marked up. The D flag stands for delegation, meaning that the control for this LSP is delegated from the PCC to the PCE. You can also see the details of the path computation, as well as information reported by the PCC. This information (Computed path and Reported path) should be equal to each other in a stable network, whereas during convergence, it might be unequal if the PCE has computed the new path and sent it to the PCC but the PCC hasn't yet installed it and therefore hasn't sent back the PCEP Report message. You might also note that all the LSPs configured on the PCC and signaled to the PCE have the **cfg_** prefix in their symbolic names.

The second type of MPLS LSP where the PCE is involved is the PCE-initiated LSP. As indicated by the name and as explained earlier in this chapter, the PCE initiated the MPLS LSP, which is why the proper SR-TE policy is configured on the PCE. Example 16-35 shows the details of this type of configuration.

Example 16-35 *Configuring the PCE-Initiated LSP on the PCC*

```
RP/0/0/CPU0:NPF-SR-PCE1(config)# show conf
Sun May 12 20:34:28.687 UTC
Building configuration...
!! IOS XR Configuration 6.5.1
pce
 segment-routing
  traffic-eng
   peer ipv4 10.0.0.33
    policy PCE_XR3_XR1
     binding-sid mpls 1000021
     color 100 end-point ipv4 10.0.0.11
     candidate-paths
      preference 20
       dynamic mpls
```

```
        metric
         type igp
        !
       !
      !
     !
    !
   !
  !
 !
!
end
```

This is the first time you have seen the PCEP peer configuration on the PCE. This configuration is necessary because the PCE needs to identify where to send the particular PCE Initiate message with the LSP details. Otherwise, the configuration of the SR-TE policy is absolutely the same as for the PCC (refer to Example 16-9).

The verification process for the PCE-initiated LSP is different from the verification process for the PCC-initiated LSP. In this case, you start with the PCE, as that is where the configuration took place. The command to obtain the necessary information is the same as for the PCC, as you can see in Example 16-36.

Example 16-36 *Verifying the PCE-Initiated LSP on the PCE*

```
RP/0/0/CPU0:NPF-SR-PCE1# show pce lsp name PCE_XR3_XR1 detail
Sun May 12 21:07:38.070 UTC

PCE's tunnel database:
----------------------
PCC 10.0.0.33:

Tunnel Name: PCE_XR3_XR1
 LSPs:
  LSP[0]:
   source 10.0.0.33, destination 10.0.0.11, tunnel ID 5, LSP ID 2
   State: Admin up, Operation active
   Binding SID: 1000021
   Maximum SID Depth: 16
   Bandwidth: signaled 0 kbps, applied 0 kbps
   PCEP information:
     PLSP-ID 0x80005, flags: D:1 S:0 R:0 A:1 O:0 C:1
   LSP Role: Single LSP
   State-sync PCE: None
```

```
PCC: 10.0.0.33
LSP is subdelegated to: None
Reported path:
  Metric type: IGP, Accumulated Metric 10
   SID[0]: Node, Label 16011, Address 10.0.0.11
Computed path: (Local PCE)
  Computed Time: Sun May 12 20:46:54 UTC 2019 (00:20:44 ago)
  Metric type: IGP, Accumulated Metric 10
   SID[0]: Node, Label 16011, Address 10.0.0.11
Recorded path:
  None
Disjoint Group Information:
  None
```

Because no constraints were set, in Example 16-36, the PCE calculates the path following the lowest IGP end-to-end metrics; therefore, the accumulated metric is equal to the metric you could find in the routing table. From the flag's perspective, it's a bit different from Example 16-34 because the LSP type is different, but the delegation flag is also set to 1, as in Example 16-34. Example 16-37 shows output from the router's (that is, the PCC's) perspective.

Example 16-37 *Verifying the PCE-Initiated LSP on the PCC*

```
RP/0/0/CPU0:NPF-XR3# show segment-routing traffic-eng policy name pcep_PCE_XR3_$
Sun May 12 21:14:51.319 UTC

SR-TE policy database
---------------------

Name: pcep_PCE_XR3_XR1 (Color: 100, End-point: 10.0.0.11)
    Status:
      Admin: up  Operational: up for 00:39:31 (since May 12 20:35:20.141)
    Candidate-paths:
     Preference 10:
       Dynamic (pce 172.16.0.1) (active)
         Metric Type: IGP,    Path Accumulated Metric: 10
           16011 [Prefix-SID, 10.0.0.11]
    Attributes:
      Binding SID: 1000021
        Allocation mode: explicit
        State: Programmed
        Policy selected: yes
```

```
    Forward Class: 0
    Steering BGP disabled: no
    IPv6 caps enable: no
    Distinguisher: 0
  Auto-policy info:
    Creator: PCEP
```

Whereas the PCE has the **cfg_** prefix, the PCE-initiated LSPs on the PCC are indicated with the **pcep_** prefix. You can also see at the end of the SR-TE policy remark in Example 16-37 that PCEP creates this prefix. There is no such remark for the locally created policies. The rest of the details on the SR-TE policy output are explained earlier in this chapter.

Summary

This chapter describes programmability in service provider networks. It covers the following topics:

- One of the focuses of programmability and automation in service provider networks is dynamic management of inter-area MPLS LSPs with various constraints, such as latency, affinity, and quality.
- The programmability suite consists of Segment Routing, BGP-LS, and PCEP.
- Segment Routing is a breakthrough MPLS protocol that is considered to be one of the first building blocks for service provider (and perhaps data center) networks.
- Segment Routing combines best-effort routing and traffic engineering capabilities by putting either a single label or the proper label stack for the MPLS LSP on the ingress MPLS router.
- BGP-LS provides a mechanism to transmit the content of the IGP domain running IS-IS or OSPF to the SDN controller, which can be outside the IS-IS or OSPF domain.
- There are three types of the routes in BGP-LS: A node route defines the entity in the traffic engineering database (TED), a link route provides connectivity between the nodes, and a prefix route associates IPv4/IPv6 prefixes with the particular nodes.
- PCEP is used to communicate the status of MPLS LSPs from the PCCs (ingress MPLS routers) to the PCE (SDN controller) and allows the PCC to request the computation of the MPLS LSP by the PCE or the PCE to request the creation of the MPLS LSP on the PCC.
- There are two major MPLS LSP types in the PCEP architecture: the PCC-initiated LSP, where the LSP is created on the PCC and the PCC asks the PCE for computation, and the PCE-initiated LSP, where the PCE computes the path and asks the PCC to establish it.

Chapter 17

Programming Cisco Platforms

As you are well aware by now, above and beyond the familiar legacy interfaces that network engineers have been using for over two decades, Cisco devices now provide a set of interfaces that are described as *programmable*. Programmable interfaces are built on top of the different components of the network programmability stack that earlier chapters discuss in a lot of detail—namely SSH, HTTP and the REST framework, JSON, XML and YAML encoding, YANG models, and the NETCONF, RESTCONF, gRPC, and native REST APIs.

This chapter introduces the programmability features of a number of Cisco platforms. It would be impossible to cover all programmability features of all platforms in one chapter, and no engineer is expected to know all APIs on all Cisco platforms. This chapter covers an invaluable skill that any network automation engineer should master—besides the fundamentals covered so far in this book: the ability to locate, read, understand, and use the API documentation provided by the vendor, in this case, Cisco.

Besides the different programmable interfaces, some platforms expose one or more Linux shells that allow a network engineer to manage a device as if it were a Linux server, using the commands and tools covered in Chapters 2, "Linux Fundamentals," 3, "Linux Storage, Security, and Networks," and 4, "Linux Scripting." Moreover, as discussed in this chapter, the Linux shells allow you to install and manage third-party software directly on the box by using typical Linux software management tools.

The purpose of this chapter is not to comprehensively cover each and every automation tool and interface available. Rather, this chapter and Chapter 18, "Programming Non-Cisco Platforms," connect the dots and show you, through application, what network programmability makes possible. These two chapters consolidate the bits and pieces covered so far in this book and illustrate how these pieces work together to enable the new paradigm of network programmability and automation on Cisco and non-Cisco platforms.

Note A note of caution before you start the chapter: Keep in mind that any product, Cisco or otherwise, may change or even become end of life (discontinued) at any point in time.

The goal of this chapter is to help you get to know the positioning of a number of different platforms in the Cisco ecosystem, what each is used for, and how each accomplishes its intended purpose. After explaining each category of platforms, this chapter provides examples or use cases of how one or more of those platforms can be managed through API calls compared to conventional methods, such as CLI or GUI. Your primary reference should always be the latest/current API documentation provided by Cisco online; where that documentation differs from this chapter in its description of any platform (especially a platform's GUI) or API, follow the documentation.

This chapter makes good use of Cisco's DevNet sandboxes. Cisco DevNet provides more than 75 sandboxes for devices in different technology areas that you can experiment with during your studies (see https://devnetsandbox.cisco.com/RM/Topology). Some of them are always on and available for immediate use, and for others you need a reservation.

API Classification

APIs can be classified in a lot of different ways. They can be classified as northbound, southbound, eastbound, or westbound APIs, which I like to call the *cardinal* classification of APIs. An API can be RESTful, partially RESTful, or not RESTful. An API may also be classified as an RPC-based API—or not. APIs can be classified based on the function they serve, such as APIs used for configuration versus APIs used to subscribe to push notifications, commonly known as *webhooks*.

Knowing the classification of an API is not nearly as important as understanding the specifications of the API, which enables you to effectively utilize the API with the tool of your choice to accomplish the task at hand. For a RESTful API, for example, you need to identify the URI to target the resource that you need to act upon (sometimes referred to as the *endpoint*), including any optional query parameters, the headers required and their values, the methods supported by the resources, and the request and response payload bodies, if any. For this reason, this chapter frequently refers to the API documentation for each platform.

Note Although an API is strictly a software interface, to keep things simple, the terms *API* and *interface* are used interchangeably throughout this chapter.

To understand the cardinal API classification, imagine placing the platforms comprising a network into a hierarchy. The term *platforms* here refers to the lowest-level and most specific data plane forwarding devices at the bottom of the hierarchy and all the way up to the highest-level and least specific operations and business support systems (OSS/BSS), including intermediate devices at all levels, such as device controllers in an SDN.

One platform at a certain level can communicate with another platform at a higher level through the lower-level device's northbound interface. On the other hand, a device may expose a southbound interface for lower-level devices to programmatically communicate with it.

Northbound APIs exposed on a platform are commonly used to communicate with a third-party system, with the third-party system attempting to retrieve information from the platform exposing the API, configure it, or execute the workflows configured on that third-party system. For example, a Python program that communicates with a router to pull the running configuration or to configure an interface on the router does so via a northbound API exposed by that router. As you may have guessed, a NETCONF, RESTCONF, or gRPC API exposed by a router or switch is a northbound API.

Southbound APIs are commonly used by a system to configure—or, more generally, to communicate with—downstream devices or controllers. For example, Cisco Meraki, DNA Center, and the ACI APIC use their southbound APIs to configure individual devices under their control.

Eastbound and westbound APIs are interfaces that systems use to integrate with other systems for exchange of information or to work together on common workflows. DNA Center integrates via eastbound and westbound APIs with other Cisco products, such as Cisco ISE and third-party IT service management (ITSM) and IP address management (IPAM) systems.

RESTful APIs are discussed in detail in Chapter 7, "HTTP and REST." As a reminder, a RESTful API is an API that adheres to six REST design constraints: client/server, stateless, cacheable, uniform interface, layered system, and code on demand. The last constraint, code on demand, is an optional constraint. Keep in mind that an API may be partially RESTful if it implements some of the design constraints only. RESTful APIs use HTTP or HTTPS at the transport layer of the programmability stack. RESTCONF is an industry-standard protocol that enables a device to expose a RESTful API. NX-API REST is a native (aka vendor-/platform-specific) RESTful API exposed by programmable Nexus switches.

RPC-based APIs are explained in Chapter 14, "NETCONF and RESTCONF." RPC is a programmatic method for a client to *call* (execute) a *procedure* (piece of code) on a different device—which is why it is labeled *remote*. An RPC message specifies an operation for the server to carry out. An operation could be, for example, retrieving the running configuration of a device or editing that configuration. As described in Chapter 14, this is exactly how NETCONF operates. This is also how gRPC operates, as discussed in Chapter 15, "gRPC, Protobuf, and gNMI."

Network Platforms

This section covers the programmability and automation features of the three major Cisco software trains that run most of Cisco's networking platforms: Open NX-OS, IOS

XE, and IOS XR. It covers four use cases: Linux shells and NETCONF on each of the three platforms and NX-API CLI and NX-API REST on Nexus switches.

Networking APIs

This section describes, at a high level, the programmability and automation capabilities of each of the three Cisco network operating systems.

Open NX-OS Programmability

Open NX-OS is Cisco's network operating system for the programmable models of the Nexus line of switches, which are commonly used in data center networks. Open NX-OS is based on a customized version of the Wind River Linux distro. The Linux Foundation started the Yocto project in 2010 to customize Linux distros for embedded systems, and the Wind River Linux distro is one of them.

Open NX-OS runs as an application on top of that Linux distro. In addition, an NGINX HTTP server runs, also as an application on top of Linux, and handles all communications with the switches that use HTTP/HTTPS. The Linux OS and the NGINX HTTP server provide a foundation for many of the programmable NX-OS interfaces.

Note For the sake of brevity, moving forward, Open NX-OS will simply be referred to as NX-OS only.

The following is a non-comprehensive list of programmable interfaces available for managing a Nexus switch running NX-OS:

- **Bash and Guest shell access:** Programmable Nexus switches expose two on-box Linux shells that can be used to manage a Nexus switch in a fashion similar to managing a Linux server. The first, the Bash shell, provides access to the actual Linux OS on which NX-OS is running as an application, and the second, the Guest shell, provides access to a separate execution space that is decoupled from NX-OS. The Guest shell runs in a Linux Containers (LXC) container.
- **NX-API CLI:** This API enables a switch to accept CLI and Bash commands encoded in JSON or XML, execute those commands on box, and then send back the results, encoded in either JSON or XML. The use of the NX-API CLI is made easier through the Developer Sandbox, a web application that runs on a Nexus switch and provides several facilities for testing this API, including converting CLI commands into XML- and JSON-encoded API calls. The Developer Sandbox can also send these calls to the switch and display the responses.
- **NX-API REST:** This native RESTful API can be used to fully manage a Nexus switch.
- **Model-based industry-standard APIs:** NX-OS can expose NETCONF, RESTCONF, gRPC, and gNMI APIs.

- **Configuration management automation:** Ansible includes modules for configuring NX-OS devices. Nexus switches have built-in support for Puppet and Chef agents.
- **OpenStack Neutron ML2 support:** Nexus switches provide a plug-in that allows an OpenStack implementation to manage a switch running NX-OS as part of a complete ecosystem of network, compute, storage, and many other components that constitute an on-premises cloud.
- **Application hosting:** The Guest shell can be leveraged to run Python scripts on-box or to install and run 64-bit Linux applications packaged in RPM format on the switch. This is facilitated by the fact that the **yum** package manager is included by default in the Guest shell. NX-OS devices also come with a preinstalled Docker daemon that is used to run on-box containers in the Bash shell on which a 64-bit Linux application may be hosted.
- **Telemetry:** NX-OS supports model-driven streaming telemetry transported using JSON over UDP or GPB over gRPC (over HTTP/2).

> **Note** Not all the listed interfaces are available on all Nexus switches. At the time of writing this chapter, most of these interfaces are available on most programmable Nexus switches (3000 and 9000 Series) running version 9.3 or later of Open NX-OS. Make sure to read the configuration guide, programmability guide, and release notes for the specific hardware model and software version of your platform to identify which interfaces are available for that specific platform and which are not.

IOS XE Programmability

IOS XE is Cisco's network operating system for enterprise-grade network devices. Some flavor of IOS XE runs on most enterprise routers, switches, SD-WAN, or wireless devices. IOS XE is based on a customized version of the Wind River Linux distro.

As with NX-OS, an NGINX HTTP server runs on top of the Linux kernel and handles all HTTP/HTTPS-based communications with the devices.

The following is a non-comprehensive list of programmable interfaces available for managing a device running IOS XE (but note that not all interfaces are applicable to all hardware platforms or software versions):

- **Guest shell access:** IOS XE devices expose a containerized Linux OS shell that can be used for running on-box scripts such as Python programs. Some IOS XE devices run a full-fledged Guest shell similar to the one exposed by NX-OS where RPM packages can be installed; some IOS XE devices run a Lite version of the Guest shell that has different capabilities than the full shell. In both cases, the Guest shell runs in an LXC container on the device.
- **Model-based industry-standard APIs:** IOS XE can expose NETCONF, RESTCONF, gRPC, and gNMI APIs.

- **Configuration management automation:** Ansible includes modules for configuring IOS XE devices. IOS XE has built-in support for both Puppet and Chef agents.
- **Application hosting:** Through the IOx (IOS + Linux) framework, also called the Cisco Application Framework (CAF), IOS XE devices support on-box KVM and LXC containers on which an application may be hosted.
- **OpenFlow:** IOS XE devices support OpenFlow, and a device can be controlled from a third-party OpenFlow controller.
- **Telemetry:** IOS XE supports model-driven streaming telemetry. Subscriptions to telemetry data items can be established using NETCONF, RESTCONF, or gNMI, and the actual telemetry stream is sent to the receivers using the YANG push mechanism over a NETCONF session.

IOS XR Programmability

IOS XR is Cisco's network operating system for the ASR, NCS, and 8000 Series routers, and it is used primarily in service provider environments. Starting with Version 6.x, IOS XR is based on a customized version of the Wind River Linux distro. Platforms running IOS XR Version 6.x run IOS XR inside an LXC container on top of the Wind River distro. The administrative plane also runs in its own LXC container. Starting with Version 7.x, IOS XR runs directly as a number of processes on top of the Wind River distro without a container.

The following is a non-comprehensive list of programmable interfaces available for managing an IOS XR–based router running IOS XR Version 7.x (but note that not all interfaces are applicable to all hardware platforms or software versions):

- **Bash shell access:** IOS XR devices expose the underlying Linux system on which the IOS XR software runs as a group of processes. IOS XR does not provide a Guest shell out of the box. You can, however, create LXC or Docker containers as required on top of the Bash shell.
- **Model-based industry-standard APIs:** IOS XR exposes three model-based APIs: NETCONF, gRPC, and gNMI.
- **Service layer APIs:** IOS XR exposes the same service layer APIs that the router's management plane uses to speak with its own control plane, which is more formally referred to as the *service adaptation layer*. These internal APIs are exposed such that you can make an API call to modify the device's control plane directly. For example, you may run your own routing protocol on a device, and this routing protocol would follow an algorithm of its own to calculate the best path to a route. This protocol may then inject routes into the RIB directly, without having to go through configuration changes that eventually reflect on the routing table entries. These routes would be labeled with an A in the routing table to signify that these are application routes, versus, for example, OSPF routes (which are labeled with an O).

- **Application hosting:** IOS XR devices come with a preinstalled Docker daemon used to run on-box containers on which an application may be hosted. The devices also support user-created LXC containers.
- **Configuration management automation:** Ansible includes modules for configuring IOS XR devices. IOS XR devices have built-in support for Puppet and Chef agents. These agents come as native RPM packages and run as processes on the Wind River distro.
- **Telemetry:** IOS XR supports model-driven streaming telemetry transported using JSON over TCP or UDP or using GPB over gRPC (over HTTP/2).

Use Cases

This section presents four use cases of programmability and automation for network platforms. The first two cover the Bash and Guest shells and the other two discuss the NX-API CLI and the RESTful NX-API REST APIs.

Use Case 1: Linux Shells

NX-OS runs as a set of processes in the user space on top of a Wind River Linux distro. As of this writing, NX-OS Version 9.2.1 runs on Linux kernel Version 4.1. Nexus switches running NX-OS provide access to two Linux shells: the Bash shell and the Guest shell. Both shells are, technically, Bash shells.

The Bash shell provides shell access to the actual Linux OS that runs a switch. This is referred to as the *underlying* Linux OS. The Guest shell provides access to a lightweight Linux OS running in an LXC container on top of the underlying Linux OS.

Since the Bash shell provides full access to the underlying OS running the switch, you get full access to all aspects of the switch, much as you would when running Linux on a regular server. Any operation done in the Bash shell will impact the functionality of the switch.

On the other hand, the containerized Linux OS through the Guest shell runs in a semi-isolated environment and provides limited access to the switch hardware and some of the other software running on the switch, including NX-OS, which itself is a group of processes running on top of the underlying Linux OS.

The Guest shell provides an environment that enables you to run Linux-based applications without having to interact directly with the underlying Linux system that runs the box. This means that the environment through the Guest shell may be customized based on the requirements of the software you plan on running there (for example, a specific version of Python). In addition, whatever you run there will minimally impact the switch functionality, since this environment and all the software running on it will be running in the user space of the underlying Linux system—and not in the kernel space.

Figure 17-1 illustrates the software architecture of a Nexus switch running NX-OS.

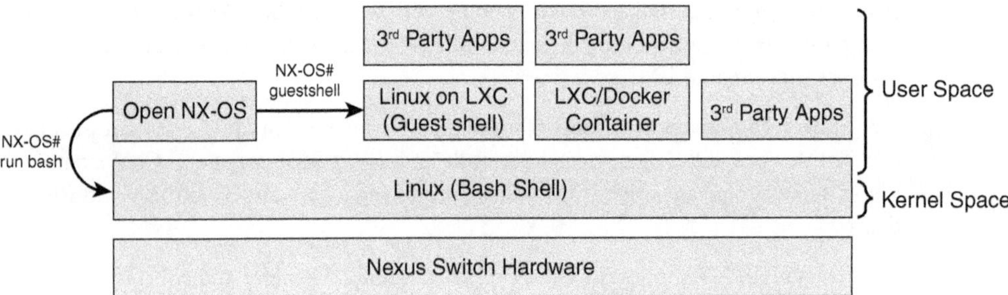

Figure 17-1 *NX-OS Software Architecture*

Before you can access the Bash shell, you need to enable it by using the command **feature bash-shell** and then start the shell by using the command **run bash**, as shown in Example 17-1.

Example 17-1 *Enabling the Bash Shell and Accessing It on NX-OS*

```
sbx-n9kv-ao# config terminal
Enter configuration commands, one per line. End with CNTL/Z.
sbx-n9kv-ao(config)# feature bash-shell
sbx-n9kv-ao(config)# show feature | in bash
bash-shell                1          enabled
sbx-n9kv-ao(config)# exit
sbx-n9kv-ao# run bash
bash-4.3$
bash-4.3$ exit
exit
sbx-n9kv-ao#
```

Example 17-2 shows the output of the **uname -a** command as well as the contents of the /etc/os-release file. As you can see, the switch is running on a Wind River Linux distro (cisco-wrlinux) Version 8, based on, as of this writing, Linux kernel Version 4.1.

Example 17-2 *Bash Shell Details on NX-OS*

```
bash-4.3$ uname -a
Linux sbx-n9kv-ao 4.1.21-WR8.0.0.25-standard #1 SMP Tue Jul 17 15:34:01 PDT 2018
  x86_64 x86_64 x86_64 GNU/Linux
bash-4.3$ cat /etc/os-release
ID=nexus
ID_LIKE=cisco-wrlinux
NAME=Nexus
VERSION="9.2(1)I9(1)"
VERSION_ID="9.2(1)I9"
```

```
PRETTY_NAME="Nexus 9.2(1)I9"
HOME_URL=http://www.cisco.com
BUILD_ID="9.2(1)I9(1)"
CISCO_RELEASE_INFO=/etc/os-release
bash-4.3$ exit
exit
sbx-n9kv-ao#
```

A few things are immediately noticeable when you run the Bash shell: The familiar [*user@hostname* ~]$ prompt that you saw in Chapter 2 is not present unless you switch to the root user. And if the directory is changed using the **cd** command, the prompt does not change to reflect the current directory. Instead, the **id** and **whoami** commands can be used to identify the current user, and the **pwd** command can be used to identify the current working directory, as shown in Example 17-3.

Example 17-3 *The whoami, id, and pwd Commands in the Bash Shell*

```
bash-4.3$ whoami
admin
bash-4.3$ id
uid=2002(admin) gid=503(network-admin) groups=503(network-admin),504(network-
  operator)
bash-4.3$ pwd
/bootflash/home/admin
! Switching to the root user
bash-4.3$ su -
Password:
root@sbx-n9kv-ao# whoami
root
root@sbx-n9kv-ao# id
uid=0(root) gid=0(root) groups=0(root)
root@sbx-n9kv-ao# pwd
/root
root@sbx-n9kv-ao#
```

Notice, however, that the prompt ending changes from the $ sign to the # sign when you switch to the root user, as expected.

Getting help in the Nexus Bash shell can be tricky. Despite the fact that you frequently get a message asking you to use **man** {*command*} or **info** {*command*} to check the man or info pages for a command, the man and info pages may not actually exist on some platforms. In such cases, you can use {*command*} **--help** to get some help on the use of a command.

Apart from these caveats, the Bash shell should feel familiar to you. The vast majority of the directory and file management commands covered in Chapters 2 through 4 should work just fine in the Bash shell. You should experiment with the Bash shell by creating, moving, copying, and deleting files and directories to see what works and what doesn't. Keep in mind, however, that deleting some files or directories may leave you with a nonfunctioning switch since everything else depends on the underlying Linux system to work properly.

You can manage switch components, such as the switch interfaces, from the Bash shell by using the same tools and commands used to manage a regular Linux server. Example 17-4 shows the output of the **show interface brief** command at the Nexus switch CLI.

Example 17-4 *Output of the **show interface brief** Command at the CLI*

```
sbx-n9kv-ao# show interface brief

--------------------------------------------------------------------------------
Port   VRF          Status IP Address                              Speed    MTU
--------------------------------------------------------------------------------
mgmt0  --           up     10.10.20.95                             1000     1500

--------------------------------------------------------------------------------
Ethernet      VLAN    Type Mode   Status  Reason                   Speed     Port
Interface                                                                    Ch #
--------------------------------------------------------------------------------
Eth1/1        1       eth  trunk  up      none                     1000(D)   11
Eth1/2        1       eth  trunk  up      none                     1000(D)   11

--------- OUTPUT OMITTED FOR BREVITY ---------
Eth1/127      1       eth  access down    Link not connected       auto(D)   --
Eth1/128      1       eth  access down    Link not connected       auto(D)   -

--------- OUTPUT OMITTED FOR BREVITY ---------

sbx-n9kv-ao#
```

Example 17-5 shows corresponding output from the Bash shell. In Chapter 3 you learned that the commands **ip link** and **ip address** display the status of the interfaces on a server. Example 17-5 shows the output of the first of these commands when entered in the Bash shell on the switch.

Example 17-5 *Output of the **ip link** Commands in the Bash Shell*

```
bash-4.3$ ip link
1: lo: <LOOPBACK,UP,LOWER_UP> mtu 65536 qdisc noqueue state UNKNOWN mode DEFAULT
  group default
    link/loopback 00:00:00:00:00:00 brd 00:00:00:00:00:00
2: dummy0: <BROADCAST,NOARP> mtu 1500 qdisc noop state DOWN mode DEFAULT group
  default
    link/ether fa:aa:16:00:0d:16 brd ff:ff:ff:ff:ff:ff
```

```
--------- OUTPUT OMITTED FOR BREVITY ---------

171: Eth1-127: <BROADCAST,MULTICAST> mtu 1500 qdisc noop state DOWN mode DEFAULT
  group default qlen 100
    link/ether 00:50:56:bb:ab:85 brd ff:ff:ff:ff:ff:ff
172: Eth1-128: <BROADCAST,MULTICAST> mtu 1500 qdisc noop state DOWN mode DEFAULT
  group default qlen 100
    link/ether 00:50:56:bb:ab:86 brd ff:ff:ff:ff:ff:ff
bash-4.3$ #
```

In a similar fashion, package and repository management on a Nexus switch can be managed from the Bash shell by using the familiar **rpm** and/or **yum** tools.

A useful functionality available in the Bash shell is the capability to run NX-OS CLI commands. This comes in handy if you wish to run a Bash script that directly invokes a CLI command or just want to use the Linux tools **grep**, **awk**, and **sed** (covered in Chapter 4) to filter or edit command output. Example 17-6 shows the **vsh** command being used to extract all /32 routes in the routing table, **grep** being used to match on the subnet mask, and the output being piped to **awk** to print the subnet only (without the trailing comma). This example gives you an idea of how useful it would be to be able to manipulate command output with the full arsenal of Bash commands and utilities available to you through the Bash shell.

Example 17-6 *Using Bash Utilities to Filter and Edit Command Output from the Bash Shell*

```
bash-4.3$ vsh -c "show ip route" | grep '/32' | awk -F , '{print $1}'
172.16.0.1/32
172.16.1.1/32
172.16.100.1/32
172.16.101.1/32
172.16.102.1/32
172.16.103.1/32
172.16.104.1/32
172.16.105.1/32
bash-4.3$ #
```

For a review of the **grep**, **sed** and **awk** utilities, see Chapter 4.

As mentioned earlier, the Guest shell provides access to a Linux environment that runs in an LXC container on top of the underlying Linux OS. The Guest shell provides access to the following:

- The switch interfaces through the underlying Linux OS network subsystem for monitoring only
- The switch file system

- The switch RAM (volatile tmpfs)
- The NX-OS CLI
- The NX-API REST API

You invoke the Guest shell by using the command **guestshell** at the NX-OS CLI, which initiates an SSH connection to the Guest shell Linux system. Unlike the Bash shell, the Guest shell is actually a CentOS Version 7 distro, as you can see in Example 17-7.

Example 17-7 *Invoking the Guest Shell from the CLI*

```
sbx-n9kv-ao# guestshell
[admin@guestshell ~]$ uname -a
Linux guestshell 4.1.21-WR8.0.0.25-standard #1 SMP Tue Jul 17 15:34:01 PDT 2018
  x86_64 x86_64 x86_64 GNU/Linux
[admin@guestshell ~]$ cat /etc/os-release
NAME="CentOS Linux"
VERSION="7 (Core)"
ID="centos"
ID_LIKE="rhel fedora"
VERSION_ID="7"
PRETTY_NAME="CentOS Linux 7 (Core)"
ANSI_COLOR="0;31"
CPE_NAME="cpe:/o:centos:centos:7"
HOME_URL="https://www.centos.org/"
BUG_REPORT_URL="https://bugs.centos.org/"

CENTOS_MANTISBT_PROJECT="CentOS-7"
CENTOS_MANTISBT_PROJECT_VERSION="7"
REDHAT_SUPPORT_PRODUCT="centos"
REDHAT_SUPPORT_PRODUCT_VERSION="7"

CISCO_RELEASE_INFO=/etc/shared/os-release
[admin@guestshell ~]$
```

In addition to offering limited access, the Guest shell runs on capped resources. This means that whatever runs in the Guest shell will not exceed certain limits with respect to CPU, memory, and storage, and it will therefore never adversely affect the basic functionality of the underlying Linux system or NX-OS. These limits are, however, configurable.

Both IOS XE and IOS XR provide access to Linux shells. However, IOS XR only provides a Bash shell to the underlying Linux OS on which IOS XR is running, and you can access it by running the CLI command **bash**. On the other hand, IOS XE only exposes a Guest shell that runs in a container and is isolated from the underlying Linux OS; you can access it by using the command **guestshell**.

Use Case 2: NX-API CLI

The NX-API CLI is an API exposed by NX-OS that provides the facility to encode (encapsulate) CLI or Linux Bash commands in JSON or XML and send them to the switch over HTTPS. The message body of the HTTP response, which is the command output in this case, is also received in JSON or XML. NX-API uses HTTP Basic Authentication.

In order to start using the NX-API CLI, you need to enable the feature by issuing the command **feature nxapi**. You can confirm that it is enabled by using the command **show feature | incl nxapi**. The feature should show up as **enabled**. You can also use the command **show nxapi** to check the status of the NX-API and its configuration.

You can use the NX-API CLI off-box via any HTTP client, such as Postman or Python HTTP libraries, and you can also use it on-box via a tool provided by Cisco called the *Developer Sandbox*.

> **Note** Don't confuse this with the sandboxes provided by Cisco DevNet for testing purposes. Whereas the Developer Sandbox is a feature, the DevNet sandboxes are test devices provided for testing purposes in isolation from any production network.

To access the Developer Sandbox, you use a web browser to browse to the switch name or IP address. For the DevNet always-on NX-OS sandbox, open your browser and browse to the URI https://sbx-nxos-mgmt.cisco.com. When prompted for a username and password, enter **admin** and **Admin_1234!**. You are then presented with the GUI shown in Figure 17-2. As of this writing, this particular switch runs NX-OS Version 9.3(3).

> **Note** The developer sandbox GUI may change from what is shown in Figure 17-2 with new NX-OS versions. Visit the DevNet sandboxes web page (https://devnetsandbox.cisco.com/RM/Topology) to get the updated URI and credentials for the NX-OS DevNet sandbox.

In order to understand how the developer sandbox assists you with converting CLI commands to API calls, let's examine the sandbox GUI. The GUI has three panes:

- The top pane is the Command pane, and this is where your input goes.
- The middle pane is the Request pane. The API payload body equivalent to the command that you enter in the Command pane appears in the Request pane.
- The pane at the bottom is the Response pane. This is where the response from the switch shows up when you click the Send button.

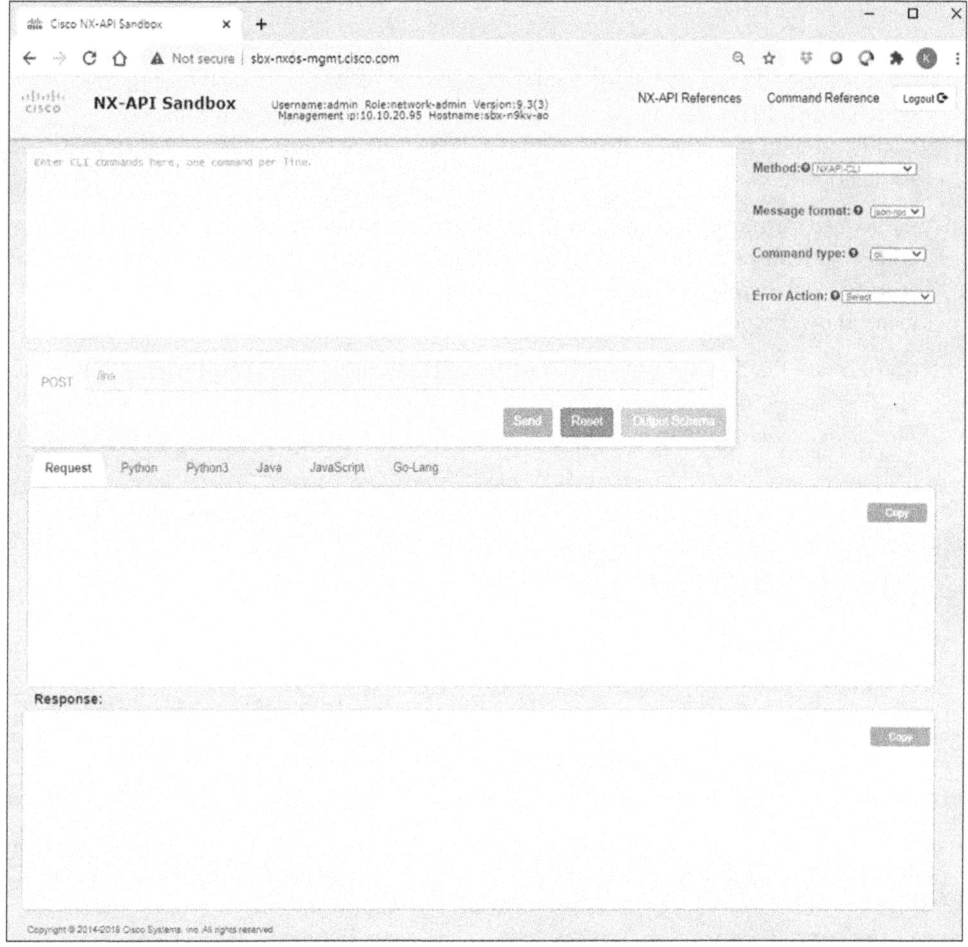

Figure 17-2 *The Developer Sandbox Graphical User Interface*

Caution As you proceed, keep in mind that any command entered in the developer sandbox and sent to the switch will actually be executed. Therefore, you should take extra care before clicking Send when using the sandbox on a network element in a production network.

To the right of the Command pane are four drop-down boxes: Method, Message format, Command type, and Error Action.

The Method drop-down enables you to select which API or protocol to work with. The three options here are NXAPI-CLI, NXAPI-REST (DME), and RESTCONF (Yang). This section covers the NXAPI-CLI option, and the next section covers the NXAPI-REST (DME) option.

When you choose NXAPI-CLI from the Method drop-down, you get three options in the Message format drop-down: json-rpc, xml, and json. Depending on which one you choose, you will be presented with up to five options for the Command type drop-down (as discussed later in this section).

You can try out this simple example to get started: Enter the command **show hostname** in the Command pane and choose json from the Message format drop-down and cli_show from the Command type drop-down. As soon as you enter the command in the Command pane, the Request pane is updated with a JSON object. This is the *payload body* of the API call to the switch. The full API details are as follows:

- **Method:** POST
- **URI:** https://sbx-nxos-mgmt.cisco.com/ins/
- **Header:**

  ```
  Content-Type: application/json
  ```
- **JSON payload:**

  ```
  {
    "ins_api": {
      "version": "1.0",
      "type": "cli_show",
      "chunk": "0",
      "sid": "1",
      "input": "show hostname",
      "output_format": "json"
    }
  }
  ```
- **Authorization:** One of the two following options:
  - Choose Basic Auth and provide username/password (admin/Admin_1234! for this example).
  - Authenticate once via a POST request by providing username/password, getting a cookie, and then adding the Cookie header in all subsequent requests.

API calls to the NX-API CLI always use the POST method and the URI **https://**{*switch_address*}**/ins/**. The header Content-Type depends on the payload *encoding*, which in turn depends on the Message format setting you choose. The payload body *content* depends on the protocol (or API) you are going to use, which again is based on your selection from the Message format drop-down. Finally, authentication is always required unless you are doing the API call on-box from the developer sandbox by clicking the Send button under the Command pane.

Now click the Send button and watch the switch response, encoded as a JSON object, appear in the Response pane. The switch hostname in this case is sbx-n9kv-ao.

To elaborate more on what exactly has happened here, you can make the same API call from Postman. Open Postman and create a new request. Edit the request attributes to match the same method, URI, headers, payload, and authentication settings shown earlier.

You should then send the request and notice the body of the HTTP response. Figure 17-3 shows a screenshot of the developer sandbox GUI and the Postman application after you make the API call from both of them. Compare the response bodies in the figure, and you see that they are identical.

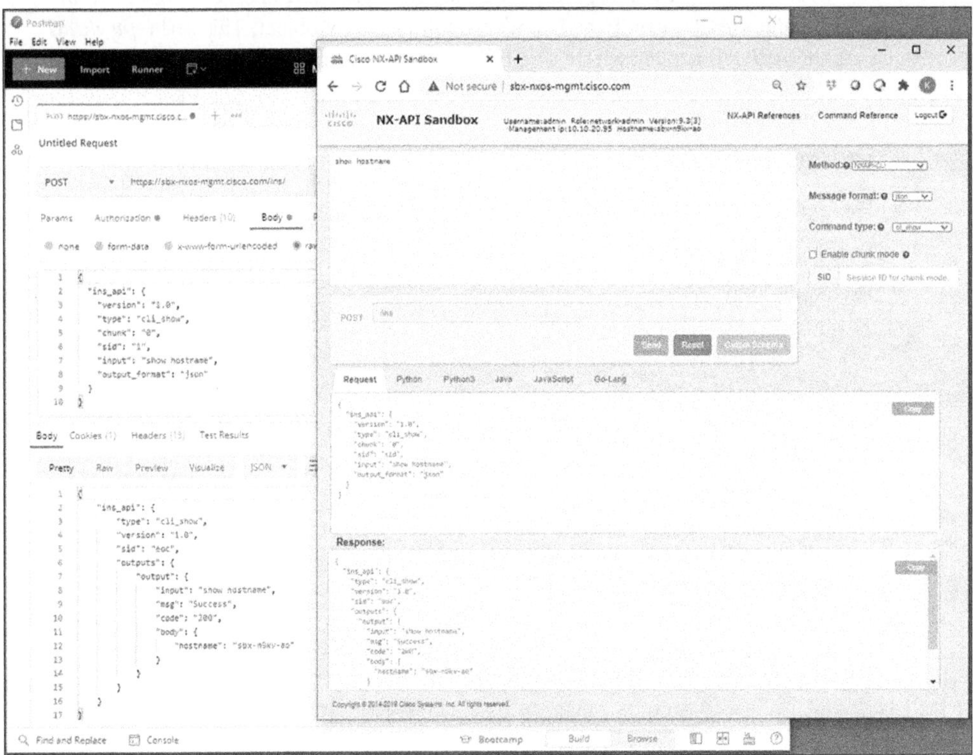

Figure 17-3 *Comparing the Body of the Response in the Developer Sandbox and Postman*

To use this API, you must provide the switch with a username and password for basic HTTP authentication. Alternatively, you might want to save a few of the processing cycles involved with authenticating each and every request by authenticating once and receiving a cookie from the server in the form of a response header field called Set-Cookie. The cookie is stored on your client and should be included in all subsequent HTTP requests to that switch, as the value of the request header field Cookie.

To authenticate and receive a cookie, send a POST request to the URI https://sbx-nxos-mgmt.cisco.com/api/aaaLogin.json with the request body content highlighted in Example 17-8. Notice that the *response* in the example has a header field called Set-Cookie. The value of this header field should be included in all subsequent HTTP *requests* as the value of the header field Cookie. The cookie value is automatically included for you in Postman as soon as you send a request to the same host from which you received the cookie. The session cookie expires after 10 minutes, and this amount of time is not configurable.

Example 17-8 *Authenticating Once to Receive a Cookie in the Set-Cookie Response Header Field*

```
! HTTP Request
POST /api/aaaLogin.json HTTP/1.1
Content-Type: application/json
Cache-Control: no-cache
User-Agent: PostmanRuntime/7.24.0
Accept: */*
Host: sbx-nxos-mgmt.cisco.com
Accept-Encoding: gzip, deflate, br
Connection: keep-alive
Content-Length: 116
{
     "aaaUser": {
       "attributes": {
         "name": "admin",
         "pwd": "Admin_1234!"
       }
     }
}

! HTTP Response
HTTP/1.1 200 OK
Server: nginx/1.13.12
Date: Wed, 01 Apr 2020 23:39:26 GMT
Content-Type: application/json
Content-Length: 891
Connection: keep-alive
Set-Cookie: APIC-cookie=DIg05JJ4w5ElHP2xG3Z5+R0eGWTcT2ZM5QDfA2OAvlx7DGY0kj70198sbnWy
  73wcOAAjELeV9nrVarLq/r9Dp8vsEjoTelhEVXI590CBjruoniT6+f1ZI3o1S7411OdDrNRjkz3DDYABLi
  NdGNXxqKdkNJ7WxNFQrVCc+NfmXsQ=; path=/; HttpOnly
--------- OUTPUT TRUNCATED FOR BREVITY ---------
```

The way the Developer Sandbox works and how it can help you when writing automation code should be clear to you by now. One very handy feature of the application is that it can also generate Python 2 and 3, Java, JavaScript, or Go code that needs minor editing to be ready for use. You can click the corresponding tab button in the Request pane (refer to Figures 17-2 and 17-3) to get the code in the language that you need. That code can then be used off-box to perform the same API call from a machine that can reach this switch.

When the Method drop-down in the Command pane is set to NXAPI-CLI, the Message Format drop-down list provides three different formats. The json-rpc option generates a payload that conforms to the standards-based lightweight protocol JSON-RPC 2.0 (defined at https:///www.jsonrpc.org/specification). The xml and json options generate a payload in XML or JSON, respectively, to be used by proprietary Cisco protocols.

In the Command type drop-down, you specify whether the command that you provide in the Command pane is a CLI **show** command, a CLI configuration command, or a Bash shell command.

When in doubt about any of the options, you can hover with your mouse pointer over the question mark to the left of a drop-down list to get a brief description of the option.

Use Case 3: NX-API REST

NX-API REST is a native RESTful API exposed by NX-OS. Like any other RESTful API, the API is defined through a set of URIs (endpoints) and the parameters in those URIs, the methods allowed on the resources represented by those URIs, header fields, the encoding of a message body, and the content of that body, as determined by the data model used by the API. (The NX-API REST API is used in the examples in Chapter 7 to demonstrate the different components of HTTP.)

The NX-API REST API uses the GET, POST, PUT, DELETE, and OPTIONS methods. It supports payload bodies encoded in either XML or JSON.

REST APIs act on resources. In Cisco lingo, these resources are called *objects*, and instances of these objects are referred to as *managed objects* (*MOs*). MOs represent configuration and state data and are organized in a hierarchical tree structure called the *management information tree* (*MIT*).

Each MO represents a resource on the switch that can be individually managed using the API. An MO is uniquely and globally identified by a *distinguished name* (*DN*). The DN is the full path to the MO and describes its location in the MIT, starting at the root of the tree; the DN therefore contains all of the MO's parent objects. As you might have guessed, the DN value constitutes most of the URI used to address the MO. The individual MO's name, excluding the hierarchical part of the DN, is called the *relative name* (*RN*). For example, if the DN of interface Eth1/1 is sys/intf/phys-[eth1/1], the RN is phys-[eth1/1]. Keep in mind that phys-[eth1/1] is an instance of the object named l1PhysIf. Also keep in mind that each node of the MIT (not only the leafs) constitutes an MO. So sys is an MO, and intf is an MO as well. You need to know this because constructing a URI involves knowing the DN of the MO you are trying to address, and constructing the body of the message involves understanding the MIT hierarchy and attributes of each MO.

The general URI format for addressing an MO is **https://**{*SW-FQDN*|*IP*}**/api/mo/**{*DN*}**.**{**json**|**xml**}[?*options*]. MOs have attributes. For example, an interface may be a layer 2 or layer 3 interface. If it is a layer 2 interface, it has its trunking mode set to either access or trunk. If it is an access port, it has a VLAN assigned, and if it is a trunk port, it has a set of allowed VLANs. The interface is the MO, and the layer, trunking mode, and VLAN numbers are some of the attributes of that MO. Some attributes have default values, and some do not.

Apart from having values, attributes have types. An MTU value is an integer. It cannot contain decimal places, and it is not a string, so it cannot contain letters. The admin state is Boolean, and it can be either up or down. A switch has an internal engine called the *Data Management Engine* (*DME*) that maintains all the attribute names and properties for all MOs, including their default values, and validates any value that you attempt to assign to these attributes.

The MIT and the DME together constitute the data model referenced by this API. (For more information on what a data model is, refer to Chapter 13, "YANG.") This means that the content of the HTTP request or response body is primarily determined by the attributes you are attempting to configure (in the case of a POST). HTTP requests used to retrieve MO information by using **GET** do not have a message body. However, the HTTP response message body follows the same data model.

How do you figure out the DN of an MO in order to build the URI? There are a few ways to do this. First, there is an on-box feature called Visore. To access Visore on the NX-OS DevNet sandbox, go to https://sbx-nxos-mgmt.cisco.com/visore.html and log in using the same credentials you use for the Developer Sandbox. In the Class or DN text box at the top of the page, type **sys** and click the Run Query button. The sys MO details then appear, as shown in Figure 17-4.

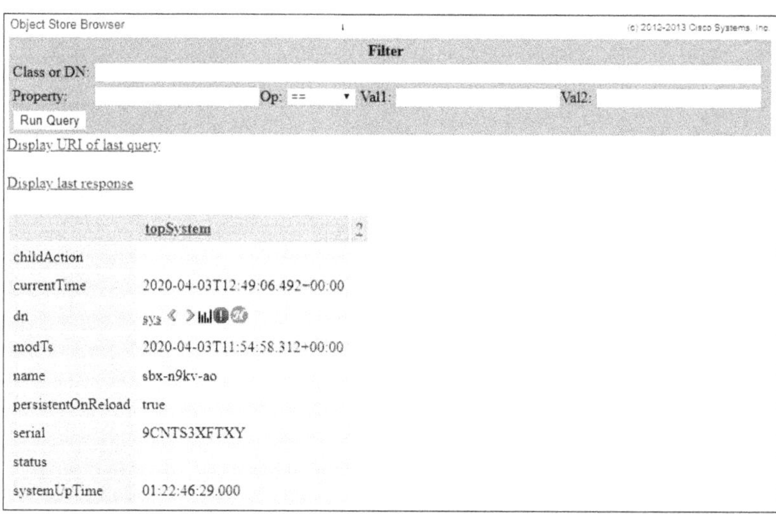

Figure 17-4 *Details of the sys MO in Visore*

Click the small green arrow to the right of sys in the dn field. You then see all the child objects under the topSystem object sys. Although it is not very efficient, you can scroll or search (by pressing Ctrl+F) through the results to find the interfaceEntity object with the RN intf. Then you can click the green arrow to the right of the DN sys/intf, and you are presented with a list of l1PhysIf objects, one for each physical interface. Again, scroll or search for your interface until you find the needed DN. (Keep in mind that Visore, like all other features and tools provided by Cisco, may at any point in time be deprecated or have its GUI changed. The description given here is valid as of this writing.)

Another way to figure out the DN of an MO in order to build the URI is to consult the Cisco Nexus 3000 and 9000 Series NX-API REST documentation at https://developer.cisco.com/docs/cisco-nexus-3000-and-9000-series-nx-api-rest-sdk-user-guide-and-api-reference-release-9-3x/. This documentation provides step-by-step instructions on how to query or configure any MO.

Now that you know how to figure out the DN of the MO, let's move to some hands-on activities.

NX-API CLI and REST use the same set of commands to enable the APIs and check their status. Use the command **feature nxapi** to enable the feature and **show nxapi** to check the status of the API, as well as which HTTP/HTTPS port the switch is listening on. The **show nxapi** command also displays the switch certificate information.

Let's go back to the earlier example of the layer 2 interface. Say that you need to configure interface Eth1/5 on the Cisco NX-OS sandbox as a trunk port allowing VLANs 1 to 100. Before configuring the interface, you should retrieve its current configuration. Referring to the API reference or Visore, you can send a GET request to the URI https://sbx-nxos-mgmt.cisco.com/api/mo/sys/intf/phys-[eth1/5].json. Example 17-9 shows the HTTP response body.

Example 17-9 *Retrieving the Interface Information for Interface Eth1/5*


```
{
    "totalCount": "1",
    "imdata": [
        {
            "l1PhysIf": {
                "attributes": {
                    "FECMode": "auto",
                    "accessVlan": "vlan-1",
                    "adminSt": "up",
                    "autoNeg": "on",
                    "beacon": "off",
                    "bw": "default",
                    "childAction": "",
                    "controllerId": "",
                    "delay": "1",
                    "descr": "",
                    "dn": "sys/intf/phys-[eth1/5]",
```

```
                        "dot1qEtherType": "0x8100",
                        "duplex": "auto",
                        "ethpmCfgFailedBmp": "",
                        "ethpmCfgFailedTs": "00:00:00:00.000",
                        "ethpmCfgState": "0",
                        "id": "eth1/5",
                        "inhBw": "4294967295",
                        "layer": "Layer2",
                        "linkDebounce": "100",
                        "linkDebounceLinkUp": "0",
                        "linkLog": "default",
                        "linkTransmitReset": "enable",
                        "mdix": "auto",
                        "medium": "broadcast",
                        "modTs": "2020-04-03T00:43:46.988+00:00",
                        "mode": "access",
                        "mtu": "1500",
                        "name": "",
                        "nativeVlan": "vlan-1",
                        "persistentOnReload": "true",
                        "portT": "leaf",
                        "routerMac": "not-applicable",
                        "snmpTrapSt": "enable",
                        "spanMode": "not-a-span-dest",
                        "speed": "auto",
                        "speedGroup": "auto",
                        "status": "",
                        "switchingSt": "disabled",
                        "trunkLog": "default",
                        "trunkVlans": "1-4094",
                        "usage": "discovery",
                        "userCfgdFlags": "",
                        "vlanmgrCfgFailedBmp": "",
                        "vlanmgrCfgFailedTs": "00:00:00:00.000",
                        "vlanmgrCfgState": "0",
                        "voicePortCos": "none",
                        "voicePortTrust": "disable",
                        "voiceVlanId": "none",
                        "voiceVlanType": "none"
                    }
                }
            }
        ]
}
```

A few fields in this output are highlighted. You can see that the interface is a layer 2 interface, in access mode, and the access VLAN is VLAN 1, which is the default interface configuration on the Nexus switch. Notice also that this MO is an instance of an l1PhysIf object, and its DN is sys/intf/phys-[eth1/5].

Referring to the references mentioned earlier, you can configure the interface as stated by executing an API call with the following details:

- **Method:** POST
- **URI:** http://sbx-nxos-mgmt.cisco.com/api/mo/sys/intf.json
- **JSON payload:**

```
{
  "interfaceEntity": {
    "children": [
      {
        "l1PhysIf": {
          "attributes": {
            "id": "eth1/5",
            "mode": "trunk",
            "trunkVlans": "1-100"
          }
        }
      }
    ]
  }
}
```

- **Authorization:** Authenticate once via a POST request by providing the username/password, getting a cookie, and then adding the Cookie header in all subsequent requests. NX-API REST does not support direct HTTP Basic Authentication.

Before proceeding, it is worth noting that one of the ways to figure out the payload for the API call is through the Developer Sandbox. Go to the Sandbox GUI and choose the NXAPI-REST (DME) from the Method drop-down and cli from the Input type drop-down. Enter the configuration commands as you would on the switch CLI, one command per line, and then click Convert. The required payload then appears in the Request pane (see Figure 17-5).

Compare what you see in the figure with what's in the bulleted list, copied from the Cisco documentation. Note that the DN + body content combination in the bulleted list is slightly different from the DN + body content from the Developer Sandbox. Both communicate the same information through an API call. The difference is that the API call in the bulleted list provides a little more hierarchy information through the URI, and the API call from the Developer Sandbox always uses the same URI (https://sbx-nxos-mgmt.cisco.com/api/mo/sys.{json|xml}) and provides all other necessary information through the message body content.

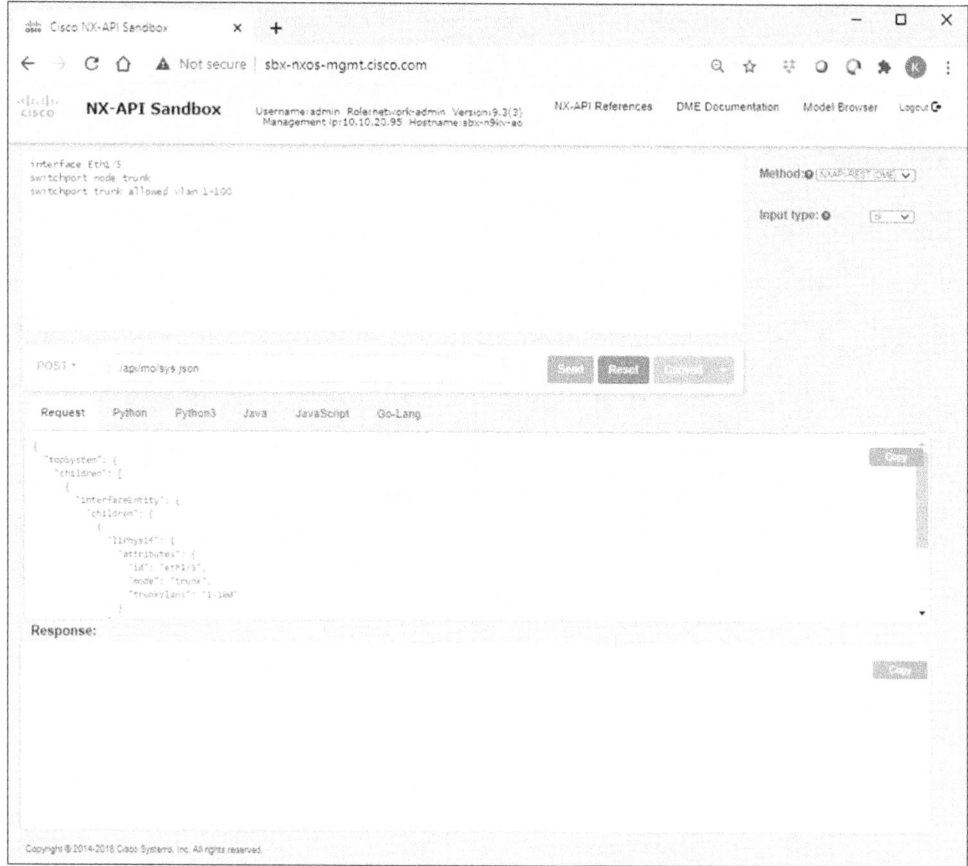

Figure 17-5 *Using the Developer Sandbox to Translate CLI Configuration Commands to an NX-API REST Payload*

Now open Postman and construct a new request, using the information in the bulleted list, and send the request. You should expect a "200 OK" response. This POST request addresses the MO named interfaceEntity, which is the parent of the MO named l1PhysIf. The DN of this parent MO is sys/intf. There is no real need to memorize either the DN or the content structure. Always refer to the Cisco documentation when needed.

Now you can send another GET request to retrieve the interface attributes. Example 17-10 shows output confirming that all went as intended.

Example 17-10 *Retrieving the New Interface Information for Interface Eth1/5 After the API Call*


```
{
    "totalCount": "1",
    "imdata": [
        {
            "l1PhysIf": {
                "attributes": {
                    "FECMode": "auto",
                    "accessVlan": "vlan-1",
                    "adminSt": "up",
                    "autoNeg": "on",
                    "beacon": "off",
                    "bw": "default",
                    "childAction": "",
                    "controllerId": "",
                    "delay": "1",
                    "descr": "Link to virt3",
                    "dn": "sys/intf/phys-[eth1/5]",
                    "dot1qEtherType": "0x8100",
                    "duplex": "auto",
                    "ethpmCfgFailedBmp": "",
                    "ethpmCfgFailedTs": "00:00:00:00.000",
                    "ethpmCfgState": "0",
                    "id": "eth1/5",
                    "inhBw": "4294967295",
                    "layer": "Layer2",
                    "linkDebounce": "100",
                    "linkDebounceLinkUp": "0",
                    "linkLog": "default",
                    "linkTransmitReset": "enable",
                    "mdix": "auto",
                    "medium": "broadcast",
                    "modTs": "2020-04-03T13:26:22.570+00:00",
                    "mode": "trunk",
                    "mtu": "1500",
                    "name": "",
                    "nativeVlan": "vlan-1",
                    "persistentOnReload": "true",
                    "portT": "leaf",
                    "routerMac": "not-applicable",
                    "snmpTrapSt": "enable",
                    "spanMode": "not-a-span-dest",
```

```
                    "speed": "auto",
                    "speedGroup": "auto",
                    "status": "",
                    "switchingSt": "disabled",
                    "trunkLog": "default",
                    "trunkVlans": "1-100",
                    "usage": "discovery",
                    "userCfgdFlags": "",
                    "vlanmgrCfgFailedBmp": "",
                    "vlanmgrCfgFailedTs": "00:00:00:00.000",
                    "vlanmgrCfgState": "0",
                    "voicePortCos": "none",
                    "voicePortTrust": "disable",
                    "voiceVlanId": "none",
                    "voiceVlanType": "none"
                }
            }
        }
    ]
}
```


The highlighted attributes in the example confirm that the configuration went through.

Use Case 4: NETCONF

This use case covers the NETCONF API on each of the networking operating systems: NX-OS, IOS XE, and IOS XR. The NETCONF protocol is covered in detail in Chapter 14. This section discusses the specific configuration details of NETCONF on each of the three platforms.

NETCONF on NX-OS

Nexus switches expose *two* NETCONF APIs. One API uses XSD models, and the other uses YANG models. This section covers the two NETCONF APIs on Nexus switches. The examples in this section use the NX-OS DevNet sandboxes at https://devnetsandbox.cisco.com/RM/Topology running Open NX-OS Version 9.x. This is a reservation-based sandbox that you will need to access through a VPN connection. Therefore, you will find that the examples address the switch using a private IP address provided by Cisco DevNet after making the sandbox reservation.

You configure the YANG-based NETCONF API, also referred to as the *NETCONF agent*, on a Nexus switch by enabling the NETCONF feature using the command **feature netconf**; you disable it by prepending **no** to the same command. You can use the command **show feature | i netconf** to make sure the feature is enabled. You can also verify the status of the NETCONF service from the Bash shell of a switch by using the command **service netconf status**. Example 17-11 shows the output of this command when the agent is running normally.

Example 17-11 *Checking the Status of the NETCONF Agent from the Bash Shell*

```
sbx-n9kv-ao# run bash
bash-4.3$ service netconf status
xosdsd (pid 30054) is running...
netconf (pid 30061) is running...
bash-4.3$
```

Two optional parameters related to NETCONF session management are **idle_timeout** and **sessions.** The first parameter, which you set by using the command **netconf idle_timeout** {*minutes*}, specifies when idle clients are disconnected, in minutes, with a default value of 5 minutes. Setting it to 0 disables timeout altogether. The second parameter, which you set by using the command **netconf sessions** {*max-sessions*}, specifies the maximum allowed number of concurrent client sessions, with a default value of 5 sessions and a maximum of 10.

To open a NETCONF session with the Nexus switch, you simply issue the command **ssh -p** {*netconf_port*} {*username*}**@**{*switch-ip-url*} **-s netconf** and, after entering the password at the password prompt, you are immediately presented with a hello message from the switch. From this point onward, everything covered in Chapter 14 is applicable here. The default port for NETCONF is 830. Example 17-12 shows the switch hello message during NETCONF session establishment.

Example 17-12 *Server Hello Message During NETCONF Session Establishment with the YANG-Based API*

```
[kabuelenain@localhost ~]$ ssh -p 830 admin@10.10.20.58 -s netconf

Welcome to the DevNet Reservable Sandbox for Open NX-OS

You can use this dedicated sandbox space for exploring and
testing APIs, explore features, and test scripts.

The following programmability features are already enabled:
  - NX-API
  - NETCONF, RESTCONF, gRPC
  - Native NX-OS and OpenConfig YANG Models

Thanks for stopping by.
Password:
<?xml version="1.0" encoding="UTF-8"?>
<hello xmlns="urn:ietf:params:xml:ns:netconf:base:1.0">
    <capabilities>
        <capability>urn:ietf:params:netconf:base:1.0</capability>
        <capability>urn:ietf:params:netconf:base:1.1</capability>
```

```
        <capability>urn:ietf:params:netconf:capability:writable-running:1.0
  </capability>
        <capability>urn:ietf:params:netconf:capability:rollback-on-error:1.0
  </capability>
        <capability>urn:ietf:params:netconf:capability:candidate:1.0</capability>
        <capability>urn:ietf:params:netconf:capability:validate:1.1</capability>
        <capability>urn:ietf:params:netconf:capability:confirmed-commit:1.1
  </capability>
        <capability>urn:ietf:params:netconf:capability:notification:1.0</capability>
        <capability>urn:ietf:params:netconf:capability:interleave:1.0</capability>
        <capability>urn:ietf:params:netconf:capability:with-defaults:1.0?basic-
  mode=report-all</capability>
        <capability>http://cisco.com/ns/yang/cisco-nx-os-device?revision=2020-07-
  20&amp;module=Cisco-NX-OS-device</capability>
    </capabilities>
    <session-id>587648866</session-id>
</hello>
]]>]]>
```

The second NETCONF API is also known as the *XML management interface*, or *XML server*, and is enabled by running the **xmlagent** service on the switch. This API is enabled by default. You can configure session timeout with the CLI command **xml server timeout** {*seconds*}, with a maximum value of 1200 seconds, which is also the default value. The maximum number of concurrent sessions can be configured by using the command **xml server max-sessions** {*sessions*}, with a maximum value of 8, which is also the default value.

You can verify the status of the XML server by using the command **show xml server status**. This command also shows all active sessions, as shown in Example 17-13.

Example 17-13 *Checking the Status of the XML Server from the CLI*

```
sbx-n9kv# show xml server status
 operational status is enabled
 maximum session configured is 8
 session: 25118, user: admin, starttime: Thu Nov 26 21:50:54 2020, sap: 9648
  timeout: 1200, time remaining: 1200 ip address: 192.168.254.11
```

Notice the highlighted session ID value in the example. You can use this value in the command **xml server terminate** {*session-id*} to terminate that active session.

NETCONF supports the concept of multiple datastores. Open NX-OS supports running configuration and candidate configuration datastores. You can apply configuration changes directly to the running configuration or choose to apply the changes to the candidate configuration first, validate the candidate configuration, and then commit it to the running configuration.

As you have read in Chapter 14, the datastore to apply the changes to is called the *target*, and it is specified in the NETCONF message from the client. You may also specify a *source*. This is required in some cases, such as when the candidate configuration is being initialized for the first time. In that case, the target is the candidate configuration, and the source is the running configuration. When initializing the candidate configuration for the first time, the source cannot be anything except the running configuration.

To access the XML server API, you can use either of these methods:

- Use SSH to the xmlagent subsystem on the switch by entering the command **ssh [-p** {*ssh_port*}] {*username*}@{*switch-ip-url*} **-s xmlagent.**
- Enter the CLI command **xmlagent** at the exec prompt of the switch.

Example 17-14 shows the NETCONF hello message from a Nexus switch running Open NX-OS Version 9.3(5) when using the XML-based API. Notice that the option **-p** was not used because the default SSH port is being used (port 22).

Example 17-14 *The Switch Hello Message Right After Initiating a NETCONF Session*

```
[kabuelenain@localhost ~]$ ssh admin@10.10.20.58 -s xmlagent

Welcome to the DevNet Reservable Sandbox for Open NX-OS

You can use this dedicated sandbox space for exploring and
testing APIs, explore features, and test scripts.

The following programmability features are already enabled:
  - NX-API
  - NETCONF, RESTCONF, gRPC
  - Native NX-OS and OpenConfig YANG Models

Thanks for stopping by.
Password:
<?xml version="1.0" encoding="ISO-8859-1"?>
<hello xmlns="urn:ietf:params:xml:ns:netconf:base:1.0">
  <capabilities>
    <capability>urn:ietf:params:xml:ns:netconf:base:1.0</capability>
    <capability>urn:ietf:params:netconf:base:1.0</capability>
    <capability>urn:ietf:params:netconf:capability:validate:1.0</capability>
    <capability>urn:ietf:params:netconf:capability:writable-running:1.0</capability>
    <capability>urn:ietf:params:netconf:capability:url:1.0?scheme=file</capability>
    <capability>urn:ietf:params:netconf:capability:rollback-on-error:1.0
  </capability>
    <capability>urn:ietf:params:netconf:capability:candidate:1.0</capability>
```

```
    <capability>urn:ietf:params:netconf:capability:confirmed-commit:1.0</capability>
  </capabilities>
  <session-id>25118</session-id>
</hello>
]]>]]>
```


As you can see, in addition to the base capabilities, the switch supports six extended capabilities.

The XSD schemas supported by the switch are located in the directory /isan/etc/schema on the switch. You can access the directory and open any of the schemas through the switch Bash shell.

Open NX-OS provides several built-in tools to assist you with constructing XML-encoded NETCONF XSD-based API messages, and it provides command output encoded in XML. While these commands may not be very helpful for the YANG-based API, they are very handy when working with the XSD-based API. These are the commands:

- **xmlin:** This is an interactive-mode tool that converts exec and config commands to their XML equivalents.
- **show** {*command*} **| xmlin:** This command provides the XML-encoded NETCONF rpc message equivalent of the **show** command.
- **show** {*command*} **| xmlout:** This command provides the XML-encoded switch output of the **show** command.

Example 17-15 shows the **xmlin** interactive tool in action.

Example 17-15 *The xmlin Interactive Tool*

```
sbx-n9kv-ao# xmlin
******************************************
Loading the xmlin tool. Please be patient.
******************************************
Cisco NX-OS Software
Copyright (c) 2002-2018, Cisco Systems, Inc. All rights reserved.
Nexus 9000v software ("Nexus 9000v Software") and related documentation,
files or other reference materials ("Documentation") are
the proprietary property and confidential information of Cisco
Systems, Inc. ("Cisco") and are protected, without limitation,
pursuant to United States and International copyright and trademark
laws in the applicable jurisdiction which provide civil and criminal
penalties for copying or distribution without Cisco's authorization.

Any use or disclosure, in whole or in part, of the Nexus 9000v Software
or Documentation to any third party for any purposes is expressly
```

```
prohibited except as otherwise authorized by Cisco in writing.
The copyrights to certain works contained herein are owned by other
third parties and are used and distributed under license. Some parts
of this software may be covered under the GNU Public License or the
GNU Lesser General Public License. A copy of each such license is
available at
http://www.gnu.org/licenses/gpl.html and
http://www.gnu.org/licenses/lgpl.html
***************************************************************************
*  Nexus 9000v is strictly limited to use for evaluation, demonstration   *
*  and NX-OS education. Any use or disclosure, in whole or in part of     *
*  the Nexus 9000v Software or Documentation to any third party for any   *
*  purposes is expressly prohibited except as otherwise authorized by     *
*  Cisco in writing.                                                      *
***************************************************************************
sbx-n9kv-ao(xmlin)# config t
Enter configuration commands, one per line. End with CNTL/Z.
sbx-n9kv-ao(config)(xmlin)# interface Eth1/10
% Success
sbx-n9kv-ao(config-if-verify)(xmlin)# switchport mode access
% Success
sbx-n9kv-ao(config-if-verify)(xmlin)# switchport access vlan 100
% Success
sbx-n9kv-ao(config-if-verify)(xmlin)# end
<?xml version="1.0"?>
<nf:rpc xmlns:nf="urn:ietf:params:xml:ns:netconf:base:1.0" xmlns="http://
  www.cisco.com/nxos:9.2.1.:configure_" xmlns:m="http://www.cisco.com/
  nxos:9.2.1.:_exec" xmlns:m1="http://www.cisco.com/nxos:9.2.1.:configure__if-
  eth-l2-non-member" xmlns:m2="http://www.cisco.com/nxos:9.2.1.:configure__if-
  ethernet-switch" message-id="1">
  <nf:edit-config>
    <nf:target>
      <nf:running/>
    </nf:target>
    <nf:config>
      <m:configure>
        <m:terminal>
          <interface>
            <__XML__PARAM__interface>
              <__XML__value>Ethernet1/10</__XML__value>
              <m1:switchport>
                <m1:mode>
                  <m1:__XML__PARAM__port_mode>
                    <m1:__XML__value>access</m1:__XML__value>
```

```
                  </m1:__XML__PARAM__port_mode>
                </m1:mode>
              </m1:switchport>
              <m2:switchport>
                <m2:access>
                  <m2:vlan>
                    <m2:__XML__PARAM__vlan-id-access>
                      <m2:__XML__value>100</m2:__XML__value>
                    </m2:__XML__PARAM__vlan-id-access>
                  </m2:vlan>
                </m2:access>
              </m2:switchport>
            </__XML__PARAM__interface>
          </interface>
        </m:terminal>
      </m:configure>
    </nf:config>
  </nf:edit-config>
</nf:rpc>
]]>]]>

sbx-n9kv-ao(xmlin)#
```

To use this tool, you enter the **xmlin** command. Inside the interactive tool, the switch prompt changes to *hostname*(xmlin)#. To enter configuration commands, you issue the command **config t**, and then, after each successful command, the switch outputs the message % Success. When all configuration commands have been entered, you issue the **end** command, and the switch immediately spits out the XML-encoded **<edit-config>** NETCONF rpc message that is equivalent to the commands you entered.

To perform the same process for a **show** command, you enter the **show** command at the **xmlin** interactive prompt, and when you press Enter, the tool immediately displays the XML-encoded NETCONF **<get>** rpc message, as shown in Example 17-16.

Example 17-16 *Using the xmlin Tool with a show Command*

```
sbx-n9kv-ao(xmlin)# show interface Eth1/10
<?xml version="1.0"?>
<nf:rpc xmlns:nf="urn:ietf:params:xml:ns:netconf:base:1.0"
  xmlns="http://www.cisco.com/nxos:9.2.1.:if_manager" message-id="1">
  <nf:get>
    <nf:filter type="subtree">
      <show>
        <interface>
```

```
          <__XML__PARAM__ifeth>
            <__XML__value>Ethernet1/10</__XML__value>
          </__XML__PARAM__ifeth>
        </interface>
      </show>
    </nf:filter>
  </nf:get>
</nf:rpc>
]]>]]>

% Success
sbx-n9kv-ao(xmlin)#
```

The **xmlin** tool converts commands to their corresponding operations as follows:

- A **show** command is converted to an rpc message that uses the <get> operation.
- Configuration commands are converted to an rpc message that uses the <edit-config> operation.
- An exec command is converted to an rpc message that uses the <exec-command> operation.

Finally, to exit the tool and return to the switch exec prompt, you use **exit**, as shown in Example 17-17.

Example 17-17 *Exiting the xmlin Tool*

```
sbx-n9kv-ao(xmlin)# exit
******************************************
****** Exited from the xmlin tool. *******
******************************************
sbx-n9kv-ao#
```

It is important to note here that the commands you enter in the **xmlin** interactive tool *are not actually applied to the switch*. This tool only shows the NETCONF equivalent of the commands you enter.

If you need the XML equivalent of a **show** command or of a **show** command's output, perhaps the easier and faster method would be to pipe the **show** command to **xmlin** for the XML-formatted NETCONF equivalent or to pipe the **show** command to **xmlout** for the XML-formatted command output. Example 17-18 shows examples of both operations.

Example 17-18 *Piping a* **show** *Command to* **xmlin** *and* **xmlout** *for the XML-Formatted Equivalents of the Command and Its Output*

```
sbx-n9kv-ao# show cdp global
Global CDP information:
    CDP enabled globally
    Refresh time is 60 seconds
    Hold time is 180 seconds
    CDPv2 advertisements is enabled
    DeviceID TLV in System-Name(Default) Format
sbx-n9kv-ao# sh cdp global | xmlin
<?xml version="1.0"?>
<nf:rpc xmlns:nf="urn:ietf:params:xml:ns:netconf:base:1.0"
  xmlns="http://www.cisco.com/nxos:9.2.1.:cdpd" message-id="1">
  <nf:get>
    <nf:filter type="subtree">
      <show>
        <cdp>
          <global/>
        </cdp>
      </show>
    </nf:filter>
  </nf:get>
</nf:rpc>
]]>]]>

% Success
sbx-n9kv-ao# sh cdp global | xmlout
<?xml version="1.0" encoding="ISO-8859-1"?>
<nf:rpc-reply xmlns="http://www.cisco.com/nxos:9.2.1.:cdpd"
  xmlns:nf="urn:ietf:params:x
ml:ns:netconf:base:1.0">
 <nf:data>
  <show>
   <cdp>
    <global>
     <__readonly__>
      <cdp_global_enabled>enabled</cdp_global_enabled>
      <refresh_time>60</refresh_time>
      <ttl>180</ttl>
      <v2_advertisement>enabled</v2_advertisement>
      <deviceid_format>DeviceID TLV in System-Name(Default) Format</deviceid_format>
     </__readonly__>
    </global>
   </cdp>
```

```
   </show>
  </nf:data>
</nf:rpc-reply>
]]>]]>
sbx-n9kv-ao#
```

As highlighted in Example 17-18, piping the output to **xmlin** results in an *rpc* message. Piping the same command output to **xmlout** results in an *rpc-reply* message.

Example 17-19 illustrates an XSD-based NETCONF session with a switch in which a hello message exchange is followed by a basic **show hostname** command.

Example 17-19 *Sample NETCONF Session via the XSD-Based API*

```
[kabuelenain@localhost ~]$ ssh -p 8181 admin@sbx-nxos-mgmt.cisco.com -s xmlagent

Welcome to the DevNet Always On Sandbox for Open NX-OS

This is a shared sandbox available for anyone to use to
test APIs, explore features, and test scripts.  Please
keep this in mind as you use it, and respect others use.

The following programmability features are already enabled:
  - NX-API
  - NETCONF, RESTCONF, gRPC
  - Native NX-OS and OpenConfig YANG Models

Thanks for stopping by.
Password:

! The switch hello message starts here
<?xml version="1.0" encoding="ISO-8859-1"?>
<hello xmlns="urn:ietf:params:xml:ns:netconf:base:1.0">
  <capabilities>
    <capability>urn:ietf:params:xml:ns:netconf:base:1.0</capability>
    <capability>urn:ietf:params:netconf:base:1.0</capability>
    <capability>urn:ietf:params:netconf:capability:validate:1.0</capability>
    <capability>urn:ietf:params:netconf:capability:writable-running:1.0</capability>
    <capability>urn:ietf:params:netconf:capability:url:1.0?scheme=file</capability>
    <capability>urn:ietf:params:netconf:capability:rollback-on-error:1.0
  </capability>
    <capability>urn:ietf:params:netconf:capability:candidate:1.0</capability>
    <capability>urn:ietf:params:netconf:capability:confirmed-commit:1.0</capability>
  </capabilities>
 <session-id>8544</session-id>
```

```
</hello>
]]>]]>

! The client hello message entered by the user starts here
<hello xmlns="urn:ietf:params:xml:ns:netconf:base:1.0">
  <capabilities>
    <capability>urn:ietf:params:netconf:base:1.0</capability>
  </capabilities>
</hello>
]]>]]>

! A get rpc message from the client to get the device hostname
<nf:rpc xmlns:nf="urn:ietf:params:xml:ns:netconf:base:1.0"
  xmlns="http://www.cisco.com/nxos:9.2.1.:sysmgrcli" message-id="1">
  <nf:get>
    <nf:filter type="subtree">
      <show>
        <hostname/>
      </show>
    </nf:filter>
  </nf:get>
</nf:rpc>
]]>]]>

! The rpc-reply message from the device to the client showing the hostname
<?xml version="1.0" encoding="ISO-8859-1"?>
<nf:rpc-reply xmlns="http://www.cisco.com/nxos:9.2.1.:sysmgrcli"
  xmlns:mod="http://www.cisco.com/nxos:9.2.1.:vdc_mgr" message-id="1"
  xmlns:nf="urn:ietf:params:xml:ns:netconf:base:1.0">
 <nf:data>
  <mod:show>
   <mod:hostname>
    <mod:__readonly__>
     <mod:hostname>sbx-n9kv-ao</mod:hostname>
    </mod:__readonly__>
   </mod:hostname>
  </mod:show>
 </nf:data>
</nf:rpc-reply>
]]>]]>
```

When the SSH connection is established, the first thing received is the hello message, which lists the switch capabilities. A hello message listing the client capabilities is sent back to the switch. You can prepare this message beforehand and just copy and paste it into the SSH session. The hello message is followed by the NETCONF rpc message for the command **show hostname**. One possible way to generate this RPC message is by using the **xmlin** tool in another SSH session. At this point, the switch outputs the rpc-reply message that contains the switch hostname. Notice that all rpc and rpc-reply messages end in the six-character sequence]]>]]>, which signals the end of that particular message.

NETCONF can also be used with Python for more scalable automation. The de facto Python NETCONF client is ncclient. The ncclient library, which is not platform specific, is covered in Chapter 14 in detail.

NETCONF on IOS XR

As of this writing, the latest IOS XR version is 7.1.2, and the commands in this section apply to this version. However, these commands may change in later versions of the software.

To enable the NETCONF agent on IOS XR, the k9sec package must be installed, and crypto keys must be generated. Then, at a minimum, these two commands need to be executed: **netconf-yang agent ssh** and **ssh server netconf**. Then, optionally, you can use any of the following commands to configure the different parameters of the agent:

- **netconf-yang agent session limit** {*number-of-sessions*}: Limits the maximum number of allowed concurrent NETCONF sessions to the router. Allowed values are 1 to 1024, and no default limit is set.
- **netconf-yang agent session absolute-timeout** {*minutes*}: Sets the maximum allowed duration for a session, regardless of whether the session is idle. Allowed values are 1 to 1440 minutes, and no default value is set.
- **netconf-yang agent session idle-timeout** {*minutes*}: Sets the maximum allowed duration for a session to remain idle. Allowed values are 1 to 1440 minutes, and no default value is set.
- **netconf-yang agent rate-limit** {*Bps*}: Sets the maximum number of incoming bytes per second per session. Allowed values are 4096 to 4294967295, and there is no rate limiting by default.
- **ssh server netconf port** {*port-number*}: Sets the port number over which the NETCONF agent will be reachable. The default port is 830.
- **ssh server netconf vrf** {*vrf-name*}: Sets the VRF instance over which the NETCONF agent is reachable.
- **ssh server netconf ipv4 access-list** {*ipv4-access-list-name*}: Sets an IPv4 access list to restrict access to the netconf agent.
- **ssh server netconf ipv6 access-list** {*ipv6-access-list-name*}: Sets an ipv6 access-list to restrict access to the NETCONF agent.

- **ssh server capability netconf-xml:** Allows the NETCONF agent to be reachable over the default SSH port (port 22).

After the NETCONF agent is configured, the following commands allow you to check the operational status of the different components of the agent:

- **show netconf-yang capabilities:** Lists the device's NETCONF capabilities. This is the same list of capabilities that the router sends out in its hello message during the NETCONF session establishment.
- **show netconf-yang clients:** Displays a list of active client sessions, each identified by its session ID, the same session ID sent out by the device in its hello message to the client.
- **show netconf-yang notification subscriptions:** Displays information about the configured telemetry subscriptions.
- **show netconf-yang rate-limit:** Displays the rate-limiting statistics as well as the number of dropped bytes as a result of rate limiting.
- **show netconf-yang statistics:** Displays statistics per client session.
- **show netconf-yang status:** Displays the status of the NETCONF agent. The agent is running normally when the status is **ready**.
- **show netconf-yang trace:** Displays the log messages generated by the NETCONF agent.

You can obtain the YANG models supported by an IOS XR–based platform by using four different methods:

- Use the **show netconf-yang capabilities** command to list the device capabilities. The command lists the YANG models supported by the device.
- Send a <get> rpc message that utilizes the <netconf-state> element, as discussed in the section "The Content Layer" in Chapter 14. The device responds with an rpc-reply message listing the supported models.
- List all supported YANG models under the corresponding directory on the switch through the Bash shell.
- Go to the GitHub repo at https://github.com/YangModels/yang/tree/master/vendor/cisco/xr and download the modules for the specific IOS XR version running on your device. However, not all modules for a specific version are supported on all device models. For example, a model listed under IOS XR Version 7.1.3 may be supported on NCS 5508 devices but not ASR9909 devices, even if both types of devices run IOS XR Version 7.1.3.

Cisco YANG modules follow the naming convention Cisco-IOS-XR-{*platform*}-{*technology*}-{*suffix*}.yang. Because several different platforms run IOS XR, the optional segment *platform* indicates the platform that this module applies to, with values such as **asr9k** or **ncs6k.** No *platform* segment indicates that the module applies to any platform running XR.

The *technology* segment indicates the technology that the module covers, such as **aaa-tacacs** or **ipv4-vrrp.**

The *suffix* segment takes one of four values:

- **cfg:** Modules defining configuration data models end with this suffix.
- **oper:** Modules defining operational data models end with this suffix. Operational submodules have the suffix oper-sub followed by an integer sequence number.
- **act:** Models defining YANG RPCs end in this suffix.
- **types:** Models defining data types not in the original YANG specification (for example, the BGP address-family datatype) end in this suffix.

For example, the module Cisco-IOS-XR-aaa-tacacs-cfg.yang defines a platform-agnostic model for the AAA/TACACS configuration data, and the Cisco-IOS-XR-asr9k-qos-oper-sub1.yang module is the first submodule of two submodules included (using an **include** statement) in the parent module Cisco-IOS-XR-asr9k-qos-oper.yang, which defines the data model for the QoS operational data for the ASR9K platform.

Platforms running Cisco IOS XR support candidate and running configuration datastores but not a startup configuration datastore. In other words, the **:startup** capability is not supported.

When you know how to enable NETCONF on IOS XR and fine-tune its parameters, and when you understand the naming conventions used for the Cisco YANG modules, working with NETCONF on IOS XR is no different than on any other platform.

NETCONF on IOS XE

As of this writing, the latest IOS XE version is (Amsterdam) 17.3.x. The commands in this section apply to this version. However, these commands may change in later versions of the software.

Devices running IOS XE generally expose a NETCONF API. Enabling NETCONF on IOS XE–based devices is as simple as issuing the CLI configuration command **netconf-yang.** To display the status of the NETCONF agent on the router, you use the command **show netconf-yang status**, as shown in Example 17-20.

Example 17-20 *Enabling NETCONF on IOS XE*

```
sr1000v-1(config)# netconf-yang

csr1000v-1# show netconf-yang status
netconf-yang: enabled
netconf-yang ssh port: 830
netconf-yang candidate-datastore: disabled
```

To optionally configure the SSH port for the NETCONF agent to a value other than the default 830, you can use the command **netconf-yang ssh port** {*port-number*}. You can also configure an IPv4 or IPv6 access list to limit the source IP addresses from which NETCONF messages may be received by using the command **netconf-yang {ipv4|ipv6} access-list name** {*access-list-name*}.

When NETCONF is enabled on IOS XE, the status of the different components of the protocol can be checked by using one of the following commands:

- **show netconf-yang datastores:** Lists the datastores that are enabled on the device and accessible via NETCONF.
- **show netconf-yang sessions [detail]:** Displays a list of active client sessions, each identified by its session ID, which is the same session ID sent out by the device in its hello message to the client. Adding **detail** to the end of the command also displays the statistics per session.
- **show netconf-yang statistics:** Displays NETCONF statistics for all client sessions.
- **show netconf-yang status:** Displays the status of the NETCONF agent. The command output also shows whether the candidate configuration datastore is enabled.
- **show platform software yang-management process:** Lists the processes (daemons) required to run NETCONF and RESTCONF on the router and the status of each.

Example 17-21 shows the output of each of the five **show** commands with two active NETCONF sessions.

Example 17-21 *Checking the NETCONF Datastores, Sessions, Statistics, Protocol Status, and Required Processes*

```
csr1000v-1# show netconf-yang datastores
Datastore Name              : running
Globally Locked By Session  : 25
Globally Locked Time        : 2020-02-01T09:55:10+00:00
Datastore Name              : candidate

csr1000v-1# show netconf-yang sessions
R: Global-lock on running datastore
C: Global-lock on candidate datastore
S: Global-lock on startup datastore

Number of sessions : 2

session-id  transport    username            source-host          global-lock
--------------------------------------------------------------------------------
20          netconf-ssh  developer           78.95.165.98         None
25          netconf-ssh  developer           78.95.165.98         R
```

```
csr1000v-1# show netconf-yang statistics
netconf-start-time   : 2020-02-01T09:26:22+00:00
in-rpcs              : 7
in-bad-rpcs          : 0
out-rpc-errors       : 1
out-notifications    : 0
in-sessions          : 7
dropped-sessions     : 0
in-bad-hellos        : 0

csr1000v-1# show netconf-yang status
netconf-yang: enabled
netconf-yang ssh port: 830
netconf-yang candidate-datastore: enabled

csr1000v-1# show platform software yang-management process
confd             : Running
nesd              : Running
syncfd            : Running
ncsshd            : Running
dmiauthd          : Running
nginx             : Running
ndbmand           : Running
pubd              : Running
```

Notice the letter **R** highlighted in the output of the command **show netconf-yang sessions.** This indicates that the session has a configuration lock on the running configuration datastore.

Most devices running IOS XE have all three datastores: running, startup, and candidate. However, as of this writing, NETCONF on IOS XE does not support the **:startup** capability, and therefore NETCONF messages cannot use **<startup/>**, either as **<source>** or **<target>**, in NETCONF messages.

The **:candidate** capability is supported on most platforms running IOS XE, but it is disabled by default, as you can see in Example 17-22.

Example 17-22 *NETCONF Support for the Candidate Datastore Is Disabled by Default on IOS XE Devices*

```
csr1000v-1# show netconf-yang status
netconf-yang: enabled
netconf-yang ssh port: 830
netconf-yang candidate-datastore: disabled
```

The candidate configuration datastore is enabled through the CLI by using the command **netconf-yang feature candidate-datastore**, as shown in Example 17-23.

Example 17-23 *Enabling NETCONF Support for the Candidate Datastore on IOS XE*

```
csr1000v-1(config)# netconf-yang feature candidate-datastore
netconf-yang and/or restconf is transitioning from running to candidate
netconf-yang and/or restconf will now be restarted, and any sessions in progress
  will be terminated

csr1000v-1# show netconf-yang status
netconf-yang: enabled
netconf-yang ssh port: 830
netconf-yang candidate-datastore: enabled

csr1000v-1# show netconf-yang datastores
Datastore Name              : running
Datastore Name              : candidate
```

When the candidate datastore is enabled, the **:writable-running** capability is not supported. Either of the capabilities may be supported at any point in time but not both. This means that after enabling the candidate configuration datastore, pushing configuration changes directly to the running configuration datastore through NETCONF is not allowed. This is evident from the list of capabilities sent back by the router on sessions started before and after enabling the candidate configuration datastore.

To terminate one of the NETCONF sessions from the CLI, you use the command **clear netconf-yang session** {*session-id*}. This command terminates the session identified in the command and releases any datastore locks this session had in place. This is the equivalent of a <kill-session> operation. To keep all sessions intact and just release a datastore lock, issue the command **clear configuration lock**. Example 17-24 shows the configuration lock held by session 25 released from the CLI.

Example 17-24 *Configuration Lock Release from the Switch CLI*

```
csr1000v-1# configure terminal
Configuration mode is locked by process '256' user 'NETCONF' from terminal '32132'.
  Please try later.

csr1000v-1# clear configuration lock
Process <256> is holding the config session lock !
Do you want to clear the lock?[confirm]
csr1000v-1# configure terminal
Enter configuration commands, one per line.  End with CNTL/Z.
csr1000v-1(config)#
```

Now that you have learned about NETCONF on IOS XE, the NETCONF material covered in Chapter 14 comes into play. Note that the examples in this section are generated using the Cisco DevNet IOS XE sandbox.

Meraki

This section discusses the Meraki offering and the associated APIs that it exposes. For the examples, this section uses the Cisco Meraki always-on sandbox located at https://devnetsandbox.cisco.com/RM/Topology. At the time of this writing, the username for the sandbox is **devnetmeraki@cisco.com**, and the password is **ilovemeraki**. Please visit the sandbox web page for updated information.

Cisco Meraki is a complete ecosystem of products that provide an integrated connectivity solution for enterprises. Cisco Meraki incorporates hardware, software, and cloud services that work together to provide one or more of the following functions: wired LAN, wireless LAN, security, SD-WAN, cellular WAN, mobile device management (MDM), security video capture and streaming, traffic collection, and cloud-based network management to manage all these functions.

Cisco Meraki is a cloud-based solution. This means that all devices, regardless of their geographic location, are fully managed using a web application that connects to the Meraki cloud over the Internet. You can manage a switch or WAN device in your branch office or a security camera in another branch office in a different country by using a web portal that you have access to anywhere in the world.

Meraki is classified as a network management platform because, at the end of the day, Meraki boils down to the cloud-management component of the ecosystem. Meraki uses out-of-band cloud management. This means that only management traffic passes through the Meraki cloud, and user traffic never does.

Meraki APIs

Cisco Meraki provides a rich set of RESTful APIs that enable the integration of the Meraki solution with any third-party software, whether the software is a simple Python program that you wrote to extract a list of clients connected to a specific AP or a full network management solution from a vendor that needs to integrate with Meraki. Meraki exposes five APIs:

- **Dashboard API:** This is the API for retrieving configuration and state data and configuring the devices managed under the Meraki cloud. This is the primary API used for managing Meraki networks and devices, and it is the most frequently used API.
- **Webhook Alerts API:** This API provides push notifications. A service subscribes to these push notifications in order to receive an alert when an event takes place on the Meraki network.

- **Captive Portal API:** This API is used for configuring external services that facilitate guest access on wireless networks managed under the Meraki cloud, such as portals that register guest details before the guest is allowed access to the network.
- **Location Scanning API:** This API provides a programmable interface to track and locate clients on Meraki wireless LANs in a particular physical space.
- **MV Sense API:** This is the primary API for managing MV Series smart security cameras under the Meraki cloud.

Meraki, as a multitenant management solution for all Meraki customers, defines organizations as the highest level in the device hierarchy. Each organization is identified by a unique ID. Under each organization are one or more networks. Under each of these networks are the devices that belong to that network. The workflow for device provisioning in the Meraki cloud starts by acquiring device serial numbers and adding those numbers under a network that belongs to the organization.

Meraki Use Case: Dashboard API

The Dashboard API can be used to push configuration to devices in a Meraki network, whether to perform configuration management for existing devices or provision new devices and networks. The Dashboard API can also be used to retrieve configuration as well as state data.

The Dashboard API is a RESTful API that uses JSON for encoding. As of this writing, XML is not supported.

Before using the Dashboard API, you need to enable it. To do so, go to Organization on the left-hand side of the Meraki dashboard and then choose Settings. Scroll to the bottom of the screen, and you see a checkbox for enabling the API. Make sure this box is checked, as shown in Figure 17-6.

The next step is to generate an API key. This key identifies a particular administrator and will be used for the authentication and authorization of every HTTP request made to the Dashboard API by that administrator. This is done by adding a header named X-Cisco-Meraki-API-Key to each HTTP request and giving it a value equal to the API key.
A maximum of two API keys per administrator are allowed.

The base URI for the Dashboard API is always https://api.meraki.com/api/v0. A resource's URI always starts with the base URI. The API version number identified by the /v0 segment at the end of the URI changes as new versions are released. (Refer to the API documentation at https://developer.cisco.com/meraki/api for the latest API specs.)

Using Postman or any other tool you feel comfortable with, retrieve the list of organizations on the Meraki sandbox by sending a **GET** request to the URI https://api.meraki.com/api/v0/organizations, as shown in Example 17-25.

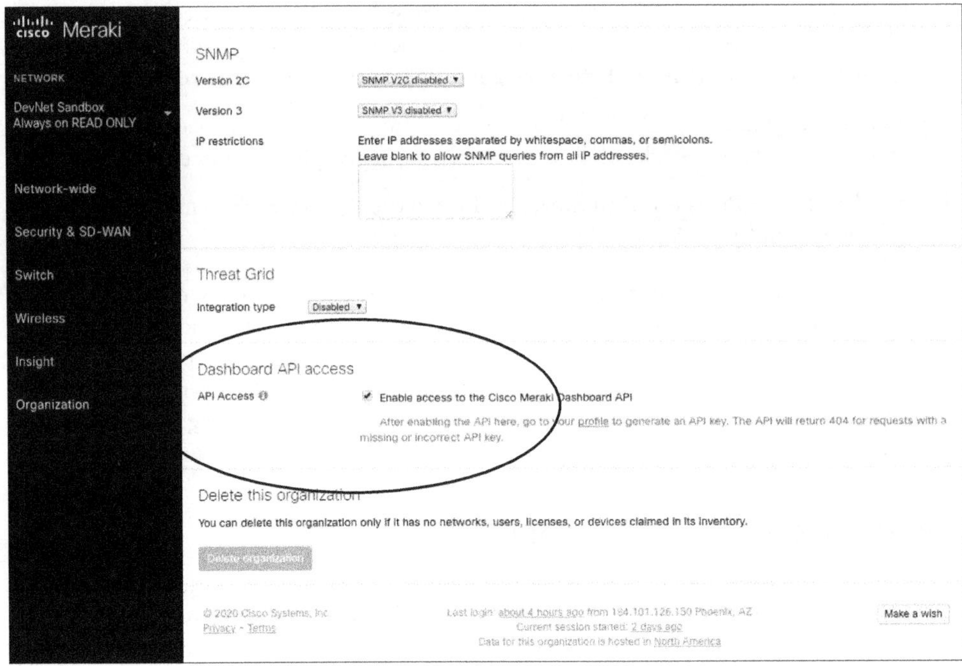

Figure 17-6 *Enabling the Dashboard API*

Example 17-25 *Listing the Organizations Under the Meraki Cloud Using the Dashboard API*

```
! HTTP Request
GET /api/v0/organizations HTTP/1.1
X-Cisco-Meraki-API-Key: 6bec40cf957de430a6f1f2baa056b99a4fac9ea0
User-Agent: PostmanRuntime/7.22.0
Accept: */*
Cache-Control: no-cache
Accept-Encoding: gzip, deflate, br
Referer: https://api.meraki.com/api/v0/organizations
Connection: keep-alive

! HTTP Response
HTTP/1.1 200 OK
Server: nginx
Date: Tue, 11 Feb 2020 22:12:51 GMT
Content-Type: application/json; charset=utf-8
Transfer-Encoding: chunked
Connection: keep-alive
```

```
Vary: Accept-Encoding
Cache-Control: no-cache, no-store, max-age=0, must-revalidate
Pragma: no-cache
Expires: Fri, 01 Jan 1990 00:00:00 GMT
X-Frame-Options: sameorigin
X-Robots-Tag: none
X-UA-Compatible: IE=Edge,chrome=1
X-Request-Id: 912df4d8b45abf4ba16a71ce61320e31
X-Runtime: 0.235174
X-XSS-Protection: 1; mode=block
Content-Encoding: gzip

[
    {
        "id": "681155",
        "name": "DeLab",
        "url": "https://n6.meraki.com/o/49Gm_c/manage/organization/overview"
    },
    {
        "id": "566327653141842061",
        "name": "ENLabs",
        "url": "https://n6.meraki.com/o/iY6FHcg/manage/organization/overview"
    },
    {
        "id": "566327653141842188",
        "name": "DevNetAssoc",
        "url": "https://n6.meraki.com/o/dcGsWag/manage/organization/overview"
    },
    {
        "id": "646829496481089588",
        "name": "DevNetMultiDomainDemo",
        "url": "https://n149.meraki.com/o/rw48vavc/manage/organization/overview"
    },
    {
        "id": "549236",
        "name": "DevNet Sandbox",
        "url": "https://n149.meraki.com/o/-t35Mb/manage/organization/overview"
    },
    {
        "id": "52636",
        "name": "Forest City - Other",
        "url": "https://n42.meraki.com/o/E_utnd/manage/organization/overview"
    },
```

```
    {
        "id": "865776",
        "name": "Cisco Live US 2019",
        "url": "https://n22.meraki.com/o/CVQqTb/manage/organization/overview"
    },
    {
        "id": "463308",
        "name": "DevNet San Jose",
        "url": "https://n18.meraki.com/o/vB2D8a/manage/organization/overview"
    }
]
```


Notice the header X-Cisco-Meraki-API-Key and its value in the request, highlighted in Example 17-25.

To retrieve the information for one particular organization, you can use the URI https://api.meraki.com/api/v0/organizations/{*organizationid*}/, where you replace *organizationid* with the actual ID of that organization.

To list the networks under an organization, send a GET request to the URI https://api.meraki.com/api/v0/organizations/{*organizationid*}/networks. Example 17-26 shows the HTTP response, with the response body containing a list of networks under the organization whose ID is 549236 and name is DevNet Sandbox. (The HTTP request is omitted in this example.)

Example 17-26 *HTTP Response Message Listing the Networks Under Organization 549236 Using the Dashboard API*

```
HTTP/1.1 200 OK
Server: nginx
Date: Tue, 11 Feb 2020 22:20:29 GMT
Content-Type: application/json
Transfer-Encoding: chunked
Connection: keep-alive
Vary: Accept-Encoding
Cache-Control: no-cache
Pragma: no-cache
Expires: Fri, 01 Jan 1990 00:00:00 GMT
X-Frame-Options: sameorigin
X-Robots-Tag: none
Last-Modified: Tue, 11 Feb 2020 22:20:29 GMT
X-UA-Compatible: IE=Edge,chrome=1
X-Request-Id: ab7da37bd159297208eb033bceb57c26
X-Runtime: 0.209099
```

```
X-XSS-Protection: 1; mode=block
Content-Encoding: gzip

[
    {
        "id": "L_646829496481104079",
        "organizationId": "549236",
        "name": "DevNet Sandbox Always on READ ONLY",
        "timeZone": "America/Los_Angeles",
        "tags": null,
        "productTypes": [
            "appliance",
            "switch",
            "wireless"
        ],
        "type": "combined",
        "disableMyMerakiCom": false,
        "disableRemoteStatusPage": true
    },
    {
        "id": "L_646829496481104279",
        "organizationId": "549236",
        "name": "DNENT3",
        "timeZone": "America/Los_Angeles",
        "tags": null,
        "productTypes": [
            "appliance",
            "camera",
            "switch",
            "wireless"
        ],
        "type": "combined",
        "disableMyMerakiCom": false,
        "disableRemoteStatusPage": true
    },

--------- OUTPUT TRUNCATED FOR BREVITY ---------
```

To get the list of devices under a particular network, use the URI https://api.meraki.com/api/v0/networks/{*networkid*}/devices, as shown in Example 17-27 for network L_646829496481104079. (The HTTP request is omitted in this example.)

Example 17-27 *Listing the Devices Under Network L_646829496481104079 Using the Dashboard API*

```
HTTP/1.1 200 OK
Server: nginx
Date: Tue, 11 Feb 2020 22:33:23 GMT
Content-Type: application/json; charset=utf-8
Transfer-Encoding: chunked
Connection: keep-alive
Vary: Accept-Encoding
Cache-Control: no-cache, no-store, max-age=0, must-revalidate
Pragma: no-cache
Expires: Fri, 01 Jan 1990 00:00:00 GMT
X-Frame-Options: sameorigin
X-Robots-Tag: none
X-UA-Compatible: IE=Edge,chrome=1
X-Request-Id: c9767d4bcbec6e27ce5df0b8f7bcebb5
X-Runtime: 0.156155
X-XSS-Protection: 1; mode=block
Content-Encoding: gzip

[
    {
        "lat": 37.4180951010362,
        "lng": -122.098531723022,
        "address": "",
        "serial": "Q2QN-9J8L-SLPD",
        "mac": "e0:55:3d:17:d4:23",
        "wan1Ip": "10.10.10.106",
        "wan2Ip": null,
        "lanIp": "10.10.10.106",
        "networkId": "L_646829496481104079",
        "model": "MX65",
        "firmware": "wired-14-40",
        "floorPlanId": null
    },
    {
        "lat": 37.4180951010362,
        "lng": -122.098531723022,
        "address": "",
        "serial": "Q2HP-F5K5-R88R",
        "mac": "88:15:44:df:f3:af",
        "lanIp": "192.168.128.2",
        "networkId": "L_646829496481104079",
```

```
        "model": "MS220-8P",
        "switchProfileId": null,
        "firmware": "switch-11-22",
        "floorPlanId": null
    },
    {
        "lat": 37.4180951010362,
        "lng": -122.098531723022,
        "address": "",
        "serial": "Q2MD-BHHS-5FDL",
        "mac": "88:15:44:60:21:10",
        "lanIp": null,
        "networkId": "L_646829496481104079",
        "model": "MR53",
        "firmware": "wireless-25-14",
        "floorPlanId": null
    }
]
```


As you can see from Example 17-27, this network is composed of three devices: an MX65 security and SD-WAN appliance, an MS220-8P switch, and an MR53 wireless access point.

Finally, to get a list of clients on a network, send a GET request to the URI https://api.meraki.com/api/v0/networks/{*networkid*}/clients.

Configuring a Meraki device is just as easy as retrieving information. You use the POST and PUT methods to create or update resources, and DELETE to delete resources.

Before a VLAN can be created on a switch, network VLANs need to be enabled. To check whether VLANs are enabled for your network, send a GET request to the URI https://api.meraki.com/api/v0/networks/{*networkid*}/vlansEnabledState.

Example 17-28 shows the VLAN's enabled status on the network from Example 17-27. (The HTTP request message and the response headers have been omitted here since there is nothing new to show.)

Example 17-28 *Querying the VLAN's Enabled Status on the Network*


```
{
    "networkId": "L_646829496481104079",
    "enabled": false
}
```

You set the VLAN's enabled status to **true** by sending a PUT request to the same URI used in Example 17-28 ending in the segment /vlansEnabledState. The message body should be a JSON structure with the enabled field only set to **true.** (**networkId** is not required in the body in this case.)

Once the VLAN's enabled state is set to true, you may refer to the Meraki API documentation at https://developer.cisco.com/meraki/api/#!create-network-vlan for information on how to create a VLAN. The page is split into three vertical sections. The middle section is split into an upper section documenting the request details titled Request Parameters. The bottom section documents the response details and is titled Responses. The request section of the page is shown in Figure 17-7.

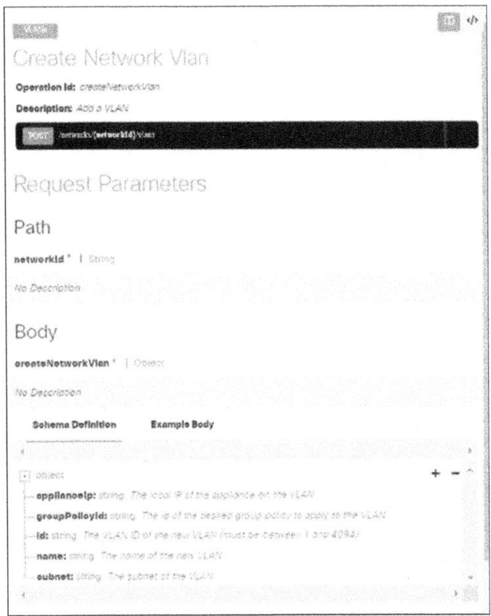

Figure 17-7 *API Documentation: Creating a Network VLAN - Request Parameters*

As you can see, in order to create a VLAN, you need to send a **POST** request to the URI https://api.meraki.com/api/v0/networks/{*networkid*}/vlans, shown without the base URI in the documentation. There are also two parameters, both of them marked with a red star, indicating that both parameters are required. The first parameter is networkId, which is of type String and is a *Path* parameter, which means it goes into the URI. The second parameter is createNetworkVlan and is a *Body* parameter, which means it goes into the message body. The createNetworkVLAN parameter is a JSON structure that consists of five fields: applianceip, groupPolicyid, id, name, and subnet. Therefore, to create VLAN 100, named DevTestVLAN, for subnet 10.0.1.0/24 on appliance 192.168.1.1 under network ID L_646829496481104079, you need to send a **POST** request to URI https://api.meraki.com/api/v0/networks/L_646829496481104079/vlans with the JSON structure in Example 17-29 as the message body. The documentation page also provides an example under the Example Body tab shown in Figure 17-7.

Figure 17-8 shows the Response section of the documentation web page. As you can see, if the VLAN is successfully configured, you should receive a "201 Created" response with a message body similar to the one shown in the figure under the Example Body tab.

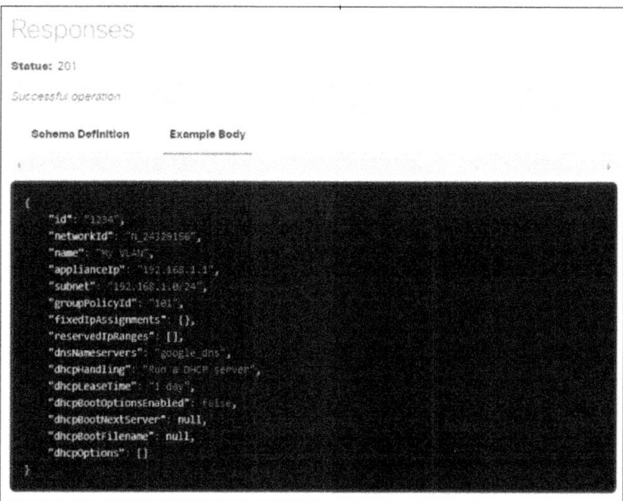

Figure 17-8 *API Documentation: Creating a Network VLAN - Response Parameters*

Example 17-29 *HTTP Request Message Body to Create VLAN 100*

```
{
  "id": "100",
  "name": "DevTestVLAN",
  "subnet": "10.0.1.0/24",
  "applianceIp": "192.168.1.1"
}
```

DNA Center

This section describes Cisco DNA Center, its positioning in the automation ecosystem, and the APIs that it exposes.

Cisco Digital Network Architecture (DNA) is Cisco's architecture framework for intent-based networking (IBN). IBN is a new network management paradigm in which the outcomes required from a network are expressed in terms of business requirements (hence *intent*), and one or more products translate these requirements into actionable configuration, implement this configuration, and then monitor the outcome, amending the configuration as required, to keep the outcomes aligned with the business intent. IBN allows the network operator to focus on what needs to be accomplished rather than how to accomplish it.

DNA Center is a Cisco product that acts as the network management system, SDN controller, and analytics engine for the IBN ecosystem for an enterprise. DNA Center has the capability to manage Cisco and non-Cisco products, physical and virtual appliances, and fabric as well as standalone devices. Input to Cisco DNA Center is *intent* that DNA Center translates into configuration that gets pushed down to the relevant managed network devices. Network devices send back *context*, which is the state of the network devices, hosts, and traffic traversing the network and is used for both reporting analytics and assurance.

When you log in to DNA Center Version 2.1.2.x, you see that the GUI has four sections: Overall Health Summary, Network Snapshot, Network Configuration, and Tools. Figure 17-9 shows the Network Configuration section.

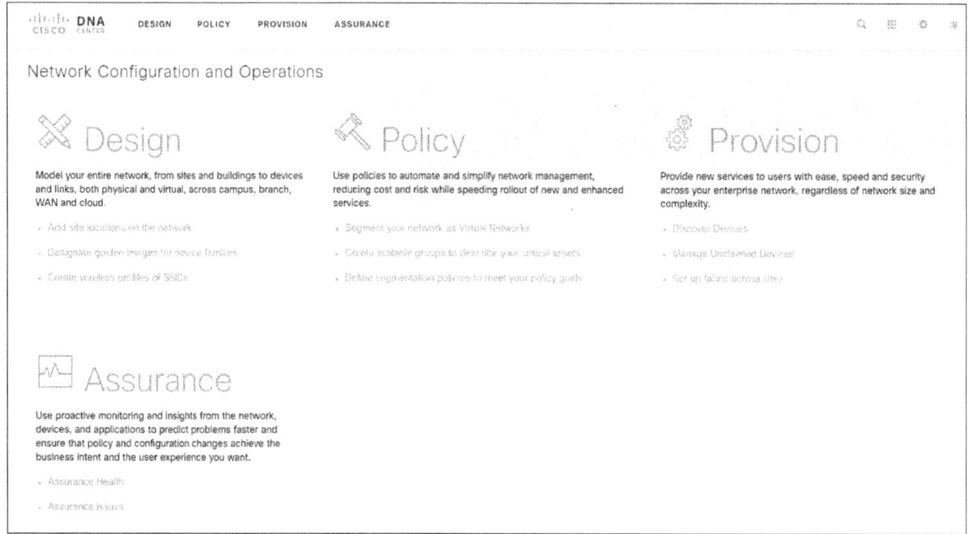

Figure 17-9 *A Section of the DNA Center GUI Showing the Different Aspects of Network Management*

In the Network Configuration section, you can see that DNA Center manages the network life cycle by managing four groups of network management tasks:

- **Design:** The tasks that you can complete from this section assist you with designing your network. You can define the geographic network hierarchy (country, state, city, building, floor, and so on), manage your network settings and services (DHCP, NTP and DNS servers, IP pools, wireless SSIDs and settings, and device credentials), manage the image repository for your devices, create network profile templates that will eventually be used to configure the wired and wireless network devices and fabrics that are managed by this DNA Center server, and manage the authentication templates for the authentication methods used for the different wired and wireless clients on the network.

- **Policy:** The tasks under this section are related to managing all the policies related to controlling application traffic, whether these policies are security policies or QoS policies. Under this section you also manage integration with the Cisco ISE server, if one exists in the network.
- **Provision:** This section allows you to complete tasks related to claiming network devices. Claiming a network device involves discovering the device and bringing it under the management supervision of this DNA Center server. This is also where you see and manage the inventory of claimed standalone and fabric devices.
- **Assurance:** In this section, you can monitor the performance of the network, applications, and hosts and manage the settings for corrective actions to take when network performance deviates from the business intent stated to DNA Center.

Note Depending on the version of your DNA Center installation, the DNA Center GUI described thus far may be different from what you see in your environment. The general concepts remain the same, and the fundamental positioning and functions of DNA Center as a product remain the same. Remember that products and their APIs change and sometimes become end of life.

DNA Center APIs

DNA Center exposes a number of APIs that can be used to programmatically accomplish most of the tasks that would otherwise be done through the DNA Center GUI. The best way to describe the APIs or interfaces that DNA Center exposes is via their cardinal classification:

- **Northbound:** DNA Center exposes a RESTful API called the Intent API that allows an application to express business intent to DNA Center through an API call and have DNA Center interpret this business intent into a low-level configuration workflow to implement this intent. The Intent API can also be used to retrieve state and configuration data from DNA Center.
- **Southbound:** DNA Center can communicate with Cisco devices under its administration via several different interfaces, including the CLI, SNMP, and NETCONF. It also provides an SDK that can be used to develop device packages to be used to integrate with other vendors' equipment.
- **Eastbound:** DNA Center provides the facility for other systems to subscribe to event notifications generated by DNA Center. These notifications are sent to the subscribing systems via a push mechanism. This is done through a RESTful API commonly referred to as a *webhook*.
- **Westbound:** DNA Center exposes a RESTful API called the Integration API that allows ITSM, IPAM, reporting, and analytics systems to integrate with DNA Center.

  The DNA Center API reference can be viewed at https://developer.cisco.com/docs/dna-center/.

Intent API

This northbound REST API uses the methods GET, POST, PUT, and DELETE and a JSON-encoded message body. This is the primary API used to communicate business intent to DNA Center, with the target of DNA Center converting this intent into actionable configuration and pushing it down to the relevant devices southbound. This API is also used to retrieve configuration and state information RESTfully from DNA Center.

The Intent API is actually a massive and continuously growing interface in DNA Center. A finer classification scheme groups all the possible Intent API calls into functional domains and subdomains. For example, the subdomain Topology under the domain Know Your Network contains the API calls for retrieving the physical, layer 2, and layer 3 topology details for the network, in addition to the overall network health information. The subdomain Software Image Management (SWIM) under the domain Site Management contains the API calls for retrieving and managing the activation and distribution of software images. Figure 17-10 illustrates the Intent API domains and subdomains hierarchy.

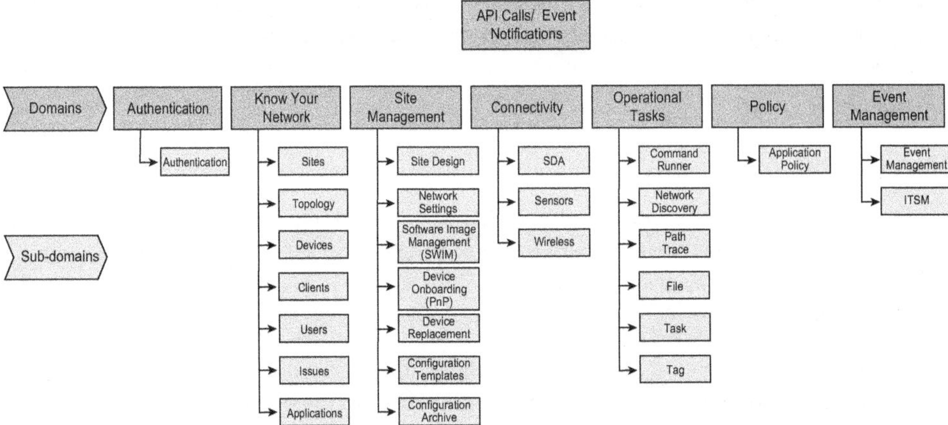

Figure 17-10 *Intent API Domains and Subdomains*

As of DNA Center Version 2.1.2.x, there are a total of 7 domains and 27 subdomains. An updated list of all the possible Intent API calls for this version of DNA Center can be found in the Intent API reference at https://developer.cisco.com/docs/dna-center/#!cisco-dna-2-1-2-x-api-overview. In addition, the use case presented later in this section elaborates on the usage of Intent APIs.

Device Management

In the southbound direction, DNA Center communicates with the Cisco devices under its administration via the CLI (over SSH or Telnet), SNMP, or NETCONF. An SDK is also available to develop device packages to manage non-Cisco devices through DNA Center. The Cisco DNA Center SDK is based on the open-source Eclipse IDE.

Event Notifications and Webhooks

Much like most other programmable products from Cisco, DNA Center provides an interface through which third-party systems can subscribe to event notifications generated by DNA Center. The end receiving a notification from DNA Center is referred to as the *notification listener*. The notification listener may be an email server that receives an email notification from DNA Center. Alternatively, the listener may be an HTTP(S) server that receives the notification in the form of a POST HTTP(S) request message from DNA Center, with a JSON payload that contains the event details. These notifications in the form of HTTP(S) POST messages are called *webhooks*.

An event notification contains information about a specific event. Events are classified into domains and subdomains, which are the same as the ones used to classify Intent API calls (refer to Figure 17-10). This information, along with the *event attributes*, Type, Category, Severity, and Workflow, is included in the notification JSON body. Each of these fields can hold one of a number of predefined values, as listed in Table 17-1.

Table 17-1 *Event Attributes and Values*

Event Attribute	Allowed Values
Type	NETWORK, APP, SYSTEM, SECURITY, or INTEGRATIONS
Category	INFO, WARN, ALERT, ERROR, or TASK PROGRESS
Severity	1, 2, 3, 4, or 5
Workflow	Incident, Problem, Event, or RFC

A potential listener may subscribe to notifications for a particular event through the DNA Center GUI or by making an Intent API call by sending a POST request to the URI https://{*DNA-Center-Address-IP*}/dna/intent/api/v1/event/subscription with a JSON-encoded body that contains the details of the event that the listener wants to subscribe to. The event details in the JSON-encoded body may be obtained from the GUI or by making another API call by sending a GET request to the URI https://{*DNA-Center-Address-IP*}/dna/intent/api/v1/events?tags=ASSURANCE, which lists all the events that you may want to subscribe to.

Integration API

One of the principles on which DNA Center operates is *integration*. DNA Center was not developed with the intention of replacing all existing tools, but rather to integrate with other tools in order to optimize the existing processes and workflows. If an ITSM system, such as ServiceNow, is doing a great job handling, among other things, incident, change, and problem management, or if an IP address management (IPAM) system such as BlueCat is already managing the IP and DHCP pools in the network, then DNA Center should be able to integrate with those tools instead of trying to replace them.

DNA Center provides out-of-the-box seamless integration with a number of certified third-party tools, such as ServiceNow, BlueCat, Infoblox, and Tableau. Cisco created software modules called *bundles* that ship with DNA Center to enable the integration of DNA Center with a number of certified third-party tools; the bundles require very limited effort from a DNA Center administrator.

In the event that a non-certified third-party tool needs to integrate with DNA Center, an Integration REST API is provided that allows this integration.

Integrating DNA Center—whether with one of the certified third-party tools or some other tool—allows DNA Center to be part of the workflows defined on those tools. For example, DNA Center can be configured to request a ticket to be opened via ServiceNow if it detects a certain condition on the managed network. Alternatively, a change that is requested and approved through the change management workflow on ServiceNow could be fulfilled by DNA Center. An IP subnet that will be used by a group of hosts and is defined on DNA Center, could automatically be exported to Infoblox, along with the DHCP pool created for that subnet, without having to go to Infoblox and explicitly creating that DHCP pool.

Use Case: Intent API

This section shows three API calls to the Cisco DevNet DNA Center reservation-based sandbox. The first API call authenticates to the sandbox and gets an authorization token. The second API call retrieves the topology of the network, and the third retrieves a list of the devices managed by this instance of DNA Center. Each API call in this section is fully documented in the Intent API reference (see https://developer.cisco.com/docs/dna-center/#!cisco-dna-2-1-2-x-api-overview).

You can reserve the sandbox through the DevNet website, at https://devnetsandbox.cisco.com/RM/Topology. As of this writing, the sandbox is reachable at 10.10.20.85 using the username **admin** and password **Cisco1234!**. As you may have guessed from the private IP address of the sandbox, you need to connect through a VPN; this is the case for all reservation-based sandboxes on DevNet. The details of this connectivity are emailed to you when the time slot you reserve comes up. Both username and password on DNA Center are case sensitive. Make sure to visit the DevNet sandbox site for the latest sandbox details.

DNA Center authenticates each HTTP request sent to its Intent API by using an authorization token. You insert this token into each HTTP request by assigning it as the value of the header field named X-Auth-Token. In order to obtain this token, you need to make an API call to the URI https://10.10.20.85/dna/system/api/v1/auth/token, which is an Intent API call defined under the Authentication domain and subdomain.

Using Postman, you can create a new request and change the method to POST. Under the Authorization tab, choose Basic Auth from the Type drop-down list and then enter the username and password, each in its corresponding text box on the right (**admin/ Cisco1234!** in this case). Click Send and then notice the response body at the bottom of the Postman window encoded in JSON, containing a Token object whose value is a string of characters.

Keep in mind that Basic Auth is nothing except the string {*username*}:{*password*}—in this case, admin:Cisco1234! encoded in Base64. This encoded Base64 string is then provided as the value of the Authorization header field in the request. This is done automatically for you in Postman. (Base64 encoding and HTTP authentication are covered in detail in Chapter 8, "Advanced HTTP.")

Now to use the token to retrieve useful information from DNA Center, you need to create a new request, this time using the default method, GET. Under the Headers tab, add a new header to your request by typing **X-Auth-Token** under Key and then copy and paste the Token value you got from the previous request into the Value field. Even better, you can create an environment variable and use that as the value for all your subsequent requests. When the token value expires, you request a new token and update it in one place only: the value of the environment variable. Postman is covered in detail in Chapter 7.

To retrieve the topology details of the network managed by this instance of DNA Center, add to the GET request you just created the URI https://10.10.20.85/dna/intent/api/v1/topology/site-topology. This URI is part of the Know Your Network domain and Topology subdomain. Example 17-30 shows the request message and part of the response message.

Example 17-30 *Listing the Sites Topology Defined in DNA Center Using an Intent API Call*

```
! HTTP Request
GET /dna/intent/api/v1/topology/site-topology HTTP/1.1
X-Auth-Token: eyJ0eXAiOiJKV1QiLCJhbGci...<Truncated>
User-Agent: PostmanRuntime/7.24.0
Accept: */*
Cache-Control: no-cache
Host: 10.10.20.85
Accept-Encoding: gzip, deflate, br
Connection: keep-alive

! HTTP Response
HTTP/1.1 200 OK
Content-Type: application/json;charset=utf-8
Transfer-Encoding: chunked
Connection: keep-alive
```

```
Date: Fri, 27 Mar 2020 17:20:05 GMT
Set-Cookie: JSESSIONID=hnppb8cevqz41nis3mfs29y6h;Path=/; Secure; HttpOnly
Expires: Thu, 01 Jan 1970 00:00:00 GMT
Server: webserver
Via: api-gateway
Cache-Control: no-store
Pragma: no-cache
Content-Security-Policy: default-src 'self' 'unsafe-inline' 'unsafe-eval' blob:
  data:
X-Content-Type-Options: nosniff
X-XSS-Protection: 1
Strict-Transport-Security: max-age=31536000; includeSubDomains
X-Frame-Options: SAMEORIGIN
```


```
{
    "response": {
        "sites": [
            {
                "id": "a7b75b75-eaee-4f7f-a2bb-53a4d36b6f6c",
                "name": "Building_1",
                "parentId": "1909e87e-75bc-4eb3-9494-b8e4e62f5773",
                "latitude": "-26.063795",
                "longitude": "28.082594",
                "locationType": "building",
                "locationAddress": "",
                "locationCountry": "South Africa",
                "displayName": "3213213",
                "groupNameHierarchy": "Global/South Africa/Gauteng/Woodlands/
  Building_1"
            },
            {
                "id": "1909e87e-75bc-4eb3-9494-b8e4e62f5773",
                "name": "Woodlands",
                "parentId": "b2ec99e3-5bbd-4bfa-8db4-1a7b6a805af3",
                "latitude": "",
                "longitude": "",
                "locationType": "area",
                "locationAddress": "",
                "locationCountry": "",
                "displayName": "3213212",
                "groupNameHierarchy": "Global/South Africa/Gauteng/Woodlands"
            },
            {
                "id": "acf4d799-f68e-41ac-a194-450c810defb3",
```

```
                "name": "Floor 1",
                "parentId": "a7b75b75-eaee-4f7f-a2bb-53a4d36b6f6c",
                "latitude": "",
                "longitude": "",
                "locationType": "floor",
                "locationAddress": "",
                "locationCountry": "",
                "displayName": "3213214",
                "groupNameHierarchy": "Global/South Africa/Gauteng/Woodlands/
  Building_1/Floor 1"
            },
            {
                "id": "41c5c785-ba04-4fcd-bf40-f0452b3b662e",
                "name": "South Africa",
                "parentId": "33fbd22e-e408-4035-a5d4-53d91732b9f7",
                "latitude": "",
                "longitude": "",
                "locationType": "area",
                "locationAddress": "",
                "locationCountry": "",
                "displayName": "3213210",
                "groupNameHierarchy": "Global/South Africa"
            },
            {
                "id": "b2ec99e3-5bbd-4bfa-8db4-1a7b6a805af3",
                "name": "Gauteng",
                "parentId": "41c5c785-ba04-4fcd-bf40-f0452b3b662e",
                "latitude": "",
                "longitude": "",
                "locationType": "area",
                "locationAddress": "",
                "locationCountry": "",
                "displayName": "3213211",
                "groupNameHierarchy": "Global/South Africa/Gauteng"
            },
--------- OUTPUT TRUNCATED FOR BREVITY ---------
        ]
    },
    "version": "1.0"
}
```

Notice the usage of the authorization token as the value of the X-Auth-Token header field, highlighted in Example 17-30. The HTTP response is a JSON object listing a number of sites. The site hierarchy is not immediately noticeable. However, note the parameter named groupNameHierarchy, which shows you the hierarchy and the relationships between the sites.

To retrieve a list of network devices claimed by the DNA Center sandbox, send a GET request to the URI https://10.10.20.85/dna/intent/api/v1/network-device. Due to the length of the response received, Example 17-31 shows the part of the response for one device only.

Example 17-31 *Listing the Devices Managed by DNA Center Using an Intent API Call*

```
HTTP/1.1 200 OK
Content-Type: application/json;charset=UTF-8
Transfer-Encoding: chunked
Connection: keep-alive
Server: webserver
Set-Cookie: JSESSIONID=4CC491036A0560A78A1E8D77D1FFC60D; Path=/apic-em-inventory-
  manager-service; HttpOnly; Secure; HttpOnly
Date: Fri, 27 Mar 2020 17:21:41 GMT
Via: api-gateway
Cache-Control: no-store
Pragma: no-cache
Content-Security-Policy: default-src 'self' 'unsafe-inline' 'unsafe-eval' blob:
  data:
X-Content-Type-Options: nosniff
X-XSS-Protection: 1
Strict-Transport-Security: max-age=31536000; includeSubDomains
X-Frame-Options: SAMEORIGIN

{
    "response": [
        {
            "memorySize": "3735220224",
            "family": "Wireless Controller",
            "type": "Cisco 3504 Wireless LAN Controller",
            "lastUpdated": "2020-03-27 12:27:31",
            "lineCardCount": "0",
            "lineCardId": "",
            "locationName": null,
            "managementIpAddress": "10.10.20.51",
            "platformId": "AIR-CT3504-K9",
            "reachabilityFailureReason": "",
            "reachabilityStatus": "Reachable",
            "series": "Cisco 3500 Series Wireless LAN Controller",
```

```
            "snmpContact": "",
            "snmpLocation": "",
            "tagCount": "0",
            "tunnelUdpPort": "16666",
            "waasDeviceMode": null,
            "apManagerInterfaceIp": "",
            "associatedWlcIp": "",
            "bootDateTime": "2019-04-10 00:53:31",
            "collectionStatus": "Managed",
            "errorCode": null,
            "errorDescription": null,
            "interfaceCount": "0",
            "roleSource": "AUTO",
            "lastUpdateTime": 1585312051211,
            "upTime": "352 days, 11:34:12.00",
            "serialNumber": "FCW2219M007",
            "macAddress": "50:61:bf:57:51:00",
            "collectionInterval": "Global Default",
            "inventoryStatusDetail": "<status><general code=\"SUCCESS\"/></status>",
            "hostname": "Cisco_57:51:02",
            "deviceSupportLevel": "Supported",
            "softwareType": "Cisco Controller",
            "softwareVersion": "8.8.111.0",
            "location": null,
            "role": "ACCESS",
            "instanceTenantId": "5be5fcaaee9a67004cf94d6b",
            "instanceUuid": "aff8a3e1-4462-4e39-b974-40ea16b609e8",
            "id": "aff8a3e1-4462-4e39-b974-40ea16b609e8"
        },
--------- OUTPUT TRUNCATED FOR BREVITY ---------
    ],
    "version": "1.0"
}
```


Retrieving the full list of devices every time you make an API call may not be very practical at times. Looking at the API documentation, under the Devices subdomain, you can see that the list of devices retrieved can be filtered by any one of several criterion, one of which is the hostname. To retrieve the details of the device whose hostname is Cisco_57:51:02, all you need to do is send a GET request to the URI https://10.10.20.85/dna/intent/api/v1/network-device?hostname=Cisco_57:51:02.

Collaboration Platforms

This section covers the programmability and automation features of Cisco's collaboration line of products, which fall into four categories: Unified Communications, Contact Center, Conferencing, and Collaboration Endpoints.

Cisco's Collaboration Portfolio

Cisco's collaboration portfolio includes the following:

- **Unified Communications:** These products provide converged solutions for voice, video, data, and mobile communication. Products in this category include the following:
  - **Cisco Webex Teams:** This solution from Cisco has the feel of a messenger or chatting application but is actually a central point for collaboration of different teams. From Webex Teams you can send text messages, share files, whiteboard, start Webex meetings, and more. Webex Teams revolves around the concepts of People (registered users of Webex Teams), Teams (groups of people with a set of rooms that are visible to all members of that team), and Spaces or Rooms (virtual meeting places where people post messages and collaborate to get work done). Several other objects, such as Devices, Events, and Places, exist in Webex Teams, but they act as the backdrop for the former three primary objects.
  - **Cisco Unified Communications Manager (CUCM):** This is the base software product from Cisco that provides the infrastructure required for IP telephony, high-definition video, unified messaging, instant messaging and presence. It is leveraged by other Cisco products, such as the Business Edition.
  - **Cisco Webex Cloud Calling:** This is a full cloud solution that provides the same functionality as on-premises CUCM, in addition to all the benefits and functionality provided by native cloud solutions.
  - **Cisco Business Edition:** This is a line of products, comprised of integrated software and hardware, that provide collaboration solutions targeting small to enterprise-grade businesses. Each solution in the Business Edition line provides different capacity, scalability, high-availability, and management options (for example, cloud versus on-premises management). This solution leverages several existing products and solutions from Cisco, including Cisco's UCS servers, CUCM, and Contact Center Express software.
- **Contact Center:** These products provide a contact center solution for customers who need to interact with their customers, whether internal or external, and provide a form of support. Contact center products expand on the function of legacy call centers in that agents interact with customers not only over the phone but via online

chat, social media, SMS, and other messaging applications. Products under this category include the following:

- **Cisco Unified Contact Center (Express or Enterprise):** This is the base software product from Cisco that provides the infrastructure for the contact center functionality. The Express offering (CCX) provides support for up to 400 agents, and the Enterprise offering (UCCE) supports up to 24,000 agents. This software provides different channels to support next-generation contact center channels to communicate with customers, such as inbound voice, outbound voice, outbound IVR, and digital channels. The Enterprise offering goes as far as supporting features such as post-call IVR, email, and web intercept surveys.
- **Cisco Webex Contact Center (Enterprise):** This is the native cloud contact center offering from Cisco. A cloud-based solution provides integrated analytics and artificial intelligence in addition to rapid deployment and minimal capital and operational cost, since the whole solution is hosted in the Cisco cloud. Webex-based cloud solutions also provide seamless integration with other Webex products, such as Webex Teams.
- **Cisco Finesse:** Through a Web 2.0 interface, Finesse provides agent and supervisor desktops in a contact center. Finesse integrates with the other products in the collaboration portfolio to provide the full contact center functionality.

- **Conferencing:** These products provide next-generation video conferencing solutions. Products in this category include the following:
  - **Cisco Webex Meetings:** This cloud-based software solution enables scheduling, running, and recording of meetings involving voice, video, messaging, whiteboarding, screen sharing, and other functions. It runs seamlessly on a number of devices, including PCs, mobiles phones, and Cisco endpoint devices.
  - **Cisco Webex Support:** This cloud-based solution enables support teams to provide remote support to their customers by facilitating tasks such gaining remote access to a customer PC. This solution requires the installation of an agent on the remote machine that requires support.
  - **Cisco Meeting Server:** This is an on-premises conferencing solution offered by Cisco.

  Other services included in this category are Webex Edge, Webex Events, Webex Training, and Webex Webcasting.
- **Collaboration Endpoints:** These are the physical endpoint appliances provided by Cisco. Products in this category include the following:
  - **Cisco Webex Board:** This is a digital whiteboard that connects wirelessly and is touch-based. It is used for meeting room presentations and integrates with the Webex line of products to extend its functionality to support conferencing. As of this writing, it comes in three sizes.

- **Cisco Webex Room Series:** This is a group of products that are geared toward running Webex Meetings in conference room settings. The product line includes the Room products, which are 4K screens fitted with microphones and cameras, and Room Kits, which are used to transform third-party 4K displays into full Webex Meetings endpoints. The Room series of products runs the programmable RoomOS software.
- **Cisco IP Phones:** This is a line of IP phones with a range of capabilities that come in both wired and wireless forms.

Collaboration APIs

Most products in Cisco's collaboration portfolio are programmable and expose a number of APIs that enable programmable management of the devices and solutions as well as integration with third-party systems. This section covers the programmability features and APIs exposed by CUCM, Webex Meetings, Webex Teams, Webex Devices, and Finesse.

Cisco Unified Communications Manager (CUCM)

CUCM exposes five APIs:

- **Administrative XML Web Service (AXL) API:** This API is used to perform CRUD operations on CUCM objects. This API is SOAP-based and uses HTTP 1.0 Basic Authentication. AXL message bodies are encoded in XML and use Web Services Description Language (WSDL) and XML Schema Definitions (XSD). AXL is the primary API used to manage CUCM programmatically and can be used to provision, retrieve the status of, update, or delete objects on the CUCM, such as phones, users, device pools, and dial plans.
- **Cisco Emergency Responder (CER) API:** The CER is an emergency communications system that manages 911 and similar emergency calls from one of the devices under CUCM administration. The CER routes emergency calls as required in addition to providing extra information, such as the caller's location. CER also automatically stores a call log of all emergency calls. The CER API, which provides programmatic access to Cisco CER, is a REST API that uses HTTP Basic Authentication and only supports the GET method and an empty message body in the requests. The message bodies of HTTP responses from this API are encoded in XML. The CER API allows third-party applications to integrate with and leverage the services provided by CER.
- **Platform Administrative Web Services (PAWS) API:** This API is meant for programmatically managing CUCM clusters. This new API is available only on Versions 9.0(1) and later. This API can be used to retrieve CUCM software version numbers or hardware details. It can also be used to upgrade the CUCM or reboot it. This is an XML/SOAP-based API.

- **CUCM Serviceability API:** CUCM Serviceability is a group of services and tools that are geared toward monitoring the status of CUCM as well as reporting, diagnosing, and resolving issues. The CUCM Serviceability API provides programmatic access to these tools via an XML/SOAP interface. Examples of data that can be retrieved from these tools includes the number of phones and devices registered to CUCM and the connection status of these endpoints. You may also retrieve the number of concurrent connections to the CUCM TFTP server (indicating the number of devices downloading new firmware) and CUCM's performance during these downloads. This API can also be used to retrieve call detail record (CDR) and CUCM logs.
- **User Data Services (UDS) API:** This API is intended for use by a specific authenticated user to manage their own experience and settings on CUCM. Calls to the UDS API may be made to retrieve general information common to all users, such as API calls to do directory searches for other users, to retrieve the CUCM time zones or to retrieve the list of nodes in the CUCM cluster. Or the calls to the API may be done to manage this user's speed dial settings or credentials. The UDS API is a REST API that uses the methods GET, PUT, POST, and DELETE.

Webex Meetings

Webex Meetings exposes four APIs:

- **XML API:** This API uses the POST method and an XML-encoded body to provide an interface to integrate custom applications with Webex Meetings. This is the primary API to use to integrate with Webex Meetings. For example, if you would like to schedule a Webex meeting, get the link to a meeting, delete a meeting, or list summary information for scheduled meetings, this is the API to call. But Meeting services is only one part of the functionality exposed by this API. This API can also be used to manage Webex Training, Webex Events, and Webex Support Services, among other functions.
- **URL API:** This API uses HTTPS requests with URIs containing PHP calls in the form of parameters. These PHP calls initiate service requests on the Webex Meetings server. The URL API provides a very limited number of functions and is often used as a lightweight alternative to the XML API.
- **Teleconference Service Provider (TSP) API:** This API provides external TSPs an interface to integrate their teleconferencing service with Cisco Webex Meetings.
- **REST API:** Cisco also provides a newly developed REST API, which will eventually expose all functionality of Webex Meetings currently exposed by the XML API.

Webex Teams

Webex Teams exposes a REST API that provides a programmatic interface to Webex Teams. Using this API, you can list, create, and delete rooms (spaces), teams, and messages and manage people and their memberships. Authentication to this API involves using an authentication token as the value of the Authorization header in the HTTP request. This token is generated by creating a developer account on https://developer.webex.com/.

This API uses the methods GET, PUT, POST, and DELETE, and the request message body is encoded in application/json or application/x-www-form-urlencoded; the responses are always encoded in application/json. The use case later in this section uses this REST API to create a new space, add participants to the space, and send messages to the space.

The Webex Teams REST API also supports webhooks. You can create a webhook so that a custom application you created receives a notification (which is actually an HTTP POST request) when a particular event occurs in Webex Teams.

Webex Devices

The majority of Webex endpoints run software called Cisco Collaboration Endpoint Software, which exposes an API called *xAPI* (short for *Experience API*). xAPI can be used to configure these endpoints or to integrate them with third-party control systems, such as Crestron, AMX/Harman, or Extron.

xAPI uses a variety of transports, each requiring its own configuration on the GUI of the software in order to be enabled. The API calls can made over SSH, Telnet, HTTP/HTTPS, WebSocket, or a serial connection. The encoding of the input and output to and from xAPI is configurable to Terminal (CLI style line-based), XML, or JSON, with Terminal being the default.

Commands to xAPI are classified into several categories. These are the main ones:

- **xCommand:** These commands direct the device to execute one or more actions, such as to join a Webex meeting, dial a phone number, or mute the microphone.
- **xConfiguration:** These commands target the device settings, such as the time zone or the IP address of the device, or the default audio level of the speaker on the device.
- **xStatus:** These commands retrieve the current status of the device, such as the current device speaker volume in dB.
- **xFeedback:** These commands specify what parts of the configuration and status hierarchies to monitor.
- **xPreferences:** These commands are used to set preferences for RS-232, Telnet, and SSH sessions.

Finesse

Cisco Finesse exposes four REST APIs. All of these APIs encode the message body, if one exists, in XML. Finesse APIs either use HTTP Basic Authentication using a Base64-encoded authorization header, or a bearer token.

Finesse Desktop APIs are used by the Finesse desktops (for both agents and supervisors) to communicate with the Cisco Finesse server or the Cisco Unified Contact Center (Enterprise or Express). The API is used for bidirectional communication of information related to the different Contact Center entities. The API calls are further broken down into the following categories:

- **User:** These are the agents and supervisors. Each user is represented by a User object that holds the information of that user, such as the first and last names, login ID and name, role, team, and status (such as logged in and ready to take calls). API calls in this category are used to sign in or sign out agents and communicate agent state information to the Finesse server.
- **Dialog:** API calls in this category are used to communicate information related to voice calls with customers and non-voice tasks, together known as *dialogs*. (Recall the difference between a legacy call center and a next-generation contact center?) Each dialog is represented by a Dialog object that holds the information of that particular dialog.
- **Queue:** API calls in this category are used to communicate information related to call queues and the statistics for those queues, such as the number of calls in queue and the start time of the longest call in queue. Each queue is represented by a Queue object that is used to hold the information for that queue.
- **Team:** A team is a group of users, such as a group of agents assigned to a specific technology or a group of agents at a certain level of the escalation hierarchy. Each team is represented by a Team object that contains information on that team, including the users assigned to the team. The API calls in this category are used to communicate team information.
- **Client Log:** The APIs in this category are used to post client-side logs to the Finesse server. These APIs are one-way only.
- **Single Sign-On:** The Finesse desktop or any other third-party desktop application that needs to integrate with the Finesse server uses the APIs in this category to manage SSO token-related operations.
- **Team Message:** The APIs in this category can be used to manage (send and retrieve) messages sent to all the users in one or more teams. This API is used by a supervisor or the Finesse server administrator.

Configuration APIs are used by Finesse administrators to configure the different Finesse entities, such as system, cluster, and database settings; reason codes and wrap-up reasons; phonebooks and contacts; team resources; and workflows and workflow actions.

Serviceability APIs are used to retrieve system information such as the installed licenses and deployment type (with CCE or CCX), retrieve diagnostic and performance data, or retrieve runtime information, such as the number of logged-in agents.

And finally, the Cisco Finesse Notifications service provides subscription-based webhook-style notifications.

Use Case: Webex Teams

This section shows how to use the Webex Teams REST API to discover the user called *networkdeveloper*, whose email is networkdeveloper@thenetdev.com. Then you will create a team called *Webex Teams Devs TEAM (via REST API)* and then add network-developer to the team. You will then create a space (room) named *Webex Teams Devs ROOM/SPACE (via REST API)*, attached to the team you just created. You will then add the user networkdeveloper to the room. Finally, you will send a message to that room. All this is accomplished solely via the Webex Teams REST API.

As stated in the previous section, you need to have an authentication token sent with every HTTP request for authorizing that request. You can get a temporary token that is valid for 12 hours by logging in to https://developer.webex.com. If you don't have a Webex Developer account, go ahead and create one. It takes only a few minutes.

When you are logged in, click the Documentation link at the top of the page and then click API Reference on the left side of the page. Scroll down and click the People section. A list of all API calls under this category appears on the right side of the page. Click the List People API: the first API in the list that uses the method GET and the URI https://api.ciscospark.com/v1/people. You are then redirected to the API documentation for that specific API call.

To the right side of each documentation page, you can see the title Header with the word Authorization under it, as shown in Figure 17-11. This is the value of the token that has to be included in each HTTP request you send. If you will use Postman, you need to add a header field in the Request Headers section with a key equal to **Authorization** and value equal to **Bearer** {*token_value*}. For the *token_value*, just click the Copy button to the right of the hidden value on the documentation page. Note that the token is valid for 12 hours or until you log off from the developer.webex.com site.

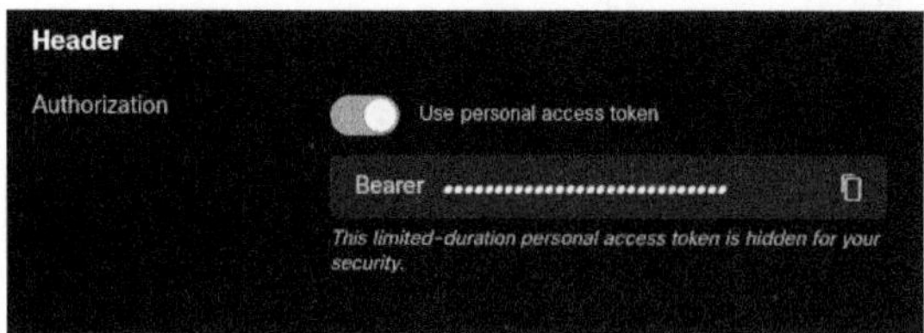

Figure 17-11 *Authorization Header Value on the API Reference Page*

API calls can be made through the API Reference web page itself or through any other HTTP client, such as Postman or cURL. If you opt for testing the API call through the page, simply fill in the fields on the right side of the page and click the orange Run button at the bottom of the page. Mandatory parameters are marked as Required under the parameter name. For this use case, Postman is a good option as it allows you to fill in all values manually and inspect the actual requests and responses in their raw format from the Postman Console.

Now open Postman and create a new request. Use the default method, GET, and enter the URI https://api.ciscospark.com/v1/people?email=networkdeveloper%40thenetdev.com. In the Headers section add the Authorization header and give it the value of the token from the API reference page. The message body will be empty for this API call. Note that the email of the user that you are querying is added to the URI as the value of the email parameter, as described in the API reference documentation. The HTTP request and response are shown in Example 17-32.

> **Note** If you need a refresher on Postman or URI query parameters, review Chapter 7. For more on HTTP authorization, review Chapter 8.

Example 17-32 *Using a GET Request to Query the User networkdeveloper by Email*

```
! HTTP Request
GET /v1/people?email=networkdeveloper%40thenetdev.com HTTP/1.1
Authorization: Bearer
  Y2MzN2IwM2YtMWY4MS00MTVhLTk2NzQtNzcwZDdmYWQ1ZTI3ZjQwMDExODEtMTM4_PF84_consumer
User-Agent: PostmanRuntime/7.24.0
Accept: */*
Cache-Control: no-cache
Host: api.ciscospark.com
Accept-Encoding: gzip, deflate, br
Connection: keep-alive

! HTTP Response
HTTP/1.1 200 OK
Cache-Control: no-cache, no-store
Via: 1.1 linkerd
Transfer-Encoding: chunked
Content-Encoding: gzip
TrackingID: ROUTER_5E825706-09B6-01BB-010F-5DA89168010F
Date: Mon, 30 Mar 2020 20:31:02 GMT
Server: Redacted
Content-Type: application/json;charset=UTF-8
Vary: Accept-Encoding
Strict-Transport-Security: max-age=63072000; includeSubDomains; preload

{
    "notFoundIds": null,
    "items": [
        {
            "id":
  "Y2lzY29zcGFyazovL3VzL1BFT1BMRS9mZTg1ODhkMi1iMjQ0LTQ2NmItYWU5ZS0xMDgwYjk0YzA0ZTk",
```

```
            "emails": [
                "networkdeveloper@thenetdev.com"
            ],
            "displayName": "Network Developer",
            "nickName": "networkdeveloper",
            "firstName": "networkdeveloper",
            "lastName": "networkdeveloper",
            "orgId": "Y2lzY29zcGFyazovL3VzL09SR0FOSVpBVElPTi9jb25zdW1lcg",
            "created": "2020-03-30T15:26:11.152Z",
            "lastActivity": "2020-03-30T20:28:29.221Z",
            "status": "active",
            "type": "person"
        }
    ]
}
```

The method, URI (including the email parameter), and Authentication header field are everything you need to perform this API call. The three objects are highlighted in the request in Example 17-32.

This API call is not entirely necessary because you may use the user's email in all subsequent requests. However, this call provides a good checkpoint to make sure the user you are trying to add to your team and space is actually registered on Webex Teams and that the first and last names are what you expected.

Now that you have retrieved the information for the user networkdeveloper, you need to create a team and add the user to it. To create a team, use the POST method and the URI https://api.ciscospark.com/v1/teams. The body of the request, at a minimum, should include the team name. For this request, you need to make sure that the Authorization header is also added. Additionally because this request contains a message body, the header Content-Type needs to be added, with the value application/json. This API call is documented under the Teams category. Example 17-33 shows both the HTTP request and response.

Example 17-33 *HTTP Request and Response for Creating a New Team*

```
! HTTP Request
POST /v1/teams HTTP/1.1
Authorization: Bearer
  MzUyYWI0ZjgtNzFmMC00OTgxLWJhMjctZWZhMWRjYjFjOWQ5NTA5YjczMDUtMDgz_PF84_consumer
Content-Type: application/json
User-Agent: PostmanRuntime/7.24.0
Accept: */*
Cache-Control: no-cache
Host: api.ciscospark.com
```

```
Accept-Encoding: gzip, deflate, br
Connection: keep-alive
Content-Length: 52
{
  "name": "Webex Teams Devs TEAM (via REST API)"
}

! HTTP Response
HTTP/1.1 200 OK
Via: 1.1 linkerd
Transfer-Encoding: chunked
Content-Encoding: gzip
TrackingID: ROUTER_5E830CAC-0AD9-01BB-00FB-5DA8916800FB
Date: Tue, 31 Mar 2020 09:26:12 GMT
Server: Redacted
Content-Type: application/json;charset=UTF-8
Vary: Accept-Encoding
Strict-Transport-Security: max-age=63072000; includeSubDomains; preload

{
    "id": "Y2lzY29zcGFyazovL3VzL1RFQU0vYTliNjc0NDAtNzMzMS0xMWVhLWFjYjktZmZm
  OGM5NGY2ODVl",
    "name": "Webex Teams Devs TEAM (via REST API)",
    "creatorId": "Y2lzY29zcGFyazovL3VzL1BFT1BMRS83ZjA0MTMzOC0xNGVhLTRiY2U
  tOTk0MS00MzUwZDgwZDRlYjM",
    "created": "2020-03-31T09:26:12.612Z"
}
```

The significant fields in the request are highlighted in Example 17-33. Notice the id field in the response, also highlighted in the example. The id value will be used in the next two API calls to identify the team that was just created.

Now to add user networkdeveloper to this newly created team, you need to use the POST method and the URI https://api.ciscospark.com/v1/team/memberships. This API call is documented under the category Team Memberships in the API reference. The body of the message, at a minimum, must include either the field personID or personEmail. Example 17-34 shows the easier option: the user's email. Make sure to include the same two headers as in Example 17-33. Example 17-34 only shows the body of the HTTP request, and not the headers, for the sake of brevity.

Example 17-34 *The HTTP Request Body for Adding the User networkdeveloper to the Team Created in Example 17-33*

```
{
  "teamId": "Y2lzY29zcGFyazovL3VzL1RFQU0vYTliNjc0NDAtNzMzMS0xMWVhLW
  FjYjktZmZmOGM5NGY2ODVl",
  "personEmail": "networkdeveloper@thenetdev.com"
}
```

The response body should look similar to the body in Example 17-35.

Example 17-35 *The HTTP Response Body Received for Making a Team Membership API Call*

```
{
   "id":
 "Y2lzY29zcGFyazovL3VzL1RFQU1fTUVNQkVSU0hJUC9mZTg1ODhkMi1iMjQ0LTQ2NmItYWU5ZS0xMDg
 wYjk0YzA0ZTk6YTliNjc0NDAtNzMzMS0xMWVhLWFjYjktZmZmOGM5NGY2ODVl",
   "teamId":
 "Y2lzY29zcGFyazovL3VzL1RFQU0vYTliNjc0NDAtNzMzMS0xMWVhLWFjYjktZmZmOGM5NGY2ODVl",
   "personId":
 "Y2lzY29zcGFyazovL3VzL1BFT1BMRS9mZTg1ODhkMi1iMjQ0LTQ2NmItYWU5ZS0xMDgwYjk0YzA0ZTk",
   "personEmail": "networkdeveloper@thenetdev.com",
   "personDisplayName": "Network Developer",
   "personOrgId": "Y2lzY29zcGFyazovL3VzL09SR0FOSVpBVElPTi9jb25zdW1lcg",
   "isModerator": false,
   "created": "2020-03-31T09:27:01.039Z"
}
```

The next step is to create a room attached to the team, and add the user networkdeveloper to that room. By navigating to the Rooms category and then to the Rooms Membership category in the API reference documentation, you should be able to figure out that you need to do two POST HTTP requests. The first, to create your room, uses the URI https://api.ciscospark.com/v1/rooms. To add the user to the room, you use the URI https://api.ciscospark.com/v1/memberships.

Keep in mind that a room is attached to a specific team, so you need the team ID that you received earlier, when creating the team. Then to add the user to the room, you need the room ID, which you should receive in the HTTP response after creating the room. Again, both requests should include the Authorization and Content-Type header fields.

When you complete all steps, the user interface of the Webex Teams application for the user networkdeveloper should be similar to Figure 17-12.

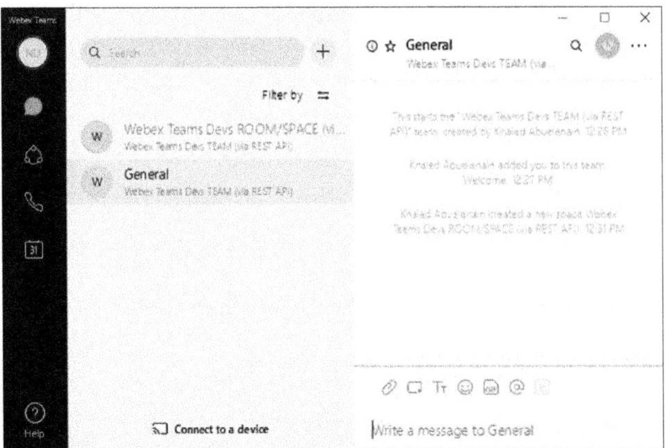

Figure 17-12 *The Webex Teams User Interface for the User networkdeveloper*

Finally, as documented under the Messages category, you need to perform an API call by using the POST method and the URI https://api.ciscospark.com/v1/messages and include both the Authorization and Content-Type header fields. The message body will, at a minimum, include the room ID and the message text that you need to send. Example 17-36 shows both the request and response.

Example 17-36 *The HTTP Request and Response for Sending a Message to a Specific Room*

```
! HTTP Request
POST /v1/messages HTTP/1.1
Authorization: Bearer
  MzUyYWI0ZjgtNzFmMC00OTgxLWJhMjctZWZhMWRjYjFjOWQ5NTA5YjczMDUtMDgz_PF84_consumer
Content-Type: application/json
User-Agent: PostmanRuntime/7.24.0
Accept: */*
Cache-Control: no-cache
Host: api.ciscospark.com
Accept-Encoding: gzip, deflate, br
Connection: keep-alive
Content-Length: 184
{
  "roomId": "Y2lzY29zcGFyazovL3VzL1JPT00vNjc4ZjEyMTAtNzMzMi0xMWVhLWJlN
  jktMTU0M2E4ZjdhNDQ5",
  "text":"This is a test message from the Webex Teams REST API to the Webex Teams
  Devs"
}

! HTTP Response
HTTP/1.1 200 OK
Via: 1.1 linkerd
Transfer-Encoding: chunked
Content-Encoding: gzip
TrackingID: ROUTER_5E830EAF-0AEE-01BB-00D1-5DA8916800D1
Date: Tue, 31 Mar 2020 09:34:40 GMT
Server: Redacted
Content-Type: application/json;charset=UTF-8
Vary: Accept-Encoding
Strict-Transport-Security: max-age=63072000; includeSubDomains; preload

{
    "id":
  "Y2lzY29zcGFyazovL3VzL01FU1NBR0UvZDhhMTRjNzAtNzMzMi0xMWVhLWEyZTQtMjk4ZmU0YzI
  0YWJm",
    "roomId":
  "Y2lzY29zcGFyazovL3VzL1JPT00vNjc4ZjEyMTAtNzMzMi0xMWVhLWJlNjktMTU0M2E4ZjdhNDQ5",
    "roomType": "group",
```

```
    "text": "This is a test message from the Webex Teams REST API to the Webex Teams
  Devs",
    "personId":
  "Y2lzY29zcGFyazovL3VzL1BFT1BMRS83ZjA0MTMzOC0xNGVhLTRiY2UtOTk0MS00MzUwZDgwZDRlYjM",
    "personEmail": "kabuelenain@gmail.com",
    "created": "2020-03-31T09:34:40.823Z"
}
```

The message you sent now appears in the Webex Teams user interface, as shown in Figure 17-13.

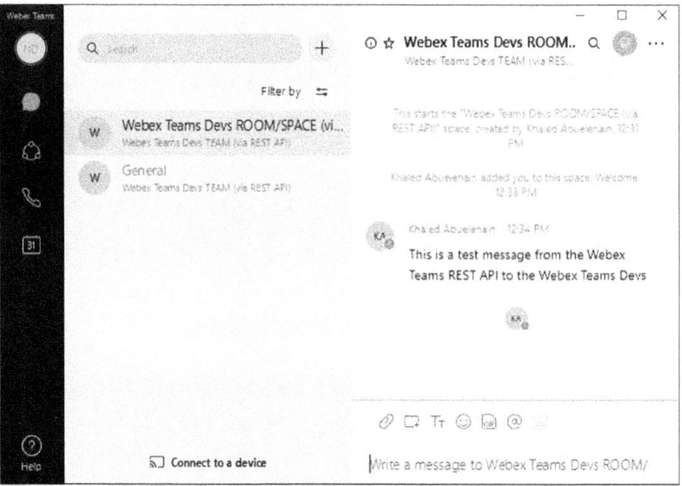

Figure 17-13 *The Teams User Interface, Showing the Message After the API Call*

Note The user performing the API calls, including the last API call that sent a message to the newly created room, is Khaled Abuelenain. The Webex Teams account in Figures 17-12 and 17-13 belongs to the user networkdeveloper. This is why in Figure 17-12 you can see the message "Khaled Abuelenain added you to this team."

Summary

This chapter explores the programmability and automation features of several Cisco platforms. The following platforms are covered under their respective domains: NX-OS, IOS XE, and IOS XR in the networks domain, Meraki in the cloud-managed networks domain, DNA Center in the network management systems and controllers domain, and the collaboration portfolio from Cisco (including an example involving Webex Teams).

The chapter presents use cases covering the following features:

- Linux shells on each of the three networking platforms
- NX-API CLI, NX-API REST and the Developer Sandbox on Open NX-OS
- NETCONF on each of the three networking platforms
- How to enable the Dashboard API on Meraki and use it to retrieve organizations, networks, and devices, as well as how to create a VLAN
- DNA Center and how to list sites and devices using its Intent API
- Cisco Webex Teams and how to create a team and a space/room, add people to the team and room, and send a message to a room using the Teams REST API

Using the information covered in this chapter, you can programmatically interface with virtually any Cisco platform using the APIs exposed by those platforms. All you need to do is understand the particulars of each API through that API's documentation, and you are good to go. Imagine the possibilities when coupling the information in this chapter with a programming language like Python that provides true automation capabilities.

The next chapter will cover the programmability and automation of a number of non-Cisco platforms.

Chapter 18

Programming Non-Cisco Platforms

In Chapter 17, "Programming Cisco Platforms," you learned about using the programmable interfaces on a variety of different platforms from Cisco, such as routers and switches running Cisco IOS XE, IOS XR, and NX-OS, as well Cisco DNA Center, Meraki, and Webex Teams. In this chapter, you will extend your knowledge to some non-Cisco network operating systems. This chapter covers some of the popular and emerging network operating systems to give you an overview of how to introduce programmability to network management practices with specific vendor platforms.

General Approaches to Programming Networks

As you have already learned in this book, you can use various interfaces to manage network platforms. Some of them are more popular or ubiquitous than others. The following sections provide an overview of several interfaces used at non-Cisco network operating systems.

The Vendor/API Matrix

When you hear about network programmability, you might be inclined to associate it with specific protocols, such as NETCONF, YANG, or HTTP/REST. However, network programmability is a much broader topic. As mentioned in Chapter 1, "The Network Programmability and Automation Ecosystem," programmability is the ability to manage platforms via *programmable interfaces* exposed by those platforms. Model-based programmability extends this paradigm to use data models. Network management involves tools and applications that add orchestration to the mix, and by using programmability, you can automate workflows involving several automated tasks performed in a specific sequence on, possibly, a number of different platforms. It's crucial that you keep this in mind and not limit yourself by unnecessary boundaries because you will run into programmability in places you never thought existed.

Programmability goes hand in hand with the different ways that network platforms can be managed. Figure 18-1 illustrates a sample API vendor mapping for a number of network operating systems. It includes Nokia SR OS and Juniper Junos OS, which, together with Cisco IOS XR, cover the majority of the service provider market in the United States, and Arista EOS and Cumulus Linux, which are very popular for big data centers and cloud providers.

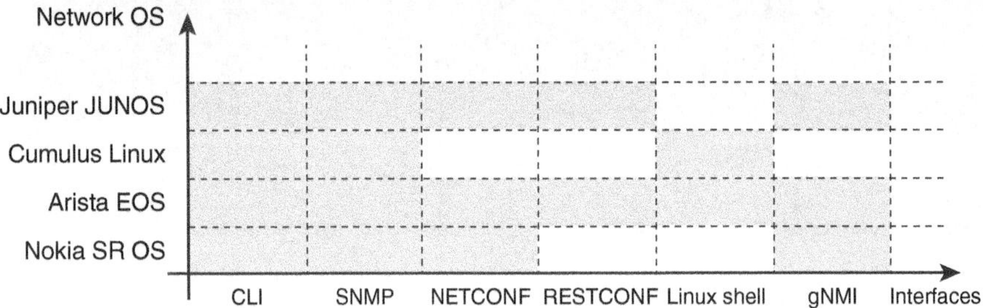

Figure 18-1 *Sample Vendor/API Mapping*

Figure 18-1 has two axes:

- The X-axis lists the types of interfaces, which allow us to interoperate with network elements.
- The Y-axis lists a subset of the vendors that exist on the market today.

If you operate a network built using a vendor not included in this figure, you should assess it based on the interfaces listed on the X-axis.

Programmability via the CLI

The most basic interface for interacting with network functions is the command-line interface (CLI). We cover the CLI under the umbrella of network programmability and automation because there are millions of legacy devices around the world that don't support NETCONF, RESTCONF, or any of the other APIs discussed so far in this book. Not being able to programmatically manage a device is certainly not a good enough reason to throw away the device if the device is performing its primary task (such routing and/or switching) well; companies do not swap these legacy devices with newer ones just to implement programmability and network automation. Therefore, the first step toward programmability and automation for such companies is to adapt their network management logic to manage legacy devices using the CLI alongside more modern devices using NETCONF, RESTCONF, gNMI, or other APIs.

When the Internet was still in its early days, finding trustworthy information on how to configure network elements was a challenging task. The number of competent network engineers was also considerably lower than it is today. The CLI was humorously referred to as the *cash line interface*. The jokes were justified, as knowledge of the CLI was a rare commodity. Today the situation is very different from the situation a couple decades ago. There are plenty of excellent resources today, including documentation covering detailed configuration for platforms from any vendor, various video trainings, and independent multivendor blogs. The newer humorous name for the CLI is *commodity line interface*. Today, the CLI is easy to understand and learn to use, and it still plays a significant role in network management.

From a software-oriented point of view, consider the following capabilities of CLI-based configuration management:

- The CLI configuration can be split into independent blocks.
- The blocks can be parametrized in terms of what is a variable and what is a fixed value.
- This configuration can be implemented in a network management system to convert the internal data modeling into the proper sequence of CLI commands.

Ansible provides a good example of CLI-based programmable network management, as you will see in Chapter 19, "Ansible." In addition, tools such as Cisco's NX-API CLI still involve using the CLI heavily to programmatically manage devices.

In short, in this era of programmability-based automation, knowledge of and ability to use the CLI are still very important.

Programmability via SNMP

For a long time, SNMP has played a crucial role in the monitoring of networks and IT infrastructure. Despite the introduction of streaming telemetry, SNMP continues to have an important role. For brand-new network equipment, streaming telemetry based on gRPC/gNMI is a much better solution. However, as a relatively new management protocol, gRPC/gNMI operates only in reasonably new software, and many legacy devices still require monitoring and rely heavily on SNMP.

SNMP was created to standardize information structures across different vendors. For example, SNMP has a standard ISO MIB tree, which is the same across all the vendors implementing it. This is quite convenient because it means you can collect the information in the same format (counter names, sizing, and so on) and using the same SNMP OID from your Cisco, Juniper, Nokia, and Cumulus devices. When this approach was created, it was a breakthrough. Even today, in the era of open-source products and collaboration, fully standardized YANG models (for example, IETF, OpenConfig) are not yet implemented across all major vendors.

Besides offering monitoring capabilities, SNMP also provides an opportunity to manage network elements. Actually, it represents the first attempt to make a network element programmable by just conveying the value of the specific parameter to a particular SNMP OID. If you think about it abstractly (not looking into a particular realization), that is what is happening today with NETCONF/RESTCONF, only via different channels.

It's essential to acknowledge that the configuration capabilities of SNMP are minimal compared to those of the CLI. In addition, there is no feature parity in terms of configuration available via the CLI and via SNMP, and the CLI is an absolute winner.

Programmability via the Linux Shell

Linux is the number-one operating system for building highly available infrastructure for the most demanding and resource-intensive applications around the world. For a long time, it was an operating system for servers; that's why Linux was not a subject of discussion in the networking arena, although each Linux distribution has a complete network stack, including routing and firewalling. Each of the most popular distributions, including Red Hat Enterprise Linux/CentOS, Ubuntu, and Debian, has a CLI, commonly referred to as the Linux shell. All the distributions are capable of running shell scripts natively, so Linux provides programmability out-of-the-box. When using a shell, you can define variables, use cycles and conditions, and perform other activities related to programming. Linux and scripting using Bash are covered extensively in Chapters 2, "Linux Fundamentals," 3, "Linux Networking and Security," and 4, "Linux Scripting." The only point that may be added here is that the Linux shell has proven to be a more programmable interface than the regular router/switch CLI, as discussed in Chapter 4.

Programmability via NETCONF

NETCONF operates on XML-wrapped data sent over SSH. For some time, the XML API was the top choice for communication between the different components of distributed applications.

In general, if you take a broader look at the IT/network ecosystem, a network device can be treated equally to any other part of the infrastructure supporting distributed applications, such as an HTTP server or a database service. Approaches and protocols to manage the network functions could be the same as between application components. This is exactly what is happening: All the protocols that were good for communication between traditional IT applications are coming to the network world. NETCONF (which is XML based) and RESTCONF (which is JSON/XML based) are perfect examples of this.

NETCONF (which is discussed in detail in Chapter 14, "NETCONF and RESTCONF") is one of the newer protocols in the network programmability arena. NETCONF has overcome the limitations of SNMP in terms of feature parity with the CLI. Depending on the vendor, the feature parity between the CLI and NETCONF could be as high as 100%. A significant factor in this success is YANG, which is covered in Chapter 13, "YANG." In the NETCONF/YANG framework, a network device is represented as a set of parameters with specific values that can be managed in individual or interdependent mode. NETCONF was the first protocol to use YANG, and so today, programmability in the network world is sometimes equated to NETCONF/YANG.

Programmability via RESTCONF and REST APIs

RESTCONF is another major programmability-related protocol. RESTCONF is a RESTful API. Today, REST APIs are a de facto standard for communication between various applications, and almost all modern applications either support them or plan to. For instance, management of Docker, the infrastructure for containers, is realized over REST APIs. As another example, InfluxDB, one of the market-leading time-series databases (a crucial component for streaming telemetry), is also managed using REST APIs; InfluxDB communicates with other components of the telemetry stack, such as a telemetry collector or visualization dashboard over REST APIs. In the network world, it is possible to manage Cisco NSO or DNA Center using REST APIs on the northbound interface.

The popularity of REST APIs in general (and RESTCONF as a specific use case) is due to the fact that it is simple, works fast, and has CRUD (create, read, update, delete) capabilities to work with the data. REST APIs (and RESTCONF) are realized over HTTP transport, typically protected by TLS. Therefore, RESTCONF has a different application layer protocol (SSH) than NETCONF (HTTP). (RESTCONF is covered in detail in Chapter 14, and HTTP, REST, and TLS are covered in Chapter 7, "HTTP and REST," and Chapter 8, "Advanced HTTP.")

RESTCONF and NETCONF are similar in their use of YANG data models. In reality, a particular network element has a single YANG data model, which defines the data structure and the interdependencies of the parameters. Given that a network device may support both NETCONF and RESTCONF interfaces, it doesn't matter how the data is transmitted: Transmission can occur over SSH/XML (NETCONF) or HTTPS/JSON/XML (RESTCONF).

However, to complete the picture, it should be noted that RESTCONF/YANG support is still in an emerging stage as of this writing. Across non-Cisco platforms, RESTCONF support is not common. For instance, Juniper Junos OS and Arista EOS support RESTCONF, and Nokia does not. Nevertheless, the general trend is toward adapting advanced and useful application concepts, and we will see more RESTCONF implementations in the next few years.

Programmability via gRPC/gNMI

Among all the protocols involved in working with YANG data models, gNMI is the most recently developed one. gNMI stands for gRPC Network Management Interface, and, as the name indicates, gNMI uses gRPC as the protocol for remote procedure calls based on HTTP/2 transport to communicate between the server and the network devices. Like RESTCONF, gNMI also has CRUD capabilities. Despite its novelty, gNMI has an extremely strong following and support in the community, and it is becoming adopted widely. Google is its main supporter and is also leading the development of both gNMI and OpenConfig YANG data models with two essential requirements in mind: low latency and scalability. As you can imagine, Google applies these two requirements to all its applications.

gNMI has a big advantage over NETCONF and RESTCONF in that its low-latency requirement and the way the data is packed for transmission make it very useful for streaming telemetry, where there is much information to be sent from each network function to the telemetry collector for processing. (See Chapter 15, "gRPC, Protobuf, and gNMI," for details.) All the major vendors, including Cisco, Juniper, and Nokia, have implemented gNMI (and therefore gRPC) as a primary protocol for streaming telemetry. There are other options available, such as TCP or NETCONF telemetry streaming, but they requires far more compute resources on the network devices to generate messages or produce more administrative traffic overhead due to inefficient serialization. Therefore, gNMI is actively used for telemetry. Due to its use for telemetry collection and network management, gNMI is becoming very popular.

gNMI adoption for the management of the network devices is expected to continue to increase. Having several management protocols—such as NETCONF, RESTCONF, and gNMI—running all together is not necessarily the best usage of a device's resources. Given that all CRUD functions can be realized using a single protocol, it might be that in future we will see unification of all processes to gNMI or RESTCONF.

Implementation Examples

Now that you have read about the available APIs, this section guides you through some real implementations with vendors other than Cisco. Some of these implementations might seem quite familiar to you, and others may not. Nevertheless, the following sections will help you follow the development of programmability in the network world.

Converting the Traditional CLI to a Programmable One

The main workhorse in the process of turning the CLI into a programmable interface is the management host. It can be an SDN controller or any other host running some application that is capable of managing the network function. In Chapter 20, "Looking Ahead," you will learn how easily you can program virtually everything in your network, even with the CLI. Ansible enables you to implement programmability easily, but even without it, you can reach some level of programmability. Earlier in this book, you learned about Linux scripting and Python programming, and you can use that knowledge to start programming network elements.

Let's say that you need to create an interface on an Arista switch. Example 18-1 shows the syntax for doing so.

Note The IP address used in this example is arbitrary, and you can use whatever IP address you need.

Example 18-1 *Creating the Loopback Interface in Arista EOS*

```
EOS1# show run int lo678
interface Loopback678
   ip address 192.168.192.168/32
!
end
```

In this example, it is important to understand the sequence of the commands you enter in order to get the interface up and running as well as the variables and the fixed text. The variables in Example 18-1 are the interface name (Loopback678 in this case) and the IP address (192.168.192.168/32). There may be another variable that you can't see in Example 18-1: the network device itself, where the interface is supposed to be configured. It can be either the hostname, if the management host knows how to reach it, or the IPv4/IPv6 address.

If you know the sequence of the commands and their syntax, you can create a simple Bash script that can create the interface for you. Example 18-2 shows an example of a possible script.

Example 18-2 *Bash Script for Creating the Interface in Arista EOS*

```
$ cat create_interface.sh
#!/bin/bash

INTERFACE_NAME=${1}
INTERFACE_IPV4=${2}
NETWORK_FUNCTION=${3}

echo "Interface with the name \"${INTERFACE_NAME}\" and IP \"${INTERFACE_IPV4}\" is
  to be created on \"${NETWORK_FUNCTION}\""

ssh aaa@${NETWORK_FUNCTION} << EOF
enable
configure terminal
interface ${INTERFACE_NAME}
ip address ${INTERFACE_IPV4}
end
show ip interface ${INTERFACE_NAME}
EOF
```

Keep in mind that this script needs to be created on a management host rather than on the network element itself. The management host could be your laptop or any jump server in your network that can reach the target network function over SSH.

This script reads a sequence of three arguments, where the first one (**${1}**) contains the name of the interface, the second one (**${2}**) contains the IPv4 address of the interface, and the third one (**${3}**) contains the hostname of the management IP address of the target network device. In this specific case, the position of the arguments is important; however, you could extend the script by adding the specific identifier as a part of the argument to tell Bash about the argument type, regardless of its position.

When the script receives all the arguments, it prints them to **stdout** for your information and then connects to the network device from the third argument by using non-interactive SSH mode and passes the configuration lines contained between the tags **<<EOF** and **EOF** created using the first two arguments. Example 18-3 demonstrates the execution of the Bash script from Example 18-2.

Example 18-3 *Creating an Interface in Arista EOS Using the Bash Script from Example 18-2*

```
$ ./create_interface.sh Loopback123 172.16.0.0/32 EOS1
Interface with the name "Loopback123" and IP "172.16.0.0/32" is to be created on
  "EOS1"
Pseudo-terminal will not be allocated because stdin is not a terminal.
Password:
Loopback123 is up, line protocol is up (connected)
  Internet address is 172.16.0.0/32
  Broadcast address is 255.255.255.255
  IPv6 Interface Forwarding : None
  Proxy-ARP is disabled
  Local Proxy-ARP is disabled
  Gratuitous ARP is ignored
  IP MTU 65535 bytes
```

In Example 18-3, you can see that the interface is successfully created using the Bash script from Example 18-2. The last command in the script creates the output of the **show ip interface** command for the created interface.

As discussed earlier, you could add many enhancements to this script, such as the one already mentioned for the sequence of the arguments or a more sophisticated configuration using loops and conditions. Two factors are crucial for such automation:

- You must know how to configure network elements with the CLI.
- You must know how to create the scripts.

The latter is particularly important because even if a script is working with one of the network vendors, it may not work with another one. One of the reasons is that the shell script expects to get the response in a certain way. For example, it might wait for the **Password:** pattern in the output before it starts entering the password. In addition, it may expect other matches, such as a **>** or **$**, before it starts sending the commands in the script. You would need to create proper updates to your script for each managed vendor.

Now say that you want to turn the script from Example 18-2 into a multivendor one. If you know the CLI and the programming/scripting, you can easily do that. Example 18-4 shows how to extend the initial Bash script so that it's capable of configuring both Arista EOS and Cumulus Linux switches.

Example 18-4 *Adding Multivendor Capabilities to the Bash Script from Example 18-2*

```
$ cat create_interface.sh
#!/bin/bash

INTERFACE_NAME=${1}
INTERFACE_IPV4=${2}
NETWORK_FUNCTION=${3}
VENDOR=${4}

echo "Interface with the name \"${INTERFACE_NAME}\" and IP \"${INTERFACE_IPV4}\" is
  to be created on \"${NETWORK_FUNCTION}\""

case ${VENDOR} in
arista*)
ssh aaa@${NETWORK_FUNCTION} << EOF
enable
configure terminal
interface ${INTERFACE_NAME}
ip address ${INTERFACE_IPV4}
end
show ip interface ${INTERFACE_NAME}
EOF
;;
cumulus*)
ssh cumulus@${NETWORK_FUNCTION} << EOF
net add interface ${INTERFACE_NAME} ip address ${INTERFACE_IPV4}
net commit
ip addr show dev ${INTERFACE_NAME}
EOF
;;
esac
```

You should already know the shell syntax used in this example. A fourth variable (**${4}**), which contains the vendor name, is used with conditional **case** syntax that defines the proper CLI commands for each vendor. (See Chapter 4 for more details on **case**.)

If you execute this script against a switch running Cumulus Linux, you see output similar to the output in Example 18-5.

Example 18-5 *Executing the Bash Script with Multivendor Capabilities*

```
$ ./create_interface.sh swp1 169.254.0.0/31 192.168.141.156 cumulus
Interface with the name "swp1" and IP "169.254.0.0/31" is to be created on
  "192.168.141.156"
Pseudo-terminal will not be allocated because stdin is not a terminal.
cumulus@192.168.141.156's password:

Welcome to Cumulus VX (TM)

Cumulus VX (TM) is a community supported virtual appliance designed for
experiencing, testing and prototyping Cumulus Networks' latest technology.
For any questions or technical support, visit our community site at:
http://community.cumulusnetworks.com

The registered trademark Linux (R) is used pursuant to a sublicense from LMI,
the exclusive licensee of Linus Torvalds, owner of the mark on a world-wide
basis.
--- /etc/network/interfaces   2019-06-10 13:24:38.928437459 +0000
+++ /run/nclu/ifupdown2/interfaces.tmp   2019-06-10 13:33:29.702733758 +0000
@@ -7,16 +7,17 @@
 auto lo
 iface lo inet loopback

 # The primary network interface
 auto eth0
 iface eth0 inet dhcp
     vrf mgmt

 auto swp1
 iface swp1
+    address 169.254.0.0/31

 auto mgmt
 iface mgmt
     address 127.0.0.1/8
     vrf-table auto




net add/del commands since the last "net commit"
================================================
User     Timestamp                  Command
-------  -------------------------  ----------------------------------------------
```

```
cumulus  2019-06-10 13:33:29.680811  net add interface swp1 ip address
  169.254.0.0/31
3: swp1: <BROADCAST,MULTICAST,UP,LOWER_UP> mtu 1500 qdisc pfifo_fast state UP group
  default qlen 1000
    link/ether 00:50:56:32:44:29 brd ff:ff:ff:ff:ff:ff
    inet 169.254.0.0/31 scope global swp1
       valid_lft forever preferred_lft forever
    inet6 fe80::250:56ff:fe32:4429/64 scope link
       valid_lft forever preferred_lft forever
```

As these examples illustrate, multivendor programmability is not very difficult. These examples illustrate another essential concept: abstraction. These examples include the same set of parameters for both Arista and Cumulus switches, correctly deployed in each network operating system. In addition, you have seen the so-called adaptor level, which translates abstract parameters into the particular syntax of the target network operating system.

Implementing similar programmability with Python or Ansible would be much easier because these solutions include relevant libraries to manage connectivity to different vendors. However, this section helps you see that programmability can be accomplished even without those tools.

Classical Linux-Based Programmability

The next step in the programmability of the various network devices is the management of Linux if it's the core operating system. As mentioned at the beginning of the chapter, as networks are moving toward including white box switches, Linux is becoming a network operating system. For example, at a high level of abstraction, Cumulus took the Debian Linux distribution and created a product that includes a unique CLI. In the vast majority of cases, networks rely on the open-source products, such as Debian Linux or the IP routing protocol suite called FRR.

A bit earlier in this chapter, you saw how to create an interface in Cumulus Linux by using its CLI (refer to Example 18-5). Cumulus Linux is a Linux distro, so all the concepts and tools explained in Chapters 2 through 4 apply to it. This means that interface configuration using a *programmable* CLI can also be reproduced using the individual files. The interfaces configuration in Cumulus Linux (and Debian in general) is stored in the file /etc/network/interfaces and looks as shown Example 18-6.

Example 18-6 *File with the Interface Configuration in Linux*

```
cumulus@cumulus:mgmt-vrf:~$ cat /etc/network/interfaces
# This file describes the network interfaces available on your system
# and how to activate them. For more information, see interfaces(5).

source /etc/network/interfaces.d/*.intf
```

```
# The loopback network interface
auto lo
iface lo inet loopback

# The primary network interface
auto eth0
iface eth0 inet dhcp
    vrf mgmt

auto swp1
iface swp1
    address 169.254.0.0/31

auto mgmt
iface mgmt
    address 127.0.0.1/8
    vrf-table auto
```

By default, only the interfaces that have non-standard configurations are listed here because the Cumulus switch used in this example has more interfaces than are shown in the file /etc/network/interfaces. This can be verified by using the standard Linux command shown in Example 18-7.

Example 18-7 *Output of the Interface Configuration in Linux*

```
cumulus@cumulus:mgmt-vrf:~$ ip link show
1: lo: <LOOPBACK,UP,LOWER_UP> mtu 65536 qdisc noqueue state UNKNOWN mode DEFAULT
  group default
    link/loopback 00:00:00:00:00:00 brd 00:00:00:00:00:00
2: eth0: <BROADCAST,MULTICAST,UP,LOWER_UP> mtu 1500 qdisc pfifo_fast master mgmt
  state UP mode DEFAULT group default qlen 1000
    link/ether 00:50:56:30:a2:99 brd ff:ff:ff:ff:ff:ff
3: swp1: <BROADCAST,MULTICAST,UP,LOWER_UP> mtu 1500 qdisc pfifo_fast state UP mode
  DEFAULT group default qlen 1000
    link/ether 00:50:56:32:44:29 brd ff:ff:ff:ff:ff:ff
4: swp2: <BROADCAST,MULTICAST> mtu 1500 qdisc noop state DOWN mode DEFAULT group
  default qlen 1000
    link/ether 00:50:56:2b:27:db brd ff:ff:ff:ff:ff:ff
5: swp3: <BROADCAST,MULTICAST> mtu 1500 qdisc noop state DOWN mode DEFAULT group
  default qlen 1000
    link/ether 00:50:56:3a:14:d8 brd ff:ff:ff:ff:ff:ff
6: swp4: <BROADCAST,MULTICAST> mtu 1500 qdisc noop state DOWN mode DEFAULT group
  default qlen 1000
    link/ether 00:50:56:29:f8:1b brd ff:ff:ff:ff:ff:ff
```

```
7: swp5: <BROADCAST,MULTICAST> mtu 1500 qdisc noop state DOWN mode DEFAULT group
  default qlen 1000
    link/ether 00:50:56:33:1a:43 brd ff:ff:ff:ff:ff:ff
8: mgmt: <NOARP,MASTER,UP,LOWER_UP> mtu 65536 qdisc pfifo_fast state UP mode DEFAULT
  group default qlen 1000
    link/ether b6:b7:20:53:a6:dd brd ff:ff:ff:ff:ff:ff
```

In Example 18-7, you can see the names of the ports available. All the ports called swp* are used for data plane forwarding. To add an IP address to any of these ports without using the CLI, you need to add the corresponding lines in the file /etc/network/interfaces and reapply the configuration by using the **ifreload -a** command. This sequence of actions forms a step-by-step procedure that you could implement directly on a network device. To do this, you would need to connect to it and use a Python or Bash script from your management host. Example 18-8 shows a Bash script that performs the file handling.

Example 18-8 *Bash Script for the Interface Configuration in Linux*

```
$ cat manage_interaces.sh
#!/bin/bash

INTERFACE_NAME=${1}
INTERFACE_IPV4=${2}
NETWORK_FUNCTION=${3}
VENDOR=${4}

echo "Interface with the name \"${INTERFACE_NAME}\" and IP \"${INTERFACE_IPV4}\" is
  to be created on \"${NETWORK_FUNCTION}\""

case ${VENDOR} in
cumulus*)
ssh cumulus@${NETWORK_FUNCTION} "sudo chown cumulus:cumulus /etc/network/interfaces"
scp cumulus@${NETWORK_FUNCTION}:/etc/network/interfaces .
echo "auto ${INTERFACE_NAME}
iface ${INTERFACE_NAME}
    address ${INTERFACE_IPV4}" >> interfaces
scp interfaces cumulus@${NETWORK_FUNCTION}:/etc/network/interfaces
ssh cumulus@${NETWORK_FUNCTION} "sudo chown root:root /etc/network/interfaces;sudo
  ifreload -a;ip addr show dev ${INTERFACE_NAME}"
;;
esac
```

The input parameters and general logic of the script in this example are the same as in Example 18-4. The difference between these examples is in the set of actions performed. This is what happens in Example 18-8:

1. The owner of the configuration file with the interface configuration is set to a value equal to the username, which is used for SSH access.
2. The configuration file is copied locally to the management host over SCP. This action allows you to get the existing set of interfaces and validate or analyze them if needed.
3. The configuration of the new interface is appended to this configuration file. This step ensures that the configuration file is accurate and complete.
4. The updated file is uploaded back to the network element so that the new validated set of interfaces is put on the device.
5. Once the file is uploaded, its owner is changed back to the root, the interfaces are reloaded, and the status of the changed interface is displayed.

Example 18-9 shows the execution of the Bash script from Example 18-8.

Example 18-9 *Programmable Management of the Linux Files*

```
$ ./manage_interaces.sh swp2 169.254.0.2/31 192.168.141.156 cumulus
Interface with the name "swp2" and IP "169.254.0.2/31" is to be created on
  "192.168.141.156"
cumulus@192.168.141.156's password:
cumulus@192.168.141.156's password:
interfaces                                                          100%  437
  602.4KB/s   00:00
cumulus@192.168.141.156's password:
interfaces                                                          100%  486
  38.1KB/s   00:00
cumulus@192.168.141.156's password:
4: swp2: <BROADCAST,MULTICAST,UP,LOWER_UP> mtu 1500 qdisc pfifo_fast state UP group
  default qlen 1000
    link/ether 00:50:56:2b:27:db brd ff:ff:ff:ff:ff:ff
    inet 169.254.0.2/31 scope global swp2
       valid_lft forever preferred_lft forever
    inet6 fe80::250:56ff:fe2b:27db/64 scope link tentative
       valid_lft forever preferred_lft forever
```

The result shown in Example 18-9 is the desired result, as the interface configured here has the correct IP address. What is not desired—and this a major drawback of using a shell—is that you need to enter the password each time you interact with the remote host on SSH/SCP. Even with this simple script, you would have to enter the password four times.

The easiest way to avoid entering a password multiple times is to use Python or Ansible, which are able to store the credentials and use them when needed. However, if you still want to use Bash, you can use SSH with RSA keys instead of passwords. To implement it, you need to generate a pair of private/public keys on your management host and send the public key to the target managed host so the management host can establish an SSH tunnel to the managed host without the password. Figure 18-2 illustrates the SSH architecture with RSA keys.

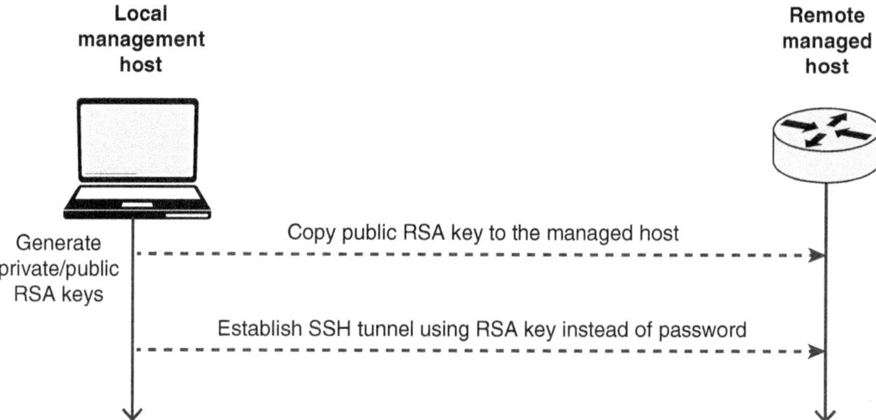

Figure 18-2 *SSH with RSA Keys*

Example 18-10 shows how you can deploy SSH access with RSA keys instead of a password.

Example 18-10 *Deploying SSH Access with RSA Keys Instead of a Password*

```
# Generate the SSH RSA Key Pair on the local management host
$ ssh-keygen
Generating public/private rsa key pair.
Enter file in which to save the key (/home/aaa/.ssh/id_rsa):
Enter passphrase (empty for no passphrase):
Enter same passphrase again:
Your identification has been saved in /home/aaa/.ssh/id_rsa.
Your public key has been saved in /home/aaa/.ssh/id_rsa.pub.
The key fingerprint is:
SHA256:dspRSyuwkcqiRBLHgItQaabOHR0c7Wgdx9IhBlKT+HY aaa@sand7.karneliuk.com
The key's randomart image is:
+---[RSA 2048]----+
|++oo+==oo..      |
|oo=..+o=.+       |
```

```
|+*  o O + o      |
|*  o B E o o     |
|o.o * o S +      |
|.+ o   o =       |
|.       o        |
|                 |
|                 |
+----[SHA256]-----+

# Create the folder for SSH keys on the remote managed host
$ ssh cumulus@192.168.141.156 "mkdir /home/cumulus/.ssh/"

# Copy the public RSA key to the remote managed host
$ scp /home/aaa/.ssh/id_rsa.pub cumulus@192.168.141.156:/home/cumulus/.ssh/
  authorized_keys
cumulus@192.168.141.156's password:
id_rsa.pub                                                    100%  405
  462.7KB/s   00:00

# Test the SSH access using the RSA keys without password to the remote managed host
$ ssh cumulus@192.168.141.156

Welcome to Cumulus VX (TM)

Cumulus VX (TM) is a community supported virtual appliance designed for
experiencing, testing and prototyping Cumulus Networks' latest technology.
For any questions or technical support, visit our community site at:
http://community.cumulusnetworks.com

The registered trademark Linux (R) is used pursuant to a sublicense from LMI,
the exclusive licensee of Linus Torvalds, owner of the mark on a world-wide
basis.
Last login: Mon Jun 10 14:19:27 2019 from 192.168.141.144
cumulus@cumulus:mgmt-vrf:~$
```

The comments in Example 18-10 help you understand each step. As you can see, you need to provide the password for the SSH command when you create the folder for SSH keys on the remote host, as well as when you copy the key file there over SCP. However, you don't need it anymore when you perform the SSH connectivity once more at the end of the output.

After applying the keys, if you now redo the execution of the configuration script from Example 18-9, the configuration process is truly automated, as shown in Example 18-11.

Example 18-11 *Programmable Management of Linux Files with SSH Using RSA Keys*

```
$ ./manage_interaces.sh swp3 169.254.0.4/31 192.168.141.156 cumulus
Interface with the name "swp3" and IP "169.254.0.4/31" is to be created on
  "192.168.141.156"
interfaces                                                        100%  486
  476.9KB/s   00:00
interfaces                                                        100%  534
  644.7KB/s   00:00
5: swp3: <BROADCAST,MULTICAST,UP,LOWER_UP> mtu 1500 qdisc pfifo_fast state UP group
  default qlen 1000
    link/ether 00:50:56:3a:14:d8 brd ff:ff:ff:ff:ff:ff
    inet 169.254.0.4/31 scope global swp3
       valid_lft forever preferred_lft forever
    inet6 fe80::250:56ff:fe3a:14d8/64 scope link tentative
       valid_lft forever preferred_lft forever
```

You might argue that the examples with the interface configuration are straightforward. The point would be fair enough. However, the core idea of any programmability is to split the whole configuration process into small and easy steps that can be templated and parametrized and then deployed in a replicable manner.

There is no right or wrong way to do automation. Different contexts require different solutions. The next section looks at a newer way to manage the network functions that might be best in some situations: by using NETCONF/YANG.

Managing Network Devices with NETCONF/YANG

Together with YANG data models, the NETCONF protocol enables you to manage network devices in a programmable way. The main difference between the NETCONF/YANG approach and the traditional CLI configuration approach is that the data structure is more consistent with NETCONF/YANG. When you use NETCONF/YANG, you define the particular node that contains the data. This operation is precise, so you don't need to take care of the sequence of the commands, as you would need to do with CLI templates.

In the examples so far in this chapter, you have learned how to manage network elements via the CLI by using shell scripts. These CLI commands are sent using non-interactive SSH sessions. A NETCONF session, on the other hand, requires extensive message exchange, so it is impossible to use shell scripts for management of network devices via NETCONF.

Let's continue our example of creating an interface with an associated IP address, but now let's look at NETCONF/YANG and another vendor. This time, let's consider the Nokia SR OS running on a Nokia SR 7750 router. Currently, Nokia supports a vendor-proprietary YANG module and a subset of the OpenConfig modules. Nokia officially published the YANG modules in October 2019, long after other vendors published their modules. Without published YANG modules, the life of a developer is difficult. Before modules are published, a developer must perform reverse engineering, which involves configuring something in the network element and then extracting the configuration over NETCONF to get the YANG model for a specific context. Example 18-12 shows an exchange of NETCONF hello messages between the management host and the Nokia router.

Example 18-12 *NETCONF Hello Exchange*

```
$ ssh  admin@nokia_router -p 830 -s netconf

admin@secgw-5.viplabs.de's password:
# NETCONF HELLO sent by the remote managed host
<?xml version="1.0" encoding="UTF-8"?>
<hello xmlns="urn:ietf:params:xml:ns:netconf:base:1.0">
    <capabilities>
        <capability>urn:ietf:params:netconf:base:1.0</capability>
        <capability>urn:ietf:params:netconf:base:1.1</capability>
        <capability>urn:ietf:params:netconf:capability:writable-running:1.0
  </capability>
        <capability>urn:ietf:params:netconf:capability:notification:1.0</capability>
        ! The output is truncated for brevity
        <capability>urn:alcatel-lucent.com:sros:ns:yang:conf-r13?module=alu-conf-
  r13&amp;revision=2019-02-13</capability>
        !
    </capabilities>
    <session-id>100</session-id>
</hello>
]]>]]>

# NETCONF HELLO sent by the local management host
<?xml version="1.0" encoding="UTF-8"?>
<hello xmlns="urn:ietf:params:xml:ns:netconf:base:1.0">
 <capabilities>
  <capability>urn:ietf:params:netconf:base:1.0</capability>
 </capabilities>
</hello>
]]>]]>
```

As you learned earlier, the character sequence]]>]]> indicates the end of the NETCONF messages (see RFC 6241. This example involves manual interaction with the remote managed host over NETCONF. Both Python and Ansible have specific modules that handle such interactions, and you only need to focus on the content of your messages. Each message begins with # and an explanation of the intent of the message.

When the exchange of the NETCONF hello messages is finished, you can start applying the configuration, as illustrated in Example 18-13.

Example 18-13 *Configuring the Loopback Interface in the Nokia SR OS Using NETCONF*

```
# NETCONF EDIT-CONFIG message with the loopback details
<?xml version="1.0" encoding="UTF-8"?>
<rpc message-id="101" xmlns="urn:ietf:params:xml:ns:netconf:base:1.0">
<edit-config>
<target>
<running/>
</target>
<config>
<configure xmlns="urn:alcatel-lucent.com:sros:ns:yang:conf-r13">
 <router>
  <interface>
   <interface-name>test_loopback</interface-name>
   <address>
    <ip-address-mask>192.168.192.168/32</ip-address-mask>
   </address>
   <loopback>true</loopback>
   <shutdown>false</shutdown>
  </interface>
 </router>
</configure>
</config>
</edit-config>
</rpc>
]]>]]>

# NETCONF OK confirmation from the remote managed host
<?xml version="1.0" encoding="UTF-8"?>
<rpc-reply message-id="101" xmlns="urn:ietf:params:xml:ns:netconf:base:1.0">
    <ok/>
</rpc-reply>
]]>]]>
```

In the case of NETCONF, it's straightforward to separate the variables from the rest of the XML message. The variables are the values inside the <> framing; these keys are the configuration nodes. The variables in Example 18-13 are the same as the variables in the previous examples: the interface name and the IPv4 addresses. In addition, in Example 18-13 you can see two more values that were not used before:

- The administrative state of the interface defines whether it's up or down. Theoretically, this value could have been defined earlier, but it was omitted for brevity. In Nokia SR OS, the newly created interface is disabled by default, however, so you need to bring it up manually.

- The interface loopback is or is not identified. Nokia SR OS handles interface naming and configuration differently than Cisco. With Nokia SR OS, you can create a Layer 3 interface with a name you like and then configure it as a loopback or map a physical port to it.

To verify that the interface is configured properly, you can check the output of the CLI from the router, as shown in Example 18-14.

Example 18-14 *Verifying the Loopback Interface Configuration on the Nokia Router*

```
*A:nokia_router# show router interface
===============================================================================
Interface Table (Router: Base)
===============================================================================
Interface-Name                   Adm        Opr(v4/v6)  Mode    Port/SapId
   IP-Address                                                   PfxState
-------------------------------------------------------------------------------
! The output is truncated for brevity
test_loopback                    Up         Up/Down     Network loopback
   192.168.192.168/32                                           n/a
! The output is truncated for brevity
-------------------------------------------------------------------------------
Interfaces : 4
===============================================================================
```

After verifying the configuration, the next step is to create a script, using Ansible or Python, to manage the network functions with the variables. Example 18-15 provides the Python script. (Ansible is covered in Chapter 19.)

Example 18-15 *Python Script to Create the Interface in Nokia SR OS*

```
$ cat nokia_netconf.py
import sys, warnings
warnings.simplefilter("ignore", DeprecationWarning)
from ncclient import manager

# Variables
NOKIA_USERNAME = 'admin'
NOKIA_PASSWORD = 'admin'
NOKIA_PORT     = 830
```

```
# User functions
def npf(host, ip_address, if_name):
    xml_conf = """<config>
                    <configure xmlns="urn:alcatel-lucent.com:sros:ns:yang:conf-r13">
                      <router>
                        <interface>
                          <interface-name>%s</interface-name>
                          <address>
                            <ip-address-mask>%s</ip-address-mask>
                          </address>
                          <loopback>true</loopback>
                          <shutdown>false</shutdown>
                        </interface>
                      </router>
                    </configure>
                  </config>""" % (if_name, ip_address)

    conn = manager.connect(host=host,
                           port=NOKIA_PORT,
                           username=NOKIA_USERNAME,
                           password=NOKIA_PASSWORD,
                           timeout=10,
                           device_params={'name': 'alu'},
                           hostkey_verify=False)

    conn.edit_config(target='running', config=xml_conf)

    conn.close_session()

# User functions
if __name__ == '__main__':
    npf(sys.argv[1], sys.argv[2], sys.argv[3])
```

The syntax of the Python is quite different from that of Bash, but the structure is similar. As you learned in Chapter 5, "Python Fundamentals," at the beginning of the snippet, you define the modules you are going to use, as well as some variables (username, password, and port). Then the function configures Nokia SR OS over NETCONF using the Nokia YANG data model. The template is the same as in Example 18-14, but this time there are two variables, **if_name** and **ip_address**, placed in the template marked with the **%s** symbol. To connect with the network function over NETCONF, the specific Python module **ncclient** (https://pypi.org/project/ncclient/) is used. This module is specially developed by the community to manage devices over NETCONF, and it includes all the relevant handlers. The function of this module in this example is to connect to the network and send the appropriate configuration to a particular datastore. If you compare Examples 18-14 and 18-15, you will see many similarities.

It is worth pointing out that parameters such as the hostname of the network function, the name of the interface, and its IPv4 address are provided as arguments during the launch of the script, as shown in Example 18-16.

Example 18-16 *Executing and Checking the Script*

```
$ sudo python nokia_netconf.py secgw-5.viplabs.de 192.168.192.169/32 npf_lo
$



*A: nokia_router# show router interface
===============================================================================
Interface Table (Router: Base)
===============================================================================
Interface-Name                   Adm         Opr(v4/v6)  Mode    Port/SapId
   IP-Address                                                    PfxState
-------------------------------------------------------------------------------
npf_lo                           Up          Up/Down     Network loopback
   192.168.192.169/32                                            n/a
! The output is truncated for brevity
test_loopback                    Up          Up/Down     Network loopback
   192.168.192.168/32                                            n/a
! The output is truncated for brevity
-------------------------------------------------------------------------------
Interfaces : 5
===============================================================================
```

If the execution of the Python script is successful, you get no notification. However, in the event of failure, as you learned in Chapter 14, you get notifications that help you understand what went wrong.

The script in Example 18-16 is straightforward, but it gives you valuable insight. If your network functions support NETCONF/YANG, you can manage the network as described here by modifying the YANG data structure in the Python script.

Managing Network Devices with RESTCONF/YANG

Recall that RESTCONF uses HTTPS as a transport protocol, with data encoded directly in JSON format; this makes RESTCONF a perfect protocol for all kinds of programmability.

There are several points you need to consider when you plan to use RESTCONF:

- RESTCONF requires SSL encryption, so you need to create either self-signed or CA-signed SSL certificates on your target network function to be able to connect to it.

- HTTPS-based applications don't use credentials to access the network devices directly; instead, they use Base64-encoded username/password pairs. Therefore, you need to transform your credentials into this format.
- RESTCONF uses HTTP transport, so you need to become comfortable with HTTP request types.

This section guides you through these considerations, using Arista EOS to configure a loopback interface.

Example 18-17 shows how to create SSL certificates and enable RESTCONF.

Example 18-17 *Preparing for RESTCONF/YANG Usage*

```
# Generate certificate/key pair
EOS1#security pki key generate rsa 4096 RESTCONF_KEY
EOS1#security pki certificate generate self-signed RESTCONF_CERT key RESTCONF_KEY
  parameters common-name "rest_test.acme.com"
certificate:RESTCONF_CERT generated


# Enable RESTCONF with created cert/key pair (only relevant output is provided)
EOS1#show run | section management
management security
   ssl profile RESTCONF_SEC_PROFILE
      certificate RESTCONF_CERT key RESTCONF_KEY
!
management api restconf
   transport https default
      ssl profile RESTCONF_SEC_PROFILE


# Verification the RESTCONF works correctly
EOS1#show management api restconf
Enabled:            Yes
Server:             running on port 6020, in default VRF
SSL Profile:        RESTCONF_SEC_PROFILE
QoS DSCP:           none


# Create credentials for remote access
EOS1#show run | grep 'username'
username aaa privilege 15 secret aaa
```

In the PKI architecture, you always need a certificate/key pair. Therefore, in Example 18-17, you need to create this as a first step. The second step is to associate the generated certificate/key pair with an SSL security profile, which in the third step is associated with the RESTCONF configuration. You can also specify a port that RESTCONF processes listen to. If you don't do this (as shown in Example 18-17), the default port value, TCP port 6020, is used. The last thing you need to do is to create the credentials that will be used with RESTCONF.

Now that the network devices are prepared for RESTCONF operation, you need to understand how to authenticate your REST requests to a network device. The REST API doesn't support the user credentials per se, as you learned in Chapter 14. However, it has the concept of the Authorization headers, which are part of each message sent to the network device. Authentication can be achieved in different ways (for example, using API tokens), and one of the easiest ways is to use a basic authorization type, such as the string *username:password* encoded in Base64 format, with this value then added to the authorization header. Figure 18-3 shows a simple way to convert credentials into Base64 format using the free online tool available at www.base64encode.org.

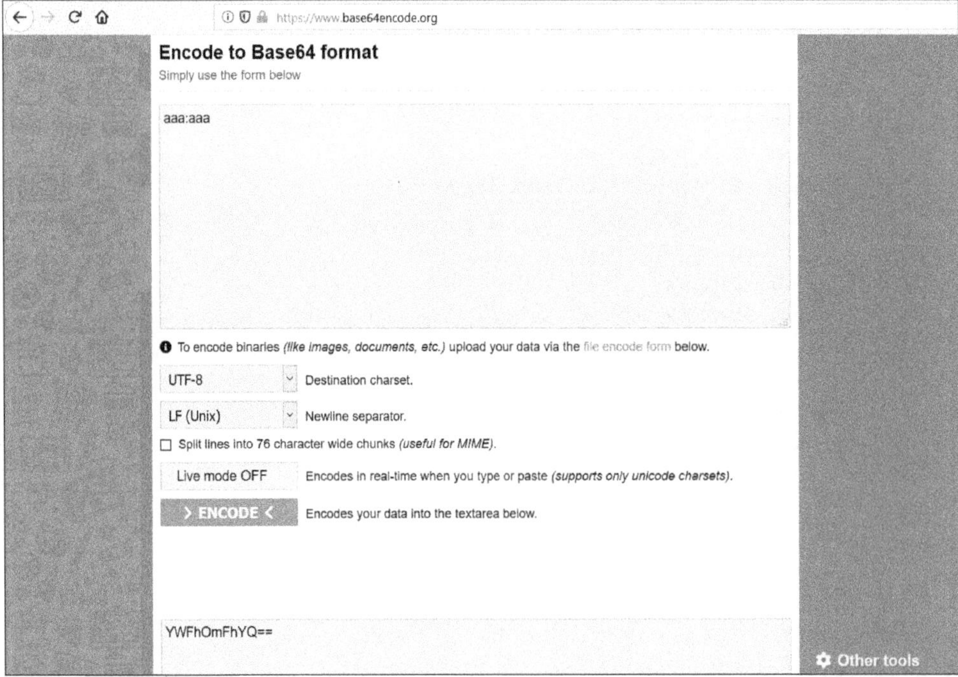

Figure 18-3 *Converting a username:password Tuple to Base64 Format*

As shown in this figure, you put your string precisely in the *username:password* form configured on the device earlier (refer to Example 18-17). Then you just click the Encode button, and at the bottom of the screen, you see the encoded value, which you can then use in the Authorization header in a RESTCONF message.

The final step before you can get or set the configuration over RESTCONF is to determine the address of the device to be configured (basically, the URI you need to access). As you learned in Chapter 14, according to RFC 8040, the URI of the node is typically an address in the format https://*hostname*/restconf/data/*yang_module:container*.

For information about supported YANG modules for a particular vendor, you can typically look at the GitHub pages or release notes for the version of the network operating system that is being used (refer to Chapter 13). The current example uses Arista, and Figure 18-4 shows the GitHub page where you can find the needed information.

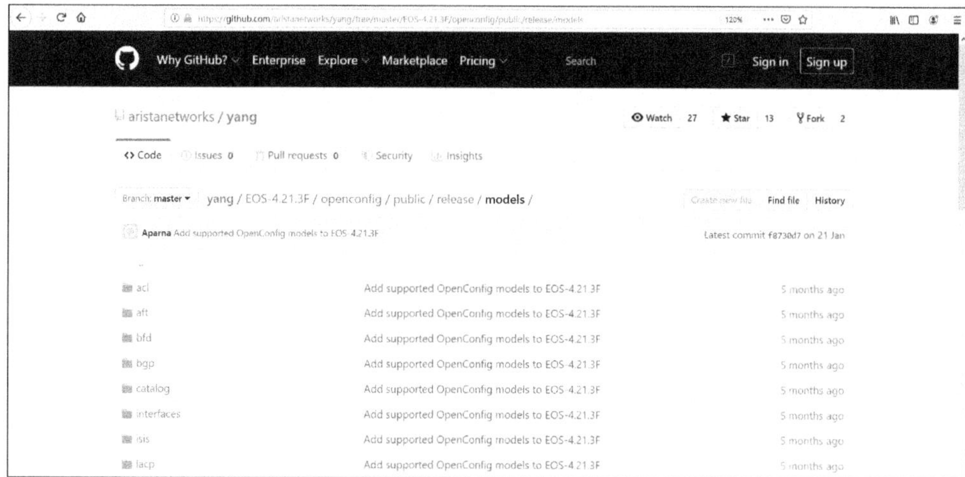

Figure 18-4 *Arista YANG Modules*

As indicated in this figure, Arista supports OpenConfig YANG modules. OpenConfig is a core YANG data model that Arista uses in its product. OpenConfig YANG data models implemented in Arista EOS have various augmentations and deviations, but there are no vendor-proprietary YANG modules.

In Chapter 13, you learned how to find the name of a YANG module and the name of a container. Using that knowledge and what you have learned about RESTCONF authorization in this chapter, you can create a RESTCONF request like the one shown in Example 18-18.

Example 18-18 *RESTCONF GET Request Using an Authorization Header*

```
$ curl -X GET https://EOS1:6020/restconf/data/openconfig-interfaces:interfaces
  --header "Authorization: Basic YWFhOmFhYQ==" --insecure | python -m json.tool
  % Total    % Received % Xferd  Average Speed   Time    Time     Time  Current
                                 Dload  Upload   Total   Spent    Left  Speed
100  2321    0  2321    0     0   9070      0 --:--:-- --:--:-- --:--:--  9101
{
    "openconfig-interfaces:interface": [{
! The output is truncated for brevity
        "config": {
            "arista-intf-augments:load-interval": 300,
            "description": "",
            "enabled": true,
            "loopback-mode": true,
            "name": "Loopback0",
            "openconfig-vlan:tpid": "TPID_0X8100",
            "type": "softwareLoopback"
        },
! The output is truncated for brevity
        "name": "Loopback0",
        "xstate": {
            "enabled": true,
            "loopback-mode": false,
            "openconfig-vlan:tpid": "TPID_0X8100"
        },
        "subinterfaces": {
            "subinterface": [
                {
                    "config": {
                        "enabled": true,
                        "index": 0
                    },
                    "index": 0,
                    "openconfig-if-ip:ipv4": {
                        "addresses": {
                            "address": [
                                {
                                    "config": {
                                        "ip": "10.0.0.22",
                                        "prefix-length": 32
                                    },
                                    "ip": "10.0.0.22",
                                    "state": {
```

```
                                    "ip": "10.0.0.22",
                                    "prefix-length": 32
                                }
                            }
                        ]
                    },
                    "config": {
                        "dhcp-client": false,
                        "enabled": true,
                        "mtu": 1500
                    },
                    "proxy-arp": {
                        "config": {
                            "mode": "DISABLE"
                        },
                        "state": {
                            "mode": "DISABLE"
                        }
                    },
                    "state": {
                        "dhcp-client": false,
                        "enabled": true,
                        "mtu": 1500
                    },
                    "unnumbered": {
                        "config": {
                            "enabled": false
                        },
                        "state": {
                            "enabled": false
                        }
                    }
                }
! The output is truncated for brevity
            }
        }
    }
  }]
}
```

Because RESTCONF works over HTTP, you can use the handy Linux tool cURL as shown in this example. The **-X** key sets the HTTP message type to **GET**, which means you collect the information already configured on the network function. Then, using the key **--header** (or **-H**), you provide the authorization data, including the credentials encoded in Base64 format. You use the **--insecure** key to avoid the certificate check, which you typically want to do with self-signed certificates. You can also see in this example that the output of the **curl** command is the input for the Python module **json.tool.** This makes the output format easy to read; without this command, the JSON output of **curl** is just a single string. Despite the fact that this string has all the correct JSON framing, it's difficult to read.

Instead of using cURL, you can use any other tool that allows you to work with a REST API. One of the most popular tools in this area is Postman, which provides a flexible way to generate the REST API commands and receive responses. (Postman is beyond the scope of this book.)

In addition to collecting data by using RESTCONF, it's also possible to create a new configuration, as discussed in Chapter 14. Although it's theoretically possible to create a shell script that uses cURL to provision a network device, this is not necessarily the best way of managing network devices over RESTCONF. Example 18-19 provides some ideas about how to create a Python script to manage the network function with a REST API.

Example 18-19 *Python Script to Manage Network Elements over RESTCONF*

```
$ cat restconf_put.py
import sys
import requests
from requests.auth import HTTPBasicAuth

# Variables
NF_USERNAME = 'aaa'
NF_PASSWORD = 'aaa'
NF_RESTPORT = 6020

# User functions
def set_interfaces(NF_HOSTNAME, NEW_INTERFACE_NAME, NEW_INTERFACE_IP):
    """
    Setting the interfaces in RESTCONF
    """
    templated_stuff = """{
                                "openconfig-interfaces:name": "%s",
                                "openconfig-interfaces:config": {
                                    "enabled": true,
                                    "name": "%s",
                                    "loopback-mode": true,
                                    "type": "softwareLoopback"
                                },
```

```
                        "openconfig-interfaces:subinterfaces": {
                            "subinterface": [
                                {
                                    "index": 0,
                                    "config": {
                                        "enabled": true,
                                        "index": 0
                                    },
                                    "openconfig-if-ip:ipv4": {
                                        "addresses": {
                                            "address": [
                                                {
                                                    "ip": "%s",
                                                    "config": {
                                                        "ip": "%s",
                                                        "prefix-length": %s
                                                    }
                                                }
                                            ]
                                        }
                                    }
                                }
                            ]
                        }
                    }""" % (NEW_INTERFACE_NAME, NEW_INTERFACE_NAME,
NEW_INTERFACE_IP.split('/')[0], NEW_INTERFACE_IP.split('/')[0],
NEW_INTERFACE_IP.split('/')[1])

    url = "https://%s:%s/restconf/data/openconfig-interfaces:interfaces/
interface=%s" % (NF_HOSTNAME, NF_RESTPORT, NEW_INTERFACE_NAME)
    set_rest = requests.put(url, auth=HTTPBasicAuth(NF_USERNAME, NF_PASSWORD),
verify=False, data=templated_stuff)

    print (set_rest)

# Main body

if __name__ == "__main__":
    set_interfaces(sys.argv[1], sys.argv[2], sys.argv[3])
```

This script is quite similar in structure to Example 18-15. At the beginning of the script, some modules are imported, and they add the function necessary for this script. The module sys, which was also used earlier, makes it possible to send variables as arguments in the CLI, and the module **requests** is in charge of interacting with the HTTP API used in RESTCONF. The **requests** module has a built-in ability to convert your credentials into Base64 encoding, so you don't need to do this conversion manually.

When the modules are imported, variables such as the credentials and RESTCONF port are provided. You can also pass these variables by using the CLI if you like. If you have the same credentials for all your devices, by storing them in the Python file, you can avoid entering them each time, and you can still provide the hostname of the target managed network device.

After the block with variables, you see the user-defined functions. This is a convenient way to structure the code because the user functions help make the code reusable. Although this structure is not needed in this small script, applying it is a good habit. Within the user-defined function **set_interfaces**, you can see the template for the interface followed by the variables. The template contains JSON data that is later used as a payload for a **PUT** message. The tricky part with the payload is that you need to provide the IP address and the subnet mask separately. Earlier in this chapter, you saw the IP address and the subnet mask together in a single line; in the OpenConfig YANG data model for interfaces, they need to appear separately. To achieve that, you use the function **split('/')**, which divides a single variable into multiple parts, using the separator provided in single quotes. When the split is complete, you can call the parts of the variable by using an index **[x]** starting from 0 for the leftmost split value.

When the template is filled in with variables, the payload for the REST API call is ready, and you can make the call by using the requests module. The type of the request is specified as **requests.put**, and you can change this request to switch **PUT** to **POST**, **PATCH**, or **GET**, depending on your needs. Within the REST API request, you need to provide the URI, which is also a template filled in with variables, the authorization data, and the payload (in this case, **data**). Because a self-signed certificate is used, you should disable the certificate check by using the key/value pair **verify=false**. The user-defined function ends by printing the output of the execution result.

The main body of the script calls the user-defined function and provides to it the variables that it receives from the CLI. Example 18-20 shows how the Python script is executed.

Example 18-20 *Execution of a Python Script to Configure the Network Function over RESTCONF*

```
$ python restconf_put.py EOS1 Loopback456 192.168.192.168/32
/home/aaa/book/non_cisco_prog/python_restconf/venv/lib/python3.7/site-
  packages/urllib3/connectionpool.py:851: InsecureRequestWarning: Unverified
  HTTPS request is being made. Adding certificate verification is strongly advised.
  See: https://urllib3.readthedocs.io/en/latest/advanced-usage.html#ssl-warnings
  InsecureRequestWarning)
<Response [200]>
```

This example launches the Python script the same way it is launched for NETCONF (refer to Example 18-15). In the output shown here, you can see that the certificate isn't verified. This is okay because you manually disabled this check in Example 18-19. However, in a production network, you should use PKI and centralized certificates to avoid security issues. The second part of the output shows the HTTP message code, which in this case is 200, which means OK. Now, by using the REST API **GET** call provided in Example 18-18, you verify the status of the newly created interface.

Summary

This chapter provides an overview of the main APIs for configuring network functions with the shell. It also provides examples of using Python to manage non-Cisco operating systems. The following are some of the specifics covered in this chapter:

- Programmability has become important in the networking industry, and many vendors have become involved with programmability.
- To begin automating your network, it is important to determine which APIs your vendor supports.
- The most popular programmable interfaces today are NETCONF, RESTCONF, and gRPC. However, you can use the CLI for programmability by using scripts.
- To successfully apply automation, you need to understand what variable will vary across different network devices' management. Based on that understanding, you can develop an API.
- The most popular and influential scripting language is Python. Nevertheless, you can use Bash, Perl, or any other scripting language that suits a particular solution.
- NETCONF, RESTCONF, and gRPC are built around a YANG data model, and they are basically just different transport and encoding protocols. You should check a vendor's supported YANG modules before you start developing automation.
- Sometimes modules aren't published. In such a case, you need to either ask your vendor for them or to do reverse engineering to extract the configuration from the network function over NETCONF/RESTCONF and analyze the YANG module.

Chapter 19

Ansible

The chapters so far in this book cover various components of the network programmability stack and how those components work together to provide a usable set of tools for network automation. This chapter covers yet another one of those tools: Ansible.

Ansible is an application that makes use of several of the components of the network programmability stack to abstract network automation tasks. As a matter of fact, the applications of Ansible extend well beyond network automation and into other domains, such as compute and application automation. The popularity of Ansible is due to the simplicity of the tool as well as the not-so-steep learning curve. Learning Ansible does not require previous knowledge of Python or any other programming language. It also does not require a deep understanding of any of the programmability protocols such as NETCONF or RESTCONF. To get started and be productive with Ansible, you don't even need to know what an API is!

By the end of this chapter, you should have a good working knowledge of Ansible and be able to write playbooks to automate everyday tasks.

Ansible Basics

Many examples related to network automation (and network programming as an inherited use case) covered so far in this book might seem complex. They require you to know some programming languages, such as Python, at a sufficiently deep level. In addition, you need to understand HTTP/REST in some detail. And then, on top of that, you need to know how to work with the different encodings as well as send and receive HTTP requests—using Python (or your language of choice). This can be a time-consuming and exhausting entry point into network automation. By this point in the book, you should have already mastered the appropriate knowledge.

But what if there is an option to approach network automation and programming in a more straightforward manner? In other words, what if there is a faster, simpler entry point into network automation?

At some point in time, the IT industry started looking for ways to simplify automation activities. It's crystal clear that the primary goal of any automation framework is to reduce the time spent on repetitive activities and to make the saved time available for something more valuable. The highest efficiency is achieved when automating tasks that must be performed across several (or several hundred or even several thousand) devices. Ansible aims to provide such efficiency.

Ansible is a relatively new tool, created in 2012 to perform simultaneous configuration of servers. Since then, it has evolved enormously, and today, perhaps, it's the first tool people think about when about it comes to IT automation in general or network automaton in particular. Several SDN controllers (including Cisco Crosswork and Juniper Contrail) use Ansible to perform configuration of network functions.

Ansible allows you to run ad hoc commands or predefined sequences of commands called *playbooks* across multiple devices simultaneously. In the context of network automation, Ansible can be heavily used for automated configuration provisioning, information collection, automated software upgrades, verification, and other activities. The functionality is practically limited only by your imagination.

Ansible, which is now owned by Red Hat, is an open-source project that is distributed under the GNU license. This means that Ansible is available for everybody to use and that everybody can contribute to its development to enrich the functionality further.

How Ansible Works

Ansible is an agentless automation tool, which means that nothing needs to be installed on the managed host besides SSH (or NETCONF, as you will see later in this chapter). If a host is capable of running Python, then Python should be installed as well. In any case, you need to install Ansible itself on the managing host, and Example 19-1 shows how you can do it on an RPM-based distro such as CentOS.

Example 19-1 *Installation of Ansible on a Managing Host*

```
$ sudo yum install -y ansible
```

When Ansible is installed on the managing host, it can immediately start managing hosts. The Figure 19-1 illustrates the call flow for a single command in Ansible.

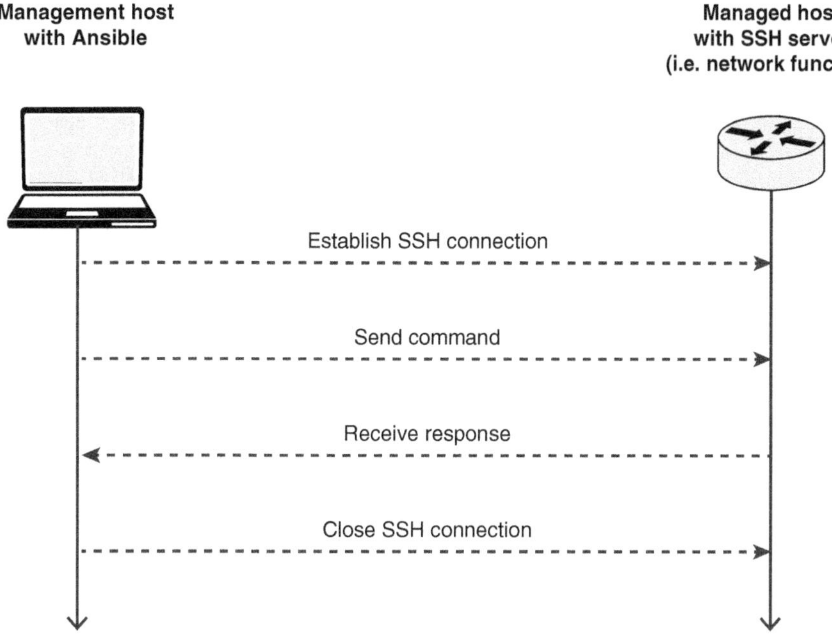

Figure 19-1 *Ansible Call Flow for a Single Command*

Figure 19-1 shows the following sequence of actions:

1. The managing host with Ansible establishes an SSH connection with the managed host.
2. The managing host sends the command(s) to execute on the managed host. For example, it could be configuration or **show** commands in the context of network functions.
3. The managing host receives the output of the command execution from the managed host. For a **show** command, this is the output of that command (meaning some operational data), whereas for a configuration command, this is empty output for a success and an error message for a failure.
4. The managing host terminates the SSH connection with the managed host.

It is important to understand where Ansible stores the configuration data that is necessary for its operation. Example 19-2 shows the use of the command **ansible --version** to find the most important locations where Ansible stores information on the system.

Example 19-2 *Reviewing the Ansible Default Configuration Parameters using Ansible Version Command*

```
$ ansible --version
ansible 2.9.11
  config file = /etc/ansible/ansible.cfg
  configured module search path = [u'/home/aaa/.ansible/plugins/modules',
  u'/usr/share/ansible/plugins/modules']
  ansible python module location = /usr/lib/python2.7/site-packages/ansible
  executable location = /usr/bin/ansible
  python version = 2.7.5 (default, Jul 13 2018, 13:06:57) [GCC 4.8.5 20150623 (Red
  Hat 4.8.5-28)]
```

In Example 19-2, the version (2.9.11 in this example) refers to the version of Ansible installed. The first digit identifies the major software version—in this case, Ansible 2.0. The second digit refers to the major update (in this case, 9), and the third digit (in this case, 11) refers to the minor update. The major version typically has some modifications, such as introduction of new modules or plugins, whereas the minor version typically contains the bug fixes or security updates.

The default configuration file is /etc/ansible/ansible.cfg. It contains all parameters relevant to Ansible functioning, such as SSH connection parameters, paths to Ansible and Python modules, and the default username. In the vast majority of automation use cases, you won't change these default parameters.

The Ansible Python module location points to the folder that contains Ansible modules. You will learn about modules later in this chapter. For now, you can think of an Ansible module as a Python program performing certain activities (for example, copying files in Linux, performing configurations on Cisco NX-OS switches). The important point for now is that modules are all installed automatically, and you don't need to worry about getting them but can just use them.

Near the end of Example 19-2, the executable location points to the folder where Ansible is installed, and you can see the Python version that is in use, which in some cases may affect the execution of Ansible modules.

In the configuration file mentioned in Example 19-2, there is a default link to the inventory, as shown in Example 19-3.

Example 19-3 *Default Path to the Ansible Inventory*

```
$ cat /etc/ansible/ansible.cfg | grep 'inventory'
#inventory      = /etc/ansible/hosts
```

The inventory is vital to the functioning of Ansible. It is the file or set of files where hostnames of the managed hosts (and possibly some other parameters) are listed and grouped in specific categories, as illustrated in Example 19-4. The inventory is the file that is used each time Ansible is launched.

Example 19-4 *Simple Ansible Inventory File*

```
$ cat /etc/ansible/hosts
[linux]
localhost

[ios]
CSR1
CSR2

[iosxr]
XR3
XR4

[nexus]
NX1
NX2
```

It is possible to run Ansible automation commands or playbooks against a single host (such as XR3), a group (such as iosxr), or all hosts together. You will learn more about this later in this chapter.

The file shown in Example 19-4 lists only groups and hostnames. You need to make sure that your managing host can reach all the listed hostnames. You can achieve this either by enabling DNS resolution or updating your Linux hosts file, as shown in Example 19-5.

Example 19-5 *The Linux Hosts File with Entries for Ansible Hosts*

```
$ cat /etc/hosts
127.0.0.1     localhost localhost.localdomain localhost4 localhost4.localdomain4
::1           localhost localhost.localdomain localhost6 localhost6.localdomain6
192.168.1.101 CSR1
192.168.1.102 CSR2
192.168.1.111 XR3
192.168.1.112 XR4
192.168.1.121 NX1
192.168.1.122 NX2
```

In some cases, you may be unable to modify the /etc/hosts file (for example, if you don't have the appropriate permissions in the system). There is an alternative way to provide details about IP addresses: by putting the IP addresses directly in the Ansible inventory file. To do so, you use the specific variable name **ansible_ssh_host**, as shown in Example 19-6.

Example 19-6 *Ansible Inventory with IP Addresses*

```
$ cat /etc/ansible/hosts
[linux]
localhost

[ios]
CSR1 ansible_ssh_host=192.168.1.101
CSR2 ansible_ssh_host=192.168.1.102
!
! Further output is truncated for brevity
```

> **Note** It is possible to define other variables in the inventory file, as you will learn later in this chapter.

Now it's time to put all the pieces together and look at a simple example of Ansible operation. Example 19-7 shows the execution of an Ansible ad hoc command.

Example 19-7 *Sample Ansible Ad Hoc Command*

```
$ ansible iosxr --user=cisco --ask-pass --connection=network_cli --module-
  name=iosxr_command --args="commands='show version | include uptime'"
SSH password:

XR3 | SUCCESS => {
    "changed": false,
    "stdout": [
        "XR3 uptime is 32 weeks, 2 days, 11 hours, 28 minutes"
    ],
    "stdout_lines": [
        [
            "XR3 uptime is 32 weeks, 2 days, 11 hours, 28 minutes"
        ]
    ]
}
XR4 | SUCCESS => {
    "changed": false,
    "stdout": [
        "XR4 uptime is 20 weeks, 4 days, 5 hours, 43 minutes"
    ],
```

```
    "stdout_lines": [
        [
            "XR4 uptime is 20 weeks, 4 days, 5 hours, 43 minutes"
        ]
    ]
}
```

By typing **ansible** at the Linux shell, you can execute an Ansible ad hoc command. With an ad hoc command, no script is created; rather, the required command is provided in {*arguments*} to the Ansible application.

Note It is also possible to use sequenced commands called playbooks, as you will learn later in this chapter, in the section "The World of Ansible Modules."

The first attribute in Example 19-7, **iosxr**, is the name of the group from the Ansible inventory. It defines the nodes that the managing host will try to reach for the execution of the command. The command itself is defined by the two attributes **--module-name=iosxr_command** and **--args="commands='show version | include uptime'"**. The first of these attributes defines which Ansible module to use, and the second one passes the arguments required for module execution.

Additional arguments can be used as well, depending on the circumstances. For example, in Example 19-7, the argument **--user=cisco** defines the username for the SSH session, and the argument **--ask-pass** instructs Ansible to ask for the password for the SSH session. The last argument in Example 19-7, **--connection=network_cli**, defines which Python plug-in is used for establishing connectivity to the managed hosts. (You will learn more about such plug-ins later in this chapter, in the section "Variables and Facts.")

Ansible's built-in help lists and describes all the available keywords, as shown in Example 19-8.

Example 19-8 *Built-in Help in Ansible*

```
$ ansible --help
Usage: ansible <host-pattern> [options]

Define and run a single task 'playbook' against a set of hosts

Options:
  -a MODULE_ARGS, --args=MODULE_ARGS
                        module arguments
  --ask-vault-pass      ask for vault password
  -B SECONDS, --background=SECONDS
                        run asynchronously, failing after X seconds
                        (default=N/A)
```

```
  -C, --check           don't make any changes; instead, try to predict some
                        of the changes that may occur
  -D, --diff            when changing (small) files and templates, show the
                        differences in those files; works great with --check
  -e EXTRA_VARS, --extra-vars=EXTRA_VARS
                        set additional variables as key=value or YAML/JSON, if
                        filename prepend with @
  -f FORKS, --forks=FORKS
                        specify number of parallel processes to use
                        (default=5)
  -h, --help            show this help message and exit
  -i INVENTORY, --inventory=INVENTORY, --inventory-file=INVENTORY
                        specify inventory host path or comma separated host
                        list. --inventory-file is deprecated
  -l SUBSET, --limit=SUBSET
                        further limit selected hosts to an additional pattern
  --list-hosts          outputs a list of matching hosts; does not execute
                        anything else

! The output is truncated for brevity
```

Let's talk for another moment about Example 19-7. After the execution of the Ansible ad hoc command, there should be some output. For each host from the group **iosxr**, there is output, which is similar to the output you would get from locally executing the CLI the command **show version | include uptime** on a Cisco IOS XR device. Two variables contain the output: **stdout** contains unformatted output, and **stdout.lines** contains output split into lines based on a standard Linux newline character. Example 19-7 does not show **stdout.lines** because there is only one line, but this variable is beneficial in extensive output.

Ad Hoc Commands and Playbooks

As mentioned earlier in this chapter, it is possible to run ad hoc Ansible commands, and it is also possible to run playbooks, which contain sequences of actions. To better understand the difference between these two approaches, in this section we solve the following tasks:

- Verify the reachability of the network functions
- Check the software version

There are plenty of ways you could complete these tasks. For example, you could first try to ping the network device (which is effectively the solution for the first task) and then connect to the network element to collect the necessary information. Alternatively, you could complete both tasks by using a single data collection operation: Run the **show version** command on a remote network device, and you know that the network is functioning if it responds to the **show version** command sent over SSH. Example 19-9 shows this approach.

Example 19-9 *An Ansible Ad Hoc Command Using the* ***iosxr_command*** *Module*

```
$ ansible iosxr --user=cisco --ask-pass --connection=network_cli --module-
  name=iosxr_command --args="commands='show version | include Cisco IOS XR'"
SSH password:

XR3 | SUCCESS => {
    "changed": false,
    "stdout": [
        "Cisco IOS XR Software, Version 6.1.4[Default]"
    ],
    "stdout_lines": [
        [
            "Cisco IOS XR Software, Version 6.1.4[Default]"
        ]
    ]
}
XR4 | SUCCESS => {
    "changed": false,
    "stdout": [
        "Cisco IOS XR Software, Version 6.1.4[Default]"
    ],
    "stdout_lines": [
        [
            "Cisco IOS XR Software, Version 6.1.4[Default]"
        ]
    ]
}
```

Instead of using ad hoc command, you can create an Ansible playbook relaying the same module as shown in Example 19-10.

Example 19-10 *An Ansible Playbook Using the* ***iosxr_command*** *and* ***debug*** *Modules*

```
$ cat npf_iosxr_show_version.yml
---
- hosts: iosxr
  connection: network_cli

  tasks:
      - name: Collect version from Cisco IOS XR
        iosxr_command:
            commands:
                - show version | include Cisco IOS XR
        register: show_output

      - name: Show results
        debug:
            msg: "{{ show_output.stdout }}"
...


$ ansible-playbook npf_iosxr_show_version.yml --user=cisco --ask-pass
SSH password:

PLAY [iosxr] ************************************************************************

TASK [Collect version from Cisco IOS XR] *******************************************
ok: [XR3]
ok: [XR4]

TASK [Show results] *****************************************************************
ok: [XR3] => {
    "msg": [
        "Cisco IOS XR Software, Version 6.1.4[Default]"
    ]
}
ok: [XR4] => {
    "msg": [
        "Cisco IOS XR Software, Version 6.1.4[Default]"
    ]
}

PLAY RECAP **************************************************************************
XR3                          : ok=2    changed=0    unreachable=0    failed=0
XR4                          : ok=2    changed=0    unreachable=0    failed=0
```

The first significant difference between these two approaches is that a playbook is a file where you compose the logic of your automation. It's written using the YAML language, which you learned about in Chapter 12, "YAML." The information in YAML format has leading --- and ending ... characters. A playbook starts with some essential statements regarding the general execution process. For instance, in Example 19-10, the **hosts** statement defines the nodes against which the playbook will be executed; in this case, the scope is **iosxr**. You can see in Example 19-9 that this information is also provided in the ad hoc command but in a slightly different format. Next, the playbook in Example 19-10 shows important information contained in the **connection** field, which defines the connectivity plug-in that should be used to connect to nodes; the ad hoc command in Example 19-9 provides the same information.

In Example 19-10, the **tasks** list shows activities to be performed. In this list, it is important to use a - symbol followed by a space before each task. Each of the tasks starts with the keyword **name**. This field is not mandatory, but it's highly recommended as it helps the reader understand the purpose of each step. The next keyword is mandatory, as it calls the particular Ansible module, such as **iosxr_command** or **debug**. Every module has some specific keys, as each has a unique set of input and output parameters.

The last important point about Example 19-10 is that it introduces the concept of variables. By default, Ansible playbooks do not print to **stdout** the result of the execution of a tasks; they print only status (OK or NOT OK), and this is entirely okay because playbooks are typically used for solving complex tasks. In this case, the output needs to be printed to the CLI, so the **debug** module is used. However, in order for the **debug** module to show something, you need to save the result of the previous module execution to some variable. This is accomplished by using the key **register**, which saves all the output of the module to a variable (**show_output** in this example).

Note The name of the variable is an arbitrary value.

After the output is saved to the variable, it can be used anywhere else in the playbook. As you can see in Example 19-10, it is called in the second task, using the {{ **show_output.stdout** }} construction. In Ansible, all variables are called by using the {{ *variable* }} format. In this case, another key in the variable is defined to filter the output further. How this variable is structured depends on the module, and you can find this information in the documentation at the official Ansible website (https://docs.ansible.com).

After a playbook is created, the next step is to execute it by using the **ansible-playbook** command. After a playbook is launched, you can follow its execution. The **name** keyword in the playbook makes it evident which tasks are successful and which ones are not. Without names, you have to count the number of the tasks to identify the status of each task. If a task is performed successfully, you see **ok:** [*hostname*] in the output. There are four possible results of task execution:

- **ok:** The task is performed successfully.
- **changed:** The task is performed successfully, and some changes are made on the remote node (which is common for configuration modules).

- **failed:** The execution of the task is unsuccessful.
- **unreachable:** The remote node isn't reachable from the managing host.

In Example 19-10, you can see at the end of the playbook execution a PLAY RECAP section, which provides a summary of all the task status information. The underlying idea with playbook execution is that the same task is performed for all defined nodes in a task-by-task fashion. If some task fails or if a node is unreachable, that host is excluded from the list of nodes for further execution in the current execution.

Note It is possible to change the standard behavior, as you will learn later in this chapter.

If you need to perform an elementary check or configuration, so that a single Ansible module is enough, you may want to use Ansible ad hoc commands. In more complicated cases, you need to use playbooks. For example, if you need to collect information about the software versions of Cisco IOS XR routers and save it somewhere using Ansible, you need to use playbooks and two operations: collect and save (refer to Example 19-10). The number of tasks you can include in a single playbook is virtually unlimited, and you can optimize each operational process, even those that are very complex.

The World of Ansible Modules

Earlier in this chapter, you saw examples of two Ansible modules, and now it's time to talk about them in more detail. Ansible is built on modules, and they are one of its strongest features. Modules are the workhorses that make Ansible such a powerful tool. In a nutshell, a *module* is a Python program with a clear structure and proper documentation that is executed within Ansible to perform a particular task. Figure 19-2 illustrates a generic Ansible module.

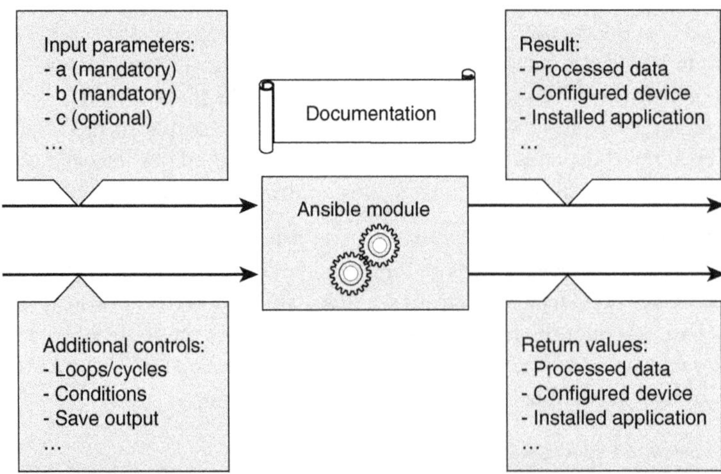

Figure 19-2 *Structure of a Generic Ansible Module*

Each Ansible module has input parameters (potentially many of them) that are necessary for its functioning. For example, earlier in this chapter, the module **iosxr_command** was used with the single defined parameter **commands**. Table 19-1, which is from the official Ansible documentation for the **iosxr_command** module, lists all the possible parameters for this module.

Table 19-1 *Input Parameters for the Ansible Module iosxr_command*

Parameter	Choices/ Defaults	Comments
commands (required)	—	Lists the commands to send to the remote IOS XR device over the configured provider. The resulting output from the command is returned. If the **wait_for** argument is provided, the module is not returned until the condition is satisfied or the number of retries has expired.
Interval	Default: 1	Configures the interval, in seconds, to wait between retries of the command. If the command does not pass the specified conditions, the **Interval** parameter indicates how long to wait before trying the command again.
match	Choices: **any** **all**	The **match** argument is used in conjunction with the **wait_for** argument to specify the match policy. Valid values are **all** and **any**. If the value is set to **all**, then all conditionals in the **wait_for** argument must be satisfied. If the value is set to **any**, then only one of the values must be satisfied.
retries	Default: 10	Specifies the number of times a command should be retried before it is considered failed. The command is run on the target device every retry and evaluated against the **wait_for** conditions.
wait_for	—	Lists the conditions to evaluate against the output of the command. The task waits for each condition to be true before moving forward. If the condition is not true within the configured number of retries, the task fails.

If a parameter that is required (for example, **commands**) doesn't have a default value, it must be explicitly configured, as shown in Example 19-10. If a parameter has a default value, you can leave it as it is; in most cases, this is what you do. If a parameter isn't marked as required and doesn't have a default value, it means it's optional and can change the behavior of the module execution, if provided.

Additional controls influence the process of module execution. None of these controls are mandatory, but you can add them to enrich the logic of an automation. For instance, Example 19-10 includes the keyword **register**, which instructs the module to save the output (whatever the module prints to **stdout**) to some variable. Table 19-2 shows some of the additional controls that are most widely used in network programming. Later in this chapter, in the section "Extending Ansible Capabilities," you will see how these controls are used in some real-life use cases.

Table 19-2 *Control Functions for Modules*

Command	Description
register	Used to save the values of a task execution to some variable for further processing within the Ansible playbook.
loop (with_items)	Used to do many things in one task, such as create a lot of users, install a lot of packages, or repeat a polling step until a certain result is reached.
when	Used to execute a task in the event that a certain condition happens (typically to compare variables with values).
ignore_errors	Used to continue the execution of a playbook for all nodes, even if the execution of a certain task fails.

The key outcome of the execution of any Ansible module is the result achieved by the execution of the task. Different modules have different purposes and therefore different results. The following are a few possible module results:

- **iosxr_command:** Gets output from the requested **show** command.
- **debug:** Prints the content of some variable to verify the correct execution of previous modules.
- **copy:** Copies a Linux file from the source to the destination path.
- **docker_container:** Creates, deletes, or modifies a Docker container.
- **netconf_config:** Configures a network function using NETCONF protocol.

If you look back at Figure 19-2, you can see that return values are an important part of a module. Return values are highly dependent on the type of module. For example, if the result of a module should include some information (such as after issuing a **show** command on a Cisco IOS XR router), this result is be stored in **stdout** as a whole and **stdout_lines** per line, as explained earlier in this chapter. If a module isn't expected to have any output, both of those keys will be missing. However, there are two keys that exist for every module: **changed** and **failed.** Both of these keys are of Boolean type, which means they can have true or false values only. These keys help you build nonlinear logic in a playbook. You might use them, for example, if you need to execute some tasks in the event that the previous task succeeds and other tasks in the event that it fails.

By now, you should have a good understanding of the structure and operation of Ansible modules in general, as well as the modules **iosxr_command** and **debug** in particular. There are several hundred Ansible modules, and each performs specific tasks. You can find them on the official Ansible website (https://docs.ansible.com), where they are split into multiple categories for ease of searching (see Figure 19-3).

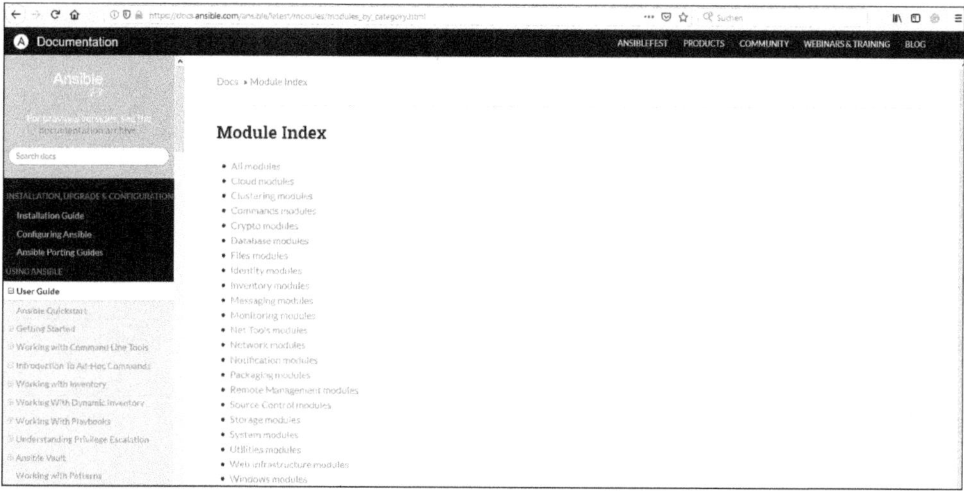

Figure 19-3 *Available Ansible Module Categories*

The modules most widely used for network automation and programming are in the categories network modules, file modules, and utility modules:

- **Network modules:** Modules in this category deal with the network stack in Ansible, including Linux and different vendors and products. Examples include modules for Cisco IOS, IOS XR, NX-OS, ASA, and ACI.
- **File modules:** This category contains modules related to file operations in Linux, such as creating, deleting, copying, and templating.
- **Utility modules:** This category contains modules responsible for the general operation of an Ansible playbook.

Several modules from these categories are covered later in this chapter, in conjunction with specific scenarios.

Extending Ansible Capabilities

As you have learned in this chapter, Ansible modules are building blocks for network automation, but you need some glue to hold these blocks together to assemble a robust network automation solution.

Connection Plugins

Recall from the earlier examples of Ansible ad hoc commands and playbooks that information about the connection type is provided in the argument **--connection=network_cli** or **connection: network_cli. network_cli** is a connection plug-in that Ansible uses to establish connectivity with a managed node. There are many additional connection plug-ins, and Table 19-3 summarizes the ones that are essential for network automation. From this table, you can see that different connection plug-ins are used in different types of interactions with network functions. The documentation for each module indicates which connectivity plug-in the module uses.

Table 19-3 *Connection Plug-ins*

Plug-in	Protocol	Requires	Persistent?	When Used
network_cli	CLI over SSH	**network_os** setting	Yes	With the **iosxr_command** module for SSH communication
netconf	XML over SSH	**network_os** setting	Yes	With NETCONF modules
httpapi	API over HTTP/HTTPS	**network_os** setting	Yes	With connectivity between a network or control function established over HTTP/HTTPS, as with RESTCONF or GRPC
napalm	NAPALM drivers over SSH	**network_os** setting	Yes	To provide connectivity to network devices using the NAPALM network device abstraction library
local	Depends on additional parameters, if defined	Additional parameters, if defined	No	To process information locally on a Linux host where Ansible is installed (no longer recommended for network function management)

An important point regarding connection plug-ins requires further clarifications. The **persistence** parameter describes how the session between the remote network device and local node is treated. If persistence has been configured, then a single SSH or HTTP/HTTPS session (depending on the connection plug-in) is established for the duration of the whole playbook execution. If persistence has not been configured, for every task in an Ansible playbook, the session has to be reestablished, and this requires the user to enter login and password information if they weren't previously saved. Even if they were saved, the operation for building and closing an SSH session requires additional computation resources. In contrast, SSH or HTTPS sessions are persistent for the duration of the playbook execution.

Another important point is that for some connection plugins, the **ansible_network_os** variable should be defined within the playbook/ad hoc command or in some variables or facts. (You will learn about this shortly.) Sometimes you don't need to define the **ansible_network_os** variable, but typically it is a good idea to define it because doing so ensures that the proper escape characters or prompt matches are used for the particular platform. In the context of this book, for Cisco devices, the well-defined types are **ios** for Cisco IOS XE, **iosxr** for Cisco IOS XR, and **nexus** for Cisco NX-OS.

Variables and Facts

Variables are some of the most critical elements of any programming or scripting logic. Defining variables is the only way you can change input parameters for some actions performed by Ansible playbooks without changing the playbooks themselves. Ansible uses Jinja2 format to define variables. (You will learn about Jinja2 later in this chapter, in the context of the templates.)

Earlier in this chapter, in Example 19-10, you saw a variable used to save the output of the execution of some commands; you might want to do this, for example, if the logic of an automation is built on the results of the previous tasks. This is one of the ways you can assign and use variables, but much more often you use variables to assign parameters that are used later in Ansible playbook tasks for configuration or information collection activities on network functions. Example 19-11 shows the most common way to define variables and assign values to them.

Example 19-11 *Defining Variables in an Ansible Playbook*

```
$ cat npf_example_simple_vars.yml
---
- hosts: linux
  gather_facts: no
  connection: local

  vars:
      interface:
          name: gig0/0/0/0
          mtu: 1500
          ip: 10.0.0.1/24
      bandwidth: 1000000
      description: Interface to Internet

  tasks:
      - name: CHECKING VARIABLES
        debug:
            msg: Interface {{ interface.name }} has IP address {{ interface.ip }},
  MTU {{ interface.mtu }}, BW {{ bandwidth }} and described as '{{ description }}'
...


$ ansible-playbook npf_example_simple_vars.yml --limit=localhost

PLAY [linux] *******************************************************************
```

```
TASK [CHECKING VARIABLES] ************************************************************
ok: [localhost] => {
    "msg": "Interface gig0/0/0/0 has IP address 10.0.0.1/24, MTU 1500, BW 1000000
  and described as 'Interface to Internet'"
}

PLAY RECAP ***************************************************************************
localhost                  : ok=1    changed=0    unreachable=0    failed=0
```

The variables are defined in the section **vars** as ordinary objects, and when they are called later on in the tasks, they are formatted in the form {{ *variable* }}. In the **vars** part, the variables can be grouped in a hierarchy (for example, **{{ interface.name }}**, **{{ interface.mtu }}**, and **{{ interface.ip }}**). There is no limit to the hierarchy depth, so you should use common sense when creating a hierarchy. Alternatively, they can be treated as independent elements, (for example, **{{ bandwidth }}** and **{{ description }}**). These two ways to define variables (structured and flat) are shown in Example 19-11 to familiarize you with both options. In real life, you are likely to use the one format that best satisfies your requirements.

Another important component of a playbook is the **gather_facts** key, which is set to the value **no**. This setting determines whether the playbook will collect facts from the destination host before running the playbook's tasks. The facts are additional information about the managed host that could help in the execution of the playbook if you make it vendor or system agnostic. Ansible originally came from the Linux management world, where the different Linux distributions have different packages (for example, **apt-get** to install packages in Ubuntu/Debian, **yum** in CentOS/RedHat up to version 8, **dnf** in CentOS 8). Knowing which Linux distro will be managed by a playbook can help you identify the proper command. Keep in mind that this mechanism is for Linux operating systems and is not applicable to network operating systems such as Cisco IOS XE and IOS XR and Juniper Junos OS.

Finally, in Example 19-11, you can see that the argument **--limit** has the value **localhost.** You use the **--limit** argument when you need to limit the scope of the playbook execution (for example, for only a specific group or a specific host). For the value of this argument, you need to provide the name of the host (or multiple hosts, separated by commas) from the inventory file.

By default, you don't define variable types because the interpreter understands the types, based on the context. There are five main variable types, as shown in Table 19-4.

Table 19-4 *Ansible Variable Types*

Type	Examples	Description
Number	**1, 23.4, ...**	Any numerical value, including floats and negative values
Boolean	**true, false**	Binary logic, when only one of two results is possible
String	**abc, interface, a3, ...**	Any type of information

Type	Examples	Description
List	**value1, value2**	Multiple entries of any other type, which are siblings to each other
Dictionary	**nested_key: nested_value**	Any nested key/value pairs (There is no limit for nesting.)

Defining variables within an Ansible playbook is possible, but it is not necessarily the best way to use variables. Typically you want to use as much automation as possible for massive-scale operations that repeat the same activities several times or several hundred times. For example, say that you need to configure a new data center fabric with IP addresses and external BGP sessions to build a leaf/spine fabric. The set of actions will be the same for each network device that is to be configured, but the network devices have unique IP addresses and BGP peers. It's straightforward to implement such logic in Ansible by using some built-in variables and importing per node variables from an external file, as shown in Example 19-12.

Example 19-12 *Importing Variables from an External File*

```
$ ls -l | grep 'npf'
-rw-------. 1 aaa aaa 418 Dec  1 14:08 npf_example_external_vars.yml
-rw-------. 1 aaa aaa 103 Dec  1 14:09 npf_NX1_variables.yml
-rw-------. 1 aaa aaa 103 Dec  1 14:09 npf_NX2_variables.yml


$ cat npf_NX1_variables.yml
---
interface:
    name: Eth1
    mtu: 1500
    ip: 10.0.0.1/24
    description: Connection to NX2
...


$ cat npf_NX2_variables.yml
---
interface:
    name: Eth2
    mtu: 1500
    ip: 10.0.0.2/24
    description: Connection to NX1
...
```

```
$ cat npf_example_external_vars.yml
---
- hosts: nexus
  gather_facts: no
  connection: local


 tasks:
      - name: IMPORTING VARS
        include_vars:
            file: npf_{{ inventory_hostname }}_variables.yml

      - name: CHECKING VARIABLES
        debug:
            msg: Interface {{ interface.name }} has IP address {{ interface.ip }}
  and described as '{{ interface.description }}'
...


$ ansible-playbook npf_example_external_vars.yml

PLAY [nexus] ***********************************************************************

TASK [IMPORTING VARS] **************************************************************
ok: [NX1]
ok: [NX2]

TASK [CHECKING VARIABLES] **********************************************************
ok: [NX1] => {
    "msg": "Interface Eth1 has IP address 10.0.0.1/24 and described as 'Connection
  to NX2'"
}
ok: [NX2] => {
    "msg": "Interface Eth2 has IP address 10.0.0.2/24 and described as 'Connection
  to NX1'"
}

PLAY RECAP *************************************************************************
NX1                          : ok=2    changed=0    unreachable=0    failed=0
NX2                          : ok=2    changed=0    unreachable=0    failed=0
}
```

The first variable in Example 19-12 is the predefined variable **{{ inventory_hostname }}**. This variable is always defined when the playbook is launched and is equal to the value contained in the inventory file associated with the hostname of the network function (refer to Example 19-4). You don't need to define it manually anywhere, but you use it a lot when building automation. As shown in Example 19-12, this variable is used to construct the proper name of the file with variables that should be imported.

Example 19-12 also introduces the module **include_vars**. As indicated by its name, this module reads the variables from an external file so that you can use it in your main playbook. The **file** parameter defines the path file, and both relative and absolute paths can be provided. In the case of a relative path, the lookup is done from the perspective of the folder from which you execute the Ansible playbook. For each network function, the playbook is executed in the appropriate context, so even though the same variable names appear in the playbook, there are no problems, and the proper values are used.

So far, you have learned two ways to define variables: in dedicated files or directly in a playbook. There is one more way to predefine variables, as shown in the Example 19-13, and it relies on the inventory file.

Example 19-13 *Defining Variables in the Inventory File*

```
$ cat /etc/ansible/hosts
[linux]
localhost

[ios]
CSR1
CSR2

[iosxr]
XR3
XR4

[nexus]
NX1 interface=Eth1 ip=10.0.0.1/24
NX2 interface=Eth2 ip=10.0.0.2/24

[nexus:vars]
ansible_network_os=nexus
ansible_user=aaa
ansible_ssh_pass=aaa


$ cat npf_example_inventory_vars.yml
---
- hosts: nexus
  gather_facts: yes
  connection: local
```

```
 tasks:
      - name: CHECKING VARIABLES
        debug:
            msg: Device {{ inventory_hostname }} is running OS '{{ ansible_network_
  os }}' and has interface {{ interface }} with IP address {{ ip }}
...


$ ansible-playbook npf_example_inventory_vars.yml

PLAY [nexus] *************************************************************************

TASK [Gathering Facts] ***************************************************************
ok: [NX2]
ok: [NX1]

TASK [CHECKING VARIABLES] ************************************************************
ok: [NX1] => {
    "msg": "Device NX1 is running OS 'nexus' and has interface Eth1 with IP address
  10.0.0.1/24"
}
ok: [NX2] => {
    "msg": "Device NX2 is running OS 'nexus' and has interface Eth2 with IP address
  10.0.0.2/24"
}

PLAY RECAP ***************************************************************************
NX1                          : ok=2    changed=0    unreachable=0    failed=0
NX2                          : ok=2    changed=0    unreachable=0    failed=0
```

Two classes of variables are used in Example 19-13:

- **group_vars:** These variables are relevant for all the devices in a specific group. In Example 19-13, they are stored in **[nexus:vars]**. This is quite a convenient way to store credentials or other general information. You can see in Example 19-13 that all the variables start with **ansible_. group_vars.** Variable names are typically predefined and have some default values, as different modules use them. You need to manually change those default values to allow modules to operate according to your needs.

- **host_vars:** These variables are relevant only for a particular host. In Example 19-13, these values are stored in the same line with the host itself in *key=value* format and divided by spaces.

There is one more way to define variables, and this method is very important for building nonlinear logic in an application. With this dynamic option, the value of a variable is defined during the execution of the Ansible playbook. Say that you want to check the version of Cisco IOS XR software running on your nodes, compare it to the target release, and automatically update it (or at least notify the operation engineers) in the event that the original software version deviates from the target. Example 19-14 shows how to set up the variable value from the output of a command.

Example 19-14 *Setting Variables Dynamically*

```
$ cat npf_iosxr_check_version.yml
---
- hosts: iosxr
  gather_facts: yes
  connection: network_cli

  tasks:
      - name: Collect version from Cisco IOS XR
        iosxr_command:
            commands:
                - show version | include Cisco IOS XR
        register: show_output
        ignore_errors: yes

      - name: debug
        debug:
            msg: The full output is {{ show_output.stdout }}

      - name: Create variable with SW value
        set_fact:
            cisco_sw: "{{ show_output.stdout | string | regex_replace('^.*Version
  (.+)\\[.*$', '\\1')}}"

      - name: debug
        debug:
            msg: Device {{ inventory_hostname }} is running Cisco IOS XR
  {{ cisco_sw }}
...
```

```
$ ansible-playbook npf_iosxr_check_version.yml

PLAY [iosxr] ***************************************************************************

TASK [Gathering Facts] *****************************************************************
ok: [XR1]
ok: [XR2]

TASK [Collect version from Cisco IOS XR] ***********************************************
ok: [XR1]
ok: [XR2]

TASK [debug] ***************************************************************************
ok: [XR2] => {
    "msg": "The full output is [u'Cisco IOS XR Software, Version 6.1.4[Default]']"
}
ok: [XR1] => {
    "msg": "The full output is [u'Cisco IOS XR Software, Version 6.1.4[Default]']"
}

TASK [Create variable with SW value] ***************************************************
ok: [XR2]
ok: [XR1]

TASK [debug] ***************************************************************************
ok: [XR2] => {
    "msg": "Device XR2 is running Cisco IOS XR 6.1.4"
}
ok: [XR1] => {
    "msg": "Device SR1 is running Cisco IOS XR 6.1.4"
}

PLAY RECAP *****************************************************************************
XR1                        : ok=5    changed=0    unreachable=0    failed=0
XR2                        : ok=5    changed=0    unreachable=0    failed=0
```

In Example 19-14, the variable is created using the module **set_fact**, which is used as a task opposite the **register** instruction, which saves the output of the execution of other modules. Within a module, you can dynamically define any number of variables you need in the form *variable*: *key*. In Example 19-14, the variable **cisco_sw** is created, and some value is assigned to it. The value is extracted from the output of the **show** command saved in the variable **show_output.stdout**. After the name of the variable, you see the rather complex construction **| string | regex_replace('^.*Version (.+)\\[.*$', '\\1')**. This construction applies two filters to the initial variable. We will look more closely at filters in the next section, but for now, you need to understand only how this particular construction works. The filter **string** is applied to an object and converts that object to a string, no matter how the variable was formatted before. The second filter, **regex_replace**, uses regular expressions to find interesting information and modify the original text. It uses standard Linux regular expressions like the ones discussed in Chapter 4, "Linux Scripting." It uses the syntax **regex_replace('*input_value*', '*output_value*')**, much like the **sed///** function in Linux.

In this section, you have learned several ways to define variables, depending on your needs:

- Using the **register** instruction to save the result of the task execution
- Using the **vars** section in a playbook
- Using the **set_fact** module
- Using the inventory file

There are no good and bad ways to define variables; the method used depends on the context.

Filters

In general, *filters* are used to manipulate data within an expression. Ansible uses both its own filters and Jinja2 filters. As with Ansible modules, the number of filters available is rather significant, and filters can perform a tremendous number of actions.

Example 19-14 shows a filter applied to a variable's value using the {{ *variable* | *filter* }} syntax, where the number of filters is not limited. Each new filter is added as | *filter*. The filters are applied sequentially one after another, so you need to pay attention to the order of the filters.

There are so many filters available that it can be difficult to foresee which ones you will use in your automation tasks. To get an idea of what filters can do for you, this section focuses on two filters that are commonly used in networking. The first of these filters allows you to generate random MAC address, and the second one provides a very flexible way of working with IP addresses. However, before you can create an Ansible playbook that uses a filter, you need to install the filter. Example 19-15 shows how to install the two filters we examine in this section.

Example 19-15 *Installing the ipaddr library*

```
$ sudo yum install -y python-netaddr
! The output is truncated for brevity
Resolving Dependencies
--> Running transaction check
---> Package python-netaddr.noarch 0:0.7.5-9.el7 will be installed
--> Finished Dependency Resolution
! The output is truncated for brevity
Installed:
  python-netaddr.noarch 0:0.7.5-9.el7
Complete!


$ sudo pip install ipaddr
Collecting ipaddr
  Downloading https://files.pythonhosted.org/packages/9d/a7/1b39a16cb90dfe491f57e1ca
  b3103a15d4e8dd9a150872744f531b1106c1/ipaddr-2.2.0.tar.gz
Installing collected packages: ipaddr
  Running setup.py install for ipaddr ... done
Successfully installed ipaddr-2.2.
```

After these filters have been installed, you can start using them with IP addresses. You can use the **ipaddr** and **random_mac** filters in any virtual environment where MAC addresses of hosts must deviate from each other and, therefore, can be random, and IP addresses must be consistent within the address allocation schema. Example 19-16 shows these two filters being used in such scenario.

Example 19-16 *Using the ipaddr and random_mac Filters*

```
$ cat npf_example_simple_vars_and_filters.yml
---
- hosts: nexus
  gather_facts: yes
  connection: local

  vars:
      interface:
          name_prefix: Eth
          mac_prefix: 00:00:5E
          ip_prefix: 10.0.0.0/24

  tasks:
      - name: CHECKING VARIABLES
        debug:
```

```
          msg: |
               interface {{ interface.name_prefix }}1
                   mac {{ interface.mac_prefix | random_mac }}
                   ip address {{ interface.ip_prefix | ipaddr('1')}}
...


$ ansible-playbook npf_example_simple_vars_and_filters.yml

PLAY [nexus] *******************************************************************

TASK [Gathering Facts] *********************************************************
ok: [NX2]
ok: [NX1]

TASK [CHECKING VARIABLES] ******************************************************
ok: [NX1] => {
    "msg": "interface Eth1\n    mac 00:00:5e:20:ce:a6\n    ip address 10.0.0.1/24\n"
}
ok: [NX2] => {
    "msg": "interface Eth1\n    mac 00:00:5e:25:13:42\n    ip address 10.0.0.1/24\n"
}

PLAY RECAP *********************************************************************
NX1                        : ok=2    changed=0    unreachable=0    failed=0
NX2                        : ok=2    changed=0    unreachable=0    failed=0
```

Before we discuss these two filters, let's return for a moment to the **debug** module. In Example 19-16, the **msg** argument of the **debug** module is provided in a different format, where it starts with a pipe (**|**) and then the text is provided as a multi-line object. This approach is the basis for template-based configuration, which is a cornerstone of massive-scale operations. (Templates are discussed in detail later in this chapter.)

The first filter in Example 19-16, **random_mac**, is used to generate the random host part of a MAC address with a given fixed OUI. As you can see, the MAC addresses for nodes NX1 and NX2 are entirely different. The second filter in this example, **ipaddr**, is applied with the argument 1, which in this context means it takes the second IP address from the initial subnet 10.0.0.0/24, which is why you see 10.0.0.1/20. Why does it take the second IP address? As you might know, in programming languages, the index of the first element in an array is always 0, so the argument 1 tells the filter to take from the array the element with index 1—that is, the second element. At this point, you might also wonder what use this filter is if both network functions NX1 and NX2 have the same IP address. You will learn more about this later in this chapter, in the section "Loops."

Conditionals

Conditionals make it possible to create if-then logic in automation, giving you the ability to react to input information with higher intelligence. In Ansible, conditionals allow you to create useful and flexible automation.

Ansible conditionals follow the standard logic of comparing one value with another one. Typically at least one value in the comparison comes from a variable because it does not usually make sense to compare one fixed value with another one. In the discussion of Example 19-14, we talked about checking the software version of the Cisco IOS XR router, but we did not look at how to compare the value collected with some other values. Example 19-17 shows how to do that.

Example 19-17 *Using a Conditional Statement in Ansible, Part 1*

```
$ cat npf_iosxr_check_version.yml
---
- hosts: iosxr
  gather_facts: yes
  connection: network_cli

  vars:
      target_cisco_sw: 6.5.1

  tasks:
      - name: Collect version from Cisco IOS XR
        iosxr_command:
            commands:
                - show version | include Cisco IOS XR
        register: show_output
        ignore_errors: yes

      - name: Create variable with SW value
        set_fact:
            cisco_sw: "{{ show_output.stdout | string | regex_replace('^.*Version
  (.+)\\[.*$', '\\1')}}"

      - name: debug
        debug:
            msg: SW upgrade is needed! Device {{ inventory_hostname }} is running
 Cisco IOS XR {{ cisco_sw }}, target release is {{ target_cisco_sw }}
        when: cisco_sw != target_cisco_sw
```

```
    - name: debug
      debug:
          msg: SW is actual, no actions are needed! Device
  {{ inventory_hostname }} is running Cisco IOS XR {{ cisco_sw }}, target release is
  {{ target_cisco_sw }}
      when: cisco_sw == target_cisco_sw
...


$ ansible-playbook npf_iosxr_check_version.yml

PLAY [iosxr] *********************************************************************

TASK [Gathering Facts] ***********************************************************
ok: [XR1]
ok: [XR2]

TASK [Collect version from Cisco IOS XR] *****************************************
ok: [XR1]
ok: [XR2]

TASK [Create variable with SW value] *********************************************
ok: [XR2]
ok: [XR1]

TASK [debug] *********************************************************************
ok: [XR2] => {
    "msg": "SW update is needed! Device XR2 is running Cisco IOS XR 6.1.4, target
  release is 6.5.1"
}
ok: [XR1] => {
    "msg": "SW update is needed! Device XR1 is running Cisco IOS XR 6.1.4, target
  release is 6.5.1"
}

TASK [debug] *********************************************************************
skipping: [XR2]
skipping: [XR1]

PLAY RECAP ***********************************************************************
XR2          : ok=4    changed=0    unreachable=0    failed=0
XR1          : ok=4    changed=0    unreachable=0    failed=0
```

At the beginning of Example 19-17, you see the variable **target_cisco_sw** defined with the value **6.5.1**, which is a string. Then the **set_fact** module is used to extract the Cisco IOS XR software version from the output of the **show** command. At the end of the automation script, based on the condition **when**, either one action or another is taken: Either a software update is needed, or it isn't. The comparison is made using syntax that is standard in many programming languages, where **==** means equal and **!=** means not equal.

As you can see in Example 19-17, the extracted value **6.1.4** is not equal to the predefined value **6.5.1**, so you are informed that an update is necessary. The task in the playbook (which isn't played in this case due to the condition) is **skipping.** Now, if the value of **target_cisco_sw** is changed to **6.1.4**, you see a different action occur, as shown in Example 19-18.

Example 19-18 *Using a Conditional Statement in Ansible, Part 2*

```
$ cat npf_iosxr_check_version.yml | grep 'target_cisco_sw:'
      target_cisco_sw: 6.1.4


$ ansible-playbook npf_iosxr_check_version.yml
! The output is truncated for brevity
TASK [debug] ***********************************************************************
skipping: [XR1]
skipping: [XR2]

TASK [debug] ***********************************************************************
ok: [XR1] => {
    "msg": "SW is actual, no actions are needed! Device XR1 is running Cisco IOS XR
  6.1.4, target release is 6.1.4"
}
ok: [XR2] => {
    "msg": "SW is actual, no actions are needed! Device XR2 is running Cisco IOS XR
  6.1.4, target release is 6.1.4"
}

PLAY RECAP *************************************************************************
XR2          : ok=4    changed=0    unreachable=0    failed=0
XR1          : ok=4    changed=0    unreachable=0    failed=0
```

When you are working with numbers, you can perform the Jinja2 comparison operations listed in Table 19-5.

Table 19-5 *Jinja2 Comparison Operations That Are Used in Ansible*

Operator	Action
==	Compares two objects for equality
!=	Compares two objects for inequality
>	*True* if the left side is greater than the right side
>=	*True* if the left side is greater than or equal to the right side
<	*True* if the left side is less than the right side
<=	*True* if the left side is less than or equal to the right side

In addition to that, in Ansible automation, you will often use two handy conditional operators that are not technically math operators. The first of these operators is used to perform a test, such as to verify whether some variable exists, as shown in Example 19-19.

Example 19-19 *Using a Conditional Statement to Check Whether a Variable Exists*

```
$ cat npf_iosxr_check_version.yml
---
- hosts: iosxr
  gather_facts: yes
  connection: network_cli

#  vars:
#      target_cisco_sw: 6.1.4

  tasks:
      - name: Check input variables for consistency
        fail:
            msg: There is no target SW defined
        when: target_cisco_sw is not defined

      - name: Collect version from Cisco IOS XR
        iosxr_command:
            commands:
                - show version | include Cisco IOS XR
        register: show_output
        ignore_errors: yes

      - name: Create variable with SW value
        set_fact:
            cisco_sw: "{{ show_output.stdout | string | regex_replace('^.*Version
  (.+)\\[.*$', '\\1')}}"
```

```
    - name: debug
      debug:
          msg: SW update is needed! Device {{ inventory_hostname }} is running
  Cisco IOS XR {{ cisco_sw }}, target release is {{ target_cisco_sw }}
      when: cisco_sw != target_cisco_sw

    - name: debug
      debug:
          msg: SW is actual, no actions are needed! Device
  {{ inventory_hostname }} is running Cisco IOS XR {{ cisco_sw }}, target release is
  {{ target_cisco_sw }}
      when: cisco_sw == target_cisco_sw
...


$ ansible-playbook npf_iosxr_check_version.yml

PLAY [iosxr] *********************************************************************

TASK [Gathering Facts] ***********************************************************
ok: [XR1]
ok: [XR2]

TASK [Check input variables for consistency] *************************************
fatal: [XR1]: FAILED! => {"changed": false, "msg": "There is no target SW defined"}
fatal: [XR2]: FAILED! => {"changed": false, "msg": "There is no target SW defined"}
        to retry, use: --limit @/home/karneliuka/de-secgw/ansible/npf_iosxr_check_
  version.retry

PLAY RECAP ***********************************************************************
XR1        : ok=1    changed=0    unreachable=0    failed=1
XR2        : ok=1    changed=0    unreachable=0    failed=1
```

Example 19-19 shows some lines of the Ansible playbook commented out with the **#** character. Comments allow you to leave notes in code for others or to temporarily deactivate some parts of your code for debugging. Example 19-19 also shows the module **fail**, which stops the execution of the playbook. Because **fail** stops a playbook, you use it only with some conditions. For example, in Example 19-19, the playbook should fail if the variable **target_cisco_sw** doesn't exist or if the way it is reflected in the code is not defined. The operator **is**, together with the predefined argument **defined**, performs this test by looking at whether such a variable is defined somewhere earlier in the playbook, is imported from another playbook, or comes from group/host variables. Example 19-19 provides an obvious example in which the variable is defined in the same file, and you can easily spot a mistake. However, if the variables are imported from another task, or even if they are dynamically set using the **set_fact** module, based on the output of the execution of some previous parts of the code, the check plays a significant role in saving resources and aiding in the development of the code. Moreover, even in Example 19-18, if you don't do a check, the playbook collects the information from the remote nodes before it fails because the last task can't be finished. Collecting the information from all the remote nodes takes time and effort, and it's best to fail earlier to save that time.

Another important operator for conditions in Jinja2 used in Ansible, the **in** operator allows you to perform a search in the text. In specific scenarios like our earlier example of software upgrades, this operator allows you to reduce the number of tasks, as shown in Example 19-20.

Example 19-20 *Using a Conditional Statement to Check Whether a Variable Contains Some Substring*

```
$ cat npf_iosxr_check_version.yml
---
- hosts: iosxr
  gather_facts: yes
  connection: network_cli

  vars:
      target_cisco_sw: 6.1.4

  tasks:
      - name: Collect version from Cisco IOS XR
        iosxr_command:
            commands:
                - show version | include Cisco IOS XR
        register: show_output
        ignore_errors: yes

      - name: debug
        debug:
            msg: SW update is needed! Device {{ inventory_hostname }} is not running
  SW {{ target_cisco_sw }}
        when: target_cisco_sw not in show_output.stdout | string

      - name: debug
        debug:
            msg: SW is actual, no actions are needed! Device
  {{ inventory_hostname }} is running SW {{ target_cisco_sw }}
        when: target_cisco_sw in show_output.stdout | string
...
```

```
$ ansible-playbook npf_iosxr_check_version.yml

PLAY [iosxr] *************************************************************************

TASK [Gathering Facts] ***************************************************************
ok: [XR1]
ok: [XR2]

TASK [Collect version from Cisco IOS XR] *********************************************
ok: [XR2]
ok: [XR1]

TASK [debug] *************************************************************************
skipping: [XR1]
skipping: [XR2]

TASK [debug] *************************************************************************
ok: [XR1] => {
    "msg": "SW is actual, no actions are needed! Device XR1 is running SW 6.1.4"
}
ok: [XR2] => {
    "msg": "SW is actual, no actions are needed! Device XR2 is running SW 6.1.4"
}

PLAY RECAP ***************************************************************************
XR1                        : ok=3    changed=0    unreachable=0    failed=0
XR2                        : ok=3    changed=0    unreachable=0    failed=0
```

The conditional operator **in** is used to find a match, and **not in** indicates that there is not a match. In a nutshell, this operator takes the value of the variable on the left side from the keyword **in** (in this case, **target_cisco_sw**) and tries to find a substring match at the beginning, middle, or end of the variable on the right side (in this case, **show_output.stdout**). If there is a match, then the result of the condition **in** is true; if there is no match, the condition **in** is false. (**not in** works the opposite way.) The filter **string** can be used for proper text processing of the output of the **show** command.

So far, you have learned about different operators used in conditional statements as well as how to apply conditionals to the tasks in Ansible playbooks. The final topic related to conditionals that we need to discuss is related to scenarios where you need to apply several conditionals simultaneously when triggering a single action—for example, to make sure that all conditions are fulfilled together (logical AND) or only partially (logical OR). Example 19-21 shows how to use these conditionals.

Example 19-21 *Using and/or Logic to Combine Multiple Conditionals*

```
$ cat npf_iosxr_check_version.yml
---
- hosts: iosxr
  gather_facts: yes
  connection: network_cli

  vars:
      target_cisco_sw: 6.1.4

  tasks:
      - name: Collect version from Cisco IOS XR
        iosxr_command:
            commands:
                - show version | include Cisco IOS XR
        register: show_output
        ignore_errors: yes

      - name: debug
        debug:
            msg: SW upgrade is needed! Device {{ inventory_hostname }} is not
  running SW {{ target_cisco_sw }}
        when: target_cisco_sw not in show_output.stdout | string or 'Cisco' not in
  show_output.stdout | string

      - name: debug
        debug:
            msg: SW is actual, no actions are needed! Device
  {{ inventory_hostname }} is running SW {{ target_cisco_sw }}
        when: target_cisco_sw in show_output.stdout | string and 'Cisco' in
  show_output.stdout | string
...


$ ansible-playbook npf_iosxr_check_version.yml

PLAY [iosxr] *********************************************************************

TASK [Gathering Facts] ***********************************************************
ok: [XR1]
ok: [XR2]
```

```
TASK [Collect version from Cisco IOS XR] ********************************************
ok: [XR2]
ok: [XR1]

TASK [debug] ************************************************************************
skipping: [XR1]
skipping: [XR2]

TASK [debug] ************************************************************************
ok: [XR1] => {
    "msg": "SW is actual, no actions are needed! Device XR1 is running SW 6.1.4"
}
ok: [XR2] => {
    "msg": "SW is actual, no actions are needed! Device XR2 is running SW 6.1.4"
}

PLAY RECAP **************************************************************************
XR1                        : ok=3    changed=0    unreachable=0    failed=0
XR2                        : ok=3    changed=0    unreachable=0    failed=0
```

To execute a task in the event that two or more conditions are fulfilled together, you need to use the keyword **and** to combine the conditions. This is equivalent to configuring routing policies in Cisco IOS with the **match-all** condition. If you want to execute a task in the event that at least one of all the provided conditions are fulfilled, you need to use the keyword **or** to combine the conditions. This is equivalent to using a **match-any** condition in routing policies in Cisco IOS (or NX-OS or IOS XR).

Example 19-21, note in the **when** section that all the variables are provided without any special syntax, like **{{** *variable* **}}**. To distinguish the variables from values (for example, any static text you might need to use), the values (static text) are framed by quotes, in the format *'value'*. In Example 19-21, you can see the value **'Cisco'** results from a search in the variable **show_output.stdout** processed with the filter **string**.

Loops

A *loop* enables you to repeat some actions with slight changes. Loops are crucial in creating templates for configuring network functions and for performing actions on remote devices. Ansible enables you to create loops with a rich set of parameters.

In Example 19-16, you saw an example of how to create a configuration for an interface of a Cisco NX-OS switch device. In that example, you could see that there were some limitations, such as the same IP addresses on the two nodes. Example 19-22 shows how to solve the duplicate IP address problem.

Example 19-22 *Using a Loop and Conditions Together*

```
$ cat npf_example_simple_vars_and_filters.yml
---
- hosts: nexus
  gather_facts: yes
  connection: local

  vars:
      interface:
          name_prefix: Eth
          mac_prefix: 00:00:5E
          ip_prefix: 10.0.0.0/8

  tasks:
      - name: CHECKING VARIABLES
        debug:
            msg: |
                interface {{ interface.name_prefix }}{{ item }}
                    mac {{ interface.mac_prefix | random_mac }}
                    ip address {{ interface.ip_prefix | ipaddr(1) }}
        loop:
            - 1/1
            - 2/1
            - 1/7
            - 1/18
        when: inventory_hostname == 'NX1'

      - name: CHECKING VARIABLES
        debug:
            msg: |
                interface {{ interface.name_prefix }}{{ item }}
                    mac {{ interface.mac_prefix | random_mac }}
                    ip address {{ interface.ip_prefix | ipaddr(2) }}
        loop:
            - 1/3
            - 1/7
            - 2/18
            - 2/23
        when: inventory_hostname == 'NX2'
...


$ ansible-playbook npf_example_simple_vars_and_filters.yml

PLAY [nexus] ************************************************************************
```

```
TASK [Gathering Facts] *****************************************************************
ok: [NX2]
ok: [NX1]

TASK [CHECKING VARIABLES] **************************************************************
ok: [NX1] => (item=1/1) => {
    "msg": "interface Eth1/1\n    mac 00:00:5e:75:8f:23\n    ip address
  10.0.0.1/8\n"
}
ok: [NX1] => (item=2/1) => {
    "msg": "interface Eth2/1\n    mac 00:00:5e:10:4d:f9\n    ip address
  10.0.0.1/8\n"
}
ok: [NX1] => (item=1/7) => {
    "msg": "interface Eth1/7\n    mac 00:00:5e:11:3f:b6\n    ip address
  10.0.0.1/8\n"
}
skipping: [NX2] => (item=1/1)
ok: [NX1] => (item=1/18) => {
    "msg": "interface Eth1/18\n    mac 00:00:5e:b9:56:59\n    ip address
  10.0.0.1/8\n"
}
skipping: [NX2] => (item=2/1)
skipping: [NX2] => (item=1/7)
skipping: [NX2] => (item=1/18)
skipping: [NX2]

TASK [CHECKING VARIABLES] **************************************************************
skipping: [NX1] => (item=1/3)
skipping: [NX1] => (item=1/7)
skipping: [NX1] => (item=2/18)
skipping: [NX1] => (item=2/23)
skipping: [NX1]
ok: [NX2] => (item=1/3) => {
    "msg": "interface Eth1/3\n    mac 00:00:5e:88:75:e2\n    ip address
  10.0.0.2/8\n"
}
ok: [NX2] => (item=1/7) => {
    "msg": "interface Eth1/7\n    mac 00:00:5e:bd:b2:05\n    ip address
  10.0.0.2/8\n"
}
ok: [NX2] => (item=2/18) => {
    "msg": "interface Eth2/18\n    mac 00:00:5e:54:74:5b\n    ip address
  10.0.0.2/8\n"
}
```

```
ok: [NX2] => (item=2/23) => {
    "msg": "interface Eth2/23\n    mac 00:00:5e:fd:84:8d\n    ip address
  10.0.0.2/8\n"
}

PLAY RECAP ***********************************************************************
NX1                        : ok=2    changed=0    unreachable=0    failed=0
NX2                        : ok=2    changed=0    unreachable=0    failed=0
```

In Example 19-22, the keyword **loop** introduces a loop after the **task** description. The loop contains a list of variables, and the task is performed sequentially for each item in the list. Actually, {{ *item* }} is also the name of a built-in variable, which takes the value from the active entry in the list. You can see how the conditions play a role here: The list contains different items, depending on the value of {{ *inventory_hostname* }}. This brings us to another critical point: The list of entries in the loop is just a list of variables, which can be defined as any other variables in the playbook or somewhere externally, as shown in the Example 19-23.

Example 19-23 *Using a Loop and Conditions Together with External Variables*

```
$ cat npf_NX1_variables.yml
---
list_of_interfaces:
    - 1/1
    - 2/1
    - 1/7
    - 1/18
...


$ cat npf_NX2_variables.yml
---
list_of_interfaces:
    - 1/3
    - 1/7
    - 2/18
    - 2/23
...


$ cat npf_example_loops_external_vars.yml
---
- hosts: nexus
  gather_facts: yes
  connection: local
```

```
  vars:
      interface:
          name_prefix: Eth
          mac_prefix: 00:00:5E
          ip_prefix: 10.0.0.0/8

  tasks:
      - name: IMPORTING VARS
        include_vars:
            file: npf_{{ inventory_hostname }}_variables.yml

      - name: CHECKING VARIABLES
        debug:
            msg: |
                interface {{ interface.name_prefix }}{{ item }}
                    mac {{ interface.mac_prefix | random_mac }}
                    ip address {{ interface.ip_prefix | ipaddr(1) }}
        loop: "{{ list_of_interfaces }}"
        when: inventory_hostname == 'NX1'

      - name: CHECKING VARIABLES
        debug:
            msg: |
                interface {{ interface.name_prefix }}{{ item }}
                    mac {{ interface.mac_prefix | random_mac }}
                    ip address {{ interface.ip_prefix | ipaddr(2) }}
        loop: "{{ list_of_interfaces }}"
        when: inventory_hostname == 'NX2'
...


$ ansible-playbook npf_example_loops_external_vars.yml

PLAY [nexus] *******************************************************************

TASK [Gathering Facts] *********************************************************
ok: [NX1]
ok: [NX2]

TASK [IMPORTING VARS] **********************************************************
ok: [NX1]
ok: [NX2]

TASK [CHECKING VARIABLES] ******************************************************
ok: [NX1] => (item=1/1) => {
```

```
    "msg": "interface Eth1/1\n    mac 00:00:5e:18:91:6e\n    ip address
  10.0.0.1/8\n"
}
ok: [NX1] => (item=2/1) => {
    "msg": "interface Eth2/1\n    mac 00:00:5e:23:64:3f\n    ip address
  10.0.0.1/8\n"
}
ok: [NX1] => (item=1/7) => {
    "msg": "interface Eth1/7\n    mac 00:00:5e:44:03:0f\n    ip address
  10.0.0.1/8\n"
}
ok: [NX1] => (item=1/18) => {
    "msg": "interface Eth1/18\n    mac 00:00:5e:14:64:72\n    ip address
  10.0.0.1/8\n"
}
skipping: [NX2] => (item=1/3)
skipping: [NX2] => (item=1/7)
skipping: [NX2] => (item=2/18)
skipping: [NX2] => (item=2/23)
skipping: [NX2]

TASK [CHECKING VARIABLES] ********************************************************
skipping: [NX1] => (item=1/1)
skipping: [NX1] => (item=2/1)
skipping: [NX1] => (item=1/7)
skipping: [NX1] => (item=1/18)
skipping: [NX1]
ok: [NX2] => (item=1/3) => {
    "msg": "interface Eth1/3\n    mac 00:00:5e:13:cc:a9\n    ip address
  10.0.0.2/8\n"
}
ok: [NX2] => (item=1/7) => {
    "msg": "interface Eth1/7\n    mac 00:00:5e:22:62:82\n    ip address
  10.0.0.2/8\n"
}
ok: [NX2] => (item=2/18) => {
    "msg": "interface Eth2/18\n    mac 00:00:5e:24:7f:20\n    ip address
  10.0.0.2/8\n"
}
ok: [NX2] => (item=2/23) => {
    "msg": "interface Eth2/23\n    mac 00:00:5e:10:e1:32\n    ip address
  10.0.0.2/8\n"
}

PLAY RECAP ***********************************************************************
NX1                        : ok=3    changed=0    unreachable=0    failed=0
NX2                        : ok=3    changed=0    unreachable=0    failed=0
```

Example 19-23 continues to use the keyword **loop**, but instead of providing a list of items directly, it calls the variable name **list_of_interfaces**, as defined in the (imported) list with variables.

We need to look at two more aspects of loops. The first aspect is that a list can contain much more information than a single entry, which means you can enrich the configuration of the interface. The second aspect is that there is a built-in counter that calculates the index of the current item. You can use this counter in any scenario you need. Take a look at the structure of the variables in Example 19-24.

Example 19-24 *Using a Loop Index and Complex List Variables*

```
$ cat npf_NX1_variables.yml
---
list_of_interfaces:
    - id: 1/1
      descr: Connectivity to Internet
    - id: 2/1
      descr: Connectivity to NX1
    - id: 1/7
      descr: Connectivity to XR1
    - id: 1/18
      descr: Connectivity to XR2
...


$ cat npf_NX2_variables.yml
---
list_of_interfaces:
    - id: 1/3
      descr: Connectivity to Internet
    - id: 1/7
      descr: Connectivity to NX1
    - id: 2/18
      descr: Connectivity to XR1
    - id: 2/23
      descr: Connectivity to XR2
```

Unlike in Example 19-23, in Example 19-24, the interface variables for each network element are now in a list containing dictionaries rather than pure values. Using the same approach as in Example 19-23, those per-device variables can be imported in the playbook during execution, as shown Example 19-25. This creates more powerful automation for configuration of the interfaces for Cisco NX-OS.

Example 19-25 *A Playbook Demonstrating the Use of a Loop Index and Complex List Variables*

```
$ cat npf_example_loops_external_vars.yml
---
- hosts: nexus
  gather_facts: yes
  connection: local

  vars:
      interface:
          name_prefix: Eth
          mac_prefix: 00:00:5E
          ip_prefix: 10.0.0.0/8

  tasks:
      - name: IMPORTING VARS
        include_vars:
            file: npf_{{ inventory_hostname }}_variables.yml

      - name: CHECKING VARIABLES
        debug:
            msg: |
                interface {{ interface.name_prefix }}{{ item.id }}
                    mac {{ interface.mac_prefix | random_mac }}
                    description {{ item.descr }}
                    ip address {{ interface.ip_prefix | ipsubnet(24, loop_index) |
  ipaddr(1) }}
        loop: "{{ list_of_interfaces }}"
        loop_control:
            index_var: loop_index
        when: inventory_hostname == 'NX1'

      - name: CHECKING VARIABLES
        debug:
            msg: |
                interface {{ interface.name_prefix }}{{ item.id }}
                    mac {{ interface.mac_prefix | random_mac }}
                    description {{ item.descr }}
                    ip address {{ interface.ip_prefix | ipsubnet(24, loop_index) |
  ipaddr(2) }}
        loop: "{{ list_of_interfaces }}"
        loop_control:
            index_var: loop_index
        when: inventory_hostname == 'NX2'
...
```

In Example 19-25, you still call the loop by using the keyword **loop** followed by the variable **{{ list_of_interfaces }}**. However, because the list has different key/value pairs, you need to call the proper value. You do this by using **{{** *item.key* **}}** syntax (for example, **{{ item.id }}** and **{{ item.descr }}** in Example 19-25). Every item should have the same set of the keys in order to work properly. You can create any further hierarchy if needed.

Another important new detail in Example 19-25 is the keyword **loop_control**, which defines different parameters relevant to the loop, including the parameter **index_var**, which, as the name suggests, is responsible for calculating the index. To use it, you need to assign some variable to it (such as **loop_index** in Example 19-25). Then this variable is used with filter **ipsubnet** to split the original subnet 10.0.0.0/8 into smaller subnets with the /24 prefix length, and the subnet number is defined based on the value of the variable **loop_index**. Example 19-26 shows that now each interface has an IP address within the subnet as well as a different subnet for each interface.

Example 19-26 *Executing the Playbook Containing a Loop Index and Complex List Variables*

```
$ ansible-playbook npf_example_loops_external_vars.yml --inventory=hosts

PLAY [nexus] *****************************************************************

TASK [Gathering Facts] *******************************************************
ok: [NX2]
ok: [NX1]

TASK [IMPORTING VARS] ********************************************************
ok: [NX1]
ok: [NX2]

TASK [CHECKING VARIABLES] ****************************************************
skipping: [NX2] => (item={u'id': u'1/3', u'descr': u'Connectivity to Internet'})
skipping: [NX2] => (item={u'id': u'1/7', u'descr': u'Connectivity to NX1'})
skipping: [NX2] => (item={u'id': u'2/18', u'descr': u'Connectivity to XR1'})
skipping: [NX2] => (item={u'id': u'2/23', u'descr': u'Connectivity to XR2'})
skipping: [NX2]
ok: [NX1] => (item={u'id': u'1/1', u'descr': u'Connectivity to Internet'}) => {
    "msg": "interface Eth1/1\n    mac 00:00:5e:ba:2f:2c\n    description
  Connectivity to Internet\n    ip address 10.0.0.1/24\n"
}
ok: [NX1] => (item={u'id': u'2/1', u'descr': u'Connectivity to NX1'}) => {
    "msg": "interface Eth2/1\n    mac 00:00:5e:57:4e:6d\n    description
  Connectivity to NX1\n    ip address 10.0.1.1/24\n"
}
```

```
ok: [NX1] => (item={u'id': u'1/7', u'descr': u'Connectivity to XR1'}) => {
    "msg": "interface Eth1/7\n    mac 00:00:5e:ea:fe:cf\n    description
  Connectivity to XR1\n    ip address 10.0.2.1/24\n"
}
ok: [NX1] => (item={u'id': u'1/18', u'descr': u'Connectivity to XR2'}) => {
    "msg": "interface Eth1/18\n    mac 00:00:5e:18:a9:09\n    description
  Connectivity to XR2\n    ip address 10.0.3.1/24\n"
}

TASK [CHECKING VARIABLES] *********************************************************
skipping: [NX1] => (item={u'id': u'1/1', u'descr': u'Connectivity to Internet'})
skipping: [NX1] => (item={u'id': u'2/1', u'descr': u'Connectivity to NX1'})
skipping: [NX1] => (item={u'id': u'1/7', u'descr': u'Connectivity to XR1'})
skipping: [NX1] => (item={u'id': u'1/18', u'descr': u'Connectivity to XR2'})
skipping: [NX1]
ok: [NX2] => (item={u'id': u'1/3', u'descr': u'Connectivity to Internet'}) => {
    "msg": "interface Eth1/3\n    mac 00:00:5e:20:06:4e\n    description
  Connectivity to Internet\n    ip address 10.0.0.2/24\n"
}
ok: [NX2] => (item={u'id': u'1/7', u'descr': u'Connectivity to NX1'}) => {
    "msg": "interface Eth1/7\n    mac 00:00:5e:ba:b8:8e\n    description
  Connectivity to NX1\n    ip address 10.0.1.2/24\n"
}
ok: [NX2] => (item={u'id': u'2/18', u'descr': u'Connectivity to XR1'}) => {
    "msg": "interface Eth2/18\n    mac 00:00:5e:1d:78:30\n    description
  Connectivity to XR1\n    ip address 10.0.2.2/24\n"
}
ok: [NX2] => (item={u'id': u'2/23', u'descr': u'Connectivity to XR2'}) => {
    "msg": "interface Eth2/23\n    mac 00:00:5e:17:08:f3\n    description
  Connectivity to XR2\n    ip address 10.0.3.2/24\n"
}

PLAY RECAP ************************************************************************
NX1                        : ok=3    changed=0    unreachable=0    failed=0
NX2                        : ok=3    changed=0    unreachable=0    failed=0
```

You should now be able to create rather advanced playbooks. So far in this chapter, you have learned how to connect to network devices by using connectivity plug-ins, how to define variables statically or dynamically, and how to use conditions and loops. However, before we look at more advanced cases with Cisco network devices, we need to examine one more crucial mass automation topic: Jinja2 templates.

Jinja2 Templates

Jinja2 is a modern and designer-friendly templating language for Python. Ansible is based on Python, and it heavily uses Jinja2. Actually, you have already seen Jinja2 used a lot. The syntax {{ *variable* }} is used to define a variable in Jinja2, and {{ *variable* | *filter* }} is also Jinja2 syntax. However, you need to learn more about Jinja2 and related modules in order to unleash the full power of automation with Ansible.

The Need for Templates

To automate any massive-scale operations, you need templates. Basically, a *template* is a predefined string (or multi-line string) that has fixed parts and variables that change in value based on what is passed to the template.

Cloud services, including AWS, Google Cloud, and THG Hosting, heavily use templates for allocating and deleting users' computing resources. Templates are also used with network devices, as typically the vast majority of the parameters in a configuration are the same across all the network functions in a network, and only a small number of them vary. Just think about the standard router configuration in an enterprise network. Let's say you are running some router protocol, like OSPF or EIGRP. It is likely that timers and areas will have the same parameters, but router IDs and interface numbers will be different. You might think that an enterprise network has a lot of specific configuration for each device, such as aggregations for EIGRP and multiple areas for OSPF, which translates to different flavors of templates. However, even such deviations can be covered using conditions and loops, as you will learn in this section. Another example that shows the power of templating is high-scale data centers and service provider networks, which have very similar configurations on a huge number of network elements.

Figure 19-4 illustrates template-based network configuration.

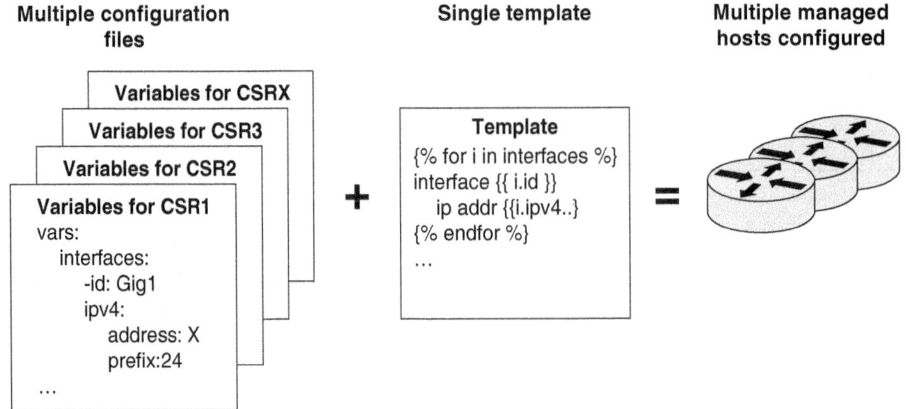

Figure 19-4 *Template-Based Approach for Network Automation*

With Ansible, there are three significant ways to interact with templates, and you are likely to use a mixture of them, depending on the particular use case or the Ansible module you use.

To see the effect of using Ansible templates, let's consider a practical example: adding new entries in /etc/hosts on Linux hosts to ease their management via hostnames. As you have already seen in this chapter, one option with Jinja2 templates is inline templates (refer to Example 19-25). An inline template usually starts with a pipe (|) as a value for some key, such as the key **msg** in the module **debug**, and then it is continued from the new string. Example 19-27 shows the structure of an inline template.

Example 19-27 *Using an Inline Jinja2 Template*

```
$ cat npf_example_inline_template.yml
---
- hosts: linux
  gather_facts: no
  connection: local
  become: yes

  tasks:
      - name: ADDING INFO TO /etc/hosts
        blockinfile:
            dest: /etc/hosts
            marker: "#{MARK} ANSIBLE MANAGED BLOCK {{ item.hostname }}"
            block: |
                {{ item.ip }}   {{ item.hostname }}
        loop:
            - { hostname: XR1, ip: 192.168.1.11 }
            - { hostname: XR2, ip: 192.168.1.12 }
            - { hostname: NX1, ip: 192.168.1.21 }
            - { hostname: NX2, ip: 192.168.1.22 }
...



$ ansible-playbook npf_example_inline_template.yml --ask-become-pass
SUDO password:

PLAY [linux] ***********************************************************************

TASK [ADDING INFO TO /etc/hosts] ***************************************************
changed: [localhost] => (item={u'ip': u'192.168.1.11', u'hostname': u'XR1'})
changed: [localhost] => (item={u'ip': u'192.168.1.12', u'hostname': u'XR2'})
changed: [localhost] => (item={u'ip': u'192.168.1.21', u'hostname': u'NX1'})
changed: [localhost] => (item={u'ip': u'192.168.1.22', u'hostname': u'NX2'})
```

```
PLAY RECAP *********************************************************************
localhost                  : ok=1    changed=1    unreachable=0    failed=0


$ cat /etc/hosts
127.0.0.1   localhost localhost.localdomain localhost4 localhost4.localdomain4
::1         localhost localhost.localdomain localhost6 localhost6.localdomain6
#BEGIN ANSIBLE MANAGED BLOCK XR1
192.168.1.11   XR1
#END ANSIBLE MANAGED BLOCK XR1
#BEGIN ANSIBLE MANAGED BLOCK XR2
192.168.1.12   XR2
#END ANSIBLE MANAGED BLOCK XR2
#BEGIN ANSIBLE MANAGED BLOCK NX1
192.168.1.21   NX1
#END ANSIBLE MANAGED BLOCK NX1
#BEGIN ANSIBLE MANAGED BLOCK NX2
192.168.1.22   NX2
#END ANSIBLE MANAGED BLOCK NX2
```

Did you notice the new entry **become: yes** at the beginning of Example 19-27? This entry forces the task to be executed from **sudo** mode in Linux; this is necessary because only the user root or another user in **sudo** mode can change the /etc/hosts file.

Now let's take a look at the content on Example 19-27. The Ansible module **blockinfile** adds some text (single-line or multi-line text) from the key **block** to the file defined in **dest**. To make it evident that Ansible has created a specific configuration, it adds the value contained in **marker** before the text insertion and after it. **marker** has a default value, and you need to be careful with it to avoid quickly deleting something you don't mean to delete. The value of **marker** is changed so that it starts and ends with the hostname of the device upon creating the entries in /etc/hosts, so that if the IP address of any host changes, it can be updated. The beginning and the end of the entry are defined by keywords **BEGIN** and **END**, which are automatically placed on the specific variable { **mark** }.

In Example 19-27, you can also see that several variables are listed in a loop statement, in a single line separated by a comma and framed by curly brackets ({}). This syntax differs from the syntax used in Example 19-25, where the key/value pairs are written once per line, but the meaning is the same. In Example 19-27, the template is created directly in the playbook, where it is used; this might be suboptimal with a long template having tens or hundreds of lines. There are alternatives to this approach, as described later in this section.

Another option is to put the Jinja2 template in a separate file and call it by using a plug-in, as shown in Example 19-28.

Example 19-28 *Using a Jinja2 Template from an External File and the* ***lookup*** *Plug-in*

```
$ cat npf_example_external_template.j2
{{ item.ip }}   {{ item.hostname }}


$ cat npf_example_external_template.yml
---
- hosts: linux
  gather_facts: no
  connection: local
  become: yes

  tasks:
      - name: ADDING INFO TO /etc/hosts
        blockinfile:
            dest: /etc/hosts
            marker: "#{mark} ANSIBLE MANAGED BLOCK {{ item.hostname }}"
            block: "{{ lookup('template', 'npf_example_external_template.j2') }}"
        loop:
            - { hostname: XR1, ip: 192.168.1.11 }
            - { hostname: XR2, ip: 192.168.1.12 }
            - { hostname: NX1, ip: 192.168.1.21 }
            - { hostname: NX2, ip: 192.168.1.22 }
...


$ ansible-playbook npf_example_inline_template.yml --ask-become-pass
SUDO password:

PLAY [linux] ***********************************************************************

TASK [ADDING INFO TO /etc/hosts] ***************************************************
changed: [localhost] => (item={u'ip': u'192.168.1.11', u'hostname': u'XR1'})
changed: [localhost] => (item={u'ip': u'192.168.1.12', u'hostname': u'XR2'})
changed: [localhost] => (item={u'ip': u'192.168.1.21', u'hostname': u'NX1'})
changed: [localhost] => (item={u'ip': u'192.168.1.22', u'hostname': u'NX2'})

PLAY RECAP *************************************************************************
localhost                  : ok=1    changed=1    unreachable=0    failed=0


$ cat /etc/hosts
127.0.0.1   localhost localhost.localdomain localhost4 localhost4.localdomain4
::1         localhost localhost.localdomain localhost6 localhost6.localdomain6
```

```
#BEGIN ANSIBLE MANAGED BLOCK XR1
192.168.1.11    XR1
#END ANSIBLE MANAGED BLOCK XR1
#BEGIN ANSIBLE MANAGED BLOCK XR2
192.168.1.12    XR2
#END ANSIBLE MANAGED BLOCK XR2
#BEGIN ANSIBLE MANAGED BLOCK NX1
192.168.1.21    NX1
#END ANSIBLE MANAGED BLOCK NX1
#BEGIN ANSIBLE MANAGED BLOCK NX2
192.168.1.22    NX2
#END ANSIBLE MANAGED BLOCK NX2
```

A Jinja2 template is stored in a file with a *.j2 extension; this means you can start directly with any text or variable, and no specific syntax is needed to define that it's a template. You can call a Jinja2 template from an Ansible playbook by using the module **lookup**; Example 19-28 shows a template being called with **{{ lookup('template', 'npf_example_external_template.j2') }}**. The path to a template can be either relative or absolute. In the example provided, the path is relative as the template is located in the same folder as the playbook.

You can instead use absolute path (for example, **lookup('template', '/home/user/templates/npf_example_external_template.j2')**) if that is more beneficial with your playbook. The main advantage of using an absolute path is that when templates are stored in a separate file, in the playbook you can focus on the logic of the execution, and in the separate template file you focus only on the quality of the template. In addition, this approach is advantageous with large templates.

A third option is to use a specific Ansible module to fill in the template with proper data and render it in the finale file, as shown in Example 19-29.

Example 19-29 *Using a Specific Ansible Module for Templating*

```
$ cat npf_example_external_template.j2
{{ item.ip }}   {{ item.hostname }}



$ cat npf_example_template_module.yml
---
- hosts: linux
  gather_facts: no
  connection: local

  tasks:
      - name: ADDING INFO TO /etc/hosts
        template:
```

```
            src: npf_example_external_template.j2
            dest: hosts_{{ item.hostname }}.txt
        loop:
            - { hostname: XR1, ip: 192.168.1.11 }
            - { hostname: XR2, ip: 192.168.1.12 }
            - { hostname: NX1, ip: 192.168.1.21 }
            - { hostname: NX2, ip: 192.168.1.22 }
...


$ ansible-playbook npf_example_template_module.yml

PLAY [linux] ********************************************************************

TASK [ADDING INFO TO /etc/hosts] ************************************************
changed: [localhost] => (item={u'ip': u'192.168.1.11', u'hostname': u'XR1'})
changed: [localhost] => (item={u'ip': u'192.168.1.12', u'hostname': u'XR2'})
changed: [localhost] => (item={u'ip': u'192.168.1.21', u'hostname': u'NX1'})
changed: [localhost] => (item={u'ip': u'192.168.1.22', u'hostname': u'NX2'})

PLAY RECAP **********************************************************************
localhost                  : ok=1    changed=1    unreachable=0    failed=0


$ ls | grep 'hosts'
hosts_NX1.txt
hosts_NX2.txt
hosts_XR1.txt
hosts_XR2.txt


$ cat hosts_*
192.168.1.21    NX1
192.168.1.22    NX2
192.168.1.11    XR1
192.168.1.12    XR2
```

As in the previous example, in Example 19-29, the Jinja2 template is stored in a separate file with a *.j2 extension. The variables are stored in separate files, one for each network device, and imported using the **include_vars** module. Then the Ansible **template** module takes a template from **src**, fills in all the variables, and creates a file in **dest**. Both the **src** and **dest** paths can be relative or absolute. The advantage of this type of module is that you see the exact text (for example, a set of configuration lines) that will be sent to a remote network device. Many Ansible configuration modules have an option to take input from external files, and the idea is that you create a template, augment it with variables, render a final configuration file, and then push this file to a network device. If you prefer to use the **lookup** plug-in, as shown in Example 19-28, you can use this template module to troubleshoot your template. (You might want to do this because not everything is straightforward with Jinja2, especially when you're new to it.)

There is one drawback to the method used in Example 19-29. You can see that for every hostname, a dedicated file is created. This occurs because the loop was created within Ansible. On the other hand, it's possible to create loops and conditions inside a template itself by using Jinja2 syntax. (This is a handy feature, and you will learn how to do it in the next section.)

So far you have learned the main ways to work with Jinja2 templates. There are no strict guidelines regarding which approach you should use in specific use cases. However, there is one general consideration you need to be aware of: You should check whether the module you are using supports input from an external file (in which case you can use the **template** module to create a temporary file) or not (in which case you need to use the **lookup** plug-in or an inline template).

Variables, Loops, and Conditions

You are already familiar with Jinja2 variables, which are represented using the syntax {{ *variable* }}. Examples 19-28 and 19-29 show this syntax for dedicated files with templates. However, this is just a small part of template capabilities, as templates support both loops and conditions inside a template. Before we jump into examining loops and conditions, note that the approaches described here are relevant for both inline templates (refer to Example 19-27) and dedicated files (refer to Examples 19-28 and 19-29). To help you better understand the approaches, this section shows examples using only one approach at a time.

The logic of loops in Jinja2 templates is very close to the logic in Ansible (as well as other programming languages). To show the syntax of loops in Jinja2, Example 19-30 shows the same example as Example 19-27, which involves the templating of entries in /etc/hosts, but now using a Jinja2 template.

Example 19-30 *A Jinja2 Template with Loop Syntax*

```
$ cat npf_example_inline_template_loop.yml
---
- hosts: linux
  gather_facts: no
  connection: local
  become: yes
```

```
 vars:
      new_hosts:
            - { hostname: XR1, ip: 192.168.1.11 }
            - { hostname: XR2, ip: 192.168.1.12 }
            - { hostname: NX1, ip: 192.168.1.21 }
            - { hostname: NX2, ip: 192.168.1.22 }

  tasks:
      - name: ADDING INFO TO /etc/hosts
        blockinfile:
            dest: /etc/hosts
            marker: "#{mark} ANSIBLE MANAGED BLOCK"
            block: |
                {% for some_var_name in new_hosts %}
                {{ some_var_name.ip }}   {{ some_var_name.hostname }}
                {% endfor %}
...


$ ansible-playbook npf_example_inline_template_loop.yml -i hosts --ask-become-pass
SUDO password:

PLAY [linux] ***********************************************************************

TASK [ADDING INFO TO /etc/hosts] ***************************************************
changed: [localhost]

PLAY RECAP *************************************************************************
localhost                  : ok=1    changed=1    unreachable=0    failed=0



$ cat /etc/host
cat: /etc/host: No such file or directory
[karneliuka@devle1automatron book]$ cat /etc/hosts
127.0.0.1   localhost localhost.localdomain localhost4 localhost4.localdomain4
::1         localhost localhost.localdomain localhost6 localhost6.localdomain6
#BEGIN ANSIBLE MANAGED BLOCK
192.168.1.11   XR1
192.168.1.12   XR2
192.168.1.21   NX1
192.168.1.22   NX2
#END ANSIBLE MANAGED BLOCK
```

You can immediately see the difference between Example 19-30 and Example 19-27: In Example 19-30, all the new entries are inserted as a single block in the /etc/hosts file rather than as individual entries, as in Example 19-27. Moreover, now you don't see the keyword **loop** associated with the module **blockinfile** because the loop is built using Jinja2 template methods. The required entries are collected in the **vars** section, in the **new_hosts** list of variables. Then, in the inline Jinja2 template, there is a construction that starts with {% **for some_var_name in new_hosts** %} and ends with {% **endfor** %}. With {% **for** %} and {% **endfor** %}, you define the beginning and the ending of the cycle. The variable {{ **some_var_name** }} has the same function as {{ **item** }} in the Ansible loop: It assigns the value of a single entry from the list, where a single entry is an abstract definition of one part of the list, even if it has a complex hierarchical structure inside. Besides the definition of the variable, there is also the keyword **in**, which points to the list from which the entries are coming. In Example 19-30, the list is called {{ **new_hosts** }}, and this is the name of the variable defined in **vars**.

The syntax in the loop in Example 19-30 is the same as the syntax for the Ansible loop in Example 19-27, and you call any particular key from the list entry using {{ *item.key* }} syntax. With Jinja2 loops, you can have a hierarchy of cycles inside the cycles. Example 19-31 shows two levels of hierarchy for configuration interfaces in Cisco NX-OS.

Example 19-31 *A Jinja2 Template with a Hierarchical Loop and Associated Variables*

```
$ cat npf_NX1_12_variables.yml
---
list_of_interfaces:
    - id: 1/1
      vlans:
          - 123
          - 234
          - 345
          - 456
    - id: 2/1
      vlans:
          - 123
          - 234
    - id: 1/7
      vlans:
          - 345
          - 456
    - id: 1/18
      vlans:
          - 123
          - 456
...
```

```
$ cat npf_template_double_loop.j2
{% for iface in list_of_interfaces %}
interface {{ interface.name_prefix }}{{ iface.id }}
    switchport
    switchport mode trunk
    switchport trunk allowed vlan add {% for v in iface.vlans %}{{ v }},{% endfor %}

{% endfor %}
```

First of all, in Example 19-31, the variables in the dedicated files for devices are structured such that the top-level variable **list_of_interfaces** is a list containing dictionaries consisting of two variables, **id** and **vlans**. As this second list is called from the first loop, it is called using the variables' names within the loop (that is, **{{ iface.vlans }}**). This is an important point, and you need to pay attention to the current level of hierarchy and call variables accordingly.

Using external files with variables, where each filename includes the name of the respective network device, as well as an external template, makes it possible to keep a playbook very small and easy to understand (see Example 19-32).

Example 19-32 *A Sample Playbook Containing External Variables and Templates*

```
$ cat npf_example_double_loops_jinja2.yml
---
- hosts: nexus
  gather_facts: yes
  connection: local

  vars:
      interface:
          name_prefix: Eth

  tasks:
      - name: IMPORTING VARS
        include_vars:
            file: npf_{{ inventory_hostname }}_l2_variables.yml

      - name: TEMPLATING CONFIG
        template:
            src: npf_template_double_loop.j2
            dest: "{{ inventory_hostname }}_intent_config.conf"
...
```

Example 19-33 shows the execution of this playbook and its outcome.

Example 19-33 *Playbook Execution and Results*

```
$ ansible-playbook npf_example_double_loops_jinja2.yml

PLAY [nexus] ***********************************************************************

TASK [Gathering Facts] *************************************************************
ok: [NX1]
ok: [NX2]

TASK [IMPORTING VARS] **************************************************************
ok: [NX1]
ok: [NX2]

TASK [TEMPLATING CONFIG] ***********************************************************
changed: [NX2]
changed: [NX1]

PLAY RECAP *************************************************************************
NX1                         : ok=3    changed=1    unreachable=0    failed=0
NX2                         : ok=3    changed=1    unreachable=0    failed=0


$ cat NX*.conf
interface Eth1/1
    switchport
    switchport mode trunk
    switchport trunk allowed vlan add 123,234,345,456,
interface Eth2/1
    switchport
    switchport mode trunk
    switchport trunk allowed vlan add 123,234,
interface Eth1/7
    switchport
    switchport mode trunk
    switchport trunk allowed vlan add 345,456,
interface Eth1/18
    switchport
    switchport mode trunk
    switchport trunk allowed vlan add 123,456,
```

From the output in Example 19-33, you can see that there is a comma at the end of each configuration line, including the VLAN list. These commas are required by CLI syntax; to see this in Example 19-31, look for the template file **npf_template_double_loop.j2**, and in the second loop you can see the string **{{ v }},** (with a comma), which is templated.

However, in Example 19-33, the comma is also presented after the last VLAN, which will be parsed by the network device and result in error. Hence, the last comma should be removed. You could solve this issue by using conditionals in a Jinja2 template.

Conveniently, that the conditional rules, operators, and notation in Jinja2 are the same as in Ansible (see the section "Conditionals," earlier in this chapter). Example 19-34 shows how to fix the problem with the last comma in the Jinja2 template shown in Example 19-33.

Example 19-34 *A Jinja2 Template with a Conditional Statement*

```
$ cat npf_template_double_loop.j2
{% for iface in list_of_interfaces %}
interface {{ interface.name_prefix }}{{ iface.id }}
    switchport
    switchport mode trunk
    switchport trunk allowed vlan add {% for v in iface.vlans %}{% if loop.index ==
  1 %}{{ v }}{% else %},{{ v }}{% endif %}{% endfor %}

{% endfor %}


$ cat NX*.conf
interface Eth1/1
    switchport
    switchport mode trunk
    switchport trunk allowed vlan add 123,234,345,456
interface Eth2/1
    switchport
    switchport mode trunk
    switchport trunk allowed vlan add 123,234
interface Eth1/7
    switchport
    switchport mode trunk
    switchport trunk allowed vlan add 345,456
interface Eth1/18
    switchport
    switchport mode trunk
    switchport trunk allowed vlan add 123,456
```

The file with the external variables and the Ansible playbook and its execution are exactly the same as in Example 19-31, so they are omitted in Example 19-34. A conditional statement is framed starting with {% **if** ... %} *action1* {% **else** %} *action2* {% **endif** %}, where *action1* occurs if the condition is fulfilled, and *action2* occurs it isn't. The condition is provided in the first {% **if** ... %} statement; in this example, **loop.index == 1**, where {{ **loop.index** }} is a built-in variable that exists in any loop context {% **for** ... %} and whose value is the number of iterations since the beginning of the cycle. The discussion of Example 19-21, earlier in this chapter, explains how to use a similar approach with Ansible loops. As you can see in Example 19-34, the string **{{ v }}** is templated for the first iteration of the loop, and then **,{{ v }}** (with a leading comma) is templated. The major difference is that in Example 19-34, the comma is added before the VLAN number and only starting from the second VLAN, whereas in Example 19-31, the comma is added after each VLAN number starting from the first one. The approach in Example 19-34 allows you to create the proper string for Nexus configuration with any number of VLANs in the list (even one).

In general, all the operators for comparison are the same as the ones described earlier in this chapter, in the section "Conditionals." In a nutshell, Ansible uses Jinja2 operators, although the Jinja2 syntax does not include the **{% if ... %}** framing.

Example 19-35 shows another operator that is called in conjunction with Example 19-34 to anticipate the case when the VLANs aren't provided explicitly.

Example 19-35 *A Jinja2 Template with Two Conditional Statements*

```
$ cat npf_NX1_12_variables.yml
---
list_of_interfaces:
    - id: 1/1
      vlans:
          - 123
          - 234
          - 345
          - 456
    - id: 2/1
    - id: 1/7
    - id: 1/18
      vlans:
          - 123
          - 456
...


$ cat npf_template_double_loop.j2
{% for iface in list_of_interfaces %}
interface {{ interface.name_prefix }}{{ iface.id }}
    switchport
    switchport mode trunk
{% if iface.vlans is defined %}
    switchport trunk allowed vlan add {% for v in iface.vlans %}{% if loop.index ==
  1 %}{{ v }}{% else %},{{ v }}{% endif %}{% endfor %}
{% endif %}
```

```
{% endfor %}


$ cat NX1_intent_config.conf
interface Eth1/1
    switchport
    switchport mode trunk
    switchport trunk allowed vlan add 123,234,345,456
interface Eth2/1
    switchport
    switchport mode trunk

interface Eth1/7
    switchport
    switchport mode trunk

interface Eth1/18
    switchport
    switchport mode trunk
    switchport trunk allowed vlan add 123,456
```

Just as in Example 19-34, the Ansible playbook isn't provided in Example 19-35 because it hasn't changed. As you can see at the beginning of Example 19-35, not every interface in the file with variables has a list of associated VLANs. It is possible that an interface may not have associated VLANs; this may be the case, for example, when the interface is used for trunking all the available VLANs. Such a case needs to be anticipated in the Jinja2 template to avoid misbehavior of the network element caused by a configuration created with syntax mistakes. In Example 19-35, this is achieved with the condition check **{% if iface.vlans is defined %}** *action* **{% endif %}**. You can see that the operator is used with a condition defined, precisely in the same way it is used earlier in this chapter, in Example 19-19.

The last important point you need to understand about conditional statements in Jinja2 is the possibility of including multiple conditional checks by using the syntax **{% if ... %}** *action1* **{% elif ... %}** *action2* **{% elif ... %}** *actionN* **{% endif %}**. This approach allows you to create a powerful template that reacts differently to different conditions. Example 19-36 extends the previous Jinja2 template with this new concept.

Example 19-36 *A Jinja2 Template with Multiple Choice Conditions*

```
$ cat npf_NX1_l2_variables.yml
---
list_of_interfaces:
    - id: 1/1
      vlans:
          - 123
          - 234
          - 345
          - 456
    - id: 2/1
    - id: 1/7
      ip: 10.0.0.0/31
    - id: 1/18
      vlans:
          - 123
          - 456
...


$ cat npf_template_double_loop.j2
{% for iface in list_of_interfaces %}
interface {{ interface.name_prefix }}{{ iface.id }}
{% if iface.vlans is defined %}
    switchport
    switchport mode trunk
    switchport trunk allowed vlan add {% for v in iface.vlans %}
  {% if loop.index == 1 %}{{ v }}{% else %},{{ v }}{% endif %}{% endfor %}
{% elif iface.ip is defined %}
    no switchport
    ip address {{ iface.ip }}
{% else %}
    shutdown
{% endif %}
!
{% endfor %}


$ cat NX1_intent_config.conf
interface Eth1/1
    switchport
    switchport mode trunk
    switchport trunk allowed vlan add 123,234,345,456
!
```

```
interface Eth2/1
    shutdown
!
interface Eth1/7
    no switchport
    ip address 10.0.0.0/31
!
interface Eth1/18
    switchport
    switchport mode trunk
    switchport trunk allowed vlan add 123,456
!
```

Note Again, the Ansible playbook in Example 19-36 is the same as defined in Example 19-31, so it is not repeated here.

Example 19-36 shows one of the advantages of templates, as you can see here the strict separation between what is done (in the Jinja2 template) and how it is done (in the Ansible playbook). By just tuning the template—and not even touching the playbook—you get different outputs.

If you take a close look at the template in Example 19-36, you can see that there are several possible conditions to match. It's important to know that only one condition at a time can be matched, which means that if the first condition is fulfilled, the rest of the conditions are not even checked. That is, the evaluation is performed until the first match is found. The template in Example 19-36 also illustrates the concept of multiple conditions in a single statement united by AND logic, which works as explained earlier in this chapter in Example 19-21.

Using Python Functions in Jinja2

As mentioned at the beginning of this chapter, Jinja2 is a templating language for Python. This means that Jinja2 and Python are tightly entwined with each other, and you can use various filters in Jinja2 expressions, as shown earlier in this chapter.

In a nutshell, *filters* are Python functions that perform various tasks. In the context of network programmability, templates are aimed at dynamically creating full-blown configuration files with sets of variables as input. Therefore, the vast majority of the filters you use with networks are focused on text processing and modification. You can find a full list of filters supported in Jinja2 at the official Jinja2 website (https://jinja.palletsprojects.com/en/2.11.x/). The following sections provide some examples of the most commonly used Python functions and filters.

The **join()** Function

The **join()** function makes it possible to merge different pieces of information; this is useful when you're processing arrays. The **join()** function may also help you more easily make templates by preventing the creation of additional loops. Example 19-37 shows how to improve the template from Example 19-36 in terms of interface templating for Cisco NX-OS.

Example 19-37 *A Jinja2 Template with the join() Function*

```
$ cat npf_template_double_loop_join.j2
{% for iface in list_of_interfaces %}
interface {{ interface.name_prefix }}{{ iface.id }}
{% if iface.vlans is defined %}
    switchport
    switchport mode trunk
    switchport trunk allowed vlan add {{ iface.vlans | join (',')}}
{% endif %}
!
{% endfor %}


$ cat npf_example_double_loops_jinja2_join.yml
---
- hosts: nexus
  gather_facts: yes
  connection: local

  vars:
      interface:
          name_prefix: Eth

  tasks:
      - name: IMPORTING VARS
        include_vars:
            file: npf_{{ inventory_hostname }}_l2_variables.yml

      - name: TEMPLATING CONFIG
        template:
            src: npf_template_double_loop_join.j2
            dest: "{{ inventory_hostname }}_intent_config.conf"
...
```

```
$ ansible-playbook npf_example_double_loops_jinja2_join.yml
PLAY [nexus] **************************************************************************
! The output is truncated for brevity
PLAY RECAP ****************************************************************************
NX1                         : ok=3    changed=1    unreachable=0    failed=0
NX2                         : ok=3    changed=1    unreachable=0    failed=0


$ cat NX1_intent_config.conf
interface Eth1/1
    switchport
    switchport mode trunk
    switchport trunk allowed vlan add 123,234,345,456
!
interface Eth2/1
!
interface Eth1/7
!
interface Eth1/18
    switchport
    switchport mode trunk
    switchport trunk allowed vlan add 123,456
!
```

It is important to note here that the result of the template execution in Example 19-37 is the same as in Example 19-36; this indicates that you have a proper configuration file. On the other hand, the new template is much more elegant and shorter, thanks to the **join** filter. Its syntax is **{{** *input_array* **| join (**'*separator*'**) }}**, and it works by merging together all the items of the **{{** *input_array* **}}** variable into a single string by using the separator value provided as an argument to the **join()** function.

The **split()** Function

The **split()** function is basically the opposite of the **join()** function: It allows you to split an input string into several pieces and manage them separately. Say that you need to install a new top-of-rack switch in a data center, wire all the servers to the proper ports, and prepare the configuration of the switch. There are a lot of fancy tools for managing network infrastructure, but table processors (such as Microsoft Excel) are still some of the most popular tools for documenting information for such an activity. Such a tool presents this information as shown in Table 19-6.

Table 19-6 *Wiring Request for a New Data Center Switch*

HOST	HOST_PORT	HOST@IP	SWITCH	PORT	VLAN
Server1	Eth0	192.168.1.10/24	NX1	1	120
Server2	Eth0	192.168.1.11/24	NX1	2	120
Server3	Ens0	192.168.2.5/24	NX1	5	130

The file formats .xls and .xlsx are not very friendly for the automation, but the .csv format works well. You are lucky if you get a task as a data_center_wiring.csv file; otherwise, you can translate a file from.xls format to .csv format. Example 19-38 shows how a .csv file is structured.

Example 19-38 *The Structure of a .csv File*

```
HOST,HOST_PORT,HOST@IP,SWITCH,PORT,VLAN
Server1,Eth0,192.168.1.10/24,NX1,1,120
Server2,Eth0,192.168.1.11/24,NX1,2,120
Server3,Ens0,192.168.2.5/24,NX1,5,130
```

You can use the **split()** function in Jinja2 templates to translate a .csv file to to a set of variables, which is ready for the configuration of a data center switch. Example 19-39 show how this works.

Example 19-39 *Using the **split()** Function in Ansible and Jinja2 Templates*

```
$ cat  npf_example_split.yml
---
- hosts: nexus
  gather_facts: yes
  connection: local

  tasks:
      - name: IMPORTING VARS
        set_fact:
            dummy_var: "{{ lookup('file','data_center_wiring.csv')}}"

      - name: TEMPLATING CONFIG
        debug:
            msg : |
                {% if item.split(',')[3] == inventory_hostname %}
                Interface Eth1/{{ item.split(',')[4] }}
                    switchport
                    switchport access vlan {{ item.split(',')[5] }}
```

```
                    description {{ item.split(',')[0] }}:{{ item.split(',')[1] }}---
  {{ item.split(',')[3] }}:Eth1/{{ item.split(',')[4] }}
                    no shutdown
                !
                {% endif %}
        loop: "{{ dummy_var.split('\n')}}"
...


$ ansible-playbook npf_example_split.yml -i hosts

PLAY [nexus] ******************************************************************

TASK [Gathering Facts] ********************************************************
ok: [NX2]
ok: [NX1]

TASK [IMPORTING VARS] *********************************************************
ok: [NX1]
ok: [NX2]

TASK [TEMPLATING CONFIG] ******************************************************
ok: [NX1] => (item=HOST,HOST_PORT,HOST@IP,SWITCH,PORT,VLAN) => {
    "msg": "\n"
}
ok: [NX1] => (item=Server1,Eth0,192.168.1.10/24,NX1,1,120) => {
    "msg": "Interface Eth1/1\n    switchport\n    switchport access vlan 120\n
  description Server1:Eth0---NX1:Eth1/1\n    no shutdown\n!\n"
}
ok: [NX1] => (item=Server2,Eth0,192.168.1.11/24,NX1,2,120) => {
    "msg": "Interface Eth1/2\n    switchport\n    switchport access vlan 120\n
  description Server2:Eth0---NX1:Eth1/2\n    no shutdown\n!\n"
}
ok: [NX1] => (item=Server3,Ens0,192.168.2.5/24,NX1,5,130) => {
    "msg": "Interface Eth1/5\n    switchport\n    swicthport access vlan 130\n
  description Server3:Ens0---NX1:Eth1/5\n    no shutdown\n!\n"
}
ok: [NX2] => (item=HOST,HOST_PORT,HOST@IP,SWITCH,PORT,VLAN) => {
    "msg": "\n"
}
ok: [NX2] => (item=Server1,Eth0,192.168.1.10/24,NX1,1,120) => {
    "msg": "\n"
}
ok: [NX2] => (item=Server2,Eth0,192.168.1.11/24,NX1,2,120) => {
    "msg": "\n"
}
```

```
ok: [NX2] => (item=Server3,Ens0,192.168.2.5/24,NX1,5,130) => {
    "msg": "\n"
}

PLAY RECAP ***************************************************************************
NX1                        : ok=3    changed=0    unreachable=0    failed=0
NX2                        : ok=3    changed=0    unreachable=0    failed=0
```

The syntax of **split()** function is {{ *variable*.**split(**'*separator*'**)**[*index*] }}, where '*separator*' is a value used to split the original text into an array, and *index* calls for particular element out of the array.

> **Note** The **split()** function is applicable not only in the context of Jinja2 templates but also with Ansible in general.

The playbook in Example 19-39 assigns all the contents of the file data_center_wiring.csv by using the **lookup** plug-in. Then this value is split into separate strings by the **split()** function with **\n** (newline) separator. In this case, the **split()** function is also used to create a loop that calls a template for every string, which is split further by the same **split()** function, this time with the ',' separator, which is used in .csv files to merge the columns into a single string. Then, in the in-line template, a conditional check allows a template to be used only in event that the {{ *inventory_hostname* }} of the device corresponds to the value *SWITCH* in the input table. If the check is successful, the template creates a configuration for a particular port by using the values from the array created using the **split()** function.

The **map()** Function

The **map()** function is handy for creating reports out of files as it searches for particular values in the list structure without using loops directly. Let's say you already have some data collected from a network or from an application, and you want to verify the elements for which the data is provided. Example 19-40 shows how you can use the **map()** function to get some insights.

Example 19-40 *Using the map() Function in a Jinja2 Template*

```
$ cat npf_example_map.yml
---
- hosts: linux
  gather_facts: no
  connection: local
  become: yes
```

```
  vars:
      new_hosts:
              - { hostname: XR1, ip: 192.168.1.11 }
              - { hostname: XR2, ip: 192.168.1.12 }
              - { hostname: NX1, ip: 192.168.1.21 }
              - { hostname: NX2, ip: 192.168.1.22 }

  tasks:
      - name: ADDING INFO TO /etc/hosts
        debug:
            msg: "{{ new_hosts | map(attribute='hostname') | join (', ') }}"
...


$ ansible-playbook npf_example_map.yml -i hosts

PLAY [linux] *********************************************************************

TASK [ADDING INFO TO /etc/hosts] *************************************************
ok: [localhost] => {
    "msg": "XR1, XR2, NX1, NX2"
}

PLAY RECAP ***********************************************************************
localhost                  : ok=1    changed=0    unreachable=0    failed=0
```

The syntax for the **map()** function is **map(*attribute*='*key*')**, where '*key*' is the key value as provided in the list. The **map()** function is often used in conjunction with the **join()** function to form the proper output format. As you can see in Example 19-40, the **map()** function searches in the initial dictionary for all '*hostname*' keys and returns their values merged in a single string by using the **join()** function with the comma separator.

As mentioned earlier, the full list of the available filters and functions is available at the official Jinja2 website (https://jinja.palletsprojects.com/en/2.11.x/). At this point, you have the knowledge you need to start automating your network with Ansible. The rest of this chapter provides examples to help you cement your knowledge.

Using Ansible for Cisco IOS XE

To automate anything with Ansible, you need at least two components: a managing host that runs Ansible and a managed host that is to be controlled. Figure 19-5 shows a simple topology with a managing host running Linux with Ansible and three managed hosts (each running a different Cisco network OS). This topology is used throughout the rest of this chapter. Because this particular part of the chapter is dedicated to Cisco IOS XE, the main focus here is on the CSR2 router.

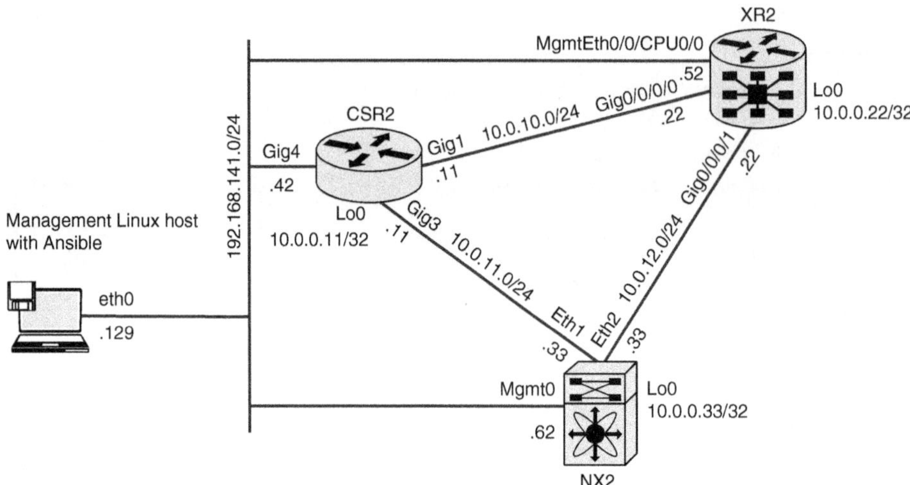

Figure 19-5 *Topology Used for Cisco Automation with Ansible*

Recall that Ansible is *agentless*, which means no agent needs to be installed on the managed host. By default, Ansible uses SSH to establish a communication channel with the host; therefore, the destination host must have an SSH server configured as well as a corresponding user/password pair. Example 19-41 shows how to prepare a Cisco IOS/Cisco IOS XE router, assuming that it is a freshly booted router without any configuration.

Example 19-41 *Preparing a Cisco IOS XE Device to Be Managed by Ansible*

```
Router# configure terminal
Router(config)# hostname CSR2
CSR2(config)# username cisco secret cisco
CSR2(config)# username cisco privilege 15
CSR2(config)# ip domain-name npf
CSR2(config)# crypto key generate rsa general-keys modulus 2048
The name for the keys will be: CSR2.npf

% The key modulus size is 2048 bits
% Generating 2048 bit RSA keys, keys will be non-exportable...
[OK] (elapsed time was 1 seconds)

CSR2(config)# ip ssh version 2
CSR2(config)# interface gig4
CSR2(config-if)# ip address 192.168.141.42 255.255.255.0
CSR2(config-if)# no shutdown
```

```
*Jan  5 18:12:41.061: %LINK-3-UPDOWN: Interface GigabitEthernet4, changed state to up
*Jan  5 18:12:42.061: %LINEPROTO-5-UPDOWN: Line protocol on Interface
  GigabitEthernet4, changed state to up
CSR2(config-if)# line vty 0 4
CSR2(config-line)# login local
CSR2(config-line)# end
CSR2(config)# copy run start
```

After this basic configuration is performed, you need to ensure that CSR2 is reachable from the managed host, and you should be able to log in to it, as demonstrated in Example 19-42.

Example 19-42 *Verifying That Cisco IOS XE Is Ready to Be Managed Using Ansible*

```
$ ping CSR2 -c 1
PING CSR2 (192.168.141.42) 56(84) bytes of data.
64 bytes from CSR2 (192.168.141.42): icmp_seq=1 ttl=255 time=0.460 ms

--- CSR2 ping statistics ---
1 packets transmitted, 1 received, 0% packet loss, time 0ms
rtt min/avg/max/mdev = 0.460/0.460/0.460/0.000 ms


$ ssh cisco@CSR2
Password:

CSR2#
```

Now that connectivity has been established, and CSR2 is ready to be automated, there is one more activity to do on the managing host: You need to update the Ansible hosts file to reflect the actual network OS versions, as well as the credentials for accessing the network. Example 19-43 shows how you do this.

Example 19-43 *Updating a File with Ansible Hosts with Additional Variables*

```
$ cat hosts
[linux]
localhost

[ios]
CSR1
CSR2

[iosxr]
XR1
XR2
```

```
[nexus]
NX1
NX2

[nexus:vars]
ansible_network_os=nxos
ansible_user=cisco
ansible_ssh_pass=cisco

[iosxr:vars]
ansible_network_os=iosxr
ansible_user=cisco
ansible_ssh_pass=cisco

[ios:vars]
ansible_network_os=ios
ansible_user=cisco
ansible_ssh_pass=cisco
```

Operational Data Verification Using the ios_command Module

Earlier in this chapter, you got a glimpse of the module **iosxr_command**, which deals with various commands (besides configuration) in Cisco IOS XR. For Cisco IOS/IOS XE, a comparable module exists: **ios_command.** Example 19-44 shows how to use this module.

Example 19-44 *Using the Ansible Module ios_command to Collect show Output*

```
$ cat npf_example_ios_command.yml
---
- hosts: ios
  connection: network_cli
  gather_facts: yes

  tasks:
      - name: COLLECTING OPEPRATION INFORMATION FROM '{{ ansible_network_os }}'
        ios_command:
            commands:
                - show inventory
                - show ip interface brief
        register: ios_output
```

```
    - name: VERIFICATION OF THE OUTPUT
      debug:
          msg: "{{ ios_output.stdout_lines }}"
...


$ ansible-playbook npf_example_ios_command.yml --limit=CSR2

PLAY [ios] ************************************************************************

TASK [Gathering Facts] ************************************************************
ok: [CSR2]

TASK [COLLECTING OPEPRATION INFORMATION FROM 'ios'] *******************************
ok: [CSR2]

TASK [VERIFICATION OF THE OUTPUT] *************************************************
ok: [CSR2] => {
    "msg": [
        [
            "NAME: \"Chassis\", DESCR: \"Cisco CSR1000V Chassis\"",
            "PID: CSR1000V          , VID: V00, SN: 9L4Z3MVC8LQ",
            "",
            "NAME: \"module R0\", DESCR: \"Cisco CSR1000V Route Processor\"",
            "PID: CSR1000V          , VID: V00, SN: JAB1303001C",
            "",
            "NAME: \"module F0\", DESCR: \"Cisco CSR1000V Embedded Services
  Processor\"",
            "PID: CSR1000V          , VID:    , SN:"
        ],
        [
            "Interface              IP-Address      OK? Method Status
  Protocol",
            "GigabitEthernet1       unassigned      YES NVRAM  administratively down
  down    ",
            "GigabitEthernet3       unassigned      YES unset  administratively down
  down    ",
            "GigabitEthernet4       192.168.141.42  YES manual up
  up"
        ]
    ]
}

PLAY RECAP ************************************************************************
CSR2                       : ok=3    changed=0    unreachable=0    failed=0
```

Because only CSR2 is part of the reference lab topology, during the execution of the Ansible playbook, the tag **--limit=CSR2** is used to avoid running the playbook against all the hosts from the ios group. Then, as credentials are provided in the hosts file and **gather_facts** is enabled, there is no need to enter any usernames or passwords during the execution of the playbook, which makes the automation smooth. In the module **ios_command**, the critical component is the section **commands**, which lists all the commands to be performed on the remote host. In Example 19-44, two commands are executed: **show inventory** and **show ip interface brief**. As these commands generate output, the output is saved in the registered value **{{** *ios_output* **}}** (as explained earlier in this chapter). Then the output is displayed using the **debug** module to verify that it's appropriately collected. As you now know, there are other options here, such as parsing values, saving them to a database (with Ansible's modules to work with databases), or reporting further. Obviously, you can use the mechanism shown in Example 19-44 to collect the running configuration from all your network elements for backup.

In addition to executing **show** commands on Cisco IOS XE devices, it's possible to perform some other commands—and they might even be interactive. Example 19-45 shows, for instance, how to clear the counters on a Cisco IOS XE device.

Example 19-45 *Using the Ansible Module* ***ios_command*** *to Clear Counters*

```
$ cat npf_example_ios_command_clear.yml
---
- hosts: ios
  connection: network_cli
  gather_facts: yes

  tasks:
      - name: COLLECTING OPEPRATION INFORMATION FROM '{{ ansible_network_os }}'
        ios_command:
            commands:
                - command: show interfaces GigabitEthernet4 | inc packets
                - command: clear counters GigabitEthernet4
                  prompt: '[confirm]'
                  answer: "\r"
                - command: show interfaces GigabitEthernet4 | inc packets
        register: ios_output

      - name: VERIFICATION OF THE OUTPUT
        debug:
            msg: "{{ ios_output.stdout_lines }}"
...


$ ansible-playbook npf_example_ios_command_clear.yml --limit=CSR2
```

```
PLAY [ios] *************************************************************************

TASK [Gathering Facts] *************************************************************
ok: [CSR2]

TASK [COLLECTING OPEPRATION INFORMATION FROM 'ios'] ********************************
ok: [CSR2]

TASK [VERIFICATION OF THE OUTPUT] **************************************************
ok: [CSR2] => {
    "msg": [
        [
            "5 minute input rate 0 bits/sec, 0 packets/sec",
            "  5 minute output rate 0 bits/sec, 0 packets/sec",
            "     681 packets input, 80415 bytes, 0 no buffer",
            "     576 packets output, 75856 bytes, 0 underruns"
        ],
        [
            "Clear \"show interface\" counters on this interface [confirm]"
        ],
        [
            "5 minute input rate 0 bits/sec, 0 packets/sec",
            "  5 minute output rate 0 bits/sec, 0 packets/sec",
            "     0 packets input, 0 bytes, 0 no buffer",
            "     0 packets output, 0 bytes, 0 underruns"
        ]
    ]
}

PLAY RECAP *************************************************************************
CSR2                       : ok=3    changed=0    unreachable=0    failed=0
```

All the commands in this example start with the key **command**, and the keys **prompt** and **answer** are introduced. The **command** key contains the pattern that is expected and the string **\r** (a carriage return) that is to be sent in response. As you can see in the playbook in Example 19-45, the counters are collected and then cleared and collected again. The second collection confirms that the counters are cleared successfully.

General Configuration Using the ios_config Module

You might say that so far you have seen no examples of real automation and network programming; you have only learned how to collect information from a remote Cisco IOS XE network device and how to use several modules for text processing/templating. Well, that's partially true, and now it's time to look at how to configure network functions in an automated way. There are plenty of modules for Cisco IOS/IOS XE devices, and they allow you to configure different aspects of a router or switch. One particular module, called **ios_config**, relies on traditional CLI commands. Therefore, to use it, you need to be proficient with the CLI. However, it allows you to automate everything, as long as you can create proper templates.

To get started with automation, let's start with some basics. Example 19-46 shows the configuration of the interface at CSR2 with all the parameters hardcoded.

Example 19-46 *Using the Ansible Module ios_config Without Variables*

```
$ cat npf_example_ios_config_simple.yml
---
- hosts: ios
  connection: network_cli
  gather_facts: yes

  tasks:
      - name: CONFIGURING THE INTERFACE
        ios_config:
            lines:
                - ip address 10.0.10.11 255.255.255.0
                - no shutdown
            parents:
                - interface GigabitEthernet1

      - name: WAITING FOR CARRIER-DELAY
        pause:
            seconds: 5

      - name: COLLECTING OPEPRATION INFORMATION FROM '{{ ansible_network_os }}'
        ios_command:
            commands:
                - show ip interface brief
        register: ios_output

      - name: VERIFICATION OF THE OUTPUT
        debug:
            msg: "{{ ios_output.stdout_lines }}"
...


$ ansible-playbook npf_example_ios_config_simple.yml -i hosts --limit=CSR2
```

```
PLAY [ios] ************************************************************************

TASK [Gathering Facts] ************************************************************
ok: [CSR2]

TASK [CONFIGURING THE INTERFACE] **************************************************
changed: [CSR2]

TASK [WAITING FOR CARRIER-DELAY] **************************************************
Pausing for 5 seconds
(ctrl+C then 'C' = continue early, ctrl+C then 'A' = abort)
ok: [CSR2]

TASK [COLLECTING OPEPRATION INFORMATION FROM 'ios'] *******************************
ok: [CSR2]

TASK [VERIFICATION OF THE OUTPUT] *************************************************
ok: [CSR2] => {
    "msg": [
        [
            "Interface              IP-Address      OK? Method Status
  Protocol",
            "GigabitEthernet1       10.0.10.11      YES manual up
  up      ",
            "GigabitEthernet3       unassigned      YES unset  administratively down
  down    ",
            "GigabitEthernet4       192.168.141.42  YES manual up
  up"
        ]
    ]
}

PLAY RECAP ************************************************************************
CSR2                       : ok=5    changed=1    unreachable=0    failed=0
```

In the **ios_config** module, the key components are the section **lines**, which contains the configuration commands, and **parents**, which contains the target context where the configuration must be applied. **parents** is essential because without it, the commands would be applied to the global configuration context. In Example 19-46, the **ios_config**, **ios_command**, and **debug** modules are used to verify that changes have been applied successfully. In addition, the module **pause** delays the execution of the Ansible playbook by a defined number of seconds. This is very useful if the results of the execution of the previous module aren't immediate. In this case, it takes roughly 2 seconds (the default carrier-delay timer of the Cisco IOS XE device) before the interface's operational state changes to up; this is why the module **pause** is used. After this timer expires, the playbook is executed further, and the verification by the **ios_command** module shows that the newly created interface is up. When you look at the log of the playbook, you can see that in the second task, called CONFIGURING THE INTERFACE, the status is changed; this means there were some changes in the configuration of the remote device.

Providing all the parameters directly in a playbook as hardcoded parameters is not the best way to automate network operations. Example 19-47 shows the use of loops and variables to achieve a higher degree of automation.

Example 19-47 *Using the Ansible Module ios_config with Loops and Variables*

```
$ cat npf_example_ios_config_extended.yml
---
- hosts: ios
  connection: network_cli
  gather_facts: yes

  vars:
      interfaces:
          - id: interface GigabitEthernet1
            ipv4:
                address: 10.0.10.11
                mask: 255.255.255.0
            state: no shutdown
          - id: interface GigabitEthernet3
            ipv4:
                address: 10.0.11.11
                mask: 255.255.255.0
            state: no shutdown
          - id: interface Loopback0
            ipv4:
                address: 10.0.0.11
                mask: 255.255.255.255
            state: no shutdown

  tasks:
      - name: CONFIGURING THE INTERFACE
        ios_config:
            lines:
                - ip address {{ item.ipv4.address }} {{ item.ipv4.mask }}
                - "{{ item.state }}"
            parents: "{{ item.id }}"
            save_when: modified
        loop: "{{ interfaces }}"
```

```
    - name: WAITING FOR CARRIER-DELAY
      pause:
          seconds: 5

    - name: COLLECTING OPEPRATION INFORMATION FROM '{{ ansible_network_os }}'
      ios_command:
          commands:
              - show ip interface brief
      register: ios_output

    - name: VERIFICATION OF THE OUTPUT
      debug:
          msg: "{{ ios_output.stdout_lines }}"
...


$ ansible-playbook npf_example_ios_config_extended.yml --limit=CSR2

PLAY [ios] ************************************************************************

TASK [Gathering Facts] ************************************************************
ok: [CSR2]

TASK [CONFIGURING THE INTERFACE] **************************************************
changed: [CSR2] => (item={u'state': u'no shutdown', u'id': u'interface
  GigabitEthernet1', u'ipv4': {u'mask': u'255.255.255.0', u'address': u'10.0.10.11'}})
changed: [CSR2] => (item={u'state': u'no shutdown', u'id': u'interface
  GigabitEthernet3', u'ipv4': {u'mask': u'255.255.255.0', u'address': u'10.0.11.11'}})
changed: [CSR2] => (item={u'state': u'no shutdown', u'id': u'interface Loopback0',
  u'ipv4': {u'mask': u'255.255.255.255', u'address': u'10.0.0.11'}})

TASK [WAITING FOR CARRIER-DELAY] **************************************************
Pausing for 5 seconds
(ctrl+C then 'C' = continue early, ctrl+C then 'A' = abort)
ok: [CSR2]

TASK [COLLECTING OPEPRATION INFORMATION FROM 'ios'] *******************************
ok: [CSR2]

TASK [VERIFICATION OF THE OUTPUT] *************************************************
ok: [CSR2] => {
    "msg": [
```

```
          [
              "Interface                IP-Address      OK? Method Status
  Protocol",
              "GigabitEthernet1         10.0.10.11      YES manual up
  up        ",
              "GigabitEthernet3         10.0.11.11      YES manual up
  up        ",
              "GigabitEthernet4         192.168.141.42  YES manual up
  up        ",
              "Loopback0                10.0.0.11       YES manual up
  up"
          ]
      ]
}

PLAY RECAP ************************************************************************
CSR2                          : ok=5    changed=1    unreachable=0    failed=0
```

Now the situation looks much better, as **vars** at the beginning of the playbook contains the dictionary with the variables that are used first to create the loop and then to create the interface configuration for each entry. In the module **ios_config**, there is a new key, **save_when**, with the value **modified**. As the name suggests, this key saves the configuration on the removed node to the startup configuration (in case the running configuration) is successfully modified.

Although the situation with the automation now is much better than it was before, there are still a lot of ways we could improve it. For instance, we haven't yet used templates. Example 19-48 shows the possible structure of the files with variables and Jinja2 templates to configure the OSPF routing protocol.

Example 19-48 *Using the Ansible Module ios_config in Conjunction with Templates*

```
$ cat CSR2_vars.yml
---
routing:
    - protocol: ospf
      id: 1
      router_id: 10.0.0.11
      interfaces:
          - id: GigabitEthernet1
            type: point-to-point
            passive: false
            area: 0.0.0.0
```

```
          - id: GigabitEthernet3
            type: point-to-point
            passive: false
            area: 0.0.0.0
          - id: Loopback0
            passive: true
            area: 0.0.0.0
...


$ cat npf_template_ios_config_pro.j2
{% if routing is defined %}
{% for rp in routing %}
{% if rp.protocol == 'ospf' %}
router {{ rp.protocol }} {{ rp.id }}
    router-id {{ rp.router_id }}
{% for r_if in rp.interfaces %}
{% if r_if.passive %}
    passive-interface {{ r_if.id }}
{% endif %}
{% endfor %}
!
{% for r_if in rp.interfaces %}
interface {{ r_if.id }}
    ip {{ rp.protocol }} {{ rp.id }} area {{ r_if.area }}
{% if r_if.type is defined %}
    ip {{ rp.protocol }} network {{ r_if.type }}
{% endif %}
!
{% endfor %}
{% endif %}
{% endfor %}
{% endif %}
```

In the same way shown in Example 19-32, the Ansible playbook for building the configuration of the Cisco IOS XR–based network device is fairly generic and, depending on the templates and variables, it could be used to create any configuration, as shown Example 19-49.

Example 19-49 *Using the Ansible Module ios_config in Conjunction with Templates, Continued*

```
$ cat npf_example_ios_config_pro.yml
---
- hosts: ios
  connection: network_cli
  gather_facts: yes

  tasks:
      - name: IMPORTING VARIABLES
        include_vars:
            file: "{{ inventory_hostname }}_vars.yml"

      - name: TEMPLATING CONFIG
        template:
            src: npf_template_ios_config_pro.j2
            dest: "{{ inventory_hostname }}_temp.conf"

      - name: CONFIGURING THE DEVICE
        ios_config:
            src: "{{ inventory_hostname }}_temp.conf"
            save_when: modified
...


$ ansible-playbook npf_example_ios_config_pro.yml --limit=CSR2

PLAY [ios] *************************************************************************

! The output is truncated for brevity

PLAY RECAP *************************************************************************
CSR2                       : ok=4    changed=2    unreachable=0    failed=0


$ cat CSR2_temp.conf
router ospf 1
    router-id 10.0.0.11
    passive-interface Loopback0
!
interface GigabitEthernet1
    ip ospf 1 area 0.0.0.0
    ip ospf network point-to-point
!
```

```
interface GigabitEthernet3
    ip ospf 1 area 0.0.0.0
    ip ospf network point-to-point
!
interface Loopback0
    ip ospf 1 area 0.0.0.0
!
```

Examples 19-48 and 19-49 show examples of many concepts you've already used to perform automation in network operations. The variables are contained in the dedicated file CSR2_vars.yml, and they are imported at the beginning of the execution of the Ansible playbook. Then, using template npf_template_ios_config_pro.j2, the final configuration file CSR2_temp.conf is created. (The contents of CSR2_temp.conf are shown at the end of Example 19-49.) As you can see, the template extensively uses loops and conditionals to build the configuration correctly. In the end, the module **ios_config** uses the key **src** with the value of the path to generate the configuration file CSR2_temp.conf instead of using **lines** and **parents**. These two methods are mutually exclusive, so you need to decide which one to use in a particular case. Example 19-50 shows the verification done directly on the router CSR2. (For brevity, the module **ios_command** is not included in this example.)

Example 19-50 *Verifying the OSPF Configuration on a Cisco IOS XE Router*

```
CSR2# show ip ospf interface brief
Interface    PID   Area           IP Address/Mask    Cost  State Nbrs F/C
Lo0          1     0.0.0.0        10.0.0.11/32       1     LOOP  0/0
Gi3          1     0.0.0.0        10.0.11.11/24      1     P2P   0/0
Gi1          1     0.0.0.0        10.0.10.11/24      1     P2P   0/0
```

In terms of a network-wide solution, Example 19-49 might be the most suitable option as the only thing you would need to do many times is to create the dedicated file with variables for each node (and even this could be automated further); the playbook and template would be created only once.

Configuration Using Various ios_* Modules

Some of the most critical goals of network programmability and automation are the simplification and acceleration of network operation processes. The engineers from Red Hat who develop Ansible are concerned with making these goals easy to reach. They have created a bunch of modules for declarative management, which works as follows: Users provide the desired state of the network, such as the state of an interface or IP addresses that should be present on a system, and the corresponding Ansible module analyzes the current operational state of the interfaces against the desired state. If any actions are needed to get the device to the desired state, they are done automatically, without additional effort from users. In a nutshell, this means that all the complexity of a particular CLI syntax is hidden from the users.

The previous section shows a declarative approach via variables defined using free syntax and templates that create proper CLI configuration based on those variables. This is the same declarative management just described, shown with implementation details. However, for specific tasks, you can use declarative modules from Ansible directly and avoid the creation of templates. You can find a full list of these modules on the official Ansible website (https://docs.ansible.com/ansible/latest/collections/index.html). This section provides examples of three such modules: **ios_interface**, **ios_l3_interface** (to compare with the earlier examples), and **ios_lldp**.

All these modules perform declarative management; that is, they compare the actual operational state of the network elements with the desired state and change the configuration only if necessary (for example, if the desired state is different from the operational state). Example 19-51 shows the use of the modules **ios_interface** and **ios_l3_interface** together.

Example 19-51 *Using the Ansible Modules ios_interface and ios_l3_interface*

```
$ cat npf_example_ios_interface_l3.yml
---
- hosts: ios
  connection: network_cli
  gather_facts: yes

  vars:
      interfaces:
          - id: GigabitEthernet1
            ipv4:
                address: 10.0.10.11
                mask: 24
            description: CSR2<--->XR2
          - id: GigabitEthernet3
            ipv4:
                address: 10.0.11.11
                mask: 24
            description: CSR2<--->NX2
          - id: Loopback0
            ipv4:
                address: 10.0.0.11
                mask: 32
            description: RID
```

```
  tasks:
      - name: CONFIGURING THE INTERFACE
        ios_interface:
            name: "{{ item.id }}"
            enabled: true
            description: "{{ item.description }}"
        loop: "{{ interfaces }}"

      - name: CONFIGURE THE INTERFACE (L3)
        ios_l3_interface:
            name: "{{ item.id }}"
            ipv4: "{{ item.ipv4.address }}/{{ item.ipv4.mask }}"
        loop: "{{ interfaces }}"
...


$ ansible-playbook npf_example_ios_interface_l3.yml -i hosts --limit=CSR2

PLAY [ios] ************************************************************************

TASK [Gathering Facts] ************************************************************
ok: [CSR2]

TASK [CONFIGURING THE INTERFACE] **************************************************
changed: [CSR2] => (item={u'id': u'GigabitEthernet1', u'ipv4': {u'mask': 24,
  u'address': u'10.0.10.11'}, u'description': u'CSR2<--->XR2'})
changed: [CSR2] => (item={u'id': u'GigabitEthernet3', u'ipv4': {u'mask': 24,
  u'address': u'10.0.11.11'}, u'description': u'CSR2<--->NX2'})
changed: [CSR2] => (item={u'id': u'Loopback0', u'ipv4': {u'mask': 32, u'address':
  u'10.0.0.11'}, u'description': u'RID'})

TASK [CONFIGURE THE INTERFACE (L3)] ***********************************************
ok: [CSR2] => (item={u'id': u'GigabitEthernet1', u'ipv4': {u'mask': 24, u'address':
  u'10.0.10.11'}, u'description': u'CSR2<--->XR2'})
ok: [CSR2] => (item={u'id': u'GigabitEthernet3', u'ipv4': {u'mask': 24, u'address':
  u'10.0.11.11'}, u'description': u'CSR2<--->NX2'})
ok: [CSR2] => (item={u'id': u'Loopback0', u'ipv4': {u'mask': 32, u'address':
  u'10.0.0.11'}, u'description': u'RID'})

PLAY RECAP ************************************************************************
CSR2                       : ok=3    changed=1    unreachable=0    failed=0
```

Example 19-51 is similar to Example 19-47, where interfaces are also configured. However, the variables have changed a bit: The state has been removed, the description has been added, and the mask has changed format from dotted decimal to prefix because the module **ios_l3_interaces** requires prefix format for the subnet mask.

The module **ios_interface** is used to configure physical parameters of an interface, its operational state, description, and some others parameters. Because no descriptions have been configured so far, you can see that the status of the Ansible task is **changed**, which means the configuration was updated. Then the module **ios_l3_interface** checks the configuration of IP addresses (it can work both IPv4 and IPv6 addresses) and updates them if they don't match. The status **ok** for this task means no changes were made; the IP addresses were configured properly earlier. If the IP addresses were missing or configured incorrectly, they would be updated to the desired values, and the status of the task would be **changed.**

The last module we need to cover for Cisco IOS XE in general and declarative management is **ios_lldp**, whose role is to configure LLDP. Example 19-52 provides details on its use.

Example 19-52 *Using the Ansible Module ios_lldp*

```
$ cat npf_example_ios_lldp.yml
---
- hosts: ios
  connection: network_cli
  gather_facts: yes

  tasks:
      - name: ENABLING LLDP
        ios_lldp:
            state: present
...



$ ansible-playbook npf_example_ios_lldp.yml -i hosts --limit=CSR2

PLAY [ios] *************************************************************************

TASK [Gathering Facts] *************************************************************
ok: [CSR2]

TASK [ENABLING LLDP] ***************************************************************
changed: [CSR2]

PLAY RECAP *************************************************************************
CSR2                           : ok=2    changed=1    unreachable=0    failed=0
```

The structure of the **ios_lldp** module is relatively easy, as it has only one key, **state**, with possible values **present** or **absent** that enable or disable LLDP globally on a Cisco IOS/IOS XE network device. Because LLDP isn't enabled by default, you can see in this example that the task ENABLING LLDP has changed state. In addition, there is not much happening in the background: The module either sends **lldp run** or **no lldp run** in global configuration mode.

Using Ansible for Cisco IOS XR

Following the same approach shown earlier for devices that run Cisco IOS/IOS XE software, a Cisco IOS XR device must be configured with the proper username, password, and SSH server in order for the managing host with Ansible to connect to it. Example 19-53 shows the preparation of the Cisco IOS XR router.

Note Refer to Figure 19-5, earlier in this chapter, for the topology information used in the following examples.

Example 19-53 *Preparing a Cisco IOS XR Device to Be Managed Using Ansible*

```
RP/0/0/CPU0:ios(config)# show configuration
Mon Jan  7 07:54:50.772 UTC
Building configuration...
!! IOS XR Configuration 6.5.1
hostname XR2
vrf mgmt
 address-family ipv4 unicast
 !
!
line console
 exec-timeout 0 0
!
control-plane
 management-plane
  out-of-band
   vrf mgmt
   interface MgmtEth0/0/CPU0/0
    allow SSH
   !
  !
 !
!
```

```
interface MgmtEth0/0/CPU0/0
 vrf mgmt
 ipv4 address 192.168.141.52 255.255.255.0
!
ssh server v2
ssh server vrf mgmt
end
RP/0/0/CPU0:ios(config)# commit
Mon Jan  7 07:55:16.530 UTC
RP/0/0/CPU0:XR2(config)# exit
RP/0/0/CPU0:XR2# crypto key generate rsa general-keys
Mon Jan  7 07:55:58.607 UTC
The name for the keys will be: the_default
% You already have keys defined for the_default
Do you really want to replace them? [yes/no]: yes
  Choose the size of the key modulus in the range of 512 to 4096 for your General
  Purpose Keypair. Choosing a key modulus greater than 512 may take a few minutes.

How many bits in the modulus [2048]: 2048
Generating RSA keys ...
Done w/ crypto generate keypair
[OK]
```

The process shown in Example 19-53 is a bit different for the process used for CSR2 (refer to Example 19-41), which has no candidate configuration. Because Cisco IOS XR does have candidate configuration, Example 19-53 shows the fully prepared candidate configuration and commit process rather than per-line entry. In addition, in Cisco IOS XR there is a management VRF instance configured, and the OOB management port MgmtEth0/0/CPU0/0 has been assigned to that instance. In Example 19-53, there is no username configured because Cisco IOS devices have a built-in account with cisco as both the username and password.

Note The Cisco IOS XE examples earlier in this chapter have no management VRF instance configuration, though you could do it as well. Whether you use a VRF instance configuration depends on your network design.

When the configuration is committed and keys are generated, you should check the connectivity from the managing host to XR2, as shown in Example 19-54.

Example 19-54 *Verifying That the Cisco IOS XR Device Is Ready to Be Managed Using Ansible*

```
$ ping XR2 -c 1
PING XR2 (192.168.141.52) 56(84) bytes of data.
64 bytes from XR2 (192.168.141.52): icmp_seq=1 ttl=255 time=1.23 ms

--- XR2 ping statistics ---
1 packets transmitted, 1 received, 0% packet loss, time 0ms
rtt min/avg/max/mdev = 1.237/1.237/1.237/0.000 ms



$ ssh cisco@XR2
Password:

RP/0/0/CPU0:XR2#
```

You can see in this output that XR2 is ready to be managed by Ansible. Recall from Example 19-43 that the Ansible hosts file has been updated for all network elements in the lab topology. Therefore, you don't need to update it again at this point.

Operational Data Verification Using the iosxr_command Module

In the same manner as for Cisco IOS XE devices, the review of the Ansible modules for Cisco IOS XR starts with the Ansible module **iosxr_command**, which is used for verification of operational information. You are already a bit familiar with it, as you used this module earlier in this chapter. Example 19-55 reminds you how it works to collect the same information collected for Cisco IOS XE earlier in this chapter.

Example 19-55 *Using the Ansible Module iosxr_command to Collect show Output*

```
$ cat npf_example_iosxr_command.yml
---
- hosts: iosxr
  connection: network_cli
  gather_facts: yes

  tasks:
      - name: COLLECTING OPEPRATION INFORMATION FROM '{{ ansible_network_os }}'
        iosxr_command:
            commands:
                - show inventory
                - show ip interface brief
        register: iosxr_output
```

```
      - name: VERIFICATION OF THE OUTPUT
        debug:
            msg: "{{ iosxr_output.stdout_lines }}"
...


$ ansible-playbook npf_example_iosxr_command.yml --limit=XR2

PLAY [iosxr] *******************************************************************

TASK [Gathering Facts] *********************************************************
ok: [XR2]

TASK [COLLECTING OPEPRATION INFORMATION FROM 'iosxr'] **************************
ok: [XR2]

TASK [VERIFICATION OF THE OUTPUT] **********************************************
ok: [XR2] => {
    "msg": [
        [
            "NAME: \"0/0/CPU0\", DESCR: \"Route Processor type (16, 0)\"",
            "PID: IOSXRV, VID: V01, SN: N/A"
        ],
        [
            "Interface                      IP-Address      Status          Protocol
  Vrf-Name",
            "MgmtEth0/0/CPU0/0              192.168.141.52  Up              Up
  mgmt     ",
            "GigabitEthernet0/0/0/0         unassigned      Shutdown        Down
  default ",
            "GigabitEthernet0/0/0/1         unassigned      Shutdown        Down
  default"
        ]
    ]
}

PLAY RECAP *********************************************************************
XR2                        : ok=3    changed=0    unreachable=0    failed=0
```

If you compare this example with Example 19-45, you can see that the only difference is that now you are using the prefix **iosxr_** instead of the prefix **ios_**. You can see the similarities in the Ansible module structures, and you can see that the Cisco IOS XE and Cisco IOS XR commands are the same.

Because the credentials and the **ansible_network_os** value are stored in the Ansible hosts file (refer to Example 19-43), connectivity to XR2 is established using the **network_cli** connection plug-in, and no additional information needs to be provided because **gather_facts** is enabled.

As you did earlier, you can now use the **iosxr_command** module again to perform some interactive commands at the CLI level. Example 19-56 shows how to use this module to clear counters.

Example 19-56 *Using the Ansible Module iosxr_command to Clear Counters*

```
$ cat npf_example_iosxr_command_clear.yml
---
- hosts: iosxr
  connection: network_cli
  gather_facts: yes

  tasks:
      - name: COLLECTING OPEPRATION INFORMATION FROM '{{ ansible_network_os }}'
        iosxr_command:
            commands:
                - command: show interfaces MgmtEth 0/0/CPU0/0 | inc packets
                - command: clear counters interface MgmtEth 0/0/CPU0/0
                  prompt: '[confirm]'
                  answer: "\r"
                - command: show interfaces MgmtEth 0/0/CPU0/0 | inc packets
        register: iosxr_output

      - name: VERIFICATION OF THE OUTPUT
        debug:
            msg: "{{ iosxr_output.stdout_lines }}"
...


$ ansible-playbook npf_example_iosxr_command_clear.yml --limit=XR2

PLAY [iosxr] ******************************************************************************

TASK [Gathering Facts] ********************************************************************
ok: [XR2]

TASK [COLLECTING OPEPRATION INFORMATION FROM 'iosxr'] *****************************
ok: [XR2]
```

```
TASK [VERIFICATION OF THE OUTPUT] **************************************************
ok: [XR2] => {
    "msg": [
        [
            "5 minute input rate 0 bits/sec, 0 packets/sec",
            "  5 minute output rate 0 bits/sec, 0 packets/sec",
            "     132 packets input, 14832 bytes, 0 total input drops",
            "     Received 1 broadcast packets, 0 multicast packets",
            "     107 packets output, 18008 bytes, 0 total output drops",
            "     Output 0 broadcast packets, 0 multicast packets"
        ],
        [
            "Clear \"show interface\" counters on this interface [confirm]"
        ],
        [
            "5 minute input rate 0 bits/sec, 0 packets/sec",
            "  5 minute output rate 0 bits/sec, 0 packets/sec",
            "     3 packets input, 286 bytes, 0 total input drops",
            "     Received 0 broadcast packets, 0 multicast packets",
            "     2 packets output, 316 bytes, 0 total output drops",
            "     Output 0 broadcast packets, 0 multicast packets"
        ]
    ]
}

PLAY RECAP *************************************************************************
XR2                        : ok=3    changed=0    unreachable=0    failed=0
```

Example 19-56 shows the process that occurs when the interface's counters are collected and then cleared and collected again to verify that clearance was successful.

> **Note** Example 19-45 and the discussion of that example provide details about the **command**, **prompt**, and **answer** entries, so refer to that example and text for clarification.

General Configuration Using the iosxr_config Module

For configuration of Cisco IOS XR devices using Ansible, there is a module called **iosxr_config** that you need to understand. This module allows you to execute a predefined set of CLI commands in a configuration context, which means you need to be familiar with the CLI syntax of Cisco IOS XR. Earlier in this chapter, you saw how to automate the implementation of the configuration for Cisco IOS XE and verify it, so this section shows only the relevant playbooks and not execution and verification. Example 19-57 shows the simplest way to configure the IOS XR interface without any variables and with all values hardcoded in the playbook.

Example 19-57 *Using the Ansible Module **iosxr_config** Without Variables*

```
$ cat npf_example_iosxr_config_simple.yml
---
- hosts: iosxr
  connection: network_cli
  gather_facts: yes

  tasks:
      - name: CONFIGURING THE INTERFACE
        iosxr_config:
            lines:
                - ip address 10.0.10.22/24
                - ipv6 address fc00:10:0:10::22/64
                - no shutdown
            parents:
                - interface GigabitEthernet0/0/0/0
...
```

If you compare Example 19-57 with the Cisco IOS XE configuration in Example 19-47, you see only two differences. The first difference is the format of the IP address, which is not related to Ansible but rather to the CLI syntax of IOS XR. (You could also provide the IP address by using a subnet mask in dotted-decimal format.) The other difference is the name of the module; IOS-XR devices use **iosxr_config** instead of **ios_config**, which is used with IOS/IOS XE devices. The similarity in the module structure allows you to focus on the content of your automation rather than on the format of different Ansible modules.

In situations where you need to provide repetitive actions, such as configuring multiple interfaces, you can use loops and Ansible variables together with the **iosxr_config** module, as shown in Example 19-58.

Example 19-58 *Using the Ansible Module **iosxr_config** with Loops and Variables*

```
$ cat npf_example_iosxr_config_extended.yml
---
- hosts: iosxr
  connection: network_cli
  gather_facts: yes
```

```
vars:
    interfaces:
        - id: interface GigabitEthernet0/0/0/0
          ipv4:
              address: 10.0.10.22
              mask: 24
          state: no shutdown
        - id: interface GigabitEthernet0/0/0/1
          ipv4:
              address: 10.0.12.22
              mask: 24
          state: no shutdown
        - id: interface Loopback0
          ipv4:
              address: 10.0.0.22
              mask: 32
          state: no shutdown
          ipv6:
              address: fc00:10::22
              mask: 128
          state: no shutdown


tasks:
    - name: CONFIGURING THE INTERFACE
      iosxr_config:
          lines:
            - {% if item.ipv4 is defined %}ip address {{ item.ipv4.address }}/{{
item.ipv4.mask }}{% endif %}
            - {% if item.ipv6 is defined %}ip address {{ item.ipv6.address }}/{{
item.ipv6.mask }}{% endif %}
            - "{{ item.state }}"
          parents: "{{ item.id }}"
      loop: "{{ interfaces }}"
...
```

You should be rather familiar with the contents of Example 19-58 because you have already learned about all the components used here. The module **iosxr_config** is looped over the entries from the dictionary **vars**, where all variables for the interfaces are stored. You can see one difference compared to **ios_config:** with **iosxr_config**, the **save_when** key is absent. It is absent because of the architecture of Cisco IOS XR, which has no concept of running and startup configurations; the configuration is saved only when it's been committed, which in the case of **iosxr_config** happens automatically. Otherwise, the structure of the variables in Example 19-58 is the same as the structure you have used for Cisco IOS XE. This illustrates the importance of being aware of platform specifics when you do the automation.

Example 19-58 introduces the concept of device abstraction. When a network device is abstracted, actions such as packet forwarding are completed in a generic way rather in terms of a particular device instance. From a network services perspective, it doesn't matter how the interfaces are internally called within the router or switch, as long as, for example, traffic can freely enter port 1 on the face plane and exit port 2. The naming conventions for the ports in Cisco IOS XE, IOS XR, and NX-OS are different. Therefore, device abstraction impacts the configuration syntax of a particular instance of a network device but not its logic (see Example 19-59).

Example 19-59 *Using the Ansible Module iosxr_config with a Jinja2 Template*

```
$ cat XR2_vars.yml
---
routing:
    - protocol: ospf
      id: 1
      router_id: 10.0.0.22
      interfaces:
          - id: GigabitEthernet0/0/0/0
            type: point-to-point
            passive: false
            area: 0.0.0.0
          - id: GigabitEthernet0/0/0/1
            type: point-to-point
            passive: false
            area: 0.0.0.0
          - id: Loopback0
            passive: true
            area: 0.0.0.0
...


$ cat npf_template_iosxr_config_pro.j2
{% if routing is defined %}
{% for rp in routing %}
{% if rp.protocol == 'ospf' %}
router {{ rp.protocol }} {{ rp.id }}
    router-id {{ rp.router_id }}
    !
```

```
{% for r_if in rp.interfaces %}
    area {{ r_if.area }}
        interface {{ r_if.id }}
{% if r_if.type is defined %}
            network {{ r_if.type }}
{% endif %}
{% if r_if.passive %}
            passive
{% endif %}
        !
    !
{% endfor %}
!
{% endif %}
{% endfor %}
{% endif %}


$ cat npf_example_iosxr_config_pro.yml
---
- hosts: iosxr
  connection: network_cli
  gather_facts: yes

  tasks:
      - name: IMPORTING VARIABLES
        include_vars:
            file: "{{ inventory_hostname }}_vars.yml"

      - name: TEMPLATING CONFIG
        template:
            src: npf_template_iosxr_config_pro.j2
            dest: "{{ inventory_hostname }}_temp.conf"

      - name: CONFIGURING THE DEVICE
        iosxr_config:
            src: "{{ inventory_hostname }}_temp.conf"
...
```

In Example 19-59, thanks to device abstraction, with the XR2 variable **XR2_vars.yml** has precisely the same structure as the similar variable for CSR2 (refer to Example 19-48). Example 19-59 does not change the variables to Cisco IOS XR syntax. Rather, the template **npf_template_iosxr_config_pro.j2** translates abstract modeling to the particular syntax of the Cisco IOS XR CLI in the same way that the template translates the syntax to the Cisco IOS XE CLI in Example 19-48. Both the module **include_vars** and the template are used without any changes from previous examples. The module **iosxr_config** also has the same structure as the module **ios_config** from earlier in this chapter in terms of providing a path to the configuration file in the key **src**.

Configuration Using Various iosxr_* Modules

Earlier in this chapter, the section "Configuration Using Various **ios_*** Modules" explains the concept of declarative management in the context of Cisco IOS XE. For Cisco IOS XR there are also a couple modules for declarative management, but their number is much smaller compared to the number of modules for Cisco IOS XE or NX-OS. This might be due to the fact that, traditionally, the skill level of network engineers at service providers was higher than the skill level in enterprises or data centers, which is why the demand for declarative management is lower in enterprises or data centers. Alternatively, it might be that the automation approaches in a service provider are different, and there are not too many requirements for Ansible declarative management modules. In any case, Example 19-60 shows how the module **iosxr_interface** is used for configuration of interfaces in Cisco IOS XR.

Example 19-60 *Using the Ansible Module iosxr_interface*

```
$ cat npf_example_iosxr_interface.yml
---
- hosts: iosxr
  connection: network_cli
  gather_facts: yes

  vars:
      interfaces:
          - id: GigabitEthernet0/0/0/0
            ipv4:
                address: 10.0.10.22
                mask: 24
            description: XR2<--->CSR2
          - id: GigabitEthernet0/0/0/1
            ipv4:
                address: 10.0.12.22
                mask: 24
            description: XR2<--->NX2
          - id: Loopback0
            ipv4:
                address: 10.0.0.22
                mask: 32
            description: RID
```

```
  tasks:
      - name: CONFIGURING THE INTERFACE
        iosxr_interface:
            name: "{{ item.id }}"
            enabled: true
            description: "{{ item.description }}"
        loop: "{{ interfaces }}"
...
```

You can see here that the variables and structure of **iosxr_interface** are the same as for CSR2 earlier in this chapter. However, there are no modules for declarative management for Cisco IOS XR that can configure the Layer 3 parts of the interface, such as IPv4 or IPv6 addresses. Also, you can see that **connection** is set to **network_cli**, which enables SSH connectivity with CLI commands. However, if a Cisco IOS XR device has a NETCONF server enabled and **connection** is set to **netconf**, the module **iosxr_interface** automatically translates the configuration in a NETCONF message by using the Cisco native YANG module.

The bottom line is that the modules **ios_command/ios_config** and **iosxr_command/iosxr_config** are almost identical, and this makes possible a unified approach to network automation using Ansible. This is especially true if you are using network device abstraction and proper templates to translate abstract network device models to particular implementations on Cisco IOS XE or Cisco IOS XR.

Using Ansible for Cisco NX-OS

Cisco NX-OS is a network operation system that is heavily used primarily in data centers but also in enterprise networks. Unlike Cisco IOS XE and IOS XR, NX-OS is built as an application on Linux. With NX-OS, it is possible to directly access the underlying Linux infrastructure and run shell or Python code directly on NX-OS switches, as discussed in Chapter 17, "Programming Cisco Platforms." When using Ansible, however, you want to be able to remotely manage devices similarly to the way you would with IOS XE and IOS XR, leveraging network device abstraction.

To automate a Cisco NX-OS network element by using Ansible, you need the same activities and information that are required as for IOS XE and IOS XR: credentials for remote access, IP connectivity, and an SSH server (see Example 19-61).

Example 19-61 *Preparing a Cisco NX-OS Device to Be Managed Using Ansible*

```
switch# configure terminal
switch(config)# hostname NX2
NX2(config)# no password strength-check
NX2(config)# feature privilege
NX2(config)# username cisco priv-lvl 15 password cisco
```

```
WARNING: Minimum recommended length of 8 characters.
WARNING: Password should contain characters from at least three of the following
  classes: lower case letters, upper case letters, digits and special characters.
WARNING: it is too short
WARNING: Configuration accepted because password strength check is disabled
NX2(config)# interface mgmt 0
NX2(config-if)# vrf member management
NX2(config-if)# ip address 192.168.141.62/24
NX2(config-if)# exit
NX2(config)# ssh key rsa 2048 force
deleting old rsa key.....
ssh server is enabled, cannot delete/generate the keys
NX2(config)#
NX2(config)# exit
NX2# copy run startup-config
[########################################] 100%
Copy complete, now saving to disk (please wait)...
Copy complete.
```

Example 19-61 shows the preparation of a freshly booted Cisco NX-OS device without any configuration applied. By default, NX-OS has enhanced security in terms of passwords, and to be able to use the insecure cisco/cisco credentials, you need to disable those security checks by issuing the **no password strength-check** command. In addition, with Cisco NX-OS, to be able use certain functionality, you need to explicitly enable specific features in the configuration context as the vast majority of features are disabled by default. For example, you need to enable **feature privilege** before you can use **priv-lvl** to define the proper access for the user. The next step is to assign an IP address and a VRF instance to the management interface. This is the final step because, by default, SSH is enabled on Cisco NX-OS devices, and if you try to enable it manually, you get an error indicating that the SSH server is enabled, and no new keys can be generated. The default key length is 1024 bytes, and if you want to improve security by extending the key length to 2048, you need to stop the SSH server, generate new keys, and then enable it again. (How to extend the key length is beyond the scope of this book.)

Example 19-43 shows the important Ansible information in the hosts file, including hostnames, credentials, and network OS values, and that information still applies with NX-OS. Example 19-62 shows the last check you need to do before starting to deal with NX2 through Ansible: You need to check reachability from the managing host.

Example 19-62 *Verifying That the Cisco NX-OS Device Is Ready to Be Managed Using Ansible*

```
$ ping NX2 -c 1
PING NX2 (192.168.141.62) 56(84) bytes of data.
64 bytes from NX2 (192.168.141.62): icmp_seq=1 ttl=255 time=0.660 ms

--- NX2 ping statistics ---
1 packets transmitted, 1 received, 0% packet loss, time 0ms
rtt min/avg/max/mdev = 0.660/0.660/0.660/0.000 ms


$ ssh cisco@NX2
Password:

NX2#
```

The output shows that NX2 is reachable. Like CSR2 and XR2 earlier in this chapter, NX2 is now ready to be automated.

Operational Data Verification Using the nxos_command Module

As with Cisco IOS XE and Cisco IOS XR, we begin here with the collection of operational data using the module **nxos_command**, as shown in Example 19-63.

Example 19-63 *Using the Ansible Module nxos_command to Collect show Output*

```
$ cat npf_example_nxos_command.yml
---
- hosts: nexus
  connection: network_cli
  gather_facts: yes

  tasks:
      - name: COLLECTING OPEPRATION INFORMATION FROM '{{ ansible_network_os }}'
        nxos_command:
            commands:
                - show inventory
                - show ip interface brief vrf all
        register: nxos_output

      - name: VERIFICATION OF THE OUTPUT
        debug:
            msg: "{{ nxos_output.stdout_lines }}"
...
```

```
$ ansible-playbook npf_example_nxos_command.yml --limit=NX2

PLAY [nexus] ************************************************************************

TASK [Gathering Facts] *****************************************************************
ok: [NX2]

TASK [COLLECTING OPEPRATION INFORMATION FROM 'nxos'] ******************************
ok: [NX2]

TASK [VERIFICATION OF THE OUTPUT] ***************************************************
ok: [NX2] => {
    "msg": [
        [
            "NAME: \"Chassis\",  DESCR: \"Nexus9000 9000v Chassis\"               ",
            "PID: N9K-9000v           ,  VID: V02 ,  SN: 99LE15NXK53         ",
            "",
            "NAME: \"Slot 1\",  DESCR: \"Nexus 9000v Ethernet Module\"          ",
            "PID: N9K-9000v           ,  VID: V02 ,  SN: 99LE15NXK53         ",
            "",
            "NAME: \"Fan 1\",  DESCR: \"Nexus9000 9000v Chassis Fan Module\"    ",
            "PID: N9K-9000v-FAN       ,  VID: V01 ,  SN: N/A                 ",
            "",
            "NAME: \"Fan 2\",  DESCR: \"Nexus9000 9000v Chassis Fan Module\"    ",
            "PID: N9K-9000v-FAN       ,  VID: V01 ,  SN: N/A                 ",
            "",
            "NAME: \"Fan 3\",  DESCR: \"Nexus9000 9000v Chassis Fan Module\"    ",
            "PID: N9K-9000v-FAN       ,  VID: V01 ,  SN: N/A"
        ],
        [
            "IP Interface Status for VRF \"default\"(1)",
            "Interface            IP Address      Interface Status",
            "",
            "IP Interface Status for VRF \"management\"(2)",
            "Interface            IP Address      Interface Status",
            "mgmt0                192.168.141.62  protocol-up/link-up/admin-up"
        ]
    ]
}

PLAY RECAP *************************************************************************
NX2                        : ok=3    changed=0    unreachable=0    failed=0
```

The module **nxos_command** plays the same role and has the same structure as **ios_command** for Cisco IOS XE and **iosxr_command** for IOS XR: It collects operational data by using **show** commands and performs some interactive commands in privileged mode. The commands themselves are provided in the **commands** dictionary. Because this module relies on the CLI commands, you need to know them. You can see in Example 19-63 that the command **show ip interface brief vrf all** is used to display IP addresses of all the interfaces, regardless of what VRF instances they belong to; recall from earlier in this chapter that for Cisco IOS or IOS XR, **show ip interface brief** is enough.

Example 19-64 provides details on issuing interactive commands in Cisco NX-OS.

Example 19-64 *Using the Ansible Module nxos_command for Interactive Commands in Privileged Mode*

```
$ cat npf_example_nxos_command_clear.yml
---
- hosts: nexus
  connection: network_cli
  gather_facts: yes

  tasks:
      - name: COLLECTING OPEPRATION INFORMATION FROM '{{ ansible_network_os }}'
        nxos_command:
            commands:
                - command: show interface mgmt 0  | include packets
                - command: clear counters interface mgmt 0
                  prompt: '[confirm]'
                  answer: "\r"
                - command: show interface mgmt 0 | include packets
        register: nxos_output

      - name: VERIFICATION OF THE OUTPUT
        debug:
            msg: "{{ nxos_output.stdout_lines }}"
...


$ ansible-playbook npf_example_nxos_command_clear.yml --limit=NX2

PLAY [nexus] *****************************************************************************

TASK [Gathering Facts] *******************************************************************
ok: [NX2]
```

```
TASK [COLLECTING OPEPRATION INFORMATION FROM 'nxos'] ******************************
ok: [NX2]

TASK [VERIFICATION OF THE OUTPUT] *************************************************
ok: [NX2] => {
    "msg": [
        [
            "1 minute input rate 0 bits/sec, 0 packets/sec",
            "  1 minute output rate 32 bits/sec, 0 packets/sec",
            "    1204 input packets 1043 unicast packets 128 multicast packets",
            "    33 broadcast packets 148020 bytes",
            "    1039 output packets 801 unicast packets 236 multicast packets",
            "    2 broadcast packets 250243 bytes"
        ],
        [
            ""
        ],
        [
            "1 minute input rate 0 bits/sec, 0 packets/sec",
            "  1 minute output rate 0 bits/sec, 0 packets/sec",
            "    3 input packets 3 unicast packets 0 multicast packets",
            "    0 broadcast packets 306 bytes",
            "    2 output packets 2 unicast packets 0 multicast packets",
            "    0 broadcast packets 604 bytes"
        ]
    ]
}

PLAY RECAP ************************************************************************
NX2                        : ok=3    changed=0    unreachable=0    failed=0
```

Note that although the values of counters are reduced in Example 19-64, they are not zero. The reason for this is that the Ansible script interacts with NX2 via this management interface. Therefore, after the counters are cleared, you send the request to collect information, and NX2 responds to that request.

The interactive management of Cisco NX-OS from privileged mode is precisely the same as it is for other Cisco operating systems. In fact, Example 19-64 was created by copying earlier examples and changing the module and registered variable name keys from **ios_** to **nxos_**. You can see that automation across different Cisco network operating systems is relatively easy if you know the CLI syntax and have adequately mastered the Ansible basics presented at the beginning of this chapter.

General Configuration Using the nxos_config Module

Automation of network devices running Cisco NX-OS starts with the **nxos_config** module, which enables you to automate the configuration of any service by using the CLI. You have already seen interface configuration for CSR2 and XR2, and now Example 19-65 shows interface configuration for Cisco NX-OS.

Example 19-65 *Using the Ansible Module nxos_config with Hardcoded Values*

```
$ cat npf_example_nxos_config_simple.yml
---
- hosts: nexus
  connection: network_cli
  gather_facts: yes

  tasks:
      - name: CONFIGURING THE INTERFACE
        nxos_config:
            lines:
                - no switchport
                - ip address 10.0.11.33/24
                - no shutdown
            parents:
                - interface Ethernet1/1
...
```

By this point in the chapter, you should readily understand what is happening in Example 19-65. The deviations from earlier examples in this chapter are minimal. With NX-OS, the first command in the **lines** dictionary, **no switchport**, is necessary because, by default, all ports on Cisco NX-OS devices are Layer 2 ports, and IP addresses can't be assigned unless they are changed to Layer 3 ports. Otherwise, the module **nxos_config** follows the same rules and has the same structure as **ios_config** and **iosxr_config.**

Example 19-66 shows the usage of loops and variables in conjunction with **nxos_config.** Note again how similar this is to the IOS XE and IOS XR examples presented earlier in this chapter.

Example 19-66 *Using the Ansible Module nxos_config with Loops and Variables*

```
$ cat npf_example_nxos_config_extended.yml
---
- hosts: nexus
  connection: network_cli
  gather_facts: yes
```

```
  vars:
      interfaces:
          - id: interface Ethernet 1/1
            mode: no switchport
           ipv4:
                address: 10.0.11.33
                mask: 24
            state: no shutdown
          - id: interface Ethernet 1/2
            mode: no switchport
            ipv4:
                address: 10.0.12.33
                mask: 24
            state: no shutdown
          - id: interface Loopback0
            mode:
            ipv4:
                address: 10.0.0.33
                mask: 32
            state: no shutdown

  tasks:
      - name: CONFIGURING THE INTERFACE
        nxos_config:
            lines:
                - "{{ item.mode }}"
                - ip address {{ item.ipv4.address }}/{{ item.ipv4.mask }}
                - "{{ item.state }}"
            parents: "{{ item.id }}"
            save_when: modified
        loop: "{{ interfaces }}"
...
```

In addition to providing the command **no switchport** for the physical interfaces, you need to add the variable **mode** to each interface. However, the **no switchport** command is not applicable to loopback interfaces, so its value is empty for those interfaces. The rest of the content and keys in the module **nxos_config** are precisely the same as for Cisco IOS XE.

The most scalable option for automation with Ansible is the use of Jinja2 templates. Earlier examples show this option for Cisco IOS XE and IOS XR, and Example 19-67 shows this option for Cisco NX-OS.

Example 19-67 *Using the Ansible Module nxos_config with Jinja2 Templates*

```
$ cat NX2_vars.yml
---
routing:
    - protocol: ospf
      id: 1
      router_id: 10.0.0.33
      interfaces:
          - id: Ethernet1/1
            type: point-to-point
            passive: false
            area: 0.0.0.0
          - id: Ethernet1/2
            type: point-to-point
            passive: false
            area: 0.0.0.0
          - id: Loopback0
            passive: true
            area: 0.0.0.0
...


$ cat npf_template_nxos_config_pro.j2
{% if routing is defined %}
{% for rp in routing %}
{% if rp.protocol == 'ospf' %}
feature ospf
!
router {{ rp.protocol }} {{ rp.id }}
    router-id {{ rp.router_id }}
!
{% for r_if in rp.interfaces %}
interface {{ r_if.id }}
    ip router {{ rp.protocol }} {{ rp.id }} area {{ r_if.area }}
{% if r_if.type is defined %}
    ip {{ rp.protocol }} network {{ r_if.type }}
{% endif %}
{% if r_if.passive and 'Loopback' not in r_if.id %}
    ip {{ rp.protocol }} passive-interface
{% endif %}
!
{% endfor %}
{% endif %}
{% endfor %}
{% endif %}
```

```
$ cat npf_example_nxos_config_pro.yml
---
- hosts: nexus
  connection: network_cli
  gather_facts: yes

  tasks:
      - name: IMPORTING VARIABLES
        include_vars:
            file: "{{ inventory_hostname }}_vars.yml"

      - name: TEMPLATING CONFIG
        template:
            src: npf_template_nxos_config_pro.j2
            dest: "{{ inventory_hostname }}_temp.conf"

      - name: CONFIGURING THE DEVICE
        nxos_config:
            src: "{{ inventory_hostname }}_temp.conf"
            save_when: modified
...
```

Thanks to network device abstraction, the variables file **NX2_vars.yml** is the same as for CSR or XR2, but the interface names are different. However, the template **npf_template_nxos_config_pro.j2** is adapted for NX-OS syntax, including activation of **feature ospf**, which is disabled by default. The playbook that ultimately executes the configuration of OSPF on NX-OS uses the module **nxos_config** with the key **src** pointing to the templated configuration.

Configuration Using Various nxos_* Modules

The number of modules for declarative management for Cisco NX-OS is much bigger than the number for Cisco IOS XE. (Remember that for Cisco IOS XR there almost no such modules.) Example 19-68 shows how to use the **nxos_interface** and **nxos_l3_interface** modules to configure physical and IP parameters of an interface.

Example 19-68 *Using the Ansible Modules nxos_interface and nxos_l3_interface*

```
$ cat npf_example_nxos_interface_l3.yml
---
- hosts: nexus
  connection: network_cli
  gather_facts: yes
```

```
vars:
    interfaces:
        - id: Ethernet1/1
          mode: layer3
          ipv4:
              address: 10.0.11.33
              mask: 24
          description: NX2<--->CSR2
        - id: Ethernet1/2
          mode: layer3
          ipv4:
              address: 10.0.12.33
              mask: 24
          description: NX2<--->XR2
        - id: Loopbacka0
          mode: layer3
          ipv4:
              address: 10.0.0.33
              mask: 32
          description: RID

tasks:
    - name: CONFIGURING THE INTERFACE
      nxos_interface:
          name: "{{ item.id }}"
          admin_state: up
          description: "{{ item.description }}"
          mode: "{{ item.mode }}"
      loop: "{{ interfaces }}"

    - name: CONFIGURE THE INTERFACE (L3)
      nxos_l3_interface:
          name: "{{ item.id }}"
          ipv4: "{{ item.ipv4.address }}/{{ item.ipv4.mask }}"
      loop: "{{ interfaces }}"
...
```

All the **nxos_*** modules for declarative management are designed to work solely with Cisco NX-OS network devices, and the specifics in the NX-OS operation must be reflected. In Example 19-68, you can see that the **vars** dictionary contains a new entry called **mode** with the value **layer3**. In the context of the **nxos_interface** module, this value is responsible for issuing the **no switchport** command. The good thing is that the declarative modules have internal validation mechanisms. For example, the presence of the **mode** key even for the loopback interface, where there is no **switchport** command at all, doesn't impact the execution, and the configuration can be applied successfully.

The last module related to declarative management that is covered in this book is **nxos_lldp**. Example 19-69 shows this module used to enable LLDP on NX-OS.

Example 19-69 *Using the Ansible Module nxos_lldp*

```
$ cat npf_example_nxos_lldp.yml
---
- hosts: nexus
  connection: network_cli
  gather_facts: yes

  tasks:
      - name: ENABLING LLDP
        nxos_lldp:
            state: present
...
```

This module enables LLDP on Cisco NX-OS network devices in much the same way the declarative management module **ios_lldp** is used to enable LLDP on Cisco IOS XE. For Cisco IOS XR, LLDP is not yet enabled because there is no such declarative module. At the end of this chapter, you will learn how to enable it using NETCONF/YANG.

At this point in the chapter, you should be familiar with the modules used for each Cisco network operating system and how to enrich their output by using Jinja2 templates and other Ansible tools. As you have seen, various modules have similar structure, and you can easily extend your skills to other platforms if you have gained enough experience with any of them.

Using Ansible in Conjunction with NETCONF

The last topic for this chapter is the use of the NETCONF/YANG network management approach in conjunction with Ansible. There are several reasons you might want to use this approach. For example, you might want to test NETCONF/YANG management in general, and Ansible makes it possible to do this. In addition, you might want to transition to NETCONF/YANG operation (especially with open-standard YANG modules) to unify the configuration and operational data formats across different network operating systems of different vendors. You may have other reasons.

Before you can use NETCONF, it must be enabled on the network devices as it's disabled by default. Example 19-70 shows how to enable NETCONF on CSR2 and verify whether it's working from the managing host.

> **Note** Refer to Figure 19-5, earlier in this chapter, for the topology information used in the following examples.

Example 19-70 *Preparing a Cisco IOS XE Host to Be Managed via NETCONF and Verifying That It Works*

```
CSR2# configure terminal
CSR2(config)# netconf ssh


$ ssh cisco@CSR2 -s netconf
Password:
<?xml version="1.0" encoding="UTF-8"?>
<hello xmlns="urn:ietf:params:xml:ns:netconf:base:1.0">
  <capabilities>
    <capability>urn:ietf:params:netconf:base:1.0</capability>
    <capability>urn:ietf:params:netconf:capability:writeable-
  running:1.0</capability>
    <capability>urn:ietf:params:netconf:capability:startup:1.0</capability>
    <capability>urn:ietf:params:netconf:capability:url:1.0</capability>
    <capability>urn:cisco:params:netconf:capability:pi-data-model:1.0</capability>
    <capability>urn:cisco:params:netconf:capability:notification:1.0</capability>
  </capabilities>
  <session-id>699879112</session-id>
</hello>
]]>]]>
```

IANA has allocated TCP port 830 to NETCONF, but some early deployments use other ports. The software release of CSR2 is 3.14.01.S, which is a bit old, and this explains why NETCONF is running on the TCP port, port 22. In Example 19-70, you can see that NETCONF is enabled using the **netconf ssh** command in Cisco IOS XE global configuration mode. NETCONF is running over SSH, so using port 22 port is not a problem in this case; however, to distinguish it from CLI-driven traffic, the NETCONF stream is marked with the string **netconf**, and you can see in Example 19-70 that the key **-s netconf** is added upon establishing the SSH session from the managing host to CSR2. In newer software versions, such as Cisco IOS XE 16.*, the configuration command is **netconf-yang**, and NETCONF runs on the TCP port, port 830, so it is important to check your version if you experience problems with the launch.

In order to manage network devices using NETCONF, it's essential to find proper YANG modules as they must be explicitly called in the NETCONF message. Chapter 13, "YANG," describes how to find the proper modules for all Cisco operating systems in different releases.

Another network function that is to be connected with the managing host is XR2 running Cisco IOS XR. Example 19-71 provides the details.

Example 19-71 *Preparing a Cisco IOS XR Host to Be Managed via NETCONF and Verifying That It Works*

```
RP/0/0/CPU0:XR2(config)# show conf
Sun Jan 13 17:16:39.792 UTC
Building configuration...
!! IOS XR Configuration 6.5.1.34I
control-plane
 management-plane
  out-of-band
   vrf mgmt
   interface MgmtEth0/0/CPU0/0
    allow NETCONF
   !
  !
 !
!
netconf-yang agent
 ssh
!
ssh server netconf vrf MGMT
end
RP/0/0/CPU0:XR2(config)# commit


$ ssh cisco@XR2 -s netconf -p 830
Password:
<hello xmlns="urn:ietf:params:xml:ns:netconf:base:1.0">
 <capabilities>
  <capability>urn:ietf:params:netconf:base:1.1</capability>
  <capability>urn:ietf:params:netconf:capability:candidate:1.0</capability>
  <capability>urn:ietf:params:netconf:capability:rollback-on-error:1.0</capability>
  <capability>urn:ietf:params:netconf:capability:validate:1.1</capability>
  <capability>urn:ietf:params:netconf:capability:confirmed-commit:1.1</capability>
  <capability>http://cisco.com/ns/yang/Cisco-IOS-XR-aaa-aaacore-cfg?module=Cisco-
  IOS-XR-aaa-aaacore-cfg&amp;revision=2018-09-04</capability>
! Further output is truncated for brevity
```

If for security reasons you don't limit access to the management plane, you can skip it and focus on the **netconf-yang agent ssh** and **ssh server netconf** commands, which are mandatory to enable NETCONF/YANG on Cisco IOS XR. As you learned in Chapter 14, "NETCONF and RESTCONF," the information about supported YANG modules is transferred in **capabilities** in the NETCONF hello message. Cisco IOS XR supports several hundred YANG modules, depending on the software version, and only a few capabilities are shown in Example 19-71. In Cisco IOS XR, the NETCONF protocol is running on its default port, port 830 (TCP), and you need to add the key **-p 830** when you check the connectivity to the NETCONF agent on XR2 from the managing host.

Last but not least, we look at the configuration of the NETCONF/YANG server on the NX2 network function running Cisco NX-OS. Example 19-72 shows how to enable NETCONF on NX2 and verify its operation.

Example 19-72 *Preparing a Cisco NX-OS Host to Be Managed via NETCONF and Verifying That It Works*

```
NX2# configure terminal
Enter configuration commands, one per line. End with CNTL/Z.
NX2(config)# feature netconf


$ ssh cisco@NX2 -s netconf -p 830
User Access Verification
Password:
<?xml version="1.0" encoding="UTF-8"?>

<hello xmlns="urn:ietf:params:xml:ns:netconf:base:1.0">
  <capabilities>
    <capability>urn:ietf:params:netconf:base:1.0</capability>
    <capability>urn:ietf:params:netconf:base:1.1</capability>
    <capability>urn:ietf:params:netconf:capability:writable-running:1.0</capability>
    <capability>urn:ietf:params:netconf:capability:rollback-on-error:1.0</capability>
    <capability>urn:ietf:params:netconf:capability:candidate:1.0</capability>
    <capability>urn:ietf:params:netconf:capability:validate:1.1</capability>
    <capability>urn:ietf:params:netconf:capability:confirmed-commit:1.1</capability>
    <capability>http://cisco.com/ns/yang/cisco-nx-os-device?revision=2018-
  07-17&amp;module=Cisco-NX-OS-device&amp;deviations=Cisco-NX-OS-device-
  deviations</capability>
! Further output is truncated for brevity
```

In Cisco NX-OS, the NETCONF server is running on the default port, port 830 (TCP), just as it does on Cisco IOS XR. To enable it, you need to enable the **netconf** feature.

Operational Data Verification Using the netconf_get Module

To collect both configuration and operational data in this case, the first step is to collect the actual information by using the module **netconf_get.** Chapter 13 explains YANG module naming as well as where these modules can be found. Example 19-73 shows how you can extract the configuration of OSPF in the Cisco IOS XR native YANG module from XR2. (All these commands are executed from the managing host that has Ansible installed.)

Example 19-73 *Using the Ansible Module* ***netconf_get*** *to Collect Configuration Information in YANG*

```
$ ls ~/Yang/yang/vendor/cisco/xr/651/ | grep 'ospf'
Cisco-IOS-XR-ipv4-ospf-act.yang
Cisco-IOS-XR-ipv4-ospf-cfg.yang
Cisco-IOS-XR-ipv4-ospf-oper-sub1.yang
Cisco-IOS-XR-ipv4-ospf-oper-sub2.yang
Cisco-IOS-XR-ipv4-ospf-oper-sub3.yang
Cisco-IOS-XR-ipv4-ospf-oper.yang
Cisco-IOS-XR-ipv6-ospfv3-act.yang
Cisco-IOS-XR-ipv6-ospfv3-cfg.yang
Cisco-IOS-XR-ipv6-ospfv3-oper-sub1.yang
Cisco-IOS-XR-ipv6-ospfv3-oper.yang


$ cat ~/Yang/yang/vendor/cisco/xr/651/Cisco-IOS-XR-ipv4-ospf-cfg.yang | grep
  'namespace'
  namespace "http://cisco.com/ns/yang/Cisco-IOS-XR-ipv4-ospf-cfg";

$ cat ~/Yang/yang/vendor/cisco/xr/651/Cisco-IOS-XR-ipv4-ospf-cfg.yang | grep '^
  container'
  container ospf {


$ cat npf_example_iosxr_netconf_get_cfg.yml
---
- hosts: iosxr
  connection: netconf
  gather_facts: yes

  tasks:
      - name: COLLECTING OPEPRATION INFORMATION FROM '{{ ansible_network_os }}'
        netconf_get:
            filter: <ospf xmlns="http://cisco.com/ns/yang/Cisco-IOS-XR-ipv4-ospf-
  cfg"/>
            display: xml
        register: iosxr_output

      - name: VERIFICATION OF THE OUTPUT
        debug:
            msg: "{{ iosxr_output.stdout_lines }}"
...


$ ansible-playbook npf_example_iosxr_netconf_get_cfg.yml --limit=XR2
```

```
PLAY [iosxr] ***************************************************************************

TASK [Gathering Facts] *****************************************************************
ok: [XR2]

TASK [COLLECTING OPEPRATION INFORMATION FROM 'iosxr'] **********************************
ok: [XR2]

TASK [VERIFICATION OF THE OUTPUT] ******************************************************
ok: [XR2] => {
    "msg": {
    "msg": [
        "<data xmlns=\"urn:ietf:params:xml:ns:netconf:base:1.0\"
  xmlns:nc=\"urn:ietf:params:xml:ns:netconf:base:1.0\">",
        "  <ospf xmlns=\"http://cisco.com/ns/yang/Cisco-IOS-XR-ipv4-ospf-cfg\">",
        "   <processes>",
        "    <process>",
        "     <process-name>1</process-name>",
        "     <default-vrf>",
        "      <router-id>10.0.0.22</router-id>",
        "      <area-addresses>",
        "       <area-address>",
        "        <address>0.0.0.0</address>",
        "        <running/>",
        "        <name-scopes>",
        "         <name-scope>",
        "          <interface-name>Loopback0</interface-name>",
        "          <running/>",
        "          <passive>true</passive>",
        "         </name-scope>",
        "         <name-scope>",
        "          <interface-name>GigabitEthernet0/0/0/0</interface-name>",
        "          <running/>",
        "          <network-type>point-to-point</network-type>",
        "         </name-scope>",
        "         <name-scope>",
        "          <interface-name>GigabitEthernet0/0/0/1</interface-name>",
        "          <running/>",
        "          <network-type>point-to-point</network-type>",
        "         </name-scope>",
        "        </name-scopes>",
        "       </area-address>",
        "      </area-addresses>",
        "     </default-vrf>",
```

```
        "       <start/>",
        "      </process>",
        "     </processes>",
        "    </ospf>",
        "   </data>"
    ]
}

PLAY RECAP *********************************************************************
XR2                        : ok=3    changed=0    unreachable=0    failed=0
```

The output in Example 19-73 is a bit long, but it provides a lot of details about how to create an Ansible playbook. First of all, you need to find the module you are going to use by looking in the folder with all Cisco IOS XR modules that you cloned from GitHub with the YANG modules. Because OSPF was configured earlier, it makes sense to extract OSPF configuration; therefore, you use **ls** to list all the files with output modification or **grep 'ospf'** to list only OSPF-related modules. Because the goal here is to get the configuration, you use the module with **cfg** in the name. The next step is to find the relevant XML namespace value and the top YANG container, which you do by parsing the content of the YANG module **Cisco-IOS-XR-ipv4-ospf-cfg.yang** for the **namespace** entry and the top container (which starts two spaces from the beginning of the new line, so **grep '^ container'** is used). Having collected both of these pieces of information that are necessary to create the body of a NETCONF message, the Ansible playbook is created.

The connection plug-in **netconf** is used for NETCONF communication. The module that allows you to collect the information in YANG format through NETCONF is called **netconf_get**. The key **filter** is the most important one in this module, as it defines precisely which information is extracted from the device. The filter is composed as a top-level container of a YANG module together with the namespace of this module. The key **display** instructs the module **netconf_get**, which is the output format (either XML or JSON) of the collected information. This output is stored in the registered variable **iosxr_output**, which is displayed using the **debug** module in the second task. After the execution of the playbook, you can see the whole OSPF configuration in the Cisco IOS XR native YANG module, which is equivalent to the CLI commands shown in Example 19-59. This approach is useful for reverse engineering, such as if you need to create XML templates for configuration of Cisco IOS XR devices, along with the **pyang** tool (refer to Chapter 13).

As mentioned earlier, it's also possible to collect operational data by using YANG modules that contain a lot of details about the network device. Example 19-74 shows how to obtain live OSPF telemetry.

Example 19-74 *Using the Ansible Module **netconf_get** to Collect Operational Data in YANG*

```
$ cat npf_example_iosxr_netconf_get_oper.yml
---
- hosts: iosxr
  connection: netconf
  gather_facts: yes

  tasks:
      - name: COLLECTING OPEPRATION INFORMATION FROM '{{ ansible_network_os }}'
        netconf_get:
            filter: <ospf xmlns="http://cisco.com/ns/yang/Cisco-IOS-XR-ipv4-ospf-
  oper"/>
            display: json
        register: iosxr_output

      - name: VERIFICATION OF THE OUTPUT
        debug:
            msg: "{{ iosxr_output.output.data }}"
...


$ ansible-playbook npf_example_iosxr_netconf_get_oper.yml -i hosts --limit=XR2

PLAY [iosxr] *********************************************************************

TASK [Gathering Facts] ***********************************************************
ok: [XR2]

TASK [COLLECTING OPEPRATION INFORMATION FROM 'iosxr'] ****************************
ok: [XR2]

TASK [VERIFICATION OF THE OUTPUT] ************************************************
ok: [XR2] => {
    "msg": {
        "ospf": {
            "processes": {
                "process": {
                    "default-vrf": {
                        "adjacency-information": {
                            "neighbor-details": {
                                "neighbor-detail": [
                                    {
```

```
                                        "adjacency-sid-protected": "false",
                                        "interface-name": "GigabitEthernet0/0/0/0",
                                       "interface-type": "mgmt-if-point-to-point",
                                        "last-oob-time": "0",
                                        "lfa-neighbor-id": "0.0.0.0",
                                        "lfa-neighbor-revision": "0",
                                        "lfa-next-hop": "0.0.0.0",
                                        "neighbor-ack-list-count": "0",
                                        "neighbor-ack-list-high-watermark": "0",
                                        "neighbor-address": "10.0.0.11",
                                        "neighbor-area-id": "0.0.0.0",
                                        "neighbor-backup-designated-router-address":
  "0.0.0.0",
                                        "neighbor-bfd-information": {
                                            "bfd-intf-enable-mode": "0",
                                            "bfd-status-flag": "1"
                                        },
! Further output is truncated for brevity
```


Note The details of how to create the filter in the **netconf_get** module are omitted here, as the process is shown in Example 19-73 example.

The information in Example 19-74 is actually telemetry data related to the OSPF process. In the full output, you can see all the neighbors, LSAs, routes, and other information related to OSPF. With telemetry, the collected data follows the chosen YANG module (in this case, Cisco native) and is transmitted using NETCONF. This is not the best way to collect telemetry, and Cisco is promoting gRPC/gNMI for telemetry collection, but if you don't have a telemetry collector, you can use NETCONF as explained in the next section. With telemetry data, it's handy to change the **display** value to **json**, as then you can save data directly in JSON format, which is easy to for any application to process.

General Configuration Using the netconf_config Module

You configure network functions via NETCONF in Ansible by using the **netconf_config** module. In Chapter 14, you learned about different operations that NETCONF can perform. The **netconf_config** module performs the **edit-config** operation, and you need to specify only the body itself, which provides the configuration. Example 19-75 shows how to enable LLDP on the Cisco IOS XR network function by using NETCONF/YANG.

Example 19-75 *Using the netconf_config Module to Push a NETCONF/YANG Configuration*

```
$ pyang -f tree -p . Cisco-IOS-XR-ethernet-lldp-cfg.yang
module: Cisco-IOS-XR-ethernet-lldp-cfg
  +--rw lldp
     +--rw tlv-select!
     |  +--rw system-name
     |  |  +--rw disable?   boolean
     |  +--rw port-description
     |  |  +--rw disable?   boolean
     |  +--rw system-description
     |  |  +--rw disable?   boolean
     |  +--rw system-capabilities
     |  |  +--rw disable?   boolean
     |  +--rw management-address
     |  |  +--rw disable?   boolean
     |  +--rw tlv-select-enter       boolean
     +--rw holdtime?              uint32
     +--rw extended-show-width?   boolean
     +--rw enable-subintf?        boolean
     +--rw enable-mgmtintf?       boolean
     +--rw timer?                 uint32
     +--rw reinit?                uint32
     +--rw enable?                boolean

  augment /a1:interface-configurations/a1:interface-configuration:
    +--rw lldp!
       +--rw transmit
       |  +--rw disable?   boolean
       +--rw receive
       |  +--rw disable?   boolean
       +--rw lldp-intf-enter    boolean
       +--rw enable?            boolean


$ cat npf_example_iosxr_netconf_config_simple.yml
---
- hosts: iosxr
  connection: netconf
  gather_facts: yes
```

```
 tasks:
      - name: CONFIGURING LLDP '{{ ansible_network_os }}'
        netconf_config:
            content: |
                <config>
                    <lldp xmlns="http://cisco.com/ns/yang/Cisco-IOS-XR-ethernet-
  lldp-cfg">
                        <enable>true</enable>
                    </lldp>
                </config>
...


$ ansible-playbook npf_example_iosxr_netconf_config_simple.yml --limit=XR2

PLAY [iosxr] ***********************************************************************

TASK [Gathering Facts] *************************************************************
ok: [XR2]

TASK [CONFIGURING LLDP 'iosxr'] ****************************************************
changed: [XR2]

PLAY RECAP *************************************************************************
XR2                        : ok=2    changed=1    unreachable=0    failed=0
```

The **pyang** tool is a very useful for configuring network elements with YANG. First of all, you build the tree to analyze how the message within the XML body should look. To enable LLDP on a Cisco IOS XR device, you can simply configure **lldp** in global configuration mode, without further details. The NETCONF/YANG equivalent of the command in the Ansible playbook **npf_example_iosxr_netconf_config_simple.yml** uses the key **content** from the **netconf_config** module. The **<config></config>** framing is mandatory, and you can use it a basis for all your configuration. The YANG module drives further internal structure within this framing. You might note that the top-level container together with the XML namespace is precisely the same as the **filter** entry used in the **netconf_get** module. This is true because when you extract the configuration, you extract exactly what is configured in a specific tree, and so the top-level container and XML namespaces are the same in both cases.

True automation of network management with Ansible is achieved through Jinja2 templates. It's possible to use them together with NETCONF as shown in Example 19-76.

Example 19-76 *Using the Ansible Module **netconf_config** to Push a NETCONF/YANG Configuration with Templates*

```
$ cat npf_template_iosxr_netconf.j2
<config>
{% if routing is defined %}
{% for rp in routing %}
{% if rp.protocol == 'ospf' %}
  <ospf xmlns="http://cisco.com/ns/yang/Cisco-IOS-XR-ipv4-ospf-cfg">
    <processes>
      <process>
        <process-name>{{ rp.id }}</process-name>
        <default-vrf>
          <router-id>{{ rp.router_id }}</router-id>
          <area-addresses>
{% for r_if in rp.interfaces %}
            <area-address>
              <address>{{ r_if.area }}</address>
              <running/>
              <name-scopes>
                <name-scope>
                  <interface-name>{{ r_if.id }}</interface-name>
                  <running/>
{% if r_if.passive %}
                  <passive>true</passive>
{% endif %}
{% if r_if.type is defined %}
                  <network-type>{{ r_if.type }}</network-type>
{% endif %}
                </name-scope>
              </name-scopes>
            </area-address>
{% endfor %}
          </area-addresses>
        </default-vrf>
        <start/>
      </process>
    </processes>
  </ospf>
{% endif %}
{% endfor %}
{% endif %}
</config>
```

```
$ cat npf_example_iosxr_netconf_config_pro.yml
---
- hosts: iosxr
  connection: netconf
  gather_facts: yes

  tasks:
      - name: IMPORTING VARIABLES
        include_vars:
            file: "{{ inventory_hostname }}_vars.yml"

      - name: CONFIGURING THE DEVICE
        netconf_config:
            content: "{{ lookup('template', 'npf_template_iosxr_netconf.j2') }}"
...


$ ansible-playbook npf_example_iosxr_netconf_config_pro.yml --limit=XR2

PLAY [iosxr] ***********************************************************************

TASK [Gathering Facts] *************************************************************
ok: [XR2]

TASK [IMPORTING VARIABLES] *********************************************************
ok: [XR2]

TASK [CONFIGURING THE DEVICE] ******************************************************
changed: [XR2]

PLAY RECAP *************************************************************************
XR2                          : ok=3    changed=1    unreachable=0    failed=0
```

The template in Example 19-76 creates a configuration in XML/YANG format to be sent via NETCONF; it is the same configuration as in Example 19-60, where the template creates a set of CLI commands to configure the OSPF process. The key **content** from the **netconf_config** module plug-in **lookup** is used to template the configuration directly to the network element, bypassing the creation of a temporary configuration file. Together, this template and network abstraction enable true automation.

Summary

In this chapter, you have learned a lot about Ansible and management of network elements running Cisco IOS XE, IOS XR, and NX-OS, including the following:

- Ansible is an agentless automation framework.
- To connect to managed devices, Ansible relies on the inventory file, which contains information about the devices' hostnames, IP addresses, and other details.
- Ansible can operate in an ad hoc manner (with individual commands) or using playbooks (that is, automation scripts).
- Ansible has myriad modules for various tasks, including modules for configuration of network elements.
- In a playbook, each task is based on a specific module; that is, there is one module for one task.
- A basic Ansible playbook defines the hosts to manage and the tasks to be executed on those hosts. It may also include variables, conditions, and loops to support sophisticated solutions.
- In Ansible, variables can be part of a playbook, they can exist in an external file, or they can be created dynamically during playbook execution.
- It is possible to control the execution of an Ansible playbook (for example, modifying the scope or passing additional variables) via additional arguments passed during launch.
- Jinja2 is a templating language that is used in Ansible. It includes filters, variables, loops, and conditions.
- Jinja2 can be used directly in Ansible playbooks inline or via a specific module leveraging external Jinja2 template files.
- Templates are handy for dynamic creation of configuration files used in network management. In conjunction with network device abstraction, Ansible and templates create a good framework for managing a multiple-OS network.
- Ansible has dedicated modules for each Cisco network OS. For configuration of network elements running Cisco IOS XE, IOS XR, and NX-OS, Ansible has modules for both imperative and declarative management.
- Via dedicated modules, Ansible supports NETCONF so that you can collect information or configure network elements by using NETCONF.

Chapter 20

Looking Ahead

Congratulations, you now have a shiny new set of tools in your automation and programmability toolbox! You know what the tools are used for, and we've given you the basics of how to use them. So, are you done? Not by a long shot.

This short final chapter provides you with some direction on how to apply what you've already learned in this book, as well as some ideas on how to enhance and advance what you've learned. This chapter, and the book, concludes with some thoughts on what automation and programmability mean for your career.

Some Rules of Thumb

You probably know a number of aphorisms about tools. You probably know a number of aphorisms about tools. The right tool for the right job. If it ain't broke don't fix it. When all you have is a hammer, every problem looks like a nail. A bad workman quarrels with his tools. The mechanic that would perfect his work must first sharpen his tools. If all you have is a hammer, it's hard to eat spaghetti.

Interestingly, most of those old saws (sorry) apply to the tools you've just acquired. No matter what book or article you pick up on network programmability and automation, you're bound to encounter at least a few rules of thumb. They're called rules of thumb—handy approximations—because they are backed by collected practical wisdom.

Let's look at a few.

Automate the Painful Stuff

Want to know where to begin applying your new-found skills? Look at your daily duties. What causes you the most pain? What tasks are the most repetitive? What jobs are the most boring? These are not only candidates for scripting, they are likely to be, by merit of being simple (but boring / repetitive / time-consuming) jobs that lend themselves to beginning scripting before you move on to more complex programming challenges.

Don't Automate a Broken Process

This is easily the most popular network automation rule of thumb. Be sure that the process you're automating is right; otherwise, your automation will only propagate a mistake faster and break your network faster.

Clean Up Your Network

This rule of thumb might strike you as less obvious than the first two. The less consistent your network is, the more complex your automation must be to deal with corner cases, "snowflake" designs, and "one-offs." Consolidate on the fewest protocols possible. Get rid of unused ACLs, prefix list entries, route maps, and so on. Make a template for your configurations and ensure that every node complies with it.

Find Your Sources of Truth

Eventually your automation is going to be extracting information from your network devices: config files, state, tables, telemetry, counters, and more. Often your automation uses this information to determine actionable data, identify symptoms and root causes for troubleshooting, or validate an intended change. The problem is, not every operating system reports this information in the same way. Even different versions of the same operating system might report information differently.

That's one of the advantages of APIs, as you've learned in this book: Normalizing data.

Distributed control planes mean many sources of truth and can complicate network automation. As mentioned in Chapter 1, "The Network Programmability and Automation Ecosystem," automation that has to reach out to every control plane and then analyze its information is problematic. This is where network abstraction comes in. Whether that abstraction is a graphical database, a repository of network data, or some other model of the network, the value of abstraction is that it becomes a single source of truth (SSoT) that you can trust for reliable automation.

An SSoT should represent both intent and network state. According to one study,[1] the most valuable data comprising the SSoT according to enterprises are:

1. Device state metrics
2. Data from shared services such as DDI (DNS, DHCP, and IPAM) and Active Directory
3. Network flows from sources such as NetFlow
4. Configuration data normalized into key/value pairs

---

1 Shamus McGillicuddy, "A Network Source of Truth Promotes Trust in Network Automation," *Enterprise Management Associates*, May 2020.

Developing an SSoT might be as simple as purchasing an automation platform that creates its own. If you are building your own platform, things might be more complicated. This is where bringing in one or more coders with much deeper programming knowledge could be cost-effective.

Avoid Automation You Can't Reuse

You don't want to invest hours and hours developing a program you are only going to run once, unless that one-time run returns extraordinary benefits. You want automation that shows value over and over. If you have followed the first rule of thumb in this section, automating the painful stuff, then by definition you're going to be writing code that you can use regularly.

Keep in mind that I'm not talking about occasionally whipping up a quick script for a single simple task that you might or might not use again. You've gained some skills, so use them. I'm talking about ensuring that the benefits of the program you write outweigh the time investment you put into writing it. You'll see more about cost/benefit analysis a little further down the list.

Document What You Do

Can anyone else use your program? Can anyone modify your program if they need to? Or is there a chance that you could return from a nice vacation to find that your associates are very unhappy with you because they couldn't figure out how to use that magic bit of automation you created? Even worse, is there a chance that they will desperately call you while you're still on vacation because no one in the office can get your software to work?

Understand What Level of Complexity You're Willing to Handle

I've already encouraged you to identify your pain points and automate them. But what if what's causing you pain is a complex workflow rather than a few simple tasks? In this case, you need to weigh what you're willing to invest to make the pain go away.

Any automation solution is going to impact you in three areas:

- People
- Time
- Money

These three factors don't exist all on their own; they influence each other. You might be able to reduce project time by adding more people, but that's going to cost you more money. You might be able to reduce cost by stretching the project time. You've participated in plenty of projects, and you have probably managed more than a few. You know this dynamic.

You might find that the people, time, and money required to address the complexity of your problem simply aren't worth the benefit and decide you can live with the pain.

Do a Cost/Benefit Analysis

As you've read through these rules of thumb, you've probably thought, "What he's telling me is to perform a cost/benefit analysis." Yep, I am.

But here's another perspective on the cost/benefit analysis: Adding automation to your network does not necessarily mean writing the program yourself. Certainly, knowing more about automation and programmability puts you in a superior position to understand the true magnitude of an automation project, but that understanding might lead you to consider alternatives to do-it-yourself (DIY) programming.

Here are your potential alternatives:

- DIY programming
- Hiring professional coders, either full time or part time
- Buying commercial ("shrink-wrapped") automation software

Each of these alternatives has pros and cons, and expense is not necessarily a determining factor here. For example, a professional coder might be able to develop in three weeks a solution that might take you—as a router jockey with some useful but basic programming experience—six months to develop. In this case, hiring the coder might be the more economical investment—especially if you are eliminating a serious operational bottleneck in three weeks instead of six months.

A commercial solution might also be cheaper than developing a solution in-house, and, if you have shopped wisely, it comes with knowledgeable software support. On the other hand, your custom-built solution is made for your specific network. You're not paying for features you don't need or a solution you have to shoe-horn into the way you run your network.

The point is, costs include more than just money, and benefits include more than just making your operations more efficient. Be sure you are considering all angles when considering which approach is right for you. And stating the blatantly obvious, keep in mind that your analysis is applicable to only one problem. DIY might be the best answer for one problem, professional coders for another, and commercial software for yet another.

What Do You Study Next?

An obvious answer to the question of what to study next is to expand on the basics we've given you in Python, Linux, APIs, modeling, and automation applications such as Ansible. You'll need them all.

But what about some ideas for branching out from the basics to take your automation toolbox to the next level? This section gives you a few ideas.

Model-Driven Telemetry

One of the practices of service management, discussed in Chapter 1, involves event and incident management. To maintain a healthy network and target minimal service downtime, it's common practice to "proactively" monitor your network in order to detect network events and incidents before they become service outages. If a network is designed properly, a network failure doesn't necessarily translate into a service outage unless the network failure is not resolved in a timely manner. For example, an interface failure on a router would not cause a service outage if there is an alternate route for the traffic to take to reach its destination. However, if another interface fails, causing that alternate route to fail as well, the service becomes unavailable. This highlights the importance of monitoring your network.

Network monitoring is usually performed by collecting logs describing the different events taking place on the network. Some of these events are simple informational messages, and others reflect critical conditions such as interface failures or, worse, resource depletion on a device, such as high CPU or memory consumption.

Until recently, syslog messages and SNMP traps were the predominant methods used to receive logs at a network monitoring station. These logs and traps are typically received by a network management station and used to create visual indicators of the status of the different network components. For metrics (versus logs), a network engineer would use a CLI and the myriad **show** commands to retrieve operational data, such as interface counters and CPU utilization. For the purpose of the discussion, these methods are labeled "legacy" network management methods.

Battle-tested legacy protocols have served us well for decades, but a number of issues render them unfit for the next era of network management. When we compare legacy SNMP and syslog with model-based telemetry, the following points stand out:

- **Resource consumption:** SNMP and syslog tend to consume significant resources on the devices on which these protocols are used, especially if SNMP polling is used in a pull-based model.
- **Speed:** Legacy methods are notably slow. If you have ever attempted to use snmpwalk with a network device, you know what we mean.
- **Ability to be integrated:** SNMP traps, syslog text-based messages, and data received as output to a **show** command through the CLI need significant grooming before they can be integrated with other systems for processing. In addition, the format of the output from CLI **show** commands is vendor and device specific.
- **Size:** In some cases, the data acquired using legacy methods is bulky, consuming substantial network bandwidth to transmit and storage to maintain. Note that this is not always the case; even with modern telemetry, data collection, storage, and transmission can be massive.

Streaming telemetry is used to receive metrics from a device at a certain cadence or event-triggered logs. It operates using push functionality and has much less impact on system resources than legacy protocols. The data retrieved using telemetry is encoded in either XML, JSON, or GBP, so the data is well formatted. GBP in particular provides the added value of being compact, especially with a flavor of GBP encoding called *compact GBP*. Data retrieved via telemetry references a data model to describe the data structure of the acquired data. This, coupled with standard encoding, makes the data ready for integration with other systems in the tool chain.

Any automation engineer involved with event, incident, or fault management (the naming varies depending on the referenced framework) should seriously start looking into model-based streaming telemetry and plan on migrating from legacy protocols as soon as feasible. Model-based streaming telemetry is the future of network monitoring (or *network visibility*, as some like to call it).

Containers: Docker and Kubernetes

The concept of virtualization is briefly covered in Chapter 1. Most engineers involved with automation have run into virtual machines at some point in their careers. However, a lesser number are familiar with the concept of containers. Although Docker containers are covered in some detail in Chapter 6, "Python Applications," the subject's importance does solicit a little more discussion here.

Whereas virtual machines abstract the host hardware and provide a virtualized version of different hardware components, such as CPU, memory, storage, and other peripheral devices, containers virtualize the operating system. More specifically, containers virtualize all software running on top of the operating system kernel.

Chapter 2, "Linux Fundamentals," introduces the concept of kernel space and user space software. Kernel space software is the core layer of the operating system that is closer to the hardware. A container is an autonomous entity that virtualizes all software components of the operating system running in the user space, including all the optional software packages that you choose to install. The container may also contain any user applications that you want to run. This means that all containers running on a system share the same hardware and kernel. So you can create and run a container that provides a virtualized version of Fedora and another container that provides a virtualized version of Ubuntu, both on the same host, since both use the same Linux kernel. However, you cannot run a Windows container on top of a Linux kernel. The difference between a virtual machine and a container should be somewhat clear by now.

A typical use case for a container is running an application that requires a specific version of an operating system with specific packages and libraries (dependencies) installed. You may need to run an Apache server and a custom Python application, both on the same host but each requiring a different OS version or the same OS version but a different set of dependencies. One solution is to run each application in its own container, where each container provides the user space OS components required to run the application software of choice.

But why containers? Containers provide a more efficient solution to virtualization than virtual machines. A container uses significantly fewer system resources than a VM, and it boots up much more quickly. You can run many more containers on a host than you can run VMs, which means they provide higher density and better utilization than VMs. Where hardware virtualization isn't required and a common kernel is not a showstopper, containers are usually the solution to the requirement of different OS environments. Different applications requiring different software dependencies to run is sometimes referred to as *dependency hell*.

The most popular container software today is Docker. Docker is open-source software and is considered the industry standard for containers. Docker has versions for Microsoft Windows Server as well as several Linux distros. Docker is composed of the core Docker Engine software and a Docker CLI for managing the Docker containers on the system. Current versions of Docker also provide an API to interface programmatically with the Docker Engine and automate tasks such as starting and stopping containers. Docker is covered in some detail in Chapter 6.

What happens when the number of containers you need to manage increases, and the applications in one container have dependencies on applications running in another container? For example, what if one container is the backup of another container, and it needs to start if the original container fails? What if you need to load balance traffic to two different containers? Several software applications on the market today provide container management and orchestration. Two of them stand out: Kubernetes and Docker Swarm. Both of these applications are open source. And, as you might expect, each of the three biggest cloud providers—AWS, Microsoft Azure, and Google—has its own cloud-native container management and orchestration software.

If you plan to work with automation software of any kind, you will more likely than not run into containers. Make sure that this subject is on your roadmap for future studies.

Application Hosting

The majority of network vendors today base the network operating system (NOS) running on their equipment on Linux. In other words, the NOS runs as user space software over some Linux distro. As mentioned in several chapters in this book, and particularly in Chapter 17, "Programming Cisco Platforms," IOX XR, IOS XE, and NX-OS all run on top of a Linux distro called Wind River. This device architecture, which is based on Linux, opens the door for a broad spectrum of innovations, including application hosting.

Software that needs to interact with a network device may be run on a remote host (that is, off-box). The software communicates with the router either over a legacy channel, such as SSH coupled with CLI commands, or over one of the APIs exposed by the device. But because most equipment is based on Linux, this software may also be run on the device itself (that is, on-box). This is application hosting. Application hosting generally can be implemented using two models:

- **Native:** This application hosting model involves developing software for the particular Linux distro running on the device. This is similar to developing software that runs natively on Windows or CentOS. The software runs only on that particular OS or OS family. This is typically done using the software development kit (SDK) provided by the equipment vendor for the particular Linux distro.

- **Containerized:** This application hosting model involves running software inside a container. For example, Cisco's IOS XR supports running on-box Docker or LXC containers. As explained in the previous section, a container constitutes the application software that you want to run as well as the OS components required to run the software. So, you may develop software that performs a global function on any Linux distro, such as collecting data from the router (not telemetry collection on the router itself, which can have serious performance impacts) or run custom functions not natively supported by IOS XR. Then you can package this software in a container, along with the OS it was developed on, and run this container on the IOS XR–based router or, better, on any network device that supports Docker containers.

The level of maturity that application hosting on network devices has reached provides innovation opportunities that were never feasible before. Cisco describes a number of very interesting use cases for using application hosting in its *Application Hosting Configuration Guides* available for a number of Cisco platforms.

One use case describes installing an iPerf server on one router and an iPerf client on another. The iPerf software measures path quality in terms of bandwidth, jitter, delay, and packet loss. Packet loss is then simulated on one path. The data provided by iPerf indicating low path quality via one interface on the router is used to increase the OSPF cost of that interface and, in the process, fail over the traffic to a different interface. This is only one example of what can be achieved using application hosting, but the sky is the limit.

Software Development Methodologies

An engineer wishing to automate the configuration of a VLAN on 100 switches can write a short Python script on a text editor such as **vim** or Notepad and then run the code on her local machine to get the task completed. However, when a team of software engineers want to develop a sophisticated multitier application, it is nearly impossible to use this method to develop software. Several software methodologies have been formulated and adopted over the past few decades to manage the process of software development in a team.

Generally speaking, the software development life cycle (SDLC) is divided into five main phases:

- Requirement specification and analysis
- Design
- Development or coding
- Testing
- Maintenance

A software development methodology is a framework that organizes the implementation of the SDLC. Several methodologies exist, such as Waterfall, Prototyping, Incremental and Iterative, Spiral, Rapid Application Development, Extreme Programming, V-Model Methodology, Scrum, Cleanroom, Dynamic Systems Development, and the Rational Unified Process.

Consider these examples:

- Waterfall is the most structured but also the most rigid methodology. It follows the analogy of a waterfall, where the water flows only downhill and never uphill. This means that each phase has a well-defined start and end and, once the phase is completed, there is no going back. So, for example, once the requirements are collected and analyzed, and the design phase starts, there is no going back to the previous phase and changing the requirements. Waterfall seemingly makes a lot of sense and is quite simple to follow, but it is hardly fit for today's development environments, where software products are in a constant state of development. Think of how frequently mobile applications such as Facebook and Google Maps get updated.
- Many of the other methodologies are described as Agile. An Agile methodology is one that conforms to the 12 principles listed in the Agile Manifesto. One of these principles describes the flexibility of such methodologies as follows: "Welcome changing requirements, even late in development." Agile methodologies also strive to produce a viable and shippable product as early as possible in the development process, and they depend on small software increments to that initial product. The principle states "Deliver working software frequently, from a couple of weeks to a couple of months, with a preference to the shorter timescale." (The 12 principles are listed at https://www.agilealliance.org/agile101/12-principles-behind-the-agile-manifesto/.) Agile methodologies are very flexible.

If you plan on getting involved in big software projects, whether as a software developer or as project manager, you need to understand the philosophies and practices involved in each of these methodologies in order to blend in with the rest of the team.

Miscellaneous Topics

The following are just a few of the areas that you might want to look into when you are done with this book:

- At some point in your software development progression, you will need some auxiliary tools to complement your programs. When the data you collect starts to be of considerable size, the data needs to be stored in a structured manner so that it can be both stored and searched efficiently. At that point, you will need to look into databases and search engines. Different types of databases exist today, and you might want to explore relational databases, graph databases, time-series databases, SQL and NoSQL databases, and software for storing and searching structured and unstructured data, such as Elasticsearch and Splunk.

- A massive potential area for further study is clouds and automation. Clouds, by definition, are platforms that automate the provisioning of resources and rent out these resources to customers. It is likely that no other area in IT utilizes automation more than cloud infrastructures. This applies to both public clouds such as AWS, Google Cloud, and Microsoft Azure and to private clouds that are custom built for specific customers.

- At some point in your programmability career, you will run into situations where you will need to learn about and/or employ advanced API features. When you do an API call and an error occurs, you need to implement proper error handling in order to isolate the users interfacing with your program from the internals of the API call. When you do an API call and the data you receive is significantly large, you may need to employ pagination to split the data received into different pages and then load subsequent pages as needed (or not). An API call may fail. You will need to look into API call retries. Caches and proxies are integral components of the Internet and some intranets. Your API calls may run into either of them.

- Chapters 17 and 18, "Programming non-Cisco Devices," cover a number of APIs exposed by Cisco and non-Cisco devices. Keep in mind that these are only examples. The vast majority of devices, systems, and networks developed and sold by Cisco and the other major vendors expose APIs. As a matter of fact, programmatic access has become part of the design requirements of any new product sold by Cisco. APIs are not an aftermath consideration anymore. Cisco is now developing products with programmatic access as a core feature. Make sure to check out the *Programmability Guide* for the product you are working on to understand the available APIs and how to work with them.

What Does All This Mean for Your Career?

When I was a young—well, younger— engineer in the late 1980s and early 1990s, teaching networking classes and working with ancient technologies like Token Ring, Frame Relay, ATM, and SNA, I came to realize that what I love about the networking field is that it was almost continually changing, and everyone was trying to figure out where the industry was going.

It was a time when one executive at a certain Ethernet hub vendor told me with great fervor that Ethernet hubs (Not switches. Hubs) were the future of the industry and would soon drive routers into obsolescence. That company ceased to exist in 1994, and while the vision of a world built around Ethernet hubs is now amusingly quaint, it highlights the struggle we all had with understanding what technologies were important to learn and what technologies were limping toward obsolescence. SNA and Token Ring were known to be on their way out, but ATM and Frame Relay were still new and cool. You had to know DECnet, IPX, XNS, and AppleTalk to pass the CCIE exam, but you didn't even have to know how to spell IPv6. Certain circles still thought OSI CLNS/CLNP would replace TCP/IP just as soon as the ISO standards committees started agreeing on something. I had to disabuse my networking students of the idea that OSPF was complicated and should only be used in complicated networks.

Abandoning my trip down memory lane and getting to the point: Networking in those days was kind of a circus. The extant technologies were not all that hard to learn, but there were *a lot* of them to learn. I was an eager learner. I loved it.

Predicting industry directions today is much easier because the role networking plays in our business and personal lives is clear. Anything that enhances that role—any technology that makes it easier to design, build, and operate networks that serve that role—is important.

I ended Chapter 1 posing a couple of questions from a couple of hypothetical engineers:

- **Older engineers:** "So I need to be a programmer now? Are software developers going to take my job if I don't?"
- **Newer engineers:** "I've invested enormous time and money into earning the certifications that will set me on the career path I want. Most of my study time has been spent configuring and troubleshooting through the CLI. Is all that a waste of time?"

The answers I gave to those questions at the end of Chapter 1:

- **Yes**, if you want to keep up with where the industry is going, you need to acquire some programming skills and understand the protocols supporting modern automation trends. This book and a mountain of other resources can help you get up to speed. If you are a seasoned engineer, none of this is different from what you have done your entire career: keeping up with new technologies by keeping up with the latest RFCs, reading the right trade journals and blogs, and attending industry events like CiscoLive! and your regional network operators' groups. If you're just starting out, you're already in deep learning mode, and you'll find that enhancing your growing skill set is not that hard at all. And I guarantee that it makes you more valuable as an engineer.
- **No**, automation and programmability do not mean that your jobs are going to be eliminated or taken over by software developers. Software developers' programming abilities go far beyond what is needed for networking, and for the most part, they know little about networking itself. You only have to know enough about programming to make your own job easier. Automating the mundane parts of your job just means you have more time for bringing your deep knowledge of networking to bear. The network is better for it, and you are most certainly the better for it.

Even if you need to bring software developers in to build automation code that is beyond your abilities or available time, you are the one who understands networking and must oversee their production. They need for you to understand what they do, and they need your superior knowledge of networking.

Learning network automation and programmability is essential to your future as a network engineer or architect. The more you know, the more valuable you are to your existing organization and the more marketable you are in the industry as a whole.

We all—Khaled, Vinit, and Jeff—hope that this book has provided you with a solid foundation for building those new skills and given you a clear-eyed insight into where your career is going.

Index

Symbols

Numbers

A

B

C

D

E

F

G

H

I

J

K

L

M

N

O

P

Q

R

S

T

U

V

W

X

Y - Z